917.404
.H632
2007

A

DATE DUE

AUG 18 2007

APR 10 2008

JUL 09 2008

GAYLORD

PRINTED IN U.S.A.

HIDDEN® New England

"Fun, informative and entertaining, this is a massive guide to the best of off-beat New England."

—*Chicago Tribune*

"*Hidden New England* is the best general guide to the region."

—*Elle*

"Really gives the flavor of each place."

—*New Orleans Times-Picayune*

"Comprehensive, well-written and filled with off-beat finds."

—*Oakland Tribune*

"Scores highly as a travel companion. It's sure to show you something new."

—*Car and Driver*

"Fun to read. Caters to those who yearn for something extra."

—*Chevron USA Odyssey*

"Helps prove there's still a treasure trove of undiscovered spots."

—*Hartford Courant*

"Fascinating. An exploration of secluded and more viable locales."

—*San Francisco Examiner & Chronicle*

HIDDEN®

New England

Including Connecticut, Maine, Massachusetts, New Hampshire, Rhode Island & Vermont

NINTH EDITION

Ulysses Press®

BERKELEY, CALIFORNIA

Copyright © 1990, 1992, 1994, 1996, 1998, 2000, 2002, 2004, 2007 Ulysses Press. All rights reserved, including the right to reproduce this book or portions thereof in any form whatsoever, except for use by a reviewer in connection with a review.

Published by:
ULYSSES PRESS
P.O. Box 3440
Berkeley, CA 94703
www.ulyssespress.com

ISSN 1090-6894
ISBN10: 1-56975-600-7
ISBN13: 978-1-56975-600-3

Printed in Canada by Transcontinental Printing

20 19 18 17 16 15 14 13

MANAGING EDITOR: Claire Chun
PROJECT DIRECTOR: Elyce Petker
COPY EDITORS: Lily Chou, Mark Woodworth
EDITORIAL ASSOCIATES: Ruth Marcus, Laurel Shane, Gail Bailey, Rebekah Morris
TYPESETTING: Lisa Kester, Matt Orendorff
CARTOGRAPHY: Pease Press
HIDDEN BOOKS DESIGN: Sarah Levin
INDEXER: Sayre Van Young
FRONT COVER PHOTOGRAPHY: © Gettyimages.com (fall foliage) and courtesy of MOTT (George Washington Statue, Boston Public Garden)
ILLUSTRATOR: Timothy Carroll

Distributed by Publishers Group West

HIDDEN is a federally registered trademark of BookPack, Inc.

Ulysses Press is a federally registered trademark of BookPack, Inc.

The author and publisher have made every effort to ensure the accuracy of information contained in *Hidden New England*, but can accept no liability for any loss, injury, or inconvenience sustained by any traveler as a result of information or advice contained in this guide.

Write to us!

If in your travels you discover a spot that captures the spirit of New England, or if you live in the region and have a favorite place to share, or if you just feel like expressing your views, write to us and we'll pass your note along to the author.

We can't guarantee that the author will add your personal find to the next edition, but if the writer does use the suggestion, we'll acknowledge you in the credits and send you a free copy of the new edition.

ULYSSES PRESS
P.O. Box 3440
Berkeley, CA 94703
E-mail: readermail@ulyssespress.com

What's Hidden?

At different points throughout this book, you'll find special listings marked with this symbol:

◄ HIDDEN

This means that you have come upon a place off the beaten tourist track, a spot that will carry you a step closer to the local people and natural environment of New England.

The goal of this guide is to lead you beyond the realm of everyday tourist facilities. While we include traditional sightseeing listings and popular attractions, we also offer alternative sights and adventure activities. Instead of filling this guide with reviews of standard hotels and chain restaurants, we concentrate on one-of-a-kind places and locally owned establishments.

Our authors seek out locales that are popular with residents but usually overlooked by visitors. Some are more hidden than others (and are marked accordingly), but all the listings in this book are intended to help you discover the true nature of New England and put you on the path of adventure.

Contents

OUTDOOR ADVENTURE SYMBOLS

The following symbols accompany national, state and regional park listings, as well as beach descriptions throughout the text.

- Camping
- Hiking
- Biking
- Horseback Riding
- Downhill Skiing
- Cross-country Skiing
- Swimming
- Snorkeling or Scuba Diving
- Surfing
- Waterskiing
- Windsurfing
- Canoeing or Kayaking
- Boating
- Boat Ramps
- Fishing

Maps

ONE

New England Sojourn

There is no more instantly recognizable scenery in the American landscape—or the American mind—than the picture-postcard image of a New England village: the white-steepled church on an emerald green ringed by white clapboard houses, the whole of it haloed by forests aflame with fall reds and golds.

No wonder people come hoping, wanting, expecting to find this metaphor for New England life. And this place of centuries past still exists, in many small towns scattered throughout the six states.

But New England is stunningly heterogeneous, possessed of countless rich dimensions. In just one state, you find old textile and industrial cities, rivers and lakes, and towering spruce forests whose denizens are moose and black bear. Visitors will discover miles and miles of white-sand beaches fringed with dunes and marsh grasses; thriving metropolises like Boston and Providence; mountain ranges with hiking and skiing trails; fishing villages hundreds of years old; Indian burial grounds; and coastal resorts where elegant yachts bob in the harbor. Standing fast before time, New England's old wooden saltbox houses have weathered into the colors of the very ground that made them.

Bounded on the north by Canada, on the east by the Atlantic Ocean, on the south by Long Island Sound, and on the west by New York, New England sits squarely in the northeastern corner of the United States. Five states border the ocean, which is never far from anyone's mind. Fishing blessed all who settled here, from the Indians and the Pilgrims to the 19th-century whalers and today's fishermen of Gloucester, New Bedford and Plymouth. New Englanders have always been premier shipbuilders and sailors, and today one of the greatest pleasures is to ride a Maine windjammer, an excursion boat or a tiny sailboat.

The ocean also tempers the weather, making summers cooler and winters less fierce. The seasons pull out all the stops here, parading four kinds of memorable variety every year. In warmer, more monotonous climates, the passing of time recedes to a blur.

New Englanders love and revere their covered bridges, their Revolutionary War–era, Federal and Greek Revival homes, and their chowder made with milk, not tomato juice, thank you. To a true New Englander, there's nothing quite like the first cider of the fall, real native maple syrup or a clambake on the beach.

To give them credit, many dour old Yankees have expanded their tastes to include the flowers, glass arcades and gourmet restaurants of Faneuil Hall Marketplace and whimsical things like balloon festivals.

Still, there is little of glitz about this region. New England simply is what it is, without apology. It's not an invented attraction but a real place, one that stands on the legitimacy and integrity of its origins.

This book was designed to help you explore this wonderful area. Besides leading you to countless popular spots, it will also take you to many off-the-beaten-path locales, places usually known only by locals. The book will tell the story of the region's history, its flora and fauna. Each chapter will suggest places to eat, to stay, to sightsee, to shop and to enjoy the outdoors and nightlife, covering a range of tastes and budgets.

The book sets out in Connecticut, taking visitors in Chapter Two through the rural outlying areas and along its pretty coastline. Chapter Three outlines tiny little Rhode Island's greatly unspoiled topography and gorgeous beaches, as well as elite Newport and historic Providence. Because of its dense population and diversity, Massachusetts is presented in four chapters. Quintessential Boston is explored in Chapter Four, from its Revolutionary War–era sites to Beacon Hill and Back Bay. Chapter Five covers all of Cape Cod, as well as the islands of Martha's Vineyard and Nantucket. Chapter Six moves along the Massachusetts Coast, from the North Shore to Plymouth and New Bedford on the South Shore. In Chapter Seven, you'll discover the Pioneer Valley and the Berkshires of central and western Massachusetts.

Chapter Eight covers Vermont, with its Green Mountains and covered bridges. Chapter Nine is dedicated to New Hampshire, land of sparkling lakes, the White Mountains and majestic Mount Washington. Last but by no means least, you'll explore the stately pine forests and rugged coast of Maine in Chapter Ten.

Wherever you choose to go, whatever you choose to see and do, you're bound to find something to like in this infinite variety. Generations of travelers have enjoyed New England's coast and mountains, forests and lakes, in all kinds of weather.

The Story of New England

GEOLOGY

Geology is destiny, you might say. Certainly this is true in the case of New England. Some of the region's most famed symbols, from stone walls, mill towns and rivers, to Bunker Hill, Walden Pond, Cape Cod and the White Mountains, sprang from geologic events.

New England is one of the oldest continuously surviving land masses on earth. In Cambrian times, half a billion years ago, New England was covered by a vast inland sea. When the earth's crust buckled and rose, it pushed up mountainous masses—the ancestors of the Berkshires and the Green Mountains. During the same era, a mass of hot molten rock gave birth to the White Mountains from deep within the earth.

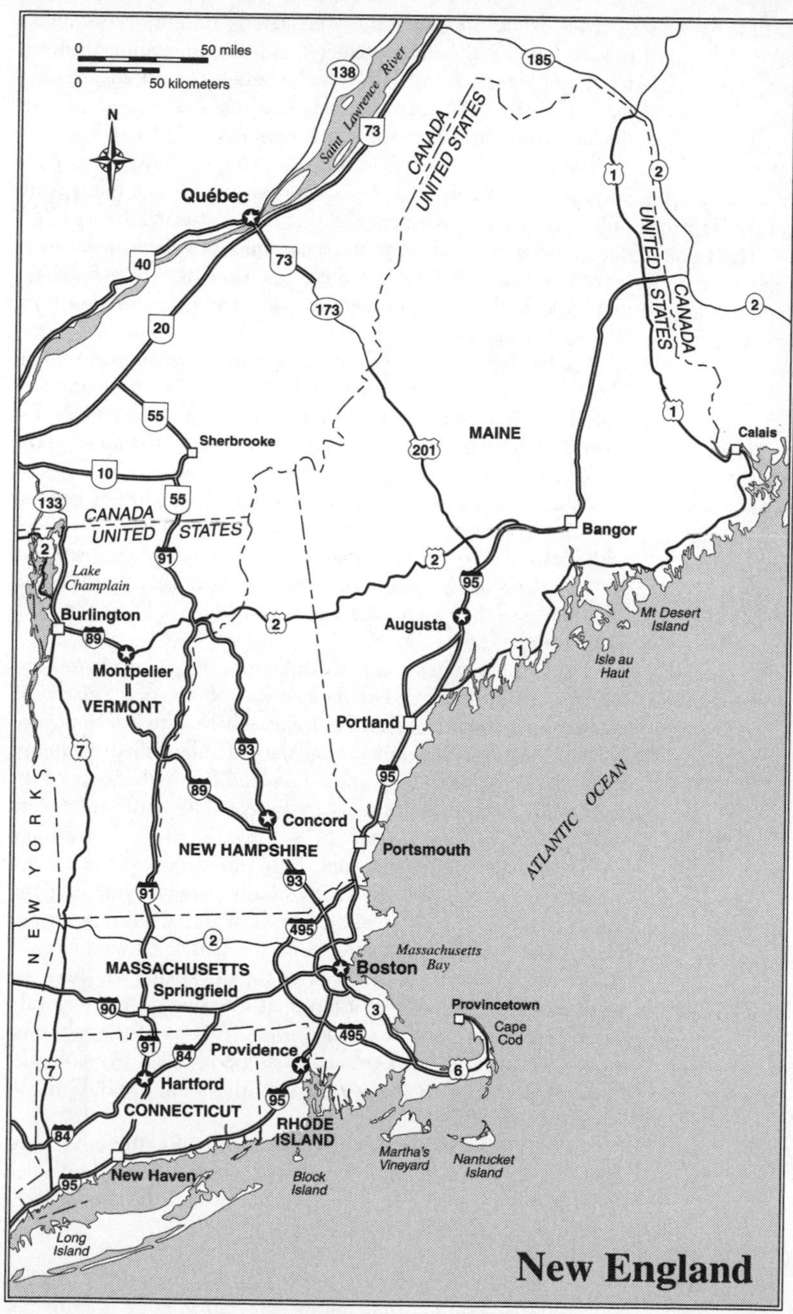
0 50 miles
0 50 kilometers
N
Québec
Saint Lawrence River
138
73
185
CANADA
UNITED STATES
40
20
173
55
Sherbrooke
10
133
CANADA
UNITED STATES
2
Lake Champlain
91
Burlington
89
Montpelier
VERMONT
7
NEW YORK
93
89
Concord
NEW HAMPSHIRE
91
2
MASSACHUSETTS
Springfield
90
91
84
Hartford
CONNECTICUT
84
95
New Haven
Long Island
Providence
95
RHODE ISLAND
Block Island
495
Boston
Massachusetts Bay
3
495
6
Provincetown
Cape Cod
Martha's Vineyard
Nantucket Island
Portsmouth
95
Portland
ATLANTIC OCEAN
Augusta
95
1
Isle au Haut
Mt Desert Island
Bangor
201
MAINE
Calais
1
2
1
2
UNITED STATES
CANADA
New England

Even while the mountains were rising, running water began to wear away at the land, leveling it and washing sediments down from the uplands. Finally all New England was reduced almost to sea level, like a flat plain. But some of the mountains survived, particularly those in the north, which was less completely leveled.

The earth's crust stirred again, 200 million to 300 million years later, but gently this time. The land rose just enough to give altitude to the slow-moving rivers of the plains, causing them to flow more swiftly, and set them off to carving out valleys. Eventually New Englanders would find these fast-flowing, powerful rivers and build mill wheels on them to run their factories and mills, which you can still see today.

The Ice Age seized the region in a frozen grip about a million years ago, gradually spreading and growing. The mass of ice finally became so vast and heavy that its own weight pushed it down and outward, and it began to move. For thousands of years, the ice cap grew, engulfing all of New England.

As it moved, the ice cap picked up boulders, some as large as houses, and carried them along with it. Fields of boulders, filled with rocks of all sizes, are common in New England. Farmers had to clear their fields of countless rocks before they could plant, and they used them to make stone walls, which still line the landscape today.

The ice moved in a southerly direction, from Canada to Long Island, paring off hills and ledges as it went. Some of the glacial till was clay, which sticks to itself more readily than to ice. Deposited clay formed into low-lying, oval-shaped hills called drumlins, many a mile or more long and a hundred feet high. Some of the region's most famous drumlins are Bunker Hill and World's End in Hingham, Massachusetts.

The glaciers came and went four times, retreating and advancing for over a million years, finally leaving New England about 10,000 to 12,000 years ago. The last glacial advance formed Cape Cod, Martha's Vineyard, Nantucket, Block Island and the Rhode Island shore. At the front of the advancing ice sheet, released rock debris built up a terminal moraine—a ridge of rubble. These islands and coasts are what remains of the morainal ridges. Watch Hill, Rhode Island, has been called by geologists "one of the finest examples of glacial dumping ground" in the eastern United States.

Large blocks of melting glacial ice formed kettle-hole lakes, deep bodies of water with a rounded shape, of which Walden Pond is a good example. It might also be said that kettle lakes make for fine ice skating and ice fishing.

HISTORY

New England is America's scrapbook, the memorabilia of a nation conceived on hardship and perseverance, faith and dreams.

It is a riveting story of high adventure and the push for freedom, of ingenuity and despotism, of victory over adverse conditions.

The opening pages tell of Pilgrims who charted a course to Greenland but were blown far southward by violent winds. The year was A.D. 1000, and, according to Norse legend, Norseman Leif Ericsson landed in a strange place, probably along Maine's rocky coast. Discovering friendly Indians and fertile land where grapes and wheat grew wild, he dubbed his find Vinland the Good and returned to Norway with tales of a fascinating world.

More than 450 years would pass before European explorers would again call on the intriguing land. Navigator John Cabot, on assignment from England's King Henry VII and seeking a Northwest Passage to the East, explored the coasts of Maine and Massachusetts in 1497. He found no pass but claimed a considerable chunk of the New World—everything north of Florida and east of the Rockies—for the British crown.

Italian explorer Giovanni da Verrazano staked out the same coast some 27 years later, claiming the territory for his employer nation, France. Just prior to his visit, navigator Miguel Corte Real had been checking out the terrain for Portugal.

Dutch sailor Adriaen Block launched a coastal investigation in 1614, calling a Narragansett Bay island "Roodt Eyland," or Red Island, a likely precursor to Rhode Island. That same year, English captain John Smith mapped the Massachusetts coast and was taken by its beauty. A soldier of fortune, Smith wrote a glowing report of the intriguing land, describing its "sandy cliffes and cliffes of rock" planted with cornfields and gardens.

Though captivated by the new region, none of these adventurers did what seemed the most logical thing: settle the place. Of course, this white man's frontier had been inhabited at least five centuries by Algonquin tribes. A peaceful people who dwelled in wigwams, they were expert growers of corn, tobacco, pumpkins and other crops. They hunted forests plentiful with moose, deer, turkey and goose, and fished the streams and ocean for bass, salmon, lobster and clams, throwing the area's earliest clambakes.

A CORNUCOPIA OF HISTORY

It would be almost impossible to find another place in the United States so densely packed with history. You can barely take a step without stumbling over a Colonial battlefield, a historic site or monument, or an 18th-century house. All that you learned in school about the birth of the United States will come to life before your eyes. And every year or so, another New England town celebrates its 350th anniversary.

The Algonquins were not populous. Small tribes, sometimes with as few as 200 Indians, were scattered among the forests and along the coast. The Pennacook tribe resided in what would become New Hampshire and Massachusetts; the Abenaki favored the New Hampshire area, too, as well as Maine. The Narrangansetts were natives of today's Rhode Island. All told, New England's Indians numbered about 25,000 when they welcomed the first permanent European settlers in 1620.

By the mid-1660s, Rhode Island received New England's first Jews and several hundred French Huguenots and Quakers.

Religious asylum, not adventure or fortune, is what those first real settlers were seeking. The Puritans, cut off from Anglican England because of their strict Protestant beliefs, read with interest John Smith's glowing report on the New World. Could it be their Utopia? They were anxious to find out.

In the spring of 1620, the Puritans struck a deal with the Plymouth Company to finance a settlement in the New World. By summer's end, 102 Puritans boarded the *Mayflower* for a rigorous, two-month journey to America. They first sighted land at Cape Cod, then cruised the coast for a month and landed at Plymouth Rock. On December 21, the Plymouth Colony was born.

That first winter proved brutal for the colonists as they fought scurvy, pneumonia and other diseases that killed nearly half their group. But springtime brought relief and the opportunity to plant crops, thanks to help from the Indians who were hospitable to their new neighbors. To celebrate the first anniversary of their friendship, the Pilgrims and Indians feasted together for three days that fall.

As word of the successful colony trickled back to England, more Puritans set out for the New World. In 1630, about 1000 Puritans on 11 ships landed at Salem during the "Great Migration." Drawn by a vast harbor filled with sea life, settlers moved southward and declared Boston their main colony. Fur-trading posts were established in Maine, and small villages sprang up in New Hampshire, Connecticut and Rhode Island.

By 1636, another 12,000 immigrants had arrived. Puritan ministers, sensing the need to train future leaders, founded Harvard College and set up a general court to govern the colonies. Local matters were dealt with by town leaders at regular meetings, the forerunners of today's town council sessions.

Ironically, those same Puritans who sought the New World for religious freedom would not tolerate other beliefs. In 1651, a visitor from the Rhode Island colony was publicly whipped for being a Baptist. Victims of English persecution, Quakers fleeing the Old World were arrested on ships in Boston Harbor before they ever set foot on the new land. Additionally, in 1659, two men and a woman were hanged in Massachusetts for espousing Quaker beliefs.

Religious dissidents fled to Rhode Island, which Puritans dubbed "the sewer of New England" and "Rogue's Island." But the tiny colony held fast to religious and social freedoms.

It was Puritan fanaticism that caused the untimely end of several other unfortunate New England souls. Witches, the Puritans said, were lurking about, possessed by demons and casting spells on innocent minds.

The accusations led to witch trials in Charlestown in 1648 and in Boston in 1655, but the most hideous ordeal occurred in Salem in 1692. After hundreds of people were imprisoned in a "Witch House," 19 were executed, including 80-year-old Giles Corey, who was pressed to death when he pled no-contest.

The Puritans were also a nightmare for the Indians. Determined to "save" them from their pagan ways, missionaries translated the Bible into Algonquin and set about converting new Christians. By the 1670s, nearly one-fourth of the Indian population had officially accepted the imposed faith. But it was not enough. The Puritans wanted not just mental converts but a race that would abandon its centuries-old customs, its very mode of existence.

As colonies expanded, the Indians got in the way. Several skirmishes ensued, but it was King Philip's War, from 1675 to 1676, that spelled the beginning of the end for the New England Indians. Pressured by colonists to abandon his land, chief Metacomet (King Philip) led a series of battles against his encroachers. He lost a decisive engagement, the "Great Swamp Fight," near Kingston, Rhode Island, when Massachusetts and Connecticut colonists burned wigwams, killing hundreds of women and children and disorganizing Indian forces.

Betrayed by a fellow Indian, King Philip was captured soon thereafter, his body beheaded and quartered. His head was displayed on a gibbet in Plymouth for 20 years as a reminder of white victory. Just four decades after the Indians had welcomed the first Puritans into their home, the Puritans had decimated them.

Eighteenth-century New England was a place of social, economic and political growth. Life centered around the ocean and rivers, as shipbuilding thrived in towns such as Portsmouth in New Hampshire, Groton in Connecticut, Kittery in Maine and, of course, Boston. Coopers, potters and furniture makers plied their trades along the waterfront, and coastal and international trade boomed.

Colleges and universities that today rank among the nation's best were established: Yale University, New Hampshire's Dartmouth College, and Rhode Island College, now Brown University. The influx of non-Puritans created a greater cultural and religious mix, and politics flourished as colonists demanded more autonomy from Mother England.

Determined to subdue its wayward child, England in 1764 imposed the Revenue Act, which levied duties on silk, sugar and some wines. Colonists rebelled and promptly boycotted the tariffs.

England didn't flinch. One year later, it slapped colonies with the Stamp Act, taxing commercial and legal papers such as newspapers and licenses. Outraged, colonists denounced the tax and refused to buy European goods. "No taxation without representation," they cried. Every Colonial stamp agent resigned, and before the law could take effect November 1, Parliament repealed the act.

But England insisted on political and economic control. Several months later Parliament passed the Townshend Acts, imposing heavy taxes on paper, glass and tea. Colonists again rebelled, and England sent troops to squelch rioting in Boston.

By 1770, hoping to rid the city of "Redcoats"—the colonists' name for the British militia—Bostonians gathered at the Customs House and began taunting the sentry. Troops arrived, and after a series of violent skirmishes, they fired shots into the crowd. When the Boston Massacre was over, five colonials lay dead on King Street, present-day State Street.

England repealed most of the Townshend taxes, leaving duties on imported tea—then the most popular drink in America. New Englanders retaliated by buying smuggled tea. In 1773, when England's Tea Act flooded the market with cheap tea, agents would not accept deliveries—except for Governor Thomas Hutchinson in Boston.

When three tea-filled ships sailed into Boston Harbor, the Committees of Correspondence and Sons of Liberty—pre-revolutionary activists—blocked the piers. Governor Hutchinson refused to let the ships return to England, so protesters invited him to a little tea party.

Disguised as Indians, 60 Sons of Liberty boarded the ships on the night of December 16, 1773 and dumped 342 chests of tea into the harbor. It was a defiant move and an ominous portent of what lie ahead: revolution was in the air.

On April 19, 1775, a single musket discharge set off America's first full-scale war. "The shot heard 'round the world" was fired at the Battle of Lexington and Concord, an effort by the Redcoats to crush revolutionary uprisings around Boston.

Forewarned by Paul Revere that the "British are coming," 77 Minutemen crouched in early morning darkness, waiting for the Redcoat attack. The British advanced, killing eight rebels and wounding ten on the present-day Lexington Green before continuing to Concord. There they destroyed a cache of arms and were finally driven out.

The colonies rallied together. Vermont's Green Mountain Boys, led by Ethan Allen and Benedict Arnold, captured Fort Ticonderoga on Lake Champlain, blocking a British invasion from Canada. On June 17, 1775, New Englanders fought the war's first major engagement—known as the Battle of Bunker Hill although it was really fought on nearby Breed's Hill—on the Charlestown peninsula near Boston. After enduring two British attacks, the Americans ran short of ammunition and retreated.

Though a technical victory for England, Bunker Hill cost the crown more than 1000 troops—over twice the Colonial losses. More important, it proved that the Minutemen volunteers were a match for the better-trained British army.

On July 4, 1776, the Declaration of Independence was adopted by the Continental Congress. The war raged on in surrounding states for six years, but New England was free.

Economic depression followed the war. Paper money was scarce, loans difficult to obtain and court foreclosures commonplace. When their new state government levied high taxes, Massachusetts farmers rose up in anger. Shays' Rebellion, which lasted from 1786 to 1787 but was unsuccessful at stopping the taxes, proved that democracy was still an elusive concept.

New England heralded the 19th century with a burgeoning shipping industry, though the War of 1812 temporarily halted matters with stiff trade embargoes. With the advent of the cotton mill in Pawtucket, Rhode Island, weavers no longer had to work at home, though their 12-hour workdays and paltry wages led to the nation's first labor strike in 1800. Eli Whitney's cotton gin revolutionized the wool industry, and mills sprang up across New England. By the 1830s, Providence alone produced 20 percent of the country's wool.

As New England grew and the railroad headed west, settlers starting moving into the interior. Wilderness areas of northern Maine, Vermont and New Hampshire were slowly penetrated, and pioneers established small farms. But unforgiving soil and unpredictable weather squelched any hopes of real agriculture, and by 1860 farming as serious business ceased to exist in these states.

AMERICAN INGENUITY

Hundreds of inventions put New England at the forefront of the industrial age. Yale graduate Samuel Morse masterminded the telegraph and his own code, Elias Howe crafted the world's first sewing machine, and Charles Goodyear developed a type of commercial rubber, though he died $200,000 in the red. In Hartford, Samuel Colt opened a munitions factory and Francis Pratt and Amos Whitney manufactured machine tools and interchangeable parts.

The Industrial Revolution sparked a mass immigration of Europeans, with hundreds arriving from England, Scotland, Italy and Portugal. Victims of the 1845 Great Potato Famine, thousands of Irish sailed to Massachusetts with dreams of a new life. By 1850, one of every ten New Englanders was foreign born. Only ten years later, 61 percent of Boston residents had been born abroad.

Not all New Englanders welcomed so many immigrants with open arms. During the 1850s, several political monsters reared their ugly heads. The Know-Nothing Party blatantly opposed all immigrants, particularly the Irish. Together with virulent anti–Roman Catholic factions in Maine, the party burned several Catholic churches. The powerful Know-Nothings managed to control governorships in several states.

At the same time, the abolition movement gripped New England. Connecticut's Harriet Beecher Stowe raised public consciousness in 1852 with *Uncle Tom's Cabin*. A fervent opponent of slavery, William Lloyd Garrison published his *Liberator* newspaper for 34 years in Massachusetts, despite being dragged through streets by angry mobs and threatened constantly.

New England was also experiencing a cultural renaissance. The great "Flowering of New England" was centered in Boston. Now called the "Athens of America," the city saw the founding of such eminent institutions as the Museum of Fine Arts, the Boston Symphony Orchestra and the Boston Pops.

Great minds thrived across the region. Artists, thinkers and literary geniuses would set the dynamic tone in New England for centuries to come. People like Nathaniel Hawthorne and Oliver Wendell Holmes, Henry David Thoreau and Julia Ward Howe, Ralph Waldo Emerson and Emily Dickinson made New England an intellectual mecca.

By the turn of the 20th century, an ethnic and political metamorphosis had taken place. The long-time bastion of Yankee Protestantism was now being run by Roman Catholics. In 1900, a majority of New England legislators were Catholic.

At the same time came a wave of corruption that would last for several decades. In Rhode Island, Republican "Boss" Charles R. Brayton built his regime by exchanging bought votes for "judge-

BAN THE BILLBOARD

Progressive New Englanders were among the first to push environmental issues to the national front, passing stringent air pollution and zoning laws. As early as the 1960s, rural Vermont banned billboards and nonreturnable bottles. Massachusetts passed the nation's earliest wetlands act.

ships and other political jobs," charged journalist Lincoln Steffens. Brayton even paid "yellow dog" Democrats to be loyal to the machine. Iniquity reached its height in Boston's James Michael Curley, elected mayor four times between 1914 and 1950 and state governor from 1935 to 1937. The "Irish Mussolini" perfected ward politics, handing out jobs, favors and money to those who guaranteed his return to office.

The Depression crushed New England. Between 1929 and 1950, more than 149,000 textile workers lost their jobs as the manufacturing industry fell prostrate. Wages were slashed in half for those lucky enough to work, and hundreds of thousands lost their homes.

New England never fully rebounded from those difficult years. During the 1960s and early 1970s, foreign imports dealt a blow to most of the manufacturing left in the area. Void of natural resources such as oil and coal, the area was especially hard hit by the 1970s recession.

But since the 1990s New England has seen a rebirth of industry and technology. Modern enterprises have flourished, producing such wonders as missile and space systems, jet aircraft engines, computers and computer equipment, and biomedical and photographic instruments. The high-tech community circles Boston along Route 128 and spills over into Hartford, southern New Hampshire, Rhode Island and even Vermont's Burlington area.

The greater Boston metropolitan area is home to around 30 newspapers, 8 television stations, 30 radio stations and many libraries and museums of national stature.

Higher education is itself a leading "industry" of Massachusetts, the site of over 120 colleges and universities—nearly half in the Boston area alone. And New England's immense beauty and rich history make tourism the number two industry, second only to manufacturing.

Today, beyond the high-tech centers and tourist attractions resounds the inescapable presence of New England's colorful past: Revolutionary War monuments, 18th-century covered bridges and statehouses, steepled churches that held this country's first congregations.

One need only explore Paul Revere's House, the Bunker Hill Monument and the Granary Burial Ground in the Boston area to recognize the sites of this country's genesis. For New England's past is America's past. And the region remains a vital part of the nation's present and future.

FLORA

The glorious flaming reds, oranges and yellows of a New England fall come from changes in its thick stands of hardwood trees, which cover more than three-quarters of the region. The most colorful displays are put on by sugar and red maples, beech, oak, birch, hickory and red oak (see "Fall Foliage: Nature's Kaleidoscope" in this chapter).

Vast and stately pine forests blanket much of the north, creating its characteristic wild and rugged look. Among them are spruce, balsam fir and hemlock. Southern New England, too, has conifers throughout, the most common being white pine. Among the tallest of eastern trees, the sun-loving white pine may live 400 years or more.

New England grows some 2000 species of flowering plants and ferns. Wildflowers bloom in colorful profusion along the roadsides and in parks and forests. The leader of the wildflowers is the long-stemmed goldenrod, which occurs almost everywhere, as do black-eyed Susans, lupine, purple asters, daisies and Queen Anne's lace. Shady, moist habitats foster several species of orchids, with the pink lady's slipper being the showiest and most common.

Three of the most spectacular wildflower displays are given by the rhododendron, flowering dogwood and mountain laurel, the state flower of Connecticut, which occurs in southern New England. The mountain laurel's lustrous, dark green leaves and six-sided, pink-and-white blossoms form a dense, impenetrable thicket in the forest, sometimes up to 13 feet high.

At the shore grow miles and miles of shrubby wild beach roses with delicate scent and fragile petals of pink, white and fuchsia. Also along the shore grow beach peas, pitch pine, huckleberry, lowbush blueberry, sheep laurel and bayberry, from which the colonists made candles.

Wetlands are prevalent throughout New England, left by glacial action. Swamps, marshes and bogs all have their own little communities of plants, specially adapted to float on the water or emerge from it. Two very characteristic swamp plants are the purplish green skunk cabbage, with a strong odor like a skunk's, and Jack-in-the-Pulpit, which looks like a miniature preacher in a covered pulpit.

In the soft, dark muck and highly organic environs of marshes grow grasses, reeds and sedges such as cattails. Purple loosestrife now covers huge expanses of marsh and wet meadows. Other common marsh plants include duckweed, the smallest flowering plant known; blue flag, a kind of native iris; Joe-pye weed and yellow pond lily.

Sphagnum moss and sedges are partial to bogs, as are knee-high evergreen shrubs, bog laurel, bog rosemary and Labrador Tea, reputedly brewed as a substitute for tea in Colonial times. In low-lying, sandy-floored bogs thrive cranberries, a mainstay of the Massachusetts economy.

FAUNA

Ubiquitous in New England is the gray squirrel, which flirts its bushy tail as it races along telephone wires, up and down trees in city parks and through backyards. Also present everywhere is the dramatically colored eastern chipmunk. Though they are pests to the gardener and the householder, rabbits and woodchucks are numerous, too.

The black bear, New England's only bear, and the moose are perhaps the region's largest land mammals, favoring wilder woodland areas in the north. The homely moose, believe it or not, is a member of the deer family and lives in the deep cover of northern forests in Maine, New Hampshire and Vermont. Another large mammal favored by hunters is the white-tailed deer, which has a bushy white tail, big ears and long legs.

The clownlike Atlantic puffin can be seen on the rocky islets of Maine, the best place in the U.S. to spot this bird, although it has been sighted to the south, as far as Maryland.

The fallow deer, a native of Asia Minor, was released on Nantucket and Martha's Vineyard. The deer became so numerous that they overran the islands and had to be thinned.

Smaller mammals include beaver, red foxes, raccoons, porcupines, skunks and possums. Pity the poor possum: he is poorly adapted to the cold, and many New England possums lose pieces of their paper-thin ears and bare tails to frostbite.

Off the rocky shores in northern coastal waters, harbor seals cavort, hauling out to sun themselves on islands and rocky shores. The coast is also home to the Atlantic white-sided dolphin and several species of whales, best seen up-close on whale-watching trips.

The arrival of spring in New England is announced vociferously by spring peepers, tiny frogs measuring little more than an inch long that climb trees to sing their lyrical nocturnal chorus.

Other native amphibians include the spotted salamander, green frog and bullfrog, a giant of native frogs, sometimes over eight inches long. Reptiles are represented by snapping turtles, painted turtles, box turtles, garter snakes and black racers. New England also has two poisonous snakes, the timber rattlesnake and the northern copperhead, although you will almost surely never see one, so rare and retiring are they.

Situated as it is right along the Atlantic Flyway, New England is a premier place for birding, especially during spring migration. More than 400 species have been sighted in New England, although more than half are transient migratories, shorebirds that rarely come ashore or accidentals carried in by storm winds. Perhaps the most characteristic bird is the gull, found everywhere along the coast.

Canada geese and cormorants have increased their range and numbers, as have ospreys, after being given special nesting platforms on Martha's Vineyard. The handsome loon rules the nor-

Text continued on page 16.

Fall Foliage: Nature's Kaleidoscope

Like nature's last fling before a long slumber, the changing hues of New England's fall foliage precede winter with a fantastic display of color gone wild. Meadows are splashed with orange and purple, lakes appear ringed with fire and whole mountains turn from green to gold.

Better than any fireworks show, this phenomenon draws at least 2.8 million visitors to New England each year. Arriving by car, train, bus and bicycle, they pitch tents in forests, settle into cabins and resorts and pack the roadways everywhere. They come not just to marvel at the scenery but to be part of an all-encompassing experience.

The show starts up around mid-September with a few hints of scarlet and gold, as if the mountains were blushing. Then slowly, the blush becomes a sea of reds and orange and purples that melt together like rivers of shimmering watercolors. Each day brings new colors, new perspectives.

What makes it all happen? Prodded by cool nights and shorter autumn days, tree leaves abandon their green veneer to reveal hues ranging from crimson and sunburst to mahogany, violet and bronze.

Of course, each tree has its own brand of color. Maples flash a brilliant red leaf. Shagbark hickory leaves turn yellow and resemble hammered gold, while witch hazel's flaxen leaves camouflage small yellow flowers. The sumac sports purple saw-toothed leaves and fuzzy twigs resembling antlers. Thin and dainty, cherry leaves go from bright purple to bright yellow.

Then there's the clever speckled alder, a swamp dweller that doesn't change color at all. Its broad green leaves provide a nice contrast to all those reds and yellows and purples.

The farther north you are, the earlier the show starts. Northern areas of Maine, New Hampshire and Vermont set things off, sending waves of color southward as fall advances. The show usually winds down around mid-October, or after the first few frosts.

Though you can "see the leaves" change almost anywhere in New England, the best leaf-peeping exists in mountain areas. Reputed as one of the best fall-foliage spots in the world, New Hampshire's White Mountain National Forest offers almost 800,000 acres of uninterrupted timberland that explodes with continuous color.

Next door, Vermont's Green Mountain National Forest has miles of dense woods, gentle mountains and rushing streams that form a spectacular foliage backdrop. In Maine, head for the area around Machias known as **blueberry barrens**. A vast sweep of blueberry fields, the barrens turn flaming red in the fall and stretch as far as the eye can see. Maine's rock-lined coast also provides extraordinary foliage pageantry, with spiraling scarlet trees set against a sea of aquamarine.

Connecticut's foliage beauty lies in its diverse forests that provide the entire spectrum of colors. Travel from the pastel-colored oaks and birches along the coast to the deep red pepperidge trees in the southwest. Then cut up to the yellow and vermilion maple trees in the northwest corner.

Tiny Rhode Island is all ablaze with fall color, though it is most concentrated in the uplands. Located on the north and west corridors, the uplands are a picture of amber rolling hills, thick timbers and nearly 300 lakes and reservoirs rimmed with rainbow hues.

For a special foliage treat, head for Massachusetts' South Shore, where **cranberry bogs** stretch just south of Boston to Bristol. During October harvests, farmers flood the bogs, forcing the berries to the top of the marsh and creating a sea of bright crimson (see "Exploring Cranberry Country" in Chapter Six).

If you'd like to take home more than photographs, gather an assortment of your favorite leaves and branches. While they're still supple, press the leaves between layers of cardboard, then secure between heavy boards or books and tie tightly with rope. Store in a warm, dry place for ten days, making sure the rope is always snug.

Branches make beautiful bouquets once preserved. Simply split the stems at the base and cover with a solution of two parts water and one part glycerine. Store in a cool, well-ventilated area until leaves show a slight change in color. Remove and hang upside down until dry.

To get the scoop on leaf-peeping conditions, call the foliage hotlines (during fall months only) sponsored by each state: New Hampshire, 800-258-3608; Vermont, 800-837-6668; Maine, 800-777-0317; Rhode Island, 800-556-2484 (route map for fall foliage); Massachusetts, 800-227-6277. Some states supply foliage guides with tips on picture-taking and leaf identification.

A word of advice: fall-foliage season is the most popular vacation time in New England, so it's important to make travel arrangements far in advance—at least six months ahead of time.

thern lakes. There are many species of ducks, in both fresh water and salt water.

Endangered species include the piping plover, roseate tern, peregrine falcon, upland sandpiper, short-eared owl and bald eagle, now nesting in the Quabbin Reservoir in central Massachusetts.

Where to Go

As with Europe, deciding what to see and where to go in New England is a tough choice. The good news is, you'll just have to keep coming back to get to know the real New England.

To help you with your decisions, we'll entice you with some brief descriptions of each state. To get the whole story, read the introductions to each chapter, then the more detailed material on the regions that appeal to you.

Connecticut packs several very different regions into its compact space. We first visit the southeastern part of the state, neighbor to New York. Failing in their effort to annex this corner, New Yorkers have nonetheless succeeded in remaking it in their own image: brimming with the fancy gourmet stores and chichi boutiques so vital to Manhattanites. The state's northwest corner offers historic villages and picturesque lakes. The capital city is Hartford, also known as the insurance capital of the world. South along the coast stands the city of New Haven, an urban industrial center whose main claim to fame is Yale University. From New Haven to the Rhode Island border, coastal Connecticut strings together one pretty fishing and sailing village after another: Essex, Old Saybrook, Mystic and Stonington. Connecticut's rural northeastern corner is the least known and developed area.

With two feet in the ocean, **Rhode Island** boasts miles of sandy beaches with rolling surf rivaling those of the Cape. The coastal villages of South County have a quiet, antique charm, while Victorian Block Island is a little island lost in time. Newport's fabled elegance still shines today in the extravagant summer "cottages" built by Gilded Age multimillionaires. Providence, a revitalized urban center, stands tall with one of the nation's finest historic districts, showcasing restored 18th- and 19th-century period houses. Farther north, the Blackstone Valley, stretching from Pawtucket to Woonsocket and west, is known as the "birthplace of American manufacturing."

With its quaint, cobblestoned streets, old-fashioned neighborhoods and big-city charms, **Boston** delights all who visit. Here is where America's most iconographic history lives on, at such sites as Paul Revere's House and the Old North Church in the North End. Much of Boston sparkles with new polish, especially the waterfront. Perennial favorites include Faneuil Hall Marketplace, the diminutive brick townhouses and sprightly gardens of Beacon Hill, the imposing brownstones of Back Bay and the soaring architecture of Copley Square. Across the Charles River sits Harvard Square, the thriving nexus of intellectual Cambridge. Rural Lexington and Concord are known for their Colonial history.

Cape Cod and the Islands explores some of the most famous and popular areas of the state. Cape Cod is a favored spot for summer vacations. The North Cape is known for its quaint historical villages, the South Cape for Hyannis, home of the Kennedy clan, the Outer Cape for its beaches and sand dunes and Provincetown for its gay life. South of the Cape lie the islands of Martha's Vineyard and Nantucket, both prosperous whaling ports in their day and now drenched in the natural beauty of windswept moors, weathered cottages, pine woods and intimate beaches.

If you plan to drive through New England in winter, be sure to clean off your head- and brake lights periodically. Your lights will be more visible if you keep them clear of the salt and sand residue from the roads.

Wending its way hundreds of miles from Boston's North Shore to New Bedford in the southeast corner of the state, the **Massachusetts Coast** is studded its entire length with lovely resorts, fine sandy beaches and small fishing villages. Gloucester, Rockport and Salem are the highlights of the exclusive North Shore. The Plymouth area is rich in Colonial history and lined with attractive fishing and farming villages with neat clapboarded 18th- and 19th-century sea captains' homes. New Bedford and Fall River have troves of whaling and textile history lore, respectively, as well as oodles of discount outlet stores.

Central and western Massachusetts includes a vast part of the state, from the old industrial city of Worcester west of Boston to the resort-oriented Berkshires on the western border. Rural hamlets, wildlife sanctuaries and state parks ring central Massachusetts, where Old Sturbridge Village re-creates the farming life of the 1840s. The Pioneer Valley stretches up the Connecticut River, through another large city with a rich industrial past, Springfield. A summer capital of music, dance and drama, the Berkshires are serene and sylvan settings of mountains, forests and lakes. Here Norman Rockwell made the streetscapes of Stockbridge famous. The Berkshires have produced a lovely commingling of luxurious resorts, charming inns, gourmet restaurants and ski havens.

No single New England state is more rural than **Vermont**, with its miles of open farmland, covered bridges, maple sugarhouses and small towns with classic village greens and general stores. Some of the best skiing in America is here, as is some of the best cheddar cheese you'll ever eat. Lying on Vermont's western border with New York is the magnificent Lake Champlain, named for explorer Samuel de Champlain and popular with boaters, swimmers and ice fishers. The most rugged region is the Northeast Kingdom, three northern counties bordering Canada that make up a realm of tiny townships, mountains, forests and isolated farms.

Though **New Hampshire**'s tiny seacoast measures a mere 18 miles, along it lies Portsmouth, a jewel of a town that is one of the most handsome refurbished antique settlements on the East Coast. Old textile mills and factories sprawl along the Merrimack River, while outlet stores and other commerce thrive in the state's prosperous, booming southern half. The northern half is a wilderness of lakes, mountains and evergreen forests. Large and beautiful bodies of water like Lake Sunapee and Lake Winnepesaukee, and the White Mountains offer sports enthusiasts numerous choices, as well as plentiful resorts. Weathered barns and country towns complete the scenery in the Monadnock Region.

Maine, the land of Downeast, has sent its most famous delicacy, Maine lobster, all over the world. In this state's wilderness and waterways live thick spruce forests, moose, black bear, loons and deer. More developed than the north, the southern coast presents low-key resort towns and outlet stores, as well as the city of Portland, a restored maritime Victorian jewel. North of Portland is the rugged, rockbound coast, the real Downeast, with its independent-minded towns of Damariscotta, Wiscasset, Camden and Castine. Out on Mount Desert Island, the old-money resort of Bar Harbor reigns, alongside the splendid Acadia National Park. Maine is also Andrew Wyeth country, as seen in the turn-of-the-20th-century world of Monhegan Island, just one of hundreds of islands in Casco Bay. To the north, the Maine woods offer an unparalleled wilderness experience, where visitors can travel for a hundred miles without spotting any sign of civilization. The lakes region provides scenic splendors and water sports galore.

When to Go

SEASONS

A constant battle wages here in New England between bristling battalions of cold, dry Canadian arctic air and laid-back, warm, humid air from the tropics. When these two mix it up, which is frequently, you have New England's legendary changeable weather. The morning may dawn fine and sunny, afternoon turn cold and foggy and nightfall bring a raging northeaster.

More than you might think, the weather varies from south to north. Weather in southeastern New England, tempered by ocean winds, is warmer. While mean temperatures for Connecticut range from 27°F in January to 73°F in July, in Vermont they go from 16° in January to 70° in July. And at the top of New Hampshire's Mount Washington, it may as well be Antarctica.

No matter how you slice it, winters are long and cold here, and the overall effect has been described as "nine months of winter and three of rough sledding." Winters are invariably colder in Vermont and Maine, where temperatures range from -10°F to 10°F and sometimes drop to -30°F. In southern New England, temperatures are more likely to hover in the 20s and 30s in winter.

In the north, snow arrives as early as Thanksgiving and stays on the ground into mid-April, but near the coast in the southeast, it's indecent of snow to put in an appearance until Christmas and subzero weather is almost unheard of. But don't be deterred by the long winter; that's what puts plenty of white stuff on the northern ski slopes.

And, inevitably, there comes the spring thaw, which in the northern country goes by the popular name of "mud season." When the frozen ground starts melting, the result is a muddy morass. Spring is a little less messy in the south, where by mid-March the songbirds are chirping away, followed by greening in another few weeks.

Summer sets in around about mid-June. Days are quite warm, with temperatures ranging from 70 to 90°F, turning to slightly cooler evenings, especially along the shore and in the mountains. Despite the tempering ocean breezes, summer can be humid, as well as foggy and rainy. The weather is hottest in central Massachusetts, in the dry valley of the Connecticut River.

Autumn may be the most wonderful season of all to visit, and certainly the most popular one. Fall colors are at their peak, and all the fall harvests of apples, cider, cranberries and pumpkins are in. Sunny days often warm up to "Indian summer" comfort, energized by cool, crisp nights. In the southeast, autumn lasts right into November.

Both autumn and winter are substantially drier than in other locales. Still, it manages to rain, snow or sleet about one day out of three, making for an annual precipitation of 42 inches and an annual snowfall in the mountains of 90 to 100 inches.

Tourists flock to New England for fall-foliage season (mid-September through October), when it can be very difficult to get

WHAT ABOUT HURRICANES?

Hurricanes, which can occur in subtropical waters any time from late June through September, occasionally veer up the Atlantic coast all the way to New England—but not often. In the 20th century, disastrous hurricanes struck in 1938, when entire coastal towns were swallowed by the sea, and 1991, when then-President George Bush's family home in Maine was demolished by Hurricane Bob. Most recently, Hurricane Ernesto menaced Florida in 2006 before dumping rain on Virginia on its way to New England, although by the time it got there it was downgraded to extratropical intensity. In fact, researchers at Brown University have found that only six hurricane-force storms have struck New England since A.D. 1400.

reservations. High summer (July through Labor Day) is also a busy time, especially along the coast. You might want to consider a visit to a seaside resort in the spring or fall, when rates are lower. Christmas, New Year's and ski season (late January through March) are other popular times with tourists. During the low seasons of April, May and late October to late December, you'll have a much less crowded vacation and a much easier time getting reservations.

CALENDAR OF EVENTS

Each year, New England celebrates its Colonial past by re-enacting historic events that took place in all six states. Other annual observances celebrate the wonderful largesse of this region: apples, maple sugar, blueberries, scallops, clams. The list of merrymaking goes on, with art, music and dance festivals, and occasions honoring many New England traditions, such as shipbuilding, quiltmaking, sheep shearing and Shaker craftsmanship.

JANUARY

Boston The **Chinese New Year** is celebrated in January or February, with three weeks of festivities.

Vermont Snow golf, ice carving, parades and lots of downhill and cross-country skiing events and even snow volleyball comprise the week-long **Stowe Winter Carnival.**

FEBRUARY

Boston The **New England Boat Show**, one of the largest on the East Coast, brings out the latest and fanciest in power and sail. Four of the city's biggest ice hockey–playing colleges (Harvard, Northeastern, Boston University and Boston College) face off in the **Beanpot Tournament.**

New Hampshire The **Dartmouth College Winter Carnival** is an exuberant expression of fun during the winter doldrums.

MARCH

Boston The **New England Spring Flower Show** has been running since 1871, giving a lift to winter-weary Bostonians. The **St. Patrick's Day Parade** thrown by the Irish of South Boston is one of the largest and most festive in America.

Maine Appropriately, the **Can-Am Crown International Sled Dog Race** takes place in the frontier town of Fort Kent.

APRIL

Boston The nation's premier running event, the **Boston Marathon** is only one of several signal events on **Patriot's Day.** Other activities commemorating Revolutionary War events include a parade plus re-enactments of Paul Revere's famous ride and the Battle of Lexington and Concord.

Cape Cod and the Islands During Nantucket's **Daffodil Festival**, hundreds of these sprightly blooms decorate shop windows.

Vermont At the **Vermont Maple Festival** in St. Albans, sample maple products, watch contests and enjoy the entertainment.

MAY

Connecticut Picnic-style lobster dinners, naturally, are the main event at the **Lobster Days** during Memorial Day weekend at Mystic Seaport.

Rhode Island **Gaspee Days** in Warwick, which often runs into June, commemorate the colonists' burning of Britain's HMS *Gaspee* in 1772—one of the first acts of hostility leading to the Revolution—with historic re-enactments, a parade, arts and crafts, food and entertainment.

Boston **Lilac Sunday** at the Arnold Arboretum finds over 500 lilacs in bloom (over 200 varieties).

Central and Western Massachusetts The **Brimfield Outdoors Antiques and Collectibles Show**, also held in July and September, draw more than 5000 dealers for week-long events in the small town of Brimfield.

Vermont Stowe's annual **Basketry Festival** hosts more than a dozen instructors teaching over 30 workshops.

JUNE

Connecticut Celebrate the blooming of over 15,000 rose bushes at the Greater Hartford **Rose Weekend** held in the Elizabeth Park Rose Garden.

Rhode Island A different area of historic Providence is on view each year during the **Festival of Historic Houses.**

Boston The **Bunker Hill Parade** features contemporary patriots dressed in Revolutionary uniforms fighting the famous battle again.

Cape Cod and the Islands At Hyannis' **Annual Chowder Festival,** you can vote for the best chowder and enjoy the live entertainment.

Massachusetts Coast Anything made with fresh strawberries can be served at the **Annual Strawberry Festival** in Ipswich.

Central and Western Massachusetts Wine and cheese on the lawn while listening to the Boston Symphony Orchestra is the attraction of the **Tanglewood Music Festival** (which runs into September) in Lenox. One of the Northeast's best-known dance festivals takes place at **Jacob's Pillow** in the Berkshires.

Vermont Hot-air balloons light up the scenery at the **Balloon Festival and Crafts Fair** in Quechee.

Maine The **Old Port Festival** brings the historic part of Portland to life with a street fair of arts and crafts, music, jugglers, children's events and ethnic foods. **Windjammer Days** in Boothbay Harbor show off these classic schooners under full sail in a dress parade.

JULY

Connecticut The **Annual Boombox Parade**, sponsored by the town of Windham, celebrates the fourth with hundreds of locals marching to the beat of their own boomboxes.

Boston Every weekend in July and August, **Italian street festivals** in the North End honor patron saints with colorful parades and festivities. The **Boston Harborfest** offers more than 200 activities celebrating the harbor at 30 sites, highlighted by a chowderfest. Local restaurants serve up heaping samples of clam chowder as they battle for the tastiest bowl of "chowdah" as determined by popular vote at the **Chowderfest** on City Hall Plaza. The **Boston Pops Fourth of July Concert** on the Esplanade's Hatch Shell promises an evening of free music and glorious fireworks.

Cape Cod and the Islands In early July, the **Annual Indian Pow Wow** is held at 55 Acres in Mashpee. The pow-wow attracts American Indians from all over the United States, as well as from Canada, Mexico and some Central and South American countries. The **Edgartown Yacht Club Regatta,** held on Martha's Vineyard, is one of New England's best and most serious yacht races.

Massachusetts Coast In Gloucester, the **Robin Hood Faire at Hammond Castle** has magic shows, music and general renaissance merriment. **Race Week** in Marblehead includes sailboat races, parades and concerts.

New Hampshire The Strawbery Banke Museum offers **An American Celebration** every July 4th with food, games, music and costumed participants.

Maine Celebrate that incredibly edible food in Pittsfield during the **Central Maine Egg Festival.** There are parades, fireworks, dances and, of course, lots of breakfast.

AUGUST

Connecticut The **Pilot Pen Tennis Women's Championships** showcases top women tennis stars in world-class play at Yale University.

Rhode Island Some of the world's best jazz musicians entertain the thousands sprawled out on the green lawns of Fort Adams State Park in Newport at the JVC **Jazz Festival**. B. B. King, Randy Newman and Leon Redbone have all performed at the **Newport Folk Festival,** also in Fort Adams State Park. A haven for independent filmmakers, the **Rhode Island International Film Festival** screens more than 150 titles in Providence.

Cape Cod and the Islands The **Falmouth Road Race** is the event of the year on the lower Cape, where the seven-mile race is run along the beach of the Vineyard Sound. On Nantucket, the **Annual Antiques Show** offers quality antiques. Imaginations go wild at the **Sandcastle & Sculpture Contest** at Jetties Beach on Nantucket. Also on Nantucket is the **Annual Billfish Tournament,** a big event where anglers compete for the biggest catch of each species. In the Vineyard's Oak Bluffs, **Illumination Night** is pure magic, with hundreds of paper lanterns strung between the Gothic homes.

Massachusetts Coast New Bedford's **Annual Feast of the Blessed Sacrament**, the largest Portuguese feast in America, features terrific ethnic food at budget prices.

New Hampshire Over 1000 car enthusiasts flock to Loudon for the annual **Vintage Celebration**, a restored-car race at the New Hampshire International Speedway. The event includes a parade of elegant vintage automobiles from around the country.

Maine A blueberry pancake breakfast is just one of the many activities at the **Union Fair** in Union, noted for its blueberry festival.

SEPTEMBER

Connecticut The South Norwalk **Oyster Festival** has something for everyone: oysters galore, seafood and ethnic foods, nationally known singers and bands, arts and crafts, tall ships and marine skills demonstrations.

Boston The **Boston Film Festival** includes feature-length movies by major studios as well as more unusual films from independent producers, students and foreign filmmakers.

Cape Cod and the Islands The **Harwich Cranberry Festival** includes a week of parades, contests, fireworks and exhibits. **Tivoli Day Festival** is held in the middle of the month in Oak Bluffs, on Martha's Vineyard, where there's a colorful street fair.

Massachusetts Coast At the **Gloucester Schooner Festival**, held on Labor Day weekend, you can watch races, a boat parade and other maritime activities.

Central and Western Massachusetts **The Big E**, or the **Eastern States Exposition**, in West Springfield is the East's largest annual fair, strong on agricultural and animal exhibits, horse shows and rides and food galore.

New Hampshire The **Scottish Highlands Games** draw thousands of people to the Hopkinton Fairgrounds; some show up in kilts for highlander games and music.

OCTOBER

Boston More than 5000 oarsmen compete in the **Head of the Charles Regatta**, now a two-day rowing spectacular. **Lowell Celebrates Kerouac** stages poetry readings and organizes "beat" tours in honor of '50s literary giant Jack Kerouac, who was born and lived in Lowell.

Massachusetts Coast If ever a place looked haunted, it would be **Hammond Castle** in Gloucester during Halloween, where ghosts and ghouls spook and delight you as you tour this romantic castle. **Haunted Happenings**, Salem's citywide Halloween festival, includes haunted-house tours, costume parades, parties, magic shows, psychics and candlelight tours with, of course, witches.

Central and Western Massachusetts The **Topsfield Fair** is another vintage event, with a petting farm, ethnic foods and midway rides.

Maine Held since the mid-1800s, the **Fryeburg Fair** sticks close to its agricultural roots during week-long festivities.

NOVEMBER

Massachusetts Coast Have a traditional turkey dinner with all the trimmings in America's hometown, Plymouth, during its annual **Thanksgiving Dinner.**

Central and Western Massachusetts Cascade mums, standard varieties and new hybrids are shown at the two-week-long **Chrysanthemum Show** at Smith College in Northampton.

DECEMBER

Connecticut Lantern light tours and a **Carol Sing** mark Christmas at the Mystic Seaport Museum.

Boston Staged by the National Center of Afro-American Artists, Langston Hughes' **Black Nativity** is a holiday spiritual tradition. Hundreds of events mark **First Night**, an alcohol-free New Year's Eve celebration held throughout the city. There's a huge pageant, plus choral groups, ice sculptures, storytellers, acrobats, puppeteers and art and drama presentations. The **Boston Tea Party Reenactment** finds patriots dressed as Indians throwing chests of tea into Boston Harbor one more time.

Cape Cod and the Islands Main Street looks like something out of Dickens when the Nantucket **Annual Christmas Stroll** takes place, with a weekend of carolers and other Yuletide festivities.

Massachusetts Coast **Salem Holiday Happenings** includes fairs, crafts, house tours, auctions, concerts and more.

New Hampshire The **Candlelight Stroll** takes place the first two weekends in December at The Strawbery Banke Museum in Portsmouth illuminates four centuries of houses.

Before You Go

VISITORS CENTERS

As well as large cities, many small towns have chambers of commerce or visitor information centers that provide detailed information about the area you wish to visit; a number of these facilities are listed in *Hidden New England* under the appropriate state or region.

Travel information on Connecticut is available from the **Office of Tourism.** ~ 505 Hudson Street, Hartford, CT 06106; 860-270-8081, 800-282-6863, fax 860-270-8077; www.tourism.state.ct.us.

For Rhode Island, contact the **Tourism Division.** ~ 315 Iron Horse Way, Suite 101, Providence, RI 02908; 401-278-9100, 800-556-2484, fax 401-273-8270; www.visitrhodeisland.com.

For Massachusetts information, contact the **Massachusetts Office of Travel & Tourism.** ~ 10 Park Plaza, Suite 4510, Boston, MA 02116; 617-973-8500, 800-227-6277, fax 617-973-8525; www.massvacation.com.

For more detailed information on Boston, contact the **Greater Boston Convention and Visitors Bureau.** ~ 2 Copley Place, Suite

105, Boston, MA 02116; 617-536-4100, 888-733-2678, fax 617-424-7664; www.bostonusa.com.

For information on vacationing in Vermont, write the **Vermont Department of Tourism and Marketing.** ~ 6 Baldwin Street, Drawer 33, Montpelier, VT 05633; 802-828-3676, 800-837-6668, fax 802-828-3233; www.travel-vermont.com, e-mail info@vermontvacation.com

In New Hampshire, contact the **Division of Travel and Tourism** for travel information. ~ 172 Pembroke Road, P.O. Box 1856, Concord, NH 03302; 603-271-2665, 800-386-4664, fax 603-271-6870; www.visitnh.gov, e-mail travel@dred.state.nh.us.

In Maine, write the **Maine Office of Tourism.** ~ 59 State House Station, Augusta, ME 04333; 888-624-6345; www.visitmaine.com.

PACKING

Packing for a visit to New England is a little trickier than for other destinations. What you must take is dictated by the fickle Yankee weather, which might change at any minute. A warm, sunny day can turn cool and foggy without so much as a by-your-leave. The best bet is to bring layers of clothing that can be added or subtracted as needed. Even in the summer, bring some long-sleeved shirts, long pants and lightweight sweaters and jackets, along with your T-shirts, jeans and bathing suit.

Fall and spring call for a full round of warm clothing, from long pants and sweaters to jackets, hats and gloves. While fall days are often sunny and warm, fall nights can turn quite crisp and cool. Bring your heaviest, warmest clothes in winter: thick sweaters, knitted hats, down jackets and ski clothes.

Boston Brahmins notwithstanding, most of New England is a pretty casual place, especially in summer, when everyone has sand in his shoes. No one will look askance if you wear your deck shoes and L. L. Bean pants to dinner at most restaurants, particularly in coastal resort areas like Kennebunkport. New England is less casual, however, than a warm-weather resort, and you can't get into most restaurants or bars without a shirt or shoes, or if you're wearing a bathing suit.

Boston is the most conservatively dressed place you'll visit. Some downtown Boston restaurants have dress codes, requiring men to wear jackets and ties and women to be "appropriately attired."

New Englanders are used to rolling up their car windows every night in summer, knowing it may rain any minute. Rain, though not usually heavy, is a big part of every season, so be sure to bring an umbrella and a raincoat, even in the summer.

Some of the streets are almost as old as New England itself. In many areas such as Boston, on these rough, cobblestone ways you need sturdy, comfortable shoes that can take this kind of beating and be kind to your feet. Women should never attempt to navigate cobblestone streets in high heels. Likewise, some New England shores can be rocky. A pair of rubber shoes or old sneakers for swimming is sometimes advisable.

Though New England is not the Caribbean, you can get just as impressive a sunburn here. Bring a good sunscreen, especially to the beach, where sand and water reflect the sun's rays more intensely. Bring insect repellent in the summertime as insurance against the greenhead flies at the shore and blackflies in the mountains.

For the northern woods of Maine and other out-of-the-way places, you'll have far fewer stores to rely on, so come prepared with whatever gear you'll be using. It's wise to consult a backpacking or camping supply store before you leave about what to bring for the weather conditions likely at the time of your travels.

No spot in New England is more than a day's drive from any other.

When you come here, you'll need nothing but the best street and road maps. Many roads in New England are winding, poorly marked or not marked at all, following an age-old philosophy that if you live here, you know where you're going, and if you don't, you have no business being here anyway.

You may want to toss in an antique guide along with your other reading; the country's oldest antiques are for sale here. Bring your camera for capturing quintessential New England vistas of lighthouses and white-steepled villages, and for heaven's sake, don't forget your copy of *Hidden New England*!

LODGING

Visiting New England is your opportunity to stay in some of the most historic lodgings this country has to offer. A number of them date to the 18th century, such as Longfellow's Wayside Inn in Sudbury, Massachusetts. Randall's Ordinary in North Stonington, Connecticut, dates to the 17th century.

New England is where the bed-and-breakfast movement gained ground in this country, and the region is thick with historic farmhouses and sea captains' homes turned into bed and breakfasts. These are often rambling, cozy affairs complete with fireplace, bookshelves and resident cat. But bed-and-breakfast booking agencies, especially in urban areas, also list host homes with a spare room, which isn't quite the same thing. Be sure to ask whether a bed and breakfast is a real inn or not.

In addition, accommodations include mom-and-pop motels, chain hotels and rustic seaside cottages where you'll awaken to the sounds of surf and crying gulls. Cities have the most deluxe highrise hotels, but outside urban areas, lodgings are generally casual and lowrise.

Whatever your preference and budget, you can probably find something to suit your taste with the help of the individual chapters in this book. Remember, rooms are scarce and prices rise in the high season, which is summer, fall-foliage time and Christmas throughout New England, and ski season in northern areas.

There are lots of special weekend and holiday packages at the larger hotels, and off-season rates drop significantly, making a week- or month-long stay a real bargain.

Accommodations in this book are organized by state or region and classified according to price. These refer to high-season, double-occupancy rates, so if you're looking for low-season bargains, be sure to inquire about them.

Budget lodgings generally cost less than $60 a night for two people and are satisfactory and clean but modest. *Moderate*-priced lodgings run from $60 to $120; what they offer in terms of luxury will depend on their location, but in general they provide larger rooms and more attractive surroundings. At *deluxe*-priced accommodations, you can expect to spend between $120 and $175. In hotels of this price you'll typically find spacious rooms, a fashionable lobby, a restaurant or two and often some shops. *Ultra-deluxe* facilities, priced above $175, are a region's finest, offering all the amenities of a deluxe hotel plus plenty of luxurious extras, such as jacuzzis and exercise rooms, 24-hour room service and gourmet dining.

If you've got your heart set on a room with a water view, be sure to pin that down. Be forewarned that "oceanside" doesn't always mean right on the beach. If you want to save money, try lodgings a block or so away from the water. They almost always offer lower rates than rooms within sight of the surf, and the savings are often worth the short stroll to the beach.

DINING

Succulent native seafood stars at legions of New England restaurants, from lobster in the rough and tender bay scallops to codfish, mussels, steamers and milky clam chowder.

Besides seafood and traditional Yankee foods, New England restaurants also serve up ethnic cuisines of every stripe, plus gourmet foods and fast food. No matter what your taste or budget, there's a restaurant for you.

Within each chapter, restaurants are organized geographically. Restaurants listed in this book offer lunch and dinner unless otherwise noted. Each entry describes the cuisine and ambience and categorizes the restaurant in one of four price ranges. Dinner entrées at *budget* restaurants usually cost $9 or less. The ambience is informal, service speedy, the crowd often a local one. *Moderate*-priced eateries charge between $9 and $18 for dinner; surroundings are casual but pleasant, the menu offers more variety and the pace is usually slower. *Deluxe* restaurants tab their entrées above $18; cuisines may be simple or sophisticated, but the decor is plusher and the service more personalized. *Ultra-*

deluxe establishments, where entrées begin at $24, are often the gourmet gathering places; here cooking is (hopefully) a fine art, and the service should be impeccable.

Some restaurants, particularly those that depend on the summer trade in coastal areas, close for the winter.

Breakfast and lunch menus vary less in price from one restaurant to another. Even deluxe establishments usually offer light breakfasts and luncheons, priced within a few dollars of their budget-minded competitors. These smaller meals can be a good time to test expensive restaurants.

TRAVELING WITH CHILDREN

New England is a wonderful place to bring children. Besides many child-oriented museums, the region also has hundreds of beaches and parks, and many nature sanctuaries sponsor children's activities year-round.

Travel agents can help with arrangements; they can reserve airline bulkhead seats where there is plenty of room and determine which flights are least crowded. If you are traveling by car, be sure to take along such necessities as water and juices, snacks and toys. Always allow extra time for getting places, especially on rural roads.

A first-aid kit is a must for any trip you embark on. Along with adhesive bandages, antiseptic cream and something to stop itching, include any medicines your pediatrician might recommend to treat allergies, colds, diarrhea or any chronic problems your child may have.

At the beach, take extra care with your children's skin the first few days, even though this is not the Caribbean. Children's tender young skin can suffer severe sunburn before you know it. Hats for the kids are a good idea, along with liberal applications of a good sunscreen. Never take your eyes off your children at the shore. If you are traveling in winter, never leave a child alone near a frozen lake.

Quite a few New England bed and breakfasts don't accept children, so be sure of the policy when you make reservations. If you need a crib or cot, arrange for it ahead of time.

All-night stores are scarce in rural areas, and stores in small towns often close early. You may go a long distance between stores that can supply you with essentials, so be sure to be well stocked with diapers, baby food and other needs when you are on the go. But all-night stores such as Store 24 and Christy's are plentiful in urban areas.

To find specific activities for children, consult local newspapers. The *Boston Globe Calendar* has especially comprehensive listings that cover a good part of New England. ~ www.boston.com/globe/calendar.

Travelers Aid Family Services is a resource for any traveler in need and maintains booths at the major transportation terminals.

Volunteers can arrange to meet young children who are traveling alone. ~ 17 East Street, off of Atlantic Avenue, Boston, MA 02111; 617-542-7286, fax 617-542-9545; www.taboston.org.

WOMEN TRAVELING ALONE

Traveling solo grants an independence and freedom different from that of traveling with a partner, but single travelers are more vulnerable to crime and should take additional precautions.

It's unwise to hitchhike and probably best to avoid inexpensive accommodations on the outskirts of town; the money saved does not outweigh the risk. Bed and breakfasts, youth hostels and YWCAs are generally your safest bet for lodging, and they also foster an environment ideal for bonding with fellow travelers.

Keep all valuables well-hidden and hold onto cameras and purses. Avoid late-night treks or strolls through undesirable parts of town, but if you find yourself in this situation, continue walking with a confident air until you reach a safe haven. A fierce scowl never hurts.

These hints should by no means deter you from seeking out adventure. Wherever you go, stay alert, use your common sense and trust your instincts. For more hints, get a copy of *Safety and Security for Women Who Travel* (Travelers Tales).

If you are hassled or threatened in some way, never be afraid to yell for assistance. It's a good idea to carry change for a phone call and to know the number to call in case of emergency. Most areas have 24-hour hotlines for victims of rape and violent crime. In the Boston area, call the **Boston Area Rape Crisis Center.** ~ 617-492-7273. In New Hampshire, contact **Sexual Assault Support Services.** ~ 603-436-4107, 888-747-7070 (in New Hampshire). In Rhode Island, **Sexual Assault and Trauma Resource Center** provides assistance. ~ 401-421-4100, 800-494-8100.

GAY & LESBIAN TRAVELERS

While New England is generally not known for its progressive attitudes, the people who live here tend to be very independent minded and not apt to stick their noses in other people's business. This allows gay or lesbian travelers to feel comfortable here. Whether you're interested in exploring the scenic rural backroads or sightseeing in the region's cities, New England has much to offer. The region also boasts several gay and lesbian hot spots to which this guidebook dedicates special "gay-specific" sections.

The first of these sections covers Boston's gay neighborhood in the city's South End. Both Boston and nearby Cambridge are home to large gay communities, with the South End area of Boston offering the greatest concentration of gay-friendly bars, nightclubs and restaurants (see "Boston Gay Scene" in Chapter Four).

Located at the tip of Cape Cod and attracting gay and lesbian travelers from all over the world is the well-known resort mecca of Provincetown (see "Provincetown" in Chapter Five).

The bucolic Pioneer Valley in central Massachusetts, which includes the college towns of Amherst and Northampton, is more commonly known in the gay community as "The Happy Valley," and has one of the largest lesbian communities in the United States (see "The Happy Valley" in Chapter Seven).

Gay and lesbian publications providing entertainment listings and happenings are available in many of the region's towns. *The Metroline*, a free bi-monthly that you can find in cafés and bookstores, covers Connecticut, Rhode Island, Massachusetts and Maine. ~ 860-231-8845, fax 860-233-8338; www.metroline-online.com, e-mail info@metroline-online.com.

Hidden New England lists gay-friendly lodging, dining and nightlife scattered throughout the six states. You can look in the index under "gay-friendly travel" to find these listings.

In Boston, you can get the weekly *Bay Windows* for entertainment listings. ~ 617-266-6670, fax 617-266-5973; www.baywindows.com, e-mail calendar@baywindows.com. Boston also has the free *IN Newsweekly*, available at cafés and bookstores. ~ 617-426-8246, fax 617-426-8264; www.innewsweekly.com.

SENIOR TRAVELERS

New England is a hospitable place for senior citizens to visit; countless museums, historic sights and even restaurants and hotels offer senior discounts that cut a substantial chunk off vacation costs. And many golden-agers from hotter climes flock to New England for its cool summers.

The **American Association of Retired Persons** offers membership to anyone over 50. AARP benefits include travel discounts. ~ 601 E Street Northwest, Washington, DC 20049; 888-687-2277, fax 202-434-7688; www.aarp.org, e-mail member@aarp.org.

Elderhostel offers many educational courses in a variety of New England locations that are all-inclusive packages at colleges and universities. ~ 11 Avenue de Lafayette, Boston, MA 02111; 877-426-8056, fax 888-426-2166; www.elderhostel.org.

Be extra careful about health matters. In New England's changeable and sometimes cold weather, seniors are more at risk of suffering hypothermia, especially during prolonged exposure to wind. Older travelers should be very careful when walking to beware of falls. Sidewalks may be poorly paved or buckled in places, and cobblestone streets are easy to lodge an ankle in.

Out-of-state prescriptions are not filled so try to bring extra of whatever medications you use. Or consider carrying a medical record with you, including your history and current medical status as well as your doctor's name, phone number and address. Make sure that your insurance covers you while you are away from home.

Travelers Aid Family Services can provide emergency financial assistance and medical and social service referrals, help find low-cost accommodations, give directions and information and train, plane and bus connections. Volunteers can arrange to meet travelers who have special needs. ~ 17 East Street, off Atlantic Avenue, Boston, MA 02111; 617-542-7286, fax 617-542-9545; www.taboston.org.

DISABLED TRAVELERS

New England has made real strides toward making its many attractions and services handicapped-accessible. Parking spaces for the handicapped are provided at most services and attractions, although few buses are handicapped-accessible.

Special escorted group tours are offered by **The Guided Tour, Inc.** ~ 7900 Old York Road, Suite 114-B, Elkins Park, PA 19027; 215-782-1370, 800-783-5841, fax 215-635-2637; www.guidedtour.com, e-mail gtour400@aol.com.

There are many organizations offering general information. Among these are:

The **Society for Accessible Travel & Hospitality** (SATH). ~ 347 5th Avenue, Suite 605, New York, NY 10016; 212-447-7284, fax 212-447-1928; www.sath.org, e-mail sathtravel@aol.com.

The **MossRehab ResourceNet.** ~ MossRehab Hospital, 1200 West Tabor Road, Philadelphia, PA 19141; 215-456-9900, 800-225-5667; www.mossresourcenet.org, e-mail staff1@mossresourcenet.org.

Also providing information for travelers with disabilities is **Travelin' Talk**, a networking organization. ~ P.O. Box 1796, Wheat Ridge, CO 80034; 303-232-2979; www.travelintalk.net, e-mail travelin@travelintalk.net. They also run **Access-Able Travel Source**, with worldwide information online. ~ 303-232-2979; www.access-able.com.

Travelers Aid Family Services can arrange for volunteers to meet disabled travelers. ~ 17 East Street, off Atlantic Avenue, Boston, MA 02111; 617-542-7286, fax 617-542-9545; www.taboston.org.

FOREIGN TRAVELERS

Passports and Visas Most foreign visitors are required to obtain a passport and tourist visa to enter the United States. Contact your nearest United States Embassy or Consulate well in advance to obtain a visa and to check on any other entry requirements.

Customs Requirements Foreign travelers are allowed to carry in the following: 200 cigarettes (one carton), 100 cigars or two kilograms (4.4 pounds) of smoking tobacco; one liter of alcohol for personal use (you must be 21 years of age to bring in alcohol); and US$100 worth of duty-free gifts that can include an additional quantity of 100 cigars. You may bring in any amount of currency, but must fill out a form if you bring in over US$10,000. Carry any prescription drugs in clearly marked containers. (You may have to produce a written prescription or doctor's statement for the customs officer.) Meat or meat products, seeds, plants, fruits and narcotics are not allowed to be brought into the United States. Contact the **United States Customs Service** for further information. ~ 1300 Pennsylvania Avenue Northwest, Washington, DC 20229; 202-354-1000; www.customs.treas.gov.

Driving If you plan to rent a car, an international driver's license should be obtained *before* arriving in New England. Some rental companies require both a foreign license and an international driver's license. Many car rental agencies require a lessee to be 25 years of age; all require a major credit card. Seat belts are mandatory for the driver and all passengers. Children under the age of 5 or 40 pounds should be in the back seat in approved child-safety restraints.

Currency United States money is based on the dollar. Bills come in six denominations: $1, $5, $10, $20, $50 and $100. Every dollar is divided into 100 cents. Coins are the penny (1 cent), nickel (5 cents), dime (10 cents) and quarter (25 cents). Half-dollars and dollar coins are rarely used. You may not use foreign currency to purchase goods and services in the United States. Consider buying traveler's checks in dollar amounts. You may also use credit cards affiliated with an American company such as Interbank, Visa, Barclay Card and American Express.

Electricity and Electronics Electric outlets use currents of 120 volts, 60 cycles. To operate appliances made for other electrical systems, you need a transformer or other adapter. Travelers who use laptop computers for telecommunication should be aware that modem configurations for U.S. telephone systems may be different from their European counterparts. Similarly, the U.S. format for DVDs (Region 1) is different from that in Europe; National Park Service visitors centers and other stores that sell souvenir DVDs often have them available in European format on request.

Weights and Measurements The United States uses the English system of weights and measures. American units and their metric equivalents are as follows: 1 inch = 2.5 centimeters; 1 foot = 0.3 meter; 1 yard = 0.9 meter; 1 mile = 1.6 kilometers; 1 ounce = 28 grams; 1 pound = 0.45 kilogram; 1 quart (liquid) = 0.9 liter.

Outdoor Adventures

CAMPING

New England offers a rich spectrum of camping experiences, from sites in the deep wilderness of the White Mountains and the Green Mountains and quiet lakeside spots to protected forests and recreational vehicle parks.

For information on camping in the Green Mountain National Forest, contact the **U.S. Forest Service.** ~ 2538 Depot Street, Manchester Center, VT 05255; 802-362-2307; www.fs.fed.us/r9/gmfl.

Brochures on camping in the White Mountains are available from the **White Mountain National Forest.** ~ 719 Main Street,

Facts and Foibles

Population—14.2 million
Square miles—69,746
Miles of coastline—6130
States with no coastline—1 (Vermont)
Square miles of lakes, rivers and streams—3660
Number of farms—27,450
Number of Fortune 500 companies—49
Percentage of college graduates—30.7
Colleges and universities
  In New England—264
  In Massachusetts—121
  In Boston—47
U.S. presidents born here—8
Percentage of native New Englanders in population—67.8
Inventive inventions—laughing gas, frozen food, sandpaper, snow-making machines, basketball, Monopoly, chocolate chip cookies
Gallons of maple syrup produced annually in Vermont—500,000
Covered bridges in Vermont—107
Pounds of Maine lobster caught annually—55–70 million
Pounds of Maine blueberries picked annually—70 million
Bushels of New Hampshire apples picked annually—1.5 million
Miles of stone walls in Connecticut—50,000
Famous cookie named for a Boston suburb—Fig Newton, for Newton
Highest natural point—Mount Washington in New Hampshire (6288 feet)
Highest manmade point—John Hancock Tower in Boston (790 feet)
Nation's first
  Highway—Route 20, Old Boston Post Road, from Boston to New York City
  Synagogue—Touro Synagogue (1759) in Newport
  College—Harvard (1639) in Cambridge, Massachusetts
  Postage stamp—printed in Brattleboro, Vermont (1846)
  Recipient of Social Security—Ida Fuller of Ludlow, Vermont, in 1940 received check #00-000-001 for $22.45
  Human Flying Stunt—John Childs (1757), using a half glider/half umbrella, jumped from the steeple of Boston's Old North Church

Laconia, NH 03246; 603-528-8721; www.fs.fed.us/r9/white_mountain.

In Connecticut, quite a few state parks and forests are open for camping. The **Bureau of Outdoor Recreation** has information on fees and regulations. ~ Department of Environmental Protection, 79 Elm Street, Hartford, CT 06106; 860-424-3200; www.dep.state.ct.us.

The beautiful Acadia National Park in Maine, as well as about half the state parks, permit camping. For information about Acadia, contact **Acadia National Park.** ~ P.O. Box 177, Bar Harbor, ME 04609; 207-288-3338; www.nps.gov/acad. Or contact the **Bureau of Parks and Lands.** ~ 107 State House Station, Augusta, ME 04333-0022; 207-287-3821. The **Maine Campground Owners Association** offers a free camping guide. ~ 10 Falcon Road, Suite 1, Lewiston, ME 04240; 207-782-5874; www.campmaine.com. At privately owned campsites, facilities range from rustic basics in wilderness areas to fairly deluxe cabins and cottages.

For information on camping at Massachusetts state forest sites, contact the **State Division of Forests and Parks.** ~ 251 Causeway Street, Boston MA 02114; 617-727-3180. Free camping guides are published by the **Massachusetts Association of Campground Owners.** ~ P.O. Box 79, Weymouth, MA 02191, 508-759-3856; www.campmass.com. Guides are also available from the **Massachusetts Office of Travel and Tourism.** ~ 10 Park Plaza, Suite 4510, Boston, MA 02116; 617-973-8500, 800-227-6277; www.massvacation.com. Camping is also permitted on several of the Boston Harbor Islands (see the "Beaches & Parks" sections of Chapter Four).

New Hampshire Camping Guide, a free guide to New Hampshire campgrounds covering private, state and White Mountain National Forest sites, is published by the **New Hampshire Campground Owners Association.** ~ 427 Route 115, P.O. Box 320, Twin Mountain, NH 03595; www.ucampnh.com, e-mail ucampnh@ucampnh.com.

In Rhode Island, the **Tourism Division** provides information on facilities and permits, and offers *The Rhode Island Outdoor Guide*, which includes a section on camping. ~ 315 Iron Horse Way, Suite 101, Providence, RI 02908; 401-278-9100, 800-556-2484, fax 401-222-2102.

The **Vermont Department of Forests, Parks and Recreation** operates 39 campgrounds with 2200 campsites. They'll also provide a list of private campgrounds in the state. ~ Agency of Natural Resources, 103 South Main Street, Waterbury, VT 05671; 802-241-3670, fax 802-244-1481; www.vtstateparks.com.

WILDERNESS PERMITS Primitive campsites are provided in certain state parks and recreation areas. While wilderness camping away from designated areas is sometimes not allowed, in other cases it is allowable without a permit.

No permit is needed for wilderness camping in either the Green Mountain National Forest or the White Mountain National Forest. But Acadia National Park does not allow camping away from designated areas.

Connecticut allows backpack camping on state lands; a wilderness permit is needed. Contact the **Department of Environmental Protection.** ~ Eastern District Office, 209 Hebron Road, Marlborough, CT 06447; 860-295-9523; www.dep.state.ct.us. Or get in touch with the DEP's **Western District Office.** ~ 230 Plymouth Road, Harwinton, CT 06791; 860-485-0226; www.dep.state.ct.us.

In Maine and New Hampshire, no permit is required to camp in wilderness areas in state forests.

Rhode Island and Massachusetts do not allow camping outside of designated camping areas in state forests.

BOATING

Boating is one of the most popular activities in New England. Sailboats, canoes, windjammers, power boats, cruise boats and ferries all ply the coastline and region's large lakes and rivers. You can bring your own boat and get your feet wet doing some New England cruising, or rent or charter a craft here. Each chapter in this book offers suggestions on how to go about finding the vessel of your choice.

Charts for boaters and divers are widely sold at marine shops and bookstores throughout New England.

Boating regulations vary slightly from state to state. In Connecticut, for a list of boating regulations and safety information, contact the **Department of Environmental Protection.** ~ Boating Safety Division, 333 Ferry Road, P.O. Box 280, Old Lyme, CT 06371; 860-434-8638.

For Rhode Island regulations, contact the **Office of Boat Registration and Licensing.** ~ 235 Promenade Street, Room 360, Providence, RI 02908; 401-222-6647.

Massachusetts boating information can be obtained from the **Division of Law Enforcement.** ~ 251 Causeway Street, Boston, MA 02114; 617-727-1843; www.state.ma.us.

Vermont boating regulations can be obtained from the **Vermont State Police.** ~ 2777 St. George Road, Williston, VT 05495; 802-878-7111 ext. 2014, fax 802-878-2742; www.dps.state.vt.us/vtsp, e-mail dbegiebi@dps.state.vt.us.

In New Hampshire, contact the **New Hampshire Marine Patrol.** ~ 31 Dock Road, Gilford, NH 03249; 603-293-2037, 877-642-9700 (in New Hampshire); www.nh.gov/safety, e-mail marinepatrol@safety.state.nh.us.

For Maine regulations inland, contact the **Department of Inland Fisheries and Wildlife.** ~ 284 State Street, Station 41, Augusta, ME 04333; 207-287-6008; www.maine.gov/ifw. For

Maine's coast, contact the **Department of Marine Resources.** ~ 21 State House Station, Augusta, ME 04333; 207-624-6550; www.maine.gov/dmr.

Canoe trails in Connecticut are described in various brochures for sale through the **Bureau of Outdoor Recreation.** ~ Department of Environmental Protection, 79 Elm Street, Hartford, CT 06106; 860-424-3555; www.dep.state.ct.us, e-mail dep.store@po.state.ct.us.

WATER SAFETY

Even in winter, you'll find diehard surfers and windsurfers riding the waves in their wetsuits. Swimming, waterskiing, jetboating and floating on inflatable rafts are popular activities in the summertime.

People have drowned in New England waters, but drownings are avoided when you respect the power of the water, heed appropriate warnings and use good sense.

Wherever you swim, never do it alone. On the ocean or in large lakes like Lake Champlain or Lake Winnipesaukee, always face the incoming waves. They can bring unpleasant surprises even to the initiated. If you go surfing, learn the proper techniques and dangers from an expert before you start out. Respect signs warning of dangerous currents and undertows. If you get caught in a rip current or any tow that makes you feel out of control, don't try to swim against it. Head across it, paralleling the shore. Exercise caution in the use of floats, inner tubes or rafts; unexpected currents can quickly carry you out to sea.

There are some jellyfish that inflict a mild sting, but that is easily treated with an over-the-counter antiseptic. If you go scalloping or musseling, swim in or wade in murky waters where shellfish dwell, wear canvas or rubber shoes to protect your feet.

Remember, you are a guest in the sea. All rights belong to the creatures who dwell there, including sharks. Though they are rarely seen and seldom attack, they should be respected. A wise swimmer who spots a fin simply heads unobtrusively for shore.

Scuba divers should always put out a visible float or flag to warn approaching boats of their presence. On a boat or a canoe, always wear a life jacket; ocean and river currents can be very powerful.

If you're going canoeing or whitewater rafting, always scout the river from land before the first trip, and check the available literature. Rivers have danger areas such as falls, boulder fields, rapids and dams.

FISHING

Ever since the Puritans discovered salt cod, New Englanders have been fishing these waters. In the 19th century, men went down to the sea in ships after bigger fish—whales.

Today many people fish just for fun, casting a line into the surf off a rock jetty for flounder, striped bass or bluefish, or perhaps going out to sea for such deep-water game fish as bluefin tuna or shark.

For tamer activities, try harvesting mussels, scallops, littleneck clams or quahogs. And anyone can throw out a lobster pot or two and bring home a tasty dinner.

Freshwater fishing in streams, lakes and ponds nets rainbow, brook and brown trout, as well as largemouth bass, northern pike, bullhead, perch, sunfish, catfish and pickerel. In cold northern lakes, you can catch lake trout, steelhead, landlocked salmon, smelt, sauger, walleye, largemouth and smallmouth bass, northern pike, muskellunge, yellow perch and channel catfish.

The most common saltwater fish are winter flounder and bluefish. Other saltwater species include striped bass, cod, tautog, mackerel, haddock, pollock, weakfish and smelt.

While all six states require a license for freshwater fishing, no license is needed for saltwater fishing, with a few restrictions.

In Connecticut, freshwater fishing licenses can be bought from town clerks or sporting goods stores. For information on fishing regulations or an angler's guide, contact the **Inland Fisheries Division.** ~ Department of Environmental Protection, 79 Elm Street, Hartford, CT 06106; 860-424-3474; e-mail dep.inland.fisheries@po.state.ct.us.

In Rhode Island, freshwater fishing licenses can be bought at bait and tackle shops, all town clerks' offices, or from the **Department of Environmental Management.** ~ 235 Promenade Street, Providence, RI 02908; 401-222-6800; www.dem.ri.gov, e-mail cheryl.kennedy@dem.ri.gov.

For fishing in Massachusetts, contact the **State Division of Fisheries and Wildlife** and ask for the Abstracts of the Fish and Wildlife Laws. (A federal saltwater permit is required for tuna fishing, and only Massachusetts residents can obtain a permit for lobster fishing.) ~ 251 Causeway Street, Suite 400, Boston, MA 02114; 617-626-1590; www.masswildlife.com, e-mail mass.wildlife@state.ma.us.

Fishing licenses in Vermont may be purchased from any town clerk or at many sporting goods stores, general stores, and state parks. The **Vermont Department of Fish and Wildlife** has details and maps in the *Vermont Digest of Fishing Laws.* ~ Agency of Natural Resources, 103 South Main Street, Building 10 South, Waterbury, VT 05671; 802-241-3700; www.vtfishandwildlife.com, e-mail fwinformation@state.vt.us.

For fishing fees and regulations in New Hampshire, contact the **New Hampshire Fish & Game Department.** ~ 11 Hazen Drive, Concord, NH 03301; 603-271-2501; www.wildlife.state.nh.us, e-mail fish@wildlife.state.nh.us.

TWO

Connecticut

Connecticut is the gateway to New England and it offers, despite its diminutive size, a sampling of everything that makes the region famous. Although it takes no more than two and a half hours to drive across the state, these 5000 square miles hold a surprising variety of riches: 250 miles of jagged shoreline; farms, woodlands, mountains and rolling hills; villages of white-clapboard houses huddled around classic greens; and cities rich in cultural offerings. Three hundred and fifty years of history are reflected in the varied architecture and in countless sites—vintage houses, museums, historical societies—that celebrate the forceful men and women who made Connecticut their home.

Shaped like a rectangle measuring about 90 miles from west to east and 55 miles north to south, Connecticut is bounded by New York State on its western border, Massachusetts to the north and Rhode Island to the east. The southern edge is traced by Long Island Sound, a sheltered arm of the Atlantic Ocean that was formerly a vital avenue of trade and transportation and is now a prime recreational asset. The state's other major waterway is its namesake: the Connecticut River, longest in New England, which roughly cuts the state in half and was the site of the earliest 17th-century settlements.

Indian names grace the rivers Housatonic, Quinnipiac and Naugatuck, as well as towns and villages like Cos Cob, Niantic, Saugatuck and Wequetequock. Most towns, however, bear names that have their roots in Great Britain—Windsor, Bristol, New Britain, Greenwich, Norwich—or in the Bible—Bethel, Goshen, Canaan, Bethlehem.

England, their land of birth, and the Puritan faith were crucial influences on the original settlers, who left the fledgling Massachusetts colony in 1633 to found the communities of Hartford, Windsor and Wethersfield on the Connecticut's fertile banks. A few years later, the three settlements joined together as the Hartford Colony—soon to become the Colony of Connecticut—and adopted the Fundamental Orders of 1639. This document, created as a framework for governing the colony, is regarded by many as the world's first written constitution. That's why the words "Constitution State" are heralded on automobile license plates.

Other, less glorious nicknames include "The Nutmeg State," a reference to the days of the itinerant Yankee peddler who went up and down the Atlantic seaboard door to door, selling anything the householder might need, including imported nutmeg, to add flavor to food. Legend has it that wily peddlers would leave the lady of the house holding a "wooden nutmeg"—a fake.

Be that as it may, few of those households could grow much of their own food, since the state's surface is largely glacial soil, too rocky for successful farming. From the beginning, many of the residents had to turn to other endeavors—commerce, shipping, insurance and, in time, manufacturing, which put the state on the map.

Towns and cities grew up around their factories—you'll see handsome brick or stone mills as you drive along the valleys of the Naugatuck, the Quinebaug and other rivers—and each locality became known by the product it manufactured. Waterbury was the brass city; New Britain was the hardware capital of the world; Danbury's fame was hats; Bristol boasted of its clocks.

As mills and factories grew, so did their need for workers. During the late 19th and early 20th centuries great waves of immigrants entered the state from Ireland, Italy, Germany, Poland—every country in Europe. The makeup of the population changed from a homogeneous nucleus of English Protestant descent to the mosaic of nationalities and ethnic groups that characterizes Connecticut's 3.4 million people today.

Industry continues to remain important to some extent: airplane parts are manufactured in East Hartford, helicopters in Stratford; in Groton, Electric Boat builds submarines. But changing patterns and needs across the nation have led to factory closings throughout the state, and to grave problems for older manufacturing cities. At the same time, a number of national corporations have moved their headquarters to Connecticut, creating new skylines and new work in cities like Greenwich, Danbury and Stamford. As a whole, the state continues to be one of the most prosperous in the country, although substantial segments of the population have been unable to share in the wealth.

Despite the importance of manufacturing, a large proportion of the land has remained rural, with vast acreage set aside for recreation and open space in more than 50 state parks and forests, as well as municipal parks and nature preserves. These peaceful oases are scattered throughout the state: along the shoreline, in the pastoral northern corners, even in the more populated valleys near the three largest cities—Bridgeport, Hartford and New Haven.

The landscape ranges from a level shoreline dotted with small beaches and coves through rolling country to the green-clad mountains of the northwest corner and gentle hills of the northeast. At the center is the Connecticut River Valley, once fertile farmland whose traditional crops, tobacco and corn, have largely given way to suburban growth in recent decades.

The central section of the state is home to several major universities: Yale in New Haven, Wesleyan in Middletown, Trinity College in Hartford. New London, on the southeastern coast, boasts Connecticut College and the Coast Guard Academy, while the University of Connecticut's main campus is in Storrs.

Though distances are short, the climate varies by several degrees from north to south, with snow and ice lasting longest in Litchfield County, the northwestern region. Winter temperatures can go below zero at times, though seldom for long;

summer can be occasionally hot and humid. And yet each season brings its own rewards and calendar of attractions. Winter turns the hilly regions into scenes of skating and ice fishing on lakes and ponds, while downhill skiers rush to half a dozen well-equipped areas and cross-country buffs head for countless trails. In spring, the dogwood's snowy blossoms brighten the roadways, and mountain laurel, the state flower, paints hillsides the very palest pink. Summer is the favorite vacation season, a time of festivals and fairs, swimming, fishing and boating, and crowds of visitors at beaches and parks. Fall, some say, shows the state at its best, with maples, oaks, dogwoods, ferns, even the dreaded poison ivy turning the countryside into a symphony of orange, red and gold.

Connecticut can be explored from several points of entry, but chances are that visitors will be coming in from New York state. With this in mind, the chapter has been organized as one lengthy, S-shaped path, going from southwest to northwest; then to the Hartford area, more or less the state's center; south to New Haven; then east along the shore with a brief jog up the Lower Connecticut Valley; finishing up with the scenic, little-known northeast corner. It's a journey that could take a few days, a week or a lifetime spent discovering the treasures of this compact state.

Southwestern Connecticut

Guidebooks tend to dismiss southwestern Connecticut, which roughly corresponds to Fairfield County, as merely a bedroom community for New York City, not worthy of a visitor's time. In fact, it's far more complex—a mix of attractive residential towns with roots in the 17th and 18th centuries, once-thriving industrial cities struggling to find new roles for themselves and clusters of tall, sleek corporate headquarters that have transformed the county's way of life. What's more, although the area is far from rural, a surprising amount of open space has been preserved in state parks and nature preserves.

SIGHTS

A brief tour to sample this variety should start in **Greenwich**, the first town encountered on crossing into the state from the southwest. Famed as an exclusive residential enclave of affluent New York commuters, this community of 58,000 has acquired an additional role as a business center. A host of corporate office buildings draws some 20,000 workers from other towns, as well as hundreds of foreign executives. The old order changeth, even here!

HIDDEN ►

The beauty of the town remains, as does the atmosphere of quiet privilege. Visitors seeking a glimpse of the **great estates** that give Greenwich its special ambience should wander the "backcountry" roads north and immediately south of the Merritt Parkway, along Lake Avenue, North Street, Round Hill Road and smaller, bucolic lanes and drives—as long as they are not guarded by stone gateposts with No Admittance signs! It's a world of white churches and manicured country clubs, ancestral trees and lavishly landscaped grounds, with mansions, neo-Tudor or Colonial Revival, barely visible behind iron gates, stone walls and fences.

One former estate that, happily, is open to the public is the renovated **Bruce Museum of Arts and Science**, housing American paintings, American Indian pottery and textiles, natural science and geologic displays and frequent exhibitions that reflect the eclectic nature of the holdings. Closed Monday. Admission (free on Tuesday). ~ 1 Museum Drive, Greenwich; 203-869-0376, fax 203-869-0963; www.brucemuseum.org.

Putnam Cottage is a late-17th-century tavern and site of General Israel Putnam's 1779 daring escape against the Redcoats—a favorite bit of local lore. Open Sunday, or by appointment. Closed January through March. Admission. ~ 243 East Putnam Avenue, Greenwich; 203-869-9697.

Also worth checking out in Greenwich is the **Cavalier Galleries**, which has a variety of contemporary paintings sculptures and photography on display. Painting styles range from highly traditional to ultramodern, and sculptures range from miniature to monumental. There's also a display of outdoor sculptures along Greenwich Avenue. ~ 405 Greenwich Avenue, Greenwich; 203-869-3664, fax 203-869-3704; www.cavaliergalleries.com, e-mail cavgallery@aol.com.

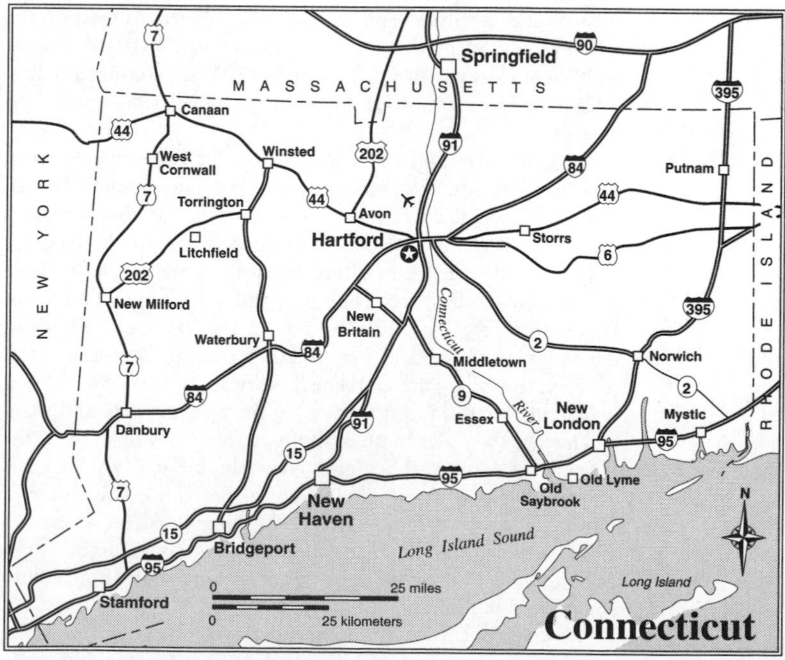

Another nearby attraction is the **Bush-Holley Historic Site and Visitor Center**, devoted to the community's long and colorful history. The 18th-century saltbox house, a boarding house for Connecticut's first art colony in the 1890s, is a National Historic Landmark. Closed Monday and Tuesday year round; closed Monday through Friday from January through February. Admission to the house. ~ 39 Strickland Road, Cos Cob; 203-869-6899, fax 203-861-9720; www.hstg.org.

Driving east from Greenwich on Route 95, you'll spot **Stamford**'s skyline, which appears as a forest of discordant office towers, huge corporate headquarters built since the 1960s that dwarf the few remaining older structures.

An interesting destination in Stamford is the **First Presbyterian Church**, a unique fish-shaped church that was designed by Wallace K. Harrison. Closed Saturday, and Sunday afternoon. ~ 1101 Bedford Street, Stamford; 203-324-9522; www.fishchurch.org.

A few miles north of downtown you'll find the **Stamford Museum and Nature Center**, perhaps the most eclectic institution in the state. Set on more than 118 acres, the center offers, in a number of widely scattered buildings, galleries devoted to art and American and natural history; an auditorium; a planetarium; an observatory; a small working farm; a unique playground; nature trails, five hiking picnic grounds and a small lake populated by all manner of geese, ducks and swans. This one's truly a treat for the whole family. Special seasonal programs are offered. Admission. ~ 39 Scofieldtown Road, Stamford; 203-322-1646, fax 203-322-0408; www.stamfordmuseum.org, e-mail smnc@stamford museum.org.

Just east of Stamford is **Darien**, one of Connecticut's most coveted addresses. Take time out to see the **Bates-Scofield Homestead**, a classic 1736 Connecticut saltbox house now used as a museum. All rooms, including the kitchen and the buttery, are fully restored with 18th-century furnishings and artwork. Open only on Wednesday and Thursday; call ahead. ~ 45 Old Kings Highway North, Darien; 203-655-9233, fax 203-656-3892; www.darien.lib.ct.us/historical, e-mail darien.historical@snet.net.

Next stop along the shoreline is **Norwalk**, a city of 80,000 that was settled in 1645 and thrived on the coastal trade and manufacturing, then went into a slump. After years of neglect, the area closest to the harbor, **South Norwalk** (known as SoNo), has been restored, gentrified and listed in the National Register of Historic Places. Its major artery, **Washington Street**, is now a stroller's mecca offering many shops and boutiques, art and craft galleries, restaurants and bars, all set in handsome 19th-century commercial buildings.

Around the corner, on five acres of riverfront, rises one of the state's top three attractions, the **Maritime Aquarium at Norwalk.**

It includes an aquarium with myriad tanks that take you from salt marsh into open sea, sharks, harbor seals and all; a maritime museum displaying classic open boats; a touch tank; a stingray petting pool; and a high-tech, 337-seat IMAX theater with a six-story screen that stretches 80 feet. Admission. ~ 10 North Water Street, Norwalk; 203-852-0700, fax 203-838-5416; www.maritimeaquarium.org.

From an adjacent dock you can board the **G. W. Tyler**, an open ferry that goes to the 1868 lighthouse on Sheffield Island. It operates on weekends only from Memorial Day to the second week of June, then daily until Labor Day. Closed Labor Day to Memorial Day. Admission. ~ 132 Water Street, Norwalk; 203-838-9444, 203-831-2898 (dock); www.seaport.org, e-mail nseaport@snet.net.

Other vessels take longer jaunts around all the islands. Information about this and other attractions is available from the **Coastal Fairfield County Tourism Information Center**. Call ahead for hours. ~ 20 Marshall Street, Suite 102, Norwalk; 203-840-0770, 800-866-7925, fax 203-840-0771; www.coastalct.com, e-mail info@coastalct.com.

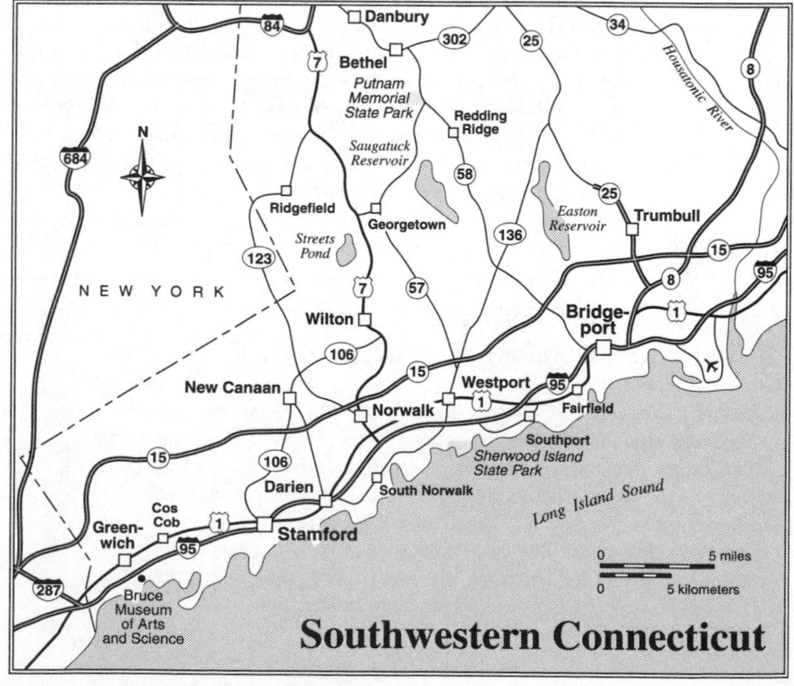

The **Lockwood-Mathews Mansion Museum** is a lavish 62-room residence built in the 1860s in French Second Empire style. It includes work by some of the finest cabinetmakers and craftsmen of the day. Saved from the bulldozer by local preservationists, it has been gradually restored room by room—stenciled ceilings, inlaid woodwork, glassed-in conservatory—and now serves as a museum of Victorian life. Closed Monday and Tuesday; closed in January and February. Admission. ~ 295 West Avenue, Norwalk; 203-838-9799, fax 203-838-1434; www.lockwoodmathewsmansion.org, e-mail lockmathew@aol.com.

Continue east and you'll soon come to **Westport**, a popular summer spot as well as a thriving community year-round. Its beaches are a magnet for visitors from inland and other parts of the coast. Take the second Westport exit northbound on Route 95 to reach **Sherwood Island**, a public beach with picnic tables, changing facilities and beachside refreshments.

A more beautiful beach—**Compo Beach**—is for Westport residents and anyone who doesn't mind paying $15 a day for parking ($30 on weekends and holidays). The price is ridiculously high, but that's what keeps the crowds from getting too big.

Westport is home to **Earth Place, The Nature Discovery Center**, a 62-acre wildlife sanctuary providing habitat for squirrels, birds, deer and other animals native to the region. The museum offers a variety of educational programs and a natural history exhibit featuring plants and animals found in Connecticut's ecosystems; the center also operates a rehabilitation program for injured animals including bald eagles and hawks. There is also an outdoor birds of prey exhibit and trails in the sanctuary. ~ 10 Woodside Lane, Westport; 203-227-7253, fax 203-227-8909; www.earthplace.org; e-mail info@earthplace.org.

From Westport, follow Greens Farms Road to Beachside Avenue, which will turn onto Pequot Avenue and take you right into

sights

AUTHOR FAVORITE

I learned much more than I thought I knew about the 19th century's greatest promoter and the preposterous cast of prodigies, dwarves, elephants, Siamese twins and others he elevated to international stardom at **The Barnum Museum** in Bridgeport. For Bridgeport, P.T. Barnum was more than the king of hoax and hokum, more than the creator of the legendary Barnum and Bailey Circus. He was a philanthropist and real estate developer, the city's mayor and its favorite son. The museum established in his will in 1891 is as flamboyant as he was, a gargoyled, towered and domed red building in the heart of the city, a reflection of his eclectic interests. See page 45 for more information.

Southport, one of Connecticut's most enchanting villages. Here you will find a stunning collection of houses, churches and public buildings crowding around the tiny Southport Harbor. Drive slowly down Pequot Avenue past the parade of homes in the Federal and Greek Revival styles and later ones in all the variations we tend to lump together as Victorian.

◄ HIDDEN

After you pass a small cluster of stores and antique shops, take a right to the harbor, the original source of the wealth that created the handsome dwellings. The vessels that traded with Boston and New York from this small, sheltered port have given way to sailboats moored at the yacht club, but the homes built by the ship's owners and captains are still lived in and lovingly maintained. Park if you can, and walk up Harbor Road for a fine view of the watery landscape.

Bridgeport, the next city along Route 95, is the largest in the state and no one's dream of a tourist attraction, but **The Barnum Museum** will delight both children and adults. Circus buffs will go straight to the third floor with its mementos of General Tom Thumb, the talented midget who achieved world fame; its big-top memorabilia; and especially the 1000-square-foot scale model of "The Greatest Show on Earth," complete with over 3000 miniatures of acrobats, clowns, elephants, trains and tents, every tiny detail hand carved by a craftsman from a nearby town. Closed Monday. Admission. ~ 820 Main Street, Bridgeport; 203-331-1104, fax 203-331-0079; www.barnum-museum.org, e-mail awestmoreland@barnum-museum.org.

Bridgeport is also home to **The Discovery Museum**, an interactive science and technology museum featuring hands-on exhibits in both disciplines. Explore light, sound, computers, electronics and nuclear energy. The Challenger Learning Center gives you the chance to go on a simulated space mission, and the planetarium offers daily shows on the stars and planets. There's also a theater that runs films on topics ranging from space exploration to dinosaurs. The museum also has rotating exhibits. Children and adults alike will love this place. Closed Monday. Admission. ~ 4450 Park Avenue, Bridgeport; 203-372-3521, fax 203-374-1929; www.discoverymuseum.org.

In addition to the towns along the shores of Connecticut's southern coast, there are a few villages just inland that merit a visit. These include New Canaan and Ridgefield.

New Canaan is a quiet residential community that was settled in 1801. Throughout the town and along the winding roads that surround it are beautifully maintained New England homes and churches. One worthwhile stop is the **Silvermine Guild Arts Center**, an art center with a school whose galleries have showcased the works of member artists and artisans since 1922. Closed

Monday. ~ 1037 Silvermine Road, New Canaan; 203-966-5617; www.silvermineart.org, e-mail sgac@silvermineart.org.

Another spot to check out is the **New Canaan Nature Center,** a 40-acre preserve that encompasses a variety of habitats, including woodland, marshes and fields. Its visitors center offers interactive, educational exhibits on animal behavior that will intrigue youngsters. A tropical greenhouse; a birds of prey exhibit; and perennial, herb and wildflower gardens are also open to the public. The building is closed Sunday but grounds are open from dawn to dusk. ~ 144 Oenoke Ridge Road, New Canaan; 203-966-9577, fax 203-966-6536; www.newcanaannature.org.

Perhaps the most idyllic town in this busy part of the state is **Ridgefield,** a quintessential New England enclave of stately homes, ancient trees and mementos of battles long past. To reach Ridgefield, a bit farther inland than New Canaan, take Route 123 through a corner of New York State to Route 35. Once a way station on the road from New York to Boston, the town provided inns for weary passengers. The tradition continues, with several old but up-to-date hostelries and one that now acts as a museum, the **Keeler Tavern Museum,** whose most famous feature is a cannonball lodged in its wall since the Battle of Ridgefield, April 27, 1777. Benedict Arnold was a hero on that day! Also on the grounds is a walled garden with a reflecting pool. Open Wednesday, Saturday and Sunday afternoons; tours on other days are available by appointment. Garden is open daily. Closed January. Admission. ~ 132 Main Street, Ridgefield; 203-438-5485, fax 203-438-9953; www.keelertavernmuseum.org, e-mail keelertavernmuseum@earthlink.net.

Not far from the tavern, another 18th-century building (from 1783, to be exact) has been transformed into the **Aldrich Contemporary Art Museum.** Currently undergoing major renovation and slated to reopen in spring 2004, the museum will boast flexible galleries to accommodate rotating exhibits of contemporary art in every medium, a performance space, an education center, and a two-acre sculpture garden. Closed Monday. Admission. ~ 258 Main Street, Ridgefield; 203-438-4519, fax 203-438-0198; www.aldrichart.org, e-mail general@aldrichart.org.

LODGING

Set proudly among the tall new office towers of downtown Stamford, the **Stamford Marriott** boasts more than 500 elegant rooms and such amenities as an indoor-outdoor pool, an in-house golf instructor and a revolving restaurant with views of Long Island Sound. It may not be everyone's ideal vacation hideaway, but its proximity to Route 95, the railroad station, cultural offerings and a major shopping mall makes it attractive. Weekends bring lower rates. ~ 2 Stamford Forum, Stamford; 203-357-9555, 800-228-9290, fax 203-324-6897; www.marriotthotels.com/stfct. ULTRA-DELUXE.

Silvermine Tavern has a special charm that spells New England, even though it's just a hop from the New York state line. Well-known for its restaurant, this picturesque cluster of rambling, circa-1785 frame buildings offers ten comfortable bedrooms appropriately but not lavishly furnished with country antiques. Overlooking the mill pond and its waterfall, the complex is at the crossroads of a woodsy residential community. Continental breakfast. ~ 194 Perry Avenue, Norwalk; 203-847-4558, 888-693-9967, fax 203-847-9171; www.silverminetavern.com, e-mail innkeeper@silverminetavern.com. MODERATE TO ULTRA-DELUXE.

A clutch of motels lines Route 1, the old Boston Post Road and now the area's crowded commercial strip. For one that's clean, quiet and operated by the same family since 1970—they live on the premises—try the **Garden Park Motel.** Their 21 units all have air conditioning, cable television, good bathrooms and firm mattresses; there's even a picnic table under a shady tree for the guests' use. Fancy it's not, but it's cheap in an area that tends to be expensive. ~ 351 Westport Avenue, Norwalk; 203-847-7303; www.gardenparkmotel.com. MODERATE.

Situated on the banks of the Saugatuck River in Westport, **The Inn at National Hall** occupies a restored, historic brick building. Its 16 rooms and suites are luxuriously decorated, with lots of trompe l'oeil, handcrafted stenciling and arched ceilings. So exquisite is this small hotel that it was featured in an *Architectural Digest* cover story. ~ 2 Post Road, Westport; 203-221-1351, 800-628-4255, fax 203-221-0276; www.innatnationalhall.com, e-mail info@innatnationalhall.com. ULTRA-DELUXE.

On the premises of The Inn at National Hall is a pricey restaurant that hosted former President Clinton and Vice President Gore on separate visits to Westport.

The Inn at Longshore is an unusual place to stay: a 12-room inn with a ballroom and banquet facilities in the midst of a town-owned golf course and park, with lawns that sweep down to Long Island Sound. The rooms (three of them are suites that can sleep four) are almost an afterthought, but they're tastefully done, with up-to-date bathrooms and views of white sails dancing on blue water. Guests may use town facilities, such as the golf course, swimming pool and tennis court, on payment of a fee. Continental breakfast. ~ 260 Compo Road South, Westport; 203-226-3316, fax 203-227-5344; www.innatlongshore.com. DELUXE TO ULTRA-DELUXE.

The **Roger Sherman Inn** is located just outside the center of New Canaan. It's a small inn that dates back to around 1740. All 17 guest rooms are decorated with cherrywood antiques, and several have sitting rooms. There is a restaurant on the premises. ~ 195 Oenoke Ridge, New Canaan; 203-966-4541, fax 203-966-0503; www.rogershermaninn.com, e-mail info@rogershermaninn.com. DELUXE.

Right next door is **The Maples Inn**, a 25-room inn that was built back in 1908. It's a grand old hotel with a wraparound porch. The large guest rooms, all with four-poster canopy beds, are furnished with antiques and reproductions. ~ 179 Oenoke Ridge, New Canaan; 203-966-2927, fax 203-966-5003; www.maplesinnct.com, e-mail info@maplesinnct.com. DELUXE.

In serene Ridgefield, set behind a wide lawn and ancient trees, sits **West Lane Inn**, a gracious dowager of a place built as a home in the mid-1800s, embellished in the Victorian era and then converted to an inn in the late 1970s. There's a wide porch that wraps around two sides, with colorful hanging baskets and black wrought-iron furniture for lazy summer days. A great carved oak staircase leads up to 18 generous-sized rooms. All show restrained elegance, and each is individually designed with plush carpeting, fine upholstered pieces and period-style furniture. Breakfast is included. ~ 22 West Lane, Ridgefield; 203-438-7323, fax 203-438-7325; www.westlaneinn.com, e-mail west_lane_inn@sbcglobal.net. DELUXE TO ULTRA-DELUXE.

Many of the great estates of Greenwich are owned by celebrities—Diana Ross and Ivana Trump among them.

The Elms Inn has been operating as an inn since 1799. Today, the famed restaurant occupies most of the main building, with two bedrooms and two suites up a steep, cramped flight of stairs. The annex offers 16 accommodations—three of them suites—that are elegantly carpeted and appointed with attractive stenciled wallpapers and period furniture. Some of the rooms offer four-poster and canopied beds. The rooms over the restaurant are more casual, with rag rugs, hand-stenciled borders on the ceilings and bathrooms sporting a "country" look. In-room continental breakfast. ~ 500 Main Street, Ridgefield; phone/fax 203-438-2541; www.elmsinn.com, e-mail innkeeper@elmsinn.com. DELUXE TO ULTRA-DELUXE.

DINING

For a glimpse of Connecticut dining at its classiest, start with **Thomas Henkelmann** at the Homestead Inn. A 1799 farmhouse turned hostelry and exquisitely restored, the inn stands on a knoll in an exclusive residential area—a treat to the eye as well as the palate. In the restaurant, the ambience is classic French and subdued; the fare is French, sophisticated and up-to-date. Tables sparkle with fine glass and unique plates designed in southern France; service is proper. In the summer, you can enjoy the outdoor verandah for dinner. No lunch on Saturday and Sunday. Dinner served on Sunday in December. ~ 420 Field Point Road, Greenwich; 203-869-7500, fax 203-869-7502; www.homesteadinn.com, e-mail events@homesteadinn.com. ULTRA-DELUXE.

Greenwich is also home to **Restaurant Jean-Louis**, a top-drawer French restaurant. Chef-owner Jean-Louis Gerin is well known in the culinary world for his masterful food preparation. The prix-fixe menu changes daily while the main menu changes seasonally and may include such dishes as seared sea scallop dressed with whipped truffle oil or beef medallions with a red wine coulis. Whatever the menu, everything is made from fresh, seasonal ingredients. The decor is very modern and showcases Parisian artists. The restaurant only accommodates 50 people, so reservations are *très* necessary. No lunch on Saturday. Closed Sunday. ~ 61 Lewis Street, Greenwich; 203-622-8450, fax 203-622-5845; www.jlrestaurant.com, e-mail jeanlouis61lewis@aol.com. ULTRA-DELUXE.

Among the myriad Italian restaurants in this part of the state, **Il Falco** is considered one of the best. Set in the heart of Stamford, this pleasant spot without glitz or pretension serves regional specialties that don't appear on every menu—gnocchi, *vitello tonnato*, fish prepared in the style of various Italian cities—all cooked with imagination and care. No lunch on Saturday. Closed Sunday. ~ 59 Broad Street, Stamford; 203-327-0002; www.ilfalco.com, e-mail vincenzo@ilfalco.com. MODERATE TO ULTRA-DELUXE.

Siena Ristorante is a noteworthy Tuscan restaurant. The kitchen serves up some of the best risotto and pasta (all homemade) you'll find in the county; the menu changes four times a year. The wonderful desserts include crème brûlée and a chocolate tart with almonds. Beautifully decorated with stucco walls and a painted mural cloud ceiling, Siena seats just 58 and has a loyal clientele, so be sure to make reservations (especially on weekends). No lunch on Saturday. Closed Sunday. ~ 519 Summer Street, Stamford; 203-351-0898, fax 203-351-0899; www.sienaristorante.net, e-mail pasquale@sienaristorante.net. DELUXE TO ULTRA-DELUXE.

A great diner to find your way to is **Bull's Head Diner**, which offers such favorites as sandwiches, stir-fry, pasta, filet mignon, seafood and roast chicken 24 hours a day. The diner also serves up Greek specialties like spinach pie, moussaka and savory sampler plates. Breakfast, lunch and dinner. ~ 43 High Ridge Road, Stamford; 203-961-1400, fax 203-961-0564. BUDGET TO DELUXE.

South Norwalk, or SoNo, a restored 19th-century neighborhood, is a good place to window-shop for lunch or dinner. On rejuvenated Washington Street and the adjoining Main Street, you can read menus in restaurant windows and decide if you're in the mood for Italian, French, Mexican, Chinese, seafood or sandwiches, funky or chic. There's been some turnover among the tenants in this historic district, but **Jeremiah Donovan's** has been a lively meeting place for over a century, a wood-paneled Victorian saloon with unpretentious, inexpensive food—good burgers, salads, sandwiches, their special New England chowder and hearty bowls of chili—and a prodigious selection of beers. A collection of vintage prizefighter photos adorns the walls, legacy of a regional champ who owned the place many decades ago. ~ 138 Washington Street, South Norwalk; 203-838-3430, fax 203-838-0136. BUDGET.

Barcelona, a Spanish tapas restaurant, attracts a crowd of fanatical regulars nightly. Step inside the stuccoed bar area and you will no longer feel as if you're in Connecticut. Elegant-looking diners crowd the bar and high-stooled tables. An outdoor courtyard is enclosed for winter. Moderately priced tapas include shrimp with garlic and sherry, spinach–chick pea dip with pita crisps and chorizo with sweet-and-sour figs. Dinner only. ~ 63 North Main Street, South Norwalk; 203-899-0088; www.barcelonawinebar.com, e-mail barcelonawinebar@aol.com. DELUXE TO ULTRA-DELUXE.

Silvermine Tavern is a landmark: a country inn, popular for decades, with several antique-filled dining rooms and a romantic terrace for summer dining, overlooking a waterfall and pond. Offerings fit the Colonial atmosphere: steak, seafood, poultry and pasta. There's live jazz on Friday and Saturday. The Silvermine also serves Sunday brunch and Thursday-night buffet. Closed Tuesday. ~ 194 Perry Avenue, Norwalk; 203-847-4558, 888-693-9967; www.silverminetavern.com, e-mail innkeeper@silverminetavern.com. DELUXE TO ULTRA-DELUXE.

Norwalk is home to a Spanish restaurant, **Meigas**. Here you can have reasonably tabbed tapas, or opt for house-cured cod with sun-dried tomatoes and black olives, braised short ribs with red wine and ginger or grilled duck breast in a citrus sauce. The dining room looks and feels like a Spanish country inn, with lots of colorful artwork, woodwork and dim lighting. Closed Monday. ~ 10 Wall Street, Norwalk; 203-866-8800, fax 203-899-0576; www.meigasrestaurant.com. DELUXE TO ULTRA-DELUXE.

For a casual bite on the water (literally on the water—the restaurant is housed in a historic barge on the Saugatuck River), grab a table at **Black Duck Café**. Offering a large selection of seafood, sandwiches, burgers and salads, this is a great choice for anyone seeking comfort food. The menu features a daily blue plate special with familiar favorites like macaroni and cheese, meatloaf,

AUTHOR FAVORITE

Donuts don't often merit hymns of praise, but at the **Coffee An' Donut Shop** they are handmade by the owner, with lots of TLC, each morning before 7 a.m. The resulting confections—glazed, sugared, twirled with cinnamon, rolled in thick chocolate or filled with raspberry jelly—have made addicts for miles around and been dubbed best in the country by food critics of national renown. ~ 343 North Main Street, Westport; 203-227-3808. BUDGET.

fried chicken and pot pie. ~ 605 Riverside Avenue, Westport; 203-227-7978, fax 203-227-9999; www.niteimage.com/clubs/blackduck. MODERATE.

For upscale Italian, **Seminara's Restaurant** is worth a visit. The fairly standard (yet well-prepared) entrées have a hint of the exotic: the founder's grandparents emigrated from Italy via North Africa, where his mother was born, and this unusual heritage creates novel tastes. The service is unobtrusive but classy; the same can be said for the decor, consisting of mirrored walls and bentwood chairs. No lunch on weekends. ~ 256 Post Road East Colonial Green, Westport; 203-222-8955, fax 203-222-0188; www.seminarasrestaurant.com, e-mail srestaurant@sbcglobal.net. DELUXE TO ULTRA-DELUXE.

In nearby Fairfield, you'll find **Centro**, a popular spot for northern Italian dishes. The menu includes a selection of daily special pastas, house pizzas and fish and chicken dishes. The caesar salad is done very well, as is the crème brûlée dessert. In addition to two main dining areas, there's a tiny bar in the rear and alfresco dining May through November. Centro is a festive place, with paper table coverings and a glass of crayons for mid-meal inspirations and explanations. Be prepared to wait on weekend nights—the restaurant does not take reservations on weekends and has quite a devoted clientele. No lunch on Sunday. ~ 1435 Post Road, Fairfield; 203-255-1210, fax 203-259-5040. MODERATE.

Parc 1070 and the hotel that houses it are stepping stones on the way to the long-awaited renaissance of downtown Bridgeport. The emphasis is on steaks, chicken and ravioli. The food is expertly prepared and served in bountiful portions—good reasons for dining in an area not previously known for its cuisine. Breakfast, lunch and dinner. ~ Bridgeport Holiday Inn, 1070 Main Street, Bridgeport; 203-334-1234, fax 203-367-1985; www.parc1070.com. MODERATE TO DELUXE.

A Fairfield County grande dame, the **Roger Sherman Inn** stands in the heart of an attractive residential community. Once a classic country inn and restaurant known for American fare, the Roger Sherman has been totally—and tastefully—renovated and is now dedicated to Continental cuisine, with grilled meats high on the list of favorites. No lunch on Monday. ~ 195 Oenoke Ridge, New Canaan; 203-966-4541, fax 203-966-0503; www.rogershermaninn.com, e-mail info@rogershermaninn.com. ULTRA-DELUXE.

A more casual find is **Tequila Mockingbird**, a Mexican-style restaurant with terra-cotta tiled floors. Menu items include all sorts of Mexican favorites. Dinner only. ~ 6 Forest Street, New Canaan; 203-966-2222, fax 203-966-8343. MODERATE TO ULTRA-DELUXE.

The **Gates Restaurant** is generally filled with "ladies who lunch" during weekdays and preppie bar-goers at night. The fare is American with a selection of salads, chicken, fish and pasta dishes. Decor is very light and airy, with lots of greenery around. ~ 10 Forest Street, New Canaan; 203-966-8666, fax 203-966-8343. MODERATE.

For a festive occasion, try the **Elms Restaurant and Tavern,** which has been greeting travelers since 1799. The handsome old white inn has changed a lot since then, needless to say. Its dining rooms are now gracious and serene, all flickering candles, flowered china and snow-white linens, and they serve impeccably prepared American cuisine. A prix-fixe menu of seafood, fowl and steak is featured. Closed Monday and Tuesday. ~ 500 Main Street, Ridgefield; 203-438-9206; www.elmsinn.com, e-mail innkeeper@elmsinn.com. ULTRA-DELUXE.

For brunch in Ridgefield, choose **Gail's on the Common**. It's a funky little restaurant within the Coppsfield Plaza where the servings are huge, healthy *and* delicious—a rare combination. Cuisine is contemporary with foreign and regional American accents. For dinner try the rainforest stir-fry (roasted cashews and brown rice in a ginger sauce) or the salmon phyllo with mushroom duxelles and lemon mayonnaise with capers. Brunch features corn-and-cheddar pancakes and skillet specials. Breakfast and lunch served daily, dinner Thursday through Saturday. ~ 103 Danbury Road, Ridgefield; 203-438-9775. MODERATE TO DELUXE.

Another good choice in Ridgefield is the **Hay Day Country Market**, a gourmet grocery store. Choose from a wonderful selection of salads, pastas and soups, as well as sandwiches such as grilled vegetables on Italian ciabatta bread and a California roll with jack cheese, alfalfa sprouts and avocado. After you've paid, you can eat your purchases at the coffee bar. ~ 21 Governor Street, Ridgefield; 203-431-4400, fax 203-894-1020; www.sutton gourmet.com. BUDGET.

HIDDEN ►

Run by an energetic local couple, busy **Ciao! Café and Wine Bar** is tucked in an unlikely spot behind Danbury's Main Street, not far from the train station. The decor in this small restaurant is simple, with black chairs, booths and tables and tables. The menu focuses on Italian dishes, with veal and inventive sauces playing major roles. Try to save room for the flourless chocolate cake. ~ 2-B Ives Street, Danbury; 203-791-0404, fax 203-730-1962. MODERATE.

Owned and run by the same couple who began Ciao!, **Two Steps Downtown Grille** is just . . . two steps away, though quite different in decor and menu. Here you will find Southwestern fare with Caribbean and Jamaican influences. Count the elaborately painted boots that hang from the ceiling; the owners, customers, staff and their friends decorated them. ~ 5 Ives Street, Danbury; 203-794-0032, fax 203-730-1962. MODERATE.

SHOPPING

Greenwich Avenue, the main street of elite Greenwich, and the adjoining blocks on **Putnam Avenue** (Route 1) present a profusion of upscale apparel shops—skiwear to prom gowns, trendy to purest Ivy League. You'll also find gifts, fine china, crystal, furniture and home accessories (check out the exquisite imported ceramics) at **Hoagland's of Greenwich**. Closed Sunday. ~ 175 Greenwich Avenue, Greenwich; 203-869-2127, 888-640-9577; www.hoaglands.com.

Fairfield County is a shopper's dream come true. Most of the shoreline towns, as well as several major cities, offer such a variety of consumer experiences that people come from far and wide to browse and buy.

In Stamford, now a mini-metropolis, you can find stylish, established department stores such as **Lord and Taylor**. ~ 110 High Ridge Road, Stamford; 203-327-6600.

Connecticut's largest city is Bridgeport, with 140,000 people, followed closely by New Haven and Hartford.

Another choice is the Cadillac of downtown shopping malls, the seven-level **Stamford Town Center**, which is anchored by **Macy's** (203-964-1500) and **Saks Fifth Avenue** (203-323-3100). What more could one wish? Well, there are trendy shops like **Aeropostale** (203-353-0028); prestigious American labels such as **Abercrombie & Fitch** (203-323-8729); **Godiva Chocolatier** (203-357-8110) with treats to satisfy the most discriminating sweet tooth; and a series of passable restaurants—all connected by high-tech escalators and glass-enclosed elevators and serviced by a mammoth parking garage. ~ 100 Greyrock Place, Stamford; 203-356-9700; www.shopstamfordtowncenter.com.

Stamford is also home to a one of Connecticut's most unique shopping experience: **United House Wrecking**. This business (since 1953) sells the salvaged remains of demolitions and estate sales—antiques, architectural items, and old lighting and plumbing fixtures. A line of reproduction furniture is also available. ~ 535 Hope Street, Stamford; 203-348-5371; www.unitedhousewrecking.com, e-mail info@unitedhousewrecking.com.

Washington Street, the heart of South Norwalk's historic district, is great for browsing through a potpourri of small shops and boutiques devoted to home furnishings, both yesterday's and today's, quirky clothing, jewelry, high-tech lighting fixtures and French ceramics. If stringing beads is something you always wanted to try, **Beadworks** will show you how and sell you all the necessary materials. Beadwork classes are also offered. ~ 139 Washington Street, South Norwalk; 203-852-9194, 800-232-2361; www.beadworks.com.

Discount outlets are located up and down nearby West Avenue and include **Loehmann's**, the grandmother of all off-price designer clothing stores. ~ 467 West Avenue, Norwalk; 203-866-2548.

You can't leave Norwalk without a trip to **Stew Leonard's**, say its fans. "The World's Largest Dairy Store" is a near-supermarket with Disneyland overtones, where bigger-than-life-size animated displays—cows, dogs, giant milk cartons—sing for your children's pleasure, if not yours. Its success is now legendary, largely because dairy products, meat, fish, fruit, veggies, baked goods and ready-cooked foods are super fresh and reasonably priced. ~ 100 Westport Avenue, Norwalk; 203-847-7214, 800-729-7839; www.stewleonards.com, e-mail stewleonard@stewleonards.com.

Back to more traditional shopping: a stroll downtown in Greenwich or in Westport provides a mall's worth of attractive shops and boutiques. On Westport's short but lively Main Street you'll find predictable fashion names like **Ann Taylor** (203-227-7557) and **Banana Republic** (203-454-0335). The street has been called "A Mall without Walls."

Westport is also home to some swanky boutiques like the very chic **Wishlist**, an upscale clothing store with a focus on stylish trends for teen girls and women. They also have a small selection of children's clothes. ~ 606 Post Road East, Westport; 203-221-7700; www.wishlistgirl.com. Family-owned and -operated **Touch of Europe** offers fine linens and gifts in a Victorian-style shop. ~ Playhouse Square, 291 Post Road East, Westport; 203-227-3355; www.touchofeurope.com.

Antique shops are ubiquitous in Fairfield County, as they are everywhere in the state. One of the most attractive spots for viewing yesterday's treasures is **Cannondale Village**, a 19th-century New England village. In the handful of small, picturesque buildings you'll also find gifts, dried floral arrangements, glassware, furniture, antiques and a tiny restaurant in an old schoolhouse. Closed Monday. ~ 28 Cannon Road, just off Route 7, Wilton; 203-761-8955.

There are also quite a few consignment stores in Fairfield County, especially on the Post Road, between Greenwich and Southport.

Another in the state's collection of oversized emporiums is **Danbury Fair Mall.** It's huge and glitzy, boasting **Macy's** (203-731-3500), **Lord & Taylor** (203-790-5115), a food court and a gaily painted carousel, in memory of the days when this vast site was the beloved Danbury Fairgrounds. ~ 7 Backus Avenue, Danbury; 203-743-3247; www.danburyfairmall.com.

NIGHTLIFE

The **Stamford Center for the Arts**, which houses the Palace Theater and the Rich Forum, presents a dazzling potpourri: classical music, plays, musical theater, dance—all performed by nationally known artists on tour. ~ 307 Atlantic Street, Stamford; 203-325-4466, fax 203-359-9108; www.stamfordcenterforthearts.org.

A cozy night spot, **Brennan's Restaurant** includes a pub and an outdoor patio. ~ 82 Iroquois Road, Stamford; 203-323-1787.

For music and dancing, follow the crowds to **Shenanigan's**. There's live entertainment nightly. This rustic brick-and-wood dancehall, located in a historic building, offers classic rock-and-roll, R&B and occasional headliners like Bo Diddley and Bonnie Raitt. Cover Thursday through Sunday. ~ 80 Washington Street, South Norwalk; 203-853-0142; www.shenanigansono.com.

Connecticut has more miles of paved highway than Alaska, the largest U.S. state.

The Black Duck Café has been a magnet for the beer-and-burger crowd since 1978. Located in a barge right on the Saugatuck River, this somewhat cramped bar is famed for its karaoke nights on Monday and Tuesday. There's live music on Friday. Cover on Friday. ~ 605 Riverside Avenue, Westport; 203-227-7978, fax 203-227-9999; www.blackduckcafe.net.

The Cedarbrook Cafe is a popular gay spot with periodic cabaret shows. Downstairs is a disco with dancefloor and loud deejay music, while upstairs is more conducive to quiet conversation and socializing. Closed Tuesday. Gay-friendly. ~ 919 Post Road East, Westport; 203-221-7429.

Downtown Cabaret Theater varies the formula by encouraging patrons to bring along their own picnic. Special children's shows are staged on weekends during the school year. ~ 263 Golden Hill Street, Bridgeport; 203-576-1636, fax 203-576-4444; www.dtcab.com, e-mail mail@dtcab.com.

In tiny Georgetown, the unpretentious **Georgetown Saloon** has acoustic open-mic on Tuesday, open-mic on Thursday, live bands on Friday and Saturday, and "family music" on Sunday. On Wednesday from July through September, they feature a Southern pig roast. Cover on Friday and Saturday. ~ 8 Main Street, Georgetown; 203-544-8003; www.georgetownsaloon.com, e-mail georgetownsaloon@aol.com.

Ives Concert Park presents an outdoor music festival during the summer that caters to most preferences: classical, pops, jazz, country and classic rock. ~ Westside Campus, Western Connecticut State University, Danbury; 203-837-9226; www.ivesconcertpark.com.

BEACHES & PARKS

SHERWOOD ISLAND STATE PARK One and a half miles of wide, sandy beach front the calm waters of Long Island Sound, with the coast of Long Island visible on a clear day. Behind the beach are extensive open fields and groves of maples and oaks that shelter picnic tables. Birding is good here; two breakwaters offer fine saltwater fishing for bluefish, striped bass and blackfish. Facilities include a nature center, a pavilion with food concession stands, restrooms, bathhouses and lifeguards (in summer only). Day-use fee (charged weekends only in May and September, daily from Memorial Day to Labor Day), $7 to $14.

Text continued on page 58.

American Indian Connecticut

Connecticut's pre-Columbian inhabitants were a tribe of Algonkian Indians known as the Pequot (the name means "destroyers"). Soon after white settlers arrived in the 1630s, smallpox decimated the tribe, reducing their number from 10,000 to 3000. In 1637, Puritans from Massachusetts declared war on the Pequot, killing more than half the tribe. Most of the survivors were sent to the West Indies as slaves, some were given to New England settlers as "servants," and still others were given to the neighboring Mohegan people, who mistreated them so badly that in 1655 the British gave the Pequot their own reservation. By then, their numbers had declined to 140—about the same as today.

Although New England's American Indian heritage is evident in tongue-twisting place names all over the region, just a few years ago it would have been easy to believe that the native people had vanished and been forgotten. Recently, however, two museums have opened on opposite sides of Connecticut to educate locals and visitors alike about the estimated 60,000 people who lived in New England before the first Europeans arrived.

The **Institute for American Indian Studies** in the Litchfield Hills contains an authentically reproduced Algonkian village that shows the various types of shelters—wigwams, longhouses and rock shelters—used by Connecticut's native people and illustrates how corn, beans and squash were grown. There's also a simulated archaeological site presenting how archaeologists excavate such sites in Connecticut fields today, as well as a museum of woodsplint baskets, bone combs, pots, art and artifacts from 10,000 years of Algonkian habitation. Native artists and craftspeople offer demonstrations, workshops and storytelling performances. Admission. ~ 38 Curtis Road, Washington; 860-868-0518, fax 860-868-1649; www.birdstone.org, e-mail iais@charter.net.

On the Pequot Indian Reservation near Mystic, the **Mashantucket Pequot Museum and Research Center** has a more elaborate full-size reproduction of a 16th-century village, complete with lifelike human figures and sound stations that describe what life in the community must have been like. Other exhibits at the tribal museum include simulations of an Ice Age glacier cave and a caribou hunt from 11,000 years ago. Admission. ~ P.O. Box 3180, 110 Pequot Trail, Mashantucket, CT 06339; 800-411-9671, fax 860-396-7013; www.pequotmuseum.org.

The most visible symbol of Indian presence in Connecticut is **Foxwoods**, the controversial site of a modern-day economic miracle. Only two elderly half-sisters lived on a 214-acre remnant of the Pequot Reservation in the 1970s, and it was feared that with their deaths the tribe would cease to exist and its land be forfeited to the state. Indian rights activist Amos George sought out all of the 55 tribal members living and working in New England, and led them in reorganizing the tribe, adopting a new constitution, and filing a successful land claim suit to regain 800 acres of land that had been taken from the tribe.

In 1992, when the federal government recognized Indian tribes' right to operate gaming casinos, the Mashantucket Pequots were quick to open the original Foxwoods Casino and High Stakes Bingo Parlor. This coincided with federal defense cutbacks that brought massive unemployment to the shipyards of nearby Mystic, making state and local government officials amenable to an ambitious expansion plan for Foxwoods. Today, **Foxwoods Resort Casino** has grown to be the largest casino on earth, with over 4500 slot machines, 233 table games, 75 poker tables and the most technologically advanced sports book in the country, as well as a 1416-room hotel and the Cinetropolis entertainment complex featuring a 360-degree wraparound movie theater, virtual thrill rides, a state-of-the-art game arcade and a high-tech dance club. ~ Route 2, Ledyard; 860-312-3000, 800-369-9663; www.foxwoods.com, e-mail information@foxwoods.com.

Though it has only about 700 members, the Mashantucket Pequot tribe is now one of the largest employers in Connecticut, with more than 12,000 employees and an annual payroll of more than $300 million. Under its revenue-sharing agreement, the casino pays more than $150 million a year to state government and has made multimillion-dollar donations to the Mystic Marine Life Aquarium, the Special Olympics World Games and the Smithsonian Institution's National Museum of the American Indian.

~ Exit 18 off Route 95 in Westport; 203-226-6983, fax 203-227-5642.

PUTNAM MEMORIAL STATE PARK This 183-acre park was the site of the Continental Army's 1776 winter encampment, under the command of General Israel Putnam. Remains of the encampment can be viewed, as well as reconstructed log buildings. A historical museum and visitors center are open daily from Memorial Day to Veterans Day. Hiking trails fan out into the woods; the pond is suitable for fishing and ice skating. There's a picnic area, swings, horseshoe pits and a historical site. ~ Route 58, three miles south of Bethel; 203-938-2285, fax 203-938-0002.

Northwest Corner

The northwestern corner of Connecticut is New England just as you pictured it. There are big old white churches, Colonial houses, covered bridges, stone walls, winding roads and woods all around. To top it all off, there are quite a few fine restaurants, historic inns and an abundance of small shops and galleries. Litchfield County encompasses most of the area and is home to dozens of small villages, including one by the same name.

From southern points the Litchfield area—often referred to as the Litchfield Hills—can be reached by taking Route 684 to Route 84 east and then following Route 7 north (Exit 7) to New Milford, or by taking Route 684 north to Route 22 and crossing over the state line on Route 55, heading into Gaylordsville.

SIGHTS

Just north of New Milford, the road turns into a shunpiker's dream, a gentle rollercoaster with views of fields and streams and vintage houses. Just before Kent, stop at **Bull's Bridge**, one of two covered bridges in the state that cars can drive through—a most picturesque spot. Washington crossed it in March 1781, and it's said that one of his horses fell into the freezing Housatonic River and had to be pulled out.

The town of Kent boasts the **Sloane-Stanley Museum**, which contains Early American farm and woodworking tools collected by Eric Sloane, artist and writer, as well as some of his own oil paintings. The grounds include the ruins of Kent Iron Furnace, one of many used for smelting the iron ore that was the mainstay of the northwest corner from the mid-18th century until the close of the next. Closed Monday and Tuesday, and from November to mid-May. Admission. ~ Route 7, Kent; 860-927-3849, fax 860-927-2152; www.cultureandtourism.org.

A few miles later, on the right of the road, the 250-foot cascade of **Kent Falls** dominates an attractive state park (see the "Beaches & Parks" section below).

Then the road splits: Route 45 goes south to **Lake Waramaug**, a zigzagged, three-mile-long body of water that has drawn visitors since the mid-1800s—by train back then. Drive all around it: the hilly, wooded shores shelter several inns, a state park and—surprise!—**Hopkins Vineyard**, with a winery housed in a restored 19th-century barn, where you can taste and buy both wines and various gourmet items. Since the late 1970s, even as dairy farms have gradually disappeared from the landscape, vineyards have sprung up, half a dozen at least and more to come. Closed Monday through Thursday from January though March. ~ 25 Hop-

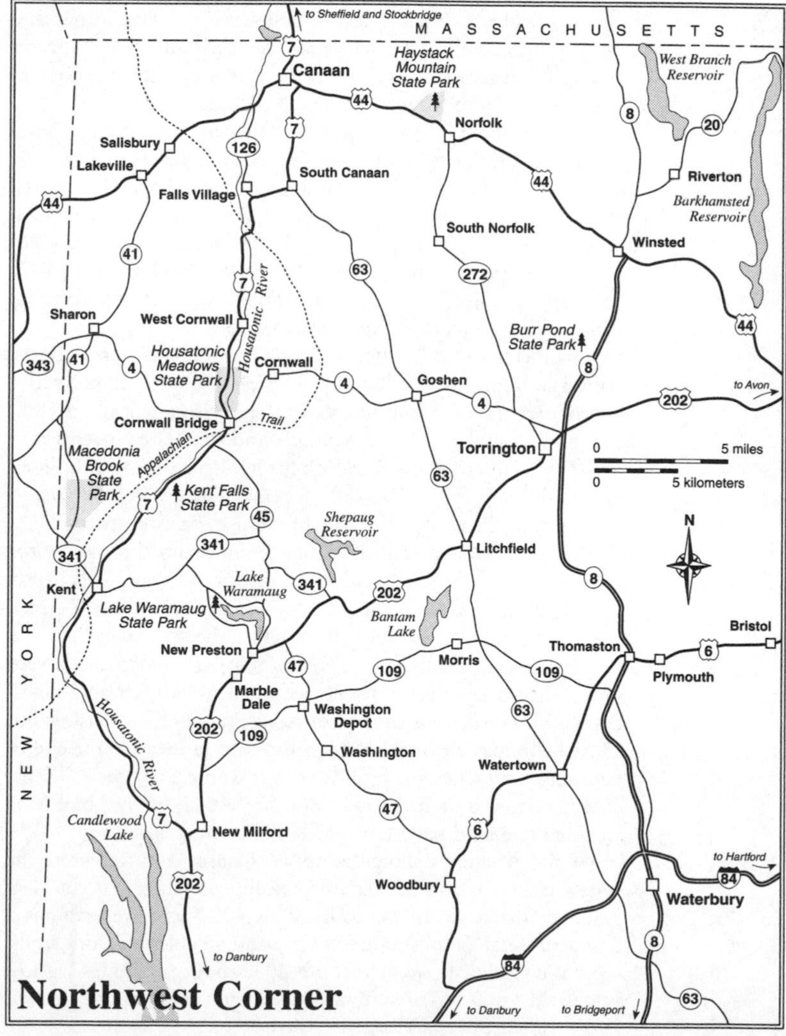

kins Road, New Preston; 860-868-7954; www.hopkinsvineyard.com, e-mail info@hopkinsvineyard.com.

From Lake Waramaug it's a short drive to **Washington**, a pristine, white hilltop residential village built around a church. Less than two miles from there, on Route 199, is the **Institute for American Indian Studies**, with excellent exhibits, including a habitat trail, a simulated archaeological site and an outdoor Indian village—a good way to learn about the region's earliest dwellers. Admission. ~ 38 Curtis Road, Washington; 860-868-0518, fax 860-868-1649; www.birdstone.org, e-mail iais@charter.net.

Litchfield is the most visited spot in the northwest corner, and its spare, graceful **Congregational Church**, built in 1828, rates among the finest in New England and is a popular photo subject. ~ Junction of Routes 202 and 118, Litchfield.

The **Litchfield Historical Society Museum** uses seven galleries of furniture, fine arts, textiles and household objects to depict the evolution of a small New England town. Closed Monday; closed from December to mid-April. Admission to the museum also admits you into the Tapping Reeve House and Law School. ~ Located on the corner of East and South streets, Litchfield; 860-567-4501, fax 860-567-3565; www.litchfieldhistoricalsociety.org, e-mail cfields@litchfieldhistoricalsociety.org.

Litchfield is home to America's first law school, **Tapping Reeve House and Law School**, founded in 1784 and now an interactive interpretive museum that re-creates the environment of an 18th-century law student. Closed Monday and from late November to mid-April. Admission. ~ 82 South Street, Route 63 South, Litchfield; 860-567-4501, fax 860-567-3565; www.litchfieldhistoricalsociety.org, e-mail cfields@litchfieldhistoricalsociety.org.

For a touring map and information on events throughout the county, contact the **Litchfield Hills Visitors Bureau.** ~ P.O. Box 968, Litchfield, CT 06759; 860-567-4506, fax 860-567-5214; www.litchfieldhills.com, e-mail info@litchfieldhills.com.

Despite its palpable concern for the past, Litchfield is very much alive and offers a variety of attractions such as **Haight-Brown Vineyard**, with winery tours, tastings and vineyard walks. Closed Monday through Friday from mid-January to the end of February ~ 29 Chestnut Hill Road, off Route 118, one mile east of Litchfield; 860-567-4045, 800-567-4045; www.haightvineyards.com, e-mail haightvineyard@aol.com.

White Memorial Foundation & Conservation Center, the state's largest nature center and wildlife sanctuary, is an ideal place for lovers of the outdoors. This 4000-acre preserve has a nature museum (admission), gift shop and 35 miles of hiking trails. ~ 80 White Hall Road, off Route 202, about two miles west of Litchfield; 860-567-0857; www.whitememorialcc.org, e-mail info@whitememorialcc.org.

Another worthwhile stop is **White Flower Farm**, a nationally known nursery with five acres of display gardens and thirty of growing fields. Closed January through March. ~ Route 63, three and a half miles south of Litchfield; 860-567-8789, 800-503-9624; www.whiteflowerfarm.com, e-mail custserv@whiteflower farm.com.

In Bristol, southeast of Litchfield, is the **American Clock & Watch Museum**, whose more than 1500 timepieces are displayed in an 1801 house. The museum boasts a permanent exhibit called "Connecticut Clockmaking and the Industrial Revolution." There is also a sundial garden and museum shop. Closed December through March, except by appointment. Admission. ~ 100 Maple Street, off Route 6, Bristol; 860-583-6070, fax 860-583-1862; www.clockmuseum.org, e-mail info@clockmuseum.org.

If matters locomotive interest you, the 1881 Thomaston Station is a worthwhile stop: The station is both the site of a railroad museum and the departure point of the **Naugatuck Railroad**. The sightseeing train trip will take you along the river to Waterville, through the Mattuck Forest, past the Black Rock Cliffs and around a series of brass mills. The trip is 20 miles and lasts about 80 minutes. The season runs from about June through October and the first three weekends in December; trains run on Tuesday, Saturday and Sunday only. ~ Thomaston; 860-283-7245, fax 860-283-7245; www.rmne.org.

In the fall, Naugatuck Railroad offers wine- and champagne-tasting rides. It's a beautiful thing to sip champagne while chugging past the New England foliage.

In nearby Waterbury, the **Mattatuck Museum Arts & History Center** exhibits artifacts such as clocks, novelty watches, art deco tableware and some of the buttons locally produced in this former "brass capital of the world." You can also visit a historic brass mill and a 19th-century boarding house highlighting immigrant memories, or peruse the galleries showcasing 18th-century furniture and American masters who have been associated with Connecticut. Closed Monday. ~ 144 West Main Street, Waterbury; 203-753-0381, fax 203-756-6283; www.matta tuckmuseum.org, e-mail info@mattatuckmuseum.org.

After enjoying the museum take the self-guided walking tour of the historic downtown district. Many buildings have been renovated thanks to the combined efforts of preservationists and developers. For further information about the Waterbury area, contact the **Northwest Connecticut Convention & Visitors Bureau**. Also available are self-guided tours of nine other historic towns in the area. Closed Saturday and Sunday. ~ 21 Church Street, Waterbury; 203-597-9527, 888-588-7880, fax 203-597-8452; www.northwestct.com, e-mail info@northwestct.com.

There's no way to see all the picturesque little towns around these parts, but you should sample the northernmost ones, such as Norfolk, surrounded by mountains and state parks. Along the

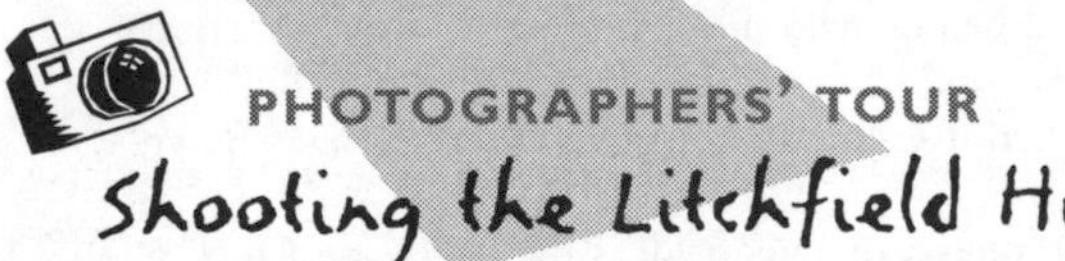

PHOTOGRAPHERS' TOUR
Shooting the Litchfield Hills

With its incomparable maze of two-lane highways winding through hundreds of quaint villages and Colonial towns, the possibilities for driving excursions in Connecticut are virtually limitless. Designed especially for travelers seeking to capture a cross-section of classic New England scenes on film, this all-day, 95-mile meander through the Litchfield Hills offers maximum country charm per mile.

LITCHFIELD Start your tour at Litchfield (page 60), one of New England's best-preserved historic towns, where the **Litchfield Congregational Church** is one of the region's most photographed churches. Nearby **White Flower Farm** (page 61) and **Topsmead State Forest** (page 72) offer great floral shots any time during the summer months.

NORFOLK From Litchfield, head north on Route 63 for six miles to the village of Goshen, turn east (right) onto Route 4, go about one and a half miles and turn north (left) onto East Street North. This idyllic country lane joins Route 272 at South Norfolk, taking you to **Dennis Hill State Park**, with one of the best panoramic views in Connecticut from its summit. In **Norfolk** (page 63), stately architecture—the Yale School of Music White House, the Norfolk Library (c. 1889), the Norfolk Academy (c. 1840) and the Church of Christ (c. 1814)—surrounds the village green.

SALISBURY From Norfolk, drive west on Route 44 for half a mile and turn south (left) on Westside Road. At the first stop sign, turn west (right) onto Mountain Road, which takes you past pretty **Wagnum Lake**. Bear left at the fork in the road, then take a right onto Under Mountain Road. Time seems to have bypassed these pastoral farm roads, which take you in about ten miles to Route 7. Turn north (right) and drive three miles

way, if you go by Route 7, you'll pass the much-photographed **covered bridge** at West Cornwall and the attractive cluster of homes and shops by its side. This section of the Housatonic River is much favored by devotees of kayaks and canoes, which can be rented both here and in **Falls Village**, a few miles to the north.

HIDDEN ► The **falls** in that town's name are channeled to provide electric power part of the year. In spring you have but to cross the bridge in the middle of town and you'll be rewarded by a dramatic rush of water to rival far more celebrated ones.

Alternatively, you could opt to drive north via the picturesque towns of Sharon, Lakeville and Salisbury, passing along the way some of the richest, most scenic farmland in the state.

on Route 7, then take a sharp left onto Sand Road to continue your scenic backroad detour. At the first fork in the road, bear right onto Boinay Hill Road, which leads to Route 44. Turn southwest (left) and continue seven miles to **Salisbury Center**, where you'll find another picture-perfect village green flanked by an old academy building, a library, and a Congregational Church (c. 1800) topped by a unique whale weathervane. The Appalachian Trail runs through town, and a hike of less than a mile takes you to the 2010-foot summit of **Bald Peak** for a spectacular 360-degree panoramic view.

CORNWALL Continue southwest for four miles on Route 44 through Lakeville and past scenic **Wononskopomuc Lake**, turning east (left) onto Route 112 for some of the best landscape views in the Litchfield Hills. At the end of the road, turn south (right) on Route 7, which follows the twists and turns of the Housatonic River, a favorite of canoers and kayakers, to **West Cornwall** (page 62), site of Connecticut's most photogenic covered bridge. Continuing south on Route 7 takes you past **Housatanic Meadows State Park** (page 73) and to **Kent Falls State Park** (page 71), where you'll find a spectacular 200-foot waterfall.

LAKE WARAMAUG Route 7 intersects Route 341 in Kent. Turn east (left) and follow Route 341 for eight miles to the turnoff to **Lake Waramaug** (page 58). The road goes completely around the lake; we suggest you follow the south shore through **Lake Waramaug State Park** (page 72) and **Mount Bushnell State Park**, turning north (left) on Route 45 at the south tip of the lake. Driving north for five miles, turn east (right) and you're back on Route 341. Just past Woodville, **Mount Tom State Park**'s Tower Trail offers another succession of great vistas. Another seven miles on Route 341 and you're back in Litchfield, where you may wish to climax your visual adventure with a visit to **White Memorial Foundation & Conservation Center** (page 60), the state's largest nature center and wildlife sanctuary.

Heading east along the swift Blackberry River, Route 44 takes you to tiny, serene **Norfolk**. Affluent families have maintained summer homes in this town since the 1880s, drawn by the cool mountain air and by the much-acclaimed **Norfolk Chamber Music Festival**, held each year from July to August. Bring a picnic dinner and enjoy the grounds before the Friday- and Saturday-night concerts at the Ellen Battell Stoeckel Estate. ~ Routes 44 and 272, Norfolk; 860-542-3000, fax 860-542-3004; www.yale.edu/norfolk, e-mail norfolk@yale.edu.

From here you can drive to several mountains with stunning views. You have to be on foot to appreciate Norfolk's exquisite green (Route 44), embellished by a fountain designed by Stanford White, eminent architect of the Gilded Age, and surrounded by graceful homes and the Congregational Church, built in 1813.

LODGING

Each of the inns studded around serpentine Lake Waramaug has a distinct personality, and its own dedicated fans. Here's a selection:

More cost-conscious travelers wishing to stay near the lake, yet who loathe roughing it at Lake Waramaug State Park, will find four quiet bed-and-breakfast rooms about a mile up the hill at **Constitution Oak Farm.** It's a rambling 1830s farmhouse whose name comes from a majestic oak tree said to descend from the legendary one in which Connecticut's Colonial charter was concealed. Two downstairs rooms have baths; the two on the second floor share. Breakfast is in the guests' own living room. The owner collects many and sundry things—a boon to some, but irksome to those who dislike clutter. ~ 36 Beardsley Road, Kent; 860-354-6495; e-mail constitutionoak@hotmail.com. BUDGET TO MODERATE.

Boulders Inn offers 20 rooms strewn throughout a picturesque, turn-of-the-20th-century main house, a carriage house and individual guesthouses, all of which are set in the hill that rises immediately behind the inn. The rooms are decorated with flair: those in the stone-and-shingle main house have antique furniture and quilts; the carriage-house rooms have antiques and stone fireplaces, while most of the guesthouses boast freestanding fireplaces. There's hiking on wooded trails and a small private beach with boats for the guests' use. ~ Route 45, New Preston; 860-868-0541, 800-455-1565, fax 860-868-1925; www.bouldersinn.com, e-mail boulders@bouldersinn.com. ULTRA-DELUXE.

The **Hopkins Inn** was named for the family who settled the northern shore of the lake in 1847, built a great rambling clapboard home and took in lodgers who came up from the city in the summer. Today, the graceful yellow bed-and-breakfast inn is

POSH PILGRIMS

The small village of Washington is home to one of the state's most exquisite inns. **The Mayflower Inn** has 30 lavishly decorated guest rooms filled with English and American antiques from the 18th and 19th centuries, some with four-poster, king-sized canopy beds. All rooms overlook the surrounding gardens and hills. The inn is a Relais & Chateaux property set on 58 acres of lawns and woods, with hiking trails, an outdoor heated pool, a tennis court, fitness center, and a spa. The service is bend-over-backwards accommodating. ~ Route 47, Washington; 860-868-9466, fax 860-868-1497; www.mayflowerinn.com, e-mail inn@mayflowerinn.com. ULTRA-DELUXE.

best known for its restaurant (closed February to early March), but it does rent eleven rooms and two apartments (that sleep up to four) on the second and third floors. The rooms are bright, with country antiques and Colonial-style wallpaper—comfortable, not dramatic. Two share a bath, the others have their own, with old-fashioned tub or stall shower. Downstairs, a shaded terrace high over the lake affords spectacular views. The adjoining hillside is owned by Hopkins Vineyards, where visitors can taste and purchase locally produced wines. ~ 22 Hopkins Road, New Preston; 860-868-7295, fax 860-868-7464; www.thehopkinsinn.com. MODERATE.

Atha House, a cozy Cape Cod–style home, is convenient to galleries and antique stores. This bed and breakfast has two rooms looking out on a big garden with evergreen, silver birch and dogwood trees as well as a Connecticut stone fence. There's a fireplace and piano in the living room. Dogs can be accommodated. ~ Wheaton Road, New Preston; phone/fax 860-355-7387; e-mail ruthpearl@sbcglobal.net. MODERATE.

For visitors who prefer to stay in Litchfield, the area's most visited town, try the **Litchfield Inn**, built circa 1980 (but Colonial in feel). The inn works hard at being graciously New England even as it highlights facilities for weddings, conferences and banquets. Its 32 guest rooms are spacious and well-appointed, with private bathrooms; two units even have a wet bar. A continental breakfast is provided, and there's an elevator—a rare commodity among country inns. ~ Route 202, Litchfield; 860-567-4503, 800-499-3444, fax 860-567-5358; www.litchfieldinnct.com, e-mail litchfieldinn@litchfieldinnct.com. DELUXE.

The **Blackberry River Inn**, built in 1763, is also listed on the National Register of Historic Places. Situated on 27 acres in the woodsy Litchfield Hills and complete with its own pool and tennis courts, the inn offers 20 guest rooms (some in the handsome, two-story main building, others in the adjoining carriage house) and a cottage. All rooms have their own bath, with an occasional clawfoot tub; some have fireplaces. The spacious public rooms are comfortable and pleasing to the eye. Complimentary breakfast is served in an attractive dining room. ~ 538 Greenwoods Road, Route 44, Norfolk; 860-542-5100, 800-414-3636, fax 860-542-1763; www.blackberryriverinn.com, e-mail blackberry.river.inn@snet.net. MODERATE TO ULTRA-DELUXE.

A bed and breakfast brimming with antiques, **The Mountain View Inn** occupies a carefully restored 1875 Victorian home. Most of its four guest rooms and suites feature four-poster beds and private baths. Relax in front of a blazing fireplace or on a cool veranda. A full gourmet breakfast is provided. ~ 67 Litchfield Road, Norfolk; 860-542-6991; www.mvinn.com, e-mail innkeepers@mvinn.com. MODERATE TO DELUXE.

The colonial design of the **Toll Gate Hill Inn & Restaurant** mirrors the comforts of a country home. Three distinctive pine buildings, one of them constructed in 1745, contain spacious accommodations appointed with pine furniture, white linens and vintage-style rugs. Many rooms have fireplaces and decks, and all guests can enjoy the inn's acres of well-manicured grounds. The Schoolhouse, once used as just that, is perfect for families with its connecting rooms. ~ 571 Torrington Road Route 202, Litchfield; 860-567-1233, 866-567-1233, fax 860-567-1230; www.tollgatehill.com, e-mail info@tollgatehill.com. MODERATE TO DELUXE.

Manor House is a sumptuous bed and breakfast, an 1898 Tudor-inspired Victorian mansion with windows designed by Louis Tiffany, a family friend. Up the handsome, carved cherry wood staircase, nine guest rooms—all with private bath, some with balcony and fireplace—have been done to a turn in period elegance. Three rooms have private jacuzzis and four have fireplaces. There's even vintage clothing hung here and there, for decoration. A classy touch: breakfast—a very hearty one—can be served in the room, even in bed. ~ 69 Maple Avenue, Norfolk; phone/fax 860-542-5690, 866-542-5690; www.manorhouse-norfolk.com, e-mail innkeeper@manorhouse-norfolk.com. DELUXE TO ULTRA-DELUXE.

In Salisbury, which is west of Falls Village and very close to the New York border, is **The White Hart**. This carefully renovated three-story inn began operating in the early 19th century. Furnishings throughout include antiques and Chippendale reproductions. The 26 guest rooms are decorated in Early American style, some with four-poster beds. In winter guests can warm up in front of the fireplace in the Hunt Room, which features dark wood paneling and overstuffed leather couches; in summer the large front porch with wicker furniture is inviting. Three meals are available daily in their restaurant. ~ 15 Undermountain Road, Salisbury; 860-435-0030, 800-832-0041, fax 860-435-0040; www.whitehartinn.com, e-mail innkeeper@whitehartinn.com. DELUXE TO ULTRA-DELUXE.

For a quiet escape, book a room in the **Cornwall Inn & Lodge**. Each of the 13 colorful accommodations includes a private bath, cable TV and wireless internet. Antiques and wrought-iron beds add a storybook quality to the inn's five rooms. Pale purple walls grace the Periwinkle Pastime Room, which has two matching queen-sized beds and dark wood furniture, while Violet's Victory Room is decorated with light blue walls, pillows and lamps. The eight lodge suites maintain a country style with wooden beds, plenty of blankets and an emphasis on comfort. Pet-friendly. ~ 270 Kent Road (Scenic Route 7), Cornwall Bridge; 860-672-6884, 800-786-6884, fax 860-672-0352; www.cornwallinn.com, e-mail info@cornwallinn.com. DELUXE TO ULTRA-DELUXE.

DINING

Petite Syrah serves New American cuisine with a French flair: sweetbread, foie gras, sirloin and seafood dishes. Located in a Cape Cod–style house, the two small dining rooms are elegantly decorated. One boasts a rustic California wine bar feel, while the other is more upscale with stark white walls and formal place settings. Closed Tuesday and Wednesday. ~ Route 202, New Preston; 860-868-7763, fax 860-868-7140. MODERATE TO ULTRA-DELUXE.

Each of the several inns around Lake Waramaug has its followers, who proclaim it the best. The **Hopkins Inn**, a rambling, many-windowed mid-19th-century house, boasts a unique location, high on a hill overlooking sparkling blue water. On a warm day, sitting under the ancient trees on the terrace would be reason enough for deep contentment, but the eclectic Continental menu casts its own spell. Austrian and Swiss traditions are emphasized; *wienerschnitzel* is a perennial favorite, as is trout, live from the inn's own tank, prepared *à la meunière* or *bleu*, the Swiss way. Closed Monday and from February through March. ~ 22 Hopkins Road, New Preston; 860-868-7295, fax 860-868-7464; www.thehopkinsinn.com. DELUXE TO ULTRA-DELUXE.

Several area places feature both lunch and take-out foods—a pleasant thought on days that call for a picnic. **The Pantry**, which doubles as a cookware shop and small restaurant, serves well-prepared entrées such as ham-and-leek quiche and apricot-almond chicken salad as part of their ever-changing menu, as well as homemade soups, salads and desserts. Closed Sunday and Monday. ~ Titus Square, Washington Depot; 860-868-0258, fax 860-868-1523; e-mail thepantry@earthlink.net. MODERATE.

The **Mayflower Inn** offers guests and passersby a highly respected restaurant. The cuisine is Continental with a Northeast

AUTHOR FAVORITE

In Woodbury, I like to feast on great food and enjoy great art at **Good News Cafe**. Works by nationally and internationally recognized artists are showcased throughout the restaurant (the exhibitions change every two months). Owned by Carole Peck, who is considered one of the best chefs in the United States, the changing menu includes creative dishes like a crisp risotto cake on a platter of roasted seasonal vegetables. Always on the menu are wok-seared shrimp with green beans, peas, olives, potatoes and garlic aioli and a grilled New York strip steak with mashed potato and crispy onion bundle. Closed Tuesday. ~ 694 Main Street South, Woodbury; 203-266-4663; www.good-news-cafe.com, e-mail carolepeck@good-news-cafe.com. DELUXE TO ULTRA-DELUXE.

accent. The salmon is hand smoked and the bacon is home cured. Dine in the garden room adorned with tapestries and feast on specialties like grilled veal with wild-mushroom sauce. Although the decor and food are elegant, dress is informal. ~ 118 Woodbury Road, Route 47, Washington; 860-868-9466, fax 860-868-1497; www.mayflowerinn.com, e-mail info@mayflowerinn.com. DELUXE TO ULTRA-DELUXE.

Food doesn't come more traditionally English on this side of the pond than at **G. W. Tavern**, where specialties include fish and chips, roast beef with Yorkshire pudding, and chicken pot pie. The tone of this Colonial-style restaurant is set by a fieldstone fireplace and a large landscape mural. In the summer, food is served on an open-air terrace overlooking the Shepaug River. Live music Thursday through Saturday nights. Reservations recommended. ~ 20 Bee Brook Road, Washington; 860-868-6633, fax 860-868-6689; www.gwtavern.com, e-mail gwtavern1@aol.com. BUDGET TO ULTRA-DELUXE.

The **West Street Grill** is a good place to people-watch as well as feast on contemporary American dishes. Try the specialty of the house—grilled New York Angus steak with rock shrimp and goat cheese, seared loin of Atlantic Salmon in a zinfandel and port wine sauce or the pan-fried seafood cakes and mixed baby greens. Closed Monday and Tuesday from January through March. ~ 43 West Street, Litchfield; 860-567-3885, fax 860-567-1374. MODERATE TO ULTRA-DELUXE.

The Bistro East at the Litchfield Inn serves New American cuisine in a country-inn atmosphere. Grilled gorgonzola-crusted New York strip steak, truffle-crusted Arctic sea bass and pan-seared pork tenderloin with fresh cranberries and shiitake mushrooms in a bourbon sauce are a few of the specialities. There's always a pasta dish and a variety of fresh fish offerings. Dinner and Sunday brunch only. ~ 432 Bantam Road, Route 202, Litchfield; 860-567-9040, 800-499-3444; www.bistroparty.com, e-mail info@bistroparty.com. MODERATE TO DELUXE.

Located in the vicinity of Bantam Lake, **Wood's Pit BBQ & Mexican Café** is a casual little eatery that serves up pretty good barbeque and a multitude of Mexican entrées thrown in for good measure. ~ 123 Bantam Lake Road, Morris; 860-567-9869. MODERATE.

59 Bank is a great dinner choice in New Milford. A cavernous space that manages to pull off being cozy, this American / Italian eatery is attentive to details. From the burnished wood throughout, to the brick walls and high tin ceilings, 59 Bank plays its role of a contemporary bistro to the hilt. Specializing in pasta dishes and grilled flatbread pizzas, menu offerings also include a wide variety of salads and tasty sandwiches. Traditional entrées include rack of pork chop with a barbecue onion ragout and pecan-crusted Atlantic salmon. Brunch served on weekends. ~ 59 Bank Street, New Milford; 860-350-5995, fax 860-350-3511; www.59bank.com, e-mail amichaelsen@59bank.com. MODERATE.

The Cornwall Inn is pure New England. Comfortable, charming and gracious, the kitchen serves up a fresh menu, and the staff will make you feel at home (the place is so quiet and remote, they seem thrilled for the company). The seasonal offerings have a French bistro flavor, with American touches (think duck confit with black currant sauce and mashed potatoes). Dinner only. Closed Monday and Tuesday, and usually during March. ~ 270 Kent Road (Scenic Route 7), Cornwall Bridge; 860-672-6884, 800-786-6884, fax 860-672-6884; www.cornwallinn.com, e-mail info@cornwallinn.com. MODERATE TO ULTRA-DELUXE.

Overlooking the river and a covered bridge, **The Wandering Moose Café** is a favorite gathering spot where friends and families come to nosh. An upscale diner of sorts, the food is a notch above what one might expect—breakfast lovers will enjoy corned beef and hash or pancakes with real maple syrup, while lunch selections include steak, fish and chips or the likes of Mandarin chicken salad. The Wandering Moose goes all out at dinner time: there's chicken with basil and roasted pepper in a sun-dried tomato pesto cream, and Bass ale baby back ribs. No dinner Monday and Tuesday. ~ 421 Sharon Goshen Turnpike, West Cornwall; 860-672-0178; www.thewanderingmoosecafe.com, e-mail russ@thewanderingmoosecafe.com. BUDGET TO MODERATE.

SHOPPING

Every little town in this fashionable rural area hosts a variety of intriguing shops and boutiques, not to mention art galleries, craft studios and antiques of all kinds.

The Silo is an uncommon enterprise, a former barn with silo that combines a handsome art gallery with changing exhibitions, a cooking school and a store that stocks everything the home chef might ever need—all in a warren of quaint little rooms.

LITCHFIELD'S LEGACY

Litchfield is as prosperous a town today as it was as an outpost and trading center; and, happily, it still centers on the handsome green that was laid out in the 1770s. The wide, maple-lined streets are edged with homes of unusual distinction, boasting past residents such as Aaron Burr, Ethan Allen and Harriet Beecher Stowe. Burr lived with his brother-in-law, Tapping Reeve; Allen was born on Old South Road, in a small privately owned house; the site on North Street where Stowe was born bears a marker—the house itself was moved some years ago.

Closed Tuesday. ~ 44 Upland Road, New Milford; 860-355-0300, 800-353-7456; www.thesilo.com, e-mail info@thesilo.com.

Historic Litchfield is a paradise for lovers of antiques who might strike gold right in the center of town, at **Thomas McBride Antiques**, for example. Hours are irregular in winter; open weekdays and by appointment on weekends the rest of the year. ~ 62 West Street, Litchfield; 860-567-5476.

Or veer a few blocks off Route 202 to visit **Toll House Antiques**, whose country-inspired merchandise reflects its 1777 location. Closed weekdays, except by appointment. ~ 38 Old Turnpike Road, Bantam; 860-567-3130.

For a complete list of antique stores in the area, contact the **Northwest Connecticut Convention & Visitors Bureau.** From mid-June to mid-October, the council runs an information booth located on Route 202. ~ P.O. Box 968, Litchfield, CT 06759; 860-567-4506, 800-663-1273, fax 860-567-5214; www.litchfield-hills.com, e-mail info@litchfieldhills.com.

You can window shop for elegant, country-style clothes or home accessories alongside the green, or half a mile west on Route 202 at Litchfield Common, an enclave of attractive shops.

Flower lovers will want to visit **White Flower Farm**, a retail and mail-order nursery known countrywide for its perennials, garden store and five acres of exquisite display grounds. Closed Halloween through March. ~ Route 63, Litchfield; 860-567-8789, 800-503-9624; www.whiteflowerfarm.com.

Alongside the picturesque covered bridge at West Cornwall, you can stroll into **Cornwall Bridge Pottery Store** and purchase attractive pots, lamps and tiles made by Todd Piker. Also for sale are handcrafted items such as clothing and wood products. Closed Tuesday through Thursday. ~ 415 Sharon Goshen Turnpike, Route 128, West Cornwall; 860-672-6545, 800-501-6545; www.cbpots.com.

TASTE OF CONNECTICUT

In addition to shops, there are vineyards and wineries in the area where you can sample and purchase local wines. Three noteworthy choices include **DiGrazia Vineyards** (closed Monday through Friday from January through March; 131 Tower Road, Brookfield; 203-775-1616; www.digrazia.com), **Haight-Brown Vineyard** (closed Monday through Friday from January through May; closed Monday and Tuesday in April; 29 Chestnut Hill Road, Litchfield; 860-567-4045; www.haightvineyards.com) and **Hopkins Vineyard** (closed Monday through Thursday in January and February, and Monday and Tuesday in March and April; 25 Hopkins Road, New Preston; 860-868-7954; www.hopkinsvineyard.com).

Should you wish to watch this fine craftsman at work, you're welcome to visit **Cornwall Bridge Pottery**. Closed Tuesday through Thursday. ~ 69 Kent Road, Route 7, one-half mile south of the junction with Route 4, Cornwall Bridge; 860-672-6545; www.cbpots.com.

Salisbury's pretty Main Street is great for gazing at 19th-century homes and window shopping innumerable small, attractive shops that feature clothes, antiques, gifts and books. There are also exotic teas to buy or sip at tiny tables at **Chaiwalla**. Closed Monday and Tuesday, and Monday through Thursday in the winter. ~ 1 Main Street, Salisbury; 860-435-9758.

One of Riverton's picture-postcard buildings is **Riverton General Store**, a historic market showcasing antiques, gifts, housewares and food items. ~ 2 Main Street, Riverton; 860-379-0811.

NIGHTLIFE

Litchfield County attracts devotees of classical music to its long-established summer festival, which features musicians of national and international renown. The **Norfolk Chamber Music Festival** lasts from July to August, with Friday- and Saturday-evening concerts. Admission. ~ Ellen Battell Stoeckel Estate, Routes 44 and 272, Norfolk; 860-542-3000; www.yale.edu/norfolk.

The **Marbledale Pub** is located five miles north of New Milford, and you'll find it lively every night, summer or winter. Locals, of the young and upscale kind, drop in before or after dinner to meet their friends, play a game of pool, and try their hand at one of the video games. ~ Route 202, Marbledale; 860-868-1496.

BEACHES & PARKS

MACEDONIA BROOK STATE PARK Many streams course through the forested 2300 acres of this park, and numerous trails traverse it. One trail reaches the crest of Cobble Mountain, almost 1400 feet, affording splendid views of the Taconic and Catskill Mountains in the adjoining states. Streams in the park are stocked in the spring with brook, brown and rainbow trout. You'll find a picnic shelter and composting toilets. ~ Macedonia Brook Road off Route 341, four miles northwest of Kent; 860-927-3238.

▲ There are 51 tent/RV sites (no hookups); $11 per night (additional reservation fee). No pets or alcohol are allowed. Closed October to mid-April.

KENT FALLS STATE PARK The foaming waterfall that cascades 250 feet here is at its peak in springtime. It's popular in summer as well, when the welcome spray brings relief from the heat, and in the fall, when the surrounding 275 acres of woods turn red and gold. You can admire it all from a grassy plain at road level, or you can view it from many different angles as you climb a wide, stepped pathway all the way to the head of the cascade. Fishing for trout is allowed at the base of the waterfall.

There are picnic grounds and restrooms. Day-use fee (weekends and holidays only), $7 to $10 per car. ~ Route 7, four miles north of Kent; 860-927-3238.

LAKE WARAMAUG STATE PARK Ninety-five wooded acres front this scenic body of water. Visitors can swim or explore countless hidden coves in kayaks and canoes that can be rented here. Fishing is good for bass, sunfish and perch. Bicycling along the quiet road around the lake is also popular, as is touring the nearby towns by car. Facilities include a picnic shelter, restrooms, food concession stands and kayak and canoe rentals. Day-use fee, $7 to $10 per car. ~ Lake Waramaug Road, off Route 45; 860-868-0220.

Visit the waterfall at Kent Falls State Park in winter, when frozen rivulets turn the mountainside to glistening abstract sculpture.

▲ There are 77 sites; $13 per night. Some sites have lake views.

BURR POND STATE PARK Five miles north of Torrington on Route 8, Burr Pond is the site of Borden's first condensed-milk factory. The 88-acre pond is very clear, and lovely for swimming in summer and skating in winter. The scenic hiking trail surrounding it is great for cross-country skiing come winter. Amenities include restrooms and a snack bar. Day-use fee, $6 to $10 per car. ~ Burr Mountain Road, five miles north of Torrington; 860-482-1817.

TOPSMEAD STATE FOREST Bequeathed to the people of Connecticut by Edith Morton Chase upon her death in 1972, this 511-acre forest is located about two miles east of Litchfield atop a 1230-foot knoll. Its main attraction is Miss Chase's summer home, an English Tudor-style cottage designed by Richard Henry Dana, Jr., in 1924. Open to the public the second and fourth weekends of each month from June through October, the house still contains most of its original furnishings. The surrounding grounds include lawns, orchards, stone walls and far-reaching views. The area is perfect for nature walking. Fires are not permitted. ~ Entrance on Buell Road, Litchfield; 860-567-5694.

WHITE MEMORIAL FOUNDATION & CONSERVATION CENTER This 4000-acre nature sanctuary bordering scenic Bantam Lake is crisscrossed by 35 miles of trails for hiking, birdwatching, horseback riding or cross-country skiing. The legacy of two visionary residents, this extraordinary preserve is dedicated to conservation education and research as well as recreation. A nature center and natural-resource museum (admission) are open to the public as are the grounds. Facilities include picnic areas, restrooms and a store. ~ White Hall Road, off Route 202, Litchfield; 860-567-0857, fax 860-567-2611; www.whitememorialcc.org, e-mail info@whitememorialcc.org.

▲ There are 68 campsites in several locations, including waterfront sites at popular Point Folly; $12.75 per night for tents, $15 per night for RVs; closed mid-October to early May. Tent-only sites are available at Windmill Hill; $8.75 per night; closed Labor Day to Memorial Day. Reservations are required. ~ 860-567-0089.

HAYSTACK MOUNTAIN STATE PARK From the stone tower atop Haystack Mountain (1706 feet above sea level) visitors can see west as far as the Catskills and north to the Berkshires' peaks in Massachusetts. You can drive halfway up the mountain, then hike a steep half-mile to the top. Fall foliage is outstanding up there, as is June's show of mountain laurel in bloom. There are picnic grounds and outhouses. Though it's closed to vehicles between the first snow and the spring thaw, the park remains open to foot traffic all year. ~ Route 272, a half mile north of Norfolk; 860-482-1817.

HOUSATONIC MEADOWS STATE PARK Encompassing 451 acres, this park is set on a former flood plain and offers flyfishing for trout and bass in the Housatonic River. Visitors will find miles of hiking trails including Pine Knob Loop Trail, which gives hikers a view of the green valley. Camping is especially good and the fall foliage is fantastic. You'll find picnic grounds and restrooms (outhouses in winter). ~ In Sharon on Route 7; 860-672-6772, 860-927-3238.

▲ There are 97 sites; $13 per night (additional reservation fee). No pets or alcohol are allowed. Note: There is no running water in winter. Closed January to mid-April.

Hartford Area

Practically smack-dab in the middle of the state is Hartford, its capital. Many people know it only because it's where they send their insurance payments. Indeed, Hartford is home to dozens of insurance companies and, in fact, is the insurance capital of the world. But it's not all business in Hartford: the city—and its surrounding towns—offers a variety of historical and cultural attractions.

SIGHTS

Route 44 heads southeast out of Norfolk, leading, some 35 miles later, to Hartford. It's a more scenic road to the state capital than the highways, one that offers the chance to stop at some attractive towns in the **Farmington Valley**. In fact, if you prefer small towns to city bustle, you could overnight there and take day trips into Hartford. For information about them, stop at the office of the **Greater Hartford Tourism District**. Closed weekends. ~ 31 Pratt Street, Hartford; 860-244-8181, 800-793-4480, fax 860-244-8180; www.enjoyhartford.com, e-mail info@ghtd.org.

HIDDEN ►

Take a brief detour south on Route 179 to the village of **Collinsville** for a glimpse of an intact 19th-century mill village—one of hundreds built across the state by the companies that gave them their names. The Collins Company was purveyor of axes and machetes to the world; the **Canton Historical Museum** features a wide array of Victorian collectibles and a charming railroad diorama circa 1900. Closed weekdays from December through March; closed Monday and Tuesday the rest of the year. Admission. ~ 11 Front Street, Collinsville; 860-693-2793; www.canton museum.org.

Continue on Route 179 into Route 4 as it follows the Farmington River into the residential town of **Farmington**, whose Main Street is a treasure trove of Colonial architecture. Just a few blocks away you'll find a little-known gem: the **Hill-Stead Museum**. Unique in many ways, Hill-Stead is a turn-of-the-20th-century Colonial revival country house built for an art-loving industrialist, Alfred A. Pope. It is furnished as if the Popes had left yesterday, and on its walls hangs a breathtaking collection of impressionist paintings—works by Monet, Degas, Manet and their American contemporaries, Cassatt and Whistler. The residence was designed by the Popes' daughter, Theodate Pope Riddle, in collaboration with an architectural firm. The personality of this pioneering woman, who went on to become an architect at a time when that profession was unheard of for a female, comes through vividly on a guided tour of the house. And there's a fine, short videotape to enlighten one further. The grounds are noteworthy as well, with hiking trails in the woods and a sunken garden designed by landscape architect Beatrix Farrand. Closed Monday. Admission. ~ 35 Mountain Road, Farmington; 860-677-4787, fax 860-677-0174; www.hillstead.org, e-mail cagenelloc@hillstead.org.

If you're intrigued by this unusual woman and her work, head north of Farmington by way of Route 10 and take a left onto Old Farms Road. In a few moments you will come to the campus of

HIDDEN ►

Avon Old Farms School, a boy's preparatory academy founded during the 1920s by Theodate Pope Riddle and designed by her in what is described as Tudor/Cotswold style—cottage-inspired buildings in reddish sandstone and dark timbers. It's private property, but nobody seemed to mind our driving through the picturesque campus. Old Farms Road winds its way north, emerging in the center of Avon, a busy suburban town that was once an agricultural community.

Not long ago, great **fields of shade tobacco** covered portions of this valley and that of the Connecticut River, a few miles to the west. Suburbanization, highways and, of course, the intense disfavor with which the evil weed is now regarded have cut sharply into this profitable business. Yet there are still some 1800 acres devoted to tobacco in the state. In summer, when the fields are

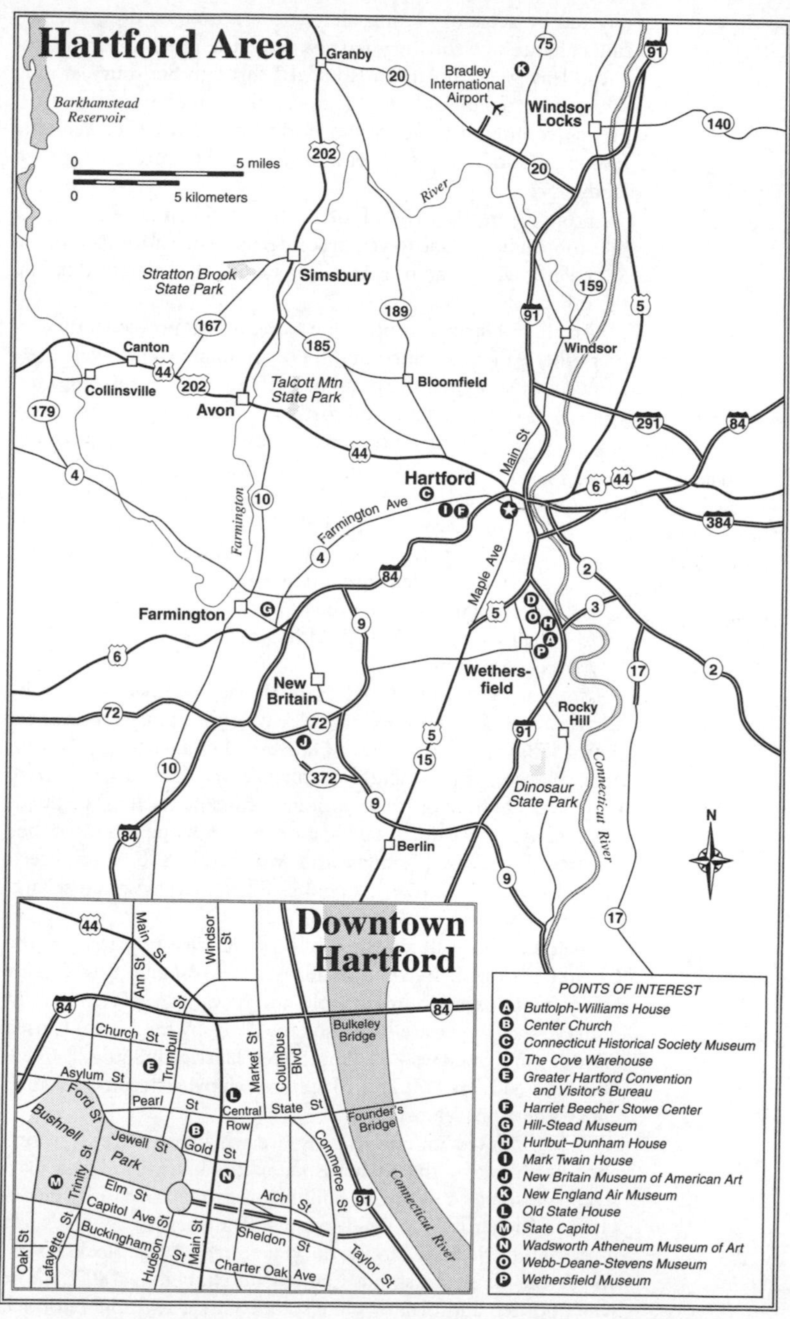

Hartford Area
Barkhamstead Reservoir
0 5 miles
0 5 kilometers
Granby
Bradley International Airport
Windsor Locks
River
Stratton Brook State Park
Simsbury
Canton
Collinsville
Avon
Talcott Mtn State Park
Bloomfield
Windsor
Main St
Hartford
Farmington Ave
Farmington
Maple Ave
Farmington
New Britain
Wethers-field
Rocky Hill
Dinosaur State Park
Connecticut River
Berlin
N
Downtown Hartford
Main St
Windsor St
Ann St
Church St
Trumbull St
Asylum St
Ford St
Pearl St
Market St
Columbus Blvd
Bulkeley Bridge
Central Row
State St
Founder's Bridge
Bushnell Park
Jewell St
Gold St
Trinity St
Elm St
Capitol Ave
Commerce St
Arch St
Connecticut River
Buckingham St
Hudson St
Sheldon St
Oak St
Lafayette St
Charter Oak Ave
Taylor St
POINTS OF INTEREST
A Buttolph-Williams House
B Center Church
C Connecticut Historical Society Museum
D The Cove Warehouse
E Greater Hartford Convention and Visitor's Bureau
F Harriet Beecher Stowe Center
G Hill-Stead Museum
H Hurlbut–Dunham House
I Mark Twain House
J New Britain Museum of American Art
K New England Air Museum
L Old State House
M State Capitol
N Wadsworth Atheneum Museum of Art
O Webb-Deane-Stevens Museum
P Wethersfield Museum

covered by acres of netting, they create a unique, dramatic setting enhanced by the long, narrow red barns used for drying tobacco leaves. Go north on Route 10 through **Simsbury**, noting the many graceful 18th- and 19th-century buildings of this prosperous community. Two miles north of the town center take Hoskins Road, and you'll get a taste of this picturesque, surreal landscape.

From Route 10, as you look to the west, you'll see a ridge of hills topped by a stone tower, the centerpiece of **Talcott Mountain State Park**, which can be reached by Route 185. Hartford lies on the other side.

Truth is, **Hartford** suffers the same image problems that afflict other American cities, and there are many well-traveled residents of the state who've never been there. They're missing a lot. Its long and distinguished history—from newborn settlement in 1635 to shipping center throughout the 18th century, industrial leader in the 19th and capital of the insurance business to this day—is reflected in its varied architecture and active cultural life. For easier sightseeing, the city can be subdivided into three separate parts: downtown; the capitol area, on the opposite side of beautiful Bushnell Park; and Asylum Hill, where Mark Twain built his celebrated mansion.

Opened in 1844 and later harmoniously enlarged, the Wadsworth Atheneum Museum of Art is America's longest continuously operating public art museum.

Start at the dignified **Old State House**, designed in 1796 by Charles Bulfinch and used as the seat of the state's government until 1878, years during which Hartford alternated as capital with New Haven. This venerable structure was almost bulldozed, until a vocal group of preservationists came to its aid. The building is now a museum. An education center is open to the public on Saturday. Closed Sunday and Monday. ~ 800 Main Street, Hartford; 860-522-6766, fax 860-522-2812; www.ctosh.org, e-mail info@ctosh.org.

Ask for the walking-tour map of the city prepared by the **Greater Hartford Convention and Visitor's Bureau.** It will guide you to two dozen landmarks, old and new. (As you've no doubt noticed, the former are being squeezed out by the latter.) Closed Saturday and Sunday. ~ 31 Pratt Street, Hartford; 860-728-6789, 800-446-7811, fax 860-293-2365; www.enjoyhartford.com, e-mail ghcvb@hartfordcvb.org.

If the printed itinerary seems overwhelming, here's a shortened list: Walk by the **Richardson**, as it is known today, a massive, handsome brownstone building designed in 1876 by Henry Hobson Richardson in his distinctive Romanesque style. It's just north of the Old State House, on Main Street. A few blocks south, and across the street, stands **Center Church**, built in 1807, whose white portico and ornate white spire contrast with the red brick of the facade. Next to it, the **Ancient Burying Ground** shelters gravestones that date back to 1640. ~ 675 Main Street, Hartford.

Across the street is the **Wadsworth Atheneum Museum of Art**, where you'll find a distinguished collection, strong in paintings of the Hudson River school, Colonial American furniture, African-American art and other works of the 20th century. Also displayed are European works from the 16th through the 18th centuries. Yet the museum doesn't overwhelm you with size and arrogance; it feels friendly, somehow. Closed Monday. Admission. ~ 600 Main Street, Hartford; 860-278-2670, fax 860-527-0803; www.wadsworthatheneum.org, e-mail info@wadsworth atheneum.org.

Nestled between the Atheneum and the fine **Municipal Building** of 1915 is **Burr Mall**, a small, endearing open space centered on Alexander Calder's giant sculpture *Stegosaurus*. The two classic buildings and the bright red steel abstract sculpture form a wonderful contrast. ◀ HIDDEN

On to the **State Capitol**, a monumental Victorian Gothic structure that can be toured, along with the legislative office building, in groups led by members of the League of Women Voters. The 1878 capitol is a sight to behold: gold-domed, turreted, mansarded, adorned with statues of Connecticut's greats (including Ella Grasso, the late governor and first woman to be elected to that post in her own right). The soaring, lavishly decorated interior is as exuberant as the facade; clearly Hartford was out to celebrate when it won the designation of sole capital over New Haven in 1875. Closed Sunday. Group reservations are required. ~ Tours and Hours: Capitol Information, 210 Capitol Avenue, Hartford; 860-240-0222, fax 860-240-8627; www.cga.ct.gov/cap itoltours, e-mail capitol.tours@cga.ct.gov.

The stately building across Capitol Avenue houses the State Library, the Supreme Court and the **Museum of Connecticut History**, which specializes in military, political and industrial history. Exhibits include a collection of historic Colt firearms and a trove of documents such as the 1662 Royal Charter. Closed Sunday. ~ 231 Capitol Avenue, Hartford; 860-757-6535, fax 860-757-6533; www.cslib.org.

Asylum Hill is where Mark Twain built his Hartford residence, along with many eminent citizens of the 1870s who fled the downtown area for what was then considered the suburb. His three-story mansion was part of Nook Farm, an enclave of writers and intellectuals that included Harriet Beecher Stowe. The **Mark Twain House** is a super-ornamented extravaganza where he wrote *Huckleberry Finn* and *Tom Sawyer*. Open to the public for guided tours only. An education and visitors center features a museum store, café, theater and exhibition galleries. Closed Tuesday from January through March. Admission. ~ 351

Farmington Avenue, Hartford; 860-493-6411; www.marktwain house.org, e-mail info@marktwainhouse.org.

You can visit the **Harriet Beecher Stowe Center**, which features Stowe's discreet Victorian "cottage" along with the Katharine Seymour Day House. Closed Monday from mid-October to the end of November and January through the Monday before Memorial Day. Admission. ~ 77 Forest Street, Hartford; 860-525-9317; www.harrietbeecherstowe.org, e-mail info@stowe center.org.

Located a few blocks away is the **Connecticut Historical Society Museum**, where a variety of lively exhibits will help you place the sights you've seen in historical context. Within the museum is a genealogy library. Library closed Sunday and Monday. Museum closed Monday. Admission. ~ 1 Elizabeth Street, Hartford; 860-236-5621, fax 860-236-2664; www.chs.org, e-mail ask_ us@ chs.org.

Hartford's surroundings offer varied attractions that can be visited on day trips. Art buffs won't want to miss the **New Britain Museum of American Art**, which features a collection spanning 250 years and is strong on Hudson River school painters and American artists of the 20th century. Closed Monday. Admission. ~ 56 Lexington Street, New Britain; 860-229-0257, fax 860-229-3445; www.nbmaa.org, e-mail nbmaa@nbmaa.org.

North of the capital, the **New England Air Museum** exhibits 75 aircrafts in three display buildings that trace the history of aviation. It is the largest museum of its type in the northeastern United States. Admission. ~ Off Route 75, Bradley International Airport, Windsor Locks; 860-623-3305, fax 860-627-2820; www.neam.org, e-mail staff@neam.org.

A mere three miles south of Hartford on Route 91, the town of **Wethersfield**, one of the original three settlements on the Connecticut River, is famed for its extensive historic district comprising 150 dwellings built before the mid-19th century. Several old Wethersfield homes are open to the public as house museums:

The **Webb-Deane-Stevens Museum** consists of three homes built, respectively, for a wealthy merchant, a diplomat and a craftsman, each representing a different style of 18th-century life. The Webb house was the setting for a conference between General George Washington and his French counterpart, Jean de Rochambeau, that led to the British defeat at Yorktown in 1781. You can wander the pretty garden behind the Webb. Closed Tuesday; closed weekdays from November through April. Admission. ~ 211 Main Street, Wethersfield; 860-529-0612, fax 860-571-8636; www.webb-deane-stevens.org, e-mail info@ webb-deane-stevens.org.

Across the street, the **Hurlbut–Dunham House** is a stylish two-story brick Georgian-style building with Victorian porches and a belvedere. It features early-20th-century collections of the Dunham family, including paintings, glassware, china and ceramics. The house retains its original wallpaper. Open weekends mid-May to mid-October. Admission. ~ 212 Main Street, Wethersfield; 860-529-7656, fax 860-563-2609; www.wethhist.org, e-mail weth.hist.society@snet.net.

The **Buttolph-Williams House**, part of the Antiquarian and Landmarks society, is a late-17th-century "mansion house" with a collection of period furnishings. Its overhanging eaves and small casement windows reflect the medieval character of the pilgrim century. Closed Tuesday and from mid-October to mid-May. Admission. ~ 249 Broad Street, Wethersfield; 860-247-8996; www.hartnet.org/als.

American Indians knew Connecticut as Quinnetukqut, "long tidal river."

The **Old Academy** is a fine 1804 brick building in the federal style housing a library with genealogy resources and several offices. Closed Sunday and Monday. ~ 150 Main Street, Wethersfield.

Nearby is the **Wethersfield Museum**, exhibiting the Wethersfield Historical Society's collection of local history. Admission. ~ Robert A. Keeney Memorial Cultural Center, 200 Main Street, Wethersfield; 860-529-7161.

At the north end of Wethersfield's Main Street, right on the Cove, is the **Cove Warehouse**. This 17th-century building is a symbol of Wethersfield's prosperous maritime past. The warehouse was one of six built in the 17th century. Hanging exhibit panels tell the complete story. Open weekends mid-May to mid-October. Admission. ~ North end of Main Street, Wethersfield; 860-529-7656.

For information on the Old Academy, the Wethersfield Museum, the Hurlbut-Dunham House or the Cove Warehouse, contact the **Wethersfield Historical Society**. ~ 150 Main Street, Wethersfield; 860-529-7656, fax 860-563-2609; www.wethhist.org, e-mail weth.hist.society@snet.net.

LODGING

For budget lodgings in the Farmington Valley, the place to go is the **Hillside Motel**, 17 miles west of Hartford. It's family-owned and -operated, and its 11 simple rooms are clean, neat and air-conditioned, though there's nothing fancy. What's more, it's close to great flyfishing in the Farmington River known as Satan's Kingdom. ~ 671 Route 44, Canton; 860-693-4951. BUDGET.

Avon Old Farms Hotel, once a small motel, has grown gradually into its present role as a major country hotel with 157 guest rooms. This multiwinged property has a dining room, an outdoor pool, an on-site fitness center, well-landscaped grounds and great views over woods and stream. You can choose from inexpensive lodging in the older original motel or more expensive options in the three-story main wing, where the rooms are done in old New England elegance and the carpeted staircase in the lofty lobby just begs for Scarlett O'Hara to sweep down it. ~ 279 Avon Mountain Road at the junction of Routes 10 and 44, Avon; 860-677-1651, 800-836-4000, fax 860-677-0364; www.avonoldfarmshotel.com, e-mail reservations@avonoldfarmshotel.com. DELUXE.

If a truly exquisite restoration makes your heart sing, then the **Simsbury 1820 House** is a must. Set on a knoll in the center of this historic small town, the three-story, four-chimney brick building was home to generations of distinguished Americans, including Gifford Pinchot, known as the father of the conservation movement. No pains were spared in transforming the graceful gray mansion and the nearby carriage house into a 33-room inn with a fine restaurant. Each room is carpeted and furnished with antiques, with imaginative use made of the nooks, crannies and arched windows. ~ 731 Hopmeadow Street, Route 10, Simsbury; 860-658-7658, 800-879-1820, fax 860-651-0724; www.simsbury1820house.com, e-mail visit@simsbury1820house.com. DELUXE TO ULTRA-DELUXE.

Behind the ornate 19th-century brick facade of the **Goodwin Hotel** in the heart of downtown, all is brand new. Once a distinguished apartment house, the local landmark was entirely rebuilt inside and appointed in a style that would have pleased Hartford-born financier J. P. Morgan, whom the hotel honors. Fine reproductions grace the 124 rooms and suites, service is personal and the ambience is gracious and subdued. Rates are expensive but lower on weekends and worth it if a touch of urban elegance fits in your plans. ~ 1 Haynes Street, Hartford; 860-246-7500, 800-922-5006, fax 860-247-4576; www.goodwinhotel.com. DELUXE.

A luxury downtown hotel offering easy access to the Civic Center's many attractions, the **Crowne Plaza Hotel Hartford-Downtown** caters largely to business travelers. The 350 guestrooms and suites are spacious and modern. There's an outdoor pool, a restaurant and a lounge on the premises. ~ 50 Morgan Street, Hartford; 860-549-2400, 877-227-6963, fax 860-549-7844; www.ichotelsgroup.com, e-mail kcyr@rosdevhotels.com. MODERATE TO ULTRA-DELUXE.

Budget accommodations can be found on the outskirts of Hartford off Route 91 at Exit 27. Of several chain hotels, the **Holiday Inn Express Hotel & Suites Convention Center** seemed the most attractive, with an airy lobby, good-size outdoor pool and 129 rooms, including 44 suites. A complimentary continental breakfast is provided. ~ 185 Brainard Road, Hartford; 860-525-1000, fax 860-525-2990; www.hartford-hotel.com, e-mail info@hartford-hotel.com. MODERATE.

Avon Old Farms Inn is just what you pictured for dinner at a country inn. Located in an 18th-century stagecoach stop, it serves large portions of traditional American food (including salmon, seabass, chicken, lamb, lobster and pasta dishes). All the baking is done on the grounds. Sunday brunch. Closed Monday. ~ 1 Nod Road, Avon; 860-677-2818, fax 860-676-0280; www.avonoldfarmsinn.com. DELUXE TO ULTRA-DELUXE.

The restaurant at **Simsbury 1820 House** is in what was once the cellar of the lovely old mansion. Room dividers give the illusion of intimate dining rooms. There are exposed brick walls with arches, and paintings by local artists. The atmosphere is casual, the cuisine Continental. An additional pleasure is a drink on the spacious veranda overlooking Talcott Mountain. Closed Friday through Sunday. ~ 731 Hopmeadow Street, Route 10, Simsbury; 860-658-7658, 800-879-1820; www.simsbury1820house.com, e-mail visit@simsbury1820house.com. MODERATE TO ULTRA-DELUXE.

Max Downtown, popular with the upscale young crowd, serves eclectic American and Continental dishes. The menu, which is written daily, might include grilled swordfish with roasted pepper sauce or roasted New Zealand rack of lamb with herbed couscous crust and harissa sauce. No lunch on weekends. ~ 185 Asylum Street, Hartford; 860-522-2530, fax 860-246-5279; www.maxdowntown.com, e-mail ssmith@maxdowntown.com. MODERATE TO ULTRA-DELUXE.

If a visit to the Wadsworth Atheneum is on your itinerary, consider staying for lunch at **The Museum Cafe**. It's an attractive, restful room off the rotunda on the main floor, enhanced by a changing selection of prints or paintings. Open only for lunch, it offers a dozen entrées that include fresh fish, chicken, sandwiches and salads with a gourmet touch. There is also a Sunday brunch and occasionally dinner on Thursday. Reservations recommended.

AUTHOR FAVORITE

Apricots fronts a lively stretch of the Farmington River. You can sit on a riverbank terrace, drink or sandwich in hand, and almost feel the water as it leaps around shiny rocks. The ground floor of the old building, a former trolley stop, is devoted to a popular pub where the "happy hour" boasts a heaping tableful of complimentary food. Upstairs is the restaurant itself, an oasis of fine American cuisine where the entrées most in demand are rack of lamb and swordfish. ~ 1593 Farmington Avenue, Farmington; 860-673-5405, fax 860-673-7138; www.apricotsrestaurant.com. DELUXE TO ULTRA-DELUXE.

Closed Monday and Tuesday. ~ 600 Main Street, Hartford; 860-278-2670 ext. 3039; e-mail info@wadsworthatheneum.org. BUDGET TO MODERATE.

Authentic Italian restaurants are hard to come by these days, but **Peppercorn's Grill** dishes up homemade gnocchi, fettuccini and ravioli in mouth-watering sauces that will have you longing for an old country getaway. This award-winning restaurant also serves such contemporary items as grilled veal with a truffle and porcini glaze. Save room for the warm chocolate bread pudding. ~ 357 Main Street, Hartford; 860-547-1714; www.peppercornsgrill.com, e-mail comments@peppercornsgrill.com. DELUXE TO ULTRA-DELUXE.

SHOPPING

Canton abounds in antique shops. For some competitive shopping, visit the Saturday auction at 7:30 p.m. at **Canton Barn Auctions.** Doors open at 5 p.m. ~ 75 Old Canton Road, off Route 44, Canton; 860-693-0601; www.cantonbarn.com.

Riverdale Farms used to provide fresh milk to Hartford County. Today it houses over 50 varied shops and services in 16 buildings, some old, some new but harmonious. There are fashions, gifts, jewelry, clothes, a day spa and specialty stores. ~ Route 10 North, Avon; 860-677-6437, fax 860-676-1021; www.riverdalefarmsshopping.com.

In downtown Hartford you will find two shopping malls. First, there is the mixed-use mall and apartment complex **Hartford 21.** ~ 210 Asylum Street; 860-525-2121. The other is the dazzling **Pavilion at State House Square.** ~ 30 State House Square, Hartford; 860-241-0100.

For unusual gifts, you might consider **The Museum Shop** at the Wadsworth Atheneum, which stocks a fine selection of art books, reproductions, prints, cards, elegant wrapping papers as well as games and books for enquiring young minds. Closed Monday. ~ 600 Main Street, Hartford; 860-278-2670; www.wadsworthatheneum.org, e-mail info@wadsworthatheneum.org.

For fabulous estate jewelry and baubles of all types, visit **Becker's.** This treasure trove of a store specializes in diamonds.

AUTHOR FAVORITE

The **Farmington Valley Arts Center** comprises 21 artists' studios, and two galleries featuring American contemporary crafts from all over the United States for sale. It's an intriguing complex of handsome brownstone buildings scattered about a landscaped park. Hours vary seasonally; call ahead. ~ 25 Arts Center Lane, Avon; 860-678-1867, fax 860-674-1877; www.fvac.net, e-mail info@fvac.net.

~ 44 Pratt Street, Hartford; 860-548-1500, 888-444-8335; www.beckers.com.

NIGHTLIFE

Bushnell Center for the Performing Arts has been a major performing-arts venue since 1930. The vast art deco auditorium is where audiences flock for concerts of the Hartford Symphony and other orchestras, the ballet and the opera, and touring dramas and musicals. ~ 166 Capitol Avenue, Hartford; 860-987-5900, 888-824-2874, fax 860-987-6080; www.bushnell.org, e-mail info@bushnell.org.

Hartford Civic Center schedules frequent, star-caliber entertainment. ~ 1 Civic Center Plaza, Hartford; 860-727-8010; www.hartfordciviccenter.com.

Brew Ha Ha Comedy Club at the City Steam Brewery Cafe features comedians from New York City on Thursday, Friday and Saturday nights. The theme here is very beer-oriented, with half a dozen homebrewed beers on tap nightly and beer decor throughout. Cover. ~ 942 Main Street, Hartford; 860-525-1600; www.citysteambrewerycafe.com, e-mail gm@brewerycafe.com.

At **Bourbon Street North** it's Top 40 and live bands on Thursday through Saturday; a deejay also fires up on Friday. Closed Sunday and Monday. Cover on Friday and Saturday. ~ 70 Union Place, Hartford; 860-525-1014; www.bourbonstreetclub.com.

PARKS

STRATTON BROOK STATE PARK An unusual feature of this 148-acre park in the Farmington Valley is a shady bicycle trail built on a former railroad bed. It travels across woodlands and along several scenic brooks, then continues through a town forest. There are also hiking trails and a pleasant pond. Facilities include a picnic shelter (by reservation only), restrooms and changing rooms. The park is completely wheelchair accessible. Closed Labor Day to Memorial Day. Parking fee, $7. ~ Off of Route 309, two miles west of Simsbury; 860-658-1388, fax 860-424-4070.

TALCOTT MOUNTAIN STATE PARK Views from this mountain, of the city of Hartford and the valleys of the Farmington and Connecticut rivers, have been favorites of painters for more than 100 years. Atop the mountain stands handsome Heublein Tower, part of a residence deeded to the state by a prominent Hartford family. A one-and-a-half-mile hike leads from the parking lot to the tower, 165 feet high; the ground floor houses a museum of local history. Closed Monday through Wednesday from Memorial Day to Labor Day; closed November to May (information, 860-677-0662). Along the trail, you might see people hang-gliding: The mountain is considered a good jumping-off place for this sport. Amenities include picnic grounds, restrooms, a museum and an observation tower. ~ Route 185, three miles south of Simsbury; 860-242-1158.

▲ There is camping nearby at the American Legion State Forest. The campground includes 30 tent/RV sites (no hookups); $15 per night. Reservations suggested. Closed mid-October to mid-April. ~ West River Road, Pleasant Valley; 860-379-0922.

DINOSAUR STATE PARK This 65-acre park, set between Hartford and New Haven, boasts a geodesic dome exhibit center enclosing a celebrated exposure of rock. The ancient rock bears some 500 tracks made by dinosaurs of the Jurassic period—200 million years ago. Visitors may make plaster casts of some tracks from May through October, but materials are not provided. Call 860-529-5816 for information about casts. Two miles of nature trails wind through the park, which offers visitors picnic grounds, restrooms and an exhibit center (closed Monday). Day-use fee, $5. ~ 400 West Street in the Rocky Hill area, one mile east of Exit 23 off Route 91; 860-529-8423; www.dinosaurstatepark.org, e-mail friends.dinosaur.prk@snet.net.

New Haven Area

Located just about midway between the borders of New York and Rhode Island, New Haven is the last major hub you reach when heading north on Route 95. The city itself is a fascinating blend of old and new, urban center and university campus—a must on any tour of the state. Just to the east is a handful of towns—including Branford, Guilford and Clinton—that are home to historic homes and museums. Just offshore are the Thimble Islands, a galaxy of tiny islands.

New Haven was founded as an independent colony in 1638, but in 1784 it merged with Hartford to become co-capital of the state, which it remained until 1875. Although it shone as an industrial center in the 19th and early 20th centuries, the special flavor that sets it apart today is due in large part to the presence of Yale University, an institution that has shared the city's fortunes since 1718.

SIGHTS

New Haven was planned around a green at its founding, and happily the 17-acre square with its trio of churches in the center has been proudly maintained as open space and still acts as focus of the downtown area. Yale University forms the backdrop to the green's western edge, along College Street and fanning out across a dozen blocks west and north of it. Most of the cultural and architectural landmarks that define this uncommon city can be seen on a walk around the immediate area.

Yale University offers free guided tours of the campus. ~ Visitor Information Center, 149 Elm Street, New Haven; 203-432-2300; www.yale.edu/visitor. The **Greater New Haven Convention and Visitors Bureau** provides maps and information on local sights and events. Closed on the weekend. ~ 169 Orange Street, New Haven; 203-777-8550, 800-332-7829, fax 203-782-7755; www.newhavencvb.org, e-mail mail@newhavencvb.org.

Three hundred years of history and architecture can be traced on these rambles. For the earliest structures, start with the three graceful clapboard homes built by late-18th-century gentry at **149, 155** and **175 Elm Street.** The three facades, set among much grander, later buildings, give a glimpse of how the city looked 200 years ago. The only structures on the green itself are the churches—**Trinity, Center** and **United**—erected between 1812 and 1815 in Gothic, Georgian and Federal styles. ◄HIDDEN

Yale's oldest remaining building, **Connecticut Hall**, is part of what is known as the old campus, which can be entered through **Phelps Gateway**, the school's massive front door at 344 College Street. It's a bulky, gambrel-roofed brick structure facing a statue of Nathan Hale, who lived there as a student.

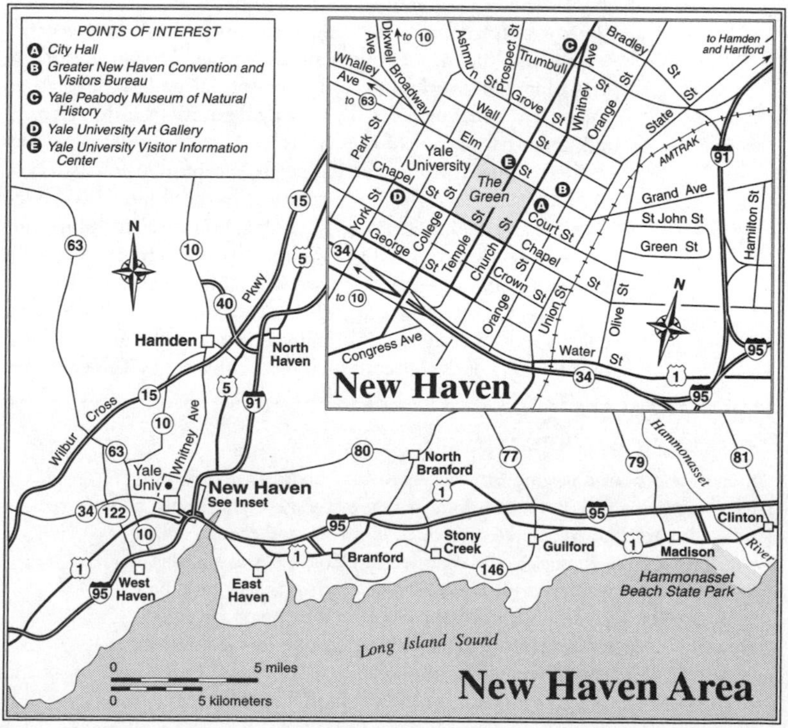

Much of the architecture for which Yale is famous is 19th- and early-20th-century Gothic Revival. By crossing the Old Campus onto High Street, the visitor can wander past **Dwight Chapel** (1842), the first Gothic design; **Harkness Tower** (1917), whose

turrets and pinnacles are a symbol of Yale itself; and **Sterling Memorial Library** (1927), a modern Gothic.

York Street, one block west of High, is also lined with Yale-related buildings, including the legendary **Mory's**, a private club celebrated in "The Whiffenpoof Song." ~ 306 York Street, New Haven.

One of the finest contemporary complexes on campus rises just west of York Street: **Morse** and **Stiles Colleges**, designed in 1960 by Eero Saarinen, contrasting yet in harmony with the older buildings.

HIDDEN ► Don't miss Claes Oldenburg's powerful sculpture **Lipstick**, an anti-Vietnam War statement that dominates the courtyard of Morse College.

Another renowned 1960s structure is Gordon Bunshaft's **Beinecke Rare Book and Manuscript Library**, a granite and translucent marble landmark that seems to float above a sunken court featuring sculptures by Isamu Noguchi. Step inside to view a Gutenberg Bible, original Audubon prints and other exhibits. Closed Sunday. ~ 121 Wall Street, New Haven; 203-432-2977, fax 203-432-4047; www.library.yale.edu/beinecke, e-mail beinecke.library@yale.edu.

Down on Chapel Street, you come upon the **Yale University Art Gallery**, known for American, European, African, Asian and pre-Columbian works, as well as a special gallery devoted to American art that includes the historical paintings of John Trumbull, the artist-patriot of the American Revolution. Designed by architect Louis I. Kahn, the gallery is exceptional for its use of interior space and light (under renovation until late 2005). One
HIDDEN ► of its most appealing features is its idyllic **outdoor sculpture garden**. Closed Monday. ~ 1111 Chapel Street, New Haven; 203-432-0600, fax 203-432-7159; www.artgallery.yale.edu.

Across the street you'll find the **Yale Center for British Art**, which was also designed by architect Louis I. Kahn and is known for the quality of its collections. It boasts canvases by Turner, Gains-

CONNECTICUT INVENTIONS

Among the products invented, or perfected, by Connecticut Yankees were hats, combs, pins, clocks, seeds, furniture, typewriters, axes, hardware of all kinds, vulcanized rubber, bicycles, textiles—both silk and cotton—silverware and firearms. Samuel Colt developed the Colt 45, "the gun that won the West," at his armory in Hartford. At his firearms factory near New Haven, Eli Whitney, who had previously invented the cotton gin, introduced the concept of interchangeable parts, which led to the flowering of the Industrial Revolution.

borough and Constable, among other renowned artists. Closed Monday. ~ 1080 Chapel Street, New Haven; 203-432-2850, 877-274-8278, fax 203-432-9628; www.yale.edu/ycba, e-mail bacinfo@yale.edu.

New Haven has suffered its share of urban ills, and efforts to upgrade its image have sometimes been ill-advised. Two of the more successful projects are the recent creation of an entertainment district on College Street, centering on the renovated **Shubert** and **Palace** theaters (see "Theater in Connecticut" in this chapter).

Another area that has been successfully restored is **Wooster Square**, between Chapel and Greene streets, six blocks east of the green. This early-19th-century enclave of graceful homes, after years of neglect, is once again a fashionable in-town address. ◄ HIDDEN

Among the many cultural and recreational facilities in New Haven are the **Yale Peabody Museum of Natural History**, with its famed dinosaur collection and a Pulitzer Prize–winning mural entitled *The Age of Reptiles*. Admission. ~ 170 Whitney Avenue, New Haven; 203-432-5050, fax 203-432-9816; www.yale.edu/peabody, e-mail peabody.admissions@yale.edu.

Nearby, the **New Haven Colony Historical Society** contains furniture and decorative arts from early New Haven homes, an art gallery, a maritime collection and industrial displays. Closed Monday; in July and August, closed Sunday and Monday. Admission. ~ 114 Whitney Avenue, New Haven; 203-562-4183, fax 203-562-2002; www.newhavenmuseum.org.

Farther out Whitney Avenue you'll find the **Eli Whitney Museum**, dedicated to the New Haven industrialist who invented the cotton gin and, on this site, an armory that helped ignite the American industrial revolution. The museum's workshop offers hands-on projects in the tradition of Yankee ingenuity. Admission. ~ 915 Whitney Avenue, Hamden; 203-777-1833, fax 203-777-1229; www.eliwhitney.org, e-mail mail@eliwhitney.org.

On a day that calls for outdoor fun, consider a trip to **Lighthouse Point Park**, with facilities for picnicking and swimming and a classic old-time carousel. Closed Labor Day through Memorial Day. Admission. ~ 2 Lighthouse Road, New Haven; 203-946-8790.

Or you may want to head for the **Shoreline Trolley Museum**, where you can ride classic, antique trolleys along a scenic one-and-a-half-mile route. Open daily from Memorial Day to Labor Day; closed January through March; call for other hours. Admission. ~ 17 River Street, East Haven; 203-467-6927, fax 203-467-7635; www.bera.org, e-mail berasltm18@sbcglobal.net.

East of New Haven, the shoreline is dotted with a string of attractive residential towns that started life as farming and fishing villages. Branford is about six miles east of town on Route 1. It's home to **Harrison House**, which was built in 1724 and is now a museum filled with 17th-, 18th- and 19th-century furnishings and artifacts. Open on Friday and Saturday from June to late September and by appointment. ~ 124 Main Street, Branford; 203-488-4828; www.branfordhistory.org.

HIDDEN ► Slightly south and just east of Branford is Stony Creek, from which cruises for the Thimble Islands sail. **The Thimbles**, some no larger than a rock that disappears at high tide, others topped by a single elaborate Victorian mansion or two, are an enchanting group of islands. They say Captain Kidd hid stolen treasures on one of these rocky outposts. You'll learn all about that, and other local legends, if you take one of the small **excursion boats** around this miniature archipelago. Seasonal. Closed Tuesday. ~ *Volsunga III*, Town Dock (203-481-3345); *Sea Mist*, Thimble Islands Cruise, Stony Creek dock, Branford; 203-488-8905, fax 203-488-3416; www.thimbleislandcruise.com, e-mail chartersea488@aol.com.

Route 146 leads from Stony Creek to Guilford, a town that has preserved many pre–Revolutionary War houses, including the **Henry Whitfield State Museum.** This home of the town's first minister, built in 1639, is said to be both the oldest stone house in New England and the oldest building in Connecticut. The green is special, generous for a town of this size and evocative of an earlier time. The museum is open Wednesday through Sunday from April to mid-March. Admission. ~ 248 Old Whitfield Street, Guilford; 203-453-2457, fax 203-453-7544; e-mail whitfieldmuseum@snet.net.

A few miles farther east you might consider a swim at **Hammonasset Beach State Park**. It's Connecticut's largest public beach, over two miles long.

A worthwhile stop in Clinton, a picturesque, little seaside village made up of Colonial Cape Cod homes, is the **Stanton House**, built in 1789. Once a general store, it now exhibits items that would have been sold in that era, such as hardware, yard goods, spices and dishware. Open Tuesday through Sunday from June through September. ~ 63 East Main Street, Clinton; 860-669-2132.

LODGING

Located just a block from the Yale campus, the **Three Chimneys Inn** is a lovely Victorian mansion (circa 1870) filled with antiques and 19th-century details. The inn also has 20th-century touches, including computer hookups and conference rooms. Its 11 guest rooms have canopy beds, oriental rugs and period furnishings. There's also a small exercise room. ~ 1201 Chapel Street, New Haven; 203-789-1201, 800-443-1554, fax 203-776-7363; www.threechimneysinn.com, e-mail chimneysnh@aol.com. DELUXE TO ULTRA-DELUXE.

The Colony is a modern, five-story hotel with 126 rooms and suites done in Colonial style. Its convenient location makes it popular with Yale visitors as well as those sampling the city's theaters and museums. The Colony has its own indoor garage, a boon in the busy downtown area, as well as a restaurant and lounge with entertainment on the weekends. ~ 1157 Chapel Street, New Haven; 203-776-1234, 800-458-8810, fax 203-772-3929; www.colonyatyale.com, e-mail info@colonyatyale.com. MODERATE.

Yet another of New Haven's many "firsts" is the frisbee: Rumor has it that in 1920, enterprising Yale students tossed a Mrs. Frisbie's Pie plate between them, giving rise to a quintessential American pastime.

The historic **Hotel Duncan**, a landmark since 1894, has probably seen better days, yet it must be the best buy in town. Behind its handsome Romanesque facade rise five floors of neatly furnished rooms with old-fashioned baths. Have the pleasure of dining in the heart of Yale and being part of a tradition. ~ 1151 Chapel Street, New Haven; 203-787-1273, fax 203-787-0160. MODERATE.

East of New Haven, the shoreline towns are well-stocked with budget- and moderate-priced motels close to Route 95. **Quality Inn**, a facility only seven miles from New Haven, has 82 guest rooms, a pool and complimentary breakfast buffet. It's also near Tweed–New Haven Airport and the popular Trolley Museum. ~ 30 Frontage Road Exit 51, East Haven; 203-469-5321, fax 203-469-2544; e-mail hotelhelp@choicehotels.com. MODERATE TO DELUXE.

DINING

The Chapel Street area is so rich in theaters, museums and scenic vistas of Yale that it's become a spawning ground for restaurants.

You'll find **Scoozzi** down a flight of stone stairs, between the British Art Center and the Yale Repertory Theatre. Location is everything, but here the high-tech setting is attractive as well, and the trendy, Italian-inspired fare pleases the customers. Sunday brunch features live jazz. Warmer months bring patio dining. Reservations are recommended. ~ 1104 Chapel Street, New Haven; 203-776-8268, fax 203-772-2124; www.scoozzi.com, e-mail scoozzi@sbcglobal.net. MODERATE TO DELUXE.

Louis' Lunch is one of New Haven's claims to fame—it seems Louis Lassen was the man who first put ground-up beef between two slices of bread, back in 1900. The small brick building is considered a landmark; in fact, it was moved in 1975 to save it from incoming bulldozers. It's old New Haven, where people talk to strangers, and the hamburger—a very fine one—is king. No dinner Tuesday and Wednesday. Closed Sunday and Monday; closed August to mid-September. ~ 261–263 Crown Street, New Haven; 203-562-5507; www.louislunch.com, e-mail jeff@louislunch.com. BUDGET.

Text continued on page 92.

Theater in Connecticut

Over the past two decades, this small state has been gaining a large reputation for excellent theater. Connecticut theater no longer means merely summer stock or road companies of successful Broadway shows. The state has seen a flowering of professional regional theaters, staging their own productions of classics and new plays and sending them forth into the national arena, where they have garnered many top awards.

New Haven, once known as a venue for New York producers testing out Broadway-bound plays, now boasts two prestigious producing companies of its own. One is the 488-seat, thrust-style **Long Wharf Theatre**. It's found in the heart of the city's wholesale market, adjacent to Route 95—a great location with no parking problems. Its season, from September through June, spans the spectrum of American and European drama and comedy, with an occasional musical—outstanding productions that have gained recognition around the country. There's a second theater on the premise called Stage II. ~ 222 Sargent Drive, New Haven; 203-787-4282; www.longwharf.org.

The other one, the prestigious **Yale Repertory Theatre**, is the professional adjunct of Yale University School of Drama. Yale Rep has produced 92 world and American premieres, 4 of which have received the Pulitzer Prize for drama. Its stage has been graced by the likes of Meryl Streep, Sigourney Weaver, Danny Glover, William Hurt, James Earl Jones and Glenn Close, to name a few. ~ 1120 Chapel Street, New Haven; 203-432-1234; www.yalerep.org, e-mail yalerep@yale.edu.

The state capital is home to the **Hartford Stage**, winner of the Tony Award for Outstanding Achievement in Regional Theater. Housed in a contemporary, 489-seat theater downtown, the company is devoted to innovative, interpretations of the classics, revivals of neglected works, as well as new works by today's hottest playwrights. The Main Stage season runs September through June, Summer Stage runs July through August, and **A Christmas Carol** runs November through December. Closed Monday. ~ 50 Church Street, Hartford; 860-527-5151, fax 860-247-8243; www.hartfordstage.org, e-mail info@hartfordstage.org.

Goodspeed Musicals at the Goodspeed Opera House is dedicated to the American musical—reviving vintage ones and inspiring the new. The legendary *Annie* as well as *Man of La Mancha* were both seen for the first time in this Victorian jewel box on the Connecticut River, as were numerous song-and-dance gems from the past that went on to Broadway. The season is April to mid-December. Closed Monday and Tuesday. ~ Route 82, East

Haddam; 860-873-8668, fax 860-873-2329; www.goodspeed.org. A second stage, the **Norma Terris Theatre**, opened in 1984 to house workshops of new musicals-in-progress. Closed Monday and Tuesday, and is only open prior to showtimes. ~ North Main Street, Chester; 860-873-8668, fax 860-873-2329; www.goodspeed.org.

The **National Theatre of the Deaf** makes its home in Connecticut, although it travels during most of the year. A professional ensemble of deaf and hearing actors, NTD combines the spoken word with sign language in unique performances that have touched the hearts of audiences in all 50 states and more than two dozen countries since 1967. ~ 139 North Main Street, West Hartford; 860-236-4193 (voice and TTY), fax 860-236-4163; www.ntd.org, e-mail ntd-info@ntd.org.

The **Eugene O'Neill Theater Center** is a nationally known playwrights workshop created on a ten-acre estate overlooking Long Island Sound. Staged readings (fee) or run-throughs of works-in-progress are open to the public from mid-June through August. Closed Saturday and Sunday in winter. ~ 305 Great Neck Road, Waterford; 860-443-5378, fax 860-443-9653; www.theoneill.org, e-mail info@theoneill.org.

These are the big guns on the theater scene, the award winners whose names are recognized by stage buffs around the land. Each year also brings new professional theater groups, such as the **Music Theatre of Connecticut**. Offerings also include performing-arts education for children and summer theater camp. ~ 246 Post Road East, Westport; 203-454-3883, fax 203-226-6629; www.musictheatreofct.com, e-mail mtcarts@aol.com.

Other showplaces present national tours of popular dramas and musicals. Foremost among them is New Haven's historic **Shubert Theater**, restored to its stylish 1914 sparkle and offering a varied fall, winter and spring season. ~ 247 College Street, New Haven; 203-562-5666; www.shubert.com.

Connecticut's straw-hat circuit—how quaint that name seems nowadays—is comprised of numerous theaters, some old, some new, that present generally lightweight fare during the summer. In the Lower Connecticut River Valley, the **Ivoryton Playhouse** offers both summer stock and winter stock. ~ 103 Main Street, Ivoryton; 860-767-8348 (summer) or 860-767-7318; www.ivorytonplayhouse.com. In the Northeast Corner the **Connecticut Repertory Theater** performs at the Harriet S. Jorgensen Theatre. ~ 2132 Hillside Road, Storrs; 860-486-4226; www.sfa.uconn.edu. The **Oakdale Theater**, located north of the New Haven area, stages works, musicals and big-name concerts year-round. ~ 95 South Turnpike Road, Wallingford; 203-265-1501; www.oakdale.com. In Southwestern Connecticut, the **Westport Country Playhouse** is one of the oldest summer theaters in the country. Plays run from April to October. Closed Monday. ~ 25 Powers Court, Westport; 203-227-4177; www.westportplayhouse.org, e-mail info@westportplayhouse.org.

Pizza on Wooster Street is a must in New Haven—you'll find no disagreement on that. But whether Pepe's is better than Sally's, or vice versa, is cause for arguments in this city that is considered the pizza capital of the state. There are numerous Italian restaurants lining the street, and all of them have lines that are long but friendly. Here are two favorites. Maybe you'll try them both, and then decide. One of the most popular is **Frank Pepe Pizzeria.** No lunch Sunday. ~ 157 Wooster Street, New Haven; 203-865-5762; www.pepespizzeria.com. BUDGET TO MODERATE.

Lobsters grow by "molting" (shedding their shells). To reach the minimum legal size of one pound, it takes about 25 molts, over the course of five to seven years.

If you're in the mood for a French meal, be sure to make reservations at the **Union League Café.** Owned by chef Jean-Pierre Vuillermet, this is one of only a few places you can get authentic French cuisine in the city. The ever-changing menu may include Provençal specialties such as rack of lamb with homemade wild mushroom tortellini. The dining room is large, open and surrounded with Tiffany-style windows. No lunch on Saturday. Closed Sunday. ~ 1032 Chapel Street, New Haven; 203-562-4299; www.unionleaguecafe.com, e-mail ulcafe@aol.com. MODERATE TO DELUXE.

A local favorite, **500 Blake Street** specializes in Tuscan style cuisine. There's something for everyone, including fish, pasta, chicken, beef and gourmet stone pies. Sunday brunch. Closed Monday. ~ 500 Blake Street, Westville; 203-387-0500, fax 203-387-7578; www.500blakestreetcafe.com, e-mail susan.500@snet.net. MODERATE TO ULTRA-DELUXE.

The **Stony Creek Market** has as many enthusiasts as do the enchanting islands it overlooks. Locals and visitors drop in and order their favorites—soups, unusual salads, breads, muffins and cookies still warm from the oven—then take their choices to a table inside or on the deck. In season, pizza is served in the evening. Food, views and friendly atmosphere vie for the raves. Breakfast and lunch year-round; dinner served Thursday through Sunday from Memorial Day to Labor Day. ~ 178 Thimble Island Road, Stony Creek; 203-488-0145. BUDGET TO MODERATE.

SHOPPING

When in New Haven, do as the Yalies do—patronize the **Yale Bookstore**, a Barnes and Noble bookstore. This mammoth complex houses 170,000 titles, 2000 periodicals, a café and even a clothing department (including children's wear). ~ 77 Broadway, New Haven; 203-777-8440; www.yalebkstore.com.

Another of the bountiful bookstores in this learned city is **Atticus Bookstore Café**, a great place to start reading that novel you just bought as you linger over a cappuccino and pastry or a sandwich. The place has the added bonus of being open until midnight every night. ~ 1082 Chapel Street, New Haven; 203-776-4040; e-mail atticusbookstore@sbcglobal.net.

The area around Chapel and College streets, home to theaters, museums and restaurants, is great for shopping, too. Some of the stores are multiples—Laura Ashley, The Gap—while others are New Haven originals. **Endleman Gallery** carries one-of-a-kind jewelry by over 100 American designers. Closed Sunday from January through October. ~ 1014A Chapel Street, New Haven; 203-776-2517; www.endleman.com. The Endleman Gallery's offspring, **Endleman Two**, presents uncommon accessories and clothes. Closed Sunday from January through October. ~ 1014 Chapel Street, New Haven; 203-782-2280.

Wander the **Boulevard Flea Market**, Connecticut's oldest, for a taste of how flea markets should be. Hidden treasures of grandma's ilk abound, as does plain old lovely junk. There's a $1 parking fee. Weekends only. ~ 500 Ella T. Grasso Boulevard (Route 10), New Haven; 203-772-1447, 877-228-7554; www.fleact.com, e-mail info@fleact.com.

NIGHTLIFE

New Haven is blessed with an outstanding theater scene (see "Theater in Connecticut" in this chapter), frequent concerts by the New Haven Symphony and visiting artists and several late-night spots that are well worth a visit.

Toad's Place headlines local and national bands. Cover. ~ 300 York Street, New Haven; 203-624-8623; www.toadsplace.com.

BEACHES & PARKS

HAMMONASSET BEACH STATE PARK Largest of Connecticut's shoreline parks, 919-acre Hammonasset offers a two-mile-long, wide sandy beach that's great for swimming, snorkeling and fishing. Patient anglers often reel in good-size bluefish, striped bass or blackfish. You can launch small sailboats on the beach, hike along numerous hiking and biking trails, and visit the nature center, which has interpretive programs. Moreover, the park is ideally located for visiting the picturesque shoreline towns. Visitors will find picnic grounds with shelter, restrooms, food concession stands and a pavilion with changing rooms. Day-use fee, $4 to $14. ~ In Madison, one mile south of Exit 62 on Route 95; 203-245-2785, fax 203-245-9201.

▲ There are 550 tent/RV sites (no hookups); most are located in open fields, a five- to ten-minute walk from the beach; $15 per night. ~ 203-245-1817, 877-668-2267.

Lower Connecticut River Valley

The Lower Valley of the Connecticut River—stretching north for some 30 miles from Old Saybrook, where the river empties into Long Island Sound—is a favorite destination for visitors from near and far. The area is studded with small scenic towns once known as shipbuilding and sea-going communities. Also blessed with numerous state parks, and sophisticated restaurants and lodgings, the Lower Valley provides a chance to get close to the longest waterway in New England, a river that was central to the development of the young nation.

SIGHTS

HIDDEN ►

Westbrook, on Long Island Sound, is a good place to begin your exploration of the valley. Take Route 1 east until it joins **Route 154**, then ramble with it past salt marshes, causeways and marinas through **Old Saybrook**, a town with shoreline along both Sound and river and many picturesque watery views.

Route 154 (natives call it the Shore Route) leads to **Essex** and points north, as does Route 9, which is speedier and beautiful in its own right, but the older road is best for antiquing and poking; it gives you more of a sense of place. Essex is one of the most visited towns in the state, and with good reason: it's a compact peninsula where the tree-lined streets end at the river and the white houses, set cheek-by-jowl, date back to 18th-century shipbuilding days. Beware of summer weekends, however: Essex's charms have been sung once too often.

At the foot of Main Street, with a river view to make you catch your breath, stands the **Connecticut River Museum**, housed in a restored 1878 warehouse where steamboats used to stop for freight and passengers on their way to Hartford or New York. Exhibits will help you place the river's role into perspective. Be sure to view the full-size replica of the ill-fated *American Turtle* (the world's first submarine), built just before the Revolutionary War. Closed Monday. Admission. ~ Steam Boat Dock, 67 Main Street, Essex; 860-767-8269, fax 860-767-7028; www.ctrivermuseum.org, e-mail crm@ctrivermuseum.org.

The **Valley Railroad** is a vintage steam train that winds its nostalgic way through the countryside. The train stops at Deep River, the next town up the line, where you may continue on by train or hop aboard a riverboat up the Connecticut River. The riverboat takes you back to Deep River, where you return to Essex. The combination train/riverboat trip takes about two and a half hours. Call for hours. Admission. ~ 1 Railroad Avenue, Essex; 860-767-0103, 800-377-3987, fax 860-767-0104; www.essexsteamtrain.com, e-mail valley.railroad@snet.net.

When you head north from Essex, go right at the turnaround at the head of Main Street and take River Road as far as Deep River—just keep bearing right when the road forks. It's a winding, narrow country road with views of quietly flowing waters and the forested banks across the way. Then back on Route 154 and on to **Chester**, a picture-postcard village with a short main street lined with charmingly eclectic buildings—a few shops, galleries and restaurants, all restored to a fare-thee-well.

Since 1769, Chester has been the site of a commuter ferry to the river's east bank. It's a few minutes' drive east of the town center, on Route 148. By all means, take it. The five-minute crossing operates continuously from 7 a.m. to 6:45 p.m. from April through November, at a minimal charge (for information call 860-347-0028). Looming above you as you stand on deck you'll see what looks like a medieval fortress atop a steep wooded hill. It's **Gillette Castle**, Connecticut's own castle-on-the-Rhine, the creation of a turn-of-the-20th-century actor/playwright who specialized in playing Sherlock Holmes. It took William Gillette five years to build his eccentric dream house, all to his own designs down to the ingenious locks for all 47 doors and the carved oak trim of the mammoth living room. At his death, it was purchased by the state, which made it the centerpiece of a popular state park with wonderful vistas, **Gillette Castle State Park.** Open daily from Memorial Day weekend to Columbus Day. Admission for castle only. ~ 67 River Road, East Haddam; 860-526-2336, fax 860-526-0807.

East Haddam, a few miles south on Route 82, holds what many consider the jewel of the valley: the **Goodspeed Opera House.** Built on the river in the elegant mansard-roofed style of 1876, this petite Victorian beauty was reopened in 1963 and dedicated to reviving American musicals of the past. Tours of the exquisitely restored interior can be taken on Saturday in July, August and September. (For performances, see the "Theater in Connecticut"

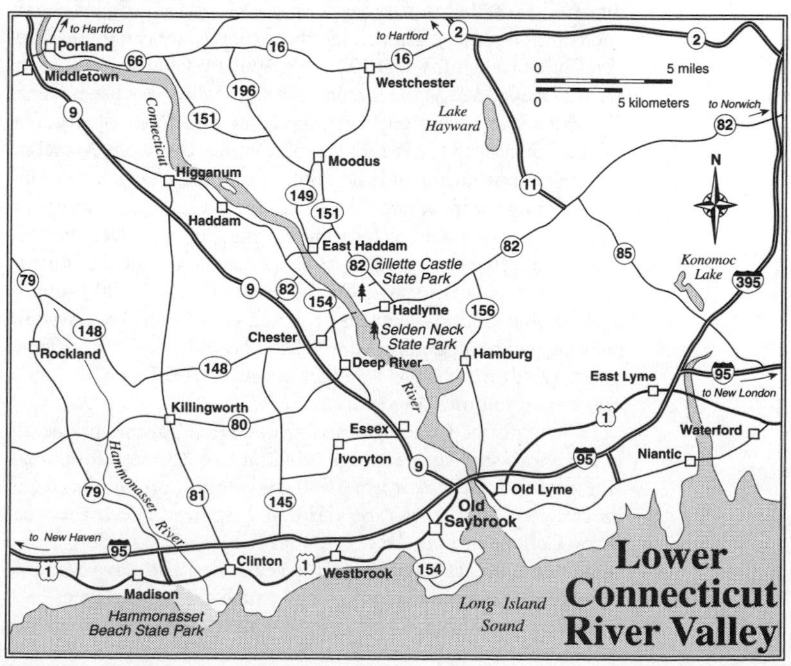

feature in this chapter.) Admission. ~ 6 Main Street, East Haddam; 860-873-8668, fax 860-873-2329; www.goodspeed.org, e-mail info@goodspeed.org.

The little town retains many well-kept buildings, reminders of the days when steamboats made regular stops, and sailing ships before them. High on a knoll is the little red schoolhouse where Nathan Hale taught in 1773–74, two years before he was hanged as a spy by the British.

Step aboard **Connecticut River Expeditions**' environmentally friendly cruise liner, *RiverQuest*, for a relaxing ride along the Connecticut River. While you venture through calm, protected waters, the captain and crew will highlight historic sites, native flora and fauna and points of interest. Each cruise lasts an hour and a half and docks back at in the Essex Harbor at the Connecticut River Museum. Closed late fall through early spring. ~ 67 Main Street, Essex; 860-662-0577, fax 860-767-7938; www.ctriverexpeditions.org.

One of Connecticut's nicknames is the "Provisions State," arising from the state's role as provider of much of the food and cannons used by the soldiers in the Revolutionary War.

Old Lyme lies due south of East Haddam, at the eastern end of the highway bridge that spans the river as it flows to the sea. The town's wealth, reflected in extraordinarily handsome, spacious homes, was born in the days of clipper ships and the China trade, but at the start of this century Old Lyme became a magnet for artists drawn by its beauty and tranquil setting. They called themselves American Impressionists: Childe Hassam, Willard Metcalf, William Chadwick and others who stayed at "Miss Florence's" boardinghouse. Miss Florence Griswold was a ship captain's daughter and lover of art. Her home, built in 1817, is today the **Florence Griswold Museum,** with period furniture and changing exhibitions. Most interesting is the dining room, where the artists painted landscape scenes on wall and door panels. A long, humorous vignette over the fireplace represents the group at an imaginary fox hunt, each member in a characteristic pose. On the premise is the 10,000 square-foot **Krieble Gallery**, featuring rotating exhibitions of sculpture, painting and photography. Closed Monday. Admission. ~ 96 Lyme Street, Old Lyme; 860-434-5542, fax 860-434-9778; www.flogris.org, e-mail tammi@flogris.org.

The imposing **Congregational Church** that appears frequently in the impressionists' paintings stands at Lyme Street's south end. Admired though it is, it is a 1910 copy, faithful in all details, of the original 1816 structure, destroyed by fire. **The Lyme Academy College of Fine Arts** continues the town's tradition with a variety of exhibits throughout the year; they also have a couple of galleries on Lyme Street. ~ 84 Lyme Street, Old Lyme; 860-434-5232, fax 860-434-8725; www.lymeacademy.edu, e-mail admissions@lymeacademy.edu.

LODGING

Westbrook is blessed with that rarest of pearls, a bed and breakfast set right on the sea. At **Talcott House**—an 1890 dormered, shingled home—guests can cross the quiet street and go swimming, or they can sit in the spacious, informal living room and admire the view. The four guest rooms face the sea, have private baths and are all tastefully done with country antiques. A hearty full breakfast is included. Closed December to mid-March. ~ 161 Seaside Avenue, Westbrook; 860-399-5020; www.talcotthouse.com, e-mail lucretiawb@aol.com. DELUXE.

◀ HIDDEN

The **Beach Plum Inn** is a woodsy, attractive poolside complex of 18 units—some with cooking facilities—and seven cottages that can be rented by the week. Guests share a picnic area and may use a sandy beach, minutes away. Pets are welcome. ~ 1935 Boston Post Road, Westbrook; 860-399-9345, fax 860-399-3403; www.thebeachpluminn.com, e-mail jc@thebeachpluminn.com. MODERATE TO DELUXE.

For many travelers, the words Connecticut Valley are interchangeable with the **Griswold Inn**. "The Gris" is a legend; a white, rambling landmark on the picture-postcard main street since 1776. Serving as a meeting place for the town, it's Olde New England to its very bones, with a taproom and restaurant, a gallery of vintage marine art and nightly musical jamborees. Four period buildings house 31 guest rooms and suites. Some are remodeled; in others, the floors list to port or starboard, as if to remind you of the town's maritime past and its nautical present as well. Continental breakfast is included. ~ 36 Main Street, Essex; 860-767-1812, fax 860-767-0481; www.griswoldinn.com, e-mail griswoldinn@snet.net. MODERATE TO ULTRA-DELUXE.

Located within easy reach of the Goodspeed Opera House and Gillette's Castle, **The Inn at Chester** is a 200-year-old homestead with plenty of modern amenities. Its 44 rooms are furnished with antiques; some have canopy beds and some have fireplaces. Other comforts include a tennis court, a library and a game room with a pool table and plenty of board games. There are also hiking trails nearby, and a restaurant on the premises. ~ 318 West Main Street, Chester; 800-526-9541, fax 860-526-1607; www.innatchester.com, e-mail innkeeper@innatchester.com. ULTRA-DELUXE.

Copper Beech Inn is a classic: a sedate, gracious country inn with an award-winning French restaurant in what was once the home of a wealthy ivory merchant—the trade that put this little town on the map. Four of the 13 rooms are in the main house, meticulously appointed, with charming old-fashioned baths. Set back near the woods, the Carriage House has been remodeled with exquisite taste and a sense of romance, and its nine bedrooms all have jacuzzis and doors leading out to a deck with sylvan vistas. Continental breakfast. Closed first week in January or February. ~ 46 Main Street, Ivoryton; 860-767-0330, 888-809-2056; www.copperbeechinn.com. DELUXE TO ULTRA-DELUXE.

Antique lovers won't know where to look first at **Riverwind Inn**. This 1800s bed and breakfast, in the center of one of the valley's quieter towns, boasts post and beam construction, charming wooden ceilings and a stone fireplace. Rates for the eight attractively furnished, hand-stenciled rooms, all with bath, include an individually served prodigious breakfast by candlelight. ~ 209 Main Street, Deep River; 860-526-2014, fax 860-526-0875; www.riverwindinn.com, e-mail innkeeper@riverwindinn.com. MODERATE TO ULTRA-DELUXE.

What could be more pleasant than to waltz up the street to **Bishopsgate Inn** after enjoying a nostalgic musical at Goodspeed Opera House? Or any time, in fact. The early-19th-century shipbuilder's house stands tall and handsome on a landscaped knoll, and the six guest rooms, all with theatrical names on the door, are done in good taste and have private baths. Breakfast is served in the spacious country kitchen. ~ Goodspeed Landing, East Haddam; 860-873-1677, fax 860-873-3898; www.bishopsgate.com. DELUXE.

The **Bee and Thistle Inn** is on every list of all-time favorites. A gambrel-roofed, mid-18th-century house, it's right next door to the Florence Griswold Museum on the town's major street, yet it's set back on extensive landscaped grounds that sweep down to the Lieutenant River, a branch of the Connecticut. Most of the ground floor is devoted to the popular restaurant. Eleven tasteful, uncluttered rooms occupy the second and third floors, each with its own decor, all with bath. Full breakfast is included. Closed Monday and Tuesday. ~ 100 Lyme Street, Old Lyme; 860-434-1667, 800-622-4946, fax 860-434-3402; www.beeandthistleinn.com, e-mail innkeeper@beeandthistleinn.com. DELUXE TO ULTRA-DELUXE.

The **Old Lyme Inn** is set in a farmhouse that dates back to the 1850s. The 13 rooms, five in the original farmhouse, are furnished with Victorian and Empire antiques. The honeymoon suites have four-poster beds, Victorian loveseats and marble-topped dressers. Guests can lounge in the library in front of the fireplace and choose from a variety of puzzles and games. A continental breakfast is served every morning. Four rooms on the first floor are wheelchair accessible. Gay-friendly. ~ 85 Lyme Street, Old Lyme; 860-434-2600, 800-434-5352, fax 860-434-5352; www.oldlymeinn.com, e-mail innkeeper@oldlymeinn.com. MODERATE TO DELUXE.

DINING

Seafood lovers think of Westbrook as the home of **Bill's Seafood Restaurant**. Here at this informal spot, fried-clam aficionados gather inside or on the terrace overlooking the salt marsh. Fish, shrimp and lobster rolls have a place on the menu, as do hot dogs and burgers, but it's the sweet, plump, lightly fried clams that are the attraction. ~ 548 Boston Post Road at the Singing Bridge, Westbrook; 860-399-7224; www.billsseafood.com. BUDGET TO MODERATE.

Restauranteur Mark Signor opened **Sig's Water Street Café** in summer 2006 with hopes of creating a casual, yet stylish establishment. The result is exactly that, with bamboo and brick accents, ample lighting and an eclectic menu. Try the coconut curry mussels with garlic crostini or grilled pork *paillard* with pickled cremini mushrooms, arugula, pine nuts, heirloom tomatoes and lemon-truffle dressing. ~ 4 Water Street, Chester; 860-526-3210, fax 860-526-9653. MODERATE TO ULTRA-DELUXE.

The Wheat Market creates gourmet sandwiches as well as changing entrées, salads, soups and a famed deep-dish pizza to eat at tables or take along on a picnic. With Gillette Castle State Park just a five-minute ferry ride away, that might be just the ticket on a nice day. Breakfast and lunch only. Closed Sunday. ~ 4 Water Street, Chester; 860-526-9347. BUDGET.

The **Copper Beech Inn** is a landmark, a longtime favorite among followers of fine French cuisine. Set in a tree-shaded, 1890 home, it breathes Old World elegance and charm. Sterling silver, fresh flowers and fine china grace the tables in the three dining rooms. Despite the high prices, you'll have to reserve well in advance, at least on weekends. Dinner only. Closed Monday all year; also closed Tuesday from January through March. ~ 46 Main Street, Ivoryton; 860-767-0330, 888-809-2056; www.copperbeechinn.com, e-mail info@copperbeechinn.com. ULTRA-DELUXE.

For years, the **Bee and Thistle Inn** has been voted the most romantic restaurant in the state by readers of *Connecticut* magazine. It's true, the rambling rooms and porches exude an air of intimacy and warmth appealing to lovers, and other mortals as well. The offerings are elegantly served and very tasty: seafood,

AUTHOR FAVORITE

Historic is a word used lightly around these parts, but surely it applies to **The Griswold Inn**, established in 1776. Go for lunch, dinner, the famous Sunday "Hunt Breakfast" or a drink so you can view the warren of wood-paneled, evocative rooms that tumble one into the other. Partake of the New England specialties and other Americana on which the "Gris" has built its reputation—it's an experience one shouldn't miss. ~ 36 Main Street, Essex; 860-767-1776, fax 860-767-0481; www.griswoldinn.com, e-mail griswoldinn@snet.net. DELUXE TO ULTRA-DELUXE.

game, poultry, meats, each flavored with fresh herbs shipped in or picked from the sunken garden just outside the windows. Reservations recommended, and jackets suggested for Saturday dinner. Closed Monday and Tuesday and for three weeks in January. ~ 100 Lyme Street, Old Lyme; 860-434-1667, 800-622-4946; www.beeandthistleinn.com, e-mail innkeeper@beeandthistleinn.com. ULTRA-DELUXE.

SHOPPING

Old Saybrook Antiques Center carries an impressive array of 18th- and 19th-century furniture and accessories, paintings, prints, porcelain dolls and many other prized collectibles. ~ 756 Middlesex Turnpike, Old Saybrook; 860-388-1600; www.oldsaybrookantiques.com.

Antiques are what most shoppers seek in this region, and every little town responds with its own array of specialized offerings.

Window shopping along Essex's lovely Main Street is a popular pastime—too popular, you might find, on summer weekends. Many of the stores' names will be familiar; some are originals, like **Swanton Jewelry**, experts in jewelry old and new. ~ 1 Griswold Square, Essex; 860-767-1271; www.swantonjewelry.com.

If gardens intrigue you, drive to the **Sundial Gardens** in tiny Higganum, where you can stroll through three gardens, including an 18th-century-style garden, then browse in the attractive barn-turned-gift-shop stocked with rare and fine teas, gourmet items, plants, books and herbs for sale. Make reservations for Saturday tea tastings and other programs and events. Closed weekdays and the last two weeks in October. Admission. ~ Route 81 to Brault Hill Road extension, Higganum; 860-345-4290, fax 860-345-3462; www.sundialgardens.com, e-mail sundial9@localnet.com.

NIGHTLIFE

The elegant **Water's Edge Resort and Spa** offers live bands in the lounge on weekends and outdoor entertainment from Memorial Day to Labor Day. ~ 1525 Boston Post Road, Westbrook; 860-399-5901, 800-222-5901; www.watersedgeresortandspa.com.

The **Griswold Inn** is a favorite meeting place after sundown. A landmark of this exquisite river town ever since 1776, "the Gris" boasts an old taproom as fine as any in the state. Nightly doings range from Dixieland to sea chanteys to traditional ballads or classic arias, all performed in a warm, friendly atmosphere. ~ 36 Main Street, Essex; 860-767-1812, fax 860-767-0481; www.griswoldinn.com.

BEACHES & PARKS

SELDEN NECK STATE PARK This one is special, a 536-acre island in the Connecticut River accessible only by water—truly a place to get away from it all. For use exclusively by campers, you can hike along woodsy trails that lead to old rock quarries, explore the shore in your kayak or canoe, or contemplate the wide, tranquil river. Canoes and kayaks can be launched at the base of Gillette Castle. The camps offer riverside and docking facilities are not provided. ~ The island is located two miles south of Gillette Castle State Park in East Haddam, which handles information and permits for both parks; 860-526-2336.

▲ Four primitive tent sites are available for one-night stops by boaters only; $4 per person. Reservations must be made in writing at least two weeks in advance by mail to 67 River Road, East Haddam, CT 06423. Closed October through May.

GILLETTE CASTLE STATE PARK One of the most popular destinations in Connecticut, this mountainside park is topped by the picturesque fieldstone structure completed in 1919 by William Gillette, a well-known actor (see "Lower Connecticut River Valley Sights" section in this chapter). Views of the Connecticut River are spectacular, and you can hike on shady trails to the water's edge and watch the ferry plying its way between Chester and Hadlyme. Picnic grounds, restrooms, food concession stands, a gift shop and a visitors center are all available here. The castle is closed Columbus Day through Memorial Day. ~ Four miles south of East Haddam, off Route 82. From the west bank of the river, take the ferry from Chester to Hadlyme and follow the signs up the mountain; 860-526-2336, fax 860-526-9768.

▲ One primitive tent site is available for one-night stops for canoers and kayakers only; $4 per person.

Mystic Area

The easternmost stretch of the Connecticut coast is lined with towns and villages with deep maritime roots. These include New London, home to the U.S. Coast Guard Academy; Groton, the "submarine capital of the world"; Mystic, where the popular Mystic Seaport is located; and Stonington, where you will find an impressive collection of 18th- and 19th-century buildings that were built for ship captains and other seafarers. Several of the east-coast towns were important whaling centers back in the early 1800s and brought great prosperity to the area.

SIGHTS

The centerpiece of this chunk of the coast is the historic Mystic Seaport, which could keep you happily amused for hours, but you'll find quite a bit to see in the towns surrounding it.

It's best to stop at the information center on I-95 at North Stonington (southbound) or contact the **Eastern Connecticut Tourism District** (Mystic area) to get the lay of the land—and of the water. Closed Saturday and Sunday. ~ 32 Huntington Street, New London, CT 06320; 860-444-2206, 800-863-6569, fax 860-442-4257; www.mysticcountry.com, e-mail info@mysticcountry.com.

New London, Groton, Mystic and Stonington grew prosperous as sea and river ports, and today the recreational uses of this jagged coastline are central to the communities' appeal. Moreover, New London and Groton are home to water-related military facilities, some of which are open to the public. At the **United States Coast Guard Academy** visitors may tour the grounds, the visitors center (closed until further notice), the museum, the chapel, some of the buildings and, when it's in port, the tall ship *Eagle*, used as a training vessel for the cadets. What a vision when she sails down the Thames River and out to sea! Call ahead for hours and restrictions. ~ 15 Mohegan Avenue (Route 32), New London; 860-444-8270, fax 860-444-8289; www.cga.edu, e-mail publicaffairs@cga.uscg.mil.

HIDDEN ►

Though the glories of whaling days are New London's main claim to fame—be sure to drive past the four magnificent 1832 temple-front mansions, known collectively as **Whale Oil Row** (105–119 Huntington Street)—the city has many strings to its bow: the lively town pier, with charter boats of all kinds; ferries that ply across the Sound to several island destinations; and some fine historic homes and museums.

Visitors of a literary bent will want to stop by the shorefront **Monte Cristo Cottage**, boyhood home of playwright Eugene O'Neill and the setting for his two autobiographical plays, *Ah! Wilderness* and *Long Day's Journey Into Night*. Call ahead for hours. Closed Labor Day through May (except by appointment). Admission. ~ 325 Pequot Avenue, New London; 860-443-0051.

The Monte Cristo cottage is part of the **Eugene O'Neill Theater Center**, an organization devoted to developing new works for the stage. Some of the play readings, performances and rehearsals are open to the public. (See the "Theater in Connecticut" feature in this chapter.) Closed Saturday and Sunday in winter. ~ 305 Great Neck Road, Waterford; 860-443-5378, fax 860-443-9653, www.theoneill.org, e-mail info@theoneill.org.

Nearby is New London's **Ocean Beach Park**, with a broad expanse of fine sand, a boardwalk and vistas of passing ships, a food court, carousel rides, a waterslide, a playground, ferries and a handsome lighthouse. Parking fee. ~ 1225 Ocean Avenue, New London; 860-447-3031, 800-510-7263, fax 860-442-1117; www.ocean-beach-park.com, e-mail blgo.bp@aol.com.

A river scene great to behold is a submarine on its way to or from the United States Naval Submarine base on the Groton side of the Thames. In Groton is the striking, steel-and-glass **Submarine Force Library and Museum**. The hands-on, up-to-date exhibits trace the history of the submarine from our friend Bushnell's *Turtle* to the sleek, high-tech models of today. Closed Tuesday from November to mid-May. ~ Exit 86 off Route 95,

Groton; 860-694-3174, 800-343-0079, fax 860-694-4150; www.ussnautilus.org.

Boat tours of the Groton–New London area offer a multitude of choices, including the two-and-one-half-hour, hands-on oceanographic cruise on the research vessel **Enviro-Lab**, where passengers learn about marine life firsthand. Trips also venture to New London's Ledge Light, or go out for a harbor seal watch in winter. Fee. ~ Project Oceanology, 1084 Shennescossett Road, Avery Point, Groton; 860-445-9007, 800-364-8472, fax 860-449-8008; www.oceanology.org, e-mail oceanology@aol.com.

Driving toward Mystic on Route 95, you'll arrive at a scenic overlook where **Mystic Seaport** comes into view. Just for a moment—as you spot the masts of tall ships in the distance and the smaller craft that ply the Mystic River—you might really believe you're entering a 19th-century New England seaport. When you (and thousands of others) get there, a little of the magic wears off. Yet it's unique, this indoor/outdoor museum on 19 riverfront acres. Admission. ~ 75 Greenmanville Avenue, Mystic; 860-572-0711, 888-973-2767, fax 860-572-5326; www.mysticseaport.org, e-mail info@mysticseaport.org.

Begun in 1929, Mystic Seaport has grown steadily, encompassing a coastal village—church, chapel, schoolhouse, pharmacy, bank, ship's chandlery—several buildings with indoor exhibits of figureheads, marine paintings and ship's models; a lively children's

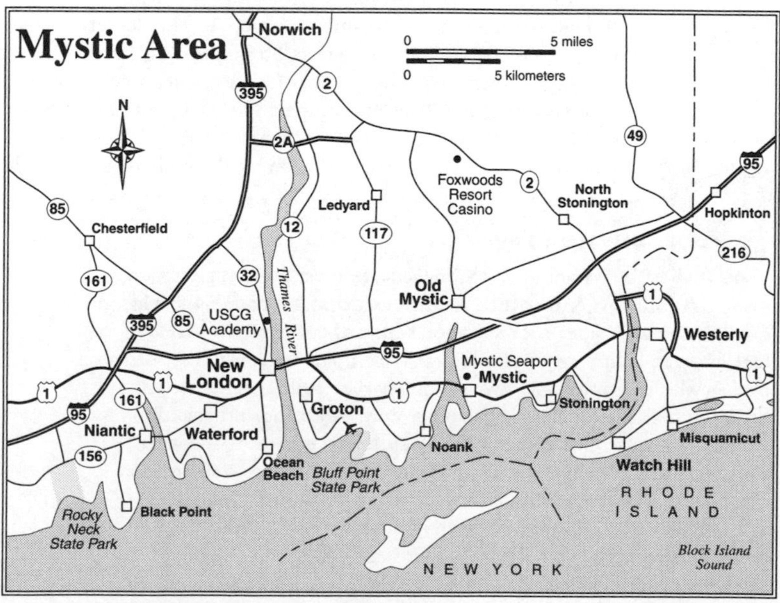

museum; a preservation shipyard where you can watch the craftsmen at work; and a collection of some 500 boats and ships headed by the *Charles W. Morgan* (1841), America's sole surviving wooden whaleship. Crowds or no crowds, you won't want to miss the opportunity to explore its decks, visit the cramped quarters where crews lived for years at a time, and watch members of the staff set sails and climb the rigging as they sing traditional chanteys. An ideal time to go is on a drizzly, misty gray day, when visitors are fewer and the atmosphere even more evocative.

Having been transported into the reconstructed past, take time to roam the town of **Mystic** itself, where vessels of all kinds, including whalers, clipper ships and pleasure boats, have been built since the 17th century. You'll find streets, such as Gravel, Clift and High, edged with early- and mid-19th-century homes of ships' owners and captains. The small downtown bustles with visitors, all watching the parade of boats passing under the rare *bascule* (that's French for "seesaw") bridge that opens hourly all summer long, while traffic stops dead. There are **windjammers** and all manner of craft available for cruises of an hour or a week. You can help sail, or not, according to the mood of the moment. For details, contact the **Eastern Connecticut Tourism District.** Closed Saturday and Sunday. ~ 32 Huntington Street, New London, CT 06320; 800-863-6569; www.mysticcountry.com, e-mail info@mysticcountry.com.

Stonington, the easternmost coastline town in the state, is thought by many to be the most attractive. The densely settled, narrow tongue of land known as Stonington Borough, part of the larger town, is home port to Connecticut's one remaining commercial fishing fleet. Its compact streets are a treasury of architectural styles dating back to the 18th and 19th centuries, when generations of seamen sailed in locally built vessels to trade

sights

AUTHOR FAVORITE

You'll want to visit Connecticut's most popular attraction, **Mystic Aquarium & Institute for Exploration**. It boasts 34 fine indoor exhibits; outdoor habitats for sea lions, seals and penguins; the World of the Dolphin, with hourly demonstrations starring trained dolphins; the Alaskan exhibit, which features Beluga whales and harbor seals; open classroom programs available for children (summer only; reservations required); an interactive exhibit, Challenges of the Deep, that illustrates the wonder and complexity of deep-sea exploration; and Swamp Things, a re-creation of a Louisiana bayou. Admission. ~ 55 Coogan Boulevard, Mystic; 860-572-5955, fax 860-572-5984; www.mysticaquarium.org, e-mail info@mysticaquarium.org.

with China and as far as Antarctica in search of whales and seals. A pleasant walking tour of Main, Water and the short diagonal streets could begin at the **Old Lighthouse Museum**, where the 1823 granite lighthouse (moved to its current location in 1840) displays maritime exhibits and artifacts of early American coastal life. Exhibits change yearly. When visiting, be sure to climb the stone steps to the top of the tower, where there is a wonderful view of three states and Long Island Sound. Closed November through April (except by appointment). Admission. ~ 7 Water Street, Stonington; 860-535-1440; www.stoningtonhistory.org.

LODGING

Don't be lulled by the abundance of accommodations around New London and Mystic; in season, a good room can still be hard to get. There's a big cluster of motels at Exit 90 off Route 95, ranging in price from moderate to deluxe (less in winter and spring). Some other options, all within a few miles of the main attractions:

The **Lighthouse Inn** was the summer home of a steel magnate who decided, in 1902, to build a Spanish-style stucco "cottage" in the meadows overlooking the sea. The meadows have been rezoned residential, but the mansion makes an opulent 50-room inn, with a fine restaurant and generous, individually designed bedrooms, some with water views, antique furnishings and unusual details. There's a private beach, outdoor pool, salon and day spa. ~ 6 Guthrie Place, New London; 860-443-8411, 888-443-8411, fax 860-437-7027; www.lighthouseinn-ct.com, e-mail reservations@lighthouseinn-ct.com. DELUXE TO ULTRA-DELUXE.

◄ HIDDEN

The cozy **Shore Inne** is a five-room bed and breakfast set among small homes right on the water—"like being in grandmother's cottage," the owner says. There are four bedrooms, each with a private bath. It's a great place to be: The views are splendid and you can walk to any of three private beaches nearby. Closed November through March. ~ 54 East Shore Avenue, Groton Long Point; 860-536-1180; www.theshoreinn.com, e-mail theshoreinn@hotmail.com. MODERATE TO DELUXE.

The Inn at Mystic is a hilltop potpourri of accommodations: a fine motel and two historic buildings for a total of some 67 rooms. Some accommodations feature balconies, fireplaces and jacuzzis. The exquisitely landscaped complex includes an exemplary restaurant, walking trails, kayaks, canoes, sailboats, a heated pool, putting greens and tennis. Despite the feeling of elegant seclusion, you're only a mile away from Mystic Seaport. ~ Routes 1 and 27, Mystic; 860-536-9604, 800-237-2415, fax 860-572-1635; www.innatmystic.com, e-mail jdyer@innatmystic.com. MODERATE TO DELUXE.

At the **Whaler's Inn** you'll find a variety of rooms housed in the inn itself and four neighboring buildings. The luxury suites come equipped with jacuzzis and fireplaces. You couldn't be more "downtown": The famed bridge is within a few feet. There's a restaurant attached to the inn, and many rooms boast fine views of the Mystic River and the Seaport, just a half mile away. ~ 20 East Main Street, Mystic; 860-536-1506, 800-243-2588, fax 860-572-1250; www.whalersinnmystic.com, e-mail sales@whalersinnmys tic.com. DELUXE TO ULTRA-DELUXE.

At first glance, the stark white Greek Revival exterior of the early 19th century **House of 1833 Bed & Breakfast** may seem imposing, but that will change as soon as guests receive a friendly greeting from the innkeepers and take in the colorful interior. The six bedroom guesthouse is beautifully appointed with antiques and reproductions throughout. Each of the guest rooms has a private bath and a wood burning fireplace, while several have canopy beds, private porches or balconies and whirlpool tubs. The decor is colorful and romantic, with flowered or pastel wallpapers, beautiful moldings and lace or flowered bedspreads. There's an outdoor pool, clay tennis courts and free use of bikes to tour the countryside. A two-course breakfast with piano accompaniment is included. ~ 72 North Stonington Road, Mystic; 860-536-6325, 800-367-1833; www.houseof1833.com, e-mail innkeeper@houseof1833.com. DELUXE TO ULTRA-DELUXE.

For a break from historic inns, give **Abbey's Lantern Hill Inn** a try. A distinctly contemporary resort, it has all of the charm one might expect to find in a New England hostelry, thanks in part to its countryside location. Each of the seven rooms is decorated according to a different theme—the downeast room has a distinctive New England feel, while the Southwest and Country rooms boast eclectic, regional furnishings. There are no less than six outdoor decks to relax on, and any one of them makes for a splendid spot to enjoy a continental breakfast on the weekdays or a full breakfast on the weekends. ~ 780 Lantern Hill Road, Ledyard; 860-572-0483, fax 860- 572-0518; www.abbeyslanternhill.com, e-mail info@abbeyslanternhill.com. MODERATE TO DELUXE.

DINING

Lunching at the **Lighthouse Inn**, you'll glimpse an intriguing view of Long Island Sound between two rows of houses. These good-size 20th-century homes seem to be dollhouses, in contrast to the baronial grandeur of the inn's dining room—dark, heavy overhead beams and dark wainscoting, great fireplaces and heavy, almost grotesque chandeliers. Yet, though the dining rooms seat more than 200, business is brisk. And with good reason: the food is well prepared, heavy on seafood—a favorite around these parts. ~ 6 Guthrie Place, New London; 860-443-8411, 888-443-8411, fax 860-437-7027; www.lighthouseinn-ct.com, e-mail reservations @lighthouseinn-ct.com. MODERATE TO DELUXE.

If you're looking for a cozy place to have dinner, **Anthony J's Bistro** is full of atmosphere. This small bistro, located just steps away from the drawbridge, serves a good mix of popular Italian dishes, such as fettuccini carbonara, chicken marsala, *lobster agnoliti* (ravioli filled with lobster meat) and stone-baked pizzas. It also has a wine bar and offers daily specials. ~ 6 Holmes Street, Mystic; 860-536-0448; www.anthonyjsbistro.com. MODERATE TO DELUXE.

Restaurant Bravo Bravo features cuisine with Italian and French accents. You may choose from entrées like veal medallions stuffed with garlic, spinach and cheese and topped with shiitake mushroom sauce, or garlic and tomato shrimp baked in a casserole. No lunch on Sunday. Closed Monday. ~ In the Whaler's Inn, 20 East Main Street, Mystic; 860-536-3228, fax 860-572-1250; www.whalersinnmystic.com/bravo. MODERATE TO ULTRA-DELUXE.

If you're spending the day at Mystic Seaport, you'll want to know about **The Seamen's Inne**, located next to the Seaport entrance. It's a large, busy place, built to resemble the New England–style structures nearby, and it specializes in the appropriate fare—basically seafood. Portions are ample. Breakfast is served on the weekend. ~ 105 Greenmanville Avenue, Mystic; 860-572-5303, fax 860-572-5304; www.mysticseaport.org, e-mail ray.kluglein@mysticseaport.org. MODERATE TO DELUXE.

High on a hill overlooking the harbor sits the **Flood Tide Restaurant**, a favorite with visitors to the town. Part of The Inn at Mystic but set apart on the unusually handsome grounds, this bright, airy dining room offers award-winning Continental cuisine with something for every taste. ~ Routes 1 and 27, Mystic; 860-536-8140, 800-237-2415, fax 860-572-1635; www.innatmystic.com, e-mail jdyer@innatmystic.com. ULTRA-DELUXE.

And then there's **Abbott's Lobster in the Rough**, a legend in its own time, a place where dining informally means sitting at waterfront picnic tables or in the simple dining room and truly using your hands for all they're worth. There's chowder, steamed clams, mussels and shrimp, but it's the lobster that has made Abbott's famous for 40 years—caught in local waters, steamed to just the

A FLAVOR FLOOD

In captivating Stonington, the **Water Street Cafe** is a wonderfully casual yet elegant spot. The cuisine is classic with an Asian twist. For example, there's a sesame-ginger roasted salmon dish and a seared tuna served with a wasabi dipping sauce. For vegetarians, there's a very tasty crispy tofu salad. It's a small restaurant—seating just about 30 people—just 15 tables and limited bar seating. ~ 143 Water Street, Stonington; 860-535-2122. MODERATE TO DELUXE.

right degree of tenderness. On a summer day, you can expect a wait, maybe a long one. But who minds waiting, when there's a harbor full of boats and a picturesque village to delight? Open daily first weekend in May to Labor Day; weekends only from Labor Day to Columbus Day and early May to Memorial Day. ~ 117 Pearl Street, Noank; 860-536-7719; www.abbotts-lobster.com. MODERATE TO ULTRA-DELUXE.

If you love to indulge in fresh seafood while gazing out on the ocean, eat in Stonington. One of the waterfront restaurants here is **Skipper's Dock,** which offers fireside dining in an elegant setting. Decorated with traditional nautical accents, Skipper's serves classic clam chowder, fish and chips, and lobster, as well as nonseafood items like the mile-high chicken focaccia sandwich. Sunday brunch. ~ 66 Water Street, Stonington; 860-535-0111; www.skippersdock.com, e-mail skippersdock@aol.com. MODERATE TO DELUXE.

SHOPPING

Olde Mistick Village is an entire community of Colonial-style structures built in 1973 to house every kind of shop and boutique known to the traveler—60 businesses on 20 landscaped acres. A bit cutesy, but it's an attractive place for browsing, with winding lanes, a stream, benches, wonderful flowers, even an authentic-looking meeting house with slender steeple and bells that soothe the weary visitor with music. ~ Exit 90 off Route 95, Mystic; 860-536-4941; www.oldemistickvillage.com, e-mail info@oldemistickvillage.com.

Within Mystic Seaport itself, the vast **Museum Store at Mystic Seaport** emphasizes things nautical and traditionally New England: gifts, clothes, jewelry, foods, books, prints, reproductions from the museum's collection. A separate section houses the prestigious Maritime Gallery at Mystic Seaport. Call ahead for hours. ~ 47 Greenmanville Avenue, Mystic; 860-572-0711, fax 860-572-5326; www.mysticseaport.com, e-mail info@mysticseaport.org.

Stonington's Water Street offers a wealth of pristine buildings to admire, good antiquing and a clutch of interesting boutiques as well. At **Hungry Palette** you'll find exclusive, locally designed fabrics and clothes. Closed Monday and Tuesday from late September to April. ~ 105 Water Street, Stonington; 860-535-2021.

Nearby on Bayview Avenue is **Fabulous Fabrics and More,** a factory outlet that carries a huge variety of designer fabrics at discount prices. It also stocks household items, gifts and furniture. ~ 22 Bayview Avenue, Stonington; 860-535-0352.

NIGHTLIFE

Ocean Beach Park presents nightly programs with top entertainment acts performing under a spacious tent close to the sea. Open Memorial Day through Labor Day. Parking fee. ~ 1225 Ocean

Avenue, New London; 860-447-3031, 800-510-7263; www.ocean-beach-park.com, e-mail bcgobp@aol.com.

Located on the Mashantucket Indian Reservation, **Foxwoods Resort Casino** is the largest casino in the world. The casino has more than 400 gaming tables, 24 restaurants and other entertainment, including the Fox Theater. The hotel has 1416 rooms and more than 340,000 square feet designated for gaming. It's open 24 hours a day, year-round. ~ 39 Norwich-Westerly Road, Route 2, Ledyard; 860-312-3000, 800-369-9663; www.foxwoods.com, e-mail information@foxwoods.com.

BEACHES & PARKS

ROCKY NECK STATE PARK The main attraction here is a half-mile sandy beach with excellent swimming and fishing, and a picturesque view of shorefront cottages across the bay. The 700-acre state park also encompasses vast salt marshes sheltering a variety of bird life that can be viewed from trails and raised viewing areas. There's a 2000-foot boardwalk along the beach. There are picnic grounds, restrooms, bathhouses and a food concession stand. Day-use fee, $7 to $14. ~ 244 West Main Street, Niantic; 860-739-5471, fax 860-739-9023.

▲ There are 160 campsites: 136 for tents and RVs, 24 for tents only (no hookups); $15 per night. Reservations: 877-668-2267; www.reserveamerica.com.

OCEAN BEACH PARK This city-owned park has a half-mile-long, crescent-shaped beach of sparkling white sand, backed by an old-fashioned boardwalk for jogging or strolling. The beach has excellent swimming. There's also miniature golf, a carousel, 14 amusement rides, a waterslide, a playground, a gift shop, snack bars, an arcade and nightly entertainment under the stars. Facilities include an olympic-sized pool, beach volleyball, picnic pavilion, restrooms and changing rooms. There's also movies shown on the beach on Tuesday and Thursday nights. Parking fee. ~ Located in New London; from Route 95, take Exit 82A northbound or Exit 83 southbound, then follow signs; 860-447-3031, 800-510-7263, fax 860-442-1117; www.ocean-beach-park.com, e-mail bcgobp@aol.com.

ADMIT ONE ADMIT ONE

AUTHOR FAVORITE

After a heavy day of sightseeing in Mystic, try the pub at the **Captain Daniel Packer Inn**. The cozy, rustic room with its old fireplace is a favorite gathering place for residents of all ages. It features live music and a relaxing atmosphere seven nights a week. ~ 32 Water Street, Mystic; 860-536-3555, fax 860-536-0597; www.danielpacker.com, e-mail captdpi@aol.com.

Northeast Corner

North of the bustling, at times crowded coastline lies the region that has dubbed itself "the quiet corner": Connecticut's little-known, unspoiled Northeast, rich in scenic and historic interest if not in per capita wealth. You'll find no corporate towers here, no hordes of tourists, but interesting small towns, some of them settled in the 18th century, and a wealth of green pastures, rolling hills, rivers and forests.

SIGHTS

The **Northeast Connecticut Visitors District** will supply information on accommodations and points of interest. ~ 877-286-9784; www.mysticcountry.com.

To reach the quiet corner from the coast, the fastest route is 395, which branches off from Route 95 west of New London. If you're in Stonington, however, and don't wish to retrace your steps, a pleasant alternative would be Route 2, which winds its way through unspoiled rural areas to Norwich, a historic city at the head of the River Thames. At the junction of Routes 2 and 169, in Norwich, the old **Leffingwell Inn**, a former Colonial "publique house" and now a museum, served as a meeting place for patriots in the Revolutionary War. Closed Sunday through Friday and from mid-October to mid-April. Admission. ~ 348 Washington Street, Norwich; 860-889-9440.

From there, Route 169 heads north and passes through the village of Taftville, past an immense, turreted brick construction

HIDDEN ►

handsome enough to serve as a king's castle. It's **Ponemah Mill**, a former cotton factory thought to have been the largest in the country and the most beautiful, many say. You won't find it on tourist itineraries—it's privately owned and now home to several companies—but it's an appropriate introduction to an area where the textile industry set the pattern of life from the mid-19th century until recent decades. When the industry moved to the South, it left behind its footprints: imposing riverfront mills, each with its village where the workers lived. Many such complexes—some shuttered and depressed, others used for new purposes—hug the banks of the Quinebaug River, which flows close to Route 169.

The road also passes graceful Colonial towns like **Canterbury**, with its neat village green where the **Prudence Crandall Museum**, a National Historic Landmark, pays tribute to the resolute young teacher who dared to open a school for "young ladies of color" in 1833. The ensuing controversy led to imprisonment—happily, brief—and to the school's closing. Fifty years later, as a restitution of sorts, the state legislature granted Crandall an annuity of $400 per year. Closed Monday and Tuesday and from mid-December through April 1. Admission. ~ Routes 14 and 169, Canterbury; 860-546-9916, fax 860-546-7803; www.chc.state.ct.us, e-mail crndll@snet.net.

The courthouse where Crandall's trial took place is a few miles north, in **Brooklyn,** where it serves as the current town hall. Near it, on Brooklyn's green, is the first **Unitarian Church** in the state, a simple, elegant white structure built in 1771, with a Paul Revere bell in its lofty belfry.

The town is known for its agricultural fair in late August, but it also holds a hidden gem: **Old Trinity Church** (1771), bypassed by time and now open just once a year on All Saints' Day. From the town center, take Route 6 east for one mile, go left on Church Street and you'll find the serene white clapboard structure, with

◄ HIDDEN

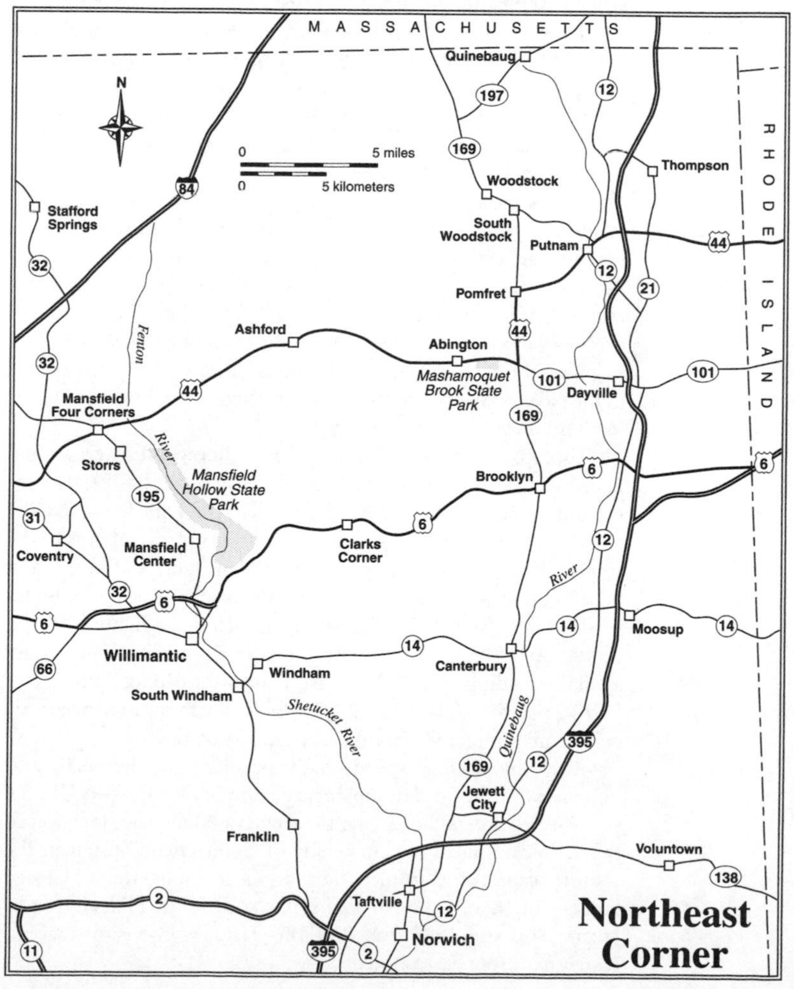

its arched windows and pedimented door, standing next to its ancient graveyard in a leafy grove, surrounded by cornfields.

Eight miles north of Brooklyn is **Pomfret**, site of an elite private school. The community has long been a magnet for affluent city families, who built substantial summer homes and landscaped gardens here.

Woodstock sits high on a hill overlooking a rich agricultural valley. Visitors come from far away to see **Roseland Cottage/ Bowen House**, a bright pink Gothic-inspired mansion built in 1846 by Henry Bowen, a local boy who grew rich in business in New York, then turned his energies toward publishing an antislavery, staunchly Republican weekly called *The Independent*. The lavish house and gardens, which remained in the family for over 100 years, are intact. Closed Monday and Tuesday June 1 through October 15 and from mid-October to the end of May. Admission. ~ 556 Route 169, Woodstock; 860-928-4074, fax 860-963-2208; www.historicnewengland.org, e-mail prusso@historicnewengland.org.

Across the Quinebaug, and just a few miles from the Rhode Island and Massachusetts lines, the town of **Thompson** boasts a magnificent 19th-century mill fronting the river, as well as a classic residential area on a hilltop—one of the finest. Today, it's as composed and tranquil as any you'll find, with its traditional green—they call it a common here—fine meeting house and white or pale-yellow homes on shady streets. It was a busy crossroads in the past: two major turnpikes intersected there, Boston to Hartford and Providence to Springfield.

Thompson's claim to fame is the **Thompson International Speedway**, a professional stock car racetrack that has been in operation since 1940. The family-owned track is home to the NASCAR Weekly Racing Series, which brings plenty of fans to the stands. If you have a couple of grand on hand and you know how to drive a racecar, you can rent the track for up to six hours to show off your skills. The site also includes a lighted driving range, an 18-hole golf course and dining facilities. No tours available. Admission. ~ 205 East Thompson Road, Thompson; 860-923-2280, fax 860-923-2398; www.thompsonspeedway.com, e-mail pitcrew@thompsonspeedway.com.

After this spell of speed, you'll be ready for the bustle and bounce of an up-to-date university campus. Route 44 will take you west to Storrs, bordering the town of Mansfield, location of the main campus of the **University of Connecticut**. Stop in at the visitors center for information about campus tours. Closed Sunday in June. ~ North Eagleville and North Hillside roads, Storrs; 860-486-4900, fax 860-486-0100; www.visitors.uconn.edu, e-mail tours@uconn.edu.

The Rose of New England

In the shadow of its more famous—and touristy—neighbors, Mystic and New London, the little town of **Norwich** is a historic gem hidden in plain sight at the mouth of the Thames River. Founded in 1659, the settlement grew to become the second-largest city in Connecticut by the mid-18th century. After the Stamp Act of 1764 brought about a boycott of English imports, Norwich evolved into one of New England's major commercial and industrial centers, eventually boasting the world's largest cotton mill complex. It also gained notoriety by association with the town's most famous native son, traitor Benedict Arnold. Dubbed "the Rose of New England" by author James Lloyd Greene, who compared the surrounding hills to the petals of a rose, Norwich's faded as the area's economic base shifted to the coast. Today the rose remains the symbol of this time-capsule town, and the **Norwich Memorial Rose Garden** (in Mohegan Park on Rockwell Street) is one of its top attractions.

A trip along Broadway, Broad Street and Washington Street reveals a wealth of stately Victorian homes, the graceful neo-Gothic **St. Patrick's Cathedral** (213 Broadway), and the extravagant French Second Empire–style **City Hall** (100 Broadway). The **Slater Memorial Museum** (108 Crescent Street; 860-887-2506), with its Richardsonian Romanesque design and landmark round tower, exhibits American Indian artifacts, Victorian furniture, plaster casts of classic sculptures, and works by regional artists. The **Old Norwichtown Burying Grounds** (Old Cemetery Lane, off Norwichtown Green) contains unusual 18th-century tombstone art by eight renowned local stone carvers. The two-mile **Heritage Walkway** makes its way from **Yantic Falls** (the cascade that drove the powerhouse where industrialism got its start in Connecticut), along the riverfront, past the large marina at **American Wharf**, to **Howard T. Brown Memorial Park**, where summer band concerts are held.

As Norwich transforms to a tourism-based economy, antique stores are springing up by the score. Two casinos, operated by the Mohegan and Mashantucket Pequot Indians, now stand on the outskirts of town, and plans have been announced for a new heritage center, a Civil War museum and a 50-acre botanical garden adjoining the rose garden.

Now a prestigious university, "UConn" was founded in 1881 as an agricultural school. The sight of emerald pastures dotted with well-fed cows across the street from massive modern buildings makes an intriguing contrast. It also makes for great ice cream, which you can buy at the Dairy Bar, made every day. Refreshed, you'll want to stop at the **William Benton Museum of Art**, where wide-ranging exhibitions are displayed in an attractive, cathedral-ceilinged gallery. The Benton has the honor of being Connecticut's state art museum—a fitting way to finish up a tour. Closed Monday and between exhibits. ~ 245 Glenbrook Road, Storrs; 860-486-4520, fax 860-486-0234; www.benton.uconn.edu, e-mail benton@uconn.edu.

LODGING

A lodging reservation service can supply additional suggestions for accommodation throughout the state. Try the **Connecticut Lodging Association** for a list of reliable establishments. ~100 Roscommon Drive, Suite 320, Middletown; 860-635-5600, fax 860-635-6400; www.ctlodgingasoc.com, e-mail info@ctlodgingassoc.com.

The posh place to stay in Norwich is **The Spa at Norwich Inn**, a Georgian-style inn on 42 acres of landscaped grounds, forest and spring-fed ponds. Guest accommodations include 49 spacious rooms in the two-story main house and suites or townhouse-style duplexes with kitchens and fireplaces in 55 luxury villas hidden along wooded roadways fronting the Norwich Golf Course. Spa facilities include a whirlpool, sauna, steam room, indoor pool and fitness center. There are tennis courts, walking trails and fitness classes including pilates and yoga. ~ 607 West Thames Street, Norwich; 860-886-2401, 800-275-4772, fax 860-886-4492; www.thespaatnorwichinn.com, e-mail spareservations@mptn.org. ULTRA-DELUXE.

The **Country Hearth Inn & Suites** makes a handy jumping-off place for exploring the "quiet corner" of the state. In decor, it tries to re-create old-time New England, but what it does best is supply 40 pleasant motel rooms and one suite, adding an outdoor pool and a restaurant for your convenience. ~ 5 Heritage Road, Putnam; 860-928-7961, 800-541-7304, fax 860-963-2463; www.countryhearthinnputnam.com, e-mail kirti@kingsinnputnam.com. MODERATE.

The 1825 **Inn at Woodstock Hill** is a Christopher Wren–style, three-story white building with black shutters. The 21 guest rooms are decorated with an assortment of antique cherry and maple furniture. Many of the rooms feature fireplaces and four-poster beds. Guests may linger at the piano in the living room or relax with a book in front of the fireplace in the library. Continental breakfast. ~ 94 Plaine Hill Road, Woodstock; 860-928-0528,

866-365-0002, fax 860-928-3236; www.woodstockhill.com, e-mail innwood@gmail.com. DELUXE TO ULTRA-DELUXE.

One bed and breakfast with a faithful following is **Altnaveigh Inn**, a 1734 farmhouse less than two miles from the University of Connecticut. The five well-cared-for rooms are located above a popular restaurant and are simply furnished. ~ Route 195, Storrs; 860-429-4490, fax 860-429-0371; e-mail gparks163@aol.com. MODERATE.

DINING

Some people plan a trip to this part of the state just to have a meal at the **Golden Lamb Buttery**. Located in a converted 1860s barn, it's country dining like you've never experienced. The menu generally includes classic American dishes and whatever's ready to be plucked from the garden. There's usually a wonderful soup to start, followed by a choice of entrées: duck, lamb, various seafood and châteaubriand. Throughout the meal a strolling guitarist lightly strums away. Closed Sunday and Monday, and from January to mid-April. ~ Wolf Den Road at Bush Hill Road, Brooklyn; 860-774-4423, fax 860-774-5225; www.thegoldenlamb.com, e-mail info@thegoldenlamb.com. ULTRA-DELUXE.

In Thompson, the **Raceway Restaurant** at the Thompson International Speedway is a step-up in small-town dining. The restaurant offers a fine selection of American cuisine and a full-service bar. Generous burgers, hot sandwiches and a variety of hor d'oeuvres are served daily. Breakfast available. Closed November through March. ~ 205 East Thompson Road, Thompson; 860-923-9591, fax 860-923-2398; www.thompsonspeedway.com. BUDGET TO MODERATE.

The Harvest bills itself as "fine country dining," and goes to great lengths to deliver. Its location in the historic Lemuel Grosvenor House, along with antique sideboards, chintz drapery, fresh flowers and flickering candlelight in the dining room, remind you that you are, after all, in a bona fide country inn. All entrées are individually prepared, and lean heavily toward seafood and meat dishes. A Japanese menu is offered on select nights,

AUTHOR FAVORITE

If you're tooling around the region and feel a sudden yen for a real, old-fashioned roadside diner, **Zip's Diner** is the answer to your prayers. It's a legacy from the 1950s with a jukebox at every booth; a true formica-and-stainless-steel classic that serves up pot roast, roast turkey, eggs any way you like, pie and ice cream and lots of hot, strong coffee. ~ Routes 12 and 101, Dayville; 860-774-6335. BUDGET.

as is an elaborate brunch on Sunday. No lunch Saturday through Tuesday. Closed Monday. ~ 37 Putnam Street, Pomfret; 860-928-0008, fax 860-928-6511; www.harvestrestaurant.com. MODERATE TO ULTRA-DELUXE.

SHOPPING

A popular shopping destination is **Caprilands Herb Farm**, most famous of its ilk. On the extensive grounds stand a bookshop, a bouquet and basket shop, a restored 18th-century barn that carries herbs and spices, a greenhouse that sells seeds and plants, and a Colonial farmhouse open for luncheon programs (by reservation only), not to mention 31 different gardens featuring vegetables, herbs and herbal flowers, framed by a meadow dotted with grazing sheep. ~ 534 Silver Street, Coventry; 860-742-7244, 800-568-7132, fax 860-742-7806; www.caprilands.com, e-mail herbs@caprilands.com.

NIGHTLIFE

A welcome addition to the area's nightlife scene is **J. D. Cooper's Fine Food and Spirits**. This triple-threat establishment comprises a restaurant, a bar and the Cooper Stadium Sports Bar, where the whole family can enjoy an oversized TV screen and video games. ~ 146 Park Road, Putnam; 860-928-0501.

The **Jorgensen Center for the Performing Arts** is the University of Connecticut's major performing center, presenting a program of music, dance and theater performed by artists of international renown. Closed June through August. ~ University of Connecticut, 2132 Hillside Road, Storrs; 860-486-4226, fax 860-486-6781; www.jorgensen.uconn.edu.

The **Bidwell Tavern** dates from the 1800s, but the music that fills this rustic spot is up-to-date, contemporary acoustic. Live music Wednesday through Sunday. ~ 1260 Main Street, Coventry; 860-742-6978.

PARKS

MASHAMOQUET BROOK STATE PARK Two major hiking trails lead to the park's most famous feature: a wolf den where, in 1742, young Israel Putnam shot a wolf that had terrorized the population. Putnam became a local hero and later gained national fame as a Revolutionary War general. The park also boasts a small pond for swimming and a brook for fishing. Located at the entrance is the Brayton Grist Mill, last in the area, with its traditional machinery intact and a display of blacksmithing tools belonging to three generations of the same family. Facilities include picnic grounds, restrooms, a concession stand and a nature trail. Day-use fee (weekends and holidays), $7 to $10. ~ Route 44, five miles southwest of Putnam; 860-928-6121, fax 860-963-2656.

▲ There are 54 tent/RV sites (no hookups); $11 per night.

Outdoor Adventures

SPORT-FISHING

Along the coast of Long Island Sound, fishing boats cast off daily with passengers eager to try their luck. Popular spots are near Block Island and Alligator Ledge. Common catches inshore (within ten miles of shore) are bluefish, blackfish, striped bass, cod and tuna. Catches offshore (50–100 miles from shore) include tuna, marlin and mako shark. Tackle can be rented on board. Among the party-fishing boats that sail on specific schedules and can be boarded on a first-come, first-served basis are the following:

MYSTIC AREA In Niantic, the 65-foot **Black Hawk II** has six-hour trips on Long Island Sound. Closed November to mid-May. ~ Niantic Bay Marina; 860-443-3662, 800-382-2824. The 87-foot **Mijoy 747** books half-day tours and more. Closed Monday and from November through May. ~ Mijoy Dock, Waterford; 860-443-0663. Half-day fishing trips, as well as lighthouse and nature cruises, are available with **Sunbeam Fleet**. ~ Captain John's Dock, Waterford; 860-443-7259; www.sunbeamfleet.com. In Groton, try the 150-passenger **Hel-Cat II**. At 114 feet, this is the largest party boat in New England; they offer half-day trips year-round and full-day trips in summer. ~ Hel-Cat Dock; 860-535-2066.

Charter fishing boats that can be booked by private groups are more numerous. You can call the **Reelin'**, a 41-foot craft that accommodates up to six people. Closed September through May. ~ New London; 860-442-7519.

LOWER CONNECTICUT RIVER VALLEY The **Sea Sprite** offers five- to eight-hour fishing charters out of Saybrook Point Marina on a 41-foot Hatteras twin diesel in search of trophy bass, bluefish and bonita. Its captain guarantees that you will catch fish or the trip is free. Closed December through April. ~ 113 Harbor Parkway, Clinton; 860-669-9613; www.captainpete.com, e-mail info@captainpete.com.

SAILING & WINDSURFING

Sailing is a way of life along the Connecticut shoreline. Each harbor, big or small, shelters its own flotilla at the ready, and yet it's hard to find sailboats for rent. Here are a few suggestions:

AUTHOR FAVORITE

For wildlife viewing, I like to set up camp by bucolic Bantam Lake in the **White Memorial Foundation & Conservation Center**, waking just after dawn to stroll along the network of trails that wends through this 4000-acre refuge teeming with great horned owls, snow geese and more than a hundred other bird species.

SOUTHWESTERN CONNECTICUT Boating is good in the Long Island Sound. The small waves at Cockenoe Island and Compo Beach are great for beginning to intermediate windsurfers. If you need a little instruction, **Longshore Sailing School** offers classes for sailing and kayaking. The school also offers an eight-hour course to obtain the required Connecticut Safe Boating Certificate. Hourly rentals are available for small sailboats, catamarans, canoes and kayaks. ~ 260 Compo Road South, Longshore Club Park, Westport; 203-226-4646; www.longshoresailingschool.com, e-mail customerservice@longshoresailingschool.com.

MYSTIC AREA **Mystic Seaport** offers a different maritime experience: a sailing education program for young people aged 15 to 19 on the 61-foot schooner *Brilliant*. Youths act as crew for six- to ten-day trips, under professional supervision. An adult version of the project involves four-day stints in spring and fall. ~ 75 Greenmanville Avenue, Mystic; 860-572-5315, 888-973-2767 ext. 5323, fax 860-572-5355; www.mysticseaport.org, e-mail education@mysticseaport.org.

CANOEING & KAYAKING

The Connecticut River lends itself to a variety of canoeing experiences, from guided overnight trips to rent-your-own. You can find out about canoe camping at three state parks by writing the **Department of Environmental Protection, State Parks Division.** ~ Office of State Parks and Recreation, 79 Elm Street, Hartford, CT 06106; 860-424-3200; www.dep.state.ct.us, e-mail dep.stateparks@po.state.ct.us.

SOUTHWESTERN CONNECTICUT Canoeing trips on rivers, lakes and the Long Island Sound are arranged by the **Mountain Workshop.** Programs run anywhere from a day to two weeks. ~ 9 Brookside Avenue, West Redding, CT 06896; 203-544-0555; www.mountainworkshop.com.

NORTHWEST CORNER For explorations of the Housatonic River by canoe, kayak or whitewater raft, contact **Clarke Outdoors.** You can also take a kayak lesson or, in the spring, a guided whitewater-rafting trip. Closed November through March. ~ 163 Route 7, West Cornwall, CT 06796; 860-672-6365; www.clarkeoutdoors.com.

HARTFORD AREA You can paddle the waters of the Farmington River in a kayak or canoe by day or on moonlit nights through the services of the **Main Stream Canoe and Kayak Corp.** There is a shuttle service available. ~ 170 Main Street, Route 44, New Hartford, CT 06057; 860-693-6791, fax 860-693-4844; www.mainstreamcanoe.com. **Farmington River Tubing** offers tubing on the Farmington River. ~ Route 44, New Hartford; 860-693-6465; www.farmingtonrivertubing.com.

MYSTIC AREA **Mystic Seaport** offers canoe and kayak rentals for use along the Mystic River. ~ 75 Greenmanville Avenue, Mystic; 860-572-0711, 888-973-2767; www.mysticseaport.org.

SKIING

The state's ski areas improve on nature with snow-making machines. Rentals and lessons are available at all the resorts listed.

NORTHWEST CORNER Downhill skiers and snowboarders can hit the slopes day or night at **Mohawk Mountain**, which has a vertical drop of 650 feet. There are six lifts for the 24 trails (20 percent beginner, 60 percent intermediate, 20 percent advanced). ~ 46 Great Hollow Road, off Route 4, Cornwall; 860-672-6100, 800-895-5222, fax 860-672-0117; www.mohawkmtn.com. Another great winter sports complex, **Woodbury Ski Area** has a double chairlift, a rope tow and two handle tows serving 18 trails (30 percent novice, 30 percent intermediate, 40 percent advanced). There's a fantastic snowboard park. There are also 2.5 kilometers of groomed cross-country trails lighted for night skiing, and a sledding, tubing and tobogganing park. ~ 785 Washington Road, Route 47, Woodbury; 203-263-2203, fax 203-263-2823; www.woodburyskiarea.com, e-mail info@woodburyskiarea.com.

Woodbury Ski Area, the first ski area in the country to allow—and promote—snowboarding, has a specially designed snowboard park including a half-mile trail with jumps and a half-pipe and slalom course with a 20-foot bank turn.

HARTFORD AREA You'll find good downhill runs and a 625-foot vertical drop at **Ski Sundown**. They're open for both day and night skiing and snowboarding. Eighty percent of the runs are beginning and intermediate slopes. ~ 126 Ratlum Road, off Route 219, New Hartford; 860-379-7669, fax 860-379-1853; www.skisundown.com, e-mail customerservice@skisundown.com.

Cross-country skiers can head to **Winding Trails Cross-country Ski Center**. Twenty kilometers of groomed trails traverse the 350-acre facility. ~ 50 Winding Trails Drive, Farmington; 860-678-9582; www.windingtrails.org.

LOWER CONNECTICUT RIVER VALLEY At an elevation of 500 feet, the family-friendly **Powder Ridge** has downhill trails and a separate snowboard park with a full-size half-pipe. There's also a designated area for snow tubing, the largest in New England. Four lifts and three surface tows serve the 17 trails (40 percent beginner, 35 percent intermediate and 25 percent advanced). They have a special ski program for kids ages four through six. (The ridge is currently closed, but is expected to re-open in 2008.) ~ 99 Powder Hill Road, Middlefield; 860-349-3454, 877-754-7434, fax 860-349-0124; www.powderridgect.com, e-mail admin@powderridgect.com.

Ski Rentals You can rent downhill and cross-country skis and snowboards at **Action Sports.** ~ 1385 Boston Post Road, Old Saybrook; 860-388-1291; www.actionsportsct.com.

GOLF

Golf courses dot the Connecticut landscape like dandelions on a lawn in spring. Most courses close in the winter. All these courses have pro shops that rent clubs and carts. Here's a selection of courses open to the public:

SOUTHWESTERN CONNECTICUT In Stamford, the **Brennan Golf Course** is open year-round. ~ 451 Stillwater Road; 203-324-4185. The Tom Fazio–designed **Ridgefield Golf Club** offers a sporty front nine holes and a challenging back nine. ~ 545 Ridgebury Road, Ridgefield; 203-748-7008.

The first telephone book ever issued was published in Connecticut in 1878. It contained only 50 names.

NORTHWEST CORNER The nine-hole **Stonybrook Golf Club** is a scenic course with stone walls and brooks. ~ 263 Milton Road, Litchfield; 860-567-9977. New Milford's **Candlewood Valley Country Club** is reputed to have the most demanding back nine holes in the state. ~ 401 Danbury Road off Route 7; 860-354-9359.

HARTFORD AREA Farmington's **Westwoods Golf Course** has a driving range and practice green. ~ 7 Westwoods Drive, Route 177, Farmington; 860-675-2548. The **Goodwin Golf Course** has a flat, nine-hole beginner course in addition to an 18-hole course. ~ 1130 Maple Avenue, Hartford; 860-956-3601.

NEW HAVEN AREA The **Alling Memorial Golf Course** was designed with the classic features of a links course. ~ 35 Eastern Street, New Haven; 203-946-8014.

LOWER CONNECTICUT RIVER VALLEY In Old Saybrook, you can tee off near the sea at the nine-hole **Fenwick Golf Course.** Bring your own clubs and a strong arm—there are no club or motorized cart rentals here. ~ 580 Maple Avenue; 860-388-2516. Farther up the river is the course at **Leisure Resort at Banner Lodge.** The front nine holes are open and wide; the back nine are woodsy, with narrow fairways. There's also a driving range. ~ 10 Banner Road, Moodus; 860-873-9075.

MYSTIC AREA Stonington's **Pequot Golf Club**'s 18-hole course features tight fairways and small greens. ~ Wheeler Road; 860-535-1898.

NORTHEAST CORNER In scenic Woodstock, the nine-hole **Harrisville Golf Course** has wide, forgiving fairways. ~ 125 Harrisville Road; 860-928-6098.

TENNIS

There's no lack of tennis courts in the state—schools, universities, clubs, hotels and municipalities are well supplied—but many are out of bounds to visitors. Each local parks and recreation department has its own rules; try calling when you come to town or ask your innkeeper or hotel desk person to make arrangements for you.

HARTFORD AREA Unlighted courts are open to the public at three of Hartford's parks. **Elizabeth Park West** offers four courts. ~ Prospect and Asylum streets. There are two courts at **Goodwin Park.** ~ South Street and Maple Avenue. **Keney Park** features four tennis courts. ~ Woodland and Greenfield streets. The city's parks and recreation department can be reached at 860-543-8877.

Outside the city, you can play at **Sycamore Hills Park** or **Avon Middle School,** with four unlighted courts apiece. ~ West Avon Road, Avon; 860-409-4332. Also check out the **Simsbury Farms Recreation Complex.** Their four lighted courts are open to the public. ~ 100 Old Farms Road, Simsbury; 860-658-3836; www.simsburyfarms.com.

NEW HAVEN AREA In New Haven, you can play at **Edgewood Park**'s seven courts (Whalley Avenue), **East Shore Park**'s eight courts (Woodward Avenue) or **Cross High School**'s eight courts (Mitchell Drive). For information call the Recreation Department at 203-946-8027.

LOWER CONNECTICUT RIVER VALLEY **Old Saybrook Racquet Club,** a private club open to nonmembers, has four indoor and four outdoor unlighted clay courts. Lessons can be taken from the club pro. Fee. ~ 299 Spring Brook Road, Old Saybrook; 860-388-5115. **Lyme Shores Sports Club** has three outdoor unlighted courts and six indoor courts. A pro is available for lessons. Fee. ~ 22 Colton Road, East Lyme; 860-739-6281; www.lymeshores.com.

MYSTIC AREA Farther east, you can play at **Toby May Field,** which has four lighted courts. ~ Ocean Avenue, New London; 860-447-5250. **Mitchell College** features four lighted courts. ~ 860-701-5049. Two courts are available at **Farquhar Park.** ~ Route 117, Groton; 860-445-0262. **Fitch Senior High** also has six lighted courts. ~ Groton Long Point Road; 860-449-7200. **Washington Park** has six lighted courts. ~ Park Avenue, Groton. For more information, call 860-446-4128.

NORTHEAST CORNER Check out the two lighted courts at **Willimantic Recreation Park.** ~ Route 14 and Main Street, Willimantic; 860-465-3046. There are six unlighted courts at the **University of Connecticut.** ~ Storrs; 860-486-2837.

BIKING

Much of Connecticut is ideal for bike touring. The relatively gentle terrain and scenic back roads lend themselves to this unhurried form of exploration—except for the hillier northwest corner, which requires some strenuous pedaling. The **Connecticut Department of Transportation** publishes a free bicycle map that indicates touring routes, loop routes and the Connecticut section of the East Coast bicycle trail. The suggested routes cover most of the state, avoiding city traffic and high-speed highways. ~ 2800 Berlin Turnpike, Newington, CT 06131; 860-594-2000; www.ct.gov/dot.

HARTFORD AREA At **Stratton Brook State Park** in Simsbury, not far from Hartford, the old railroad tracks have been replaced by an extensive bike trail traveling along a scenic brook.

MYSTIC AREA At **Haley Farms State Park** in Groton, an eight-mile trail winds its way through the picturesque old shoreline farm.

Bike Rentals A few inns and hotels keep a small fleet of bicycles for their guests. Other than that, there are no bikes for rent around Connecticut. Best to bring your own, if pedaling is your pleasure.

HIKING

Although Connecticut is densely populated, a surprising amount of open space has been preserved and provided with trails suitable for hiking. The Connecticut Blue-Blazed Hiking Trails System, established and maintained by the **Connecticut Forest and Park Association**, consists of more than 800 miles of cleared and well-marked woodland trails touching on every county. Contact them for a brochure describing the trails. Office closed weekends. ~ 16 Meriden Road, Rockfall, CT 06481; 860-346-2372, fax 860-347-7463; www.ctwoodlands.org, e-mail info@ctwoodlands.org.

In addition, a portion of the white-blazed Appalachian Trail crosses northwestern Connecticut, and many state parks and forests and nature preserves have created their own hiking routes. You may also call or write to the **Department of Environmental Protection, State Parks Division** for hiking maps and information. ~ 79 Elm Street, Hartford, CT 06106; 860-424-3200; www.ct.gov/dep, e-mail dep.webmaster@po.state.ct.us.

All distances for hiking trails are one way unless otherwise noted.

SOUTHWESTERN CONNECTICUT In **Devil's Den Preserve**, over 20 miles of interconnecting trails cover a variety of terrain, from wetland, stream and pond through mature forest to rocky knolls with wide-open vistas. Take Exit 42 from the Merritt Parkway, go north on Route 57 for five miles, then east on Godfrey Road for one-half mile; turn left on Pent Road and follow it to the end. There are no restrooms. No picnicking allowed. ~ 203-226-4991, fax 203-226-4807; www.nature.org, e-mail theden@tnc.org.

NORTHWEST CORNER In **Kent Falls State Park**, a steep trail (.5 mile) leads up the south side of the falls, across a bridge and down more gradually on the north side, through dense woods and towering hemlock trees. The south side trail hugs the cascade itself, enabling hikers to view the falls from many angles. ~ 860-927-3238.

The blue-blazed **Housatonic Range Trail** (8 miles) follows the general route of an old Indian trail along the hills above the Housatonic River. Along the way are several caves to explore; fine views of Candlewood Lake, the Housatonic and its verdant valley; occasional steep climbing; and some areas of rough scrambling over boulders. The moderate-to-strenuous trail begins one and a half miles north of New Milford on Route 7. ~ 860-567-4506.

Tories' Cave, found along the Housatonic Range Trail, is said to have sheltered Loyalists during the Revolutionary War.

Macedonia Ridge Trail (7 miles) is a loop within Macedonia Brook State Park. The trail, which begins and ends near the parking area at the southern end of the park, crosses bridges and brooks, passes old charcoal mounds and climbs Pine Hill and Cobble Mountain, both with splendid views and demanding ascents. ~ 860-927-3238.

Undermountain Trail (2.6 miles) is a steep, rugged hike to the 2316-foot summit of Bear Mountain, which reveals a vast panorama of mountains, lakes and forests in three states, as well as of turkey vultures soaring along the edge of the plateau. Take the Undermountain Trail to the Appalachian Trail—it's .75 mile on the Appalachian Trail to the top of the mountain. This hike begins on Route 41, at a small parking lot three-and-two-tenths miles north of its junction with Route 44 in Salisbury. ~ 860-927-3238.

HARTFORD AREA **Heublein Tower Trail** (1.5 miles) is an easy walk along a section of the blue-blazed Metacomet Trail, which circles around a scenic reservoir and climbs steeply up to Heublein Tower in Talcott Mountain State Park. From the tower, you'll see the skyline of Hartford and, on the clearest of days, the distant mountains of Massachusetts and New Hampshire. Before setting out, check with a ranger for detailed directions. The park entrance is on Route 185 in Simsbury. ~ 860-242-1158.

Windsor Locks Canal Trail (4.5 miles) provides a level, easy hike along the towpath that follows a historic canal built in 1829 to bypass the Enfield rapids on the Connecticut River. The trail begins on Canal Road, off Route 159.

NEW HAVEN AREA **Westwoods**, a 2000-acre open space in Guilford, is crisscrossed with hiking trails. By taking the white circle trail out and the orange one back, you'll have walked six mostly level miles along marsh boardwalks, stands of hemlock and laurel, rocks, ledges, an abandoned quarry and Lost Lake, a scenic halfway point for a picnic.

Sleeping Giant, two miles north of Hamden, is a series of mountaintops resembling an oversized reclining man. More than 32 miles of trails traverse the titan's anatomy—head, chin, chest—affording distant views of hills and cities. For a strenuous, up-and-down circuit of the major peaks (6 miles roundtrip), follow the blue-blazed trail from near the parking lot all the way to the giant's right foot, then back on the white trail, with a detour to the stone tower for the loftiest vista. ~ 203-789-7498.

LOWER CONNECTICUT RIVER VALLEY **Devil's Hopyard Trail** (15 miles) in East Haddam crisscrosses the state park of the same name, beneath ancient groves of hemlocks, across picturesque foot bridges and along Chapman Falls, which tumbles in a 60-foot cascade. This moderate-to-strenuous trail begins near the parking lot. ~ 860-873-8566.

MYSTIC AREA The easy **Bluff Point Trail** (1.5 miles), in Bluff Point State Park and Coastal Reserve, leads from the parking area to the bluffs. Wander along the rocky, pristine beach, then wind your way back on a different trail through woods and salt marshes that cover this rare, undeveloped peninsula on Long Island Sound. ~ 860-444-7591.

NORTHEAST CORNER **Wolf Den Trail** (4-mile loop) lies within Mashamoquet Brook State Park and takes you along varied terrain into Israel Putnam's celebrated cave. It also loops past a boulder known as Indian Chair and into diverse environments that include swampland and open fields, woods and streams and high ledges that offer fine vistas. The blue-blazed moderate-to-strenuous trail starts near the parking lot off Wolf Den Drive. ~ 860-928-6121.

Mansfield Hollow Trail (3.7 miles) is part of the popular blue-blazed Nipmuck Trail. This medium-difficulty trail starts in the parking lot of the Mansfield Hollow Dam Recreation Area and winds along the Fenton River, then veers steeply up a hillside to emerge at a cliff known as 50 Foot, a fine lookout with views of eastern Connecticut. ~ 860-346-8733; www.ctwoodlands.org.

Transportation

CAR

Four major highways thread their way through the state. **Route 95**, the Connecticut Turnpike, runs along the shoreline, all the way from the New York state line to Rhode Island. At New Haven, it connects with **Route 91**, which heads north through Hartford into Massachusetts. **Route 84** enters the state at Danbury and runs northeast through Hartford to join with the Massachusetts Turnpike at Sturbridge. **Route 15**, the celebrated Merritt Parkway, winds its scenic way a few miles north of Route 95, then swings north at New Haven to join with Route 91. The major highways are all linked to each other by north–south roads set at convenient intervals.

Route 1, the old Boston Post Road, goes through the heart of all the coastline communities paralleling Route 95. Unfortunately, most of Route 1 has turned into a commercial strip, with just a few old buildings here and there to recall the historic roadway it once was.

AIR

The major airport in the state is **Bradley International Airport** in Windsor Locks, 12 miles north of Hartford. Airlines flying into Bradley include Air Canada, America West, American Airlines, Continental Airlines, Delta, Delta Express, Northwest Airlines, Skyway Airlines, Southwest Airlines, United Airlines and US Airways.

Several bus and shuttle companies provide ground transportation from Bradley Airport. Call **Bradley Airport Information** for details. ~ 860-292-2000; www.bradleyairport.com.

Taxi service is available 24 hours a day from the **Yellow Cab Company.** ~ 860-666-6666.

Two smaller airports offer limited service. **Groton–New London Airport**, on the southeastern coast, is serviced by US Airways Express. ~ www.grotonnewlondonairport.com. **Tweed–New Haven Regional Airport** is serviced by US Airways Express. ~ www.flytweed.com.

Residents of the southwestern section of Connecticut tend to use New York City's two airports, **La Guardia** and **John F. Kennedy.** They are crowded and frantic, but all the airlines fly there; they are less than an hour's drive from the state line (more at peak traffic time) and connected by frequent limousine service. For information, call **Connecticut Limousine Service.** ~ 800-472-5466; www.ctlimo.com.

FERRY

Two auto ferry lines operate daily, year-round, from points on Long Island in New York state across Long Island Sound, to the Connecticut shore. On the **Bridgeport and Port Jefferson Ferry**, the trip from Port Jefferson, New York, to Bridgeport, Connecticut, takes approximately an hour and 20 minutes. Reservations are recommended if you want to bring your car along. ~ 631-473-0286, 888-443-3779; www.bpjferry.com.

The **Cross-Sound Ferry**, from Orient Point, New York, to New London, Connecticut, takes about the same amount of time. You'll need a reservation if you want to bring your car along. ~ 860-443-5281; www.longislandferry.com.

BUS

Greyhound (800-231-2222; www.greyhound.com) and **Bonanza** (800-556-3815; www.bonanzabus.com) bus lines provide scheduled interstate service for most points in Connecticut. Greyhound offers service from the following terminals: Bridgeport (203-335-1123), New Haven (203-772-2470), Hartford (860-724-1397) and New London (860-447-3841).

TRAIN

Metro-North (New Haven Line) runs hourly trains (more frequent at commute time) from New York City's Grand Central Station to New Haven, with connecting service from Stamford to New Canaan, South Norwalk to Danbury, and Bridgeport to Waterbury. ~ Reservations: 212-532-4900, 800-638-7646 (in Connecticut); www.mta.info. At New Haven, Metro-North connects with **Amtrak**'s main line to Boston, with stops at Old Saybrook, New London and Mystic. Also at New Haven, Amtrak links with service to Hartford. Amtrak's service from Washington to Boston makes Connecticut stops at Stamford, Bridgeport and New Haven. ~ Reservations: 800-872-7245; www.amtrak.com.

CAR RENTALS

At Bradley International Airport, you'll find the following car rental agencies represented: **Avis Rent A Car** (800-331-1212), **Budget Rent A Car** (800-527-0700), **Dollar Rent A Car** (800-800-4000), **Hertz Rent A Car** (800-654-3131) and **National Car Rental** (800-227-7368).

PUBLIC TRANSIT

The **Norwalk Transit District** has city buses, some of which meet Metro-North trains at the railroad station. ~ 203-299-5160.

CT TRANSIT operates frequent buses within the city of Hartford and offers service to the outlying towns of New Britain, Middletown, Manchester, Windsor and the Farmington Valley communities of Avon, Canton, Farmington and Simsbury.

CT TRANSIT also services the New Haven area with city buses as well as buses that go to East Haven, West Haven, Milford, Cheshire, Waterbury and Wallingford. ~ 203-624-0151; www.cttransit.com. **Dattco Bus Company** operates buses that go from downtown New Haven east along Route 1, making stops along the way to Old Saybrook and frequent commuter buses to the shoreline communities of Guilford and Madison. ~ 800-229-4879; www.dattco.com.

The **Southeast Area Transit District** runs buses that connect New London, Norwich, Groton, East Lyme, Montville, Waterford and parts of Mystic. ~ 860-886-2631; ww.seatbus.com.

TOURS

In New Haven, visitors can tour the **Yale University campus** on guided walks that are conducted twice daily. ~ Visitor Information Office, 149 Elm Street; 203-432-2300; www.yale.edu/gateways/visitors.

Heritage Trails offers daily scheduled tours of Hartford and vicinity, as well as less-frequent visits to other parts of the state and dinner tours of historic Farmington sites. Reservations required. ~ P.O. Box 138, Farmington, CT 06034; 860-677-8867; www.charteroaktree.com.

THREE

Rhode Island

Rhode Islanders don't think of their state as small; they see it as compact, easy to get around in. They point out with great pride that no place in the state is more than a 45-minute drive away from anywhere else. In fact, one of the quirky traits that sets Rhode Islanders apart from the rest of us is their reluctance to drive "long" distances. (Any commute longer than ten minutes is considered grounds for changing either one's job or one's residence.)

It's not only the locals who benefit from all this cozy proximity. Rhode Island's easy-to-reach destinations make it an ideal state for visitors. In a single day, it's possible to swim in Narragansett Bay, lunch in Newport, tour a mansion or two and still be in Providence in time for dinner.

Rhode Island, as every schoolchild knows, is the smallest state in the union—a mere 1214 square miles to be exact. But crammed into this tiny package is an overload of good things. The state's statistics are impressive: 400 miles of coastline (and this in a state that measures only 48 miles from north to south) with over 100 public beaches, some 18,000 acres of parklands, 12 institutions of higher learning, as well as a statewide storehouse of historically significant spots.

Having mentioned some of the state's obvious attributes, let's peek at some of its hidden virtues. Perhaps the best-kept secret about Rhode Island is the immense diversity within its modest boundaries. Some of its sites are well-known throughout the world. Surely everyone has heard of the glittering mansions of Newport, but how many tourists know it is also possible to hike through a natural "cathedral of forest" near the historic village of Hopkinton? And while probably every sailor on the East Coast has discovered the seaport haven of Block Island, how many have ventured north into Narragansett Bay to set sail for the solitary splendor of Prudence or Patience Islands? Those travelers who seek an individual path could not have found a more appropriate state than this one founded on an individual search for religious freedom. Back in 1636 Roger Williams settled this territory after he could no longer tolerate the religious constraints of the early Boston Puritans. Migrating south with his wife and daughters, he stopped to settle with the friends he had made among the Narragansett Indian tribe. After years of setbacks and negotiations, in 1663 Williams succeeded in wresting a royal charter from England for his new territory, one that would also allow him to unite Providence with several other settlements nearby.

A truly enlightened clergyman, Williams' religious tolerance was universal; his new state embraced all faiths. Although Williams founded his own Baptist Church in 1638 (the building in Providence can still be toured), Quakers, Jews and any other group seeking religious freedom were wholeheartedly welcomed. (Touro Synagogue in Newport, built in 1763, stands today as the oldest Jewish house of worship in continental America.)

This sense of tolerance endured. Although Rhode Island did participate in the infamous "triangle trade" (slaves traded for molasses traded for rum), it was also the first colony to prohibit slavery. Rhode Island was also the first colony to declare independence from Great Britain. And at the end of the Revolutionary War, it was the last of the original 13 colonies to ratify the new Constitution, holding out until the Bill of Rights, guaranteeing individual liberties, was added.

America's industrial revolution began in Rhode Island in 1790, when Samuel Slater started operating the first water-powered cotton mill. That power was provided by the mighty Blackstone River, and the rest is American history. Other successful industrial endeavors in the state have included jewelry and silver manufacturing, both of which have drawn immigrants here from all over the world. The newcomers brought along ethnic riches that can still be found in the state's cuisine, architecture and even the spoken word.

During "La Belle Époque" right before the turn of the 20th century, the seaside town of Newport became the darling of America's newly rich and famous, a status-conscious group who lavished their untaxable millions on opulent "summer cottages." Folks like the Vanderbilts, the Astors and the Belmonts vied to one-up each other architecturally in the designs of these palaces, as well as with the opulent furnishings within. It was truly a gilded age, the spoils of which we can all still marvel over.

But palaces of the past are only part of the splendor of today's Rhode Island, much of it to be found away from the cities. One glance at a map reveals why Rhode Island is nicknamed the "Ocean State": its flamboyant coastline can only be the handiwork of a creative sea. While its interior boundaries are the work of man (they are pure New England—ruler-straight and right-angled), it's a different story along the coast, where the relentless surf has carved out a wild, exotic profile, etching miles of extravagant bays and barrier beaches into the shores, capriciously sprinkling the expanse with an explosion of islands.

South County's coastal villages reflect this watery whimsy. From the westernmost reaches of Watch Hill up to Greenwich in the east, each small town harbors its unique bit of history and maintains its individual personality, yet each is linked to the others by common bonds—silken beaches that edge the coastline and a dependence on the sea.

Thirteen miles off this coast lies Block Island, offshore but very much a part of the makeup of South County. Aggressively underdeveloped (the resident islanders intend to keep it this way!), Block Island is a haven in the true sense of the word, with no traffic lights, no fast-food places and no neon. Peace, quiet and nature are the touristic lures here, combined with some world-class fishing and sailing.

Connected to South County by bridges across the broad expanse of Narragansett Bay is Newport County, occupying the islands the Indians named Conanicut and Aquidneck. Today visitors travel to Jamestown on little Conanicut Island, and the big draw on Aquidneck is Newport.

Although Newport is famous for its mansions and breathtaking beaches, the town has another, little-known side—its close proximity to relaxed country life. A mere ten-minute drive from all the glamour and the clamoring crowds of tourists

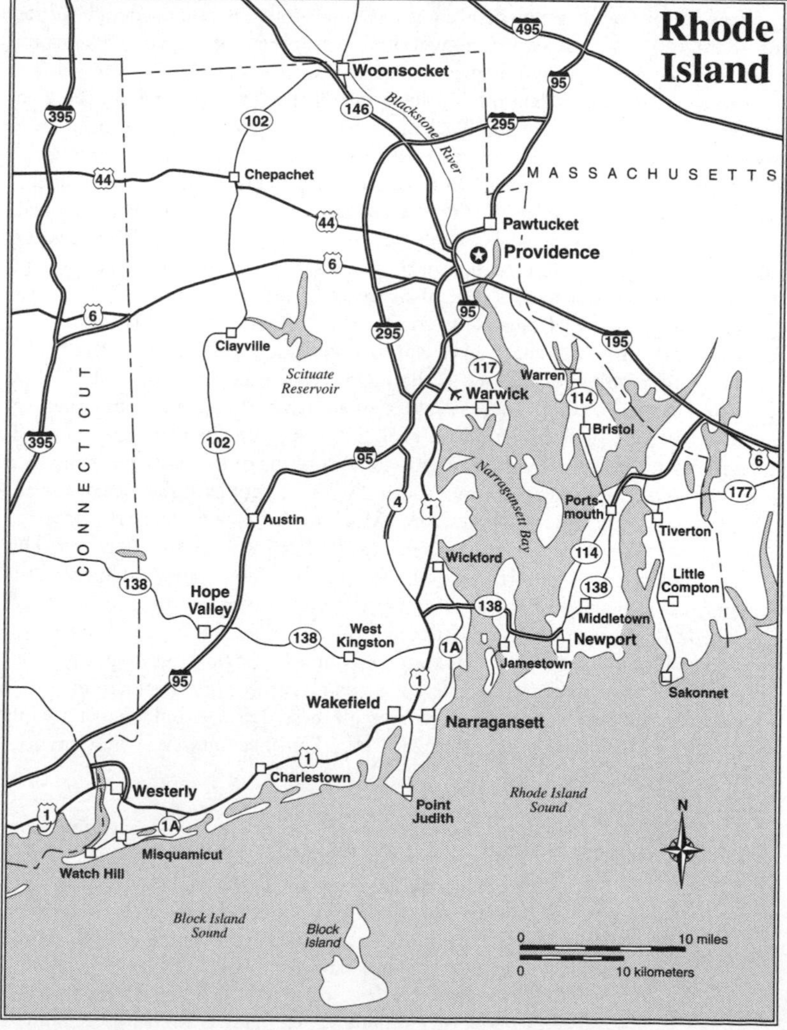

along Bellevue Avenue stretch miles of bucolic farmlands, wilderness areas, deserted beaches and even a vineyard. A short drive to the postcard-perfect villages of Tiverton and Little Compton reveals a pastoral way of life that remains centuries removed from the glittering tourist passions of Newport.

Northwest of Newport, in the center of Rhode Island and representing its metaphysical heart as well, stretches the Greater Providence area. A get-acquainted visit to Providence helps first-time visitors establish a sense of place; the capitol building is here, as are Brown University and the Rhode Island School of Design, along with scores of historic buildings, some dating back two or three centuries to the original colony.

Providence combines the best of big-city/small-town; it's small enough for residents to know each other, yet large enough to support top-rate restaurants and one of the country's outstanding small museums.

Above Providence along the northern tier of the state, throughout the great rectangle of land known as the Blackstone Valley, folks have been gearing up to show off their special blend of treasures to the world. But for the moment, this densely forested river valley is yours to discover, its bounties still largely "hidden."

The Blackstone River itself is the key to this area. Its history includes a starring role in America's industrial revolution, and its future includes landmark status as a federally funded recreation heritage preserve. For the immediate present, the mighty Blackstone awaits your pleasure and your exploration.

Statewide, it is this appealing combination of big-city sophistication and country-style hospitality that makes Rhode Island such an intriguing place to discover. You'll note these qualities in the people you meet; they combine the best of both. Oh yes, and don't overlook their innate sense of independence—that legendary strength of will that surpasses even the rock-bound, generic version attributed to most Yankees. This rugged individuality—one of the principles on which Rhode Island was founded—comes naturally to the people of the Ocean State.

Weatherwise, temperate is the word. Much of the state lies near the ocean or Narragansett Bay, which plunges northward through Rhode Island's center. This watery influence results in light winter snowfalls and temperatures that reach the freezing mark only in January. In summers, the average temperature is around 72°.

Rhode Island has another nickname, "America's First Resort." We're confident you will enjoy discovering this state for yourself. The only question is whether or not you'll want to share the tales of your adventures in this newfound playground. You may decide you want to keep all these treasures hidden just a while longer, before the word gets out and Rhode Island becomes everyone's favorite place in New England.

South County

Officially, this southern tier of the state—extending from Connecticut along Block Island Sound and reaching into Narragansett Bay—is called Washington County. But you will have trouble finding even one resident who calls it that. Rhode Islanders know this area as South County, and so should you if you want to be understood.

South County truly *is* resort country; beach lovers from all over flock here every summer. Even many native Rhode Islanders maintain vacation homes in this coastal area, which provides great seaside escapes from urban pressures.

The sometimes unpronounceable names of many of South County's villages and waterways—Misquamicut, Cocumscussoc, Pettaquamscutt—reflect the region's American Indian heritage. Roger Williams befriended the Indians when he settled Rhode Island and divided his time between Providence and North Kingstown (in South County), where he lived with his wife and two children from 1644 to 1650. The rolling farmlands and white-sand beaches of today's South County—a bucolic landscape mercifully lacking in high-rise condos and fast-food stores—make this history seem ancient indeed.

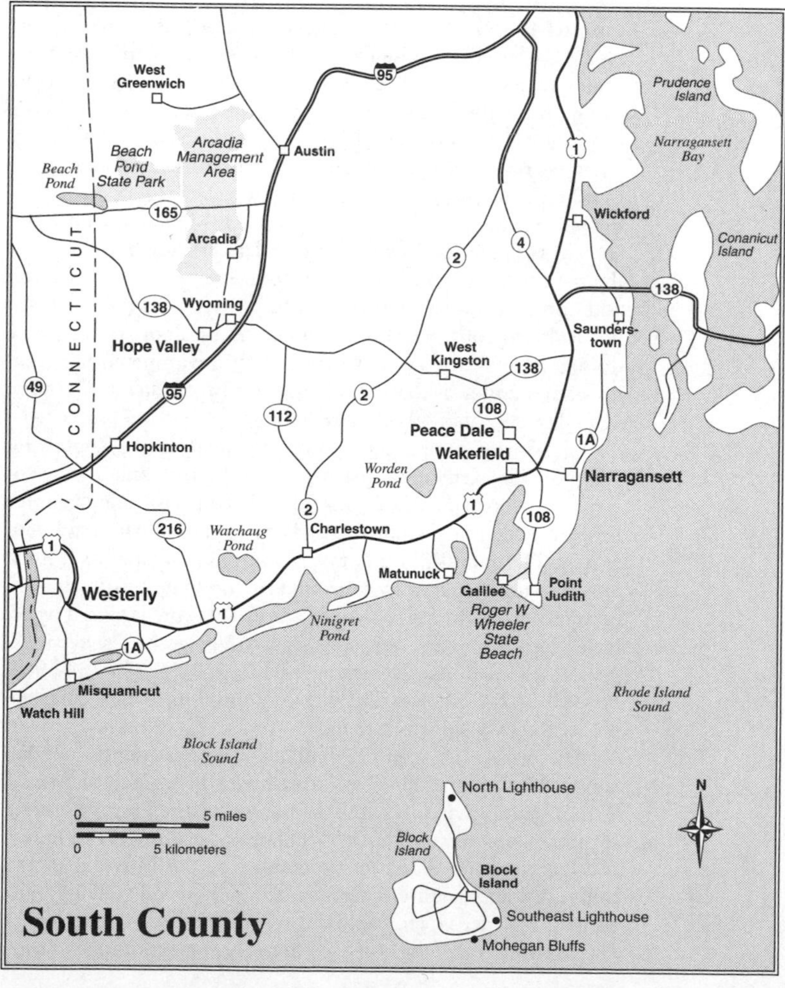

SIGHTS

Among the more high-profile residents of South County's villages are those who live in **Watch Hill**. (This select group strives for seclusion and anonymity, but their lavish dwellings continue to pique the imaginations of outsiders.) Although there's no formal "sightseeing route," many visitors love to drive through Watch Hill's quiet country lanes to ogle the tastefully lavish summer estates of these rich and reclusive folks. It seems that every turn in the road reveals a more elaborate, more imposing "summer cottage." Although most were built decades ago, there are one or two new additions to the "Millionaires' Colony."

Local custom decrees that as soon as a child's feet can touch the floor, he is too old to ride Watch Hill's "Flying Horse Carousel."

In town, at the foot of Bay Street, the country's oldest **carousel** is still spinning its magic. Locals call it the "Flying Horse Carousel" because its gaily painted ponies are hung from chains that spin outward, so the horses "fly." Pint-sized riders still grab for the brass ring, squealing in triumph as they store less valuable rings on their horses' pointed ears for safekeeping.

In the nearby town of Westerly, **Wilcox Park**, a 14-acre haven right in the heart of town, has been an oasis for locals and visitors alike since 1898. Designed by Warren Manning, who was a student of Frederick Law Olmsted and an artist in his own right, the park is listed in the National Register of Historic Places. In addition to strolling by the beautiful flower beds (with labeled horticultural collections), you can attend outdoor concerts here during the summer. The park also boasts a war memorial, granite statues and a historic fountain. ~ 44 Broad Street, Westerly; 401-596-2877, fax 401-596-5600.

Inland from South County's coastal areas, along Route 138, lies the 1886 **Kenyon's Grist Mill**. Run by the same family for years, Kenyon grinds the cornmeal that is the basic ingredient for proper Rhode Island johnnycakes. Proprietors Paul Drumm Junior and Paul Drumm III love to talk about their mill and its history. Drop by for a chat, a look around or for some tips, recipes or cornmeal from the mill's country store. The store is closed weekdays from September through May. ~ Village of Usquepaugh, Glen Rock Road, West Kingston; 401-783-4054, 800-753-6966, fax 401-782-3564; www.kenyonsgristmill.com, e-mail customer service@kenyonsgristmill.com.

The history of American Indians in South County stretches some 12,000 years; this whole area is rich in artifacts and trails. A four-page driving tour through some of the best sightseeing territory—complete with drive guides, detailed maps and historical commentary—has been assembled by the **Museum of Primitive Art and Culture**. There are also self-guided walking tours of Mill Village. Open Tuesday through Thursday from Labor Day to Memorial Day; open Wednesday (by appointment only) the rest of the year. Admission. ~ 1058 Kingstown Road, Peace Dale; 401-783-5711; www.primitiveartmuseum.org.

Back along the coast, you may want to stop in at the **South County Tourism Council**, where the folks can help with maps, brochures and information on the entire county. Closed weekends. ~ 4808 Tower Hill Road, Wakefield; 401-789-4422, 800-548-4662; www.southcountyri.com.

From here the coast road starts winding north along Narragansett Bay. Just north of Wickford, you'll find the building known as **Smith's Castle**. Although not a castle by fairy tale standards, this centuries-old woodframe house does harbor some impressive history, and 1.8 of its 23 acres are a National Historic Landmark. Roger Williams preached to the Indians here in the mid-1630s, and he and Richard Smith conducted a little business when the site was a trading post. Rebuilt in 1678 after a fire, it became one of the largest Rhode Island slave-holding plantations in the mid-18th century. Today, this era is memorialized by the 17th- and 18th-century architecture and household furnishings throughout the building. Open May through October from Friday to Sunday, and also Thursdays during the summer months. Admission. ~ 55 Richard Smith Drive, Wickford; 401-294-3521; www.smithscastle.org, e-mail smithscastle@earthlink.net.

On a newsworthy note: Experts at Brown University believe that America's oldest mass burial ground may lie beneath Smith's Castle property. In 1675, in the Great Swamp Fight with warring local Indian tribes, many colonists and Indians—including women and children—were killed. Archaeologists have conducted a dig at the site, where many of the colonists were buried.

Also near Wickford stands the **Gilbert Stuart Museum**. Sounds like an unlikely combination, but the famous George Washington portraitist was born here in this 1750 gambrel-roof house, in the museum where his dad owned and operated America's first snuff mill. Also on-site is a 1662 grist mill and a nature trail that leads to a small Indian burial ground. Closed Tuesday and Wednesday. Admission. ~ 815 Gilbert Stuart Road, Saunderstown; 401-294-3001, fax 401-294-3869; www.gilbertstuartmuseum.com.

Although Block Island is considered part of South County, this highly independent bit of territory 13 miles offshore marches to its own drummer. From its earliest days, when the native Narragansetts called it "Manisses," meaning "God's Little Island," this spirit has prevailed. (Dutch explorer Adriaen Block, in a 1614 visit, gave it his own name.) Many have compared Block Island's landscape to that of Ireland or Scotland. It's renowned for sightseeing of the natural kind; the island's remote location offers a unique closeness to nature. (See "Rhode Island's Favorite Island" in this chapter.)

LODGING

While visitors can always find one or two cookie-cutter chain hotels clustered near the larger towns, it is the rambling Victorians and out-of-the-way inns one remembers, and that tend to become a cherished part of the South County experience. As with most New England resort areas, many lodgings here close for the winter. Rates, too, are seasonal; those indicated below reflect the heady rates of the peak summer season. Because of the crush of visitors, many places will also require two- or three-day minimum stays during high season and holiday weekends.

Guests at **Pleasant View House** get the full ocean treatment. The wide swath of beach unfolds like a carpet just at the edge of the hotel's manicured lawns. The rambling, white wood exterior is accented with sail-blue canvas fronting each private deck. The atmosphere is vintage seaside; dining rooms and a lounge front the ocean, as do many of the rooms. Don't look for posh appointments; rooms are decorated in basic motel. But they're clean, comfortable and air-conditioned. The views from the private decks are well worth the price. There's also an outdoor heated pool, sauna and fitness room. Closed Columbus Day through April. ~ 65 Atlantic Avenue, Misquamicut; 401-348-8200, 800-782-3224, fax 401-348-8919; www.pvinn.com, e-mail info@pvinn.com. DELUXE TO ULTRA-DELUXE.

The **Shelter Harbor Inn** looks exactly the way a seaside country inn should look: a spanking white clapboard main building with contrasting window shutters, well-manicured and welcoming. This 1800s farmhouse, its landscaped grounds defined by rustic stone fences, is an inn as well as a popular restaurant. There are ten guest rooms in the main building (each with private bath and some with private sun deck), ten more in the converted barn

AUTHOR FAVORITE

I feel it's worth making reservations far in advance—and saving up—for a sojourn to **Hotel Manisses**. Presiding like a grande dame over all she surveys, the hotel rules with Victorian splendor. Built in 1870 and restored by the Abrams family, innkeepers well-known locally, the Manisses seems to personify Block Island's unique charm and individualism. In the wicker-appointed parlor leaded-glass windows rainbow the sunlight. There are a few surprises: several of the 17 guest rooms, like the Princess Augusta, feature jacuzzis; the Antoinette room opens directly onto the front porch; the Pocahontas has its own deck. Closed November through March. ~ Spring Street, Block Island; 401-466-2421, 800-626-4773, fax 401-466-2858; www.blockislandresorts.com, e-mail biresorts@riconnect.com. ULTRA-DELUXE.

nearby and four in the coach house. In each room antiques gleam with care, and bedsteads complement the period decor. The public rooms include a cozy library just off the sun porch bar. Breakfast included. ~ 10 Wagner Road, Westerly; 401-322-8883, 800-468-8883, fax 401-322-7907; www.shelterharborinn.com, e-mail reservations@shelterharborinn.com. DELUXE TO ULTRA-DELUXE.

Not all of South County's inns reflect a Yankee heritage. **The Villa,** with its Italianate decor and colorfully decorated swimming pool, is decidedly Mediterranean in ambience. All the rooms have jacuzzis; four have fireplaces. Enjoy a full breakfast around the pool. No children or pets allowed. ~ 190 Shore Road, Westerly; 401-596-1054, 800-722-9240, fax 401-596-6268; www.thevillaatwesterly.com, e-mail villa@riconnect.com. ULTRA-DELUXE.

Lazing on the wraparound porch of the **Grandview Bed and Breakfast,** congratulating yourself on your thrifty accommodations, you may think you'll never move again. And then the table games begin to beckon, the VCR and movie library chime in and the sweeping grounds seal the deal. If the activities at this turn-of-the-20th-century estate aren't enough for you, you'll find a golf course, tennis courts and lovely beaches nearby. A continental breakfast, served on the sun porch, is included. ~ 212 Shore Road, Westerly; 401-596-6384, 800-447-6384; www.grandviewbandb.com, e-mail info@grandviewbandb.com. MODERATE.

Set on one-and-a-half pastoral acres, the **Sugar Loaf Hill Bed and Breakfast** features four individually themed rooms with provincial touches. Book the comfortable Fireplace Room, which boasts starched white curtains, brick-red linens and accents, and a fireplace. A stay in the larger Cozy Room includes a private deck, a skylight and cable TV. Before heading out, enjoy a hearty, country breakfast. ~ 607 Main Street, Wakefield; 401-789-8715; www.sugarloafhillbandb.com, e-mail sugarloaf@efortress.com. MODERATE TO DELUXE.

Victorian is the word for most of the lodgings on Block Island. Imposing, gingerbread-trimmed structures dominate the island's ocean skyline. A word of caution: some "modernizations" may not please everyone. One such example might be the National Hotel's trendy front-porch scene. Although this place is well-known and located in the middle of the action, its amplified music and noisy camaraderie are not everyone's idea of an idyllic island vacation.

The **1661 Inn and Guest House** combines Victorian charm with sweeping views of Old Harbor. Rooms with water views also sport private decks (the Ackurs room even has its own kitchenette). Guest quarters are antique-filled and sunny. The inn is known for its huge breakfast buffet, served overlooking the water. ~ Spring Street, Block Island; 401-466-2421, 800-626-4773, fax

Text continued on page 138.

Rhode Island's Favorite Island

When describing Block Island, some liken it to Ireland. Many choose to rhapsodize over its bucolic charms, while others see it as being in a Victorian time warp. Block Island is all these—and more. A modest triangle of land lying 13 miles off the coast of Rhode Island, it measures a scant three miles wide by seven miles long. Yet captured within its 11 square miles are vistas that do indeed recall Ireland at its best: verdant, rolling hills, neatly defined by rambling stone fences; grassy meadows strewn with wildflowers; ponds—over 365 of them (one for every day of the year); and always, the wild Atlantic crashing just offshore.

As you approach Block Island by ferry, you'll first spot the chalky cliffs that rise 200 feet in a straight vertical from the thundering waves of the sound. It was from these cliffs that the resident Narragansett Indians once dispatched a band of off-islanders who attempted to conquer them; in a now famous battle, they pushed a band of invading Mohegans over the bluffs onto the rocks below.

As the ferry slides into Old Harbor, passengers are greeted by an imposing phalanx of ornate Victorian buildings that stand shoulder-to-shoulder, facing out to sea. These grande-dame structures are really most welcoming, offering bed and board to the island's multitudes of summer visitors—the same throngs who swarm the sidewalks of Old Harbor, slurping up mountains of homemade ice cream, purchasing enough "I ❤ Block Island" T-shirts to clothe the entire population of an emerging nation, and generally soaking up the festive salt-air island mood.

Do not misunderstand: Block Islanders are not about to let their idyllic spot fall prey to tourist trappings. There are no fast-food chains and not a glint of neon anywhere. No traffic lights wink on this island; in fact, there is no traffic to speak of. Visitors can get around in local taxis, or they can rent bikes or mopeds. (Mopeds, however, are discreetly discouraged.)

This is an island for travelers who truly want to commune with nature. Just minutes (even by bike) from the bustle of Water Street in Old Harbor, the island's only town (apart from New Harbor, which materializes in the summer), lies a three-mile swath of sand known as **Crescent Beach**. As the island's most popular bathing and sunning beach, Crescent may become too "crowded" for a loner's tastes. No problem: simply pick up your towel and mosey a few yards to the north where an isolated stretch of sand awaits.

Bikers are delighted to find the island's rolling hills offer just the right amount of challenge. The quiet roads wind past a handful of weathered-shingle cottages and a clapboard Victorian or two. But mostly, it is nature that's on view: brushy bayberry and scrub pines, grassy moors punctuated by ponds.

An astute naturalist will observe that there are very few trees standing on this island. Once there were many. That was back in the mid-1600s, when the first white settlers arrived. They felled the island's forests for lumber for their houses and barns, and for fuel. When that ran out, they burned peat from the marshes. Life has never been easy for islanders anywhere; but these early island dwellers had to cope not only with stern New England winters but also with the resident Indians who took a dim view of the new arrivals.

You might want to visit the **Southeast Lighthouse** or **North Lighthouse**. The Southeast Lighthouse features a museum as well as occasional guided tours. The North Lighthouse has been renovated and now houses an interpretive exhibit on Block Island.

History teaches that several explorers "discovered" Block Island, among them Italian Giovanni Verrazano, who named it "Claudia," in honor of the mother of his patron, Francis I of France. But it was the Dutch navigator Adriaen Block who, in 1614, claimed this bit of land as his own, dubbing it "Adriaen's Eylant."

Today's Block Island is available to visitors on a limited basis. We mainlanders will never really belong; that privilege is only for the handful whose ancestors first settled here. But we are welcome to enjoy the bounties nature has bestowed: the wildlife that inhabits the marshy ponds; the quiet countryside; the pebbly beaches that ring the coastline and the migrating birds that swarm here each spring and fall.

At the entrance to Rodman's Hollow, an ancient glacial crevice that is now a wildlife refuge, locals have posted a hand-carved sign that admonishes all visitors: "This land has been dedicated for preservation in its natural state . . . please respect it so that all human, creature and plant life may share in its peace and beauty." A fitting sentiment that could easily be applied to all of Block Island.

The **Block Island Chamber of Commerce** can fill you in on anything else you want to know about the island. Closed Sunday off-season. ~ Drawer 1, Water Street, Block Island, RI 02807; 401-466-2982, 800-383-2474, fax 401-466-5286; www.blockislandchamber.com, e-mail info@blockislandchamber.com.

401-466-3162; www.blockislandresorts.com, e-mail biresorts@riconnect.com. DELUXE TO ULTRA-DELUXE.

DINING

People "in the know" eat at the **Olympia Tea Room.** Sit in the old mahogany booths or at the sidewalk café and watch the local world go by. Owners Jack and Marcia Felber stress a modern American cuisine with an emphasis on fresh seafood and an extensive wine list. The menu is both homey and eclectic; the Olympia is as famous for its littleneck clam and sausage dish as for its dainty dessert pastries shaped like swans. Closed November through March. ~ 74 Bay Street, Watch Hill; 401-348-8211; www.olympiatearoom.com, e-mail jack@olympiatearoom.com. MODERATE TO ULTRA-DELUXE.

If you've got a craving for Caribbean food with an Asian flair, stop by **Paddy's Restaurant**. The place provides a series of exotic mixed drinks, and you can't beat the prices or location (it's right on the beach). Closed Labor Day through May. ~ 159 Atlantic Avenue, Westerly; 401-596-2610; www.paddysbeach.com, e-mail info@paddysbeach.com. MODERATE TO DELUXE.

Haute cuisine served in rarified surroundings greets visitors to **Basil's.** With striped awnings outside and delicate floral wallpaper inside, Basil's is a tiny gem of European-style dining. The service is formal, and guests tend to dress up for the occasion (unusual in a seaside area). The menu includes many usual Continental favorites (beef Stroganoff, scallops Provençal), but owner and chef Vasilios Kourakis has an inspired hand with herbs and spices, so old favorites tend to become new favorites at first bite. Dinner only. Closed Monday and Tuesday in winter; closed Monday in summer. ~ 22 Kingston Road, Narragansett; 401-789-3743. MODERATE TO ULTRA-DELUXE.

Eating at **George's of Galilee** has become a Rhode Island tradition located on its very own beach. Diners at this casual, wood-

AUTHOR FAVORITE

I found the ideal country dining experience alive and well at **Shelter Harbor Inn**. Meals are served in several small rooms, with stone fireplaces, burnished wooden chairs and wildflowers at every table. The creative American cuisine reflects the local harvest, changing every season. Seafood, as you will have come to expect in this area, is fresh and excellent. Pasta dishes are well seasoned and imaginative. Try a wine from the local vineyards. And for dessert, sample the Indian pudding, which arrives warm and fragrant. Breakfast, lunch and dinner. ~ 10 Wagner Road, Westerly; 401-322-8883, fax 401-322-7907; www.shelterharborinn.com, e-mail reservations@shelterharborinn.com. MODERATE TO DELUXE.

paneled spot usually sit before huge windows that offer views of the fishing boat dock or its open-air deck. Fare is a traditional mix of clam cakes, lobster, fish and pasta, plus beef and poultry items. ~ 250 Sand Hill Cove Road, Narragansett; 401-783-2306, 800-399-8477; www.georgesofgalilee.com, e-mail contact@georgesofgalilee.com. MODERATE TO DELUXE.

Most visitors to Block Island feel they have stepped back in time, into a gentler era. Among Block Island's bevy of Victorian mansions, the favored lodging is also the preferred dining spot. In summer the **Hotel Manisses** focuses its meal service on the flower-studded outdoor patio; when chill winds blow in off the Atlantic, the focus shifts indoors, where crackling fires warm the spirits. Seafood is featured, with seasonal variations. Appetizers include a selection of clams and oysters. Closed November through March. ~ Spring Street, Block Island; 401-466-2421, fax 401-466-3162; www.blockislandresorts.com, e-mail biresorts@riconnect.com. DELUXE TO ULTRA-DELUXE.

Whether you fancy a sandy beach or a clifftop ocean view, picnics will become an important part of your Block Island experience. Pick up your favorites at **Rebecca's Take Out**, which stays open some nights until 2 a.m. in July and August. Closed mid-October to mid-May. ~ 435 Water Street, Old Harbor, Block Island; 401-466-5411. BUDGET.

◄ HIDDEN

Late-fall and early-spring daytrippers who come over to Block Island for a few hours of biking or hiking are often surprised to find the hotels and restaurants closed for the season. No problem. Just join the locals who head for **Bethany's Airport Diner**, which serves basic breakfast- and lunch-counter meals all day, every day. Specialties are quesadillas, eggs Benedict and garden burgers. ~ State Airport, Block Island; 401-466-3100. BUDGET.

◄ HIDDEN

SHOPPING

The **Sun-Up Gallery** introduces the wonderful world of dazzling and upscale made-in-America crafts, jewelry and wearable-art fashions to this staid and conservative community. They also have a paint-your-own pottery studio during peak season only. Closed February. ~ 95 Watch Hill Road, Avondale; 401-596-3430; www.sunupgallery.com.

Antique lovers take heart; there are more than 25 traditional antique dealers located in South County, including **Granite Hill**, with glassware, china, silver, lamps and jewelry from the 18th, 19th and 20th centuries. Closed Tuesday in winter. ~ 50 High Street, Westerly; 401-348-2838, 860-572-6000.

Another antique dealer in the area is **Top Shelf Antique Decoys**, specializing in a must-have for any collector of the unusual—duck decoys. Some date back all the way to the 1800s. By appointment only. ~ 20 Gray's Point Road, Charlestown; 401-364-3844.

For a brochure listing every shop, contact the **South County Tourism Council.** ~ 4808 Tower Hill Road, Wakefield, RI 02879; 401-789-4422; www.southcountyri.com.

Near the waterfront, **Scarlet Begonia** is the place to go for quilts, pillows, jewelry, rugs and other handicrafts. Closed Christmas to Easter; call ahead for hours. ~ Dodge Street, Old Harbor, Block Island; 401-466-5024.

NIGHTLIFE

A dancefloor and deejay make the otherwise-ordinary **Andrea Hotel** bar a lively locale for evening entertainment. The music plays seven nights a week in summer months and on some weekends during the rest of the year. Occasionally live bands perform. ~ 89 Atlantic Avenue, Westerly; 888-318-5707.

If a younger, energetic crowd is more your speed, check out **193 Degrees Coffee House** at the University of Rhode Island. On any given night, the place might rock out with live funk, rock, punk, hip-hop, open-mic and deejay music. At this student-run nonprofit establishment, the only charge will be for a cup of Joe. ~ URI Memorial Union, South Kingston; 401-874-5060.

BEACHES & PARKS

There are 19 government-managed preserves, state parks, beaches and forest areas in South County. The stretch of coastline from Watch Hill to Narragansett is made up almost entirely of sandy beaches.

HIDDEN ►

NAPATREE POINT BARRIER BEACH This Watch Hill spit of land evokes a true wilderness feeling; cars are barred from this ecologically fragile, half-mile-long sandy fishhook, allowing the many species of shorebirds and human visitors to enjoy a peaceful coexistence. ~ At the westernmost end of Watch Hill.

MISQUAMICUT STATE BEACH One of the largest and most popular beaches in New England, this is a good family beach, with surf that is usually mild and a gradual drop-off. The wide beach is equally good for lazing or walking, and the sand is of fine quality, although August can bring in an excess of seaweed. There are picnic tables, a pavilion, snack bars, restrooms, lifeguards during summer, a bathhouse and changing rooms. Closed Labor

SATISFY YOUR SWEET TOOTH

The **Hack and Livery General Store** is everything you ever dreamed a country store would be: more than 50 varieties of penny candy arrayed in glass canisters. Bet you can't walk out with only one of those tiny paper bags full of goodies. They also have a selection of collectibles. Closed Monday and Tuesday from January through June, open daily from July through December. ~ 1006 Main Street, Hope Valley; 401-539-7033.

Day to Memorial Day. Day-use fee, $12 to $14. ~ Along Atlantic Avenue in Misquamicut; 401-596-9097.

NINIGRET CONSERVATION AREA (EAST BEACH) A four-mile-long swath of broad, sandy barrier beach between Ninigret Pond and Block Island Sound, this is considered by many to be the most beautiful in the state because of its undeveloped expanse of dunes and scrub pines. (The 1938 hurricane blew away all houses, and the state now forbids any development.) The beach is usually not crowded because the state strictly limits parking in the entire conservation area. (Get there early in the morning on weekends for a parking spot.) The beach has a rocky bottom with a steep drop-off about three feet out. There is a lifeguard in a designated area, but this beach can be dangerous for small children. Because of drop-off, waves tend to break hard close to shore. There are portable toilets here. ~ At the foot of East Beach Road, off Route 1 in Charlestown; 401-322-0450.

▲ Permitted for four-wheel camper vehicles only on barrier beach; $14 per night for residents, $20 for nonresidents. Closed November through April.

ARCADIA WILDLIFE MANAGEMENT AREA Thousands of inland wilderness acres have been set aside in the northwest corner of South County and can be enjoyed by outdoor lovers at Rhode Island's largest recreation area. The management area offers some excellent hiking opportunities. There's also boating and swimming along the sandy beaches of Beach Pond (no boat launches allowed) during the summer months, and fishing in the freshwater pond and streams and rivers for trout and bass. You'll find picnic areas at Browning Mill Pond. ~ The main entrance is located off Route 165; 401-539-2356, fax 401-539-1157.

▲ The park has free hike-in tent camping and $15-a-night shelter camping. Camping requires a permit (free) available at park headquarters (260 Arcadia Road, Arcadia). If you don't find sufficient camping in the park, there's always *Oak Embers* (219 Escoheag Hill Road, West Greenwich; 401-397-4042), a private campground nearby. There are 50 seasonal RV sites with sewer hookups and 30 year-round RV hookup sites (both $30 per night), as well as tent sites ($28 per night).

EAST MATUNUCK STATE BEACH One mile of nice shoreline, sand dunes and, on a clear day, a nice view of Block Island are yours at this popular family beach. A gradual drop-off makes East Matunuck a good place to take the kids. Facilities include picnic tables, bathhouse, restrooms, concessions and lifeguards. Closed Labor Day to Memorial Day. Day-use fee, $6 to $14 per car. ~ On Succotash Road off Route 1 in South Kingstown; 401-789-8585; www.riparks.com/eastmatunuck.htm.

ROGER W. WHEELER STATE BEACH Lying within the protective breakwater of Point Judith Harbor of Refuge, this wave-free spot known locally as Sand Hill Cove is an ideal swimming beach for families. The sand is fine and white, waters are calm and the drop-off is so gradual that it is often necessary to wade great distances just to reach waist-deep water. There are picnic tables, restrooms, lifeguards, showers and a playground. Open weekends in May and from Memorial Day to Labor Day. Day-use fee, $6 to $14 per car. ~ Off Sand Hill Cove Road in Narragansett, near Galilee; 401-789-3563.

NARRAGANSETT TOWN BEACH Voted the "best swimming beach in the state" by *Rhode Island Monthly* magazine, this swath is visible from every point in town and from every turn along the local stretch of scenic Route 1A. Just south of the elite Dunes Club, it's a quintessential New England beach with miles of fine white sand in a broad sweep from waterline to dune and rollers that can kick up enough to lure surfers in rough weather. The Northeast Surfing Championships are held here every fall; for wanna-be surfers, lessons are given by the pros every summer. Other activities offered include aerobics or yoga on the beach. You'll find a bathhouse and lifeguards (seasonal). ~ On Route 1A, two miles east of Route 1; 401-783-6430, fax 401-788-2553.

Newport Area

You'll really understand just how much diversity Rhode Island crams within its tiny borders as you leave mellow South County and cross over Narragansett Bay to Newport, with its abundance of high-powered millionaires' yachts and extravagant mansions. These, of course, are the very elements that set Newport apart from other New England resort towns.

Modern-day Newport does retain its fair share of Colonial history and landmarks, however. Founded in 1639 by settlers from Providence, the town became an important shipbuilding center and seaport, a landing site for the infamous "triangle trade" in molasses, rum and slaves. By the time of the Revolution, Newport was already prospering.

That prosperity would reach staggering heights during the next century, when wealthy families from New York and Philadelphia started building their summer mansions in this idyllic spot. It is really the lavish excesses of these "gilded age" palaces that everyone flocks here to see; we want an insider's glimpse into the lifestyles of the long-ago rich and famous.

SIGHTS

The **Preservation Society of Newport County** maintains eleven historic house museums, including some of the most opulent mansions of the Gilded Age. In each, the one-hour tours are well organized and quite thorough, given by guides who obviously love their work. Two of the mansions offer self-guided audio tours. You'll see examples of mind-boggling wealth and extravagance, holdovers from a pre–income tax era when families with Vanderbilt-like reputations to uphold could squander vast fortunes on palatial "summer cottages." The Society offers individual and multiple-house tour tickets. Mansions are open daily from mid-April through December, seasonal hours the rest of the year. ~ 424 Bellevue Avenue, Newport; 401-847-1000, fax 401-847-1361; www.newportmansions.org, e-mail info@newport mansions.org.

Hammersmith Farm was a working farm in the 1600s. More recently the farm's cottage and its 50 waterfront acres (landscaped by Frederick Law Olmsted) served as summer home to young Jacqueline Bouvier and as a "Summer White House" to her husband, John F. Kennedy. Now a private residence, the house is closed to the public. ~ Ocean Drive, Newport.

WALKING TOUR

Mansions of Newport

It's not possible to tour all the mansions that are open to the public on the same day, since each one takes almost an hour. This walk lets you hit the high points in a day and covers about four miles, not counting the vast interiors of the mansions. Start around 10 a.m. at the **Preservation Society of Newport County**. Buy a $31/adult ($10/youth 6 to 17) combination tour ticket for five mansions (saving $23 over individual admission), called the Newport Mansion Experience. You need not use the ticket at all houses on the same day; it's good for the entire season. ~ 424 Bellevue Avenue; 401-847-1000, fax 401-847-1361; www.newportmansions.org, e-mail info@newportmansions.org.

CHATEAU-SUR-MER Follow Bellevue Avenue South to the nearby Chateau-sur-Mer with its distinctive mansard roofline. Built in 1852 for William Wetmore, who made his fortune in the China trade—hence the Chinese "moongate" in the south wall—the mansion incorporates most of the major design trends of the Victorian era. Its broad parklike grounds shaded by copper beech trees were the scene of *fêtes champêtres*, elaborate picnics attended by as many as 2000 guests.

ROSECLIFF TO BELCOURT Walking south on Bellevue Avenue, across Ruggles Avenue, you'll come to **Rosecliff**, architect Stanford White's version of the Grand Trianon at Versailles. It was completed in 1902 for the heiress to the Comstock silver lode, one of the richest silver finds in history. Next in line, **The Astors' Beechwood** (not one of the Preservation Society mansions—call 401-846-3772) offers living-history tours by costumed actors appearing as guides, gossipy servants, eccentric house guests and even an Astor or two. Closed Monday through Wednesday from December through mid-May. Closed January. Beyond the Astor mansion, **Marble House** was the first of the Vanderbilt mansions in Newport (William Vanderbilt gave it to his wife as a present on her 39th birthday). Its interior boasts virtually no surface left ungilded, unmarbled or unembellished. It incorporates features from the Grand and Petit Trianons in Versailles and has a colorful Chinese teahouse over-

The name **Newport Casino** refers not to gambling but to the elegant resort built in 1880 that now houses the **International Tennis Hall of Fame and Museum**, as well as famed championship grass courts and court tennis (the "sport of kings"). Admission. ~ 194 Bellevue Avenue, Newport; 401-849-3990, 800-457-1144, fax 401-849-8780; www.tennisfame.com, e-mail newport@tennisfame.com.

looking the Atlantic. Near the south end of Bellevue, **Belcourt Castle** (not a Preservation Society mansion—call 401-846-0669; www.belcourt castle.com; admission) is a Louis XIII–style palace built in 1894 and filled with art treasures and antiques from around the world.

CLIFF WALK TO THE BREAKERS Past the Belcourt estate, Bellevue Avenue makes a sharp right. Near the corner of Coggeshall Avenue, Cliff Walk goes off to the south toward a rocky point. From the point, the trail turns north and winds its sometimes precarious way above the crashing waves, providing "hidden" views of the back yards and facades of the great mansions you've visited so far. Keep to the inside of the path—erosion has weakened the outer edges in some sections. A little less than two miles along, you'll come to Ochre Point Avenue and **The Breakers**, the grandest of the Newport mansions. Cornelius Vanderbilt II commissioned architect Richard Morris Hunt to design this full-scale replica of a 16th-century Italian palace. After touring the Great Hall, with its 45-foot ceiling and the rest of the splendid interior, visitors can ramble through the 13-acre grounds overlooking the sea.

CHEPSTOW AND THE ELMS Continue north on the Cliff Walk for another half-mile to Narragansett Avenue. Along the way you'll pass **Ochre Court**, a former summer home built in 1892 that now serves as the administration building for Salve Regina University. At Narragansett, turn inland to the two-story white Italianate **Chepstow**, which houses the art and historical document collections of the Morris clan, one of America's founding families. Continue on Narragansett back to Bellevue, then turn right to **The Elms**. The summer home of coal tycoon Edward Julius Berwind, it was modeled after the mid-18th-century French chateau d'Asnieres and was famed for its classical gardens, which have been restored.

ADDITIONAL HOMES The Preversation Society operates several other historic houses, including **Kingscote**, a smaller early-19th-century residence that was among the first on Bellevue Avenue, as well as the **Isaac Bell House**, one of the finest examples of shingle-style architecture in America, **The Breakers Stable and Carriage House** on Coggeshall Avenue, **Hunter House** (page 147) on Washington Street, and **Green Animals** (page 146) in Portsmouth.

Not *everything* in Newport has to do with gilded monuments and big bucks—the city is one of the oldest in the United States and has an intriguing history stretching back three centuries. One spot that has attracted a horde of historical theories yet remains a mystery is the **Old Stone Mill**. Some believe it was erected by Norsemen in the days of Leif Ericsson. Others date it to the 17th century or believe it to be the remains of a 17th-century windmill. ~ Bellevue Avenue and Mill Street in Touro Park, Newport.

America's oldest Jewish house of worship, **Touro Synagogue** dates back to 1763. The first members of Newport's Jewish community—Sephardic Portuguese whose families had fled to the New World to escape the Catholic Inquisition—had arrived in Newport a century earlier, drawn by Rhode Island's then-unique policy of universal religious tolerance. Although not large, the Georgian-style brick structure is considered the crowning achievement of Peter Harrison, 18th-century America's leading architect. It embodies features typical of Sephardic temples in Spain and Portugal, such as the seating arrangement and the massive columns, each carved from a single tree, that support the women's gallery. Twelve in number, they symbolize the twelve tribes of Israel. The synagogue is set at an angle on the property so that worshippers standing in prayer before the Holy Ark containing the Torah face east toward Jerusalem. No tours on Saturday. Admission. ~ 85 Touro Street, Newport; 401-847-4794 ext. 23, fax 401-845-6790; www.tourosynagogue.org, e-mail info@tourosynagogue.org.

The Newport Historical Society's **Museum of Newport History** provides a context for the city's architectural marvels. Artifacts, graphics, old photographs and audiovisual programs reveal the origins of Rhode Island's policy of religious tolerance and show the lifestyles of the wealthy, the artists, writers and architects and the diverse ethnic subcultures that shaped Newport's cultural heritage. Among the exhibits are model ships, Colonial silver and the printing press used by Benjamin Franklin's brother James. A reproduction omnibus offers a video tour of Bellvue Avenue in the Gilded Age. Open daily mid-June through Labor Day, and Thursday through Sunday from September to the end of December. Call for hours. Admission. ~

sights

AUTHOR FAVORITE

Of all the fabulous mansions in the Newport area, none brings a smile to my face like **Green Animals,** a whimsical garden of more than 80 century-old trees and shrubs sculpted in the European manner to resemble dogs, camels, goats, roosters, bears, sailboats and even a man on horseback. It's a treat for kids, a mecca for horticulture buffs. A Victorian toy collection is housed inside the country estate's 19th-century white clapboard house. Admission. ~ 380 Cory's Lane, Portsmouth; 401-847-1000, fax 401-847-1361; www.newportmansions.org, e-mail info@newportmansions.org.

127 Thames Street, Newport; 401-846-0813, fax 401-846-1853; www.newporthistorical.org.

The oldest library building in the U.S., the **Redwood Library and Athenaeum** was founded in 1747 and today boasts an important collection of books and paintings, including several by Gilbert Stuart. View the extensive renovations that restored the library to its original condition. ~ 50 Bellevue Avenue, Newport; 401-847-0292, fax 401-841-5680; www.redwoodlibrary.org, e-mail redwood@redwoodlibrary.net.

Nearby stands the **Great Friends Meeting House**, a Quaker worshipping place since it was built in 1699. The original large English Gothic structure received two Colonial-style additions in 1729 and 1807. The meeting house is open from mid-June through Labor Day and by appointment only the rest of the year. Admission. ~ Marlborough and Farewell streets, Newport; 401-846-0813, fax 401-846-1853; www.newporthistorical.org.

The oldest restored home in Newport, the **Wanton-Lyman-Hazard House** dates to 1697 and has seen a wealth of history all by itself. Several Colonial governors called the place home, but its claim to fame was as the site of a riot following passage of England's infamous Stamp Act of 1765. It seems an outspoken Loyalist lived in this house, which was heavily damaged by a distraught mob of patriots. Today the house features period pieces and an archaeological dig in its backyard. Admission. ~ 17 Broadway, Newport; 401-846-0813, fax 401-846-1853; www.newporthistorical.org, e-mail info@newporthistorical.org.

A fine Colonial mansion dating to 1748, **Hunter House** was saved from demolition in 1945 by the Preservation Society of Newport County. Today it is a restored National Historic Landmark with an excellent collection of 18th-century Colonial furnishings, as well as paintings and other decorative objects. Open late June through early September. Admission. ~ 54 Washington Street, Newport; 401-847-1000, fax 401-847-1361; www.newportmansions.org, e-mail info@newportmansions.org.

A good stress-buster is **Viking Tours**, which helps you beat Newport's summertime gridlock traffic. The bus tour leaves from the Newport Visitor Center (located on America's Cup Avenue) and stops at mansions and major attractions. Closed Sunday through Friday from January through March. Fee. ~ 401-847-6921, fax 401-848-5773; www.vikingtoursnewport.com, e-mail info@vikingtoursnewport.com.

Newport County Convention & Visitors Bureau (Gateway Center) is a bustling hub of traveler's information: helpful staff; brochures, maps and guides; multimedia video; and bus, trolley and tourist train terminal. ~ 23 America's Cup Avenue, Newport; 401-849-8048, 800-976-5122; www.gonewport.com.

Across from the Visitors Bureau, hop aboard the historic **Old Colony & Newport Scenic Railway**. During the ten-mile, 80-minute roundtrip you'll pass a number of the island's maritime sites. It's an interesting and comfortable way to get the lay of the land. Open Sunday only. Fee. ~ 19 America's Cup Avenue at Bridge Street, Newport; 401-624-6951; www.ocnrr.com.

The towns of Middletown and Portsmouth share Aquidneck Island with Newport. In Middletown, the **Norman Bird Sanctuary** encompasses over 300 acres of extraordinarily beautiful wilderness. Wildlife (pheasant, nesting birds, rabbit and fox) inhabits the 30 acres of hay fields; there are woodlands, salt marshes and craggy ridges. An extremely active program includes guided trail walks, educational workshops, children's programs and themed hikes. Trail fee, $4. ~ 583 Third Beach Road, Middletown; 401-846-2577, fax 401-846-2772; www.normanbirdsanctuary.org, e-mail info@normanbirdsanctuary.org.

Across the Sakonnet River from Portsmouth lie the bucolic towns of Tiverton and Little Compton. Comparable to the fashionable bedroom communities found near any urban center, these towns have their fair share of power residents who share the country scene with gentlemen farmers. Everything is peaceful here; strict zoning laws and sky-high real-estate prices conspire to keep things that way.

HIDDEN ► **Sakonnet Vineyards** is the oldest of Rhode Island's three vineyards. Established in 1975, Sakonnet now produces a southeastern New England selection including their popular chardonnay and vidal blanc. There are guided tours and winetastings. ~ 162 West Main Road, Little Compton; 401-635-8486, 800-919-4637, fax 401-635-2102; www.sakonnetwine.com, e-mail info@sakonnetwine.com.

Sakonnet's vineyards and its scenic acres are an altogether idyllic picnic setting. After buying a bottle of wine at Sakonnet's tasting room, stop by the **Provender at Tiverton Four Corners**, a gourmet food emporium housed in an old mansard-roofed general store, to assemble your dream lunch, complete with fresh-baked bread. Closed January through February; closed Monday from September through March. ~ 3883 Main Road, Tiverton; 401-624-8096.

LODGING

The Wayside is a trim beige-brick Georgian mansion just across Bellevue Avenue from the famous Elms. Owner Dorothy Post has restored this sprawling 1896 home, creating seven guest rooms blessed with antique furnishings and majestic proportions—and each with its own private bath. There's a two-bedroom cottage apartment over the carriage house and a heated pool in the back garden. ~ 406 Bellevue Avenue, Newport; 401-847-0302, 800-653-7678, fax 401-848-9374; www.waysidenewport.com, e-mail info@waysidenewport.com. DELUXE.

The 1855 **Marshall Slocum Guest House** sits on a tree-lined, Norman Rockwell kind of street. An American flag flies overhead, and on the spacious front porch rocking chairs await your leisure. Inside, the recently renovated rooms are cheery and graced with antiques. Your gregarious innkeepers, Mark and Diana Spring, who are creative both in the kitchen (fresh-baked quiches and muffins every breakfast) and in decorating, have chosen sunny yellows and marine blues to balance the house's original dark woods. Two of the five upstairs guest rooms have fireplaces and all have private baths. A full breakfast is served on the deck overlooking the sunny back garden in warm weather. ~ 29 Kay Street, Newport; 401-841-5120, 800-372-5120, fax 401-846-3787; www.marshallslocuminn.com, e-mail info@marshallslocuminn.com. DELUXE TO ULTRA-DELUXE.

The **Newport Marriott** is big, modern and on the harbor in downtown Newport. A number of the newly renovated 319 rooms and seven suites command sweeping views of Newport Harbor or feature atrium balconies with views of Narragansett Bay. Glass-fronted elevators (often exasperatingly slow to arrive) seem to double as kinetic sculpture, providing space-age mobility to the lobby's plant-filled atrium design. Rooms feature contemporary nautical decor and the usual complement of electronic equipment. Among the definite pluses: a health club and indoor pool in the hotel; the Gateway Center (Convention & Visitors Bureau) next door; and shopping and waterfront dining within easy walking distance. ~ 25 America's Cup Avenue, Newport; 401-849-1000, 800-228-9290, fax 401-849-3422; www.newportmarriott.com. ULTRA-DELUXE.

Hotel Viking is Newport's grande dame, a 1920s National Historic Landmark in red brick trimmed in white. The understatement of the tidy four-column entrance is deceptive; inside, the hotel is a sprawl of rooms and levels. There are 209 guest rooms, a dining room and a spa and pool. Rooms are a bit cramped, crammed with heavy antique reproduction four-posters and furniture. In summer, dining at the Garden Patio Café offers a charming alternative to the somewhat overpowering hotel at-

MANSION FOR RENT

In addition to the usual chain hotels, Newport has an abundance of small bed and breakfasts. As one islander observed, "In this town, almost everyone has an extra room or two to rent." Don't be fooled by that gem of Yankee understatement; we have observed that, in this town where extravagant landmark mansions are almost the norm, the bed and breakfasts tend to follow suit.

mosphere inside. ~ 1 Bellevue Avenue, Newport; 401-847-3300, 800-556-7126, fax 401-848-4864; www.hotelviking.com, e-mail contactus@hotelviking.com. ULTRA-DELUXE.

Castle Hill Inn & Resort sits on 40 acres of secluded peninsula overlooking Narragansett Bay. Built in 1874 for international naturalist Alexander Agassiz, this weathered, shingled inn today retains most of its original Victorian charm. Its rambling structure yields nine guest rooms of unique shapes, bursting with antique decor. Bedrooms are furnished with oriental carpets and Chinese antiques, authentic washstands and upholstered slipper chairs, and are paired with large, modern baths. Six more guest rooms are found in cliffside harbor houses behind the main building, and beachfront cottages (closed in winter) draw repeat visitors every year (weekly rates in the summer, nightly rates in the spring). Individually decorated beach houses are their premier units, offering large sitting areas, kitchens, stone fireplaces, entertainment centers, two-person jacuzzis, and private decks on the beach. Guests like to gather before the unique marquetry fireplace in the downstairs sitting room. All accommodations include breakfast and an afternoon tea service. ~ 590 Ocean Drive, Newport; 401-849-3800, 888-466-1355, fax 401-849-3838; www.castlehillinn.com, e-mail info@castlehillinn.com. ULTRA-DELUXE.

Built in 1880 as a summer home for Maryland governor Thomas Swann, the **Cliffside Inn** is ideally located—a block from Cliff Walk and within easy reach of the beach and Newport's mansions. But in this case, location is not everything. The inn is a beautiful Victorian building with 16 guest rooms, all furnished with antiques and boasting fireplaces or whirlpools. At one point, it was home to artist Beatrice Turner, whose paintings can be seen throughout. No smoking and no pets. Children over 13

SERVING TIME . . . COMFORTABLY

For an overnight stay that will make a good story to tell friends later, spend the night in an 18th-century jail. Located in the heart of downtown Newport a block from the harbor, the **Jailhouse Inn** was built in 1772 as the town lockup. Beautifully renovated, the dining room and common areas are furnished with antiques for a homelike feel. Many of the 22 guest rooms and suites emphasize the jailhouse motif with convict-striped bedspreads and upholstery. No jail cell was ever so spacious, though, as these rooms with their king- or queen-size beds, dormer windows and premium cable TV. Rates include afternoon tea and a continental breakfast buffet. Closed January through mid-March. ~ 13 Marlborough Street, Newport; 401-847-4638, 888-427-9444, fax 401-849-0605; www.historicinnsofnewport.com, e-mail vacation@jailhouse.com. DELUXE TO ULTRA-DELUXE.

only; two-day minimum stay on weekends, three-night minimum on holidays. ~ 2 Seaview Avenue, Newport; 401-847-1811, 800-845-1811, fax 401-848-5850; www.cliffsideinn.com, e-mail reservations@legendaryinnsofnewport.com. ULTRA-DELUXE.

The graceful Victorian **Adele Turner Inn** was built in 1855 by Captain Augustus Littlefield. Its 13 rooms have elaborate beds and private baths, and the entire inn is air-conditioned (which is welcome during Newport's steamy summers). Each room is individually decorated, some with arched windows, others with gaslight and window nooks; all have fireplaces. ~ 93 Pelham Street, Newport; 401-847-1811, 800-845-1811; www.adeleturnerinn.com, e-mail reservations@legendaryinnsofnewport.com. ULTRA-DELUXE.

Named after the vessel responsible for smuggling liquor into Newport during Prohibition, the 1870 **Black Duck Inn** maintains a historic, country look. With a Laura Ashley–inspired style of floral patterns and light colors, the eight rooms, (six with private baths), are elegant and comfortable; many are appointed with distinctive, dark wood beds. Deluxe suites with jacuzzis and fireplaces are available as well. A country breakfast in the quaint dining area is included. ~ 29 Pelham Street, Newport; 401-841-5548, 800-206-5212, fax 401-846-4873; www.blackduckinn.com, e-mail marya401@aol.com. DELUXE TO ULTRA-DELUXE.

The **Admiral Fitzroy Inn** has 17 rooms, each with a private bath, an elevator, and a roof deck with a harbor view. Admiral Fitzroy commanded the *Beagle* during Charles Darwin's *Origin of the Species* voyage to the Galápagos Islands. Breakfast is included. ~ 398 Thames Street, Newport; 401-848-8000, 866-848-8780, fax 401-848-8006; www.admiralfitzroy.com. DELUXE TO ULTRA-DELUXE.

During the Revolution, the **Admiral Farragut Inn**, built in 1702, housed two of the aides-de-camp of General Rochambeau, the French general who assisted George Washington throughout the war. The ten-room inn maintains its Colonial air, with wide plank floors, 12-over-12 paned windows, and original cave mouldings. Some of the rooms have jacuzzis or fireplaces ~ 31 Clarke Street, Newport; 401-848-5300, 800-524-1386, fax 401-847-7630; www.innsofnewport.com, e-mail newportinn@aol.com. MODERATE TO ULTRA-DELUXE.

Within easy walking distance of the mansions is **The Hydrangea House Inn**, named after the blossoms so abundant in Newport. The ten-room inn was built in 1876 and has been carefully restored. The guest rooms—which are all non-smoking—are variously decorated with antiques and original artwork; some have jacuzzis and fireplaces. The rate includes a breakfast of fresh-ground coffee, just-squeezed orange juice, home-baked bread and granola, plus pancakes or scrambled eggs; the formal dining room has a fireplace, chandelier and 13-foot mahogany dining table. The inn is right on Bellevue Avenue, about a five-minute walk to the waterfront. ~ 16 Bellevue Avenue, Newport; 401-846-4435, 800-945-4667, fax 401-846-6602; www.hydrangeahouse.com, e-mail hydrangeahouse@cox.net. ULTRA-DELUXE.

Spring Seasons Inn offers three bed-and-breakfast accommodations situated in the heart of Newport. One suite features an over-sized jacuzzi, a cathedral ceiling and a private deck. There are regular jacuzzis in each of the other suites. All units in this 1870s Greek Revival building have air conditioning. ~ 86 Spring Street, Newport; 401-849-0004; www.springseasonsinn.com, e-mail innkeeper@springseasonsinn.com. DELUXE TO ULTRA-DELUXE.

The **Ivy Lodge** is an eight-room inn housed in a large Victorian. All rooms are individually decorated in Victorian style. All have their own bathrooms, a rarity at most bed and breakfasts; most rooms have fireplaces and a whirlpool tub. Breakfast is always a treat; you'll enjoy the homemade muffins and other baked goods in addition to a different main dish each day. Call ahead for winter hours. ~ 12 Clay Street, Newport; 401-849-6865, 800-834-6865, fax 401-849-0704; www.ivylodge.com, e-mail innkeepers@ivylodge.com. DELUXE TO ULTRA-DELUXE.

Not everything in the Newport area is rarified and expensive. The **Newport Inn and Spa** offers clean, comfortable and affordable lodgings. The 147 guest rooms are large and decorated with modern furnishings. Amenities include no-smoking rooms, a lounge, a heated indoor pool and the Captain's Table Restaurant and Lounge. ~ 936 West Main Road, Middletown; 401-846-7600, 800-846-8322, fax 401-849-6919; www.newportspa.com. DELUXE TO ULTRA-DELUXE.

DINING

As you might expect, the restaurant scene in this posh town can get quite fancy and expensive. For those who prefer a more laid-back approach, there are many waterfront places that specialize in seafood, harbor views and relaxed enjoyment.

Non-guests are welcome to enjoy the legendary Sunday brunch (lunch and dinner also available) at **Castle Hill Inn & Resort**. This three-story, weathered-shingle 1874 Victorian, with its peaked roof and turrets, overlooks the bay from its own peninsula. Inside, the chestnut paneling shines in the glow of Victorian lamps. Oriental rugs accent hardwood floors. Brunch, served on the lawn or indoors in a gazebo setting of green and white, combines just the right mix of formal and alfresco eating as you sit peacefully watching the sailboats on Narragansett Bay. The vast spread offers everything from breakfast items such as eggs Benedict to tempting entrées such as pan-roasted salmon and pork tenderloin. ~ 590 Ocean Drive, Newport; 401-849-3800,

888-466-1355; www.castlehillinn.com, e-mail info@castlehillinn.com. DELUXE TO ULTRA-DELUXE.

An atmosphere of elegance prevails at the **White Horse Tavern,** a restored 1673 Colonial landmark. Although it's America's oldest tavern, don't expect a typical pub scene; this is one of Newport's finest restaurants. The White Horse's interior, too, remains true to its Colonial heritage with huge fireplaces and exposed beams. While the menu varies with the season, you can count on always finding native seafood specialties like fresh lobster and grilled salmon or terra-firma dishes such as beef Wellington. Service is formal, lending additional panache to the upscale Continental cuisine. ~ 26 Marlborough Street, Newport; 401-849-3600; www.whitehorsetavern.com, e-mail thewhitehorse1@aol.com. ULTRA-DELUXE.

While not strictly hidden, **Canfield House and Canfield Pub** are decidedly a couple of finds. Relying primarily on satisfied diners to spread its good word, Canfield maintains a discreet elegance. An unpretentious Victorian building tucked away in a tiny alley off the main street, Canfield began as a gambling casino, the joy and toy of Richard Canfield, a colorful figure in the gaming world of the early 1900s. Today's diners enjoy Continental classics in the main casino, under a vaulted ceiling of intricately carved cherry. Service is upscale-casual and attentive. Visitors and locals (many of whom come to celebrate special occasions) enjoy dressing up to complement the surroundings. Closed Mondays. ~ 5 Memorial Boulevard, Newport; 401-847-0416, fax 401-848-5178; www.canfieldhousenewport.com. DELUXE TO ULTRA-DELUXE.

◄ HIDDEN

AUTHOR FAVORITE

After a day of marveling at the old-fashioned opulence along Newport's Bellevue Boulevard, I'm ready to splurge for a seat on **The Newport Dinner Train.** Two lavishly refurbished railroad cars roll sedately along tracks paralleling Narragansett Bay, making a two-and-a-half-hour journey to nowhere and back, allowing ample time for the four-course meal. Diners choose from entrées of pork, chicken or fish and have the option to take part in a murder-mystery show on Friday evenings or a children's event on Thursday and Saturday in the summer. The mood is festive, with many parties celebrating a special occasion. Reservations required. Closed January through March. ~ Newport Depot, 19 America's Cup Avenue, Newport; 401-841-8700, 800-398-7427, fax 401-841-8724; www.newportdinnertrain.com, e-mail info@newportdinnertrain.com. ULTRA-DELUXE.

For 25 years, locals and tourists have flocked to the **Brick Alley Pub**. The casual downtown restaurant also serves an assortment of steaks, fresh local seafoods, pastas and seasonal specials. The decor consists mainly of walls full of award plaques the restaurant has won since it opened in 1980. ~ 140 Thames Street, Newport; 401-849-6334, fax 401-848-5640; www.brickalley.com, e-mail info@brickalley.com. MODERATE TO ULTRA-DELUXE.

With slick black leather booths, bright red accents and white linen tablecloths, **The Fifth Element** offers a classy dining environment with a youthful edge. Creative entrées (seared fennel-spiced yellowfin tuna with artichoke-chickpea cake) and decadent desserts (white chocolate and ginger cheesecake) add to the restaurant's flair. The kitchen closes by 10, but the bar doesn't wind down until 1. Closed the first three weeks in January. ~ 509 Thames Street, Newport; 401-841-0011, fax 401-841-0015; www.5eri.com, e-mail info@5eri.com. DELUXE TO ULTRA-DELUXE.

The exquisite two-story **Pronto Restaurant** has a penchant for the posh. The downstairs dining room is decked out in rich red, floor-to-ceiling curtains and shimmering chandeliers, while the upstairs area resembles more of a French country home with pale yellow walls and floral table runners. Start off with a seafood crêpe topped with pine nuts and work your way to the North African braised lamb shank served over white lentils and sautéed greens. Paired with an extensive wine list, the Pronto menu will not disappoint. ~ 464 Thames Street, Newport; 401-847-5251; www.prontonewport.com, e-mail prontonewport@aol.com. DELUXE TO ULTRA-DELUXE.

Decorated in solid beach tones, **The Mooring** is reminiscent of a luxury sailboat. With deep blue accents and warm woods, this waterfront restaurant suggests all the calm of the ocean, as well as the comfort of a day at the beach. The upscale menu includes beef and lobster with shiitake demiglace and vanilla butter, and also creative specialties such as Georges Bank scallops en casserole with toasted pecans, wild mushrooms and sweet potato. Three-time winner of *Wine Spectator* magazine's coveted "Best of Award of Excellence," the wine list is exceptional. ~ Sayer's Wharf, off America's Cup Avenue, Newport; 401-846-2260, www.mooringrestaurant.com, e-mail info@mooringrestaurant.com. ULTRA-DELUXE.

A very worthwhile French restaurant, **Le Bistro** specializes in Provençal cooking, using lots of herbs and oils. Everything is made from scratch here including the sauces (which are lighter than traditional French sauces) and baked goods. Le Bistro is located on the waterfront, offering views of the water from the dining areas. ~ 41 Bowen's Wharf, Newport; 401-849-7778, fax 401-846-9279; www.lebistronewport.com, e-mail bistroman@aol.com. MODERATE TO ULTRA-DELUXE.

A great little place for breakfast or a simple lunch, **Annie's** serves wonderful homemade muffins and delicious omelettes. The lunch menu includes sandwiches, soups, burgers and salads. The restaurant—a cross between a diner and a bakery—has booths and a counter area perfect for settling in with a meal and a newspaper. ~ 176 Bellevue Avenue, Newport; 401-849-6731. BUDGET.

Sea Fare Inn dazzles with festive opulence: chandeliers glitter, and tables (as well as patrons) are decked in Sunday best. The cuisine is American regional of the unabashedly haute classical variety—the kind that requires (and receives) similarly haute service and attention to detail. Whether you're seated in the large, formal, pillared dining room or in what once was the sun porch of this Victorian mansion, you'll catch the festive spirit of the place. Dinner only. Closed Sunday and Monday; closed for two weeks in February. ~ 3352 East Main Road, Portsmouth; 401-683-0577, fax 401-683-2910; www.seafareinn.com. DELUXE TO ULTRA-DELUXE.

◄ HIDDEN

The beachside line of people waiting to get into **Flo's Drive-in** is the first clue. A true "clam shack" and the best of the genre, this beachfront haven sells huge, puffy clamcakes, fried steamers and spicy "stuffies" (stuffed clams). Open Thursday through Sunday from April to December. ~ Island Park, Portsmouth. BUDGET.

SHOPPING

In Newport, even the shopping malls sport a nautical/historical air. **Bowen's Wharf** is a mix of 18th-century wharf buildings and 19th-century brick warehouses that make up today's complex of open-air restaurants, fashion boutiques and import shops. ~ Just off America's Cup Avenue, Newport; 401-849-2120; www.bowenswharf.com.

Brick Market Place is a four-acre complex of more than 30 shops and restaurants along a—you guessed it—brick road. The

YULETIDE FARMERS

Christmas trees are a $6 million-a-year business in Rhode Island, which has more Christmas tree farms than any other New England state. The industry has proved to be ideal for this tiny state, because the trees—balsam fir, Douglas fir, Fraser fir, noble fir, Scotch pine, Virginia pine and white pine—can be grown on relatively small farms on land that is only marginally productive for other crops. Besides being more profitable than timbering for lumber, Christmas trees are ready for harvest (six feet tall) in about seven years, compared to 20 to 30 years for timber. Most Christmas tree farms along Rhode Island highways welcome visitors, and as the holiday season approaches many farms let customers choose and cut their own trees.

original building, which used to be the site of the market and granary built in 1762, is now a National Historic Landmark that also houses the Museum of Newport History. ~ Between Thames Street and America's Cup Avenue, Newport; e-mail info@brickmarketnewport.com.

Picture frames, stationery, etiquette books and elegant trinkets abound at **Papers**, a charming boutique with a variety of custom gifts. ~ 178 Bellevue Avenue, Newport; 800-660-9670; www.papersnewport.com.

Tiverton Four Corners is a gathering of some very chic merchandise presented in attractive old-fashioned surroundings. On one corner, the 1829 Josiah Wilcox House is home to **Peter's Attic**, which specializes in country antiques. ~ 8 Neck Road; 401-625-5912. Nearby, **Provender at Tiverton Four Corners** purveys gourmet imports as well as fresh-baked goods and fancy take-outs. Closed January through February and closed Monday from September through March. ~ 3883 Main Road, Tiverton; 401-624-8096.

NIGHTLIFE

In summer, Newport's nightlife assumes world-class proportions with its famous festivals: the **Newport Folk Festival** (401-847-3700), held the first week in August; the JVC **Jazz Festival/Newport** (401-847-3700), the second week of August; and the **Newport Musical Festival** (401-846-1133), the second and third weeks in July, which features classical concerts at some of the most spectacular mansions of Bellevue Avenue.

The **Newport Playhouse & Cabaret Restaurant** offers dinner theater and cabaret Friday through Sunday. Tuesday, Wednesday, Thursday, Saturday and Sunday matinees are available as well. Closed in January. ~ 102 Connell Highway, near the foot of the Newport Bridge, Newport; 401-848-7529; www.newportplayhouse.com.

Something is always going on at the **Rhino Bar & Grille** on the weekends. Thursday through Saturday, live bands play in the Rhino Bar Room while deejays spin tunes in the Mamba Room.

AUTHOR FAVORITE

Even if you can't afford to buy an original work of art, it's a delight to shop at **William Vareika Fine Arts**. Browsing the 300 years worth of American paintings, prints and drawings—many of Newport and Narragansett Bay—is like strolling through a museum. A gallery featuring five centuries of international artwork has been added to the store. Poster and reproductions are available for those a bit light in the pocketbook. ~ 212 Bellevue Avenue, Newport; 401-849-6149; www.vareikafinearts.com, e-mail info@vareikafinearts.com.

Call ahead if you don't like reggae; it's often the theme of the night. ~ 337 Thames Street, Newport; 401-846-0707; www.therhinobar.com.

BEACHES & PARKS

Although not quite technically an island, Aquidneck Island has water along almost every inch of its four sides and an enviable selection of ocean, bay and river beaches.

FORT ADAMS STATE PARK Built in 1824 to protect the entrance to Newport Harbor, Fort Adams stands now as a National Historic Landmark, its stone fortress open for tours (fee); its 21 acres of parklands offer a recreational haven for all. The park lies at the toe of Aquidneck Island's boot, facing Narragansett Bay. This vast grassy meadow—home to the Newport Jazz and Folk festivals and other summer concerts—matches great sounds with spectacular sights such as views of the bay and its active boating scene. Tours of the Fort are offered hourly from 10 a.m. to 4 p.m. from mid-April to mid-October. Facilities include picnic groves with grills, restrooms and lifeguards. ~ Located at the end of Fort Adams Road on Ocean Drive; 401-847-2400, fax 401-841-9821.

EASTON'S BEACH (FIRST BEACH) This swath has a real public beach atmosphere, the only one you're likely to find in the area; a mostly young crowd comes here. This stretch of beach curves, with rougher waves for surfers on the outer edges and calmer waters on the broad inner arc. The sand is fine and very soft, the beach wide. There are restrooms, showers and lifeguards, as well as a concession stand, an aquarium, a small skate park and a boardwalk with a carousel. There's also a children's playground. Parking fee, $8 to $15. ~ Located along Memorial Boulevard, from the northern end of the Cliff walk eastward to Middletown; 401-845-5810, fax 401-846-3627.

SACHUEST BEACH (SECOND BEACH) Its two miles of rolling dunes, fine sand and waves for surfing at one end make Sachuest the favorite local beach, and singles tend to congregate here. Beautiful views include St. George's School in the distance. The beach abuts the 21 shoreline acres of the Norman Bird Sanctuary. Facilities include picnic tables, restrooms, showers, lifeguards, outdoor grills and a concession stand. Parking fee, $10 to $20. ~ On Sachuest Way, Middletown; 401-849-2822, fax 401-845-0404.

▲ The campground (401-846-6273) offers 44 sites with full hookups. Reservations are necessary. Daily fees are $31.25 to $37.50 per site, with weekly and monthly discounted rates. Closed October to mid-May.

PEABODY BEACH (THIRD BEACH) This spot is ideal for families because it fronts the calm waters of the

Sakonnet River. Its profile includes high dunes and a beach that's more soil than sand. It's also popular with windsurfers. The view across the river includes Little Compton's sweep of rolling hills. Portable restrooms are the only facilities here. ~ Off Third Beach Road, Middletown.

Providence Area

At a glance Rhode Island seems comprised of water first and land second. The reason for this is Narragansett Bay. Twisting southward from Providence and the Blackstone River, the bay permeates the state's rocky landscape, then spills into the Atlantic at Newport. If you follow this waterway you will see that it defines Rhode Island. The communities it touches thrive on fishing, shipbuilding and sailing. From the busy port of Providence to the Herreshoff Boatyard in Bristol (builders of the first torpedo boat in 1887) to the resorts and beaches of Warwick, the Narragansett is a saltwater net that holds the state together.

Within the city limits of Providence are enough historical treasures to satisfy even the most insatiable culture buffs—from the architectural beauties of Benefit Street to the marble dome of the State House, which gleams like a beacon above the skyline. The lofty College Hill area is home to Brown University and to a resulting Cambridge-like neighborhood of bookstores, boutiques and trendy restaurants. Revitalized sections—such as Corliss Landing—are springing up like mushrooms almost overnight, bringing new life and lifestyles into forgotten parts of town. There's a vitality, a zingy balance of past and future, to this place.

This capital city of Rhode Island was also its first, established in 1636 by Roger Williams, founder of the Baptist Church, "in commemoration of God's Providence." Williams' religious bent extended even to the naming of local thoroughfares; visitors today walk along Benefit, Church, Benevolent, Hope and Friendship streets.

SIGHTS

Seven hills and the Providence River give the city its geographic complexity. Most fashionable addresses lie on the east side of town (not to be confused with the neighboring town of East Providence). College Hill is a steep incline dotted with many historic sites and crowned by the Brown University complex.

It is fitting to begin at the corner of North Main and Waterman streets, site of Williams' **First Baptist Church**, built in 1775 (although his first congregation was founded in 1638). The 185-foot church steeple, visible from just about anywhere in town, was inspired by designs of Sir Christopher Wren. The church is the largest of all-wooden structures in New England and has a 1792 Waterford crystal chandelier hanging in the sanctuary. Actively used by its local congregation, the building is open to visitors Monday through Friday. ~ 75 North Main Street, Providence; 401-751-2266, fax 401-421-4095; www.fbcia.org, e-mail info@fbcia.org.

Nearby is the **Museum of Art, Rhode Island School of Design,** considered one of America's finest museums of its size. Housed within a deceptively unimposing 1926 seven-story, Federal-style brick structure, attached to the Daphne Farago Wing, are three floors of artistic masterpieces with dates ranging from the ancient Egyptian period to the present. Throughout the galleries, you'll encounter clutches of students studying and creating their own artwork; this museum is a treasured storehouse for RISD (pronounced Rizz-dee) students and faculty. Don't miss: the satiny Goddard-Townsend block and shell masterpiece (a 1760s mahogany desk and bookcase, one of only 12 still in existence, whose sibling piece fetched $12 million at a Christie's auction); the Bab-

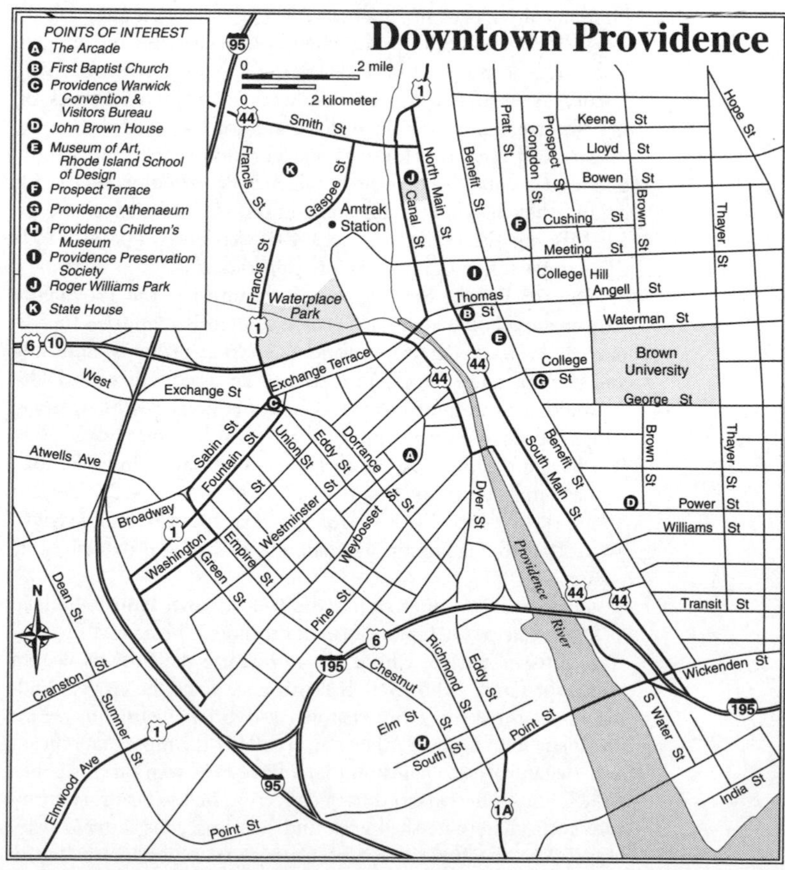

ylonian lion bas-relief (605 B.C.); the impressionists (Manets and Monets); and the Rodin sculptures. Step into the Daphne Farago Wing for a look at the contemporary art collection, or wander through the museum's interior sculpture garden. Closed Monday. Admission. ~ 224 Benefit Street, Providence; 401-454-6500, fax 401-454-6556; www.risdmuseum.org, e-mail museum@risd.edu.

If you're interested in seeing art by RISD students, head over to the **Rhode Island School of Design's Woods-Gerry Gallery**. Undergraduate students show their work here in ever-changing exhibitions. It's located in the three-story Woods-Gerry Mansion, designed by Richard Upjohn in 1860. Opening times vary with semester schedules; best to call ahead for exact hours. ~ 62 Prospect Street, Providence; 401-454-6141; www.risd.edu.

Benefit Street, which traces a path across College Hill's vertical pitch, boasts a "Mile of History," regarded by scholars as one of the highest concentrations of Colonial- and Federal-era buildings anywhere in America. Along this miracle mile are restored 18th- and 19th-century buildings, all carefully maintained. They are also homes and businesses, for this is a street of *living* history as well. During the first weekend in June, houses on Benefit Street and in other historic areas are opened during the "Festival of Historic Houses," a celebration that includes tours and food events. Contact the **Providence Preservation Society** for details; they also have maps and pamphlets. Closed weekends. ~ 21 Meeting Street, Providence; 401-831-7440, fax 401-831-8583; www.ppsri.org, e-mail info@ppsri.org.

One of Benefit Street's historic beauties is the **Providence Athenaeum**. Founded in 1753 as one of this country's first libraries, it sits in Grecian splendor, looking properly imposing and scholarly. The Greek Doric structure was completed in 1838. A wealth of rare and historic volumes is housed within, along with a bit of famous romantic history. It was here that Edgar Allan Poe met, loved and lost Sarah Helen Whitman. Closed Sunday in the summer, and the first two weeks of August. ~ 251 Benefit Street, Providence; 401-421-6970, fax 401-421-2860; www.providenceathenaeum.org, e-mail cbevilacqua@providenceathenaeum.org.

A few blocks south stands the **John Brown House**, built in 1786 for one of the famous Brown brothers. The name "Brown" is an integral part of Rhode Island history: the Browns were a merchant family who lived in Providence since the city's founding. This three-story brownstone and brick Georgian, which President John Quincy Adams once called "the most magnificent and elegant private mansion that I have ever seen on this continent," houses an extraordinary collection of 18th-century furniture such as its nine-shell desk and bookcase, the latter considered to be the finest piece of American Colonial furniture in existence today. Closed Sunday through Thursday from January through March. Admission. ~ 52 Power Street, Providence; 401-273-7507, fax 401-751-2307; www.rihs.org.

Brown University is indeed king of the hill, the nation's seventh-oldest university, founded in 1764. ~ College Hill, end of College Street, Providence; 401-863-1000.

You'll feel the Ivy League influence throughout the sprawl of gothic and beaux-arts structures and commons areas, dominated by the enormous **John D. Rockefeller, Jr., Library**, which houses Brown's general collections. ~ Prospect and College streets, Providence; 401-863-2167.

University Hall, a National Historic Landmark, served as a barracks and hospital for American troops during the Revolutionary War. ~ Prospect Street, Providence.

Before leaving College Hill, stop off at **Prospect Terrace**, the site of the Roger Williams Memorial, which overlooks downtown Providence. A tiny park is maintained here, making an ideal place for a picnic lunch. Enjoy the panoramic view while you digest all the history you've just seen and prepare to tour the city's other neighborhoods. ~ Congdon Street at Cushing Street, Providence.

Providence's downtown area is dominated by the **State House**, considered by some to be the most beautiful capitol building in America. The classic structure's white marble exterior dazzles in the sunlight. Its self-supported marble dome is the fourth largest in the world. A full-length portrait of George Washington, painted by Rhode Island's own Gilbert Stuart, hangs in the State Reception Room. Closed weekends. Free tours of the capitol are given on weekday mornings. ~ Smith Street, Providence; 401-222-2357, fax 401-222-1356; www.state.ri.us.

Several blocks south, you'll find **The Arcade**, an 1828 Greek Revival–style National Historic Landmark that is now a three-story shopping mall. Closed Sunday. ~ 65 Weybosset Street, Providence; 401-598-1199, fax 401-598-4784.

A GREAT PLACE TO RETIRE

Rhode Island's reputation for championing personal freedoms is once again evidenced in today's newest minority: senior citizens. The state is second only to Florida in its over-65 population percentage. It's especially curious that many of these seniors have moved here from other states, choosing to move to a place far from the Sunbelt's climate. Whatever the reasons for the influx (state statisticians are still puzzling over this one), it becomes fairly obvious that Rhode Island's winters cannot be regarded as a negative factor.

Nearby is the **Providence Children's Museum**, located in an enormous, old brick jewelry factory in the Jewelry District. Nine major hands-on exhibit areas include one called "Littlewoods"—appropriate for infants up to four years old. There, children climb trees, discover a cave and explore to their hearts' content. Elsewhere in the museum, you can brush a giant mouth, travel back through Rhode Island history, walk through a kaleidoscope and solve a skeleton puzzle. Closed Monday June through September. Admission. ~ 100 South Street, Providence; 401-273-5437, fax 401-273-1004; www.childrenmuseum.org, e-mail provcm@childrenmuseum.org.

For more information on this area contact the **Providence Warwick Convention & Visitors Bureau.** Closed Sunday. ~ 1 Sabin Street, Providence; 401-751-1177, 800-233-1636, fax 401-521-3465; www.providencenightandday.com, e-mail info@pwcvb.com.

A short drive away is **Roger Williams Park**, Providence's favorite park since 1871, when Betsy Williams bequeathed her 102-acre farm to the city. Today this spacious parkland combines wilderness areas with such people pleasers as a zoo, complete with a community of penguins and 130 other species on display (admission), a lake and picturesque boathouse (now housing the park's administrative offices), a lakeside bandstand, a carousel, paddleboats, pony rides and a greenhouse of exotic plants and flowers. All this amid landscaped, wooded parklands in the heart of the city. ~ 1000 Elmwood Avenue, Providence; park information 401-785-9450, zoo information 401-785-3510, fax 401-941-3988; www.rogerwilliamsparkzoo.org, e-mail info@rwpzoo.org.

Also in Roger Williams Park is the **Museum of Natural History**, which has a planetarium, cultural and wildlife exhibits and changing exhibits. Admission. ~ 401-785-9457; www.providenceri.com/museum, e-mail info@musnathist.com.

Across the Providence River lies the serene haven of **Blithewold Mansion, Gardens & Arboretum**. Jutting spectacu-

FOURTH OF JULY EXTRAVAGANZA!

Nowhere in America is July 4th given such notice as in Bristol, where they've been celebrating since 1785, adding a bit more each year. Now, more than 250,000 visitors flood this tiny village in July (regular population: 21,625) to participate in its Independence Day celebration. The country's oldest parade marches along Route 114 (which features a red, white and blue stripe all year), and the festivities continue for days. For more information about this area, contact the East Bay Chamber of Commerce. Closed weekends. ~ 16 Cutler Street, Suite 102, Warren; 401-245-0750, 888-278-9948, fax 401-245-0100; www.eastbaychamberri.org.

larly into Narragansett Bay, Blithewold dazzles with verdant acres and landscape gardens that border the water. A 17th-century-style manor house, all stone with steep pitched roofs, plays centerpiece to this bucolic setting. Here lived the Van Wickle family from 1894 until the last heir, Mrs. Marjorie Van Wickle-Lyon, died in 1976 and willed the estate to the Heritage Trust of Rhode Island. Visitors today can tour some of the Van Wickle's private rooms and wander around their gardens. New England's tallest giant sequoia stands here, 90 feet tall, a century old and thriving far from its West Coast homeland. Tour the 33 acres of grounds, including a rose garden, a rock garden, a display garden and a water garden. Even winter is special here, with the mansion decked in bows and baubles and an 18-foot Christmas tree stretching past the balcony to the second-floor ceiling. Grounds open year round. House closed on Monday and Tuesday, and from January to mid-April. Admission. ~ 101 Ferry Road, Bristol; 401-253-2707, fax 401-253-0412; www.blithewold.org, e-mail info@blithewold.org.

A short drive away, across the horseshoe cove of Bristol Harbor, is **Coggeshall Farm Museum**, a living-history museum that represents a Rhode Island coastal farm in the 1790s. A costumed guide is often on hand to answer questions about the farm. The seasonal special programs—maple sugaring, 18th-century crafts demonstrations—are worth checking out. Closed Monday. Admission. ~ Adjacent to the Colt State Park, Route 114, Bristol; 401-253-9062.

Across Narragansett Bay from Bristol lies **Warwick**, the second-largest city in Rhode Island. Home to the state's only commercial airport as well as to the largest concentrations of hotels and retail stores, it bills itself as "Rhode Island's Host City."

One of Warwick's most popular family attractions is the **John D. Florio Memorial Park**. Operated by a nonprofit children's charity, the park is known as the "impossible dream" to accentuate the positive. There are manual merry-go-rounds, a life-size doll house, a castle, a miniature golf course, swings and slides. All rides and the playground are wheelchair accessible. Closed mid-October to mid-April. ~ 575 Centerville Road, Warwick; 401-823-5566; www.impossibledreaminc.com, e-mail drmimp@aol.com.

LODGING

There are some large, urban hotels in the capital city, with several more under construction.

The **Westin Providence**, a 364-room, 25-story hotel, is a favorite among business travelers and others seeking all the amenities of a full-service hotel. There's a fitness center and a small indoor pool. Rooms are standard big-city hotel rooms with coordinated light and airy fabrics. ~ 1 West Exchange Street, Providence; 401-

598-8000, fax 401-598-8200; www.westin.com/providence, e-mail provi@westinprovidence.com. ULTRA-DELUXE.

The **Providence Biltmore** has traditionally been the area's biggest and best. The 291 guest rooms are quite grand, with stately mahogany and dark green decor. The lobby's grand staircase and glass-cage elevator continue to impress, as does the view from the Grand Ballroom. ~ 11 Dorrance Street, Providence; 401-421-0700, 800-294-7709, fax 401-455-3050; www.providencebiltmore.com. ULTRA-DELUXE.

Judging from the number of briefcases and power suits, the **Providence Marriott** is a favorite site for local business meetings as well as a familiar setting for out-of-town visitors. The all-over design is classic Marriott, although the sprawling layout requires quite a hike to reach the guest room elevators. Rooms are standard issue, modern and clean, with no surprises either good or bad. The lobby bar tends to be very popular and noisy at night. The indoor/outdoor pool is also a gathering spot. ~ Charles and Orms streets, Providence; 401-272-2400, 800-228-9290, fax 401-273-2686. ULTRA-DELUXE.

The **Old Court Bed & Breakfast Inn** is an antique buff's delight. The building, which began as an Episcopal church rectory in 1863, was restored in 1985. Today each of its ten guest rooms is decorated in authentic treasures: Chippendale desks and antique beds and china. All rooms have private baths. Reserve early; this inn is quite popular. ~ 144 Benefit Street, Providence; 401-351-0747, fax 401-272-4830; www.oldcourt.com, e-mail reserve@oldcourt.com. DELUXE.

Located in the heart of Warren's Historic District, the **Wren & Thistle Bed & Breakfast** is perfect for a couple or an individual seeking privacy or solitude. With only a single suite, this gem offers an intimate two-story space that's appointed with romantic touches such as swooping white curtains and hardwood furniture. The suite also includes a private entrance and an enclosed garden. A European-style breakfast is left outside your door. ~ 19 Market Street, Warren; 401-247-0631; www.wrenandthistle.com, e-mail wrenthistleantq@fctvplus.net. MODERATE.

Radisson Airport Hotel Providence is the practicum facility for Johnson & Wales University, a hotel, tourism and culinary institute. Opened in 1989, this state-of-the-art hotel offers such wide-ranging facilities and amenities as a helpful staff, a restaurant, a lounge, a whirlpool in each suite and free airport shuttle service. Even better, guests can be sure that the entire staff will be trying extra hard to please; many are students, and they are being graded on their performance. Continental breakfast included. ~ 2081 Post Road, Warwick; 401-739-3000, 800-333-3333, fax 401-732-9309; www.radisson.com/warwickri. DELUXE TO ULTRA-DELUXE.

Best Western Airport Inn, a 103-room economy motel, offers excellent value. Guests can look forward to complimentary continental breakfasts and airport shuttle service. ~ 2138 Post Road, Warwick; 401-737-7400, 800-528-1234, fax 401-739-6483; www.bestwestern.com, e-mail bestwesternairportinn@gmail.com. MODERATE.

DINING

In keeping with its role as state capital, university town and business center, Providence has developed into a sophisticated dining arena. The many local yuppie types demand it, and visitors can enjoy it. Happily, the focus on upscale eateries has not banished the plenitude of casual, ethnic restaurants.

Overlooking a small lake called Spectacle Pond, **Twin Oaks** serves seafood, steak and Italian dishes in its classic Rhode Island eatery south of Providence. The restaurant offers three contemporary indoor dining areas with lake views. Closed Monday. ~ 100 Sabra Street, Cranston; 401-781-9693, fax 401-941-7890. MODERATE.

Rhode Island is home to more than 20 percent of all Registered Historic Landmarks in the entire country.

Fine American bistro cuisine with an international twist fills the menu at **Rue de l'Espoir**. Specials change nightly and might include entrées like Australian sea bass with a Niçoise olive and lemon salsa. Their "small plates" are popular and everything is served with hot bread from the oven. The casual French-country decor features hardwoods and tables topped with red tile. The Saturday and Sunday brunch is a must. Breakfast, lunch and dinner. Reservations recommended. ~ 99 Hope Street, Providence; 401-751-8890, fax 401-751-8896; www.therue.com, e-mail ruedeb@ids.net. MODERATE TO ULTRA-DELUXE.

Al Forno was the inspiration of two local innovative foodies, George Germon and Johanne Killeen. Al Forno is renowned for its grilled pizzas (*al forno* means "from the oven"). The atmosphere is casual but the food is serious, hearty and, most of all, good. Dinner only. Closed Sunday and Monday. ~ 577 South Main Street, Providence; 401-273-9760; www.alforno.com, e-mail mail@alforno.com. DELUXE TO ULTRA-DELUXE.

Next door, the **Hot Club**, housed in what was once a factory boiler room, serves lighter fare like grilled chicken breast sandwiches, hamburgers and grilled zucchini. When the Hot Club moved here, it caused the waterfront area of Corliss Landing to become gentrified, elevating it to the status of "in" spot. ~ 575 South Water Street, Providence; 401-861-9007. BUDGET.

The Fish Company, which shares a common outdoor boardwalk along the river with the Hot Club, is a casual, trendy and romantic spot at sundown for appetizers and predinner drinks on the deck, where you can watch the boats pass. ~ 515 South Water Street, Providence; 401-421-5796. BUDGET.

Cuban Revolution is part café, part political headquarters. With vibrant reds, yellows and greens decorating both the café and the menu, this unique establishment offers delicious entrées such as Havana chicken served on a bed of black beans and rice, as well as a decor conveying myriad facts about Cuban history and U.S. politics. ~ 50 Aborn Street, Providence; 401-331-8829; www.thecubanrevolution.com, e-mail info@thecubanrevolution.com. MODERATE.

In a building that resembles a huge Rubik's Cube, **Hemenway's** serves what some consider the area's best seafood. The room's simple high-ceilinged decor does not detract from the cuisine, although the spectacular views of the river do tend to vie strongly for one's attention. ~ 1 Providence Washington Plaza, 121 South Main Street, Providence; 401-351-8570, fax 401-351-8594; www.hemenwaysrestaurant.com. MODERATE TO ULTRA-DELUXE.

Federal Hill, Providence's "Little Italy," is fairly bursting with wonderful ethnic restaurants; most are family-oriented with menus priced accordingly. A local favorite is **Angelo's Civita Farnese Restaurant.** The decor in the front room is strictly luncheonette (and includes a photo-collage of celebrity customers) with more traditional decor in the back. The service is friendly and family-style and the cuisine is traditional, hearty and wholesome, with dishes like veal with roasted peppers and a variety of pasta specials. ~ 141 Atwells Avenue, Providence; 401-621-8171, fax 401-273-6943; www.angelosonthehill.com. BUDGET TO MODERATE.

For a more upscale venue in the same neighborhood, you might sample the fine Italian cuisine at **Camille's.** No dinner on Sunday. Closed Monday. ~ 71 Bradford Street, Providence; 401-751-4812; www.camillesonthehill.com. MODERATE TO ULTRA-DELUXE.

Across the Providence River in Bristol County is **Stella Blues Restaurant and Lounge**, which overlooks the Warren River. Located on the corner of Miller and Water streets, the cleanly styled restaurant is comfortable and chic. The menu offers classic entrées such as chicken marsala, seafood jambalaya and pasta primavera, as well as house-made specialties like the antipasto skewer of olives, artichokes, roasted peppers, provolone, pep-

GOING OUT TO STAY HOME

Cable Car Cinema and Café shows classic and foreign films in at-home comfort; half the regular theater seats have been replaced with overstuffed two-seater couches. A café serves sandwiches and pastries right in the theater building, with outdoor seating during good weather. ~ 204 South Main Street, Providence; 401-272-3970; www.cablecarcinema.com. BUDGET.

peroncini, prosciutto, marinated mushrooms and fresh mozzarella. Closed Monday. ~ 50 Miller Street, Warren; 401-289-0349, fax 401-289-2132; www.stellabluesri.com. MODERATE TO DELUXE.

SHOPPING

Although there are a couple of vertical malls in downtown Providence, the best of the city's shopping is found in independent shops and boutiques all over town.

The **Peaceable Kingdom** is a quirky little store that stocks one-of-a-kind folk art, including American Indian crafts, Haitian paintings, oriental rugs and Hmong story cloths. Closed Sunday and Monday. ~ 116 Ives Street, Providence; 401-351-3472.

The Arcade, which occupies three floors of an 1828 majestically columned granite National Historic Landmark building, bills itself as America's first shopping mall. It may be the oldest, but it's far from the nation's finest or most well-stocked. There are lots of small specialty shops to browse but nothing to lure the serious shopper. Closed Sunday. ~ 65 Weybosset Street, Providence; 401-598-1199, fax 401-598-4784.

The **Rhode Island School of Design Museum Gift Shop** offers a wealth of reproductions as well as jewelry, cards, textiles, sculptures, prints and books focusing on the art treasures exhibited throughout the museum. Closed Monday. ~ Museum of Art, Rhode Island School of Design, 224 Benefit Street, Providence; 401-454-6500; www.risd.edu.

NIGHTLIFE

Two major theater experiences in town offer audiences both local repertory and touring company productions. **Trinity Repertory Company**, in operation since 1964, is going strong. This Tony Award–winning repertory company supports a talented group of resident artists and also encourages audience participation. ~ 201 Washington Street, Providence; 401-351-4242; www.trinityrep.com, e-mail info@trinityrep.com.

Providence Performing Arts Center showcases national touring companies' road shows of Broadway and other hit productions. The PPAC is located in the landmark Loew's Theater, a 1920s beauty complete with vintage velvet seats and gilded ceiling. ~ 220 Weybosset Street, Providence; 401-421-2787, fax 401-421-5767; www.ppacri.org.

The beautiful people show up in swarms at the popular nightclub **Ultra**, which features throbbing deejayed hip-hop and dance music. Thursday is college night (dress code). Closed Monday through Wednesday. Cover. ~ 172 Pine Street, Providence; 401-454-5483; www.ultrathenightclub.com, e-mail christy@ultrathenightclub.com.

MiraBar is a gay nightspot that cranks all week long. Monday is Karaoke night, and deejays spin high-energy dance music the remaining six nights. Cover on the weekend. ~ 35 Richmond Street, Providence; 401-331-6761.

Dunkin' Donuts Center Providence is the site of family shows, concerts and sporting events. ~ 1 LaSalle Square, Providence; 401-331-6700; www.dunkindonutscenter.com.

BEACHES & PARKS

COLT STATE PARK Formerly the private estate of the Samuel Pomeroy Colt family, this Bristol park now provides a 464-acre outdoor haven to all families. A three-mile shore drive traces Narragansett Bay, and a network of bike paths (which links up with the "East Bay Bike Path") crisscrosses the wooded park. There's excellent saltwater fishing. Visit the popular Chapel-by-the-Sea. You'll find picnic areas and restrooms. There are disabled-accessible boat ramps ~ Along Route 114, Bristol; 401-253-7482, fax 401-253-6766; www.riparks.com/colt.htm.

GODDARD MEMORIAL STATE PARK This beachfront park is beautifully maintained and provides outdoor recreation year-round. The old carousel building on the shore now serves as a performing-arts center for band and jazz concerts during the summer. Spread throughout the nearly 500 wooded acres are 18 miles of bridal trails, an equestrian show area, a nine-hole golf course and a picnic gazebo. There are picnic areas, lifeguards during the summer, horse rentals, a bathhouse and concession stands. ~ On Ives Road, about one mile south of East Greenwich; 401-884-2010, fax 401-885-7720; www.riparks.com/goddard.htm.

Blackstone Valley

To help pinpoint the Blackstone Valley area, visualize the state of Rhode Island as a layer cake: the Blackstone Valley forms the entire top layer. (And the icing, too, its fans would add.) The Blackstone River surges through the eastern portion of this layer with a force powerful enough to have altered the course of our country's history.

America's industrial revolution began in the Blackstone Valley. In 1793, Samuel Slater harnessed the potential of mighty Blackstone River (which subsequently became known as "the hardest working river in America"), creating the first factory in America able to produce cotton yarn by using water power.

Today this entire "top-layer" area is Rhode Island's undiscovered gem, a region dotted with historic industrial towns that lie within huge tracts of rural and forested wilderness areas. You'll drive along scenic country roads that meander past historic sites, charming villages, meticulously restored Colonial homes, antique stores and farm stands.

SIGHTS

The city of **Pawtucket**, at the extreme southeastern edge of the region, is home to Mr. Slater's mill, the place where it all began.

Fourth-largest city in the state, Pawtucket (an Indian term meaning "falls of water") sits at the upper tidewaters of Narragansett Bay.

The Old Slater Mill was the site of the 1793 mill and cotton factory, featuring the first water-powered cotton spinning mill in the U.S. Today, the **Slater Mill Historic Site** is a National Historic Landmark. Visitors to this wooden building, resplendent in its original vivid yellow hue, can tour the museum, with its huge looms still intact. Next door is the original rubblestone 1810 Wilkinson Mill that houses the 16,000-pound waterwheel. The Slater Mill has recently changed to a living museum format, with costumed interpreters and a wide variety of hands-on activities, including weaving cotton and making bobbins. Admission. ~ 67 Roosevelt Avenue, Pawtucket; 401-725-8638, fax 401-722-3040; www.slatermill.org, e-mail info@slatermill.org

Nearby **Slater Memorial Park** is fun for children and adults. The oldest "stander carousel" in the world is located here (closed November through March). This gem is a genuine Charles Looff creation and one of the few that remain of this master craftsman's handiwork. Built in 1895, it was installed in Slater Park in 1910 and has been thrilling children ever since. The park has ball fields, bike trails, a pond full of ducks and even a regulation lawn bowling green. Daggett Farm, located in the heart of the 200-acre park, features farm animals and a greenhouse. Also located within the park is the **Daggett House** (admission), a 1685 farmhouse and the oldest home in Pawtucket. The Daggett House is open by appointment. ~ Newport Avenue, Pawtucket; 401-728-0500 ext. 251, fax 401-729-4712.

A few minutes' drive north of Pawtucket is **Diamond Hill Vineyards**, which lies nestled in the beautiful Cumberland coun-

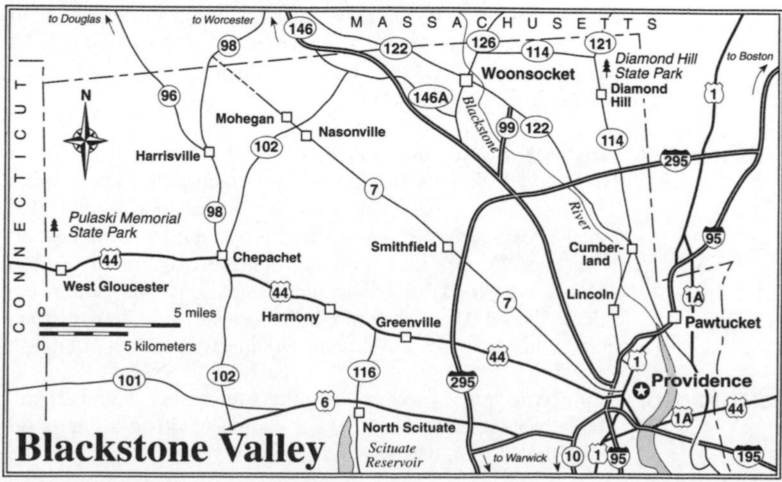

tryside. After a jostling drive over the private road that runs through fields of vines, you arrive at the trim, gray, 1780 home of the owners, the Berntson family, who welcome visitors and invite them to use the spacious porch and rolling front lawn for picnics. Inside there's a tasting room and gift shop. You can even design your own customized labels (complete with photos, personal messages or whatever else) to affix on gift bottles of their grape and fruit wines or nonalcoholic ciders here. Call ahead for hours. ~ 3145 Diamond Hill Road, Cumberland; 401-333-2751, 800-752-2505, fax 401-333-8520; www.favorlabel.com.

For a listing of all the area's factory outlets, contact the Blackstone Valley Tourism Council. ~ 175 Main Street, Pawtucket; 401-724-2200; www.tourblackstone.com.

While you're in the area, you might want to stop by the **Blackstone Valley Tourism Council** for maps, brochures and information about Blackstone Valley and its activities. ~ 175 Main Street, Pawtucket; 401-724-2200, 800-454-2882, fax 401-724-1342; www.tourblackstone.com, e-mail info@tourblackstone.com.

A bit farther north lies Woonsocket, whose residential North End holds an unexpected treasure—the **B'nai Israel Synagogue.** This house of worship has Milanese hand-blown glass chandeliers as well as a series of spectacular stained-glass windows designed by a disciple of Marc Chagall. It's listed in the *Encyclopedia Judaica* as one of America's premier synagogues. Closed Tuesday, Saturday and Sunday. ~ 224 Prospect Street, Woonsocket; 401-762-3651, fax 401-767-5243; www.shalom-cbi.org, e-mail synagogue@cbi.necoxmail.com.

LODGING

Surprises await at the **Comfort Inn** in Pawtucket. It features a pool and 138 newly renovated rooms with amenities, including Nintendo video games. The hotel also has a staff so courteous and helpful you'll be glad you stayed. Continental breakfast included. ~ 2 George Street, Pawtucket; 401-723-6700, 800-228-5150, fax 401-726-6380; www.comfortinn.com, e-mail manager@comfortinnri.com. DELUXE.

DINING

Wright's Farm Restaurant is the undisputed king of the "chicken family-style" dinners that are unique to the Blackstone Valley. This meal must always include macaroni, roast chicken, salad, french fries and dessert—served and served until you can't eat another bite. Wright's Farm's dining room can accommodate 1200, so expect busloads of fellow diners, groaning boards and low prices. Closed Monday through Wednesday. ~ 84 Inman Road, Harrisville; 401-769-2856; www.wrightsfarm.com. BUDGET.

SHOPPING

From basic housewares to specialty soy candles, Cumberland's **Toadally Country** store stocks a variety of down-home goods and gifts. Clocks, wreaths and sewing supplies are easily within reach at this clapboard shop. ~ 1255 Mendon Road, Cumberland; 401-334-3800; www.toadallycountry.com.

HIDDEN

There are about a dozen antique stores in the tiny village of Chepachet in the town of Gloucester, but the undisputed star of the group is the **Brown & Hopkins Country Store**. As country stores go, this one is the genuine article; it's also one of the oldest continuously operated stores in America. Opened in 1809, Brown & Hopkins retains much of the old while giving today's customers what they want (gourmet foods, hand-dipped candles, even penny candies). The antiques are displayed throughout the store and replica home furnishings, curtains, linens and lighting are sold on the second floor. Owner Liz McIntyre also stocks popular wheels of Vermont cheddar cheese. ~ 1179 Putnam Pike, Gloucester; 401-568-4830; www.brownandhopkins.com.

NIGHTLIFE

The **Gamm Theatre** puts on five plays a year, ranging from dramas to comedy, classics to contemporary works. The season runs from September to June. Performances are held Wednesday through Sunday with matinees on Sunday. ~ 172 Exchange Street, Pawtucket; 401-723-4266, fax 401-723-0440; www.gammtheatre.org, e-mail info@gammtheatre.org.

Chan's is, in addition to being a popular Asian restaurant, renowned throughout New England for showcasing international jazz and blues artists. Host John Chan invites only the best to perform. Shows are usually on Friday and Saturday nights. Cover. ~ 267 Main Street, Woonsocket; 401-765-1900, fax 401-766-2627; www.chanseggrollsandjazz.com.

BEACHES & PARKS

LINCOLN WOODS STATE PARK Over 600 acres of woodland make up this popular recreation area north of Providence. Visitors can swim in Olney Pond and hike or ride horses along the oak-bordered trails surrounding it. In the winter, people come here to skate, cross-country ski and snowmobile. Facilities include restrooms, a bathhouse, playing fields, lifeguards and a concession stand; horse rentals are available right outside the park at Sunset Stables (401-722-3033). Picnic tables and sites can be rented for $2 to $35 a day (April 15th to September 16th.) ~ Entrances are located on Great Road, Route 123, and Twin River Road off Route 146 in Lincoln; 401-723-7892, fax 401-724-7951; www.riparks.com/lincoln.htm.

DIAMOND HILL PARK This woodsy hill is skirted by a mile-long ledge of quartz, thus the park's moniker. The 373-acre spot, crossed by hiking trails, has a picnic area and restrooms. ~ Off Route 114 on Diamond Hill Road in Cumberland; 401-334-9996, fax 401-334-1313.

PULASKI MEMORIAL RECREATION AREA A part of the 4000-acre George Washington Management Area, Pulaski has 100 acres of red pine, white pine and oak woods that skirt Peck Pond, whose beach is a main attraction for visitors here. Fishing is good for bass, perch and trout; swimming is excellent. You can also hike or cross-country ski on trails through the forest area or get a game going at the ball field. You'll find a picnic area, restrooms, a changing room and lifeguards. ~ Pulaski Road, off Route 44 six miles west of Chepachet; 401-568-2085, fax 401-568-2045.

Outdoor Adventures

FISHING

Known as the Ocean State, Rhode Island is an angler's paradise. The New England Offshore Sportfish Tournament is held here every summer, with weigh-ins at the Ram Point Marina in Port Judith. Local waters teem with tuna, bluefin, albacore, marlin and shark. Charter boats abound, sailing from every port along the coast. The best seasons to fish are summer and fall.

SOUTH COUNTY **Snug Harbor Marina Booking Service** charters trips on Narragansett Bay or Block Island Sound. Offshore excursions for shark and tuna are also available. ~ 410 Gooseberry Road, Wakefield; 401-783-7766. On Block Island, **Bent Rod Fishing** has trips on a 28-foot diesel boat for striped bass, flukes and bluefish. ~ 401-524-2235.

SAILING

While not every Sunday sailor gets to crew during Newport's famed America's Cup races, Rhode Island's bays, sounds and open ocean lure boating fans of all degrees of expertise. In fact, you don't even have to know how to sail: plenty of vessels come complete with their own crews.

NEWPORT AREA **Newport Sailing School and Tours** offers lessons and popular harbor cruises. Closed November through May. ~ Goat Island Marina, Newport; 401-848-2266; www.newportsailing.com, e-mail newportsail@aol.com.

CANOEING & KAYAKING

Paddling the inland waterways is an increasingly popular sport in Rhode Island. A number of places not only rent boats but offer instruction as well; some host group trips.

SOUTH COUNTY The **Kayak Centre at Wickford Cove** offers kayak rentals and sales, instruction and harbor tours. ~ 9 Phillips Street, Wickford; 401-295-4400, 888-732-5292; www.kayakcentre.com.

NEWPORT AREA **Island Sports** is a haven for water activity supplies, offering everything from wetsuits and goggles to wakeboards. In the summer, they rent kayaks. ~ 86 Aquideck Avenue, Middletown; 401-846-4421; www.islandsports.com.

CROSS-COUNTRY SKIING

During winter months when areas in the state are blanketed by snow, cross-country skiing is a popular pastime. Though most ski centers are located in Eastern Massachusetts, several state parks have ungroomed trails that are available to skiers, including **Lincoln Woods State Park** and South County's **Arcadia Management Area.** The **George Washington Management Area** in Blackstone Valley has groomed trails.

WIND-SURFING

This sport, which requires both sailing and surfing skills to master, is also pretty to watch. All along Rhode Island's beaches, the colorful windsurfing sails add to the beauty of the ocean views.

NEWPORT AREA **Third Beach** in Newport is a popular windsurfing spot. If you'd like to give it a try, **Island Sports** offers lessons and rents and sells boards and gear. ~ 86 Aquidneck Avenue, Middletown; 401-846-4421, 888-639-7529.

GOLF

Throughout the state, many public courses welcome visitors.

SOUTH COUNTY **Winnapaug Country Club** is semiprivate and features an 18-hole course designed by Donald Ross. ~ 184 Shore Road, Westerly; 401-596-1237. Tee off at **Weekapaug Golf Club**'s semiprivate nine-hole course, but don't get stuck on their signature fourth hole, which shoots over a saltwater pond. ~ 265 Shore Road, Westerly; 401-322-7870. In Hope Valley, try **Lindhbrook Country Club**, the only par-3 course in Rhode Island. ~ 299 Woodville-Alton Road, Hope Valley; 401-539-8700.

NEWPORT AREA The semiprivate **Green Valley Country Club** has a course full of long and difficult par 4s and 5s. ~ 371 Union Street, Portsmouth; 401-847-9543. **Montaup Country Club** has an 18-hole, semiprivate course. ~ 500 Anthony Road, Portsmouth; 401-683-0955.

PROVIDENCE AREA **Triggs Memorial Golf Course** is a beautiful, 18-hole, Donald Ross–designed public facility overlooking the Providence River. ~ 1533 Chalkstone Avenue; 401-521-8460.

RIDE INTO THE SUNSET

Given Rhode Island's wealth of superb wilderness and parklands, one might expect to find a similar abundance of stables offering horseback rentals, but there are relatively few. Guided rides in Arcadia Management Area are offered by appointment only at **Stepping Stone Ranch**. They also offer overnight camping trip rides. ~ 201 Escoheag Hill Road, West Greenwich; 401-397-3725; www.steppingstoneranch.com. Lincoln's **Sunset Stables** also provides guided 45-minute rides through Lincoln Woods State Park. ~ 1 Twin River Road, off Route 146, Lincoln; 401-722-3033.

TENNIS

Courts range from the modest playground variety to the grassy splendor of Newport's venerable Casino. Regardless of status, most require advance reservations.

SOUTH COUNTY On Block Island, **The Atlantic Inn** has two courts. Fee. ~ 401-466-5883.

NEWPORT AREA At the **International Tennis Hall of Fame**, you can play on the world-famous Newport grass courts from mid-May through September. There are also year-round indoor courts and outdoor hard courts available to the general public. Lessons available; reservations required. Fee. ~ 194 Bellevue Avenue; 401-849-3990; www.tennisfame.com.

PROVIDENCE AREA **Roger Williams Park** has a beautiful clay court. ~ 1000 Elmwood Avenue; 401-785-9450.

BIKING

Rhode Island is a biker's paradise. There are bike lanes everywhere.

SOUTH COUNTY For strong cyclists who can handle the hills, Block Island can be biking heaven, with its pristine byways and incredible views.

NEWPORT AREA In Newport, you can cycle the lovely 15-mile Bellevue Avenue and Ocean Drive route that hugs the Atlantic. Across the Sakonnet River, there are 25 to 35 miles of quiet routes that meander through the peaceful villages of Tiverton and Little Compton. As you travel the state's multitude of country lanes, you'll understand why so many Rhode Islanders are avid cyclists.

PROVIDENCE AREA A special ten-foot-wide, 14.5-mile-long "East Bay Bicycle Path" runs from East Providence to Bristol along scenic shoreline routes and through several state parks.

Bike Rentals Disappointingly few shops rent bikes in the state. However, the state's biking possibilities are superior enough to warrant bringing your own bike if you don't want to chance a rental.

In South County, **Narragansett Bikes** rents mountain bikes, tandems and hybrids. ~ 1153 Boston Neck Road, Route 1A, Narragansett; 401-782-4444. On Block Island, visit **Old Harbor Bikeshop**, which rents tandems and mopeds. ~ Off Water Street in the ferry parking lot, Old Harbor; 401-466-2029.

In Newport, **Ten Speed Spokes** rents comfort mountain bikes and hybrids. ~ 18 Elm Street; 401-847-5609; www.tenspeedspokes.com.

HIKING

The entire state of Rhode Island holds wonderful surprises both for serious hikers as well as for those who simply enjoy meandering through the great outdoors. In the northern tier of the state, a unique two-state federal project, the Blackstone River Valley National Heritage Corridor, will develop miles of new trails along the banks of the river and the original tow paths along the canal. Even though not fully completed, this linear park offers endless opportunities to those who celebrate wilderness beauty. All distances listed for hiking trails are one way unless otherwise noted.

SOUTH COUNTY The lowlands of South County are studded with great tracts of protected wilderness areas that are ideal for the hiking enthusiast.

Arcadia Management Area's **Yellow Dot Trail System** can be followed via yellow spots painted on trees. It features over 30 miles of trails, ranging from 1.6 to 9.6 miles long, and crosses much of the park's wooded wilderness. ~ 401-539-2356.

In the 29-acre Kimball Wildlife Refuge near Charlestown, the **Orange Trail** (1.5 miles roundtrip) leads through postglacial forests of oaks and maples and passes Toupoyesett Pond. This easy, leisurely walk is maintained by the Audubon Society for hiking, birding and photography. ~ 401-949-5454; www.asri.org, e-mail kimball_refuge@cox.net.

On Block Island, venture upon **The Greenway Nature Trail** (25 miles), a silent wilderness of intersecting trails where you'll encounter rolling hills, coastal shrub lands and open meadows. Along the way you'll espy the foundation of an old mill and a cemetery—remnants of an old farm. The only sounds heard are bird calls; this glacial land mass provides sanctuary for over 200 species of migratory birds. There are trailheads at many different parts of the island, with moderate hiking that has sections of steep climbs. For more information and trail maps, contact The Nature Conservancy. ~ P.O. Box 1287, Block Island, RI 02807; 401-466-2129, fax 401-466-2511; www.nature.org.

NEWPORT AREA The famous **Cliff Walk** (3.5 miles) in Newport must be counted as unique, if not the ultimate in hikes. Beginning at the Memorial Drive gate and winding its sometimes precarious way along and above the crashing waves, this scenic path provides "hidden" views of the front yards and facades of the town's great mansions, as well as sweeping views of Rhode Island Sound. Keep to the inside of the path because erosion has weakened the outer edges of some sections at the end of the trail.

AUTHOR FAVORITE

I was a little skeptical of the claim that the **Long Pond–Ell Pond Trail** is "the most beautiful walk in Rhode Island"—until I saw for myself. Now I'm a believer. This four-and-a-half-mile trail leads to three ponds through what locals call a "cathedral forest" of wild rhododendrons and hemlocks. Located in Hopkinton, this area is listed in the Registry of Natural Landmarks. Trailheads are located off North Road and off Cahouchet Road in Hopkinton.

There are a dozen varied trails through the 450 acres of the Norman Bird Sanctuary in Middletown, ranging from the brief **Woodcock Trail** (.5 mile) that leads through level shrublands and a forest of black cherry and black locust, to the 300-million-year-old Paradise Rock formation known as **Hanging Rock Trail** (1 mile), along a 70-foot-high rocky ridge that overlooks the ocean, Gardiner's Pond and the marshlands.

HIDDEN ►

BLACKSTONE VALLEY The **Blackstone River Valley National Heritage Corridor** encompasses both the canal tow paths as well as the river area itself. Covering over 45 miles in the region, the corridor will eventually contain miles of hiking trails. Although not yet a formal "hiking trail," a two-mile stretch of canal tow path in Lincoln provides a feel of what the finished park will offer. It's a flat walk bordered by flood plain meadows and dense forest; you will see great blue herons, woodchucks, rabbits and turtles along the way. ~ To get there, take Exit 10 off of Route 295 to Route 122S (also called Mendon Road). Continue on for about one and one half miles to Martin Street. Cross two bridges. Park in the pull-off at the second bridge. Skirt the orange guard rail and turn right. After one mile of hiking, you will see the old Captain Kelly house, the Ashton Mill and the dam. Turn back here. ~ 401-724-2200, 800-454-2882, fax 401-724-1342; www.tourblackstone.com.

Three marked trails crisscross the 120-acre Powder Mill Ledge's Wildlife Refuge in Smithfield. Owned by the Audubon Society of Rhode Island, this refuge is home to many species of animals in forests of white pine, hickory, butternut and chestnut trees. The **Orange Trail** (1 mile) is graded "easy" and the **Blue Trail** (1.5 miles) and the **Yellow Trail** (2 miles) are a bit more difficult. In winter, the Orange and Blue trails are groomed for cross-country skiing and snowshoeing. ~ 401-949-5454; www.asri.org, e-mail audubon@asri.org.

Transportation

CAR

Route 95 traverses the state north and south, connecting Rhode Island to Connecticut and to the rest of New England. Along the coast, scenic **1A** hugs the ocean shoreline, a slower but more beautiful drive.

AIR

T. F. Green Airport in Warwick is the state's only commercial airport. Regularly scheduled service is provided by Air Canada, American Airlines, Cape Air, Continental Express, Delta Airlines, Northwest Airlines, Southwest Airlines, United Airlines and US Airways Express. ~ www.pvd-ri.com.

New England Airlines operates daily 12-minute commuter flights between Block Island and Westerly. ~ 401-596-2460, 800-243-2460.

Several limo and van companies link the airport to cities throughout the state: **Airport Taxi and Limousine** runs to and from Warwick. ~ 401-737-2868. **Cozy Cab** runs daily shuttles to and from Newport. ~ 401-846-2500, 800-846-1502.

FERRY

Ferry service between Block Island and Newport and New London is provided by **The Interstate Navigation Company.** Cars and passengers are transported on a year-round basis from Point Judith and Newport, although the schedule is abbreviated during off-season. Reservations for cars are essential year round. ~ Galilee; 401-783-4613, 866-783-7996; www.blockislandferry.com, e-mail info@blockislandferry.com.

BUS

Scheduled and charter bus services connect all points within the state. **Archway Bus Lines** is based in West Warwick. ~ 76 Industrial Lane, West Warwick; 401-828-4100. **Rhode Island Public Transit Authority** (RIPTA) operates throughout the state. ~ 265 Melrose Street, Providence; 401-781-9400; www.ripta.com.

TRAIN

Amtrak's (800-872-7245; www.amtrak.com) Northeast Corridor service connects Rhode Island with Boston and New York City. There is frequent service to and from Providence at Union Station (100 Gaspee Street; 401-727-7389) and less frequent service to Kingston Station (Railroad Avenue, West Kingston; 401-783-2913).

CAR RENTALS

Major car-rental agencies at the Warwick airport include **Budget Rent A Car** (800-527-0700) and **Hertz Rent A Car** (800-654-3131). Across the street from the airport are **Dollar Rent A Car** (800-800-4000) and **Thrifty Car Rental** (2329 Post Road; 800-367-2277).

PUBLIC TRANSIT

Bus service throughout the state is provided by **Rhode Island Public Transportation Authority** (RIPTA). These buses can connect airport passengers with the Block Island ferry in Galilee, as well as direct service from Providence to Newport, Westerly and the South County beaches. ~ 401-781-9400; www.ripta.com.

FOUR

Boston

A stately dominion of brick and brownstone, parks and trees, river and harbor, Boston has stood as the preeminent New England city for more than three and a half centuries. Holding fast to the tip of a tiny peninsula jutting into the Atlantic, the city grew and spread south and west through the centuries, but it's still compact and eminently walkable. Despite its tiny size, Boston has played a mighty role in history, a history etched in the minds of all Americans. For this is the birthplace of our nation, where Paul Revere made his dashing midnight ride, where "the shot heard 'round the world" was fired.

A city of fanatical Puritan roots, Boston has been mocked and scorned by more worldly others as dull, pious and provincial, no match for New York or Los Angeles in sophistication. Rich in artistic and intellectual life, Boston has still been notched down on the big-city scoresheet for its lackluster shopping, dining and hotel accommodations.

But Boston is changing its face. While still revering its history and roots, the city is searching for a new identity as a modern, stylish metropolis. In the 1980s, world-renowned chefs set up shop here, winning over Bostonians and food critics alike. The palatial shopping emporium Copley Place opened, anchored by flashy Dallas retailer Neiman Marcus, which would never have dared show its face here in the 1950s. A building boom pushed up skyscraping: First-class hotels like the Westin, the Boston Harbor Hotel and the Four Seasons, as well as gleaming Financial District office towers, add to the city's skyline. At the same time, old treasures like South Station and the Ritz-Carlton Hotel received much-needed facelifts. Change continued in the 1990s. In 1995, the Boston Public Library completed a $50 million restoration project, and the FleetCenter, a $160 million contemporary sports arena, opened to replace the antiquated Boston Garden. In 2002, the CMGI Field Stadium opened to replace Foxboro—home of New England Patriots and the New England Revolution teams.

The push for class continues with a grand project called the "Big Dig" begun in the early 1990s, which involves carving a giant tunnel to allow for the ugly, elevated Central Artery expressway underground. The project's completion will bring light and spaciousness to the downtown area. And the city's main eyesore—the burlesque district known as the Combat Zone—has all but disappeared. Trendy restaurants, cafés and shops have sprung up in Boston's efforts to demolish the Combat Zone (known to some as the "Ladder District") and expand the nearby theater district. The area has surprisingly become a spot for hip jazz clubs and excellent people watching. Boston's ambitious facelift includes the redevelopment of the Seaport District, a convention center, hotel, shopping and restaurant zone that will replace existing warehouses and will feature a harborfront walkway.

The city's Puritan past took root in 1630, when a small band of English Puritans led by Governor John Winthrop arrived and settled on the peninsula. The colonists found Boston waters teeming with cod and, by the 1640s, were shipping dried cod to the West Indies and the Mediterranean. In exchange, they received sugar, gold and molasses. By the 1670s, Boston dominated the West Indian shipping business, and by 1700 it was the third busiest port in the British realm, after London and Bristol.

But Britain resented this young upstart colony and began to impose trade and tax restrictions. The growing city resisted, and soon colonial anger erupted into riots. The British responded by sending troops to occupy the city in 1768. Anti-crown tensions climaxed in the Boston Massacre in 1770, a clash between British soldiers and colonists in which five American men were killed.

More signal events on the road to independence followed in rapid succession. In the 1773 Boston Tea Party, 200 men dressed as Indians tossed three shiploads of tea into Boston Harbor as a protest against the English tea tax. King George closed the port and sent more troops to Boston.

The Revolution began in earnest in and around Boston. The first shots were fired at nearby Lexington and Concord in 1775. In the Battle of Bunker Hill, the British drove off the heavily outnumbered Americans, but only after sustaining severe losses. When George Washington fortified Dorchester Heights in a single night, the British were ousted forever. They evacuated the city on March 17, 1776, and fighting never again touched Boston.

With the ink dry on the Declaration of Independence, thoughts turned to commerce. But lost British markets pushed the city into a depression, and Boston began looking toward the Far East for trade, bringing in silks, spices and porcelain.

The city grew and thrived in the years after the Revolution. Fortunes were made by Boston's more prosperous merchants, a group of influential families who came to be known as the "codfish aristocracy." They dubbed themselves Boston Brahmins, smugly adopting the title of India's priestly caste. This small group counted among them the names of Cabot, Lowell and Hancock. They ruled the city with an unapproachable elitism, letting it be known that "the Lowells speak only to the Cabots, and the Cabots speak only to God."

The Brahmins built brick monuments to their prosperity on Beacon Hill, an elite residential district that defined the social character of Boston throughout the mid-19th century. Beacon Hill was home to such intellectuals as Francis Parkman, William James, Henry Wadsworth Longfellow, James Russell Lowell, Bronson Alcott, Julia Ward Howe and Horace Mann.

In the 1850s Boston become the premier builder of clipper ships, sending these graceful crafts around the world. To accommodate the growing trade, the city built many wharves along its waterfront. But the clipper era was cut short by the rise of steam-powered ships, which conservative Bostonians did not trust and would not build. Merchants shifted their capital to manufacturing, and the harbor went into a long decline.

The mid-19th century also saw the founding of some of Boston's most famed cultural institutions, among them the Boston Public Library, the Boston Symphony Orchestra, the Massachusetts Institute of Technology and Boston University, the first to admit women on an equal basis. The cultural richness produced a new nickname for the city: "The Athens of America."

Into this bustling urban area swarmed thousands of immigrants, led in the 1840s by the Irish, who had been forced from their homeland by the potato famine. The influx of Irish changed the character of this Yankee city forever. First blatantly discriminated against by old-line Bostonians ("No Irish need apply"), they grew in numbers great enough to win political power. The first Irish mayor was elected in 1885.

Boston bloomed into an ethnic rainbow in the 1880s, when waves of Italians, Poles and Russians arrived, multiplying the population thirty-fold. At the same time, the city's area was itself multiplying. In the mid-19th century, Boston had begun filling in the bay between Beacon Hill and Brookline, a neighborhood now known as Back Bay. Other swampy land to the south was also filled and became the South End. By the turn of the century, Boston had tripled its size with landfill.

But soon after, Boston's economy suffered a tremendous decline that would last until the 1960s. The city lost its major port status to New York and Baltimore, and its textile, shoe and glass mills moved south in search of cheaper labor and operating costs. Population shrank in the 1940s and '50s, with Boston the only large city to decline in numbers during the postwar baby boom years. The city languished in the throes of this decline for decades.

Good times returned suddenly in the 1960s, as the Protestant elite and Irish Catholics finally cooperated in managing city affairs. Urban renewal projects created the new Government Center and the landmark Prudential and Hancock towers. The technological revolution of the 1970s and '80s enriched Boston's economy, with computer companies and think tanks springing up in Cambridge and Greater Boston.

With prosperity came urban problems. In the early 1970s, court-ordered busing among racially imbalanced schools sparked rioting and protests, particularly in South Boston and Charlestown. The crisis lasted several years. Racial strife eased somewhat in the 1980s and 1990s as African Americans began to gain more power in local and state government and in private business.

Today Boston has a Democrat-controlled legislature and a reputation for liberalism, spearheaded by the reigning scion of the Kennedy clan, Senator Ted Kennedy. Breaking the Irish tradition, today's top city official—Thomas Menino—is the city's first Italian mayor.

Boston the city is home to a scant 581,616 souls. Many are under 30; thousands of students flood the city each September, injecting it with vitality and youthfulness.

Text continued on page 184.

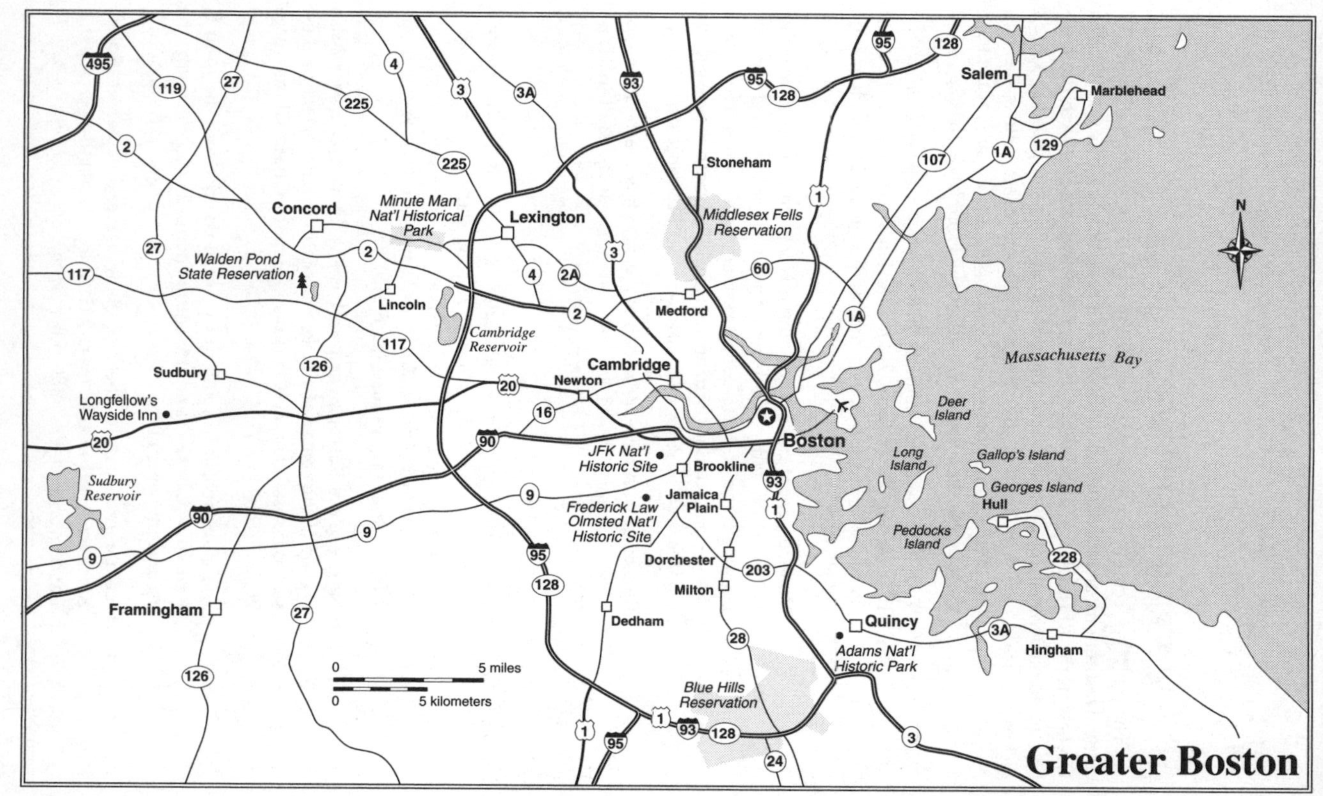
Greater Boston
N
Massachusetts Bay
Salem
Marblehead
Stoneham
Middlesex Fells Reservation
Concord
Minute Man Nat'l Historical Park
Lexington
Walden Pond State Reservation
Lincoln
Medford
Cambridge Reservoir
Cambridge
Sudbury
Newton
Longfellow's Wayside Inn
Boston
Deer Island
Long Island
Gallop's Island
Georges Island
Hull
JFK Nat'l Historic Site
Brookline
Sudbury Reservoir
Jamaica Plain
Frederick Law Olmsted Nat'l Historic Site
Peddocks Island
Dorchester
Milton
Framingham
Dedham
Quincy
Adams Nat'l Historic Park
Hingham
Blue Hills Reservation
0
5 miles
0
5 kilometers
495
119
27
4
3
3A
93
95
128
225
2
107
1A
129
1
117
60
126
20
16
90
9
228
203
28
24
3A
3

Three-day Weekend

Boston and Environs

Day 1

- Explore historic Boston on the **Freedom Trail** (pages 194–95). This string of pre-Revolutionary buildings echoing with the footsteps of Samuel Adams and young Ben Franklin provides a good excuse to wander the streets of the city center. Along the way, you're sure to be sidetracked by other attractions such as the huge **Quincy Market** (page 196) at Faneuil Hall Marketplace.
- Take a lunch break midway through your walking tour at The **Blackstone Grill** (page 206), a hidden alternative to the usual Freedom Trail tourist haunts such as the Union Oyster House and Durgin Park.
- Continue under the freeway to the North End to see where Paul Revere rode. Today the North End is an Italian neighborhood boasting some of Boston's best restaurants. Why not try the *pollo arrabbiata* at **Lucia Ristorante** (page 189), where the ceilings are covered with frescoes by local latter-day Michelangelos.
- Take in a play this evening at one of the city's fine theaters, then top off your history-packed day with a nightcap at the **Bell in Hand Tavern** (page 210), Boston's oldest bar.

Day 2

- Learn more about some of the ethnic subcultures that have helped shape Boston's unique character. A good place to start is Beacon Hill, once the heart of the city's early-day free black community. Visit the **Museum of African-American History** and the **African Meeting House** (page 215).
- Next explore Boston's compact, bustling Chinatown, a very Asian enclave in the center of a Yankee city. Stop in for lunch at the best seafood restaurant in Chinatown, **Grand Chau Chow** (page 208).
- This afternoon, head south to Columbia Point to visit the **John F. Kennedy Library and Museum** (page 242), celebrating the accomplishments of the 20th-century's most famous Bostonian.
- Before returning to the city, enjoy a steak dinner at **South Kitchen & Wine Bar** (page 243), a long-established eatery that was a favorite of JFK and brother Bobby.

- Take your choice among the many nightclubs that have made Boston a music mecca.

Day 3

- Cross the river to Cambridge and explore the hallowed halls of **Harvard** (page 245), America's premier university.
- It's an amazing experience just to sit in Harvard Yard, read a book and watch students strolling by. To make a full day of it, visit some of the university's world-class museums. We recommend the **Peabody Museum of Archaeology and Ethnology** (page 247), the **Arthur M. Sackler Museum** (page 246) and the **Fogg Art Museum** (page 246).
- Complete your visit with a special dining experience **Upstairs on the Square** (page 252), steeped in Harvard tradition and one of greater Boston's finest restaurants.

The weather is infinitely changeable, varying from warm, humid summers when temperatures range from the 60s to the low 90s, to dry, crisp falls hovering in the high 40s (and the low 70s during Indian summer), to very cold winters when temperatures dip to the 20s and 30s, occasionally falling below zero.

The nucleus of Boston proper is a pear-shaped peninsula. At its northernmost tip stands the North End, a small Italian enclave clustered with shops, cafés and restaurants. The downtown area takes up most of the peninsula, winding between the waterfront and Boston Common from north to south and encompassing a Chinatown that is tiny yet rich in tradition.

A booklet of tickets to six of the most popular sights in Boston, CityPass may save you money and waits in line. ~ 888-330-5008; www.citypass.net, e-mail info@citypass.com.

High above Boston Common in regal splendor sits Beacon Hill, crowned by the State House and graced with bowfront brick homes, window boxes and hidden gardens. To the west of Beacon Hill lies its cousin, stately Back Bay, a place of wide boulevards and imposing brownstones. Back Bay also encompasses the architectural jewels of Copley Square: the Public Library, Trinity Church and the John Hancock Tower. Farther west is the Fenway, sprawling around its marshy gardens and home to baseball's famous Fenway Park.

A bit farther south lies the city's largest neighborhood, the South End, another 19th-century brick residential area in the process of gentrification. Cut off from eastern downtown by the Fort Point Channel, South Boston (not to be confused with the South End) is a primarily commercial area, home to the city's fish piers.

The residential neighborhoods, harking back to English architecture, have led to Boston's being characterized "America's most European city." But since Boston has added new space-age layers to the urban quiltwork of centuries, the city wears a more American and international face. Though the city took its time, it has come a long way from its Puritan roots and the days when books by male and female authors were separated on different shelves.

The North End

The North End is Boston's oldest, most colorful neighborhood. Today it's a tightly knit, homogeneous Italian community, established after a gradual takeover from pockets of Irish, Portuguese and Jewish residents starting in the late 19th century. The North End's mostly one-lane streets are crowded cheek-by-jowl with Italian restaurants and food stores. Many residents still greet each other in the language of the Old Country and hang their wash out between the alleys. All summer long, Italians celebrate their patron saints with picturesque weekend parades and street festivals.

On the roundish peninsula that is Boston, the North End juts north into Boston Harbor and is cut off from downtown by the elevated Southeast Expressway, which helps keep it a place unto itself. It's a spot where Boston history still lives.

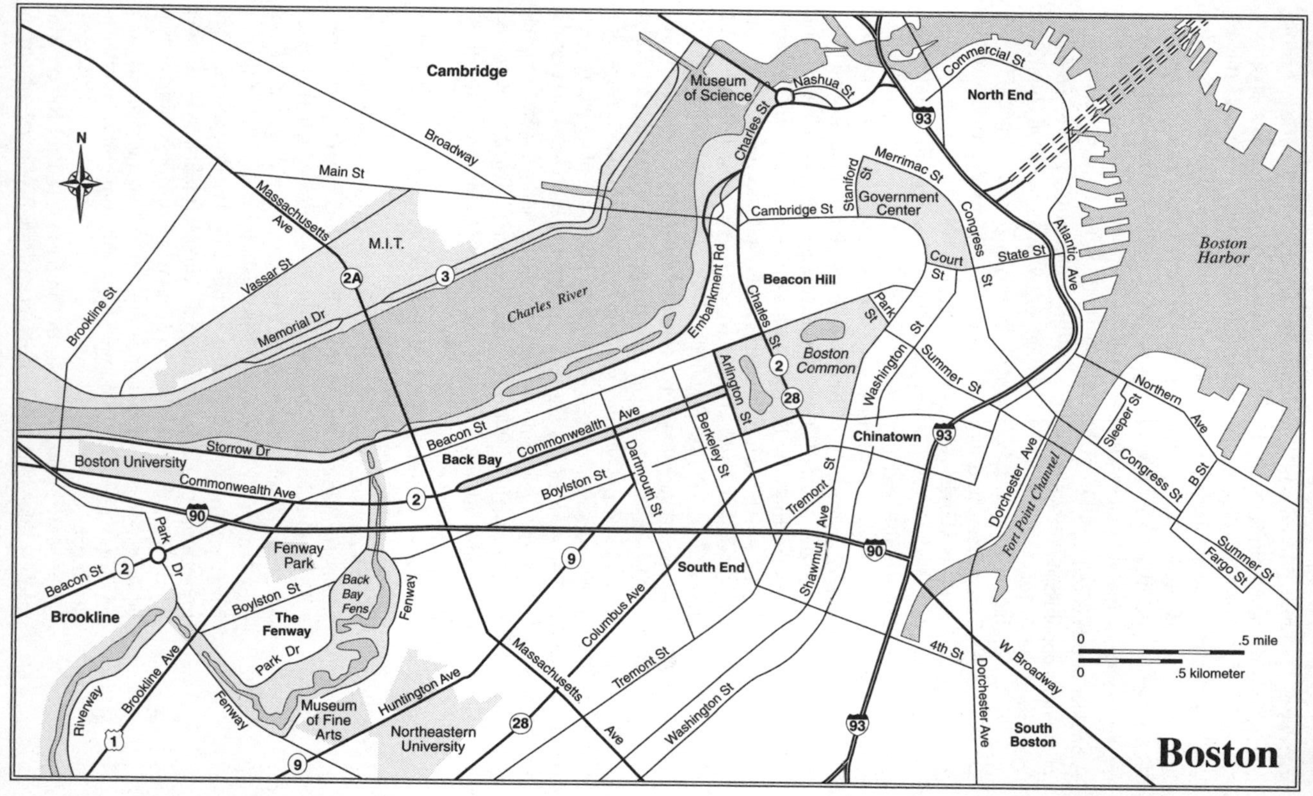
Boston
0 .5 mile
0 .5 kilometer
N
Cambridge
Museum of Science
Nashua St
Commercial St
North End
Broadway
Main St
Massachusetts Ave
M.I.T.
Charles St
Merrimac St
Staniford St
Government Center
Cambridge St
Congress St
Atlantic Ave
Boston Harbor
Court St
State St
Vassar St
Brookline St
Memorial Dr
Charles River
Embankment Rd
Beacon Hill
Park St
Boston Common
Washington St
Summer St
Arlington St
Berkeley St
Northern Ave
Sleeper St
Congress St
B St
Beacon St
Commonwealth Ave
Storrow Dr
Boston University
Back Bay
Chinatown
Dorchester Ave
Fort Point Channel
Dartmouth St
Boylston St
Commonwealth Ave
Tremont St
Shawmut Ave
Summer St
Fargo St
Park Dr
Beacon St
Fenway Park
Back Bay Fens
Fenway
South End
Brookline
Boylston St
The Fenway
Columbus Ave
Park Dr
Massachusetts Ave
Tremont St
4th St
W Broadway
Riverway
Brookline Ave
Fenway
Museum of Fine Arts
Huntington Ave
Northeastern University
Washington St
Dorchester Ave
South Boston
93
90
2
28
9
3
2A
1

SIGHTS

Probably no name evokes more romance in American history than Paul Revere. His famous ride warning of the British attack in 1775 has been chronicled the world over. The quiet little expanse of North Square, lined with cobblestones and black anchor chain, is where you come upon the **Paul Revere House**. This simple little two-story house with gray clapboards and leaded-glass, diamond-paned windows looks almost out of place in Boston today, and well it might. Built in 1680, it's the only example left in downtown Boston of 17th-century architecture. Revere lived here from 1770 until 1800, although not with all of his 16 children at the same time. Inside are period furnishings, some original Revere family items and works of silver. Closed Monday from January through March. Admission. ~ 19 North Square; 617-523-2338, fax 617-523-1775; www.paulreverehouse.org, e-mail staff@paulreverehouse.org.

Next door to Paul Revere's house and entered through the same courtyard is the **Pierce-Hichborn House.** Built around 1711 for glazier Moses Pierce, it's one of the earliest remaining Georgian structures in Boston. It later belonged to Paul Revere's cousin, boatbuilder Nathaniel Hichborn. Guided tours only; call for schedule. Closed Monday from January through March. Admission. ~ 29 North Square; 617-523-2338, fax 617-523-1775; www.paulreverehouse.org, e-mail staff@paulreverehouse.org.

Also in North Square are the **Seamen's Bethel** (12 North Square) and the **Mariner's House** (11 North Square). An anchor over the door announces the Mariner's House, a place where, since 1838, a seaman has always been able to get a cheap meal and a bed for the night. Said the sailor-preacher of the Seamen's Bethel, "I set my bethel in North Square because I learned to set my net where the fish ran." Once a place where sailors worshipped, it's now a rectory office.

On a street noted for "gardens and governors" lived John F. "Honey Fitz" Fitzgerald, one of Boston's Irish "governors," a ward boss, congressman and mayor. His daughter Rose Kennedy was born in this plain brick building at **4 Garden Court Street.**

The **Old North Church** is the one from which the sexton hung two lanterns the night of Paul Revere's midnight ride ("one if by land, two if by sea"). This beautiful church has Palladian windows and a white pulpit inspired by London designs. The four trumpeting cherubim atop the choir loft pilasters were taken from a French pirate ship. Replicas of the steeple's lanterns may be viewed in the adjacent museum. ~ 193 Salem Street; 617-523-6676, fax 617-725-0559; www.oldnorth.com, e-mail tours@oldnorth.com.

Directly behind Old North Church in the **Paul Revere Mall** stands a life-sized statue of Revere astride his horse—one of the city's most photographed scenes.

On the other side of the mall you'll come to **St. Stephen's Church**, a brick Federal-style church designed by the man who established that style, Charles Bulfinch, America's first native-born architect. The only Bulfinch-designed church still standing in Boston, St. Stephen's has a bell and copper dome cast by Paul Revere. Inside are wedding cake–white fluted pillars, balconies and Palladian windows, a pewter chandelier and an 1830s pipe organ. ~ Hanover and Clark streets.

Copp's Hill Burying Ground served as the cemetery for Old North Church in the 17th century. Set high on a little green knoll, it overlooks Boston Harbor and Charlestown, which was bombarded by British guns placed here during the Battle of Bunker Hill. Its simple gray headstones bear pockmarks from British target practice. Buried here are Increase and Cotton Mather, Puritan ministers who wielded considerable political clout. ~ Hull and Snowhill streets.

The widest street in all the North End is **Hanover Street**, a major center for shops and restaurants. Walking south on Hanover Street leads you straight to the **Haymarket–North End Underpass**, which leads under the Southeast Expressway to downtown. The underpass is lined with bright, primitive mosaics done by North End children, a kind of urban folk art. The walls of the

◄HIDDEN

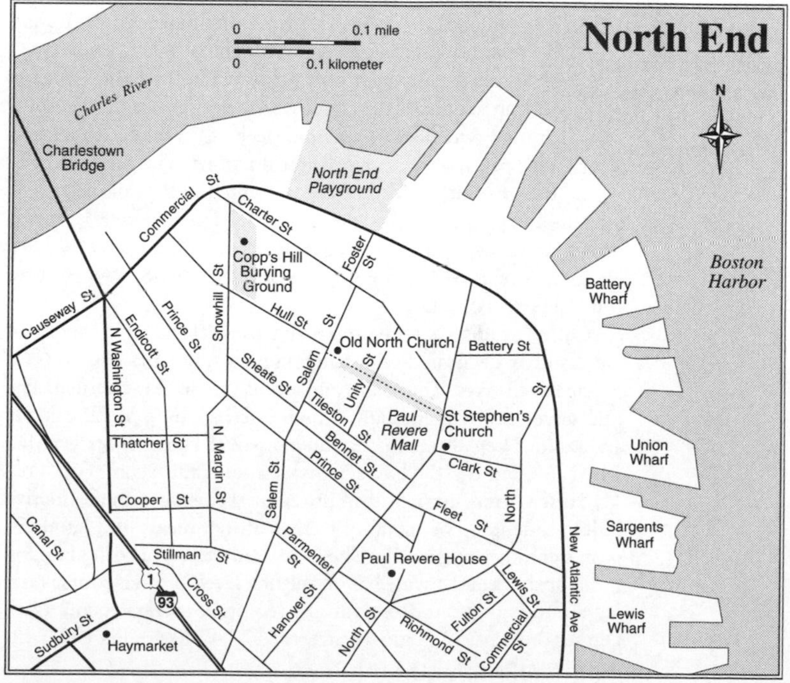

underpass also sport the work of Sidewalk Sam, a well-known local sidewalk artist who paints brightly colored reproductions of works by the Italian masters.

Boston by Foot gives regular walking tours of many of the city's fascinating neighborhoods. Hour-and-a-half tours take place from May through October, rain or shine. Fee. ~ 77 North Washington Street; 617-367-2345, 617-367-3766, fax 617-720-7873; www.bostonbyfoot.com, e-mail bbfoot@bostonbyfoot.com.

DINING

In the Italian North End, you can feast on pasta and regional dishes from one end to the other, stopping at neighborhood "red-sauce" cafés, plush formal dining rooms or late-night espresso bars. Some of the best deals in Boston dining are here, with many restaurants offering moderate prices.

Mamma Maria is the queen of North End gourmet. Highly regarded, it's set in a ritzy townhouse bedecked with brass chandeliers, mirrors and taupe-and-cocoa walls. An upstairs atrium overlooks Paul Revere's little house. Mamma Maria's menu is refreshingly free of red sauce, featuring the lighter, reduced-sauce dishes of Tuscany and Piedmont, which might include hand-rolled gnocchi with fresh Maine crab meat, local greens and shaved black truffle. Dinner only. ~ 3 North Square; 617-523-0077, fax 617-523-4348; www.mammamaria.com, e-mail mammamaria@bicnet.net. DELUXE TO ULTRA-DELUXE.

Book a tour with North End resident Michele Topor, who offers an insider's look of her neighborhood's culinary nooks and crannies. ~ 617-523-6032; www.micheletopor.com.

In business for only a few years, **Bricco** has already won scores of coveted awards and praise. The restaurant's two floors include a sleek main dining room and an upstairs area for private functions. The menu is classic Italian, but the dishes are presented with a modern flair for simplicity and elegant presentation. The clientele is super-fashionable, especially at the full bar. Dinner only. ~ 241 Hanover Street; 617-248-6800, fax 617-367-0666; www.bricco.com. DELUXE TO ULTRA-DELUXE.

Caffé Paradiso is a favored haunt of local Italians. There's an espresso bar decorated with hanging plants, mirrors and colorful Italian cake boxes. The gelato and *granite* are freshly churned. The café serves desserts and light Italian fare including pizza, calzone and salad. They also feature a full bar. ~ 255 Hanover Street; 617-742-1768, fax 617-742-7317; www.caffeparadiso.com. BUDGET.

Tresca offers authentic, multiregional cuisine with destinctive Italian touches. The menu of fresh seafood, meats and hand-cut pastas changes seasonally. The restaurant boasts a formal dining room upstairs and a wine bar on the first level. A three-course tasting menu is popular. Reservations required; jackets encouraged. Dinner only. ~ 233 Hanover Street. 617-742-8240, fax 617-742-8246. DELUXE TO ULTRA-DELUXE.

Caffe Vittoria is the most colorful of the espresso bistros. It might have been shipped here straight from Italy, so Old World is it. A massive and ancient espresso machine stands in the window, and latticework, marble floors and a mural of the Italian coast add to the feeling. Here's the place to indulge in a late-night espresso, cappuccino or Italian liqueur, accompanied by gelato or cannoli. There's also a downstairs cigar lounge. ~ 296 Hanover Street; 617-227-7606, fax 617-523-5340. MODERATE.

If you can't visit the Sistine Chapel, you can still see its transcendent frescoes covering the ceiling at **Lucia Ristorante.** Art critics come to rave and art students to stare in awe. More magnificent ceiling frescoes show Marco Polo's visit to China, the 12 Apostles and the Last Supper. Lucia's chef hails from Abruzzo and prepares specialties from all over Italy, robust to light dishes, something for everyone. Try the *pollo arrabbiata* or *maccheroni Chittara Filippo.* ~ 415 Hanover Street; 617-367-2353, fax 617-367-8952; www.luciaristorante.com. MODERATE.

Pizza is all that's been served at **Pizzeria Regina** since 1926, and that's fine with the loyal clientele who jam the doorway at lunch and dinner waiting for one of the few tables inside. When you get in, you'll sit on high-backed benches at long, heavy wooden tables, where you'll eat slice after slice of pizza served with pitchers of beer, soda or house wine. The service is fast, if sometimes curt, but that's the North End style. Cash only. ~ 11½ Thatcher Street; 617-227-0765, fax 617-227-2662. BUDGET TO MODERATE.

At **La Famiglia Giorgio,** the portions are so big and the prices so reasonable, you can't believe it. Locals do believe, and they pack the uproarious place nightly to feast on gargantuan helpings of spaghetti and meatballs, lasagna, linguine with clam sauce and a sautéed seafood platter. As the name suggests, the small, bright low-decor eatery is family-owned. Reservations are required for parties of six or more. ~ 112 Salem Street; 617-367-6711, fax 617-367-6174. BUDGET TO MODERATE.

SHOPPING

The North End is a food lover's shopping dream, chock full of wine and cheese shops and bakeries.

Since **Bova's Bakery,** at the corner of Salem and Prince streets, is open 'round the clock, it's a great place to satisfy late-night hunger pangs. It's also an ideal spot to hear local gossip. The well-connected Bova family owns shops and apartments all over the North End, and the bakery serves as an apartment-hunters' clearinghouse for folks who are in the know. ~ 134 Salem Street; 617-523-5601.

For a pungent whiff of Old World ambience, head for **Polcari's Coffee Store,** a tiny shop brimming with open bags of cornmeal and flour, wooden bins of nuts and jars of coffee beans.

Closed Sunday. ~ 105 Salem Street; 617-227-0786; www.northendboston.com/polcaricoffee.

Overwhelming, tantalizing smells hit the nose in the **Modern Pastry Shop**, which dates to 1931. It's hard to choose among the *pizzelle*, *torroncini*, amaretto biscotti and macaroons. ~ 257 Hanover Street; 617-523-3783; modernpastry.com.

Mike's Pastry is a popular spot for North End–residing yuppies to pick up a boxful of pastries for breakfast meetings downtown. A warning: The volume of goods available here far outweighs their consistent quality, so take your time to peruse the offerings. ~ 300 Hanover Street; 617-742-3050, fax 617-523-2384; www.mikespastry.com.

Downtown

The downtown area comprises several distinct neighborhoods that sprawl around the peninsula and loop around Beacon Hill and the Boston Common. Although Boston's compactness makes it very easy to sightsee on foot, there is no convenient way to see these neighborhoods, and you'll find yourself doubling back more than once.

SIGHTS

For visitors who would rather combine all their historic sightseeing into one trip, the **Freedom Trail** (see "Walking Tour," pages 194-95) is Boston made simple. But if you only follow the red line, you'll have missed many of Boston's riches. For visitors with more time and energy, the following tour provides an in-depth look at Boston, old and new. It loops northward from the North End to the old West End, back down through Government Center and Quincy Market, and out to the Waterfront. Then it goes up State Street, down through the Financial District to Chinatown and the Theater District, and finally back up Washington Street to Boston Common. Since all these neighborhoods are so small, there's no need to treat them as separate geographic areas. But when a sight lies within the boundaries of a particular downtown neighborhood, we'll be sure to let you know.

When you come out the North End Underpass, you'll be crossing Blackstone Street, home to **Haymarket** (covering several blocks of Blackstone Street), the country's oldest market, in operation more than 200 years.

HIDDEN ►

You'll find the **Boston Stone** easily enough by looking behind the Boston Stone Gift Shop. A round brown stone embedded in the rear corner of the house and dated 1737, it was brought from England and used as a millstone to grind pigment. A tavern keeper named it after the famous London Stone and used it as an advertisement. ~ Marshall and Hanover streets.

Behind Marshall Street is the **Blackstone Block**, tiny alleyways that are the last remnants of Boston's 17th-century byways, the old-

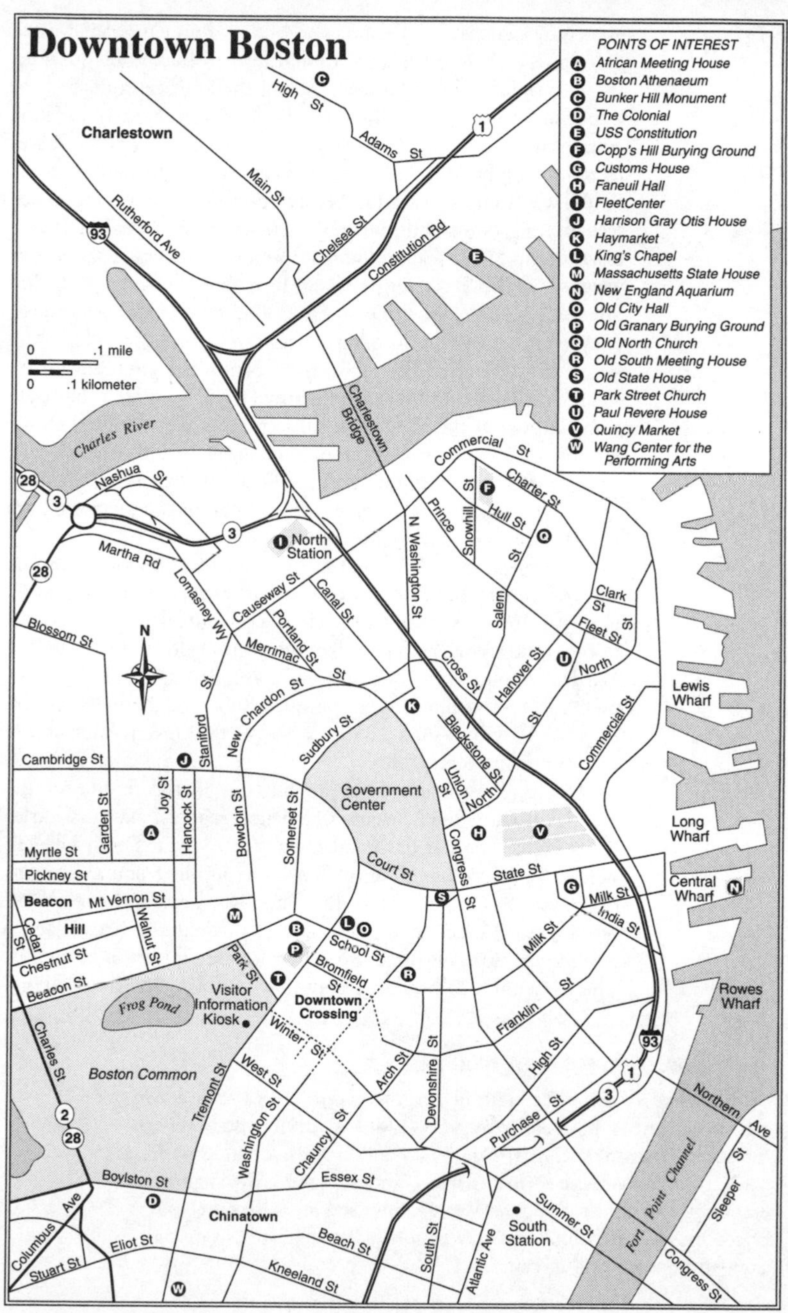
Downtown Boston
POINTS OF INTEREST
A African Meeting House
B Boston Athenaeum
C Bunker Hill Monument
D The Colonial
E USS Constitution
F Copp's Hill Burying Ground
G Customs House
H Faneuil Hall
I FleetCenter
J Harrison Gray Otis House
K Haymarket
L King's Chapel
M Massachusetts State House
N New England Aquarium
O Old City Hall
P Old Granary Burying Ground
Q Old North Church
R Old South Meeting House
S Old State House
T Park Street Church
U Paul Revere House
V Quincy Market
W Wang Center for the Performing Arts
Charlestown
Charles River
North Station
Government Center
Beacon Hill
Frog Pond
Boston Common
Visitor Information Kiosk
Downtown Crossing
Chinatown
South Station
Lewis Wharf
Long Wharf
Central Wharf
Rowes Wharf
Fort Point Channel
0 .1 mile
0 .1 kilometer

est commercial district. Their names, Marsh Lane, Creek Square and Salt Lane, represent the early topography of Boston's landscape.

The **Union Oyster House**, built in the 18th century, became a restaurant in 1826, making it the oldest continuously working restaurant in America. Here Daniel Webster drank a tall tumbler of brandy and water with each half-dozen oysters, and he rarely had fewer than six plates. Before it was a restaurant, exiled French King Louis Philippe taught French here to wealthy ladies. Upstairs in 1771, Isaiah Thomas published *The Massachusetts Spy*, one of the first newspapers in the United States. ~ 41 Union Street; 617-227-2750, fax 617-227-2306; www.unionoysterhouse.com, e-mail info@unionoysterhouse.com.

At the western edge of Boston's peninsula, stretching from the Southeast Expressway to Storrow Drive, is an area that used to be known as the West End. Once rich in many-quilted ethnic groups, it's now a mostly commercialized neighborhood. The area around North Station and the Boston Garden has begun to sprout new restaurants, while a few of the old-time sports bars have become trendy hangouts for a younger crowd.

Located next to the site of the hallowed Boston Garden is the state-of-the-art **TD Banknorth Garden**. Featuring 19,600 seats, luxury suites, restaurants, spacious concourses and air conditioning, the arena is a far cry from Boston's beloved but outdated Garden. Home to the Boston Celtics and Bruins, the shiny complex still sports the famous parquet floor and banners. ~ 100 Legends Way; 617-624-1050, 617-624-1000 (event line); www.tdbanknorthgarden.com.

Not on the peninsula at all but out in the middle of the Charles River is the **Museum of Science**, reached via the Charles River Dam. The star of the museum is the Mugar Omni Theater, whose 76-foot domed screen and surrounding sound systems make you feel as though you're actually whizzing down Olympic slopes on skis, moving underwater through the Great Barrier Reef or breaking through the Antarctic's icy underwater depths. The museum also houses live animal exhibits, the Charles Hay-

sights

AUTHOR FAVORITE

Whether it's in Mexico or Marrakesh, I am always drawn to the excitement of an open-air market—and that goes for Boston's centuries-old **Haymarket**, where, on Friday and Saturday, open-air vendors hawk fruits and vegetables, meats, fresh fish and crabs, crowding over several blocks. Ancient hanging metal scales are used to weigh purchases. Prices are good here, but don't try to touch anything without permission—the vendor will scream.

den Planetarium and changing displays on foreign cultures. Admission. ~ Science Park, O'Brien Highway; 617-723-2500; www.mos.org, e-mail information@mos.org.

The **Harrison Gray Otis House** was the first of three Boston houses Charles Bulfinch designed for his friend Otis, a prominent lawyer and member of Congress. Built in 1796, the three-story brick house is classically symmetrical, with rows of evenly spaced windows and a Palladian window. Inside is one of the most gorgeous interiors in Boston, rich with imported wallpapers, opulent swag curtains and carpeting, gilt-framed mirrors, Adams mantels and neoclassical motifs framing every doorway and window. Surviving abuse as a bathhouse, Chinese laundry and rooming house, the building became the headquarters of the Society for the Preservation of Historic New England in 1916. Closed Monday and Tuesday from June 1 through October 15. Admission. ~ 141 Cambridge Street; 617-227-3956, fax 617-227-9204; www.historicnewengland.org.

Right next door is the **Old West Church**, a handsome Federal-style brick building with a cupola and pillars on three stories. The British tore down its original steeple to prevent signaling across the river during the siege of 1776. Rebuilt in 1806, it houses a Charles Fisk organ; there are free organ concerts on Tuesday evenings from June through August. ~ 131 Cambridge Street; 617-227-5088, fax 617-227-7548, www.oldwestchurch.org, e-mail staff@oldwestchurch.org.

A short walk up Cambridge Street brings you to **Government Center**, a sprawling brick plaza with multilevel stairs and fountains designed by I. M. Pei, an architect who was to change the face of the city in the 1960s, leaving his imprint on many key buildings. The plaza contains two of Boston's most important government structures, the **John F. Kennedy Federal Building** and **City Hall**, a modernistic-looking inverted pyramid. An abstract sculpture entitled *Thermopylae*, inspired by Kennedy's book *Profiles in Courage*, stands facing the JFK Building. A mass of twisting forms, it takes its name from a Greek battle in which the Spartans fought the Persians to the last man.

Some say the **Steaming Teakettle**, a huge copper kettle hung outside the doorway at 65 Court Street at the edge of Government Center, is America's oldest advertising sign. It once announced the operations of the Oriental Tea Company, Boston's largest tea company. Made by city coppersmiths, it holds 227 gallons, two quarts, one pint and three gills. It gives you a warm feeling to see the teakettle steaming away, especially on a cold day.

For a figure so flamboyant as **James Michael Curley**, one statue is not enough. The colorful but corrupt Curley dominated Boston politics for years, from 1914 to the late 1940s, serving as mayor, congressman and governor and figuring prominently in

WALKING TOUR
The Freedom Trail

This two-and-a-half-mile, one-way route, marked by a red brick or painted line on the sidewalk, links 16 major historical places from downtown to Beacon Hill, the North End and Charlestown. It takes two to three hours to walk, though you can easily spend all day. Guided tours are also available, leaving every half hour from the National Park Service visitors center at 15 State Street opposite the Old State House.

BOSTON COMMON Start your walk at Boston Common, one of the oldest public parks in the U.S., which has served during its 250-year history as a British Army encampment, a cow pasture and the site of public hangings. Freedom Trail maps are sold at the **Visitor Information Kiosk** on the southeast side of the park, near the Park Street Station. ~ 147 Tremont Street; 617-426-3115. At the corner of the park, **Park Street Church** is often called the "church of firsts"; here, the first Sunday school in the U.S. was held, William Lloyd Garrison gave his first public anti-slavery speech and "My Country 'tis of Thee" was sung for the first time. ~ Park and Tremont streets; 617-523-3383. Behind the church, governors, mayors and three signers of the Declaration of Independence lie in the **Old Granary Burying Ground**.

SCHOOL STREET Walk northeast on Tremont, past the Granary Burying Ground, to School Street and turn east (right). **King's Chapel**, at the corner, was the first Anglican church in New England and the first church in Boston to have an organ (the Puritans didn't believe in music in church). ~ 58 Tremont Street; 617-523-1749. One block up the street, at the corner of Province Street, is the site of the **Boston Latin School**, the first public school in America, where Benjamin Franklin attended classes. The **Ben Franklin Statue** stands behind the school in Old City Hall Plaza.

Edwin O'Connor's novel *The Last Hurrah*. This four-term mayor was loved by the poor and fond of calling Boston bankers the "State Street Wrecking Crew." Behind City Hall, two very lifelike bronze statues immortalize Curley, one sitting on a park bench, the other standing right on the brick pavement with no pedestal. Tourists have been seen patting the stomach of the standing Curley, so temptingly portly is it. ~ Union and Congress streets.

If you walk down the stairs at the rear of Government Center and across Congress Street, you'll be entering Faneuil Hall Marketplace, one of Boston's most popular destinations.

OLD HOUSES Turn south (right) on Washington and walk one short block to the **Old South Meeting House**, where Samuel Adams and his co-conspirators plotted the Boston Tea Party. Admission. ~ 310 Washington Street; 617-482-6439. Across Milk Street is the house where Benjamin Franklin was born. ~ 17 Milk Street. Next, do an about-face and walk two blocks north to the **Old State House** (c. 1713), the oldest surviving public building in Boston, which is now a museum. Admission. ~ 206 Washington Street; 617-720-3290. Right next door, **Boston National Park Visitor Information** has maps, tour books and brochures. ~ 15 State Street; 617-242-5642.

FANEUIL HALL Turn east (right) on State Street and walk one block to the corner of Congress Street. Here, a circle of cobblestones marks the **Boston Massacre Site**, where British soldiers killed five colonists, triggering the Revolutionary War. Turn north (left) on Congress. Across the street from the present City Hall, Faneuil Hall Marketplace has been a public market and meeting hall since 1742—and still is. Patriots gave speeches that inspired the American Revolution at Faneuil Hall.

THE NORTH END Follow the red tour route line carefully as it takes you about one mile north along Union, Marshall and Salem streets to loop around the North End. At the intersection of Salem and Hull streets stands the **Old North Church** (c. 1723); its 191-foot steeple was the tallest structure in Boston when Robert Newman signaled the approach of British troops with his lanterns, launching Paul Revere's midnight ride. ~ 193 Salem Street; 617-523-6676. To find the **Paul Revere House**, follow Tileston Street east past the Paul Revere Mall, take a little jog south at Hanover and Fleet streets, and go south (right) for one and a half blocks. The simple house is the only remaining residence in Boston dating back to the 17th century. Closed Monday from January through March. ~ 19 North Square; 617-523-2338. To complete your tour, return to Salem Street via Richmond Street or catch any bus with a "Downtown" sign back to Boston Common.

Faneuil Hall was the city's central market in the mid-18th century. The second floor of Faneuil Hall became known as the "Cradle of Liberty," as it resounded with the patriotic rhetoric of James Otis and Samuel Adams in the years leading to the Revolution. On the fourth floor is a museum and armory of the **Ancient and Honorable Artillery Company**, the nation's oldest military group, founded in 1638. Look up to see the four-foot-long gilded copper grasshopper weathervane, a familiar Boston landmark and symbol. Museum closed weekends. ~ Off Congress Street; www.cityofboston.gov.

Quincy Market is another historic marketplace, built in 1826 by Mayor Josiah Quincy to expand Faneuil Hall. In a move that has been imitated by almost every major city, Faneuil Hall Marketplace, which includes Quincy Market along with its twin flanking arcades, the North and South Markets, was renovated in the 1970s into shops and restaurants that have become a major tourist draw for the city. The cobblestoned mall is a street festival by day, a lively nightspot in the later hours. It's wonderfully decorated during the holidays. ~ Off Congress Street.

If you walk out the rear of the marketplace and under the Southeast Expressway across busy Atlantic Avenue, you'll arrive at the waterfront.

When Atlantic Avenue was built in the 1860s, it sliced right through the center of many of the great old wharves, including **Long Wharf**, the oldest existing one in Boston. Built in 1711, Long Wharf was named for its length—formerly 1800 feet. The British marched up Long Wharf when they occupied the city in 1768, only to retreat back down it when they were evacuated in 1776. Long Wharf also saw the departure of the first missionaries to Hawaii in 1819 and played a role in the 1850s California gold rush, when thousands of New Englanders departed for San Francisco.

If you're here for the world-famous Boston Marathon, bring a plastic bag and cut holes for your arms and head. You can wear it in the race if it's raining and then simply throw it away.

Buildings imitating Renaissance palazzos and Greek temples were built in the 19th century along Rowes, India, Central, Long, Commercial, Lewis, Sargent's and Union wharves. **Lewis Wharf**, formerly Clarke's Wharf, was once owned by a Mr. John Hancock. Nathaniel Hawthorne served for a time as a customs inspector at Long Wharf. By the mid-19th century, the wharves were a center of clipper trade with China, Europe, Australia and Hawaii.

Some of the old wharf buildings, which once housed ships' chandlers and sail riggers, have been renovated into shops, offices and restaurants, including the **Pilot House**, **Mercantile Wharf** and **Chart House**, the only surviving late-18th-century building on the waterfront. ~ Off Atlantic Avenue.

Central Wharf is home to the **New England Aquarium**, just a short walk from Faneuil Hall Marketplace. Bostonians like to congregate to watch the harbor seals in the outdoor pool. Inside, the Giant Ocean Tank is home to more than 120 species of exotic reef fish, sea turtles, sharks and moray eels. In the Aquarium Medical Center, you can observe medical check-ups of the sea life from behind a glass window. An IMAX theater is on the premises. Admission. ~ Central Wharf, off Atlantic Avenue; 617-973-5200, fax 617-367-6615; www.neaq.org.

Christopher Columbus Waterfront Park is a neatly landscaped pocket park with brick walkways and benches that offers a lovely harbor view along with respite. Dedicated to the late matriarch of the Kennedy clan, the Rose Fitzgerald Kennedy Garden is a lovely spot at any time of year, but especially when it is in full bloom early in the summer. It's not far from Mrs. Kennedy's birthplace in the North End. ~ North of Long Wharf on Atlantic Avenue.

From the wharves, you can take cruises of Boston Harbor, a great way to while away an afternoon or evening and see the city skyline. The boat line servicing the harbor is **Massachusetts Bay Lines.** ~ 60 Rowes Wharf; 617-542-8000, fax 617-951-0700; www.massbaylines.com.

If you're into intrigue and humor, book passage with the **Boston Harbor Mystery Cruise** put on by the Mystery Café. These three-hour dinner cruises depart from Long Wharf and feature a comic murder mystery. Closed November through April. ~ 63 Long Wharf; 781-793-9700, 800-697-2583; www.mysterycafe.com, e-mail boxoffice@mysterycafe.com.

From Long Wharf, walk up State Street. In a couple of blocks, you'll come to the granite Greek Revival **Customs House**, built between 1837 and 1847, where inspectors once examined all cargoes arriving at the wharves. Incongruously, this building also became Boston's first skyscraper in 1915, when the great clock tower was added. The clock, broken for many years, was restored in the late 1980s and its bright blue and gold face now glows handsomely at night, visible from great distances. ~ McKinley Square at State and India streets.

The **Cunard Building** was built in 1902 for the Cunard Steamship Line, owners of the ocean liner *Queen Elizabeth II*. Twin brass anchors flank its doors, festooned with dolphins and seashells. ~ 126 State Street.

The **Old State House** is a pretty little brick building dwarfed by the surrounding skyscrapers. The bronze lion and unicorn atop its gables stand as symbols of the English crown. Until the American Revolution, this was the seat of British government. A ring of cobblestones outside marks the site of the Boston Massacre, the signal event launching the Revolution. A museum since 1881, the Old State House features winding galleries of exhibits on the building's history and architecture, early Boston and maritime history, including memorabilia, a model ship, paintings and prints. Admission. ~ 206 Washington Street, corner of State Street; 617-720-1713, fax 617-720-3289; www.bostonhistory.org, e-mail oldstatehouse@bostonhistory.org.

An outdoor flower market fronting the brick, Colonial-style **Old South Meeting House** adds to its charms. Built in 1729, Old South has high-arching Palladian windows, a white pulpit and a candlelight chandelier. Many crucial meetings leading to the American Revolution took place here, including the debate that launched the Boston Tea Party. Countless notables spoke here, including Samuel Adams, John Hancock and, later, Oliver Wendell Holmes. Though Old South was repeatedly ravaged—the British turned it into a riding school complete with jumping bar, and it was forced to serve as a temporary post office after a devastating fire in 1872—it has been restored to its 18th-century look. Audio taped presentations re-create the famous Tea Party debate and others. This building offers historical and architectural programs and hands-on exhibits, and still serves as a public forum for community events. Admission. ~ 310 Washington Street, corner of Milk Street; 617-482-6439, fax 617-482-9621; www.oldsouthmeetinghouse.org.

The Boston Irish gave us such political leaders as former Speakers of the House John W. McCormack and Tip O'Neill, James Michael Curley and the Kennedy clan.

Milk Street leads into the heart of the Financial District, a warren of streets stretching south from State Street to High Street and east to Washington Street. Dominated by towering banks and office buildings, the Financial District was considerably built up in the 1980s with bold new buildings, provoking controversy over their design in tradition-minded Boston. One of these—the **BankBoston**—is laughingly called Pregnant Alice because of its billowing shape. ~ 100 Federal Street.

In its marching devastation, the **Great Fire of 1872** leveled 60 acres of downtown Boston. The spot where the fire was arrested on its northeastward path is noted on a **bronze plaque** on the front of the U.S. post office at Post Office Square. ~ Corner of Milk and Devonshire streets.

HIDDEN ►

Two bonanzas await in the lobby of the **New England Telephone building**. One, a massive mural called *Telephone Men and Women at Work*, encircles the rotunda and depicts decades of telephone workers, from 1880s switchboard operators to later engineers, cable layers and information operators. The other reward is Alexander Graham Bell's Garret, a dark little corner filled with memorabilia surrounding the birth of the telephone in Boston in 1875. The garret looks much as it did when Bell worked in it at its original location at 109 Court Street. (A **bronze plaque** at Government Center in front of the John F. Kennedy Federal Building marks that spot, where sound was first transmitted over wires in the fifth-floor garret.) ~ 185 Franklin Street.

Walk south down Summer Street until you come to **South Station**. In its day, South Station was a grand old station house, in fact the largest in the world at the turn of the 20th century. After a thorough restoration completed in 1989, this pink granite beauty stands tall and proud. Ionic columns, a balustrade and a clock with eagle decorate the curved beaux-arts facade stretching for two blocks. South Station today serves as a transportation hub for subway, rail and bus connections. The interior, designed to resemble a European market square, sparkles with polished marble floors and brass railings and is filled with restaurants, shops and pushcart vendors. ~ Summer Street and Atlantic Avenue.

Across the street, you'll see the **Federal Reserve Bank**, which processes millions of dollars worth of currency every day. The Fed's unusual design—it looks like a giant white washboard, and there's a gap where the fifth floor should be—is intended to withstand down drafts and wind pressures. The Fed, which boasts a lobby full of sculpture and murals, also hosts jazz and classical concerts and changing art and crafts exhibits. For a performance schedule, call 617-973-3453. The Fed is not currently open to the public. Prescheduled educational tours are available to groups of ten or more, and must be booked at least a month in advance. Included is the Fed's **New Economic Adventure**, an interactive presentation dealing with economic history. ~ 600 Atlantic Avenue, corner of Summer Street; 617-973-3097, fax 617-973-3511; www.bos.frb.org, e-mail publiccomm.affairs-bos@bos.frb.org.

Winthrop Lane, a tiny brick-lined channel between Arch and Devonshire streets, contains one of the most interesting pieces of public art in Boston, entitled *Boston Bricks: A Celebration of Boston's Past and Present*. In 1985 artists Kate Burke and Gregg Lefevre created bronze reliefs of various Boston personages, scenes and stories and placed them along this red-brick shortcut that's used by folks who work in the Financial District. Take the time to peruse the bricks here; you'll recognize some things—the Red Sox, the swan boats in the Public Garden lagoon—and wonder about others. ◄HIDDEN

South Station is just a hop, skip and a jump from **Chinatown**, bounded by Essex and Washington streets and the Southeast Expressway. See "A Taste of China" for more information.

Few people know that **Edgar Allan Poe** had a long history in Boston, so in 1989 a memorial bronze plaque was erected in his memory at the corner of Boylston Street and Edgar Allan Poe Way. Born here, Poe was the son of actors at the Boston Theatre. He published his first book, lectured and enlisted in the Army in Boston.

The **Grand Lodge of Masons** is decorated with blue and gold mosaics of masonic symbols, and its grand lobby houses a small exhibit of masonic memorabilia. Closed weekends. ~ 186 Tremont Street, corner of Boylston Street; 617-426-6040, fax 617-426-6115; www.glmasons-mass.org, e-mail grandsec@glmasons-mass.org. ◄HIDDEN

From Tremont Street head south. In short order you'll be in the Theater District, centered on Tremont Street, Warrenton Avenue and Charles Street South. Boston has a lively and prestigious theater scene, with many tryouts moving on to Broadway. Among the half dozen or so nationally known theaters is the **Colonial**, the oldest continuously operated theater in Boston, built in 1900. At that time the sumptuously decorated Colonial was considered one of the most elegant theaters in the country, with its 70-foot Italian-marble vestibule and foyer rich with ceiling paintings, cupids, plate mirrors, bronze staircases and carved wood. George M. Cohan, Noel Coward, Fred Astaire, Katharine Hepburn and the Marx Brothers have trod its boards, and the original writing table that Rodgers & Hammerstein used when they wrote *Oklahoma!* is located outside the ladies' lounge. ~ 106 Boylston Street; 617-426-9366, 617-880-2400, fax 617-880-2455; www.broadwayacrossamerica.com, e-mail boston service@broadwayacrossamerica.com.

Formerly the Metropolitan Theatre, the splendid **Wang Center for the Performing Arts** was built in 1925 as a palace for first-run movies in the Roaring Twenties. Restored to its original grandeur, it is opulently decorated with gold leaf, crystal, mirrors and Italian marble, and was designed to be reminiscent of the Paris Opera and Versailles. This 3610-seat theater is one of the largest in the world, and has hosted a variety of artists including Yo-Yo Ma, Luciano Pavarotti, Robin Williams, Lauryn Hill and the Alvin Ailey American Dance Theater. The Center is listed on the National Register of Historic Places. ~ 270 Tremont Street; 617-482-9393, fax 617-451-1436; www.citicenter.org, e-mail info@citicenter.info.

Eliot Norton Park, with bright lights and green lawns, stands where Chinatown and the Theater District meet Bay Village. The park is appropriately dedicated to the dean of American drama critics. ~ Corner of Tremont Street and Charles Street South.

Boston's famed **Combat Zone** on lower Washington Street should be added to the endangered species list. As the pace of development quickened in the late 1970s, its former horde of topless lounges, sleazy bars and adult bookstores and movies shrank to a pathetic few blocks that would be the scorn of any true big-city habitué.

Downtown Crossing is the heart of downtown shopping. Lunchtime shoppers crowd the brick pedestrian mall fronting on Macy's. Downtown Crossing is street entertainment at its most diverse. Pushcart vendors and street musicians—one day a Peruvian folk band, the next a rock group—vie for space in the crowded mall. A one-man band is a permanent local fixture. ~ Corner of Washington and Summer streets.

Old City Hall, a grand French Second Empire building, was renovated in the 1970s into offices and a French restaurant. As one of the first 19th-century Boston buildings to be recycled, it helped spark the preservationist movement. In front of Old City Hall stands the **Franklin Statue**, an eight-foot bronze tribute to Benjamin Franklin. Relief tablets at the base illustrate scenes from his career as printer, scientist and signer of the Declaration of Independence. ~ 45 School Street.

A Taste of China

Compared to Chinatowns in other major cities, Boston's is geographically quite small, just a few blocks long. But this Chinatown was much larger decades earlier, before the Southeast Expressway was built, cutting a wide swath through the district. The Tufts New England Medical Center, too, took a great chunk of Chinatown land when it was built. Now hemmed in by the Expressway and the Combat Zone, Chinatown has little room to grow. But don't be fooled by its physical size: Boston's densely populated Chinatown makes it the third largest Chinese neighborhood in the country.

The Chinese were first brought to Boston to break a shoe industry strike in the 1870s, coming by train from the West Coast. They settled close to South Station because of the convenience of the railroad. First living in tents, the Chinese eventually built houses or moved into places previously inhabited by Syrians, Irish and Italians.

Despite its small size and recent influx of Thai and Vietnamese immigrants, Chinatown is intensely and authentically Chinese. Signs are in Chinese characters, and the area is densely packed with Chinese stores and restaurants. Even the phone booths are covered with Chinese pagodas.

The **Chinatown gates**, a bicentennial gift from Taiwan, stand at the intersection of Beach Street and Surface Road, marking the entrance to Chinatown. White stone with a massive green pagoda on top, they are guarded fore and aft by stone Chinese Foo dogs and sport gold Chinese characters on green marble. The classic characters are not readily translatable in modern Chinese, but they embody such moral principles as propriety, righteousness, modesty and honor.

The large **Unity/Community Chinatown Mural**, painted in 1986, depicts the history of the Chinese in Boston. Among its pigtailed Chinese figures are construction workers, a launderer and women at sewing machines. Other scenes show the Chinese learning to read, protesting to save their housing and gaining access to professional careers. ~ Corner of Harrison Avenue and Oak Street.

During January or February, make sure to plan for the **Chinese New Year's Celebration Parade**. Swarms of people descend on Chinatown for the oversized, dancing puppet dragons, vibrant flags, firecrackers, music and food.

Bromfield Street, a short lane located between Washington and Tremont streets, is chock-full of tiny camera shops, jewelers and watchmakers, stamp traders, pawnshops and a couple of tiny cafés. There are some interesting historical buildings sprinkled along the street, including the home of Revolutionary War hero Thomas Cushing, who held meetings here with the Adamses, Thomas Paine and other cronies.

The **Omni Parker House** is the oldest continuously operating hotel in America, first opening in 1855. Soon after, it became a hangout of the Saturday Club, a literary group whose members included Nathaniel Hawthorne, Ralph Waldo Emerson, Henry Wadsworth Longfellow, James Russell Lowell, Oliver Wendell Holmes and John Greenleaf Whittier. This little group founded the *Atlantic Monthly*. ~ 60 School Street; 617-227-8600, 800-843-6664, fax 617-227-9607; www.omniparkerhouse.com.

King's Chapel looks morosely like a mausoleum. Its steeple was never finished so its Ionic columns flank a bare, squat granite building. The inside, however, is gorgeous, with carved Corinthian columns and pewter chandeliers. The first Anglican church in New England, King's Chapel eventually became the first Unitarian church in the United States. The chapel is closed to the public Sunday, Tuesday and Wednesday from Memorial Day through Labor Day; the rest of the year they're open on Saturday only. ~ Corner of Tremont and School streets; 617-227-2155, fax 617-227-4101; www.kings-chapel.org, e-mail admin@kings-chapel.org.

Beside the church is **King's Chapel Burying Ground**, the oldest cemetery in Boston. It contains the graves of John Winthrop, the colony's first governor, and William Daws, the minuteman who helped Paul Revere warn the colonists the British were coming.

Park Street Church is one of Boston's most beautiful churches, with its white Christopher Wren spire and brick exterior. It was known as Brimstone Corner during the War of 1812 because gun powder was stored in its basement. ~ Park and Tremont streets; 617-523-3383, fax 617-523-0263; www.parkstreet.org, e-mail info@parkstreet.org.

Next door is the **Granary Burying Ground**, which took its name from a large grain storehouse the Park Street Church replaced. Buried here are Paul Revere, Boston's Mother Goose (Elizabeth Ver Goose, who became known for her nursery rhymes) and three signers of the Declaration of Independence, including John Hancock. You can't see exactly where each is buried, however, since the headstones were rearranged for the convenience of lawn mowing. Death's heads, skeletons and hourglasses were popular headstone motifs here.

Times have changed considerably at **Boston Common**, a large tract of forested green, America's oldest public park. In 1634, its acres served as pasture for cattle, training grounds for the militia and a public stage for hanging adulterers, Quakers, pirates and witches. A few steps from the visitor kiosk is **Brewer Fountain**, brought from Paris by Gardner Brewer in 1868 for his Beacon Hill home and later donated to the city. Notable among the statuary on the Common is the **Soldiers and Sailors Monument** high on a hill, whose figures represent history and peace.

Today, downtown office workers use the crisscrossing paths as shortcuts to work, and it's a popular spot for jogging, Frisbee tossing, dog walking, concerts and community events. You might wander into **Park Street Station**, the first station built on the nation's oldest subway, which opened in 1897.

Leaving the edge of Boston Common, you can walk up Park Street, which brings you to Beacon Hill.

LODGING

A boutique luxury hotel with 201 rooms, the **Millennium Bostonian Hotel** stands right next to Faneuil Hall Marketplace. In its lobby are two Colonial artifact exhibits. Besides one of the city's top-rated restaurants, the Bostonian has a terraced atrium, as well as a fitness suite. A typical room might have a rose carpet and contemporary furnishings like glass-topped tables and white love seats. The bathroom is spacious, with double sinks and a large oval tub. Eleven rooms even have hot tubs and fireplaces. ~ North and Blackstone streets; 617-523-3600, 866-866-8086, fax 617-523-2454; www.millenniumhotels.com, e-mail bostonian@mhrmail.com. ULTRA-DELUXE.

The **Boston Harbor Hotel** is simply the most visually stunning hotel to be built in Boston in many years. Set right on the harbor and designed in grand classical style, the brick structure is pierced with an 80-foot archway. The waterfront side is lined

GREENER PASTURES

Boston Common is the first jewel in Boston's **Emerald Necklace**, a seven-mile tracery of green that loops through and around the city, all the way to Jamaica Plain, Brookline and Fenway. It was designed in the late 1800s by famed landscape architect Frederick Law Olmsted (designer of New York City's Central Park), who believed that parks could provide a psychological antidote to the noise, stress and artificiality of city life. The Emerald Necklace also includes the Public Garden, the Commonwealth Avenue Mall, the Back Bay Fens, the Muddy River, Olmsted Park, Jamaica Pond, Franklin Park and the Arnold Arboretum. The Boston Park Rangers (617-635-7383, fax 617-635-7418) conduct periodic walking and bicycling tours of the entire Emerald Necklace; www.cityofboston.gov/parks.

with Venetian-style piers and crowned with a copper-domed rotunda observatory. A cobblestone courtyard reaches toward the ornate marble-floored and crystal lobby. Many of the 230 guest rooms have magnificent water views and feature dark wood furniture in a green decor and marble-topped nightstands. The hotel has a health club and spa, sauna and lap pool, 40-slip marina, and an award-winning restaurant and bar. ~ Rowes Wharf; 617-439-7000, 800-752-7077, fax 617-330-9450; www.bhh.com, e-mail reservations@bhh.com. ULTRA-DELUXE.

One of New England's top-rated hotels, the 273-room **Four Seasons Hotel** overlooks the Public Garden. The recently renovated interiors reflect the contemporary residential character of Beacon Hill, with a grand staircase leading up from the lobby and, in the rooms, leather-topped writing desks, fresh flowers in the bathroom and marble-topped vanities. There's a spa, whirlpool, exercise room, masseur and lap pool with a view of Beacon Hill. ~ 200 Boylston Street; 617-338-4400, 800-332-3442, fax 617-351-2051; www.fourseasons.com. ULTRA-DELUXE.

The posh **Langham Hotel, Boston** is one of the country's most highly acclaimed hotels. It opened in 1981 in the former Federal Reserve Bank, built in 1922, a Renaissance Revival granite and limestone structure modeled after a Roman palazzo. Many original interior architectural details remain, including elaborate repoussé bronze doors, gilded, coffered ceilings and sculpted bronze torchières. The Julien Lounge is dominated by two massive N. C. Wyeth murals depicting Abraham Lincoln and George Washington. The hotel has 326 rooms, two restaurants, a bar, an indoor lap pool and health club facilities with whirlpool and sauna. The generous-sized rooms are elegantly cozy, with varied color schemes. A matching two-toned silver embroidered sofa and club chair contrast a black lacquer writing desk, and you will find granite vanities and marble floors in the bathrooms. ~ 250 Franklin Street; 617-451-1900, 800-791-7761, fax 617-423-

CELEBRITY SLEEPOVER

Omni Parker House is a fabled Boston institution. Many celebrities have stayed here, from Charles Dickens and John Wilkes Booth to former Presidents John F. Kennedy and Bill Clinton. Its lobby is decorated in the grand old style, with carved wood paneling and gilt moldings, a carved wooden ceiling, bronze repoussé elevator doors and candlelight chandeliers. In the heart of downtown, it's just steps away from Faneuil Hall Marketplace. Rooms have writing desks and wing chairs, floral spreads and marble baths. ~ 60 School Street; 617-227-8600, 800-843-6664, fax 617-742-5729; www.omniparkerhouse.com. ULTRA-DELUXE.

2844; www.langhamhotels.com, e-mail bos.concierge@langham hotels.com. ULTRA-DELUXE.

The 500-room **Hyatt Regency Boston** is run with efficiency and hospitality. Conveniently located to everything, the hotel has every luxury you could ask for: 24-hour room service, bathroom telephones, a spa, an Olympic-size pool with outdoor terrace, a sauna, an exercise room, one restaurant and a lounge. The decor mixes Colonial and European styles, with impressive antique furniture and paintings, Waterford crystal chandeliers and imported marble. Rooms are smartly finished in green, mocha or rose. ~ 1 Avenue de Lafayette; 617-912-1234, 800-233-1234, fax 617-451-2198; www.hyattregencyboston.com. ULTRA-DELUXE.

There are at least half a dozen bed-and-breakfast agencies in Boston, offering accommodations in host homes from downtown to Cambridge and the suburbs.

Bed & Breakfast Associates Bay Colony has rooms in 150 homes, most with continental breakfast and private bath, many offering Waterfront, Midtown, Back Bay or Beacon Hill locations. Accommodations range from a bow-windowed room with pine floors, antique brass bed and fireplace in a South End Victorian townhouse, to Beacon Hill and Back Bay homes close to the Public Garden. One of the best deals for the money. ~ P.O. Box 57166, Babson Park Branch, Boston, MA 02457; 781-449-5302, 888-486-6018; www.bnbboston.com, e-mail info@bnbboston.com. MODERATE TO DELUXE.

Personal attention is always given when rooms are booked through **Greater Boston Hospitality**, which offers dozens of options; many are in Back Bay, South End, Brookline and Cambridge. Host homes include a converted Georgian carriage house in Brookline and a classic 1890 Back Bay brownstone appointed with 18th-century mahogany furniture and floors and oriental rugs. Gay-friendly. ~ P.O. Box 525, Newton, MA 02456, 617-393-1548 fax 617-277-7170; www.bostonbedandbreakfast.com, e-mail info@bostonbedandbreakfast.com. BUDGET TO DELUXE.

DINING

Downtown dining covers a wide spectrum, from traditional Yankee bastions to sprightly outdoor cafés and inexpensive ethnic eateries.

HIDDEN

Haymarket Pizza fronts right on Haymarket, a weekend open-air food market, and the surrounding crowds make it hard to get in the door. But if you do, you'll find some of the best cheap pizza in Boston. Cash only. Closed Sunday. ~ 106 Blackstone Street; 617-723-8585. BUDGET.

If you want to be treated like a local, go to **Durgin Park**. Noisy and chaotic, Durgin Park is legendary for its rude waitresses and community tables set with red-and-white-checked cloths. A Boston institution founded in 1827, it dispenses such solid and hefty Yankee fare as prime rib, corned beef and cabbage, franks and beans, corn bread and Indian pudding. ~ 30 North Market, Faneuil Hall; 617-227-2038, fax 617-720-1542; www.durgin-park.com, e-mail seanadpark30@ad.com. MODERATE TO DELUXE.

Far above the crowded bustle of Faneuil Hall Marketplace, you can dine in removed splendor at **Seasons**, one of Boston's top-rated restaurants. Widely spaced tables, designer show plates, mocha banquettes, crisp white napery and mirrored ceilings add to the mood. A creative New American menu is served, changing seasonally, which might include butter-brushed lobster with shiitake mushrooms, seared scallops with prosciutto, or herb-roasted New Zealand rack of lamb. No dinner Sunday or Monday; no lunch on weekends. ~ 24 North Street, Faneuil Hall, in the Millennium Bostonian Hotel; 617-523-4119, fax 617-523-2454. ULTRA-DELUXE.

HIDDEN ►

Southern-style comfort food from a tony eatery? You'll get that and much more from **Anthem**, located a stone's throw from the FleetCenter. With floor-to-ceiling windows and massive velvet curtains, Anthem caters to both well-heeled business people and sports fans alike. Its ambitious menu is a successful marriage of pure nostalgia and continental cuisine. Sharing equal billing on the dinner menu is meatloaf, pan-crisped salmon, crispy skin chicken, and pappardelle pasta. Lunch offerings include tuna casserole and a Cuban pork sandwich. A standout is the mac and four cheeses with cheddar, parmesan, fontina and roquefort—it's even coated in bread crumbs, like mom used to make. Reservations recommended. ~ 138 Portland Street; 617-523-8383. MODERATE TO DELUXE.

Most tourists walk right by the **Blackstone Grill** on their way to the picturesque Union Oyster House, the famous hostelry just down the street. Locals prefer this less crowded and less expensive alternative in a pocket of cobblestoned streets and brick sidewalks. Large portions of chowder, fish and chips, burgers and icy cold beer—all excellent—are served by friendly staff with thick Bahston accents. ~ 15 Union Street; 617-523-9396, fax 617-523-8163. MODERATE.

You can't beat the **Union Oyster House** for historic atmosphere. In 1742 it was a dry goods store and in 1775 it became a center for fomenting revolutionary activity. The restaurant, recently designated a National Historic Landmark, opened in 1826, and Daniel Webster was fond of slurping down oysters at its U-shaped oyster bar, still standing today. Little alcoves with wooden booths and bare wood tables wend around the several wood-paneled dining rooms, and there are ship's models, a mahogany bar and antique wooden pushcarts in this casual and boisterous eatery. The menu features chowders, seafood and

New England shore dinners. Reservations are recommended. ~ 41 Union Street; 617-227-2750, fax 617-227-6401; www.unionoysterhouse.com, e-mail info@unionoysterhouse.com. DELUXE TO ULTRA-DELUXE.

The **Boston Sail Loft** stretches back and back, out onto the harbor for some wonderful views. Some of the best potato skins in town are to be had here, along with burgers, sandwiches, pastas and fish plates, in a nautical atmosphere. ~ 80 Atlantic Avenue; 617-227-7280. BUDGET TO MODERATE.

The **Chart House** is one of Boston's most historic restaurants. Set on cobblestoned Long Wharf, it was built in 1760 and served as John Hancock's counting house. His black iron safe is embedded in the upstairs dining room wall. The Chart House carries a marine motif all the way, with gilt-framed black-and-white pictures of ships, as well as model ships. Famed for its dense mud pie, Chart House also dishes up hearty steaks and seafood. Dinner only. ~ 60 Long Wharf; 617-227-1576, fax 617-227-5658; www.chart-house.com. MODERATE TO ULTRA-DELUXE.

So, you want it kosher? You can get it at the **Milk Street Café**, a cozy Financial District cafeteria that dishes up some of the best inexpensive homemade vegetarian food in the city: soups, sandwiches, salads, muffins, bread and desserts such as homemade brownies and cookies. No dinner. Closed weekends. ~ 50 Milk Street; 617-542-3663, fax 617-451-5329; www.milkstreetcafe.com, e-mail feedback@milkstreetcafe.com. BUDGET.

The blue glow of fish tanks and the mouth-watering smell of spices greet you upon entering **Penang**. Located on the edge of Chinatown, this upbeat eatery serves up spicy Malaysian dishes, blending Thai, Chinese, Indian and Portuguese flavors. If you're game, try an exotic dish such as sautéed frog with kung pao sauce or chicken feet and mushroom casserole. Too wild? Tamer concoctions of poultry, beef, pork and seafood are available. ~

AUTHOR FAVORITE

When I want to indulge myself with top-notch cooking, I reserve a table at **Radius**. Chef Michael Schlow blends seasonal goods and modern French cooking into sublime creations. You might start off with California squab *en pot au feu*, then proceed to Maine diver scallops or loin of venison. For dessert, you can't go wrong with a pear poached in red wine. As one would expect, this epicurean delight will lighten your wallet considerably. ~ 8 High Street; 617-426-1234, fax 617-426-2526; www.radiusrestaurant.com, e-mail info@radiusrestaurant.com. ULTRA-DELUXE.

685 Washington Street; 617-451-6373, fax 617-451-6300; www.penangboston.com. BUDGET TO MODERATE.

HIDDEN ►

The best Chinese seafood restaurant in Boston's tiny Chinatown district is **Grand Chau Chow**. The decor is cafeteria-minimalist, and the well-meaning staff is practically non-English speaking, but Bostonians of all ethnicities ignore the communication problem—they queue up in long lines for fabulous shrimp, crab, sea bass and other delectables. ~ 45 Beach Street; 617-292-5166, fax 617-292-4646. BUDGET.

A thoroughly Chinese lobby greets diners at the **Imperial Seafood** in the heart of Chinatown, with Chinese lanterns and gold dragons. Known for its dim sum, the restaurant also serves Mandarin cuisine to lots of locals. ~ 70 Beach Street; 617-426-8439, fax 617-889-1468. BUDGET TO DELUXE.

Representative of the Southeast Asian immigration to Chinatown is **Pho Pasteur**, an inexpensive Vietnamese restaurant. You can choose from noodle dishes, a variety of soups and excellent seafood entrées. ~ 682 Washington Street; 617-482-7467. BUDGET.

China Pearl specializes in Cantonese and Mandarin cuisine. Locals form long lines for their dim sum and seafood specialties. ~ 9 Tyler Street; 617-426-4338, fax 617-426-8427; www.chinapearlrestaurant.com. MODERATE.

Silvertone Bar & Grill's comfort food has been drawing crowds for years. The basement eatery, styled with mid-century photographs and movie posters, offers dozens of reasonably priced dishes, though it's hard to go wrong with the marinated steak tips, roast chicken, or super-popular mac and cheese. A good selection of beer and cocktails creates a lively bar scene. Frequent waits; no reservations accepted. Closed Sunday. ~ 69 Bromfield Street; 617-338-7887, fax 617-338-7890. MODERATE.

Taken together, the restaurants at the Chinatown Eatery offer some 400 items, covering Szechuan, Hunan, Mandarin, Cantonese, Vietnamese and Thai cuisines.

When **Locke-Ober Café** opened shop in 1875, Ulysses S. Grant was president. The menu and decor at this Brahmin landmark have changed little over the last century, though in 2001 new owner/chef Lydia Shire refurbished the interior and selectively updated the menu. Gleaming wood-paneled walls, private dining-room options, and a mirrored basement bar set the scene for wienerschnitzel à la Holstein, rum-and-tobacco-smoked salmon, and that long-lost classic, Indian pudding. Jackets and ties preferred. Reservations strongly recommended. Closed Sunday. ~ 3 Winter Place; 617-542-1340, fax 617-542-6452; www.lockeober.com, e-mail info@lockeober.com. ULTRA-DELUXE.

Swank **Mantra** draws crowds with French- and Indian-inspired entrées such as rack of lamb in a lentil ragout with mint glaze, and rainbow trout with coconut chutney and toasted almond milk. There's an extensive wine list and some inventive cocktails (consider a pomegranate martini). And be sure to check out the hookah den. Closed Sunday. ~ 52 Temple Place; 617-542-8111; www.mantrarestaurant.com, e-mail info@mantrarestaurant.com. DELUXE TO ULTRA-DELUXE.

A visit to **Excelsior**, is a guaranteed gastronomic adventure. The food's billed as "bold contemporary American cuisine," and chef Eric Brennan is unafraid to take chances—menu offerings in the main dining room include five-spiced wild chinook salmon, duck with marsala-fig sauce, pork with maple-ginseng and braised red cabbage, and beef short ribs with Thai spices and pumpkin gnocchi. A more casual bar menu allows diners to flirt with innovative cuisine at a moderate price. Reservations recommended. Dinner only. ~ The Heritage on the Garden, 272 Boylston Street; 617-426-7878; www.excelsiorrestaurant.com. ULTRA-DELUXE.

Be sure to ask for a table by the window at **Aujourd'hui** so you will have a view of the Public Garden below. The dining room boasts a 1930s Paris art-deco feel, complete with silver leaf ceilings. The modern French menu features game, poultry and seafood dishes. There's also a low-cholesterol menu. In addition to the regular menu, you can try the nightly tasting menu, either traditional or vegetarian, which offers five or six courses of the chef's evening specialties. One block from the theater district, this is a great place *après* theater. Dinner only. ~ 200 Boylston Street, in the Four Seasons Hotel; 617-351-2037, fax 617-351-2293. ULTRA-DELUXE.

SHOPPING

The biggest tourist shopping bonanza in Boston continues to be **Faneuil Hall Marketplace**. A Boston institution since 1826, Quincy Market is the centerpiece of three shopping arcades filled with more than 150 shops and two dozen food stands and restaurants. Outside the market are a profusion of cheery flower and balloon stands, and under its glass-canopied sides are pushcart vendors selling novelty products.

Flanking Quincy Market are two more arcades, the North Market and the South Market.

Feel the Irish eyes smiling at **Celtic Weavers**, an importer of Irish goods. You can set yourself up with clothing, jewelry and perfume, or take home some music, pottery and food. ~ 316 Faneuil Hall, North Market; 617-720-0750; www.celticweavers.com.

For such a small area, Chinatown has more shops than you might imagine. If you've never experienced Chinese pastries, your mouth will water for them at **Hing Shing Pastry**. ~ 67 Beach Street; 617-451-1162.

◄ HIDDEN

Another delicious option is **Eldo Cake House**, which specializes in soft and spongy cakes with a variety of fruits. ~ 36 Harrison Avenue; 617-350-7977.

For an extensive selection of books on Chinese culture, language, cooking, martial arts and tradition, head to **Silky Way**, a second-floor shop that is reliably stocked. ~ 38 Kneeland Street; 617-451-5719.

Downtown Crossing is the heart of downtown shopping. A brick pedestrian mall at the intersection of Washington and Summer streets, it fronts on **Macy's**. ~ 450 Washington Street; 617-357-3000.

No shopping tour would be complete without a visit to **Filene's Basement**, the country's oldest bargain store (founded in 1908), which has made a legend out of off-price shopping. In the 1940s, 15,000 women once stormed the doors to get the last dresses to leave Paris before the German occupation. Detractors say merchandise slipped during the 1980s, when the Basement opened 22 stores in six states. But the Basement is always crowded with women, who used to try on clothes in the aisles until dressing rooms were installed in 1989, and who don't mind the flaking paint and exposed piping when they can pick up designer dresses for less than ten percent of retail price after three markdowns. Or, on occasion, an $80,000 sable coat for $5000. ~ 426 Washington Street; 617-542-2011, fax 617-348-7915; www.filenes basement.com.

In the market for a bridal gown? Once a year, Filene's Basement holds a designer wedding gown sale where dresses that are normally priced up to $9000 go for the rock-bottom price of $249.

NIGHTLIFE

Boston's arts scene has rich centuries of history behind it and is expanding all the time. The **BosTix Booth** at Faneuil Hall Marketplace offers half-price tickets for many performance events on the day of the show, cash only, first-come, first-served. Tickets go on sale at 10 a.m. Closed Monday. ~ 617-723-5181.

THE BEST BARS There's a Boston bar for everyone downtown: young singles, bricklayers and stevedores, the State House crowd, Financial District workers, Cambridge academics, sports fans, the Irish.

The **Bell in Hand Tavern** is America's oldest tavern, opened in 1795, and retains a cozy, colonial feeling. There's live music nightly. Cover Thursday through Saturday. ~ 45 Union Street; 617-227-2098.

Irish brogues roll so thickly at the **Black Rose** that it sounds like Dublin. Irish beers, nightly Irish folk music and a rollicking good time are house specialties. Cover on the weekends. ~ 160 State Street; 617-742-2286; www.irishconnection.com.

Silvertone is a popular retro bar frequented by young urbanites. Fashioned after an art deco–era diner, the black-and-white photos on the wall herald the age of supper clubs and big band music. The raspberry martini is the signature drink of choice. Closed Sunday. ~ 69 Bromfield Street; 617-338-7887, fax 617-338-7890.

The **Littlest Bar** is just that—Boston's smallest tavern. There are 15 stools at the bar and a tiny bench behind them. The noise from the television is often deafening, but this is a fun place to have a quick drink before dinner; most locals haven't heard of it, either. ~ 47 Province Street; 617-523-9766; www.celticweb.com/littlestbar.

◄ HIDDEN

The Good Life specializes in retro cocktail drinks like cosmopolitans, Manhattans and sidecars. The drab '70s decor doesn't deter large after-work crowds or music enthusiasts who enjoy live deejays downstairs Wednesday through Saturday. Closed Sunday. ~ 28 Kingston Street; 617-451-2622, fax 617-451-5146; www.goodlifebar.com, e-mail info@goodlifebar.com.

NIGHTCLUBS AND CABARETS One of the nation's premier comedy venues, **Comedy Connection** has showcased talent such as Chris Rock, Rosie O'Donnell, Dennis Miller and Margaret Cho. ~ Faneuil Hall Marketplace, 245 Quincy Market; 617-248-9700; www.comedyconnectionboston.com.

The **Orpheum Theater** hosts nationally known rock performers. ~ One Hamilton Place off Tremont Street; 617-679-0810 (tickets), 617-931-2000.

Seemingly transplanted from New York City is **Felt**, a swanky pool hall/restaurant/lounge/dance club. Early evening brings in the business-suit crowd; after 10 p.m. you'll find a younger, well-dressed clientele in their 20s and 30s. Occasionally closed Sunday. ~ 533 Washington Street; 617-350-5555; www.feltclubboston.com.

The Roxy is a beautiful and elegant art deco–style club with a 360° balcony overlooking the floor below. Dress code. Open Friday and Saturday nights for dancing. Cover. ~ 279 Tremont Street; 617-338-7699; www.roxyboston.com, e-mail andrea@hotmail.com.

The **Bristol Lounge** is an American bistro that offers late-night bites and live jazz piano Thursday through Sunday. ~ 200 Boylston Street, Four Seasons Hotel; 617-351-2037.

THEATER AND DANCE Boston's theater district is tightly clustered on lower Tremont Street and several blocks west. Many of these host pre-Broadway tryouts and national touring companies. One such venue is the **Colonial Theatre.** ~ 106 Boylston Street; 617-426-9366; www.broadwayacrossamerica.com. Popular contemporary plays are offered by the **Wilbur Theatre.** ~ 246 Tremont Street; 617-931-2787; www.broadwayacrossamerica.com.

The opulent theater of the **Wang Center for the Performing Arts**, formerly a Roaring Twenties movie palace, sponsors extravaganzas in dance, drama, music and film. ~ 270 Tremont Street; 617-482-9393; www.citicenter.org.

Also operated by the Wang Center, the **Shubert Theatre** stages broadway plays, opera and performances presented by community nonprofit organizations. ~ 265 Tremont Street; 617-482-9393; www.citicenter.org.

The **Boston Ballet** performs classics like *The Nutcracker* and contemporary works at the Wang Center. ~ 19 Clarendon Street; 617-695-6950; www.bostonballet.org.

Musical comedies are the specialty at the **Charles Playhouse.** ~ 74 Warrenton Street. On **Stage I**, the innovative Blue Man Group wows audiences with eye-popping performance art and fun-filled escapades. ~ 617-426-6912; www.blueman.com. **Stage II** (downstairs) is home to the country's longest-running nonmusical play, *Shear Madness*, a comedy whodunit. ~ 617-426-5225; www.shearmadness.com.

Beacon Hill

Beacon Hill got its name from a beacon that stood atop it in 1634 to warn colonial settlers of danger. "The Hill" used to be much taller; it was leveled by 60 feet to make way for residential building in the 19th century.

After a building boom, Beacon Hill fast became the most elite section of the city, home to doctors, lawyers, writers and intellectuals. Oliver Wendell Holmes called it "the sunny street that holds the sifted few." The first formal residents of the neighborhood were John Singleton Copley and John Hancock. Later residents included Daniel Webster, Louisa May Alcott, William Dean Howells, Henry James and Jenny Lind.

SIGHTS

No single section of town is more elegant than Beacon Hill. This charming area still looks like a 19th-century neighborhood with its gas lamps, brick sidewalks and narrow, steep streets that wind up and down the hill. Its brick rowhouses were designed in fine Federal and Greek Revival style, with symmetrical windows, fanlight door windows, black shutters and restrained black iron grillwork. Beacon Hill residents love windowboxes and gardens, and many of the houses have beautiful hidden walled gardens. About a dozen of these are opened to the public on the third Thursday in May. This self-guided walking tour of the **Hidden Gardens of Beacon Hill** is sponsored by the Beacon Hill Garden Club. ~ P.O. Box 302, Charles Street Station, Boston, MA 02114; 617-227-4392; www.beaconhillonline.com.

The crown of Beacon Hill, at its summit, is the **Massachusetts State House**, a grand replacement for the old State House downtown. After the American Revolution, state leaders wanted a more elegant home for the prosperous new government. Charles Bulfinch designed it for them in 1795 in Federal style, with a gold dome, brick facade, Palladian windows and white Corinthian columns and trim. A free weekday tour of the interior is well worthwhile, but be sure to make advance reservations. An impressive rotunda, floors made of 13 kinds of marble, unique "black lace" iron grillwork stair railings, stained-glass windows and decorated vaulted ceilings are all part of the appointments. Don't miss the Sacred Cod in the House of Representatives, a wooden fish hung there in 1784 to symbolize the importance of the fishing industry to Massachusetts. Closed on the weekend, call ahead. ~ Beacon and Park streets; 617-727-3676.

The **Old (John Adams)Court House,** now the Suffolk County Courthouse, has a grand rotunda with vaulted ceilings decorated with gilt rosettes and figures of cherubs, urns, scrolls and trumpet-blowing figures. Stone caryatids line the rotunda, representing Justice, Fortitude, Punishment, Guilt, Reward, Wisdom, Religion and Virtue. ~ Pemberton Square.

Many come to admire **Louisburg Square** for its sheer beauty. The centerpiece of the square is a serene oval park with a tall black iron fence, ringed with brick bowfront houses. Louisburg Square looks so much like London that a British film company produced *Vanity Fair* here in the 1920s. Louisa May Alcott lived at number 20. ~ Between Mt. Vernon and Pinckney streets.

Tiny one-lane **Acorn Street**—just south of Louisburg Square between Cedar and Willow streets—is one of the few old cobblestone streets left on Beacon Hill, and a very picturesque one it is. Coachmen and servants for nearby mansions used to live here.

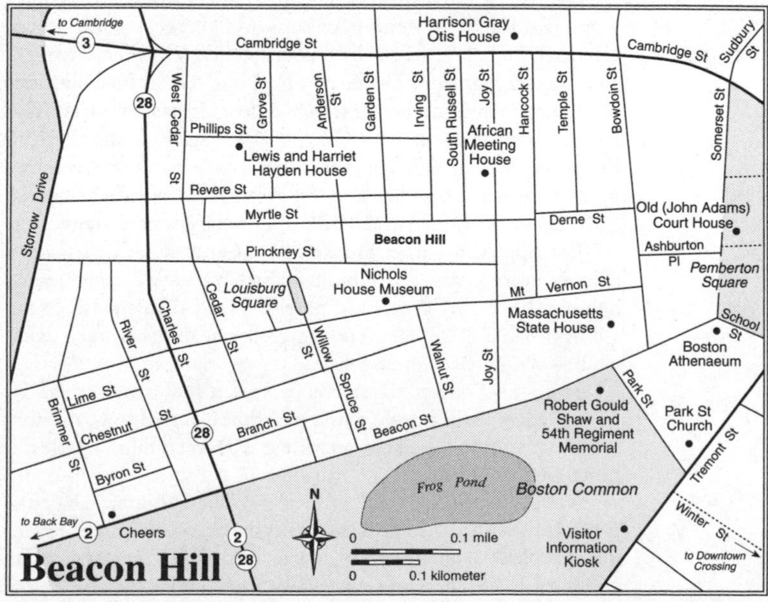

Although the **Nichols House Museum** was not fashionable for its time, the interior is a fine example of the late-19th-century townhouse of historic Beacon Hill. Rose Standish Nichols was quite a personage in her day. A noted landscape architect and pacifist, she traveled around the world and was a friend of Woodrow Wilson. Designed by Charles Bulfinch, her home is filled with rare antiques such as Renaissance Flemish tapestries, works by noted American sculptor Augustus Saint-Gaudens and unusual imitation leather gilded wallpaper. Tours run during operating hours. Open Tuesday through Saturday from April through October, and Thursday through Saturday from November through March. Admission. ~ 55 Mt. Vernon Street; 617-227-6993, fax 617-723-8026; www.nicholshousemuseum.org, e-mail nhm@earthlink.net.

There are two ideal times to stroll along Marlborough Street: on a snowy winter night and on a bright, warm spring morning when the magnolias are in bloom.

The house at **85 Mt. Vernon Street** was Harrison Gray Otis' second Bulfinch-designed home, while **45 Beacon Street** was his third, an unheard-of extravagance.

A grander library than the **Boston Athenaeum** would be hard to find. The interior features high, vaulted ceilings, pillared archways, scores of marble busts, solid wood reading tables and red-leather, brass-studded armchairs. Founded in 1807 by a group including the Reverend William Emerson, father of Ralph Waldo Emerson, it's one of the country's oldest independent libraries. Its picture gallery and sculpture hall served as Boston's first art museum, and the library still maintains an impressive collection of art today, including works by Gilbert Stuart, John Singer Sargent and Chester Harding. The library is also noted for its collections of 19th-century American prints, Confederate state imprints and books from the libraries of George Washington, General Henry Knox and Jean Louis Cardinal Cheverus. Public tours are given by appointment Tuesday and Thursday. ~ 10½ Beacon Street; 617-227-0270, fax 617-227-5266; www.bostonathenaeum.org.

The **Appleton-Parker Houses**, twin Greek Revival structures alike in every detail, were built for two wealthy merchants. At number 39, Fanny Appleton married Henry Wadsworth Longfellow in 1843. Number 40 is now the home of the Women's City Club. ~ 39–40 Beacon Street.

At 63–64 Beacon Street you can see a few panes of the famous **Beacon Hill purple glass**, with hues caused by a reaction of sunlight. It acquired cachet, along with everything else traditional on "the Hill."

While most people think of Beacon Hill as a Brahmin bastion, in the 19th century its north slope was the heart of Boston's emerging free black community. Blacks arrived in Boston as slaves in 1638. By 1705, there were over 400 slaves and a few free blacks who settled in the North End. In the 19th century, most blacks lived in the West End and on Beacon Hill, between Joy and Charles streets. The free blacks worked hard to provide decent housing and education for their own, and to help end slavery.

◄ HIDDEN

A number of their houses and public buildings still stand, and you can see them on the 14-stop **Black Heritage Trail.** A guide leads daily scheduled trips (617-742-5415).

Walking-tour maps of the trail are available at the Boston Common Visitor Information kiosk, as well as at the **Museum of African-American History**, the last two stops on the trail. The museum is closed on Sunday. Admission. ~ 46 Joy Street; 617-725-0022, fax 617-720-5225; www.afroammuseum.org, e-mail history@afroammuseum.org.

Among the public buildings on the Black Heritage Trail is the **African Meeting House**, the oldest standing black church in America. Built in 1806, it was known in the abolitionist era as the Black Faneuil Hall. It was here, in 1832, that the New England Anti-Slavery Society was founded, with a few black leaders, and white abolitionist William Lloyd Garrison and others speaking from the platform. ~ 46 Joy Street.

A stirring tribute to the first black regiment recruited for the Civil War stands at the corner of Beacon and Park streets and marks the start of the Black Heritage Trail. A bas-relief sculpture by Augustus Saint-Gaudens, the **Robert Gould Shaw and 54th Regiment Memorial** shows the regiment on the march leaving Boston with their young white leader, Bostonian Robert Gould Shaw, and an angel flying overhead. The black military role in the Civil War won new recognition with the release of the film *Glory*, which chronicles the story of the Massachusetts 54th Regiment.

The trail also takes you to one of the first schools for black children and to homes built by free blacks, among them the **Lewis and Harriet Hayden House**, which served as an Underground Railway station and was visited by Harriet Beecher Stowe. ~ 66 Phillips Street.

On an entirely different note, television history is also alive and well in Beacon Hill. Like homing pigeons, all tourists head for "Cheers," so we may as well get it out of the way. The setting for the television show was the Bull and Finch Pub. Now appropriately renamed **Cheers**, it's a basic sports bar with televisions, pub fare, and, of course, officially licensed "Cheers" merchandise. It is, however, a bar with real atmosphere. Originally an English pub, it was dismantled and shipped here, complete with old leather and walnut paneling. ~ Downstairs at 84 Beacon Street; 617-227-9605, fax 617-723-1898; www.cheersboston.com, e-mail pubmanager@cheersboston.com.

Yet another point of television trivia can be found in Beacon Hill. Private eye Spenser of *Spenser: For Hire* lived above a

Boston firehouse, which he entered through a bright red door. The firehouse is right next to the Charles Street Meeting House on Mt. Vernon Street, at the corner of River Street.

LODGING

Beacon Hill Bed & Breakfast, located in a pretty six-story brick rowhouse, is in a quiet residential neighborhood on the lower slope of Beacon Hill, just two blocks west of Charles Street. Each of the two high-ceilinged guest rooms has a decorative fireplace and a private bath. One room has a view of the Charles River; another looks out over the lovely Gothic Revival Church of the Advent, across the street. ~ 27 Brimmer Street; 617-523-7376; e-mail bhillbb@gmail.com. ULTRA-DELUXE.

A real find, far less pricey than downtown hotels, is the **John Jeffries House**. It offers 46 spacious studio apartments and suites, most with kitchenettes, in a renovated turn-of-the-20th-century house overlooking Charles Street. Guest quarters are furnished in tasteful pastels, with dark reproduction furniture, large windows and contemporary bathrooms. There is also a large and comfortable lobby. ~ 14 David G. Mugar Way; 617-367-1866, fax 617-742-0313; www.johnjeffrieshouse.com. DELUXE.

DINING

Along with its chic boutiques, Charles Street is lined with restaurants representing many ethnic cuisines.

Step into a Tuscan village at **Ristorante Toscano**, whose dining room has exposed brick walls hung with paintings of the Italian countryside and antique Italian cookware and pottery. Feast on Florentine cuisine including homemade pastas and game dishes. The tiramisu is a dessert standout. No lunch on Sunday. ~ 47 Charles Street; 617-723-4090, fax 617-720-4280. ULTRA-DELUXE.

The bakers at **Café Vanille** learned their craft in Paris and now bring the secrets of French pastry-making to this large Charles Street café. Try a cranberry-walnut or apricot croissant; if you're in the mood for something more substantial, go for a made-to-order sandwich or a slice of quiche. ~ 70 Charles Street; 617-523-9200; www.cafevanilleboston.com. BUDGET.

Good and spicy Thai food stars over the decor at **King and I**. Start off your meal with satay and Thai rolls, then move on to

COFFEE ON CHARLES STREET

Café Bella Vita is a great coffeehouse where you can linger over an espresso or cappuccino and feel welcome in a European way. Its café chairs are always crowded with young students munching on hearty Italian sandwiches. Specialties are desserts such as fresh gelato or chocolate cheesecake. ~ 30 Charles Street; 617-720-4505. BUDGET.

dancing squids, seafood *panang* or any number of chicken, duck, beef, tofu and noodle dishes. No lunch on Sunday. ~ 145 Charles Street; phone/fax 617-227-3320. BUDGET TO MODERATE.

Located in the quaint Beacon Hill Hotel, the **Beacon Hill Bistro** has an expanded menu almost large enough to qualify it as a full-scale restaurant. A warm, stylish eatery, the Beacon Hill's decor offers polished mahogany paneling, a roaring fireplace and mosaic tile flooring. The café serves three meals a day—while breakfast and lunch are an American/Continental affair, dinner entrées consisting of chicken, fish and meat dishes have a heavy French influence. Menus change seasonally. ~ 25 Charles Street; phone/fax 617-723-7525; www.beaconhillhotel.com. MODERATE TO DELUXE.

SHOPPING

At the foot of Beacon Hill, little Charles Street is thickly lined with antique shops, art galleries and specialty stores.

Black Ink caters in "unexpected necessities" for the home, office and child. This is the place for frog-shaped tape dispensers, spinning tops, rubber stamps, kaleidoscopes and other novel knicknacks. ~ 101 Charles Street; 617-723-3883.

If you stop by **Rouvalis Flowers** you can take home an exotic plant or flower. The shop has a wonderful selection of topiary trees and orchids as well as unusual seasonal varieties. Shipping is available. Closed Sunday. ~ 40 West Cedar Street; 617-720-2266, 800-397-2555, fax 617-720-2636.

The retail outlet of a local paper manufacturer, **Rugg Road Paper Co.** carries virtually every paper good you can imagine, from exclusive handmade paper to custom stationery and invitations to hand made books. ~ 105 Charles Street; 617-742-0002, fax 617-742-0008.

An amazing selection of beautifully colored and embroidered Western-style leather boots awaits at **Helen's Leather**, along with stylish leather coats, briefcases and belts. Western apparel such as shirts and buckles are also available. ~ 110 Charles Street; 617-742-2077; www.helensleather.com.

You ought to be able to find the perfect brass drawer pull at **Period Furniture Hardware**, which carries a full line of reproduction hardware. Closed Sunday. ~ 123 Charles Street; 617-227-0758.

NIGHTLIFE

Despite its fame as the "Cheers" bar, **Cheers**, formerly known as the Bull and Finch Pub, is a watering hole with character. The venerable English pub features big brews, burgers and an uproarious crowd. ~ Downstairs at 84 Beacon Street; 617-227-9605; www.cheersboston.com, e-mail pubmanager@cheersboston.com.

If you need more "Cheers" atmosphere, they've opened a second location: **Cheers Faneuil Hall**. The new bar features a near-perfect replica of the Hollywood set, complete with Tiffany lamps and a central island bar. ~ Faneuil Hall Marketplace; 617-227-0150, fax 617-227-8416.

The **Sevens Ale House** is a better Boston neighborhood bar than nearby Cheers. Decorated in dark, mellowed wood and with photos of patrons finishing the Boston Marathon and other local events, the Sevens is small and lively, lacks tourists, and is blessed with some of the friendliest staff we've ever met. ~ 77 Charles Street; 617-523-9074.

Back Bay

Although it started life as a mud flat, Back Bay fast became a fashionable neighborhood. As the city grew, it started running out of room in its original peninsula surrounding Boston Common, so it began filling in the tidal flats of the Back Bay in 1858, the largest land reclamation project of its time. Some 450 acres of marshland were turned into usable land over 20 years.

Given all this room to plan, Back Bay is the only place in town laid out with any perceivable logic. Streets follow an orderly grid, with cross streets named alphabetically for palatial ducal mansions: Arlington, Berkeley, Clarendon, Dartmouth, Exeter, Fairfield, Gloucester and Hereford.

SIGHTS

The centerpiece of this grand reclamation project is **Commonwealth Avenue**. Patterned after the Champs Élysées, it's a wide boulevard with a grass strip mall that runs right through the heart of the Back Bay. "Comm Ave," as it's called by natives, is lined with stately brownstones and many historic buildings. Newbury, Beacon and Marlborough streets parallel Comm Ave. Stylish Newbury Street is lined with chic boutiques, expensive jewelry, fur and clothing stores, art galleries, antique stores and loads of restaurants. Back Bay crosses Massachusetts Avenue, which natives shorten to "Mass Ave," and ends at Kenmore Square.

To the north, the Back Bay ends at the Charles River, where the wide, grassy Esplanade is a popular sunning spot in warm weather. Also on the Esplanade is the **Hatch Memorial Shell**, where the Boston Pops Symphony Orchestra performs summer concerts.

If Boston Common is Boston's Central Park, then the **Public Garden** is its Tuileries, the first botanical garden in the country. Lavishly landscaped with flowers and trees, it's home to the **swan boats,** which circle the weeping willow–draped lagoon in season. The famous boats were launched in 1877 by Robert Paget, who was inspired by the swan-boat scene in Wagner's opera *Lohengrin*. The same family continues to operate them. Also in the Public Garden is some notable statuary: George Washington on horseback and abolitionist Wendall Phillips. ~ Bordered by Beacon, Charles, Arlington and Boylston streets.

If you walk straight through the Public Garden gates at the corner of Beacon and Charles streets, you'll come upon **Mrs. Mallard and her brood of eight ducklings** stretched out in a row behind her, all heading for the pond. Placed here in 1987, the bronze, larger-than-life statues represent the ducks made famous in Robert McCloskey's children's story *Make Way for Ducklings*. Every Mother's Day, the ducklings are feted on Duckling Day with a parade and festival. ◄ HIDDEN

Ever since opening in 1927, the Ritz-Carlton has catered to a select clientele. It was recently purchased and renamed **Taj**, but its splendor and elegance remain the same. The 17-story brick building overlooking the Public Garden, while not particularly striking on the outside, is the epitome of old elegance inside, where the lobby is graced with a large curving staircase and antique touches such as an exquisite brass railing. The original owner would never permit a reservation without researching the client's reputation in the Social Register or business directories. Many notable people have lived at the Ritz, including Charles Lindbergh and Winston Churchill. Many more have stayed here, among them Rodgers & Hammerstein, Albert Einstein, the Duke and Duchess of Windsor, Tennessee Williams and John F. Kennedy—even Lassie and Rin Tin Tin. ~ 15 Arlington Street; 617-536-5700, fax 617-536-1335; www.lhw.com/tajboston.

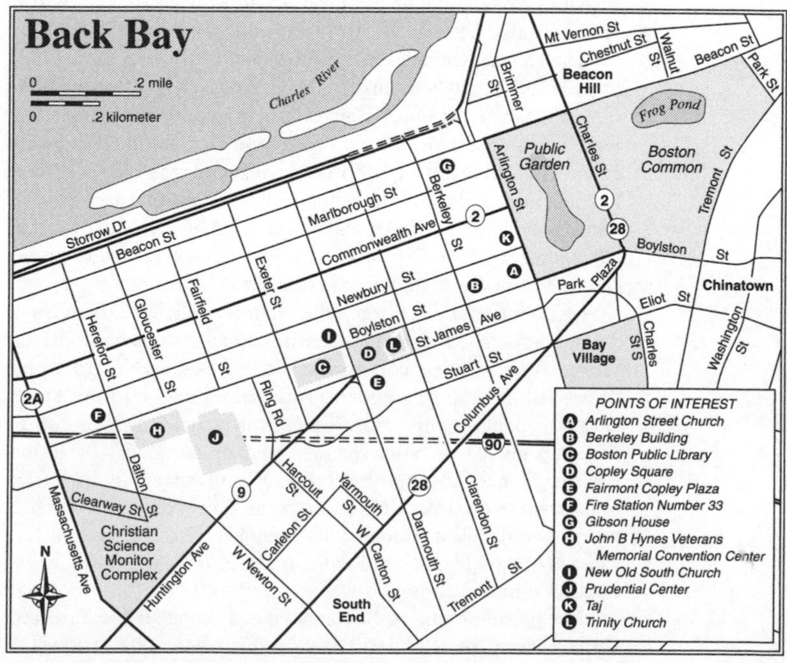

Down the street, the Georgian-style **Arlington Street Church** features a tall and graceful steeple fashioned in the style of Christopher Wren. ~ Arlington and Boylston streets.

The beaux-arts **Berkeley Building** looks like a wedding cake, so curlicued and beribboned is its frothy white bas-relief terracotta molding. Tiers of windows are trimmed in sea green, and a black marble entrance sign is flanked with dolphins and sea serpents. Built in 1905 and beautifully restored in 1988, it formerly housed Boston's design center. ~ 420 Boylston Street.

The **New Old South Church** is where the congregation of the Old South Meeting House moved in 1875, after they decided their Washington Street neighborhood had become too noisy to hear the sermon. The Gothic facade is dominated by a tower and carved stone rosettes. Inside the church are Venetian mosaics and 15th-century stained-glass windows depicting the Prophets, the Evangelists, the miracles and the parables. ~ Corner of Boylston and Dartmouth streets.

The Boston Library System is the oldest library system in the United States.

The heart of this area is gorgeous **Copley Square**, named for artist John Singleton Copley. Boston's religious and intellectual center at the end of the 19th century, the square is dominated by two architecturally imposing structures, Henry Hobson Richardson's Trinity Church and Charles McKim's Boston Public Library. ~ The square is on Boylston Street, located between Clarendon and Dartmouth streets.

The French-Romanesque, medieval-style **Trinity Church**, built in 1877, is visually stunning inside and out. One of Richardson's most brilliant creations, Trinity Church has an enormous tower reminiscent of the domes of Venice and Constantinople. Inside, rich colors and exquisite Moorish details cover the vaulted ceiling, rotunda and walls, and there are gorgeous John LaFarge frescoes and stained-glass windows. Public tours are available daily. ~ 206 Clarendon Street; 617-536-0944, fax 617-536-8916; www.trinitychurchboston.org, e-mail info@trinitychurchboston.org.

Much more than a library, the **Boston Public Library** in Coley Square houses art and architectural treasures. A wide marble staircase, Corinthian columns and frescoes grace its grand entrance hall (at the side door). Inside are murals by John Singer Sargent, paintings by John Singleton Copley, sculptures by Augustus and Louis Saint-Gaudens and bronze doors by Daniel Chester French. Inspired by Italian Renaissance palaces, it was opened in 1895. Take time to sit in the lovely central courtyard, where you'll find a fountain and benches. Art and architecture tours are available. ~ 700 Boylston Street; 617-536-5400; www.bpl.org, e-mail info@bpl.org.

The grande dame of Boston's vintage hotels is the **Fairmont Copley Plaza**, built in 1912 in high Victorian style. It boasts a wide stone facade, whose curving center echoes the bowfront homes of Back Bay and Beacon Hill. Inside, marble and crystal appointments set off an elegant lobby topped with a trompe l'oeil painting of the sky. The internationally known Fairmont Copley Plaza has served as a resting place for a nearly every president since Taft and European royalty. ~ 138 St. James Avenue; 617-267-5300, fax 617-267-7668; www.fairmont.com, e-mail boston@fairmont.com.

The **Skywalk Observatory** at the Prudential Tower gives you a bird's-eye view of downtown, this time a 360° one. Commonly called "the Pru," the Prudential Center was built in the early '60s as another piece of urban renewal. It houses shops and offices, and in front of it is a cast bronze statue called *Quest Eternal*, representing man reaching for the heavens. The tower is accessible for daylight or starlight viewing, from 10 a.m. to 10 p.m., or until 8 p.m. in winter. Admission. ~ 800 Boylston Street, Prudential Center; 617-859-0648, fax 617-859-0056.

The **Burrage House** was created in the 1920s in an 1899 mansion modeled after a Loire Valley château. Its medieval-looking exterior has sculptured stone cherubs and gargoyles looking down from its battlements. Inside the building you will find spectacular bas-relief mahogany walls, gold-leaf carved ceilings, stained-glass windows and an ornately carved marble staircase. ~ 314 Commonwealth Avenue.

Nowhere is the opulence of the Back Bay Victorians more amply evidenced than at the **Gibson House**, now a museum and location of the Victorian Society in America, New England chapter. Built for the prominent Gibson family in 1859, the Italian Renaissance Revival home retains its kitchen, scullery, formal dining and family quarters as well as the original Gibson family furniture and personal possessions. Tours are available Wednesday through Sunday. Admission. ~ 137 Beacon Street; 617-267-6338, fax 617-267-5121; www.gibsonmuseum.org, e-mail info@thegibsonhouse.org.

A major convention hall, the **John B. Hynes Veterans Memorial Convention Center** was extensively renovated and rebuilt in the late 1980s. Call for a schedule of the numerous conventions and expositions, including a college-fest weekend and a bridal expo. ~ 900 Boylston Street; 617-954-2000, fax 617-954-2299; www.mccahome.com, e-mail info@massconvention.com.

LODGING

The vintage 1927 Ritz-Carlton building, now called **Taj**, sparkles more than ever. A standard room is spacious and airy, with a high ceiling, brown floral drapes and spread and French provincial furnishings. On the walls are prints of antique engravings of Boston and Bunker Hill. The bathroom has polished white marble floors and antique fixtures. Besides an in-house health and fitness facility with massage, the 293-room hotel has three restaurants, an afternoon tea lounge and a bar. ~ 15 Arlington Street; 617-536-5700, 800-241-3333, fax 617-536-1335; www.lhw.com/tajboston. ULTRA-DELUXE.

The grande dame of Boston hotels is the **Fairmont Copley Plaza,** built in 1912. The hotel was famed for throwing such sumptuous affairs as an "Evening in Venice," with gondolas floating on the parquet floor, converted to the Grand Canal. Every president since Taft (except George W. Bush, but that could easily change) has visited, as well as royalty from eight countries. JFK was a regular visitor. The Fairmont Copley Plaza's elegant lobby is appointed with coffered gold ceilings adorned with a trompe l'oeil painting of the sky, marble columns and floors, crystal chandeliers and French provincial furniture. The hotel has two restaurants and two bars. The 383 guest rooms and suites are residential in style and feature rich fabrics and sumptuous decor. Bathrooms feature vintage marble and chrome fixtures. ~ 138 St. James Avenue; 617-267-5300, 800-441-1414, fax 617-437-0794; www.fairmont.com, e-mail boston@fairmont.com. ULTRA-DELUXE.

Built in 1891, the vintage stone **Copley Square Hotel,** completely renovated, draws lots of families and Europeans to its cozy, friendly 143 guest rooms. Though the rooms are on the smallish side, they're comfortably appointed with modern furniture and fabrics in blues, greens and mauves. ~ 47 Huntington Avenue; 617-536-9000, 800-225-7062, fax 617-267-3547; www.copleysquarehotel.com. ULTRA-DELUXE.

Real working fireplaces add to the numerous vintage charms of the **Lenox Hotel.** Opening at the turn of the 20th century, the 212-room Lenox was popular with such entertainers as Enrico Caruso, who pulled his private streetcar up to the door. The lobby wears its original Gilded Age elegance of soaring white columns, gold-leaf moldings, marble fireplace and handsome wood furniture. A typical room has a Colonial-style chandelier, a rocking chair, high ceilings and a Colonial ambience. The top floor, however, has been renovated in French Provincial decor. ~ 61 Exeter Street; 617-536-5300, 800-225-7676, fax 617-267-1237; www.lenoxhotel.com, e-mail info@lenoxhotel.com. ULTRA-DELUXE.

HIDDEN ►

One of the city's most charming hotels, the **Eliot Suite Hotel** was built in 1925 by the family of Charles Eliot, a Harvard president. The hotel has a warm, welcoming feeling. Its soft green-colored lobby is set with Queen Anne chairs, sofas and crystal wall sconces. Its 16 deluxe rooms and 79 suites are furnished with antique-style furniture and chintz fabric. ~ 370 Commonwealth Avenue; 617-267-1607, 800-443-5468, fax 617-536-9114; www.eliothotel.com, e-mail email@eliothotel.com. ULTRA-DELUXE.

The first independent luxury hotel built in Boston since the 1950s, the **Colonnade Hotel**, which opened in 1971, sparked the citywide hotel building boom a decade later. Recognized for its contemporary European atmosphere, The Colonnade has 285 rooms with classy mahogany and oak furnishings with copper or rose accents. The hotel has a restaurant as well as Boston's only rooftop pool. ~ 120 Huntington Avenue; 617-424-7000, 800-962-3030, fax 617-424-1717; www.colonnadehotel.com, e-mail reservations@colonnadehotel.com. ULTRA-DELUXE.

For less expensive lodging in Boston, rent a furnished apartment from **Comma Realty, Inc.** Units with kitchens, rented weekly, have twin beds and funky bathroom fixtures. ~ 371 Commonwealth Avenue; 617-437-9200; www.commarealty.com. MODERATE TO DELUXE.

DINING

For Southwest dining in the Northeast, check out **Cottonwood Restaurant and Cafe**. To start, consider the "snakebites" (fried jalapeños stuffed with shrimp and jack cheese, served with fresh cilantro mayonnaise) or the "cowboy pot stickers" (chicken dumplings paired with a four-chili sauce). Round two, there's steaks, seafood and Tex-Mex options, including enchiladas verdes and chicken breast stuffed with cilantro pesto and a goat cheese relleno. The award-winning margaritas are a fine way to wash down the award-winning cuisine. ~ 222 Berkeley Street; 617-247-2225; www.cottonwoodboston.com, e-mail info@cottonwoodboston.com. MODERATE TO DELUXE.

◀ HIDDEN

Off the beaten path of Newberry Street restaurants, **Café Jaffa** is a neighborhood haunt where those in the know frequently take friends and guests. This Middle Eastern eatery does a brisk business serving garlicky hummus plates, crispy falafels, lemony grape leaves and shawarmas. Portions are large enough to enjoy a second time around. ~ 48 Gloucester Street; 617-536-0230. BUDGET TO MODERATE.

A swank steakhouse with a dark and clubby atmosphere, **Grill 23** is a gathering spot for discerning carnivores. Prime, dry-

AUTHOR FAVORITE

If you're a fan of Indian curries but your dinner companion tends to be unadventurous, try the smallish **Bombay Café**. There will be enough spicier selections to satisfy you, and your pal will probably be pleased with the milder items, such as stuffed *naan* or chicken *tikka*. ~ 175 Massachusetts Avenue; 617-247-0555, fax 617-247-0434; www.bollywoodlex.com. BUDGET TO MODERATE.

aged beef is king here—there's slow-roasted beef tenderloin, prime sirloin, Kobe beef, prime rib and steak au poivre, among others. If you feel your blood's iron level is acceptable, try the Alaskan butterfish with vanilla and watermelon radish, or the à la carte organic chicken. Reservations are suggested. Dinner only. ~ 161 Berkeley Street; 617-542-2255, fax 617-542-5114; www.grill23.com. ULTRA-DELUXE.

Skipjack's Seafood Emporium boasts one of the biggest and most varied seafood menus in Boston—over two dozen kinds of fresh fish daily, ranging from tuna, trout and salmon to lesser-known moonfish and parrot fish. The decor is nautical, reminiscent of a ship's belly: glass block, wooden beamed ceilings, rich mahogany booths and changing exhibits by local artists. ~ 199 Clarendon Street; 617-536-3500, fax 617-969-6161; www.skipjacks.com, e-mail info@skipjacks.com. DELUXE TO ULTRA-DELUXE.

The first Boston Marathon took place in 1897 and had only 15 runners. The winner ran 24.5 miles in 2:55:10. Today, more than 20,000 participants aspire to break the current record: 2:07:14 for 26.2 miles.

The beautiful people dine at **Davio's Northern Italian Steak House**, a stylish Italian restaurant with primo service and real panache. It's a massive 9000-square-foot dining space with wall-to-wall windows, soaring ceilings and hardwood floors. Davio's offers superb creations such as grilled porterhouse veal chop with creamy Yukon potatoes and vintage port puccini sauce, and free-range chicken with sauteed spinich and whipped potatoes. No lunch on weekends. ~ 75 Arlington Street; 617-357-4810, fax 617-357-1997; www.davios.com. DELUXE TO ULTRA-DELUXE.

Sonsie is where you go to see and be seen. A nice perk is the food—here the elite meet to eat, and eat well. The menu has a bit of everything, from Italian pasta dishes to American staples. It features a wine room with over 200 choices, most of which are available by the glass. There's sidewalk dining in good weather, the better to drape yourself around Parisian-style café tables and look elegant. Brunch on Saturday and Sunday. ~ 327 Newbury Street; 617-351-2500, fax 617-351-2565; www.sonsieboston.com. DELUXE TO ULTRA-DELUXE.

SHOPPING

Back Bay is another of the city's densest shopping districts, concentrated on fashionable Newbury Street, lined from end to end with chic boutiques.

Shreve, Crump & Lowe, a Boston jeweler since 1796, has always been the place to go for fine gold and silver jewelry. Closed Sunday. ~ 440 Boylston Street; 617-267-9100; www.shrevecrumplowe.com.

Alan Bilzerian is a chic shop filled with classic-style and avant-garde clothing for men and women. The store carries designs by

Issei Miyake, Yohji Yamamoto and Ann Demeulemeester. Closed Sunday. ~ 34 Newbury Street; 617-536-1001, fax 617-236-4770; alanbilzerian.com.

Located in the neo-Gothic Church of the Covenant, **Gallery NAGA** showcases the work of New England painters (as well as the occasional photographer and sculptor), and some of the country's most highly regarded studio furniture makers. Closed Sunday and Monday. ~ 67 Newbury Street; 617-267-9060; www.gallerynaga.com.

Who would mind buying used men's and women's clothing when it's as fashionable and "gently worn" as that at **The Closet, Inc.** Only the latest clothes in the finest condition are accepted. ~ 175 Newbury Street, downstairs; 617-536-1919.

Founded in 1897, the **Society of Arts and Crafts** is the oldest nonprofit craft organization in the United States. It maintains two galleries where you can buy whimsical animal sculptures, ceramics, glass and furniture with real personality, as well as pottery and jewelry. ~ 175 Newbury Street, 617-266-1810, fax 617-266-5654; www.societyofcrafts.org, e-mail retailgallery@societyofcrafts.org.

London Lace specializes in reproduction Victorian lace patterns made on the only Victorian machinery left in Scotland. Items include lace curtain panels, table runners, tablecloths, antique furniture and accessories. Closed Sunday and Monday. ~ 89 West Concord Street; 617-267-3506, 800-926-5223, fax 617-267-0770; www.londonlace.com.

The shopping jewel of this area is brass- and marble-bedecked **Copley Place** on upper Huntington Avenue, resplendent with indoor waterfalls and trees. The Copley Place complex also includes the Westin and Marriott hotels, and the shopping mall is in-between the two, connected to both hotel lobbies. A glass pedestrian bridge carries shoppers over Huntington Avenue to the Prudential Center.

Opened in the mid-1980s, Copley Place holds 100 upscale stores, anchored by classy Dallas import **Neiman Marcus** (617-536-3660). Copley Place also houses outlets of **Polo** (617-266-4121), **Gucci** (617-247-3000), **Bally** (617-437-1910) and **Louis Vuitton** (617-437-6519). ~ Huntington Avenue and Dartmouth Street; 617-369-5000; www.shopcopleyplace.com.

The best place in the city to buy new rock CDs is **Newbury Comics**, where prices are typically lower than the giant chain stores. A selection of comic books and kitschy knickknacks round out the inventory. ~ 332 Newbury Street; 617-236-4930; www.newburycomics.com.

Copley Place's much older cousin is the **Prudential Center**, anchored by **Saks Fifth Avenue** (617-262-8500) and **Lord & Taylor** (617-262-6000). The Pru's stylish interior includes a network of glass-roofed pedestrian streets lined with shops. ~ 800 Boylston Street.

NIGHTLIFE The ornate **Oak Room** was built in 1912; you can still sidle up to its original brass-and-wood bar. Cabaret and jazz are performed Tuesday through Saturday. ~ 138 St. James Avenue, in the Fairmont Copley Plaza; 617-267-5300; www.fairmont.com.

Though a bit touristy, the Prudential Tower's **Top of The Hub** offers a breathtaking view of Boston's skyline (you are on the 52nd floor, after all). Enjoy a nightcap at the lounge, where cocktails and a full lounge menu are served up along with live nightly jazz. ~ 800 Boylston Street; 617-536-1775; www.prudentialcenter.com/dine/topofthehub.html.

Boston nightlife doesn't get more local than the **Pour House**, where an uproarious underground bar features blues and psychedelic music. ~ 907 Boylston Street; 617-236-1767; www.pourhouseboston.com.

Your search for the classy, plush, quiet cocktail lounges of old can end now. You've found **The Wine Room**, the downstairs lounge at Sonsie's restaurant. Sink into bordello-red chairs as you clink wine glasses. They have an impressive list of single-malt scotches and serve appetizers as well. Closed Sunday. ~ 327 Newbury Street; 617-351-2500, fax 617-351-2565; www.sonsieboston.com.

The **Lyric Stage Company of Boston**, Boston's oldest resident professional theater company, performs revivals and premieres. ~ 140 Clarendon Street, Copley Square; 617-585-5678; www.lyricstage.com.

Theater-goers and other performing-arts fans may purchase half-price, day-of-show tickets at **BosTix**. Shaped like an enormous webbed wooden mushroom, the booth also serves as a full-service box office and Ticketmaster outlet for performing-arts events in and around Boston. Half-priced tickets are cash only, first-come, first-served. Tickets go on sale at 10 a.m. ~ On the northwest corner of Copley Square.

The Fenway

The western side of Massachusetts Avenue edges over to the Fenway, the area surrounding the Back Bay Fens, another piece of the Emerald Necklace. Fens, from an Old English word meaning low wetlands or marshes, describes the area aptly. Along its sprawling length are several creeks and ponds, a rose garden and private garden plots, remnants of Boston's wartime "Victory Gardens."

SIGHTS No one thinks of the Fenway without **Fenway Park**, the home of the Boston Red Sox and the Green Monster, the famous left-field wall. Fenway Park remains one of the homiest and most old-fashioned ballparks in the country. Built in 1912, it is one of the few baseball parks with a playing surface of real grass. The Green Monster is there to protect the ballfield from the Massachusetts

Turnpike, and vice versa. ~ 4 Yawkey Way; 617-267-1700, fax 617-236-6640; www.redsox.com.

The campuses of two well-known Boston colleges are also in the Fenway—**Boston University**, along Commonwealth Avenue, and **Northeastern University**, south of Huntington Avenue.

Visible from Kenmore Square is the brightly lit, red-white-and-blue **Citgo Sign**, a gasoline advertisement and relic of the 1950s. It is the last of six similar signs in the United States.

Housed in a 15th-century-style Venetian palazzo, the **Isabella Stewart Gardner Museum** is a little jewel of a museum. It contains the personal collection of Mrs. Isabella Stewart Gardner, amassed over a lifetime of travel to Europe. "Mrs. Jack," as she came to be called, was considered somewhat eccentric and outrageous by proper Bostonians, and she collected what she liked. Her booty includes Italian Renaissance, 17th-century Dutch and 19th-century American paintings, as well as sculpture, textiles, furniture, ceramics, prints and drawings. The museum offers weekly chamber music concerts from September through May. Closed Monday. Admission. ~ 280 The Fenway; 617-566-1401, fax 617-232-8039; www.gardnermuseum.org, e-mail information@isgm.org.

The Boston University Bridge on Commonwealth Avenue is said to be the only place in the world where a boat can sail under a train traveling under a car driving under an airplane.

Not far from the Gardner Museum is the **Museum of Fine Arts**, world-famous for its exceptional collections of Asian, Greek, Roman, European, Egyptian and American art. The MFA also holds impressionist paintings and works by such American masters as John Singer Sargent, John Singleton Copley and Winslow Homer. The MFA regularly attracts mega-exhibitions, such as Gauguin and art deco works. Don't miss the Japanese gardens and the little first-floor café. Admission. ~ 465 Huntington Avenue; 617-267-9300, fax 617-236-0362; www.mfa.org, e-mail pr@mfa.org.

LODGING

◄ HIDDEN

The Buckminster, a friendly lodging house with 94 rooms, is an inexpensive alternative to the higher-priced inns and hotels in nearby Back Bay. The hotel is on six floors of a nice old building in the heart of the vibrant Kenmore Square area. Guest rooms and suites tend to be large; all are furnished with reproduction furniture. The Buckminster's prime attraction is its thoughtful convenience to travelers who are staying for more than one night—each floor has a kitchen and full laundry facilities. If only there were hotels like this in every city! ~ 645 Beacon Street; 617-236-7050, 800-727-2825, fax 617-262-0068; www.bostonhotel buckminister.com. MODERATE TO ULTRA-DELUXE.

The best deal for budget-minded travelers in Boston just has to be **Florence Frances'** 1840s brownstone, with four guest rooms that share baths. Florence has traveled around the world and decorated each room individually with an international flair. The Spanish Room, done in red, black and white, has a display of Spanish fans on the wall. The living and sitting rooms are beautifully furnished with antiques and a collection of Royal Doulton figurines. There is also a community kitchen. ~ 458 Park Drive; 617-267-2458. MODERATE.

Hostelling International—Boston represents the rock bottom of Boston accommodations in terms of price. Amenities are certainly not luxurious. Dormitory-style rooms hold six beds, with men and women kept separate, although coed rooms are available. There are also 11 private, air-conditioned rooms available. Non-AYH members can stay by paying a small extra charge for an introductory membership. The hostel can accommodate up to 205 people. There are laundry and kitchen facilities and a lounge with a piano, and internet access. ~ 12 Hemenway Street; 617-536-9455, 800-909-4776, fax 617-424-6558; www.bostonhostel.org, e-mail bostonhostel@bostonhostel.org. BUDGET TO MODERATE.

The **YMCA** welcomes both male and female guests during the summer; men only the rest of the year. Generously appointed, the YMCA has a wood-paneled lobby, an indoor pool, laundry facilities and cafeteria. Rooms are cell-like and furnished with Salvation Army–style furniture. ~ 316 Huntington Avenue; 617-536-7800, fax 617-267-4653; www.ymcaboston.org. MODERATE.

DINING

You'll halfway expect the girl from Ipanema to stroll into **Buteco**, so Brazilian and laidback is it. Framed photos of Brazil line its white walls, and tables are simply set with oilcloth covers and fresh yellow primroses. A standout is the *feijoada*—the Brazilian national dish, a stew of black beans with pork, sausage and dried beef, served with rice (available on weekends only). There is also a wide variety of chicken and vegetarian dishes. Also try the homemade soups and desserts. ~ 130 Jersey Street; 617-247-9508. BUDGET TO MODERATE.

Betty's Wok and Noodle Diner serves up fast, tasty meals at wallet-friendly prices. This retro eatery, with its space-age facade and sleek interior (red banquettes, black tables, neon lights) melds Asian and Latino flavors into dishes such as beef won tons with a Cuban citrus dip, fried plantains with tomatillo-lime sauce and pork ribs with a *sake-hoisin* glaze. Noodles are made to order with seven tasty sauces to choose from. ~ 250 Huntington Avenue; 617-424-1950, fax 617-638-3242; www.bettyswokandnoodle.com. BUDGET TO MODERATE.

SHOPPING

The music of '50s jazzmen, psychedelic '60s groups, and other performers of yesteryear rules at **Looney Tunes**, where you can buy used records on the cheap. ~ 1106 Boylston Street; 617-247-2238.

On the border of Brookline and Fenway sits the **Boston Book Annex**, a fine purveyor of used books. With over 100,000 volumes in stock, this funky little shop is the perfect place to while away an afternoon. ~ 906 Beacon Street; 617-266-1090.

NIGHTLIFE

Avalon, one of the city's largest danceclubs, plays progressive and Top-40 sounds for avid dancers, and hosts top names like Eric Clapton and Prince. Closed Monday through Thursday. Cover. ~ 15 Lansdowne Street; 617-262-2424; www.avalonboston.com, e-mail dave@avalonboston.com.

Next door, one of the trendiest danceclubs is **Axis**, featuring house and techno music. Monday is gay night, though a real mixed crowd turns out at both Axis and Avalon, especially on Friday, when the doors that separate the clubs are opened. Closed Sunday, Tuesday, Wednesday and Thursday. Cover. Gay-friendly. ~ 13 Lansdowne Street; 617-262-2437, fax 617-437-7147.

Upscale **Jake Ivory's** has dueling pianos playing rock from the '50s to the present. Closed Sunday through Wednesday. Cover. ~ 9 Lansdowne Street; 617-247-1222; www.jakeivorysboston.com.

Bill's Bar specializes in loud music of all kinds and live performances six nights a week. Featuring nationally famous and local

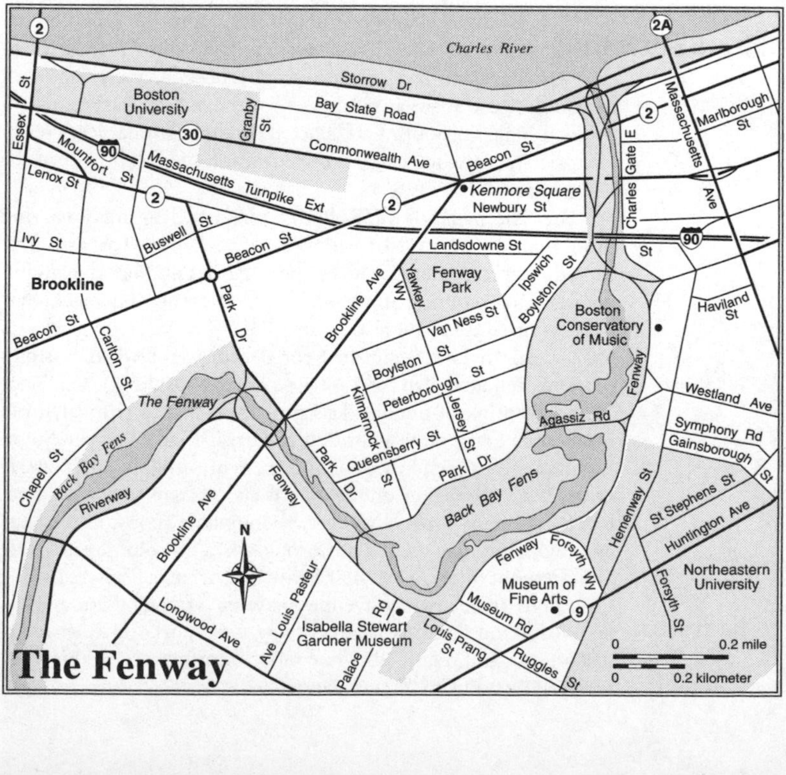

The Fenway

underground bands, this "Dirty Rock Club" is sure to be packed. Cover. ~ 5½ Lansdowne Street; 617-421-9678; www.billsbar.com.

A little farther out of the neighborhood is another club. **The Paradise** draws SRO crowds for its national headliners who perform live rock music and dance. Local bands also play here. Cover. ~ 967 Commonwealth Avenue; 617-562-8800.

CLASSICAL MUSIC & THEATER The prestigious **Boston Symphony Orchestra** presents more than 250 concerts annually. ~ 301 Massachusetts Avenue; 617-266-1492; www.bso.org.

The Symphony's **Boston Pops,** with the youthful Keith Lockhart as conductor, perform lighter favorites in spring and free outdoor summer concerts at the Hatch Shell on the Esplanade.

The **Handel and Haydn Society** is the country's oldest continuously active performing-arts group, started in 1815. They perform instrumental and choral music, including Handel's *Messiah* at Christmas. ~ 300 Massachusetts Avenue; 617-266-3605; www.handelandhaydn.org, e-mail info@handelandhaydn.org.

The **Huntington Theatre Company,** Boston University's resident company, specializes in classics, comedies and musicals. There are no summer performances. ~ 264 Huntington Avenue; 617-266-7900; www.huntingtontheatre.org

The South End

Boston's largest neighborhood is also the least known. Like the Back Bay, it was built on filled land, preceding Back Bay by more than a decade. Victorian brick rowhouses rose apace as residences for the middle class and well-to-do. Today, the South End is listed on the National Register of Historic Places as the largest concentration of such houses in the United States.

After the panic of 1873, banks foreclosed on the area, and those who could afford to moved to Back Bay. The area was carved up into rooming houses and factories and became an immigrant ghetto of more than 40 nationalities, notably black, Syrian, Latino and Lebanese.

The South End languished for decades, but when Boston's economy rebounded in the 1960s, so did this neighborhood. Since 1965, an influx of middle-class professionals has renovated old rowhouses and partly gentrified the area. Not all of the South End has risen again, however, and there are still blighted, unsafe areas. But today the neighborhood is a vital center of creative activity, and many artists live here. Fashionable shops, restaurants and nightclubs line the main thoroughfares of Columbus Avenue and Tremont Street, as well as Shawmut Avenue. The area along Columbus and Shawmut avenues between Massachusetts Avenue and Arlington Street is a largely gay neighborhood with many restaurants and nightclubs. For more information on this area, see the "Boston Gay Scene" below.

SIGHTS

The South End is a largely Victorian neighborhood that covers one square mile, bounded roughly by the Massachusetts Turnpike, the Southwest Corridor, Albany Street and Northampton Street. Although the South End is a massive area to explore on foot, an annual house tour is given in October by the **South End Historical Society.** Call ahead. Admission. ~ 532 Massachusetts Avenue; 617-536-4445, fax 617-536-0735; www.southendhistoricalsociety.org, e-mail admin@southendhistoricalsociety.org.

At the corner of Huntington Avenue and Massachusetts Avenue is the famous **Symphony Hall.** Designed in 1900, it's so acoustically perfect it's known worldwide as a "Stradivarius among halls." The Boston Symphony Orchestra celebrated its 100th anniversary here in 1981. Tours take place Wednesday and the first Saturday of the month from October through May. ~ 301 Massachusetts Avenue; 617-266-1492, 888-266-1200, fax 617-638-9436; www.bso.org.

Prolific television producer David E. Kelley (Mr. Michelle Pfeiffer) grew up in the Boston area and set three of his series here: *Ally McBeal, The Practice* and *Boston Public.*

The **First Church of Christ, Scientist** is the world headquarters of Christian Science, founded in 1879 by Mary Baker Eddy. The mother church is topped by an imposing dome and set in a brick pedestrian plaza with a reflecting pool designed by I. M. Pei. Take a walk through the echoing **Mapparium** in the Christian Science Monitor building, a unique 30-foot stained-glass globe with a footbridge through it, for a peek at how the world looked in 1935. Church services are open to the public Wednesday and Sunday. ~ 175 Huntington Avenue; 617-450-2000, 800-288-7155, fax 617-450-3554; www.tfccs.com.

The **Boston Center for the Arts** operates the Cyclorama, the center of South End arts activity. Built in 1884 to exhibit a huge cylindrical painting, *The Battle of Gettysburg* (now in Pennsylvania), it's also where Albert Champion developed the spark plug. Its large rotunda hosts art exhibits, plays, festivals and an annual antique show. ~ 539 Tremont Street; 617-426-5000, fax 617-426-5336; www.bcaonline.org, e-mail info@bcaonline.org.

Also part of the Boston Center for the Arts is the **Mills Gallery,** which specializes in exhibits by Boston artists. These might include mixed media, sculpture and paintings, and are always intriguing. Closed Monday and Tuesday. ~ 549 Tremont Street; 617-426-8835, fax 617-426-5336; www.bcaonline.org.

◄ HIDDEN

Once second in size only to the U.S. Capitol, the building that formerly housed the **Piano Craft Guild Apartments,** now a craft guild, has been a Boston landmark since 1853. The pianos made here until 1929 were played not only in Victorian drawing rooms but in the concert halls of Europe and South America. Founder Jonas Chickering was said to be just like his pianos: "upright, grand and square." The building now serves as living, work and exhibition space for artists, musicians and professionals. ~ 791 Tremont Street; 617-536-2622, fax 617-859-7794.

LODGING

The **Berkeley Residence/YWCA** offers the most basic of accommodations near to Copley Square and the subway system, the T. Rooms have twin beds, and bathrooms are down the hall. There are laundry facilities, a lovely garden and a cafeteria. Full breakfast is included ~ 40 Berkeley Street; 617-375-2524, fax 617-375-2525; www.ywcaboston.org, e-mail rooms_berkeley@ywcaboston.org. MODERATE.

DINING

Ever since yuppies began moving into the South End in the 1970s and 1980s, restaurants have been springing up left and right, from small inexpensive cafés to upscale eateries.

A popular, upscale eatery, **Icarus Restaurant** serves up contemporary American cuisine. There's a great bar to wet your palate, and appetizers to whet your appetite. Start with the parsnip soup or polenta with braised exotic mushrooms. The seasonal fare includes braised rabbit with porcini, leeks and red wine, pepper-crusted venison steak with pomegranate sauce, and halibut filet with stuffed lobster tail. Dinner only. ~ 3 Appleton Street; 617-426-1790; www.icarusrestaurant.com, e-mail greatfood@icarusrestaurant.com. ULTRA-DELUXE.

HIDDEN ►

Tourists will feel like a local insider at the **Franklin Cafe**, a warm, sophisticated eatery in the South End. The hearty, New American menu may include polenta-crusted swordfish with carrot risotto, grilled sirloin with chive mashed potatoes and turkey meatloaf with fig sauce. The appetizers work well for a midnight snack (the café serves food until 1:30 a.m.). Come early or late—just nine tables, a small bar area and a no-reservations policy make the wait here ridiculously long during peak dinner hours (7 to 10 p.m.). Dinner only. ~ 278 Shawmut Avenue; 617-350-0010, fax 617-350-5115. MODERATE.

HIDDEN ►

Don't look for silverware at **Addis Red Sea Ethiopian Restaurant**. A very African decor features authentic basketweave straw tables in a bright geometric pattern, low, carved wooden chairs, and paintings of African villagers; this was the nation's first authentic Ethiopian restaurant. Platters of food cover the entire table surface. Ethiopian *injera* bread is served with chicken, lamb, beef and vegetarian dishes. The chef uses all-natural herbs and spices. No lunch Monday through Friday. ~ 544 Tremont Street; 617-426-8727; www.addisredsea.com. BUDGET TO MODERATE.

The heavenly scent of freshly baked pastries, breads, cakes and pies are the draw at **Garden of Eden**. This bakery/café was voted the Best of Boston neighborhood sandwich shop, serving

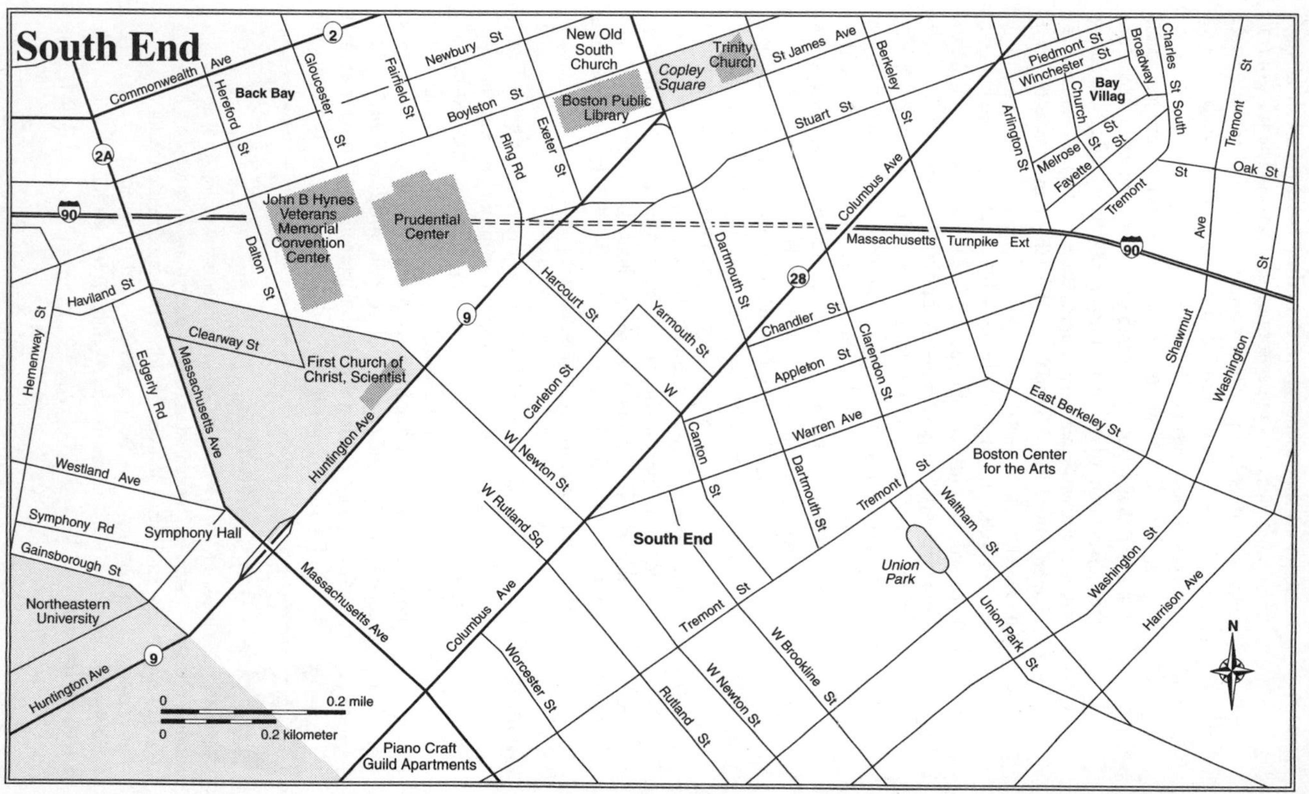
South End
Commonwealth Ave
Back Bay
Hereford St
Gloucester St
Fairfield St
Newbury St
Boylston St
Ring Rd
Exeter St
New Old South Church
Boston Public Library
Copley Square
Trinity Church
St James Ave
Berkeley St
Stuart St
Arlington St
Piedmont St
Winchester St
Church St
Bay Villag
Melrose St
Fayette St
Broadway
Charles St South
Tremont St
Oak St
Tremont St
Ave
St
Shawmut
Washington
Massachusetts Turnpike Ext
Columbus Ave
Dartmouth St
Clarendon St
Chandler St
Appleton St
Warren Ave
East Berkeley St
Boston Center for the Arts
Tremont St
Waltham St
Union Park
Union Park St
Washington St
Harrison Ave
N
W Brookline St
W Newton St
Rutland St
Tremont St
Canton St
South End
Yarmouth St
W
Harcourt St
Carleton St
W Newton St
W Rutland Sq
Worcester St
Columbus Ave
John B Hynes Veterans Memorial Convention Center
Prudential Center
Dalton St
First Church of Christ, Scientist
Huntington Ave
Massachusetts Ave
Clearway St
Haviland St
Hemenway St
Edgerly Rd
Westland Ave
Symphony Rd
Symphony Hall
Gainsborough St
Northeastern University
Huntington Ave
Massachusetts Ave
0
0.2 mile
0
0.2 kilometer
Piano Craft Guild Apartments
2
2A
9
28
90

scrumptious sandwiches (including the "Garden Of Eden" vegetarian sandwich) on copper-topped café tables. The full gourmet market proffers unique cheeses and pâté. ~ 571 Tremont Street; 617-247-8377, fax 617-247-8493; www.goeboston.com, e-mail gardenofedencafe@aol.com. MODERATE.

Decorated in Christmas kitsch, Elvis busts and retro paraphernalia, the **Delux Cafe & Lounge** features a cheap, eclectic and tasty assortment of pub grub until 11:30 every night. The changing menu always features staples such as fish or sandwiches. Dinner only. Closed Sunday. ~ 100 Chandler Street; 617-338-5258. BUDGET TO MODERATE.

One of the South End's favorite breakfast and lunch hangouts is **Charlie's Sandwich Shoppe**. The walls are lined with photographs of satisfied patrons—local politicians, famous actors and jazz greats of decades past. Open early in the morning, it's a delightful place for homebaked muffins, pancakes, sandwiches, burgers and conviviality, since you'll be sharing a table. No dinner. Closed Sunday. ~ 429 Columbus Avenue; 617-536-7669; e-mail charlies@tiac.net. BUDGET TO MODERATE.

The charming **Columbus Cafe** is a cozy neighborhood establishment featuring outstanding fare blending South American and Mediterranean cuisine. Entrées might include grilled marinated lamb chop with Tunisian coriander eggplant purée and braised cod with kalamata olives. Columbus Cafe is also famous for its weekend brunch. The lounge here serves light, late-night fare. Brunch Sunday. ~ 535 Columbus Avenue; 617-247-9001; www.columbuscafeboston.com. MODERATE TO DELUXE.

SHOPPING

You can find things to decorate your nest with at **Fresh Eggs**, a home-furnishings store that carries furniture and kitchen appliances. In addition it proffers high-end gifts handcrafted by local artists. Mexican church candles, astro resin frames, aluminum bottle stoppers, unique bath accessories and much more are sold here. Closed Monday. ~ 58 Clarendon Street; 617-247-8150.

You're sure to find a deliciously aromatic souvenir at **Aunt Sadie's Candles**. Don't let the old-fashioned name fool you—hip

ADMIT ONE ADMIT ONE

AUTHOR FAVORITE

Founded in 1947, **Wally's Café** has been showcasing local and national artists for decades. The crowded joint is everything an old-time jazz club should be—small, dark and host to lots of talented musicians, including plenty of students from the Berklee School of Music, which is just a few blocks away. ~ 427 Massachusetts Avenue; 617-424-1408; www.wallyscafe.com.

candles in seasonal scents (lilac, apple pie, fresh-cut grass) each come in a stylish glass votive painted with flowers, animals or retro patterns. You'll also find bath products, lotions, mugs and bags. ~ 18 Union Park Street; 617-357-7117; www.auntsadies inc.com.

NIGHTLIFE

At the **Delux Cafe & Lounge** the cool crowd consists of rockers and artists, both gay and straight. The decor is funky, the drinks are cheap and the music ranges from Frank Sinatra to the Sex Pistols. Closed Sunday. ~ 100 Chandler Street; 617-338-5258.

Boston Gay Scene

Boston's gay community is continually growing, and its collection of gay spots is always expanding. While gay activities and nightlife are found throughout Boston (like Back Bay and the Fenway), the highest concentration is found in the South End, one of the city's most diverse neighborhoods. Bounded by Columbus and Shawmut avenues, Arlington Street and Massachusetts Avenue, this area is home to an array of gay restaurants, cafés, bars and nightclubs.

SIGHTS

At the very northeast corner of the South End lies **Bay Village**, which used to be known as South Cove. This cluster of narrow little streets displays the most charmingly antique character in the area. Gaslights stand on the sidewalks outside these Victorian rowhouses decorated with black shutters and windowboxes, black iron grilled doorways and hidden, sunken gardens in backyards. ~ Bordered by Arlington, Tremont and Stuart streets and Charles Street South.

LODGING

Greater Boston Hospitality is a reservation service with dozens of bed-and-breakfast listings. It can help you find the perfect lodging in Boston, many of which are located in Back Bay, South End, Charlestown, Beacon Hill and Cambridge. Gay-friendly. ~ P.O. Box 525, Newton Branch, MA 02456; 617-393-1548, fax 617-277-7170; www.bostonbedandbreakfast.com, e-mail info@bostonbedandbreakfast.com. BUDGET TO DELUXE.

A pretty streetside patio and stately brownstone facade greet guests of the **Newbury Guest House**. Besides its superb location on fashionable Newbury Street in the Back Bay, the restored 1882 inn offers 32 guest rooms with pine plank floors, high ceilings and reproduction Victorian furnishings. Some have bay windows, and all have private baths, televisions and telephones—rarities in a small inn. Full breakfast included. ~ 261 Newbury Street; 617-437-7666, 800-437-7668, fax 617-670-6100; www.newburyguesthouse.com, e-mail newbury@hagopianhotels.com. DELUXE TO ULTRA-DELUXE.

Text continued on page 238.

Boston Area Bookstores

Boston is a book lover's delight, brimming with bookstores full of quirky personality, charm and the imprint of history. These shops display a colorful individual stamp, with secondhand shelving, hand-lettered signs and perhaps a beat-up leather chair or two or a resident dog.

Rare and fine books are the specialty at **Peter L. Stern & Company** (55 Temple Place; 617-542-2376) and the **Lame Duck Books** (12 Arrow Street, Cambridge; 617-407-6271). Here you can get first editions, 19th- and 20th-century literature and private-press books. Peter L. Stern is closed Sunday.

The **Brattle Book Shop** claims the title of being the successor to America's oldest continuous antiquarian bookshop, dating from the 19th century. Used books sit on battered gray steel shelving and range from fiction, humor and poetry to history, genealogy and heraldry. Old *Life* magazines dating to 1936 march up the stairway and through history, covered with the faces of Marilyn Monroe, John Kennedy, and Ted Williams. Closed Sunday. ~ 9 West Street; 617-542-0210, 800-447-9595, fax 617-338-1467; www.brattlebookshop.com, e-mail info@brattle bookshop.com.

Good food and good books go hand in hand, and never more so than at **Trident Booksellers & Café**. Trident claims the prize for being funky: the province of young hipsters dressed in black, a plethora of Third World, gay and alternative publications, and a recently expanded menu featuring homemade soups and sandwiches tailored to a struggling writer's budget. It also sells incense and myrrh, self-improvement videos and campy black-and-white postcards. ~ 338 Newbury Street; 617-267-8688, fax 617-247-1934; www.tridentbookscafe.com, e-mail trident@tridentbookscafe.com.

An astonishing 25 bookshops surround Harvard Square. Established in 1856, **Schoenhof's Foreign Books, Inc.** is America's oldest comprehensive foreign-language bookstore. It carries reference books in over 700 languages and dialects, among them Swahili, Urdu, Tibetan, Navajo and classical Greek and Latin, whatever you need to complete a master's or Ph.D. Still, the shop is not too pedantic to sell children's favorites like *Le Petit Prince*, *Babar* and even *Harry Potter* in over 40 languages. Closed

Sunday. ~ 76-A Mt. Auburn Street, Cambridge; 617-547-8855; www.schoenhofs.com, e-mail info@schoenhofs.com.

Where else but Cambridge could a poetry-only bookshop survive? The **Grolier Poetry Book Shop Inc.**, founded in 1927, is America's oldest continuously operating poetry bookshop, carrying more than 15,000 titles from all periods and cultures. Supported by friends of Conrad Aiken, who lived next door in 1929, the shop grew into a meeting place for such poets as Ezra Pound, Marianne Moore and T. S. Eliot. The shop sponsors an annual poetry prize and a reading series of unpublished poets each semester. Closed Sunday and Monday. ~ 6 Plympton Street, Cambridge; 617-547-4648, 800-234-7636; www.grolierpoetrybookshop.com, e-mail grolierpoetrybookshop@compuserve.com.

Many Harvard Square bookshops specialize in rare and out-of-print books. Among them is **James & Devon Gray Booksellers**, featuring rare books—in any language or on any subject—published before 1700. Among the obscure and hard-to-find volumes are a first edition of Edmund Spenser's *The Faerie Queene* and manuscripts by John Dryden. Closed Sunday and Monday. ~ 12 Arrow Street, Cambridge; 617-868-0752; www.graybooksellers.com, e-mail info@graybooksellers.com.

Seven Stars breathes New Age culture. Besides such titles as *Everyday Zen*, *The Biggest Secret* and *Passport to the Cosmos*, the shop sells tarot cards, incense and gorgeous chunks of amethyst and other crystals, which some believe have healing powers. ~ 731 Massachusetts Avenue, Cambridge; 617-547-1317.

A couple of miles out from Harvard Square, **Kate's Mystery Books** is a mecca for mystery lovers and writers. Opening on Friday the 13th in 1983, the store has a black cat logo and walls lined with several hundred black cat figurines. About 10,000 new and used titles range from Dashiell Hammett and Agatha Christie to Tony Hillerman and Robert Parker. A special section focuses on mysteries set in New England. Mystery Writers of America, New England Chapter, meets here, as does the local chapter of Sisters in Crime. Kate's hosts author readings and signings at least once a week. Closed Monday and Tuesday. ~ 2211 Massachusetts Avenue, Cambridge; 617-491-2660; www.katesmysterybooks.com, e-mail katesmysbks@earthlink.net.

This is just a sampling of Boston's bookstores, large and small. In this area of scholars and writers, there's a bookstore for everyone, with almost 300 listed in the Yellow Pages. That's almost one for every 2000 inhabitants.

Popular with gay visitors, **463 Beacon Street Guest House** also draws a mixed clientele. Twenty rooms, all equipped with a microwave and refrigerator, make this turn-of-the-20th-century brownstone an excellent value. The five-story walk-up also offers short-term lodging in Back Bay, business services and a laundry. ~ 463 Beacon Street; 617-536-1302, fax 617-247-8876; www.463beacon.com, e-mail info@463beacon.com. MODERATE TO DELUXE.

The circa-1860 **Oasis Guest House** caters to a gay crowd but all are welcome. Some of its 30 rooms feature antiques and queen-sized beds. Located on a quiet street in the Back Bay, the inn serves continental breakfast in the living room. ~ 22 Edgerly Road; 617-267-2262, 800-230-0105, fax 617-267-1920; www.oasisgh.com, e-mail info@oasisgh.com. MODERATE.

The **Chandler Inn** offers 56 clean, decently appointed rooms in blues and greens and oak furniture, with all the basic amenities. The bar is a popular gay hangout in the South End. ~ 26 Chandler Street; 617-482-3450, 800-842-3450, fax 617-542-3428; www.chandlerinn.com, e-mail inn3450@ix.netcom.com. MODERATE TO DELUXE.

Christmas wasn't a legal holiday in Massachusetts until 1856. Residents made up for lost time, however, by implementing the tradition of sending holiday cards.

Also in the South End is the **Clarendon Square Bed & Breakfast**, a well-run, friendly B&B. Housed in a six-story building dating to the 1860s, the three open and airy rooms are eclectic and individually decorated. Most have working fireplaces, and bathrooms offer limestone floors, French fixtures and two-person showers or whirlpool tubs. A rooftop sundeck complete with hot tub is a great place to unwind and contemplate Boston's skyline. ~ 198 West Brookline Street; 617-536-2229; www.clarendonsquare.com. ULTRA-DELUXE.

DINING

The South End has no shortage of places to eat, but one standout is **Don Ricardo's Restaurant**, which serves authentic South American cuisine. Traditional favorites—empanadas, churrasco and paella—are available alongside lesser-known dishes such as *albondigas rellenas* (ground beef with olives and eggs), *moqueca de peixe e camarão* (fish and shrimp cooked in coconut milk) and *seco de cordero* (lamb in a beer-cilantro sauce). ~ 57 West Dedham Street; phone/fax 617-247-9249; www.donricardorestaurant.com. MODERATE.

A local favorite for fresh, tasty food is the always-crowded **Jae's Café and Grill**. The health-conscious menu travels the Far East with selections from Korea, Japan and Thailand. Try the *kalbi* (marinated barbecued beef spareribs), crispy *pad thai* noodles or a sampling of tidbits from the downstairs sushi bar. Closed Sunday and Monday. ~ 520 Columbus Avenue; 617-421-9405, fax 617-247-6140; www.jaescafe.com. MODERATE.

Gays and straights alike head over to **224 Boston Street** to nosh on sandwiches, pasta, pizzettas and salads in a lively setting. Entrées at this gay-owned restaurant are traditionally eclectic urban cuisine and change quarterly. Offerings include a wide variety of seafood, meat and poultry dishes as well as pasta. Dinner only. ~ 224 Boston Street, Dorchester; 617-265-1217, fax 617-825-4738. MODERATE TO DELUXE.

SHOPPING

Located inside the gay club indelicately named Ramrod, **THE-PX** is your friendly neighborhood leather store. Here you'll find leather pants, vests and chaps, as well as latex and vinyl gear, and some body toys we'll leave to your imagination. Open 10 p.m. to 2 a.m., Thursday through Sunday. ~ 1256 Boylston Street; 508-345-3621; www.the-px.com.

NIGHTLIFE

Spot the carved eagle above the doorway, and you know you've arrived at the **Boston Eagle**. Although a bit divey, the Eagle is a typical chat-and-cruise bar that attracts mostly 30-somethings. There's a pool table, a pinball machine and a friendly atmosphere. ~ 520 Tremont Street; 617-542-4494.

For deejay-generated disco music in the theater district, gays head to **Chaps**. Women are also welcome at this high-energy club, which includes a separate lounge off the throbbing dancefloor. Closed Monday and Tuesday. Cover. ~ 100 Warrenton Street; 617-695-9500.

The leather and Levi's crowd likes to cruise down to **The Boston Ramrod** in the Fenway. There's a special two-stepping night at this gay-only bar that also offers pool. If leather is not your scene, you can go dancing at the **Machine** (cover on weekends), which attracts all types. Cover Sunday. ~ 1254 Boylston Street; 617-266-2986, fax 617-536-1950; www.ramrodboston.com.

Club Café, an avant-garde social complex, attracts a primarily gay and lesbian crowd with its art deco style and amusing diversions. Down a few drinks in the video bar (located in the back) and catch live blues or oldies (and occasional cabaret acts) in the lounge from Thursday to Saturday. ~ 209 Columbus Avenue; 617-536-0966; www.clubcafe.com, e-mail clubcafe@aol.com.

Fritz, in the Chandler Inn, is a casual gay sports bar that's usually crowded with regulars. ~ 26 Chandler Street; 617-482-4428.

Jacque's Cabaret has something for everyone, as long as you enjoy female impersonators mixed with your live rock. The clientele is diverse—gay, straight and lesbian couples and groups of gawkers. Cover. ~ 79 Broadway, Bay Village; 617-426-8902; www.jacquescabaret.com.

South Boston

Not to be confused with the South End, South Boston lies directly east of it. Despite its name, South Boston juts farther east into the Atlantic than any other point in the city, cut off from Boston by the Southeast Expressway and the Fort Point Channel. Everyone here calls it "Southie," especially the Irish who call it home.

The Irish poured into South Boston in the early 19th century, attracted by the work opportunities of the glass, iron and shipping industries. They stayed, and today this is the most predominantly Irish community in Boston, evidenced by the riotous St. Patrick's Day parade. The Irish are fiercely proud of their L Street Brownies, a local swim club that has won national publicity for swimming every day, even in January.

Though South Boston has historically been a conservative, family-oriented neighborhood, there has been a recent influx of young, single professionals to the area. Close to downtown with reasonably priced housing, this migration trend is sure to continue.

SIGHTS

Ideally positioned for shipping, the peninsula is lined with commercial fishing and shipping piers. The **Fish Pier**, near the World Trade Center and Jimmy's Harborside on Northern Avenue, is a lively scene at dawn, when the fishing boats return to port to unload their catch. The fresh catch is sold at a lively auction right off the boats to retailers.

The **Institute of Contemporary Art** has won an international reputation for its wide-ranging artistic events, held here for more than half a century. Housed in an old Boston police station, the ICA often shows experimental or controversial works, among them art exhibits, films, videos, music events, lectures and literary readings. Closed Monday and between exhibitions. Admission. ~ 100 Northern Avenue; 617-478-3100, fax 617-266-4021; www.icaboston.org, e-mail info@icaboston.org.

Three bridges link South Boston with downtown: the Summer Street Bridge, the Northern Avenue Bridge and the Congress Street Bridge, with its Chinese lantern–style, wrought-iron lamps.

When you cross the Congress Street Bridge, you may not quite believe your eyes, but the first thing you'll see is a giant milk bottle. The 30-foot **Hood Milk Bottle** was a vintage lunch stand from the 1930s and sells snacks again today.

The Hood Milk Bottle signals the beginning of Museum Wharf, a mini-park of several museums. The **Children's Museum** is housed in a brick building, a former wool warehouse whose large windows and wool bays lend themselves nicely to exhibit spaces. You don't have to be a kid to enjoy this gigantic toy box filled with four floors of hands-on fun where you can make giant bubbles, scramble up a rock-climbing wall or participate in a play production at the interactive theater. There's also a real Japanese house and a two-story maze. Admission. Closed for renovations until spring of 2007. ~ 300 Congress Street; 617-426-8855, fax 617-426-1944; www.bostonkids.org, e-mail info@bostonkids.org.

Nearby is the **Boston Tea Party Ship & Museum**, a floating museum where you can board a two-masted brig and throw your own chest of tea into the harbor (it'll be retrieved by an attached rope for another visitor to heave). Displays are lively and informative, explaining the events surrounding the 1773 dumping of 342 chests of tea overboard, a tax protest that was one of many spurs to the American Revolution. Closed January and February. Due to fire damage, the ship is closed until spring 2008. Admission. ~ Congress Street Bridge; 617-338-1773, fax 617-338-1974; www.bostonteapartyship.com.

A spanking white building with a flag-lined boulevard, the **Seaport World Trade Center** replaced the drab old Commonwealth Exhibition Hall in the 1980s. It hosts many of Boston's biggest trade shows. ~ 200 Seaport Boulevard; 617-385-5000, fax 617-385-5090; www.wtcb.com, e-mail info@wtcb.com.

Four kinds of granite decorate the exterior of the **Boston Design Center**, New England's major design center. Architects and designers come here from miles away to search out the latest and chicest in interior designs. Outside the building stands an imposing cast of Auguste Rodin's sculpture *Cybèle*. Closed weekends.

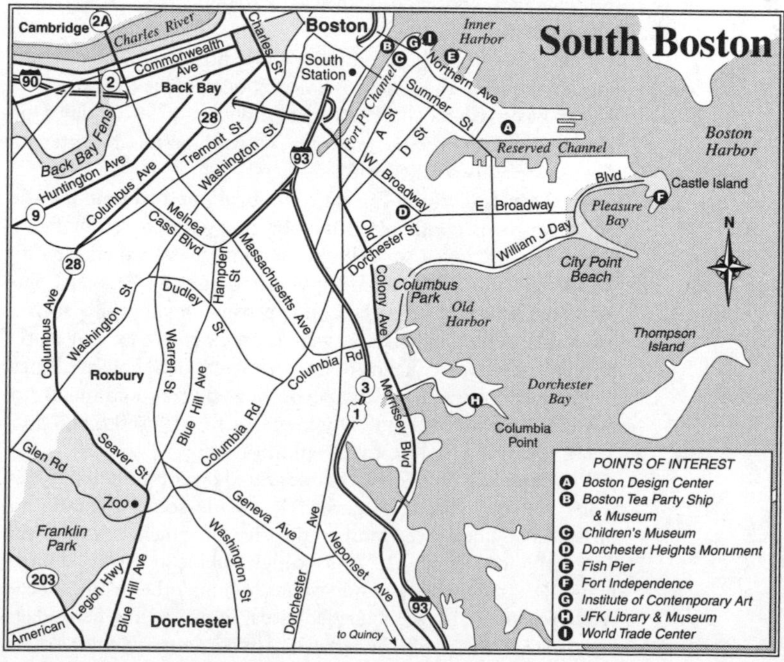

~ 1 Design Center Place; 617-338-5062, fax 617-482-8449; www.bostondesign.com.

The work of painters, photographers, sculptors and others is on view at the **Fort Point Arts Community Gallery**. Gallery showings are free and open to the public. Call for showings and times. Closed Sunday. ~ 300 Summer Street; 617-423-4299; www.fortpointarts.org, e-mail gallery@fortpointarts.org.

Dorchester Heights Monument is where George Washington set up his guns and forced the British to evacuate Boston in 1776, never to return. The British were astounded to see these guns, which had been dragged 300 miles by oxen from Fort Ticonderoga. A 115-foot marble tower marks the spot. The monument is open from mid-April to the end of September. Tours of the monument are conducted from the visitors center. ~ 15 State Street; 617-242-5675, fax 617-242-6006.

More artists live in the old high-ceilinged, industrial buildings of the Fort Point Channel area than anywhere else in the city.

Out at the very tip of South Boston, **Castle Island** is a windswept place of green lawns and high granite ramparts, a fine spot for picnicking and exploring. A series of eight forts has stood here since 1634, making it the oldest continuously fortified site in North America. The island was held by the British during the Revolution until Washington forced them out from his vantage point at Dorchester Heights. The current fort, the star-shaped **Fort Independence**, was built in 1851. ~ End of Day Boulevard.

On a peninsula just south of South Boston lies **Dorchester**, once the home of the country's oldest chocolate manufacturer, the Walter Baker Chocolate Factory, founded in 1780. Today Dorchester is a quiet, residential area known for its characteristic three-story houses called triple deckers.

Don't miss the **John F. Kennedy Library and Museum**, a stirring place to visit both inside and out. In a parklike setting by the ocean that JFK loved so well, the striking, glass-walled building was designed by I. M. Pei. The museum houses JFK's papers, photographs, letters and speeches, and personal memorabilia such as his desk and rocking chair, as well as an extensive exhibit on the former first lady, Jacqueline Kennedy. Also housed here are Ernest Hemingway's papers, which may be viewed by appointment. Admission. ~ Columbia Point, Dorchester; 617-514-1600, 866-535-1960, fax 617-514-1593; www.jfklibrary.org.

The **Franklin Park Zoo** was once rated one of the country's ten worst zoos by *Parade* magazine. It's made some dramatic improvements since then, most impressive of which is an African Tropical Forest. Inside the 75-foot-high bubble live tropical birds, mandrils, a pygmy hippo and gorillas, among other tropical denizens. You may also see amur leopards, lions and the Serenghetti Crossing exhibit, as well as a seasonal exotic butterfly tent. Admission. ~ 1 Franklin Park Road, Boston; 617-541-5466, fax 617-989-2025; www.zoonewengland.org.

DINING

As you walk east on Northern Avenue, it becomes the Fish Pier, a crowded place of fish-processing plants and wharves. Not surprisingly, the Fish Pier is home to a spate of seafood restaurants, some of them among the city's finest.

Located right here on the Fish Pier, two of Boston's most famous restaurants, Jimmy's Harborside and Anthony's Pier 4, have waged a decades-long battle for supremacy in harborside seafood dining. Both eateries offer a long list of fresh fish, from Boston scrod to steamed, boiled or baked lobster, as well as floor-to-ceiling windows with smashing views of Boston Harbor.

Albanian immigrant Anthony Athanas started life in Boston as a shoeshine boy and built the reputation of his **Anthony's Pier 4** with backbreaking work. The smiling Anthony has posed with Liz Taylor, Red Skelton, Gregory Peck and Richard Nixon, whose photos gaze down from the walls. Despite its fame, Anthony's has its detractors, who say the seafood doesn't live up to its reputation, although Anthony's owns its own lobster company. Still, Anthony's has the largest wine list in Boston, and there is outdoor seaside dining on yellow-awninged terraces. ~ 140 Northern Avenue; 617-482-6262, fax 617-426-2324; www.pier4.com, e-mail pier4@pier4.com. MODERATE TO ULTRA-DELUXE.

◄ HIDDEN

Largely undiscovered, **Sebastian's Café** is one of the least expensive places to eat with a view in Boston. Grab a sandwich or homemade soup or salad to eat overlooking Boston Harbor and the skyline. Closed weekends. ~ 157 Seaport Boulevard; 617-563-8358; www.sebastians.com/cafes. BUDGET.

The **No-Name Restaurant** not only has no name, it has no decor either. Famed for the freshness of its fish bought right off the boats, the No-Name always has long lines, though we've had some complaints that the less-than-stellar service is a turn-off. ~ 15½ Fish Pier; 617-338-7539. BUDGET TO DELUXE.

South Kitchen & Wine Bar brings a bit of downtown sophistication to South Boston. Grilled Kobe flatiron steak with a wild mushroom demiglace, crispy salmon with basil sauce and herbed pork loin with dried fruit chutney are just a sampling of the bistro's regional American cuisine. Sunday brunch. ~ 77 Dorchester Street; 617-269-7832; www.southkitchenbar.com. MODERATE TO DELUXE.

Charlestown

Across the river but still considered part of Boston, Charlestown is an area that has become increasingly popular among the yuppie set. This is the oldest part of town. It was founded in 1630 by a small band of Puritans who later abandoned it, moving across the river to Boston. Much of Charlestown was destroyed by the British in the Battle of Bunker Hill, so few 18th-century houses stand today.

SIGHTS

A walk over the river on the Charlestown Bridge brings you to the Charlestown Navy Yard, the berth of the **USS Constitution**, the oldest commissioned vessel in the world. It won its nickname of Old Ironsides when British cannon fire bounced off its sturdy oak hull in the War of 1812. While you can tour the decks and down below, lines are always long; try going at lunchtime. Closed Monday through Wednesday during winter. ~ 617-242-5671, fax 617-242-2308; e-mail njps1@navtap.navy.mil.

A handsome black-and-white frigate, the USS *Constitution* once required 400 sailors to hoist its sails.

Across the yard from Old Ironsides is the **USS Constitution Museum**, which houses exhibits on Old Ironsides' many voyages and victories, memorabilia and paintings. Interactive exhibits allow visitors to load and fire a cannon and command the *USS Constitution* in battle via computer. ~ Charlestown Navy Yard, Building 22; 617-426-1812, fax 617-242-0496; www.ussconstitutionmuseum.org, e-mail exhibits@ussconstitutionmuseum.org.

Nearby is the **Commandant's House**, a handsome Federal-style brick mansion where Navy officers lived. ~ Charlestown Navy Yard.

The **Bunker Hill Monument** actually stands atop Breed's Hill, where the Battle of Bunker Hill was in fact fought. This encounter became legend with the words of Colonel William Prescott to his ammunition-short troops: "Don't fire until you see the whites of their eyes." The cornerstone of the 221-foot Egyptian Revival granite obelisk was laid in 1825 by General Lafayette, with Daniel Webster orating. There are 294 steps to the observatory, which affords a magnificent view of the city and the harbor. ~ Monument Square; 617-242-5641, fax 617-241-2258; www.nps.gov/bost, e-mail bost_email@nps.gov.

Companion exhibits at the **Whites of Their Eyes, Bunker Hill Pavilion** include a multimedia slide show with 14 screens and costumed storytellers re-enacting the battle. Musket demonstrations are offered April through October. Admission. ~ 55 Constitution Road; 617-241-7575, 800-868-7482, fax 617-269-8018.

DINING

Mention Charlestown to a Bostonian and chances are you'll find yourself at **Olives**. The food is New England with northern Italian and Mediterranean twists. Dinner only. ~ 10 City Square; 617-242-1999, fax 617-242-1333; www.toddenglish.com. DELUXE TO ULTRA-DELUXE.

The **Warren Tavern** dates to 1780, and the small, clapboard house with gaslights was patronized by Paul Revere and George Washington. The inside appears dark and Colonial, with a heavy beamed ceiling, wood-planked floors, candelabra wall sconces, punched-tin lights and a roaring fire. The solid fare includes steaks, seafood and a tavern burger with peddler fries. The tavern also makes homemade tavern chips. Lunch, dinner and weekend brunch. ~ 2 Pleasant Street; 617-241-8142, fax 617-242-0667; www.warrentavern.com, e-mail contact@warrentavern.com. MODERATE.

Cambridge

Everyone thinks of Cambridge and Boston together, as if they were two sides of the same coin. While Cambridge is actually a separate city, the lives of the two are very much entwined, linked by a series of foot and vehicular bridges.

Cambridge was founded in 1630, originally named New Towne, and was the colony's first capital. In 1638, two years after the founding of Harvard, the nation's oldest university, the city was renamed after the English university town where many Boston settlers had been educated. Contrasting with Harvard's ivy-covered brick eminence is the city's other major center of learning, the Massachusetts Institute of Technology, which moved across the river from Boston in 1916.

Today Cambridge remains very much an intellectual center, home to Nobel Prize winners, ground-breaking scientists and famous writers, among them John Kenneth Galbraith, David Mamet and Anne Bernays. Cambridge became the heart of what came to be nicknamed "Silicon Valley East" when high-tech companies blossomed here during the 1960s and 1970s, as well as in outlying towns scattered along the Route 128 beltway. These think tanks and computer companies fueled a boom in the Massachusetts economy and population.

But not all of Cambridge is serious or intellectual. It's given life and vitality by throngs of young students, protesters handing out leaflets, cult followers and street musicians.

SIGHTS

The heartbeat of Cambridge is **Harvard Square**, where life revolves around the many bookstores, coffee shops, boutiques and newsstands. In the very center stands the **Out of Town Newspapers** kiosk, a Harvard Square landmark for many years, famous for its thousands of national and foreign periodicals. ~ 617-354-7777, fax 781-643-2622.

Right next to it you'll find the **Cambridge Office for Tourism**, which dispenses tourist information and walking maps. ~ 617-441-2884, 800-862-5678, fax 617-441-7736; www.cambridge-usa.org, e-mail info@cambridge-usa.org.

No one would come to Cambridge without taking a walk through **Harvard Yard.** A stroll of the yard's winding paths, stately trees, grassy quadrangles and handsome brick buildings is a walk through a long history of higher education. Seven U.S. presidents have graduated from Harvard.

Enter the main gate by crossing Massachusetts Avenue. On the right, you'll see **Massachusetts Hall**, built in 1718, the college's oldest remaining hall. In the quadrangle of the historic Old Yard, on the left, tucked between Hollis and Stoughton Halls, is a little jewel of a chapel. **Holden Chapel**, built in 1744, has blue gables decorated with scrolled white baroque cornices, ahead of its time in its ornateness.

Along the diagonal path that cuts across Old Yard is the **Statue of John Harvard** by Daniel Chester French, called the statue of the "three lies." Besides giving the wrong date for Harvard's founding, the statue is actually not of John Harvard at all, but of a student model instead; and John Harvard is not the college's founder but its first great benefactor.

Harvard's famed **Widener Library** stands in the New Yard, a massive building with a wide staircase and a pillared portico. With nearly three million books, Widener ranks as the third largest library in the United States, second only to the Library of Congress and the New York Public Library. Unfortunately, Widener is not open to the public, but its steps are still a popular spot for taking pictures.

Straight across from it is the **Memorial Chapel**, built in 1931 with a Bulfinch-style steeple in memory of the young men of Harvard who died in World War I. Their names are engraved on the walls.

Harvard is also home to a spate of museums known the world over for their esoteric collections, including three art museums (one fee is good for admission to all three museums; tours are offered Monday through Friday):

The **Busch-Reisinger Museum** is noted for central and northern European works of art from the late 19th and 20th centuries. Admission. ~ 32 Quincy Street; 617-495-2317; www.artmuseums.harvard.edu/busch.

The **Fogg Art Museum** showcases European and American artwork, with a particularly notable impressionist collection. Admission. ~ 32 Quincy Street; 617-495-9400; www.artmuseums.harvard.edu/fogg.

Ancient, Asian and Islamic art are the specialties at the **Arthur M. Sackler Museum**. Admission. ~ 485 Broadway at Quincy Street; 617-495-9400; www.artmuseums.harvard.edu/sackler.

Harvard Museum of Natural History consists of three natural history museums. The **Botanical Museum** holds the internationally famed handmade Glass Flowers, showcasing more than 700 species. At the **Museum of Comparative Zoology**, the development of animal life is traced from fossils to modern man. The **Mineralogical and Geological Museum** has a collection of rocks and minerals, including a 3040-carat topaz. ~ 26 Oxford Street; 617-495-3045, fax 617-496-8206; www.hmnh.harvard.

edu, e-mail hmnh@oeb.harvard.edu. The **Peabody Museum of Archaeology and Ethnology** displays artifacts from the world over, including Mayan and American Indian relics. Admission. ~ 11 Divinity Avenue; 617-496-1027, fax 617-495-7535; www.peabody.harvard.edu.

Under the spreading chestnut tree/ The village smithy stands;/ The smith a mighty man is he/With large and sinewy hands. These words from Longfellow's famous poem "The Village Blacksmith" were written about a real blacksmith who lived in a house in Boston built in 1811. It's now the **Hi-Rise Pie Co.** with an outdoor café in warm weather and upstairs seating in cooler weather. Old World pastries and cakes are made here the same way they have been for decades. Brunch and lunch are served. Closed Sunday in winter. ~ 56 Brattle Street; 617-492-3003, fax 617-876-8761.

Harvard Lampoon Castle, a funny-looking building with a round brick turret and a door painted bright red, yellow and pur-

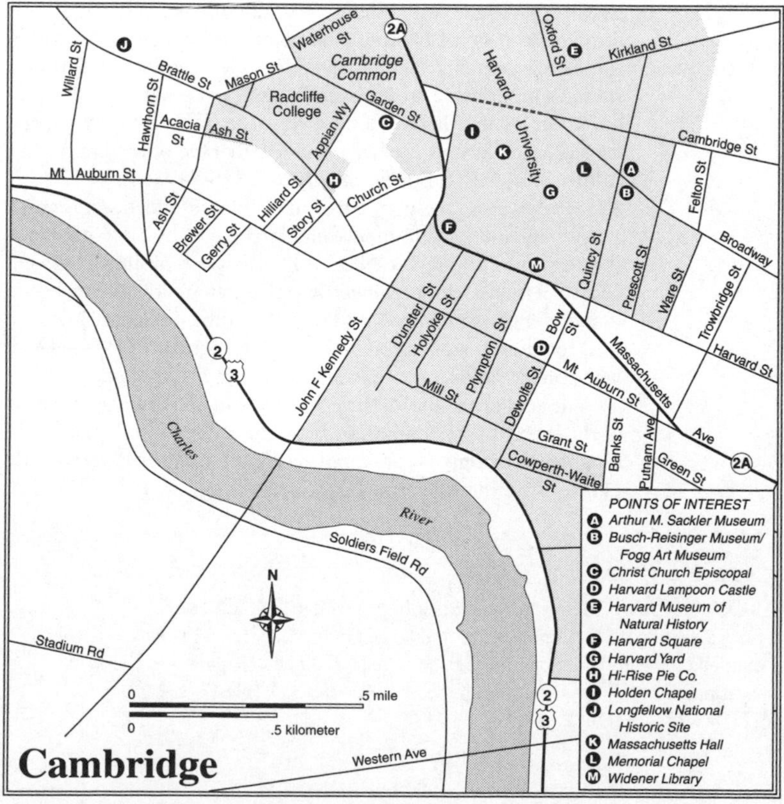

ple, befits its occupants: the publishers of Harvard's longstanding satirical magazine, the *Harvard Lampoon*. ~ 57 Mt. Auburn Street at Bow Street.

Christ Church Episcopal, a simple gray-and-white structure with a squat steeple, is Cambridge's oldest church building. George and Martha Washington worshipped here on New Year's Eve 1775. ~ Zero Garden Street; 617-876-0200, fax 617-876-0201; www.cccambridge.org.

Under an elm tree on the grassy **Cambridge Common**, General Washington took command of the Continental Army in 1775. A plaque and monument to Washington mark this spot. Nearby are three old black cannons, abandoned by the British at Fort Independence when they evacuated in 1776. ~ Massachusetts Avenue and Garden Street.

The **Longfellow National Historic Site** is where poet Henry Wadsworth Longfellow lived for 45 years and wrote most of his famous works. Painted a cheery yellow and accented with dark green shutters, the house was built in 1759 for a well-to-do Loyalist and years later was used by Washington as his headquarters during the siege of Boston. The house has many fine Victorian furnishings, among them Longfellow's desk, quill pen and inkstand. The house also contains Longfellow's personal 10,000-book library and his 600,000-piece collection of family papers. Closed Monday and Tuesday; closed end of October to mid-May. Admission. ~ 105 Brattle Street; 617-876-4491, fax 617-497-8718; www.nps.gov/long, e-mail frla_superintendent@nps.gov.

A handsome, slate-blue Colonial revival house with black shutters, the **Hooper-Lee-Nichols House** was built by a physician named Richard Hooper. Later it was the home of Joseph Lee, a founder of Christ Church, and then the home of George Nichols. Call for hours. Admission. ~ 159 Brattle Street; 617-547-4252; www.cambridgehistory.org, e-mail info@camhistory.com.

The western end of Brattle Street is called **Tory Row** because of the lovely homes built there by wealthy Tories in the 18th century. A fine example is at Number 175, the **Ruggles Fayerweather House**, first the home of Tory George Ruggles, later of patriot

EXTRA! EXTRA!

The **Out of Town Newspapers** kiosk has been declared a National Historic Landmark. Set right in the middle of Harvard Square and surrounded by traffic, the kiosk carries more than 3000 newspapers and magazines from all over the world. ~ Zero Harvard Square; 617-354-7777, fax 781-643-2622.

Thomas Fayerweather. The house served as an American hospital after the Battle of Bunker Hill.

Just down the street sits **Radcliffe College**, once a women's branch of Harvard but now fully integrated into the university. The gates to **Radcliffe Yard** are entered off Brattle Street, between James Street and Appian Way. As you walk the path, the four graceful brick main buildings of the campus will be in a semicircle to your right. First is **Fay House**, a mansion built in 1807, the administrative center. Next you'll find Rieman Dance Center, home of the Radcliffe Dance Program. Third is **Agassiz House**, fronted by white classical pillars, which holds a theater, ballroom and arts office. Last is the college's renowned **Schlesinger Library**, which contains an outstanding collection of books and manuscripts on the history of women in America, including papers of Susan B. Anthony, Julia Ward Howe and Elizabeth Cady Stanton.

A few miles east of Harvard Square lies Cambridge's other famous college, the **Massachusetts Institute of Technology** (M.I.T.). Offering a premier education in engineering and technology since 1865, M.I.T. draws students from all over the world, including China, Japan and Vietnam. In distinct contrast to the hallowed ways of Harvard, M.I.T. students are famed for their witty irreverence and contests they engage in to outdo each other in intellectual pranks. One of their episodes involved placing a car on top of a campus building. Fittingly, the campus looks modern and high-tech, with geometrical buildings designed by Eero Saarinen.

LODGING

Set in an office tower and shopping complex, the 294-room **Charles Hotel** is just steps away from Harvard Square. Rooms are styled in grays and blues, with Shaker-style beds, upholstered loveseats and armchairs, and oak armoires; many have views of the river. Every room features an LCD television screen that disappears when turned off. There are two restaurants and one of the city's best jazz bars, as well as a health spa with steam room, sauna and whirlpool. ~ 1 Bennett Street at Eliot Street; 617-864-1200, 800-882-1818, fax 617-864-5715; www.charleshotel.com. ULTRA-DELUXE.

A convenient place to stay in Cambridge is the **Harvard Square Hotel**. Although some rooms are on the smallish side, this 73-room private hotel has nicely appointed digs with contemporary furniture and floral spreads. ~ 110 Mt. Auburn Street; 617-864-5200, 800-458-5886, fax 617-864-2409; www.harvardsquarehotel.com, e-mail reservations@theinnatharvard.com. ULTRA-DELUXE.

The **Inn at Harvard** is wonderfully situated, only a couple blocks from Harvard Square. The label "inn" seems a little inappropriate, however, since it's more of a standard hotel. Even so, it has its charms: there's a wonderful atrium lobby area that's four stories high, open to balconies and guest rooms—very much like a Renaissance palazzo. The 113 rooms are well appointed with cherry furnishings and original artwork from the Harvard Fogg Museum. ~ 1201 Massachusetts Avenue; 617-491-2222, 800-458-5886, fax 617-520-3711; www.theinnatharvard.com, e-mail reservations@theinnatharvard.com. ULTRA-DELUXE.

Boutique hotels are hard to come by in this university town, and **The Kendall Hotel** fills this void nicely. The oldest building in Kendall square, what was once an 1893 Victorian firehouse, is now a boutique hotel with attentive touches throughout. The rooms are decorated with a blend of original and reproduction antiques, warm pastel walls and oriental rugs. Its prime location within walking distance of downtown Boston makes it an ideal home base—or you can simply sink into one of the welcoming armchairs. Breakfast buffet and high-speed internet included ~ 350 Main Street; 617-577-1300, 866-566-1300, fax 617-577-1377; www.kendallhotel.com, e-mail stay@kendallhotel.com. DELUXE TO ULTRA-DELUXE.

Some of the least expensive, albeit plainest, accommodations are to be had at the **Irving House** near Harvard Square. This wood-frame walk-up offers 44 plain but clean rooms. Your best bets are the top-floor units featuring skylights in the rooms or bathrooms, private baths and wall-to-wall carpets or hardwood floors. Breakfast is included. ~ 24 Irving Street; 617-547-4600, 877-574-4600, fax 617-576-2814; www.irvinghouse.com, e-mail reserve@irvinghouse.com. MODERATE TO ULTRA-DELUXE.

The stepped, pyramidal walls of the **Hyatt Regency Cambridge** sit right on the banks of the Charles River, offering splendid views of the Boston skyline from many rooms. The 14-story atrium lobby has a semitropical feeling, from the Australian finches in a glass cage to a large fountain and towering potted plants and trees. Lighted glass elevators whoosh you up through the atrium, past a trompe l'oeil mural of an Italian villa and a 100-foot-high glass wall. The 469-room hotel has two restaurants, a lap pool and a health club with sauna, whirlpool and steam bath. The fair-sized rooms have natural woods, contemporary furnishings and carpeting, plus marble vanities in the bathroom. ~ 575 Memorial Drive; 617-492-1234, 800-233-1234, fax 617-491-6906; www.cambridge.hyatt.com. DELUXE TO ULTRA-DELUXE.

HIDDEN ►

A 20-minute walk from Harvard Square, **A Cambridge House, Bed & Breakfast Inn** is a special place to stay. A private home built in 1892 with a wide pillared porch, it's listed on the National Historic Register. Beautifully restored and richly furnished with floral print fabrics, patterned wallpapers, period antiques and oriental rugs, the living room and den offer guests luxurious spaces. Each of the 15 rooms is individually decorated with antiques and has a private bath. The room we saw had a canopied bed and a working fireplace. Breakfast is complimentary, as are the evening hors d'oeuvres. Homemade brownies, cookies and fresh fruit are always available. No children under seven allowed. ~ 2218 Massachusetts Avenue; 617-491-6300, 800-232-9989, fax 617-868-2848; www.acambridgehouse.com, e-mail innach@comcast.net. DELUXE TO ULTRA-DELUXE.

DINING

HIDDEN

A retrofit, '50s-style decor of diner stools, neon and a black-and-white-tiled floor enlivens the **East Coast Grill & Raw Bar**. The Southern grilled ribs, pork and chicken are served with coleslaw, baked beans, corn bread and watermelon, and hot drinks to match: blue, green and gold margaritas. Grilled seafood with a tropical twist are other specialties. Appetizers are equally muscular, notably the "sausage from hell." Dinner only except for Sunday brunch. ~ 1271 Cambridge Street; 617-491-6568, fax 617-868-4278; www.eastcoastgrill.net, e-mail ecgrill@aol.com. MODERATE TO ULTRA-DELUXE.

It would be hard to find a friendlier place than the **Casa Portugal**, one of only a handful of Boston Portuguese restaurants. Imbibe the Latin mood set by black iron lanterns, red-vested waiters and folk-art murals of bullfights and musicians. *Courico* arrives in a small flaming grill, followed by spicy dinners of marinated pork cubes with potatoes or mussels, *paelha a Marinheiro*, and squid stew, all served with thickly cut Portuguese french fries. There's a good selection of Portuguese wines and beers, and espresso and cappuccino to top it all off. ~ 1200 Cambridge Street; 617-491-8880, fax 617-354-6832; www.restaurantcasaportugal.com. MODERATE TO DELUXE.

Look for some 20 artworks from the Arts on the Line Project at the Harvard, Porter, Davis and Alewife T stations.

At **Magnolia's Southern Cuisine**, chef John Silberman, a former student of Cajun master chef Paul Prudhomme, serves up Southern-inspired creations like fried green tomatoes with tomatillo salsa and shrimp with sherry scallion sauce. You can also order fiery jambalaya, grilled duck with orange-chipotle sauce, pecan pie and praline parfait. Dinner only. Closed Sunday and Monday. ~ 1193 Cambridge Street; 617-576-1971; www.magnoliascuisine.com. MODERATE TO DELUXE.

The family-owned **La Groceria Italian Restaurant** looks like an Italian trattoria, with its striped awning, lattice ceiling and exposed brick wall. Famed for its hot antipasti and homemade pasta, La Groceria does old-style Southern Italian dishes such as lasagna, eggplant parmigiana and a seafood marinara that must be eaten to be believed. Seafood and other Mediterranean dishes have also made their way onto the menu. Its splendid dessert case offers cannoli, *tartufo* and *tiramisu*. ~ 853 Main Street; 617-876-

4162, fax 617-864-9566; www.lagroceriarestaurant.com, e-mail lagroceria@aol.com. MODERATE.

African folk art hangs on the walls of the green, black and white dining room of **Asmara**, one of the many Ethiopian and Eritrean eateries in Greater Boston. Chicken, lamb, beef, fish and vegetarian entrées are to be eaten without silverware, in the Ethiopian manner. ~ 739 Massachusetts Avenue; 617-864-7447, fax 617-628-0663. MODERATE.

The first ever World Series was held in 1903 here in Beantown; the Boston Pilgrims (predecessor to the Red Sox) beat the Pittsburg Pirates in a best-out-of-nine series.

Upstairs on the Square offers two different dining experiences in one location. The Monday Club Bar on the first level is an eclectic bistro serving lighter (and cheaper) fare than the upstairs Soirée Room, which offers one of the top contemporary American dining experiences in Greater Boston. The à la carte menu selections include fresh local seafood, rack of lamb and rabbit. Soirée room closed Sunday and Monday. ~ 91 Winthrop Street; 617-864-1933, fax 617-864-4625; www.upstairsonthesquare.com, e-mail info@upstairsonthesquare.com. MODERATE TO ULTRA-DELUXE.

HIDDEN ►

Run by a group of transplanted Londoners, **Shay's** is a fairly authentic English-style pub right in the heart of Crimson territory, with a good selection of international draft beers and pub grub. ~ 58 John F. Kennedy Street; 617-864-9161. BUDGET.

The **Algiers Coffeehouse** is one of Cambridge's most bohemian eateries. With its 50-foot domed ceiling, white stucco walls and copper embellishments, it feels like a cross between a Moroccan palace and a mosque. The menu has a Middle Eastern flavor, with lentil falafel and *baba ganoosh*. There are 16 kinds of coffees and hot beverages, teas, iced drinks and Arabic pastries. ~ 40 Brattle Street; 617-492-1557. BUDGET.

The café/bar area and dining room of **Casablanca** sport murals of Rick, Ilsa and the rest of the "As Time Goes By" gang. The Mediterranean flavor continues with several exotic seating options in the café—the "love baskets" curve up to form a roof and a cocoon-like feeling. For the most part, the food is quite good. The lunch and dinner menus include steak, seafood, vegetarian dishes, lamb and beef. ~ 40 Brattle Street; 617-876-0999, fax 617-661-1373; www.cbrestaurant.com, e-mail sari@casablanca-restaurant.com. DELUXE.

HIDDEN ►

Tucked a few blocks away from busy Harvard Square, **Café Pamplona** is a tiny basement-level café that serves Spanish dishes and tapas, pastries and strong coffee. During the summer, there are tables outside on a brick patio. ~ 12 Bow Street; 617-492-0352. BUDGET.

HIDDEN ►

Just over the Cambridge–Somerville line, in a somewhat scruffy neighborhood, **Dalí** is as flamboyant as the artist it's named after. Who would've guessed that inside this vibrant periwinkle building awaits the best Spanish food in the metropolitan area. The interior, radiant with red hues, is eccentrically decorated. Make a meal of several different tapas and a bottle of hearty Iberian wine, or dig into entrées such as *piedra* (grill your own food tableside), paella, and *pescado a la Sal*. Dinner only. ~ 415 Washington Street, Somerville; 617-661-3254; www.dalirestaurant.com, e-mail dalirestaurant@verizon.net. MODERATE TO ULTRA-DELUXE.

SHOPPING

Harvard Square offers a wealth of shopping, from eclectic boutiques to upscale chain stores. Most notable in this intellectual bastion are the many bookshops surrounding the square. (See "Boston Area Bookstores" on page 236.)

The **Harvard Coop** holds three floors of men's and women's clothing, books and an astonishing selection of art prints, posters, and plenty of dorm supplies. The Coop (pronounce it as in "bird coop" to avoid student ridicule) was formed in 1882 by several Harvard students as a cost-saving measure. ~ 1400 Massachusetts Avenue; 617-499-2000, fax 617-441-2814; www.thecoop.com.

The Harvard Square annex of the **Globe Corner Bookstore** is a beautiful, bright shop. There's a high percentage of travel books here as well as plenty of guides to the immediate area. ~ 90 Mount Auburn Street; 617-497-6277, 800-358-6013; www.globecorner.com, e-mail info@gcb.com.

Jasmine Sola is your best source for up-to-the-minute shoes that are wearable as well as fashionable. The accessories selection is extensive, too, particularly the wall stocked full of women's hosiery. They also have huge gift and jewelry departments. ~ 39 Brattle Street; 617-354-6043, fax 617-547-2057; www.jasminesola.com.

Colonial Drug is like a European perfume shop, with more than a thousand kinds of fragrances. Closed Sunday. ~ 49 Brattle Street; 617-864-2222.

If you're a knitter, you'll enjoy **Woolcott & Co.** There are enormous binders full of carefully organized patterns and helpful staff members who are accustomed to talking novices through knitting traumas. ~ 61 John F. Kennedy Street; 617-547-2837; www.woolcottandcompany.com.

HIDDEN

The products of local and national artists are for sale at the **Cambridge Artists Cooperative**, a treasure trove of whimsical and beautiful things: handblown glass fish, pink flamingo earrings made of tin, wearable art, quilts and handmade paper, to name a few. ~ 59-A Church Street; 617-868-4434, fax 617-868-5966; www.cambridgeartistscoop.com, e-mail cacart@gis.net.

In the M.I.T. neighborhood, urban trendsetters and conventional dressers alike appreciate the **Garment District**, where you can pick up the vintage '60s and '70s clothing as well as more traditional officewear. Downstairs is a room full of clothes, shoes and purses for $1.50 a pound. ~ 200 Broadway; 617-876-5230; www.garmentdistrict.com.

Whether you're looking for estate jewelry or a Wonder Woman action figure, try the **Cambridge Antique Market**. Over 150 dealers operate out of this four-story building, where elegant furniture sits side by side with retro decorative pieces. Closed Monday. ~ 201 Monsignor O'Brien Highway (Route 28); 617-868-9655.

NIGHTLIFE

Grendel's Den Restaurant and Bar is a comfy pub in the basement of the old Pi Eta Club building in Harvard Square, with brick walls, plank floors, and a bar you can really lean on. Lunch and dinner are served on the outdoor patio in good weather. ~ 89 Winthrop Street; 617-491-1160 or 617-491-1050, fax 617-491-9299; www.grendelsden.com.

Since 1958, **Club Passim** has been going strong as a showcase for acoustic folk performers, including Tracy Chapman, Jimmy Buffett and Joan Baez, in a clean-cut, no-alcohol basement coffeehouse. Reservations for performances are suggested. Cover. ~ 47 Palmer Street; 617-492-7679; www.clubpassim.org, e-mail staff@passimlanter.org.

Harvard's professional theater company, **American Repertory Theatre** produces world premieres and classical works, often taking a nontraditional approach. They also sponsor productions in more intimate venues throughout Cambridge and Boston. ~ 64 Brattle Street; 617-547-8300 (box office), 617-495-2668; www.amrep.org, e-mail information@amrep.org.

Scullers is in an unlikely place—on the second floor of the Doubletree Guest Suite Hotel in one of the uglier buildings along the Charles. Don't let the location or the architecture dissuade you—this classy jazz club (with a terrific view of the Charles) has big-name acts. Cover. ~ 400 Soldiers Field Road, Boston; 617-562-4111; www.scullersjazz.com, e-mail info@scullersjazz.com.

The **Plough and Stars** is that rare thing, an uncorrupted working-class bar where habitués are logo-capped, burly types

ADMIT ONE ADMIT ONE

AUTHOR FAVORITE

One of the best jazz showcases in Greater Boston, the **Regattabar** offers an intimate jazz experience in a sophisticated club environment. The Regattabar regularly features such headliners as McCoy Tyner, Mike Stern, and The Bad Plus. Closed Sunday and Monday. Cover. ~ Charles Hotel, 1 Bennett Street; 617-661-5000, 617-395-7757 (performance schedule and tickets), fax 617-661-5053; www.regattabarjazz.com, e-mail gherbst@charleshotel.com.

who belly up for live, boisterous entertainment. Black-and-white caricatures of neighborhood regulars line a whole wall. Cover Wednesday through Saturday. ~ 912 Massachusetts Avenue; 617-576-0032; www.ploughandstars.com.

You never know what you'll hear on open-mic nights (Sunday through Wednesday) at the **Cantab Lounge**, but the rest of the time it's soulful rhythm-and-blues or bluegrass bands in a let-it-all-hang-out playpen. Cover Friday and Saturday. ~ 738 Massachusetts Avenue; 617-354-2685.

For the last several years, the coolest area in metro Boston has been in Cambridge—Harvard Square's scruffy cousin, Central Square, which is about two-thirds of the way down Massachusetts Avenue from Harvard to M.I.T. *The* nightspot in this haven of coolness is **The Middle East**, which has four venues for live music: Upstairs, Downstairs, Zuzu and the Corner. There's a mix of music and clientele here—from Turbo Negro to The Rapture, for example, as far as national acts go—and you're as likely to see college kids as graying rock fans. Cover on most nights. ~ 472–480 Massachusetts Avenue; 617-492-1886, fax 617-547-3930; www.mideastclub.com, e-mail upstairs@mideastclub.com.

An industrial danceclub with a flair for art, **Man Ray/Campus** serves up progressive and alternative music. Wednesday is goth night and Thursday is gay night. Creative (read fetish) attire is encouraged, but when in doubt wear black. Closed Sunday through Tuesday. Cover. The club is undergoing renovations until summer 2007. ~ 21 Brookline Street in Central Square; 617-864-0400; www.manrayclub.com, e-mail manray@manrayclub.com.

Named for the carved wooden amphibians overlooking the bar, **Toad** teems with music lovers of all ages enjoying live bands seven nights a week. Aimee Mann (formerly of 'Til Tuesday) has even been spotted in this tiny no-cover hotspot. ~ 1912 Massachusetts Avenue; 617-497-4950.

Pat Metheny got his start at **Ryles**, which features nightly jazz, rhythm-and-blues, Latin music and big band nights in a casual atmosphere. Closed Monday. Cover. ~ 212 Hampshire Street; 617-876-9330; www.rylesjazz.com.

Outlying Areas

Although many tourists never leave the bounds of Boston and Cambridge, there is much of interest in the surrounding towns, many of which serve as bedroom communities for Boston workers and have rich colonial histories, too.

SIGHTS

Due west of the city and bordering the Fenway, **Brookline** is one of the more prestigious and wealthy residential surrounding towns. The architect of Boston's Emerald Necklace lived and worked in a little house in a quiet Brookline neighborhood, where he often took his work outside to a landscaped hollow.

President John F. Kennedy was born in Brookline in 1917, in a little house now restored to its period appearance as the **John F. Kennedy National Historic Site**. The house holds much JFK memorabilia, including furnishings and artifacts evoking his boyhood years. Open Wednesday through Sunday from May to October. Admission. ~ 83 Beals Street, Brookline; 617-566-7937, fax 617-730-9884; www.nps.gov/jofi.

South of Brookline lies **Jamaica Plain**, which is technically part of Boston. The star of Jamaica Plain is the **Arnold Arboretum of Harvard University**, one of the more remarkable green strands in Boston's Emerald Necklace. The 265-acre preserve was established in 1872, and growing here are more than 15,000 scientifically labeled trees and plants from around the world. The arboretum has one of the oldest and largest lilac collections in North America, 200-year-old bonsai trees and rare specimens from China. A two-mile walk along a nature trail takes visitors through meadows and over valleys and hills, offering serene and secluded vistas in any season. Maps are available for $1. ~ 125 Arborway, Jamaica Plain; 617-524-1718, fax 617-524-1418; www.arboretum.harvard.edu, e-mail arbweb@arnarb.harvard.edu.

To the southeast, the working-class city of **Quincy** may look uninteresting, but it happens to be the "City of the Presidents"—birthplace of John Adams and his son John Quincy Adams, the second and sixth U.S. presidents. There are several sights surrounding the Adams family history. But before you make a trip through history, be sure to stop at the **Discover Quincy** visitors center or call ahead to make necessary tour arrangements. ~ 1250 Hancock Street, Quincy; 617-657-0527, fax 617-471-3132.

At the **Adams National Historical Park** stands an elegant gray Colonial house built in 1731; it's home to four generations of Adamses. The house is set on several acres strikingly set off with formal gardens that create a beautiful profusion of color in spring and summer. Inside the house are many original furnishings, including portraits of George and Martha Washington, Waterford candelabra and Louis XV furniture. There is also a cathedral-ceilinged library with 14,000 original volumes. As the Adams family prospered, John and his wife Abigail, who moved into the house in 1787, enlarged it from 7 to 20 rooms. The National Park Service gives excellent tours of this dwelling. Closed November 10 to April 19. Admission. ~ 135 Adams Street, Quincy; 617-770-1175, fax 617-472-7562; www.nps.gov/adam, e-mail adam_visitor_center@nps.gov.

Nearby and part of the same site are the **John Adams** and **John Quincy Adams Birthplaces**, a pair of simple saltbox houses where the two presidents were born, built in 1663 and 1681. Closed November 10 to April 19. Admission. ~ 133 and 141 Franklin

Street, Quincy; 617-770-1175, fax 617-472-7562; www.nps.gov/adam, e-mail adam_visitor_center@nps.gov.

East of the Adams National Historical Park, and on the National Register of Historic Places, lies the **Quincy Homestead,** home to four generations of Edmund Quincy's, the family of Dorothy Hancock. The fourth Quincy daughter, Dorothy, married John Hancock, who was born in Quincy. A Colonial-style herb garden and authentic period furnishings embellish the 1686 house, and one of Hancock's coaches is displayed. Closed during winter. Call ahead. ~ 34 Butler Road, Quincy; 617-773-1177.

The 1872 Gothic Revival **Adams Academy** was founded by an endowment from John Adams and is home to the **Quincy History Museum**. Exhibits show the city's industrial history. Closed Sunday. ~ 8 Adams Street, Quincy; 617-773-1144, fax 617-472-4990.

Dominating downtown Quincy Square is a beautiful granite church, **United First Parish Church,** designed by Alexander Parris and built in 1828. Also known as The Church of the Presidents, its crypt holds the remains of John Adams, John Quincy Adams and their wives. Open for tours mid-April to mid-November. Admission. ~ 1306 Hancock Street, Quincy; 617-773-1290, fax 617-773-7499.

Across the street is **City Hall**, designed in 1844 in Greek Revival style by Bunker Hill architect Solomon Willard. Near City Hall is the **Hancock Cemetery**, dating to about 1640, where John Hancock's father is buried, as are Quincy and Adams ancestors.

A few miles south of Quincy lies one of the region's most attractive coastal communities, **Hingham**, settled in 1635. Sailing yachts bob in its picturesque harbor, and the downtown retains the characteristics of a small village, with mom-and-pop shops, restaurants and a vintage movie theater surrounding **Hingham**

sights

AUTHOR FAVORITE

If, like me, you find a certain thrill in lying down with literary lions, then curl up with a volume of Henry Wadsworth Longfellow's poetry at **Longfellow's Wayside Inn**. Open since 1716, the inn was made famous by Longfellow's cycle of poems, *Tales of a Wayside Inn*, which includes "Paul Revere's Ride." Historic structures include an 18th-century–style grist mill and the little red schoolhouse of "Mary Had a Little Lamb" fame. Restored in 1923, it's a fully functioning inn and restaurant. ~ 72 Wayside Inn Road, Sudbury; 978-443-1776, 800-339-1776, fax 978-443-8041; www.wayside.org, e-mail history@wayside.org.

Square. A drive along the long and wide **Main Street** rewards you with views of stately 18th- and 19th-century homes sporting neat black shutters. A number of them are on the National Register of Historic Places. These houses are private, but many are open to the public during the **Hingham Historical Society's** annual house tour in June, reputed to be the oldest historical house tour in the country, held since 1924. Cover. ~ P.O Box 434, Hingham, MA 02043; 781-749-1851; www.hinghamhistorical.org, e-mail info@hinghamhistorical.org.

The Old Ordinary, circa 1688, numbered among its many owners tavern keepers who provided an "ordinary" meal of the day at fixed prices. Halfway on the day-long stagecoach ride from Plymouth to Boston, the Old Ordinary did a brisk business. Additions were made to the house in the mid-18th century. Now a museum of Hingham history, the house has an 18th-century taproom, complete with wooden grill, pewter plates and rum kegs. There's also an 18th-century kitchen outfitted with large hearth and butter churn, and a den, dining room and front parlor. Upstairs are four bedrooms furnished in period style. There are a number of rare objects among the collection, including "mourning" samplers, embroidered to honor the dead; a 17th-century Bible box; an 18th-century Queen Anne mirror; and paintings of Hingham ships that sailed to China. The Old Ordinary is open for public tours mid-June to mid-September. Closed Sunday and Monday, and mid-September to mid-June. Admission. ~ 21 Lincoln Street off historic Hingham Square, Hingham; 781-749-0013 or 781-749-0664; www.hinghamhistorical.org, e-mail info@hinghamhistorical.org.

The Puritan congregation of the **Old Ship Church** gathered in 1635. Built in 1681, it is the oldest building in continuous ecclesiastical service in the United States, and the nation's only surviving Puritan meetinghouse. Crafted by ships' carpenters, the building has curved oak roof frames like the knees of a ship, and the unusual roof structure resembles an inverted ship's hull. Closed weekends in July and August; open by appointment only the rest of the year. ~ 90 Main Street, Hingham; 781-749-1679; www.oldshipchurch.org.

Not far from Hingham, on a peninsula jutting out into Boston Harbor, is **Hull**, site of **Boston Light**, the oldest lighthouse in America. Immediately south, on Jerusalem Road, is **Cohasset**, known for magnificent homes with sweeping ocean views.

Surrounding the Route 128 beltway are several more towns of interest to the traveler. A large and urbanized town about 20 miles west of Boston, **Framingham** offers a lovely respite within

HIDDEN ►

the **Garden in the Woods**, the largest collection of native plants in the Northeast. You can meander along 45 acres of woodland trails, planted with some 1500 varieties of flora, including more than 200 rare and endangered species. There are specially designed garden habitats, including woodland groves, a lily pond, bog, limestone garden, pine barrens and meadows. Closed November to mid-April. Admission. ~ 180 Hemenway Road, Framingham; 508-877-7630, fax 508-877-3658; www.newfs.org, e-mail newfs@newfs.org.

Unlike later New England churches with white spires and sides, Old Ship Church is built of mustard-colored wooden clapboards in Elizabethan Gothic style, as its Puritan worshippers saw fit.

A few miles north of Framingham lie the endearing green Colonial towns of **Sudbury** and **Lincoln**, still quite rural in character.

Walter Gropius, founder of the Bauhaus school of art and architecture in Germany, had his family home in the rolling green hills of Lincoln. The first house he designed upon his arrival in the United States in 1938, **Gropius House** embodies those principles of function and simplicity that are hallmarks of the Bauhaus style. The house has works of art and Bauhaus furnishings. Closed Monday and Tuesday from June to mid-October; open weekends only from mid-October through May. Admission. ~ 68 Baker Bridge Road, Lincoln; 781-259-8098, fax 781-259-9722; www.historicnewengland.org, e-mail dmoore@historicnewengland.org.

Set in a wooded, green, 35-acre park that recently underwent extensive landscaping, the **DeCordova Museum and Sculpture Park** showcases modern and contemporary art by internationally acclaimed regional artists. A café serves light fare. The museum is closed on Monday. Admission. ~ 51 Sandy Pond Road, Lincoln; 781-259-8355, fax 781-259-3650; www.decordova.org, e-mail info@decordova.org

LODGING

There's a great deal of historic ambience to **Longfellow's Wayside Inn**, which the poet made famous in his *Tales of a Wayside Inn*. The innkeepers have kept a number of the original rooms furnished with period items. Of the inn's ten rooms, only two are in the older part of the inn. Eight are in a modern addition and feature Colonial reproduction furniture (as well as original pieces), traditional colors of cranberry and green, and oak floors. The two rooms in the original inn have wide-planked floors and hand-hewn ceiling beams, but they have tiny bathrooms with cramped showers. The inn has a wonderful restaurant that serves traditional country fare. A full breakfast is included in the rates. ~ 72 Wayside Inn Road, Sudbury; 978-443-1776, 800-339-1776, fax 978-443-8041; www.wayside.org, e-mail frontdesk@wayside.org. DELUXE.

DINING

If you're looking for a funky, East Village–esque night on the town, give **Bella Luna** a try. The pizza parlor is loud and energetic and the food's pretty good, although service can be slow. But there's plenty to look at, from the eclectic patrons to the rotating art exhibits to the open kitchen. And if your patience wears thin, pop downstairs to the nightclub/bowling alley and knock over a few pins. ~ 405 Centre Street, Jamaica Plain; 617-524-6060.

Don't be deterred by the strip-mall surroundings of **La Paloma in Quincy**, complete with sub shop and package store. La Paloma has won several awards from *Boston* magazine, including six "Best Mexican Restaurant" awards. People line up outside the doors on weekends for the first-rate food, including beef and chicken fajitas, Mexican paella and *gorditos* (fried tortillas topped with homemade sausage and sour cream). The dining room feels as warm and festive as a Mexican village, with peachy-colored walls, dim lantern light, airy latticework, tiled floors and Mexican paintings and folk art. Closed Monday. Dinner only on Sunday. ~ 195 Newport Avenue, Quincy; 617-773-0512, fax 617-376-8867; www.lapalomarestaurant.com. BUDGET TO MODERATE.

Great Blue Hill, the highest point on the Massachusetts coast south of Maine, is the site of the oldest weather station in North America.

Even Southerners recommend **Tennessee's** for some of the best barbecue in the area. Beef brisket, baby-back ribs, chicken wings and pulled pork are all smoked then dry-rubbed with a blend of spices. Sides include barbecued beans, cucumber salad, corn bread, mac and cheese, corn on the cob and watermelon. Collard greens, dirty rice and sweet potato pie round out the Southern selections. ~ 341 Cochituate Road, Framingham; 508-626-7140; www.tennbbq.com. MODERATE TO DELUXE.

Visions of Longfellow will come to mind immediately when you enter **Longfellow's Wayside Inn**. Before lunch or dinner, you can tour the period rooms of the original inn and several historic buildings on the grounds. Ask for a table in the small and intimate Tap Room, which has a truly Colonial ambience with two fireplaces, ladderback chairs and brown-and-white-checked tablecloths. The menu features hearty game and seafood dishes such as those an 18th-century wayfarer might have dined on: prime rib, rack of lamb, roast duckling, goose and sole. For dessert, there are deep-dish apple pie and baked Indian pudding. ~ 72 Wayside Inn Road, Sudbury; 978-443-1776, 800-339-1776, fax 978-443-8041; www.wayside.org, e-mail frontdesk@wayside.org. DELUXE.

SHOPPING

Shop for a good cause at **Boomerangs**, a fundraising venue for the AIDS Action Committee that's chockfull of recycled housewares and clothing. Brand-name quality goods are also donated by such retailers as Filene's Basement and Urban Outfitters. ~ 716 Centre Street, Jamaica Plain; 617-524-5120; www.aac.org, e-mail boomerangs@acc.org.

NIGHTLIFE

If you've ever thought a nightclub in a bowling alley would be a great idea, someone beat you to it. **The Milky Way Lounge & Lanes**, downstairs from the Bella Luna pizza parlor, is a big room split in half; you can bowl on one side, or sit at the bar or on sofas on the other. There's pool; live bands entertain some nights, deejays on others. ~ 405 Centre Street, Jamaica Plain; 617-524-3740; www.milkywayjp.com.

Ballroom dancers from 18 to 80 love **Moseley's on the Charles** for its large ballroom, complete with sparkling ceiling globe. Available for rent every weekday but Wednesday. Wednesday is open ballroom, Saturday and Sunday are reserved for private functions. Cover. ~ 50 Bridge Street, Dedham; 781-326-3075; www.moseleysonthecharles.com.

BEACHES & PARKS

BOSTON HARBOR ISLANDS Over 30 islands lie in Boston Harbor, scattered along the coast from Boston south to Quincy, Hingham and Hull, with 10 of them comprising a state park. Each island has a unique flavor and character.

HIDDEN

Peddocks Island, a 184-acre preserve of woodlands, salt marsh, rocky beaches and open fields, has a turn-of-the-20th-century fort, a wildlife sanctuary and an old cottage community, as well as a visitors center with displays detailing the island's history.

Peaceful and primitive **Lovells Island** is characterized by long beaches and diverse wildlife, rocky tidepools and sand dunes. This is the only island where swimming is allowed.

The smaller **Georges Island**, the most developed in the park, is dominated by Fort Warren, a National Historic Landmark built between 1833 and 1861. Construction was overseen by Sylvanus Thayer, the "Father of West Point."

Other islands in the park system include **Gallops, Grape** and **Bumpkin.** (Gallops is currently closed to the public.) Swimming is permitted on Lovells Island only. Fishing is good from the rocky shores and public piers on all the islands except Peddocks; you'll find lots of flounder, cod, haddock, pollack and striped bass. Picnic areas, restrooms, park rangers, nature trails, fort tours, historical programs, boat docks and a concession stand are available on Georges Island. Georges Island also serves as the entrance to the park and provides free interisland water taxis from Memorial Day to Labor Day. (The islands are also accessible through **Boston Harbor Cruises.** ~ 1 Long Wharf; 617-227-4321. **The Friends of Boston Harbor Islands** sponsors special boat trips and tours. ~ P.O. Box 690187, Quincy; 781-740-4290.) Closed Columbus Day to Memorial Day. ~ 617-223-8666, fax 617-223-8671; www.bostonislands.com, e-mail boha_information@nps.gov.

▲ There are primitive sites on Peddocks, Lovells, Grape and Bumpkins islands ($8 per night; reservations required). No water or electricity; composting toilets available. ~ 877-422-6762.

HIDDEN ►

BELLE ISLE MARSH This preserve holds 241 acres of one of the largest remaining salt marshes in Boston. Typical of the wetlands that once lined the shores of the Massachusetts Bay Colony, Belle Isle Marsh is a special place where you can see lots of wildlife and salt marsh plants, a rare experience in an urban area. Facilities include a boardwalk, nature trails and a couple of observation towers. ~ At Bennington Street in East Boston; phone/fax 617-727-5350; www.state.ma.us/mdc, e-mail geoffwood5@comcast.net.

NANTASKET BEACH Once a classy mid-19th-century resort with grand hotels rivaling those in Newport, the Nantasket Beach area later declined into a tacky strip of bars, fast-food stands and Skeeball arcades. Still, this three-and-a-half-mile barrier beach is one of the nicest in the area, with clean white sand and a wide open vista of the Atlantic Ocean. The water is always good for swimming, and after a storm there's enough surf to go bodysurfing or windsurfing. There are picnic areas, restrooms, lifeguards, shade pavilions, a boardwalk, a carousel, restaurants and snack stands. Parking fee, $3. ~ On Nantasket Avenue, at the terminus of Route 228 in Hull; 617-727-5290, fax 617-727-8252.

The Puritans used the Boston Harbor Islands for pastureland and firewood, and there are tales of buried pirate treasure and ghosts haunting old Civil War forts.

WOLLASTON BEACH RESERVATION Come high tide, the beach virtually disappears, so narrow is this two-mile stretch of sand. The beach is backed by a wide seawall and a parking strip along its entire length. Here people like to sunbathe in lawn chairs or draped across the hoods of their cars, and to walk their dogs, giving this beach a distinctly urban feel. The sand here is gravelly and often crowded, but the beach does have a splendid view of the Boston skyline. You'll find picnic areas, restrooms, bathhouses and a playground; snack bars and restaurants with great fried clams are across the street. ~ On Quincy Shore Drive, south on Route 3A from Neponset Circle, Quincy; 617-727-1680, fax 617-727-9905.

BLUE HILLS RESERVATION This 7000-acre park is the largest open space within 35 miles of Boston. The reservation comprises dozens of hills, forested land and also several lakes and wetlands, as well as 150 miles of hiking, ski touring and bridle trails. There's the **Trailside Museum** (admission), a natural-history museum with live animals and exhibits. Closed Monday and Tuesday. ~ 1904 Canton Avenue, Route 138, Milton; 617-333-0690, fax 617-333-0814; www.massaudubon.org, e-mail bluehills@massaudubon.org.

Houghton's Pond, with its calm waters and sandy bottom, offers particularly good swimming for children. Ponds are stocked with trout, bass, bullhead, perch and sunfish. Facilities include picnic areas, restrooms, lifeguards, a snack bar, tennis courts, a golf course, a small downhill ski run with rentals and ballfields. ~ Reservation headquarters are on 695 Hillside Street next to the state police station in Milton, where maps are available; 617-698-1802, fax 617-727-6918.

▲ The Appalachian Mountain Club operates 20 cabins and 2 campsites on Ponkapoag Pond (781-961-7007 for reservations); camping rate is $15 per night, cabin rates are $140 to $200 per week (there are only weekly rentals in the summer). Reserve these well ahead of time. There are outhouses; no electricity. ~ 617-523-0655, fax 617-367-8878; www.outdoors.org.

MIDDLESEX FELLS RESERVATION "Fells" is a Scottish word meaning wild, hilly country, which aptly describes the 2000-plus-acre terrain of this reservation. These rugged highlands were first explored in 1632 by Governor Winthrop, first governor of the Massachusetts Bay Colony. They were acquired as public parkland in 1893, and a 19th-century trolley line brought in droves of picnickers. The region has been used for logging, granite quarrying, ice harvesting and water power for mills that manufactured the first vulcanized rubber products. Fifty miles of hiking trails and old woods roads run through the Fells. For anglers, Fellsmere, Doleful, Dark Hollow and Quarter Mile ponds hold sunfish, catfish, perch, pickerel and bass. Horses are allowed, though there are no stables. Biking trails are seasonal. Facilities include picnic areas, a skating rink and a swimming pool. ~ Six miles north of Boston, off Exits 33 and 34 from Route 93; 617-727-5380, fax 617-727-8228; www.mass.gov/dcr/parks/metroboston/fells.htm.

◄ HIDDEN

Lexington & Concord

Just outside Cambridge, the two towns of Lexington and Concord are forever linked by the historical events of April 19, 1775, when the first battle of the Revolutionary War took place. The British planned to advance on Concord from Boston to seize the colonials' stash of military supplies. Warned by Paul Revere the night before, farmer/soldier Minutemen had mustered early before dawn on the Lexington Green.

About 77 men at Lexington Green, and hundreds more at Concord, fought off 700 highly trained British regulars. With heavy casualties, the British retreated back to Boston. "The shot heard 'round the world" had been fired, launching the American Revolution.

SIGHTS

Between the two towns you can spend a couple of days visiting battle sites and monuments. When you arrive in Lexington, a few miles north of Lincoln off Route 128, stop first at the **Lexington Visitors Center** for maps and brochures, and to see a diorama of the battle. ~ Lexington Green, 1875 Massachusetts Avenue, Lexington; 781-862-2480, fax 781-862-5995; www.lexingtonchamber.org.

Across from Lexington Green, in the center of town, stands the **Minuteman Statue**, a simple bareheaded farmer holding a musket. The statue's rough, fieldstone base was made of stone taken from the walls the American militia stood behind as they shot at the British. This statue has become symbolic of Lexington history. ~ Battle Green, intersection of Massachusetts Avenue and Bedford Street, Lexington.

On the green next to the Visitors Center is the yellow, woodframe **Buckman Tavern**, built in 1709. This is where the Minutemen gathered to await the British after Revere's warning. Friendly costumed guides lead you through the house, with its wide-planked floors and 18th-century furniture and musket displays. Call for hours. Closed November through March. Admission. ~ Lexington Green, 1 Bedford Street, Lexington; 781-862-5598 or 781-862-1703, fax 781-862-4920; www.lexingtonhistory.org, e-mail info@lexingtonhistory.org.

A short walk north of the green is the **Hancock-Clarke House**, where Samuel Adams and John Hancock were staying that fateful night. Revere stopped here to warn them. John Hancock's father built this pretty little woodframe house with 12-over-16 windows around 1700. Call for hours and group tours. Closed late October to April. Closed weekdays April through June. Admission. ~ 36 Hancock Street, Lexington; 781-862-1703, fax 781-862-4920; www.lexingtonhistory.org, e-mail info@lexingtonhistory.org.

The little red **Munroe Tavern**, built in 1695, served as British headquarters and housed wounded British soldiers after the battle. The tavern has been maintained as it was, and there are mementos of a 1789 visit by George Washington. Closed weekdays April through June. Closed November through March. Admission. ~ 1332 Massachusetts Avenue, Lexington; 781-862-1703, fax 781-862-4920; www.lexingtonhistory.org, e-mail info@lexingtonhistory.org.

The **Jonathan Harrington House**, now a private residence, was the home of Minuteman fifer Jonathan Harrington, who died in his wife's arms after being fatally wounded in the battle. ~ Harrington Road, Lexington.

The **Museum of Our National Heritage** has changing exhibits on American history in four galleries. Past programs have included retrospectives on George Washington, American Indians and topics such as diners, neon, folk art and textiles from different periods. There are also permanent exhibits on the American Revolution and Masonic history. There's also a small café in an airy, bright atrium featuring light sandwiches, snacks and coffee.

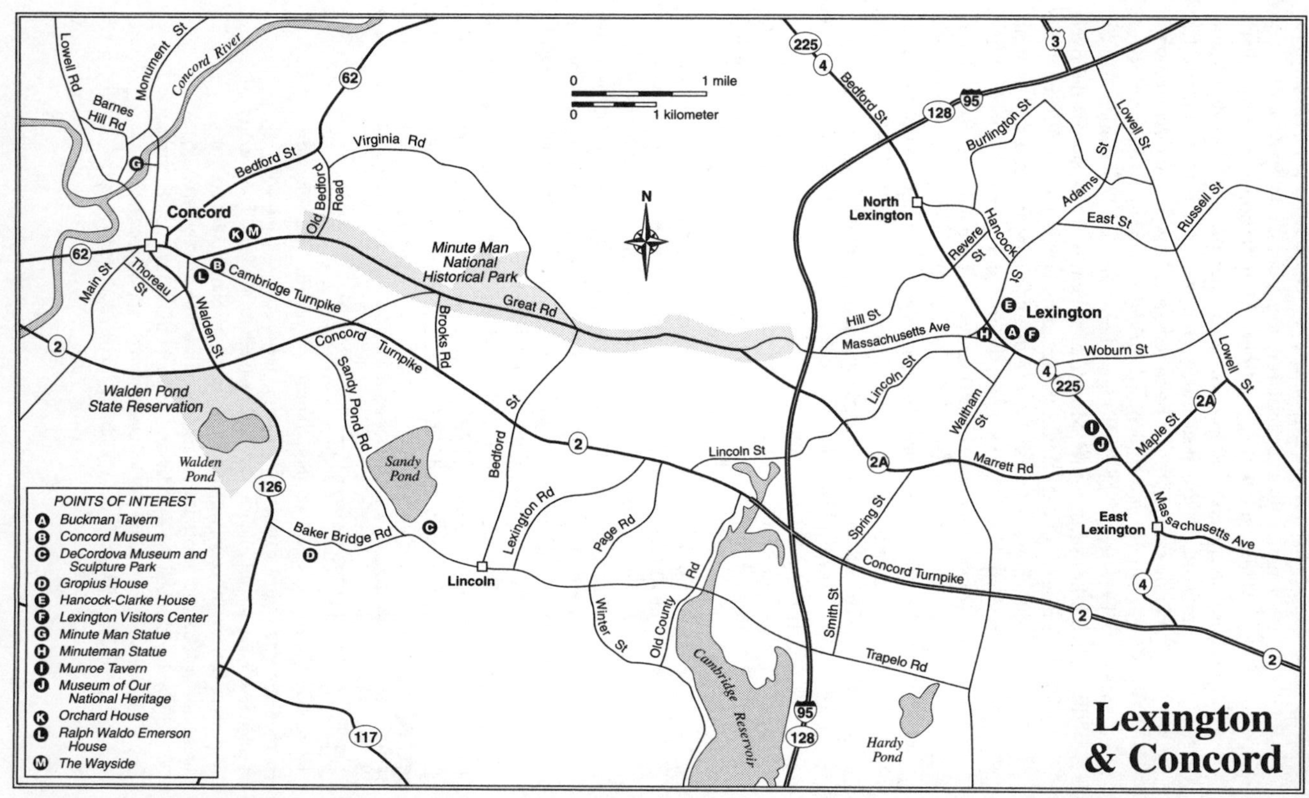
Lexington & Concord
POINTS OF INTEREST
A Buckman Tavern
B Concord Museum
C DeCordova Museum and Sculpture Park
D Gropius House
E Hancock-Clarke House
F Lexington Visitors Center
G Minute Man Statue
H Minuteman Statue
I Munroe Tavern
J Museum of Our National Heritage
K Orchard House
L Ralph Waldo Emerson House
M The Wayside
Concord
Lexington
North Lexington
East Lexington
Lincoln
Minute Man National Historical Park
Walden Pond State Reservation
Walden Pond
Sandy Pond
Hardy Pond
Cambridge Reservoir
Concord River
0
1 mile
0
1 kilometer
N
Lowell Rd
Barnes Hill Rd
Monument St
Main St
Thoreau St
Walden St
Bedford St
Old Bedford Road
Virginia Rd
Cambridge Turnpike
Great Rd
Brooks Rd
Concord Turnpike
Sandy Pond Rd
Baker Bridge Rd
Bedford St
Lexington Rd
Page Rd
Winter St
Old County Rd
Lincoln St
Smith St
Spring St
Trapelo Rd
Hill St
Massachusetts Ave
Revere St
Hancock St
Burlington St
Adams St
East St
Russell St
Lowell St
Woburn St
Waltham St
Marrett Rd
Maple St
2
2A
3
4
62
95
117
126
128
225

~ 33 Marrett Road, Lexington; 781-861-6559, fax 781-861-9846; www.nationalheritagemuseum.org, e-mail info@monh.org.

Within the 970-acre **Minute Man National Historical Park** are several more sites involved in the Battle of Lexington and Concord. In this peaceful, sylvan spot, it's hard to picture the bloody carnage of the historic battle. A wide, pine-scented path leads to the site of the **North Bridge** spanning the Concord River, a 1956 replica of the bridge where Concord Minutemen held off the British. Another **Minute Man Statue** stands across the river, made of melted cannon, designed by Daniel Chester French. This one shows a farmer with gun and plow in hand and is well-known from U.S. Savings Bonds and as the symbol of the National Guard. The five-and-a-half mile Battle Road Interpretive Trail enables visitors to follow remnants of the historic Battle Road and visit historic houses, farming fields, wetlands and forests. ~ 174 Liberty Street, Concord; 978-369-6993, fax 978-318-7800; www.nps.gov/mima, e-mail mima_info@nps.gov.

At the **Minute Man Visitor Center** are a film and exhibits. ~ Route 2A, Lexington; 781-862-7753; www.nps.gov/mima.

Concord is also famed as the home of four great literary figures of the 19th century: Nathaniel Hawthorne, Ralph Waldo Emerson, Henry David Thoreau and Louisa May Alcott.

The **Old Manse** was home not only to Emerson but also to Hawthorne, who lived there with his wife for three years while writing *Mosses from an Old Manse*. The restored house is filled with Emerson and Hawthorne memorabilia. Closed November to mid-April. Admission. ~ 269 Monument Street, near North Bridge, Concord; 978-369-3909, fax 978-287-6154; www.oldmanse.org, e-mail oldmanse@ttor.org.

The Alcott family lived at **Orchard House** for almost 20 years. Here Louisa May Alcott wrote her most famous novels, *Little Women* and *Little Men*. The 300-year-old home is also the

sights

AUTHOR FAVORITE

A trip to Concord should include a visit to **The Wayside**. Former home to the Alcotts and Nathaniel Hawthorne, this historical residence is now part of Minute Man National Historical Park. The Alcotts lived there for several years when Louisa was a girl. Hawthorne bought the house in 1852 and wrote his biography of Franklin Pierce here. Closed Monday through Wednesday and from late October to Memorial Day. Call for hours. Admission. ~ 455 Lexington Road, Concord; 978-318-7825, 978-369-6993 (off-season), fax 978-318-7800; www.nps.gov/mima.

site of special events, workshops and family programs. Closed the first two weeks in January. Admission. ~ 399 Lexington Road, Concord; 978-369-4118, fax 978-369-1367; www.louisamayalcott.org, e-mail info@louisamayalcott.org.

Ralph Waldo Emerson House is where Emerson lived for almost 50 years, with Thoreau, Hawthorne and the Alcotts as his frequent guests. Almost all furnishings are original. Closed Monday through Wednesday and from mid-October to mid-April. Admission. ~ 28 Cambridge Turnpike, Concord; 978-369-2236.

The **Concord Museum** contains Revolutionary War artifacts, literary relics and other historic items associated with Concord. Emerson's study was reconstructed and moved here, and the Thoreau Room holds the simple furniture Thoreau made for his cabin at Walden Pond. Admission. ~ Cambridge Turnpike, Concord; 978-369-9763, fax 978-369-9660; www.concordmuseum.org, e-mail cm1@concordmuseum.org.

Few places have been more indelibly stamped by the presence of one individual than **Walden Pond State Reservation.** "I went to the woods because I wished to live deliberately, to front the essential facts of life, and see if I could not learn what it had to teach, and not, when I came to die, discover that I had not lived," wrote Thoreau in his famous account of his two years spent in a little cabin in these woods, beginning in 1845. Thoreau occupied himself studying nature, fishing and hoeing his bean crop. Today, Walden Pond offers less solitude—it's almost always crowded. But you can swim or fish in the pond, or perhaps try a little rowboating. Nature trails wind around the pond. You can also visit the little cairn of stones that marks the cabin site, and see a replica of the house. Parking fee, $5. ~ Route 126 off Route 2; 978-369-3254, fax 978-371-6438.

LODGING

If you're looking for an inexpensive place to stay right in the middle of Lexington, you might stop at the **Battle Green Inn & Suites.** The 96 rooms in this L-shaped motel surround two courtyards graced with tropical plants and a heated swimming pool. Inside, guest rooms sport Colonial decor. ~ 1720 Massachusetts Avenue, Lexington; 781-862-6100, 800-343-0235, fax 781-861-9485; www.battlegreeninn.com, e-mail manager@battlegreeninn.com. MODERATE.

Concord is greener and more rural than Lexington, making it a more restful place to stay. You can't stay there without stumbling over history.

The **Hawthorne Inn,** built around 1870, is situated on land that once belonged to Emerson, the Alcotts and Hawthorne, and stands right across the street from the Hawthorne and Alcott houses. This homey inn has seven rooms, all furnished with canopied or four-poster beds covered with handmade quilts, as well as original artwork and antique furnishings. The private baths are large and nicely redone. Rates drop significantly during the off-season. Continental breakfast and afternoon tea are included. No smoking. ~ 462 Lexington Road, Concord; 978-369-5610, fax 978-287-4949; www.concordmass.com, e-mail inn@concordmass.com. ULTRA-DELUXE.

Right on the town green, the **Colonial Inn** dates to 1716. The original part of the house was once owned by Thoreau's grandfather. Although the inn has 56 rooms, few are in the historic old inn. Twenty rooms are in a newer wing added in 1970 and are comfortable but bland. The 15 rooms in the original part of the house are larger and have a more historic ambience, with wide-planked floors, hand-hewn beams and four-poster beds. The inn has three restaurants and a tavern. ~ 48 Monument Square, Concord; 978-369-9200, 800-370-9200, fax 978-371-1533; www.concordscolonialinn.com, e-mail colonial@concordscolonialinn.com. DELUXE TO ULTRA-DELUXE.

Among other things, Concord is known for Concord grapes, developed and cultivated here by Ephraim Wales Bull.

In nearby Bedford, the contemporary **Bedford Glen Hotel** occupies 24 piney acres, offering a bit of a resort experience. The 284 rooms are all decorated with modern furnishings. Facilities include indoor and outdoor tennis courts, a fitness center, a whirlpool and sauna. The hotel works well both as a family-friendly accommodation (rooms are child-proof) and as a business hotel (there are meeting rooms and a business center). ~ 44 Middlesex Turnpike, Bedford; 781-214-4545, 866-651-5500, fax 781-275-8956; www.bedford.dolce.com. DELUXE TO ULTRA-DELUXE.

DINING

Yangtze River Restaurant specializes in Polynesian cuisine as well as Szechuan and Cantonese favorites. The dining room is noisy and casual, with a jungle of greenery and exposed brick walls. ~ Depot Square, Lexington; 781-861-6030, fax 781-861-0410. MODERATE.

For some traditional Yankee fare in a historic setting, try the **Colonial Inn**. Built in 1716, the original part of the house was once owned by Thoreau's grandfather. There are three restaurants, each with its own Colonial-inspired decor. The menu includes prime rib, steak, and lobster. ~ 48 Monument Square, Concord; 978-369-9200; www.concordscolonialinn.com, e-mail colonial@concordscolonialinn.com. MODERATE TO ULTRA-DELUXE.

Located in Concord's turn-of-the-20th-century firehouse, **Walden Grille** offers a well-rounded menu of meat- and seafood-based fare. Dine in the formal dining room or the more laid-back bar area. For appetizers, consider the duck sausage or goat cheese bruschetta. Entrées include cumin-and-fennel grilled salmon, braised haddock in a lobster-tomato sauce, and a variety of chicken, lamb, pork, steak and veal options. Reservations recommended. ~ 24 Walden Street, Concord; 978-371-2233; www.waldengrille.com. DELUXE TO ULTRA-DELUXE.

Outdoor Adventures

SAILING

Sailing the blue waters of the Charles on a breezy day with views of both the Boston and Cambridge skylines is an experience to be savored. **Community Boating** rents windsurfers, kayaks, sonars and more to visitors who pass a test and buy a two-day membership. Closed November through March. ~ 21 David G. Mugar Way; 617-523-1038; www.community-boating.org. You can charter captained sailboats at the **Boston Sailing Center**. Closed November to May. ~ 54 Lewis Wharf; 617-227-4198; www.bostonsailingcenter.com. Experienced sailors can rent 23- to 39-foot boats from the **Boston Harbor Sailing Club**. ~ Rowes Wharf; 617-720-0049; www.bostonharborsailing.com.

WHALE WATCHING

Boston is within easy reach of Stellwagen Bank, a major feeding ground for whales. You can go whale watching from April through November with the **New England Aquarium.** ~ Central Wharf; 617-973-5200; www.neaq.org. **Boston Harbor Cruises** also offers day trips in the area around Stellwagen Bank. Trips run from July through October. ~ 1 Long Wharf; 617-227-4321, 877-733-9425; www.bostonharborcruises.com. **Beantown Whale Watch** offers half-day outings on their multideck vessels. Don't spot a whale?—the next trip's on them. ~ 60 Rowes Wharf; 617-542-8000; www.massbaylines.com.

JOGGING

Running is very big in Boston, where half the population seems to be in training for the Boston Marathon. The most popular running paths are along both sides of the green strips paralleling the Charles River; these run more than 17 miles. For information, call **USA Track & Field.** ~ 2001 Beacon Street, Brookline; 617-566-7600; www.usatfne.org, e-mail office@usatfne.org. Another safe place to jog is **Breakheart Reservation**'s two- and three-mile paved roads. ~ 177 Forest Street, Saugus; 781-233-0834.

ICE SKATING

Skaters have been tracing the curves of the lagoon in the Public Garden and the Boston Common's **Frog Pond** for more than 200 years. Skate rentals available. Closed April through October. Admission. ~ 617-635-2120. The Charles River is almost never frozen hard enough for skating, but **The Department of Conservation and Recreation** maintains 20 public indoor rinks, some with rentals available. Closed mid-March to mid-November. Admi ssion. ~ 617-626-1250; www.mass.gov/dcr/recreate/skating.htm.

The Skating Club of Boston also has public skating and rentals. Call for times and age restrictions. Admission. ~ 1240 Soldiers Field Road; 617-782-5900; www.scboston.org.

SKIING Cross-country skiers have a number of options. The **Weston Ski Track** has two kilometers of gently sloping trails that are machine generated and run over a golf course; lessons and rentals (including snowshoes) are available. They operate from mid-December to mid-March. ~ 200 Park Road, Weston; 781-891-6575; www.ski-paddle.com. The **Middlesex Fells Reservation** has a free six-mile trail, suiting a variety of skill levels, but you have to pay for the trail maps. ~ 4 Woodland Road, Stoneham; 781-662-5214. **Wompatuck State Park** has seven miles of fairly hilly cross-country trails, with free trail maps at the park headquarters. ~ Union Street, Hingham; 781-749-7160.

GOLF In Hyde Park, visit the 18-hole **George Wright Golf Course.** Designed by Donald Ross, the championship course rents carts and clubs. ~ 420 West Street; 617-364-2300. The par-5 **Presidents Golf Course** has 18 holes. Their signature 15th hole lands even the most experienced golfers in the water. ~ 357 West Squantum Street, Quincy; 617-328-3444. The 18-hole **Braintree Municipal Golf Course** is open for play. ~ 101 Jefferson Street, Braintree; 781-843-9780. The public **Newton Commonwealth Golf Course**'s second hole is a difficult par 5 around a creek on an elevated green. Lessons are available. ~ 212 Kenrick Street, Newton; 617-630-1971. There are two 18-hole courses at the **Stow Acres Country Club.** ~ 58 Randall Road, Stow; 978-568-1100; www.stowacres.com. A natural marsh surrounds the **Colonial Golf Club**'s course. Closed in winter. ~ 1 Audubon Road, Wakefield; 781-245-0335.

TENNIS **The Department of Conservation and Recreation** (DCR) maintains about 45 courts in the city and greater Boston. ~ 251 Causeway Street; 617-727-1680. Cambridge, too, has more than ten outdoor public courts. ~ Parks and Recreation: 617-349-6231.

There are numerous private clubs; one open to the public is the **Sportsmen's Tennis Club**, offering both indoor and outdoor courts. Fee. ~ 950 Blue Hill Avenue, Dorchester; 617-288-9092; www.sportsmenstennisclub.org.

BIKING Biking is popular around Boston's scenic waterways, including the Charles River, although we wouldn't recommend it in the narrow, congested downtown streets. The Charles River Esplanade,

AUTHOR FAVORITE

If you're up for a really challenging bike route, try the 135-mile **Claire Saltonstall Bikeway.** The first segment runs from Boston to Bourne at the entrance to Cape Cod; continuing segments follow the Cape Cod Rail Trail all the way to Provincetown at the tip of the Cape.

on the Boston side of the Charles River, has the well-marked, 18-mile **Dr. Paul Dudley White Bike Pathway,** which goes from Science Park through Boston, Cambridge and Newton, ending in Watertown. The **Stony Brook Reservation Bike Path** runs four miles through forests in West Roxbury/Hyde Park. ~ Turtle Pond Parkway, West Roxbury, Hyde Park; 617-698-1802. The **Mystic River Reservation** also has a nice bike path (3.5 miles) that runs from the Wellington Bridge in Somerville along the Mystic River to beyond the Wellington Bridge in Everett.

For information on area biking, contact the **Massachusetts Bicycle Coalition** (MassBike). ~ 171 Milk Street, Boston; 617-542-2453; www.massbike.org, e-mail bikeinfo@massbike.org.

Bike Rentals Mountain bike and hybrid rentals (locks and helmets included) are available at the **Community Bike Shop.** ~ 496 Tremont Street; 617-542-8623; www.communitybicycle.com. Near Copley Square, **Back Bay Bike and Board** rents mountain bikes, hybrids, cruisers and tandems and has trail maps. ~ 362 Commonwealth Avenue; 617-247-2336; www.backbaybicycles.com.

Transportation

CAR

If you arrive in Boston by car, you'll have to watch closely for road markings; routes change numbers and names frequently. Also, roads will be tied up by a major project designed to construct a third harbor tunnel and to depress the Central Artery underground. This project, known as the "Big Dig," is nearly complete. No one in his right mind would want to bring a car to downtown Boston, where narrow, confusing streets are ruled by legendarily homicidal drivers. Save the car for touring the suburbs of Greater Boston or outlying areas.

From the north, **Route 95** follows a curving, southwesterly path to Boston, changing to **Route 128** as it forms a beltway around the city. **Route 93** runs directly north–south through Boston; its downtown portion is called the Central Artery, and it's known as the John Fitzgerald Expressway and the Southeast Expressway between Boston and Route 128 in Braintree. **Route 90,** the Massachusetts Turnpike, heads into and through Boston from the west. It also directly connects to Logan International Airport From the south, you can reach Boston by Route 95, **Route 24** or **Route 3.**

AIR

Logan International Airport, the busy and crowded main airport serving Boston, is two miles north of the city in East Boston. Numerous domestic and international carriers fly in and out of Logan, including Aer Lingus, Air Canada, Air France, Alitalia Airlines, America West, American Airlines, British Airways, Continental, Delta Air Lines, Icelandair, JetBlue Airways, Lufthansa Airlines, Northwest Airlines, Swiss International Airlines, United Airlines, US Airways and Virgin Atlantic Airways. ~ www.massport.com.

Limousines and buses take visitors to numerous downtown locations, including **Carey Worldwide Chauffeur Services** (617-623-8700), **Commonwealth Limousine Service** (617-787-5575) and **Peter Pan Bus Lines** (800-237-8747).

You can also take the subway from the airport by taking a free Massport bus to the Blue Line stop. The slickest way to get downtown is to hop the **Harbor Cruise**, bypassing traffic altogether for a short, scenic ride across Boston Harbor. ~ 617-227-4321.

BUS

Greyhound Bus Lines has bus service to Boston from all over the country. The main downtown terminal is at South Station. ~ 700 Atlantic Avenue; 800-231-2222; www.greyhound.com. **Peter Pan Bus Lines** runs between Boston and New York, New Hampshire and Cape Cod. ~ 700 Atlantic Avenue; 800-237-8747; wwwpeterpanbus.com. **Concord Trailways** runs from points in New Hampshire and Maine only. ~ 700 Atlantic Avenue; 617-426-8080, 800-639-3317; www.concordtrailways.com.

TRAIN

Amtrak services many destinations from Boston including San Francisco, Chicago and New York. ~ 2 South Station, Summer Street at Atlantic Avenue; 800-872-7245; www.amtrak.com.

CAR RENTALS

Parking grows scarcer and ever more expensive, and you can easily see Boston on foot, but if you must rent a car, you can do so in the airport terminal at **Alamo Rent A Car** (800-327-9633), **Avis Rent A Car** (800-831-2847), **Budget Rent A Car** (800-527-0700), **Dollar Rent A Car** (800-800-4000), **Hertz Rent A Car** (800-654-3131), **National Car Rental** (800-227-7368) and **Thrifty Car Rental** (800-367-2277).

Used-car rentals in the area include **U-Save Auto Rental** (617-254-1900) and **Adventure Rent A Car** (617-783-3825).

PUBLIC TRANSIT

Boston's subway system is operated by the **Massachusetts Bay Transportation Authority**, MBTA, popularly called the "T." The T has four lines, the Red, Blue, Green and Orange, which will get you almost anywhere you want to go quite handily. The basic fare is $1.70. Special multiple-day discount passes can be bought at many T stations and the visitor booths throughout the city.

The MBTA also runs a fleet of buses providing extensive coverage of Boston and Cambridge. Exact change required for the $1.25 fare. ~ 617-222-3200; www.mbta.com, e-mail feedback@mbta.com.

TAXIS

Several cab companies serve Logan Airport, including **Boston Cab** (617-536-5010), **Cambridge Taxi Company** (617-492-1100), **Checker Cab** (617-497-1500) and **Town Taxi** (617-536-5000).

FIVE

Cape Cod and the Islands

Every year starting in June, close to 3.5 million people invade this foot-shaped peninsula, grappling with horrendous traffic and crowded beaches just to be on their beloved Cape Cod. It's easy to understand why.

The Cape has it all: silver-gray saltbox cottages, historic villages, sports, seafood, art, first-rate theater and more. But those attributes aren't the real reason people come here. It's the land itself. With its ethereal light, comforting woodlands and 300 miles of majestic, untamed shoreline, Cape Cod reaches deep into the soul. Formed 12,000 years ago from an enormous glacier that left in its wake a unique and magical landscape of sand dunes, moors, salt marsh and ocean vistas, the Cape has a staggering number of utterly beautiful beaches and natural parks.

Linked to the Cape in the minds of many travelers (although definitely *not* in the minds of residents) are the nearby islands of Martha's Vineyard and Nantucket, wealthy enclaves where celebrities find retreat and make their homes along quiet or dramatic seascapes, beside purple heath or in museum-perfect villages dotted with historic buildings. Following in the footsteps of Lillian Hellman and Dashiell Hammett, folks like Walter Cronkite have moved to Martha's Vineyard. Smaller Nantucket has one lovely town filled with museums, galleries and history, plus great wild beaches and backroads. Everyone calls Nantucket and Martha's Vineyard "the Islands"—except the people who live there. Don't even *suggest* that the "islanders" are connected to the Cape unless you want to start a row.

The Cape's first visitors were the Pilgrims, who landed near Provincetown just long enough to write the Mayflower Compact before heading off to Plymouth. As Massachusetts thrived after the Revolution, Nantucket and Martha's Vineyard joined other coastal areas as major whaling ports.

In the 1800s, artists and writers such as Henry David Thoreau discovered the Cape. Tourists were soon to follow, and these once-isolated fishing communities were never the same again.

Tourism has taken its toll. The Cape has a commercial side, complete with tired-looking shopping malls, pizza parlors, video arcades, tract houses and ugly motels. But it's easy to avoid all that if you know where to go.

The 70-mile-long Cape projects out into the ocean in an east–west direction for about 35 miles, then becomes narrower and turns northward. Practically everything worth seeing here lies along the shore, so an ideal way to explore is to follow the northern coast along Cape Cod Bay to the tip in Provincetown, then go back down along Nantucket Sound to Falmouth and Woods Hole. This is the route we will take.

We have labeled the first segment the North Cape, which follows scenic Route 6A along the north shore past some of the Cape's most charming historic villages. Route 6A eventually joins with busy Route 6 and soon arrives at Eastham. Here begins the Outer Cape area, the region known for sand dunes, rolling moors, impressive beaches and the bohemian and tourist enclave of Provincetown. Route 28 runs back along South Cape past a couple of attractive villages and some of the region's less scenic commercial areas (including Hyannis, home to the Kennedy clan). This section ends at the scientific community of Woods Hole, noted for its oceanographic institute. We then journey to those two pearls off the Cape's southern coast, Martha's Vineyard and Nantucket.

Touring this area, perhaps you'll understand what inspired Thoreau to write *Cape Cod*. There's something here, though, that can't be put into words—a special chemistry and charisma that draw people back year after year, generation after generation.

The North Cape

Hugging Cape Cod Bay along Route 6A are the beautiful historic villages of Sandwich, Barnstable, Yarmouth, Dennis and Brewster. Once known as Olde Kings Highway, Route 6A is a tree-lined road that dips and turns past lovely old homes, sweeping lawns, stone walls, duck ponds, museums, elegant restaurants and antique stores.

SIGHTS

Sandwich, the first town we reach, is very green, woodsy and English looking. It dates back to 1639 and has a 17th-century grist mill. Sandwich has more sights than any town on the Cape except Brewster. Maps are available at the **Cape Cod Canal Region Chamber of Commerce**. The four information booths are closed mid-October to April. ~ 70 Main Street, Buzzards Bay; 508-759-6000, fax 508-759-6965; www.capecodcanalchamber.org, e-mail info@capecodcanalchamber.org.

Near the heart of the village stands the **Hoxie House**, one of the oldest houses in Sandwich. Built around 1675, this modest saltbox structure has furnishings that are impressive in their simplicity and ingenuity. A 1701 Connecticut blanket chest with inlay is spectacular; chairs turn into tables and benches into beds. Closed mid-October to mid-June. Admission. ~ Water Street (Route 130), Sandwich; 508-888-1173; e-mail hoxieemail@yahoo.com.

Heritage Museums & Gardens has a 1912 carousel, an antique car collection (including a stunning Dusenberg once owned by actor Gary Cooper), an American history museum and an art museum. If cars, folk art or military history interest you, you'll be impressed. The American history museum has memorabilia from the Cape Cod Baseball League Hall of Fame's heyday. The art museum includes an impressive collection of antique weather vanes, early American primitive and Western art, and cigar-store carved figures. The musuem's 100 acres of gardens are so perfectly manicured they look artificial. There's also diverse concerts and programs. Closed January through March. Admission. ~ Pine and Grove streets, Sandwich; 508-888-3300, fax 508-888-9535.

In the heart of Sandwich village is the **Sandwich Glass Museum.** In 1825 Deming Jarves, a Bostonian, built a glass factory in Sandwich because of its convenient water access to Boston and abundant wood supply for the furnaces, and also because he thought his employees wouldn't squander their money on city temptations, as they had in Boston. His formula worked, and in no time Sandwich became renowned for its glass.

The museum's collection includes everything from jars, nursing bottles and tableware to saucers, vases and candlesticks. A lot of the glass is displayed on shelves in front of large picture

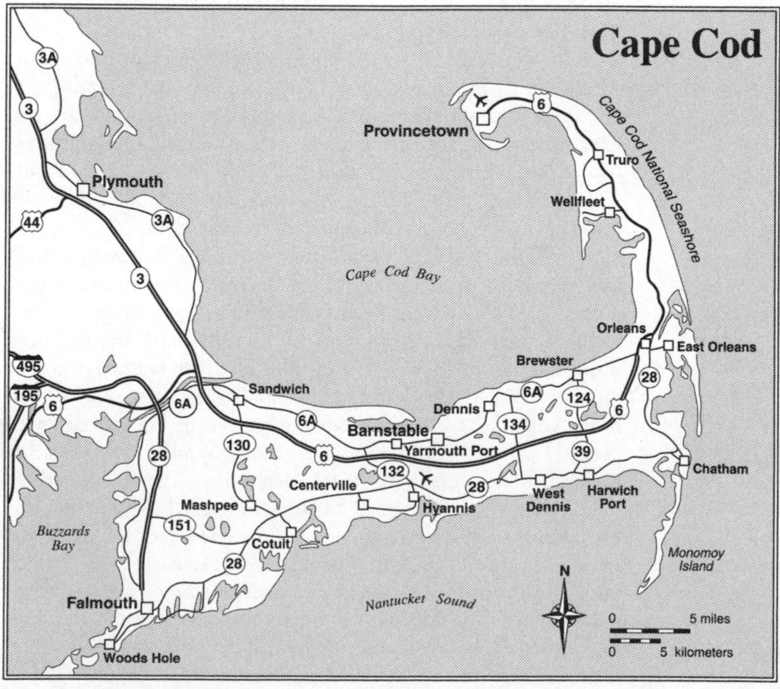

windows. Sun illuminates the glass, and it lights up the museum in a kaleidoscope of sparkling colors. There's a glass-blowing demonstration area and a theater that features a presentation about the town of Sandwich pre-industrial revolution, as well as interactive children's exhibits and a gift shop. Closed Monday and Tuesday from February through March; closed in January. Admission. ~ 129 Main Street, Town Hall Square, Sandwich; 508-888-0251, fax 508-888-4941; www.sandwichglassmuseum.org, e-mail glass@sandwichglassmuseum.org.

The **Green Briar Nature Center and Jam Kitchen** and the **Old Briar Patch Conservation Area** are east of the center of town. "'Tis a wonderful thing to sweeten the world which is in a jam and needs preserving," wrote Thornton W. Burgess to Ida Putnam. As a boy Burgess roamed the woods around Ida's jam kitchen. Today, the Burgess Society produces natural jams, pickles and jellies from Ida's recipes (you can observe the process from April to December only). Nestled in the woods next to a pond, the old-fashioned kitchen looks like an illustration from one of Burgess' books. Peter Rabbit and his animal friends would have loved it here. The Jam Kitchen is closed from January through March; the Nature Center is closed Sunday and Monday from January through March. ~ 6 Discovery Hill Road, Sandwich; 508-888-6870, fax 508-888-1919; www.thorntonburgess.org, e-mail tburgess@capecod.net.

East of Sandwich lies the popular resort town of **Barnstable,** where some of the Cape's most beautiful inns and tempting restaurants and shops are located. For information on local sights and happenings, contact the **Hyannis Area Chamber of Commerce.** Closed Sunday from mid-October to Memorial Day. ~ 1481 Route 132, Hyannis; 508-362-5230, 877-492-6647, fax 508-362-9499; www.hyannis.com, e-mail chamber@hyannis.com.

You'll find the **U.S. Coast Guard Heritage Museum,** a brick structure built in 1856, which was once a custom house, then a post office. Named after a local patriot and historian, the museum includes the largest collections of Coast Guard art, artifacts, memorabilia and books dating from the 18th century into the modern era. Next to the museum stands the oldest wooden jail in the United States (circa 1690), whose walls are covered with graffiti written by seamen. Closed Monday, and from December to April. Admission. ~ Route 6A, Barnstable; 508-775-5308.

Farther along Route 6A, **Yarmouth Port** is the site of two historic homes with impressive antiques. A white Greek Revival home with black shutters, **Captain Bangs Hallet House** provides a peek into 19th-century American life. It features special annual theme exhibits with fine porcelain, antique toys and maritime oil paintings. Open Thursday through Sunday from June to mid-October; group appointments available during off-season. Admission. ~

HIDDEN ►

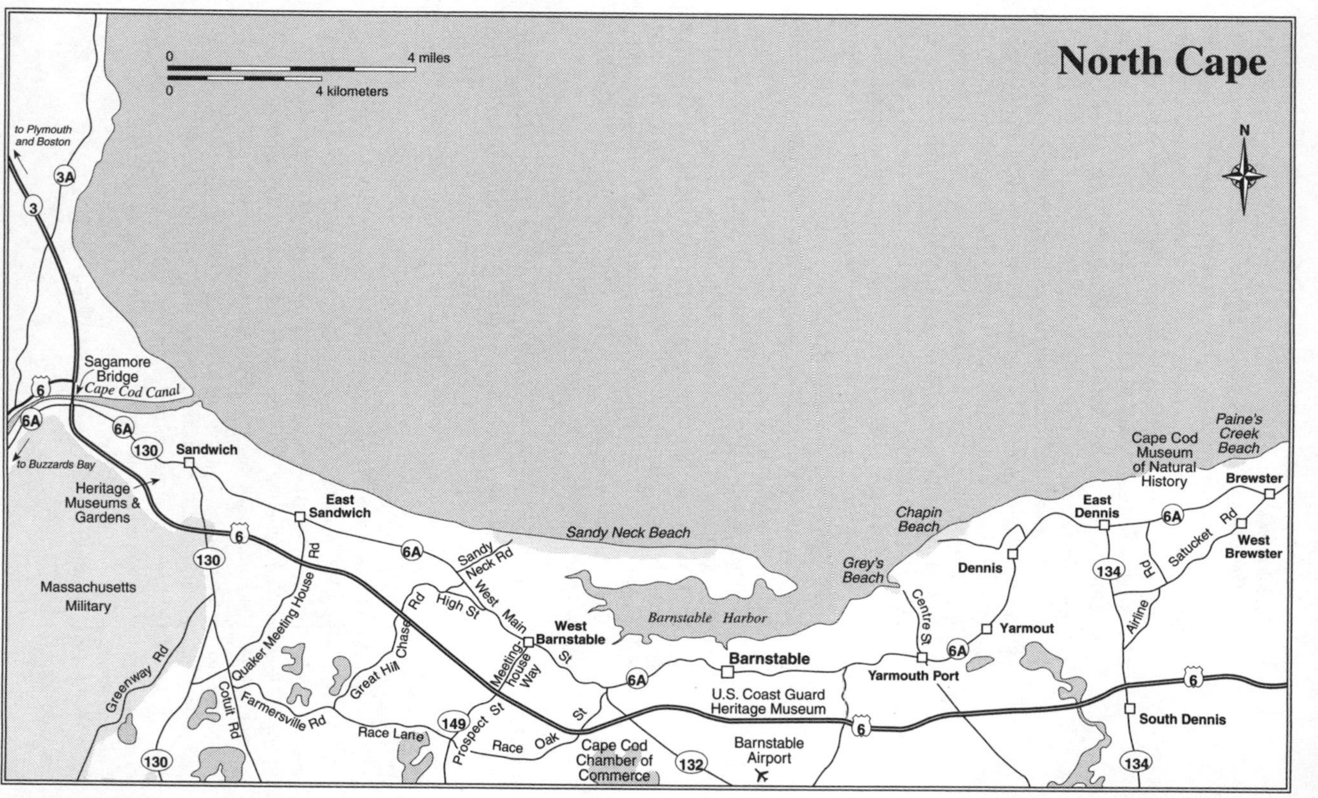
North Cape
0
4 miles
0
4 kilometers
N
to Plymouth and Boston
3A
3
Sagamore Bridge
Cape Cod Canal
6
6A
to Buzzards Bay
130
Sandwich
Heritage Museums & Gardens
East Sandwich
Sandy Neck Beach
Massachusetts Military
Quaker Meeting House Rd
Greenway Rd
Cotuit Rd
Farmersville Rd
Great Hill Chase Rd
Race Lane
High St
Sandy Neck Rd
West Main St
West Barnstable
Meeting-house Way
149
Prospect St
Race Oak St
Cape Cod Chamber of Commerce
132
Barnstable Airport
Barnstable Harbor
Barnstable
U.S. Coast Guard Heritage Museum
Grey's Beach
Chapin Beach
Centre St
Yarmouth Port
Yarmout
Dennis
East Dennis
134
Airline Rd
Satucket Rd
Cape Cod Museum of Natural History
Paine's Creek Beach
Brewster
West Brewster
South Dennis

11 Strawberry Lane, Yarmouth Port; 508-362-3021; www.hsoy.org, e-mail info@hsoy.org.

The 1780 **Winslow Crocker House**, a shingled Georgian with handsome wood paneling and an impressive walk-in fireplace, has a rare 17th-century wooden cradle and blanket chest, a Windsor writing chair and many more valuable antiques. Tours available. Open weekends only. Closed mid-October through May. Admission. ~ 250 Route 6A, Yarmouth Port; 617-227-3957; www.spnea.org.

With four permanent galleries and a rotating special exhibits gallery, the **Brewster Historical Society Museum** maintains an excellent collection of historical items. Paintings, archives, furniture and clothing tell the story of Brewster as it was in the 1800s. Next to the museum are additional buildings owned and restored by the historical society, including the Higgins Farm Wind Mill and the Harris-Black House, two 18th-century structures. Closed Sunday through Wednesday from mid-October to mid-June. ~ 3171 Main Street, Route 6A, Brewster; 508-896-9521; www.brewsterhistoricalsociety.org, e-mail brewsterhistoricalsociety@comcast.net.

The **Cape Cod Museum of Natural History** hosts guided walks through the salt marsh behind the museum, as well as kayaking trips, lectures and overnight stays at Monomoy Island. The hands-on exhibits are popular with both children and adults. Closed Monday and Tuesday from October to June. Admission. ~ Main Street (Route 6A), Brewster; 508-896-3867, fax 508-896-8844; www.ccmnh.org, e-mail info@ccmnh.org.

LODGING

Located in the heart of Sandwich Village, **The Belfry Inne** is a veritable compound comprising three distinctly different buildings. The Village House is an 1860s Federal-style bed and breakfast with six guest rooms. The place is strewn with antiques, and

sights

AUTHOR FAVORITE

Even during my first visit to Cape Cod, I felt an air of nostalgia evoked by the **Thornton W. Burgess Museum**. Dedicated to the author of *Old Mother West Wind* and other children's tales, this shrine to childhood is filled with the children's books that my grandparents read to my parents. The three-quarter Colonial building overlooking the idyllic Canadian geese and swan–friendly Shawme Pond contains a large collection of books by Burgess, beautiful old book illustrations and a gift shop with children's books. The museum offers animal storytimes in July and August. Closed November through March. ~ 4 Water Street, Sandwich; 508-888-4668, fax 508-888-1919; www.thorntonburgess.org, e-mail tburgess@capecod.net many of the rooms are graced with flowered wallpaper. A stay at the Abbey promises a unique experience. As its name suggest, this hostelry is an ex-abbey, and each of its six guest rooms is named after one of the days of the week (Sunday, the Lord's day, is excluded, of course). The rooms offer vaulted ceilings, skylights, balconies and whirlpool tubs. Built as a rectory in 1879, the Painted Lady offers nine spacious guest rooms with working fireplaces and antique tubs. The Belfry Meetinghouse, built in 1638, was the first public building on the Cape. Today it's a B&B; the four rooms have two-person whirlpool tubs, fireplaces and TVs with DVD players. ~ 8 Jarvis Street, Sandwich; 508-888-8550, 800-844-4542, fax 508-888-3922; www.belfryinn.com, e-mail info@belfryinn.com. DELUXE TO ULTRA-DELUXE.

The **Dan'l Webster Inn** is a full-service hotel on Main Street. The Federal-style, 53-room inn is so much bigger than most of the other buildings in Sandwich, it looks a little out of whack. But the inside is very warm and cozy. Guest rooms are done in muted shades like smoke and rose, and are decorated with reproduction Colonial furniture and wingback chairs; some beds have canopies, and some of the rooms have fireplaces and whirlpool tubs. Brick paths lead through graceful flower gardens to a gazebo and pool area. The hotel boasts five dining rooms, an informal tavern, a gift shop, a bar, a spa for both men and women and, in a nod to modern times, free wi-fi. Rates are available with or without breakfast and dinner. Closed on Christmas Day. ~ 149 Main Street, Sandwich; 508-888-3622, 800-444-3566, fax 508-888-5156; www.danlwebsterinn.com, e-mail info@danlwebsterinn.com. DELUXE TO ULTRA-DELUXE.

Built in 1750, the Federal-style **Inn at Sandwich Center** is listed on the National Register of Historic Places and features an outside hot tub (inside a gazebo surrounded by woods) and in-room spa services (by appointment). Guest have their choice of five rooms, each with a private bath and wireless internet, and some with fireplaces. The inn is also within walking distance of the water, art galleries, antique shops and several museums. ~ 118 Tupper Road, Sandwich; 800-249-6949; www.innatsandwich.com, e-mail info@innatsandwich.com. DELUXE.

The **Beechwood** is one of the prettiest inns on Route 6A. An ancient weeping beech tree shades a good portion of this buttery yellow, gabled Queen Anne Victorian and its lovely wraparound porch. The entire house is furnished with fine antiques. In the Cottage Room you'll find a rare 1860 handpainted bedroom set, in the Marble Room a graceful marble fireplace and 19th-century brass bed. The Garret Room on the third floor has steeply angled walls and a half-moon window overlooking Cape Cod Bay, while the popular Rose Room features a fainting couch at the foot of an antique canopy bed and a working fireplace. It doesn't matter where you stay—all six guest rooms are wonderful. They all have private baths and air conditioning. A full breakfast is served in the wood-paneled dining room and tea on the porch. ~ 2839 Main Street, Barnstable Village; 508-362-6618, 800-609-6618, fax 508-362-0298; www.beechwoodinn.com, e-mail info@beechwoodinn.com. DELUXE TO ULTRA-DELUXE.

Located in Yarmouth Port's historic district is **Gull Cottage**, a guest house that has a predominantly gay male clientele. The three guest rooms with shared bath are on the lower level of this 1790s house and are decorated mostly with antiques. The cottage is a mile from the beach and five miles from the boat docks. Closed January through April. ~ 10 Old Church Street, Yarmouth Port; 508-362-8747, fax 508-362-5488; e-mail sallie@ccsnet.com. BUDGET.

As romantic as it is historic, the over-200-year-old **Inn at Cape Cod** exudes class and sophistication. The nine guest rooms (all with private baths) are decorated with antiques, gold-framed mirrors and hand-carved furniture. Some rooms provide a view of the rose garden, while four of the suites boast fireplaces. A gourmet breakfast buffet is served in the elegant pale yellow dining room. ~ 4 Summer Street, Yarmouth Port; 508-375-0590; www.innatcapecod.com, e-mail theinn@gis.net. DELUXE TO ULTRA-DELUXE.

A large inn located on a tree-lined street, the **Colonial House Inn & Restaurant** is a grand hostelry with 21 refurbished rooms with private baths. Most have canopy beds and are individually decorated with period antiques. All boast views of the grounds and adjacent historic homes. The inn features include a heated pool, jacuzzi, an on-call massage therapist (fee), a free business computer center and wireless DSL. A lovely garden complete with waterfall rounds out the amenities. A light breakfast in included, as is a dinner entrée from the gourmet restaurant. A two-night minimum stay is sometimes required on the weekend; call ahead. ~ 277 Main Street (Route 6A), Yarmouth Port; 508-362-4328, 800-999- 3416, fax 508-362-8034; www.colonialhousecapecod.com, e-mail info@colonialhousecapecod.com. DELUXE.

The **Isaiah Clark House**, an 18th-century sea captain's home, is surrounded by three acres of gardens, fruit trees and wild berry patches. Impeccably appointed with Shaker and Colonial antiques, many of the seven guest rooms have stenciled walls, canopy beds, sloping pine floors and fireplaces. Breakfast is served in an appealing room with an enormous fireplace—guests linger here all morning. Impromptu musical entertainment is offered by innkeepers/professional musicians Jan and Dale Melikan. Closed January and February. ~ 1187 Main Street, Brewster; 508-896-2223, 800-822-4001, fax 508-896-2138; www.isaiahclark.com, e-mail innkeeper@isaiahclark.com. DELUXE.

A large turn-of-the-20th-century gray-and-white-trimmed house, the **Old Sea Pines Inn** used to be a girls' finishing school. The spacious lobby and 24 guest rooms are comfortably furnished with antique wicker, slipcovered chairs and sofas; 19 rooms have private baths. Each of the five suites can accommodate a family of four, and three of the units have adjoining bedrooms. A wrap-around porch with rockers, perfect for reading or snoozing, overlooks a yard canopied by pine and beech trees. Breakfast is served on a bright sunporch with many skylights or on the canopied side deck. Several gardens are open for meandering. Guests can also enjoy dinner and a Broadway musical review on Sunday in the summer. Closed December to April. ~ 2553 Main Street, Brewster; 508-896-6114, fax 508-896-7387; www.oldseapinesinn.com, e-mail innkeeper@oldseapinesinn.com. MODERATE TO DELUXE.

Luxury is the bottom line at **Brewsters by the Sea**, an inn and resort with six guest rooms and two suites. Designed as a European spa, Brewsters offers all the amenities you'd expect, plus additional pampering such as fireside massages. Four of the rooms are located in a farmhouse built in 1896 and include whirlpool tubs and fireplaces. All rooms have private baths. ~ 716 Main Street, Brewster; 508-896-3910, 800-892-3910, fax 508-896-4232; www.brewsterbythesea.com, e-mail info@brewsterbythesea.com. ULTRA-DELUXE.

DINING

The **Dan'l Webster Inn** is so Colonial looking, you expect it to serve traditional New England fare, but the food is rather diverse. While the menu changes yearly, specials change every four to six weeks and cover a wide range of tastes. The award-winning restaurant boasts an extensive wine cellar and over 20 different wines by the glass. Meals are served in the very formal Webster Room with peach walls, mahogany chairs and brass chandeliers; in the intimate Heritage Dining Room with brass chandeliers; the light and airy Music Room with a fireplace and grand piano; or in the Conservatory overlooking the garden and gazebo. The **Tavern at the Inn Grille & Winebar** offers casual, reasonably

SANDWICH FOR BREAKFAST

The place to go for breakfast in Sandwich is **Marshland**. A diner-cum-bakery, it's locally famed for its reasonably priced, hearty and reliably good food. It has all the customary breakfast dishes plus lots of daily specials like pancakes, omelettes and hash. Be sure to order a homebaked muffin; they're celestial. ~ 109 Route 6A, Sandwich; 508-888-9824, fax 508-888-8201. A second location (Marshland Too) is located at 315 Cotuit Road, Sandwich; 508-888-9747. BUDGET.

priced meals that include wood-grilled pizzas, sandwiches, burgers and salads. Breakfast is also available. ~ 149 Main Street, Sandwich; 508-888-3622, 800-444-3566; www.danlwebsterinn.com, e-mail info@danlwebsterinn.com. MODERATE TO ULTRA-DELUXE.

Barnstable Restaurant and Tavern serves Cape-American fare with seafood stew, grilled ribeye and a variety of pasta. Located in a small complex of shops, the restaurant creates a pleasant Early American feeling with Windsor chairs, folk art and brass light fixtures. The friendly bar is a good place for a drink, and different varieties of wine are served by the glass. ~ 3176 Main Street (Route 6A), Barnstable; 508-362-2355, fax 508-362-9012; www.barnstablerestaurant.com. MODERATE TO DELUXE.

HIDDEN

Mattakeese Wharf, a quintessential summer resort eatery that is literally on the wharf in Barnstable Harbor, is a bit overpriced, but the million-dollar view will be well worth the cost of a meal. Try to get here before sunset and linger over cocktails while you watch fishermen and waterskiing families come and go in this quiet, lovely harbor. Entrées include large swordfish steaks, burgers, generous portions of mussels and boiled lobster, naturally. Closed November through April. ~ 271 Mill Way, Barnstable; 508-362-4511, fax 508-362-8826; www.mattakeese.com, e-mail mattakeese@aol.com. MODERATE TO ULTRA-DELUXE.

Abbicci serves contemporary Mediterranean cuisine in an 18th-century Cape Cod cottage on one of the prettiest stretches of historic Route 6A. A good spot for a special lunch or dinner, the restaurant has an imaginative, occasionally changing menu. Dishes have included grilled beef tenderloin with black truffle butter, roasted rack of lamb with tomato chutney, and pan-seared diver scallops with white truffle cream. Cozy yet sophisticated and contemporary, it has a number of small dining rooms with low ceilings, Windsor chairs and white tablecloths. ~ 43 Main Street

AUTHOR FAVORITE

The **Bramble Inn** is one of those restaurants people (including me) always rave about. Housed in a Greek Revival farmhouse on scenic Route 6A, the place offers a prix-fixe menu that changes every three weeks. Dinner is served in five small dining rooms complete with Queen Anne chairs, fresh flowers and antiques. Innovative dishes have included grilled seafood in curry sauce, smoked bluefish pâté, and rack of lamb with garlic and rosemary. An à la carte menu is available as well. Dinner only. Closed January to mid-April. ~ 2019 Main Street (Route 6A), Brewster; 508-896-7644, fax 508-896-9332; www.brambleinn.com, e-mail brambleinn@aol.com. DELUXE.

(Route 6A), Yarmouth Port; 508-362-3501; www.abbicci.com, e-mail abbicci@comcast.net. DELUXE TO ULTRA-DELUXE.

Seafood is the specialty at **Oliver's**, where you can start off with crab-stuffed mushrooms then proceed to broiled scrod or seafood alfredo. Veal parmigiana, charbroiled sirloin and chicken cordon bleu are options for meat eaters. ~ Route 6A, Yarmouth Port; 508-362-6062; www.oliverscapecod.biz, e-mail olivers@oliverscapecod.biz. MODERATE.

Gina's By The Sea, a sweet little white-shingled restaurant located within walking distance of Chapin Beach, is far more sophisticated than it looks. The predominantly Italian menu features daily specials and includes entrées like shrimp scampi, mussels marinara, chicken, veal and pasta dishes. Ruffled curtains, white tablecloths and plain wooden chairs create a casual elegance. Dinner only. Closed December to April. ~ 134 Taunton Avenue, Dennis; 508-385-3213; www.ginasbythesea.com. MODERATE TO DELUXE. ◄HIDDEN

The food is hearty and predictable, the service fast and friendly at **Marshside Restaurant**, a casual restaurant popular with locals. Omelettes, bagels, pancakes and french toast are some of the breakfast offerings. Lunch items include lobster salad, quesadillas and fried clams. At dinner it's fried clams, stuffed shrimp, steak, chicken piccata and daily specials. The decor is kitchen-cute with bentwood chairs and ruffled curtains. The back room has a spectacular view of a salt marsh meadow. ~ 28 Bridge Street, East Dennis; 508-385-4010, fax 508-385-4038. BUDGET TO DELUXE. ◄HIDDEN

The painted wood floors, linen drapes, ceiling fans and cloth napkins of the **Brewster Fish House Restaurant** creates a quaint and casual atmosphere. Its small, imaginative menu features dishes such as calamari with tomato-red aïoli and sesame-crusted flounder and five-spice grilled lobster with lotus root and vanilla-ginger nage. Menu changes seasonally. ~ 2208 Main Street (Route 6A), Brewster; 508-896-7867, fax 508-896-7344. MODERATE TO ULTRA-DELUXE. ◄HIDDEN

Elegant and expensive, **Chillingsworth** has been repeatedly praised by the *New York Times* and *Esquire*. The menu changes daily, utilizing seasonal and fresh ingredients. The food is eclectic American, with a seasonal menu that may include dishes such as seared diver scallops with asparagus risotto and lemon butter; and seared tuna tournedos with fresh foie gras, sautéed spinach, and horseradish smashed potato and morel sauce. Located in a tree-shaded 1689 Colonial house, the restaurant has dining areas combining modern and traditional decorative touches such as contemporary artwork, antique mirrors and white tablecloths. Lunch, brunch and bistro dinners are served in the greenhouse room. After lunch, browse in the restaurant's adjacent antique and pastry shop. The seven-course dinner is served at two seatings. The main dining room, closed on Monday, is ultra-deluxe. Bistro dining in the garden is moderate to deluxe. Closed Monday year-round and Tuesday from Labor Day to late November, and from Thanksgiving through Mother's Day. Reservations are recommended. ~ 2449 Main Street (Route 6A), Brewster; 508-896-3640, 800-430-3640; www.chillingsworth.com, e-mail info@chillingsworth.com. MODERATE TO ULTRA-DELUXE.

SHOPPING

Some of the Cape's best shopping is along Route 6A, which is lined with antique stores and artists' studios selling pottery, weavings, handcrafted furniture and more.

Design Works specializes in antique Scandinavian pine armoires, mirrors, chairs, settees, and white linen and lace napkins, tablecloths and bed accessories. ~ 159 Main Street (Route 6A), Yarmouth Port; 508-362-9698; www.designworkscapecod.com.

The Cape Cod Antique Market, a large gathering of antique and collectibles dealers, takes place year-round at the First Congregational Church in Barnstable.

Originally a general store that also housed a church on its second floor, **Parnassus Book Service** has a wealth of maritime and Cape Cod book titles, among countless others. ~ 220 Route 6A, Yarmouth Port; 508-362-6420; www.parnassusbooks.com, e-mail bmuse@parnassusbooks.com.

One of the nicest sights on Route 6A is the vibrant display of fresh produce and flowers at **Tobey Farm Country Store**. Stop here in the summer for fresh native corn, peaches and plums, and in the fall for pumpkins and apples. The white clapboard farm also sells reasonably priced dried wreaths made from German statice, rose hips, lavender, yarrow, dried pink rosebuds, baby's-breath, purple statice and eucalyptus. In October, the store sponsors "scary" and "not-so-scary" hayrides. Hours vary; call ahead. Closed January to mid-April. ~ 352 Main Street (Route 6A), Dennis; 508-385-2930.

A hodgepodge of arts and crafts by over 30 New England artists, **By-the-Bay-Designs** in the Lemon Tree Village has something for everyone. Offerings include glasswork, jewelry, pottery and wall hangings. All pieces are unique and hand crafted. Closed January to March. ~ 1073 Main Street, Brewster; 508-896-1800; www.artbythebay.com; e-mail shop@artbythebay.com.

The **Strawberry Patch** is located in a charming, white 1870s barn with red shutters and red painted strawberries, near the Brewster General Store. It offers infant and child clothing, gifts, household items, dolls and handmade quilts. A life-size horse waits by the front entrance, which is fitting since the shop items are all displayed in the original barn stalls. ~ 2550 Main Street, Brewster; 508-896-3744; www.brewsterstore.com/strawberry_patch.

The Spyglass is a wonderful salty-dog store filled to its dark brown rafters with antique telescopes, microscopes, opera glasses, barometers, nautical antiques, paintings and tools. Closed Sunday during winter. ~ 2257 Main Street, Brewster; 508-896-4423.

NIGHTLIFE

Heritage Plantation Concerts offers a diverse program throughout the summer, including jazz, ethnic and folk music, banjo music, Scottish pipe bands, chorale groups and big bands. ~ Pine and Grove streets, Sandwich; 508-888-3300; www.heritagemuseumsandgardens.org.

Barnstable Comedy Club Community Theater, founded in 1922, is the oldest amateur theater group on the Cape. Throughout the year it gives major productions and workshops. Kurt Vonnegut, an alumnus of the Club, acted in many of its earlier productions. ~ Route 6A, Barnstable Village; 508-362-6333; www.barnstablecomedyclub.com.

Established in 1927 and America's oldest professional summer theater, **The Cape Playhouse** presents well-known plays and musicals such as *The Sound of Music*, *Ain't Misbehavin'* and *Noises Off*, performed by Hollywood and Broadway stars. Lana Turner, Gregory Peck and Henry Fonda have been on stage here; Bette Davis, an usher, was plucked from her job to fill a small role as a maid in a play here. Nostalgic and romantic-looking, the Playhouse is in an 1838 meetinghouse surrounded by graceful lawns, gardens and a Victorian Gothic ticket booth. On Friday morning, the group presents children's theater. Closed mid-September to mid-June. ~ 820 Route 6A, Dennis; 508-385-3911, 877-385-3911; www.capeplayhouse.com, e-mail tickets@capeplayhouse.com.

The Cape Museum of Fine Arts' **Reel Art**, on the grounds of The Cape Playhouse, shows quality films—new, old, foreign, independent—such as *Henry V* with Laurence Olivier, *Ginger and Fred* and *House of Games*. Films are shown during the winter. ~ Route 6A, Dennis; 508-385-2503; www.capecinema.com.

BEACHES & PARKS

North Cape beaches are on protected Cape Cod Bay. They tend to be quiet and calm, with gentle surf and scenic vistas of soft sand dunes and salt marsh.

SANDY NECK BEACH & THE GREAT MARSHES This area has all the ecological treasures for which the Cape is known. Very straight and long, beautiful Sandy Neck Beach offers an expansive view of the ocean and rippling sand dunes bordered by the Great Marshes, 3000 acres of protected land harboring many species of marine life and birds. The sand is ideal for beachcombing, and trails meander through the dunes and marsh. Facilities are limited to restrooms and a snack bar. Parking fee, $15 (Memorial Day to

Text continued on page 288.

The Land of Lighthouses

Massachusetts' prominence as a shipping and fishing center made lighthouses essential early in its history. The first lighthouse in America was built in Boston Harbor on Little Brewster Island in 1716. During the years to follow, 60 more were built all along the coast.

The majority of lighthouses have been well preserved, and many are still in use, although the lighthouse keeper has gone the way of time. Today, lighthouses are automated and unmanned. Lighted buoys, radio communications, radar and high-tech navigational equipment, electronic fog signals and the Coast Guard offer additional protection to seafaring vessels. Shipwrecks are practically unheard of these days.

A few beacons are privately owned, but most are maintained by the Coast Guard or local historic organizations. What follows is a guide to some of the most beautiful and historically significant lighthouses.

Built in 1867, **Highland Museum and Lighthouse Station** in Truro, Cape Cod, is better known as Cape Cod Highland Light. It stands on clay bluffs overlooking an area once known as "the graveyard of the Atlantic" because hundreds of vessels went aground here before the lighthouse was built. Visible 20 miles out to sea, this classic white-and-black lighthouse is surrounded by scenic Cape Cod National Seashore and commands a magnificent view. Open May through October. ~ phone/fax 508-487-1121; www.trurohistorical.org, e-mail highlandlight@earthlink.net.

Located within the Cape Cod National Seashore, **Race Point Lighthouse**, built in 1816, guards the entrance to Provincetown Harbor. Surrounded by wild, windswept dunes, it is accessible only by four-wheel-drive vehicle or by foot. Even after the lighthouse was built, from 1816 to 1946 more than 100 shipwrecks occurred in this treacherous area. ~ 508-487-9930; e-mail racepointlighthouse@comcast.net.

Plymouth Lighthouse, established in 1768, is located on a beautiful bluff at the end of a peninsula that stretches from Duxbury to Plymouth Harbor. During the Revolutionary War, a British ship fired a cannonball at the lighthouse, but it barely made a dent. Destroyed by fire in 1801, it was rebuilt in 1843 and is one of Massachusetts' most scenic lighthouses.

On the road to Nauset Beach is **Nauset Light**, a classic red-and-white lighthouse, one of Cape Cod's most photographed sights. ~ Off Route 6, at the end of Cable Road and along Nauset Light Beach Road, Eastham; 508-349-3785; www.mps.gov/caco.

Scituate Lighthouse, built in 1811 on Cedar Point at the entrance to Scituate Harbor, is maintained by the Scituate Historical Society. It's no longer in use, but an event that took place here during the War of 1812 gave this lighthouse historic distinction. In September 1814, Rebecca and Abigail Bates, the lighthouse keeper's young daughters, were alone in the lighthouse, when they spotted British war ships heading for the harbor. Frantic to do something, they started playing military songs on a drum and fife. The music made the British think the American Army was amassing, and they hightailed it back to the high seas. The girls became local heroes. Admission. Call ahead for time. ~ 781-545-1083, fax 781-544-1249; www.scituatehistoricalsociety.org, e-mail scituatehist@aol.com.

Minot's Lighthouse, which dates to 1850, is built on a ledge one mile offshore from Cohasset. The ledge can only be seen at low tide. Most of the time the lighthouse looks as if it's floating in water. Since it was built in a highly dangerous area, men working on the lighthouse were washed out to sea by strong waves and currents. In 1851, a ferocious storm destroyed the lighthouses and two keepers died. Because of these tragedies the lighthouse was thought to be haunted by the ghosts of those who perished at sea. A museum in Cohasset contains many artifacts and historical information on the lighthouse.

Annisquam Harbor Lighthouse is on Wigwam Point at the mouth of Annisquam River on the North Shore. Built in 1801, this lighthouse doesn't have historic significance, but it is one of the most scenic in all of Massachusetts. It's off the beaten path: to get there, take Route 127 to Annisquam and turn right at the village church, then right into Norwood Heights and follow the road to the water.

Farther out to sea, Nantucket has three lighthouses. Near the town of Nantucket, **Brant Point Light** was the second lighthouse built in America (1746); since then it has been rebuilt eight times. **Sankaty Head Lighthouse**, one mile north of Siasconset, dates back to 1850 but is now endangered because erosion is undercutting the cliff on which it stands. In 1987 this lighthouse was fitted with a modern airport beacon, and its original lens can now be seen in the Nantucket Whaling Museum. The **Great Point Light**, only 15 years old, is a reproduction of an earlier lighthouse built in 1817. Its battery-powered light is recharged by solar cells. ~ The end of Wauwinet Road, off Polis Road, at the northeast end of the island.

Labor Day only). ~ Take Sandy Neck Road off Route 6A in Sandwich to the beach in Barnstable; 508-362-8300, fax 508-362-6517; www.town.barnstable.ma.us/sandyneck.

GREY'S BEACH This small, quiet beach is perfect for children. But the main reason people come here is to stroll along the long, elevated walkway stretching across the marsh that skirts the beach. The walkway permits a close-up view of marsh flora and fauna, and from a distance it appears to be floating in grassy water. This area is quite beautiful, especially at sunset. Facilities here include picnic tables, a playground, restrooms, lifeguards in summer and a pier for fishing and watching the sunset. ~ Off Route 6A on Centre Street, Yarmouth Port; for information, call the Yarmouth Chamber of Commerce, 508-778-1008, fax 508-778-5114.

At Paine's Creek Beach, children love the tidepools that form when the water recedes almost two miles into the bay.

CHAPIN BEACH The sand-strewn road leading to Chapin Beach passes gentle sand dunes and small, unpretentious, summer cottages. A pleasant spot for walks along the shore, the thin, slightly curved, dune-backed beach has soft, white sand ideal for clean, comfortable sunbathing. Occasionally, daredevils (armed with the proper permits) ride their four-wheel-vehicles on the beach's off-road areas (riding on the dunes is illegal). Chase Garden Creek at the back of the beach is fun for canoers; you can shore fish for striped bass. Facilities are limited to portable toilets. Parking fee, $15; call ahead (from mid-June to Labor Day only). ~ Off Route 6A on Taunton Road, Dennis; 508-394-8300, fax 508-394-8309.

HIDDEN ►

PAINE'S CREEK BEACH There are better beaches nearby for sunning and swimming, but Paine's Creek is ideal for quiet walks through timeless scenery bathed in golden light. Weather-beaten skiffs are moored along the shore, and Paine's Creek, a gentle slip of a stream, winds through a salt marsh meadow down to a narrow strip of soft beach surrounded by tiny coves and inlets. At low tide the beach becomes part of the Brewster Flats, exposing tide pools and an additional mile of beach to explore. Parking fee, $10 (mid-June to Labor Day only); parking stickers are only available at the Brewster Visitor Center (2198 Main Street). Be prepared for a miniscule parking lot at the beach. Closed weekends in winter. ~ Off Route 6A on Paine's Creek Road, Brewster; for information, call the Brewster Chamber of Commerce at 508-896-3500, fax 508-896-1086; www.brewstercapecod.org.

NICKERSON STATE PARK This 2000-acre park looks more like the Berkshires than Cape Cod. Dense pine groves, meadows and jewel-like freshwater ponds with beaches are home to abundant wildlife including red foxes and white-tailed deer. There is so much to do here—hiking, biking, motor boating, canoeing—it gets very crowded in the summer. Quiet beaches and hiking trails can be found around Little Cliff, Big Cliff, Higgins and Flax ponds. In winter there's cross-country skiing on the ponds. Catch-and-release fishing is excellent at all four ponds, which are stocked annually with trout; salmon can be caught for keeps at Big Cliff Pond. You can swim in the freshwater ponds. You'll find canoe rentals, picnic areas, restrooms, showers, a ranger station and interpretive programs. ~ Route 6A, Brewster; 508-896-3491; www.mass.gov/dcr.

▲ There are 418 tent/RV sites (no hookups); 168 are available on a first-come, first-served basis; 250 require reservations six months in advance; $15 to $17 per night. Five yurt-style buildings that accommodate four to six adults rent for a week at a time during the summer for $30 to $40 per night. Call 877-422-6762 for reservations during the spring and summer; www.reserveamerica.com.

The Outer Cape

Route 6A ends at Orleans, where it intersects with Route 6 and leads to Eastham. At this point the character of the landscape changes dramatically. The woods disappear and the sky opens up to reveal towering sand dunes, miles of silver marsh grass and windswept moors. At the very tip is Provincetown, one of the Cape's largest communities.

About 50 percent of the Outer Cape is under the jurisdiction of the Cape Cod National Seashore, a natural playground with miles of bicycle paths, hikes and the Cape's most dramatic beaches (see the "Beaches & Parks" and "Hiking" sections in this chapter).

SIGHTS

Fort Hill in Eastham offers a mesmerizing view overlooking Nauset Marsh that's so beautiful it doesn't seem real. Once productive farmland, the marsh today is laced with wavy ribbons of water that wind through downy, soft green-gold marsh grass past old farmhouses, stone walls and ponds complete with adorable ducks. Trails meander through this area, which is a special resting place for blue herons. This private residence and inn is surrounded by the Cape Cod National Seashore. ~ 75 Fort Hill Road, Eastham; 508-240-2870; www.forthillbedandbreakfast.com, e-mail gordon@forthillbedandbreakfast.com.

After Eastham is **Wellfleet**, an unpretentious, wiggle-your-toes-in-the-sand kind of place with a surprising number of good art galleries and gourmet restaurants. On Saturday nights in the summer, many galleries have openings that feel like neighborhood block parties. Wellfleet has many year-round residents, and they all seem to know each other.

Before heading into town, stop at the **Wellfleet Chamber of Commerce** for a gallery guide. Closed Monday through Thursday from mid-May to late June and from Labor Day to mid-October; closed mid-October to mid-May. ~ Route 6; 508-349-2510, fax 508-349-3740; www.wellfleetchamber.com, e-mail info@wellfleetchamber.com.

In the center of town is **Uncle Tim's Bridge**, a low wooden boardwalk that goes over a field of silvery marsh grass to a small wooded hill. A dreamy sort of place shrouded in delicate mist in the morning and soft mellow light in the afternoon, it's perfect for a picnic or quiet walk.

North of Wellfleet lies magnificent **Truro**, a vast treeless plain of rolling moors surrounded by water and some of the state's most impressive sand dunes. Named after an area of Cornwall, England, that's similar in appearance, Truro is a wonderful area for picture taking.

LODGING

HIDDEN ►

To capture the essence of Wellfleet, stay at the **Holden Inn**, a long, white farmhouse-style building. There's nothing fancy about the place, but like Wellfleet, it has an easy, casual feeling. Located on a shady country lane five minutes from the wharf, the inn offers 27 well-kept rooms (some with shared bath) with ruffled white curtains and floral wallpaper or wood paneling. Closed November to mid-May. ~ 140 Commercial Street, Wellfleet; 508-349-3450; www.theholdeninn.com, e-mail info@theholdeninn.com. BUDGET TO DELUXE.

DINING

Restaurants on the Cape fall into three categories: expensive French/nouvelle cuisine, surf and turf, and coffee shop fare. If you crave variety, head for the Outer Cape. Wellfleet has a surprising number of excellent, imaginative restaurants.

Right on Wellfleet's pretty harbor, the **Bookstore & Restaurant** lets you browse through regional titles while you wait for a table. The fare is almost entirely seafood, ranging from Cajun shrimp and steamed littleneck clams to boiled lobster and charbroiled swordfish. Breakfast, lunch and dinner. Closed mid-December to mid-February. ~ 50 Kendrick Avenue, Wellfleet; 508-349-3154; www.wellfleetoyster.com, e-mail bookstre@cape.com. MODERATE.

The Lighthouse is a Wellfleet institution. If you want to mingle with the locals, come here in the morning for breakfast. The ambience is strictly coffee shop, as is the food, which includes french toast, bacon and eggs, fried seafood, sandwiches, hamburgers and the like. Located in the center of town, it has a kitschy miniature lighthouse on its roof that is impossible to miss. Breakfast, lunch and dinner are served. ~ 317 Main Street, Wellfleet; 508-349-3681, fax 508-349-1411; www.mainstreetlighthouse.com, e-mail lighthouserestaurant@gmail.com. MODERATE TO ULTRA-DELUXE.

Sweet Seasons is an exceptionally pretty restaurant overlooking an idyllic duck pond surrounded by rushes, flagstone paths, locust trees and woods. The restaurant serves dishes such as shrimp and scallop in phyllo on a mushroom *duxelle* with a lobster sauce, shrimp with feta cheese, tomatoes and ouzo, petite rack of lamb and duck breast. Dinner only. Closed Monday and from mid-September to late June. ~ The Inn at Duck Creeke, 70 Main Street, Wellfleet; 508-349-6535; www.innatduckcreeke.com, e-mail info@innatduckcreeke.com. DELUXE TO ULTRA-DELUXE.

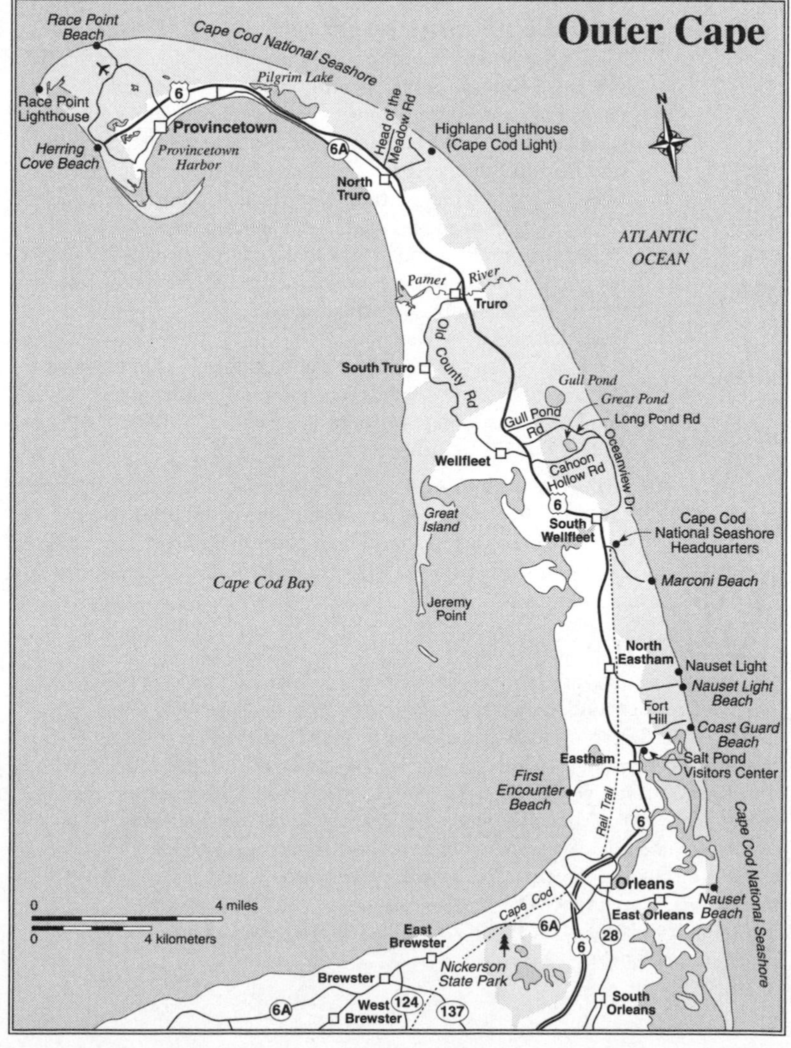

BEACHES & PARKS

FIRST ENCOUNTER BEACH This is where the Pilgrims first encountered the Wampanoag Indians, who were not exactly happy to see them. Six years earlier an English slave dealer had kidnapped some of them to sell in Spain. When the Pilgrims arrived a mild skirmish broke out, but no one was hurt and the Pilgrims made a hasty retreat. Sandy paths lead through dense green grass to this striking beach bordered by a vast marsh meadow and brilliant sky. The long, wide beach attracts a relatively quiet crowd in the summer. Facilities are limited to restrooms. Day-use fee, $15. ~ Take Samoset Road off Route 6, Eastham; 508-240-7211, fax 508-240-1291.

CAPE COD NATIONAL SEASHORE This 44,000-acre ecological wonderland includes endless stretches of unbelievably beautiful beaches, 60-foot sand dunes, steep cliffs, wind-bitten moors, salt marsh, freshwater ponds and woodlands. Undisturbed and undeveloped, the area runs from Chatham to Provincetown and is laced with some of the Cape's finest hiking and bicycle trails (see "Cape Cod by Bike" and the "Hiking" section in this chapter). There's great fishing offshore and in the ponds. Canoe and kayaks can be rented in Provincetown and Eastham. There are lifeguards and restrooms in beach areas (summer only). Parking fee, $15, $45 for a season pass (mid-June to Labor Day only).

What follows are some of the National Seashore's most renowned beaches and ponds. For more information visit the **Salt Pond Visitors Center**. ~ Route 6, Eastham; 508-255-3421, fax 508-349-9052; www.nps.gov/caco.

COAST GUARD BEACH "On its solitary dune my house faced the four walls of the world," wrote Henry Beston of the place he built in 1927 on this extraordinary beach. In 1978 the house washed away in a storm, but Beston's experiences are

AUTHOR FAVORITE

My idea of camping tends more towards lazing than hiking. Lucky for me, **Paine's Campground** has wooded campsites 1.25 miles' walk from Cape Cod National Seashore and the ocean. Nearby, crystal-clear kettle ponds offer freshwater swimming. Toward the front are trailer and RV sites with water and 30-amp electric hookups. A family section has limited hookups and room for multiple tents or a tent and a camper. Quiet couples have tent sites without hookups. There are central restrooms, and water is available throughout the camp. Reservations are recommended during the summer. Closed Labor Day to Memorial Day. ~ 180 Old County Road, South Wellfleet; 508-349-3007, fax 508-349-3007; www.campingcapecod.com. BUDGET.

chronicled in *The Outermost House*, available at most Cape Cod bookstores. Rugged and wild, Coast Guard Beach goes on for as far as the eye can see. Bordered by cliffs, marsh grass and tributaries, a historic red-and-white coast guard station (now an environmental education center) sits on a bluff overlooking the beach. The beach is ideal for long walks, sunbathing, swimming (although the sea can be rough at times) and surfing. Among the amenities are restrooms, showers and lifeguards (summer only). A shuttle bus runs between the parking area and the beach (summer only). Parking fee, $10 (mid-June to Labor Day, and weekends from Memorial Day to mid-October). ~ Take Nauset Road off Route 6 in Eastham.

NAUSET LIGHT BEACH & MARCONI BEACH These impressive beaches are bordered by towering, shrub-covered cliffs. Long, steep wooden stairways descend to the clean, white-sand beaches. The imposing cliffs and expansive vistas make you feel very small and in awe of it all. Walk north along the shore for a quiet spot in the summer, when the beaches get crowded. Swimming is excellent in the protected area, but watch the undertow; swimmers are urged to make sure a lifeguard is on duty before taking the plunge. On the road to Nauset Light Beach is Nauset Light, a classic red-and-white lighthouse, one of the most photographed sights on Cape Cod. There are restrooms, showers and summer lifeguards. Day-use fee, $15 per vehicle or $45 for a season pass. ~ Nauset Light is off Route 6 at the end of Cable Road and along Oceanview Drive in Eastham. Marconi is off Route 6 on Marconi Beach Road, Wellfleet.

GREAT POND & GULL POND Wellfleet has some of the most idyllic freshwater ponds on the Cape. Less than a mile from wild-looking shoreline, these two offer a completely different nature experience. Densely wooded and pine-scented, they look like mountain ponds. The sparkling water is fresh and invigorating. Gull Pond has a lovely shaded grassy area with picnic tables, a small sand beach and a float in the water. Great Pond is approached via wooden steps leading down from the parking lot overlooking the pond. It has a pretty sandy beach. Half-hidden houses lie along some of the shore. You must live or be staying in Wellfleet to park at either pond, and nonresidents must purchase a permit and furnish proof of stay; there are paddleboat concessions at Gull Pond (508-349-9808). Restrooms and picnic tables are available to visitors. ~ To reach Great Pond, take Calhoon Hollow Road off Route 6 in Wellfleet; for Gull Pond, take Gull Pond Road off Route 6 in Wellfleet; for information (late June through Labor Day only), call the Beach Sticker House, 508-349-9818; or call Wellfleet Chamber of Commerce, 508-349-2510, fax 508-349-3740.

◄ HIDDEN

Provincetown

Provincetown, at the Cape's outer tip, is nestled on a hill overlooking the bay. Everything good and bad about Cape Cod can be found here: elegant sea captains' mansions, a honky-tonk wharf, dazzling beaches, first-rate museums, schlocky galleries, hamburger joints and gourmet restaurants.

The people are equally diverse. Provincetown has a large gay population, as well as artists and writers, Portuguese fishermen, aristocrats, beer-guzzling rabble-rousers and plenty of tourists. Similarly, Provincetown's many attractions draw all types of visitors, but the town is particularly popular among gay travelers. The gay scene is everywhere, ranging from the beaches to the boulevards to the bars. Every hotel and restaurant in the area welcomes gays and lesbians and in many cases caters primarily to them, as is noted in the listings below.

Provincetown is so small and parking is such a hassle that everything is (luckily) within walking distance.

Of all the towns on the Cape, Provincetown has the most interesting history. The Pilgrims landed here in 1620 before going to Plymouth, and in the 18th and 19th centuries it was a prominent whaling and fishing port, attracting many Portuguese settlers who still fish the waters today.

Around the turn of the 20th century, artists and writers, such as Eugene O'Neill, started moving to Provincetown, and it became one of America's most renowned artists colonies. A renaissance period flourished until about 1945, when tourism evolved and many artists scattered for quieter parts of the world.

SIGHTS

To immerse yourself in Provincetown's artistic past, get a map of the town and a guide to a complete listing of the art scene in Provincetown, including a calendar of events and listings for various art organizations, from the **Provincetown Chamber of Commerce.** Call ahead for off-season operating hours. ~ 307 Commercial Street, near MacMillan Wharf; 508-487-3424, fax 508-487-8966; www.ptownchamber.com, e-mail info@ptownchamber.com.

For a free directory of gay- or lesbian-owned hotels, restaurants, bars, shops and services, visit the **Provincetown Business Guild** online or call. ~ P.O. Box 421-94, Provincetown, MA 02657; 508-487-2313, 800-637-8696; www.ptown.org, e-mail info@ptown.org.

Walk east on Commercial Street, the main drag, to the **Provincetown Art Association and Museum** for the best art on the Cape. The museum exhibits work by noted Provincetown artists. Call ahead for days and times. Admission. ~ 460 Commercial Street; 508-487-1750, fax 508-487-4372; www.paam.org, e-mail paam@capecod.net.

For a picture-postcard view of Provincetown and the surrounding seashore and sand dunes, visit the **Pilgrim Monument and Provincetown Museum.** The 252-foot all granite tower was

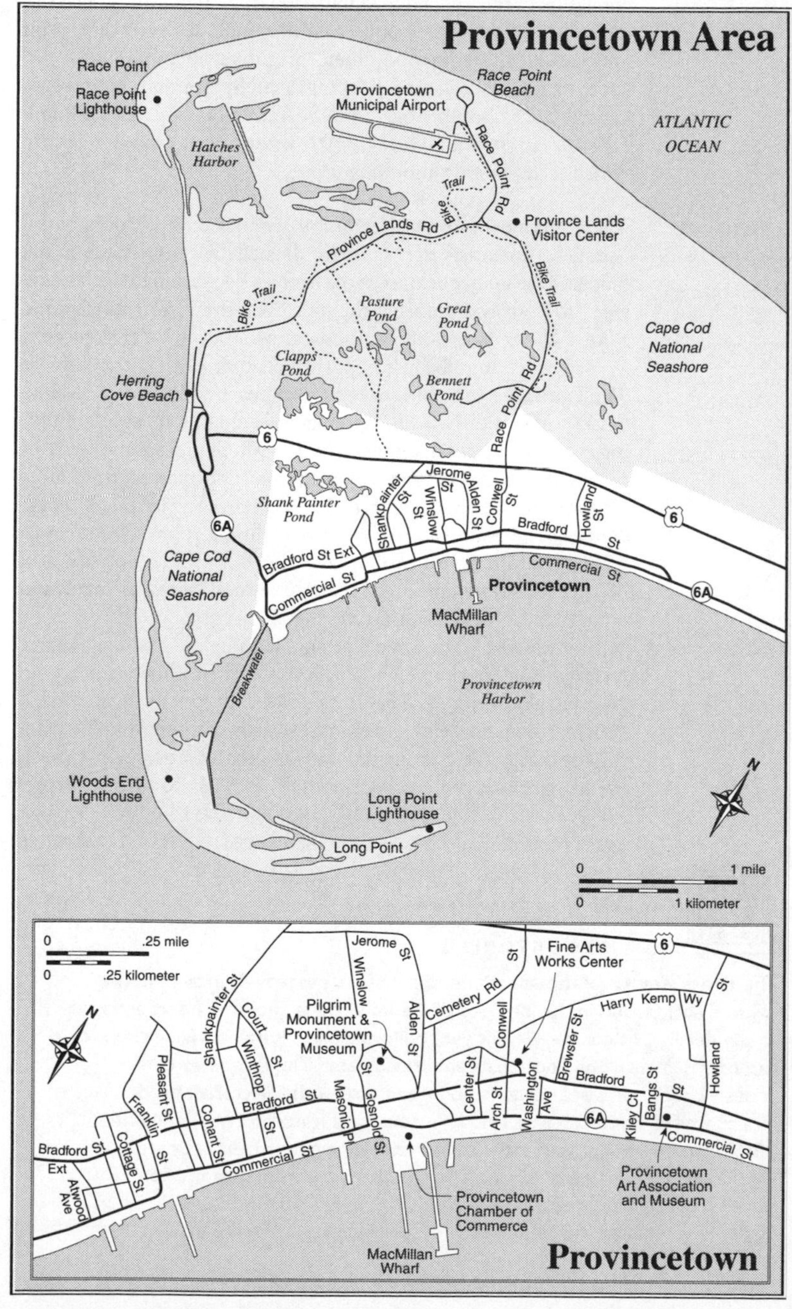

Provincetown Area
Race Point
Race Point Lighthouse
Hatches Harbor
Provincetown Municipal Airport
Race Point Beach
ATLANTIC OCEAN
Race Point Rd
Bike Trail
Province Lands Visitor Center
Province Lands Rd
Pasture Pond
Great Pond
Clapps Pond
Bennett Pond
Cape Cod National Seashore
Herring Cove Beach
Shank Painter Pond
Jerome St
Shankpainter St
Winslow St
Alden St
Conwell St
Howland St
Bradford St
Bradford St Ext
Commercial St
Provincetown
MacMillan Wharf
Breakwater
Provincetown Harbor
Woods End Lighthouse
Long Point Lighthouse
Long Point
N
0
1 mile
1 kilometer
.25 mile
.25 kilometer
Fine Arts Works Center
Cemetery Rd
Harry Kemp Wy
Pilgrim Monument & Provincetown Museum
Court St
Winthrop St
Pleasant St
Franklin St
Conant St
Cottage St
Atwood Ave
Masonic Pl
Gosnold St
Center St
Arch St
Washington Ave
Brewster St
Kiley Ct
Bangs St
Provincetown Chamber of Commerce
Provincetown Art Association and Museum
Provincetown

copied from the Torre del Mangia tower in Siena, Italy. The museum houses an eclectic collection that includes everything from antique dolls, Wedgwood china, primitive portraits and scrimshaw to figureheads and a captain's cabin from a whaling ship. Closed December through March. Admission. ~ High Pole Hill; 508-487-1310, fax 508-487-4702; www.pilgrim-monument.org, e-mail info@pilgrim-monument.org.

LODGING

The Outermost Hostel offers dorm-style accommodations in five cottages. Amenities are standard hostel: common kitchen and lounge. One unique feature is the hostel's key system, which allows entry to your room during the day. Closed mid-October to mid-May. Gay-friendly. ~ 28 Winslow Street; 508-487-4378. BUDGET.

Set in a carefully restored 18th-century sea captain's home, **The Fairbanks Inn** comprises a charming building and fairly extensive amenities (working fireplaces in most and air conditioning in all of the rooms, for example). There are 15 guest rooms, two with a kitchen. Wide plank floors and wainscoting, large, airy rooms and four-poster beds complete the picture. A deluxe continental breakfast is offered in the dining room. Gay-friendly. ~ 90 Bradford Street; 508-487-0386, 800-324-7265, fax 508-487-3540; www.fairbanksinn.com, e-mail info@fairbanksinn.com. DELUXE TO ULTRA-DELUXE.

HIDDEN ►

Built in 1825, the **Snug Cottage**, with its cedar shingles, shutters and nursery-rhyme garden, looks like an illustration from a Mother Goose book. The cottage, one of the most inviting in Provincetown, has eight guest rooms with working fireplaces and private baths. A continental breakfast and afternoon refreshments are served. Gay-friendly. ~ 178 Bradford Street; 508-487-1616, 800-432-2334, fax 508-487-5123; www.snugcottage.com, e-mail info@snugcottage.com. DELUXE TO ULTRA-DELUXE.

AUTHOR FAVORITE

The **Brass Key Guesthouse** is one of the area's best gay-friendly inns. The owner's background in the high end of the hotel trade shows in his attention to the details that count—elegant yet comfortable furniture, sparkling clean bathrooms, meticulous landscaping and friendly staff. The Brass Key comprises 42 rooms in a sea captain's home and three other Victorian buildings, as well as three cottages. The large courtyard features a pool and hot tub. All rooms have private baths and air conditioning; many have private whirlpool baths and gas fireplaces. There is also a beautiful cabana poolside. ~ 67 Bradford Street; 508-487-9005, 800-842-9858, fax 508-487-9020; www.brasskey.com, e-mail ptown@brasskey.com. ULTRA-DELUXE.

The lesbian-owned **Heritage House** offers great people watching and harbor views from the upper veranda. This centrally located Cape Cod–style home, which dates from 1856, has seven rooms furnished with an eclectic assortment of antiques. Expanded continental breakfast buffet included. ~ 7 Center Street; 508-487-3692, fax 508-487-9299; www.heritageh.com, e-mail info@heritageh.com. MODERATE TO DELUXE.

Built in 1820, the **Watership Inn** is popular with gay men and women. Located on a quiet street yet close to everything, the inn features 15 guest rooms with arched beamed ceilings and antiques and two ultra-deluxe-priced two-bedroom apartments. Some have private decks. Continental breakfast is served on an outdoor deck or in an attractive living room with vaulted ceilings, a wood stove. There's a yard where volleyball and croquet are played in the summer. The inn offers terrific off-season bargains. ~ 7 Winthrop Street; 508-487-0094, 800-330-9413; www.watershipinn.com, e-mail info@watershipinn.com. DELUXE.

Located in the heart of Provincetown, the **Beaconlight Guesthouse** was home to a local sea captain in the 1850s. This charming, gay-friendly inn offers guests an eclectic setting, mixing modern and antique furnishings to create a cozy, friendly atmosphere. Common areas include a roof deck, a hot tub, a living room with a fireplace and grand piano and an open kitchen where a continental breakfast is served each morning. ~ 12 Winthrop Street; phone/fax 508-487-9603, 800-696-9603; www.beaconlightguesthouse.com, e-mail info@beaconlightguesthouse.com. ULTRA-DELUXE.

Within easy reach of all of P-Town's attractions, yet a bit removed, is the **Ampersand Guesthouse**. Catering to a mix of gay and straight clientele, it's a Greek-revival house whose nine guest rooms and one studio are decorated with a combination of antique and contemporary furnishings; all have private baths. Some have views of the water. There's a great sundeck with a view of the bay. ~ 6 Cottage Street; 508-487-0959, 800-574-9645; www.ampersandguesthouse.com, e-mail info@ampersandguesthouse.com. DELUXE.

DINING

Provincetown restaurants serve everything from Italian, French, vegetarian and Continental to nouvelle, meat-and-potatoes and bistro-style fare.

Ciro & Sal's is one of Provincetown's most legendary restaurants. Established in 1951 as a coffeehouse for artists, it grew into a full-fledged restaurant serving classic northern Italian food. In 1959 Sal left and opened his own restaurant (described below), and in 2000 the place was bought by a former employee who continues the traditions begun by its founders. Dripping with atmosphere, the basement dining room resembles an Italian wine cellar with a low ceiling, slate floor and candle-lit tables. An upstairs dining room overlooks a garden. Popular dinner entrées include *abbruzzese;* linguine with seafood in a plum tomato sauce and *vitello piccato*—thin slices of veal with mushrooms in a light cream sauce with lemon. Dinner only. Closed Monday through Thursday from November through May; and closed in January. ~ 4 Kiley Court; 508-487-6444; www.ciroandsals.com, e-mail info@ciroandsals.com. MODERATE TO ULTRA-DELUXE.

Sal's Place is cozy and intimate, with Italian ambience: Chianti bottles hang from the low-beamed ceiling, bay windows are draped with lace curtains and a Modigliani poster adorns a wall. The southern Italian menu includes pasta, veal dishes and inventive seafood entrées such as *brodetto* (seafood medley) and broiled salmon with balsamic vinegar and capers. Try the homemade *tiramisu* or chocolate mousse for dessert. Dinner only. Closed November through April. ~ 99 Commercial Street; 508-487-1279, fax 508-349-6243; www.salsplaceofprovincetown.com, e-mail piazzanavona@comcast.net. MODERATE.

HIDDEN ►

A short jaunt off of the beaten path from Commercial Street restaurants, **Napi's** attracts locals and out-of-towners alike. The two-story eatery is filled with local art, including antique stained glass and carousel horses. A woodstove contributes to its homey, down-to-earth feel. Napi's serves dishes of duckling Santa Clara, cod almandine and vegetarian offerings. ~ 7 Freeman Street, Provincetown; 508-487-1145, 800-571-6274; www.napis-restaurant.com, e-mail info@napis-restaurant.com. DELUXE.

Café Heaven is located on a part of Commercial Street away from the touristy hoopla. Housed in an old storefront with large picture windows, the restaurant is bright and uncluttered, with white wooden tables and wooden floors. Colorful paintings by artist John Grillo adorn one wall. The food is hearty and all-American—bacon and eggs, Portuguese french toast, omelettes, tasty scones, lusty sandwiches, gourmet burgers and salads such as chicken tarragon. This popular hangout for gays and lesbians is open for breakfast, lunch and dinner. Closed January through March. ~ 199 Commercial Street; 508-487-9639. MODERATE.

TIME FOR A TEA DANCE

During the summer a popular activity for the gay crowd is the afternoon tea dance at **The Boatslip Beach Club**, a full-service resort on the beach. The afternoon dances run daily through Labor Day and Saturdays only in September and October. Closed November to mid-April. Cover. ~ 161 Commercial Street; 508-487-1669, fax 508-487-6021; www.boatslipresort.com.

The **Mews Restaurant & Café** has two levels of dining right on the waterfront. Elegant dinners and brunches are served downstairs, while upstairs is more casual. The cuisine is intercontinental, the fresh seafood especially good. They also offer more than 225 varieties of vodka. There's an open-mic coffeehouse on Monday from November to mid-May, and brunch on Sunday. Reservations recommended. ~ 429 Commercial Street; 508-487-1500, fax 508-487-3700; www.mews.com, e-mail info@mews.com. MODERATE TO ULTRA-DELUXE.

SHOPPING

Marine Specialties sounds like a straightforward place, but it's not. Housed in a barnlike room, this eclectic shop is jammed with all sorts of reasonably priced oddball nautical and military items such as antique brass buttons, old-fashioned oars, bells, baskets, antique diving gear, fog horns, vintage shoe carts, Army and Navy clothing, flags, bicycle lights, shells and fishing nets. Even people who hate to shop love this place. Closed weekdays in January and February. ~ 235 Commercial Street; 508-487-1730, fax 508-487-3095.

Remembrances of Things Past is fun to explore even if you aren't in the mood to buy. It's full of nostalgic memorabilia from the '20s to the '80s—jewelry, sports memorabilia and vintage photographs of Elvis, Marilyn and Lucy. Closed most weekdays after Halloween. ~ 376 Commercial Street; 508-487-9443; www.thingspast.com.

NIGHTLIFE

Provincetown has first-rate gay and lesbian entertainment—everything from afternoon tea dances, cabaret and ministage productions to piano bars, discos, you name it. Here are some of the most popular hotspots, a few of which draw straights and gays alike.

The hottest gay bar and disco in town is the **Atlantic House**. You can join in on the "manhunt" on Thursday or a specialty theme on Friday. There are three bars: a dance bar, a small jukebox bar and a leather bar. Cover for dance bar only. ~ 4–6 Masonic Place; 508-487-3821; www.ahouse.com.

The **Pied Bar** is a mixed gay bar with a waterfront deck and a big, open dancefloor. Locals say the best time to go is after 6 p.m. for the after-tea dances. Closed November through March. Occasional cover. ~ 193-A Commercial Street; 508-487-1527; www.thepiedbar.com.

Drag shows are a hit at the **Crown and Anchor Inn**, housed in a historic waterfront building. There are loads of different cabaret and comedy shows. This place attracts gays, lesbians and straights. Cover. ~ 247 Commercial Street; 508-487-1430; www.onlyatthecrown.com.

The Post Office Cabaret is the spot for lesbians and gays in the summer, when it presents noted female performers such as Teresa

Trull. The restaurant, located downstairs, is a good place to hang out. Cover. ~ 303 Commercial Street; 508-487-3892.

BEACHES & PARKS

RACE POINT BEACH & HERRING COVE BEACH "Here a man may stand, and put all America behind him," wrote Thoreau in his book *Cape Cod*. Located at the end of the Cape, both beaches have magnificent 360° views of brilliant sky, ocean, dunes and a silver sea of beach grass. On cloudy days, the winds shift, the colors change and a minimalist environment unfolds. When the sun shines, everything shimmers. Both beaches offer long stretches of clean white sand surrounded by acres of untouched land. Bicycle paths and hiking trails are everywhere. There are restrooms, showers and lifeguards, as well as a snack bar at Herring Cove. Day-use fee, $15 per vehicle (mid-June through Labor Day only). ~ To reach Race Point, take Race Point Road off Route 6; for Herring Cove, go to the end of Route 6 and follow the signs; 508-487-1256.

The South Cape

This part of the Cape is a hodgepodge of scenic villages, inexpensive motels, mini-malls and gas stations. To explore it from Provincetown, head back on Route 6 to Route 28 in Orleans, a pleasant yet unassuming residential area. At Chatham, Route 28 swings around to the west and runs along the south shore of the Cape along Nantucket Sound.

SIGHTS

Chatham, one of the most stylish towns on the Cape, has exquisite inns, good restaurants and beautiful shops. It's a very Ralph Lauren kind of place where everyone looks as though they play tennis.

Chatham's **Information Booth** is in the middle of town. Closed mid-October to mid-May. ~ 533 Main Street, Chatham; 508-945-5199, 800-715-5567; www.chathaminfo.com, e-mail chamber@chathaminfo.com. For year-round information, you can stop by the **Bassett House**. ~ Intersection of Route 137 and Route 28.

At the end of Main Street, you run into **Shore Road**, lined with graceful oceanfront homes and a classic lighthouse across from the Coast Guard station.

HIDDEN ►

The **Old Atwood House Museum** is an unassuming 1752 shingled house exhibiting antiques, seashells and Sandwich glass. Right next to the house, a barn displays compelling murals by realist painter Alice Stallknecht. The murals depict Chatham townspeople of the 1930s in religious settings, such as Christ preaching from a dory below the Chatham lighthouse. There's also a maritime exhibit and autobiographical material of Chatham's 19th-century sea captains. Open Tuesday through Saturday from mid-June to mid-October. Admission. ~ 347 Stage Harbor Road, Chatham; 508-945-2493; www.chathamhistoricalsociety.org, e-mail chathamhistoricalsociety@verizon.net.

Monomoy National Wildlife Refuge includes Morris and two other sandy islands immediately off the coast of Chatham, and is home to over 300 species of birds, some on the threatened and/or endangered species list. Harbor and gray seals also thrive here; over 3000 gray seals inhabit this area. The islands, which were actually one island before it split in 1978, are accessible by private boat or seasonal ferry service (North and South islands). Only Morris is accessible by car (headquarters). Parts of them are off limits to the public during certain seasons. ~ 30 Wikis Way, Chatham; 508-945-0594, fax 508-945-9559; monomoy.fws.gov.

West of Chatham is Harwich Port, a lovely residential area, followed by Dennis Port, West Dennis, West Yarmouth and Hyannis, considerably less attractive spots. This stretch of Route 28 is mostly gas stations, coffee shops and cheap motels. But if you've had it up to here with history and quaint villages, this area is great for slumming. There are 11 miniature golf courses in the region, and one of the best is **Pirates Cove**. The Trump Tower of miniature golf, it has an elaborate pirate ship in a lagoon surrounded by terraced rock cliffs, gushing waterfalls and caves complete with plaques featuring pirate tales and lore. Closed November to mid-April. Admission. ~ 728 Main Street, South Yarmouth; 508-394-6200, fax 508-394-5252; www.pirates cove.net.

Because the Kennedys live in **Hyannis**, people usually expect it to be glamorous and beautiful, but most of the town is very commercial. The Kennedys live in the one nice area. People come to

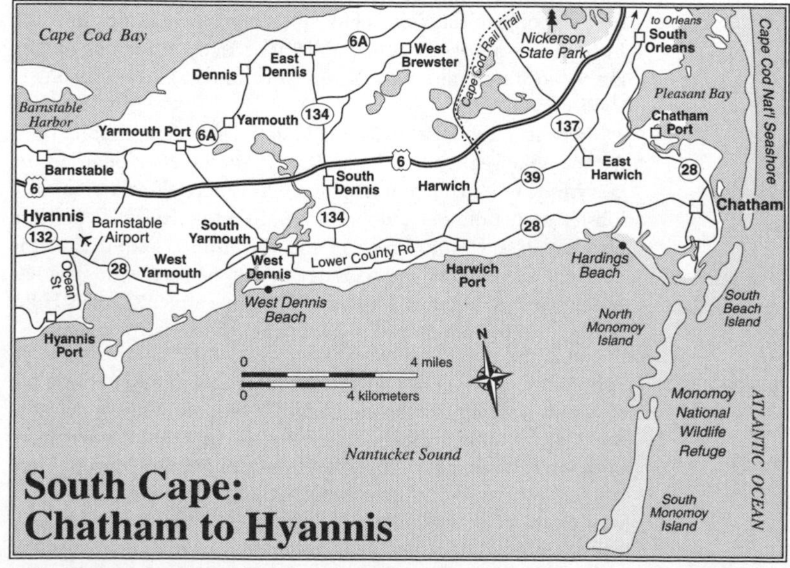

Hyannis for three reasons: the airport, ferries to the Islands, and spying on the Kennedys.

At the western end of the South Cape is **Falmouth**, a charming New England town with a beautiful village green surrounded by some of the Cape's loveliest historic homes. One of these, which houses the **Falmouth Historical Society**, is a creamy yellow, hip-roofed 1790 Colonial building with a widow's walk. Closed Sunday and Monday, and from early October to mid-June. ~ 65 Palmer Avenue (across from Village Green), Falmouth; 508-548-4857; www.falmouthhistoricalsociety.org, e-mail fhs@cape.com.

HIDDEN ►

Six miles north of town, **Ashumet Holly & Wildlife Sanctuary** offers self-guided nature trail walks through its 49 acres. A variety of holly and wildlife abound. Admission. ~ Off Route 151 and Currier Road, East Falmouth; 508-362-1426; www.massaudubon.org, e-mail longpasture@massaudubon.org.

The rest of downtown Falmouth isn't as scenic, but it does have a number of beautiful, high-quality clothing and home furnishing stores. The **Falmouth Chamber of Commerce**, right off Main Street, can provide more information. ~ 20 Academy Lane, Falmouth; 508-548-8500, 800-526-8532, fax 508-548-8521; www.falmouthchamber.com, e-mail info@falmouthchamber.com.

Immediately south of Falmouth is **Woods Hole**, a small, deeply wooded, hilly village that's primarily a scientific community. It looks and feels like a small university town, with a good bookstore, craft galleries and cafés. This is also where you can catch a ferry for the islands—Martha's Vineyard and Nantucket. It's also home to the **Woods Hole Oceanographic Institution**. The Institution isn't open to the public; it's strictly a research facility ranked in stature alongside Scripps Institute of Oceanography in California.

However, the nearby **Woods Hole Science Aquarium** is open to the public year-round. In its effort to preserve regional species, everything in its 16 major display tanks is native to the area: cod, lobster and, flounder among other sea animals. The aquarium also has a seal tank. Proof of identification is required at the door. Closed Sunday and Monday in summer, weekends the rest of the year. ~ Corner of Water and Albatross streets, Woods Hole; 508-495-2267, fax 508-495-2382; aquarium.nesfc.noaa.gov.

LODGING

A romantic, dark brown 1810 farmhouse, the **Nauset House Inn** is within walking distance of beautiful beaches. One of the inn's most memorable features is a magnificent 1907 conservatory with white wicker furniture, exotic plants and grapevines. Each of the 14 guest rooms is individually decorated, and may feature tiny floral-print wallpaper, stenciling and antiques such as a handpainted Victorian cottage bed. Most of the guest rooms in the main house and carriage house have private baths. Full breakfast included. Closed November to March. ~ 143 Beach Road, East Orleans; 508-255-2195, 800-771-5508, fax 508-240-6276; www.nausethouseinn.com, e-mail info@nausethouse inn.com. MODERATE TO DELUXE.

Motels aren't known for beautiful landscaping, but **Pleasant Bay Village Resort**'s will be a welcome surprise. It boasts impeccably maintained Asian rock and flower gardens that are so lush you hardly notice the 58 nondescript guest rooms and apartments. It is, however, only one-eighth of a mile away from a warm-water bay beach and there are guest laundry facilities. Closed November through April. ~ 1191 Orleans Road, Route 28, Chatham Port; 508-945-1133, 800-547-1011, fax 508-945-9701; www.pleasantbayvillage.com, e-mail info@pleasantbayvillage.com. DELUXE TO ULTRA-DELUXE.

Chatham Bars Inn, one of Cape Cod's most luxurious grand resorts, looks like the kind of place where everyone should be wearing white linen and playing croquet. Built in 1914 as a hunting lodge, the horseshoe-shaped gray-shingled inn sits high on a gentle hill overlooking Pleasant Bay. An expansive brick veranda runs the length of the inn. The inviting lobby, luxurious rooms and comfortable cottages reflect the original beauty of this historic building with antique reproductions and period pieces like Vanderbilt Casablanca fans, authentic Victorian mantels and Hitchcock chairs. The 25-acre resort has a private beach, heated swimming pool, spa, fitness room, tennis courts, fishing, golf, magnificent theme gardens and three restaurants. ~ 297 Shore Road, Chatham; 508-945-0096, 800-527-4884, fax 508-945-6785; www.chathambarsinn.com, e-mail welcome@chathambars inn.com. ULTRA-DELUXE.

Since 1860, the **Chatham Wayside Inn** has set the casually elegant tone of the busiest part of Main Street. Each of the inn's 56 rooms has air conditioning, a private bath and reproduction period furniture. Some rooms have a canopied or four-poster bed. If you're planning to be in Chatham on a Friday night dur-

LIVE LIKE A NATIVE

The Cape has some of the most beautiful inns in the country, plus hundreds of other accommodations in every price range, location and style imaginable. Contact the **Cape Cod Chamber of Commerce** for names of realtors handling rentals in a particular area. ~ Junction of Routes 6 and 132, Hyannis, MA 02601; 508-862-0700, 888-332-2732, fax 508-862-0727; www.capecodchamber.org, e-mail info@capecodchamber.org.

ing the summer, try to reserve a suite with a private deck overlooking Kate Gould Park, where Chatham's famous band concerts are held. ~ 512 Main Street, Chatham; 508-945-5550, 800-391-5734, fax 508-945-3407; www.waysideinn.com, e-mail info@waysideinn.com. ULTRA-DELUXE.

Seashore-inspired décor sets the tone at the **Beach House at Chatham**. All three guest rooms include private baths and have clean white walls and white furnishings with blue or red accents. The ambience is calm and refreshing in both the private rooms and the common areas, such as the beach-colored living room with blue and white arm chairs. Breakfast is served in the bright dining room with hardwood floors and furniture. ~ 812 Main Street, Chatham; 508-945-3150; www.beachhouseatchatham.com, e-mail info@beachhouseatchatham.com. ULTRA-DELUXE.

Even though the Kennedy compound (near Ocean Street in Hyannis) is surrounded by tall hedges, all day long tour buses prowl this area, hoping to catch a glimpse of one of the clan. Their efforts are almost always in vain.

Another nearby option is **The Bradford Inn of Chatham**. The 42 guest rooms and suites (all with private baths) are cheerfully decorated; many have balconies or fireplaces. There's an outdoor heated pool. A continental breakfast is included. Children over 12 only. ~ 26 Cross Street, Chatham; 508-945-1030, 800-562-4667, fax 508-945-9652; www.bradfordinn.com, e-mail info@bradfordinn.com. DELUXE TO ULTRA-DELUXE.

Most of Chatham's hotels are expensive, but not the **Bow Roof House**. Located in the heart of the high-rent district, a five minute drive from the beach, this cozy late-18th-century sea captain's house feels comfortable and casual. A patio overlooking a scenic, winding road makes an ideal spot for afternoon tea or cocktails. The six guest rooms are appointed with Colonial bedspreads and furniture, but they're far apart and private. ~ 59 Queen Anne Road, Chatham; 508-945-1346. MODERATE.

Accommodations in Harwich Port are limited and expensive, but **Harbor Walk Guest House** is an exception. The white 1880 bed and breakfast with gingerbread trim is within walking distance of the town's exclusive beaches. Six guest rooms (two with shared bath) are decorated with new and antique furnishings. A porch runs the length of this house overlooking the yard. A full breakfast is included. Pets are welcome. Closed in off-season. ~ 6 Freeman Street, Harwich Port; 508-432-1675; www.harborwalkguesthouse.com. MODERATE TO DELUXE.

HIDDEN ►

A more standard option is the **Cape Cod Wishing Well Bed & Breakfast**. With floral curtains, blue bedspreads and white wicker furniture, the rooms are comfortable, but offer little more than typical hotel accommodations. All rooms include private baths, and discounts are provided for reduced maid service. ~ 212 Route

28, Harwich; 508-432-2150, 888-996-9530; www.capecodwishingwell.com, e-mail info@capecodwishingwell.com. BUDGET TO DELUXE.

On a quiet, tree-lined street, with its own private stretch of Nantucket Sound beach, **Alyce's Dunscroft By The Sea**, a 1920 Dutch Colonial inn, offers seven rooms plus a cottage suite. All are romantically decorated in designer linens and each room has its own bath. Some feature fireplaces and jacuzzis. There's a sitting room and screened porch to be enjoyed by all. Adults only. A full breakfast is included. ~ 24 Pilgrim Road, Harwich Port; 508-432-0810, 800-432-4345, fax 508-432-5134; www.dunscroftbythesea.com, e-mail dunscroft@comcast.net. ULTRA-DELUXE.

HIDDEN

Route 28 from Dennis Port to Hyannis is dotted with one indistinguishable motel after another. However, if you head south toward the beach you will find some nice alternatives, like **The Lighthouse Inn**. This sprawling, 68-room, Old World resort is remarkably affordable for Cape Cod. Located on the ocean, the inn is formed around a lighthouse that stood at nearby Bass River during the 19th century. The ambience is friendly and unpretentious. Activities include shuffleboard, horseshoes, miniature golf, tennis, swimming in the pool or ocean and nightly entertainment. A children's program provides daily family activities, as well as day and evening babysitting in July and August. Guest rooms in the main inn are simply furnished, and separate cottages are also available. Full breakfast is included in the rates. Closed November through April. ~ 1 Lighthouse Inn Road, West

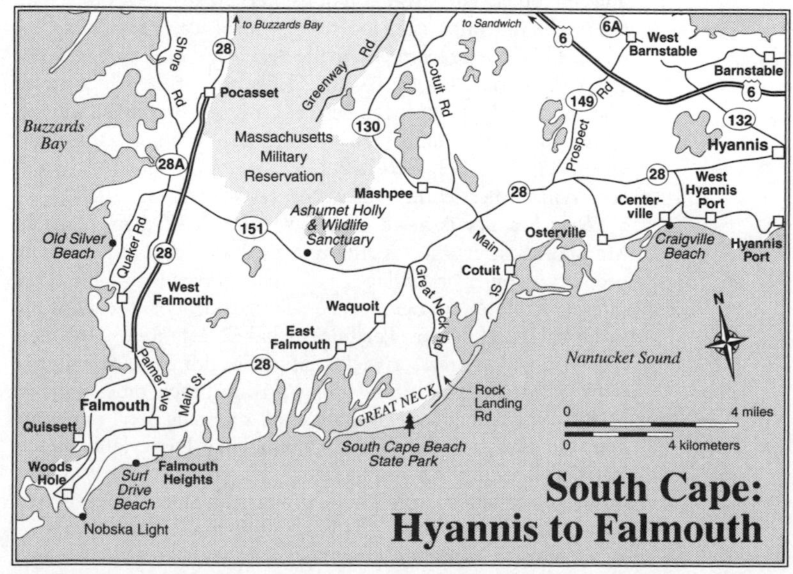

Dennis; 508-398-2244, fax 508-398-5658; www.lighthouseinn.com, e-mail inquire@lighthouseinn.com. ULTRA-DELUXE.

Located in quaint and historic Hyannis Port, the **Simmons Homestead Inn** was once a private estate. Built in 1800, this gracious inn is furnished with quality antiques, canopy beds, white wicker and brass. Sweeping porches overlook gardens leading down to Simmons Pond. The inn also has ten-speed bikes for guest use, a hot tub, a billiards room and a collection of 50 classic red sports cars housed in adjoining Toad Hall Museum. Unlike those in most old inns, the ten rooms and four bedrooms in the original barn are fairly large and have individual animal themes. The barn is also home to over 30 cats, none of which are allowed in the inn. Pets allowed. Full breakfast and evening wine are included in the rates, which drop on weekdays. ~ 288 Scudder Avenue, Hyannis Port; 508-778-4999, 800-637-1649; www.simmonshomesteadinn.com, e-mail simmonshomestead@aol.com. DELUXE TO ULTRA-DELUXE.

Craigville Realty rents a wide variety of homes within a mile of Craigville Beach in Centerville. The houses, available by the week, are clean, well equipped and situated in quiet neighborhoods. ~ 648 Craigville Beach Road, West Hyannis Port; 508-775-3174, fax 508-771-5336; www.craigvillebeach.com, e-mail rentals@craigvillebeach.com. DELUXE TO ULTRA-DELUXE.

Centerville Corners is a pleasant motel of 48 spacious rooms, all with private bath and some with kitchenettes. The decor and furnishings are rather ordinary, but the place is clean, comfortable and quiet. The attraction of Centerville Corners, other than the reasonable rates, is its location in the peaceful center of Centerville, half a mile from Craigville Beach and directly across the street from Four Seas Ice Cream. Other amenities include an indoor pool and a lawn that's perfect for croquet and badminton. Closed October to mid-April. ~ 369 South Main Street, Centerville; 508-775-7223, 800-242-1137, fax 508-775-4147; www.centervillecorners.com, e-mail ccorners@cape.com. DELUXE.

New Seabury is more of a town onto itself than a part of Mashpee. Scattered across the resort's 2300 acres of shorefront property, groups or "villages" of small gray-shingled buildings offer a variety of configurations. All apartments and condos are furnished with kitchens. Facilities include 2 restaurants, 16 tennis courts, 2 golf courses, a well-equipped health club, an outdoor pool, a three-and-a-half-mile-long private beach on Nantucket Sound, bike rentals and trails, a small shopping area, miniature golf and activities for children. Sound like Disneyland on the Cape? Believe me, you're not far off. Three-night minimum stay during the summer, two-night minimum off-season. ~ Great Neck Road, Mashpee; 508-477-9111, 800-999-9033, fax 508-477-9790; www.newseabury.com. ULTRA-DELUXE.

In 1849 Captain Albert Nye built **La Maison Cappellari Mostly Hall** for his Southern bride, who refused to live in a traditional Cape Cod house. Typical of houses in New Orleans' garden district, this raised Italian-style Greek Revival mansion (aptly named for its 35-foot center hall) has ten-foot windows, louvered shutters, a wraparound veranda and a wrought-iron fence. Only steps away from Falmouth's village green, this elegant inn is set well back from the road and hidden from view by trees and bushes. The six rooms are spacious and airy, furnished with antiques, including canopied, four-poster beds. Bikes are available for guest use. No smoking. A full breakfast is included. ~ 27 Main Street, Falmouth; 508-548-3786, fax 508-457-1572; www.mostlyhall.com, e-mail stay@mostlyhall.com. DELUXE TO ULTRA-DELUXE.

DINING

A popular local hangout, especially on Saturday nights, **Land Ho** is a fish and chips place. The white clapboard restaurant has red-and-white checked tablecloths, dark wood walls and nautical decorative touches. The menu offers classic Cape Cod fare (fried and broiled seafood, hearty salads, fries and burgers), as well as locally famous stuffed clams and kale soup. The bar is a friendly watering hole. There is live music on Thursday and Saturday. ~ Route 6A and Cove Road, Orleans; 508-255-5165, fax 508-240-2621; www.land-ho.com, e-mail info@land-ho.com. BUDGET TO MODERATE.

◄ HIDDEN

On their days off, chefs from the Cape's most noted restaurants often dine at **Nauset Beach Club Restaurant**, on the road to beautiful Nauset Beach. The small gray-shingled restaurant offers consistently good, reasonably priced Northern Italian fare such as roasted local oysters with herbed crust, or lobster fettuccini; ingredients are usually local and always fresh. They also have an

REPAST AT THE ROADHOUSE

A great find in Hyannis is the **Roadhouse Café**. With four dining rooms, some with fireplaces, it can seat 200, but the restaurant has a small, intimate feel with lots of antiques, hardwood floors and oriental rugs. The menu features local seafood (whatever's in season), plus beef, veal and Italian specialties. Diners can choose from the regular dinner menu or a lighter bistro menu, for salads, sandwiches and thin-crust pizza. There's an impressive wine list and over three dozen types of beers, plus desserts—all made on the premises. There's live jazz on Monday and piano on Friday and Saturday. Dinner only. ~ 488 South Street, Hyannis; 508-775-2386, fax 508-778-1025; www.roadhousecafe.com, e-mail contact@roadhousecafe.com. MODERATE TO ULTRA-DELUXE.

excellent wine selection. Dinner only. ~ 222 Main Street, East Orleans; 508-255-8547; www.nausetbeachclub.com, e-mail info@nausetbeachclub.com. ULTRA-DELUXE.

The **Impudent Oyster** is the place to go for traditional or exotic seafood in an informal setting next to a park. The menu changes seasonally. A few of the dishes have Chinese or Mexican ingredients, such as Szechuan beef and *hangzhou* satay. There are also some excellent non-seafood items, such as the steak *au poivre*. The cheerful restaurant has skylights, a cathedral ceiling and stained-glass panels. Prices are much lower in the winter. ~ 15 Chatham Bars Avenue, Chatham; 508-945-3545, fax 508-945-9319. MODERATE TO ULTRA-DELUXE.

In historic Chatham village, **Christian's** draws an attractive tennis and yachting crowd. The bar, a regular watering hole for many locals, does as much business as the restaurant. A semiformal, nonsmoking dining room on the ground floor, appointed with oriental rugs, dark wood floors and linen napkins, serves dishes such as baked cod with spinach, cranberries and cheddar, seafood sauté, chicken parmesan and filet mignon topped with a zinfandel demiglace. In addition to the downstairs menu items, the informal, wood-paneled piano bar on the second floor serves appetizers and pizzas. Closed Sunday through Wednesday from December through April and Tuesday and Wednesday in May. ~ 443 Main Street, Chatham; 508-945-3362, fax 508-945-9058; www.christiansrestaurant.com. MODERATE TO DELUXE.

The **Chatham Bars Inn**, one of the Cape's most luxurious resorts, also boasts an excellent restaurant. The food, service and location are superb, the crowd elegant old money. The large dining room overlooking the water is decorated in soothing shades

AUTHOR FAVORITE

It took some searching among the trendy nouveau cuisine and northern Italian restaurants that are Cape Cod's norm, but I finally found timeless New England cooking in an equally classic setting. Housed in an 18th-century, red-and-white inn on the edge of a duck pond, the **Coonamesset Inn** serves seafood Newburg, oysters on the half shell, quahog chowder, Indian pudding and other classic native New England dishes. The Cahoon Room, one of three dining rooms, features primitive paintings by artist Ralph Cahoon depicting life on Cape Cod. The inn and restaurant are tastefully decorated with Shaker and Colonial furnishings. ~ Jones Road and Gifford Street, Falmouth; 508-548-2300, fax 508-540-9831; www.capecodrestaurants.org, e-mail coonamessett.inn@verizon.net. DELUXE TO ULTRA-DELUXE.

of beige, rose and navy. In the summer the restaurant offers a menu of healthful dishes such as steamed halibut, plus a regular dinner menu—stuffed haddock, filet mignon with a truffle port sauce and duck à l'orange. Reservations are required if you aren't a guest at the inn. Dinner served from mid-May to mid-November; breakfast is served year-round. ~ 297 Shore Road, Chatham; 508-945-0096, fax 508-945-5491; www.chathambarsinn.com, e-mail welcome@chathambarsinn.com. ULTRA-DELUXE.

It looks like something out of a Popeye cartoon. Half of **The Lobster Boat Restaurant** is a gray-shingled Cape Cod cottage with cheerful red window boxes, and the other half is an enormous red, white and blue lobster boat that seems to have grown out of the restaurant's side. The dining room overlooks a small harbor, and the decor is very yo-ho-ho with captains chairs, dark wood and rope. The atmosphere is free and easy, and the menu features lobster as well as a variety of fried, sautéed and broiled seafood. Closed November through April. ~ 681 Main Street, West Yarmouth; 508-775-0486, fax 508-778-6110. BUDGET TO DELUXE.

Best known for their award-winning clam chowder, **Captain Parker's Pub** has a wide range of seafood options, including blackened salmon with dill dijonnaise sauce, as well as grilled pork chops, London broil and baked stuffed chicken. Sunday brunch is also available. ~ 668 Route 28, West Yarmouth; 508-771-4266; www.captainparkers.com, e-mail info@captainparkers.com. MODERATE

Yarmouth House Restaurant has been a Cape Cod favorite for many years. The dark furniture, red tablecloths, and working water wheel give it an old-time ambiance. And while this family-owned eatery specializes in seafood and beef, this is no ordinary surf-n-turf. Options include sirloin sauteéd in shallot butter with cognac and lobster cooked in butter, sherry and brandy. ~ 335 Main Street, Route 28, West Yarmouth, 508-771-5154, fax 508-790-2801; www.yarmouthhouse.com, e-mail yarhse@aol.com. MODERATE TO DELUXE.

Founded in 1934, **Four Seas** serves traditional sandwiches such as peanut butter and jelly, lobster salad and tuna salad, but is best known for its ice cream. Owners Doug and Peggy Warren insists on using only the freshest ingredients in the ice cream; for example, they won't make their famous peach flavor (reportedly the favorite of the Kennedy clan, who live down the street) until the fruit is ripe enough. The small dining area is decorated with photos of the all American–looking summer crews, newspaper articles about Four Seas and framed odes from its many fans. Closed September to May. ~ 360 South Main Street, Centerville; 508-775-1394, fax 508-775-6964; www.fourseasicecream.com, e-mail dugger@fourseasicecream.com. BUDGET TO MODERATE.

Oyster Too offers a variety of meat and seafood in an atmosphere complemented by a fireplace and piano bar. Appetizing starters include the poached-pear-and-prosciutto salad with gorgonzola and pecans. For entrées you'll find braised lamb shank with grilled eggplant and rice pilaf, as well as Cape Bay scallops sautéed with shiitake mushrooms and apple-smoked bacon in a cream sauce. Arrive before 5:30 and you'll have the option of an early-bird special at a significant price reduction. ~ 876 East Falmouth Highway, East Falmouth; 508-548-9191; www.oysterstoo.com, e-mail oysterstooha@yahoo.com. DELUXE TO ULTRA-DELUXE.

The Regatta of Cotuit is considered one of the top restaurants on the Cape. Housed in a Federal-style mansion that dates back to 1790, it specializes in New American cuisine with European and Asian touches. Dinner selections, served in one of the eight candlelit dining rooms, include cast-iron-seared premium filet mignon with port wine demiglace, roasted potatoes and grilled sweet Vidalia onions. A signature menu item is the trilogy of fresh fish and shellfish served with unique sauces, vegetables and evening starches, a selection that changes nightly. They also do wonderful things with buffalo tenderloin. A dessert not to miss is the Chocolate Seduction Cake with sauce *framboise* and *crème anglaise*. Dinner only. ~ Route 28, Cotuit; 508-428-5715; www.regattarestaurant.com, e-mail regattaofcotuit@verizon.net. DELUXE TO ULTRA-DELUXE.

HIDDEN ►

At **Moonakis Cafe** delicious food is served, and plenty of it. If you have your breakfast or lunch here, it's likely that you won't feel any hunger pangs until well into the afternoon. Indulge in fluffy omelettes stuffed with sausage, onions, bacon or Brie. Or try a stack of fresh blueberry pancakes, thick french toast or eggs Benedict. Lunch favorites include the homemade corned beef hash and clam chowder. No lunch on Sunday. ~ 460 Route 28, Waquoit; 508-457-9630. BUDGET.

The best part about the **Firefly Woodfire Grill and Bar** is its open kitchen, where diners can watch rib-eyes and native swordfish prepared over a wood-burning fire or Chatham scrod and rack of lamb baked in a stone oven. Gourmet pizzas and an extensive vegetarian selection are also available. Closed Sunday and Monday. No lunch from Labor Day to Memorial Day. ~ 271 Main Street, Falmouth; 508-548-7953; www.fireflywoodfiregrill.com; e-mail fireflywoodfiregrill@hotmail.com. DELUXE TO ULTRA-DELUXE.

The Clam Shack serves fantastic seafood in genuine seaside ambience. Unfortunately, there's not enough room to sit down inside; the tiny place is taken up with cooking vats. That's OK—walk around the building to the back deck, have a seat on a bench and watch the fishing and sailing vessels coming and going from

Falmouth's Inner Harbor. Closed Labor Day to Memorial Day. ~ 227 Clinton Avenue, Falmouth; 508-540-7758. MODERATE.

Pie in the Sky is a great source of strong coffee, scrumptious pastries and pies, and thick deli-style sandwiches. ~ 10 Water Street, Woods Hole; 508-540-5475; e-mail etgura@aol.com. BUDGET.

The place to go for a raw bar in Woods Hole is **Shuckers Raw Bar**. It's a bustling little spot, on the water, with table service provided by college students. In addition to raw bar offerings, you can choose from a tempting selection of seafood dishes and lobster rolls that just hit the spot. Shuckers serves its own home-brewed beer, Nobska Light. Closed Monday through Friday from mid-September to mid-October; closed mid-October to mid-May. ~ 91-A Water Street, Woods Hole; 508-540-3850, fax 508-540-8919; www.woodshole.com/shuckers, e-mail shuckersrb@aol.com. MODERATE.

SHOPPING

Aptly named **Bird Watcher's General Store** sells anything having to do with birds—field guides, binoculars, 25 kinds of birdbaths, bath heaters, birdfeeders and carving kits. It also has coffee mugs, T-shirts, floor mats and pot holders adorned with birds. ~ 36 Route 6A, Orleans; 508-255-6974, 800-562-1512; www.birdwatchersgeneralstore.com.

HIDDEN

The Odell Studio/Gallery—Tom and Carol Odell, metalsmith and painter, respectively—run a gallery out of the lovely old house that they live and work in. Carol's colorful abstract oils are an interesting and flattering complement to Tom's metalwork, which includes fine jewelry, bronze vases and outdoor sculpture. Closed Sunday. ~ 423 Main Street, Chatham; 508-945-3239; www.odellarts.com.

Isaiah Thomas Books has an enormous selection (over 70,000 volumes) of first edition and slightly used books collected in a peppermint-pink Victorian house. A sampling of categories: bodice rippers, thesauri, military shipping, and children's books, divided by age group and interest. The dealer, a highly

AUTHOR FAVORITE

Looking for a little joie de vivre? I recommend **Tony Andrew's Farm Stand**, a wonderful spot to be alive during strawberry season (late May to early June). Pick your own berries and pick up some other produce, too; all are reasonably priced (especially the fruit you pick yourself). You can pick your own sunflowers as well, or drop by with the kids for the Harvest of Horror in September for corn-picking, hay rides and Halloween-themed festivities. ~ 394 Old Meeting House Road, East Falmouth; 508-548-4717.

knowledgeable antique-book enthusiast, also offers appraisals, restoration and repair services. Hours vary by season; call ahead. Open weekends in winter. ~ 4632 Falmouth Road, Cotuit; 508-428-2752; www.isaiahthomasbooks.com, e-mail isthomas@aol.com.

NIGHTLIFE

Musical acts, comedies and plays are presented at the **Academy Playhouse**, in a former town hall built in 1837. ~ 120 Main Street, Orleans; 508-255-1963; www.apa1.org.

The **College Light Opera Company**'s energetic college-student company has risen to the challenge of providing live entertainment for area visitors. Music and theater-arts students from across the country audition by cassette tape. Those who are accepted perform nine shows in nine weeks, from Gilbert and Sullivan operettas to American musical comedies, from mid-June to late August. Box office is closed the rest of the year, and on Sunday. ~ 58 Highfield Drive, at the top of Depot Avenue next to Highfield Hall, Falmouth; 508-548-0668; www.collegelightopera.com.

BEACHES & PARKS

South Cape beaches are usually big and wide with huge parking lots and ample facilities. Located in residential neighborhoods, they're popular with college students and families. Because this is the ocean side of the Cape, the water tends to be rougher than on the North Cape.

HARDINGS BEACH Big, straight and long, this popular beach attracts a gregarious crowd of kids. Expensive houses on a hill overlook Hardings, a spot good for swimming, sunning and hanging out with the neighbors. You can surf fish for blue fish and striped bass, though there are limits on when and where. There are restrooms, showers, lifeguards and a snack bar open from July to Labor Day. Parking fee, $15 per vehicle (July to Labor Day only). ~ Take Barn Hill Road off Route 28 to Hardings Beach Road, Chatham; 508-945-5158, fax 508-945-3550.

WEST DENNIS BEACH The view at the end of this sprawling beach, where the Bass River empties into the Atlantic, is of old summer houses with green lawns spilling down toward docks dotted with boats. West Dennis Beach attracts big summer crowds; its parking lot can accommodate 1600 cars. Popular with surfers, families and teens, this wheelchair-accessible beach is bordered by flat salt marsh laced with tributaries from the river. Surf fishing is good for bass and bluefish, and this windy beach is known locally for good kite surfing. There are restrooms, showers, a boardwalk, lifeguards, swings and a snack bar. Day-use fee, $15. ~ Take School Street off Route 28 to Lighthouse Road, West Dennis; 508-760-6143, 800-243-9920, fax 508-760-5212; e-mail dpineau@town.dennis.ma.us.

HIDDEN

ASHUMET HOLLY & WILDLIFE SANCTUARY A treat for birdwatchers and botany enthusiasts, this 49-acre reserve abounds with many varieties of holly grown by the late Wilfred Wheeler. You're definitely out in the wilds here, and nothing looks manicured or fussed over. The reserve features a rare ecosystem grassy pond, which is unique to the cape. An easy-to-maneuver trail goes past a pond, forest, dogwoods, rhododendrons and a grove of Franklinia, an unusual, fall flowering shrub discovered in Georgia in 1790. Wildlife includes catbirds, so named because they make a meowing sound, barnswallows, belted kingfishers and pond critters such as ribbon snakes, catfish and painted turtles with bright yellow heads and dark shells. Day-use fee, $4. ~ 286 Ashumet Road (off Currier Road and Route 151), East Falmouth; 508-362-1426; www.massaudubon.org, e-mail longpasture@massaudubon.org.

Since 1935, a barn on the Ashumet Holly & Wildlife Sanctuary's property has been a nesting site for swallows. Every spring up to 44 pairs arrive to nest, then depart in late summer.

OLD SILVER BEACH This spot, popular with a college-aged crowd and locals, doesn't look like a typical Cape Cod beach. A large, modern resort is situated on the north end, and most of the beach houses in the immediate area are fairly new. A lovely cove to the south is protected by wooded cliffs jutting down to the shore. Swimming is calm; lessons are available. You'll find restrooms, showers, lifeguards, and a snack bar from late June to early September. Parking fee, $20. ~ Off Route 28A on Quaker Road, Falmouth; 508-548-8623, fax 508-457-2511; www.town.falmouth.ma.us, e-mail beach@town.falmouth.ma.us.

Martha's Vineyard

With its museum-perfect villages, Gothic Victorians and scenery that mimics the coast of Ireland, it isn't any wonder this enchanting island swells from around 14,000 year-round residents to more than 100,000 in the summer months.

Discovered in 1602 by the English explorer Bartholomew Gosnold, it was named by him for its proliferation of wild grapes. Who Martha was is anybody's guess, but legend has it she may have been Gosnold's daughter or his mother.

An active whaling port in the 19th century, "the Vineyard," as it's often called, became a popular summer resort in the 20th century. Today it is a summer home to an impressive number of celebrities fiercely protected from ogling tourists by proud locals. Vacationing notables such as former President Bill Clinton, Spike Lee and Michael J. Fox have also spent time on the Vineyard.

One way not to impress the natives is to rent a moped. In the summer these noisy (but fun to drive) motorized bicycles sound like swarms of angry bees. They're considered a menace on the road, and bumper stickers that read "Outlaw Mopeds" are everywhere.

Only 20 miles long and 10 miles wide, the Vineyard can easily be toured in a day. Ferries dock at Oak Bluffs or Vineyard Haven, or you can fly in (see the "Transportation" section at the end of this chapter). The Vineyard's three major towns—Vineyard Haven, Oak Bluffs and Edgartown—are on the northeast side of the Island. The western end, known as "up-island," comprises bucolic farmland, moors and magnificent beaches.

SIGHTS

In the '30s, Lillian Hellman and Dashiell Hammett spent their summers in **Vineyard Haven,** and ever since writers have been coming to this friendly, unpretentious town. Vineyard Haven has never attracted tourists like Edgartown, the island's main resort town, and therein lies its charm. It has the best bookstore (Bunch of Grapes), attractive shops, restaurants and a handful of wonderful inns. It's also home to the **Martha's Vineyard Chamber of Commerce.** ~ Beach Road, Vineyard Haven; 508-693-0085, fax 508-693-7589; www.mvy.com, e-mail mvcc@mvy.com.

It is believed that humans first came to the Vineyard after the Ice Age but before melting glaciers raised the sea level, separating it from the mainland. Remains of Indian camps from around 2270 B.C. have been discovered on the Island.

One historical sight of note here is the **Martha's Vineyard Seafaring Center,** established in 1893 to provide spiritual guidance to seamen and a refuge to shipwreck victims. Today it is part of a larger organization, the Boston Seaman's Friend Society that still offers social services and ministry to seafarers. A small museum houses a collection of seafaring artifacts. Closed in winter. Call for hours. ~ 110 Main Street, Vineyard Haven; 508-693-9317, fax 508-693-1881.

Oak Bluffs is only a couple of miles away. A must-see here is the **Martha's Vineyard Camp Meeting Association,** also known as **Cottage City,** right off the main drag through town. In 1835, Methodist church groups started holding annual summer meetings in Oak Bluffs, with hundreds of families living in tents for the occasion. Over time the tents were replaced by tiny whimsical cottages with Gothic windows, turrets, gables and eaves dripping with gingerbread and painted in a riot of colors—pink, green and white; peach, yellow and blue. Called "campground Gothic Revival," this is the only architectural style native to the Vineyard. In mid-August, on Illumination Night, a custom dating back to 1870, hundreds of colorful glowing oriental lanterns are strung up all over the cottages, creating a dazzling display of light. ~ Off Circuit Avenue, Oak Bluffs; 508-693-0525, fax 508-696-8661; www.mvcma.org, e-mail tabernacle@adelphia.net.

With the exception of Cottage City and Ocean Park—a genteel neighborhood of Queen Anne Victorians overlooking the water on the road to Edgartown—most of Oak Bluffs is hamburger restaurants and T-shirt and souvenir shops. It has a funky, salt-water-taffy kind of charm. In the center of town is the **Flying Horses Carousel**, an antique, hand-carved wooden carousel (the oldest in the country) still in operation. In the glass eye of each horse is a replica of a small animal. Grab the brass ring as your horse passes by and receive a free ride. The carousel is closed from Columbus Day weekend to Easter weekend. Admission. ~ Lake Street at Circuit Avenue, Oak Bluffs; 508-693-9481.

Not far from Oak Bluffs is elegant **Edgartown.** With its narrow streets, brick sidewalks, graceful yachts and pristine Greek Revival and Federal-style architecture, it looks like a living museum. Prim, proper and perfect, Edgartown can sometimes appear a bit too perfect.

Edgartown has always been a town of considerable wealth and power. Prosperous whaling captains retired here, building magnificent homes along **North Water Street** that can still be seen today. Today's residents include many Boston Brahmin families. Life revolves around the formidable yacht club, where expert sailor Walter Cronkite reigns supreme.

The main thing to do in Edgartown is walk along its tree-lined streets window shopping and admiring the homes. The **Martha's Vineyard Museum**, tucked away on a beautiful side street, comprises several buildings, including the early 1700s **Cooke House.** This fine example of pre-Revolutionary architecture once served as a customs house. The house, which has undergone little renovation since the mid-19th century, contains exhibits relating to all chapters of the island's history. The 1854 Fresnel lens from the Gay Head Lighthouse is housed here; it's

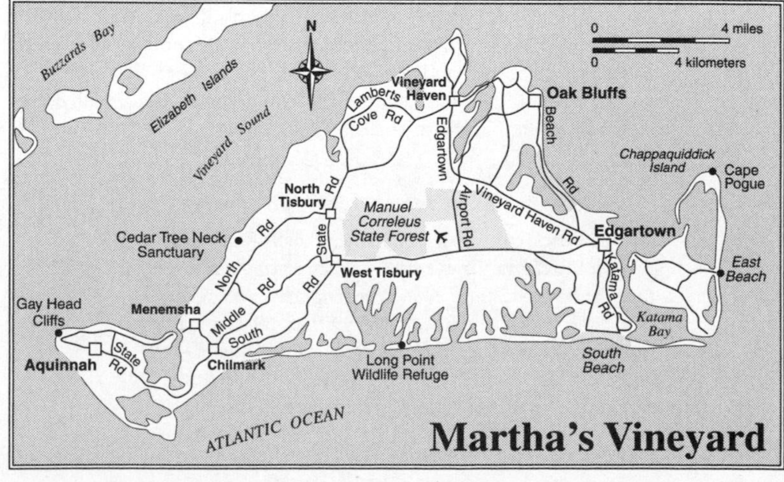

illuminated for a few hours each night. The museum also houses exhibits such as the Wampanoag Gallery, focusing on the history of the Wampanoag Tribe, and Vineyard Voices, with oral histories and photos of islanders. Call for operating hours. Admission. ~ Cooke and School streets, Edgartown; 508-627-4441, fax 508-627-4436; www.marthasvineyardhistory.org, e-mail info@marthas vineyardhistory.org.

With exquisitely preserved details that include an enclosed cupola, roof and porch balustrades, shallow hipped roof, large window panes and a portico, the 1840 **Dr. Daniel Fisher House** is the Vineyard's best example of Federal-period architecture. Dr. Fisher was Martha's Vineyard's 19th-century Renaissance man—he was a doctor, whaling magnate, banker, merchant and miller. The house is now the headquarters of the Martha's Vineyard Preservation Trust, which saves, restores, and makes self-sufficient any important island buildings that might otherwise be sold for commercial purposes or radically remodeled. Dr. Fisher's house is open (and tours are conducted) daily from mid-June to mid-September. Admission. ~ 99 Main Street, Edgartown; 508-627-4440, fax 508-627-8088;www.mvpreservation.org.

Right off the coast of Edgartown is **Chappaquiddick Island.** Called "Chappy" by locals, it is accessible by ferry (see the "Transportation" section at the end of this chapter). There's not much to do here except go to the beach and take long walks. The island, of course, is noted for the tragic auto accident involving Senator Edward Kennedy that resulted in the death of a young woman. Chappaquiddick Road ends at Dyke Bridge, site of the mishap, which has now fallen apart and is off limits to cars and people. The island's only other road, Wasque Road, leads to Wasque Point, a beautiful natural area.

The up-island section of the Vineyard includes West Tisbury, Chilmark and Aquinnah, bucolic rural areas sporting lush green farms, meadows and scenic harbors. To explore this area from Edgartown, take the Edgartown–West Tisbury Road, which cuts through the middle of the island.

WINERIES IN MASSACHUSETTS?

From Menemsha head back to Vineyard Haven via North Road and State Road, which goes by **Chicama Vineyards**. Massachusetts' first winery, it offers guided tours and winetastings in an appealing shop that sells wine, homemade jam, mustard, herb vinegar and many other delights made on site. Tour availability and hours vary. Call ahead for winter hours. ~ 191 Stoney Hill Road, West Tisbury; 508-693-0309, fax 508-693-5628; www.chicamavineyards.com, e-mail info@chicamavineyards.com.

About the only thing in West Tisbury is **Alley's General Store**, where locals sit on the front porch drinking coffee and glaring at tourists. It's the oldest running store in Martha's Vineyard, first opened in 1858. ~ State Road, West Tisbury; 508-693-0088, fax 508-693-3315. ◄HIDDEN

On Saturday mornings, the big social event is the outdoor produce market at **Grange Hall**, down the road from Alley's. Don't be fooled by the casual way the locals are dressed. Look closely and you'll see Rolex watches, $600 cowboy boots and maybe, if you're lucky, James Taylor. This area of the island is where many accomplished writers, musicians and artists make their homes. ◄HIDDEN

From West Tisbury, follow the road to **Chilmark**. At the center of Chilmark, **Beetlebung Corner** is an intersection of the main up-island roads: Middle Road, South Road, State Road and Menemsha Cross Road. The intersection was named for a grove of beetlebung trees, the New England name for tupelo trees, which are unusual in the northeastern United States. A very tough wood, tupelo proved to be excellent for making wooden mallets, or beetles, and plugs, or bungs, that stopped up the holes of the wooden barrels used to store whale oil.

At Beetlebung Corner, bear left onto South Road, heading toward Aquinnah. After a mile, you'll pass over a bridge. Nashaquitsa Pond, or Quitsa, depending on who's talking, will be on your right, and Stonewall Pond on your left. About one-tenth of a mile farther, the road heads up a hill. Halfway up the hill, pull over to the wide spot on the side of the road. This is called the **Quitsa Overlook**. Step out of the car to look out over Quitsa and Menemsha ponds. Past the ponds is the tiny village of Menemsha, then Vineyard Sound, the Elizabeth Islands and Woods Hole and Falmouth on the mainland. ◄HIDDEN

About half a mile farther along on the road to Aquinnah, there's another wide spot in the road with room on both sides for two or three cars to pull over safely. This is where the locals park their cars and bikes, then walk over to drink from a fresh, sweet **aquifer**. This water is considered an antidote for various afflictions, from stress to the common cold to the occasional hangover. ◄HIDDEN

The road ends at **Gay Head Cliffs**, towering ocean cliffs formed by glaciers over 10,000 years ago. Laced with multicolored bands of rust, lavender, wheat and charcoal, constant erosion over the millennia has washed away most of the vibrant hues. This popular tourist attraction is approached by a path lined with chowder and gift shops owned by the native Wampanoag people.

Leave the Gay Head Cliffs area via Lighthouse Road, then turn left onto State Road. When you get to Beetlebung Corner, turn right onto Menemsha Cross Road, which takes you out to **Menemsha Creek** and **Dutcher's Dock**, a lovely fishing village of simple, weathered gray shingled houses and short, sturdy docks. The channel seems to be impossibly narrow to be a working harbor, yet it's nearly constantly used by hardworking fishing folks.

LODGING **Crocker House Inn** is tucked away on a quiet side street within walking distance of Vineyard Haven and the harbor, and dotted with gardens, patios and cobblestone walkways. The eight country-cozy, air-conditioned guest rooms in this shingled Victorian are masterfully decorated; all feature private baths, entrances and decks. For those who can't live without the comforts of home, all rooms have flat-screen TVs with cable and DVD players, stereos complete with CDs and wi-fi. For serious getaways, try a room with gorgeous harbor views and a balcony. A full breakfast is served, as well as cookies in the afternoon. ~ 12 Crocker Avenue, Vineyard Haven; 508-693-1151, 800-772-0206, fax 508-693-1123; www.crockerhouseinn.com, e-mail info@crockerhouseinn.com. ULTRA-DELUXE.

Only minutes from the beach stands the picturesque white colonial **1720 House**, a beautifully restored mansion surrounded by gardens. Once home to prominent Martha's Vineyard families, the inn now offers six guest suites with vintage Americana furnishings, such as flag pillows and red and blue accents. The fittingly named Lincoln Room features peach-colored walls and a portrait of the former president, along with an antique wood dresser and a plush goose-down comforter. Four of the rooms have private baths (one with a clawfoot tub). Complimentary bicycles are provided for quiet rides into town or to the beach, and a continental breakfast and afternoon beverages are served. ~ 152 Main Street, Vineyard Haven; 508-693-6407; www.1720house.com, e-mail info@1720house.com. DELUXE TO ULTRA-DELUXE.

HIDDEN ► A classic 1918 Craftsman-style main house, a Cape Cod–style shingled carriage house, and a private cottage make up the **Thorncroft Inn**, which rests on a quiet, tree-lined residential street. There is nothing very craftsman-like about the decor, which leans toward country Colonial. Catering to couples on romantic getaways, most of the 14 guest rooms have working fireplaces and four-poster lace-canopy beds; some have jacuzzis and hot tubs. One of the best things about Thorncroft is its enormous breakfast of breakfast burritos with baked tomato and asparagus, bacon, french toast, quiche, Belgian waffles and more. If you don't mind the crumbs, they'll serve you a substantial continental breakfast in bed. ~ 460 Main Street, Vineyard Haven; 508-693-3333, 800-332-1236, fax 508-693-5419; www.thorncroft.com, e-mail innkeeper@thorncroft.com. ULTRA-DELUXE.

Just up the road from the center of Oak Bluffs is the **Admiral Benbow Inn**. What makes it stand apart from many inns is that it has all the New England touches, but not a don't-put-your-drink-on-this-table attitude. The 1800s house is a beauty. All seven rooms are attractively furnished with some antique pieces, big comfortable beds and private baths. A continental breakfast is served. ~ 81 New York Avenue, Oak Bluffs; 508-693-6825, fax 508-693-7820; www.admiral-benbow-inn.com, e-mail innkeepers@admiral-benbow-inn.com. DELUXE TO ULTRA-DELUXE.

Right across the street from busy, picturesque Oak Bluffs Harbor, the **Wesley Hotel** is the last of the seven large oceanfront hotels that graced Oak Bluffs during the turn of the 20th century. The Carpenter Gothic–style building, a traditional Gothic design elaborately constructed with wood, is wrapped with a wide, welcoming veranda. The hotel's 95 fairly large bedrooms are comfortably furnished. Closed mid-October through April. ~ 70 Lake Avenue, Oak Bluffs; 508-693-6611, 800-638-9027, fax 508-693-5389; www.wesleyhotel.com, e-mail info@wesleyhotel.com. ULTRA-DELUXE.

At the top of Circuit Avenue, you can't miss the **Oak Bluffs Inn**—it's the pink building on the left with an enormous cupola atop the third story. Guests are encouraged to climb (escorted) up to the cupola to take in the view of Oak Bluffs' rooftops and the ocean beyond. The inn's guest rooms and common areas are filled with fine examples of Victorian-style furniture, prints and wall coverings. All nine accommodations have private baths, bright bathrooms, air conditioning and views of charming Oak Bluffs. Continental breakfast served. Closed November through April. ~ Corner of Circuit and Pequot avenues, Oak Bluffs; 508-

AUTHOR FAVORITE

One look at the **Captain R. Flander's House** and I understood why it was featured in Martha Stewart's *Wedding Book*. The rambling, 18th-century farmhouse sits on a grassy knoll overlooking ancient stone walls, rolling meadows, grazing horses, a sparkling pond, ducks and woodlands. Chilmark is so peaceful and bucolic, it's no wonder the rich and famous have chosen to live here. The inn is simply furnished, but with scenery like this who needs decoration? Guest accommodations (some with shared bath) are comfortable and sparsely appointed with antiques and country-style furnishings—no TVs or phones in the room. Two ultra-deluxe-priced cottages are available. Guests are given passes to Martha's Vineyard's two private beaches. Two-night minimum. Continental breakfast is served. Closed November through May. ~ North Road, Chilmark; 508-645-3123; www.captainflanders.com. ULTRA-DELUXE.

693-7171, 800-955-6235, fax 508-693-8787; www.oakbluffs inn.com, e-mail bmyguest@oakbluffsinn.com. ULTRA-DELUXE.

The shingled, gingerbreaded 1872 **Oak House** is appropriately named—there's oak, oak everywhere, from the walls to the ceilings to the fine examples of antique oak furniture. The large wraparound veranda has wonderful rocking chairs and swings where many guests spend a lot of time relaxing and looking out across Seaview Avenue to the ocean. Many rooms have private balconies. All eight guest rooms and both suites have private baths and air conditioning. Continental breakfast and afternoon tea are provided. Closed mid-October to mid-May. ~ Corner of Seaview and Pequot avenues, Oak Bluffs; 508-693-2966, 800-245-5979, fax 508-696-7293; www.vineyardinns.com, e-mail inns@vineyard.net. ULTRA-DELUXE.

The **Arbor Inn** is a quintessential New England cottage, fresh and white with a winsome vine-clad arbor, brick path and English garden. Located a couple of blocks away from Edgartown's shopping district, the inn offers nine guest rooms simply but attractively appointed with antiques and fresh cut flowers, as well as a one bedroom house that is available for rent on a weekly basis. A continental breakfast is served in the old-fashioned formal dining room or in the garden. Closed November through April. ~ 222 Upper Main Street, Edgartown; 508-627-8137, 888-748-4383, fax 508-627-9104; www.arborinn.net, e-mail info@arbor inn.net. DELUXE TO ULTRA-DELUXE.

Built in 1840 by Edgartown's leading physician, Dr. Clement Frances Shiverick, the **Shiverick Inn** is a fantastic example of the high Greek Revival style. Inside, the recently remodeled common areas and ten guest rooms are furnished with fine antiques and pieces period art. All guest rooms have private baths and air conditioning; six have fireplaces. The library on the second floor has a terrace that looks out over the Old Whaling Church. In the backyard, there's a small flagstone terrace and flower garden. A full gourmet breakfast is served in the airy Garden Room, as is afternoon tea; both are included in the price of accommodation. Dogs are welcome. Gay-friendly. ~ 5 Pease's Point Way, Edgartown; 508-627-3797, 800-723-4292, fax 508-627-8441; www.shiverickinn.com, e-mail shiverickinn@vineyard.net. ULTRA-DELUXE.

Edgartown Commons has 35 comfortably furnished efficiencies, from studios to one- and two-bedroom apartments. Outside, there are grills and picnic tables, a play area for the kids and an outdoor swimming pool. Closed late October to early May. ~ 20 Pease's Point Way, Edgartown; 508-627-4671, 800-439-4671, fax 508-627-4271; www.edgartowncommons.com. ULTRA-DELUXE.

The **Harbor View Resort** is Edgartown's only waterfront resort with conference facilities. Its 124 rooms, suites and cottages all have private bath, telephone and cable TV. Rooms are generously proportioned, and decorated with four-poster beds, armoires, antique prints and watercolor landscapes by local artists. The hotel's gazebo is one of the most-photographed structures on the Edgartown waterfront. True to its name, the Harbor View does indeed have some of the best views of the harbor. ~ 131 North Water Street, Edgartown; 508-627-7000, 800-225-6005, fax 508-627-7845; www.harbor-view.com. ULTRA-DELUXE.

The Aquinnah Wampanoag tribe and the town of Gay Head voted to change the town name back to Aquinnah in 1998.

If you want a peaceful hideaway that's still close to the sights, the cheerful accommodations of the **Edgartown Lodge** are ideal. Each of the eight rooms has bright blue walls, large beds with colorful quilts, and private decks overlooking the landscaped grounds. Two one-bedroom suites feature private kitchens and comfortably fit up to five people. The downtown location is perfect for a day of sightseeing, or you can stay in and throw a picnic or barbeque in the back garden. ~ 68 Winter, Edgartown; 508-627-1092, fax 508-627-7493; www.edgartownlodge.com, e-mail edgartownlodge@aol.com. DELUXE TO ULTRA-DELUXE.

For an inn with such a prestigious address, the **Shiretown Inn** has pretty good prices. Some rooms are furnished with antiques and have private entrances and air conditioning; others, especially those in the carriage houses in the back of the inn, are quite plain, rather than quaint. A cottage rents weekly and features a full kitchen. All have private bathrooms. ~ 44 North Water Street, Edgartown; 508-627-3353, 800-541-0090; www.shiretowninn.com, e-mail paradise@shiretowninn.com. DELUXE TO ULTRA-DELUXE.

HIDDEN

With its elaborate windows and dormers, the **Victorian Inn** looks formal from the outside, but it's an easygoing place located one block from Edgartown harbor. Guests enjoy the cool, private garden in the summer. The 14 guest rooms are sweet and tidy with canopy beds, floral wallpaper, antiques and some antique reproductions; a few rooms have private balconies. Full breakfast included. Closed January to mid-February. ~ 24 South Water Street, Edgartown; 508-627-4784; www.thevic.com, e-mail victorianinn@thevic.com. ULTRA-DELUXE.

The **Charlotte Inn** is one of the most elegant and luxurious inns in America. A sparkling white 1860 sea captain's house, it is nestled amid a profusion of flowers, lawns, wisteria and latticework. Guests check in at a gleaming English barrister's desk. Twenty-five meticulous guest rooms are appointed with fine English antiques, handpainted china and equestrian prints. Suites, located in separate buildings, are quite extravagant—one has its own English cottage garden, another a bedroom balcony and palladium window. A continental breakfast is served in the inn's dining room. ~ 27 South Summer Street, Edgartown;

508-627-4751, fax 508-627-4652; e-mail charlotte@relais chateaux.com. ULTRA-DELUXE.

HIDDEN ► The homey, unpretentious **Summer House** is a place for vacationers who enjoy staying in a B&B that really is someone's home. There's a big, beautiful, very private front yard with a wonderful ivy-covered wall as a backdrop. The two large guest bedrooms have king-sized beds. A rustic summer cottage is located in the back with its own brick terrace and garden. Full continental breakfast is served. Closed October to mid-May. ~ 96 South Summer Street, Edgartown; 508-627-4857; www.summerhouse mv.com, e-mail chloenolan@msn.com. DELUXE TO ULTRA-DELUXE.

Hostelling International—Martha's Vineyard is an ideal place to stay on the Vineyard if you want to spend a lot of time biking. It's on the edge of the Correleus State Forest, which is crisscrossed with bike paths. The hostel was the first purpose-built youth hostel in the U.S. when it was built and opened in 1955. Sleeping areas are dormitory-style bunk beds and are separated by sex. All linen is provided and no sleeping bags are allowed. Bathrooms are large, as they are shared by all (also segregated by sex). There's also a fully equipped kitchen as well as a common room with a fireplace. Hostels aren't for everyone, but if you know what to expect, this is a good one. Reservations recommended. Closed mid-October to mid-April. ~ 525 Edgartown–West Tisbury Road, West Tisbury; 508-693-2665, 888-901-2087, fax 508-693-2699; www.hiayh.org, e-mail mvhostel@yahoo.com. BUDGET.

HIDDEN ► Talk about off the beaten path. **Lambert's Cove Inn and Restaurant** is down a long country road deep in the woods. Surrounded by vine-covered stone walls and expansive lawns, the white clapboard inn is appointed with English-style antiques. Some of the 15 guest rooms have private decks, and one has a greenhouse sitting room. Amenities include a plush pool and spa. Guests have access to Lambert's Cove Beach, one of the Vineyard's most beautiful private beaches. Full breakfast included. Three-night minimum stay required in summer. Closed January through March, but open Valentine's weekend. ~ Lambert's Cove Road, West Tisbury; 508-693-2298, fax 508-693-7890; www.lambertscoveinn.com, e-mail lambinn@gis.net. ULTRA-DELUXE.

The emphasis is on the peaceful surroundings at **Menemsha Inn and Cottages**, which is situated on 14 acres of tranquil forest in beautiful Menemsha. There are six luxurious rooms in the Carriage House, nine smaller, bright and lovely rooms in the inn's main building, and twelve housekeeping cottages. There's also a two-bedroom, two-bath suite, complete with kitchen. All rooms and cottages have private bath, and each cottage has a screened-in porch, fully equipped kitchen, outdoor shower, barbecue and wood-burning fireplace. There's a tennis court and fitness room. Closed early December to mid-April. ~ North Road between Menemsha Cross Road and Menemsha Harbor, Menemsha; 508-645-2521, fax 508-645-9500; www.menemshainn.com, e-mail info@innatmenemsha.com. ULTRA-DELUXE.

HIDDEN

Duck Inn is a health-oriented B&B that offers a variety of luxuries, including massages, post-massage relaxation in the inn's outdoor hot tub, all-natural fibers on the comfortable beds, and delicious breakfasts that accommodate vegetarians and vegans. Some of the island's most spectacular beaches are but a few minutes' walk through the waving beach grass. The five guest rooms are furnished eclectically with a duck motif and ethnic prints. The suite in the basement has a large fireplace; all rooms have private baths and saunas. ~ 10 Duck Pond Way, Aquinnah; 508-645-9018, fax 508-645-2790; www.gayheadrealty.com. MODERATE TO ULTRA-DELUXE.

The Outermost Inn is on a 20-acre piece of land that has the island's second-most spectacular ocean view. (For the best, walk a few hundred yards up the hill to the Aquinnah lighthouse.) The inn has six guest rooms and one suite, all with private bath and one with a private whirlpool. Unpainted furniture, subdued colors and natural fabrics suit the inn's location perfectly; nothing detracts from the location or the views. This is one of the most romantic inns in coastal New England; it's worth the splurge. Closed October through April. ~ 81 Lighthouse Road, Aquinnah; 508-645-3511, fax 508-645-3514; www.outermostinn.com, e-mail inquiries@outermostinn.com. ULTRA-DELUXE.

DINING

Only Edgartown and Oak Bluffs serve liquor, but you can bring your own when you dine in other towns.

A gray-shingled saltbox overlooking the harbor, rustic **Black Dog Tavern** is a Vineyard institution popular with the waterfront crowd. The best place to sit in the summer is an enclosed porch with beautiful harbor views. The changing menu is traditional—quahog chowder, codfish, dry-aged Delmonico steak—with an

AUTHOR FAVORITE

For me, walking along the beach trying to eat an ice cream cone before it melts just about epitomizes summer. The island's best homemade ice cream is at **Mad Martha's**, a bright, noisy, crowded spot that's full of families and college kids from spring through fall. ~ 12 Circuit Avenue, Oak Bluffs; 508-693-9151; e-mail mvmad@aol.com. BUDGET.

emphasis on fresh seafood. Breakfast, lunch and dinner are served. The restaurant is BYOB. ~ Beach Street Extension, Vineyard Haven; 508-693-9223; www.theblackdog.com, e-mail info@theblackdog.com. DELUXE TO ULTRA-DELUXE.

HIDDEN ► It's a bit off the beaten track in busy Vineyard Haven, but maybe that's why the locals go to **Louis'** for pizza and take-out salads and pasta dishes. ~ 350 State Road, Vineyard Haven; 508-693-3255, fax 508-696-7436. BUDGET TO MODERATE.

HIDDEN ► **Giordano's** is a classic family-style restaurant, and yes, there usually are a lot of large families here, with diners gobbling up what some people insist are the Vineyard's best fried clams. There's also an Italian restaurant on the premises, serving up traditional fare. Closed late September to late May. ~ Lake and Circuit avenues, Oak Bluffs; 508-693-0184; www.giosmv.com, e-mail gio@giosmv.com. MODERATE.

The homey **Linda Jean's** serves fantastic, thick pancakes and other delicious breakfast items, as well as such lunch and dinner fare as baked stuffed chicken, pork chops, fresh fish and meatloaf. Check the blackboard for daily specials. ~ 24 Circuit Avenue, Oak Bluffs; 508-693-4093, fax 508-693-7139. MODERATE.

HIDDEN ► Small, casual **Jimmy Sea's Pan Pasta** has enormous portions of delicious pastas ranging from raviolis, zitis to flat pastas—all cooked to order and served in the pan. The *frutti di mare* is for those who can't get enough of shellfish (all types of shellfish with red sauce over linguini). If you're only moderately hungry, you may be able to get two meals out of one dinner—many people carry doggy bags out of Jimmy's. Closed November through April. Dinner only. ~ 32 Kennebec Avenue, Oak Bluffs; 508-696-8550, fax 508-696-0282; e-mail jimmyseas@vineyard.net. MODERATE TO ULTRA-DELUXE.

David Ryan's Restaurant is the kind of place where you stop for a drink and end up staying for hours. It's a restaurant/bar where you can order anything from a burger to filet mignon to striped bass. Downstairs is informal with high stools situated around tall tables and a bar; upstairs is bistro style with an intimate martini bar. ~ 11 North Water Street, Edgartown; 508-627-4100, fax 508-627-9673; www.davidryans.com. MODERATE TO ULTRA-DELUXE.

The Coach House is a traditional New England brasserie. Breakfast might include eggs benedict or a cured salmon omelette and blueberry pancakes. For lunch, try a lobster roll or visit the raw bar; for dinner, choose from striped bass with lentils and a seven-herb salad. Only locally grown and caught greens and seafood are used. No dinner Sunday and Monday from mid-October through Memorial Day. ~ 131 North Water Street, Edgartown; 508-627-3761, fax 508-627-8417; www.harborview.com/coach_house. DELUXE TO ULTRA-DELUXE.

L'êtoile, one of the finest dining establishments in New England, is perfect for a special occasion. In this romantic, fantasylike environment, contemporary French cuisine is served. The prix-fixe menu offers fresh game and seafood entrées. Sauces are light and aromatic, flavored with fresh herbs, exotic fruit, wines and liquors. À la carte and light bar menus are also offered. Dinner only. Limited off-season hours. ~ 22 North Water Street, Edgartown; 508-627-5187, fax 508-627-6059; www.letoile.org. ULTRA-DELUXE.

Carly Simon, James Taylor, Caroline Kennedy Schlossberg, Diana Ross, Beverly Sills, Walter Cronkite and Mike Wallace all have homes on "the Vineyard."

Even if you're not knocked out the by the prix-fixe surf-and-turf menu (steak, salad, lobster, etc.) at **Home Port**, come here for the mesmerizing view. The rustic, brown-shingled restaurant overlooks sand dunes, rolling green pastures and idyllic Menemsha harbor. An outdoor patio is available for summer dining. Dinner only. Closed mid-September through Memorial Day. ~ 512 North Road, Menemsha; 508-645-2679, fax 508-645-3119. ULTRA-DELUXE.

Small, exclusive **Beach Plum Inn** is easy to miss. A narrow dirt road leads you to the inn, which has a lovely terraced rock and flower garden. Once you've figured out where to go, you'll be glad you came. The intimate dining room has large picture windows overlooking Menemsha Harbor. The cuisine features items such as steamed lobster, grilled swordfish with coconut lime sauce and roasted rack of lamb. Breakfast and dinner served. Closed December through April. ~ North Road, Menemsha; 508-645-9454, 877-645-7398, fax 508-645-2801; www.beachpluminn.com, e-mail info@beachpluminn.com. ULTRA-DELUXE.

Perched next to the cliffs at Gay Head, the **Outermost Inn Restaurant** serves dinner only; it's extremely popular, and reservations are essential. The prix-fixe meals, a variety of gourmet and home-style American and French-inspired foods, are scrumptious. Closed October to May. ~ 81 Lighthouse Road, Aquinnah; 508-645-3511; www.outermostinn.com, e-mail inquiries@outermostinn.com. ULTRA-DELUXE.

The **Aquinnah Restaurant**, a slightly shabby establishment that's perched on top of the highest of the Gay Head Cliffs, has a breathtaking view of the cliffs, the ocean, Noman's Land and the Elizabeth Islands. The food varies from good—chowder, lobster, scallops and whole fried clams—to uninspired, but you may not notice what you're eating as you indulge in the view. Closed Columbus Day to Easter. ~ On the Cliffs, Aquinnah; 508-645-3867, fax 508-605-7853. DELUXE TO ULTRA-DELUXE.

SHOPPING

Bunch of Grapes Bookstore Inc. is a writers' and readers' hangout. The best bookstore on Martha's Vineyard, it has shelves well-stocked with quality fiction and poetry. The store regularly hosts autograph parties. ~ 44 Main Street, Vineyard Haven; 508-693-2291, 800-693-0021; www.bunchofgrapes.com.

Linen, antique English pine furniture, handpainted coffee mugs and nubby hand-knit sweaters can be found at **Bramhall & Dunn**. ~ 23 Main Street, Vineyard Haven; 508-693-6437.

In the Woods, a cavernous red brick room, sells handsome hand-crafted wooden spoons, plates, bread platters, bowls, cutting boards, Christmas ornaments, tables and benches. Prices are reasonable, and the craftsmanship is superb. Open only in the summer. ~ 55 Main Street, Edgartown; 508-627-8989.

The Great Put-On has the Vineyard's most stylish line of clothing for men and women. Closed December through April. ~ 1 Dock Street, Edgartown; 508-627-5495.

HIDDEN ►

Penumbra Photographs has a fascinating selection of top-quality vintage photographs spanning from the 1850s to the 1960s that will interest amateurs and collectors alike. Open July, August and early September; closed Monday. ~ 33 North Summer Street, Edgartown; 508-627-9002.

NIGHTLIFE

Throughout the year, the **Vineyard Playhouse**, the Island's only professional theater, presents an interesting selection of new works and classics. ~ 24 Church Street, Vineyard Haven; 508-693-6450, 508-696-6300 (summer box office); www.vineyardplayhouse.org.

Old Whaling Church Performing Arts Center offers cultural lectures, classic films, concerts and plays throughout the year. Located in an 1843 Greek Revival church, the center has featured stars such as Patricia Neal, Andre Previn and Victor Borge. Folk artists such as Arlo Guthrie have also graced the stage. ~ Old Whaling Church, 89 Main Street, Edgartown; 508-627-4442.

BEACHES & PARKS

FELIX NECK WILDLIFE SANCTUARY A 350-acre haven for wild animals, birds, flora and fauna, the sanctuary has four miles of easy walking trails through salt marshes, thick forests and

BEACH TIPS

Beaches in rural West Tisbury, Chilmark and Aquinnah are dramatic, untamed and less crowded than beaches near the Vineyard's three towns. But the parking lots are for residents only, and in the summer guards check to see if cars have resident stickers. Nonresidents ride bikes to these beaches. Shore fishing is excellent from all south shore beaches.

open meadows of wildflowers. The area is owned and managed by the Massachusetts Audubon Society. There are activities for children and adults, including guided nature walks and bird-watching trips geared toward novices and experts alike. You'll find restrooms, an interpretive exhibit center and a gift shop. Admission (free for Massachusetts Audubon Society members). ~ Felix Neck Drive, three miles from the center of Edgartown off the Edgartown–Vineyard Haven Road; 508-627-4850, fax 508-627-6052; www.massaudubon.org, e-mail felixneck@massaudubon.org.

NANTUCKET SOUND BEACHES Strung together along protected Nantucket Sound are Oak Bluffs Town Beach, Joseph A. Sylvia State Beach, Bend-in-the-Road Beach and Lighthouse Beach. Swimming lessons are offered at some of the beaches, and bicycle paths run alongside the shore, which is bordered by ponds, salt marsh and summer homes. A stately lighthouse overlooks Lighthouse Beach. You can expect lifeguards but not much else. ~ Along Beach Road between Oak Bluffs and Edgartown.

SOUTH BEACH Also called Katama South, this popular, mile-long, Atlantic-facing beach runs into Norton Point Beach on one end and a privately owned beach on the other. Wide, expansive and flat, it is surrounded by heath dotted with 20th-century homes—a rare sight in Martha's Vineyard. In the summer the air is soft and warm from southwesterly winds. The beach allows swimming (watch out for the undertow), and fishing is excellent; you might be able to surf or windsurf if the waves or wind show up. You'll find restrooms, changing rooms and lifeguards. ~ Off Katama Road, south of Edgartown. You may take a shuttle bus from the center of town; 508-627-6145.

FULLER STREET BEACH A favorite among the many young folks who spend the summer in Edgartown, it's a quick bike ride away and a great place to take a break from Edgartown's other, more crowded beaches. There are no facilities or lifeguards. Parking is extremely limited. ~ At the end of Fuller Street; 508-627-6165, fax 508-627-6123.

CAPE POGE WILDLIFE REFUGE & WASQUE RESERVATION HIDDEN If you want to get away from it all, take the two-minute car and passenger ferry from Edgartown to these wilderness areas on Chappaquiddick Island, an undeveloped peninsula of vast, empty beaches and moors. (Be prepared: There are often long ferry lines.) The refuge and reservation are adjacent to each other and form the eastern shoreline of the Vineyard. Both offer an assortment of low dunes, ponds, tidal flats and cedar thickets. Wildlife abounds, including noisy least terns, piping plovers, common terns and American oystercatchers. East Beach, part of the Cape Poge Wildlife Refuge, is the best spot for swimming (although it is sometimes rough), and is a great spot to catch blue fish. Wasque Point is a world-renowned fishing area that teems with bonito, striped bass and more. There are seasonal restrooms. Day-use fee, $3 per person; parking fee, $3. ~ Cape Poge is at the end of Chappaquiddick Road on the other side of Dyke Bridge. Wasque Point is at the end of Wasque Road; 508-693-7662, fax 508-693-7717.

MANUEL CORRELEUS STATE FOREST Right in the center of the Vineyard lie over 5000 acres of towering evergreens and scrubland. Laced with bicycle and horseback-riding paths, as well as hiking trails carpeted with soft, thick pine needles, the cool, hushed forest offers a peaceful respite from the Vineyard's wind-bitten moors and wide-open beaches. Beware of ticks. ~ Off Barnes Road between West Tisbury and Edgartown; phone/fax 508-693-2540.

LONG POINT WILDLIFE REFUGE A never-ending, loosen-your-teeth dirt road is the only way to get to this mystical, magical wildlife refuge. The road forks here and there; just follow the signs and eventually you come to a small parking lot (seasonal parking with a fee). Shortly beyond lies an endless grass and huckleberry-covered heath that looks like a prairie with two enormous ponds. Tisbury Great Pond and Long Cove are home to black ducks, bluebills, ospreys, canvasbacks and swans. Beyond the ponds you'll discover a sea of silver beach grass and a white sand beach. Swimming and fishing are good, although the waters can get rough and there are no lifeguards on duty. Facilities are limited to portable toilets and a freshwater pump. Day-use fee, $3 per person; parking fee, $10. ~ This place is very difficult to find. It's three-tenths of a mile west of Martha's Vineyard Airport off Edgartown–West Tisbury Road on Waldrons Bottom Road, a deeply rutted dirt road without a sign; look for ten mailboxes in a row and the sign for Long Point. It's best to ask locals for directions; 508-693-7392, fax 508-696-0875; e-mail longpoint@ttor.org.

MOSHUP BEACH Adjacent to the multicolored Gay Head Clay Cliffs, a national landmark off-limits to the public, this long, flat, sandy beach is extremely popular in the summer. Moshup Beach is great for sunning, fishing, swimming and beachcombing, but be cautious of the surf. You can pay a hefty fee to park at the lot behind the dunes (508-645-2300), but you may be better off taking the Up Island Shuttle Bus that runs in the summer. There are restrooms and snack bars nearby. Parking fee, $15. ~ At the western tip of the Vineyard at Moshup Trail; 508-627-7141, fax 508-627-7415.

CEDAR TREE NECK SANCTUARY The raucous chirping of kingfishers, osprey, terns and Carolina wrens is the first thing to greet you at this 300-acre preserve. This is their kingdom, and what a spectacular place it is. Follow one of several well-marked paths through hilly woods of beech, sassafras, red maple, hickory oak and beetlebung. Soon the sky opens up, and, out of nowhere, extraordinary vistas appear of deep ponds, rolling sand dunes and the ocean beyond. Paths lined with ferns, moss and mushrooms lead down through the woods to an elevated catwalk and the shore. Unfortunately, picnicking is not allowed, and swimming and fishing are prohibited in the sanctuary. ~ From State Road in West Tisbury, take Indian Hill Road to a dirt road with a Cedar Tree Neck sign. The road goes down a hill to the parking lot; 508-693-5207, fax 508-693-0683; www.sheriffsmeadow.org, e-mail info@sheriffsmeadow.org.

◄ HIDDEN

Nantucket

Thirty miles out to sea from Cape Cod, this magical, fog-shrouded island is a study in contrasts. With its historic homes and cobblestone streets, Nantucket looks like storybook land, circa 1800. Yet it has quite a number of sophisticated New York City/San Francisco–style restaurants and Madison Avenue shops. Outside town, Nantucket is a bittersweet world of rolling moors, wild roses and windswept saltbox cottages that appear to have sprouted from the earth itself.

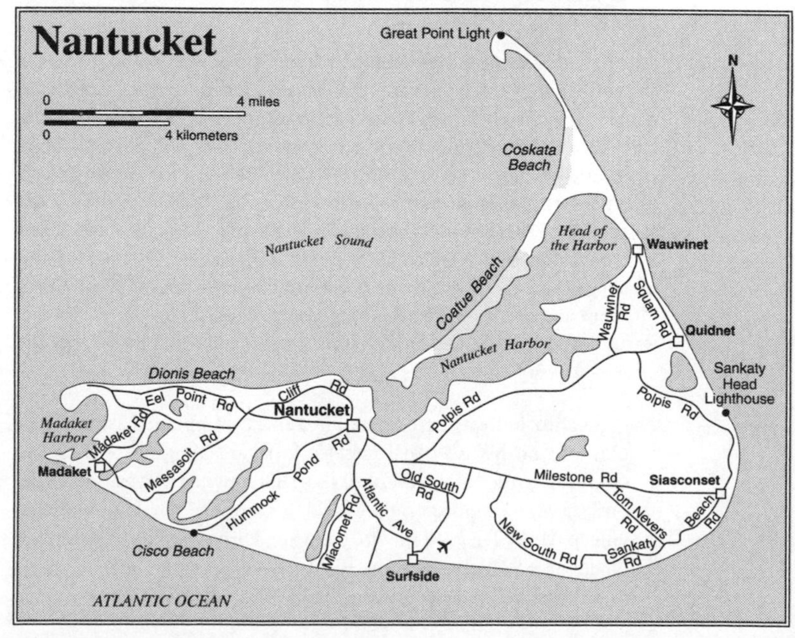

WALKING TOUR

Historic Nantucket

This easy walk through the streets of old Nantucket takes in more than a dozen historic sites from the town's 18th- and 19th-century whaling heyday. It takes about two and a half hours to walk.

THOMAS MACY WAREHOUSE Start your walk at the Thomas Macy Warehouse (c. 1846) on the waterfront. Originally a storehouse for whaleship supplies, it now houses a commercial shop.

BROAD STREET Walk one block west to South Water Street, then north (right) two blocks to Broad Street and the **Whaling Museum**. A former candleworks with enormous cross beams, this rustic old building contains a 47-foot sperm whale skeleton, a lighthouse lens, a whaleboat, a scrimshaw collection and relics from the *Essex*, the ship rammed by an enraged sperm whale that inspired Herman Melville's *Moby Dick*. Admission. Call for late fall and winter hours. ~ 5 Broad Street; 508-228-1736, fax 508-228-5618; www.nha.org. Next door, the **Peter Foulger Museum** traces Nantucket's human history from American Indian habitation to the present. Visitors can purchase a handy pass covering the sites on this walking tour. Closed in winter. ~ 15 Broad Street; 508-228-1894.

MAIN STREET Leaving the museums, walk one block west on Broad Street and turn south (left) on Federal, then west (right) onto the picturesque, cobblestoned Main Street. A fire destroyed most of the town in 1846, and some buildings, such as the public library, have only recently been restored. Two blocks up on Main, turn south (left) on Fair Street and go one block to the **Friends Meeting House** (c. 1838), which has been preserved by the historical society for more than a century and is still used as a house of worship by the island's Quakers. An annex to the meeting house, the **Fair Street Museum** originally housed the Whaling Museum and now contains changing historical exhibits. ~ 7 Fair Street. Returning to Main Street, turn west (left) again and continue for another

Nantucket was first sighted in 1602 by Captain Bartholomew Gosnold on his way to Martha's Vineyard. English settlers and Quakers farmed the land until the 1830s, when it was one of the busiest whaling ports in the world, a fact noted by Herman Melville in *Moby Dick*. In the 1870s, when kerosene started to replace whale oil as a fuel source and whales were becoming scarce, the industry started to decline. As a result, Nantucket lost 60 percent of block to Walnut Street. Turn north (right) and go one block to Liberty Street to the **Macy-Christian House** (c. 1740), a pre-Revolutionary merchant's home where a guided tour takes you through rooms of period furnishings. ~ 12 Liberty Street. Returning to Main Street, walk two more blocks west to tour the **Hadwen House** (c. 1845), one of the most elegant mansions on the island; the local garden club maintains period-style gardens here. ~ 96 Main Street.

MILLS AND MOORS Turn south (left) on Pleasant Street and go four blocks to South Mill Street, then turn west (right) and climb the hill to the corner of Prospect Street to see the **Old Mill** (c. 1746), a Dutch-style sailed windmill with wooden gears. It still grinds corn into meal, which is offered for sale to visitors. ~ Mill and Prospect streets. Returning north on Pleasant Street, turn west (left) on Mill Street. Passing the private **Moor's End** mansion (c. 1839) and the **1800 House** (c. 1801, closed for restoration), continue one block to New Dollar Lane.

GARDNER STREET Turning north (right), walk one block and turn west (left) onto Vestal Street. Continue for one and a half blocks to the **Old Gaol** (c. 1805), used to incarcerate prisoners for nearly 130 years before a rash of escapes prompted the town council to build a new jail. ~ Vestal Street. Returning the way you came, turn north (left) onto Gardner Street and walk two blocks, past the **Civil War Monument** at the corner of Main Street, to the **Hose-Cart House** (c. 1886), the last of several fire stations housing hand-pumped fire carts that were built throughout town after the devastating fire of 1846. ~ 8 Gardner Street.

JETHRO COFFIN HOUSE From the corner of Gardner and Main, you can return to your starting point at the Thomas Macy Warehouse by walking six blocks east on Main Street. For a longer walk—ten minutes each way—continue north on Gardner Street, which becomes North Liberty Street; turn east (right) on West Chester Street, then north (left) onto Sunset Hill Lane to see the Jethro Coffin House (c. 1686), Nantucket's oldest house. It's a classic saltbox, characteristic of late-17th-century Massachusetts Bay Colony homes. Open mid-May to mid-October. ~ Sunset Hill; 508-228-1894. West Chester becomes Centre Street and returns you to Main Street three blocks from the visitor center.

its population. A depression followed, but around the turn of the century tourism blossomed and the island prospered once again.

Nantucket is so small and flat you can zip across it on a bicycle in about two hours or by car in 30 minutes. There are almost as many bicycle paths as roads, and bicycle rental shops abound on the wharf where the ferries dock. Like Martha's Vineyard, the only way to get here is by ferry or plane (see the "Transportation" section at the end of this chapter). If you come here in summer, you *must* have reservations beforehand—competition is intense, and anti-camping laws are actively enforced.

SIGHTS

There is only one town, Nantucket, but it can occupy you for hours or days if you enjoy historic homes, museums, fine restaurants, shopping and gallery hopping.

At the **Nantucket Island Chamber of Commerce**, you can pick up the 288-page color guidebook, *Official Guide to Nantucket*, a comprehensive resource guide. Benches abound, so you can sit and map out an itinerary or just people watch. During summer the town is packed with tanned college kids, prosperous-looking couples, families on vacation and some wide-eyed daytrippers from the Cape and nearby Martha's Vineyard. Tail-wagging dogs wander about, and the local gentry stand on corners sipping coffee and chatting. Closed weekends. ~ 48 Main Street; 508-228-1700, fax 508-325-4925; www.nantucketchamber.org, e-mail info@nantucketchamber.org.

The **Nantucket Historical Association** maintains a number of historical properties, including the Jethro Coffin House (also known as the Oldest House), the Hadwen House, the Quarter Meeting House, the Whaling Museum and the Old Mill. Individual passes are available at each property or a combination pass may be purchased for all sites. The Whaling Museum is open year round and all other properties are open on a seasonal basis from mid-May to mid-October. ~ P.O. Box 1016, Nantucket, MA 02554; 508-228-1894, fax 508-228-5618; www.nha.org, e-mail nhainfo@nha.org.

If you walk up Main Street past the shops, you'll find many elegant mansions built during the heyday of whaling.

Nearby stands the **Maria Mitchell Science Center**. Mitchell, a Nantucket native, was the first American woman to discover a comet with a telescope, and the first female member of the American Academy of Arts and Sciences. The center, named in her honor, includes a natural science museum with an impressive insect and bird collection, an aquarium, and the house in which Mitchell was born. The library is currently closed for renovations. Call to receive updated status. The center conducts summer field trips and discovery classes, as well as bird and marine walks. Call for hours. Closed October to mid-June. Admission. ~ Vestal and Milk streets; 508-228-9198, fax 508-228-1031; www.mmo.org.

For a heady dose of Nantucket country life, visit **Siasconset,** a doll-sized hamlet of 17th-century pitched-roofed cod fisher shanties transformed into beguiling summer homes. In spring and early summer this endearing village looks as though it's been attacked by roses. Everywhere you look wild pink roses are climbing over fences, up sides of houses and over roofs, creating a dusty pink, gray and sage landscape.

Called "Sconset" by nearly everyone, the village lies seven and a half miles from Nantucket town on Milestone Road, which is bordered by a smooth, flat bicycle path. There isn't much to do here except enjoy the scenery and go to the beach. Sconset has a couple of restaurants, including renowned Chanticleer, and Summer House, one of Nantucket's prettiest inns.

On the way back to town, take scenic Polpis Road. It goes past **Sankaty Head Lighthouse** and **The Moors**, magnificent, windbitten low-lying land that resembles a Persian carpet in the fall.

◄HIDDEN

The road also passes the windswept **cranberry bogs**, where you can watch cranberries being harvested in the fall (see "Exploring Cranberry Country" in Chapter Six for information about cranberry growing on the South Shore).

The rest of Nantucket is all huckleberry-covered heath dotted with houses surrounded by spectacular beaches (see "Beaches & Parks" below).

LODGING

Nantucket has an astonishing number of inns and bed and breakfasts, but perhaps the most well-known is the **Jared Coffin House.** Built in 1845 by wealthy shipowner Jared Coffin, it features guest and public rooms appointed with antiques, oriental rugs, crystal chandeliers, period wallpaper, marble fireplaces and canopy beds. All guest rooms have private baths; some are air-conditioned. A busy, festive establishment, it feels like a big city hotel of the 19th century. Forty-three guest rooms span two different buildings. ~ 29 Broad Street; 508-228-2400, 800-248-2405, fax 508-228-8549; www.jaredcoffinhouse.com. ULTRA-DELUXE.

AUTHOR FAVORITE

The Summer House, a rose-covered structure overlooking the ocean, is quintessential Nantucket, the kind of place you dream about but rarely find. Not surprisingly, it once graced the cover of *New York* magazine. Quaint little low-slung, vine-clad cottages surrounding the main house look as though they were designed by and for elves. But they're much bigger and lighter than they seem, and the decor blends just the right mix of rustic country charm. Rooms have features such as fireplaces, jacuzzis, rough-hewn beams, painted wood floors and hand-painted borders. There is a lively restaurant, as well as an oceanfront pool. Closed November to mid-April. ~ 17 Ocean Avenue, Siasconset; 508-257-4577, fax 508-257-4590; www.thesummerhouse.com, e-mail reservations@thesummerhouse.com. ULTRA-DELUXE.

Right down the street from the Jared Coffin House is one of the island's few bargain spots, the **Nesbitt Inn**. The white Victorian was built in 1872 and much of the original furniture remains. One room has a wood-rimmed bath tub that accommodates two. There are 12 guest rooms, each with a sink and shared bath. The inn's porch is a great place for people watching. Closed January and February. ~ 21 Broad Street; 508-228-0156. MODERATE.

Right next door is the **Centerboard Guest House**, a restored 1840 Victorian residence with seven rooms, all decorated with period furnishings. At an inn of this sort, it's surprising to find modern amenities such as air conditioning and refrigerators in each guest room, as well as newly renovated bathrooms and LCD-panel TVs. Continental breakfast included. ~ 8 Chester Street; 508-228-9696; www.centerboardguesthouse.com, e-mail relax@centerboardguesthouse.com. ULTRA-DELUXE.

Anchor Inn, a narrow gray clapboard house with green shutters and window boxes, is typical of Nantucket's many bed and breakfasts. Old and quaint, with narrow halls and sloping wood floors, it offers 11 cozy guest rooms, some hidden under dormers and eaves in small irregular spaces. Each has a private shower and air conditioning and some have canopy beds. Once the home of the Gilbreth family (of Frank Gilbreth's *Cheaper by the Dozen*), the Anchor is furnished with Colonial- and Shaker-style antiques. A continental breakfast is served in a cheerful blue-and-white breakfast room, or out on a brick patio. ~ 66 Centre Street; 508-228-0072; www.anchor-inn.com, e-mail info@anchor_inn.com. ULTRA-DELUXE.

The **Woodbox at 36 Fair** offers lodging inside an old ship captain's house. Located in the historic district, it's within walking distance of every Nantucket amenity. The six suites all have private baths. Closed mid-October to Memorial Day. ~ 36 Fair Street; 508-228-0587, fax 508-228-7527. DELUXE.

The Wauwinet, a lavish resort outside town, is decorated to the hilt with country pine antiques, green wicker, primitive folk art, Victorian carpet runners, white wainscotting and pickled floors. The 33 guest rooms sport gentle sea-breeze colors like pale smoke, sage and cream; five cottages sleep up to six people each. White wicker furniture sits prim and proper on a vast lawn overlooking Nantucket Bay, and cushioned wicker furniture lines a bayside porch. Guests are transported to and from town in a shuttle bus. The Wauwinet is one of the most expensive inns on the island, attracting a well-heeled young crowd. There's a full-service restaurant on the premises. Closed November to early May. ~ 120 Wauwinet Road; 508-228-0145, 800-426-8718, fax 508-228-6712; www.wauwinet.com. ULTRA-DELUXE.

HIDDEN ►

If you haven't stayed in a youth hostel since you gave up your backpack, you might want to try it again when you see **Hostelling**

International—Nantucket. Located across from Surfside Beach, this historic wooden A-frame building looks like a cross between a Swiss chalet and a church. Originally a lifesaving station, it today attracts a lot of young people, Europeans, senior citizens and cycling groups. Volleyball is played in a large yard in back bordered by a marshland. The rows of bunk beds inside remind most people of camp. As with most youth hostels, Nantucket's is closed to guests during the day. Two of the three dormitory-style rooms and restrooms are segregated by sex; there is a good-sized kitchen, dining room and common room. Closed mid-October to mid-April. ~ 31 Western Avenue; 508-228-0433, fax 508-228-5672; www.capecodhostels.org, e-mail nantuckethostel@yahoo.com. BUDGET.

DINING

Among Nantucket's astonishing number of sophisticated restaurants, one of the best is **Le Languedoc**. Elegant and hushed, the upstairs has bistro-style dining with yellow and pale red walls, contemporary art and dark carpeting that are strictly big-city. The downstairs resembles a pied-à-terre with navy-and-white checked tablecloths and Windsor chairs that add a touch of French country. There is also an outdoor patio in the summer. Chilled lobster and warm foie gras salad, seasonal sweetbreads, *noisette* veal loin, and shrimp and jambalaya risotto may be found on the deluxe bistro menu, along with parsnip chips over pan-roasted lobster and soft-shell crab. A lot of care goes into the presentation. Advance reservations strongly suggested for upstairs; no reservations accepted for downstairs. Dinner is served nightly. ~ 24 Broad Street; 508-228-2552; www.lelanguedoc.com, e-mail languedoc@nantucket.net. DELUXE TO ULTRA-DELUXE.

Nantucket is an island, a county and a town. As if that weren't enough, it's also the only place in the United States with the same name for all three distinctions.

Learn all about Nantucket while you dine at **The Brotherhood of Thieves**, named after an 1844 pamphlet condemning slavery. The upstairs walls showcase a historical tour of the island, while the large downstairs bar looks much as it has looked since it was frequented by whalers in the 1840s. Settle in for a leisurely meal, starting with a selection from the cheese menu. It may be tempting to fill up on gourmet burgers, sandwiches, soups and salads, but be sure to leave room for a cup of alcohol-infused coffee and a chocolate brownie a la mode for dessert. ~ 23 Broad Street; 508-228-2551, fax 508-228-6168; www.brotherhoodofthieves.com. MODERATE TO DELUXE.

American Seasons serves American regional cuisine such as mesquite-smoked sweetbreads and herb-crusted tuna with root-vegetable gratin. The restaurant is in a white, two-story building with window boxes spilling a variety of seasonal blossoms. The interior is romantically lit with hurricane lamps, and jazz plays softly in the background; the fully covered outdoor patio has copper tables to dine on. The crowd is young, happy and casual. Dinner only. Closed mid-December to mid-April. ~ 80 Centre Street; 508-228-7111, fax 508-325-0779; www.americanseasons.com. ULTRA-DELUXE.

The Atlantic Café is on a street that should be called Hamburger Row. Every restaurant on this block serves the same thing—burgers, beer and rock-and-roll. You can smell the fried food before you get here. The restaurant attracts families with small kids. The Atlantic is a clean-looking establishment with white walls, wood beams and a bar in the middle surrounded by wooden chairs and tables. Steak and seafood specials round out the menu. Closed for a couple of weeks around the holidays. ~ 15 South Water Street; 508-228-0570, fax 508-228-8787; www.atlanticcafe.com, e-mail theac@nantucket.net. BUDGET TO DELUXE.

One of Nantucket's most beautiful and versatile restaurants, the **Boarding House** has a shady brick patio that's perfect for people watching and a lovely bar and café. (A woman could come to the bar alone and feel totally at ease.) A formal dinner is served in the cellar, a grottolike, candlelit room with cream-colored arched walls. Dishes change frequently. Popular offerings, many served in both the café and dining room, include butter-poached lobster tails with handmade pasta, summer corn and vanilla beurre blanc. A comprehensive wine list is featured. Lunch Thursday through Sunday in season. Closed from mid-December through April. ~ 12 Federal Street; 508-228-9622, fax 508-325-7109; www.boardinghouse-pearl.com, e-mail info@boardinghouse-pearl.com. ULTRA-DELUXE.

Tiny **Sconset Café** has an enticing menu any time of day. The café's patrons are the lucky taste-testers of new recipes and variations on old favorites, which are best termed New American. Try the lamb Dijon or the baby vegetable risotto. Closed mid-October through April. ~ Post Office Square, Siasconset; 508-257-4008; www.sconsetcafe.com, e-mail rc@sconsetcafe.com. DELUXE TO ULTRA-DELUXE.

The Chanticleer is one of New England's most romantic restaurants. In spring, the many-windowed, gray-shingled house is covered with climbing roses, and the garden is a riot of pink, white and lavender flowers. The menu features traditional French cuisine—foie gras, lobster soufflé, fresh figs in sweet white wine and herbs, trout with salmon mousse and lobster ginger sauce. Many locals prefer the restaurant for lunch in the rose garden. Closed Monday and from November to mid-May. ~ 9 New Street, Siasconset; 508-257-6231; www.thechanticleerinn.com, e-mail besusans@msn.com. ULTRA-DELUXE.

SHOPPING

Hoorn-Ashby Gallery, one of Nantucket's most beautiful galleries, sells American and European contemporary paintings, antique handpainted blanket chests, French-country porcelain and more in a sun-filled room with wood-paneled walls, tall columns, wainscoting and high ceilings. Closed Monday through Friday in November and December, closed January through April. ~ 10 Federal Street; 508-228-9314, fax 508-228-6178; www.hoornashby.com.

Woven lightship baskets and carved scrimshaw items were crafts created in the 18th century by lighthouse keepers and sailors with idle time on their hands.

Many shops in Nantucket sell handwoven goods, but at **Nantucket Looms** the blankets, throws, shawls and home decor are a cut above the rest. Popular designs include voluminous, fluffy white throws with thin navy stripes, and blankets in all colors of the rainbow. Closed Sunday from late December through March. ~ 16 Federal Street; 508-228-1908, fax 508-228-6451; www.nantucketlooms.com, e-mail info@nantucketlooms.com.

Four Winds Craft Guild specializes in the island's two oldest crafts: antique and new lightship baskets and scrimshaw. The former are tightly woven, bowl-shaped baskets used as purses or decorative items; scrimshaw are items decoratively carved from whale bone and teeth. Lightship purses are a status symbol among the island's conservative ladies. The older the basket, the better. Closed January through February. ~ 15 Main Street; 508-228-9623, fax 508-228-8958; www.sylviaantiques.com.

Brimming with hidden delights, **Vis-A-Vis** offers an eclectic mix of goods ranging from hand-knit sweaters, bathing suits and antique hooked rugs, to quilts, shoes and jewelry. Women can find something to wear to the beach, a wedding or an evening on the town. Closed Sunday through Thursday in January and February. ~ 34 Main Street; 508-228-5527, fax 508-228-5901; www.visavisnantucket.com, e-mail visavis@nantucket.net.

NIGHTLIFE

In summer, **Nantucket Musical Arts Society** gives classical concerts in the First Congregational Church located at 62 Centre Street. ~ P.O. Box 897, Nantucket, MA 02554; 508-228-1287.

The best place to catch a movie is the **Starlight Theatre**, which shows first-run and independent movies, and occasionally hosts film festivals. Forget about popcorn and soda; grab some food and a bottle of Italian wine or local beer from the attached café and bring it in with you. ~ 1 North Union Street; 508-228-4479; www.starlightnantucket.com, e-mail info@starlightnan tucket.com.

Fun, funky and informal, **The Chicken Box**, a bar with live entertainment, presents a variety of bands—rock-and-roll, reggae, rhythm-and-blues and others. They perform nightly in the summer, on weekends only in the winter. Cover for bands. ~ 14 Daves Street; 508-228-9717; www.thechickenbox.com.

BEACHES & PARKS

Bicycle paths go to Madaket, Dionis, Surfside and Siasconset beaches, and fishing is great from those on the south shore. Nantucket doesn't have parks, per se, but the **Nantucket Conservation Foundation** owns and manages more than 8500 acres (28 percent of the island's land area) of undeveloped land open to the public to explore. Foundation land is identified by roadside maroon posts topped with a wave and seagull logo. If you want to know more, stop in and talk to the foundation folks, a friendly group of people who are happy to discuss the island's flora and fauna. They'll also commiserate about the rapid growth on the island, and the frightening amounts being paid for land. ~ Larsen-Sanford Center, 118 Cliff Road; 508-228-2884. The **Nantucket Park and Recreation Commission** oversees Dionis, Madaket, Surfside and Siasconset beaches. ~ 2 Bathing Beach Road; 508-228-7213, fax 508-325-5347; e-mail parkrec@nantucket.net.

The beaches of the Nantucket Sound are where the movie *Jaws* was filmed, but don't panic—this isn't shark country. The narrow, gently curved shoreline has clean sand and calm water.

Surfers take note: Surfing is *not* permitted in lifeguarded areas. Furthermore, lifeguarded areas are subject to frequent change. Before dragging your gear out, you might want to call **Upperdeck and Indian Summer Surf Shop** (508-228-3632, fax 508-228-4211) and ask where people are surfing.

DIONIS BEACH If it weren't for a big white rock, you'd never find this beach, which faces the bay and is ideal for swimming, picnics and cookouts (fire permits available from the Nantucket fire station). Beyond the large dirt parking lot, a bike path leads through tall sand dunes to the beach. These are dunes protected from natural erosion and people by a fence. During low tide, a sand bar stretches out into the water quite a distance. There are restrooms and lifeguards in summer. ~ Three miles west of town off Eel Point Road, Dionis; 508-228-7213, fax 508-325-5347; e-mail parkrec@town.nantucket.net.

JETTIES BEACH If you have the kids in tow, head for this popular bayside beach with gentle surf. This beach has it all: windsurf, sailboat and kayak rentals, changing rooms, bathrooms, playground, tennis courts, volleyball nets, lifeguards and shuttle service during the summer. ~ Bathing Beach Road, three-quarters of a mile west of town; 508-228-7213, fax 508-325-5347; e-mail parkrec@town.nantucket.net.

HIDDEN ►

CISCO BEACH The road to this out-of-the-way beach goes past scenic Hummock Pond and rolling heathlands.

The wide-open beach is a free and easy place where you can walk for miles on white sand. It's popular with seasoned beach rats and young surfer types. Lifeguards are not always available, so call ahead to check. ~ At the end of Hummock Pond Road in Cisco, four miles southwest of town; 508-228-7213, fax 508-325-5347; e-mail parkrec@town.nantucket.net.

SURFSIDE Narrow sand paths lace the moors leading to this massive beach. Because Surfside is only three miles from town, it gets very crowded in the summer. But it's a great beach—big, long and wide with the best surf on the island. Surfside attracts families and college students. To get away from the crowds, walk east along the shore toward Siasconset and soon you'll discover long stretches of blissfully empty beach. There's a bike path. Summer facilities include restrooms, showers, lifeguards, a snack bar and a shuttle service. ~ At the end of Surfside Road, three miles south of town; 508-228-7213, fax 508-325-5347; e-mail parkrec@town.nantucket.net.

SIASCONSET BEACH This lovely eastern-facing beach seven miles from town is in the village of Siasconset. People make a day out of bicycling or driving here to explore the beach and the village; you can catch a shuttle bus from town in summer. Part of the beach is surrounded by grassy cliffs and dunes, then the land dips and becomes flat. To the left of the beach is Sankaty Lighthouse and the summer community of Quidnet. Walk south along the beach for an empty spot. Because of the wind, seaweed can be a problem. Keep an eye on small children: this beach gets very deep about 20 feet out. There are lifeguards in summer. ~ Seven miles east of town at the end of Milestone Road, Siasconset; 508-228-7213, fax 508-325-5347; e-mail parkrec@town.nantucket.net.

GREAT POINT, COSKATA & COATUE BEACHES If you really want to leave civilization, consider exploring this narrow stretch of uninhabited land that wraps around Nantucket Harbor. It's like one giant sand dune surrounded by water. Driving through this desertlike landscape is an adventure, and those who make the trek can swim in calm waters lapping a deserted white-sand beach and view a nesting ground for piping plovers, clam and oyster ponds, a century-old cedar forest and the Great Point Lighthouse. There's fantastic shore fishing for fluke, Spanish mackerel, bluefish and bass at Great Point, the northernmost point of land; swimming is calm on Nantucket Sound but not recommended on the Atlantic side, where the current and undertow are rough. Driving in this area requires an expensive ($25 per day for rental vehicles; $125 for private vehicles for the year) permit and a four-wheel-drive vehicle equipped with everything you need to dig yourself out of a deep sand rut. Permits are avail-

◄HIDDEN

Text continued on page 342.

Cape Cod by Bike

Cape Cod, Martha's Vineyard and Nantucket are a cyclist's paradise. The flat landscape is laced with miles of smooth, paved bicycle paths that meander past sand dunes, salt marsh, woods and pastures. What follows is a modest sampling of some of the best rides. Local chambers of commerce can provide more comprehensive information. *Short Bike Rides*, by Edwin Mullen and Jane Griffith (Globe Pequot Press) is a handy little book that describes 31 bike rides on Cape Cod, Nantucket and Martha's Vineyard.

NORTH CAPE The **Cape Cod Rail Trail**, an eight-foot-wide bicycle path, runs about 30 miles along the old Penn Central Railroad tracks from Route 134 in South Dennis to six miles off Locust Road in Eastham, past classic Cape Cod scenery—ponds, forest, saltwater and freshwater marsh, cranberry bogs and harbors.

OUTER CAPE **Head of the Meadow**, a moderately hilly bicycle path in the Cape Cod National Seashore in Truro, traverses some of the Cape's most dramatic scenery, including The Highlands' vast expanses of grassy knolls. The two-mile path starts at Head of the Meadow Road off Route 6 and ends at High Head Road.

PROVINCETOWN Talk about dramatic scenery. The **Province Lands Bike Trail** dips and turns past towering sand dunes, silvery mounds of wavy beach grass, two magnificent beaches and the Province Lands Visitors Center. The five-mile loop starts at Herring Cove Beach parking lot at the end of Route 6 and includes many places where you can stop and picnic.

SOUTH CAPE The **Shining Sea** bicycle path between Falmouth and Woods Hole is popular with experienced cyclists because it's hilly in some areas and very scenic. The 3.3-mile path runs along Palmer Avenue in Falmouth, then down a hill past deep woods and historic homes, ending at Woods Hole Harbor.

MARTHA'S VINEYARD The **Oak Bluffs–Edgartown–Katama Beach** bike path on Martha's Vineyard is smooth and easy, even though it's nine miles long. Departing from Oak Bluffs, the flat path runs along the shore past lovely old homes, beaches, ponds and salt marsh to historic Edgartown, then through heathland dotted with occasional houses to magnificent Katama Beach.

From Vineyard Haven, the hale and hearty can bicycle to **Menemsha** and **Aquinnah** via State Road to West Tisbury, then Middle Road to the end. The ride is hilly in parts, but the scenery is breathtaking. The beaches in this area have residents-only parking lots, so bicycling is the only way a nonresident can enjoy them.

NANTUCKET Aside from the downtown hazards of cobblestone streets, narrow roads and heavy traffic, bicycling on Nantucket is a snap. Smooth, flat bike paths parallel the island's two main roads. The 6.2-mile **Madaket** bicycle path is the more scenic, dipping and winding past moors and ending at Madaket Beach, the western tip of the island. The 8.2-mile **Siasconset** path is a straight, flat line that goes past barren scrub pine and sandy scenery, ending at the village of Siasconset on the eastern end of the island.

A 3.5-mile bike path leads to the ever-popular **Surfside Beach** and offers lovely scenery. The ten-mile **Polpis Bike Path**, an alternate route to Siasconset, features views of Nantucket Harbor.

Bike Rentals Practically every town on Cape Cod has a couple of bike rental shops. Most are closed November through April.

Along with sales and service, **The Little Capistrano Bike Shop** rents cruisers, hybrids and mountain bikes; helmets and locks cost extra. ~ 341 Salt Pond Road, Route 6, Eastham; 508-255-6515; www.capecodbike.com. In Provincetown, check out **Arnold's** for repairs, sales or rentals (hybrids, kids' bikes, mountain bikes). Locks are included; helmets are extra (except for children). ~ 329 Commercial Street; 508-487-0844. Falmouth Heights' **Holiday Cycles** rents seven-speed cruisers, hybrids, mountain bikes, quadracycles, recumbent bikes, tandems and kids' bikes, as well as four-wheeled surreys. Repairs and sales are undertaken, and knowledgeable staff will direct you to a suitable bike path. ~ 465 Grand Avenue; 508-540-3549.

Martha's Vineyard has **Anderson's Bike Rentals** in Oak Bluffs. Choose from mountain and kids' bikes, hybrids and tandems; helmets and locks are included. Free road service for broken bikes is provided. You can also get the necessary repairs done here, or just buy a new bike. ~ 23 Circuit Avenue Extension; 508-693-9346. In Edgartown, there's **R.W. Cutler Bicycle Shop**. Rental bikes (mountains and hybrids) come with locks and helmets. They sell and repair bikes as well. ~ 1 Main Street; 508-627-4052; www.edgartownbikerentals.com.

Nantucket's wharf has many bicycle rental shops; one of the biggest outfits is the full-service **Young's Bicycle Shop**, whose rental bikes (tandems, hybrids, mountain, full-suspension) include helmets and locks. Closed January through mid-February. ~ 6 Broad Street, Steamboat Wharf; 508-228-1151; www.youngsbicycleshop.com

able at the Wauwinet Gate House on Wauwinet Road (508-228-5646). Tours are advertised in the local paper. Be forewarned, the beaches are subject to closure at any time. ~ The end of Wauwinet Road off Polpis Road, at the island's northeast end.

HIDDEN ► **SANFORD FARM, RAM PASTURE AND THE WOODS** Owned by the Nantucket Conservation Foundation, this former dairy farm and hunting preserve consists of 779 acres of protected conservation land. A magical place for quiet walks and private picnics, it has 6.6 miles of trails meandering through rare grasslands and heathlands that look like Scotland. Follow the trail past long and winding Hummock Pond down to the empty beach overlooking the Atlantic Ocean on the island's south shore. In spring and summer the property is lush with wildflowers, but its most beautiful time is fall, when the land is a tapestry of burgundy, sage, rose, gold and ivory. Deer can be spotted early in the morning and at dusk. Turtles live in the pond. To minimize damage, visitors are urged to stay on trails and roadways. Motorized vehicles are prohibited. The property is open from dawn to dusk. ~ West of town off Madaket Road near the intersection of Cliff Road and Madaket; 508-228-2884, fax 508-228-5528; www.nantucketconservation.org, e-mail info@nantucketconservation.org.

Outdoor Adventures

Cape Cod, Martha's Vineyard and Nantucket offer a staggering number of opportunities for fishing, boating and other water sports, as well as cycling, golf, tennis and more.

FISHING

Bluefish, striped bass, tuna, cod and flounder are abundant. No license is required to fish, and tackle shops are everywhere. For detailed information on what to catch when, where and how, check the website of the **Massachusetts Division of Marine Fisheries.** ~ www.mass.gov/marinefisheries.

NORTH CAPE Among the hundreds of charter and party boat outfits on Cape Cod, one of the most reputable is the 52-foot **Albatross.** ~ Sesuit Harbor, East Dennis; 508-385-3244; www.albatrossfishing.com. The 60-foot **Naviator** also comes highly recommended; sea bass and blackfish are common catches. ~ Wellfleet town pier; 508-349-6003; www.naviator.com. **Teacher's Pet** has a good reputation, offering bluefish and striped bass excursions. Closed November to mid-May. ~ Hyannis Harbor; 508-362-4925; www.teacherspetfishing.com.

MARTHA'S VINEYARD **Larry's Tackle Shop** has shore guides and charter services. The four-hour trips can be small (one person) or large (six people). ~ 258 Upper Main Street, Edgartown; 508-627-5088, fax 508-627-5148.

NANTUCKET The **Albacore** will take you out for bluefish, bass, shark or tuna. Private charters only. Closed November to May. ~ Slip 17, Straight Wharf, Nantucket; 508-228-5074; www.albacorecharters.com.

WATER SPORTS

Cape Cod abounds with marinas and harbors where you can rent sailboats, windsurfing equipment, canoes and more. The bay and ponds around the area are good for canoeing and kayaking, while the ocean whips up fine surfing waves.

OUTER CAPE **Jack's Boat Rental** has four locations for canoe, kayak, boogieboard and surfboard rentals. Sailing lessons are available. Closed mid-September to mid-June. ~ Route 6, Wellfleet, 508-349-9808; Gull Pond, Wellfleet, 508-349-7553; Flax Pond, Brewster, 508-896-8556, Nickerson State Park, Brewster, 508-896-8556; www.jacksboatrentals.com.

PROVINCETOWN **Flyer's Boat Rental** can outfit you with powerboats, sailboats and kayaks. Closed mid-October to mid-May. ~ 131-A Commercial Street; 508-487-0898; www.flyersboats.com.

SOUTH CAPE **Cape Water Sports** rents Hobie cats, Sun-fish and kayaks. ~ Route 28, Harwich Port; 508-432-5996; www.capewatersports.com.

MARTHA'S VINEYARD For sailboat rentals, as well as kayaking and windsurfing rentals or lessons, there's **Wind's Up**. Rentals and lessons during summer only. ~ 199 Beach Road, Vineyard Haven; 508-693-4252; www.windsupmv.com. **Ayuthia Charters** offers half-day sails on a 48-foot ketch. Closed October through April. ~ Coastwise Wharf, Vineyard Haven; 508-693-7245.

NANTUCKET **Nantucket Island Community Sailing** rents windsurfing gear, kayaks and sailboats, and gives lessons. Closed September to end of June. ~ North Beach Street on Jetties Beach; 508-228-5358; www.nantucketcommunitysailing.org.

WHALE WATCHING

May through October is the season to catch sight of humpbacks and minkes. Among the many excursions departing from Cape Cod is **Hyannis Whale Watcher Cruises**. Whale spotting is guaranteed, which takes 400 passengers out on a 138-foot triple decker boat. ~ Millway Marina, Barnstable Harbor, Barnstable; 508-362-6088; www.whales.net. In Provincetown, **Dolphin Fleet Whale Watch** also guarantees whales. A naturalist is on board one of the three 100-foot boats to provide insight. Closed October to mid-April. ~ MacMillan Pier; 508-255-3857; www.whalewatch.com.

SCUBA DIVING

Lobsters, starfish, crabs and skates are common sights when diving in Cape Cod waters. Cape Cod Bay and Sandwich Town Beach are recommended spots.

GOLF

NORTH CAPE Clientele primarily consists of resort guests at the 18-hole **Ocean Edge**, but everyone is welcome. Carts are required. ~ 832 Village Drive, Brewster; 508-896-5911; www.oceanedge.com.

OUTER CAPE Located on the Cape Cod National Seashore, **Highland Golf Links** is a nine-hole public course that requires tee times. You'll get views of Cape Cod Lighthouse as well as the seashore. ~ Lighthouse Road, Truro; 508-487-9201; www.truro capecod.com.

SOUTH CAPE The **Harwich Port Golf Club** has a nine-hole course. ~ Forest and South streets, Harwich Port; 508-432-0250. The public 18-hole **Fairgrounds Golf Course** on the South Cape features a driving range, a pro shop, and a restaurant and lounge. ~ 1460 Route 149, Marstons Mills; 508-420-1142; www.obf golf.com.

MARTHA'S VINEYARD **Mink Meadows Golf Club** is a semiprivate, nine-hole course featuring wooded, rolling terrain. ~ Golf Club Road off Franklin Street, Vineyard Haven; 508-693-0600; www.minkmeadows.com. The 18-hole, semiprivate **Farm Neck Golf Course** offers beautiful scenery. Closed January to April. ~ County Road, Oak Bluffs; 508-693-2504.

NANTUCKET The 18-hole public **Miacomet Golf Club** has a driving range and a practice putting green. ~ 15 West Miacomet Road; 508-325-0333; www.miacometgolf.com. Or play your nine holes at **Siasconset Golf Club**, one of the oldest courses in the country. This public links-style course resembles Scotland Yard. Closed Columbus Day to Memorial Day. ~ Milestone Road, Siasconset; 508-257-6596; www.siasconsetgolf.com.

TENNIS

Most Cape Cod towns have tennis courts in schools and resorts.

NORTH CAPE A privately owned club, **Mid-Cape Racquet & Health** has nine courts, all lighted. They rent racquets and offer lessons. ~ 193 White's Path, South Yarmouth; 508-394-3511; www.midcaperacquet.com.

PROVINCETOWN **Bissell Tennis Courts** is a privately owned facility with five clay courts. Pros here can show you the swing of things. Closed mid-October to mid-May. ~ 21 Bradford Street Extension; 508-487-9512; www.bisselltennis.com.

MARTHA'S VINEYARD Tennis is very popular on Martha's Vineyard. Municipal courts are at Church Street in Vineyard Haven, Niantic Park in Oak Bluffs, Robinson Road in Edgartown, Old Country Road in West Tisbury and the Chilmark Community Center on South Road.

NANTUCKET **Jetties Beach Tennis Courts** accepts walk-ins and reservations for its six courts. Lessons also offered. ~ 2 Bathing Road; 508-325-5334.

BIKING

For biking listings see "Cape Cod by Bike" in this chapter.

HIKING

Otherworldly sand dunes, heaths that recall those across the Atlantic, sheltering forests and salt marshes are just a few of the environments available to hikers on Cape Cod and the Islands. You can trek through wilderness areas or stick to spots close to town. For more information on hikes throughout the state, contact the **Massachusetts Department of Conservation and Recreation.** ~ 251 Causeway Street, Boston; 617-626-1250; www.mass.gov/dcr. All distances listed for hiking trails are one way unless otherwise noted.

NORTH CAPE **Talbot's Point Salt Marsh Trail** (1.5 miles), off Old Country Road in Sandwich, offers excellent views of the Great Marsh. The trail winds through red pine forest, along the fern-filled marsh, and past cranberry bogs and the state game farm, where thousands of quail and pheasant are raised.

OUTER CAPE **Nauset Marsh Trail** (1-mile loop) offers some of the Cape's lushest scenery. The trail starts at the Salt Pond Visitors Center in North Eastham and goes past the shoreline of Salt Pond and Nauset Marsh, then rises through pastoral farmland filled with beach plums, bayberries and cedars.

A mesmerizing view of salt marsh and the bay beyond greets you at **Goose Ponds Trail** (1.4-mile loop) in the Wellfleet Bay Wildlife Sanctuary. The path leads through forest down a slight grade past Spring Brook to a salt marsh. A wooden boardwalk leads to secluded tidal flats. There are many species of bird life nesting in bird houses in one part of the sanctuary. Admission. ~ 508-349-2615; www.wellfleetbay.org.

Great Island Trail (3 miles), a wind-bitten wilderness, is best in the morning when the sun isn't too intense. Starting at the end of Chequesset Neck Road in Wellfleet, this challenging trail borders tidal flats, grassy dunes, pitch pine forest, the ocean and meadows where purple marsh peas and fiddler crabs flourish. Great for solitary beachcombing, the trail offers a number of spectacular views. Sections are occasionally submerged, depending on the tide.

TRANSPORTATION TIPS

For information on every conceivable way to get to Martha's Vineyard, Nantucket and Cape Cod short of walking on water, call the **Massachusetts Office of Travel and Tourism** and order a free *Getaway Guide*. In addition to transportation details, the guide lists outdoor adventure possibilities, lodging choices and sightseeing highlights. ~ 10 Park Plaza, 4th floor, Boston; 617-973-8500, 800-227-6277; www.mass-vacation.com.

PROVINCETOWN You'll find hikers on the moderately difficult **Beech Forest Trail** (1 mile). Most of the trail wanders through cool beech forests and around freshwater ponds. It starts at the Beech Forest parking lot off Race Point Road in Provincetown. ~ 508-487-1256.

MARTHA'S VINEYARD **Felix Neck Wildlife Sanctuary Trail System**, off the Edgartown–Vineyard Haven Road, provides habitat for animals such as ducks, swans, otters, muskrats, deer, osprey, voles, moles, harrier hawks and other wildlife. The easy trails wind past waterfowl ponds, salt marsh, the tip of a peninsula, wetland vegetation and oak forest. Most start at the sanctuary's exhibit building, which has aquariums, wildlife displays, a library and a naturalist gift shop. Admission. ~ 508-627-4850.

NANTUCKET The island's only marked hiking trail is the **Sanford Farm–Ram Pasture Walking Trail**, offering 15 miles of moors. The Nantucket Conservation Foundation also owns parcels of moors the public can explore. For more on this, see the "Beaches & Parks" sections in this chapter. Following are two of the most scenic areas in which to hike:

Tupancy Links, off Cliff Road immediately west of town, is laced with paths that overlook Nantucket Sound. A former golf course, today this marked trail system traverses a big, open, grassy field offering dramatic views.

Alter Rock, off Polpis Road in the central moors, is crisscrossed by unmarked paths and rutted dirt roads. Dotted with kettle hole ponds, rocks and scrub oak thicket, the scenery is classic heathland. A four-wheel-drive is required if driving. (Use caution: it's easy to get lost here).

Transportation

CAR

Route 6 cuts through the middle of Cape Cod, ending at Provincetown. **Route 6A** runs along the north side of the Cape, and **Route 28** runs along Nantucket Sound. Both routes connect with Route 6 in Orleans.

AIR

Five airports serve Cape Cod and the Islands: **Logan International Airport** (800-235-6426) in Boston, Barnstable Airport and Provincetown Municipal Airport on Cape Cod, Martha's Vineyard Airport and Nantucket Memorial Airport.

Barnstable Airport in Hyannis is served by Cape Air, Colgan Air, Island Air, Nantucket Airlines and US Airways Express.

Cape Air services **Provincetown Municipal Airport** (508-487-0241).

Flying into **Martha's Vineyard Airport** (508-693-7022) are Cape Air and US Airways Express.

Nantucket Memorial Airport (508-325-5300) is serviced by Cape Air, Colgan Air, Continental, Island Air, Nantucket Airlines and US Airways Express.

For ground transportation from Barnstable Airport to Logan Airport and areas throughout southern Massachusetts, contact **King's Coach** (508-747-6622; www.kingscoach.com).

Taxis and car rentals listed below provide ground transportation to all other airports except Logan.

FERRY & BOAT

Ferries and boats between Cape Cod, Martha's Vineyard and Nantucket require reservations during the summer. Throughout the year, the **Steamship Authority** provides service out of two mainland ports. Year-round service to Martha's Vineyard operates out of Woods Hole. Year-round ferry service to Nantucket operates out of Hyannis. ~ 508-477-8600; www.steamshipauthority.com.

The following ferries and boats operate seasonally and do not transport cars: **Hy-Line Cruises** takes passengers to and from Hyannis, Nantucket and Oak Bluffs on Martha's Vineyard. ~ Ocean Street Dock, Hyannis; 508-775-7185; www.hylinecruises.com. **The Island Queen** goes between Falmouth and Oak Bluffs on Martha's Vineyard. Trips run from late May to mid-October. ~ 75 Falmouth Heights Road, Falmouth; 508-548-4800; www.islandqueen.com. The **Chappaquiddick Ferry**, universally known as the "Chappy ferry," travels between Edgartown and Chappaquiddick Island year-round. ~ Dock and Daggett streets, Edgartown, Martha's Vineyard; 508-627-9427.

BUS

Greyhound Lines offers frequent service to Newburyport and Boston. ~ 700 Atlantic Avenue, South Station, Boston; 617-526-1801, 800-229-9424; www.greyhound.com.

Bonanza runs buses to and from Logan Airport, Hyannis, Woods Hole, Falmouth, Bourne, New Bedford, Fall River, Connecticut, Rhode Island and New York. ~ 59 Depot Avenue, Falmouth; 508-548-7588; www.bonanzabus.com.

Plymouth and Brockton Street Railway Company has year-round express service to and from Boston's Logan Airport and local service along Route 6 on Cape Cod from Hyannis to Provincetown. ~ The Plymouth terminal is at exit 5 off Route 3, Plymouth, 508-746-0378; the Hyannis terminal is at Center and Main streets, Hyannis, 508-775-6502; www.p-b.com.

Peter Pan Bus Lines offers service to Springfield, Newton and Worcester. ~ 700 Atlantic Avenue, Boston; 800-343-9999.

CAR RENTALS

Car-rental agencies at Barnstable Airport include **Avis Rent A Car** (800-331-1212), **Budget Rent A Car** (800-527-0700), **Enterprise Rent A Car** (800-736-8222) and **Hertz Rent A Car** (800-654-3131).

Martha's Vineyard has **Thrifty Adventure Car and Moped Rentals** (508-693-1959), **Budget Rent A Car** (800-527-0700) and **Hertz Rent A Car** (800-654-3131).

Nantucket Memorial Airport agencies include **Budget Rent A Car** (800-527-0700), **Hertz Rent A Car** (800-654-3131) and **Nantucket Windmill Auto Rental** (800-228-1227).

PUBLIC TRANSIT

Cape Cod Regional Transit Authority offers door-to-door minibus service (reservations required) and makes six daily roundtrips between Barnstable and Woods Hole, Hyannis and Orleans, and Hyannis and Barnstable Harbor (winter only). There are expanded daily rounds during the summer. ~ 215 Iyannough Road, Hyannis; www.thebreeze.info.

Nantucket doesn't have public transportation. Most people get around with rental cars or bicycles.

TAXIS

Taxis serving airports on the coast are as follows: Barnstable Airport, **Town Taxi of Cape Cod** (508-771-5555); Provincetown Airport, **Mercedes Cab** (508-487-3333); Martha's Vineyard Airport, **Adam Cab** (508-627-4462); Nantucket Memorial Airport, **A-1 Taxi** (508-228-3330).

SIX

Massachusetts Coast

Immortalized by Herman Melville in *Moby Dick*, the Massachusetts coast today remains fertile territory for the imagination. This magnificent stretch of windswept coast abounds with historic seaside villages, vintage lighthouses, glorious beaches and history that reads like an adventure story complete with witches and pirates, authors and artists, Pilgrims and American natives, sea captains and Moby Dick.

An ethnic melting pot of Portuguese fishermen, Yankee blue bloods, old salts and the Irish (who seem to be everywhere), coast residents are very proud of where they live. North Shore loyalists wouldn't think of moving to the South Shore, and vice versa. What unifies everyone is the sea. Rich and poor alike have mini weather stations on their roofs to determine wind direction, and everyone reads tide charts. Kids learn how to fish, sail and dig for clams when they're five years old.

That all-encompassing sea is, of course, what lured Europeans to these shores in the first place. One hundred years before the Pilgrims set foot on Plymouth Rock, English adventurers fished the waters around the Massachusetts coast. Between 1600 and 1610, explorers Samuel de Champlain and Bartholomew Gosnold sailed to Gloucester.

Aboard the *Mayflower*, 102 Pilgrims landed in Plymouth in 1620, establishing the first permanent settlement in New England. By 1640, about 2500 of the new settlers lived in eight communities. Although they came to America to seek religious freedom, the Pilgrims persecuted Quakers and anyone else who didn't adhere to their strict Puritan religion. Their intolerant thinking helped fuel one of the most infamous pieces of American colonial history—the Salem witch trials of 1692. Salem had been founded six years after Plymouth. Here the Puritans tried to impose their religious laws on rowdy fishermen who lived in nearby Marblehead, but adultery and drunkenness won out. The Puritans were more successful in their witch hunt—in a single year 20 people, most of them women, were executed for practicing "witchcraft."

The gruesome trials took place during a time when witchcraft was thought to be the cause for any unexplained event. Similar trials and executions occurred throughout New England and Europe, but Salem had the dubious distinction of executing the most women in the shortest amount of time.

Fortunately, by the 1700s the focus was more on commerce than religion. Salem sailing vessels had opened routes to the Orient, thus establishing the famous China trade and Salem's reputation as a major port.

For the next 150 years, shipbuilding, the China trade and commercial fishing flourished along the Massachusetts coast, particularly in the towns north of Boston. Concurrently, New Bedford, near Rhode Island, became a leading whaling port.

All this maritime activity brought great prosperity to the coast. Fortune and adventure lay in wait for any man willing to risk his life on a whale boat or ship bound for the Orient to obtain ivory, spice, silver and gold. It was an exciting, swashbuckling time, filled with tall tales and tragedy. The widows' walks on many historic homes in towns such as Newburyport are a sad reminder of the men who never returned from the sea.

Evidence of the wealth gleaned during these years is apparent in the amazing number of 18th- and 19th-century mansions built by sea captains that dot the coast. Impeccably restored by a people in love with the past, these coast homes make up an architectural feast bulging with Greek Revival, Federal, Queen Anne, Victorian Gothic, Colonial and classic saltbox structures. Historic villages and buildings throughout the area enable visitors to see the evolution of America's unique architectural style.

By the mid-1800s everything along the Massachusetts coast started to change. Salem's prominence as a seaport was over. Its harbor was too shallow for the new, faster clipper ships, and railroads provided cheaper and more rapid shipping service. The whaling industry also started to decline as petroleum replaced whale oil and whales became scare. Eventually the entire industry vanished, plummeting New Bedford and other whaling ports into serious depressions.

The Industrial Revolution came along in the nick of time, and manufacturing businesses started to sprout along the Massachusetts coast and throughout New England. In the late 1800s, New Bedford and Fall River became leading textile manufacturers, but this prosperity was short lived. Prior to the Depression, union problems and cheaper labor in the South wiped out the textile industry.

While the coast economy was transforming itself in the mid-1800s, two other developments were evolving that would change the flavor of the coast forever. Tourism began to bloom on Cape Cod, and artists and writers discovered the inspirational charms of the coast.

Rudyard Kipling and Winslow Homer lived north of Boston in Rocky Neck, one of the country's oldest artist colonies. Nathaniel Hawthorne wrote about Salem, which he called home, in the *House of the Seven Gables*. Melville immortalized whaling in New Bedford. To this day, creative people are drawn to the Massachusetts coast, now supported by light industry, fishing and a tourist industry that just keeps growing.

We have divided the coast into two geographic areas. The North Shore (everything above Boston to the New Hampshire border) and the South Shore (Plymouth and the area from Cape Cod to the Rhode Island border). Cape Cod and the Islands have always attracted the lion's share of tourists, but the North Shore and South Shore offer more opportunities to discover hidden villages, inns, restaurants, beaches and more.

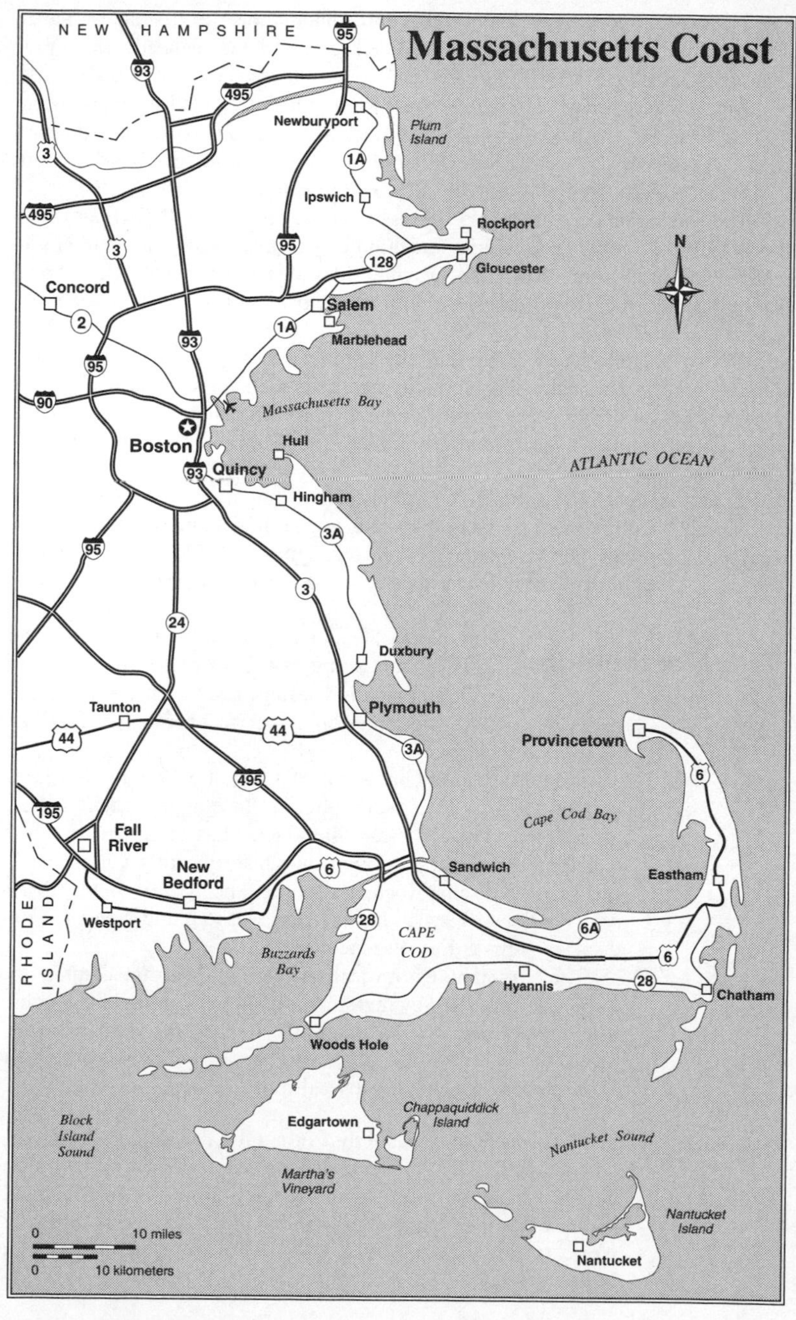
Massachusetts Coast
NEW HAMPSHIRE
RHODE ISLAND
Newburyport
Plum Island
Ipswich
Rockport
Gloucester
Concord
Salem
Marblehead
Massachusetts Bay
Boston
Hull
Quincy
Hingham
ATLANTIC OCEAN
Duxbury
Plymouth
Taunton
Provincetown
Cape Cod Bay
Fall River
New Bedford
Sandwich
Eastham
Westport
CAPE COD
Buzzards Bay
Hyannis
Chatham
Woods Hole
Block Island Sound
Edgartown
Chappaquiddick Island
Nantucket Sound
Martha's Vineyard
Nantucket Island
Nantucket
N
0 10 miles
0 10 kilometers

The North Shore wears many faces. Immediately north of Boston are the affluent commuter towns of Magnolia, Manchester and Marblehead, where prep schools, yachts and turn-of-the-20th-century seaside mansions are a way of life.

Beyond these towns are Salem, known for architecture, witches and maritime museums; Gloucester, a major fishing port; Rockport, an artist-colony-turned-resort; Essex and Ipswich, pastoral areas with antiques and seafood; and Newburyport, a scenic 19th-century town near the New Hampshire border.

The South Shore is a patchwork of wealthy commuter towns, Portuguese neighborhoods, blue-collar communities and cranberry farms. Its three main towns include Plymouth, "America's Home Town," New Bedford and Fall River. You'll find Pilgrim lore, factory outlets, whaling museums, scenic ports, winding rivers and coastal pastures.

The coast has milder weather than the rest of the state. Summer temperatures range from the 60s to the 80s. Humidity can be a problem, especially along the North Shore, although ocean breezes keep things from getting too unbearable. In the fall temperatures range from the around 45° to 65°. Rain is unpredictable and can happen any time of year.

Traditionally the Massachusetts coast has been a summer destination, but more people are starting to visit in the fall, when prices decline along with the crowds. But no matter when you visit you're bound to be impressed. The scenery is unparalleled, the architecture magnificent, the history fascinating, the seafood plentiful.

The North Shore

The North Shore is a real sleeper. Unspoiled and relatively uncommercial, it's a place where you can still discover hidden inns, restaurants, beaches and parks. An explorer's destination, it's perfect for people who like to go it on their own.

From Marblehead immediately north of Boston to Newburyport on the New Hampshire border, this craggy stretch of coast offers tremendous diversity. Marblehead has magnificent yachts; Salem means witches and maritime history; gritty Gloucester is filled with old salts; Rockport has art and beautiful inns; Essex offers antiques; Ipswich has the best seafood; and Newburyport displays 19th-century elegance.

The North Shore is a vacation area and bedroom community to Boston populated by investment bankers, Yankee blue bloods, fishermen, artists and history buffs. In the 18th and 19th centuries, the country's most magnificent ships were built in North Shore towns, bringing great wealth to the area.

SIGHTS

HIDDEN ►

In Marblehead, head directly to the Old Town historic district, where you'll find **Abbot Hall**, the Victorian town hall that houses the famous historic painting The Spirit of '76 by Archibald Willard. Visitors are free to wander in and view his dramatic work of art. Closed weekends from November through Memorial Day. ~ 188 Washington Street, Marblehead; 781-631-

0000, fax 781-631-8571; www.marblehead.org, e-mail tonys@marblehead.org.

Located right down the street is the **Jeremiah Lee Mansion**, a Georgian home built in 1768 for Colonel Lee, a Revolutionary War activist. The entrance hall adorned with elaborate woodwork and an extra-wide stairway, was the largest and most opulent in New England. The original wallpaper is the only 18th-century hand-painted English scenic paper in the world still in place. There are lovely historic gardens for wandering. Closed Sunday and Monday, and from November through May. Admission. ~ 161 Washington Street, Marblehead; 781-631-1768, fax 781-631-0917.

Salem is so civilized and proper looking, it's hard to believe the 1692 witchcraft trials ever took place here. This macabre piece of American history began in a very innocent way. A group of teenage girls, who had learned black magic from a West Indian

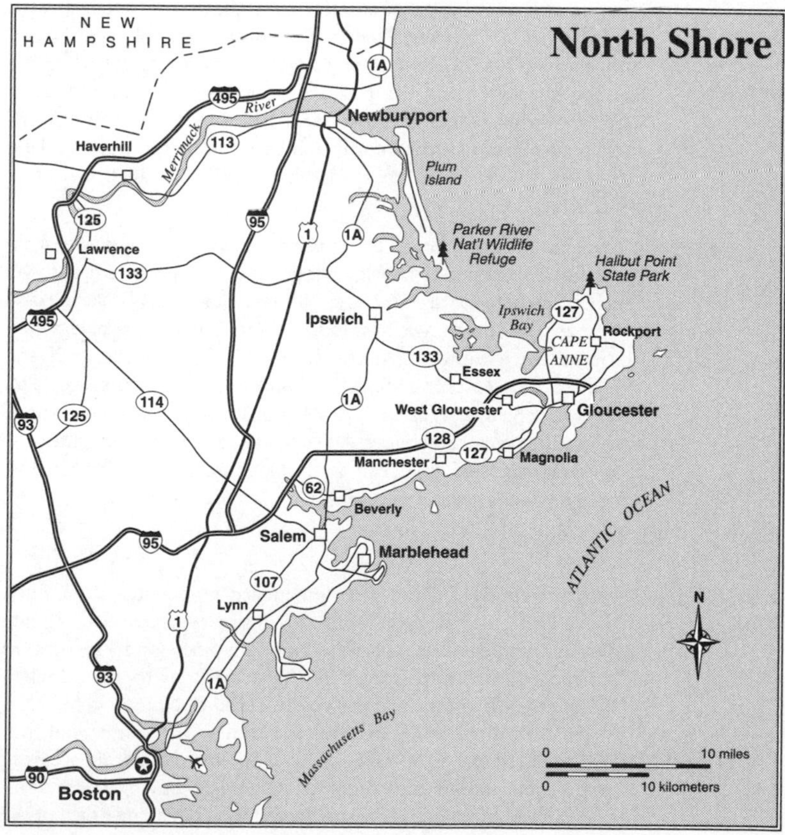

SCENIC DRIVE

The North Shore

This 80-mile day trip from Boston provides a chance to explore the North Shore in all its diversity and quiet charm. Start by taking the Callahan Tunnel (Route 1A) north through the suburbs, where it becomes the McClellen Highway, then North Shore Road, and finally Lynnway before the divided roadway ends at East Lynn, a distance of ten miles.

MARBLEHEAD Take the east fork in the highway and follow Route 129 for six miles to **Marblehead**, a small village of clapboard houses, hollyhocks and cobblestone streets. Marblehead is sailboat country. All summer long the harbor is alive with some of the most sophisticated racing vessels in America. A good place to picnic and watch them is high on a hill in **Crocker Park** at the western end of Front Street. Marblehead's **Old Town**, which surrounds the harbor, dates back to before the Revolution and is a pleasant place to stroll, with interesting shops and casual restaurants. The **Marblehead Chamber of Commerce** maintains a visitor information booth at Pleasant Street (781-639-8469). ~ 62 Pleasant Street, Marblehead; 781-631-2868; www.marbleheadchamber.org.

SALEM Salem, the largest North Shore town, is only ten minutes away from Marblehead on Route 114, which rejoins Route 1A just south of town. People come here for architecture, maritime museums, Nathaniel Hawthorne and, of course, witches. Tourist information is available at the **National Park Service Visitor Center**. ~ 2 New Liberty Street, Salem; 978-740-1650. Or contact the **Chamber of Commerce**. ~ 265 Essex Street, Suite 101, Salem; 978-744-0004; www.salem-chamber.org, e-mail scc@salem-chamber.org. An easy way to see historic sights is to follow **Salem's Heritage Trail**, a self-guided walking tour indicated by a red line painted on the sidewalks.

woman named Tituba, were diagnosed as bewitched. All hell broke loose, and everyone started accusing everyone else of being a witch. In the nine months to follow, 14 women (and 5 men) were hanged and 150 imprisoned. The hysteria came to an end when the wives of prominent men were accused of being witches.

Salem's three witch exhibits are somewhat commercial, but kids love them. Every day in the summer, children wearing pointed black hats and capes purchased at nearby witch boutiques stand in long lines waiting to get in. The saving grace of the

GLOUCESTER Northeast of Salem, turn off Route 1A again onto scenic Route 127, which hugs the coast and takes you through the wealthy residential towns of Manchester and Magnolia. Right off Route 127, about 14 miles north of Salem, you'll spot **Hammond Castle** perched on the edge of a steep, windswept cliff, looking like the setting for a Gothic novel. Three miles beyond the castle is Gloucester, the oldest seaport in the United States. Home port to approximately 200 fishermen, it has a salty-dog ambience that brings you back to the real world after the castle. Overlooking the harbor stands the town's famed **Gloucester Fisherman** statue, *Man at the Wheel*, commemorating "They that go down to the sea in ships." There's not much to do in Gloucester; information on the town and local services is available at the **Cape Ann Chamber of Commerce**, the largest tourist information center on the North Shore, in the center of town. ~ 33 Commercial Street, Gloucester; 978-283-1601; www.capeannvacations.com, e-mail info@capeannchamber.com.

ROCKPORT A short hop from Gloucester off Route 127 is **Rocky Neck Art Colony**, one of the country's oldest artist colonies, dating back to the 18th century. Winslow Homer and Rudyard Kipling lived here. Today it is a quainter than quaint seaside village with tiny houses, restaurants and galleries. Ten minutes farther along on Route 127 is Rockport, the quintessential New England seaside village and the North Shore's only resort town. Until the mid-19th century, Rockport was a quiet fishing village. Then artists discovered its scenic charm, and the proverbial seascape was born. Today tourists flock to Rockport in the summer. The town is rather commercial, but the beautiful harbor and windswept rocky coast that originally attracted artists are still here to enjoy.

BACK TO BOSTON From Rockport, continue on Route 127 for nine more miles as it loops around the peninsula and joins Route 128, a divided freeway that connects to Routes 1 and 95 and can put you back in downtown Boston in less than an hour. Or, to extend your North Shore outing, leave Route 128 after four miles at Exit 14, detour through **Essex** and **Ipswich** (page 358) on Route 133, and return to Boston via Route 1A.

exhibits is that they are in historic buildings—not re-creations of haunted houses.

Salem Witch Museum is an audio-visual sound-and-light show. Life-size dioramas are spotlighted during the show to illustrate the events of the 1692 witch trials. They also have a more cerebral exhibit that examines the new views and multiple meanings of "witch." Admission. ~ 19½ Washington Square North, Salem; 978-744-1692, fax 978-745-4414; www.salemwitchmuseum.com, e-mail faq@salemwitchmuseum.com.

Witch House is the restored 1642 home of witch trial judge Jonathan Corwin, and the only structure still standing in Salem with direct ties to the witch trials. A narrated tour describes the style of life during this era and examines Judge Corwin's role in the trials. Closed mid-November to early May. Admission. ~ 310½ Essex Street, Salem; 978-744-8815, fax 978-741-0578; www.salemweb.com/witchhouse, e-mail info@corwinhouse.org.

Witch Dungeon Museum re-enacts the witch trials and offers a tour of the dungeon. Closed December through March. Admission. ~ 16 Lynde Street, Salem; 978-741-3570, fax 978-741-1139; www.witchdungeon.com, e-mail salemwitchpirate@aol.com.

Although mostly known for its witch trial tragedies, Salem has also had to endure piracy. Highlights of a visit to the **New England Pirate Museum** include a recreated dock-side village and pirate ship. Admission. Closed December through May. ~ 274 Derby Street, Salem; 978-741-2800; www.piratemuseum.com.

A tourist information booth is located at the **Central Wharf Warehouse** on Derby Wharf.

To understand the real story of Salem, which was a major port in the 18th and 19th centuries, visit the **Peabody Essex Museum.** The museum houses a treasure trove of objects from China, Japan, Korea, the Pacific Islands and India in over 30 galleries. The collection includes maritime art, American decorative art, photographs, portraits, costumes and furniture. The museum campus includes numerous parks, period gardens and 24 historic properties. The three houses that can be toured are fascinating, especially if visited in chronological order, and the architecture and craftsmanship are superb. Admission. ~ East India Square, Salem; 978-745-9500, 866-745-1876, fax 978-745-7550; www.pem.org, e-mail pem@pem.org.

Chestnut Street is one of the most architecturally significant avenues in America. Many of its mansions were designed by Salem's famed Federal-period architect and woodcarver, Samuel McIntire. These brick-and-wood houses are simple in their design, yet the overall effect is graceful and elegant.

Pickering Wharf, a short walk from Chestnut Street, is a new but made-to-look-old commercial development of tourist shops and chain restaurants. About a block east stands **Derby Wharf**—a good area for strolling along the harbor.

Even though it's often crowded with tourists, there's something romantic and compelling about the **House of Seven Gables**, located down the street from Derby Wharf. Built in 1668, the dark, almost black house is framed by ocean and sky. The tall, imposing gables look a bit like witch hats (although this thought probably wouldn't come to mind in another town). Inside, a labyrinth of cozy rooms with low ceilings, narrow passageways and secret stairs add to the ancient feeling of the place. The guided tour includes a good short film about how the house inspired Nathaniel Hawthorne to write his famous novel. Year-round guided tours are available. Closed the first three weeks of January. Admission. ~ 54 Turner Street, Salem; 978-744-0991, fax 978-741-4350; www.7gables.org.

Northeast of Salem on scenic Route 127, which hugs the coast, are the residential towns of **Manchester** and **Magnolia,** known for their old money, private schools and magnificent mansions.

HIDDEN

Right off Route 127 is **Hammond Castle Museum**, a popular spot in Gloucester. Built by John Hays Hammond, Jr., creator of the radio remote control, the house features an eccentric collection of medieval to early American artifacts. Closed November to Memorial Day; open weekends only from Labor Day through October. Admission. ~ 80 Hesperus Avenue, Gloucester; 978-283-2080, fax 978-283-1643; www.hammondcastle.org.

Beauport, the Sleeper McCann House, is a sprawling oceanfront English manor formerly owned by noted decorator Henry Davis Sleeper. From 1907 to 1934 Sleeper spent a fortune decorating all 40 rooms with a vast collection of American and European antiques, tapestries, wood paneling from abandoned old homes and much more. An informal pale green dining room has a worn brick floor and two long wooden tables set with a beautiful collection of colored glassware that reflects the light coming in from a bank of ocean-facing windows. Surprisingly, the overall effect is of an intimate English cottage. Closed mid-October to early June, and weekends from early June to mid-September. Admission. ~ 75 Eastern Point Boulevard, East Gloucester; 978-283-4484; www.historicnewengland.org, e-mail beauport house@historicnewengland.org.

Bearskin Neck, a narrow peninsula jutting out into the ocean, is one of Rockport's main tourist attractions. It is lined with Lilliputian-sized wooden fishing shacks transformed into restaurants, shops and galleries selling everything from T-shirts and seascapes in every style imaginable to model ships made of cut-up beer cans. Overlooking the harbor, off Bearskin Neck, is **Motif #1**, a red lobster shack so named because it has been painted by many artists.

"HOW DRY I AM . . ."

Rockport is a dry town, thanks to Hannah Jumper, a temperance supporter. In 1856 after a raucous Fourth of July celebration, Hannah convinced town fathers to outlaw liquor. Even today you can't buy it in a store or order it in a restaurant. But you can buy liquor in Gloucester, which is only ten minutes away, and bring it to any Rockport restaurant.

About one mile south of downtown Rockport is the **Rockport Chamber of Commerce Information Booth**. Closed from mid-October to mid-May. ~ 170 Main Street, Rockport; 978-546-6575, 888-726-3922, fax 978-546-5997; www.rockportusa.com, e-mail info@rockportusa.com.

The folks here can point out the local sights, such as the eccentric **Paper House.** At first it looks like a normal cottage, but it's made entirely out of newspaper. Even the furniture and fireplace mantle piece are rolled paper. Elis F. Stenman, its creator, started the house in 1920; it took 20 years to complete. Admission. Closed mid-October to March. ~ 52 Pigeon Hill Street, Rockport; 978-546-2629; www.paperhouserockport.com.

The Massachusetts coast is dotted with majestic sea captains' homes, many of them now inns.

The rural villages of **Essex** and **Ipswich** are about 30 minutes north of Rockport. Essex is famous for its antique stores (see the "Shopping" section below), Ipswich for its clams. A pleasant day can be spent antiquing and enjoying fresh, affordable seafood at one of the many roadside eateries in this area.

This route takes you right past **Whipple House Museum**, a steeply pitched-roofed house built circa 1677 and occupied by the Whipple family for over 200 years. As did many colonists, the Whipples built their home in the post-Elizabethan style popular in England at the time. It has a lovely Colonial-style garden and is located in a semirural area close to other historic buildings. Closed Monday and Tuesday and from November through April. Admission. ~ 54 South Main Street, Ipswich; 978-356-2811, fax 978-356-2817; www.ipswichmuseum.org, e-mail info@ipswichmuseum.org.

Just before the New Hampshire border, about 30 minutes north of Ipswich, lies the handsome 19th-century town of **Newburyport.** When the fog rolls in and the smell of brine and fish fills the air, you can walk along narrow streets bearing names like Neptune and imagine what it was like 100 years ago when this was a major shipbuilding center.

In the late 1970s the downtown area overlooking the harbor was renovated from top to bottom. Today, Newburyport's 19th-century brick buildings are so spit-and-polish clean, the town literally sparkles. As in many European towns, there's a central plaza overlooking the harbor where you can sit and watch the world go by. The shops and restaurants are quite tasteful; T-shirt and souvenir shops are the exception. **Greater Newburyport Chamber of Commerce** is in the heart of downtown. Closed weekends from Memorial Day to Columbus Day. ~ 38R Merrimac Street, Newburyport; 978-462-6680, fax 978-465-4145; www.newburyportchamber.org, e-mail info@newburyportchamber.org.

High Street (Route 1A) offers a view of every architectural style from the pilgrim era to the present. It is lined with immaculate 19th-century Federal-style mansions built by sea captains and includes houses built from the 1690s to the 1850s. For a peek inside, visit **Cushing House Museum**, home of the Historical Society of Old Newbury. It has 19th-century antiques, plus a genealogical library, a 19th-century garden and a carriage house. Closed Sunday and Monday and from May through October. Admission. ~ 98 High Street, Newburyport; 978-462-2681, fax 978-462-0134; www.newburyhist.com, e-mail hson@greennet.net.

LODGING

Many of the North Shore's accommodations are in the resort town of Rockport. A sprinkling of motels can be found along Route 127, but they're short on charm and expensive.

Marblehead's historic 1910 bed and breakfast **Darci's Parkside Inn** offers complete comfort in a romantic homestead. With pillow-top mattresses, vintage furniture, wireless internet, cable TV and private baths, all five guest rooms provide a welcoming safe haven for relaxation. Three of the suites include two-person jacuzzi tubs and working fireplaces. The ultra-plush Marblehead Suite is the absolute in luxury with all the amenities, set in a two-level lodging with a loft and private balcony. ~ 4 Wyman Road, Marblehead; 781-631-5733, 888-273-7704; www.dpinn.com, e-mail info@dpinn.com. MODERATE TO ULTRA-DELUXE.

◄ HIDDEN

A modest-looking green clapboard house, **The Nautilus Guest House** doesn't have a sign outside. "People just know about it," says the owner. Four plain and simple guest rooms with quaint furnishings occupy the second floor (no private baths). The house stands on a narrow street across from the busy harbor and the Driftwood, a colorful, sea shanty–style restaurant popular with fishermen and locals. ~ 68 Front Street, Marblehead; 781-799-5338; www.brassandbounty.com/nautilus.htm, e-mail info@shiplights.com. MODERATE.

If you can't live without a phone, color TV, air conditioning and room service, stay at **The Hawthorne Hotel.** One of the few real hotels on the North Shore, this impeccably restored Federal-style building is located across from Salem Common. Its 93 rooms are tastefully decorated with reproduction Colonial antiques. Elegant public rooms have wood paneling, brass chandeliers and wingback chairs. ~ 18 Washington Square West, Salem; 978-744-4080, 800-729-7829, fax 978-745-9842; www.hawthornehotel.com, e-mail info@hawthornehotel.com. DELUXE TO ULTRA-DELUXE.

Within easy reach of Singing Beach is the **Old Corner Inn,** a small, unpretentious and very casual inn in a building that dates back to 1865. The nine rooms (six with private baths) are simply but comfortably furnished with some antiques. A couple of rooms have four-poster beds and working fireplaces; the bathroom of room number one has a ball-and-claw bathtub. Advance reservations are a must in the summer months, since it's the only inn in Manchester. ~ 2 Harbor Street, Manchester; 978-526-4996, 800-830-4996, fax 978-526-7671; www.theoldcornerinn.com, e-mail theoldcornerinn@aol.com. MODERATE TO DELUXE.

There is something inexpressibly lovable about the **White House**, a cross between an inn and a motel. Surrounded by a well-coifed lawn steps away from the heart of little Magnolia, it has a total of 16 rooms, 6 fitting beautifully into the charming-inn category (antique furnishings and all sorts of little Victorian touches), and another 10 rooms that are traditional motel accommodations. The latter are actually quite comfortable, most with two big double beds, a television, a private entrance, a private bath and a parking spot—a welcome change from the inns that sometimes compromise on privacy. Limited rooms available in the winter. A continental breakfast is included. ~ 18 Norman Avenue, Magnolia; 978-525-3642; www.whitehouseofmagnolia.com. MODERATE TO DELUXE.

Beach lovers enjoy the **Blue Shutters Inn**, a lovely old house on Good Harbor Beach, one of the North Shore's most beautiful strips of sand. It's situated on the outskirts of a secluded, affluent residential area overlooking the ocean and a vast expanse of scenic salt marsh. Blue and white throughout, the inn offers 22 rooms, most with ocean views and sporting furnishings that are homey, simple and sparkling clean. Breakfast included. ~ 1 Nautilus Road, Gloucester; 978-283-1198; www.blueshuttersbeachside.com, e-mail ejciii@rcn.com. MODERATE TO DELUXE.

Only a ten-minute walk from Gloucester's famed fisherman statue, **The Manor Inn** has economical accommodations to satisfy all tastes. The main guest house, a lovely Victorian built in 1900, has 11 B&B-style guest rooms, some with turret-shaped ceilings and oversized beds. Next to the guest house are one-story motel units, some of which overlook the Annisquam River, a salt marsh and estuaries. The decor is plain and unobtrusive.

AUTHOR FAVORITE

Witches aside, one of the best reasons I can think of to visit Salem is the **Stephen Daniels House**, which is like a trip back in time. Built in 1667 by a sea captain, it is one of the few bed and breakfasts around here furnished entirely with museum-quality antiques. The four guest rooms have enormous walk-in fireplaces, low beamed ceilings and age-worn pine floors. It's located on a quiet, historic street within walking distance of everything, although the sign outside is small and easy to miss. ~ 1 Daniels Street, Salem; 978-744-5709. DELUXE.

Closed January through April. ~ 141 Essex Avenue, Gloucester; 978-283-0614, 877-626-6746; www.themanorinnofgloucester.com, e-mail themanorinn@prodigy.net. MODERATE TO DELUXE.

A 1771 Georgian-Federal bed and breakfast, **The Inn on Cove Hill** is a five-minute walk from Bearskin Neck, Rockport's main tourist attraction. Seven guest rooms have wide pine-plank floors, beautiful restored moldings, antiques, queen-sized canopy beds and country quilts. No smoking on the premises. ~ 37 Mount Pleasant Street, Rockport; 978-546-2701, 888-546-2701, fax 978-546-1095; www.innoncovehill.com, e-mail betsy25@verizon.net. MODERATE TO DELUXE.

JFK and Jackie once slept at the **Yankee Clipper Inn**, one of Rockport's finest hostelries. The main inn, a stately white oceanfront mansion, has magnificent wood-paneled public rooms appointed with model ships, oriental rugs, paintings and elegant yet comfortable furniture. The Quarterdeck, a separate building built in 1960, has panoramic ocean views and a traditional look. Most of the 16 guest rooms are nondescript, but what they lack in decor is made up for by location. The inn has a swimming pool, gazebo and nature paths. Breakfast included. Closed Monday through Friday from December through March. ~ 127 Granite Street, Rockport; 978-546-3407, 800-545-3699, fax 978-546-9730; www.yankeeclipperinn.com, e-mail info@yankeeclipperinn.com. ULTRA-DELUXE.

The **Peg Leg Inn**, a white clapboard Colonial, is only steps away from the beach. Both of the inn's buildings are on the ocean and offer spectacular views and a large, sweeping lawn. The 14 guest rooms are furnished with chenille bedspreads, braided rugs and reproduction Colonial furnishings and wallpaper. A continental breakfast is included in the rates. Closed late October to mid-April. ~ Corner of Beach and King streets, Rockport; 978-546-2352, 800-346-2352; www.thepegleginn.com. DELUXE TO ULTRA-DELUXE.

Located on a quiet street in the center of town, the **Linden Tree Inn** has 18 rooms with private baths. Twelve antique-furnished rooms are in the main house; the rest are motel-style accommodations in the carriage house. The inn is named after an enormous linden tree on the grounds. Full buffet breakfast is included, complete with legendary scones. ~ 26 King Street, Rockport; 978-546-2494, 800-865-2122, fax 978-546-3297; www.lindentreeinn.com, e-mail ltree@shore.net. DELUXE.

Rockport's **Seaward Inn**, a rambling brown-shingle building, sits on a beautiful bluff overlooking the ocean and is surrounded by flower gardens, lawns and stone walls. Twenty-three guest rooms, some with ocean views and fireplaces, are simply appointed with homey-looking Colonial-style furnishings. The Adirondack-style chairs on a grassy knoll overlooking the windswept shore are perfect for relaxing and reading. Rates include a full breakfast. Closed late October to mid-April. ~ 44 Marmion Way, Rockport; 978-546-3471, 877-473-2927, fax 978-546-7661; www.seawardinn.com, e-mail info@seawardinn.com. ULTRA-DELUXE.

A reasonably priced bed and breakfast in the heart of Rockport is hard to come by, but **Lantana House** fits the bill. The three-story cedar shake-shingled inn has five charming guest rooms, each with distinctive decor. There are two decks where guests can enjoy breakfast or a quiet afternoon. All rooms have private baths and air conditioning, and continental breakfast is included. ~ 22 Broadway, Rockport; 978-546-3535, 800-291-3535; www.thelantanahouse.com, e-mail lantana_house@yahoo.com. MODERATE.

Guests at the **George Fuller House** will get the full Essex treatment. The house was built in 1830 by shipwrights who built many of the fishing schooners that plied Cape Ann's waters during the whaling era. Many of the original Federal-style details have been preserved, including the interior folding shutters, paneling and carved fireplace mantels. The seven rooms are furnished with antiques and reproductions; all have private baths, some have canopy beds and five have working fireplaces. The innkeeper serves a full breakfast every morning in the dining room, and tea is available on the porch or in the living room in the late afternoon. ~ 148 Main Street, Route 133, Essex; 978-768-7766, 800-477-0148, fax 978-768-6178; www.cape-ann.com/fuller-house, e-mail georgefullerhouse@verizon.net. MODERATE TO DELUXE.

The **Clark Currier Inn** is a beautiful 1803 Federal home in the square style of the period. The woodwork and other details throughout the house are splendid, and the antiques and reproductions are, for the most part, true to the Federal period. The eight rooms are individually named for former owners or well-known visitors. Some rooms have canopy beds, and some have twin beds or are convertible to suites for parents who would rather have their children sleeping in an adjoining room. Children staying at the inn must be over 11. All rooms have private baths. The backyard boasts a lovely garden and a gazebo. ~ 45 Green Street, Newburyport; 978-465-8363; www.clarkcurrierinn.com. DELUXE.

HIDDEN ►

The **Morrill Place Inn**, a three-story, 1806 Federal-style mansion, stands on historic High Street, where wealthy shipbuilders lived in the 19th century. The inn's 12 spacious guest rooms are beautifully decorated. The Henry W. Kinsman room (named for a former owner) is a rich hunter green with an enormous white canopy bed, while the Daniel Webster room has a four-poster antique bed and sleigh dresser. Rooms on the third floor are less formal but charming in their own way, with Colonial-style antiques. Some rooms share baths. ~ 209 High Street, Newburyport; 978-462-2808, 888-594-4667, fax 978-462-9966. MODERATE TO DELUXE.

DINING

Rockport has the majority of restaurants on the North Shore, but few are outstanding. Restaurants with a steady local clientele in nearby towns are generally better.

The Landing features entrées like lobster basilico and baked scrod, plus non-seafood options like tenderloin medallions or pasta primavera, in a nautical-themed setting. The waterfront deck juts out over Marblehead Harbor. Sunday brunch is also offered. ~ 81 Front Street, Marblehead; 781-639-1266; www.thelandingrestaurant.com, e-mail thenewlanding@aol.com. MODERATE TO ULTRA-DELUXE.

The **Driftwood Restaurant** is something of an institution. Homey, friendly and colorful, it attracts fishermen in the wee hours (it opens at 5:30 a.m.) and young professionals late on weekend mornings. The fare is traditional and plentiful: ham and eggs, pancakes, fried dough, clam chowder, burgers, fried seafood. The interior of this modest little establishment is plain and simple with red-and-white checked tablecloths. Tables are jammed close together, and there's a counter. No dinner. ~ 63 Front Street, Marblehead; 781-631-1145. BUDGET.

If the diner urge strikes, head for **Red's Sandwich**. Its booths and two horseshoe-shaped bars are always crowded with regulars who all seem to know one another. The menu includes all the diner favorites, from pancakes at breakfast to hamburgers for lunch. ~ 15 Central Street, Salem; 978-745-3527. BUDGET.

Located in the Hawthorne Hotel, **Nathaniel's** is an elegant choice for American and European classics, including swordfish with cilantro-mango salsa, bacon-wrapped filet mignon and pumpkin-seed haddock. The appetizers (sashimi tuna napoleon, grilled lamb lollipops) are rich enough for a meal. ~ 18 Wash-

AUTHOR FAVORITE

If you have a ravenous sweet tooth, don't leave Salem without stopping off at **Harbor Sweets**, which carries Sweet Sloop chocolates (a combination of white and dark chocolate with almond butter crunch) that are frighteningly delicious. You can take a tour of the factory if you call ahead for an appointment. Fortunately, Harbor Sweets does mail-order, so before leaving fill out an address card to receive mailings. At Valentine's Day you can order a dozen tiny red boxes of Sloops for all the loves in your life. Closed Sunday. ~ 85 Leavitt Street, Salem; 978-745-7648, 800-243-2115, fax 978-741-7811; www.harborsweets.com, e-mail contact@harborsweets.com.

ington Square West, Salem; 978-825-4311, 800-729-7829, fax 978-745-9842; www.hawthornehotel.com, e-mail info@hawthornehotel.com. DELUXE TO ULTRA-DELUXE.

The Rudder is a quaint waterfront restaurant with low-beam ceilings and a natural wood decor that creates a casual dining atmosphere. On any given night, you may find fresh local seafood, beef, chops and daily specials. For those who travel by boat, the restaurant has its own dock. Closed Columbus Day through April. Dinner only. ~ 73 Rocky Neck Avenue, Gloucester; 978-283-7967, fax 978-281-7004; www.rudderrestaurant.com, e-mail therudderrestaurant@hotmail.com. MODERATE TO ULTRA-DELUXE.

Portions of *The Perfect Storm* were shot in Gloucester. The movie, starring George Clooney, focused on a swordfishing crew that set out to sea in 1991, never to return.

Passports is the perfect place to bring picky kids. Their international menu features just about every kind of cuisine imaginable, from Adriatic stew to Southwestern pasta to steak *au poivre*. Daily lunch and dinner specials include pasta, seafood and sandwiches. ~ 110 Main Street, Gloucester; 978-281-3680. MODERATE TO DELUXE.

The stylish **Franklin Cape Café** attracts locals with its friendly atmosphere and tasty American cuisine. Each meal in this cavernous but warm, candle-lit restaurant begins with pita and hummus—and, for many, one of the special martinis. Dinner then progresses to entrées such as cassoulet of crispy duck confit, smoked sausage and white beans, or grilled Atlantic salmon with caramel apple in a curry sauce. ~ 118 Main Street, Gloucester; 978-283-7888; www.franklincafe.com. DELUXE TO ULTRA-DELUXE.

The Greenery, located near the entrance to Bearskin Neck, has sandwiches, bakery goods and desserts to go. The back dining room facing the harbor serves all these dishes plus entrées such as pesto pizza, lobster, crab quiche and grilled swordfish. The restaurant is appointed with blond wood, brass light fixtures and touches of green throughout. ~ 15 Dock Square, Rockport; 978-546-9593. MODERATE TO ULTRA-DELUXE.

Portside Chowder House & Grill is a good place for a cup of chowder on a cold, blustery day. Cozy and tiny, the dark wood restaurant has low-beamed ceilings, harbor views and a fireplace. Specialties include New England and corn chowders, crab and chicken. Lunch is served year round; call for dinner hours. ~ 7 Tuna Wharf, Rockport; 978-546-7045, fax 978-546-3104. BUDGET TO MODERATE.

Follow Bearskin Neck as far as it goes (resisting the urge to stop for a lobster roll or bowl of chowder along the way) and you reach **My Place By-the-Sea.** Here the view of the ocean competes with the food for your attention. If the weather's nice, grab a table outside: this is Cape Ann's prettiest dining spot. For both lunch and dinner you'll find lots of seafood specialties, including lobster prepared several different ways. The lunch menu also includes an array of salads and sandwiches. Closed winter and early spring. ~ 68 South Road, Bearskin Neck, Rockport; 978-546-9667, fax 978-546-2033; www.myplacebythesea.com. MODERATE TO ULTRA-DELUXE.

Downhome and lively, **Woodman's** hasn't changed anything except the prices since it opened in 1914. This roadside institution claims to have created the fried clam. The menu includes steamers, lobster, clam cakes, scallops and corn on the cob. Sit inside at old wooden booths or outside at picnic tables in back. There's a raw bar upstairs and a full liquor bar downstairs. Locals like to come here after a day at nearby Crane's Beach. ~ 121 Main Street, Route 133, Essex; 978-768-6057, 800-649-1773; www.woodmans.com, e-mail yankeetradition@woodmans.com. BUDGET TO DELUXE.

Tom Shea's is a quality seafood restaurant with large picture windows overlooking Essex River—a perfect spot for watching the sunset. The wooden interior gives the restaurant an understated, nautical look. The fare includes baked stuffed lobster, fried clams, seafood risotto, pasta, and some beef and chicken dishes. ~ 122 Main Street, Route 133, Essex; 978-768-6931, fax 978-768-7907; www.tomsheas.com, e-mail tomsheas@cove.com. DELUXE.

The **Clam Box of Ipswich** has been frying up seafood (clams, oysters, calamari, haddock) since 1953, and the crowds have been coming back for just as long. They also serve burgers, hot dogs, lobster rolls and chicken sandwiches. Closed mid-December to mid-February. ~ 246 High Street, Ipswich; 978-356-9707; e-mail dale61@comcast.net. BUDGET TO MODERATE.

The **Purple Onion** is a funky little joint that serves a variety of fresh, made-to-order food. Popular starters, soups may include black bean or sweet-and-sour tomato. Fare includes salad bowls and an assortment of specialty and Mexican wraps. No dinner on Saturday; closed Sunday. ~ 44 Inn Street, Newburyport; 978-465-9600, fax 978-462-0562; www.thepurpleonion.com, e-mail info@thepurpleonion.com. BUDGET.

Grog is a large, dark, woody college bar–type place in a non-college town. The burgers and caesar salads are particularly good, and the cheerful staff may entice you into hanging out for longer than you'd planned. There's live music Thursday through Sunday. Occasional cover. ~ 13 Middle Street, Newburyport; 978-465-8008; www.thegrog.com, e-mail enjoy@thegrog.com. MODERATE TO DELUXE.

Housed in what is rumored to have once been an old stagecoach stop, **Joseph's Winter Street Café** is popular with locals looking for a special night out. A lovely dining room, white linen tablecloths, soft lighting, a new cocktail lounge with couches by the fire and a jazz pianist set the mood. The constantly evolving menu might include rack of lamb, seafood couscous, Portuguese seafood stew, or artichoke-crusted halibut. No lunch on Saturday. ~ 24 Winter Street, Newburyport; 978-462-1188, 800-698-3463; www.josephswinterstcafe.com. MODERATE TO ULTRA-DELUXE.

SHOPPING

Located in a former tavern, **Antique Wear** offers beautiful earrings, stick pins, broaches, pendants and tie pins made out of antique buttons, some dating back to the 18th century. ~ 82–84 Front Street, Marblehead; 781-639-0070.

HIDDEN ►

One of Salem's biggest attractions is a witch shop once owned by Jody Cabot, the city's most illustrious witch. **Crow Haven Corner** is filled with gargoyles, unicorns, crystal balls, magic wands and the full assortment of herbs, powders and seeds necessary for attracting good spirits or warding off bad ones. ~ 125 Essex Street, Salem; 978-745-8763.

When the Revolutionary War broke out in 1775, America didn't have a navy, so Salem sea captains armed their merchant vessels and fought the British.

In Salem, the **Peabody Essex Museum Gift Shop** offers a wonderful assortment of reproductions from around the world, as well as posters and regional history books. You'll also find children's books, Indian jewelry and ceramic plates from China. ~ 137 Essex Street, Salem; 978-745-1876; www.pemshop.com.

Across from the House of Seven Gables is **Ye Olde Pepper Candy Companie**. Established in 1806, it claims to be the oldest candy company in America. Specialties include gibralters, black jacks and other old-fashioned candies made on site. ~ 122 Derby Street, Salem; 978-745-2744; www.yeoldepeppercandy.com.

HIDDEN ►

Nearby is the **Pickering Wharf Antique Gallery**, which at first glance looks like your garden-variety antique shop. Upon closer examination you'll find an astounding arena for dozens of antique dealers. ~ 69 Wharf Street, Salem; 978-741-3113.

Hanna Wingate sells French country furniture and accessories. Open weekends January through March. ~ 11 Main Street, Rockport; 978-546-1008; www.hwfrenchcountryfurniture.com.

Rockport has almost as many galleries as bed and breakfasts. The majority sell seascapes—some good, many bad. For an excellent selection of Cape Ann art, visit the **Rockport Art Association**. All the work on view is for sale. Closed January; closed Monday from October through May. ~ 12 Main Street, Rockport; 978-546-6604; www.rockportartassn.org.

HIDDEN ►

Walker Creek, a real find, offers reasonably priced, finely crafted wood tables, hutches, four-poster beds, one-of-a-kind pieces and custom work loosely based on Shaker or Colonial designs. Closed Monday. ~ 57 Eastern Avenue, Route 133, Essex; 978-768-7622; www.walkercreekfurniture.com.

Essex's 25 antique dealers run the price-range gamut. Always ask an antique dealer if you can do better on a price—you're expected to bargain. Don't hope for major savings, however. The **White Elephant** is bargain-basement heaven. ~ 32 Main Street, Essex; 978-768-6901. At the high end of the spectrum is **A. P. H. Waller & Sons,** which carries quality American and European antiques from the 18th and 19th centuries. ~ 140 Main Street, Essex; 978-768-6269. **The Scrapbook** specializes in historical and decorative prints, and maps from the 16th to 19th centuries. In winter open weekends only. ~ 34 Main Street, Essex; 978-768-7922. **Main Street Antiques** carries accessories, jewelry and textiles from the late-18th to the mid-19th centuries. ~ 44 Main Street, Essex; 978-768-7039. **North Hill Antiques** has 18th- and 19th-century furniture. ~ 155 Main Street, Essex; 978-768-7922.

If you've ever spent a lengthy period of time in the British Isles and you miss such examples of British cuisine as Bovril, Ir'nbru or Smarties, you'll have a ball at **Best of British**, which imports a variety of English, Scottish, Irish and Welsh goods for Anglophiles who just can't do without 'em. ~ 22 State Street, Newburyport; 978-465-6976.

NIGHTLIFE

◄HIDDEN

Most Sunday afternoons, Le Grand David and his Spectacular Magic Company perform a highly skilled magic show at the **Cabot Street Cinema Theatre**, featuring levitations, vanishing acts, comedy skits and energetic song-and-dance routines, complete with lavish costumes and sets. (The magic show is closed August to mid-September.) The rest of the week the theater shows first-rate foreign and domestic films. ~ 286 Cabot Street, Beverly; 978-927-3677; www.legranddavid.com.

Symphony by the Sea concerts take place at Abbot Hall in Marblehead, October through May, and in the Peabody Museum's spectacular East Indian Marine Hall in January. Formal winter concerts are concluded by a reception with the musicians. ~ P.O. Box 1425, Marblehead, MA 01945; 978-745-4955; www.symphonybythesea.org.

The **Gloucester Stage Company**, formerly under the artistic direction of playwright Israel Horovitz, stages first-rate plays in an old Gorton's fish warehouse from June through October. Check out a new director for the 2007 season. ~ 267 East Main Street, Gloucester; 978-281-4433, fax 978-281-0550; www.gloucesterstage.org, e-mail info@gloucesterstage.com.

The **Rockport Chamber Music Festival** performs in the Hibbard Gallery of the Rockport Art Association for four weeks in June and also offers evening concerts in July. Music ranges from baroque to contemporary. ~ 12 Main Street, Rockport; 978-546-7391; www.rcmf.org, e-mail info@rcmf.org.

Every Thursday, from July to August, **Castle Hill Picnic** presents a wide range of summer picnic concerts on the manicured grounds of the Crane Estate. ~ 290 Argilla Road, Ipswich; 978-356-4351, fax 978-356-2143; www.craneestate.org, e-mail castle hill@ttor.org.

The Grog is an attractive restaurant and cabaret with live entertainment ranging from reggae, rock and rhythm-and-blues to oldies and dance bands. Occasional cover. ~ 13 Middle Street, Newburyport; 978-465-8008; www.thegrog.com.

BEACHES & PARKS

DEVEREUX BEACH On the causeway leading to scenic Marblehead Neck, Devereux is a small, clean beach. There's a lot to see here. The affluent town lies immediately behind the beach on a hill, while across the street lies a windsurfing cove and busy Marblehead harbor. Devereux is popular with families and teens, yet, unlike most North Shore beaches, it isn't always packed on summer weekends. Swimming and fishing are good here. You'll find picnic areas, restrooms, a playground, a bike rack and a lifeguard from mid-June to Labor Day. Parking fee, $5. ~ Located on Ocean Avenue, to the south of Marblehead harbor; 781-631-3551, fax 781-639-3420.

HIDDEN ►

SALEM WILLOWS Don't be thrown off by the tawdry-looking Chinese take-out joints and arcade you see when you enter the parking lot. Salem Willows holds some pleasant surprises, including a nostalgic old amusement park overlooking Salem Sound that is shaded with graceful willow trees planted in 1801 to provide a protected area for smallpox victims. Next to the park is a small beach. People come here to stroll in the park, admire the view and fish from the shore or a short pier. The waters are a little rough, and may not be ideal for swimming. Locals swear by the popcorn and chop suey sandwiches sold in the parking lot. Facilities include picnic areas, restrooms and a snack bar from mid-April to mid-October. ~ Located at the end of Derby Street, Salem; 978-744-0180, fax 978-740-9299.

SINGING BEACH This jewel of a beach, only a quarter mile long, has pristine sand that literally squeaks underfoot. Hidden away in a lovely affluent neighborhood, the beach is surrounded by steep cliffs and spectacular mansions. The crowd matches the conservative neighborhood—blond and preppy. The parking lot is for residents only, and parking in the immediate area is impossible. But that doesn't keep out-of-towners away. Bostonians like this beach so much, they take the commuter train to Manchester, then walk one long, sweaty quarter mile to the shore. There are restrooms, a lifeguard and a snack bar Memorial Day through Labor Day. Day-use fee, $2 on Friday and weekends. ~ At the end of Beach Street, Manchester-by-the-Sea; 978-526-2019, fax 978-526-2001.

GOOD HARBOR BEACH Located in a spectacular natural setting outside of Gloucester proper, this sweeping, half-mile beach is all ocean, sand dunes, marsh grass and big sky. A small shrub-covered island, positioned between two rocky headlands and accessible at low tide, is fun to explore. The beach is raked clean every day in the summer. There are restrooms, showers and a snack bar. All garbage should be packed out. No lifeguards are on duty from early September to Memorial Day. Parking fee, $20 to $25. ~ On Thatcher Road, East Gloucester; 978-281-9785, fax 978-281-3896.

WINGAERSHEEK BEACH This gentle, sloping, fine sand beach on Ipswich Bay is surrounded by rocks, tall marsh grass and homey summer cottages hidden in the woods. There are also tidepools to explore. The beach is quite close to downtown Gloucester and Rockport, but it feels as though it's far out in the country. There are restrooms, showers, lifeguards and a snack bar. This is also a pack-out-your-trash beach. No lifeguards are on watch from early September to Memorial Day. Parking fee, $20 to $25. ~ On Atlantic Street, West Gloucester; 978-281-9785, fax 978-281-3896.

◄ HIDDEN

Families with young children frequent Wingaersheek Beach because it has good climbing rocks that aren't too slippery.

ROCKPORT BEACHES Rockport has two small beaches right in the heart of town. **Front Beach**, a favorite with small children, has a parallel sidewalk that gives everyone in town a perfect view of the beach. **Back Beach** is on the other side of a small bluff and is much more private. Restrooms can be found at both beaches. ~ Both beaches are on Beach Street, Rockport; 978-546-3525, fax 978-546-3562.

HALIBUT POINT STATE PARK This wild and rugged 62-acre oceanfront park, formerly the site of a granite quarry, has one of the most spectacular views on the North Shore. A walking path goes past the old quarry down a gentle incline to a vast, treeless plain of scrub thicket and wildflowers overlooking the ocean. The stark, rugged shoreline has tidepools and smooth granite rocks large enough for a group of people to picnic on. Swimming is permitted, but not recommended since the shore is covered with big, slippery rocks. There is also a World War II observatory tower. Amenities include restrooms, walking trails and guided tours. Occasional parking fee, $2. ~ Three miles north of Rockport off Route 127; 978-546-2997, fax 978-546-9107; e-mail halibut.point@state.ma.us.

◄ HIDDEN

THE COX RESERVATION Formerly the home of famed muralist Allyn Cox, this 27-acre salt marsh farmland is now headquarters for the Essex County Greenbelt Association. Peaceful and pastoral, it has paths leading through gardens of perennials and roses, salt marsh, woods, orchards and open farmland down to winding Essex River. Artists come here in the late afternoon when the river and graceful marsh grass are bathed in a soft

◄ HIDDEN

golden light, creating a dreamlike environment. It's easy to see why a muralist lived in this romantic and private place. ~ Off Route 133, Essex; 978-768-7241, fax 978-768-3286; www.ecga.org, e-mail ecga@ecga.org.

CRANE BEACH MEMORIAL RESERVATION This massive, four-mile, dune-backed beach is surrounded by over 1000 acres of salt marsh, shrub thicket and woods. In the off-season, the wide beach seems to go on forever. Nature and beachgoers coexist peacefully, however. At certain times of the year, sections of the beach are fenced off to protect nesting birds. A boardwalk leading to the beach protects sand dunes and marsh grass. There are restrooms, showers, lifeguards, picnic areas and a seasonal snack bar. Parking fee, $15 to $22, in summer. ~ Located on Argilla Road, Ipswich; 978-356-4351, fax 978-356-2143; www.craneestate.org.

PARKER RIVER NATIONAL WILDLIFE REFUGE This magnificent oceanfront wildlife refuge on Plum Island is only about ten minutes from downtown Newburyport, but it feels very far away from civilization. One third of Plum Island is covered with ramshackle summer beach houses; the rest is the refuge—salt and freshwater marshes, cranberry bogs, maritime forest, sand dunes and beach. It's a good beach for surf fishing, although a strong undertow discourages swimming. Several boardwalks lead to the beach, and a few trails meander throughout the refuge. The abundant wildlife includes seals, waterfowl, deer, coyote and over 300 species of birds including the piping plover. From April through August, most of the beach is closed to accommodate nesting piper plovers. Parker River is dearly loved by Newburyport residents. The only facilities are restrooms. Slated to open in summer 2007 is a visitor facility with an exhibit hall, an auditorium and environmental education classrooms. Entrance fee, $5. ~ On Plum Island, Newburyport; 978-465-5753, fax 978-465-2807; parkerriver.fws.gov, e-mail fw5rw_prnwr@fws.gov.

The South Shore

The South Shore is a mix of cranberries and Pilgrim history, small scenic villages, pastoral farmland, clean beaches and one main town, Plymouth, about 50 minutes south of Boston. Each town has a different personality and history. Plymouth, of course, is where the Pilgrims landed. New Bedford, an active fishing port, was once the whaling capital of the world. Fall River, a factory-outlet mecca, was a leading textile manufacturer at the turn of the 20th century.

Sights, accommodations and restaurants are limited in Fall River and New Bedford. People usually visit these towns on their way to and from Cape Cod or Boston. Plymouth draws over one million tourists annually. It has enough historic sights to occupy an entire weekend, although most people can't take more than a day of Pilgrim lore.

SIGHTS

To reach Plymouth from Boston, drive south on Route 3 or take scenic Route 3A. It winds along the coastline past beautiful, affluent commuter villages with lovely coves and harbors, historic lighthouses, stately mansions and winding streets.

Right before Plymouth is wealthy **Duxbury**, an aristocratic residential area of elegant homes. Stop by the **King Caesar House**, one of the state's most beautiful historic homes, located off Route 3A on a winding coastal road. A fresh yellow and white Federal-era mansion with green shutters, a sweeping lawn and climbing roses, the house stands across from a massive stone wharf where ships were once rigged. The house has finely crafted wood cornices, moldings, fanlights and balustrades, plus original handpainted French wallpaper and fine antiques. Open Wednesday through Sunday from June through August, and weekends only in September. Admission. ~ King Caesar Road, Duxbury; 781-934-2378, 781-934-6106, fax 781-934-5730; www.duxburyhistory.org, e-mail pbrowne@duxburyhistory.org.

◄ HIDDEN

At Plimoth Plantation, there's not one contemporary detail in sight—just the village, the ocean and settlers going about the daily tasks of the time, tending the vegetable garden or building a house with 17th-century tools.

From Duxbury head south for **Plymouth**. "America's Home Town" can't seem to make up its mind whether to be a tourist trap or a scenic, historic village. The town is a jarring mix of historic homes, cobblestone streets, '50s-style motels, souvenir shops, a tacky waterfront and tour buses everywhere you look. It's not particularly scenic in parts, yet the town is rich with history.

Plymouth is small, and without trying you bump into everything there is to see. The **Plymouth Area Chamber of Commerce** has walking-tour maps. ~ Water Street, Plymouth; 508-830-1620, fax 508-830-1621; www.plymouthchamber.com, e-mail info@plymouthchamber.com. So does **Destination Plymouth**. ~ 800-872-1620, fax 508-757-7535; www.visit-plymouth.com.

The first thing everyone heads for is **Plymouth Rock** on Water Street on the harbor. Believed to be the landing place of the Pilgrims, it is housed inside a Greek canopy with stately columns. Don't expect to see a big impressive rock; it's only large enough to hold two very small Pilgrims.

Right next to the rock is the **Mayflower II**, a brightly painted reproduction of the real *Mayflower* that looks like the pirate ship at Disneyland. The self-guided tour is worthwhile, even though there's occasionally a line to get in. The *Mayflower* is shockingly small. It's hard to imagine how 102 people ever survived 66 days at sea in such cramped quarters. Closed December through March.

Admission. ~ State Pier, Plymouth; 508-830-6021, fax 508-746-7037; www.plimoth.org.

For more Pilgrim lore, head for **Pilgrim Hall Museum**, on the main drag. Continuously operating since 1824, the museum houses the nation's largest collection of Pilgrim possessions, including richly styled Jacobean furniture and the relic of a ship that brought colonists to America. Its hull is made out of naturally curved tree trunks and branches, a crude but effective design. Closed in January. Admission. ~ 75 Court Street, Plymouth; 508-746-1620, fax 508-747-4228; www.pilgrimhall.org.

Three miles south of Plymouth is **Plimoth Plantation**, a "living history museum" where men and women in period costumes portray the residents of a 1627 Pilgrim village, as well as a Native Wampanoag homesite. This sounds contrived, but it's authentic and well-done. The re-created village, situated on a dusty, straw-strewn road overlooking the ocean, is composed of many wooden dwellings with deeply thatched roofs. The villagers speak in period dialect, and you can ask them questions about anything—including the politics of the 17th century. The Wampanoag Indian site is staffed by modern native people and re-creates a typical native encampment with woven and bark dome-shaped dwellings. Interpreters demonstrate native cooking and handicrafts. There is also a crafts center where reproductions are made by artisans and are for sale in the gift shop. Closed December through March. Admission. ~ Route 3A, 137 Warren Avenue, Plymouth; 508-746-1622, fax 508-746-4978; www.plimoth.org, e-mail info@plimoth.org.

HIDDEN ►

From Plymouth go west on Route 44, then south on Route 58 to rural **Carver**, cranberry capital of the world. In the fall the harvesting process, a breathtaking sight, can be witnessed from the road. (See "Exploring Cranberry Country" in this chapter.)

About a half-hour's drive southeast of Carver lies the former whaling town of New Bedford, which gained immortality in Herman Melville's *Moby Dick*. It still looks and feels a lot like a 19th-century whaling city, with a bustling waterfront and large Portuguese population.

Until the early 1980s the waterfront area was in disarray. Then, to attract tourists, the town restored more than 100 buildings. Fortunately New Bedford didn't go overboard with cute, contrived tourist attractions. Today it has a number of fine museums, restaurants, antique shops and galleries alongside the harbor. There's something genuine and tasteful about this miniature city.

The **New Bedford National Park Visitor Center** offers brochures, maps and tours. ~ 33 William Street, New Bedford; 508-996-4095, fax 580-984-1250; www.nps.gov.

The **Rotch-Jones-Duff House and Garden Museum** is a 19th-century Greek Revival with a picturesque rose garden that be-

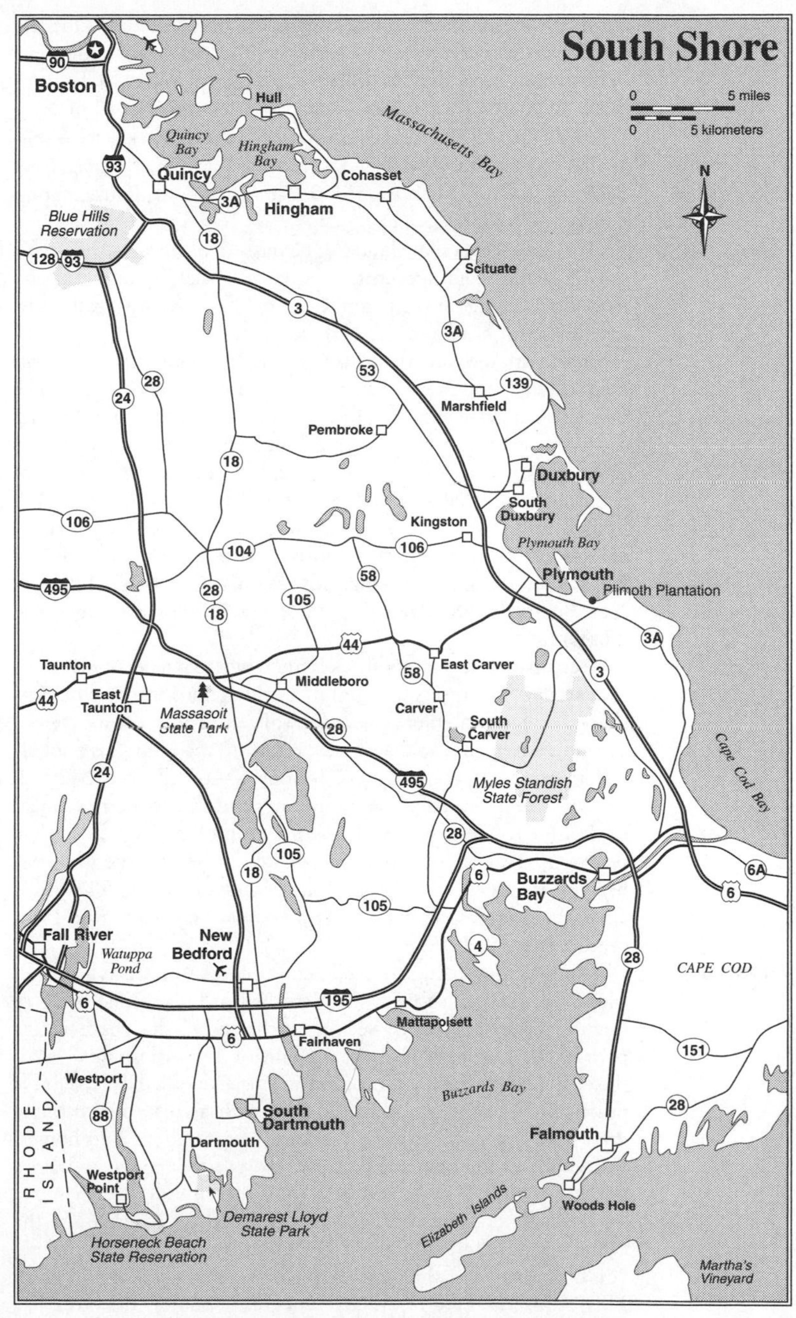
South Shore
0 5 miles
0 5 kilometers
N
Boston
Hull
Massachusetts Bay
Quincy Bay
Hingham Bay
Quincy
Cohasset
Hingham
Blue Hills Reservation
Scituate
Marshfield
Pembroke
Duxbury
South Duxbury
Kingston
Plymouth Bay
Plymouth
Plimoth Plantation
Taunton
East Taunton
Massasoit State Park
Middleboro
East Carver
Carver
South Carver
Myles Standish State Forest
Cape Cod Bay
Buzzards Bay
CAPE COD
Fall River
Watuppa Pond
New Bedford
Mattapoisett
Fairhaven
Westport
RHODE ISLAND
South Dartmouth
Dartmouth
Buzzards Bay
Falmouth
Westport Point
Woods Hole
Elizabeth Islands
Demarest Lloyd State Park
Horseneck Beach State Reservation
Martha's Vineyard

comes a Christmas showplace during the holidays and is the site of summer concerts, lecture series and educational programs. Named for three families who owned the property, it features many of their fine antiques and chronicles the history of New Bedford. This 28-room mansion is one of the region's best. A self-guided audio tour is available. Admission. ~ 396 County Street, New Bedford; 508-997-1401, fax 508-997-6846; www.rjdmuseum.org, e-mail info@rjdmuseum.org.

For three sights that shouldn't be missed, begin with the Whaling Museum. Continue on to Seaman's Bethel, a church across from the whaling museum, and County Street, where wealthy sea captains built homes in the 19th century.

Start with the **New Bedford Whaling Museum**, then enter Seamen's Bethel, and New Bedford won't look the same again. The museum depicts whaling's profound impact on this town, telling the story beautifully with large, dramatic paintings of life aboard whaling ships and an enormous mural created in 1848. You can climb aboard a half-scale model of a fully rigged whaling ship housed in a large room with harpoons and figureheads. There's also a 66-foot complete skeleton of a blue whale. The museum is spacious, airy and absorbing. Admission. ~ 18 Johnny Cake Hill, New Bedford; 508-997-0046, fax 508-997-0018; www.whaling museum.org.

Across the street is **Seamen's Bethel**, where whalers prayed before setting out to sea. The pulpit of this plain, sturdy church is shaped like a ship's bluff bows. Its walls are covered with memorial tablets to men who died at sea. A visit to this church is a sobering experience. ~ Located at 15 Johnny Cake Hill, New Bedford.

HIDDEN ►

"Nowhere in America will you find more patrician-like houses," wrote Herman Melville of **County Street**, located a few blocks up a slight hill from the whaling museum. The impeccably restored Federal-style mansions and elaborate Victorians along this picturesque street illustrate how grand life was in 19th-century New Bedford.

HIDDEN ►

For a unique change of pace, consider visiting **Cuttyhunk**, an island 14 miles offshore from New Bedford accessible by ferry (see the "Transportation" section at the end of this chapter). It's part of the Elizabeth Islands, a chain of 16 tiny islands, 14 of them owned by the Boston Brahmin Forbes family. The island is practically all sand and scrub bushes with a rocky beach but it does have a general store, 2 restaurants and about 100 homes. Cuttyhunk is the opposite of busy, crowded Cape Cod—there's nothing to do but walk and fish—and therein lies its charm.

Immediately southwest of New Bedford off Route 6 are the affluent rural communities of **Dartmouth** and **Westport**, where you'll find some of the most exquisite coastal farmland in all of Massachusetts. Like Kentucky bluegrass country, this area has miles of ancient stone walls, lovely old houses, shingled dairy barns, rolling pastures and elegant horse farms.

Off Slocums Road in South Dartmouth sits **Padanaram**, a fashionable yachting resort on Apponagansett Bay. It's home to the famous boatyard Concordia, where beautiful old wooden yachts are restored. The village is only two blocks long, but it has a number of fine restaurants and shops.

Not far from Padanaram, where the Slocum River meets Buzzards Bay, is the **Lloyd Center for Environmental Studies**, a nonprofit organization that studies coastal and estuarine environments. Open to the public are an aquarium with an Interactive Touch Tank, five miles of walking trails through woods and salt marshes, and changing exhibits featuring such work as naturalist photography. The best thing here is the dazzling view from the observation deck, which on a clear day offers views of Cuttyhunk and other Elizabeth islands. The center offers weekly walks, canoe and kayaking trips and educational programs. Closed Monday; closed Sunday and Monday from November to April. ~ 430 Potomska Road, South Dartmouth; 508-990-0505, fax 508-993-7868; www.thelloydcenter.org, e-mail admin@thelloydcenter.org.

◄ HIDDEN

Wealthy mill owners built their mansions on Columbia Street in the 1830s, but by the late 1850s, immigrants began to settle here to be closer to the mills and the owners moved up the hill to Fall River.

Heading back to New Bedford, you can take Route 195 west to Fall River 15 minutes away. Factory outlets (see the "Shopping" section below) and Battleship Cove are this town's claims to fame.

At the turn of the 20th century **Fall River** had more than 100 textile mills, but in 1927 the industry sagged and the town went through hard times. Today its large granite mills are occupied by electronics and metals firms and factory outlets, but the effects of the depression still linger.

Fall River's downtown has been spruced up, but so many "for lease" signs are tacked to its grand 19th-century buildings that the town looks a little lost.

Columbia Street, the Portuguese section of downtown, is a colorful place to stroll, sample treats from the many good bakeries and discover the beautiful mosaic sidewalks. Television chef Emeril Lagasse grew up here, and can occasionally be spotted in the midst of this vibrant ethnic community. For travel information, call the **Bristol County Convention and Visitors Bureau.** ~ 70 North 2nd Street, New Bedford; 508-997-1250, 800-288-6263, fax 508-997-9090; www.bristol-county.org, e-mail info@bristol-county.org.

◄ HIDDEN

There's also an information center at **Battleship Cove**, a harbor and park area right in town off Route 195 at Exit 5. Docked in the water at Battleship Cove are a World War II battleship, de-

Text continued on page 378.

Exploring Cranberry Country

Hidden away in Carver, a scenic rural area ten minutes east of Plymouth, is one of Massachusetts' most spectacular and least-known autumn attractions—**cranberry harvesting**. If you think fall foliage is a beautiful sight, wait until you see this dazzling display of color.

Cranberries are the state's number-one agricultural product, valued at about $100 million annually. Around 500 growers, with several hundred employees, work more than 14,400 acres of cranberry bogs. Little Carver alone produces one third the nation's crop, while Cape Cod and Nantucket also have cranberry farms.

One of the few fruits native to North America, cranberries were known to Indians as sassamenesh. They ate the tart red berries raw and mixed them with venison and fat to make small cakes called pemmicans. The cranberry's slender, cone-shaped flower reminded early European settlers of the beak of a crane—hence the present name. Nineteenth-century sea captains sailing from New England ports supplied cranberries to their crews because it was the most readily available source of vitamin C to prevent scurvy.

The popularity of cranberries was limited to a harvest time until 1930, when a Massachusetts lawyer-turned-cranberry-grower joined with two other growers to form a marketing cooperative promoting demand for cranberry juice cocktails. The cooperative, which became Ocean Spray Cranberries, now has 904 members—more than 90 percent of all independent cranberry growers—and continues to explore ways to boost demand by touting the berries' health benefits and trying to popularize them in other countries. The co-op held a near-monopoly until the 1990s, when the Wisconsin-based Northland Corporation went public, raising investor capital to buy up bogs around Cape Cod, and quickly became the world's largest cranberry producer. Today, a "cranberry war" rages between the two companies, while cranberry surpluses have reached unprecedented levels.

Harvest time starts September 15 and continues until the first week of November. During this time, restaurants and bakeries in southern

Massachusetts use the berry in a number of creative dishes, ranging from cranberry horseradish and salsa to cranberry soup, bread, muffins, sorbet and tarts. Other innovative recipes involve mixing cranberries with applesauce, wild rice and cole slaw. To experience the full range of creative cranberry cookery, head for the **Massachusetts Cranberry Festival**, held in South Carver on Columbus Day weekend.

To explore the cranberry bogs, from Plymouth take Route 44 east to Route 58 south. Bogs line both routes, and the harvest process is easy to see from the road. Many farmers don't mind if you observe from the elevated dirt paths bordering the bogs, as long as you stay well out of their way.

The short, dark green vines are grown in shallow bogs surrounded by deep woods. When the cranberries are ripe, they are picked by either dry or wet harvesting. Dry-picked berries are often sold fresh, while wet-picked fruit usually becomes juice or canned cranberry sauce.

Dry-harvested berries are combed off the vine with a machine. But it's wet harvesting that's the real treat to watch. First the bogs are flooded with about 18 inches of water. Then farmers in bright yellow slickers beat the fruit off the vine with large water reels that look like giant eggbeaters stirring up a waterfall of crimson berries. The buoyant berries float to the water's surface, creating a scarlet sea surrounded by a fiery ring of woods ablaze with fall colors.

The wind blows the floating berries to one end of the pond, where they are corralled with wooden brooms. Giant vacuum cleaners then suck the berries into dechaffing machines. Helicopters and trucks transport the berries to packing houses, where they are graded according to size, color and quality.

Plymouth Colony Winery, off Route 44, is in a former berry-screening house in the middle of a ten-acre cranberry bog. It offers free tastings. Closed January; open weekends only February through March. ~ 56 Pinewood Road, Plymouth; 508-747-3334, fax 508-747-4463.

stroyer, attack submarine and PT boat that you can tour. Not surprisingly, these vessels, which are in excellent condition, are filled with children playing war. Hundreds of scout troops make pilgrimages to this John Wayne playground. Admission for boat tours. ~ 5 Water Street, Fall River; 508-678-1100, 800-678-1100, fax 508-674-5597; www.battleshipcove.org, e-mail battleship@battleshipcove.org.

Next to the boats is the **Fall River Heritage State Park Visitors Center**. It has an attractive 8.5 acre waterfront park and hosts numerous concerts, festivals and outdoor movies in the summer. Open very limited hours. Call ahead. ~ 200 Davol Street, Fall River; 508-675-5759, fax 508-676-5773.

LODGING

The Plymouth area has an abundance of very ordinary motels that attract families and tour groups, but there is also a sprinkling of hidden bed and breakfasts that is quite special.

HIDDEN ►

For a romantic getaway try the **Winsor House Inn**, 15 minutes north of Plymouth. This graceful 1812 inn stands on a street lined with houses listed on the National Register of Historic Places, and it's next to a classic white-steepled church. Down the street are a few elegant little shops, a French bakery and a small wharf. Winsor House has two tastefully decorated guest rooms and two beautiful suites. All guest rooms are furnished with Shaker- and Colonial-style antiques. A cozy restaurant on the ground floor looks like an ancient seafaring tavern. A full breakfast is included. ~ 390 Washington Street, Duxbury; 781-934-0991, fax 781-934-5955; www.winsorhouseinn.com, e-mail info@winsorhouseinn.com. DELUXE TO ULTRA-DELUXE.

Route 3A in Plymouth is lined with indistinguishable motels, but the **Best Western Cold Spring** is one of the most attractive. This motel is in pristine condition and beautifully landscaped. In the summer, thick yellow marigolds border brick paths leading to the 60 units. These are spacious and tastefully appointed. There's a heated pool, and a continental breakfast is included. Closed December through March. ~ 188 Court Street, Plymouth; 508-746-2222, 800-678-8667, fax 508-746-2744; www.bwcoldspring.com, e-mail coldspring@yahoo.com. MODERATE TO DELUXE.

The **John Carver Inn**, a large, imposing, Colonial-style hotel, gets very crowded in the summer. But it's in the most scenic part of Plymouth, across the street from a row of 17th-century historic homes and a beautiful grist mill. Seventy-nine rooms and six suites are pleasantly decorated in soft shades and Colonial-style reproduction antiques. A full-service hotel, it has a restaurant, a lounge, a gift shop and an indoor pool with a waterslide and whirlpool. ~ 25 Summer Street, Plymouth; 508-746-7100, 800-274-1620, fax 508-746-8299; www.johncarverinn.com, e-mail info@johncarverinn.com. DELUXE.

In the heart of cranberry country, **On Cranberry Pond** is a great place to stay if you want to get away from the crowds in Plymouth (which is just 25 minutes away). The house is surrounded by ponds, horse pastures and cranberry bogs. The six high-ceilinged bedrooms are furnished with country decor. One of the rooms includes a master suite with a kitchenette and a whirlpool bath. The enormous back porch is a great place to while away a morning or an afternoon. A gourmet breakfast is included in the rates. ~ 43 Fuller Street, Middleboro; 508-946-0768, fax 508-947-8221; www.oncranberrypond.com, e-mail oncranberrypond@aol.com. MODERATE.

HIDDEN

Off-the-beaten-path **Kinsale Inn** is in a scenic little seaside village of doll-sized clapboard houses with white picket fences and window boxes. Its village, which is only four blocks long, consists of a small dock, a bookstore/café, a picnic area, a museum and the inn. This yellow-clapboard inn with green shutters, right across the street from the harbor, has a restaurant and pub on the ground floor. Its three spacious guest rooms on the second floor have queen beds and are neat, clean, bright and comfortable; they share a balcony overlooking the ocean. ~ 13 Water Street, Mattapoisett; 508-758-4922, fax 508-758-4924; www.kinsaleinn.com, e-mail info@kinsaleinn.com. MODERATE.

It takes more than 4000 cranberries to produce a gallon of juice—good thing that nearly 640 million pounds are harvested in the U.S. annually.

A 1760 brown-shingle bed and breakfast, **The Edgewater** is so close to the water you'd swear you were on a boat when you look out the window. The inn seems miles away from civilization, yet it's only a five-minute drive from New Bedford's Whaling National Historic Park. A perfect spot for romance, the handsome house has soft taupe walls and crisp white arched moldings. The blue-and-white Captain's Suite, the best room in the house, has a sitting room, fireplace and spectacular views. The other five guest rooms are attractive and comfortable. All are appointed with contemporary and antique furnishings. Most of the rooms have a water view, and one has a kitchenette. ~ 2 Oxford Street, Fairhaven; 508-997-5512; www.rixsan.com/edgewater, e-mail kprof@aol.com. MODERATE TO DELUXE.

DINING

You may have to wait to get a table at the crowded **Run of the Mill Tavern**, but it's worth the wait for golden battered onion rings and their famous burgers. ~ 6 Spring Lane, Plymouth; 508-830-1262. MODERATE.

For traditional New England–style fare, swing by **Isaac's**. They bake, they fry—they even prepare some Italian dishes such as chicken Milan. You'll also find steak, lamb and seafood on the menu. ~ 114 Water Street, Plymouth Harbor; 508-830-0001, fax 508-830-0758. MODERATE.

Though a magnet for tourists, **The Lobster Hut** should not be avoided. Here you can feast on clam chowder, fried clams and lobster at outdoor picnic tables overlooking the harbor, or you can eat inside, though the atmosphere may be a bit too fast-food for your liking. Closed in January. ~ On the Town Wharf, Plymouth Harbor; 508-746-2270, fax 508-746-5655. DELUXE.

The Hearth 'n Kettle Restaurant at the John Carver Inn serves three meals a day in a casual, colonial-style space with wood beamed ceilings, a fireplace and blond wooden furnishings. Breakfast consists of a variety of egg dishes, the lunch menu is stocked with burgers and sandwiches, while dinner offerings consist of rib-sticking entrées such as prime rib, seafood medleys and fresh-baked desserts. ~ 25 Summer Street, Plymouth; 508-746-7100, 800-274-1620, fax 508-746-8299; www.johncarverinn.com, e-mail info@johncarverinn.com. MODERATE.

Candleworks is housed in an 1810 granite candle factory half a block from New Bedford's major sights. An atriumlike room in front is appointed with wooden tables and Windsor chairs. The main dining room has a low-beamed ceiling and rich wood. The menu features Northern Italian cuisine and a wide variety of American food including veal medallions sautéed with lobster and asparagus; breast of chicken stuffed with prosciutto, provolone and roasted peppers and served with a pesto cream sauce; and grilled swordfish with lemon butter. ~ 72 North Water Street, New Bedford; 508-997-1294, fax 508-990-1739; www.thecandleworksrestaurant.com. MODERATE TO ULTRA-DELUXE.

Padanaram Village Café is a funky little 50s-style diner with black-and-white checkered tile, and walls painted in brilliant pastel hues and adorned with Beatles memorabilia. A closer look will reward you with Paul McCartney's guitar pick, and a slew of original photographs and posters. The food is standard diner fare—eggs, breakfast meats, burgers, sandwiches, clubs, fish-and-chips and salads. ~ 7 Bridge Street, South Dartmouth; 508-984-1400. BUDGET.

AUTHOR FAVORITE

There are many Portuguese restaurants in New Bedford, but my favorite is **Café Portugal**. A large, festive restaurant popular with Portuguese families, it features house specialties such as an enormous platter of succulent shrimp and marinated steak served with eggs on top. With its acoustical tile ceiling and plastic flower arrangements, Café Portugal looks a little bit like a banquet hall. ~ 1280 Acushnet Avenue, New Bedford; 508-992-8216. MODERATE TO DELUXE.

It may look like a coffee shop, but **Bayside** serves classic clambar fare as well as such specials as chicken burritos and eggplant parmigiana. More "in" than it seems, the restaurant has a clientele ranging from construction workers, senior citizens and families to yuppies and arty types dressed entirely in black. Bayside overlooks salt marsh, stone walls and the ocean. Call ahead for winter hours. ~ 1253 Horseneck Road, Westport; 508-636-5882, fax 508-636-6496; e-mail earlofcod@aol.com. BUDGET TO MODERATE.

◄ HIDDEN

SHOPPING

This is outlet country. Fall River has over 100 outlets, and New Bedford has quite a few, too. Until the 1980s these were novel, but today there are so many discount shopping places across the country that they don't seem unique. Choices are somewhat limited because the same brands are sold everywhere: Bass, Farberware, American Tourister, Jonathan Logan, Van Heusen and Vanity Fair to name a few.

Driving the expressway in Fall River, you can't help but notice the mammoth, six-story granite textile mills transformed into factory outlets—**Fall River Outlets**. All the outlets are close together, and each building has between 50 and 100 retailers selling clothes, dishes, sheets, towels, jewelry, handbags and more. Prices are rock bottom, and the merchandise is pretty low-end. Natural fiber clothing is difficult to find. ~ To visit them from Route 195, which runs through town, take Route 24 south to the Brayton exit and follow the signs.

Salt Marsh Pottery specializes in handpainted pottery and tiles designed with wildflower motifs. Closed Sunday in winter. ~ 1167 Russells Mills Road, South Dartmouth; 508-636-4813, 800-859-5028; www.saltmarsh.com.

NIGHTLIFE

Occasional free summer concerts at the **Village Landing Gazebo** range from swing bands to Irish balladeers and children's performances. ~ Water Street, Plymouth.

Live bands can be heard free on Friday and Saturday at **The Pub**. ~ In the Radisson behind Village Landing, 180 Water Street, Plymouth; 508-591-5036.

Zeiterion Theatre presents a wide range of year-round musical and dramatic performances—everything from *Singin' in the Rain* to *The Nutcracker*. Located in historic downtown New Bedford, the Zeiterion is a masterfully restored 1923 vaudeville theater with gilded Grecian friezes, elaborate crystal light fixtures and a glamorous atmosphere. The box office is closed Sunday and Monday. ~ 684 Purchase Street, New Bedford; 508-994-2900; www.zeiterion.org, e-mail info@zeiterion.org.

BEACHES & PARKS

DUXBURY BEACH This five-mile stretch of clean white sand is one of the finest barrier beaches on the Massachusetts coast.

The beach juts out into Cape Cod Bay and is bordered by a little harbor on one side and the Atlantic on the other. Stretches are dotted with salt marsh, and parts are accessible only by four-wheel-drive vehicles. Located in an affluent residential neighborhood, it attracts a well-heeled crowd. There are restrooms, showers, a changing room, lifeguards, a snack bar and a restaurant. No dogs allowed. Parking fee, $5 to $8. ~ Off Route 3 on Route 139 West in Duxbury, north of Plymouth; 781-837-3112; www.duxburybeachpark.com.

MYLES STANDISH STATE FOREST Locals joke that once you're in this 16,000-acre park, you'll never find your way out again. The park is enormous, and the roads winding through the forest and meadows seem to go on forever. Because of its size, it feels remote and peaceful even in the summer. You can fish most of its 15 ponds and swim at College Pond. Motorized vehicles are not allowed off-road. Bicycle, bridle and hiking paths wind through the forest. Non-motorized boats are allowed. Among the amenities are picnic areas, restrooms and interpretive programs. Day-use fee, $5. ~ Long Pond Road, off Route 3, Plymouth; 508-866-2526, fax 508-866-5043; www.mass.gov/dcr.

There are 416 tent/RV sites (no hookups) with restrooms, hot showers, fireplaces and picnic tables; $12 per night for state residents, $14 per night for visitors. ~ 877-422-6762.

PLYMOUTH BEACH Located in a half-rural, half-residential area, this straight, three-mile beach dotted with beach grass and clear stretches of sand serves as a nesting ground for migratory shore birds such as terns and plovers. The nesting area is fenced off for protection, but the birds are easily observed. In summer this busy beach attracts families and local kids. Facilities included are restrooms, lifeguards and a snack bar. Parking fee, $10 on weekdays, $15 on weekends. ~ Off Route 3A, three miles south of Plymouth; 508-747-1620, fax 508-830-4062; www.plymouth-ma.gov.

HIDDEN ►

HORSENECK BEACH STATE RESERVATION This vast, breezy beach is one of the state's most spectacular and least known. Bordered by fragile dunes that create a barrier between the huge parking lot and the beach, it has crunchy white sand and fine waves. **Gooseberry Island** is a narrow, mile-long stretch of land jutting out into the ocean and laced with paths. There's an abandoned World War II lookout tower at the end. Right before Gooseberry Island is a small parking lot and a tiny beach popular with windsurfers. There are also restrooms, a playground, basketball and volleyball courts, showers, a concession stand and seasonal lifeguards. Day-use fee, $2. ~ At the end of Route 88, Westport Point; 508-636-8816.

▲ Permitted in 100 RV sites (no hookups); $15 to $17 per night. ~ 877-422-6762.

DEMAREST LLOYD STATE PARK This little-known state park has everything: natural grassy areas for picnics, rambling hills of beach grass, winding rivers, abundant wildlife—deer, hawks, egrets—and a fairly isolated beach. At low tide a long sand bar juts out into the calm, warm waters. Located in the bucolic Dartmouth area, Demarest is a real find. Closed from Labor Day through Memorial Day. Facilities include picnic areas, restrooms, showers and lifeguards. Day-use fee, $7. ~ Barney Joy Road, Dartmouth; 508-636-3298 in summer, 508-636-8816 in winter.

Outdoor Adventures

FISHING

Bluefish, striped bass, tuna, cod and flounder are abundant on the Massachusetts coast. No license is required to fish, and tackle shops are everywhere. For detailed information on what to catch when, where and how, call the **Massachusetts Division of Marine Fisheries.** ~ 251 Causeway Street, Suite 400, Boston, MA 02114; 617-626-1520; www.state.ma.us/dfwele/dmf, e-mail marine.fish@state.ma.us.

NORTH SHORE **Hilton's Fishing Dock** is a fishing, bait and tackle shop. ~ 54-R Merrimac Street, Newburyport; 978-465-9885.

About five miles north of Newburyport in the town of Salisbury is **Clipper Fleet**, which offers all-day excursions and "Ladies' Day" trips (bring your gal, and she fishes for half price). ~ Route 1, Salisbury; 978-465-7495, 800-404-4575; www.clipperfleet.com.

SOUTH SHORE Half- and full-day cod fishing trips are available through **Captain John Boats.** ~ Town Wharf, Plymouth; 508-746-2643, 800-242-2469; www.captjohn.com. **Captain Leroy Inc.** charters cabin boats for fishing and full-day party boat excur-

AUTHOR FAVORITE

The more chances I have to encounter whales up close, the happier I am that we humans are learning to interact with them instead of killing them. In fact, these days whale watching seems to be Gloucester's main industry. **Yankee Fleet** is the oldest and largest whale-watching outfit, with trips to Stellwagon Bank and Jefferey's Ledge (May through October). Charter and fishing party excursions are also available. ~ 75 Essex Avenue; 978-283-0313, 800-942-5464, fax 978-283-6089; www.yankeefleet.com, e-mail office@yankeefleet.com.

sions. ~ Route 6, on the Fairhaven Bridge, New Bedford; 508-992-8907.

SAILING

Marblehead, on the North Shore, is sailboat country. **Coastal Sailing School** has boats for excursion rides. Lessons are available from May through September. ~ P.O. Box 1001, Marblehead, MA 01945; 781-639-0553; www.coastalsailingschool.com.

WHALE WATCHING

The Massachusetts coast offers an enormous number of whale-watching excursions, some conducted by naturalists. The season starts in May and runs through October.

NORTH SHORE Gloucester is the North Shore's gateway to whale watching. **Cape Ann Whale Watch** has a half-day trip to Stellwagen. ~ 415 Main Street, Gloucester; 978-283-5110, 800-877-5110; www.caww.com. The **Newburyport Whale Watch** runs half-day trips twice daily. They also organize dinner cruises. ~ Hilton's Fishing Dock, 54 Merrimac Street, Newburyport; 978-499-0832; www.newburyportwhalewatch.com.

SOUTH SHORE **Captain John Boats** books whale-watching trips to Stellwagen Bank, deep-sea fishing excursions, harbor cruises and ferry service to Provincetown on four 85-foot boats. ~ Town Wharf, Plymouth; 508-746-2643; www.captjohn.com. **Captain Tim Brady & Sons** departs daily (June to August) for Stellwagen Bank. Fishing trips are also offered. ~ 16 Plantation Road, Plymouth; 508-746-4809; www.fishchart.com.

CANOEING & SEA KAYAKING

NORTH SHORE One of the most beautiful canoe trips in New England is along the North Shore's Ipswich River, through the 2500-acre **Ipswich River Wildlife Sanctuary**. Here you can spot deer, beaver and fox, among other animals, on a naturalist-guided half-day trip. ~ 87 Perkins Row, Topsfield; 978-887-9264; www.massaudubon.org. For canoe rentals, contact **Foote Brothers Canoes**. You can enter the Ipswich River on Route 97. Closed November through March. ~ 230 Topsfield Road, Ipswich; 978-356-9771; www.footebrotherscanoes.com.

SOUTH SHORE South of New Bedford, near Dartmouth, are many rivers ideal for canoeing. **The Lloyd Center for Environmental Studies** organizes day-long guided canoe and kayaking

ICE SAILING

A tradition on Watuppa Pond in Fall River is ice sailing. This graceful sport takes tremendous skill and specially designed sailcrafts. Rentals aren't available, but it's a delight to watch these lighter-than-air boats glide along the icy pond.

trips that focus on the natural history of local rivers. ~ 430 Potomska Road, South Dartmouth; 508-990-0505; www.lloydcenter.org. **Canoe Passage Outfitters** rents kayaks and canoes and provides half-day narrated trips. Shuttles are available. ~ 120 Ingell Street, Taunton; 508-824-1146, 800-689-7884; www.canoepassage.com.

GOLF

NORTH SHORE Public golf courses are rare on the North Shore, but there is one beautiful semiprivate, 18-hole course surrounded by deep woods, the **Beverly Golf and Tennis Club**. The signature par-3 15th hole is called the Wedding Cake. ~ 134 McKay Street, Beverly; 978-922-9072. **Harwich Port Golf Club** is a nine-hole public course of par 3s and par 4s that offers pull carts. ~ Forest and South streets, Harwich Port; 508-432-0250.

SOUTH SHORE Golfing opportunities on the South Shore are limited. There aren't any public golf courses close to Plymouth, but about 30 minutes out of town is the par-71 **Pembroke Country Club**, a semiprivate 18-hole course. ~ 94 West Elm Street, Pembroke; 781-826-3983; www.pembrokecc.com. **Bay Pointe Country Club** is nearby and offers a full course with an island hole—completely surrounded by water. ~ 19 Bay Pointe Drive, off Onset Avenue, Onset; 508-759-8802, 800-248-8463; www.baypointecc.net.

TENNIS

NORTH SHORE A few municipal courts are available throughout the North Shore towns. The best spot here is the **Beverly Golf and Tennis Club**. It has 12 clay courts open to the public; a tennis pro is available for lessons. Fee. ~ 134 McKay Street, Beverly; 978-922-9072; www.competitiveedgetennis.com.

SOUTH SHORE Six clay municipal tennis courts can be found in New Bedford's woodsy **Buttonwood Park**. ~ Rockdale and Hawthorne avenues. **Hazelwood Park** is a city park with playgrounds and five lighted courts. ~ Brock Avenue, New Bedford; 508-991-6295.

BIKING

The North Shore and South Shore have limited bicycling areas, but a few choice spots are described below.

NORTH SHORE Cyclists in the area recommend scenic **Route 127** between Beverly, Manchester and Magnolia. The tree-lined road dips and turns past seaside mansions and historic homes. It's cool and peaceful in the summer.

SOUTH SHORE The **Westport** and **Dartmouth** area on the South Shore doesn't have many cars, and the flat country roads wind past elegant horse farms, pastures and ocean. From Route 195, take Exit 12 and head south to Chase or Tucker Road. At this point it doesn't matter which road you take; they're all lovely, and as long as you head south you'll wind up at the beach.

Bike Rentals On the North Shore, you can rent mountain bikes and hybrids at **Seaside Cycle**. Accessories and repairs are also available here. Closed Sunday. ~ 23 Elm Street, Manchester; 978-526-1200; www.seasidecycle.com.

HIKING

The Massachusetts coast offers excellent opportunities to hike through salt marsh, forest, sand dunes and moors bordering freshwater ponds and the ocean. Many of these hikes are short and easy. The rest of the Massachusetts coast has a limited number of marked trails. All distances listed for hiking trails are one way unless otherwise noted.

For more information on hikes throughout the state, contact the **Massachusetts Department of Conservation and Recreation.** ~ 251 Causeway Street, Boston; 617-626-1250.

NORTH SHORE **Art's Trail** (1 mile), in Dogtown Common, a 3000-plus-acre park in Gloucester, winds through red oak forest past a highland of scrub oak, gray birch, blueberries and huckleberries. Several low areas flood in late winter and spring, forming frog-breeding ponds. Of moderate difficulty, the trail is rocky in parts and requires careful walking.

Also in Dogtown Common, **Whale's Jaw Trail** (4.5 miles) is a rugged, rocky, hilly hike starting at Blackburn Industrial Park off Route 128. The trail meanders through former grazing land and past Babson Reservoir, birch groves and cattail marsh. It ends at the top of a hill, where you'll see an enormous split granite boulder that looks like a whale's jaw.

SOUTH SHORE **East Head Reservoir Trail** (3 miles roundtrip) starts behind the Myles Standish State Forest headquarters building in South Carver. The best thing about this hike is that it covers the full spectrum of habitats in the over 14,000-acre park. The relatively flat trail winds past deep forest, marsh, hardwood and soft wood groves and a pristine pond. A pamphlet available at headquarters explains the flora and fauna of each environment. A couple of benches are located along the way.

The **Peter Adams Trail** (3 miles) in Massasoit State Park in East Taunton meanders through white-pine forest and hardwoods and past swamps and brooks. Skirting Lake Rico, it ends at a large, secluded sandy beach. No swimming is allowed. Along the way, you might spot deer, fox, turkey and owls. To get a map, call 508-822-7405.

Transportation

CAR

On the North Shore, **Route 128** is the main artery connecting Salem, Manchester, Magnolia, Gloucester and Rockport. **Route 95** is the major north–south artery to Essex, Ipswich and Newburyport.

Route 3 links Boston to Plymouth and ends at the Sagamore Bridge to Cape Cod. **Route 195** is the main east–west artery connecting Fall River and New Bedford.

AIR

Many people visiting this area come into **Logan International Airport** in Boston (see Chapter Four). Also serving the southern coastal area is the **New Bedford Regional Airport.** Cape Air flies into New Bedford Regional Airport.

FERRY & BOAT

Ferries and boats between Boston, Plymouth, New Bedford, Cape Cod, Martha's Vineyard and Nantucket require reservations during the summer.

The following ferries and boats operate seasonally and do not transport cars:

Captain John Boats goes between Plymouth and Provincetown. ~ State Pier, Plymouth; 508-747-2400, 800-242-2469; www.captjohn.com. The **Steamship Authority** offers year-round service to Martha's Vineyard out of Woods Hole and seasonal service out of New Bedford. ~ 508-477-8600; www.steamshipauthority.com. The **Cuttyhunk Ferry Service** connects New Bedford and Cuttyhunk Island. ~ 66B State Pier, South Bulkhead, New Bedford; 508-992-0200; www.cuttyhunkferry.com.

BUS

Greyhound Bus Lines offers frequent service to Newburyport and Boston. ~ 617-526-1801, 800-231-2222. **Peter Pan** runs buses to and from Logan Airport, Hyannis, Woods Hole, Falmouth, Bourne, New Bedford, Fall River, Connecticut, Rhode Island and New York. ~ 700 Atlantic Avenue, South Station, Boston, 800-343-9999; 59 Depot Road, Falmouth; www.peterpanbus.com.

PUBLIC TRANSIT

Many Boston commuters live on the North Shore; hence **Massachusetts Bay Transportation Authority** runs numerous buses from Boston's Haymarket Square and trains from North Station to Salem, Beverly, Gloucester and Rockport. ~ 617-222-3200; www.mbta.com. **Cape Ann Transit Authority** provides bus service from Gloucester and Rockport. ~ 978-283-7916; www.canntran.com.

Plymouth does not have public transportation. **South Eastern Regional Transit Authority** provides bus service throughout Fall River, Westport and New Bedford. ~ 508-997-6767; www.srtabus.com.

TAXIS

The New Bedford Regional Airport is serviced by **Yellow Cab** (508-999-5213).

SEVEN

Central & Western Massachusetts

Take a good long breath once you arrive in this region, and prepare for a relaxing mix of the rural and the urbane: rolling hills and acres of cornfields, winding country roads that meander along rivers and streams, small museums, old houses, historic villages and college towns with maple-lined streets.

Don't bother to bring your high heels or tuxedo to central and western Massachusetts unless you're spending a weekend in a fancy Berkshire resort. The mood here—and the dress code—is casual.

Culturally, economically and socially, this area has always been strongly defined by its landscape. The forests, fields and vistas of the Berkshire hills attracted poets and authors of a naturalist bent in the 19th century, and they in turn attracted the rich and famous, who built the elaborate estates of the so-called "Gilded Age." The majestic Connecticut River provided a transportation route as well as water power to generate the mills and factories in the 1800s. Those factories, along with the fertile soil along the Connecticut's shores, attracted immigrant mill workers and farmers, who helped make the area the breadbasket of New England for decades.

Europeans who first arrived here found primeval forestland as well as large, treeless stretches that had been settled by the Mohegan Indians, hunters who had journeyed from the Hudson River area, and by the Mohawks farther north.

Development first came to central and western Massachusetts in the early 17th century, as small forts like Deerfield were built and trading posts like Springfield sprang up along the Connecticut River. These settlements were significant to our nation's history, as they marked the first movement of the colonists into the interior of the Northeast and served as models for further exploration west.

In the 1800s, canals and mills were built in the southern end of the Pioneer Valley at South Hadley Falls. Within 30 years of its founding in 1850, the city of Holyoke, the first planned city in the country, would become the "Queen of Industrial Cities" and soon after "Paper City of the World."

Thousands of immigrants from Canada and Europe came to central and western Massachusetts in the late 19th century to work in the mills and factories, and to the east, Worcester was experiencing its historical pinnacle as a city where industrial innovation and forward thinking flourished.

As New England's manufacturing economy ebbed in the 20th century, so did the fortunes of the flourishing cities of Holyoke and Worcester, as well as the smaller rural mill towns. Other areas of the state found new economic life in high-technology industries, but for central and western Massachusetts, it's been a struggle. The area continues to rely largely on smaller manufacturing, education, agriculture and the service industries. As a result, there is a different standard of living in this region than in wealthier areas near Boston.

Today, though the three areas in this chapter are not so far apart geographically, each has its own identity. Central Massachusetts, with Worcester and Sturbridge as its hubs, is made up of small rural and mill towns. The Pioneer Valley, stretching up the Connecticut River, is shifting from an agricultural area into a bedroom community for Springfield and Hartford. The Berkshire area takes its influences more from New York City than from Boston, and it, too, is seeing changes as the manufacturing jobs that once served as the mainstay of the local economy have disappeared.

Many residents of eastern Massachusetts are unaware of just how rural this area is, and "westerners" often quip that the state ends at Route 495, which makes a large semicircle around Boston. Every once in a while a local politician brings up the idea of secession for central and western Massachusetts, partly because of the claim that the smaller cities and towns of the region don't get their fair share of state funds.

But it's also because people in this part of the state have a different way of thinking. There's a streak of high-mindedness and independence here that was already evident back in 1787 when Daniel Shays, a farmer from Hatfield, started the nation's first tax insurrection. It continues up to this day, with nearly a hundred citizens in the region who refuse to pay their taxes in protest of U.S. military policy.

Over the centuries, the region has drawn many writers: from Nathaniel Hawthorne (a Salem man who didn't like the Berkshires) and Herman Melville (a Pittsfield man who did). Comedian Bill Cosby has a home in the hills surrounding the Pioneer Valley, and Poet Laureate Richard Wilbur resides in Cummington, carrying on the tradition of poets William Cullen Bryant, who lived in the same town, and Emily Dickinson, who wrote in her home in the center of Amherst in the 19th century.

What all these people have found is a place that's close enough to city amenities and resources—New York is less than four hours away, Boston two—but far enough from the urban smog, crime and high cost of living.

Many current residents in this area first came here as students. In the 1960s, western Massachusetts was a haven for the "back to the landers," who found cheap land and stimulating political activities on the University of Massachusetts campus in Amherst. Like every place else, the area has mellowed, but for many, political activism remains an important part of life. Most municipal decisions, except in the cities, are made at traditional New England town meetings. The region is also rich with craftspeople and artists, drawn here for the area's natural beauty and solitude, and their works fill galleries and studios in even the smallest towns.

Education is big business in these parts: Worcester is home to Holy Cross, Clark University and Assumption College, while the Pioneer Valley boasts the so-called "Five Colleges"—the University of Massachusetts, Smith, Mount Holyoke, Hampshire and Amherst—as well as a number of prestigious private schools like Deerfield Academy and Northfield Mount Hermon. Williams College is in the Berkshire village of Williamstown.

This is a special place, best taken at a slow pace. Don't try to do too much here; take the time to loll in a sidewalk café in Northampton or to lose yourself in any of the fine museums of Springfield, Worcester or Williamstown. Although summer is the closest thing to paradise in this region, other seasons have their special pleasures as well. Spend an autumn day climbing a mountain to see the foliage colors, or a winter weekend cross-country skiing at a cozy inn in the Berkshires.

Mark Twain's adage "If you don't like New England weather, wait a minute" applies here, and the weather can vary in locations only 20 miles apart in the Berkshires. Expect anything in winter, from brilliant, 50° days after a snowstorm, to stretches when the thermometer doesn't get above 20°. Early spring—maple sugaring season—will bring warmer days and freezing nights, while summer generally offers 70° to 80° days and, oftentimes, thunderstorms in the early evening. Indian summer is truly one of the most beautiful times in this area, with crystal blue skies, stunning foliage and temperatures that range in the 50s and 60s.

A visit to this region can put you in touch with life's simple pleasures. Like the pleasure of being outdoors and listening to the silence. The exhilaration of a hike down a forested trail. The fun of getting onto a backcountry road and not knowing where you'll end up.

If you're looking for an area that combines the serene pleasures of country life with abundant recreational and cultural opportunities, you will want to return again and again to this scenic refuge.

Central Massachusetts

All too often travelers whiz through Central Massachusetts on the Mass Pike (Route 90) completely missing the attractions of the area. What a shame. This part of the state is home to several truly worthwhile attractions, including several museums in the city of Worcester (pronounced WUS-ter); Old Sturbridge Village, a living-history museum in Sturbridge; and the tiny town of Brimfield, which has been called the "flea-market capital of the world."

Thanks to Route 90, Central Massachusetts is a breeze to reach. In fact, Worcester is only an hour's drive west of Boston. People are often surprised to learn that Worcester's the second-largest city in New England. Perhaps even more surprising are its impressive contributions to education and commerce. It's home to a dozen colleges and was the birthplace of the ingenious machines that were the first to weave carpets and fold envelopes. The Valentine card was invented here, as were the cotton gin and the birth control pill. Abbie Hoffman, father of the Yippies, was born here, as was Clara Barton, mother of the Red Cross. Isaiah Thomas, publisher of the *Massachusetts Spy*, the country's first

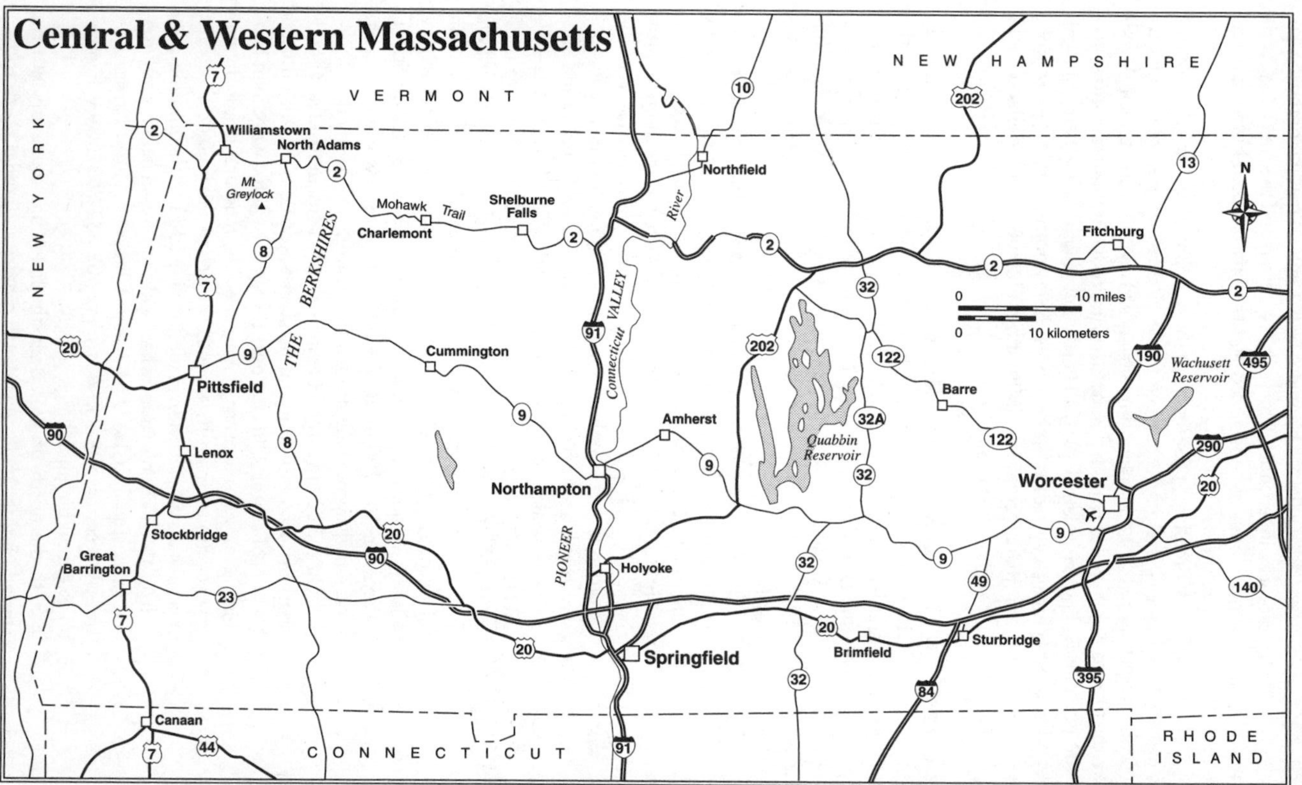
Central & Western Massachusetts
NEW YORK
VERMONT
NEW HAMPSHIRE
CONNECTICUT
RHODE ISLAND
Williamstown
North Adams
Mt Greylock
Mohawk Trail
Charlemont
Shelburne Falls
Northfield
River
THE BERKSHIRES
Pittsfield
Lenox
Stockbridge
Great Barrington
Canaan
Cummington
Connecticut VALLEY
Northampton
PIONEER
Holyoke
Springfield
Amherst
Quabbin Reservoir
Barre
Brimfield
Sturbridge
Fitchburg
Worcester
Wachusett Reservoir
0 10 miles
0 10 kilometers
N

newspaper, gave the premiere New England reading of the Declaration of Independence here in Worcester, and the American Antiquarian Society he founded was the first national historical society in the country.

Worcester's proximity to Boston hasn't helped its cultural image, and its recent economic history has not been quite as grand. Like its neighbor Springfield to the west, the city's fortunes faded with the manufacturing economy, and it is still struggling to redefine itself. There's not much doing here, but the downtown area is in the process of restoration and revitalization, and there are some interesting museums and sights spread throughout the city.

SIGHTS

The **Worcester Historical Museum** is housed in a Georgian Revival–style building and features a collection that details the settlement of the Worcester area. The library here has materials and books on local history for use by researchers. Closed Sunday and Monday. ~ 30 Elm Street, Worcester; 508-753-8278, fax 508-753-9070; www.worcesterhistory.org, e-mail info@worcesterhistory.org.

Founded in 1812 by Isaiah Thomas, the **American Antiquarian Society** was this country's first national historical society. Its remarkable collection of printed material includes books, manuscripts, newspapers and ephemera produced in the United States before 1877. It also houses Thomas' printing press. Access to the library is limited, but hour-long tours of the collection and its conservation lab are offered on Wednesday. Closed Saturday and Sunday. ~ 185 Salisbury Street, Worcester; 508-755-5221, fax 508-753-3311; www.americanantiquarian.org, e-mail library@mwa.org.

The **Worcester Art Museum** has a fine reputation as one of the best art museums in New England and features a fine collection of European, Middle Eastern, Asian and early American works. Closed Monday and Tuesday. Admission. ~ 55 Salisbury Street, Worcester; 508-799-4406, fax 508-798-5646; www.worcesterart.org, e-mail webmaster@worcesterart.org.

On the outside, the **Higgins Armory Museum** is a steel-and-glass art deco building, but inside it's a castle filled with dozens of suits of armor collected over the years by John Woodman Higgins, who was a local steel magnate. The museum details the history of armor from the year 2000 B.C. to the present, and even features a suit of armor made for "Hell-Mutt" the hunting dog. There's a children's room where kids can try on helmets and medieval costumes. Closed Monday. Admission. ~ 100 Barber Avenue, Worcester; 508-853-6015, fax 508-852-7697; www.higgins.org, e-mail higgins@higgins.org.

To the north of Worcester, the landscape opens up into the broad Nashua Valley. It's worth the drive 20 miles north to visit the **Fruitlands Museums.** Fruitlands is an overlooked gem, with four small museums spread out on a hillside offering an expansive view of the valley. It was once the home of Bronson Alcott, father of Louisa May and founder of the transcendental movement of the 1840s, which espoused individualism and self-reliance, among other things, and included in its disciples Ralph Waldo Emerson and Henry David Thoreau. The **Fruitlands Farmhouse** has exhibits detailing the movement, while the **Shaker House** provides a look at Shaker life during the 19th century. The **Picture Gallery**, built by the museums' founder, Boston Brahmin Clara Endicott Sears, houses her collection of landscapes by several Hudson River School painters. The **Indian Museum** has dioramas and artifacts relating to New England's Indians, including Thoreau's collection of arrowheads. The grounds here are quite spectacular, so bring a picnic lunch and spend the day if you can. ◄HIDDEN

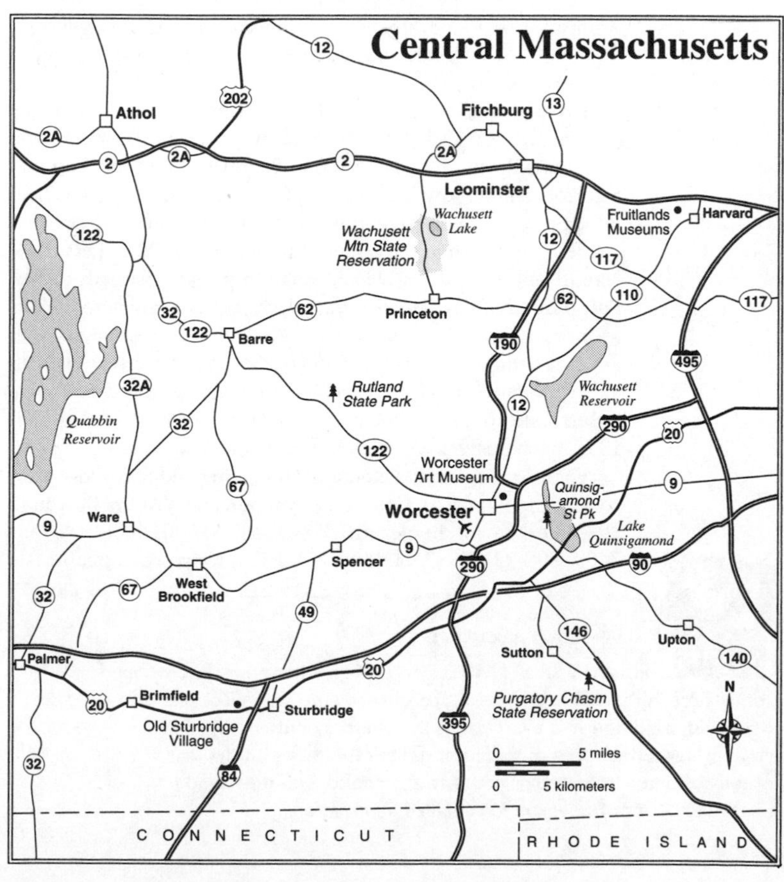

The museums are closed from the end of October to mid-May but the grounds are open year-round. Admission. ~ 102 Prospect Hill Road, Harvard; 978-456-3924, fax 978-456-8078; www.fruitlands.org.

West of Worcester, the land becomes less developed. You've now arrived in the real country. A good introduction to the history of this area comes in **Old Sturbridge Village**. Traveling the paths that wind through some 200 acres of the small village, gardens, farms and fields, you can learn how 19th-century potters, blacksmiths, weavers and other craftspeople created their wares. Every activity here is designed to bring the visitor back to the 1800s. They host a variety of special events, some of which are based on the seasons and include cider making, preparation and eating of special Thanksgiving dinners, and craft and antique weekends. A good place for families, this is a must-stop on any tour of the region. Closed Monday from mid-March to late-May. Admission. ~ 1 Old Sturbridge Village Road, Sturbridge; 508-347-3362, 800-733-1830, fax 508-347-0375; www.osv.org, e-mail osv@osv.org.

Driving west from Sturbridge on Route 20, you're on the open highway, traveling past forests and ponds to the small town of Brimfield, home of the famous **Brimfield Outdoor Antiques and Collectible Show**, a week-long flea market extravaganza held three times a year, in May, July and September. Spread out along a mile-long stretch in the center of town, over 5000 dealers come here to sell their wares, which range from old postcards to fine European antiques. *The Brimfield Exchange* is a guide to the different exhibitors, available at any local coffee shop or newsstand. For a schedule and general information, send $5 to Quaboag Valley Chamber of Commerce. Closed weekends. ~ 3 Converse Street, Suite 103, Palmer, MA 01069; 413-283-6149, fax 413-289-1355; www.quaboag.com, e-mail info@quaboag.com.

For more information about the Worcester and Sturbridge area, contact the **Worcester County Convention and Visitors Bureau.** ~ 30 Major Taylor Boulevard, Worcester, MA 01608; 508-755-7400, 800-231-7557, fax 508-754-2703; www.worcester.org.

sights

AUTHOR FAVORITE

Imagine a small New England village where time just stopped somewhere in the 1830s, and you'd probably conjure up a place like **Old Sturbridge Village**. It is a fascinating living-history museum that recreates New England life of that period, from the shoes on the feet of the costumed interpretive guides to the rooftops of the 40-odd restored buildings. See above for detailed information.

LODGING

Located near the busy University of Massachusetts Medical Center, the **Beechwood Hotel** is one of the town's newer hotels. The large round building has a lobby crowned with magnificent antique stained glass. There's an opulent ballroom with cathedral ceilings and alabaster light fixtures, painted in gold and rose. The Beechwood offers 73 spacious guest rooms, including some fireplace suites, each individually decorated and featuring wall-to-wall carpeting. The restaurant here has earned high praise from local food critics for its classic American cuisine. ~ 363 Plantation Street, Worcester; 508-754-5789, 800-344-2589, fax 508-752-2060; www.beechwoodhotel.com. DELUXE.

Worcester has its share of chain motels, but Sturbridge, 18 miles southwest, offers a better variety of accommodations.

A local institution, the **Publick House on the Common** was originally founded in 1771 by Colonel Ebenezer Crafts. The original building, which is listed on the National Register of Historic Places, has 17 rooms plus several restaurants and shops. It's surrounded by other accommodations, including the next-door Chamberlain House (a six-suite building) and a 96-room motor lodge. Free wi-fi is available throughout the main inn. ~ Route 131 on the Common, Sturbridge; 508-347-3313, 800-782-5425, fax 508-347-5073; www.publickhouse.com, e-mail info@publickhouse.com. MODERATE TO DELUXE.

Offering 54 basic, modern motel rooms, **America's Best Value Inn** has nicely kept grounds and a swimming pool and is convenient to Sturbridge, Worcester and Brimfield. ~ 408 Main Street, Route 20, Sturbridge; 508-347-7327, fax 508-347-2954. MODERATE.

Five ornately decorated accommodations await guests at **Yankee Cricket**, a bed and breakfast brimming with country comforts. Each suite includes its own special touches such as an in-room sink in the white and blue appointed Patriots Room and a private entrance in the warm, peach-colored Garden Room. There are also four common areas designed for relaxation, from the Keeping Room with a large fireplace to the Three Seasons Porch with white wicker furniture and checkered floor tile. ~ 106 Five Bridge Road, Brimfield; 413-245-0030; www.yankeecricket.com, e-mail wsimonic@charter.net. MODERATE.

Berkshire Folkstone Bed and Breakfast is a reservation service that matches travelers with a number of small country inns in the Pioneer Valley, Sturbridge and North and South County Berkshires areas. ~ 101 Mulberry Street C-1, Springfield; 413-247-5800, 800-762-2751, fax 413-731-5775.

DINING

The Sunburst features natural foods for breakfast and lunch in a coffee-shop atmosphere. The muffins are excellent, as is the quiche and granola. Other items include fresh fruit bowls, sandwiches and "nogs," seasonal fruit mixed with milk and eggs. No dinner. ~ 484 Main Street, Sturbridge; 508-347-3097. BUDGET.

A local dining institution, the **Salem Cross Inn** is a restored 1705 New England farmhouse filled with collections of antiques and photographs. The Salem family specializes in some unique eating events that include drinks in the old tavern downstairs, and hayrides and sleigh rides through their 600-acre farm. In the summer, their Drover's Roasts serve up a large side of beef, slowly cooked as it was in the 1700s, over a fieldstone open pit. In winter, the weekend Fireplace Feasts feature prime rib cooked on a 1700s roasting jack in the fieldstone fireplace and apple pie baked in the inn's 1699 brick beehive oven. These meals are worth rearranging your schedule for. Reservations are required. Closed Monday. ~ Route 9, West Brookfield; 508-867-8337, fax 508-867-0351; www.salemcrossinn.com, e-mail info@salemcrossinn.com. MODERATE TO DELUXE.

SHOPPING

The gift shop at the **Worcester Art Museum** is a great place to find small, quality gifts including reproduction jewelry, coffee-table books, calendars and toys. ~ 55 Salisbury Street, Worcester; 508-799-4406, fax 508-798-5646; www.worcesterart.org, e-mail information@worcesterart.org.

The **Museum Gift Shop** and **New England Bookstore at Old Sturbridge Village** are two outstanding shops that feature crafts made at Sturbridge Village, as well as reproductions of early American items for the home. The bookstore features a wide selection of books about New England history, life and lore, including gardening and the home arts. Closed Monday mid-March to late-May. ~ Route 20, Sturbridge; 508-347-3362, 800-733-1830, fax 508-347-0369; www.osvgifts.org, e-mail osvmgs@osv.org.

NIGHTLIFE

Worcester's **DCU Center**, formerly the Worcester Centrum, is a 14,800-seat arena offering rock and pop music concerts, as well as hockey and basketball games and conference events. ~ 50 Foster Street, Worcester; 508-755-6800; www.dcucenter.com.

Mechanics Hall, one of the finest pre–Civil War concert halls in the country, is especially noted for its beauty and fine

AUTHOR FAVORITE

Spag's 19 is a Worcester institution, with three large buildings and an assortment of tents filled with, well, *stuff* of all kinds, from small appliances to clothing to groceries. It's a warehouse-type operation where customers actually line up to get in the place. If you plan to do any heavy shopping, bring a tote or knapsack—vendors don't give out shopping bags. ~ Route 9, Worcester.

acoustics. The hall draws folk, jazz, country and classical performers and is frequently used for the recording of compact discs and records. ~ 321 Main Street, Worcester; 508-752-5608; www.mechanicshall.org, e-mail info@mechanicshall.org.

Sh'boom's is a danceclub with disc jockeys spinning "oldies" on Wednesday, and house, techno and the like Thursday through Saturday. Also here is **Polyester**, a "commercial party music" (read: hip-hop and reggae) club accessible through Sh'boom's. Cover Thursday through Saturday. ~ 213 Main Street, Worcester; 508-752-4214.

VIP's Lounge has live bands with dancing on Saturday nights from Labor Day to Memorial Day. ~ Sturbridge Host Hotel, 366 Main Street, Sturbridge; 508-347-7393.

Those in search of more low-key nightlife should try the popular **Ugly Duckling Loft**, the loft of the Whistling Swan. The place has a warm and relaxed atmosphere amid brass and wood decor, with live entertainment, including piano music and acoustic guitar, seven nights a week. ~ 502 Main Street, Sturbridge; 508-347-2321, fax 508-347-3361; www.thewhistlingswan.com.

BEACHES & PARKS

PURGATORY CHASM STATE RESERVATION This park offers 960 acres of forestland, including the dramatic and unusual Purgatory Chasm. The chasm itself is a quarter-mile-long granite fissure, a sharp valley filled with huge boulders that have detached from the walls. Geologists can't seem to agree on exactly how the chasm was formed, and its mystery adds to the allure of the place. There are hiking trails, including a difficult one through the chasm, as well as picnic areas, a visitors center and restrooms. ~ On Purgatory Road, off Route 146, Sutton; 508-234-3733, fax 508-234-9610.

QUINSIGAMOND STATE PARK This 51-acre preserve is an urban park, offering a grassy, midday break for visitors to the Worcester area. There are several beaches, including Regatta Point and Lake Park. Crew teams from the area's colleges can often be found at Regatta Point, while Lake Park offers tennis courts and a track. Fishing is good for stocked trout and salmon. Picnic areas and restrooms (open seasonally late April through October) are found here. Weekend parking fee, $5 Memorial Day through Labor Day. ~ On Lake Avenue off Plantation Street exit from Route 290; 508-755-6880, fax 508-755-5347; www.mass.gov/der, e-mail mass.parks@state.ma.us.

▲ Nearby, at the Sutton Falls Camping Area (90 Manchaug Road, West Sutton; 508-865-3898; www.suttonfalls.com), there are 100 tent/RV sites (hookups available); $21 to $32 per night. Closed October to mid-April.

Pioneer Valley

The Pioneer Valley, actually a section of the Connecticut River Valley, stretches from the city of Springfield in the south to Brattleboro, Vermont, and beyond. Here you'll find an eclectic mix of old mill cities, semi-chic college towns and country villages, with tobacco, hay and cornfields in between. The farther north you travel from Springfield, the more country you'll find. Northampton and Amherst offer good restaurants and shops, while the towns in the surrounding hills are much more rural and relaxed, some with town commons and white-steepled churches, others with old iron bridges and brick factories along the rivers, remnants of the days when cutlery factories and paper mills fueled the region's economy.

Today, housing developments are starting to encroach on farmland, but the area is still remarkably rural in some parts. This area is known for its unique mix of Yankee stubbornness, ethnic influences and a '60s political outlook that remains even today.

SIGHTS

THE LOWER VALLEY Founded by fur trader William Pynchon in 1636, **Springfield** is the oldest settlement and the largest city in western Massachusetts, as well as the commercial hub of the region. Though it is a city that tries hard, Springfield's glory days seem to lie in the past. It does have a good collection of museums, however, that makes it worth spending a rainy day here.

Overlooking the Connecticut River is the **Naismith Memorial Basketball Hall of Fame Museum.** Basketball was invented here in Springfield in 1891, and this museum is enjoyable even if you're not a sports fan. There are videos, a full-size regulation court and plenty of interactive displays, including one where guests can become sportscasters or another where they can pay on-on-one in virtual hoops against some of today's best players. Admission. ~ 1000 West Columbus Avenue, Springfield; 413-781-6500, 877-446-6752, fax 413-781-1939; www.hoophall.com.

Court Square is a pleasant green space in the heart of Springfield bordered by the **Hampden County Courthouse**, the **Old First Church** and **Symphony Hall.** ~ Main Street, between Court and Elm streets, Springfield.

From here it's a short hike up the hill to **Springfield Museum at the Quadrangle**, which features four museums (one admission charge admits you to all four). Closed Monday. ~ Springfield Museums, 21 Edwards Street, Springfield; 413-263-6800, 800-625-7738, fax 413-263-6807; www.springfieldmuseums.org.

The **George Walter Vincent Smith Museum** houses a collection of Asian art, as well as 19th-century European and American paintings. Closed Monday. ~ 21 Edwards Street, Springfield; 413-263-6800, 800-625-7738, fax 413-263-6807; www.springfieldmuseums.org.

Across The Quadrangle is the **Museum of Fine Arts**, which features works from the early Renaissance to the 20th century. One gallery is devoted to impressionist, expressionist and early modern European works. Of special interest are the works of local 19th-century portrait artist Erastus Salisbury Field, whose gigantic *Historical Monument of the American Republic* is a mind-boggler. Closed Monday. ~ 21 Edwards Street, Springfield; 413-263-6800, 800-625-7738, fax 413-263-6807; www.springfieldmuseums.org.

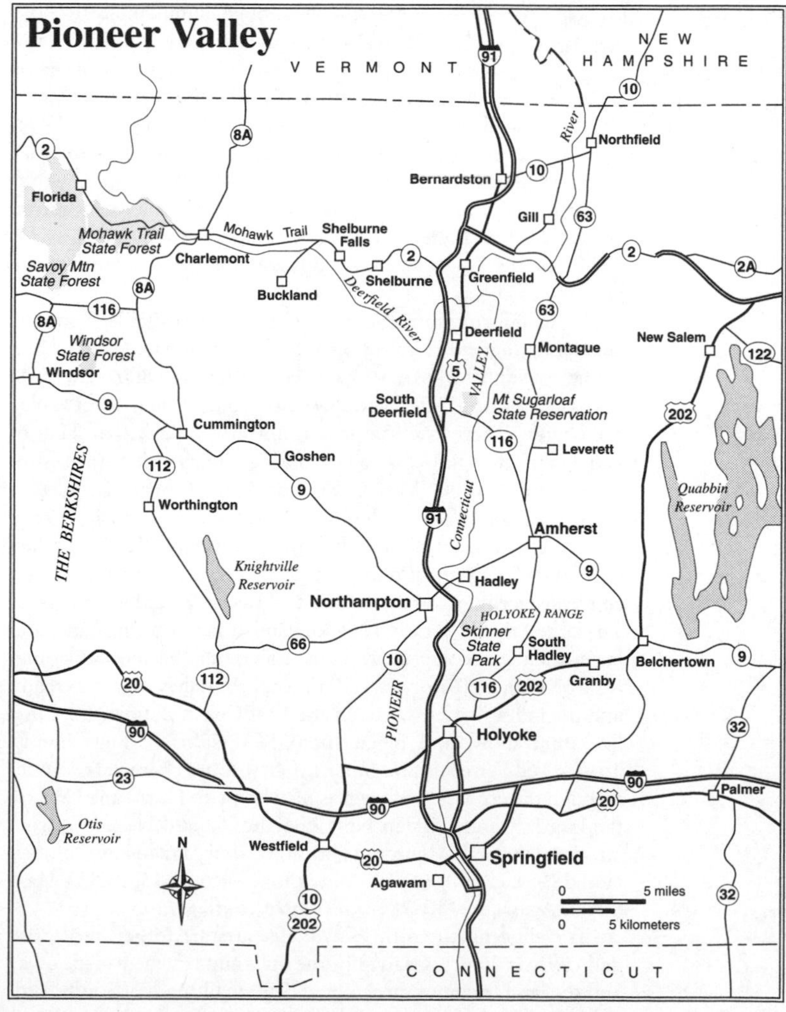

The **Springfield Science Museum** offers exhibits in the natural and physical sciences, including hands-on exhibits for children and the Seymour Planetarium. Closed Monday. ~ 21 Edwards Street, Springfield; 413-263-6800, 800-625-7738, fax 413-263-6807; www.springfieldmuseums.org.

The **Connecticut Valley Historical Museum** offers a glimpse of the social and economic history of the Connecticut River Valley. They also offer a genealogy and local history library. Closed Monday. ~ 21 Edwards Street, Springfield; 413-263-6800, 800-625-7738, fax 413-263-6807; www.springfieldmuseums.org.

The Mount Holyoke College campus was designed by Frederick Law Olmsted, designer of Central Park, who used a variety of rare trees to provide form, beauty and consistency.

Up the hill from The Quadrangle, on the campus of Springfield Technical Community College, is the **Springfield Armory National Historic Site**, established at a spot chosen by George Washington in 1794. The Springfield Armory produced the first U.S. military small arms—the Springfield rifle—bringing skilled workers to the area and setting the scene for the valley's industrial growth. Call for hours. ~ 1 Armory Square, Springfield; 413-734-8551, fax 413-747-8062; www.nps.gov/spar, e-mail spar_interpre tation@nps.gov.

More information about Springfield is available from the **Greater Springfield Convention and Visitors Bureau.** ~ 1441 Main Street, Springfield, MA 01103; 413-787-1548, 800-723-1548, fax 413-781-4607; www.valleyvisitor.com, e-mail info@valley visitor.com. There is also a location near the Basketball Hall of Fame that offers information on Springfield as well as the rest of the region. ~ 1200 West Columbus Avenue, Springfield; 413-750-2980, fax 417-750-2984.

The venerable, if slightly shabby, old Riverside Park was taken over in 1999 by the Premier Parks Inc. conglomerate, given a complete facelift, and reopened in 2000 as **Six Flags New England.** The largest theme park in New England, it features ten, bigger and faster-than-ever roller coasters including the 208-foot Superman Ride of Steel, a 20-story freefall ride appropriately named Scream! and the tallest Ferris wheel on the East Coast. Batman stars in a live stunt show, and bigger-than-life versions of Bugs Bunny, Tweety and Sylvester and other Looney Tunes characters wander through the crowds. Six Flags is also home to Hurricane Harbor, the largest water park in New England. Closed weekdays from late April through Memorial Day and Labor Day to late October; closed November to April. Admission. ~ Route 159, 1623 Main Street, Agawam; 413-786-9300; www.sixflags.com.

Traveling north from Holyoke, you start to get into farm-and-college country. Gradually, the mills and tenements fade away and the land becomes more open. The small town of South Hadley is the home of **Mount Holyoke College**. Established by Mary

Lyon in 1837, Mount Holyoke is one of the oldest women's colleges in the country. A maple-lined road leads the traveler through the 800-acre campus, between two campus ponds and up to the wooded Prospect Hill, which has bridle paths and a lawn for picnics. There's a lovely botanical garden and art museum on the college grounds. ~ 50 College Street, South Hadley; 413-538-2000; www.mtholyoke.edu.

On the Granby town line on Route 116 farther north is the funky and fascinating **Nash Dinosaur Land**, where 200-million-year-old dinosaur tracks were discovered in 1933 by geologist Carleton Nash. His son Cornell now runs the business his father established in 1939 and built up until his death in 1999, excavating the tracks and building a small museum and shop to display the prints, some as tiny as chicken feet. The Nashes boast the largest footprint quarry in the world, as well as the largest footprints from the early Jurassic period; many pieces are for sale. Kids will love this place. Open in winter by appointment. Admission. ~ Route 116, South Hadley; 413-467-9566. ◄HIDDEN

THE UPPER VALLEY **Northampton** counts among its past residents Calvinist minister Jonathan Edwards and President Calvin Coolidge, who also served as mayor. Sylvester Graham invented the graham cracker here, and in the early 1800s the place was a thriving industrial center for wool, buttons, paper and, later, cutlery.

Today, it is perhaps the most cosmopolitan town in western Massachusetts (some locals say too much so), with its mix of restored old buildings, galleries, restaurants and trendy Main Street boutiques. The home of Smith College, the town is a pleasant and lively place year-round but especially nice in summer, when the students have gone home.

Smith College is located just outside the town's center. One of the so-called "Seven Sisters" (as is Mount Holyoke), Smith's campus is quintessentially old-money New England, with old Gothic buildings and beautifully tended gardens. Among its attractions is the **Lyman Plant House**, a rambling, old-fashioned greenhouse filled with hundreds of different flowers, plants and trees and open to the public. The annual bulb show in early spring is a favorite visitor destination. Another idyllic spot is **Paradise Pond**, framed by weeping willows and elm trees and ideal for an afternoon picnic.

The **Smith College Museum of Art** houses works by Picasso, Cézanne, Rodin and Thomas Eakins as well as rotating exhibitions in a wide variety of mediums throughout the year. Closed Monday. ~ 76 Elm Street at Bedford Terrace, Northampton; 413-584-2760, fax 413-585-2782; www.smith.edu/artmuseum, e-mail artmuseum@smith.edu.

Calvin Coolidge, the nation's 30th president, attended Amherst College and settled in Northampton, where he practiced law and began his political career. Coolidge lived with his wife at **21 Massasoit Street**, and after his presidency the couple retired to The Beeches, a stately home located on Hampton Terrace. Both homes are private.

For an example of Gothic architecture, visit the **Academy of Music**, a former opera house built in 1890 that now serves as a movie theater with occasional live performances. ~ 274 Main Street, Northampton; 413-584-8435, fax 413-587-0936; www.academyofmusictheatre.com, e-mail academyofmusic@yahoo.com.

Historic Northampton operates three homes that highlight local history and daily life in Northampton over the past three centuries. The **Isaac Damon House** (46 Bridge Street) was built circa 1813 by Damon, a prominent New England architect of the day. The house includes an 1820 parlor display and changing exhibitions. A modern addition houses the Damon Education Center, which features a permanent exhibit, delineating Northampton's history from the 17th century to the 20th century. Built in 1730, the **Parsons House** (58 Bridge Street) features an architectural tour; look inside the walls to see the various layers of wallpaper and paint from the 19th century. The **Shepherd House** (66 Bridge Street) is furnished with the Shepherd family collection, including travel souvenirs from around the world. There is a museum gift shop located in a renovated 1820s barn on site. Admission. Closed Monday. ~ 66 Bridge Street, Northampton; 413-584-6011, fax 413-584-7956; www.historic-northampton.org, e-mail mailbox@historic-northampton.org.

For more information on the Northampton area, contact the **Greater Northampton Chamber of Commerce**. Closed on weekends from November through April. ~ 99 Pleasant Street, Northampton; 413-584-1900, fax 413-584-1934; www.explorenorthampton.com, e-mail info@explorenorthampton.com.

Follow Route 9 east across the Coolidge Bridge and you will reach Hadley, a farming town once noted for its asparagus and tobacco but now fast becoming a suburb. The **Hadley Farm Museum** is housed in a 1782 barn moved to the spot in 1930. The museum features a wonderful collection of farm tools, an 18th-century stagecoach, wagons and home utensils used during the 18th and 19th centuries, including a broom-making machine. Closed Monday and Tuesday and from mid-October to mid-May. ~ Junction of Route 9 and Route 47 (behind Town Hall), Hadley; 413-584-3120; www.hadleyonline.com/farmmuseum.

Amherst is a pretty college town with shops and restaurants spread out along a maple-lined town common. Although it has been influenced by the gentrifier's wrecking ball, there's still a spark of politics in its downtown area, with tie dye–clad students joining activist locals in petitioning against U.S. military policy or in favor of animal rights.

Founded in 1821, **Amherst College** gracefully borders the southern side of the Amherst common. With about 1650 students, Amherst is one of the smaller "Little Ivy" colleges, and its campus architecture includes a rich mix of old ivy-covered halls and newer buildings. ~ 413-542-2000, fax 413-542-2040; www.amherst.edu, e-mail info@amherst.edu.

One of the newer buildings houses the **Robert Frost Library**, named for one of the college's better-known faculty members. Open daily when school is in session. ~ 413-542-2373, fax 413-542-2662; www.amherst.edu/library.

At the other end of Amherst is the **University of Massachusetts.** With an enrollment of about 25,000 students, it is one of the largest universities in New England. ~ 413-545-0111; www.umass.edu.

"UMass" has come a long way from its beginnings as an agricultural land-grant college in 1863, and its campus buildings reflect that stretch, from the Romanesque-Revival **Old Chapel** to the 26-story **W. E. B. Du Bois Library** that stands beside it. The library, as well as the **Top of the Campus** restaurant at the **Murray D. Lincoln Campus Center**, offer fine views of the Holyoke range.

The Campus Pond is the center of fair-weather activities, and the **Fine Arts Center** presents varied performances in theater, dance and music. ~ 413-545-2511; www.umass.edu/fac.

For more information on the Amherst area, contact the **Amherst Area Chamber of Commerce**. Closed weekends. ~ 28 Amity Street, Amherst; 413-253-0700, fax 413-256-0771; www.amherstarea.com, e-mail info@amherstarea.com.

Travel north on Route 116 and you'll leave the college towns behind. Here the landscape is punctuated by the long, faded red tobacco barns and cornfields whose crop will feed the area's dairy cows. Just off Routes 5 and 10 is **Historic Deerfield.** ~ Deerfield; 413-775-7214, fax 413-775-7220; www.historic-deerfield.org, e-mail info@historic-deerfield.org.

It's almost jarring to turn off the busy highway and onto the tree-lined main street of Deerfield because you have, in a sense,

THE "BELLE OF AMHERST'S" FAMILY HOME

The **Emily Dickinson Homestead** is composed of the Dickinson Homestead, home of "The Belle of Amherst" (reclusive poet Emily Dickinson) and the Evergreens, home of the poet's brother and sister-in-law. Owned by Amherst College, the museum has become a mecca for poetry lovers. The home is open to the public March to mid-December. Call ahead for hours. Admission. ~ 280 Main Street, Amherst; 413-542-8161; www.emilydickinsonmuseum.org, e-mail info@emilydickinsonmuseum.org.

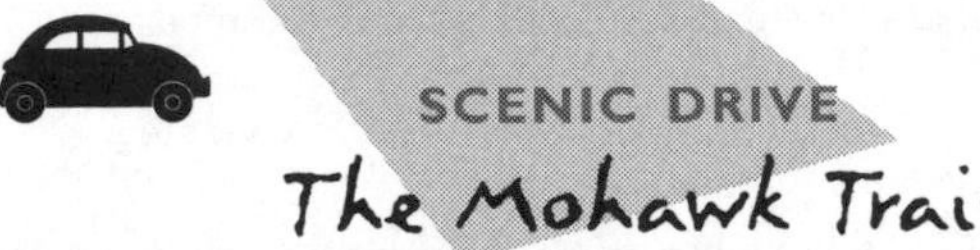

SCENIC DRIVE
The Mohawk Trail

The Mohawk Trail is one of the region's oldest and finest touring roads, winding past farm towns, forests and some of the best scenic views in western New England. The trail is dotted with remnants of the 1950s heyday of automobile touring: cabins, old Indian souvenir shops and several spots with lookouts boasting multistate views. It is particularly popular in fall, when its hills offer spectacular foliage viewing. While the trail officially runs for some 60 miles across Massachusetts from Lexington to the New York state line, by far the most beautiful part is the 28-mile segment described here.

SHELBURNE From the town of Greenfield on Route 5 or Route 91 Exit 26, drive west on Route 2. Six miles along, at Shelburne Falls, take time to visit the lovely **Bridge of Flowers**, a former trolley bridge across the Deerfield River that has been converted into an incredible flower garden in bloom three seasons out of the year. Across the bridge, follow the signs to **Salmon Falls**, where you'll find the **Glacial Potholes**, carved out of rock during the Ice Age.

CHARLEMONT Fourteen more miles bring you to the village of Charlemont, and a couple of miles farther on, the **Hail to the Sunrise Statue**, a 900-pound bronze figure depicting a Mohawk Indian with arms upraised to the east, memorializing the people who used this route for their annual migration in ancient times. A nearby pool contains 100 inscribed stones from tribes throughout the United States. As you travel farther, the curves deepen in the road as it enters the

left the modern world behind. The mile-long main street of this late-17th-century village (it's just called "The Street") is flanked by a dozen restored Colonial and Federal-style houses, all painted in the reds, blues and grays of bygone days. Here you can get a sense of the emerging Connecticut Valley architecture, which was different from the styles in England as well as the coastal New England towns. And the interiors at Historic Deerfield are just as faithful to the past as the exteriors; the village's collection of decorative arts and architecture has been compared to that of historic Williamsburg and the Winterthur Museum in Delaware.

Surrounded by farmland and meadows, Deerfield began in the 17th century as a tiny frontier outpost. The town was nearly destroyed by Indians in the Bloody Brook Massacre during the King Philip's war in 1675, and again by a later attack by the

Mohawk Trail State Forest (page 412), one of the most scenic woodland areas in Massachusetts, where you can hike a portion of the original Mohawk foot trail.

FLORIDA North of the highway near the town of Florida is the east entrance of the **Hoosac Tunnel**. One of the great engineering accomplishments of the mid-19th century, the railroad tunnel runs nearly five miles through the mountain and took 20 years to complete. Soon after passing Florida, Route 2 reaches the mountain pass the tunnel was designed to avoid—2272-foot **Whitcomb Summit**, the highest point on the Mohawk Trail, from which you can see parts of Massachusetts, New York, Vermont and New Hampshire. Descending the western slope, **Hairpin Turn** affords another breathtaking view of the Hoosac Valley and the Berkshire Hills. For more information, contact **The Mohawk Trail Association**. ~ P.O. Box 1044, North Adams, MA 01247; 413-743-8127; www.mohawktrail.com.

NATURAL BRIDGE STATE PARK Just before arriving in **North Adams** (page 414), the Mohawk Trail brings you to the intersection with Route 8 and Natural Bridge State Park, site of the only natural marble bridge in North America, formed by the raging waters of melting glaciers millions of years ago. Also interesting to look at are the carvings done by quarrymen and visitors, many dating back to the 1800s.

BIRTHPLACE OF SUSAN B. ANTHONY To continue this drive as a scenic loop, from North Adams take Route 8 south for six miles to Adams and follow Route 116 back to Route 91/Route 5 at South Deerfield, a distance of 36 miles with few specific points of interest—other than the birthplace of Susan B. Anthony in Adams—but plenty of pastoral beauty.

French and Indians in 1704. Testimony to that fateful day still stands: there's a door with a hatchet hole in it at the **Memorial Hall Museum**, one of the oldest local historical museums in the country. Closed November through April. Admission. ~ Memorial Street, Deerfield; 413-774-7476, fax 413-774-5400; www.old-deerfield.org, e-mail info@old-deerfield.org.

The town recovered, and Deerfield went on to prosper as a center for commerce and agriculture, as well as an exchange post for travelers between Boston and points west. In 1952, Mr. and Mrs. Henry Flynt established Historic Deerfield, Inc. to carry out the restoration of the town, one of the first such undertakings in the country.

The **Flynt Center** features rotating exhibits of its collection of decorative arts. Closed January through March. Admission. ~

37D Old Main Street, Deerfield; 413-775-7214, fax 413-775-7220; www.historic-deerfield.org, e-mail info@historic-deerfield.org.

The lookout tower at Whitcomb Summit once appeared as an illustration on the cover of the *New Yorker.*

The **Sheldon House** is the best-preserved Deerfield building from the 18th century, and the dark-stained, clapboard structure is one of the oldest houses in town, dating back to 1755. The interior woodwork is intact, and some of the furnishings are original Deerfield pieces. The Sheldon displays New England furniture, European brass and English ceramics, while the **Wells-Thorn House** features a series of period rooms that illustrate the influence of the local economy and changing styles in home life in Deerfield from 1725 to 1850. One admission fee (good for two days) will admit you into all the individual houses and museums. ~ 413-775-7214, fax 413-775-7220; www.historic-deerfield.org, e-mail info@historic-deerfield.org.

The Connecticut River is the backbone of this region, and from June to mid-October, the **Quinnetukut II Riverboat** cruises a six-mile section of the river, giving you a look at the geology, history and natural beauty of the area. Closed Monday and Tuesday. Admission. ~ Northfield Mountain Recreation and Environmental Center, 99 Miller's Falls Road, Northfield; 413-659-3714, 800-859-2960, fax 413-659-4460; www.nu.com/northfield/riverboat.asp.

If you're lucky enough to be in the area in the late summer or early fall, check out one of the region's many agricultural fairs. The **Eastern States Exposition** represents all six New England states and features music, food, agricultural contests, animal shows and much more. The exposition is held for three weekends in September in West Springfield. The **Cummington Fair** is another small-town beauty, held the last week of August. This fair's highlights are its old engine display, square dancing and fireworks. The **Northampton Fair** is held during Labor Day weekend at the Three-County Fairground on Bridge Street in Northampton. The **Franklin County Fair** is the first weekend after Labor Day, held at the Franklin County Fairgrounds on Wisdom Way in Greenfield.

For a complete listing of agricultural fairs around the state, write to the **Department of Agricultural Resources**. ~ 251 Causeway Street, Boston, MA 02114; 617-626-1700, fax 617-626-1850; www.mass.gov/agr.

HIDDEN ►

If you're traveling the Mohawk Trail (see "Scenic Drive") in early spring, **Gould's Sugar House** is a tasty stop. You're likely to find Edgar Gould out in the back boiling sap to make maple syrup, while his wife and grandchildren are in the restaurant serving it on waffles and pancakes. (Dill pickles are served on the side to cut the sweetness of the syrup!) In foliage season, the family also sells their apples, pumpkins and excellent pies. Closed during summer; call ahead for hours. ~ Mohawk Trail, Shelburne; 413-625-6170, fax 413-625-8681; www.goulds-sugarhouse.com, e-mail info@goulds-sugarhouse.com.

There are many opportunities for picnicking along the Deerfield River, and you may want to stop in Shelburne Falls for supplies. **McCusker's Market** has a good deli and a supply of health foods as well as Bart's ice cream, a local favorite. ~ Bridge of Flowers, Shelburne Falls; 413-625-9411; www.mccuskersmarket.com, e-mail info@mccuskersmarket.com.

LODGING

The Springfield area offers a large selection of chain motels and luxury hotels, while accommodations in the upper Pioneer Valley include more motels, country inns and bed and breakfasts. Advance reservations are strongly recommended in June, when college graduations and the American Council Crafts Fair are held, and in September, when the Eastern States Exposition and fall foliage bring a flurry of visitors.

The most elegant hostelry in the Pioneer Valley, the **Sheraton Springfield Monarch Place** has a plush lobby highlighted by marble, a 12-story atrium and amenities like an indoor pool with a sun deck. The 325 spacious guest rooms and suites are decorated in soft pastels. You'll also find a restaurant, a lounge and a health club with jacuzzi, weight room and sauna. Ask for a room with a view of the Connecticut River. ~ 1 Monarch Place, Springfield; 413-781-1010, 800-426-9004, fax 413-747-8065; www.sheratonspringfield.com, e-mail info@sheratonspringfield.com. DELUXE TO ULTRA-DELUXE.

The **Yankee Pedlar Inn** has 28 guest rooms in four separate buildings on a busy street in Holyoke. Rooms are individually decorated in Early American decor, with period pieces and antiques along with canopy and four-poster beds. The Pedlar has a Colonial-style tavern and a restaurant (closed Monday). Although not an isolated country inn, this is a popular place for business travelers, and its location just off Route 91 makes it convenient to all parts of the Pioneer Valley. ~ 1866 Northampton Street, Holyoke; 413-532-9494, 800-413-3771, fax 413-536-8877; www.yankeepedlarinn.com, e-mail info@yankeepedlarinn.com. MODERATE.

Near downtown Northampton and right next to the Smith campus, the **Autumn Inn** is a simple, comfortable 29-room hostelry. Guest rooms are large, clean and individually decorated with wall-to-wall carpeting, Colonial reproductions, brass lamps, Hitchcock rockers and prints from the owner's collection. Extras include an outdoor pool and a dining room with a large fireplace. The place has attracted a regular clientele due to its location and attention to detail. Continental breakfast is included. ~ 259 Elm Street, Northampton; 413-584-7660, fax 413-586-4808; www.hampshirehospitality.com, e-mail innoho@javanet.com. MODERATE TO DELUXE.

The 1927 **Hotel Northampton** has undergone a facelift, converting a once middle-aged downtown hotel into something with a touch of class. There are 106 rooms and suites here, including some with fireplaces. The lobby is nicely decorated in a late-Georgian motif, and the hotel has become a favorite for Smith College parents because of its accommodations and its proximity to the campus. Reservations advised. Continental breakfast is included. ~ 36 King Street, Northampton; 413-584-3100, 800-547-3529, fax 413-584-9455; www.hotelnorthampton.com, e-mail info@hotelnorthampton.com. ULTRA-DELUXE.

Standing in the center of Amherst, the **Lord Jeffery Inn** has been a fixture in this college town for decades. Many of its 48 rooms are decorated with antiques, and some overlook the lovely town common. The inn has the sedate feel of an Ivy League faculty club, with an elegant dining room and tavern, as well as several cozy public sitting rooms, comfortable arm chairs and a fireplace. It's located within walking distance of the shopping area and Amherst College. ~ 30 Boltwood Avenue, Amherst; 413-253-2576, 800-742-0358, fax 413-256-6152; www.lordjefferyinn.com, e-mail info@lordjefferyinn.com. DELUXE.

HIDDEN ►

Allen House Victorian Inn is a wonderful bed and breakfast (seven rooms, all with private baths), set in an 1886 Victorian. The owners have painstakingly restored it to its original form, earning it the Historic Preservation Award from the Amherst Historical Commission. It's set on three wooded acres within walking distance of town. A five-course country breakfast and afternoon tea are included. ~ 599 Main Street, Amherst; 413-253-5000, fax 413-253-7625; www.allenhouse.com, e-mail allenhouse@webtv.net. DELUXE.

The **Campus Center Hotel** offers 116 rooms with standard low-cost hotel decor in a concrete highrise on the University of Massachusetts campus. The ambience is nothing special, but the hotel is convenient for visitors to the university, and the view of the Holyoke range and the campus is great. ~ University of Massachusetts, Amherst; 413-549-6000, fax 413-545-1210; www.aux.umass.edu/hotel, e-mail doconnor@mail.aux.umass.edu. MODERATE TO ULTRA-DELUXE.

One of the few elegant old country inns in the northern Pioneer Valley is the **Deerfield Inn**, an original historic inn built in 1884, which stands along a lovely, tree-lined street in Deerfield. Its 23 rooms are decorated in antiques and Graeff fabric wallpaper. There's a comfortable sitting room with a fireplace to enjoy pre-dinner drinks, and a good restaurant. The regular clientele from Boston and New York enjoy the ambience as well as the services of innkeepers Karl and Jane Sabo, themselves urban refugees. Breakfast and afternoon tea are included. ~ 81 Old Main Street, Deerfield; 413-774-5587, 800-926-3865, fax 413-775-7221; www.deerfieldinn.com, e-mail information@deerfield inn.com. ULTRA-DELUXE.

DINING

What the Pioneer Valley lacks in fancy eateries it makes up for with a solid roster of good, moderately priced restaurants, including a number of ethnic and vegetarian spots.

Traditional New England fare is served at the **Yankee Pedlar Inn**, including clam chowder, chicken pot pie, crab cakes, a large selection of seafood and chicken marsala. The dining room is a handsome Colonial-style scene with wood-planked walls. Closed Monday. ~ 1866 Northampton Street, Holyoke; 413-532-9494, 800-413-3771; www.yankeepedlarinn.com, e-mail info@yankee pedlarinn.com. BUDGET TO DELUXE.

Joe's Café is a quintessential dive, with peeling paint and great Italian food: eggplant parmigiana, spaghetti and a marvelous vegetarian pizza primavera. Mingle with the locals and college students over pitchers of beer and try to figure out exactly what that mural on the wall means. Joe's is an oasis in an area fast succumbing to culinary gentrification. No lunch on weekends from Memorial Day to Labor Day. ~ 33 Market Street, Northampton; 413-584-3168. MODERATE.

At the other end of the Italian food spectrum is **Spoleto**, a local favorite. This place is a real find, with imaginative Italian dishes at reasonable prices. Dishes include a sublime chicken rollatini, homemade pasta served with shrimp, scallops, mussels and calamari, eggplant terrine and veal scallopine. Desserts are homemade, and the espresso is strong. Dinner only. ~ 50 Main Street, Northampton; 413-586-6313, fax 413-585-0978; www.fundin ing.com, e-mail denise@fundining.com. MODERATE TO DELUXE.

Paul and Elizabeth's has a local following for its healthy lunches and dinners. You might be tempted by their salads—

JUDIE'S POINT OF VIEW

Judie's is an Amherst dining institution, noted for its sun-room view of the comings and goings of downtown Amherst, its chic clientele and wonderful desserts. The cuisine here is "nouvelle à la Judie" and includes some unusual dishes like Southwest steak and a basil pesto chicken breast stuffed into an oversized popover. Desserts include chocolate decadence treat and fried bananas and ice cream. Closed Monday. ~ 51 North Pleasant Street, Amherst; 413-253-3491; www.judiesrestaurant.com. MODERATE.

tabouli, spinach and egg—good soups, fish broiled with tamari, a vegetable and seafood tempura, sandwiches or pasta. Decor is light and airy; some nights the place can be bursting with vegetarian baby boomers and their vegetarian babies, but the staff always keeps its cool. ~ Thorne's Market, 150 Main Street, Northampton; 413-584-4832, fax 413-582-7999. BUDGET TO MODERATE.

The dining room at the **Lord Jeffery Inn** is a good choice for a more formal meal (though in Amherst, a college town, *formal* means anything except jeans). It's a big Colonial-style room with a fireplace; tables are lit by oil lamps. Menu items include such dishes as herb-seared shrimp, duck breast and braised lamb shank plus some house specialties, including a wonderful lobster ravioli as an appetizer. ~ 30 Boltwood Avenue, Amherst; 413-253-2576, 800-742-0358, fax 413-256-6152; www.lordjefferyinn.com, e-mail info@lordjefferyinn.com. MODERATE TO DELUXE.

SHOPPING

Holyoke Mall at Ingleside has over 185 specialty and department stores, including **Macy's** (413-538-7360), **JC Penney** (413-536-3963), **Banana Republic** (413-533-8223) and the **GAP** (413-538-7064). ~ 50 Holyoke Street, Holyoke; 413-536-1440; www.holyokemall.com.

A favorite Sunday excursion for locals is the **Yankee Candle** flagship store, with its fragrant assortment of hundreds of hand-dipped candles along with a remarkable Christmas shop featuring ornaments and toys from around the world. Two cafés offer light lunches, and afterwards you can wander through their candle-making museum. ~ Routes 5 and 10, South Deerfield; 413-665-8306, 800-243-1776, fax 413-665-4815; www.yankeecandle.com, e-mail info@yankeecandle.com.

> Pioneer Valley is noted for its craftspeople, who continue traditions started in the 17th century.

The Pioneer Valley is especially noted for the large number of craftspeople who make their home here, and their presence is reflected in several fine shops in Northampton and beyond.

In Northampton, **Pinch** carries a wide variety of handmade pottery, ceramics and related gifts. ~ 179 Main Street, Northampton; 413-586-4509; www.epinch.com.

Thorne's Marketplace is an old department store renovated into five floors of shops and boutiques, including a record store, a hair salon, clothing stores and toy shops, as well as a natural-foods restaurant. ~ 150 Main Street, Northampton; 413-584-5582; www.thornesmarketplace.com.

Valley Antiques carries a wide range of items from stained glass lamps and mirrors to mahogany pieces and Victorian reproductions. They also stock a variety of mission-style antiques.

Closed Sunday through Tuesday. ~ 15 Bridge Street, Northampton; 413-584-1956.

Check out the **Salmon Falls Artisans Showroom**, set in a late-19th-century post-and-beam granary overlooking the famous Bridge of Flowers. The works of nearly 200 artisans are showcased. ~ 1 Ashfield Street, Shelburne Falls; phone/fax 413-625-9833.

NIGHTLIFE

Concerts, entertainment and sporting events are held regularly at the **Mass Mutual Center**, formerly the Springfield Civic Center. ~ 1277 Main Street, Springfield; 413-787-6610; www.mccahome.com.

Every Friday and Saturday, **Cafe Lebanon** offers two nightly belly dancing shows. Order a drink at the bar or make dinner reservations and enjoy. ~ 1390 Main Street, Springfield; 413-737-7373; www.cafelebanon.com, e-mail info@cafelebanon.com.

For a wide array of folk, blues, African, Caribbean and Celtic music nightly in a coffeehouse setting, check out the **Iron Horse Music Hall**. There's a restaurant, a good dancefloor and a wide selection of imported beers at this intimate spot. Cover. ~ 20 Center Street, Northampton; 413-584-0610; www.iheg.com.

Northampton is also home to the **Academy of Music**—the sixth oldest continuously operating theater in the country. ~ 274 Main Street, Northampton; 413-584-8435.

Pearl Street Night Club features local and nationally known rock, jazz, blues, reggae and funk performers in an art deco–style nightclub. Check its website for calendar of events and ticket sales. Cover. ~ 10 Pearl Street, Northampton; 413-586-8686; www.iheg.com.

The **Fine Arts Center** at the University of Massachusetts offers concerts, plays, lectures and dance events during the regular school year. ~ Amherst; 413-545-2511.

BEACHES & PARKS

SKINNER STATE PARK Located atop the Holyoke Range, this park offers a view of the Connecticut River that Thomas Cole make famous in his 1836 painting, *The Oxbow*, depicting an ancient bend in the river. Here the Summit House, a Victorian-style hotel built in 1851, has been restored as a visitors center. Birdwatchers can view hawk migrations in mid-April and mid-September. A picnic area, restrooms and the Summit House are available Memorial Day through October. Day-use fee on weekends and holidays, $2. ~ Off Route 47 on Mountain Road, Hadley; 413-586-0350, fax 413-586-5380; www.mass.gov/dcr, e-mail mass.parks@state.ma.us.

▲ Nearby, at Daughters of the American Revolution State Forest (Route 112, 78 Cape Street, Goshen; 413-268-7098), there are 51 tent/RV sites (no hookups); $12 per night for Massachusetts residents, $14 per night for non-residents. Regular campsites closed Columbus Day to Memorial Day, but winter sites are available. ~ 877-422-6762; www.reserveamerica.com.

MOUNT SUGARLOAF STATE RESERVATION Jutting up out of the Connecticut River Valley farmland like a huge monument to nature, Mount Sugarloaf shows a red sandstone face and varied natural life. This forested, 532-acre reservation overlooks the Connecticut River from on high and is a foliage season favorite. You'll find picnic areas, restrooms and a lookout tower. Closed in winter. ~ 103 Sugarloaf Street, Deerfield; 413-665-2928.

MOHAWK TRAIL STATE FOREST One of the state's well-kept secrets, this forest covers over 6000 acres spread along the Deerfield and Cold Rivers. The old Indian Trail used by Mohawks to travel from upstate New York to the Pioneer Valley is etched into the woods here, and open fields and meadows lead down to the river. Fish for trout on the Deerfield River and take a dip in a sheltered, sandy pool off the Cold River, or in the small waterfalls downstream. This park has a regular camping clientele because of its size and the range of activities available. Facilities include picnic areas, showers and restrooms. ~ Route 2, three miles west of Charlemont; 413-339-5504, fax 413-339-6682; www.mass.gov/dcr, e-mail mass.parks@state.ma.us.

▲ There are 56 tent/RV sites (no hookups), $12 per night for Massachusetts residents, $14 per night for non-residents. ~ 877-422-6762; www.reserveamerica.com.

The Happy Valley

To its many inhabitants with alternative sexual orientations, the Pioneer Valley is fondly referred to as "The Happy Valley." Originally coined in the 1960s, the name was adopted by the gay community to describe this vibrant lesbian enclave. A scenic rural retreat with fine inns and restaurants, the Pioneer Valley is a relaxing vacation spot. With the second-largest lesbian population in the country (after the San Francisco Bay Area) and a sizable population of gay men, the Valley offers a rural version of the gay-friendly atmosphere found in such cities as New York or San Francisco.

HAPPY AND GAY

The Happy Valley's five colleges—especially Smith and the University of Massachusetts—sponsor gay dances and events just about every weekend. *The Five College Bulletin* (available in campus buildings and at bus-stop racks) is a good resource, or you can check flyers on campus to find out what's happening.

A number of the Valley's happy denizens are spread out along quiet backroads and in the outskirts of towns, enjoying the peace of the country; many of the gay establishments, consequently, are also widely dispersed throughout the area. Northampton (or "Noho" to locals) serves as the pulse of the Valley's gay scene. It's here that you'll find the concentration of gay clubs, restaurants and inns. You can pick up a copy of *The Metroline*, a free biweekly, at local cafés. Or you can get the Boston-based weekly, *Bay Windows*.

LODGING

Relax at the **Old Mill on the Falls Bed and Breakfast**, a pale yellow country inn maintained by friendly innkeeper Ted Jarrett. All nine rooms include private baths and many have windows looking out on the front rose bushes and patio tables. The full breakfast provided is prepared by a veteran chef and served on the deck overlooking a waterfall. European travelers will feel at home because, between the innkeeper and the chef, five languages are spoken, including Italian and French. ~ 87 School Street, Hatfield; 413-247-3301; www.oldmillbnb.net. MODERATE TO DELUXE.

DINING

For gourmet vegetarian food, try lesbian-owned **Bela**. A lively, casual eatery, Bela features an eclectic variety of healthful entrées. This is a popular spot. Closed Sunday and Monday. ~ 68 Masonic Street, Northampton; 413-586-8011. BUDGET TO MODERATE.

The crowded, happening **Haymarket Cafe** serves coffee, tea and pastries and has a fresh juice bar. In addition, the kitchen whips up tantalizing vegetarian and vegan fare using Eastern, Latin American and other ethnic flavors. Open for lunch and dinner. ~ 185 Main Street, Northampton; 413-586-9969. BUDGET.

Named after the inventor of the graham cracker, Dr. Sylvester Graham, **Sylvester's Restaurant** is popular among both gays and straights. One dining room has a coffee bar. The other is modern and airy with lots of windows. Lunch entrées include soups, salads and sandwiches. No dinner. ~ 111 Pleasant Street, Northampton; 413-586-5343; www.sylvestersrestaurant.com, e-mail sylvestersrestaurant@verizon.net. BUDGET.

SHOPPING

One of the area's best bookstores, **Northampton Pride & Joy** has an excellent selection of feminist and gay/lesbian titles as well as gifts, clothing, jewelry, music, videos and locally made crafts. ~ 20 Crafts Avenue, Northampton; 413-585-0683, fax 413-584-4848; www.nohoprideandjoy.com, e-mail info@nohoprideandjoy.com.

The **Food for Thought** bookstore is well-stocked with gay/lesbian and progressive political material. ~ 106 North Pleasant

Street, Amherst; 413-253-5432, fax 413-256-8329; www.foodforthoughtbooks.com.

NIGHTLIFE The motto at **Diva's Nightclub** is "dance like no one is watching." And judging by the sweat and smiles on the mixed crowd, that's exactly what Diva-goers do. Deejay music and drinks encourage the festivities. Closed Sunday and Monday. Cover on Friday and Saturday. ~ 492 Pleasant Street, Northhampton; 413-586-8161; www.divasofnoho.com.

The Berkshires

The lay of the land is different in the Berkshires. It's more rural than the Pioneer Valley and central Massachusetts, with more broad, open valleys and stretches of farmland and forest. There are three kinds of towns here: old mill towns like Dalton and Great Barrington, which have their own red-brick, utilitarian beauty; small country towns like New Ashford and Monterey, with tree-lined greens, a general store or two and a white church; and tourist towns like Lenox and Stockbridge, whose identities are closely tied to a plethora of cultural activities. Despite the tourism and second-home building boom of the 1980s, the area is still remarkably rural, and you can find yourself in a Lenox traffic jam one minute, and a few minutes later on the open road with nothing but lush green scenery around you.

The Berkshires have a noteworthy cultural heritage as well. For years, the hills' natural beauty and remoteness drew authors, poets and artists. The rich followed. At the turn of the 20th century, the area was nicknamed the "inland Newport" for the large number of wealthy families who built their ornate "cottages" (actually, they were 20-odd-room mansions!) here as summer retreats.

SIGHTS The gateway to the northern Berkshires, the city of **North Adams** was once a thriving manufacturing center of textiles and electrical components. Today, the old mills lie idle, and North Adams is a bit down-at-the-heels. The city may be on the comeback trail, however, thanks to the construction of the **Massachusetts Museum of Contemporary Art** (MASS MoCA). The town converted an abandoned 27-building mill complex into the world's largest contemporary art museum. Its galleries feature rotating exhibits and a packed schedule of performing-arts events. The complex is listed on the National Historic Register. Closed Tuesday from September through June. ~ 87 Marshall Street, North Adams; 413-664-4481, fax 413-663-8548; www.massmoca.org, e-mail info@massmoca.org.

Natural Bridge State Park is the site of the only natural marble bridge in North America, formed by the raging waters of melting glaciers millions of years ago. Also interesting to look at are the many carvings done by quarrymen and visitors, a num-

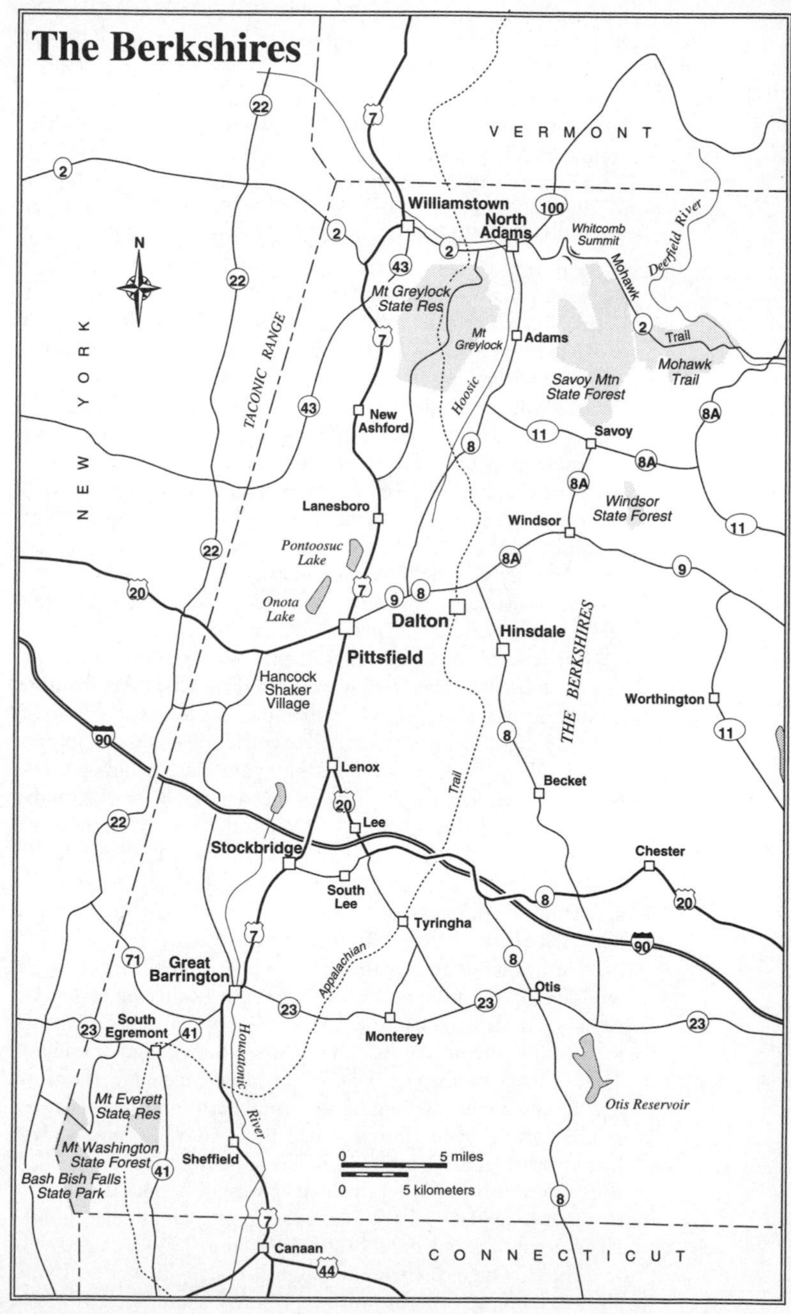
The Berkshires
VERMONT
NEW YORK
CONNECTICUT
TACONIC RANGE
THE BERKSHIRES
Williamstown
North Adams
Whitcomb Summit
Deerfield River
Mohawk
Trail
Mohawk Trail
Mt Greylock State Res
Mt Greylock
Adams
Hoosic
Savoy Mtn State Forest
New Ashford
Savoy
Windsor State Forest
Windsor
Lanesboro
Pontoosuc Lake
Onota Lake
Dalton
Hinsdale
Pittsfield
Hancock Shaker Village
Worthington
Lenox
Lee
Becket
Stockbridge
South Lee
Chester
Tyringha
Appalachian
Great Barrington
Otis
Monterey
South Egremont
Housatonic River
Otis Reservoir
Mt Everett State Res
Mt Washington State Forest
Bash Bish Falls State Park
Sheffield
0 5 miles
0 5 kilometers
Canaan

ber of them dating back to the 1800s. Closed Columbus Day to Memorial Day. Parking fee. ~ Route 8, North Adams; 413-663-6392, 413-663-8469 (off-season).

Traveling into downtown North Adams, you'll pass huge mills—monuments to bygone days. **Western Gateway Heritage State Park Visitors Center**, located in a former railroad yard, has a fascinating exhibit on the construction of the four-and-three-fourths-mile Hoosac Tunnel between North Adams and Rowe. The tunnel opened rail traffic between Boston and Albany, and, at the time of its construction in the mid-19th century, was considered an engineering wonder. ~ Off Route 8 at Furnace Street Bypass (between State and Furnace streets), North Adams; 413-663-6312, fax 413-664-0033; www.mass.gov/dcr/wghp, e-mail western.gateway-hsp@state.ma.us.

The **Williams College Museum of Art** is in an octagonal building inspired by Monticello and a wing designed by Charles Moore. The museum is one of the best college art museums in the country, with changing exhibitions as well as a strong collection of older and contemporary watercolors, oils, photographs, fabric art and sculpture. Works by Charles and Maurice Prendergast provide a look at 19th-century seaside New England. Closed Monday. ~ Route 2, Williamstown; 413-597-2429, fax 413-458-9017; www.wcma.org, e-mail wcma@williams.edu.

Just west of the center of Williamstown, you'll find another fine-art museum. The **Sterling and Francine Clark Art Institute**, located on parklike grounds with expansive lawns, picnic areas and walking trails, has an extensive collection of French impressionist, Old Master, and 19th-century paintings, including works by Renoir, Monet, Degas, Sargent and Homer. Closed Monday from September through June. ~ 225 South Street, Williamstown; 413-458-2303; www.clarkart.edu, e-mail info@clarkart.edu.

If you love the furniture and crafts of the Shakers, you may also enjoy learning more about how they lived, with a visit to **Hancock Shaker Village**. Restored in the 1960s, the Shaker settlement at Hancock was the third of 19 communities to be established by the followers of Mother Ann Lee in the early 19th century. At its height in the 1840s, the population in Hancock reached 300 members, divided into six groups called "families." The Shaker economy was built on agriculture, including the growing, processing and selling of medicinal herbs and seeds, as well as the crafting of furniture for which they have become so well known. The guides stationed in the buildings are an excellent source of information on the Shaker way of life. Crafts demonstrations take place on a regular basis in many buildings, and the village's round stone barn, originally built in 1826, is a real sight to behold. Open year-round but call ahead in winter. (Note: Visitors coming from the north on Route 7 should be aware that

Hancock Shaker Village cannot be reached through the town of Hancock. Keep heading south toward Pittsfield and take Route 20 west.) Admission. ~ Route 20, Pittsfield; 413-443-0188, 800-817-1137, fax 413-447-9357; www.hancockshakervillage.org, e-mail info@hancockshakervillage.org.

With a population of about 50,000, **Pittsfield** is the largest city in Berkshire County but it's not the most attractive. One exception to Pittsfield's otherwise dull demeanor is the **Berkshire Museum**, which is devoted to art, natural science and history, with family-friendly interactive exhibits. Established in 1903 by Zenas Crane, a member of the Crane paper family, the museum has 18 galleries of permanent and changing exhibitions, including works by a number of Hudson River School painters and early American portraits by Bierstadt, Copley and Peale. There are also classic and modern sculptures as well as an aquarium with a touch tank. Admission. ~ Route 7, Pittsfield; 413-443-7171, fax 413-443-2135; www.berkshiremuseum.org, e-mail info@berkshiremuseum.org.

Pittsfield is also home to **Arrowhead**, the house where Herman Melville wrote *Moby Dick* while living here from 1850 to 1863. Headquarters for the Berkshire County Historical Society, the house displays exhibitions and vintage furnishings. There is also a gift shop. Open Friday through Wednesday from Memorial Day through Columbus Day, and by appointment the rest of the year. Admission. ~ 780 Holmes Road, Pittsfield; 413-442-1793, fax 413-443-1449; www.mobydick.org.

"The **Lenox** and **Stockbridge** region is Berkshire in its best dress suit and evening gown," wrote the authors of a Federal Writers Project book on the Berkshires in 1939. The writers were no doubt assessing the remnants of the so-called "Gilded Age" in the days

THE BEST STAGE OF SUMMER

In summer, the 2002 Tony Award recipient **Williamstown Theatre Festival** draws crowds from around the country. One of the nation's finest summer theater offerings, the festival showcases productions that are weightier than the average summer stock, such as *The Legend of Oedipus* and works by Anton Chekhov and Tennessee Williams. Regulars include Joanne Woodward and Paul Newman, Dianne Wiest and Olympia Dukakis. The schedule is usually announced in mid-May, and it's a good idea to order tickets as early as possible. Season runs from July to late August. ~ P.O. Box 517, Williamstown, MA 01267; 413-597-3400 (box office), 413-597-3200 (information line), fax 413-458-3147; www.wtfestival.org, e-mail wtinfo@wtfestival.org.

before income taxes, when the Vanderbilts, Carnegies, Westinghouses and others frolicked at their famous "Berkshire Cottages."

These estates, with their ornate architecture, elaborate furnishings and lovely gardens hold an allure even for the staunchest of socialists. For your viewing pleasure are 20 to 25 summer mansions from the time when Lenox was known as the "Inland Newport." Among these estates are:

The Mount was the home of Pulitzer Prize–winning author Edith Wharton from 1902 to 1911. Wharton, in her day a recognized expert on interior design, architecture and gardens, designed the interior as well as the gardens; the home is the only complete example of her design theories. The white American Classical mansion has marble floors and fireplaces, elaborate molding and plaster ceilings, and beautiful grounds. Closed November through April. Call for tour schedule. Admission. ~ 2 Plunkett Street, Lenox; 413-637-1899, 888-637-1902, fax 413-637-0619; www.edithwharton.org, e-mail admin@edithwharton.org.

Chesterwood is an 1898 Colonial Revival mansion that served as the summer estate of Daniel Chester French, sculptor of *The Minute Man* and the Lincoln Memorial. French traveled widely, and his home is decorated with a remarkable collection of European and American furnishings, antiques and sculptures gathered in his travels. The grounds feature country gardens and woodland walks, and his studio houses the small-gauge railroad track that French used to move his sculptures into the natural light for viewing. The plaster casts of the Lincoln statue were made here and, as you'll see, still dominate the interior. Closed mid-October to mid-May. Admission. ~ Off of Route 183, Stockbridge; 413-298-3579, fax 413-298-3973; www.chesterwood.org.

sights

AUTHOR FAVORITE

Although there are "Norman Rockwell museums" in other places around New England, the **Norman Rockwell Museum** is the only collection of original paintings authorized by the Rockwell family. The museum houses the largest collection of Rockwell art in existence, including selections from his *Saturday Evening Post* covers, portraits and advertising works and the famous Four Freedoms and Main Street at Christmas. As a center devoted to the art of illustration, the museum also exhibits the works of contemporary and past artists. The museum is open daily year-round. Rockwell's original Stockbridge Studio, located on-site, is open May through October. Admission. ~ Route 183, Stockbridge; 413-298-4100, fax 413-298-4145; www.nrm.org, e-mail postmaster@nrm.org.

Naumkeag, designed by Stanford White, was built in 1885 for Joseph Choate, the ambassador to England. The stately home remains an excellent example of turn-of-the-20th-century design, in its architecture as well as its landscaping and furnishings. Although it is not the largest of the mansions, Naumkeag's collection of antiques and porcelain from the Far East make it worth a visit. And, like those of the other cottages, the gardens and grounds are magnificent. Closed Columbus Day to Memorial Day. Admission. ~ Prospect Hill Road, Stockbridge; 413-298-3239, fax 413-298-5239; www.thetrustees.org, e-mail westregion@ttor.org.

Route 7 south of Lenox takes you through another piece of lovely farmland, where you'll get a sense of just how rural this area is. Before too long you'll come to the town of Stockbridge, a pretty, if increasingly glossy, small town whose tree-lined main street is dominated by small shops and the rambling wooden Red Lion Inn. Stockbridge has been immortalized in popular culture in two very different ways: as the setting for Arlo Guthrie's song "Alice's Restaurant" and as the subject of works by its most famous former resident, artist Norman Rockwell.

Stockbridge center, with many shops and a few galleries, is worth a stroll. An interesting stop is the **Image Gallery**, owned by photojournalist Clemens Kalischer. ~ Main Street, Stockbridge; phone/fax 413-298-5500; e-mail inform@bcn.net.

The home of poet William Cullen Bryant, **Great Barrington** is a departure from the country-style villages of Stockbridge and Lenox. Its funky downtown looks as though it came straight out of an old Jimmy Stewart movie.

For a scenic country drive, take Route 23 east from Great Barrington to Monterey, and head north to the town of Tyringham.

For further information on the Berkshires, contact the **Berkshire Visitors Bureau.** ~ Colonial Theater Annex, South Street, Pittsfield; 413-443-9186, 800-237-5747, fax 413-443-1970; www.berkshires.org, e-mail bvb@berkshires.org.

LODGING

This area offers a large selection of elegant accommodations and small bed and breakfasts. Restrictions are common here, however, and some of the room rate cards are as complicated as life insurance policies. In a nutshell: rates are highest (and they do get high!) on weekends in summer and fall; most places near Lenox require a two-night minimum stay on weekends during Tanglewood season, from mid-June to early September.

A resort built around a country-inn motif, **The Orchards** offers 49 rooms individually decorated in English antiques and fancy bedspreads, some with fireplaces, refrigerators and marble-floored bathrooms. The ambience here is one of quiet elegance, despite the inn's incongruous proximity to the Route 2 commercial strip. Tea is served each afternoon in the graciously appointed lobby, and guests get a chocolate chip cookie with their turned-down beds each evening. On-site amenities include a whirlpool, a sauna, concierge service and a restaurant. ~ Route 2, Williamstown; 413-458-9611, 800-225-1517, fax 413-458-1977; www.orchardshotel.com, e-mail reservations@orchardshotel.com. ULTRA-DELUXE.

The **Maple Terrace Motel** is a budget-conscious traveler's find. The 17 rooms are clean and cozy and the Maple Terrace, set back from the street, is quieter than others along the highway. Behind the motel is a two-acre field with a spacious heated swimming pool, picnic tables, a playground and several large weeping willow trees. This is a good place for families and is within walking distance of the Williamstown Theatre Festival, shopping and restaurants. Continental breakfast. ~ 555 Main Street, Route 2, Williamstown; phone/fax 413-458-9677; www.mapleterrace.com, e-mail stay@mapleterrace.com. MODERATE.

HIDDEN ►

River Bend Farm is a historic bed and breakfast set in a tavern built in 1770 by Colonel Benjamin Simonds, one of the founders of Williamstown. The place has been meticulously restored and has shared baths and four rooms, each individually decorated in Colonial antiques. Its location makes it convenient to the Williams College campus. Expanded continental breakfast. Closed November through March. ~ 643 Simonds Road, Williamstown; 413-458-3121; www.riverbendfarmbb.com. MODERATE.

Canyon Ranch in the Berkshires is an East Coast version of a famous Tucson fitness resort. It's housed at the 120-acre estate called Bellefontaine, one of the most ornate of the original Berkshire "cottages" and a replica of Petit Trianon at Versailles, built by Louis XV. The 126-room renovated resort is geared for busy

AUTHOR FAVORITE

Red Lion Inn is a New England classic. Originally built in 1773 as a stagecoach stop, the inn was destroyed by fire and rebuilt in 1897. Today, the rambling wooden structure is one of the few remaining old wood hotels in the country. An icon of the Berkshires, the Red Lion serves as the centerpiece of Stockbridge center. The lobby/parlor, with its fireplace, comfortable old couches and rich Oriental rugs, is always full of people. And there may be no finer place to enjoy a summer afternoon drink than from a rocking chair on the front porch. There are 108 rooms (some with shared bath), including some suites with parlors, decorated with antiques and reproductions. Although it offers modern amenities like an outdoor pool, the Red Lion is an elegant old lady of a place that conjures up images of a bygone era. ~ 30 Main Street, Stockbridge; 413-298-5545, fax 413-298-5130; www.redlioninn.com. MODERATE TO ULTRA-DELUXE.

city folk looking for a bit of down time away from it all. There's a full fitness program, complementary lectures on health and wellness topics, gourmet "spa cuisine," indoor and outdoor pools, walking trails and gardens. ~ Bellefontaine, Kemble Street, Lenox; 413-637-4100, 800-742-9000, fax 413-637-0057; www.canyonranch.com. ULTRA-DELUXE.

A very homey Berkshire cottage, **Garden Gables Inn** is a lovely white clapboard house built in 1780. Although it is located within walking distance of downtown Lenox, the inn is quiet and relaxed, with nice gardens and a swimming pool. The inn's 18 rooms are individually decorated in a mix of styles, and all have private baths; some have jacuzzis or fireplaces, others balconies with a view of the pool. A welcoming porch is ideal for lazing about. The inn has many regular long-term visitors. Full breakfast is offered in a cozy dining room. ~ 135 Main Street, Lenox; 413-637-0193, fax 413-637-4554; www.lenoxinn.com, e-mail innkeeper@lenoxinn.com. DELUXE TO ULTRA-DELUXE.

The **Village Inn** is an 18th-century hostelry with 32 rooms, all with private baths. All rooms are furnished with country antiques and reproductions, some with working fireplaces and four-poster beds. This Federal-style building has served as an inn since 1775, and the innkeepers have restored and modernized it without destroying its integrity. The low-beamed tavern downstairs offers a full bar. This place has a comfortable, homey feel despite its size and is conveniently located in the center of Lenox. ~ 16 Church Street, Lenox; 413-637-0020, 800-253-0917, fax 413-637-9756; www.villageinn-lenox.com, e-mail info@villageinn-lenox.com. DELUXE TO ULTRA-DELUXE.

Located right in the village of Lenox but on three very private acres, the **Walker House Inn** is a gay-friendly hostelry with eight rooms (all with private baths). It's a lovely house, built in 1804 with an addition built in 1906. The rooms are named after composers and decorated individually. There are lots of antiques around and fireplaces in many of the guest rooms. The parlor has a grand piano and another fireplace, and movies are shown on a 12-foot-wide screen in the library. ~ 64 Walker Street, Lenox; 413-637-1271, 800-235-3098, fax 413-637-2387; www.walkerhouse.com, e-mail walkerhouse.inn@verizon.net. MODERATE TO ULTRA-DELUXE.

The **Historic Merrell Inn** wears its age well, having welcomed guests since 1794, when it was the next-to-last stop on a busy stagecoach route between northwestern Connecticut and the Berkshires. Original furnishings, such as the wooden birdcage bar in the dining room, the only complete and unmodified one of its kind in the country, adorn the inn. The ten guest rooms are luxurious and, for the most part, quite large, although a few of the bathrooms are small but adequate. Some beds have canopies, ◄ HIDDEN and four of the rooms have working fireplaces. The owners continually search for antique furnishings that complement the inn's historic past. Take a look at the book in the dining room that records the names of the inn's visitors and their horses on the corresponding date in the early 19th century. ~ 1565 Pleasant Street, South Lee; 413-243-1794, 800-243-1794, fax 413-243-2669; www.merrell-inn.com, e-mail info@merrell-inn.com. DELUXE TO ULTRA-DELUXE.

For a bed and breakfast that focuses on informal hospitality—the innkeeper calls it a "chintz-free zone"—spend a night or two at **Race Brook Lodge** in the southwestern corner of Massachusetts. It's a restored barn with a variety of 30 rooms (all with private bath). It also has suites, which are perfect for a small group. The country decor—quilts, understated stenciling and hooked rugs on plank floors—allows the beauty of the building to speak for itself. Swim in the pool, take a walk from the lodge to the Race Brook waterfall, then up to the Appalachian Trail. You can also enjoy meals in the historic Stagecoach Tavern Thursday through Saturday. Or poke around in the nearby antique shops: Sheffield is a mecca for antiquing fiends from all over New England. ~ 864 South Under Mountain Road/Route 41, Sheffield; 413-229-2916, 800-725-6343, fax 413-229-6629; www.rblodge.com, e-mail rblodge@adelphia.net. DELUXE.

The 1780 **Egremont Inn** is a cozy country inn with 20 rooms decorated in 19th-century furnishings. A feeling of subdued elegance is conveyed by a long white porch where guests enjoy coffee, cocktails and dinner during summer months. A Colonial-era tavern with a low, beamed ceiling serves dinner Wednesday through Sunday and adds to the ambience. The inn also has a pool and tennis courts. Modified American plan offered. Three-night minimum stay required in summer. ~ 10 Old Sheffield Road, South Egremont; 413-528-2111, 800-859-1780; www.egremontinn.com, e-mail info@egremontinn.com. ULTRA-DELUXE.

Days Inn offers proximity to southern Berkshire attractions in a motel setting. For those who like to stay in places with tele-

BERKSHIRES BUDGETING TIPS

Budget lodging is virtually impossible to find in the Berkshires. One economical strategy is to make a home base in towns slightly away from the often-crowded and expensive Lenox–Stockbridge area. To the north, Williamstown offers a wider price range of motels and inns, with fewer restrictions. Just south of Stockbridge, the small towns of South Egremont, Sheffield and Great Barrington have many historic and pretty inns and bed and breakfasts.

visions (63 rooms), this is one of the few such motels in the region. ~ 372 Main Street, Great Barrington; phone/fax 413-528-3150, 800-329-7466; www.daysinn.com. MODERATE TO DELUXE.

The Turning Point offers a nonsmoking environment in a handsome, 1790s brick inn that served as a stagecoach stop in the 19th century. The inn has six rooms (two share a bath) and a fully equipped two-bedroom ultra-deluxe-priced cottage, with lovely grounds and hiking trails through the surrounding woods and fields. There are two chefs on the premises, so prepare to eat well. Breakfast (included) is served daily; dinner is available on Saturday with prior arrangements. ~ 3 Lake Buel Road at Route 23, Great Barrington; 413-528-4777, fax 413-528-7799; www.turningpointinn.com, e-mail turningpointinn@aol.com. MODERATE TO ULTRA-DELUXE.

Berkshire Folkstone Bed and Breakfast can match you up with small country inns in the Berkshire and Pioneer Valley areas. ~ 101 Mulberry Street C-1, Springfield; 413-247-5800, 800-762-2751.

DINING

There are many restaurants to choose from in the Berkshires, roughly divided into two classes: the expensive, fancy places that draw weekenders and tourists, and the places where locals eat, which are generally cheaper, casual and strong on all-American, meat-and-potatoes menus.

Church Street Cafe offers an eclectic lunch and dinner menu in a pleasant outdoor café or indoor setting in the heart of Lenox's shopping district. The menu changes over four times a year, and lunch may feature sandwiches and burgers, as well as more exotic fare like Louisiana gumbo, tabouli salad and bean quesadillas; dinner features Thai beef salad, Jamaican "jerked" chicken and red chile pasta with corn, peppers, cilantro and jalapeños. Closed Sunday and Monday from Columbus Day to Memorial Day. ~ 65 Church Street, Lenox; 413-637-2745; www.churchstreetcafe.biz, e-mail churstcafe@aol.com. MODERATE TO ULTRA-DELUXE.

Wheatleigh is a restaurant of some renown, within walking distance of Tanglewood. It's a special spot, known for fine food and formal service, located in a restored 19th-century Italian palazzo built for a countess. The decor recalls the splendor of the Gilded Age, with a fireplace and crystal chandeliers. Wheatleigh serves Americanized French cuisine in four-course and six-course prix-fixe meals, and the menu may include such imaginative items as citrus-marinated Scottish salmon on a wild-rice blini with Osetra caviar and seared breast of free-range duck with potato, vegetables and fresh black huckleberries. Reservations required; jackets for men are preferred. Open daily during the summer; abbreviated hours the rest of the year. ~ Hawthorne

Road, Lenox; 413-637-0610; www.wheatleigh.com, e-mail info@wheatleigh.com. ULTRA-DELUXE.

The **Red Lion Inn** has a menu that is contemporary New England, featuring roast turkey and clam chowder. You can choose the Colonial-style formal dining room, with pink-and-rose wallpaper, Norman Rockwell prints on the walls, and fresh flowers on the table. Or try the more casual tavern, with its publike atmosphere, wide-plank floorboards and beamed ceiling. In good weather, meals can be enjoyed outside. ~ 30 Main Street, Stockbridge; 413-298-5545, fax 413-298-5130; www.redlioninn.com, e-mail info@redlioninn.com. DELUXE TO ULTRA-DELUXE.

The **Castle Street Cafe** is a lively bistro known for its creative pastas and grilled fish dishes. It's a handsome spot with an exposed brick wall. There's a full jazz bar in the back. Dinner only. Closed Tuesday. ~ 10 Castle Street, Great Barrington; 413-528-5244; www.castlestreetcafe.com, e-mail info@castlestreetcafe.com. DELUXE.

Once an old blacksmith's shop, and yes, even an old mill, **The Old Mill** is now one of the nicer restaurants in the southern Berkshires. The menu includes roast Portland cod with lobster sauce and mashed Yukon golds in addition to chicken, calf's liver, steaks and chops. The building itself is a handsome one, set on a river, with large beams, a cozy bar and a double-sided fireplace. Dinner only. Closed Monday from November through May. ~ Route 23, South Egremont; 413-528-1421, fax 413-528-0007. DELUXE TO ULTRA-DELUXE.

SHOPPING

Serious antique hunters head to the southern Berkshires and the towns of Egremont, South Egremont and Sheffield. There are dozens of shops in this corner of the state, featuring pieces from early American to European to deco to plain old junk.

AUTHOR FAVORITE

Gateways Inn & Restaurant is one of the most highly acclaimed dining spots in Lenox. The restaurant is located on the first floor of the small and elegant Gateways Inn, built in 1912 as the summer mansion of Harley Procter of Procter and Gamble. The entranceway is graced with a sweeping mahogany staircase, rich tapestries and beautiful flower arrangements. Gateways offers American cuisine with a European influence such as roasted rack of baby New Zealand lamb, and homemade yukon potato gnocchi. Save room for the *tiramisu* (or sorbet if you possess restraint). No lunch in the winter. Closed Monday. ~ 51 Walker Street, Lenox; 413-637-2532, fax 413-637-1432; www.gatewaysinn.com, e-mail innkeeper@gatewaysinn.com. ULTRA-DELUXE.

Vintage furniture, lamps and housewares overflow at **Corner House Antiques**, a picturesque two-story barn on a country road. While you can spend plenty of time on the first floor eyeing the elegant glass light fixtures and mahogany book cases, you'll want to head upstairs to view their specialty pieces—wicker. Literally floor-to-ceiling, antique wicker furniture hangs overhead while rockers, chairs and tables are stacked high or set up for easy browsing. Call ahead for hours. ~ Route 7, Sheffield; 413-229-6627; www.americanantiquewicker.com.

NIGHTLIFE

On weekends **The Orchards** features soft rock by a pianist in its pub. ~ Route 2, Williamstown; 413-458-9611.

Lenox is the summer home to the **Boston Symphony Orchestra**, which performs through the summer months. ~ 297 West Street, Lenox; 617-266-1492 or 413-637-1600 (between June and September); www.bso.org.

Shakespeare & Company offers theatrical performances during its May-through-October season. Call ahead for schedule. ~ 70 Kemble Street, Lenox; 413-637-1199; www.shakespeare.org.

Jacob's Pillow Dance Festival produces summer dance performances featuring companies from a variety of distant lands, including Cambodia, Indonesia, Europe and Africa. Closed September to late June. ~ 358 George Carter Road, Becket; 413-243-0745; www.jacobspillow.org, e-mail info@jacobspillow.org.

The **Lion's Den** regularly showcases folk music with occasional bluegrass, blues and jazz. ~ Red Lion Inn, Main Street, Stockbridge; 413-298-5545.

BEACHES & PARKS

SAVOY MOUNTAIN STATE FOREST Nearly 11,000 acres, this popular retreat bordering on the Berkshire hills is favored by families. North and South ponds offer fishing and swimming, and campsites are in an old apple orchard. The park has miles of hiking trails, including a route to Tannery Falls. The dramatic set of cascading waterfalls that once powered small mills is now one of the prettiest spots in western Massachusetts. There's good trout fishing in North Pond, and trout and bass are found in Burnett and Bogg ponds. North Pond and South Pond have swimming beaches. Non-motorized boats are allowed. There are picnic areas, restrooms and a nature center. Parking fee, $5. ~ Off Routes 2 and 116, Savoy; 413-663-8469, fax 413-664-8614; www.mass.gov/dem/parks/svym.htm.

▲ There are 45 tent sites; $12 per night for Massachusetts residents, $14 per night for non-residents. Closed mid-October to mid-May. There are also cabins available year-round that sleep up to four people ($30 per night); reservations are required and are taken up to six months in advance.

Text continued on page 428.

The Sounds of Music in Rural Massachusetts

It's said that New England has only two seasons, July and winter. That's not exactly true, of course, but folks here do try to pack as much as possible into the fleeting periods of good weather. Case in point: the large number of concerts and music festivals held in this area during summer and autumn, many spreading out under the warm, open skies. In central and western Massachusetts, visitors have some rich choices when it comes to music, from Cuban jazz under the stars to chamber music in a church.

The undisputed king of the music festivals in this region, and perhaps in the whole country, takes place at the 600-acre Lenox summer home of the Boston Symphony Orchestra. ~ Before mid-June, contact Symphony Hall, Boston, MA 02115; 617-266-1492. After mid-June, contact West Street, Lenox, MA 01240; 413-637-1600; www.bso.org.

Tanglewood takes its name from a story by Nathaniel Hawthorne, and, with its tall and stately pine trees, rolling lawns and nearby mountains, the place is renowned for its physical beauty as well as the quality of the musicians and composers who perform there. These have included Leonard Bernstein, John Williams, Yo-Yo Ma, Itzhak Perlman and jazz performers like Ella Fitzgerald and Ray Charles.

Weekend symphony concerts are held Friday through Sunday in July and August, and chamber music concerts take place most Thursdays and other selected weeknights. Saturday morning rehearsals are open to the public (admission), providing an opportunity to see music-making in a more relaxed setting. Seating is available in the Shed, a covered, open-air theater, or, more reasonably, on the lawn. The tradition on the lawn is to bring a blanket or lawn chairs and an elaborate picnic lunch or dinner, complete with candelabra and champagne.

Tanglewood is just one of many music series and festivals in this region, offering all types of music in some spectacular settings. A sampling of some others:

South Mountain Concerts, a chamber music series running from September to mid-October, takes place in the acoustically superb, 400-seat South Mountain Concert Hall, built in 1918 and listed in the National Historic Register. ~ Box 23, Pittsfield; 413-442-2106, fax 413-442-2171.

Stockbridge Summer Music Series includes light opera, classical music, cabaret and jazz concerts held in a turn-of-the-20th-century mansion (Seven Hills Country Inn in Lenox). A mix of prominent regional and international artists performs Monday and Tuesday in July and August. ~ 40 Plunkett Street, Lenox; 413-443-1138; www.stockbridgesummermusic.org, e-mail info@stockbridgesummermusic.org.

Music in Deerfield offers chamber music from October through April in Northampton and historic Deerfield. ~ P.O. Box 75, Shelburne Falls, MA 01370; 413-774-4200; www.musicindeerfield.org, e-mail info@musicindeerfield.org.

Mohawk Trail Concerts offers summer chamber music concerts in the intimate setting of a charming old white clapboard Federated church on the Mohawk Trail in Charlemont. ~ 75 Bridge Street, Shelburne Falls, MA 01370; 413-625-9511, 888-682-6873; www.mohawktrailconcerts.org, e-mail info@mohawktrailconcerts.org.

Although it's always a good idea to reserve tickets ahead of time for most of these events, last-minute seats are generally available. Check out the local newspapers for concert dates and times, and bring a sweater for those summer evenings that can turn cool once the sun goes down.

WINDSOR STATE FOREST This spot is known for the spectacular Windsor Jambs, a half-mile-long series of waterfalls that travel through sheer granite cliff gorges of up to 80 feet. There are many old roads and trails for hiking and a good 100-foot beach on a dammed-up spot on the Westfield River. There's good trout fishing in the West Branch of the river. This is a popular place for families with small children. You'll find picnic areas and restrooms. Closed Labor Day through Memorial Day. Day-use fee, $5. ~ On River Road off Route 9, Windsor; 413-684-0948 (summer), 413-442-8928 (winter), fax 413-442-5860.

▲ There are 24 sites, for tents only; $8 per night for Massachusetts residents, $10 per night for non-residents.

MOUNT GREYLOCK STATE RESERVATION If you have time for a visit to only one park on your tour, this is the one to see. This 12,500-acre reserve is atop the state's highest mountain. Immortalized by Thoreau, Hawthorne and Melville, Mount Greylock is noted for the number of rare species of bird and plant life, and the views in all directions are truly breathtaking. Hiking trails—including a stretch of the Appalachian Trail—and Nordic ski trails are plentiful. Facilities include picnic areas on the summit and restrooms; Bascom Lodge Visitors Center (closed Columbus Day to Memorial Day; 413-743-1591) has a snack bar and offers dinners by reservation. ~ Off Route 7 in Lanesboro or off Route 2 in North Adams; 413-499-4262, fax 413-442-3364; www.mass.gov/dcr.

Bash Bish Falls State Park, within Mt. Washington State Forest, is home to Bash Bish Falls, featuring 80-foot drops and cascading pools, along with a serene view of farmland.

▲ There are 35 sites; $8 to $10 per night. Reservations: 877-422-6762.

MT. WASHINGTON STATE FOREST This 4000-acre expanse on the New York–Connecticut–Massachusetts border spreads out over mountainous, densely wooded land, and there's a feeling of isolation and solitude here. Even during daylight, watch for deer as you drive into the area; they seem to be everywhere. You can also angle for trout in brooks and streams. All this provides a great escape from the sometimes-madding crowds of Stockbridge and Lenox. Non-motorized boats only. There are picnic areas and restrooms. ~ Off Route 41, Mount Washington; 413-528-0330.

▲ There are 15 hike-in wilderness sites; no fee.

Outdoor Adventures

FISHING

A fishing license is required for all freshwater fishing in Massachusetts. You're likely to hook trout and bass in the numerous lakes and streams. The Deerfield, Connecticut and Westfield rivers are some of the more popular spots.

PIONEER VALLEY Try **Pipione's Sport Shop** for all your fishing equipment needs. ~ 101 Avenue A, Turner Falls; 413-863-4246.

Allure Outfitters has flyfishing trips in the Berkshires. ~ 66 Norman Avenue, Pittsfield; 413-499-2096; www.allure-outfitters.net

CANOEING & KAYAKING

The large number of lakes, ponds and rivers in this region provide ample opportunities for paddlers.

CENTRAL MASSACHUSETTS Canoe, kayak and rowboat rentals are available at **Fin and Feather Sports.** ~ Route 140, Upton; 508-529-3901.

PIONEER VALLEY **Zoar Outdoor** offers raft trips, kayak rentals and canoe and kayak instruction on the Deerfield River. Closed November through March. ~ Mohawk Trail (Route 2), Charlemont; 413-339-4010, 800-532-7483; www.zoaroutdoor.com.

THE BERKSHIRES Canoe and kayak rentals are available through **Berkshire Outfitters.** ~ Route 8, Adams; 413-743-5900; www.berkshireoutfitters.com.

SKIING

The downhill ski areas in this region are tame compared to their sisters to the north, but lift lines are often shorter, the ambience less pretentious and lift tickets cheaper. Lessons and rentals are available at most sites; they're good places to take the family. Those who prefer cross-country will find wonderful spots in the region, from open farmland to wooded state parks. Some state parks' trails are groomed by the ubiquitous (and noisy) snowmobile crowd.

PIONEER VALLEY In Princeton, hit the slopes at **Wachusett Mountain,** which has a 1000-foot vertical drop. Downhill skiing as well as snowboarding are available on this ski area, serviced by 22 trails. ~ 499 Mountain Road, off Route 140; 978-464-2300; www.wachusett.com, e-mail info@wachusett.com.

In Charlemont, **Berkshire East** has a 1180-foot vertical drop. Snowboarders share the runs with downhill skiers, though there is a half pipe on one slope, Exhibition. ~ Mohawk Trail; 413-339-6617; www.berkshireeast.com.

There are twenty-five miles of wide, well-groomed Nordic trails crosshatching **Northfield Mountain.** ~ Route 63, Northfield; 413-659-3714; www.nu.com/northfield.

For a more rustic ski on narrower cross-country paths through the woods, try **Stump Sprouts Guest Lodge and Cross Country Ski Center,** with 25 kilometers of trails. There are also groomed trails for more traditional skiing. ~ West Hill Road, Hawley; 413-339-4265; www.stumpsprouts.com.

THE BERKSHIRES In New Ashford, try the runs of family-friendly **Jimmy Peak Tubing at Snowy Owl Resort,** known for being the highest skiing elevation in Massachusetts at 2700 feet.

Four double chair lifts serve 30 percent beginner, 45 percent intermediate and 25 percent expert trials. A snow park is open to boarders. ~ Route 7; 413-443-4752; www.skibrodie.com, e-mail info@jimmy.com.

In Hancock, test the slopes at **Jiminy Peak, the Mountain Resort**, with an elevation of 2380 feet and a vertical drop of 1150 feet, eight lifts, and more than 11 miles of trails. ~ Corey Road; 413-738-5500; www.jiminypeak.com, e-mail info@jiminy.com.

Two terrain parks cover **Ski Butternut**, which has an elevation of 1800 feet and a vertical drop of 1000 feet. Ten chair lifts (three of which are quads) carry skiers throughout the 22 trails—rated 20 percent beginner, 60 percent intermediate and 20 percent expert. There's also a tubing park for the less adventurous. The season runs from late November to early April. ~ Route 23, Great Barrington; 413-528-2000; www.skibutternut.com, e-mail info@skibutternut.com.

GOLF

Wide-open spaces make for several good golfing spots in the region. Club and cart rentals are available at these 18-hole courses.

CENTRAL MASSACHUSETTS Tee off at **Crumpin-Fox Club**, a semiprivate course. Closed mid-November to mid-April. ~ Parmenter Road, Bernardston; 413-648-9101; www.golfthefox.com. The challenging **Green Hill Golf Course** is located at the second-highest point in Worcester. Golfers enjoy spectacular views of the city down below. Closed mid-December through March. ~ Marsh Avenue, Worcester; 508-799-1359; wwwci.worcester.ma.us/tpw.

BIKING

PIONEER VALLEY The Amherst–Northampton area offers some fairly flat and easy rides. The **Northampton Bicycle Path** begins at the end of State Street and ends up 2.3 miles later in Look Park. Several local bicycle groups also offer weekend day trips, including the **Franklin-Hampshire Freewheelers** of western Massachusetts and Connecticut. Overnight camping trips are also occasionally arranged. Schedules for the group's trips and events are available in local bike shops. ~ 413-548-9435; www.freewheelers.org.

Bike Rentals Bikes, repairs and accessories are found at each of these locations. No bicycle tours are offered; however, information about trips in the area is available. In the Pioneer Valley, **The Spoke** specializes in sales and repairs. ~ 279 Main Street, Williamstown; 413-458-3456; www.spokebicycles.com. **Plaine's Bike Ski Snowboard** rents bicycles by the day, week or month. ~ 55 West Housatonic Street, Pittsfield; 413-499-0294; www.

plaines.com. For mountain bikes, comfort bikes and helmets in the Berkshires, try **Berkshire Outfitters**. They also rent canoes and kayaks. ~ Route 8, Adams; 413-743-5900; www.berkshire outfitters.com.

HIKING

There's no better way to experience the natural beauty of the hills and mountains of this region than on your own two feet—particularly during fall foliage season, when the highways can seem like parking lots. Hiking opportunities abound at any of the region's state parks and conservation areas.

Some private companies offer tours geared to the serious hiker. **New England Hiking Holidays** leads hiking tours of the Berkshires as well as other New England locales. Trips range from two to eight days. Lodging and meals are included. ~ P.O. Box 1648, North Conway, NH 03860; 603-356-9696, 800-869-0949; www.nehikingholidays.com, e-mail nehh@aol.com.

The steep mountains of western Massachusetts make two-wheeled travel between regions difficult, but once you're settled in, bicycling is a great way to explore the country backroads.

All distances listed for hiking trails are one way unless otherwise noted.

CENTRAL MASSACHUSETTS The **Mid-State Trail** (91 miles) travels from Mount Watatic at the New Hampshire state border through Worcester County to the Rhode Island border. The trail offers a mixed bag of central Massachusetts scenery, traveling along old cart roads, through forests and across open fields. You can pick up stretches of the trail at any of several spots in the Worcester area, including Douglas State Forest and Rutland State Park.

Wachusett Mountain State Reservation offers a comprehensive network of 18 trails (total 17 miles) through nearly 2300 acres, with some steep-going in parts. Trails wend through hardwood forests of oak and maple, past stands of mountain laurel, spring wildflowers, ponds and meadows. You may see wildlife on the mountain, and this area offers some good trails for fall foliage vistas. ~ Mountain Road, Princeton; 978-464-2987.

PIONEER VALLEY At Arcadia Wildlife Sanctuary, owned by the Massachusetts Audubon Society (413-584-3009) in Easthampton, the **Fern Trail** (1 mile) takes you past many different types of ferns and includes an observation tower for birdwatching. It is one of many self-guided trails that wind through some 750 acres of forests on an ancient oxbow of the Connecticut River.

The **Enfield Lookout Trail** (3 miles) at Quabbin Park leads up to the Enfield Overlook, from which you can spot eagles in the winter months. The trail is part of a 22-mile network that takes you through the state's largest piece of wilderness land.

At Northfield Mountain Recreation and Environmental Center (413-659-3714), the **Hidden Quarry Nature Trail** (1-mile loop) offers a minicourse in the geology and natural history of the upper Pioneer Valley. The trail winds past the ancient beds of Lake Hitchcock, as well as porcupine dens, woods wildflowers and stands of eastern white pine.

THE BERKSHIRES **Pike's Pond Trail** (.5-mile loop), at Pleasant Valley Wildlife Sanctuary (413-637-0320) in Lenox, cuts through fields and forest and circles the beaver habitat on the pond. Other trails at the sanctuary run past meadows, a hemlock gorge and a hummingbird garden.

One of the Berkshires' better-known hiking spots is Bartholomew's Cobble, a rock-topped hill named for 18th-century farmer George Bartholomew. The **Bailey Trail** (1 mile) at the Cobble is a large loop that leads into the **Sparrow Trail** (1 mile). It's a gentle walk along the flood plain of the Housatonic River, through silver maple groves and rich deciduous woods and past an old oxbow. The Cobble offers wonderful views of the Housatonic Valley and, in late April and early May, a beautiful array of wildflowers.

Transportation

CAR

This area is easily accessible from **Route 90**, the **Massachusetts Turnpike**, which runs the entire length of the state's southern half and has exits at Worcester, Sturbridge, Springfield and Stockbridge.

From Boston, **Route 2** offers a scenic highway route to the famed Mohawk Trail and the northern portions of central and western Massachusetts.

AIR

Many people fly into Boston's **Logan International Airport** (see Chapter Four). The area is also served by **Bradley International Airport** in Windsor Locks, Connecticut (see Chapter Two), near Hartford. Those who are combining a trip to the Berkshires with a visit to Vermont may want to use **Albany County Airport** in Albany, New York; (518-242-2222; www.albanyairport.com).

Peter Pan Bus Lines (800-343-9999; www.peterpanbus.com) provides regular shuttles between Bradley International and the Springfield Bus Terminal at 1776 Main Street.

BUS

All long-distance bus lines operate from terminals at 75 Madison Street, Worcester, and 1776 Main Street, Springfield.

Greyhound Bus Lines (800-231-2222; www.greyhound.com) links Worcester and Springfield with the Berkshires, Boston and New York City. **Peter Pan Bus Lines** (800-343-9999; www.peterpanbus.com) provides transportation to Boston; points west, including Springfield, Amherst, Northampton, the Berkshires and Albany; and points south, including Hartford and New York

City. **Bonanza Bus Lines, Inc.** (888-331-7500; www.peterpanbus.com) connects Springfield with the Berkshires, Albany and Providence, Rhode Island.

TRAIN

Amtrak serves the Worcester area from New York City and Albany. A train leaves New York City daily with stops in Amherst, and there are several trains daily between Springfield and New York's Pennsylvania Station. ~ 2 Washington Square, Worcester; 66 Lyman Street, Springfield; 800-872-7245; www.amtrak.com.

CAR RENTALS

From both Logan and Bradley International Airports, you can rent a car from **Alamo Rent A Car** (800-327-9633), **Avis Rent A Car** (800-831-2847), **Budget Rent A Car** (800-527-0700), **Enterprise Rent A Car** (800-325-8007), **Hertz Rent A Car** (800-654-3131), **National Car Rental** (800-227-7368) or **Thrifty Car Rental** (800-847-4389).

PUBLIC TRANSIT

In central Massachusetts, **Worcester Regional Transit Authority** has bus service to local destinations within Worcester County. ~ 508-791-9782; www.therta.com. In the Pioneer Valley, **Pioneer Valley Transit Authority** offers frequent service throughout greater Springfield, Holyoke, Northampton and Amherst. ~ 413-781-7882; www.pvta.com. During the school year, the **Five-College Bus Service** links the campuses of the University of Massachusetts, Smith College, Mount Holyoke College, Amherst College and Hampshire College. Information on how to obtain passes may be obtained by calling 413-781-7882 or 413-586-5806. ~ 413-545-0056; www.umass.edu/bus. **Greenfield Montague Transportation Area** provides bus service throughout greater Greenfield, Amherst, Montague and Turners Falls. ~ 413-773-9478; www.gmta-transit.org.

In the Berkshires, **Berkshire Regional Transit Authority** links Pittsfield with Williamstown, North Adams, Lenox, Lee, Stockbridge and Great Barrington. ~ 413-499-2782.

EIGHT

Vermont

Vermont offers a soothing dose of old-fashioned Americana, a carefully tended piece of pastoral utopia that's down-home, uphill and intrinsically genuine. Here, dreams are lived, farms are cultivated and children are raised the traditional ways. Vermonters are at peace with their land—and it shows.

Its candid beauty is unpretentious and beguiling, a patchwork of slumbering red barns, tangled country roads and old covered bridges riveted against a backdrop of emerald mountains that twist through the heart of the state. Forming the backbone of Vermont's terrain, those towering Green Mountains—New England's oldest range—burst forth some five billion years ago when the earth's crust trembled and buckled.

Though only 9614 square miles in size, Vermont explodes with soul-gripping tableaux—alpine ridges and surging rivers, sporadic flatlands and miles of untamed wilderness. Skinny at the bottom and wide on top, this New England wedge spans an easy 159 miles in length and ranges in width from 37 miles at the Massachusetts border to 89 miles at the Canadian line.

But more than just a spot to behold, Vermont is a place to *be*. For its magic persists not only in its glorious scenery but also in its illustrious history and fastidious Yankee ideals and uncomplicated mode of existence.

Vermont may be the only landlocked New England state (a detail many Vermonters remain quite touchy about), but travelers need only scan the shores of vast Lake Champlain to find a coastline whose beauty parallels any Atlantic Ocean vista.

It was, in fact, that extraordinary lake that seduced the state's first European explorers back in 1609. Frenchman Samuel de Champlain, accompanied by native Algonquian Indians, who told great tales of mysterious waters, led an expedition from Canada and instantly claimed the lake (modestly naming it for himself) and surrounding lands for France.

During the next two centuries, the French, British and Dutch grappled to control the waterway, the sixth largest freshwater lake in the United States. The scrap was finally settled during the War of 1812, when an American naval fleet won a battle off Valcour Island.

Vermont found itself entangled in a different kind of tug-of-war during the mid-1700s, when its territory was claimed by both New York and New Hampshire. England eventually ruled in favor of New York, prompting settlers who had come from New Hampshire to organize a Vermont military force known as the Green Mountain Boys. This troupe, led by Ethan Allen, harassed New York landholders and went on to defeat the British in several decisive American Revolution battles, including the Battle of Bennington.

A flamboyant patriot determined to conquer any who attempted to steal his precious state, Allen vowed to preserve the independence of Vermont or "retire with my hardy Green Mountain boys into the caverns of the mountains and make war on all mankind."

Though New Hampshire inevitably surrendered its claims to Vermont, New York persisted. In July of 1777, Vermonters called a convention in the town of Windsor, drew up a constitution and declared their independence.

Drafted by 72 delegates who met for seven arduous days in a town tavern, the constitution prohibited slavery and was the first to establish suffrage for all men. According to local lore, the Windsor document was nearly abandoned by the delegates, who were about to dash off to fight advancing British forces at the state's west border when a fierce storm arose and prevented their departure.

Despite pleas to the Continental Congress for recognition as a state, Vermont was forced to remain an independent republic for 14 years because of boundary disputes with New York. Finally, in 1791, both sides acquiesced and Vermont became the 14th state.

Early 19th-century Vermont was a land of milk and honey, where cows outnumbered people and people took to fashioning grand Victorian estates and lobbying for abolition. But prosperous times turned tumultuous during the Civil War, as half of Vermont's young men headed for the battlefield. When it was all over, Vermont had lost a larger percentage of its men than any other state. The four-year war caused population and economic devastation that affected the state for more than 40 years.

Tourism eventually helped set things straight during the early 1900s, when word got out that Vermont was "The Switzerland of North America." Well-to-do New Yorkers set up fancy summer estates, developers threw up dozens of roadside attractions and interstate highways helped fuel the influx. Suddenly, the land boom was on.

By the 1950s, yet another new breed of visitors—the kind with skis—arrived en masse. Much to the dismay of firmly rooted Vermonters, dozens of ski runs were carved in the mountainsides, and resorts were planted where dense forests once thrived.

Today, ski resort areas remain the only real tokens of full-scale development in Vermont, often called the most rural state in the nation. Yankee conservatism has spawned a rigorous array of zoning and antipollution laws meant to stave off mass growth. Vermonters' sentiments toward development were summed up by former Governor Thomas P. Salmon in 1973 when he declared: "Vermont is not for sale."

Forests still cover 78 percent of the state, and a 1960s law banning all roadside billboards has worked wonders for Vermont's highways, which remain pristine and untainted by commercialism. In the 1980s, Vermont became the first state to prohibit automobile air conditioners that use chlorofluorocarbons, chemicals known to damage the ozone layer.

Through the years, Vermont's feisty independence and great beauty have attracted dozens of national and international artists, writers and folk heroes, including Norman Rockwell, Dorothy Canfield Fisher, Robert Frost and Rudyard Kipling, to name a few.

Today's new artisans follow in the footsteps of those early protagonists of Vermont history, fleeing America's big cities for a simpler existence among the quiet mountains. Together with the die-hard Republicans, patriotic farmers, leftover hippies and well-heeled elite, they form a curious, independent populace, united by their laissez-faire attitudes and unwavering devotion to free living.

Sprinkled on hillsides and straddling mountain streams, the quaint villages of Vermont often cling to the social values of times past and harbor historic legacies and colorful personalities.

With a population just over 616,000, Vermont is the nation's third smallest state, though its exquisite forested mountains and shimmering lakes and rivers pack as much beauty per square mile as any of the other 49.

Best of all, the terrain reveals four distinct faces as the seasons change. Fall brings a sacred occurrence, and during the season—usually from mid-September to mid-October—the entire state is covered by resplendent colors, and the temperature hovers around a crisp 50° to 60°.

Winter delivers a Currier-and-Ives backdrop, with carpets of plush white snow that weave through the country and temperatures that plunge toward 0°.

Waterfalls thaw and gush forth in spring, and millions of maple trees give up their candied sap for that wonderful Vermont maple syrup. Summer is pure green, a panorama of verdant forests, lucid lakes and blissful, breezy days when the thermometer reads about 75°.

Vermont's enchantment exists not only in its fanciful seasons and scenery but in the 242 small towns that comprise the essence of this state. Their very structures spell tradition: each town will almost certainly have a Main Street, a village square, a general store and a cemetery where you're apt to discover tombstones from the 1700s.

Each region of the state maintains its own intriguing personality. Southern Vermont is a mingling of forests, ski resorts and small cities that have been heavily influenced by neighboring New York, Massachusetts and New Hampshire. In central Vermont, "The Marble City" of Rutland has churned out tons of smooth stone for more than a century, its marble-plated buildings a testament to this vital industry. Nearby Woodstock is the state's center of prosperity, a summer playground of majestic estates, trendy shops and restaurants and total gentility.

Crawling through the upper center of the state, the Northern Mountain Region thrives as an alpine haven of ski centers and maple sugarhouses, obscure mountain hamlets and fields of wildflowers.

Gorgeous Lake Champlain wanders along the western border, edged by New York's Adirondack Mountains and Vermont's fertile Champlain Valley, and supports the state's largest city. Burlington—home to a mere 40,000 people—is a dynamic

Text continued on page 440.

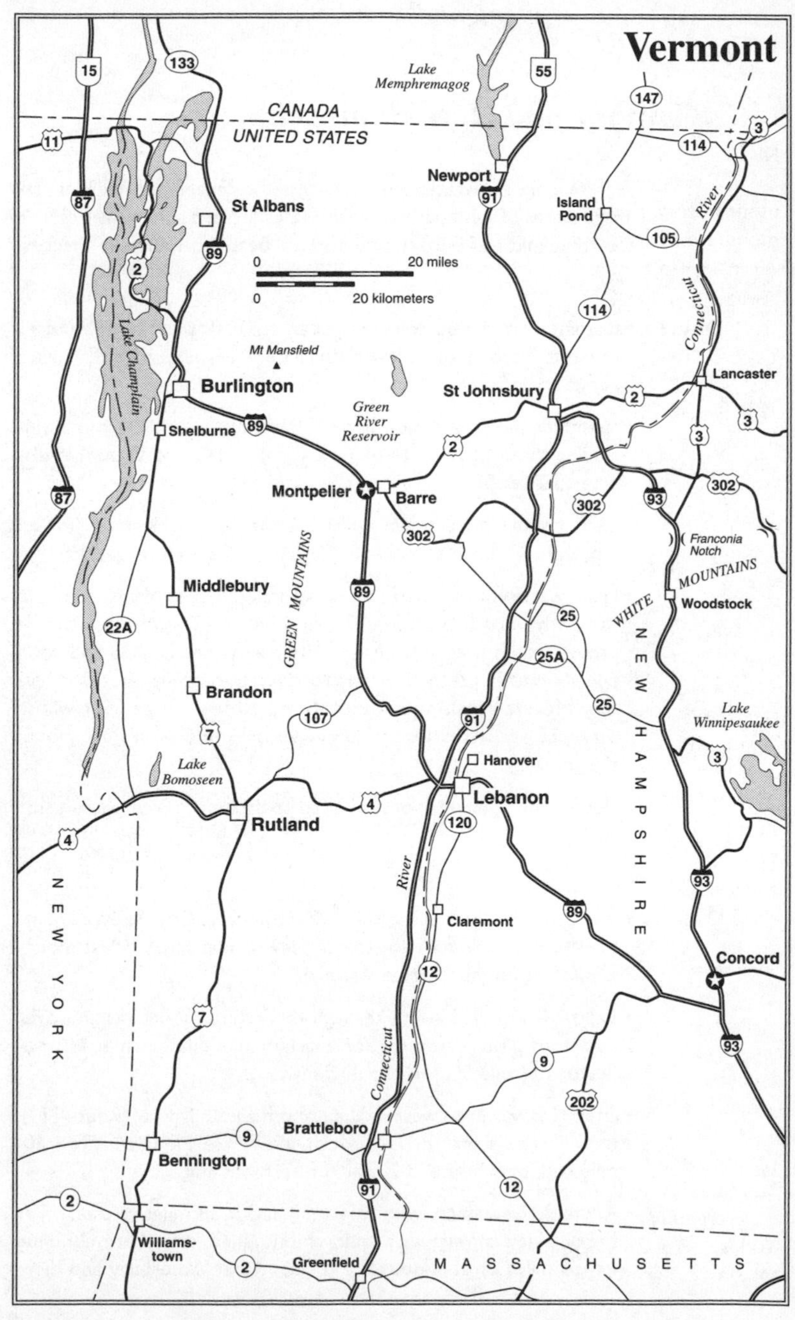
Vermont
Lake Memphremagog
CANADA
UNITED STATES
Newport
Island Pond
St Albans
Connecticut River
0 20 miles
0 20 kilometers
Lake Champlain
Mt Mansfield
Burlington
Shelburne
Green River Reservoir
St Johnsbury
Lancaster
Montpelier
Barre
Franconia Notch
GREEN MOUNTAINS
WHITE MOUNTAINS
Middlebury
Woodstock
NEW HAMPSHIRE
Brandon
Lake Winnipesaukee
Lake Bomoseen
Hanover
Lebanon
Rutland
Claremont
NEW YORK
Concord
Brattleboro
Bennington
Williams-town
Greenfield
MASSACHUSETTS

Three-day Weekend

Vermont and New Hampshire

This itinerary showcases the diversity of the deceptively small mirror-image states of Vermont and New Hampshire in a spectacular driving tour that links half a dozen of the states' best sights and experiences.

Day 1

- Coming from the Boston area, get an early start and take Route 95 north to Portsmouth, New Hampshire, a 66-mile drive that takes about an hour.
- Spend the morning exploring the historic homes of Portsmouth, including those of **John Paul Jones** (page 514) and **Daniel Webster** (page 515).
- Take a short drive down coastal Route 1A to Hampton for an atmospheric lunch at **Widow Fletcher's Tavern** (page 519).
- Head west on Route 101 for 43 fast miles, bypass Manchester and then drive north on Route 93 for 76 miles. The two-hour drive proves worth it as you turn off the freeway at Exit 35 and soon find yourself in pretty Bretton Woods at the turn-of-the-20th-century **Mount Washington Hotel and Resort** (page 558), whose opulence surpasses that of any mansion you saw in Portsmouth this morning.
- Devote the remainder of the day to luxuriating in your elegant surroundings.

Day 2

- In the morning, ride the **Mount Washington Cog Railway** (page 554) to the 6288-foot summit of New Hampshire's tallest mountain (don't forget to dress warmly).
- Follow Route 302 south through the White Mountains and over Crawford Notch, stopping for a fashionable pub lunch at **Horsefeathers** (page 560) in North Conway.
- From Conway, head west on the Kancamagus Highway (Route 112), the ultimate scenic drive through the White Mountains. The 60-mile trip joins Route 302 near the Vermont state line.
- Route 302 connects with Route 89 about 38 miles farther on at the outskirts of Vermont's capital, Montpelier. From there, continue for 14 miles on the interstate to Exit 10 at Waterbury and drive

south on Route 100 to Waitsfield. You ought to arrive at just the right time to check in at the **Lareau Farm** (page 472) for a quintessential Vermont farm stay.

Day 3

- Head back north to the interstate, stopping in Waterbury for a tour and tasting at **Ben & Jerry's Ice Cream Factory** (page 468).
- Drive south on Route 100 for about 60 miles along the eastern slope of the **Green Mountains**, one of Vermont's most beautiful excursions.
- When you reach the intersection with Route 4, turn west and drive seven miles to Mendon for an Alpine lunch at **Countryman's Pleasure** (page 462).
- Returning east on Route 4, turn off to the south on Route 100 for a visit to **President Calvin Coolidge State Historic Site** (page 458) in Plymouth Notch, an idyllic village that time seems to have forgotten.
- All good things must end. Return via Route 100A to Route 4, where a drive of 16 miles will return you to Route 89 near the New Hampshire state line. From there, a 131-mile, two-hour freeway drive will bring you back to Boston in time for dinner.

port and culture center whose well-groomed cityscapes and obvious lack of pollution make it a splendid place to tarry.

The Northeast Kingdom is undoubtedly Vermont's last stand, a 2000-square-mile piece of rural wonderland snuggled against Canada and New Hampshire. Here, craggy peaks hover above dozens of glacier-dug lakes, evergreen spires ache toward the clouds and man and nature exist together simply and peacefully.

But of all Vermont's jewels, perhaps none is so extraordinary as its people. Amiable, generous and always interested, Vermonters know how to make a person feel right at home.

In fact, visiting Vermont is a lot like coming home: Once you're there, you feel like you've always belonged. Once you leave, you'll yearn to go back.

Southern Vermont

Edged by New York, Massachusetts and New Hampshire, this southerly precinct serves predominately as a gateway for skiers, weekenders and other seekers of pleasure and solace. Here, spun into one fine geographical web, are all the components that typify the state of Vermont—wooded mountain corridors, lazy farmlands, bucolic villages and a cornucopia of history.

Two of Vermont's largest cities, Brattleboro and Bennington, anchor the state corners and bring culture, politics and manufacturing into the region. In between are several towns that were founded in the 18th century as frontier outposts.

SIGHTS

Nestled nicely between the Connecticut River and a string of western mountain ledges, **Brattleboro** debuted as a sparse colony in 1724, making it Vermont's first permanent settlement. Today, Brattleboro owes its importance to health care and educational centers, as well as wholesale distribution facilities.

The **Brattleboro Chamber of Commerce** carries helpful information. Closed Sunday. ~ 180 Main Street, Brattleboro; 802-254-4565, 877-254-4565, fax 802-254-5675; www.brattleborochamber.org, e-mail info@brattleborochamber.org.

Located in a 1915 native stone railroad station, the **Brattleboro Museum and Art Center** has dynamic rotating exhibits and educational and family programs woven together with an annual theme. Closed Tuesday and in March and April. Admission. ~ Main and Vernon streets, Brattleboro; 802-257-0124, fax 802-258-9182; www.brattleboromuseum.org, e-mail info@brattleboromuseum.org.

Back in 1892, Rudyard Kipling put down roots just north of Brattleboro in the village of Dummerston. Here, in an odd, ship-shaped house called **Naulakha**, he lived for four years with his wife, Vermont native Carrie Balestier, and penned *Captains Courageous* and two *Jungle Books*. Now available for week-long rentals, the dwelling is set back from the road and cloaked in tall trees. ~ Kipling Road, two miles north of Black Mountain Road.

To experience the rural rhythms of this state, head north on Route 30 to **Newfane.** Settled in 1774, this beguiling village is a paradigm of Vermont culture, showcasing 40 exquisite buildings that harken back to the 1700s. White clapboard houses mingle with graceful maple and elm trees and vast green. The grand **Windham County Courthouse** (802-365-4257), a Greek Revival design with enormous pillars, edges the green and is the village focal point. Closed Saturday and Sunday. Across the green rests the **Old Newfane Inn** (802-365-4427), a venerable 1787 Colonial building trimmed in white lattice porches and chimneys.

A drive northward on Route 30 and then Route 35 will put you smack in the middle of back country, a piece of terrain laced with mountain brooks and meandering meadows, occasional farms and one-room schoolhouses.

If you're like Ulysses S. Grant and Oliver Wendell Holmes, you'll make a pit stop in Grafton at the **Old Tavern at Grafton,** an 1801 Colonial-style inn that's filled with marvelous antiques and Old World character. Once a popular stagecoach layover, the tavern also hosted the likes of Ralph Waldo Emerson and Rudyard Kipling. Closed late March through April. ~ 92 Main Street at

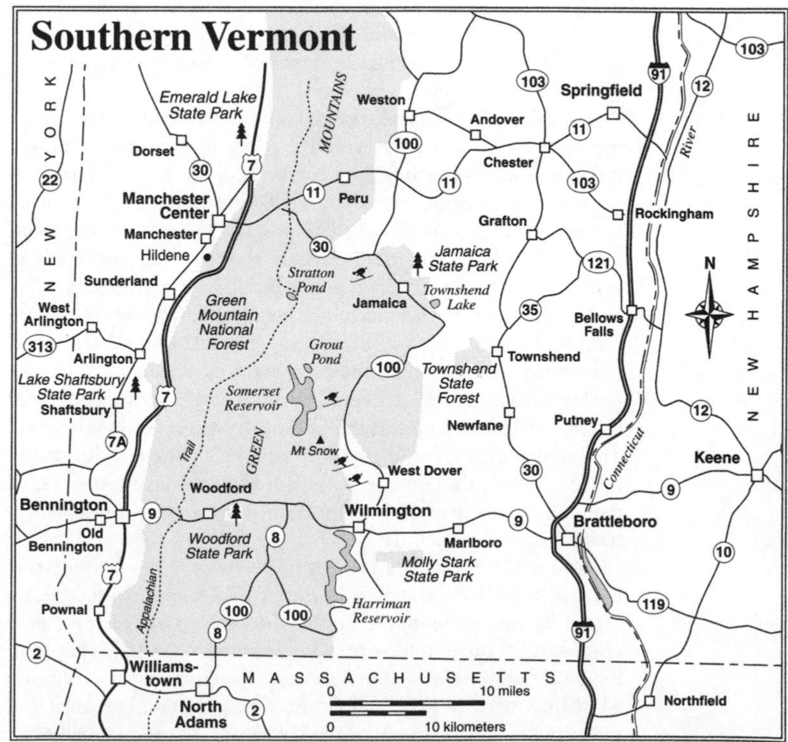

Route 121, Grafton; 802-843-2231, 800-843-1801, fax 802-843-2245; www.old-tavern.com, e-mail oldtavern@vermontel.net.

Some say **Grafton** got its name in a bidding contest—won with $5 and a flask of rum—back in 1791, though the village owes its existence to sheep farming (15,000 grazed here during the 1800s). Grafton now boasts two covered bridges, 250 year-round residents and a network of well-preserved, white-frame buildings.

In Old Bennington you'll find more than 80 well-preserved 18th- and 19th-century buildings, comprising a sort of outdoor museum.

Exquisite views await back along Route 9, to the west of Brattleboro, where the road climbs 2350 feet to the top of **Hogback Mountain**. This captivating plateau, surrounded by lofty spires of spruce and fir trees, affords a 100-mile panorama across New Hampshire and Massachusetts' Berkshires.

The **Southern Vermont Natural History Museum** contains a vast collection of unusual birds and animals "stuffed" by taxidermist and naturalist Luman Nelson. The winged collection alone is staggering: more than 600 different birds, including a large eagle and owl collection, the albino deer and skunks, and the extinct passenger pigeon and heath hen. If you tire of viewing immobile wildlife, visit the live hawks and owls exhibit. Open late May to late October; call for winter hours. Admission. ~ Hogback Mountain, Route 9, Marlboro; 802-464-0048; www.vermontmuseum.org.

Continue through this forested mountain wonderland, traveling west on Route 9, and you'll descend into the town of **Wilmington**. Long a juncture between Brattleboro and western Bennington, this bucolic town of 1800 swells to 15,000 during winter when skiers pack nearby **Haystack Mountain** and **Mount Snow**. Of course, summer activities abound, too, and you can learn about these and other leisure pursuits at the **Mount Snow Valley Chamber of Commerce**. ~ Route 9 (Main Street), Wilmington; 802-464-8092, 877-887-6884, fax 802-464-0287; www.visitvermont.com, e-mail info@visitvermont.com.

Heading west toward Bennington, Route 9 cuts through the broad, verdant expanse of the **Green Mountain National Forest**. This sinuous, heady trail explodes with brilliant color during fall foliage season, though the views border on amazing the rest of the year, too. Keep an eye out for bears, coyotes and moose, which roam the area frequently.

You can see it before you get to Bennington, an intimidating limestone obelisk looming over the city like some celestial figure. The 306-foot **Bennington Battle Monument**, the region's geographical frame of reference, pays tribute to the 1777 Battle of Bennington, a decisive conflict during the American Revolution. Though American general John Stark organized his troops and supplies here in Bennington, the battle was actually waged eight miles away on a New York hill. Closed November to mid-April. Admission. ~ 15 Monument Circle, Old Bennington; 802-447-0550, fax 802-447-6421; www.historicvermont.org/bennington, e-mail marylou.chicote@state.vt.us.

Bennington is Vermont's southwesternmost city and the first town chartered in the state, though residents didn't arrive until 12 years later in 1761 because of fierce raids during the French and Indian War. Suffused with culture and Revolutionary War history, the city is flanked by the Green Mountains and the Taconic range, a setting that's nothing short of spectacular.

The downtown area is pretty but naturally quite commercialized, so you'll want to spend most of your time in **Old Bennington.** Draped across a hill on the city's west quadrant, this pristine borough harbors marvelous expressions of early American history.

Before you start exploring, pick up a walking tour map and an area guide from the **Bennington Area Chamber of Commerce.** Closed Saturday and Sunday from November through April. ~ 100 Veterans Memorial Drive, Route 7, Bennington; 802-447-3311, 800-229-0252, fax 802-447-1163; www.bennington.com, e-mail chamber@bennington.com.

American history becomes an enthralling experience at the **Bennington Museum.** This historic 1855 building—one of New England's finest museums—evokes America's past with American Revolution artifacts, the famous Bennington flag (one of the oldest Stars and Stripes in existence), the largest public collection of Grandma Moses paintings and a genealogical library. It also showcases the frame schoolhouse, moved from Eagle Bridge, New York, that Grandma Moses attended as a child. Adjacent to the museum is Hadwen Woods, with a nature trail and pavilion. Closed Wednesday. Admission. ~ Main Street, Bennington; 802-447-1571, fax 802-442-8305; www.benningtonmuseum.org, e-mail krielly@benningtonmuseum.org.

West on Main Street rests Vermont's Colonial shrine, the **Old First Church** (also known as the First Congregational Church), erected in 1805 and now a much-photographed sight. Nestled on the green in Old Bennington, the simple white building has columns formed with single pine trees, arched Romanesque windows and well-preserved pine box pews. In this state of tradition, some of today's church members are descendants of the original founders. Open for tours on weekends from Memorial Day weekend through June 30. Open daily from July 1 to mid-October. ~ Monument Avenue, Bennington; phone/fax 802-447-1223; www.oldfirstchurchbenn.org, e-mail oldfirst@sover.net.

Beside the church on a shady knoll, symmetrical rows of granite comprise the **Old Burying Ground,** where you can stroll peacefully among tombstones dating back to the 1700s. Many epitaphs are intriguing ruminations of early settlers and soldiers who toiled here under a more difficult life, but perhaps the most reflective endures on the grave of poet Robert Frost: "I had a lover's quarrel with the world."

Head north from Old Bennington on Fairview Street, cross one of three quaint covered bridges, and you'll arrive at **Bennington College.** A medley of Colonial designs, the campus lazes peacefully across 470 acres on a pretty hill overlooking mountains and valleys. ~ Route 67A, Bennington; 802-442-5401, fax 802-440-4269; www.bennington.edu.

The rigorous scholastic and artistic exercises Bennington students must endure are often referred to as "The Bennington Experience."

Since its founding in 1929, the tiny liberal-arts school has initiated some of the country's most progressive teaching styles, employing accomplished (and oftentimes renowned) artists, writers and musicians to act as both teachers and colleagues to students. Among the more famous who have graced these halls are dancer and choreographer Martha Graham and author Bernard De Voto.

Perhaps the most intriguing sight on campus is **Jennings Hall,** a grand three-story structure carved of solid granite. Built in the mid-1800s, the building was home to the Frederic B. Jennings family, who donated their estate to the college.

The cozy pastoral spirit and thoughtful personalities of **Arlington,** 16 miles north of Bennington off Route 7A, remain preserved on *Saturday Evening Post* covers, sketched by Norman Rockwell when he lived here during the 1940s and early 1950s.

HIDDEN ►

Rockwell's farm and studio are now the **Inn on Covered Bridge Green,** a scenic resting place nestled among apple orchards and dairy farms. ~ River Road at Covered Bridge Road, four and a half miles west of Route 7A, West Arlington; 802-375-9489, 800-726-9480; www.coveredbridgegreen.com, e-mail cbg@sover.net.

You can chat with some of the local people Rockwell painted if you stop by the **Norman Rockwell Exhibit,** a 19th-century church where several hundred *Saturday Evening Post* covers, illustrations and prints are displayed. Closed January. Admission. ~ Route 7A, Arlington; 802-375-6423.

Meander north on Route 7A to Sunderland, then head west on **Skyline Drive** toll road for a hair-raising, five-mile trek to the top of **Mount Equinox.** At 3816 feet up, the panorama is inspiring, the air brisk and the feeling serene.

On the slope of the mountain, stop at the **Southern Vermont Art Center** for a tryst with culture and nature. A beautiful early 1900s Georgian mansion holds ten galleries that display about 300 pieces (paintings, graphic art and photography) by contemporary artists; there's also a museum with changing exhibits. Set on 375 acres of forest and pastureland, the center also boasts a performing arts pavilion for indoor concerts, an extensive botany trail and a sculpture garden sprinkled with wildflowers. Closed

Monday. Admission. ~ West Road, Manchester; 802-362-1405, fax 802-362-3274; www.svac.org, e-mail sva@svac.net.

On Route 7A lies **Manchester**, which made its imprint in the 19th century as a thriving summer resort town and in the 20th century as a nucleus for designer outlet stores. But its main claim to fame is a former resident, Robert Todd Lincoln, eldest son of Abraham Lincoln, who built a Georgian Revival mansion here in 1905 and called it **Hildene, the Lincoln House**. Possibly one of New England's finest historic scenes, Hildene, the Lincoln House offers a glimmer of the gilded, intriguing life of Robert Lincoln, an attorney, minister to Great Britain, and U.S. Cabinet member. On 412 acres of beautiful formal gardens, evergreen trees and nature trails, the 24-room mansion is extremely well-preserved and filled with original furnishings and possessions including a grand 1908 Aeolian pipe organ once played by the Lincoln women. Closed Tuesday and Wednesday from November to June. Admission. ~ Route 7A, Manchester; 802-362-1788, 800-578-1788, fax 802-362-1564; www.hildene.org, e-mail info@hildene.org.

Avid fishers—and even nonanglers—will get a kick out of the **American Museum of Fly Fishing**. Peruse more than 30,000 flies and 1000 rods and reels, tracing the history of this intriguing sport. You'll see what anglers through the ages used to snag a fish, along with artifacts from famous rod-makers like Thomas and Orvis. Don't miss the oldest documented flies in the world. A real treat for anyone fishing for fun. Admission. ~ Route 7A, Manchester Village; 802-362-3300, fax 802-362-3308; www.amff.com, e-mail amff@amff.com.

LODGING

Art deco in Vermont? Just check out **The Latchis Hotel**, a 1938 deco charmer in the heart of downtown. This four-story find sparkles with bright terrazzo floors and curved chrome designs and boasts 30 guest rooms in soft pastels offset by black lacquer furniture and restored 1930s pieces. The best part is that many rooms peek a view at the Connecticut River. There's also a movie theater and microbrewery on the premises. Continental breakfast included. ~ 50 Main Street, Brattleboro; 802-254-6300, 800-798-6301, fax 802-254-6304; www.latchis.com, e-mail reservations@latchis.com. MODERATE.

The sophisticated serenity of the **Four Columns Inn** has long drawn celebrities (Mick Jagger, Tom Cruise and Nicole Kidman among them) seeking a quiet reprieve from life's fast lane. Set amid 150 forested acres, the 19th-century Greek Revival inn sports a swimming pool enveloped in flowers and a cobblestone path that wends across brooks and meadows. Its trademark is four majestic columns that bestride the loggia—a marvelous place to mellow out and listen to birds chirp. The 15 guest rooms offer wide plank floors, lace curtains and a mix of canopy and four-poster beds. Six suites are also available. Breakfast is included. Closed Christmas week. ~ 21 West Street, Newfane; 802-365-7713, 800-787-6633, fax 802-365-0022; www.fourcolumns inn.com, e-mail innkeeper@fourcolumnsinn.com. DELUXE TO ULTRA-DELUXE.

The Old Tavern is possibly the most renowned spot in historic Grafton, and rightly so, since guest rooms are scattered in eight historic buildings throughout the village. The main house is an 1801 Colonial design brimming with lovely antiques, pine floors and pewter and brass. Formerly a popular stagecoach stop, the tavern boasts a notable guest list that included Ulysses S. Grant and Ralph Waldo Emerson. The 46 rooms and 6 suites feature period antiques and include private baths and sitting areas. Four houses accommodate larger groups and contain full kitchens and living areas. Closed in April. ~ 92 Main Street at Route 121, Grafton; 802-843-2231, 800-843-1801, fax 802-843-2245; www.old-tavern.com, e-mail oldtavern@vermontel.net. ULTRA-DELUXE.

A stay at the **Inn at Woodchuck Hill Farm**, set at the end of a provincial road, ensures full country comfort. With guest accommodations in the main house, the wood frame barn and the cozy spruce cottage, the inn abounds in country quilts, antiques and hardwood furniture. The Studio Suite in the main house is bright with floral wallpaper and blue trim and has a full kitchen and private deck. In the barn's wood-paneled Residential Suite, guests can enjoy plush lodging with a private entrance, reserved parking and spacious rooms that overlook an apple orchard. ~ P.O. Box 223, Grafton; 802-843-2398; www.woodchuckhill.com, e-mail marks.gabriel@gmail.com. DELUXE TO ULTRA-DELUXE.

Tucked away on ten acres dotted with pine and maple trees is a country inn that could very well double as Grandmother's holiday home through the woods—but much bigger. The Smith family's **Trail's End Inn**, a 15-room bed and breakfast with light wood furnishings and ultracomfortable bedding, even offers specialty child care. Decorated in Laura Ashley–inspired tones, all rooms include private baths, six boast wood-burning fireplaces and some have whirlpool tubs. An extensive country breakfast is served with choice of french toast or pancakes, along with fresh fruit and eggs. ~ 5 Trails End Lane, Wilmington; 802-464-2055, 800-859-2585; www.trailsendvt.com, e-mail reservations@trail sendvt.com. DELUXE TO ULTRA-DELUXE.

Skiers seeking close proximity to the slopes should check out **The Grand Summit Resort Hotel**, a lodge at the base of Mount Snow. There are 200 rooms and suites, and the hotel offers ski-to-front-door skiing. A golf course and a mountain biking school should please summertime guests. Other amenities include a spa and sauna, a pool, a hot tub and a fitness center. ~ 89 Mountain Road, West Dover; 802-464-7788, 800-245-7669, fax 802-464-4070; www.mountsnow.com, e-mail info@mountsnow.com. ULTRA-DELUXE.

Thirteen miles west of Wilmington, the **Greenwood Lodge Hostel** lolls peacefully in a picturesque wooded glen. Rustic but tidy, the mountain lodge has 16 beds in four rooms, two of them available for private use. There's a fireplace and community kitchen, plus fishing ponds, canoeing, swimming, boating and 40 wooded campsites. Closed late October to mid-May. ~ Route 9, adjacent to Prospect Ski Mountain, Woodford; phone/fax 802-442-2547; www.campvermont.com/greenwood, e-mail campgreen wood@aol.com. BUDGET.

A gorgeous Victorian mansion cloaked in a sea of trees, the **South Shire Inn** is positively dazzling. The first floor is a series of parlors and sitting rooms with mahogany woods, leaded-glass doors, high carved ceilings and a knockout staircase; one guest room with an antique double bed and a fireplace is situated downstairs; upstairs, four guest accommodations, some equipped with original fireplaces, are decorated in period pieces. Four more contemporary-styled rooms with whirlpool tubs and fireplaces are in the carriage house. All rooms have private baths. Full breakfast is included. ~ 124 Elm Street, Bennington; 802-447-3839, fax 802-442-3547; www.southshire.com, e-mail relax@ southshire.com. DELUXE.

Relaxation is at the heart of the **Samuel Safford Inne**, a 1774 Victorian mansion rumored to be the oldest home in East Bennington. The charming bed and breakfast does not shy away from color; rooms are decorated in rich burgundy and dark blue. Hand-carved furniture and period antiques add to the ambience

AUTHOR FAVORITE

Something about the **Old Newfane Inn** makes me instantly feel as though I've come home. Perhaps it's the lazy wraparound porch with rocking chairs, the warm parlors with brick hearths or the wonderful old general store across the street. It could be the eight rooms, decorated without pretension in rich woods and country wallpapers, or the massive maple trees that stand across the front lawn. Whatever the reason, the magic is there—and has been since this venerable country inn opened way back in 1787. Closed November to mid-December and April to mid-May; closed Monday. ~ Village Common, Route 30, Newfane; 802-365-4427, 800-784-4427; www.oldnewfaneinn.com. DELUXE.

in both the spacious rooms and common areas. Guests can also curl up in front of the large fireplace or can lounge on the glass-enclosed porch. Reservations strongly recommended, especially in fall. ~ 722 Main Street Route 9, Bennington; 802-442-5934; www.samuelsaffordinne.com, e-mail samuelsaffordinne@verizon.net. BUDGET TO MODERATE.

Surrounded by mountains and bordered by the Battenkill River, **Hill Farm Inn** is a gay-friendly B&B attracting both gays and straights. Its two vintage farmhouses contain 15 recently revamped guest rooms, with quilts on every bed and hand-painted stenciling. Enjoy the breeze on the new cedar deck. In the summer months, four cabins are also available. All rooms have private baths. Nearby, you'll find hiking, biking, canoeing, kayaking, fishing and (come winter) skiing and skating. Breakfast and afternoon tea and cookies included. ~ 458 Hill Farm Road, Arlington; 802-375-2269, 800-882-2545, fax 802-375-9918; www.hillfarminn.com, e-mail stay@hillfarm.com. DELUXE TO ULTRA-DELUXE.

The scenic Battenkill River runs in front of the five-acre grounds at the Inn on Covered Bridge Green, surrounded in all directions by apple orchards and tranquil horse and dairy farms.

"Who is there, I wonder, who doesn't want to escape from the speed and rudeness of today's living . . . ?" When Norman Rockwell penned those words, he likely had in mind his secluded farmhouse in West Arlington. Today, the 1792 timber house is HIDDEN the **Inn on Covered Bridge Green**, a beguiling bed and breakfast offering a glimmer of the rural cheer that Rockwell's paintings so cleverly depicted. There are ten units (one of which is a two-bedroom suite) set off by broad pine floors and provincial antiques. ~ 3587 River Road, four and a half miles west of Route 7A, West Arlington; 802-375-9489, 800-726-9480; www.coveredbridgegreen.com, e-mail cbg@sover.net. DELUXE TO ULTRA-DELUXE.

Ira Allen and his Green Mountain Boys checked into **The Equinox** once for a little rest and relaxation. It was the late 1700s, and the hotel was *the* place to stay. Centuries later, the place still draws history-makers, as well as anyone seeking indulgent surroundings. A main four-story building, fronted by Greek Revival columns, features over 175 rooms graced with white Vermont pine furniture and country-style accents. An adjoining building offers 9 one- and two-bedroom suites with fully stocked kitchens and elegant country decor. Other features include a pool, an 18-hole championship golf course, a spa, indoor and outdoor tennis courts, horseback riding, and three restaurants. For those interested in learning a new skill there is a falconry school as well as an off-road driving school. In the winter you can ice skate and go snowmobiling. All this is set on 1100 acres etched with cross-country ski trails. Who could ask for more? ~ 3567 Main Street Route 7A, Manchester Village; 802-362-4700, 800-362-4747, fax 802-362-4861; www.equinoxresort.com, e-mail reservations@equinoxresort.com. ULTRA-DELUXE.

For close proximity to Manchester's factory outlet stores, consider **Barnstead Inn**. Built in 1830, the post-and-beam hay barn has been converted with all its charm intact. Fourteen tidy bedrooms are outfitted with old-time furniture and wall-to-wall carpets, and there's a pool and a hot tub out back. ~ Route 30, Manchester; 802-362-1619, 800-331-1619, fax 802-362-0288; www.barnsteadinn.com, e-mail barnstead@sover.net. DELUXE TO ULTRA-DELUXE.

DINING

The diminutive venue of **T. J. Buckley's** is the last place you'd expect to find some of the city's finest gourmet fare. But here it is, served in an adorable Worcester diner with eclectic decor and only eight tables. Four entrées are offered nightly on an ever-changing menu. Selections might include diver scallops served with roasted fennel and buckwheat polenta, roasted duck breast in an artichoke stew, or beef tenderloin with a shallot-rosemary reduction. No credit cards. Dinner only. Closed Monday and Tuesday. ~ 132 Elliot Street, Brattleboro; 802-257-4922. ULTRA-DELUXE.

Things take on a subdued pace at **Peter Havens**, a tiny but sophisticated eatery obscured beneath streetside awnings. Continental fare focuses on fresh seafood, including curried shrimp, sea scallops Provençal and grilled swordfish with Geneva butter. Linen tablecloths, original artwork and only ten tables make this a cozy spot. Dinner only. Closed Sunday and Monday; closed the last two weeks of March, July and November. ~ 32 Elliot Street, Brattleboro; 802-257-3333. DELUXE TO ULTRA-DELUXE. ◄HIDDEN

Located in the Colonial Motel is **Max's**, a surprisingly fine restaurant serving upscale Italian fare. The menu varies from classic four-cheese pasta to specialty dishes such as Tuscan-style cauliflower with linguini, garlic, onion, chiles, mint and pecorino. Gorgonzola-stuffed pork loin and grilled salmon filet are also available, along with an extensive wine list. Brunch served on Sunday. Closed Tuesday. ~ 889 Putney Road, Brattleboro; 802-254-7747; www.maxsrestaurant.com, e-mail mcconde@sover.net. DELUXE TO ULTRA-DELUXE

A majestic country establishment built in 1787, the **Old Newfane Inn** possesses quite an impressive restaurant. The surroundings are pure Vermont: dark pine floors, high beamed ceilings and wallpapered walls sprinkled with beautiful antiques. The bill of fare includes an array of highbrow delights such as smoked goose pâté and frogs' legs Provençal. Dinner only. Closed Monday; closed in November and April. ~ Route 30 on the village common, Newfane; 802-365-4427; www.oldnewfaneinn.com. DELUXE TO ULTRA-DELUXE.

Charm and elegance embrace at the **Four Columns Inn** restaurant, renowned across the region for its exceptional native cuisine. Built in 1839 of hand-hewn timbers, the Colonial-style inn exhibits four grand columns across its loggia. Inside, candlelit tables are arranged cozily around a brick fireplace accented by windows draped in lace sheers. Try the rack of lamb served with capers, eggplant and goat cheese; seared venison loin in a zinfandel sauce; or Basque-style fish stew with sausage. Closed Tuesday and Christmas week. ~ 21 West Street, Newfane; 802-365-7713, 800-789-6633, fax 802-365-0022; www.fourcolumnsinn.com, e-mail innkeeper@fourcolumnsinn.com. ULTRA-DELUXE.

The Old Tavern imparts a warm formality that reveals its rich heritage. Indeed, the inn's handsome pine floors and beam ceilings, which date back to the late 1700s, have seen the likes of Oliver Wendell Holmes and Henry David Thoreau. Two lavish dining rooms are decorated with antiques and American portraits, while a sunny greenhouse affords picturesque views of gardens. The menu focuses on local fare such as Green Mountain lamb, smoked pork loin and New England salmon. Breakfast and dinner only. Closed in April. ~ 92 Main Street at Route 121, Grafton; 802-843-2231, 800-843-1801; www.old-tavern.com, e-mail stay@old-tavern.com. DELUXE TO ULTRA-DELUXE.

West Dover's **Inn at Sawmill Farm** is fashioned from a 1797 barn. The ever-changing Continental menu usually includes a variety of fresh fish dishes and a selection of meat, poultry and game dishes. It also has one of the most impressive wine lists in the northeast, with a 28,000-bottle cellar. A newly built patio enables guests to dine outside. Dinner only. Reservations required. Closed late March to late May. ~ 7 Crosstown Road at Route 100, West Dover; 802-464-1133, 800-493-1133, fax 802-464-

FOOD WITH A VIEW

Sip one of five local microbrews while lounging on the open-air deck of the **Riverview Café**, located in downtown Brattleboro. Overlooking the Connecticut River, the comfortable restaurant prides itself on casual elegance and delivers just that. Guests can dine on one of two outdoor patios or within the panoramic-windowed indoor café. Vegetarian and children's options are available along with traditional seafood, pasta, salad or steak dishes, all of which feature local produce. Three meals served daily. ~ 36 Bridge Street, Brattleboro; 802-254-9841; www.riverviewcafe.com. MODERATE TO DELUXE.

1130; www.theinnatsawmillfarm.com, e-mail sawmill@sover.net. ULTRA-DELUXE.

A prominent black stone fireplace warms the dining room of the **Red Shutter Inn and Restaurant**. With white linen tablecloths, wood-backed chairs and old country décor, Red Shutter manages to balance good taste with a good time. While the managers maintain a sense of casual comfort, the cuisine is top-notch with seasonally rotating entrées such as seared apricot duck with vegetable spring rolls and apricot cognac demiglaze served with cranberry and thyme risotto. You'll want to save room for the European and Vermont cheese plate or a homemade fruit pie with vanilla ice cream. Reservations recommended. ~ 41 West Main Street Route 9, Wilmington; 802-464-3768, 800-845-7548; www.redshutterinn.com, e-mail innkeeper@redshutterinn.com. ULTRA-DELUXE.

You'll find plenty of local color at **Poncho's Wreck**, a pub-style eatery with nautical decor and stained-glass windows. The food is dependably good and ranges from Mexican fare and steaks to seafood. The mood is casual but festive, particularly during ski season. No lunch Monday through Friday. ~ 10 South Main Street, Wilmington; 802-464-9320, fax 802-464-5058; www.ponchoswreck.com, e-mail wfponwrk@sover.net. MODERATE TO ULTRA-DELUXE.

SHOPPING

For the most part, Vermont shops are down-home and unpretentious, a smattering of country gift marts, antique nooks and epicure emporiums with locally made cheeses and maple syrup. To assist with shopping excursions, the **Capital Region Visitors Center** has excellent brochures on where to find antiques, designer outlets, cheese and Christmas trees (in case you brought the car). ~ 134 State Street, Montpelier, VT 05602; 802-828-5981; www.vermontvacation.com.

Pick up your brand-name outdoor clothes and supplies at reasonable prices at **Sam's Department Store**, a downtown institution housed in a ruddy brick building. ~ 74 Main Street, Brattleboro; 802-254-2933; www.samsoutfitters.com.

The fun and funky selections at **Bartleby's Books & Music** reflect the owner's love of fiction, history, Vermont, cooking and classical music. ~ North Main Street, Wilmington; 802-464-5425.

At **Taddingers**, visitors will step into a store that's more like a country home. Small carved wooden figures, tin lanterns, antiques, jams, teddy bears, blankets and pictures are arranged to please the eye. ~ Route 100, Wilmington; 802-464-6263, 800-528-3961, fax 802-464-1223; www.taddingers.com.

Bennington Potters has everything you need to set the perfect country table. All pottery is made on location, and factory tours are offered if you'd like to see how your purchases were created. ~ 324 County Street, Bennington; 802-447-7531, 800-205-8033, fax 802-442-6080; www.benningtonpotters.com.

The outstanding **Bennington Museum Shop** features Grandma Moses prints, historical literature, salt-glazed pottery and works by local artisans. ~ 75 West Main Street (Route 9), Bennington; 802-447-1571, fax 802-442-8305; www.benningtonmuseum.org.

Panache is equipped with contemporary women's clothing, gifts and accessories. ~ 457 Main Street, Bennington; 802-442-8859.

NIGHTLIFE

A marvelous neighborhood bar, **McNeill's Brewery** features a vast selection of draught beers brewed on the premises. The bartender has control of the musical selections, which range from jazz to punk to hip-hop. ~ 90 Elliot Street, Brattleboro; 802-254-2553.

Locals go underground at **Mole's Eye Cafe**, a noisy, crowded nook with booths and occasional rock bands. Cover on Friday and Saturday. Closed Sunday. ~ 4 High Street, Brattleboro; 802-257-0771.

Deegan's Tavern, near Wilmington, is a wood-and-glass tavern where skiers stop off for a cold brew. There's live rock-and-roll and blues on weekends during winter. Cover on Friday and Saturday. ~ Route 100, West Dover; 802-464-8600.

Smack in the middle of ski action, **The Snow Barn** draws huge winter crowds with live rock-and-roll on Friday and Saturday. Weekend cover. ~ In the Snow Lake Lodge, South Access Road, Mount Snow; 802-464-3333; www.mountsnow.com.

One of the most prestigious thespian groups in Vermont, **Oldcastle Theatre Company** stages dramas, comedies and musicals in their arts center from June through October. ~ Performing in the regional Bennington Center for the Arts, Route 9 and Gypsy Lane, Bennington; 802-447-0564, fax 802-442-3704; www.oldcastletheatreco.org.

BEACHES & PARKS

GREEN MOUNTAIN NATIONAL FOREST This colossal tract of greenery constitutes the spine of Vermont, uniting over 400,000 acres that slice through the center of the state. Technically, it's divvied into two big chunks, starting at the Massachusetts border and climbing to the town of Wallingford, then picking up again in Mendon and heading northward to Bristol. Dense, verdant and pristine, the forest provides asylum for thousands of animals and birds, including black bears, coyotes, moose, white-tailed deer, wild turkeys, raptors and the protected peregrine falcons. You can spot these intriguing inhabitants by exploring miles of nature trails and canoeing the waters.

The trees themselves—those great sweeps of maple, beech and birch, intermingled with black cherry, white ash, balsam firs and occasional hemlock forests—are no less enthralling. Swimming is excellent at several spots, including **Hapgood Pond** and **Grout Pond**, a developed but rustic site in Stratton on Kelley Stand Road, six miles west of Route 100. There's excellent fishing from 440 miles of rivers and tributaries. Anglers ply the Otter Creek for brook trout and the White, Deerfield and nearby Battenkill and West rivers for rainbow and brown trout. To see everything the national forest offers would take several weeks, though there are several choice spots perfect for an afternoon rendezvous. Non-motorized boats only. Facilities include picnic areas and restrooms; nature trails and ranger stations are dispersed throughout the forest. Day-use fee, $4. ~ Route 7 scales the west side of the forest, while Route 100 borders the east side. In between, Routes 73, 125, 9, 11 and 30 slice through the middle. Along these roads are all 32 access points for trails, waterfalls, ponds, rivers and campgrounds. Before you go, contact the Green Mountain National Forest (231 North Main Street, Rutland, VT 05701-2417; 802-747-6700, fax 802-747-6766) for maps and information on the huge forest network.

◄ HIDDEN

At the Green Mountain National Forest, rivers gush forth from the mountains, giving rise to lovely waterfalls and tiny, pebble-studded brooks perfect for wading.

▲ Several good campsites exist, in five developed campgrounds; four accommodate RVs (no hookups). Most sites are on a first-come, first-served basis and are $5 per night. Try Hapgood Pond, on Hapgood Road in Peru, five miles from the intersection of Routes 11 and 30; and Moosalamoo, a developed campground on Ripton-Goshen Road, 3.2 miles from Route 125 and one mile east of Ripton. In addition, visitors are welcome to throw up a tent anywhere, as long as it's at least 200 feet from roads, trails and waterways. The developed campgrounds are closed from Labor Day to Memorial Day. Call for information on backcountry camping.

FORT DUMMER STATE PARK Stashed along some sylvan back roads, this 217-acre, heavily forested park is named after the first white settlement in Vermont, established in 1724. There's a small shaded clearing for picnicking and a mile of nature trails that ramble through evergreens to a view of the Connecticut River. Picnic tables, restrooms and a playground round out the amenities. Closed October to Labor Day. Day-use fee, $2.50. ~ From Routes 91 and 5 in Brattleboro, take Route 5 north one-tenth of a mile to Exit 1 and go to the first set of lights. Take a right here onto Fairground Road, then follow the road until it ends. Take a right to the stop sign. Here you'll see a sign for the park. Continue to the park's entrance; 802-254-2610.

◄ HIDDEN

▲ There are 61 wooded sites (no hookups), including ten lean-tos, with showers and fireplaces; $14 per night for tent/RV sites, $21 per night for lean-tos. Reservations: 888-409-7579.

TOWNSHEND STATE PARK Resting amidst a slew of craggy green mountains, this fine park spans 856 acres and borders the scenic West River. For delightful views, take a hardy hike 1100 feet up to the top of Bald Mountain; for sunbathing, swimming and canoeing, take a one-mile trek down to the **Townshend Dam Recreation Area** (802-365-7503), where an 1800-foot thread of tawny sand stretches lazily along the river. Try by the dam for brook trout, walleye and smallmouth bass. You'll also find nice nature trails near the dam. Picnic tables and restrooms are available. Closed mid-October to mid-May. Day-use fee, $2.50. ~ State Forest Road, three miles south of Route 30 near Townshend; 802-365-7500.

▲ Permitted at 34 sites (eight for RVs) with fireplaces and showers but no hookups. Rates are $14 per night for tent/RV sites, $21 per night for lean-tos. Reservations: 888-409-7579.

LIVING MEMORIAL PARK As municipal parks go, this one is tops. Blanketing 53 acres of gentle hills, this shady sanctuary teems with recreational opportunities, including a swimming pool (fee) and ice-skating rink (fee), two outdoor tennis courts, an indoor rink for rollerblading and inline hockey and an expansive playground with some state-of-the-art equipment. Families love this place, and it's one of the few parks that manages to be packed (or even open) year-round. There are picnic pavilions, lifeguards, a snack bar, softball fields, tennis and basketball courts, a beginner's downhill ski hill, and a sledding hill. ~ Guilford Street, off Route 9 a quarter of a mile west of Route 91, near Brattleboro; 802-254-5808, fax 802-257-2310.

MOLLY STARK STATE PARK Magnificent stands of maple and birch blanket this pristine area, marked by beavers, deer and rabbits. There's a broad clearing that affords cool picnicking and a one-and-a-half-mile roundtrip hike to the summit of Mount Olga. Once you're there, climb the abandoned fire tower and be rewarded with a view into New Hampshire. Facilities include a playground and picnic tables and shelters. Closed mid-October to mid-May. Day-use fee, $2.50. ~ Route 9, about four miles east of Wilmington; 802-464-5460.

▲ There are 34 sites, including 11 lean-tos, with showers and fireplaces (no hookups); $14 per night for tent/RV sites, $21 per night for lean-tos. Reservations: 888-409-7579.

JAMAICA STATE PARK The arrow-straight, wide, rocky West River plows right through this beautiful park, creating a cool, 756-acre playground for outdoor lovers. A short cord of gravel forms a semibeach against the river, where you can swim or roll up your pants legs and explore. You can also cast a rod for walleye, trout and panfish. There's a wooded trail leading up to Hamilton Falls, where eons of torrential water flow have formed curious miniature bathtubs among slippery rocks. You'll find restrooms, picnic tables and a playground. Closed mid-October to late April. Day-use fee, $2.50. ~ Off Route 30, Jamaica; 802-874-4600.

The best part of Jamaica State Park is a trail along an old railroad bed that leads to the Ball Mountain Dam, a monstrous structure that's unleashed twice a year for popular canoe and kayak races.

▲ There are 41 tent sites ($16 per night) and 18 lean-tos ($23 per night) with showers and fireplaces but no hookups. Some sites accommodate RVs. Reservations: 888-409-7579.

WOODFORD STATE PARK Certainly one of the most picturesque parcels in the state, this 398-acre mountain woodland teems with wildflowers and all sorts of wildlife, from moose, deer and bear to very active beavers. Much of the activity centers around Adams Reservoir, dotted with small boats and canoes and rimmed by a small beach with coarse gray sand. You can swim, though the water can be murky at times. When the reservoir is stocked, the trout are biting. At 2400 feet up, the setting is cool and serene. Facilities include picnic areas, boat and canoe rentals and a nature trail. Closed October to mid-May. Day-use fee, $2.50. ~ Route 9, ten miles east of Bennington; 802-447-7169.

▲ Some of the most extensive in the state, with 103 sites and 20 lean-tos, with fireplaces and hot showers. A third of the sites accommodate RVs (no hookups). Rates are $16 per night for tents, $23 per night for lean-tos. Reservations: 888-409-7579.

SHAFTSBURY STATE PARK Situated along a fine, clear lake, this park possesses 84 acres sprinkled with evergreens and maple trees, nature trails and those industrious beavers. Locals fancy the 600-foot beach of fine, ginger-colored sand that allows great sunbathing and swimming. You can fish along parts of shore or from boats for bass and rainbow trout. Boat and canoe rentals and available, as are picnic areas and a playground. Closed September to mid-May. Day-use fee, $2.50. ~ Route 7A, Shaftsbury; 802-375-9978 (summer), 802-483-2001 (winter); www.vtstateparks.com.

EMERALD LAKE STATE PARK True to its name, this body of water glistens with a green glow and is so clear you can see much of its sandy bottom. A choice thread of tawny sand forms a popular beach, while nature trails crisscross the hillside terrain. Here you'll also find some of the tallest (more than 100 feet) maple trees in Vermont. In the lake you can cast a rod for panfish, small- and largemouth bass and northern pike. Amenities include a playground, restrooms, a snack bar and canoe and boat rentals. Closed mid-October to late May. Day-use fee, $2.50. ~ Route 7, Dorset; 802-362-1655.

▲ There are 105 sites, including 36 lean-tos, with showers and fireplaces but no hookups. Lean-tos are $23 per night; all other sites are $16 per night. Reservations: 888-409-7579.

Central Vermont

Sprawled across the lower waist of the state is a diverse lot of mining cities, picturesque mountain hamlets, ski areas and affluent riverside towns. Driving through this fertile area, you'll encounter a variety of lifestyles and people—fifth-generation farmers, descendants of European immigrants, small-time merchants and established aristocrats.

On the region's west side, Rutland and nearby villages are pocked with marble quarries that have churned the wheels of industry for two centuries. Eastward, Woodstock is a meld of tree-lined streets and gracious 19th-century architecture that owes its affluence and elegance to a line of wealthy partisans, including Laurance S. Rockefeller and railroad magnate Frederick Billings. Beyond Woodstock rambles the lazy Connecticut River, a natural divider between Vermont and New Hampshire.

SIGHTS

HIDDEN ►

Just south of Rutland and off Route 7 is a mandatory side trip (via a few dirt roads) to **Shrewsbury** (North Shrewsbury Road, about eight miles east of Route 7), a quiescent village of 800 that seems buried at the end of the world.

Northward lies **Rutland**, which earned the name "Marble City" during the mid-1800s when local marble mining exploded, though it was also the state's largest railroad junction. This commercial city—Vermont's second largest with 17,292 people—bears a handful of marble-plated buildings, but much of its marble was used for more than 250,000 headstones at Arlington National Cemetery in Virginia as well as the Lincoln Memorial in Washington, D.C., and the U.S. Supreme Court.

The **Rutland Region Chamber of Commerce** will assist with sightseeing in the area. Closed Saturday and Sunday. ~ 256 North Main Street, Rutland; 802-773-2747, 800-756-8880, fax 802-773-2772; www.rutlandvermont.com, e-mail info@rutlandvermont.com.

The marble bridge, sidewalks and high school are a testament to more than a century of serious quarrying in nearby Proctor, where you can check out the **Vermont Marble Exhibit**, a series of intriguing marble displays with history to boot. Admission. Closed

November to mid-May. ~ 52 Main Street, Proctor; 802-459-2300, 800-427-1396; www.vermont-marble.com, e-mail info@vermont-marble.com.

A short (and very worthwhile) trip north on Route 7 will bring you to the town of **Brandon**, where you'll find one of the state's best expressions of 19th-century architecture. This fertile farming town, lined with serene, shady streets, was chartered in 1761. Excellent walking-tour maps are available at the **Brandon Area Chamber of Commerce's information booth.** ~ Corner of Routes 7 and 73 East, Brandon; 802-247-6401; www.brandon.org, e-mail info@brandon.org.

A sensational drive along Route 73, **Brandon Gap** cuts through precipitous mountains and miles of forest and gurgling brooks. While you're there, why not take a hiking or biking tour of the area? You can book reservations with **Country Inn Along the Trail.** They offer customized tour planning. ~ 3128 Forest Dale Road, Brandon; 802-326-2072, 800-838-3301; www.inntoinn.com, e-mail office@inntoinn.com.

East of Rutland, **Killington** and **Pico** constitute the state's largest and perhaps most popular ski area, though the resort scene seems quite contrived when compared to the genuine quaintness of surrounding villages (as most any native Vermonter will quickly point out).

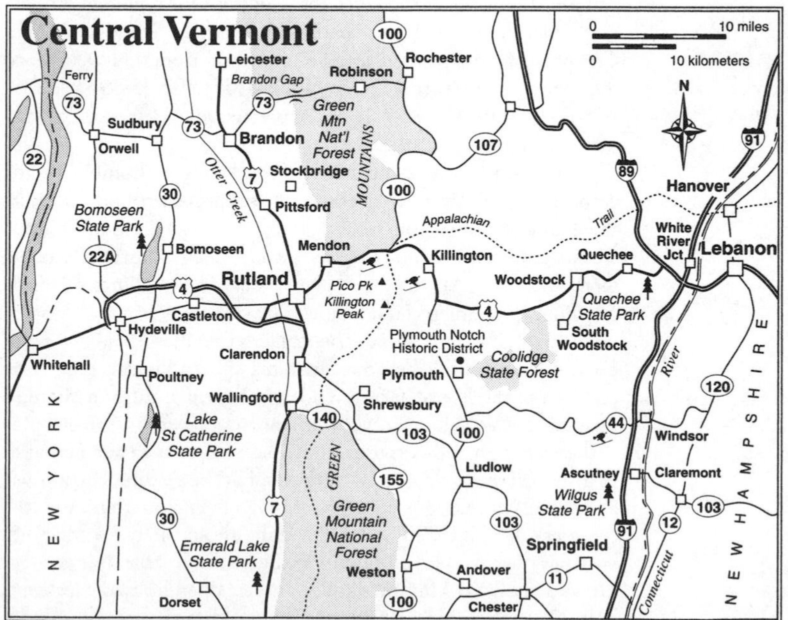

From Killington, go east on Route 4 to Route 100S, then it's just a few miles to **Plymouth Notch**. This gloriously remote mountain hamlet harbors the **President Calvin Coolidge State Historic Site**, where the 30th president was born and spent a lot of his time. The entire scene is quite striking, a thread of well-preserved white clapboard buildings and gravel lanes set against stalwart trees and mountain peaks. There's a general store once operated by Coolidge's father, the 1924 Summer White House with all its original furnishings and the home where, following President Harding's sudden death, he took his 2:47 a.m. presidential oath. The Wilder Barn houses one of the country's best collections of late-19th- to early-20th-century agricultural equipment. A restaurant on the premises that serves lunch, and offers an enclosed picnic area. Closed mid-October to late May. Admission. ~ Route 100A, Plymouth Notch; 802-672-3773, fax 802-672-3337; www.historicvermont.org/coolidge.

Brandon was the birthplace of Stephen A. Douglas, the famous Illinois debater who lost the 1860 presidential race to Abe Lincoln.

A short drive east on Route 4 transforms you from bucolic byroads to overt affluence and centuries of prosperity in **Woodstock**. Superb red-brick and white clapboard buildings skirt the beautiful oval green, fashionable shops and restaurants line side streets and a chalkboard called the **Woodstock Town Crier** (Central and Elm streets) provides the scoop on local goings-on.

For more detailed information, stop by the **Woodstock Area Chamber of Commerce**. Closed Sunday and from mid-October to mid-May. ~ 18 Central Street, Woodstock; 802-457-3555, 888-496-6378, fax 802-457-1601; www.woodstockvt.com, e-mail info@woodstockvt.com.

While some Vermonters bash Woodstock as bombastic, the community's attempts to preserve the natural surroundings shine through any pretensions that may exist. Power lines are hidden from sight, thanks to donations from resident Laurance Rockefeller, and rural beauty has been preserved at **Billings Farm & Museum**, a premiere Jersey dairy farm.

A railroad magnate and Rockefeller's grandfather-in-law, Frederick Billings established the farm in 1890 and began importing cows from the Isle of Jersey. Today, the farm features a championship herd of Jersey cows, draft horses, sheep and oxen, plus daily programs and activities. Extensive exhibits depict activities that shaped the lives of rural Vermonters. The restored farmhouse showcases the farm office, the family living quarters and the creamery. Down the hill, you can learn about the uses of historic varieties of vegetables and herbs in the heirloom vegetable garden. Open daily from May through October; open holiday weekends only November and December. Admission. ~ Route 12, Woodstock; 802-457-2355, fax 802-457-4663; www.billingsfarm.org, e-mail info@billingsfarm.org.

Picturesque and subtly beguiling, neighboring **Quechee** lolls across the banks of the Ottauquechee River and claims a large concentration of resort estates. These grand mansions and sprawling country villas serve as summer homes for members of society's upper echelons and as eye-pleasing spectacles for passersby.

Even more inspiring than the resort estates is **Quechee Gorge,** a mammoth rocky chasm chiseled by the Ottauquechee River. Maple and fir trees skate down the rocky walls of the 165-foot-deep gorge, carved by glaciers during the Ice Age. It's a mile walk to the bottom, but the trek is scenic, cool and rewarding. ~ Route 4, ten miles north of Routes 89 and 91.

LODGING

There's plenty of room in the apartmentlike suites at **Best Western Inn & Suites**, a modern hostelry just outside downtown. Set at the foot of the mountains, the medley of two-story frame buildings is accented by generous landscaping and a broad seasonal swimming pool. Expect one- and two-bedroom suites with vaulted ceilings, queen-sized sofabeds, distinctive windows and kitchens with modern appliances. Motel rooms available. ~ 1 Route 4, Rutland; phone 802-773-3200, 800-828-3334, fax 802-773-6615; www.bestwestern-rutland.com. MODERATE TO DELUXE.

Nestled on a bank of rolling hills between Rutland and Killington, **The Vermont Inn** is a congenial 1840 farmhouse trimmed in chimneys and red-and-white awnings. The whole place is terribly cozy, a timeless structure of rubbed pine floors and cherrywood furniture. Bedrooms follow suit with eyelet quilts, private baths and fireplaces. Some rooms have either a fireplace or a jacuzzi tub or both. Closed mid-April to Memorial Day ~ Route 4, Mendon; 802-775-0708, 800-541-7795, fax 802-773-2440; www.vermontinn.com, e-mail relax@vermontinn.com. DELUXE.

The Grey Bonnet Inn mixes new and old with 41 modern rooms decorated in country motifs and accompanied by amenities such as indoor and outdoor pools, tennis courts, a hot tub, a sauna, a small reading library, a game room and an exercise room. Outside the two-story building, wood shingles scale the walls, while inside the lobby is an intimate affair donned in carved wood beams, antique spinning wheels and other period pieces. Cross-country ski through the lodge's 25 acres, or take on Killington's slopes about four miles away. Guests can also hike to the nearby Appalachian Trail. Closed from the end of October to mid-November and mid-April through May. Complimentary full breakfast. ~ 83 Route 100 North, Killington; 802-775-2537, 800-342-2086, fax 802-775-3371; www.greybonnetinn.com, e-mail innkeep@together.net. MODERATE TO ULTRA-DELUXE.

Daniel Boone would have felt right at home in the **Inn at Long Trail**, a woodsy resting place with big country throw rugs, rustic furniture, pine tree pillars and a fieldstone fireplace. Vermont's original ski lodge, it has six fireplace suites with wood furniture, and 14 smaller rooms with private baths and cozy decor. But what ol' Dan would have liked best is the "relaxation room" fitted with a huge redwood hot tub. The inn is closed for awhile after ski season, usually from mid-April to mid-June. ~ 709 Route 4, Sherburne Pass, Killington; 802-775-7181, 800-325-2540, fax 802-747-7034; www.innatlongtrail.com, e-mail ilt@vermontel.net. MODERATE TO ULTRA-DELUXE.

Ski zealots will want to plant themselves at the **Mountain Green Ski and Golf Resort**, a maze of 216 alpine-style condominiums skirting the foot of Killington Peak. Here, convenience and amenities are stressed: lifts are within walking distance, and so are the heated outdoor pool (summer only), health spa and video arcade. Other on-site amenities include a mini-mart, fireplaces and fully equipped kitchens. ~ 133 East Mountain Road, Killington; 802-422-3000, 800-336-7754; www.mtgreen.com, e-mail stay@mtgreen.com. ULTRA-DELUXE.

Despite its name, the large country-style **Cortina Inn** is actually a full-service resort. Its 96 rooms are individually decorated by the innkeepers. You'll find all the comforts here, including an indoor heated pool and fitness center with a hot tub and saunas. Some of the accommodations have fireplaces or jacuzzis and some have decks. There are two restaurants on the premises. The Killington ski area is six miles away. The inn is home to both Killington School for Tennis and Vermont Golf Vacations. ~ Route 4, Killington; 802-773-3333, 800-451-6108, fax 802-775-6948; www.cortinainn.com, e-mail cortina1@aol.com. DELUXE TO ULTRA-DELUXE.

About 16 miles north of Rutland, the lovely town of Brandon is a labyrinth of beautiful historic buildings, shade-giving maple trees and fine-trimmed lawns. Stashed away high in the mountains above Brandon, the **Churchill House Inn** is a fetching 1871 farmhouse known best to cross-country skiers, hikers and bikers. Three stories tall and fashioned in the Federal style, the inn features a swimming pool set in a perennial garden and ample fireplaces in the common rooms, as well as a 24-hour hot and cold beverage bar. Rates include full country breakfasts. Dinner is available at an additional cost. Closed the last two weeks of November and the first three weeks of April. ~ Route 73 East, Brandon; 802-247-3078, 877-248-7444; www.churchillhouseinn.com, e-mail stay@churchillhouseinn.com. DELUXE TO ULTRA-DELUXE.

The quintessence of Old World luxury exists at **The Canterbury House Bed & Breakfast**, an elegant 1880 Victorian townhouse within walking distance of Woodstock's best sights and activities, as well as the restaurants and shops on the Village Green. Named after the *Canterbury Tales* (there's a Parson's Tale and Monk's Tale), seven air-conditioned bedrooms and a suite are decorated with refinement: antique spool and brass beds, pedestal sinks and old-fashioned clawfoot tubs. ~ 43 Pleasant Street, Woodstock; 802-457-3077, 800-390-3077; www.thecanterbury house.com, e-mail stay@thecanterburyhouse.com. DELUXE TO ULTRA-DELUXE.

Perhaps no other Vermont inn has received so much acclaim as the **Woodstock Inn & Resort,** partly because of all the luminaries who frequent the place. The other part is that it's just plain wonderful to look at and, of course, *be* at. Nestled against the Village Green, the grand, Colonial-style estate sports a ten-foot stone fireplace in its lobby and needlework rugs, solid wood beams and columns, and artwork from the Rockefeller collection. Most of the 142 refurbished rooms are furnished rather simply, but extensive amenities include a huge health and fitness center complete with spa, a golf course, a ski area and a ski touring center. ~ Route 4 on the Village Green, Woodstock; 802-457-1100, 800-448-7900, fax 802-457-6699; www.woodstockinn.com, e-mail email@woodstockinn.com. ULTRA-DELUXE.

Vermont supposedly acquired its name on top of Killington Peak in 1763 when the Reverend Samuel Peters ascended on horseback and proclaimed the area *Vert Mont,* French for "green mountain."

The 28-room **Kedron Valley Inn** is a haven for well-heeled escapees who need a shot of gentrified country life. A few antique quilts adorn the guest rooms and common areas, and several rooms have private decks and terraces. Some also have fireplaces and jacuzzis. Depending on the season, guests may stroll around the 15 acres, take a walk in nearby Woodstock, ski at one of the nearby resorts, take a horse or carriage ride, swim in the inn's enormous swimming pond or laze away a few hours on the front porch. Closed in April and the ten days immediately preceding Thanksgiving. Breakfast and dinner may be included for an additional fee. ~ Route 106, South Woodstock; 802-457-1473, 800-836-1193, fax 802-457-4469; www.kedronvalleyinn.com, e-mail info@kedronvalleyinn.com. DELUXE TO ULTRA-DELUXE.

The Parker House Inn is a meticulously renovated Victorian mansion with eight generously proportioned guest rooms (all with private bath) that are furnished with period antiques. Two of the rooms look out over the Ottauquechee River. Once the home of Senator Joseph Parker, this 1856 home is now a National Historic Site. Be sure to inspect the painstakingly preserved original stenciling on the plaster walls in the entrance hall. The French bistro features fresh produce, and guests may dine on the porch during ◄ HIDDEN warmer weather. Full breakfast included. ~ 1792 Quechee Main Street, Quechee; 802-295-6077, fax 802-296-6696; www.theparkerhouseinn.com, e-mail info@theparkerhouseinn.com. DELUXE.

A sprawling 1793 farm that was home to Vermont's first lieutenant governor, **The Quechee Inn** radiates a spirit all its own. Relax in the rustic common room, complete with fireplace and grand piano, with a game or nightcap. Dine by candlelight in the restaurant on some of Vermont's own harvest. Retire to one of 25 rooms, each with private bath and air-conditioning, individually decorated with period furnishings. During the day, play tennis, swim, canoe, bike or ski on the property that surrounds a scenic lake. A full breakfast is included. ~ 1119 Quechee Main Street, Quechee; 802-295-3133, 800-235-3133, fax 802-295-6587; www.quecheeinn.com, e-mail info@quecheeinn.com. DELUXE.

Nearly half a million people flock to Vermont to take in the fall foliage.

DINING

The surrounding Green Mountains make a perfect setting for the Austrian-style **Countryman's Pleasure**. Delicate pine chairs, pink draperies and straw wreaths complete this restored 1824 farmhouse-style interior, creating a soothing effect reminiscent of the majestic Alps. The impressive menu boasts roast duck with raspberry sauce, veal medallions, fiddleheads (a Vermont specialty), venison and grilled salmon. Dinner only. Closed on Sunday, except for the holiday season. ~ Off Route 4E on Town Line Road, Mendon; 802-773-7141, fax 802-747-4959; www.countrymanspleasure.com, e-mail hentinger@verizon.net. MODERATE TO DELUXE.

Appealing to our health-conscious side, **Back Home Again** whips up entrées with organic produce and high-quality, free-range meats. Frequently mobbed by regulars, with salads and sandwiches, including a nostalgic peanut butter, banana and honey sandwich for lunch. Dinner usually includes a fish and pasta special, and all bread is baked fresh in the restaurant's own upstairs bakery. Diners lounge in a casual and creative atmosphere comprised of lots of wood, plants, paintings, murals, and of course, macrame. ~ 23 Center Street, Jutland; 802-775-9800; www.backhomeagaincafe.com. MODERATE.

Just east of Killington in Stockbridge is the large and welcoming **Peavine Family Restaurant & Thirsty Bull Pub**. Solid wood tables, low-hanging lamps and eclectic country items afford the place an instantly comfortable character. Ample servings of traditional favorites such as teriyaki chicken, barbecue ribs and grilled sirloin treat diners like family. Kids will feast on their own dishes of chicken tenders, pasta primavera or pepperoni pizza. ~ Route 107, Stockbridge; 802-234-9434; www.peavinerestaurant.com, e-mail email@peavinerestaurant.com. MODERATE.

Beautifully prepared, innovative cuisine has garnered **Hemingway's** quite a reputation around these parts. Everything is fresh and scrupulously served among elegant surroundings of white tablecloths and crystal. The prix-fixe three- or four-course meal highlights regional cuisine, while the á la carte menu might include lobster and corn chowder with vanilla, sauté of Vermont pheasant with wild mushrooms or poached salmon in pea broth. grilled striped bass with spring vegetables. The desserts are true works of art. Usually closed Monday and Tuesday, mid-April to mid-May and the first two weeks of November. ~ 4988 Route 4, Killington; 802-422-3886, fax 802-422-3468; www.hemingwaysrestaurant.com, e-mail hemwy@sover.net. ULTRA-DELUXE.

It began as a modest greenhouse that later took on a soda fountain. Now **Bentley's** is the local noshing post, an uptown eatery decked in antiques, lace curtains and fringed lampshades. You can show up in casual or dressy attire and feast on treats such as scampi *pescatore*, beef stew and daily pasta dishes. Brunch on Sunday. ~ 3 Elm Street, Woodstock; 802-457-3232, fax 802-457-3238; www.bentleysrestaurant.com, e-mail info@bentleysrestaurant.com. MODERATE TO DELUXE.

Simon Pearce Restaurant affords an unusual blend of sophisticated cuisine and artistic talent. Glassblower Simon Pearce—who's quite well known around New England—has fashioned beautiful stemware and globes that rest on formal tablecloths. His creative American cuisine menu is a perfect accompaniment, highlighted by roast duck with mango chutney and horseradish-crusted cod with crisp fried leeks. The brick building—a story in itself—was an 1830s mill that produced the country's largest supply of wool flannel. Reservations recommended for dinner. ~ Main Street, Quechee; 802-295-1470, fax 802-295-2853; www.simonpearce.com, e-mail qrestaurant@simonpearceglass.com. DELUXE TO ULTRA-DELUXE.

SHOPPING

Camille's Experienced Clothing is the place to go for high-end second-hand clothing. This store carries everything from designer cocktail dresses and furs to cashmere, leather, and kids' and men's clothing. ~ 44 Merchants Row, Jutland; 802-773-0971.

For unusual hand-crafted items, check out **Truly Unique Gift Shop**. Also available are various Vermont food products. ~ Route 4E, Rutland; 802-773-7742, fax 802-773-7378.

For fun and unusual kitchenware, head to **Aubergine**, an eclectic shop purveying tools for the amateur chef and amusing gifts. Specializing in unique items, the store also stocks an array of useful household gadgets as well as colorful ceramic and glass dishes. ~ 1 Elm Street, Woodstock; 802-457-1340, 800- 458-1340; www.purple-eggplant.com.

Great kitchen treasures await at **F. H. Gillingham & Sons**, where you can pick up picnic baskets, costly wines and frou-frou cooking devices. ~ 16 Elm Street, Woodstock; 802-457-2100, fax 802-457-2101; www.gillinghams.com.

Woodstock Folk Art Prints & Antiquities displays paintings, prints and ceramics by established and up-and-coming artists from around the country and Vermont. Of note are works by Sabra Field, who designed the state's centennial stamp, and Woody Jackson of Ben & Jerry's truck art fame. ~ 6 Elm Street, Woodstock; 802-457-2012; www.woodstockfolkart.com.

Vermont-style paraphernalia, from maple products and cheese to wicker baskets and country cookbooks, are all jammed under one big red roof at the vast **Quechee Gorge Village**. ~ Route 4W, Quechee; 802-295-1550; www.qgv.com.

NIGHTLIFE

As its name suggests, **The Wobbly Barn** is an old, crooked wooden building and a very popular après ski hangout. There's live music that cranks nightly, ranging from Blues and rock to 70s disco. Cover. ~ On Kelvington Road between the lifts and the access road, Kelvington; 802-422-6171; www.wobblybarn.com.

On Saturday night during ski season, skiers jam into the **Pickle Barrel**, where you'll find late-night rock, a huge dancefloor and a barnlike environment. Closed May through September. Cover. ~ Killington Access Road, Killington; 802-422-3035; www.picklebarrelnightclub.com.

BEACHES & PARKS

GREEN MOUNTAIN NATIONAL FOREST See "Beaches & Parks" in the Southern Vermont section.

LAKE ST. CATHERINE STATE PARK With a three-mile shoreline, St. Catherine is one of Vermont's largest and most beautiful lakes. The 117-acre park borders only part of the lake, but its 250-foot beach draws large crowds, particularly on weekends. Swimming in the lake is exceptional and there are great opportunities to catch rainbow and lake trout, smelt, yellow perch, northern pike, bullhead and small- and largemouth bass. There's also a trail where you're apt to see deer, raccoons and rabbits. Facilities include picnic areas, a playground, a snack bar

AUTHOR FAVORITE

The heart of trendiness, **Bentley's** is (and has been, forever) the town noshing spot, decked in lace curtains, antique lamps, and one long, polished bar. There's live music (in winter) on Friday night, and dancing to a three-piece jazz band on Saturday night. ~ 3 Elm Street, Woodstock; 802-457-3232, 877-457-3232; www.bentleysrestaurant.com, e-mail info@bentleysrestaurant.com.

and boat rentals. Closed mid-October to mid-May. Day-use fee, $2.50. ~ Route 30, three miles south of Poultney; 802-287-9158.

▲ There are 50 tent/RV sites ($16 per night) with hot showers, fireplaces and 11 lean-tos ($23 per night); no hookups. Reservations: 888-409-7579.

BOMOSEEN STATE PARK This vast area harbors Vermont's largest lake, Lake Bomoseen, along with an incredible stretch of forest sprinkled with dormant slate quarries. The park spans 365 acres, part of the 2940-acre Bomoseen State Forest, and contains yet another large freshwater body called Glen Lake. There's a nice long tawny beach on Bomoseen, plenty of surrounding nature trails, plus a visiting naturalist who conducts bird and wildflower walks and other programs. Swimming and fishing are exceptional at both lakes, with possibilities for panfish, yellow perch, bass and trout. Facilities include picnic areas, a snack bar, and boat and canoe rentals. Closed September to mid-May. Day-use fee, $2.50. ~ Off Route 4 on West Shore Road, about four miles north of Hydeville; 802-265-4242.

▲ There are 66 sites with hot showers, fireplaces and 10 lean-tos but no hookups. Rates are $16 to $18 per night for tent/RV sites and $23 to $25 per night for lean-tos. Reservations: 888-409-7579.

COOLIDGE STATE FOREST The 30th president spent most of his life in this incredibly scenic, remote swath of forest, which spans close to 17,000 acres and now serves as a nucleus for hiking, snowmobiling and relaxation. Nearby, but not within the forest, are the dusky Black River and the gurgling Broad Brook—great for wading and stone collecting—which cut through dense, cool pine stands. Trails will lead you to magnificent views atop Shrewsbury and Killington peaks. Within the forest is the 500-acre **Coolidge State Park**, where you'll find camping and hiking opportunities. There are picnic tables, restrooms, hiking and nature trails, and an extensive snowmobile network; the historic Calvin Coolidge Homestead is only a few miles away. Closed mid-October to mid-May. Day-use fee, $2.50. ~ Route 100A, two miles north of the intersection with Route 100, Plymouth; 802-672-3612.

▲ The state park has 25 tent/RV sites ($14 per night) and 35 lean-tos ($21 to $23 per night), with hot showers and fireplaces but no hookups. Reservations: 888-409-7579.

CAMP PLYMOUTH STATE PARK There's gold in them thar hills—at least in this park. Believe it or not, this 295-acre wooded spread attracts a sprinkling of gold diggers who wade ankle-deep and pan the silty bottom of the Buffalo Brook. Of course, no one has struck it rich lately, but who cares? This hilly park's other claim to fame is shimmering Echo

Lake, which possesses a very pretty but small slice of cinnamon-colored sand. You can swim or try for smelt, trout, bass and yellow perch. Facilities include picnic tables, a playground, restrooms, a snack bar, volleyball, nature trails and boat rentals. Four cabins (they each sleep six) are available for rent by the week; $80 per night. Closed Labor Day to Memorial Day. Day-use fee, $2.50. ~ Off Route 100 just north of Ludlow in the town of Tyson; 802-228-2025.

▲ There are six primitive lean-tos that serve as horse camps; $4 per person. Reservations: 888-409-7579.

WILGUS STATE PARK This 100-acre park draws life from the wide, fertile Connecticut River. Most of the area is heavily wooded, but a small clearing allows for cool picnicking and nice views across the river to New Hampshire. There's no beach, but an opening in the steep river banks makes way for canoes. The strong currents discourage swimming. Facilities include picnic areas, restrooms, a playground, canoe rentals and nature trails. Closed mid-October to mid-May. Day-use fee, $2.50. ~ Route 5, south of Ascutney; 802-674-5422.

Plymouth-born Calvin Coolidge was the only president born on the 4th of July (1872).

▲ There are 19 tent/RV sites ($14 per night) and 6 lean-tos ($21 per night) with hot showers and fireplaces. Reservations: 888-409-7579.

QUECHEE STATE PARK This is one of the most visited parks in Vermont, and rightly so, since it provides access to the geological phenomenon called Quechee Gorge. Carved by glaciers during the Ice Age, the 163-foot gorge provides a cool, scenic milieu along the Ottauquechee River. Quite large, the 611-acre park mostly skirts calmer, flatter parts of the river and provides asylum for plenty of white-tailed deer. For anglers, this area is trout land. There are picnic tables, a playground, restrooms and top-notch nature trails. Closed October to Memorial Day. ~ Route 4, three miles west of Exit 189 in Quechee, six miles from White River Junction; 802-295-2990.

▲ There are 47 tent/RV sites ($14 per night) and 7 lean-tos ($21 per night), with hot showers and fireplaces but no hookups. Reservations: 888-409-7579.

Northern Mountain Region

Seemingly limitless forests of maple trees, or "sugarbushes," have earned this region its image —along with a handsome maple syrup industry. Indeed, the entire region evokes a sense of ultimate Vermont charm, a place crisscrossed with valley farms and corn fields, winding country roads, hidden swimming holes and the whizzing Mad River that inspires virtually every part of local life.

Most of the tranquil villages here can trace their roots to the early 1800s (some even further back), making them a delight to visit and investigate. Tiny, endearing Montpelier, the state capital, was established in 1805 after Vermont's legislature roamed for almost 30 years. Austria-like Stowe, its great alpine peaks forming a sea of green, harkens back to 1833 when it was a crossroads for travelers on horseback.

While longtime Vermonters surely appreciate the region's idyllic aura, it's the flatlanders—natives of New York, Massachusetts or any other place that's not Vermont—who have lately sought out the serenity of these vertical reaches. Typically owners of small businesses or bed and breakfasts, these "immigrants" have left the so-called good life in big cities for what they say is a better life among Vermont's Green Mountains.

SIGHTS

Though the Sugarbush ski resort area churns up the most activity, the real local beauty lies in **Warren** (off Route 100 east of Lincoln Gap Road) and **Waitsfield** (northward along Route 100), a pair of pastoral towns with covered bridges, general stores and friendly, down-home folks.

The region's alpine setting and excellent thermal currents make it a splendid place for **gliding**, also known as **soaring. Sugarbush Soaring** will allow you to ride the air currents 7500 feet up and secure a bird's-eye view of farmlands and mountaintop beaver ponds. Flights are offered at the **Warren–Sugarbush Airport**, where a pilot will take one passenger at a time for rides lasting 20 to 30 minutes. Rides are offered from mid-May to the end of October. ~ Airport Road off Route 100; 802-496-2290; www.sugarbushsoaring.com, e-mail soar@sugarbushsoaring.com.

East on Route 89 lies **Montpelier**. With a population of only a little over 8000, Montpelier is the smallest state capital in the nation, though its grand old buildings and manicured cityscapes may well be the country's most charming. To direct you around town—and the state—the **Capital Region Visitors Center** provides an impressive array of information on sights as well as history, culture and economy. ~ 134 State Street, Montpelier; 802-828-5981; www.1-800-vermont.com. For a guided walking tour, lasting one and a half hours, contact Margot George. Tours available by group appointment only from mid-May to mid-October. Call ahead. ~ 802-229-4842.

Montpelier's sister city is **Barre**, though no two siblings could be less alike. Barre is the rough-and-tumble one of the pair, a working-class town put on the map by the granite industry. During the late 1800s, thousands of European and Canadian immigrant stoneworkers flocked to town, making Barre quite a bustling place and along the way producing frequent labor disputes and strong movements toward socialism.

Today, this self-proclaimed Granite Capital of the World harbors the largest deep-hole, dimension granite quarry, known as **E. L. Smith Quarry**, owned and operated by The Rock of Ages Corporation. This colossal stony pit, which plunges nearly 600 feet down and spans 50 acres, is an active quarry in which workers may be viewed as they wrest titanic blocks of granite from its depths. You can sandblast your own granite souvenir at the Cut-In-Stone Activity Center. Open Memorial Day to mid-October, weather permitting. Admission for tours. ~ 558 Graniteville Road, off Route 14, Graniteville; 802-476-3119, 866-748-6877, fax 802-476-0329; e-mail visitor@barre.rockofages.com.

Some of the granite found its final resting place at the **Hope Cemetery**, a fascinating collection of memorial art. The delicate engravings of granite craftspeople (often designed for their deceased coworkers) survive on everything from small headstones and ornate monuments to giant mausoleums. There are scrolls, hearts, religious sculptures and even a large soccer ball. ~ 175 Maple Avenue, Barre.

Remember those two crazy guys named Ben and Jerry who hit the big time with an ice cream recipe? Here's where you'll find them, smack in the middle of Vermont rural country, at **Ben & Jerry's Ice Cream Factory Tours**. The factory—the state's number-one tourist attraction—is a lesson in American free enterprise. You'll see the creamy stuff being made, get free samples in their tasting room, watch a short film and learn about two guys who haven't let success stand in the way of having fun. Ben and Jerry are revered around this state, and not surprisingly, since one out of ten Vermont families bought stock in their corporation when they went public. Tours are offered daily, but no ice cream is made on weekends or holidays. Admission. ~ 1281 Waterbury-Stowe Road, Waterbury; 802-882-1240, 866-258-6877; www.benjerry.com.

Another fun stopover is the **Cold Hollow Cider Mill**, an old barn that houses a small apple cider mill and a vast country gift shop. You can watch the apple presses at work year-round. There's a winery and a live beehive. ~ 3600 Waterbury-Stowe Road Route 100 Waterbury Center, Waterbury; 802-244-8771, 800-327-7537, fax 802-244-7212; www.coldhollow.com, e-mail info@coldhollow.com.

Northward along Route 100 lies picturesque, alpine **Stowe**, a country town augmented by a bustling ski resort area and set against a deep green necklace of mountains.

The busy "downtown" area, situated at the crossroads of Route 100 and Mountain Road, is a pleasing meld of 19th-century buildings and contemporary marts and restaurants. All the ski action awaits up Mountain Road, a seven-mile jog lined with hotels and inns, shops, pubs and eateries of every culinary calling.

Vermont's highest peak, **Mount Mansfield**, looms 4395 feet above the town and presents an incredible backdrop, its craggy profile resembling the silhouette of a human face. In summer, you can take an auto toll road or a gondola ride to the summit of Mount Mansfield, ride down the thrilling **alpine slide**, jump on the bungee trampolines or race through the inflatable obstacle course. Admission. ~ Mountain Road; 802-253-3000, 800-253-4757, fax 802-253-3439; www.stowe.com, e-mail info@stowe.com.

The Stowe Land Trust was established during the 1980s by a group of Stowe citizens dedicated to preserving the rural quality of life in and around this picturesque mountain village. One of the trust's conservation projects is the **Wiessner Woods**, 80 acres of woods, streams and meadows that overlook the Stowe valley from Edson Hill. If you keep your eyes open and your conversation quiet, you're likely to see partridge, thrush, falcons and perhaps even an owl. From Mountain Road, turn right onto Edson Hill Road, three and a half miles from the village. Pass the entrance to the Stowehof Inn. Take the next drive on the right. Park on the left in the marked parking area. From here follow signs to the Wiessner Woods trailhead.

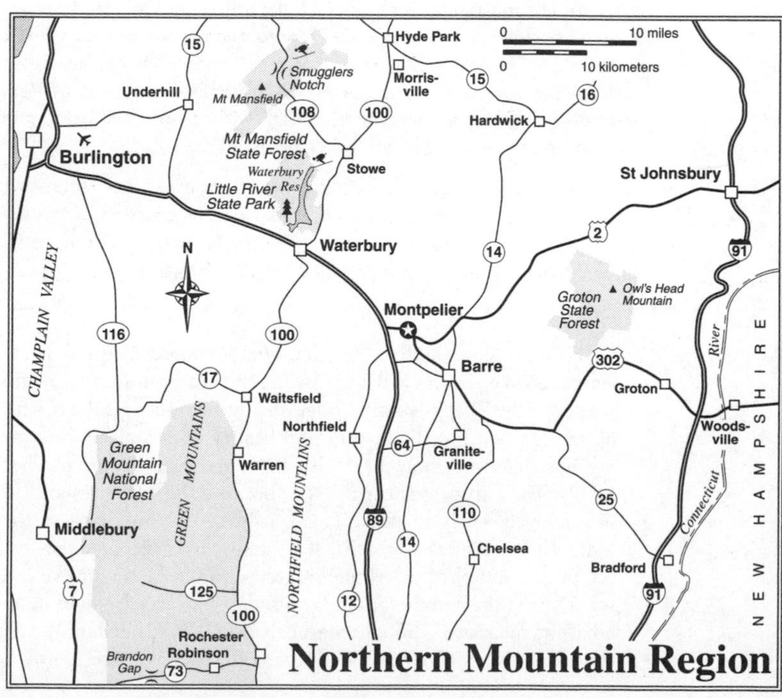

Northern Mountain Region

WALKING TOUR

Montpelier's State Street

A casual walk down State Street, the main street along the north shore of the Winooski River, reveals the architectural charms of America's smallest state capital. Simply start at the **Capital Region Visitors Center** (134 State Street; 802-828-5981; www.1-800-vermont.com) by the Bailey Avenue Bridge and walk east.

CAPITAL BUILDINGS The **State House** (c. 1859), with its gold-leaf dome resting dramatically against the evergreens of Hubbard Park, easily takes center stage with its portico. Modeled after the Greek temple of Theseus, the granite granddaddy sports a statue of Ceres, Roman goddess of agriculture. Take a free tour (late June to mid-October) or wander around and muse over the Civil War paintings and flags, Victorian decor and quotations by Theodore Roosevelt, Ethan Allen and other national legends. Closed Saturday from November through May and closed Sunday. ~ 115 State Street; 802-828-2228, 800-322-5616, fax 802-828-2424; www.leg.state.vt.us. Across the street, the **State Agriculture Building** (c. 1891), originally built as the home office of the National Life Insurance Company, features a Romanesque red-brick facade, a conglomerate of roof styles, fanciful turrets and arched, convex windows. ~ 116 State Street. In contrast is another former insurance building, the symmetrical and stately **Vermont Department of Personnel** (c. 1870), an elegant Victorian with a mansard roof and Corinthian columns. ~ 110 State Street.

STATE STREET The Pavilion Building, which houses the **Vermont Historical Society Museum**, is a modern reconstruction of the exterior of the Pavilion Hotel of 1876, an elegant Steamboat Gothic structure with inviting piazzas that provided lodging for legislators during ses-

Several decades after the film *The Sound of Music* was released, Stowe visitors still keep asking the same question: how do we get to the **Trapp Family Lodge**? Certainly much of the town's appeal is bound to the history and beauty of this place, built as a singing camp during the 1940s by Maria Von Trapp and her family. The baroness chose the spot because she said it resembled her beloved Austrian Alps. The Tyrolean-style buildings of the lodge sit high on a mountain, surrounded by 2800 acres of forest, ponds and pasture. Alpine ridges extend as far as the eye can see. During the summer, popular Sunday concerts are held in an adjacent meadow. Though Maria died in 1987, her family still runs the lodge. ~ 700 Trapp Hill Road off Mountain Road, Stowe;

sions. The museum presents exhibits of fine and decorative arts, farm and industrial equipment and memorabilia that imaginatively traces the state's history. Closed Monday year round and Sunday from November through April. Admission. ~ 109 State Street; 802-828-2291; www.vermonthistory.org. The three grand brick homes—one partly hidden by a service station—at **107, 99 and 89 State Street** are remnants of the vanished era of the 1820s, when the street was lined with high Federal style architecture.

SINNERS AND SAINTS The Greek Revival **Washington County Courthouse** (c. 1844 and 1880), with its classic clock tower, is the county's third courthouse. After the second was destroyed by fire, this one was built from local granite. Its interior has been modernized, but the original wooden stairway remains intact. ~ 65 State Street. Behind the courthouse is the **Jailhouse Common** (c. 1857). The difference in brick between the first and second stories reveals that it was expanded in 1911. ~ 22–24 Elm Street. Across the street from the courthouse stands the Gothic **Episcopal Church** (c. 1867), more striking inside than out because its spire was removed for safety reasons after a fire and flood in 1927. ~ 64 State Street.

BUSINESS BUILDINGS The simple-frame **Langdon Building** (before 1853) represents the kind of storefront that was typical in most Vermont towns before brick came into wide use in the mid-19th century. ~ 4 Langdon Street. The bank building at **41–45 State Street** (c. 1874), with its turn-of-the-20th-century mansard roof, has always been a bank, though its exterior has been modernized at least twice. Finally, the Italianate **Walton Block** (c. 1879), with its stamped sheet metal ornaments and cast-iron columns, typifies the style of storefronts in the late 19th century. It was the first structure in Montpelier to undergo historical restoration, beginning in 1967. ~ 17 State Street.

802-253-8511, 800-826-7000, fax 802-253-5740; www.trappfamily.com, e-mail resstaff@trappfamily.com.

There's no sign for **Bingham Falls**, but you won't want to miss this pristine look at nature's handiwork. A rocky footpath winds a quarter mile through the evergreen forest, culminating at a scenic gorge where rushing, gurgling water swirls around large boulders. A great swimming hole, if you don't mind chilly waters. ~ Off Mountain Road, a few miles north of The Lodge resort.

LODGING

The closest proximity to downhill skiing can be found at **Sugarbush Village Condominiums**, where you can choose from 150 condos (many ski-in and ski-out) sprinkled about the base of

Sugarbush North and South. Most accommodations are modern apartment style, though they vary widely from small studios and loft apartments to townhouses and four-bedroom condos. ~ Sugarbush Access Road, Warren; 802-583-3000, 800-451-4326, fax 802-583-2781; www.sugarbushvillage.com, e-mail sugarbush village@yahoo.com. DELUXE TO ULTRA-DELUXE.

You can get a true feel for Vermonters and their lifestyles if you stay at **Lareau Farm**, a picturesque 67-acre spread hugging the Mad River. The owner is convivial and genuine, ready to show you local customs and all the town has to offer. The 1832 farmhouse is quintessential New England: big gracious rooms with wide-plank floors, a living room with a fireplace, a fabulous gazebo-style porch overlooking the mountains and 12 very comfortable bedrooms with antique beds and plush handmade quilts. Closed early November and late April. ~ Route 100, Waitsfield; 802-496-4949, 800-833-0766, fax 802-496-7979; www.lareaufarminn.com, e-mail clay@lareaufarminn.com. MODERATE TO DELUXE.

Call it pastoral luxury or rural fancy, but the **1824 House Inn** is the place to indulge while soaking up the country sights. Set on 16 scenic acres in the Mad River Valley, this two-story gabled farmhouse is awash with beautiful antiques, Oriental and dhurrie rugs, and a distinct air of elegance and precise design. There are eight bright and airy bedrooms, all with private baths, plus a gracious dining room where guests get treated to an extensive breakfast. Gourmet dinners are served nightly in the renovated, circa 1870 barn. Closed the first two weeks of November and May. ~ 2150 Main Street, Waitsfield; 802-496-7555, 800-426-3986, fax 802-496-7559; www.1824house.com, e-mail stay@1824house.com. DELUXE.

The most eloquent place to stay in the state capital is **The Inn at Montpelier**, a pair of stately antebellum buildings that breathe history. There are high ceilings and beautiful Victorian furnishings, ten fireplaces and an enormous wraparound porch dotted

SMUGGLERS NOTCH

Perhaps the area's ultimate nature encounter occurs at **Smugglers Notch** (Mountain Road), a slender, sensational pass through the mountains with dramatic sheets of silver rock on either side. Used as a secret passage between Canada and the U.S. during the War of 1812, the notch harbors dozens of intriguing rock formations (check out the singing bird and elephant head) and a rock crevasse where the summer temperature hovers around 49°. Keep an eye out for rock climbers who navigate the cliffs and rappel down.

with hanging plants and fan-back chairs. Lavishly decorated, the 19 guest rooms feature mirrored armoires, Queen Anne and teak poster beds and polished pedestal sinks. Well worth the price. No smoking. ~ 147 Main Street, Montpelier; 802-223-2727, fax 802-223-0722; www.innatmontpelier.com, e-mail innatmontpelier@comcast.net. DELUXE TO ULTRA-DELUXE.

The prow-like roofline of the **Stowehof Inn** is deceptive: there's nothing remotely marine about this large, luxurious hotel. Perched on a hillside that overlooks the dips and swells of the Stowe valley, the Stowehof's generous spaces are attentively fitted out, with comfortable chairs in the lounge area and drapes on the bedroom windows for guests to block out the bright morning light. Room decor varies: When you call for a reservation, ask about the range of rooms available during your visit (and unless you really want one, request a room without a mirrored wall). Although most travelers associate the Stowe area with winter sports, the Stowehof is a true four-season resort: In addition to the miles of cross-country trails and sleigh rides available right from the hotel during the winter, there's a fitness complex; an indoor and outdoor swimming pool and four tennis courts are available for guests' use during warmer weather. Breakfast included. ~ 434 Edson Hill Road, Stowe; 802-253-9722, 800-932-7136, fax 802-253-7513; www.stowehofinn.com, e-mail discover@stowehofinn.com. MODERATE TO ULTRA-DELUXE.

Butternut Inn on the River is one of those inns that tries to be homey and elegant at the same time—and pulls it off swimmingly. Wrought with dozens of beautiful American country antiques, the four-story lodge is practically a museum. There's even more refinement outside, where twinkling lights meander through evergreens, and a gazebo overlooks a swimming pool and perennial gardens. There are two swimming holes and many that lace trails through the inn's eight-acre landscape. The fireside breakfasts, cozy game room, hot tub, river and mountain views and warmly decorated bedrooms suggest quite a snug lodging experience. A few of the rooms have fireplaces and whirlpool tubs. A full country breakfast is included, as is afternoon tea accompanied by homemade cookies. ~ 2309 Mountain Road, Stowe; 802-253-4277, 800-328-8837, fax 802-253-5263; www.butternutinnvt.com, e-mail innstowe2@aol.com. MODERATE TO ULTRA-DELUXE.

Ten Acres Lodge, a huge 1836 red inn with white trim, is perched on a hill in picturesque Stowe. Guestrooms are bright with floral wallpaper and quilts, flower garlands and warm-toned furnishings; all include a private bath, cable TV and a sitting area. The lodge also boasts its own movie theater with a nine-foot screen, a spa and a swimming pool, as well as a fine restaurant. For a more intimate setting, a pet-friendly, two-bedroom cottage with a fireplace is also available. ~ 14 Barrows Road, Stowe; 800-

327-7357, fax 802-253-6589; www.tenacreslodge.com, e-mail info@tenacreslodge.com. DELUXE TO ULTRA-DELUXE.

Endless waves of mountains and evergreen valleys create a milieu that's nothing short of sensational at the **Trapp Family Lodge**. This peaceful, 2800-acre slice of nirvana was set up as a 1940s singing camp by Maria Von Trapp. Tyrolean in style, the enchanting buildings have flowerpots that brim with kaleidoscopic colors and 96 guest rooms simply adorned in dark woods and muted colors and featuring modern amenities. There are also motel-style units and rooms available in outlying guesthouses. You can't miss the scenic pond, two swimming pools edged with lawn, greenhouse and gardens—and many more sightseers than guests. ~ 700 Trapp Hill Road, Stowe; 802-253-8511, 800-826-7000, fax 802-253-5740; www.trappfamily.com, e-mail resstaff@trappfamily.com. ULTRA-DELUXE.

A serene French Provincial manor obscured down a winding mountain road, **Edson Hill Manor** offers 225 acres of solitude amid majestic surroundings. Featuring hewn-wood ceilings and Oriental rugs, the main house offers nine spacious rooms—five with beautiful fireplaces—while a carriage house contains 16 guest rooms. You'll also find a terraced swimming pool, riding stables, nature trails and plenty of cross-country skiing possibilities. Full breakfast and dinner included in the rates. ~ 1500 Edson Hill Road off Mountain Road, Stowe; 802-253-7371, 800-621-0284, fax 802-253-6580; www.edsonhillmanor.com, e-mail info@edsonhillmanor.com. DELUXE TO ULTRA-DELUXE.

DINING

This is ski country, and most restaurants cater to those tired skiers with hearty appetites. Oftentimes you'll find a cauldron of soup steaming over a blazing hearth, and cushy chairs for snuggling.

The refinement and understated elegance of **The Common Man** has earned it a solid culinary reputation across Vermont. Situated in a 19th-century barn, the place is simply romantic. Pretty chandeliers hang from high beam ceilings, while well-spaced tables hug a large stone hearth. The cuisine is *très* gourmet, with an accent on native offerings. There's a variety of offerings that include duck, veal, lamb, salmon, rabbit, game hen, shrimp, filet, pasta and vegetarian entrées. Dinner only. Closed Sunday through Monday from mid-April to mid-December. ~ 3209 German Flats Road, Warren; 802-583-2800; www.commonmanrestaurant.com, e-mail info@commonmanrestaurant.com. MODERATE TO DELUXE.

A charming 1850s structure, the **Millbrook Inn and Restaurant** truly captures the flavor of Vermont. The decor is warm and inviting, with wide-plank floors, country antiques and paintings of local life. A congenial couple acts as manager and chef, serving hand-rolled pastas and very special pies. Entrées include two fresh fish specials every day, an "innkeeper's choice" of roast meat, *badami* *rogan josh* (lamb) and several curry dishes. Closed April, May and November. Closed Tuesday in summer. ~ 533 Mill Brook Road (Route 17), Waitsfield; 802-496-2405, 800-477-2809; www.millbrookinn.com, e-mail gorman@millbrookinn.com. MODERATE.

The swank, contemporary **Purple Moon Pub** contains neither country antiques nor historic furnishings. Martinis and appetizers are the order of the hour all evening long at this chic tavern. Grilled panini sandwiches, goat cheese fondue and fresh green salads pair easily with the full bar and on-tap selections. A classic burger and sirloin steak round out the small, but complete, menu. For a bite of hip atmosphere, stop here. ~ Route 100, Waitsfield (a half mile south of the junction of Routes 17 and 100); 802-496-3422, fax 802-496-7232; www.purplemoonpub.com, e-mail info@purplemoonpub.com.

In Montpelier, the New England Culinary Institute operates three restaurants where you'll discover very vogue cuisine. The most upscale is the **Chef's Table**, which serves innovative and classic American cuisine in an intimate setting. The red walls, antique oil paintings and low lighting create a Baroque effect and a romantic atmosphere. The menu changes daily and features gourmet dishes such as warm goat cheese Napoleon and hickory-smoked duck. No lunch on Saturday. Closed Sunday. ~ 118 Main Street, Montpelier; 802-229-9202; www.necidining.com. DELUXE.

For more casual surroundings, visit the Culinary Institute's **Main Street Grill & Bar** downstairs. This casual bistro offers hearty contemporary American fare amidst eclectic country decor. There is a seasonal menu, but try the portobello mushroom sandwich or the herbed roast chicken with garlic mashed potatoes. The outdoor patio is open in the summer. Closed Monday. ~ 118 Main Street, Montpelier; 802-223-3188; www.necidining.com. MODERATE.

At **La Brioche Bakery and Café**, also run by the Institute, you can pick up puffy croissants, gourmet cookies, napoleons and other baked goodies. ~ 89 Main Street, Montpelier; 802-229-0443, fax 802-229-6462; www.necidining.com. BUDGET.

BREAKFAST BRIGHT AND EARLY

To experience the true flavor of **McCarthy's**, get there just after dawn when local farmers arrive dressed in overalls and straw hats. This congenial breakfast and lunch café offers friendly service, huge portions and great prices. You'll find apple and blueberry pancakes with real Vermont syrup, country eggs Benedict, sticky buns and pumpkin bread. Surroundings are modern and airy with Irish country touches. ~ 2043 Mountain Road, Stowe; 802-253-8626. BUDGET.

HIDDEN ► For top-notch Tex-Mex fare, check out **Julio's**. This serene downtown niche offers up basic south-of-the-border entrées plus interesting selections such as Mexican pizzas, ribs and egg rolls. There's an oak bar and walls covered with Mexican prints and local art. ~ 54 State Street, Montpelier; 802-229-9348; www.julioscantina.com. BUDGET TO MODERATE.

Mulligan's is a popular town rendezvous with real flair. The two-story, ranch-style eatery is flanked by wagon wheels and exhibits walls smothered in old license plates and farm tools. An Irish pub with a hint of Tex-Mex, they serve burritos, burgers, stacked sandwiches and salads. Closed Sunday. ~ 9 Maple Avenue, Barre; 802-479-5545. BUDGET.

The beautiful **Trapp Family Lodge** boasts one of the area's most renowned dining rooms. Situated in a marvelous mountain setting, the restaurant is simple yet elegant, with picture windows, draped hanging plants and light oak tables. The food is gourmet Continental with Austrian touches. Try the *zwiebelrostbraten* (Viennese onion steak) or the *wienerschnitzel* (breaded and sautéed veal cutlets). The menu is prix-fixe, with your choice of a three- or five-course meal. No lunch. Reservations recommended for dinner. ~ 700 Trapp Hill Road, Stowe; 802-253-8511, 800-826-7000, fax 802-253-5740. ULTRA-DELUXE.

SHOPPING

Absolutely don't miss **The Warren Store**, a former stagecoach inn that's like Grandpa's general store. The place starts with a jumble of wines, jams, homemade honey and baskets, continues with a wonderful bakery and deli, then finishes upstairs with housewares, clothing, jewelry and leather goods. ~ 284 Main Street, Warren; 802-496-3864, fax 802-496-7233; www.warrenstore.com, e-mail info@warrenstore.com.

Even if you leave empty-handed, don't miss a trip to **The Store**, a bi-level, cook's fantasy world of gourmet gadgets galore. They also feature accessories for the home, as well as American and English antiques. ~ Route 100, Waitsfield; 802-496-4465; www.vermontstore.com.

Outside of ski season, the main industry in Stowe appears to be the creation of quality arts and crafts. While galleries abound, the widest selection of work by local and other artisans can be

AUTHOR FAVORITE

More than 50,000 books crowd **The Yankee Paperback Exchange**, where I've found everything from old classics and out-of-print gems to volumes on religion, cooking and lifestyles. Closed Sunday. ~ 11 Langdon Street, Montpelier; 802-223-3239.

found at the **Stowe Craft Gallery**, where wares range from delicate crystal and custom stained-glass lamps to Judaica, African art and handmade furniture. ~ 55 Mountain Road, Stowe; 802-253-4693, 877-456-8388; www.stowecraft.com.

Women won't need to vacillate at **Decisions, Decisions**, where they can choose among beautiful sleepwear, lingerie and snug winter items, as well as casual daywear. ~ 1056 Mountain Road #7, Stowe; 802-253-4183.

NIGHTLIFE

Local theater in Vermont tends to be high quality, and such is the case at **Valley Players Theater**, which focuses on drama, comedy and children's productions performed in a 200-seat, two-story brick building. ~ Route 100, Waitsfield; 802-496-9612 or 802-583-1674; www.valleyplayers.com.

Politicians rub elbows at **The Thrush Tavern**, a tiny watering hole with framed old photos and occasional live folk music. ~ 107 State Street, Montpelier; 802-223-2030; www.thrushtavern.com.

Grab a frosty beverage at the worn pine bar at **Charlie O's**. This pool hall has live music on the weekend and a sound system that cranks. ~ 70 Main Street, Montpelier; 802-223-6820.

The **Main Street Grill & Bar** is a comfortable basement bar (completely smoke-free) with exposed flagstone walls, original artwork and one of the state's largest collections of wine, beer and liquor. ~ 118 Main Street, Montpelier; 802-223-3188.

One of the hottest night spots in town is **The Rusty Nail**, with live bands and dancing on weekends; it's packed to the rafters during ski season. Occasional cover. ~ 1190 Mountain Road, Stowe; 802-253-6245; www.rustynailbar.com.

The Matterhorn Restaurant & Nightclub, a voluminous rock-and-roll bar perched near the base of Mt. Mansfield, occasionally hosts big-name rock groups and local acts during the ski season. Occasional cover. ~ 4969 Mountain Road, Stowe; 802-253-8198; www.matterhornbar.com.

BEACHES & PARKS

GREEN MOUNTAIN NATIONAL FOREST See "Beaches & Parks" in the Southern Vermont section.

LITTLE RIVER STATE PARK A dense, bushy area within Mount Mansfield State Forest, this park spans 60 acres of the 12,000 forest acres of maple, birch and fir and a big manmade body of water called the Waterbury Reservoir. There are two campers-only beaches—one in a wooded camping area and the other in a large picnic clearing. Nature lovers will revel in the excellent gridwork of trails. Swimming and fishing (for perch, rainbow trout, and small and bigmouth bass) are good all over the reservoir. Facilities include picnic tables, restrooms, a playground and boat rentals. Closed mid-October to Memorial Day. Day-use fee, $2.50. ~ From the junction of Routes 100 and 2, take Route 2 one and a half miles west to Little River Road and go north for three and a half miles; 802-244-7103.

▲ There are 81 tent/RV sites ($16 per night) and 20 lean-tos ($23 per night) with hot showers and fireplaces but no hookups. Reservations: 888-409-7579.

GROTON STATE FOREST This 25,625-acre wonderland harbors several natural jewels. Fishing is good at the campgrounds, but the best place in the forest is Seyon Ranch State Park. One of the most popular forest activities is the hike to the summit of Owl's Head Mountain, where incredible views stretch across Camel's Hump Forest. ~ Access points are located off Routes 302 and 232 northwest of Groton; 802-748-6687.

Montpelier is the only state capital in the United States without a McDonald's.

▲ Groton Forest has five camping areas, including primitive, group and developed campgrounds. All of the areas mentioned below have camping except Boulder Beach, which is day-use only. Reservations: 888-409-7579.

Seyon Lodge State Park There's outstanding flyfishing here; you'll find a trout pond and rowboat rentals. Boating is only allowed for fishing. Day-use fee, $2.50. ~ Located just off Route 302 three miles west of Groton; 802-582-3829 (summer), 802-479-4280 (winter).

Ricker Pond State Park This camping-only facility has a boat launch and rentals (canoes, kayaks, rowboats). Anglers hook perch, bass and pickerel. Swim at your own risk—there are no lifeguards. Fireplaces, restrooms and showers are available. Closed Memorial Day to Columbus Day. Visitor fee, $2.50. ~ Route 232, three miles northwest of Route 302; 802-584-3821.

▲ Campers choose from 27 tent/RV sites ($16 to $18 per night), 23 lean-tos ($23 to $25 per night), five cabins ($46 per night) and a cottage with a kitchenette and bathroom ($60 per night). There are showers but no hookups.

Boulder Beach State Park At this picturesque beach, bulky rocks dot the coarse, cream-colored sand that edges Lake Groton. Small boats laze across the water, surrounded by mighty stands of evergreen trees. Swimming is excellent along a calm, shallow shelf at Boulder Beach. There are picnic areas, restrooms, boat rentals, a snack bar and a pavilion. Nearby is the **Groton Nature Center** (802-584-3827), which houses interesting displays of plant and animal life. Closed September to late May. Day-use fee, $2.50. ~ From Groton, go two miles west on Route 302, then six miles northwest on Route 232, then two miles east on Boulder Beach Road; 802-584-3823 (summer), 802-479-4280 (winter).

Stillwater State Park Facilities at Stillwater include picnic tables, fireplaces, boat rentals, a dock, a boat launch, a playground and showers. Closed mid-October to mid-May. Visitor fee, $2.50. ~ From Groton, go two miles west on Route 302, then six miles northwest on Route 232, then a half mile east on Boulder Beach Road; 802-584-3822.

▲ There are 62 tent/RV sites ($16 per night) and 17 lean-tos ($23 per night). There are showers but no hookups.

New Discovery State Park New Discovery (on Osmore Pond) offers a scenic clearing for picnicking. You'll find boat rentals, picnic tables, restrooms, showers and pavilions. Closed September to mid-May. Day-use fee, $2.50. ~ Route 232, nine and a half miles northwest of Route 302; 802-241-3655; e-mail parks@state.vt.us.

▲ There are 47 tent/RV sites ($14 per night) and 14 lean-tos ($21 per night) with showers but no hookups.

SMUGGLERS NOTCH STATE PARK Wedged at the apex of two stony, sheer mountains, Smugglers Notch offers idyllic surroundings of rock ledges and formations, fern grottos and damp caves for exploring. The park itself comprises 25 acres of shady, brookside picnic grounds, but you can walk to many choice sights outside the park grounds. There are picnic tables, restrooms and hiking trails. Closed mid-October to mid-May. Visitor fee, $2.50. ~ Route 108 (Mountain Road) in Stowe, about eight miles north of the Route 100 junction; 802-253-4014. ◄ HIDDEN

▲ There is a small area with 20 tent/RV sites ($14 per night) and 14 lean-tos ($21 per night); hot showers and fireplaces but no hookups. Reservations: 888-409-7579.

UNDERHILL STATE PARK Remote and rustic, this pretty park lies in the midst of back country, smothered in maple and birch trees and filled with moose, bear, deer and rabbits. It lies within the 34,000-acre Mt. Mansfield State Forest and features four popular trails that ascend the western flank of Mount Mansfield. The park also holds rare, federally protected arctic tundra, which can only be viewed from specific trails. To get here, you'll have to tackle three miles of steep gravel road—but it's well worth it. There is a picnic shelter and restrooms. Closed late October to late May. Day-use fee, $2.50. ~ From the town of Essex Junction, go nine miles east on Route 15, then four miles east on Pleasant Valley Road, then three miles east on gravel Mountain Road (there's a sign at this point); 802-899-3022.

▲ Camping is at a small primitive area with 11 tent sites ($14 per night) and 6 lean-tos ($21 per night). Reservations: 888-409-7579.

Champlain Valley

A great big meeting of mountains, water and islands, the Champlain Valley is a prosperous, breathtaking region that ambles leisurely along Vermont's northwestern edge. Lake Champlain, the area's frame of reference, stretches 130 glistening miles and divides Vermont's flat, irregular lakefront border from New York's Adirondack Mountains. Back in 1609, French explorer Samuel de Champlain discovered the lake, named it for himself and laid the groundwork for its flourishing maritime history. Champlain Valley is also home to Vermont's most populated city, Burlington, which was founded in 1763.

SIGHTS

The state's most popular attraction lies in this region. Just south of Burlington, the **Shelburne Museum** is really a *collection* of buildings—39 to be exact. It takes two days to tackle this amazing 45-acre trek through Vermont and New England history. There's something for everyone here, from the 220-foot sidewheel steamboat and toy shop to the 1786 sawmill. Kids and adults will love the circus building with its carousel ride and remarkable 500-foot miniature circus parade that took 30 years to complete. The museum's Owl Cottage Family Activity Center has a children's dress-up exhibit, historical puzzles and toys. The Electra Havemeyer Webb Memorial Building contains artwork from Degas, Monet, Manet and Cassatt. A 168-foot covered bridge, built in 1845 and moved to the museum from Cambridge, Vermont, is the United States' only remaining two-lane bridge with a footpath. If snipes, loons and yellowlegs are your bag, stop in the wildfowl decoy exhibit, where an eye-popping 1000 specimens line the walls. A marvelous place to muse, the hat and fragrance textile gallery has hat boxes, costumes, perfumes, quilts and textiles dating back to the early 1800s. You'll also find the state's largest collection of folk art, divided among several buildings. Closed November to early May; call ahead. Admission (good for two consecutive days). ~ Route 7, Shelburne; 802-985-3346, fax 802-985-2331; www.shelburnemuseum.org, e-mail info@shelburnemuseum.org.

Board a covered wagon for a tour of **Shelburne Farms**, a vast land empire that gives new meaning to the term "pastoral aristocracy." Sprawled across 1400 acres along Lake Champlain, the estate was designed back in the 1800s for Dr. William Seward Webb and wife Lila Vanderbilt. Their 24-room Queen Anne house is still one of the largest in Vermont and operates as a seasonal inn. The beautiful grounds—a series of free-flowing perennials, statues and fountains—were designed with the assistance of Frederick Law Olmsted, architect of New York City's Central Park. This National Historic Landmark boasts extensive walking trails, scenic picnic sites and a children's farmyard. Closed mid-October to mid-May.

Admission. ~ 1611 Harbor Road, off Route 7, Shelburne; 802-985-8686, fax 802-985-8123; www.shelburnefarms.org.

Five miles south of the Shelburne Museum is the **Vermont Wildflower Farm,** which sells more wildflower seeds than any other flower farm in the eastern United States. If you're not allergic to pollen, take an hour or so to wander along the paths that cross the six acres. There's a stupendous array of flowers sure to yield some surprises for even the most discerning floral connoisseur. Closed late December to April. Admission. ~ Route 7, between Burlington and Middlebury; 802-985-9455; www.americanmeadows.com.

Just north of Shelburne, skirting the lake and reigning over the valley, is Vermont's Queen City, **Burlington.** With a population of 40,000, it's the state's largest city but one that manages to maintain an intimate milieu. Burlington's remarkable alliance of mountain and water vistas were lauded by none other than Charles Dickens when he landed here back in the mid-1800s. Today, art centers, innovative theater, a university and four colleges add to the cultural mix of this spirited, youthful metropolis. In the last couple of years, the waterfront area has flourished. A community boathouse provides boat rentals and a seven-mile path has been created along the lake shore for bikers, joggers and walkers. Restaurants and shopping abound, making the lakefront a very pleasant place for a stroll. In fact, nearly half of Burlington's population is made up of college students, many of whom attend the statuesque hilltop campus of the **University of Vermont.** ~ Off University Place and Colchester Avenue, Burlington; 802-656-3131; www.uvm.edu.

The university's **Robert Hull Fleming Museum,** a grand Colonial Revival building, houses an excellent collection of European and American paintings, decorative artworks and costumes, and ethnographic objects from around the world. Closed Monday. Admission. ~ 61 Colchester Avenue, Burlington; 802-656-0750, fax 802-656-8059; www.flemingmuseum.org.

To help get you started in the area, stop by the **Lake Champlain Regional Chamber of Commerce.** ~ 60 Main Street, Burling-

sights

AUTHOR FAVORITE

I'm living proof that you don't have to be a kid to love the largest folk-art collection in New England at the wonderful **Shelburne Museum,** with its miniature circus parade, a thousand duck decoys, a steamboat, a costume collection and countless other curiosities. See page 480 for detailed information on this must-see destination.

ton; 802-863-3489, 877-686-5253, fax 802-863-1538; www.vermont.org, e-mail vermont@vermont.org.

The city's best side exists, naturally, on glittering Lake Champlain. Stroll along **Lake and Battery streets** and peer across the water to New York's Adirondack Mountains, then take a two-hour roundtrip **ferry** (May to October only) from Burlington over to Port Kent, New York, while absorbing all the scintillating views. ~ Ferry: King Street Dock, King and Battery streets; 802-864-9804, fax 802-864-6830; www.ferries.com, e-mail lct@ferries.com.

Most of the day and nighttime activity occurs at **Church Street Marketplace**, a thriving pedestrian mall jammed with outdoor cafés, trendy shops, strolling musicians and magicians and graced with 19th-century architecture. The effect is European, to say the least. ~ Church Street between Main and Pearl streets.

Northward, the **Champlain Islands** comprise Vermont's own "seacoast," a virgin outpost of apple orchards and dairy farms, rustic lakeside retreats and shores lined with anglers casting their nets. Though today there's a causeway linking these isles to Burlington, 19th-century residents had to make do with small skiffs and winter weather, when a frozen lake afforded the best access to the mainland. Route 2 traces a 30-mile path over water and land through this quiescent, largely undeveloped archipelago.

Revolutionary War veteran Jedediah Hyde, Jr., built a log cabin on the largest island, Grand Isle, back in 1783. Today the **Hyde Log Cabin** is thought to be the oldest log cabin in the country, a one-room alcove of rough-hewn beams held together by clay and straw. Amazingly, some of the original furniture and farm tools remain intact. ~ Route 2.

Up on Isle La Motte, 19th-century stone houses and a meandering rocky coastline form quite a beautiful tableau. The **St. Anne Shrine** denotes the site of Fort St. Anne—Vermont's earliest settlement—built in 1666 by Captain Pierre La Motte. ~ Off Route 129.

LODGING

Near the southern end of the Champlain Valley lies the vibrant college town of Middlebury. Here, the **Swift House Inn** reposes among enormous locust and maple trees and broods with New England history. The 1814 main house, a Federal-style building that was home to former Vermont Governor John W. Stewart, has ten rooms with poster beds and some marble fireplaces. An 1876 Victorian carriage house offers six cozy rooms with fireplaces and whirlpool tubs, while the gatehouse features five rooms with a mixture of reproductions and antiques. ~ Route 7 and 25 Stewart Lane, Middlebury; 802-388-9925, 866-388-9925, fax 802-388-9927; www.swifthouseinn.com, e-mail info@swifthouseinn.com. MODERATE TO ULTRA-DELUXE.

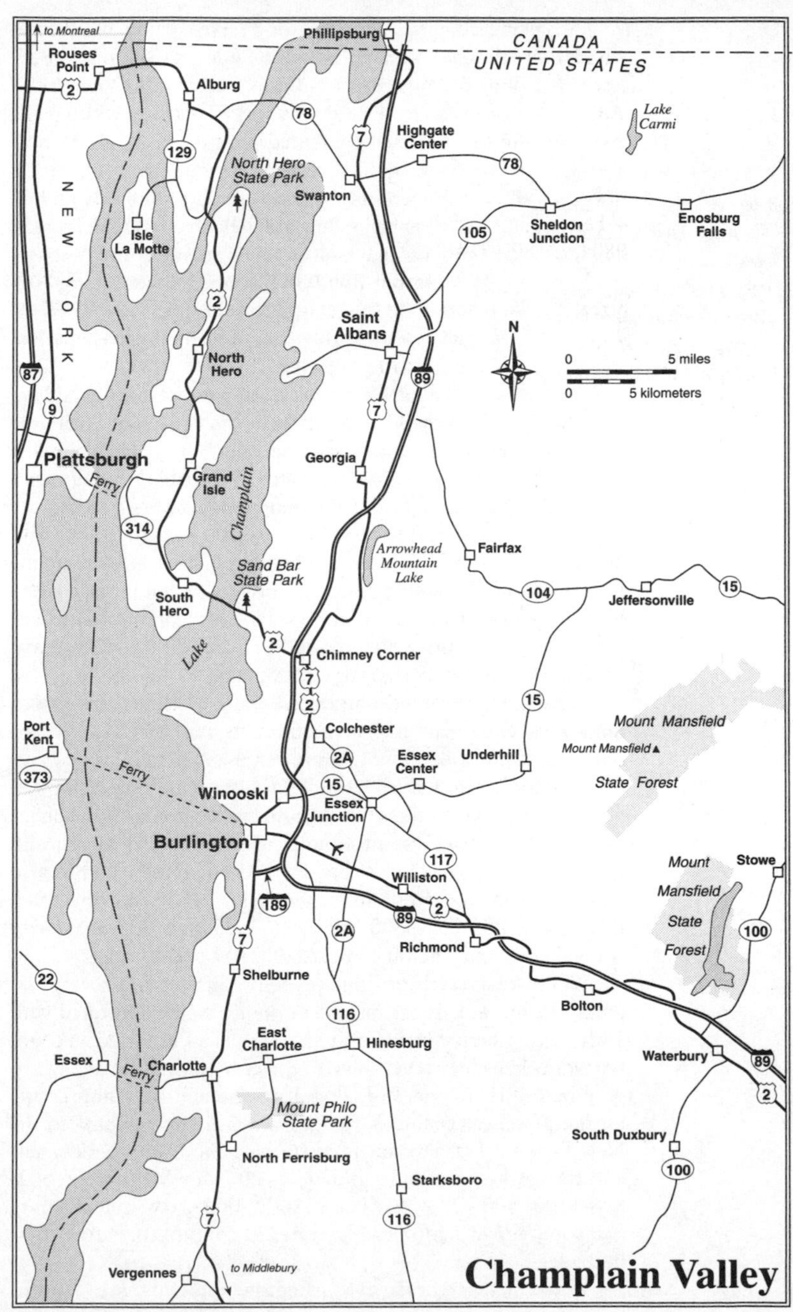
Champlain Valley
to Montreal
Phillipsburg
CANADA
UNITED STATES
Rouses Point
Alburg
Lake Carmi
Highgate Center
North Hero State Park
Swanton
Isle La Motte
NEW YORK
Sheldon Junction
Enosburg Falls
Saint Albans
North Hero
N
0 5 miles
0 5 kilometers
Plattsburgh
Ferry
Grand Isle
Georgia
Champlain
Arrowhead Mountain Lake
Fairfax
Sand Bar State Park
South Hero
Jeffersonville
Lake
Chimney Corner
Mount Mansfield
Mount Mansfield
State Forest
Port Kent
Colchester
Essex Center
Underhill
Winooski
Essex Junction
Burlington
Williston
Mount Mansfield State Forest
Stowe
Richmond
Shelburne
Bolton
East Charlotte
Hinesburg
Essex
Charlotte
Waterbury
Mount Philo State Park
South Duxbury
North Ferrisburg
Starksboro
Vergennes
to Middlebury

Occupying a choice 700 acres along Lake Champlain, the **Basin Harbor Club** has been a prime waterside getaway since 1886. Sprinkled along the lake banks and peeking across to New York's Adirondack Mountains are 38 rooms and 77 cottages with simple, cozy furnishings. This self-contained retreat boasts an 18-hole golf course, a swimming pool, tennis courts, two top-notch restaurants and an airstrip. Pets are welcomed in the cottages. Closed mid-October to mid-May. ~ Basin Harbor Road off Route 22A, Vergennes; 802-475-2311, 800-622-4000, fax 802-475-6545; www.basinharbor.com, e-mail info@basinharbor.com. ULTRA-DELUXE.

Keep your eyes peeled for "Champ," Lake Champlain's own Loch Ness Monster, whose bulky outline and distinct humps were first sighted by Samuel de Champlain and recorded in his ship's log.

Perhaps the most distinguished lodging address in all the Champlain Valley is the **Inn at Shelburne Farms**. Formerly home to Lila Vanderbilt Webb, the 1899 brick manor has all the Vanderbilt trimmings: incredible Lake Champlain and mountain vistas, 24 guest rooms and 2 cottages with opulent furnishings and 1400 acres of lovely farmlands sprinkled with 19th-century buildings. Settle in, soak up the history of this fascinating place and pretend you'll never have to leave. Closed mid-October to mid-May. ~ Harbor and Bay roads, off Route 7, Shelburne; 802-985-8498, fax 802-985-1233; www.shelburnefarms.org. DELUXE TO ULTRA-DELUXE.

Burlington, Vermont's largest city, offers little in the way of homey bed and breakfasts and quaint inns, but does have a smattering of motor lodges, motels and hotels.

At the **Sheraton Burlington Hotel and Conference Center**, you will find 309 spacious rooms with contemporary furnishings, marble vanities and distant mountain views, as well as a health club with a removable glass atrium over the pool. There is also a large interior courtyard and a sundeck. ~ 870 Williston Road, Burlington; 802-865-6600, 800-325-3535, fax 802-865-6670; www.sheratonburlington.com. DELUXE TO ULTRA-DELUXE.

Within easy reach of downtown Burlington and several ski areas, the **Inn at Essex** features 121 rooms, some decorated with 18th-century period-style furniture, some in an Ethan Allen country motif. Half the rooms have fireplaces. The suites have whirlpool baths. There's an 18-hole golf course and six tennis courts on the premises. Dining is top-drawer: The inn is home to the New England Culinary Institute. In fact, the institute's kitchens and classes are right under the inn. ~ 70 Essex Way, Essex; 802-878-1100, 800-727-4295, fax 802-878-0063; www.vtculinaryresort.com, e-mail innfo@vtculinaryresort.com. DELUXE TO ULTRA-DELUXE.

Two miles northeast of Burlington, the **Days Inn** is a no-nonsense place where you can get a clean, modern-style room with a moderate price. The three-story design is generic motel with 74 rooms, though the decor is a notch above, with cushy couches, designer draperies and cedar siding. There's also an indoor pool. ~ 124 College Parkway, Colchester; 802-655-0900, 800-329-7466, fax 802-655-6851. DELUXE TO ULTRA-DELUXE.

DINING

Tully and Marie's perches on the bank of Otter Creek in the middle of pretty Middlebury. The restaurant is three stories high, with floor-to-ceiling windows that make even the rainiest day seem bright to indoor diners. During warm weather, try to get a table on the outdoor deck. Fresh ingredients star in most dishes, which run the gamut from American to Thai to Mexican. Among the offerings are pad thai, grilled-seafood risotto, tofu curry with mango, and pan-seared duck breast. ~ 7 Bakery Lane, Middlebury; 802-388-4182, fax 802-388-0813; www.tullyandmaries.com. MODERATE TO DELUXE.

Not only is Burlington Vermont's largest city, it's also its restaurant capital. Not surprisingly, you'll find a medley of choice dining establishments. Some of the best can be found on Church Street's four-block Marketplace, a brick-lined pedestrian mall packed with outdoor cafés and college students.

A rare Vermont sushi bar is part of the **Marketplace at Sakura**, a simple but cheery restaurant with two tatami rooms and small wooden tables that peek out over the street. The sushi and sashimi are fresh and served on wooden trays with pretty designs. If you prefer a hot Japanese meal, opt for the *yakitori* (broiled chicken on skewers) or *gyoza* (meat dumplings) or select from the host of teriyaki and tempura entrées. ~ 2 Church Street, Burlington; 802-863-1988, fax 802-860-0496; www.sakuravt.com, e-mail sakuravt@aol.com. MODERATE.

The place for fresh New England seafood is the **Ice House**, a restored harborside building with a venerable seafaring aura. There's a wharf and ferry station a stone's throw away. Specialties include grilled swordfish and salmon, filet mignon and a shrimp, calamari and sea scallop combination. The place is draped in wood and stone and features two outdoor decks. ~ 171 Battery Street, Burlington; 802-864-1800, fax 802-864-1801. MODERATE TO DELUXE.

Located in nearby Essex, **Butler's** features New American cuisine prepared and served by students of the prestigious New England Culinary Institute. The menu changes nightly and usually includes a selection of fish and meat dishes with international influences. There is always a vegetarian dish. They're good for breakfast and lunch, too. ~ Inn at Essex, 70 Essex Way, Essex; 802-878-1100, 800-727-4295, fax 802-878-0063; www.innatessex.com. MODERATE TO ULTRA-DELUXE.

Both gourmet and adorable, **Sneakers Bistro & Café** strikes an excellent balance of delicious cuisine offered in a comforting, small-town atmosphere. Hot breakfasts, such as Kahlua-batter-dipped french toast with fresh fruit or a breakfast burrito with homemade bean pesto, add to the luxury of a lazy morning. Lunch entrées range from tuna melts and burgers to veggie wraps and salads. This small eatery serves brunch every day. ~ 36 Main Street, Winooski; 802-655-9081; www.sneakersbistro.com, info@sneakersbistro.com. BUDGET TO MODERATE.

SHOPPING

HIDDEN ►

It nearly takes a miracle to find **Authentica African Imports**, but once you're there, it's worth it. More than just a shop, this place offers a look at African styles and customs, with jewelry from West, South and East African nations, Mali blankets, Ethiopian rugs, Zulu clay pots, fertility statues from Malawi and much more. Closed Sunday through Wednesday except by appointment. ~ 2190 Greenbush Road about three quarters of a mile north of the Old Brick Store on Ferry Road, Charlotte; phone/fax 802-425-3137.

Stroll Burlington's four-block **Church Street Marketplace** and you'll be rewarded with a bevy of fine, trendy shops. ~ Church Street between Main and Pearl streets, Burlington; 802-863-1648; www.churchstmarketplace.com.

NIGHTLIFE

The **Flynn Center for the Performing Arts**, a 1453-seat 1930 art deco palace and old vaudeville house, offers international and Broadway theater and major symphony and dance performances. ~ 153 Main Street, Burlington; 802-863-5966; www.flynncenter.org.

A dark cubbyhole with a crowd predominantly in their 30s, **Nectar's** serves up top-notch live blues and rock nightly. ~ 188 Main Street, Burlington; 802-658-4771; www.liveatnectars.com. Upstairs you'll find **Club Metronome**, where there's live music, including blues, funk, ska and hip-hop. Cover.

The hottest night scene pulses in Burlington, where 16,000 college students feed a multitude of discos, progressive clubs and bebop joints.

Sweetwaters is undeniably the area's most upscale meeting place, where patrons linger around a shiny bar and observe all the street activity through large glass windows. There's acoustic music once a month. ~ 120 Church Street, Burlington; 802-864-9800; www.sweetwatersbistro.com.

Clearly one of the hippest places in town for the 20-something crowd, **Red Square** is part music venue, part pub and part art gallery. With chic touches like handmade matchbooks, this place has a following because it offers a consistent lineup of local performers and a genuinely cut-loose atmosphere. ~ 136 Church Street, Burlington; 802-859-8909; www.redsquare.com, e-mail info@redsquare.com.

Late-nighters flock to **The Vermont Pub and Brewery**, a spacious but cozy brew house with brick walls, archways, mirrors and hanging plants. There's usually live music Thursday through Saturday in summer. ~ 144 College Street, Burlington; 802-865-0500; www.vermontbrewery.com.

BEACHES & PARKS

MOUNT PHILO STATE PARK Resting right on top of Mount Philo, this park rewards those who tackle its very steep but paved road with astonishing panoramas. From here, you can peer across Lake Champlain into New York's Adirondacks and farther. A total of 150 acres, most of the park is vertical and forested. There is a nice picnic area with tables, and the park's hiking trails are splendid. Closed mid-October to mid-May. Day-use fee, $2.50. ~ Off Route 7, six miles north of Route 22A near North Ferrisburg; 802-425-2390.

▲ There are 10 tent sites ($14 to $16 per night) and three lean-tos ($21 per night), with hot showers and fireplaces (firewood is for sale). Reservations: 888-409-7579.

SAND BAR STATE PARK One of the flattest areas in the state, this ever-popular locale borders Lake Champlain and a waterfowl refuge. Families and college students crowd the coarse, mocha-colored sand and grassy areas lining the lake, while windsurfers and sailboats whiz along just offshore. The views across the lake of the Adirondack Mountains are exceptional. The water is waist-deep at least 100 yards out and is popular with swimmers. Anglers catch perch, sunfish, salmon and bass. There are picnic facilities, a bathhouse, volleyball courts, boat rentals and a snack bar. Closed Labor Day to Memorial Day. Day-use fee, $2.50 to $3.50. ~ Route 2, four miles north of Route 89, Milton; 802-893-2825 (summer), 802-879-5674 (winter).

NORTH HERO STATE PARK From its perch on a thickly wooded peninsula, this 400-acre park captures a prominent view of Lake Champlain and glances backward on North Hero Island. Though it actually borders two miles of lake, the only real accessible shore is a small but pretty shale beach at the peninsula's tip, a secluded spot favored by Canadians and local sailboaters. Swimming is good, but you must wade out past a rim of slippery rocks. Immense Lake Champlain provides superb fishing opportunities, from bass and pike to perch, walleye and pickerel. You'll find picnic tables, restrooms, a playground and rowboat and canoe rental; a store is four miles southwest on Route 2. Closed September to mid-May. Day-use fee, $2.50. ~ From Alburg, go six miles south on Route 2 and cross the bridge to North Hero Island. Take an immediate left onto Bridge Road. Follow Bridge Road two miles to Lakeview Drive and take a left onto Lakeview. Go one mile on Lakeview, and the entrance will be on your left; 802-372-8727.

▲ There are 99 tent/RV sites ($14 per night) and 18 lean-tos ($21 per night) with hot showers and fireplaces but no hookups. Reservations: 888-409-7579.

Northeast Kingdom

This vast rural outback could well contain the largest stretch of splendid scenery in all of Vermont. A broad land inhabited by log cutters, cattle drivers and mountain folk, it forms a fine skein of glacier-dug lakes, mellow ponds and rivers, untamed evergreen forests and abrupt alpine ridges. Fall foliage first peeks out its gorgeous head up here, snow falls early and huge bodies of water turn to compact ice.

Beginning in St. Johnsbury and extending northward to the Canadian border, the Northeast Kingdom could well be termed Vermont's last stand. Its thin population and lack of major industry perpetuate considerable unemployment (by Vermont's standards), though firmly rooted residents vow their rugged country living surpasses that in southern ski meccas any day.

SIGHTS

St. Johnsbury, the region's largest city, is a quaint, mostly blue-collar town located where the Moose and Sleepers rivers flow into the Passumpsic River. The local **Northeast Kingdom Chamber of Commerce Welcome Center** will provide walking-tour maps and regional information. ~ 51 Depot Square, St. Johnsbury; 802-748-3678, 800-639-6379, fax 802-748-0731; www.nekchamber.com, e-mail nekinfo@nekchamber.com.

A perfect spot to learn about local history is the **Fairbanks Museum and Planetarium**, where exhibits are imaginative and informative. The extensive wildlife collection includes stuffed condors and owls, pythons and a tiger, and monstrous Kodiaks and a polar bear. The building itself, with a barrel-vaulted ceiling and Romanesque designs of red sandstone, is marvelous. Closed Monday from October through April. Admission. ~ 1302 Main Street, St. Johnsbury; 802-748-2372, fax 802-748-1893; www.fairbanksmuseum.org, e-mail info@fairbanksmuseum.org.

HIDDEN ►

Tucked in the back of a beautiful 1871 library, the **St. Johnsbury Athenaeum Art Gallery**, a National Historic Landmark, is a step back in time. The place bills itself as the "oldest unaltered art gallery in the United States," and indeed, its collection has not changed since the mid-1920s. The 100-plus paintings feature an American landscape scene by Albert Bierstadt and other famed Hudson River School artists. The library, a lovely Victorian-style masterpiece, has seen minimal architectural change since its inception. Closed Sunday. ~ 1171 Main Street, St. Johnsbury; 802-748-8291, fax 802-748-8086; www.stjathenaeum.org, e-mail inform@stjathenaeum.org.

Take Route 5A north to Route 105, then backtrack south on a splendid trek revealing yet another flawless meld of mountain and water. Gaze at the hilltop homes that scope out scenic views, at the farmers bailing hay and at old frame homes with laundry draped across their porches.

Soon you'll come to the town of **Island Pond,** where bait shops, log cabins and a gas station form an earthy setting. The town green overlooks the water and was the site of the first international railroad in North America. There's also a Civil War cannon and a World War II monument.

Head toward Canada again, traveling north along Route 111, and you'll quickly feel the French vibes of our northern neighbor. Enormous **Lake Memphremagog** shares its waters (nearly equally) with Vermont and Quebec.

Newport is a special town, resting on a procession of hills that skirt the lake and crowned by the spires of beautiful **St. Mary Star of the Sea Church.** ~ 191 Clermont Terrace, Newport; 802-334-5066, fax 802-334-5067; www.stmarystarofthesea.org, e-mail stmarynewport@verizon.net.

Downtown offers a nice array of shops and restaurants and a beautiful lakeside boardwalk. A helpful **Chamber of Commerce Information Booth** will load you up with information. ~ 246 The Causeway, Newport; phone/fax 802-334-7782, 800-635-4643; www.vtnorthcountry.com, e-mail chamber@pshift.com.

There are three dirt roads that lead to the valley hamlet of **Brownington,** though the less adventurous will opt for the one that's paved. Here awaits an enchanting museum called **The Old**

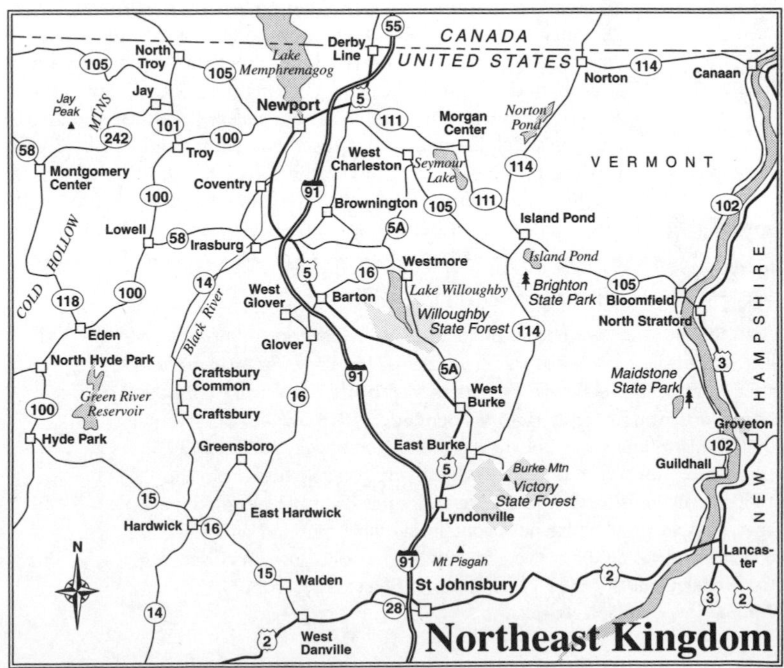

Stone House, built as a school dormitory in 1836 by the Reverend Alexander Twilight, the country's first black college graduate and legislator. Twenty-three rooms are filled with inspiring memorabilia that form endearing snapshots of early American life. Nearly everything here was donated by local families, including the 18th-century furniture, 19th-century military uniforms (worn by Brownington men) and a wonderful collection of 1800s newspapers. Across the road is the 1830 Federal-style home of Twilight (now a visitors center) and an 1840 barn with agricultural exhibits. Closed Monday and Tuesday and from October 15 through May 15. Admission. ~ Brownington Village near Orleans; 802-754-2022, fax 802-754-9336; www.oldstonehousemuseum.org, e-mail information@oldstonehousemuseum.org.

HIDDEN ►

A block from the Old Stone House is **Prospect Hill Observatory**, a wooden tower perched atop a grassy hill. Climb a short flight of stairs and be rewarded with a 360-degree panorama of rolling mountains and evergreen spires. A splendid way to remember Vermont, for sure. Closed May through October. ~ Take the dirt road beside Brownington Congregational Church.

LODGING

Children, animals and dramatic scenery abound at the **Wildflower Inn**, part of a 500-acre estate that's a great place to spend more than one night. All accommodations have private bathrooms and a mix of antique and reproduction furniture. Fourteen of the 24 units are suites; the honeymoon cottage is complete with a jacuzzi built for two. For the kids, there's a playroom with a chestful of dress-up clothes and a petting barn with several horses, a pony, a cow, a goat, a rabbit and a sheep. Breakfast and an afternoon snack are included. Closed November and April. ~ 2059 Darling Hill Road, Lyndonville; 802-626-8310, 800-627-8310, fax 802-626-3039; www.wildflowerinn.com, e-mail info@wildflowerinn.com. MODERATE TO ULTRA-DELUXE.

sights

AUTHOR FAVORITE

Vermont does wonders for my sweet tooth, if not my waistline. Just when I think I've recovered from Ben & Jerry's world headquarters, along comes **Maple Grove Farms of Vermont**, the world's oldest and largest maple sugar candy factory. Founded in 1915 by two local women, the little farmhouse was bought out and a factory was built in 1929. Tours take visitors through the factory, where vintage equipment from the 1930s is still in use and where large quantities of maple syrup are packaged. The old sugar house now contains a maple museum, and a third building features an extensive gift shop. Admission. Museum closed late December through May. ~ 1052 Portland Street, St. Johnsbury; 802-748-5141; www.maplegrove.com.

Standing by Lake Willoughby, the **Willough Vale Inn** offers spectacular views and a rustic elegance. Though built in 1987, the Colonial-style inn harkens to yesteryear with stained-wood floors, antiques and Oriental rugs. Most of the eight rooms in the main inn snatch a lake view and are enhanced with simple oak and cherry furniture and country prints; two suites feature fireplaces, jacuzzis and kitchenettes. There are also four fully furnished lakeside cottages, each with a kitchen and living room, in front of the inn. Occasionally closed in April and November; call ahead. ~ Route 5A South, Westmore; 802-525-4123, 800-594-9102, fax 802-525-4514; www.willoughvale.com, e-mail info@willoughvale.com. DELUXE TO ULTRA-DELUXE.

The Inn on the Common is an impeccable inn in the impeccable little town of Craftsbury Common. There are a total of 16 rooms in three separate buildings, one of which is on the village green; the others are steps away. Several are furnished with antiques and attractive floral fabrics. At the back of the main building are formal gardens and a far-reaching view of the surrounding Northeast Kingdom countryside. Breakfast is included in the room rate. Closed in April and November. ~ Craftsbury Common; 802-586-9619, 800-521-2233, fax 802-586-2249; www.innonthecommon.com, e-mail info@innonthecommon.com. MODERATE TO ULTRA-DELUXE.

At the end of a long dirt road in the hilly Northeast Kingdom, the **Rodgers Country Inn** takes in a few visitors at a time. Once a working dairy farm, you can now take a walk through the pretty countryside, where you'll see that this corner of Vermont is a haven for family-run farms. There are five guest rooms; guests share three large bathrooms. Two cabins are on the property. In winter, you can cross-country ski, snowmobile or snowshoe right on the property. Breakfast is included. ~ Call for directions, West Glover; 802-525-6677, 800-729-1704, fax 802-525-1103; www.virtualvermont.com/rodgers, e-mail jnrodger@together.net. BUDGET.

A stunning three-story mansion, **Maple Manor B&B** offers accommodations on 250 sweeping acres lined with maple trees. Floral is the theme throughout the inn, with wreaths adorning the walls and flower patterns covering much of the furniture. The three guest rooms are appointed with antiques, and each one has a storybook feel, with teddy bears and pastel colors. Romance is almost overwhelming in Sandra's Secret, the largest guest room, where white and floral patterns bedeck every square inch. Breakfast is a three-course, candle-lit feast in the dining room. ~ 77 Maple Lane, West Glover; 802-525-9591; www.maple-manor.com, e-mail mplmnr@together.net. DELUXE TO ULTRA-DELUXE.

The Inn on Trout River is a great find for travelers who find themselves in the Jay area of northern Vermont. Skiers will be es- ◄HIDDEN pecially satisfied with the flannel-sheeted queen beds, large bathrooms with clawfoot tubs, the publike bar and the substantial discount on lift tickets to Jay Peak. During the summer, visitors can take advantage of the excellent fishing in the area's many rivers and streams. Breakfast is included. ~ 241 Main Street, Montgomery Center; 802-326-4391, 800-338-7049, fax 802-326-3194; www.troutinn.com, e-mail info@troutinn.com. MODERATE TO DELUXE.

Rudyard Kipling invented snow golf while living in Vermont. The prolific Brit painted the balls red so they would be visible against the snow.

In Montgomery Center, at the base of Jay Peak, stands the 1882 **Phineas Swann Bed and Breakfast and Antiques Gallery**, a stunning gingerbread Victorian owned and run by gay men. Absolutely every inch of this house is beautiful—hardwood floors, canopy beds, Vermont antiques, hand-carved furniture. There are seven guest rooms, all with private baths. Breakfast is quite an event here, with all homemade dishes including sausage and preserves from the blueberries and strawberries grown on the property. It's accompanied by big-band music and candlelight. The room rate also includes afternoon tea with fresh-baked scones on the front porch. Gay-friendly. Closed mid-April to mid-May. ~ Route 118, Montgomery Center; phone/fax 802-326-4306; www.phineasswann.com, e-mail axperkins@aol.com. MODERATE TO DELUXE.

DINING

Cuisine here reflects the ruggedness of the land, and though restaurants are far apart they're certainly worth the scenic drive.

Nestled serenely on a glacier-carved lake, the **Willough Vale Inn and Restaurant** affords some of Vermont's most scintillating views. The dining room, which overlooks captivating Lake Willoughby, serves steak, seafood and other American fare. Reservations required. Dinner only. Closed Sunday through Wednesday from January to mid-March; call for summer hours. ~ Route 5A, Westmore; 802-525-4123, 800-594-9102; www.willoughvale.com, e-mail info@willoughvale.com. MODERATE TO DELUXE.

Lemoine's, located in The Inn on Trout River, offers a varied menu for all palates—fresh fish, leg of lamb and good homemade soups, as well as an innovative "wholesome choices menu" for guests with special dietary needs. Try to sit near the fireplace; the carved mantel is intricate and worth a closer look, as are the moldings and wainscoting throughout the inn. Dinner only. Closed Monday through Wednesday, June through September. Closed Monday from December through April. Closed from mid-September through November and in May. ~ Main Street, Montgomery Center; 802-326-4391, 800-338-7049; www.troutinn.com, e-mail info@troutinn.com. MODERATE TO DELUXE.

The **Parkside Restaurant** is one of those nondescript blueish-gray eateries off the side of the highway that everyone in town seems to know about. It has nothing in the way of atmosphere, but the food is cheap, plentiful and pretty good—always a winning combination. Breakfast at this family spot is served all day long, and specials are served Thursday through Saturday, ranging from all-you-can-eat meatloaf to chicken, fish, or spaghetti. ~ 408 Western Avenue, Newport; 802-334-2486. BUDGET TO MODERATE.

SHOPPING

Going fishing, perhaps? **The Great Outdoors of Newport** has loads of fishing gear, plus mountain bikes and skis. ~ 177 Main Street, Newport; 802-334-2831; www.greatoutdoorsvermont.com.

The Landing Clothing Company not only has men's formal attire but also jeans and sportswear for both sexes. Closed Sunday from late December to Mother's Day. ~ 138 Main Street, Newport; 802-334-2953, fax 802-334-0265.

NIGHTLIFE

Other than a few motel lounges and pool halls, this remote mountain area is short on nightlife.

Have a drink by the lake at **The Eastside**. In the summer you can enjoy the views from the outdoor deck; in the winter, relax by the fire in the nautical-themed bar. ~ 47 Landing Street, Newport; 802-334-2340, fax 802-334-7363.

Canada and the United States share the **Haskell Opera House**, a marvelous, ornate 1901 building that hosts comedy, musicals and drama as well as symphony, jazz and ballet. Open from the end of April to the beginning of October. Closed Sunday and Monday. ~ 93 Casswell Avenue, Derby Line; 802-873-3022 (U.S.), 819-876-2020 (Canada); www.haskellopera.org, e-mail haskelllibrary@adelphia.net.

BEACHES & PARKS

PROUTY BEACH This popular municipal park corners the market on local views. Situated along tranquil Lake Memphremagog, Prouty preens across the water to the city of Newport, with its quaint downtown and historic church spires. A 100-foot sliver of sand skirts the lake, protected by a row of weeping willows. Try from shore or on a boat for trout, salmon, pike and bass. And with lighted tennis and basketball courts as well as football and soccer fields, who could get bored? Facilities include picnic pavilions and restrooms. Closed mid-October to mid-May. Day-use fee, $3.50. ~ On Veterans Avenue in Newport; 802-334-6345.

There are 4 tent sites ($20 per night) and 52 RV sites ($24 per night) with water and electrical hookups. Sixteen of those sites also have sewer hookups and are $25 per night. Amenities include washers, dryers and showers as well as a dumping station for RVs.

MAIDSTONE STATE PARK Ringed with majestic mountain peaks and tucked in the middle of nowhere, this gorgeous preserve possesses a very special feature: the crystal-clear Maidstone Lake. It's enough to just sit and gaze at reflections of trees in the water, but the more adventurous might choose to sunbathe on a generous stretch of cream-colored sand. People swim here, though the water is quite chilly, even in the summer. Fishing is excellent for lake and rainbow trout as well as salmon. You may see loons and moose while you're here. Don't be intimidated by the remoteness of this park. Once you're here, you'll be thankful you made the drive. Facilities include picnic tables, restrooms, boat and canoe rentals and a nature center. Closed September to mid-May. Day-use fee, $2.50. ~ From Bloomfield, go south along the Connecticut River for five miles on Route 102, then turn southwest at the State Forest Highway (it's marked). This is a gravel road that extends six miles to the state park; 802-676-3930.

▲ There are 45 tent sites ($16 per night) and 37 lean-tos ($23 per night) with fireplaces and hot showers but no hookups. Reservations: 888-409-7579.

HIDDEN ►

BRIGHTON STATE PARK Even with the fiercest of competition, this has to be the prettiest park in all of Vermont. The setting is absolutely magnificent, the mood incredibly serene. Nestled along poignant Spectacle Pond, Brighton claims a sliver of crystalline tawny beach and 582 acres packed with spruce, firs, pines and many other very green, very big trees. There's also a nature museum and plenty of forested trails that scale the billowy terrain. There's excellent fishing for trout on Island Pond and bass on Spectacle Pond. Facilities include picnic tables, restrooms, showers, fireplaces and canoe rentals. Closed mid-October to mid-May. Day-use fee, $2.50. ~ Off Route 105, two miles east of Island Pond; 802-723-4360.

▲ There are 61 tent/RV sites ($16 per night) and 23 lean-tos ($23 per night) with showers but no hookups. Reservations: 888-409-7579.

Outdoor Adventures

SKIING

The thrills of downhill and cross-country skiing draw tens of thousands of enthusiasts to Vermont every year. Ski resort villages all over the state offer a variety of challenges and settings that cater to families, singles and the elderly.

Before you go, send for the *Ski Vermont Magazine* brochure from the Vermont Ski Areas Association. ~ P.O. Box 368, 26 State Street, Montpelier, VT 05601; 802-223-2439; www.skivermont.com, e-mail info@skivermont.com.

The varied terrain of gentle hills and fields, old carriage roads and frozen ponds—combined with an excellent gridwork of trails—attract vast numbers of cross-country skiers to Vermont. In fact, tiny Vermont boasts more Nordic ski centers than any western state. Though many of the state parks are closed in the winter, most allow cross-country skiing on ungroomed trails. The best time for cross-country skiing is mid-December through March.

A black line divides the Haskell Opera House building nationally, with half of the wooden seats in Vermont and the other half and the stage in Quebec.

For a list of ski centers, write for the *Best of Cross-Country Skiing*, available from Cross-Country Ski Areas Association. The $3 charge covers postage and handling. Or you can check out their website, which has more information. ~ 259 Bolton Road, Winchester, NH 03470; 603-239-4341; www.xcski.org, e-mail ccsaa@xcski.org.

SOUTHERN VERMONT **Mount Snow** climbs 3600 feet and boasts a large array of alpine villas, condos and restaurants. Here you'll find 106 trails (many quite difficult), 19 lifts and a vertical drop of 1700 feet. Twenty percent of the trails are novice, sixty percent are intermediate and the rest are expert runs. The mountain has four terrain parks and one half-pipe, as well as a tubing park open weekends. ~ 12 Pisgah Road Route 100, West Dover; 802-464-3333, 800-245-7669; www.mountsnow.com, e-mail info@mountsnow.com.

CENTRAL VERMONT The place to be in central Vermont is **Killington**, a sprawling, seven-mountain network with 31 lifts and a vertical drop that plummets 3150 feet. Killington offers the Rams Head mountain, which is devoted to family activities, ten alpine and snowboard parks and a gondola. The 200 trails are a third beginner, a third intermediate and a third expert. They also house a skiing and snowboarding school. Closed late May to late October. ~ Off Routes 4 and 100; 802-422-6200, 800-621-6867; www.killington.com, e-mail info@killington.com.

NORTHERN MOUNTAIN REGION **Sugarbush**, a six-mountain area with 111 trails and 16 lifts, maintains a congenial atmosphere with its quaint shops and medley of fine restaurants and lodging. Half of the Sugarbush area is intermediate, with more than a third rated advanced. Snowboarders can enjoy a new jibbing halfpipe and a newly designed terrain park. ~ Sugarbush Access Road, off Route 100, Warren; 802-583-6300, 800-537-8427; www.sugarbush.com, e-mail info@sugarbush.com.

Nearby **Stowe** harbors Vermont's highest peak, 4395-foot Mt. Mansfield, and a stunning alpine milieu with 48 trails and 12 lifts, including a terrain park with a half-pipe. Stowe also offers 35 kilometers of groomed cross-country trails and 40 kilo-

Text continued on page 498.

Vermont Maple Syrup

It begins quite subtly during the first hint of spring: a tiny sprig of green sprouts, a bird chirps gaily and the sap inside a maple tree breaks free from its icy chamber and trickles ever so gently toward the warm ground.

Squirrels, rabbits and other forest dwellers scurry to lap up the sweet elixir, a welcome indulgence after a long, frigid winter. Along comes another mountain inhabitant, a farmer, who pierces the maple trunk with a plastic tap, drawing the sticky sap into a clear plastic tube. The farmer does this hundreds, perhaps thousands of times, tapping trees and connecting them with little tubes until their sap trickles harmoniously down the mountain.

And so it goes. Each spring, millions of Vermont maple trees surrender their gooey, candied essence for the sake of that sought-after substance known as maple syrup. Called "sugarbushes" or "maple orchards," these grand stands of trees blanket the mountains with their stalwart trunks and burgeoning canopies of delicate toothed leaves.

Vermont is the country's largest supplier of maple syrup, producing an annual average of half a million gallons. Though the harvesting processes are fairly simple, they've changed quite a bit since American Indians cooked sap over an open fire back in the 1500s.

Today, most farmers use plastic tubes, drawing sap by gravity or with a vacuum system, but some still opt for the time-honored metal bucket system. In this method, sap drips from trees into large buckets, which are carted on sleds down the mountains.

Back at the sugarhouse, sap is boiled all day (and sometimes all night) in huge metal pans until it's reduced to a smooth syrup. It takes an average of 40 gallons of sap to net a single gallon of syrup.

All the cooking takes place in hundreds of wooden sugarhouses—characterized by vented roofs to help steam escape—that dot verdant mountains and valleys. You can peek in on all the action by visiting large syrup mills, but for the most rewarding experience, stop in on a family-owned operation. Here, cordial folks will bring you up to snuff on the sweet stuff as well as share their lifestyles and family histories.

You'll discover small, family-owned farms all over the state, and while many display a small sign that says "Maple Syrup," others have no sign at all (these you can find out about at the local general store). The Vermont Department of Agriculture supplies dandy, free brochures such as *Maple by Mail* and *Vermont Farms* for those looking for mail-order syrup or just want to visit a farm. Listings are by region and provide information on number of taps, size of sugarhouses, methods of operation and tours. ~ 116 State Street, Drawer 20, Montpelier, VT 05620; 802-828-2416; www.vermontmaple.org.

The **New England Maple Museum** promises "The Sweetest Story Ever Told" if you visit its displays of maple sugar nostalgia. A great place to bone up on syrup history, the museum stocks old artifacts like wooden buckets and taps and horsedrawn sleds used for toting sap. The best part, though, is the free syrup and Vermont specialty foods tastings. Closed January to mid-March. Admission. ~ Route 7, Pittsford; 802-483-9414; www.maplemuseum.com, e-mail info@maplemuseum.com.

Or, immerse yourself in syrupy activities at the **Vermont Maple Festival**, held each April in St. Albans, north of Burlington. Feast on pancakes smothered in syrup, take in the fiddlers' contest and savor the honeyed flavor of assorted syrup varieties. ~ Contact the Vermont Maple Festival Council, P.O. Box 255, St. Albans, VT 05478; 802-524-5800; www.vtmaplefestival.org.

Plan to visit from late February (southern areas) through mid-April (northern areas). The choicest syrup, a fancy golden extract, is harvested first. As the season progresses, syrup turns a medium amber, then a dark amber and finally a bitter, murky consistency that's seldom edible.

Of course, the finer things in life always cost more, and such is the case with maple syrup. Usually double and triple the price of blended syrups, the real stuff can cost you from 40 to 60 cents per ounce.

But be forewarned. Those accustomed to blended syrup shall unwittingly be seduced by the pure maple kind, a victim of their own newly enlightened taste buds. Syrupoholics say it's sort of like switching from jug wine to fine wine: once you've tasted the good stuff, it's impossible to go back.

meters of backcountry trails. ~ Route 108; 802-253-7311, 800-253-4754; www.stowe.com.

Several cross-country trails connect inns around Warren and Waitsfield in the Sugarbush area.

NORTHEAST KINGDOM Vermont's best-kept ski secret is **Burke Mountain**, nestled in the outposts of the Northeast Kingdom. Here you'll find excellent skiing in an uncrowded (no lift lines!) place, along with 45 trails, four lifts and a nice vertical drop of 2011 feet. ~ Off Route 114, East Burke; 802-626-7300; www.skiburke.com, e-mail info@skiburke.com.

Another scenic route traverses the farmlands and forests between the **Craftsbury Nordic Center** near Craftsbury Common and the Highland Lodge in Greensboro. ~ 802-586-7767.

Since **Jay Peak** regularly gets more natural snow than any other ski area in the northeast, you might well expect it to be packed—but it's not. The trek from any major city is a long one, and the weather can be pretty nasty up here; consequently, few New England skiers come, and lift lines are almost unheard of, especially since recent upgrades include two lifts, a quad chair and a moving carpet. Experienced skiers who are looking for a challenge should head for Jay's glade areas when the snow is deep enough. If it's not, the runs on the smaller of the two mountains are more challenging than the curving trails that descend from the tram, on the higher peak. ~ 4850 Route 242, Jay; 802-988-2611, 800-451-4449, fax 802-988-4049; www.jaypeakresort.com, e-mail info@jaypeakresort.com.

SLEIGHING

Sleigh rides afford wonderful opportunities to meet local folks and take in the beautiful countryside. They are usually offered from mid-December to mid-March.

CENTRAL VERMONT In Wilmington, **Adam's Farm** runs hour-and-a-half horsedrawn sleigh trips with a midway stop at a log

ARE WE THERE YET?

Known as the "Longest Backcountry Ski Trail in North America," the **Catamount Trail** stretches 300 miles across the length of Vermont. Along the way, the trail connects 11 of Vermont's finest Nordic centers and bypasses many country inns. The trail is accessible to skiers of all levels and offers terrain ranging from breathtaking mountain climbs to gently rolling hills and woodlands. For further information on the Catamount Trail, or to order a guidebook on the trail, call 802-864-5794, fax 802-864-5710, or check out www.catamounttrail.org, e-mail info@catamounttrail.org.

cabin in the woods for hot chocolate. ~ 15 Higley Hill Road; 802-464-3762; www.adamsfamilyfarm.com. **Hawk Inn and Mountain Resort** has shorter sleigh rides. ~ Route 100, Plymouth; 802-672-3811; www.hawkresort.com. In Castleton, **Pond Hill Ranch** offers hour-long rides. ~ Pond Hill Ranch Road; 802-468-2449; www.pondhillranch.com.

NORTHERN MOUNTAIN REGION The **Trapp Family Lodge** offers short horsedrawn wagon rides Saturday through Monday. ~ 700 Trapp Hill Road, Stowe; 802-253-8511, 800-826-7000. **Lajoie Stables** offers one-hour sleigh rides and horseback riding in the Smuggler's Notch area. ~ 922 Pollander Road, Jeffersonville; 802-644-5347; www.lajoiestables.com.

FISHING

From salmon and trout to shad and walleye, Vermont's extensive network of streams, rivers and lakes teem with fine fishing opportunities. The general fishing season lasts from April to October.

To find out where the fish bite, contact the **Vermont Fish and Wildlife Department**. ~ Information and Education Division, 103 South Main Street, Waterbury, VT 05671; 802-241-3700; www.vtfishandwildlife.com.

SOUTHERN VERMONT Half- and full-day guided flyfishing trips on the Connecticut River are available from **Strictly Trout**. Closed November through April. ~ Off Route 121 just south of Saxton River Village; 802-869-3116; www.sover.net/~deenhome, e-mail deenhome@sover.net.

CENTRAL VERMONT Several outfits will set you up with rental boats and/or fishing equipment.

The Vermont Fly Fishing School offers early-morning and evening guide service for flyfishing for trout on the White River and smallmouth bass on the Connecticut River. ~ The Quechee Inn, Main Street, Quechee; 802-295-7620; e-mail wildernesstrails@valley.net. **Duda Water Sports** rents small fishing boats, canoes, kayaks, mopeds, speedboats, ski boats and pontoon boats. ~ Creek Road, Hydeville; 802-265-3432. **Sailing Winds Marina** rents sailboats, motorboats, kayaks and canoes. ~ Route 30, Wells; 802-287-9411; www.sailingwindsmarina.org, e-mail boat_rentals@sailingwindsmarina.com.

NORTHERN MOUNTAIN REGION **The Fly Rod Shop** operates year-round and outfits four-hour trips, mostly on the Winooski and Lamoille rivers, for trout and bass. ~ Route 100, Stowe; 802-253-7346; www.flyrodshop.com, e-mail angler@flyrodshop.com.

CHAMPLAIN VALLEY Half- and full-day guided fishing trips are available at **Green Mountain Troutfitters**. They also offer both gear and watercraft rentals. ~ 233 Mill Street, Jeffersonville; 802-644-2214, 800-495-4271; www.gmtrout.com.

CANOEING

Whether you're in it for sightseeing or for rugged adventure, canoeing through Vermont can be an idyllic experience. The season usually lasts from May through October.

SOUTHERN VERMONT **Vermont Canoe** rents canoes, kayaks and a rowboat. Closed in winter. ~ Putney Road, Brattleboro; 802-257-5008. You can also try **Battenkill Canoe** for canoe rentals and shuttle services along the Battenkill River. ~ Route 7A between Arlington and Manchester; 802-362-2800.

CENTRAL VERMONT In Wells, **Sailing Winds Marina** rents canoes and kayaks. ~ Route 30; 802-287-9411. **Wilderness Trails** offers half- and full-day canoeing float trips down the White River, the Connecticut River and the Ottaquechee River. They also offer kayak and guided fly-fishing excursions as well as canoe and kayak rentals. ~ The Quechee Inn, Main Street, Quechee; 802-295-7620; www.wildernesstrailsvt.com.

Ice fishing has become increasingly popular all over the state but particularly in the Northeast Kingdom, where northern pike, smelt and perch can be plucked from frozen lakes.

NORTHERN MOUNTAIN REGION **Clearwater Sports** rents canoes and kayaks for the Mad, Winooski and White rivers. Guided trips are also available and shuttles are provided. ~ 4147 Main Street Route 100, Waitsfield; 802-496-2708; www.clearwatersports.com.

CHAMPLAIN VALLEY **Green Mountain Troutfitters** rents tandem canoes and water gear. They also rent pontoon boats and float tubes. ~ 233 Mill Street, Jeffersonville; 802-644-2214, 800-495-4271; www.gmtrout.com.

NORTHEAST KINGDOM For canoes and kayaks, try **The Village Sport Shop**. ~ 511 Broad Street, Lyndonville; 802-626-8448, 800-464-4315; www.villagesportshop.com.

GOLF

You can tee off at numerous public courses across the state. They generally operate between April and November.

SOUTHERN VERMONT The **Sitzmark Golf Course** is a par-3 executive course surrounded by woods. ~ East Dover Road off Route 100, Wilmington; 802-464-3384. There's a semiprivate course at the **Mount Anthony Country Club**. ~ 180 Country Club Drive, Bennington; 802-447-7079.

CENTRAL VERMONT Surrounded by trees and brooks, the **Killington Golf Course** is a difficult Jeffrey Cornish–designed green. Closed November through April. ~ Killington Access Road, Killington; 802-422-6700. **Neshobe Golf Club** has a course with rolling fairways. ~ Town Farm Road, Brandon; 802-247-3611.

NORTHERN MOUNTAIN REGION **Resort Sugarbush** has a Robert Trent Jones, Sr., mountain course. ~ Sugarbush Golf Course, Warren; 802-537-8427. The **Stowe Country Club**'s course has a view of Mt. Mansfield and Camel's Hump. Open May through

October. ~ Cottage Club Road off Cape Cod Road, Stowe; 802-253-4893.

CHAMPLAIN VALLEY Don't land in the water on the fifth hole at **Kwiniaska Golf Club.** ~ Spear Street, Shelburne; 802-985-3672; www.kwiniaska.com.

NORTHEAST KINGDOM **St. Johnsbury Country Club**'s 18-hole course features lush fairways and marshlands. ~ Route 5, St. Johnsbury; 802-748-9894, fax 802-748-1591; www.stjohnsburycountryclub.com.

TENNIS

Tennis fans will find outdoor and indoor courts across the state.

SOUTHERN VERMONT **Mount Anthony Country Club** has three outdoor courts. Fee. Closed January through the end of March. ~ 180 Country Club Drive, Bennington; 802-442-2617; www.golfingvermont.com. **Manchester Parks and Recreation** has three outdoor courts. Fee. ~ Off Route 30, Manchester; 802-362-1439.

CENTRAL VERMONT Two courts are open to the public at **Vail Field.** Closed in winter. ~ Route 106 behind the Woodstock Inn, Woodstock. For information, call 802-457-1502.

NORTHERN MOUNTAIN REGION **The Bridges Family Resort and Tennis Club** has two indoor clay courts, eight outdoor clay courts and two outdoor hardtop courts. Fee. ~ Sugarbush Access Road, Warren; 802-583-2922; www.bridgesresort.com.

CHAMPLAIN VALLEY Eight tennis courts are open to the public at **Leddy Park.** ~ North Avenue, Burlington; 802-864-0123.

NORTHEAST KINGDOM **Prouty Beach** offers four lighted courts in Newport. Fee. ~ Veterans Avenue; 802-334-6345.

RIDING STABLES

What could be more exciting than tromping on horseback through the unspoiled Vermont countryside? Plenty of stables will provide horses and directions to the best trails.

CENTRAL VERMONT Try **Kedron Valley Stables** for lessons and escorted trail rides in the woods. Overnight trips, with inn accommodations, are also offered. ~ Route 106, South Woodstock; 802-457-1480; www.kedron.com. **Pond Hill Ranch** provides guided trips on mountain trails. ~ Pond Hill Road, Castleton; 802-468-2449; www.pondhillranch.com. The **Vermont Icelandic Horse Farm** offers trips on scenic back roads and mountain trails. ~ North Fayston Road, Fayston; 802-496-7141; www.icelandichorses.com, e-mail horses@icelandichorses.com.

CHAMPLAIN VALLEY In Chittenden, **Mountain Top Inn Stables** leads one-hour guided excursions in the Green Mountain National Forest. Closed mid-November to late May. ~ Mountain Top Road; 802-483-2311, 800-445-2100; www.mountaintopinn.com.

Lajoie Stables offers guided trailrides lasting one, one-and-a-half or two hours. Reservations are required. ~ 992 Pollander Road, Jeffersonville; 802-644-5347; www.lajoiestables.com, e-mail lajoiestables@aol.com.

BIKING

Vermont's mountains and abundance of back roads create a perfect environment for bicycling.

NORTHERN MOUNTAIN REGION In the **Sugarbush** area there's a 16-mile excursion along Route 100 and East Warren Road, winding through the scenic Mad River Valley and taking in the quaint towns of Warren and Waitsfield.

CHAMPLAIN VALLEY You can take an easy but lengthy 51-mile trek through the fertile **Champlain Valley**, meandering among apple orchards and cornfields and skirting beautiful Lake Champlain. Stick to Routes 125, 17 and 23, picking up Lake Street along the lake.

Bike Rentals In southern Vermont, **Brattleboro Bike Shop** has rentals, sales and repairs. ~ 165 Main Street; 802-254-8644, 800-272-8245; www.bratbike.com. **Green Mountain Rentals** rents mountain bikes and sells accessories. ~ 158 North Main Street, Rutland; 802-775-0101. In central Vermont, **Wilderness Trails** rents mountain bikes (helmets, locks and maps included) and offers guided tours. ~ The Quechee Inn, Main Street, Quechee; 802-295-7620. In the Northern Mountain Region, **Clearwater Sports** rents mountain bikes. ~ 4147 Main Street Route 100, Waitsfield; 802-496-2708; www.clearwatersports.com. **The Ski Rack** has road, mountain, tandem and hybrid bikes; trail maps are also available. ~ 85 Main Street, Burlington; 802-658-3313, 800-882-4530; www.skirack.com. Up in the Northeast Kingdom, **Village Sport Shop** provides road and mountain bike rentals and repairs. ~ 511 Broad Street, Lyndonville; 802-626-8448; e-mail villagesport@kingcon.com.

Bike Tours To help get you started, **VBT Bicycle Tours and Vacations** offers tours with all levels of difficulty and will help build tours for groups of 14 or more. ~ 614 Monkton Road, Bristol, VT 05443; 802-453-4811, 800-245-3868; www.vbt.com, e-mail vbtinfo@vbt.com. For touring around the Champlain Valley, **Bicycle Holidays** rents mountain bikes for their custom-designed self-guided tours. ~ 1394 Munger Street, Middlebury; 802-388-2453, 800-292-5388; www.bicycleholidays.com, e-mail cyclevt@sover.net. **Bike Vermont** runs tours for all levels that last up to seven days. They'll rent you a bike, or you can bring your own. ~ P.O. Box 207, Woodstock, VT 05091; 802-457-3553, 800-257-2226; www.bikevt.com.

HIKING

With more than 700 miles of splendid hiking terrain—including 512 miles on state and national forest lands—Vermont is a hiker's nirvana. The best time to go, of course, is early summer to late fall, avoiding the spring "mud season" from mid-April to late May.

Vermont's hiking authority, **The Green Mountain Club**, can supply books, brochures and guidance on the subject, as well as information on biking, snowshoeing and Nordic skiing. ~ 4711 Waterbury-Stowe Road, Waterbury Center, VT 05677; 802-244-7037; www.greenmountainclub.org, e-mail gmc@greenmountain club.org.

All distances listed for hiking trails are one way unless otherwise noted.

The longest uninterrupted trek exists on the aptly named **Long Trail** (270 miles), a strenuous, primitive footpath that crawls along the crest of the Green Mountains from Massachusetts to Canada. Nature-lovers enjoy the abundance of wildlife and foliage on this trek, which ambles through dense evergreen forests and shaded glens and alongside quiescent ponds and rivers. An inspiration for the Appalachian Trail, which links the mountains from Georgia to Maine, the Long Trail includes 175 miles of side trails and climbs as high as 4393 feet.

SOUTHERN VERMONT **Bald Mountain Trail** (2.5 miles), off Route 9 in Bennington, makes a loop past an alder swamp and a cascading brook and through a hemlock forest. There are some fine mountain views along the way.

A nice, short hike in southern Vermont can be found along **Harmon Hill Trail** (1.7 miles) off Route 9 east of Bennington. There's a steep then moderate climb to the summit, where views of Bennington and Mt. Antone are fabulous.

A few miles north, **Baker Peak** and **Lake trails** (3.3 miles), off Route 7 near Danby, wind through brooks and streams then scale Baker Mountain for a magnificent look at the Otter Creek Valley and marble quarry on Dorset Peak.

CENTRAL VERMONT A dramatic crevice can be seen along the **Clarendon Gorge and Airport Lookout Viewing Area** (.2 miles), which picks up off Route 103 east of Route 7 near Clarendon.

SWITZERLAND ON MY MIND

Travel north of St. Johnsbury on Route 5 to Route 5A and you'll arrive at what may be the state's single most stupendous vista. **Lake Willoughby**, an incredible expanse of water chiseled by glaciers, known as the "Lucerne" of the United States, shimmers peacefully beneath the craggy peaks of Mounts Pisgah and Hor. Rimmed with rocky shoreline, fine carpets of grass, and inns and lakefront cabins (not too many due to the foresightedness of local leaders), the lake dispenses all the beauty the eye can handle.

A path crosses a suspension bridge over the Mill River, then ascends steadily to a nice vantage point with views of the Otter Creek Valley and Bird and Herrick mountains.

For a history lesson capped by great scenery, take one of three trails at **Mt. Independence** past well-preserved remains of Revolutionary War fortifications built back in 1775. You'll also discover superb views of Lake Champlain, Fort Ticonderoga and surrounding valleys. The trail begins off Route 73A west of Orwell Village.

Apparently Vermont hogs are pickier than one might think. Fed ice cream waste from Ben & Jerry's, the hogs liked all the flavors but mint Oreo.

Abbey Pond Trail (1.9 miles) affords a close look at beautiful wilderness areas teeming with marsh plants, deer, rabbits, bears and other wildlife. Follow the trail from Route 53, near Forest Dale, past a series of cascades to a view of the twin peaks of Robert Frost Mountain.

The **Skylight Pond Trail** (2.6 miles) commences at Steam Mill Clearing, a pretty meadow and former logging camp, and meanders easily up Battell Mountain, then continues to picturesque Skylight Pond. Pick up the trailhead off Forest Road 59 seven and a half miles east of East Middlebury.

NORTHERN MOUNTAIN REGION For a 180-degree view of the Champlain Valley and New York's Adirondack Mountains, opt for the **Battell Trail** (2 miles), a western-slope approach to the Long Trail. Hiking enthusiasts can continue 2.9 miles north to the Mt. Abraham summit for a look at the alpine vegetation. The entrance is located off Route 100 in the scenic Lincoln Gap.

Mount Mansfield is Vermont's highest peak (4393 feet) and naturally the most hiked. The easiest trek is via the **Long Trail** (4.6 miles), while the most ghoulish endures along **Hell Brook Trail** (1.5 miles), a supersteep rocky climb recommended only for experienced hikers. Both trailheads begin off Route 108 in Stowe.

One of the most beautiful, secluded spots on the Long Trail is at **Devil's Gulch Trail** (2.6 miles), an interesting rock defile and fern grotto. The trailhead is along Route 118 five miles west of Eden.

CHAMPLAIN VALLEY Take a hike to Lake Champlain on the **Red Rocks Park Trails** (2.5 miles), a series of short paths through cool pine woods that lead to vantage points on the lakeshore. The park is off Queen City Park Drive west of Route 189 in South Burlington.

Open only to campers using the campgrounds, the **Grand Isle State Park Trail** (.3 mile) is short on distance but long on views. The path cuts through a lush thicket and makes a loop over a low bluff to an observation tower. You can see Lake

Champlain in the distance. The park is on Route 2 one mile south of Grand Isle.

Knight Point State Park Trail (1 mile) follows Lake Champlain's shoreline through a dense hardwood forest. You'll find the trail on Route 2 in North Hero.

NORTHEAST KINGDOM **Mount Pisgah Trail** (1.7 miles) crosses this 2751-foot mountain via thick forests and wooden walkways over beaver ponds. There are exceptional views packed into this trek, including a 60-mile panorama from Lake Memphremagog and Jay Peak to beyond Camel's Hump. The trail starts along Route 5A, about six miles from West Burke.

The remote Northeast Kingdom offers some glorious hikes, including the **Wheeler Mountain Trail** (1.3 miles), which creeps through meadows and woods and across open rocks to a 2371-foot summit. Along the way, you'll catch splendid views of Mount Mansfield and Lake Willoughby. The trail picks up off Route 5 east of Barton.

Transportation

CAR

Automobile travel is quickest (though not very scenic) on **Routes 91** and **89**, Vermont's two interstate highways. Route 91 cuts in from Massachusetts and follows Vermont's eastern border, while Route 89 starts at the New Hampshire line and snakes across the northern center of Vermont to Quebec.

From New York, opt for **Route 7** or **Route 4**, entering on Vermont's western edge. Though not a major highway by any means, **Route 100** is the picturesque thoroughfare slicing north–south through the center of the state.

AIR

Burlington International Airport, a small and easily accessible facility in Burlington, is the major air gateway for Vermont. Carriers serving it are Continental Airlines, Delta Air Lines, JetBlue, Northwest Airlines, United Airlines and US Airways.

Burlington Airport Information Desk provides details on traveling from the airport to anywhere in the state. ~ 802-863-1889; www.burlingtonintlairport.com.

BUS

Vermont Transit Lines provides extensive service throughout New England, with major Vermont stops. For general information, call 800-642-3133 (in Vermont), 800-451-3292 (outside Vermont); www.vermonttransit.com. Stations are in Brattleboro at the Junction of Routes 5, 9 and 91, 802-254-6066; in Montpelier at 1 Taylor Street, 800-229-9220; in White River Junction at Sykes Avenue, 802-295-3011; in Rutland at 102 West Street, 800-552-8737; in Burlington at 345 Pine Street, 802-864-6811; and in Bellow's Falls at 7 Square, 802-463-3069.

TRAIN

Amtrak offers direct service from Washington, D.C., Philadelphia, New York, Connecticut and Montreal. The train stops in Vermont at White River Junction (Railroad Row), Montpelier (Junction Road and Short Road), Waterbury-Stowe (Park Row) and Burlington–Essex Junction (29 Railroad Avenue, near Burlington). ~ 800-872-7245; www.amtrak.com.

CAR RENTALS

If you arrive at Burlington International Airport, you'll find the following rental companies: **Avis Rent A Car** (800-331-1212), **Budget Rent A Car** (800-527-0700), **Hertz Rent A Car** (800-654-3131), and **National Car Rental** (800-227-7368). **Thrifty Car Rental** (800-367-2277), is located near the terminal and provides free airport transfers.

NINE

New Hampshire

New Hampshire. It's a heart-stopping collage of sculpted mountains, stony profiles, seamless country roads, expansive lakes and broad beaches. A place you yearn to clutch tightly, to safeguard and to proclaim.

A slender fragment of Yankee domain framed by Vermont, Maine and Massachusetts, New Hampshire is all this and much, much more. It is a region that seems not quite real when you first reach the state, yet you're certain you've been there before. New Hampshire's daunting landscape flirts with the imagination; its spirit roams wild around untamed timberland, wilderness expanses and riots of flowers.

Born of molten granite and giant glaciers, the state's geologic surface was but a labyrinth of smoke, dust and ice sheets some 300 million years ago. Hot rock hissed beneath the earth, forced its way up and drove the ground to buckle and split. Advancing ice sheets smoothed the rock, forming it into hills and mountains, then swiftly melted to create rivers and lakes.

Along the way, these icy torrents deposited thousands of granite chunks. All that stone gives today's New Hampshire a rugged veneer, as well as its moniker of "The Granite State." Boulders lie strewn across farmlands, jut out into the sea and loom atop mountains, their mystic profiles often evocative of some familiar face or object.

Human rumblings in this area go back at least 8000 years, when the Abenaki and Pennacook Indians roamed the lands. Members of Algonquin tribes, they fished the swift rivers, hunted forests for game and fruit and culled maple sugar from the trees. Their first European visitor, British captain Martin Pring, sailed up the Piscataqua River in 1603, though it was not until 1623 that the first settlement was founded at Odiorne Point in present-day Rye.

Several towns soon sprang up along the coast and river. Strawbery Banke, now Portsmouth, became the capital and commercial center of New Hampshire life as fishers, coopers and shipbuilders plied their trades there. In 1643, a greedy Massachusetts annexed the settlements into its Bay Colony, holding them for 36 years until England declared New Hampshire a royal province.

Thick forests, bitter winters and unforgiving earth made life difficult for those who tried to tame New Hampshire's interior. Even worse, previously friendly Indians came to resent white intrusion and exploitation, and a series of violent skirmishes ensued. In one infamous incident, Indians captured a settler named Hannah Dustin, a 39-year-old mother of 12, and took her to River Islet, near present-day Concord. During the night, Dustin killed and scalped her ten sleeping captors, escaping with her life.

In the mid-1700s, settlers struggled to cultivate the rocky soil that became bloodied by French and Indian conflicts. The French and Indian War finally settled the matter in 1763, though the subsequent American Revolution only brought more strife to a battered land.

New Hampshire entered the Revolution with a vengeance. In December 1774, when patriots received word from Paul Revere that British soldiers would soon be at Portsmouth, they stormed Fort William and Mary. Six months later, England's governor was driven from the colony.

After the war, people gave up on agriculture and turned to textile manufacturing. But an even more lucrative source of income was about to arrive: the stream of pleasure seekers who, lured by bewitching landscapes and a bevy of natural resources, started coming to New Hampshire in droves. Exclaimed one well-traveled visitor: "There is no doubt but the scenery of New Hampshire is more varied and beautiful than can be found in any other state in the Union."

Thousands of new arrivals, known as "summer people," converged on the land. Those with money built grand estates or lavish hotels, while the majority put up frame houses and white picket fences and settled on their front porches for the summer. All of a sudden, New Hampshire's first tourist industry was raging.

By the late 1800s, a different kind of industry had emerged. Virtually overnight, logging businesses penetrated the White Mountains and cleared thousands of acres of trees to feed a voracious lumber demand. Within 20 years, barren patches scarred the mountainsides and wildlife was dwindling.

It might have been the undoing of New Hampshire's precious mountains had not public outcry prompted Congress to halt the destruction. The Weeks Act of 1911 called for federal purchase of most of the state's forest lands, which today make up the 768,000-acre White Mountain National Forest.

Now forests cloak 84 percent of the state, while some 1300 lakes form pockets of beauty and intrigue. Shaped like a skinny triangle that points toward Canada, New Hampshire spans only 168 miles from top to bottom and 90 miles at its broadest point. Its 9304 square miles cover six geographic regions so disparate you might think they existed in separate states, though together they create a powerful display of nature.

The wind-whipped seacoast ambles a mere 18 miles from Massachusetts to Maine, though its dramatic jetties, swirling tidepools and generous stretches of sand pack a state-sized dose of beauty. Northern Portsmouth, one of the finest ports in New England, brims with culture and commerce and endearing remnants of history.

The Merrimack Valley crawls up the lower spine of New Hampshire, its old textile mills clinging to the shores of the Merrimack River. The valley claims its largest city, Manchester, and seat of government, Concord.

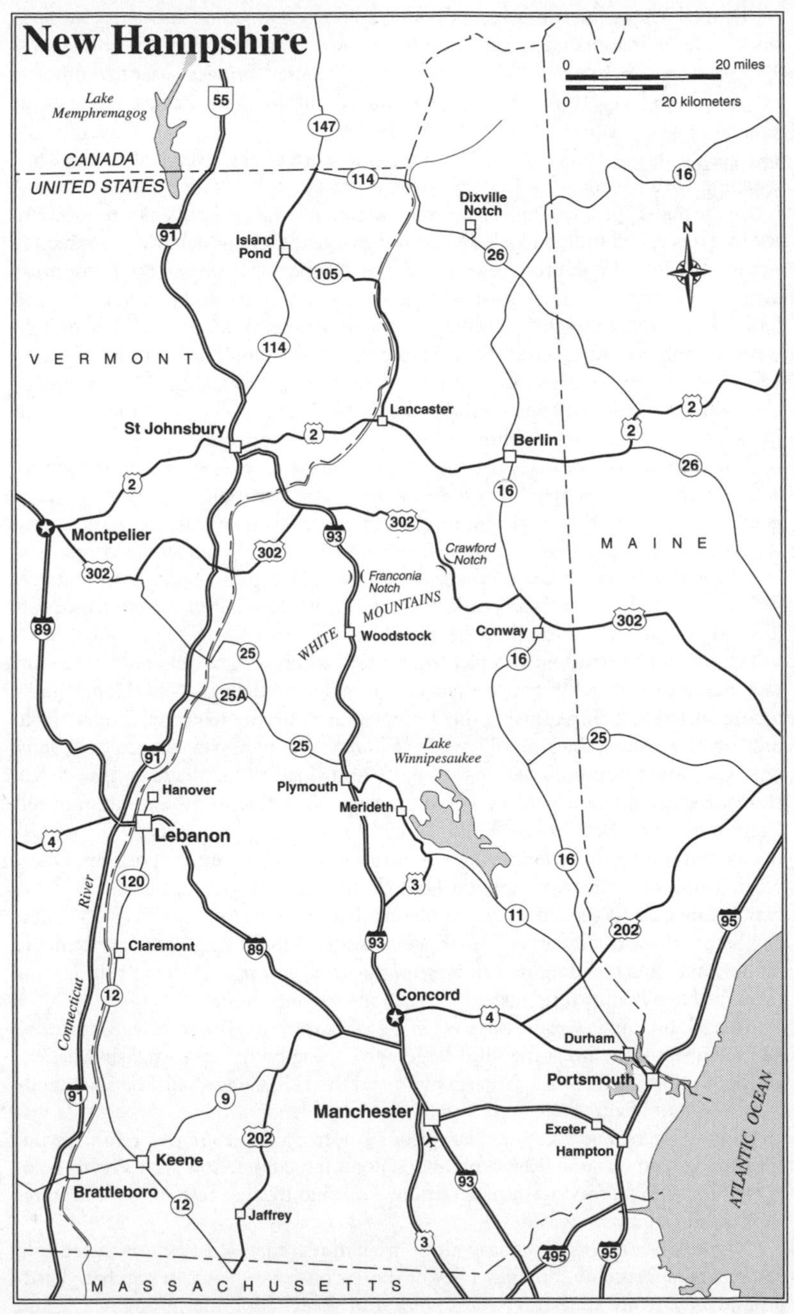
New Hampshire
Lake Memphremagog
CANADA
UNITED STATES
VERMONT
MAINE
MASSACHUSETTS
ATLANTIC OCEAN
0 20 miles
0 20 kilometers
N
Island Pond
Dixville Notch
St Johnsbury
Lancaster
Berlin
Montpelier
Crawford Notch
Franconia Notch
WHITE MOUNTAINS
Woodstock
Conway
Lake Winnipesaukee
Plymouth
Merideth
Hanover
Lebanon
Connecticut River
Claremont
Concord
Durham
Portsmouth
Manchester
Exeter
Hampton
Keene
Brattleboro
Jaffrey
55
147
114
91
105
16
26
2
302
93
89
25
25A
4
120
3
11
202
95
12
9
495

Draped across the southwest corridor are lone mountains known as monadnocks. The Monadnock Region embodies a perfect canvas of rural New England, speckled with covered bridges, weathered barns and charming country towns that seem locked in the 18th century.

In January 1776, New Hampshire became the first independent American state.

The state's midwestern edge, flanked by the Connecticut River, is graced with cornfields, subtle mountains and the culture of Dartmouth College. Nearby Lake Sunapee and its attendant sentinel, Mount Sunapee, are a year-round playground for lovers of the outdoors.

A tryst of twinkling azure water and gentle peaks, the Lakes Region is altogether captivating and soothing. A total of 273 bodies of water bundle together across New Hampshire's heartland. Their names—many were given by the Indians—conjure up romance and exotica. Lake Winnipesaukee, with 283 miles of coast and 274 habitable islands, is the sixth largest lake lying wholly in the United States.

Towering above the lakes are the White Mountains, overwhelming in appearance and massive in scope. Life slows down up here as people tend to small farms and businesses and raise their families. There are pockets of tourism, particularly ski resorts, nestled between canopies of evergreens and remote country roads.

In addition to its obvious aesthetic appeal, New Hampshire basks in the nation's political limelight every four years. Since 1915, it has secured the edge on presidential primaries, holding the first one in each election.

This claim to firstdom has yielded the tiny state considerable political clout, as candidates frequently gauge their campaigns according to New Hampshire's mood. In 1988, George Bush gained momentum after he trounced Robert Dole in New Hampshire. Back in 1976, a little-known Jimmy Carter earned credibility after a warm reception in the first primary. And since 1952, New Hampshire has chosen the candidate who would go on to be president, with the exception of Bill Clinton in 1992 and George W. Bush in 2000.

It's certain that New Hampshire aims to keep its first-primary position. Once, when Vermont mentioned it might hold elections earlier than its neighbor, New Hampshire quickly passed a law mandating that its primaries be held on the Tuesday before those of any other New England state. Wily Massachusetts once made the mistake of scheduling its primary on the same day as New Hampshire's. Indignant, New Hampshire pushed its elections up one week.

Indeed, politics is serious business in New Hampshire. The state legislature has 424 members—making it the third-largest governing body in the English-speaking world (behind Great Britain's Parliament and the U.S. Congress). The state tends to vote Republican.

"Live Free or Die" is New Hampshire's motto, as every native reminds you. It's emblazoned on state license plates, on not a few homes and across some businesses. But despite this constant assertion of autonomy, the state still sees fit to restrict itself in curious ways.

Nightclubs and bars standing alone are banned; they must be connected to a restaurant, sports club, bowling alley or similar business. You can purchase hard-liquor only from state-run stores, many of which dot major highways and interstates. These cobwebbed laws have been in place since Prohibition and don't seem likely to change in the near future.

For the most part, freedom to New Hampshire inhabitants means no sales tax and no personal income tax. Not surprisingly, these particular freedoms have lured throngs of people who now live in New Hampshire but work in nearby states. Miffed at the situation, Maine responded by taxing its workers who live in New Hampshire—as well as their spouses who live and work in New Hampshire. Needless to say, the two states continue a classic Yankee feud.

Today's New Hampshire is home to a new band of artists, as well as the factory workers and bankers, innkeepers and small business people who run the general stores. Its thriving tourism and aesthetic surroundings make the state a desirable place to live for its 1.2 million residents.

Despite some apparent modernization, New Hampshire still clings to its founding principles. It is a world focused on clapboard houses and slender steeples, Yankee ingenuity and memories of Pilgrims, town halls and the freedom to worship and vote.

Over the years, New Hampshire changes—yet somehow stays quite the same. Lifestyles and customs are passed on through generations firmly rooted in its granite soil. With a seashore, mountains and lakes that remain poignant and timeless, this state is a glorious place under the sun.

The Seacoast

Despite its diminutive size—only 18 miles in length—New Hampshire's seacoast is one of the state's most revered possessions. And rightly so, for its alliance of pounding surf, rocky headlands and tidepools, stately mansions and nature preserves offers a wealth of beauty and continuous intrigue.

Naturally the dramatic seaboard is a driver's paradise, which explains why it remains perpetually clogged with traffic. Warm summer breezes and sunshine draw the most crowds—particularly on weekends—though locals claim that winter snow falling on the sand is truly a sight to behold.

SIGHTS

Just north of the Massachusetts line, whiffs of salty marsh air announce the town of **Seabrook**. Families favor this small oceanside nook for its amusement centers and pretty beaches, though the main attraction is **Seabrook Greyhound Park**. More than 1000 agile racing dogs call this fast track home, performing for bettors year round. ~ Route 107, Seabrook; 603-474-3065; www.seabrookgreyhoundpark.com.

Since 1976, Seabrook has received national attention because of the controversial **Seabrook Station Nuclear Power Plant**. Although citizens groups and the state of Massachusetts waged a long and costly battle to block the opening of the plant, it began operating in March 1990—three years after the 1150-megawatt, $6.5 billion facility was completed. The controversy continues today. Its science and nature center welcomes visitors by appointment only. ~ Routes 107 and 1, Seabrook; 603-474-9521, 800-

338-7482; www.seabrookstation.com, e-mail seabrookstation@fpl.com.

Traveling northward on Route 1A, you'll notice the scenery changing from marshlands to wide, open beaches as you approach the seacoast's most animated stretch of sand, **Hampton Beach**. Mobbed by hundreds of thousands of vacationers every year, this heavily developed tract is one giant pleasure center, its nucleus an oceanside promenade that reels with constant activity.

Start out by walking the promenade, a three-mile human fiesta extending along Ocean Boulevard from Dumas Avenue to Hampton Beach State Park, taking in the well-strolled boardwalk jammed with trinket and T-shirt vendors, low-slung motels and the aroma of carnival food. This is people-watching at its best, a place where a whole spectrum of humanity—drifters, beach bums and the highbrow—converges on one long slab of concrete.

There's a constant hum of cars, joggers, bicyclists and curious sightseers who stop to ponder the **New Hampshire Marine War Memorial**, a tribute to soldiers lost at sea. The granite statue features a forlorn maiden draped in rolls of stone cloth and clutching a wreath. ~ Ocean Boulevard and Nudd Avenue, Hampton Beach.

Great Boars Head, a rocky bulkhead in the ocean, projects an imposing silhouette just north of Hampton Beach. Topped with grand old mansions and seaside homes, Boars Head is particularly intriguing at sunrise, when the day's first light and the ocean mist produce a surreal portrait. ~ Ocean Boulevard and Dumas Avenue.

To help get you organized with local sightseeing, stop by the **Hampton Area Chamber of Commerce**. Their headquarters are located a couple of miles west of Hampton Beach. They also run an information booth (180 Ocean Boulevard, Hampton), open in the summer. ~ 603-926-8718, 800-438-2826; www.hamptonbeach.org, e-mail hamptonbeachinfo@comcast.net.

A ten-minute drive west will land you in the rural respite of **Applecrest Farm Orchards**, where 200 acres of apple trees and pumpkin patches bask along the hillsides. Show up from Labor Day to mid-October and pick your own, or check out the applemart, an 1812 barn stocked with apple ciders, pies, butter, sauce and other great-smelling goodies. During the summertime, strawberries and blueberries come ripe for pickin'. ~ Route 88, west of Route 1, Hampton Falls; 603-926-3721, fax 603-926-0006; www.applecrest.com.

Hop back over onto Route 1A, heading north along this roving high road flanked on one side by a turgid ocean and on the other by regal New England mansions known as "Millionaire's Row" for the old-monied families who live here.

The largest tract of undeveloped coastline exists at **Odiorne Point State Park**, which wanders along two oceanfront miles and covers 135 acres. Back in 1623, New Hampshire's first white settlers landed here and found thick vegetation and whistling winds. The park includes grave sites, old stone walls, remains of a formal garden and several World War II fortifications. **The Seacoast Science Center**, located on the park's premises, offers a look at the area's natural and social history. (A separate admission fee is charged.) Open daily April to October with fee; open weekends only with no fee the rest of the year. Admission during summer and weekends. ~ Route 1A, Rye; 603-436-7406, fax 603-436-1036 (park), 603-436-8043 (Seacoast Science Center); www.seacoastsciencecenter.org, e-mail info@seacenter.org.

From here you can peer out to sea and spy the stony profile of the **Isles of Shoals**, an archipelago that harbors great mysteries and torrid tales of pirates, treasures and wrecked ships. In 1614, Captain John Smith dubbed the isles "barren piles of rocks with a few scrub cedar," and they've seen minimal change since. Blackbeard and Captain Kidd supposedly stashed their loot among the rocky crevices, the former abandoning his wife there in 1723. Some say her spirit still roams the shores.

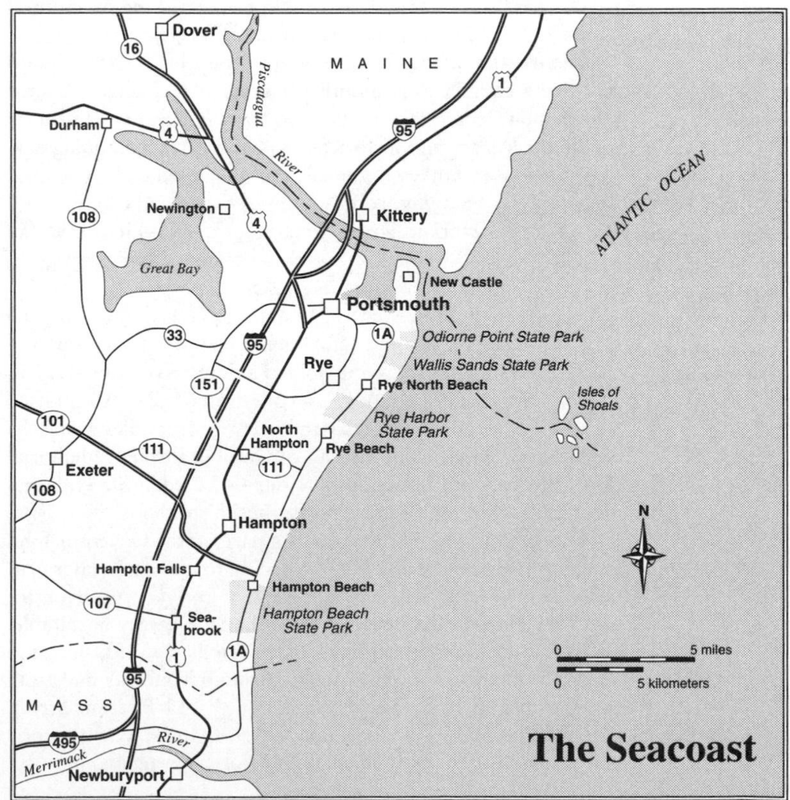

The Seacoast

The isles later drew many artists and writers, including Nathaniel Hawthorne and Childe Hassam. Today, you can visit the islands via the **Island Cruises**, which offers narrated tours seasoned with history. It offers ferry trips to Star Island, Saturday-evening island tours and a Star Island walkabout. Closed October through May. Admission. ~ Rye Harbor State Marina, Route 1A, Rye; 603-964-6446; www.uncleoscar.com, e-mail info@uncleoscar.com.

Anchoring the northern end of the seacoast, **Portsmouth**, with its rich maritime history, has long played a critical role in the state's prosperity and development. Lying at the mouth of the Piscataqua River, the city seems like some profound old sage, locked in a bygone era yet quite vibrant and progressive at the same time.

Stone sidewalks and ivy-clad brick buildings, their walls holding two centuries of memories, gather stoically along the harbor. In central downtown, known as Market Street, immaculately restored 18th- and 19th-century enclaves mingle with sleek new highrises. Young artists and professionals continue to arrive from Boston, New York and Maine, polishing the cultural patina and dynamic night scenes of this port city.

There's so much to see here, and the best place to get organized is the **Greater Portsmouth Chamber of Commerce Visitor Information Center**. Pick up the *Portsmouth Harbour Trail*, a resource book featuring historical facts and a map outlining several self-guided tours. Closed Saturday and Sunday from Columbus Day to mid-May. ~ 500 Market Street, Portsmouth; 603-436-3988, fax 603-436-5118; www.portsmouthchamber.org, e-mail info@portsmouthchamber.org.

At the John Paul Jones House you'll find a room arranged with marvelous wedding gowns worn in the 1800s as well as the oldest piano in the United States.

Built between 1716 and 1807, the houses vary architecturally and enjoy their own special museums and personalities. At the **John Paul Jones House**, a 1758 Georgian design, there's a collection of Civil War guns, a nifty wooden bathtub, and oars and paddles from the South Seas. Closed from the end of October through Memorial Day. Call ahead for hours. Admission. ~ 43 Middle Street, Portsmouth; 603-436-8420; www.portsmouthhistory.org.

George Washington dropped by a party at the **Governor John Langdon House** back in 1789. According to memos he later penned, George found the home quite warm and its proprietor, future New Hampshire Governor John Langdon, very hospitable. Today, beautiful wood carvings and precious period furnishings adorn the interior. Closed Monday through Thursday and from mid-October through May. Admission. ~ 143 Pleasant Street, Portsmouth; 603-436-3205, fax 603-436-4651; www.historicnewengland.org, e-mail pmichaud@historicnewengland.org.

One treat that goes with the Portsmouth Trail is the opportunity to meet the congenial docents (many are Portsmouth natives) who fill you with history and interesting anecdotes. Most of the trail homes close during winter and open only a few days each week the rest of the year, so call ahead.

To find out what makes Portsmouth tick, stroll southeast on Market Street down to the **docks**, where the Piscataqua River laps at the city's edge. Back in the 18th and 19th centuries, furniture makers, potters, coopers and shipbuilders gathered along the waterfront to ply their trades, while a flourishing sawmill industry provided Great Britain with thousands of ships' masts. Today, tugboats, fishing vessels and sailboats scoot across the dark waters that flow to nearby Kittery, Maine.

From here you can catch a harbor cruise or take a longer jaunt to the Isles of Shoals. **Isles of Shoals Steamship Co.** provides trips from April through October. Cruises inland for fall foliage tours. ~ 315 Market Street, Portsmouth; 603-431-5500, 800-441-4620; www.islesofshoals.com, e-mail customerservice@islesofshoals.com. **Portsmouth Harbor Cruises** offers trips from mid-May to late October. A tour of the inland rivers is also featured. ~ 64 Ceres Street, Oar House Dock, Portsmouth; 603-436-8084, 800-776-0915, fax 603-436-4337; www.portsmouthharbor.com, e-mail phc@portsmouthharbor.com.

Follow the water northwest to Marcy Street, where you'll discover Portsmouth's most prized gem, **Strawbery Banke**, site of the original settlement. Sheltered within ten acres of rambling gardens and Colonial buildings is a wonderful lesson on New England architecture through 1943 and the struggles and lifestyles of America's founders. The area gets its moniker from the profusion of berries found here in 1630 by the city's first English settlers.

Thanks to the foresight of local leaders, the banke's 42 buildings, dating from 1695 to 1954, were spared demolition in the 1950s. Every place offers some fascinating historical insight, and it takes a full day to see it all. There's the **Daniel Webster House** (not open to the public), where Webster and his wife Grace lived from 1814 to 1816, as well as the boyhood home of author Thomas Bailey Aldrich, whose book *The Story of a Bad Boy* inspired Mark Twain to write *Tom Sawyer*. Open for guided tours only, November through April. Admission. ~ Entrance off Marcy Street south of Court Street, Portsmouth; 603-433-1100, fax 603-433-1115; www.strawberybanke.org, e-mail sbrooks@strawberybanke.org.

The **Strawbery Banke Museum** offers an intimate peek at four centuries of New England work and life by interpreting the living history of those who settled Portsmouth. There are exhibits as well as live demonstrations of artisans plying traditional

New England trades such as potting, cooking, needlepoint, coopering and wooden boat building. Closed weekdays from November through April. Admission. ~ Marcy and Hancock streets, Portsmouth; 603-433-1100, fax 603-433-1115; www.strawberybanke.org, e-mail sbrooks@strawberybanke.org.

The 1766 **Pitt Tavern**, perhaps the banke's most historically significant building, was a meeting place for loyalists and then patriots. Revolutionary War strategies were devised within these walls, which now display ads from 1770s newspapers announcing those historic meetings.

Before you leave town, stop by the **North Cemetery**, purchased by the town for £50 in 1753. Buried on this unassuming grassy swell are John Langdon, former New Hampshire governor and signer of the Constitution, and General William Whipple, signer of the Declaration of Independence. ~ Maplewood Avenue and Russell Street, Portsmouth.

The coastline bustle takes on a gentler cadence as you head north of Portsmouth. **Dover**, a working-class mill town with charm, was founded by fishermen during the early 1600s and remained independent until 1642, when it joined the Massachusetts Bay Colony. Route 9 trundles right through town, flanked by huge mansions sporting multiple chimneys, many built in the 19th century by wealthy mill owners.

You can mull over the town's beginnings at the **Woodman Institute**, which houses an excellent display of New Hampshire and New England memorabilia, wildlife and natural history. The institute also includes a 19th-century colonial garrison house. Closed Monday and Tuesday and from February through March. Admission. ~ 182 Central Avenue, Dover; 603-742-1038.

Travel south on Route 108 to the college town of Durham, where the **University of New Hampshire** provides a restful haven for strolling. The campus is surrounded by 3000 acres of fields and woodlands, crisscrossed with walking trails. ~ 1 Main Street, off Route 155A, Durham; 603-862-1234; www.unh.edu.

West on Route 108, **Durham Landing** recalls the venue of a bloody battle in 1694, when more than 200 Indians attacked about 100 settlers, destroying their houses and garrisons along the Oyster River.

In nearby Exeter, you'll find a constant drum of traffic and human motion caused by the presence of exclusive **Phillips Exeter Academy**. One of the oldest and most renowned preparatory schools in the country, the academy has aged beautifully. Founded in 1781, the school boasts lovely brick buildings that lay masked in tangled ivy and are edged by green lawns and maple trees. Through the years, its hallowed halls have seen students like Daniel Webster, historian George Bancroft and Booth Tarkington. ~

20 Main Street, Exeter; 603-772-4311, fax 603-777-4384; www.exeter.edu, e-mail info@exeter.edu.

LODGING

Toward the north (and somewhat quieter) end of Hampton Beach, the **Hampton House Hotel** offers very comfortable accommodations amid contemporary surroundings. A breezy lobby edges the busy beachfront street and comforts with soothing ocean views from the floor-to-ceiling glass windows. Three floors of spacious guest rooms feature wall-to-wall carpets, modern wood furnishings and private balconies that yield some fine ocean views and people-watching opportunities. Two-night minimum. ~ 333 Ocean Boulevard, Hampton Beach; 603-926-1033, 800-458-7058, fax 603-926-3473; www.hamptonhousehotel.com. ULTRA-DELUXE.

Wander into **D.W.'s Oceanside Inn** and you'll enter a world of superb 19th-century Victorian designs. In the breakfast room, handsome pine floors show off period furniture and braided rugs. Each of ten rooms (including two that face the ocean) is named after Hampton Beach citizens of historic or literary importance, and boasts elegant period decor; some are appointed with handpainted wallpaper or murals. A full breakfast is included. Closed mid-October to mid-May. ~ 365 Ocean Boulevard, Hampton Beach; 603-926-3542, 866-623-2674, fax 603-926-3549; www.oceansideinn.com, e-mail info@oceansideinn.com. DELUXE TO ULTRA-DELUXE.

The Inn at Hampton and Conference Center possesses all the charm and detail of a fancy bed and breakfast. The guest rooms offer such personal touches as mirrored armoires, quilted headboards and dust ruffles, vaulted pine ceilings and scents of jas-

AUTHOR FAVORITE

Comprising two adjacent 19th-century buildings fronted by white picket fences and connected by a flower-lined path, the **Martin Hill Inn** has all the romance and charm of a country inn. The Main House is a Federal-style affair with three guest rooms. The Guest House's decor leans more towards country Victorian, and is reflected in the soft colors and florals that grace its four guest rooms. Period pieces abound throughout, and all seven guest rooms boast antique writing desks as well as canopy, brass or four-poster beds. Be sure to relax in the greenhouse or take a stroll along the winding paths of the perennial and water gardens. The inn is only a ten-minute walk from downtown. A gourmet breakfast is served. ~ 404 Islington Street, Portsmouth; 603-436-2287; www.martinhillinn.com, e-mail reservations@martinhillinn.com. DELUXE.

mine. Among the other niceties of this family-fun inn are an indoor pool and jacuzzi, an exercise room and, of course, a congenial staff. Continental breakfast is included. ~ 815 Lafayette Road, Hampton; 603-926-6771, 800-423-4561, fax 603-929-2160; www.theinnofhampton.com. DELUXE TO ULTRA-DELUXE.

For the charm of a country inn with the luxuries of a large hotel, consider the **Sise Inn**. Set in an 1881 Queen Anne home within walking distance of most downtown Portsmouth sights, the hostelry features a lobby that soars three stories and is highlighted by pretty butternut banisters and oriental rugs. Oversized guest rooms are suited with bay windows, four-poster beds, showers *and* tubs (some with whirlpools) and nice extras like VCRs. ~ 40 Court Street, Portsmouth; 603-433-1200, 877-747-3466, fax 603-431-0200; www.siseinn.com, e-mail info@siseinn.com. ULTRA-DELUXE.

The **Bow Street Inn** claims an unusual location: a second floor above a performing-arts center in central downtown. Not to worry—all ten guest rooms are nicely soundproofed and come with accoutrements like brass beds, plush carpets and ruffled curtains. A brewery during the 19th century, the ruddy brick building peers across the Piscataqua River. ~ 121 Bow Street, Portsmouth; 603-431-7760, fax 603-433-1680; www.bowstreetinn.com, e-mail info@bowstreetinn.com. DELUXE.

Around 1800, Christian ship captains—anxious to separate themselves from military captains—settled in modest homes west of downtown Portsmouth. Now the **Inn at Christian Shore** harkens back to those early days with simple, Federal-style design and sunny ambience. Five bedrooms are cheerfully outfitted with wallpaper and antique furniture. The dining room, with its low-slung beam ceilings and large fireplace, is quite cozy. Full breakfast is included in the rates. ~ 335 Maplewood Avenue, Portsmouth; 603-431-6770, fax 603-373-8421; www.innatchristianshore. MODERATE TO DELUXE.

DINING

For superb seafood amidst some hopping beach action, try the dining room at **The Ashworth by the Sea**. Lobster fiends will revel in the ten different lobster entrées such as baked stuffed lobster pie, lobster Newburg and a sinful baked lobster stuffed with extra lobster. For non-seafoodites, there's veal and chicken plus roast Vermont turkey. In July and August, a buffet for breakfast and dinner is available. Sunday brunch is offered from late October to mid-May. ~ 295 Ocean Boulevard, Hampton Beach; 603-926-6762, fax 603-926-2002. MODERATE TO DELUXE.

Possibly the finest seafood restaurant on New Hampshire's 18-mile coast is popular **Ron's Landing**. Elegant yet quite relaxed, the restaurant sits across the street from the ocean; the Atlantic views are marvelous from its second-floor deck. Small tables draped in starched cloth and perfectly folded napkins create an intimate atmosphere. The Continental menu features a generous seafood selection plus interesting chicken, duck, beef and pasta entrées. Dinner only, except for Sunday brunch from October to April. ~ 379 Ocean Boulevard, Hampton Beach; 603-929-2122, fax 603-926-3167; www.ronslanding.com. DELUXE TO ULTRA-DELUXE.

The **Galley Hatch** is a bright, cheerfully modern restaurant offering something for every taste. The menu has everything from soup and salad to the freshest seafood. Also available are pasta, pizza and a full steakhouse menu. The on-site store carries fine wines and cheeses, fresh flowers and seasonal gift items. ~ 325 Lafayette Road, Hampton; 603-926-6152, fax 603-929-4490; www.galleryhatch.com. MODERATE.

The Carriage House provides a curious mix of Colonial and seaside ambience—and pulls it off swimmingly. The two-story casual nook rests across the street from Jenness Beach but looks like a mountain eatery. Early American wood tables and booths encircle a big hearth downstairs, while upstairs a smaller room promises great views of the beach. The Continental-style bill of fare offers gems like steak *au poivre*, veal *pasquale*, sea scallops florentine, and lobster flamed in pernod. Dinner only. ~ 2263 Ocean Boulevard, Rye; 603-964-8251; www.carriagehouserye.com, e-mail info@carriagehouserye.com. MODERATE TO ULTRA-DELUXE.

The **Blue Claw** offers waterfront dining right on the dock, with clear views of the ocean and passing tugboats. While they serve an array of seafood (fish and chips, shrimp, and clams), it's the lobster that makes them shine. The lobster roll, a quarter-pound of fresh meat on a grilled Piantadosi roll, is a local favorite. Sandwiches, salads and ribs are also available. There's no

AUTHOR FAVORITE

Back in 1764, a 26-year-old grenadier named Thomas Fletcher reportedly died of fever after drinking a hot beer. Forlorn and eager for companionship, his widow turned their tiny frame home into a tavern. Today, **Widow Fletcher's Tavern** remains one of New England's supreme pubs, framed in hand-hewn wood beams and booths and wide plank floors worn to a perfect late-18th-century patina. Fare goes a step beyond standard tavern food, with entrées such as seafood linguine, broiled haddock, and a slew of excellent salads, sandwiches and appetizers. No lunch Monday through Friday; Sunday brunch is served. ~ 401 Lafayette Road, Hampton; 603-926-8800. MODERATE.

indoor seating, so be sure to stop here when it's warm. Closed December through April. ~ 58 Ceres Street, Portsmouth; 603-427-2529; www.theblueclaw.com, e-mail theblueclaw@yahoo.com. MODERATE TO DELUXE

HIDDEN ►

A departure from traditional New England fare can be found at **The Wellington Room.** Here, international cuisine takes center stage. The broad menu includes items such as exotic mushroom crepes and New Zealand lamb with mint blackberry honey. All pastries are made fresh in house. It's all served in a stylish second-floor dining room overlooking the river. Dinner only. Closed Monday and Tuesday. ~ 67 Bow Street, Portsmouth; 603-431-2989; www.thewellingtonroom.com. DELUXE TO ULTRA-DELUXE.

The place for sushi is **Sakurabana**, a small but airy downtown nook that serves up fresh *maki* rolls and sashimi, tempura and teriyaki dishes, and interesting appetizers like soft-shell crabs. The decor borders on plain, with a small sushi bar, wood tables and railings, but it's neat as a pin. Very popular with the business set. No lunch Saturday through Monday. ~ 40 Pleasant Street, Portsmouth; 603-431-2721. MODERATE TO DELUXE.

Despite its stringent liquor laws—which mandate that bars must be part of restaurants, ski lodges or similar businesses—New Hampshire manages an ample share of lively establishments.

The **Harbor's Edge Restaurant** captures a superb view of the harbor amidst romantic surroundings. Decked in hues of emerald and rose, the eatery conveys an air of refinement with crystal and flower-topped linen tablecloths. Cuisine falls in the American and nouvelle categories, with seafood and mixed grill items. ~ In the Sheraton Portsmouth, 250 Market Street, Portsmouth; 603-431-2300, fax 603-443-5649; www.sheratonportsmouth.com, e-mail info@sheratonportsmouth.com. DELUXE.

Portsmouth's famous old spaghetti house is **The Rosa**, a great family-style place that opened back in 1927. Adorned with dimly lit wood booths and old-time photographs, the restaurant serves up those heart-stopping, traditional Italian favorites like parmigianas and cacciatores, lasagna, ravioli, tortellini and thin-crust pizza. ~ 80 State Street, Portsmouth; 603-436-9715, fax 603-436-6930; www.therosa.com. MODERATE.

East of Hampton Beach, the town of Exeter is home to Phillips Exeter Academy, one of the country's most renowned and oldest preparatory schools. Here, the student population sustains a happy array of quaint street cafés, one of the best being **The Loaf and Ladle.** Everything is homemade and fresh, served cafeteria-style by friendly young people. You'll find black-bean soup, country pâté, stacked sandwiches and cheesecakes. ~ 9 Water Street, Exeter; 603-778-8955. BUDGET.

SHOPPING

For shopping in Hampton Beach, you can slum it on the boardwalk, bartering with vendors for jewelry, T-shirts and endless assorted souvenirs. The main action is along **Ocean Boulevard** from Nudd Avenue to Haverhill Avenue, where you can snag everything from leather jackets and tattoos to fake photo IDs and suntans (in tanning salons, of course).

Bona fide mallaholics should head straight for **Fox Run Mall,** where over 100 stores and eateries provide quality browsing amid fashionable surroundings. ~ Fox Run Road off Spaulding Turnpike, Newington; 603-431-5911; www.shopfoxrun.com.

It's so much fun to stroll Portsmouth's colorful, funky shops that you'll likely forget you're spending money.

Spacious and entertaining, **G. Willikers!** has enough toys, stuffed animals and other kid paraphernalia to make a tot go crazy. ~ 13 Market Street, Portsmouth; 603-436-7746; www.gwillikers.com.

The Lollipop Tree is a specialty food manufacturer that churns out goodies along the lines of pepper jellies, artisan bread mixes, glazing sauces, dressings, jams and syrups. Closed Sunday. ~ 319 Vaughan Street, Portsmouth; 603-436-8196, 800-842-6691, fax 603-436-0282; www.lollipoptree.com.

A noteworthy art stop, **N. W. Barrett Gallery** proffers wood, handblown glass and other crafts by local and nationally acclaimed artists. On the second floor, there's a fine-art gallery with original and limited-edition prints, as well as unique wedding and engagement rings. ~ 53 Market Street, Portsmouth; 603-431-4262; www.nwbarrett.com.

The **Strawbery Banke Museum Shop** has all sorts of gifts, including reproductions of museum items, pottery, books, cards, toys and candy. Closed late October to May. ~ Marcy and Hancock streets, Portsmouth; 603-433-1114; www.strawberybanke.com.

NIGHTLIFE

The 1800-seat **Hampton Beach Casino Ballroom,** one of those great old big-band clubs built in the 1920s, headlines top-name rock-and-roll, jazz, country-and-western and comedy. The season runs from March through October. ~ 169 Ocean Boulevard, Hampton Beach; 603-929-4100, fax 603-926-3501; www.casinoballroom.com, e-mail info@casinoballroom.com.

At **Paddy's American Grille,** a low-key bar-and-grill with a full bar and 18 televisions, the billiard room has eight professional pool tables. They also present a summer concert series. ~ 27 International Drive, Portsmouth; 603-430-9450, fax 603-334-6218; www.paddysgrille.com, e- mail karen@paddysgrille.com.

Have a home-brewed beer (and watch it being brewed) at **Portsmouth Brewery.** Enjoy a laidback evening in the downstairs bar, playing pool, shuffleboard or just lounging in the oversized padded booths. ~ 56 Market Street, Portsmouth; 603-431-1115; www.portsmouthbrewery.com.

Dolphin Striker resides above an underground tavern built around a spring-fed well. Hang out for a bite to eat, or relax to nightly live acoustic music. ~ 15 Bow Street, Portsmouth; 603-431-5222, fax 603-431-2573; www.dolphinstriker.com.

Set in a 19th-century brick brewery, the **Seacoast Repertory Theatre**, housed in the beautiful Bow Street Theatre, stages Shakespearean plays and other drama, major musicals and comedy in an intimate, under-300-seat pit theater. Closed Monday. ~ 125 Bow Street, Portsmouth; 603-433-4472; www.seacoastrep.org, e-mail info@seacoastrep.org.

BEACHES & PARKS

For the most part, New Hampshire's parks are open only for the summer, usually from Memorial Day through Labor Day. During the off-season, contact the **New Hampshire Division of Parks and Recreation.** ~ Box 1856, Concord, NH 03302; 603-271-3556.

HAMPTON BEACH STATE PARK One of the most popular parks in all New Hampshire, this place boasts a quarter mile of broad pewter-colored beach flecked with smooth stones. A jetty shoots several feet into the ocean, and there's a long row of sand dunes, some of the few remaining in the state. From here, you have tremendous views northward of Great Boars Head and an opportunity to fish from the jetty for flounder. You'll find a gazebo with picnic tables, restrooms, a bathhouse, a snack bar and lifeguards. Closed mid-September to early May. Day-use fee, $10. ~ On Route 1A at the southern tip of Hampton Beach; 603-926-3784.

There's an RV campground with 28 full hookup sites; $42 to $47 per night.

HAMPTON SEASHELL STATE PARK This is *the* liveliest sand in New Hampshire. For six months a year, thousands jam a three-mile stretch of fine ashen grains whipped by waves and surrounded by street action. The boardwalk, with its sidewalk vendors, carnival food and trinket shops, follows the beach and creates constant activity. Despite the size of this beach, the crowds do follow a certain order: families cluster around the north end, older folks lay claim to the south tip and the skimpy-suited, let's-party group stakes out the middle near the Beach Patrol Station. There are restrooms, a playground, lifeguards, a pavilion, an amphitheater and a band shell. Closed November through April. ~ In Hampton Beach along Ocean Boulevard between M Street and Great Boars Head; 603-926-6705.

NORTH BEACH A thick seawall hides this beach from the roadway, though rough waves occasionally send salt water over the top and onto passing traffic. The narrow cord of hard-packed sand, stretching one and a half miles, is submerged during most high tides, when locals congregate atop the wall for prime wave watching. This is the most popular spot in New Hampshire to surf; it's best around Great Boars Head, a rocky bulkhead on the northern end of the beach. Restrooms are available. ~ In Hampton Beach along Ocean Boulevard between Great Boars Head and 19th Street; 603-436-1552.

◄HIDDEN

PLAICE COVE BEACH Strewn with gray boulders and pebbles, this volcaniclike beach is encased in sand as silver as gunpowder. Small but picturesque, it rests before beautiful homes and appears to be a private beach. Locals know it as one of the quietest spots around and assemble here at low tide when the sand area is widest. Seagulls hang around the north end, scurrying about seaweed patches and constant ocean sprays. Swimming is okay at low tide during summer, though water is frequently quite rough. ~ Take the unmarked footpath that starts on Route 1A, across from Ron's Beach House restaurant just north of the intersection of Route 101C in Hampton Beach. The path leads between two houses down to the beach.

NORTH HAMPTON STATE BEACH Stretching 1000 feet along the ocean, this fine sliver of mocha sand covers a short lapse between seaside neighborhoods. Families favor the park for its subdued tone and gentle waves. Lovely Little Boars Head, a rocky ocean spur, looms to the north. You'll find restrooms (open Memorial Day to mid-September) and lifeguards (June to late August). ~ Along Ocean Boulevard just south of Little Boars Head in North Hampton; 603-436-1552.

SOUTH RYE BEACH This so-called "beach" consists solely of millions of silvery pebbles (bad for the back but pretty to look at) that extend about one-quarter mile. Dedicated sunbathers set up lawn chairs and wear sturdy shoes, but the real action centers around surfing. Board toters call this beach "Rye on the Rocks" and arrive en masse anytime there's a whiff of wind. Stores are less than a mile away in Rye. ~ Route 1A, south of Causeway Road in Rye.

On a clear day at Rye Harbor State Park, the historic Isles of Shoals hover in the distance.

RYE HARBOR STATE PARK Situated on Ragged Neck Peninsula, this park offers commanding views of Rye Harbor and a 200-foot jetty for prime fishing (flounder and pollack) and sightseeing. There's no beach, but a grassy lawn is flecked with trees. Picnic areas and restrooms are available. Closed Columbus Day through Memorial Day. Day-use fee, $3 per person. ~ Route 1A at Rye Harbor Road in Rye; 603-436-1552.

WALLIS SANDS STATE BEACH Wild and scenic, Wallis Sands boasts one of the coast's choicest swaths of copper-colored sand punctuated by a dramatic jetty. On windy days, waves slash the rocks, sending sprays as high as 60 feet. Only five acres in size, the park features soft patches of grass and a concrete walkway that edges the beach. Get there at low tide, when the beach spans up to 800 feet. When the tide comes in, the sand shrinks back to 150 feet—the only drawback of this beautiful place. Restrooms, lifeguards, a bathhouse, showers and a store are available to beachgoers. Closed Labor Day to Memorial Day. Day-use fee, $10. ~ Route 1A, Rye; 603-436-9404.

ODIORNE POINT STATE PARK You can spend days exploring all the goodies Odiorne Point State Park offers, including old grave sites and stone walls, three World War II bunkers and the remains of a formal garden. New Hampshire's first settlers landed amid these rocky headlands and marshes back in 1623. Today, the natural sanctuary accounts for 330 acres and three-fourths of a mile of shoreline—the largest undeveloped tract on the coast. You can explore their five miles of trails, two ponds, fishing for bass and flounder in spring and fall, dozens of tidal pools, and the Sea Coast Science Center with wildlife exhibits, bookstore and local history displays. Besides

HIDDEN ►

historical secrets, the park harbors a secluded beach on **Frost Point**. There's no sand here, only grass and pebbles and total seclusion. Just north of the point, sandy shores draw larger crowds. Facilities include a visitors center, restrooms and a bathhouse, and are available only from Memorial Day through Columbus Day. Day-use fee, $3 per person. ~ There are two entrances on Route 1A in Rye. To get to Frost Point, park at the north entrance and take the rocky trail about a quarter mile through the woods; 603-436-7406.

GREAT ISLAND COMMON Picturesque and serene, this municipal beach belongs to the tiny island of New Castle, near Portsmouth. Swampy meadows share the shoreline with hard-packed sand and several rocky beaches. There's a spacious grassy area for excellent picnicking and a series of jetties that offers interesting tidepooling. A lighthouse hovers in the distance, occasionally sounding its foghorn. You'll find picnic areas, restrooms and a playground. Day-use fee, $3 per adult. ~ Route 1B, New Castle; 603-431-6710, fax 603-433-6198.

Merrimack Valley

For the last two centuries, towns have grown alongside the Merrimack River, their inhabitants making use of its swift waters first for fishing, then for running textile mills. Today many of New Hampshire's 1.1 million residents call the Merrimack Valley home, making the area a seat of commerce and the state government.

This industrial region takes in a string of sizable cities, including Nashua, often called a "suburb" of nearby Boston, as well as the metropolis of Manchester and the capital, Concord. Spiraling out from these cities are bedroom communities and fragments of endearing rural areas.

SIGHTS

Scenic Route 111 twists its way southwest from Exeter to one of the state's most peculiar phenomena. **America's Stonehenge**, also known as Mystery Hill, may seem like a big pile of rocks. To archaeologists and astronomers, who've pored over its contents for 50 years, it presents an unsolved puzzle. How old is it and where did it come from? Spread across 30 acres, the erratic stone walls and bizarre rock formations are reputed to be an astronomical site of an ancient civilization—some claim it goes back 4000 years. England's Stonehenge it's not, but it's worth a look. Admission. ~ 105 Haverhill Road, off Route 111, Salem; 603-893-8300; www.stonehengeusa.com, e-mail info@stonehengeusa.com.

A short drive northward will land you in **Manchester**, New Hampshire's largest city with a population of over 100,000. This once-industrial city is undergoing a renaissance, and you can get a feel for this by strolling Elm Street, the main drag, lined with brick buildings and coffee shops and crowded with businesspeople. The **Greater Manchester Chamber of Commerce** can point you to the best local sights. Closed Saturday and Sunday. ~ 889 Elm Street, Manchester; 603-666-6600, fax 603-626-0910; www.manchester-chamber.org, e-mail info@manchester-chamber.org.

The valley's other large city, **Concord**, is the state capital and probably best known for its Concord Coach. Drop by the **Museum of New Hampshire History** for a peek at the coaches that helped connect America's East and West during the 19th century. Closed Monday from mid-October through November and from January through June. Admission. ~ 6 Eagle Square, Concord; 603-226-3189; www.nhhistory.org.

sights

AUTHOR FAVORITE

It's enough just to stand outside and ogle the **Currier Museum of Art**, with its lustrous limestone facade and gorgeous mosaics that resemble a Renaissance palace. But step inside and your eyes will feast on a series of archways and vaulted ceilings, then trail off to a substantial collection of artwork ranging from the Renaissance era to modern times. There's also a fascinating collection of glass and photography. The Currier ranks as one of the finest small museums in the country. It's closed for expansion until early 2008; call for status. ~ 201 Myrtle Way, Manchester; 603-669-6144, fax 603-669-7194; www.currier.org, e-mail visitor@currier.org.

Pick up a copy of *The Historic Downtown Concord Walking Tour*, which will direct you to the city's choicest sites. It's available at the **Greater Concord Chamber of Commerce**, which also supplies general information on Merrimack Valley. ~ 40 Commercial Street, Concord; 603-224-2508, fax 603-224-8128; www.concordnhchamber.com, e-mail info@concordnhchamber.com.

Locals are fond of saying the carpets are rolled up at dusk in this very conservative city. The streets do clear out around dinner time, and except for a couple of watering holes, you'll be hard-pressed to find much activity around here.

Of course, people who go to Concord looking for action will ultimately be sidetracked by the **State House**, a beautiful 1819 building made of smooth granite and capped with a gold-leaf dome. Inside this grand old edifice throbs the pulse of the city, setting the political, social and oftentimes cultural agenda for the entire state. It's the nation's oldest state house and oldest continuously used legislative chambers. Closed weekends. ~ 107 North Main Street, Concord; 603-271-1110, fax 603-271-1097; www.nh.gov.

After you've roamed the capital streets, head north for the wilds of **Canterbury Shaker Village**. Stashed way out in an agrarian sanctuary, this insightful place will hold your attention for hours. Founded in 1784 by one very progressive woman named Ann Lee, the religious sect lived in self-contained villages and aspired to create a utopia. Each of Canterbury's 25 buildings reflects principles of efficiency: drawers are built into walls and wall pegs eliminate floor clutter.

Exhibits highlight the Shakers' inventive ingenuity; the collection includes a bell cast by Paul Revere. Shakers believed in equal rights, shared work and celibacy, the last of which may have caused their virtual disappearance by the early 1900s. More likely, the decline of the group was caused by the onset of the Industrial Revolution, a modern market in which the Shakers found it impossible to compete. The museum is open mid-May through October. Admission. ~ 288 Shaker Road off Route 106, Canterbury; 603-783-9511, fax 603-783-9152; www.shakers.org, e-mail info@shakers.org.

LODGING

Small chain motels are the most frequent accommodations along New Hampshire's industrial combe, though you will find a few very special inns and bed and breakfasts.

One of the nicest chain motels, **Fairfield Inn by Marriott** mingles the new and old with its Federal-style red-brick design and its many modern amenities. There's a swimming pool out back and a lobby fashioned with reproductions of Victorian antiques and framed prints of hunting scenes. You'll find more antiques in the 116 guest rooms, along with designer wallpapers and a crisp,

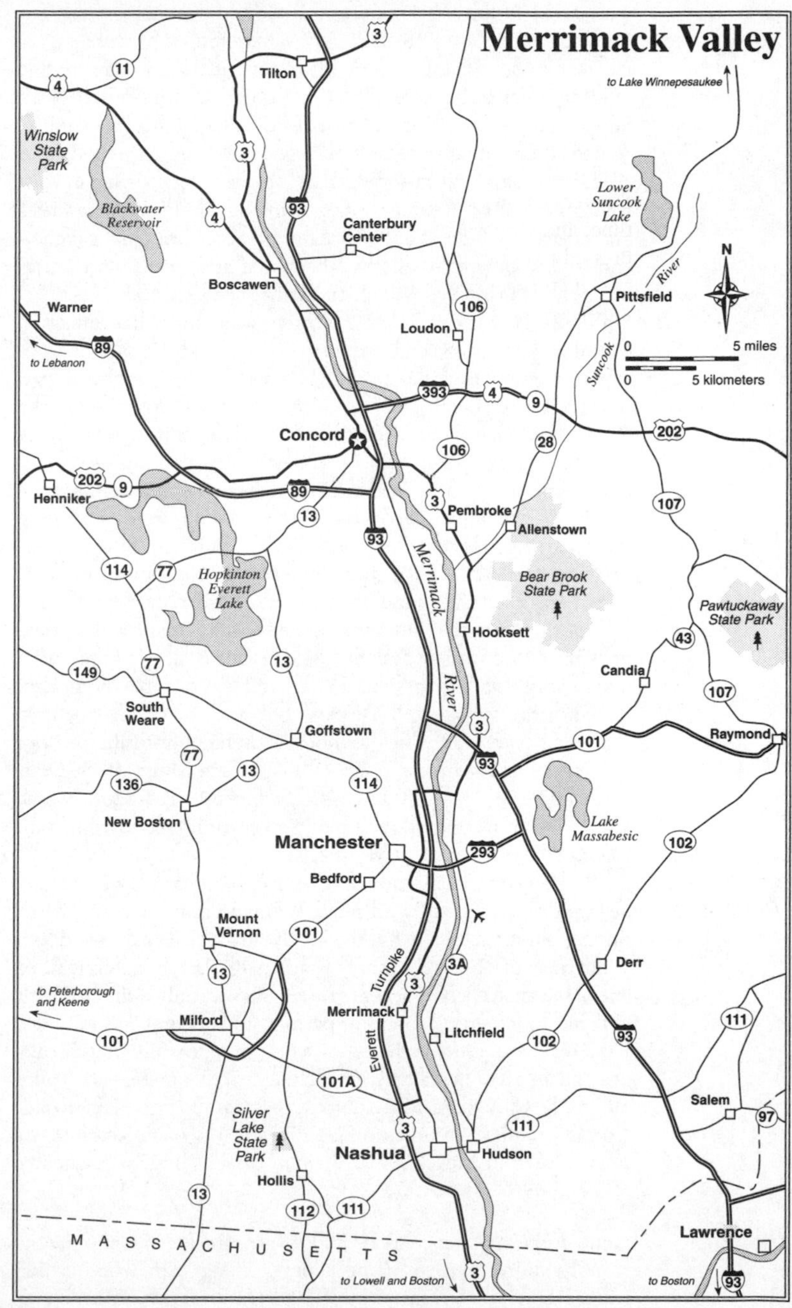
Merrimack Valley
to Lake Winnepesaukee
Tilton
Winslow State Park
Blackwater Reservoir
Lower Suncook Lake
Canterbury Center
Boscawen
Warner
to Lebanon
Loudon
Pittsfield
Suncook River
N
0 5 miles
0 5 kilometers
Concord
Henniker
Pembroke
Allenstown
Hopkinton Everett Lake
Bear Brook State Park
Merrimack River
Hooksett
Pawtuckaway State Park
Candia
South Weare
Goffstown
Raymond
New Boston
Lake Massabesic
Manchester
Bedford
Mount Vernon
Everett Turnpike
Derr
to Peterborough and Keene
Merrimack
Milford
Litchfield
Salem
Silver Lake State Park
Nashua
Hudson
Hollis
Lawrence
MASSACHUSETTS
to Lowell and Boston
to Boston

manicured feeling. ~ 4 Amherst Road, Merrimack; phone/fax 603-424-7500, 800-228-2800; www.marriott.com. MODERATE.

Think about it this way: with rooms offering Italian marble whirlpool baths, big-screen TVs and gorgeous four-poster beds, how could you *not* adore **The Bedford Village Inn**? This vanilla-coated estate, a medley of Colonial-style buildings, barns and grain silos, is a lesson in ultra-indulgence, a place where staying in your room may well be preferred to venturing out. Wet bars, pine chests and huge bay windows are also standard accessories in the higher-end rooms, or opt for the two-bedroom apartment with a fireplace and whirlpool. ~ Village Inn Lane, Bedford; 603-472-2001, 800-852-1166, fax 603-472-2379; www.bedfordvillageinn.com, e-mail guestservices@bedfordvillageinn.com. ULTRA-DELUXE.

Accommodation choices in Manchester are generally limited to motel and hotel chains. Nicely situated downtown, the **Radisson Manchester at Center of New Hampshire** caters mostly to business travelers and thus features plenty of extras like an indoor pool, a sauna, a health club, a bar and two restaurants. Expect upscale motel decor in 250 rooms and 6 suites, including plush carpets and marble countertops. ~ 700 Elm Street, Manchester; 603-625-1000, fax 603-206-4000; www.radisson.com/manchesternh, e-mail admin@centerofnh.com. DELUXE.

For exploring the state capital, the **Holiday Inn** provides prime proximity to downtown sights. The layout is classic hotel, with a four-story, nondescript exterior and 122 comfortable rooms decorated with wall-to-wall carpets and standard conveniences. There's also an indoor heated pool, a sauna, a hot tub, in-room spa service and a fitness room. ~ 172 North Main Street, Concord; 603-224-9534, 800-465-4329, fax 603-224-8266; www.holidayinn.com/concordnh, e-mail reservations@concordhi.com. MODERATE TO ULTRA-DELUXE.

HIDDEN ►

Standing amid acres and acres of rambling meadows and gardens and surrounded by hillsides, **Wyman Farm** is a place worth finding. Built back in 1783, the lovely farmhouse awaiting down a labyrinth of obscure country roads is the family homestead of one of the innkeepers. There are three suites warmly fashioned with old pine floors, sitting rooms or parlors, and oriental or hook rugs. For a real treat, request the room with the copper tub. Full breakfast and an evening tea tray are included. To get there, take Route 106 to the Clough Pond Road exit, then turn left on Flagg Road. Go eight-tenths of a mile on Flagg Road to Wyman Road, a dirt road. Closed in March. ~ 22 Wyman Road, Loudon; phone/fax 603-783-4467. MODERATE.

DINING

Housed in a spacious, circa-1800 tavern, **Buckley's Great Steaks** is much more than its name claims. Along with wood-grilled steaks, the elegant restaurant also serves inventive, upscale cuisine such as roasted miso-marinated salmon with Korean cucumber salad, and lobster stroganoff simmered in white wine and mushrooms. White tablecloths and chic, contrasting black linen napkins add to the sophisticated ambience. Live music serenades diners on Sunday, Monday and Friday nights. ~ 438 Daniel Webster Highway Route 3, Merrimack; 603-424-0995, fax 603-424-0997; www.buckleysgreatsteaks.com, e-mail info@buckleysgreatsteaks.com. ULTRA-DELUXE

For a taste of Italy, enjoy a meal at **Florence's Restaurant**, a casual eatery with checkered tablecloths. Pizza, pork chops and pasta fill the menu, along with a fine selection of seafood and Italian favorites, such as the steak mafioso (top sirloin sautéed with potatoes, peppers, mushrooms and onions in a white wine or tomato sauce). They also offer a variety of meats prepared in their signature Florentine style, which includes a butter, garlic and white wine sauté tossed with ziti, broccoli and grated Parmesan cheese. Closed Monday. ~ 465 Daniel Webster Highway, Merrimack; 603-424-4010; www.florencesitalian.com. MODERATE TO DELUXE

The firehouse tower at the Canterbury Shaker Village was used for drying the fire hoses.

In a world of Americanized Mexican restaurants, it's rare to strike authentic south-of-the-border cuisine. That, of course, is what makes **Hermanos** so very special. Here, surrounded by Aztec murals and paraphernalia, you discover hefty burritos, enchiladas, quesadillas and tostadas, served with verve and panache. The specials are interesting, too—try the *carne estufa* (spicy stew), Mexican pizza and *taco pastor* (soft-shelled tacos stuffed and wrapped in grilled corn tortillas). Enjoy live jazz in the lounge five nights a week. No smoking. No lunch on Sunday. ~ 11 Hill's Avenue, Concord; 603-224-5669, fax 603-226-2635; www.hermanosmexican.com, e-mail hermanosmexican@comcast.net. BUDGET TO MODERATE.

SHOPPING

Pompanoosuc Mills proffers handcrafted contemporary Shaker-style furnishings such as plush couches and silk arrangements and oak dressers. ~ 3 Eagle Square, Concord; 603-225-7975; www.pompy.com.

HIDDEN

It's well worth a trip into the countryside to peruse the **Museum Store** at Canterbury Shaker Village, an 1825 carriage house stocked with Shaker reproductions and literature, as well as cookbooks, handmade sweaters and crafts. Open mid-May through October and weekends only in November. ~ 288 Shaker Road, Canterbury; 603-783-9511; www.shakers.org, e-mail info@shakers.org.

NIGHTLIFE

The best place to catch top-quality international and national plays is the **Palace Theatre**, an ornate, 864-seat downtown arena that also hosts musicals, ballet and concerts. ~ 80 Hanover Street, Manchester; 603-668-5588; www.palacetheatre.org.

The **Majestic Theatre Trust** (MTT) produces a year-round season of family-oriented entertainment. Offerings run the gamut from children's shows to original works to musicals. They perform at the Hevey Theatre, a local 300-seat house. ~ 281 Cartier Street, Manchester; 603-669-7469; www.majestictheatre.net.

BEACHES & PARKS

SILVER LAKE STATE PARK Locals mob this place on summer weekends for one reason: a very special sliver of sand. These toffee-colored granules extend 1000 feet along Silver Lake and churn up a storm of activity. The 34-acre lake itself is also quite stunning, sheltered by a cascade of grassy knolls and gracious pine trees. Facilities here include a picnic area, restrooms, lifeguards, a bathhouse, a play field and a refreshment stand. No pets allowed. Day-use fee, $3. ~ Route 122, one mile north of Hollis; 603-465-2342; e-mail nhparks@dred.state.nh.us.

PAWTUCKAWAY STATE PARK Tucked just outside the bustle of several major cities, this 5500-acre park has it all. There's 803-acre Lake Pawtuckaway with its broad mocha beaches and islands, a vast oak and hickory forest and hemlock ravine, 25 acres of wooded picnicking spots and the Pawtuckaway Mountains, surrounded by curious rock formations carved some 275 million years ago. There are extensive trails for hiking, snowmobiling and cross-country skiing. Swimming and bass fishing are excellent. You need to explore all three areas to get a good feel for this diverse park, so plan to spend some time. No pets are allowed. You'll find a picnic area, restrooms, a small store, a playground, boat rentals and a pavilion. Closed Labor Day to early June. Day-use fee, $3. ~ Off Route 156, three and a half miles north of Route 101 in Nottingham; 603-895-3031.

▲ Horse and Big islands and Neals Cove offer 195 tent sites, many right on the lake. Reservations are recommended. Most take RVs (no hookups); $19 to $27 per night. The campground is open from early May through Columbus Day. Reservations: 603-271-3628.

BEAR BROOK STATE PARK This mammoth place, dense with red and white pines, covers 10,000 acres and offers a slew of activities. Of the park's five ponds, Catamount Pond attracts the most activity with its wide beach, ball fields and picnic facilities for 1500 people. You'll also find more than 40 miles of hiking trails, a physical fitness course, a snowmobile museum, a nature center, the Civilian Conservation Corps Museum, a family camping museum and an archery range. Fishing is excellent for trout, perch, bass and pickerel in lakes and streams. Archery Pond is reserved for fly fishing. You can swim in Beaver and Catamount ponds (restricted to campers only at Beaver Pond). Facilities include picnic areas, pavilions, a small store, boat rentals, restrooms and bathhouses. Day-use fee, $3. ~ Off Route 28, five miles northeast of Hooksett; 603-485-9874.

▲ Beaver Pond features 98 tent/RV sites (no hookups); $18 to $23 per night. The campground is open from May 15 through Columbus Day only. Information: 603-485-9869; reservations: 603-271-3628.

WINSLOW STATE PARK After a 1820-foot climb (via auto) up Mount Kearsarge, the park rewards with magnificent panoramas that stretch into Vermont. The park was named for Civil War admiral John Winslow. A steep, one-mile hike takes you to the peak—2937 feet up. A picnic area and restrooms are available. Closed early November to mid-April. Day-use fee, $3. ~ Off Route 11, three miles south of New London in Wilmot Flat. You can also take Exit 10 off Route 89 and follow the signs to Winslow State Park; 603-526-6168.

Monadnock Region

Curled along the southwest bend of New Hampshire, the Monadnock Region makes up a collage of all the virtues one associates with New England. White steepled churches and old covered bridges, itinerant country roads edged by miles of wild woods and lazy lakes, and lovable Currier and Ives towns all mesh to give this domain a warm Yankee flavor.

SIGHTS

General stores, coffee shops and old-time pharmacies line the streets of **Peterborough**, founded in 1738 and believed to be the model for Thornton Wilder's *Our Town*. It's easy to see why Wilder may have taken to this mountain hamlet, which has spawned old saltbox homes and very congenial townsfolk.

Behind the Colonial Meeting House rests a shaded cemetery and the graves of novelist Willa Cather and Amos Fortune, an African-born slave who purchased his freedom.

At the **Peterborough Historical Society Museum**, you can walk through rotating exhibits of the town and Monadnock region's life and history, including thriving agriculture and manufacturing industries and, lately, publishing. In addition, the museum displays re-creations of a Colonial kitchen, along with a graphic timeline of the town's history. Closed Sunday and Monday. Admission. ~ 19 Grove Street, Peterborough; 603-924-3235, fax 603-924-3200; www.peterboroughhistory.org, e-mail director@peterborough history.org.

South on Route 202, **Jaffrey** purports to be the only Jaffrey in the world but more importantly is home to **Mount Monadnock**, which looms 3165 feet over the region like an astute sentinel. This imposing butte has become world famous as the most-climbed peak; myriads ascend its 40 miles of trails each year.

Henry David Thoreau and Ralph Waldo Emerson scaled Monadnock, now part of **Monadnock State Park**, where you'll also find an environmental center with historical and geological displays. (See "Beaches & Parks" section below.) Admission. ~ Off Route 124, Jaffrey; 603-532-8862.

Just east of the park you'll encounter Jaffrey's grandest man-made structure, the **Colonial Meeting House**. Its huge clock and bell tower, built in 1773, are framed by Mount Monadnock, an arousing sight for sure. ~ Route 124, Jaffrey.

Some of Monadnock's choicest views can be had at **Cathedral of the Pines**, a wood and stone shrine built by local parents for a son who was slain in World War II. There are guided tours offering a look at the Altar of the Nation, composed of stones from every state in the Union and from every president since Truman. A piece of the Rock of Gibraltar is here, along with a hunk from the Blarney Stone. You'll also see personal medals and war memorabilia donated by families of deceased military. When these carillon bells ring, they reverberate down the mountain and make melodies for miles. There's a quaint, five-bedroom bed and breakfast on the grounds. Closed November through April. ~ Off Route 119, Rindge; 603-899-3300, 866-229-4520, fax 603-899-3311; www.cathedralpines.com, e-mail info@cathedralpines.com.

Nature has surely blessed the Monadnock Region, and nowhere is it more evident than at **Rhododendron State Park**. Arrive in mid-July and be rewarded with 16 acres smothered in fields of wild rhododendrons. There's a half-mile trail through this riot of color. (See "Beaches & Parks" below.) ~ Rhododendron Road, off of Route 119, Fitzwilliam; 603-532-8862.

LODGING

Nestled in a marvelous Currier and Ives setting, **The Birchwood Inn** oozes history and enchantment. Fashioned of deep red brick, the 1775 Federal-style building brandishes twin chimneys and lazes across from a white steepled church and a grassy hill topped with war memorials. Murals of itinerant artist Rufus Porter spread across dining room walls, while seven bedrooms exhibit different themes and eclectic decor. An "editorial room" features newsprint wallpaper, while a "music room" is arranged with musical instruments. Lose yourself in the 18th century at this place. Full breakfast is included. Closed for two weeks in the spring and one week in November. ~ Route 45, Temple; 603-878-3285, fax 603-878-2159; www.thebirchwoodinn.com, e-mail info@thebirchwoodinn.com. MODERATE.

The three quaint rooms inside **The Currier's House** are as charming as the 1810 bed and breakfast appears from the outside. Stately, yet comfortable, the inn offers guest rooms with private baths and country décor. Cozy beds with floral quilts provide a welcoming atmosphere in which guests can curl up with a book or linger under the covers on a snowy morning. A full breakfast of omelettes, pancakes and other favorites is provided in the small dining room. ~ 5 Harkness Road, Jaffrey; phone/fax: 603-532-7670; www.thecurriershouse.com, e-mail info@thecur riershouse.com. MODERATE.

For up-to-date motel accommodations, consider **Jack Daniel's Motor Inn**. A single, two-story building covered with wood shingles, the inn maintains 17 quite modern guest rooms with plush carpets, high-back chairs, large showers and upstairs balconies. Some rooms overlook the pretty Contoocook River. Guests also have access to free wi-fi internet. ~ Concord Street North Route 202, Peterborough; 603-924-7548, fax 603-924-7700; www.jack danielsinn.com, e-mail innkeeper@jackdanielsinn.com. MODERATE.

◄ HIDDEN

The ultimate New Hampshire hideaway may well be **Woodbound Inn**, a captivating retreat stashed deep in a mountain forest. Here you have the trying task of choosing between several accommodations: early American–style bedrooms housed in a 19th-century farmhouse; contemporary rooms with brass beds in the annex; or cozy lakeside cabins with fireplaces. It's easy to kick back in any of the three, or explore the inn's 165 acres thick with pines and firs. There are also a nine-hole, par-3 golf course, numerous cross-country ski trails, a clay tennis court and a superb restaurant. Full breakfast is included. ~ 247 Woodbound Road,

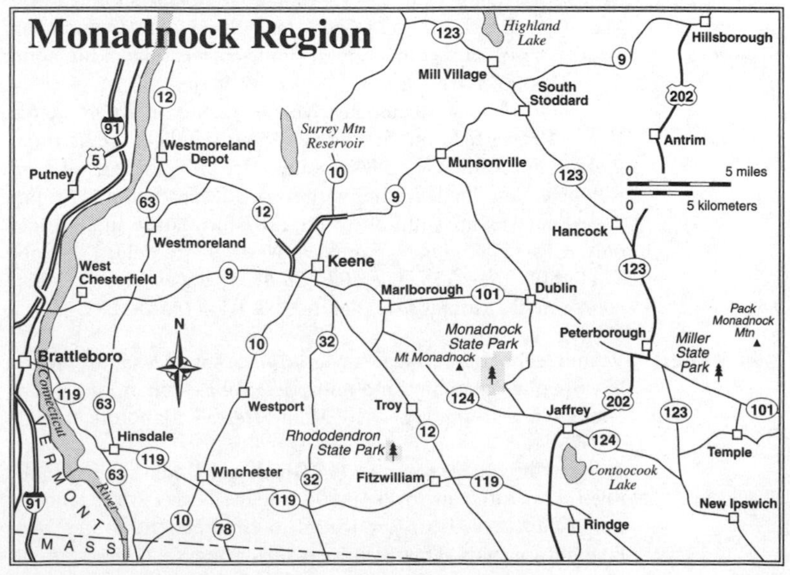

Rindge; 603-532-8341, 800-688-7770, fax 603-532-8341; www.woodbound.com, e-mail info@woodbound.com. MODERATE TO DELUXE.

The Hancock Inn radiates an ancient aura, and rightly so—it's the state's oldest continuously operating inn. Braided rugs rest atop the 1789 floor, bouquets of fragrant flowers bask on old tabletops and walls sport early-19th-century Rufus Porter murals and Moses Eaton stencils. Upstairs in 14 bedrooms, sunlight streams in through rows of windows, and antique chests and beds provide a cozy demeanor. Breakfast is included and features homemade breads and granola. ~ 33 Main Street, Hancock; 603-525-3318, 800-525-1789, fax 603-525-9301; www.hancockinn.com, e-mail innkeeper@hancockinn.com. DELUXE TO ULTRA-DELUXE.

DINING

For quick, affordable Italian pies, try the **Jaffrey Pizza Barn**, a modest downtown cubbyhole with rows of orange formica booths. Thick- or thin-crusted pizzas come with a good selection of toppings (including steak and eggplant); there are hot and cold grinders, too. ~ 6 Blake Street, Jaffrey; 603-532-8383; www.jaffreypizzabarn.com, e-mail pangiotesn@netscape.net. BUDGET.

The Hancock Inn doles out some of the best Yankee cookin' around, serving a prix-fixe New England dinner. The Shaker cranberry pot roast is always on the menu. Set in New Hampshire's oldest operating inn (circa 1789), the three dining rooms feature cultured country decor and face a rambling flower garden. Dinner only. ~ 33 Main Street, Hancock; 603-525-3318, 800-525-1789, fax 603-525-9301; www.hancockinn.com, e-mail innkeeper@hancockinn.com. ULTRA-DELUXE.

The famous story "The Devil and Daniel Webster" was based on real-life politician/orator/statesman Daniel Webster—also a New Hampshire native.

About 20 minutes west of Keene on Route 9, the **Chesterfield Inn** has a very elegant, candlelit dining room looking out at the Green Mountains. The unfailingly good food is largely New England, but with some adventure to it. The dining room was an addition to an 1787 farmhouse inn. Dinner only. Closed Sunday. ~ Route 9, West Chesterfield; 603-256-3211, 800-365-5515, fax 603-256-6131; www.chesterfieldinn.com, e-mail chstinn@sover.net. DELUXE TO ULTRA-DELUXE.

SHOPPING

Wanna feel better? **Maggie's Marketplace** supplies natural foods like organic corn chips and no-cholesterol ice cream, plus cookbooks. Closed Sunday. ~ 14 Main Street, Peterborough; 603-924-7671.

Your literary layover is **The Toadstool Bookshop**, a small-town shop with new (over 60,000) and used (over 20,000) books ranging from warship catalogues to children's titles and New England journals. They also carry CDs. There's a coffee shop on the premises. ~ 12 Depot Square, Peterborough; 603-924-3543; www.toadbooks.com, e-mail books@ptoad.com.

It's mall shopping 19th-century style at **Colony Mill Marketplace.** Located in a refurbished 1838 mill, the aesthetic trading center houses a medley of stores offering clothes, gifts, cards, home decor items and books. ~ 222 West Street, Keene; 603-357-1240, fax 603-352-5826; www.colonymill.com.

NIGHTLIFE

One of the most respected theater troupes in New England, the **Peterborough Players** perform in a marvelous converted barn from mid-June to mid-September. ~ 55 Hadley Road off Middle Hancock Road, Peterborough; 603-924-7585; www.peterborough players.org.

BEACHES & PARKS

MILLER STATE PARK New Hampshire's oldest state park was settled back in 1891 and named for General James Miller, a hero of the War of 1812. It rests atop the 2290-foot summit of South Pack Monadnock Mountain, a one-and-a-half-mile semivertical drive with numerous hairpin curves. The Wapack and Marion Davis trails wander from the base to the summit of the mountain. Incredible vistas extend to the skyscrapers of Boston. Spring and fall are excellent times to view hawk migration from the summit. Facilities include a picnic area and primitive restrooms. Day-use fee, $3 per person. ~ Off Route 101, three miles east of Peterborough; 603-924-3672.

◄ HIDDEN

CONTOOCOOK LAKE PUBLIC BEACH It's a rare find indeed, this tiny but choice spot. Edging the shore of beautiful Contoocook Lake, a sliver of beach features glistening white sand as soft as talcum powder. During the summer, the town closes part of the road and spreads sand across it, making it a great spot for small children. There are picnic areas, restrooms, lifeguards and a concession stand in the summer. ~ From the junction of Routes 124 and 202 in Jaffrey, take Stratton Road southeast to Howard Hill Road. Head east on Howard Hill Road and you'll soon arrive at the beach; 603-532-7863.

MONADNOCK STATE PARK The lonely, imposing peak of Mount Monadnock has long inspired poets and intrigued all those who cast eyes upon it. Frequently called the world's most-climbed mountain, its barren granite pinnacle has been scaled by Mark Twain, Ralph Waldo Emerson, Henry David Thoreau and thousands of others. Today, the 5000-acre park remains a hiker's mecca, crisscrossed with 40 miles of trails enriched by views of every New England state. No pets are allowed. You'll find a picnic area, restrooms, a refreshment center and a visitors center (all are closed weekdays in winter). Day-use fee, $3. ~ Off Route 124, four miles west of Jaffrey; 603-532-8862, fax 603-532-4373.

▲ There are 28 tent sites; a few accommodate RVs (no hookups); $18 per night for two, $9 for each additional person. Reservations: 603-271-3628.

RHODODENDRON STATE PARK No doubt, this place is extra special. Arrive around mid-July and revel in the explosion of rhododendrons that form a pink-and-white canopy across 16 acres. A one-mile trail meanders up Little Mount Monadnock, ensuring a feast for the senses and lovely views of Mount Monadnock. Other jewels bloom here, too, including the jack-in-the-pulpit, trillium, mountain laurel and pink lady's slipper. The Wildflower Trail (.6 mile) offers views of stunning patches of wildflowers clearly marked by the Fitzwilliam Garden Club. No pets allowed. You'll find a picnic area and pit toilets. Day-use fee, $3. ~ On Rhododendron Road, off Route 119, two and a half miles north of Fitzwilliam; 603-532-8862.

Lake Sunapee–Dartmouth Area

The area north of the Monadnocks—edged on the west by the Connecticut River—is a long, lazy union of cornfields and hills and big tufts of wildflowers tossed against Vermont's western border. Bustling mill towns, Ivy League schools and Colonial hamlets bless this region. Inland, Lake Sunapee exists as a world unto itself, stretching ten glittering miles beaded with sylvan villages and a statuesque mountain crisscrossed with ski trails. Life here is lived slowly, a welcome pace for travelers seeking bona fide tranquility.

SIGHTS

In the summer of 1777, General John Stark, commissioned by New Hampshire's legislature, organized a military force in **Charlestown**, the first town we visit in this area. That 1500-man troop marched westward across Vermont's border and defeated British-German forces in the famed Battle of Bennington. Now a **historical marker** (Route 12) pays homage to these local heroes.

Of course, Charlestown had its own share of skirmishes, as you'll see over at **The Fort at No. 4**, a re-creation of the great log stockade village built by pioneers in 1744. The fort suffered a three-day attack in 1747 by French and Indian forces, who were staved off by a 31-man garrison. Today, a medley of log cabins, barns, blacksmith shop and saw pit are displayed alongside original 18th-century tools. A nice trip back in time. Open Wednesday through Sunday from May to the end of November. Admission. ~ Route 11, Charlestown; 603-826-5700, 888-367-8284, fax 603-826-3368; www.fortat4.com, e-mail info@fortat4.com.

North of Charlestown along the Connecticut and Sugar rivers, the industrial town of **Claremont** sustains a maze of centuries-old mills, weaving sheds and mansions. The folks in this blue-collar town are quite congenial. Stop by the **Claremont Chamber of Commerce** for a walking-tour map of the **Historic Mill District**, which is bounded generally by Main, Spring and Central streets. Closed weekends. ~ Moody Building, 24 Tremont Square, Claremont; 603-543-1296, fax 603-542-1469; www.claremontnhchamber.com, e-mail chamber@adelphia.net.

From here, the Lake Sunapee area presents an obvious side trip and promises panoramas of small towns, rocky coastlines, rhyth-

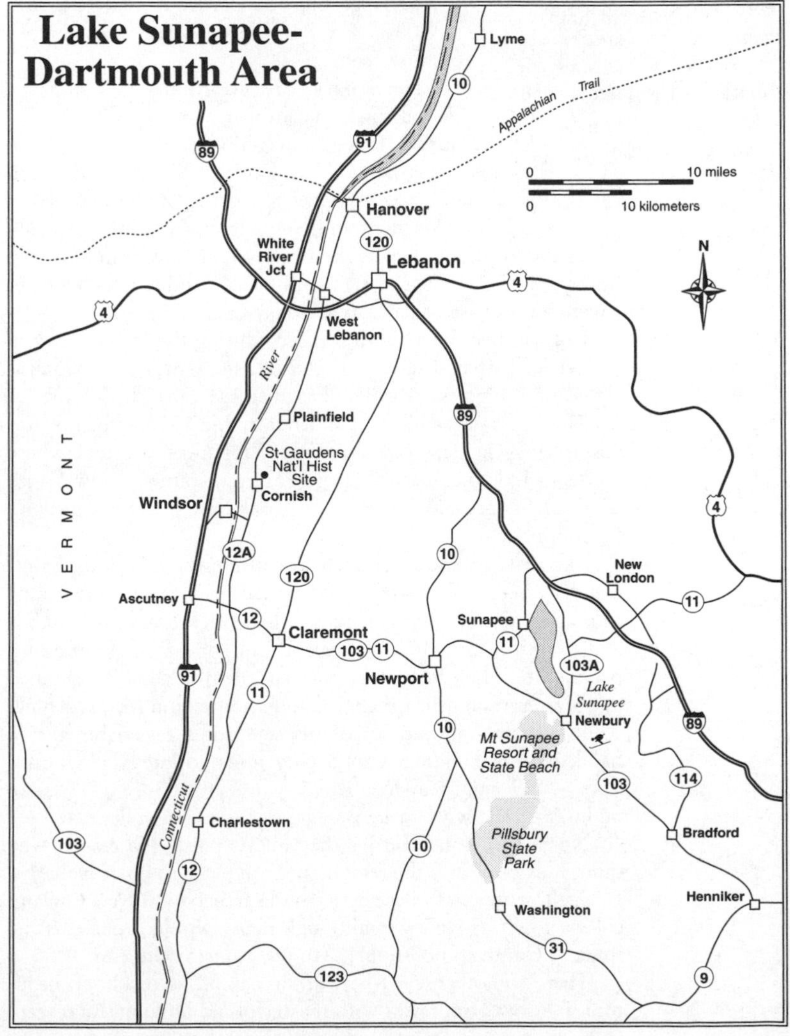

mic beaches and distinguished lighthouses. Tourism has certainly hit this outdoor playground, but it's not yet overwhelming. Start by rounding the lake on Routes 11 and 103, gazing across pristine waters at the windsurfers and small boats and gentle backdrop of forest-covered Mount Sunapee.

The **M.V. Mount Sunapee II** offers daily narrated tours of the lake from mid-May through Labor Day. Go during fall foliage season to appreciate the area at its peak. Closed Columbus Day to mid-May. Fee. ~ Sunapee Harbor, off Route 11; 603-763-4030, fax 603-938-5671; www.sunapeecruises.com.

Novelist Winston Churchill, poets Percy MacKaye and Witter Bynner, former *New Republic* editor Herbert Croly, landscape painter Willard Metcalfe and actress Ethel Barrymore all took up residence in Cornish.

Head back east to Route 12A and the hushed town of **Cornish**, where you'll find the country's longest covered bridge. Just in sight of the cornfields, the **Cornish-Windsor Covered Bridge** arches 470 feet across the Connecticut River, linking Vermont and New Hampshire. Built in 1866, it was the fourth at the site, the first two falling victim to raging floodwaters. An ancient sign still warns today's travelers to "Walk your horse or pay a two-dollar fine."

Cornish became a cultural mecca during the late 1800s and early 1900s when a series of noted artists, writers, poets, musicians and sculptors arrived and formed the Cornish Colony.

This mass migration was spurred by the 1885 arrival of Augustus Saint-Gaudens, one of America's foremost sculptors, whose works include the Admiral David Farragut statue in New York's Madison Square and the statue of Abraham Lincoln in Chicago's Lincoln Park.

Those artists and writers left Cornish long ago, but the **Saint-Gaudens National Historic Site** survives as a marvelous tribute to that great era. Saint-Gaudens' white brick house, his studios and beautiful formal gardens afford an endearing glimpse of a prolific life. High hedges of pine and hemlock and birch-lined paths are a testament to Saint-Gaudens affection for gardening, while originals and copies of his sculptures reveal his gift of hand. Exhibit buildings closed November to late May. Admission. ~ 139 Saint-Gaudens Road, Cornish; 603-675-2175, fax 603-675-2701; www.nps.gov/saga, e-mail saga@valley.net.

North of Cornish throbs the valley's pulse, *the* reason why thousands pour into the region, and *the* place to go at night. Ivy League **Dartmouth College** exists in the archetypical New England college town of Hanover, although many would argue it *is* the town. ~ Hanover; 603-646-1110; www.dartmouth.edu.

There's no other way to say it: this campus is absolutely beautiful. It at once impresses with masterful old buildings that seem to go on forever. Stately red-brick Federal styles stand next to softer Georgian architecture, erected in the late 1700s and so unaffected by age or wars or government strife.

Dartmouth was actually started in Lebanon, Connecticut, in 1755 as a school for American Indians, called Moor's Indian Charity School. A donation of 3300 Hanover acres—plus a generous sum of money from England's second Earl of Dartmouth—put the school on its current site in 1769. Its charter, dated that year, can still be found in the hallowed halls of **Baker Library**, as can celebrated murals by Mexican painter José Clemente Orozco. ~ 603-646-2560; library.dartmouth.edu.

The **Hopkins Center for the Arts** is a must-see. The exterior of Hopkins resembles the Lincoln Center in New York City (and was actually designed by the same architect), while inside, barreled ceilings, dramatic plants and various works of art combine to make this a work of great beauty. ~ Wheelock Street, Hanover; 603-646-2422; www.hop.dartmouth.edu, e-mail hopkins.center@dartmouth.edu.

Next door at the **Hood Museum of Art**, you'll encounter a splendid small museum with a diverse permanent collection featuring works by American and European masters such as Coneley, Eakins, Thomas Sully, Rembrandt and Dürer. There are also excellent examples of African, American Indian and Oceanic art, Assyrian reliefs and Chinese bronzes and ceramics. Closed Monday. ~ Wheelock Street, Hanover; 603-646-2808, fax 603-646-1400; www.hoodmuseum.dartmouth.edu, e-mail hood.museum@dartmouth.edu.

Dartmouth's distinguished life, combined with over 5000 students, spills over nicely into the town of Hanover. Gracious tree-lined streets, underground pubs and polished shops make the town a great place for strolling. For more information, stop by the **Hanover Area Chamber of Commerce**. (During the summer you can stop at the visitors booth on the Dartmouth College Green.) ~ 47–53 South Main Street, Hanover; 603-643-3115; www.hanoverchamber.org, e-mail hacc@hanoverchamber.org.

LODGING

HIDDEN

No signs even hint of **Goddard Mansion**. Pity those who bypass this camouflaged treasure, a European-style estate that exudes elegance and refinement. The expansive, ornate living rooms and parlors feature high-beamed ceilings, carved mantles and a baby grand piano. A breezy porch overlooks the manicured lawn, croquet court and tea house, and ten bedrooms are designed to gratify. Several rooms command views of mountains all the way to Vermont. ~ 25 Hillstead Road and Route 12, Claremont; 603-543-0603, 800-736-0603, fax 603-543-0001; www.goddardmansion.com, e-mail deb@goddardmansion.com. MODERATE TO DELUXE.

Lingering in the shadows of Mount Sunapee, **The Back Side Inn** tenders home-style accommodations in an 1835 farmhouse-cum-inn. Resting on 120 acres, the inn is enveloped in pines; ten comfortable bedrooms featuring pretty antiques and wall-to-wall carpets or stenciled wood floors. A hot tub on the back deck offers beautiful sunset views. You can walk to a 49-acre pond or take the five-minute drive to sprawling Lake Sunapee. Full breakfast is included. ~ 1171 Brook Road off Routes 103 and 10, Goshen; 603-863-5161, fax 603-863-5007; www.backsideinn.com, e-mail info@backsideinn.com. MODERATE.

Barely 12 miles from Lake Sunapee, **New London Inn** is one place that has grown beautiful with time. Built back in 1792, the three-story clapboard inn overlooking the town green and bandstand is surely the prototype of gracious New England sojourns. Spacious porches wrap around the lower floors, wood hallways lead to carpeted rooms, and beams crisscross ceilings. Twenty bedrooms have personality and flair, adorned with brass or wicker beds and lovely antique dressers and chairs. Continental breakfast is included. ~ 353 Main Street, New London; 603-526-2791, 800-526-2791, fax 603-526-2749; www.newlondoninn.net, e-mail newlondoninn@excite.com. MODERATE TO DELUXE.

Snuggled nicely against the upper Connecticut River, **The Sunset Motor Inn** tenders simple accommodations. The configuration is standard motel L shape, with 18 modest but clean rooms. Expect industrial-grade carpets and formica furniture; most rooms have splendid views across the river and mountains. ~ 305 North Main Street, Route 10, West Lebanon; 603-298-8721. MODERATE.

The place to stay in Hanover is **The Hanover Inn**. For one, it's right across from (and owned by) Dartmouth College, thereby drawing all sorts of Ivy Leaguers. For another, it's one of those beautiful old buildings that absolutely commands respect. Graced in red brick and crowned by a sloping shingled roof, this granddaddy has been accommodating the rich and prestigious since the late 1700s. Four floors of guest rooms reflect early Colonial designs but throw in amenities such as cable TV, air conditioning and a fitness room. ~ Main and Wheelock streets, Hanover; 603-643-4300, 800-443-7024, fax 603-643-4433; www.hanoverinn.com. ULTRA-DELUXE.

Check your worries at the door when you book a room at **Breakfast on the Connecticut**. Before you even arrive, a custom basket of champagne and cookies (or the goodies of your choice) can be prepared and placed in your suite. The 15 rooms all include a private bath and TV; some even boast a whirlpool tub or gas fireplace. With contemporary country décor, guests can comfortably lounge in the brightly lit suites or common areas or soak in the outdoor spa. A separate guesthouse is more rustic and does not include breakfast. ~ 651 River Road, Lyme; 603-353- 4444, 888-353-4440, fax 603-353-4391; www.breakfastonthect.com, e-mail breakfast.connecticut@valley.net. MODERATE TO DELUXE.

DINING

For standard American, family-style dining, **Dimick's** is your destination. The menu includes sandwiches—grilled chicken, tuna melt, roast beef—and entrées such as steak, pork chops, fried chicken and baked haddock. If available, ask for one of the three tables that overlook the Sugar River. Breakfast is only served on Sunday. Closed Monday. ~ Lower Main Street, Claremont; 603-542-6701. MODERATE.

Fashioned as a country inn, the **Millstone American Bistro and Wine Bar** is a congenial restaurant embellished with bow-back chairs and local artwork. Freshness is the key word on this varied menu, and it keeps showing up in the seafood, game, vegetables, pasta and herbs. The winelist offers more than 50 selections by the glass. Reservations recommended. ~ 74 Newport Road, New London; 603-526-4201, fax 603-526-2933; www.millstonerestaurant.com, e-mail info@millstonerestaurant.com. MODERATE TO DELUXE.

HIDDEN

You'll swear you've reached the outer limits of the universe by the time you arrive at **Home Hill**. Stashed three miles up a wooded sinuous road, the restored mansion conceals a French restaurant with a serious following. The dining room is intimate, with plank floors and blazing hearths. A prix-fixe menu changes seasonally, offering delights such as *daurade royale*, a Mediterranean fish entrée and veal in a morel mushroom sauce. Closed Monday and Tuesday and two weeks in January. ~ River Road, off Route 12A, Plainfield; 603-434-6700, fax 603-675-5220; e-mail homehill@relaischateau.com. ULTRA-DELUXE.

If cooking is your passion, stop in Board & Basket for the latest kitchenware gadgets, cookbooks and gourmet foods. ~ Powerhouse Plaza, West Lebanon; 603-298-5813; www.boardandbasket.com.

It's hard to miss the big bubble windows of **Molly's Restaurant & Bar**, a chic little nook that has "yuppie" written all over it. There's an expansive oak bar in the middle. Choose from seating in the cozy booths or the outdoor patio. The cuisine runs the gamut from stacked deli sandwiches and burgers, soups and salads to meatloaf and pasta dishes. ~ 43 South Main Street, Hanover; 603-643-2570; www.mollysrestaurant.com, e-mail info@mollysrestaurant.com. MODERATE.

SHOPPING

Powerhouse Mall is like a fairyland, adorned with barreled ceilings and colored strands of light. The 30-plus stores are imaginative and often feature a single theme. **Artifactory** (603-298-6010), for instance, leans toward the unusual with whimsical gifts like wizard-shaped candles and 14-karat gold jewelry. ~ Glen Road off of Route 12A, West Lebanon; 603-298-5236.

NIGHTLIFE

The historic **Claremont Opera House**, with its arched stained glass and scrolled columns, is a superb place to see all types of entertainment—jazz, Broadway musicals, family shows, magic and dance. ~ Tremont Square, Claremont; 603-542-4433 or 603-542-0064; www.claremontoperahouse.com.

Dartmouth College nightlife sizzles on the underground circuit. Among the best below-ground pubs, **Five Olde Nugget Alley** features a long, battered maple bar, a round of maple tables and piped-in contemporary music. ~ 5 Olde Nugget Alley, off Wheelock and Main streets, Hanover; 603-643-5081.

Dartmouth College's dazzling **Hopkins Center for the Arts** hosts major drama, musicals, concerts and films in three auditoriums. ~ Wheelock Street, Hanover; 603-646-2422; www.hop.dartmouth.edu.

BEACHES & PARKS

PILLSBURY STATE PARK A 9000-acre wilderness of forests, ponds and subtle hills, Pillsbury was once a bustling village of sawmills and frame homes. Today there's no hint of that 18th-century activity as loons, ducks, deer and other wildlife roam the moist hammocks and dense thickets. Hiking and picnicking are superb; nine ponds provide excellent stillwater canoeing and havens for serious fishers hoping to reel in bass, pickerel, or perch. There are 30 miles of hiking trails and 50 miles of biking trails, as well as picnic areas, canoe and kayak rentals and pit toilets. Day-use fee, $3. ~ Off Route 31, four miles north of Washington; 603-863-2860.

▲ There are 40 primitive sites bordering all nine ponds (2 accessible by canoe only); $16 per night. Warning: not suitable for big RVs. Campground closed from late October to late April. Reservations: 603-271-3628.

MOUNT SUNAPEE RESORT AND STATE BEACH This ever-popular resort and park is a year-round recreation haven that caters to swimmers and sunbathers, hikers and skiers, ice fishers and sightseers. The resort operates chair lifts that cruise up 2743-foot Mount Sunapee for downhill skiing and lovely views of Lake Sunapee and the surrounding alpine mountains. There's a cafeteria up here (during winter only) and another at the mountain's base, where you'll find a sun terrace and exhibition trout pool. Spring-fed Lake Sunapee is re-

COUNTRYSIDE CREATIVITY

The state's unswerving individualism, coupled with its bucolic settings, have enticed some of the country's most creative minds. Robert Frost, Nathaniel Hawthorne, Ralph Waldo Emerson, Thornton Wilder, sculptor Augustus Saint-Gaudens and many other talents employed New Hampshire's rural reaches as their studios.

nowned for trout and salmon fishing. And there's more: the 2700-acre park claims a ski school and shop, a nursery and a lineup of events like state craft shows and sporting events. Across the street, Sunapee State Beach is a 900-foot ribbon of crystalline sand edging the lake. You'll find picnic areas, restrooms, bathhouses, lifeguards, cafeterias and snack bars. Day-use fee, $3. ~ Route 103, three miles west of Newbury; 603-763-2356 (resort), 603-763-5561 (state beach), fax 603-763-5989; www.mtsunapee.com.

The Lakes Region

Strewn across New Hampshire's heart like a strand of aquamarine beads, some 273 lakes range from sealike to pondlike. Skirted by olive hills and sheltered coves, the lakes weave about 39 towns and three cities and engender a slew of outdoor pursuits. Many of the lakes bear Indian names, including Kanasatka, Ossipee, Squam and Winnipesaukee, queen of them all.

SIGHTS

One of the westernmost—and least visited—lakes is **Newfound,** whose fine sandy shores are covered by spiraling evergreens, sand and chimney-topped cabins. It lies along Route 3A.

HIDDEN

The town of Hebron, on the northwest corner, harbors an unexpected treasure known as **Sculptured Rocks**. This geological treat comprises dozens of undulating rocks carved into designs by thousands of years of swift water. There's a frowning face, a seal, a camel and other interesting sculptures. ~ Sculptured Rocks Road, a gravel road off North Shore Road, just southwest of Hebron town center.

HIDDEN

Tucked away in North Groton you'll find a darling clapboard cottage that was the **Mary Baker Eddy Historic House**. Eddy, an astute woman who founded the Christian Science religion and *Christian Science Monitor*, lived here from 1855 through 1860. The house has been nicely maintained and features her old iron pot-bellied stove and bed strung with ropes. (Tours of this structure begin at Eddy's Rumney home.) The house is closed for reconstruction until June 2007. Closed Monday and from November through April. Admission. ~ Hall's Brook Road, North Groton; 603-786-9943.

HIDDEN

Eddy left North Groton in 1860 and moved to nearby Rumney, where her **Rumney House** rests behind a white picket fence. Here she penned the poem "Major Anderson and Our Country" in response to the Civil War and waged her own war against slavery. The late-1700s house is adorned with relics like a banjo clock, melodian piano and unusual wall drawers used to store ammunition. The house is closed for reconstruction until June 2007. Closed November through April. Admission. ~ 58 Stinson Lake Road, Rumney; 603-786-9943.

From here, head east though the mountains and cut over to **Squam Lake**, speckled with fishing skiffs, sailboats and loons. Antique shops, decoy stores, rustic cabins and miles of tall trees give this area a peaceful milieu, a setting that no doubt attracted makers of the 1981 movie *On Golden Pond*, parts of which were filmed here.

Get close to those crazy loons at the **Squam Lakes Natural Science Center**, a 200-acre wildlife preserve near Squam Lake. From the trails here (and behind protective glass) you can spot whitetail deer, black bears, mountain lions and bald eagles, visit ponds and view otter and raptor (bird of prey) exhibits. Kids love the hands-on nature exhibits, games and puzzles. Closed November through May. Admission. ~ Route 113, Holderness; 603-968-7194, fax 603-968-2229; www.nhnature.org, e-mail info@nhnature.org.

South on Route 25, **Meredith** is a very lucky place. Resting on a finger of Lake Winnipesaukee, it also touches Lakes Wicwas, Waukewan, Pemigewasset and Winnisquam. The town bears a charming demeanor with cosmopolitan touches like small shopping malls, antique shops, art galleries and numerous restaurants and motels. The **Meredith Area Chamber of Commerce** has sightseeing information on the town and surrounding areas. Closed weekends during winter. ~ 272 Daniel Webster Highway, Meredith; 603-279-6121, fax 603-279-4525; www.meredithcc.org, e-mail meredith@lr.net.

Drawing more people than any shopping mall, **Annalee's Doll Museum and Gift Shop** stocks every doll imaginable (and even those you can't imagine). Displays are colorful and creative, featuring animals, presidents, Indians, spiders and witches, a Christmas section that would impress Santa himself, and much more. But more fascinating is the story of Annalee Thorndine, a housewife who began making dolls at her kitchen table in the 1950s. Today, her doll business is a nationally recognized and hotly collected brand. Museum closed Columbus Day to Memorial Day. ~ Annalee Place and Hemlock Drive, Meredith; 603-279-6542, 800-433-6557, fax 603-279-6659; www.annalee.com.

Lake Winnipesaukee (pronounced Win-a-peh-SAW-kee), which translates as either "the smile of the great spirit" or "smiling water in a high place," is by far the state's largest and most impressive lake, spanning 72 square miles with 283 miles of shoreline and 274 habitable islands. If you care to explore the big lake by train, show up at **Winnipesaukee Scenic Railroad** and catch the next choo-choo south to Weirs Beach. Of course, you can hop on at the Weirs Beach station (Lakeside Avenue) for the return trip. From mid-May to late June and from Labor Day to late October, the railroad is open only on weekends. Except for a few "Santa Express" rides during the Christmas season, the railroad is closed late October to mid-May. Admission. ~ Route 3, Meredith; 603-279-5253, fax 603-745-9850; www.hoborr.com.

At **Weirs Beach**, New Hampshire's own little Coney Island, a well-roamed boardwalk extends several blocks along Lake Winnipesaukee, sprinkled with arcades and bumper cars, pizzerias and souvenir shops. There's also a dock where you board the **M.S. Mount Washington**, a 230-foot passenger ship that glides across the lake on sightseeing excursions. Closed November to mid-May. ~ Weirs Beach; 603-366-5531; www.cruisenh.com, e-mail info@cruisenh.com.

Winnipesaukee's southeastern joints shelter miles of wooded estuaries and broad water vistas; you can wind your way around on Routes 11 and 28. You will soon land in **Wolfeboro**, a busy little town wedged between lakes Winnipesaukee and Wentworth. The village harkens back to 1763, when Governor John Wentworth built the country's first known summer resort here.

Scattered under some maple and elm trees, the **Clark House Museum Complex** is a trio of buildings that recall Wolfeboro's earlier years. There's a one-room clapboard schoolhouse built in 1805, a 1778 Cape Cod–style house with painted plank floors and marvelous antiques, and a replica 1862 fire station with period fire equipment. Open in July and August and by appointment the rest of the year. Closed Sunday through Tuesday. Admission. ~ South Main Street, Wolfeboro; 603-569-4997;

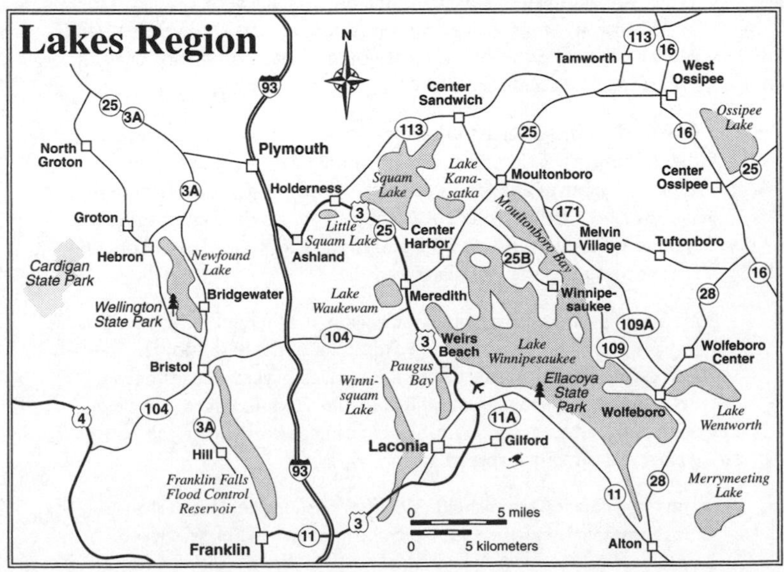

Text continued on page 548.

The Roads Less Traveled

They crisscross the state like a tangle of veins, concealing treasures that can be unlocked only by foraging through unfamiliar terrain. The **roads less traveled** may not be the shortest way to get there from here, but you can bet they're the most scenic.

New Hampshire's byroads exist everywhere, yet they are chosen by very few. They link towns and lakes, clamber up mountains, trundle through isolated villages and navigate miles of wild forest. They sometimes lead to nowhere, but they always harbor a special price: an 18th-century cemetery, a glistening pond or beach, a wildlife hollow or perhaps a vista to ignite your spirit.

To natives, these tireless country routes are known as "shunpikes," used to "shun" crowded main roads and highways. During fall foliage time, shunpikes are ripe with brilliant splashes of red and gold and purple leaves that form one incredible spectacle. They undoubtedly provide the best leaf-peeping seats in the house.

You'll discover glorious back roads in all of New Hampshire's six regions:

When you get tired of battling traffic on coastal Route 1A, take a jog on **Willow Avenue**, which starts just north of Little Boars Head, and relish a peaceful ride that explores grand 19th-century mansions and manicured lawns and gardens.

Few think of the seacoast in terms of fruit farms and old barns, but they're here, right along **Routes 88** and **84**. These roads twist through 1700s farmhouses and lonely stretches of pastureland, apple orchards and raspberry farms (where you can pick your own). Both begin in Hampton Falls. Take Route 88 from Route 1 to Route 101C; Route 84 starts at Route 1 and Wild Pasture Road.

New Hampshire's most populated region, the Merrimack Valley, manages to have some fine less-traveled roads. One of the best, **North Pembroke Road** snakes through five miles of rural scenes between Route 28 near Allenstown and Route 106. It winds past a cornfield, wildflower farm, several log cabins, an old cemetery and a sap house where you can buy maple syrup.

The Monadnock Region shelters dozens of shunpikes, but perhaps the most beautiful is **Route 119**, which hovers near the Massachusetts border between Routes 202 and 10. Wend your way through the bucolic town of Rindge, then along remote Pearly Pond, where lakefront homes peek out from evergreen forests and reflect against the water. At sunset, bright orange light bands ignite the pond and make it appear to be on fire.

For unmatched views of Mount Monadnock, veer off Route 124 onto **Webb Depot Road** in Marlborough. Here you'll spy an old stone bridge and wonderfully clear vistas across open fields toward the vast summit.

Way out in the boondocks of the Lake Sunapee–Dartmouth area, **Stage Road** is one shunpike worth finding. It scouts out the soul of this fertile region, fording three brooks and a covered bridge and miles of hardwoods and idle hills. You'll find this gem between Route 120 in Meriden and Route 12A.

In the Lakes Region, seek out **West Shore Road** along the west side of Newfound Lake. A series of hairpin curves through patched tar and forest, the road frequently squeezes between the mountains and lake and dispenses unobstructed water vistas. With views of Squam Lake, **Route 113** and **Route 109** will take you past classic New England landscapes with villages, farms and old estates in Sandwich Notch.

Scenic Drive is like a secret pass along the west brink of Lake Winnipesaukee. Prized by local residents for its peaceful, uncongested feeling, this shady bypass affords breathtaking panoramas of one of New England's most prominent lakes. It picks up just south of Weirs Beach.

In the White Mountains, **Bear Notch Road** is a cool, misty tryst with nature, a natural high of rock grottos, evergreen spires and tiny patches of blue sky. Keep your eye out for the pretty sandy cove along the Swift River, a solitary respite for those lucky enough to uncover it. The road runs from the Kancamagus Highway at Passaconaway to Route 302.

Route 116 from Jefferson to Franconia is the archetype of New England tranquility. Cows graze on grassy knolls, windmills twirl across hayfields and old farmhouses repose against the mountains. During fall foliage season, maple and elm trees flail their yellow and orange canopies across the road, truly a sight to behold.

Before you take the roads less traveled, get a good map, and when in doubt, ask for directions at a local general store. Shunpiking is primarily a summer and fall sport, since many byroads are jammed with snow the rest of the year. Don't be afraid to venture upon these foreign passages. It's virtually impossible to get lost, and if you do, there's always someone to set you straight again.

www.wolfborohistoricalsociety.org, e-mail protopipnit@adelphia.net.

One local resident has nicely catalogued Wolfeboro goings-on, and the results can be seen at the **Libby Museum**, a natural-history collection with a refreshing funky flavor. Here you'll find rows of stuffed birds, fish, animals and other native wildlife, relics from the long-destroyed Governor Wentworth mansion, and great Indian artifacts. New England artists exhibit from June through August, and children's science and nature programs are featured. Closed Monday and from mid-September to May. Admission. ~ Route 109, Wolfeboro; 603-569-1035, fax 603-569-2246; www.wolfeboro.com/libby, e-mail libbymus@metrocast.net.

HIDDEN ►

Tucked in a forest off the road, **Abenaki Tower** is one place you can have all to yourself. The post-and-beam tower, erected by local townsfolk, will seduce you with stirring vistas of surrounding lakes and random wooded islands. ~ Route 109, about five miles north of Wolfeboro in Melvin Village.

Castle in the Clouds is an incredible place, cloaked in secrets and almost magical in design. Fashioned as a medieval castle, it sits high on a mountain and gives the illusion that it's floating. The castle's maker, shoe magnate Thomas Gustave Plant, bought 6300 acres—including seven mountains—and paid $7 million to have his dream built between 1913 and 1914.

The 16 rooms and 8 bathrooms add to the mystique with their five- and eight-sided designs, doors of English lead, an enormous skylight, fluted windows and the curious absence of any nails. Plant had 12 closets and a secret reading room seen by others only after his death. At one time, he was worth $21 million. But on the advice of friend Teddy Roosevelt, Plant invested heavily in Russian bonds during the 1930s. In 1941, he died a penniless man. Closed mid-October through April. Call ahead. Admission. ~ Route 171, Moultonboro; 603-476-5900, fax 603-476-2512; www.castleintheclouds.org, e-mail info@castleintheclouds.org.

LODGING

HIDDEN ►

Along placid Newfound Lake rests a grand old summer house and former stagecoach station called **The Inn on Newfound Lake**. Here you'll discover great vistas, fabulous sunsets, friendly innkeepers and a completely unhurried pace. The 31 rooms are casually decorated in an eclectic mixture of antiques. During summer, there's a sandy lakefront beach across the street; during winter, the lake freezes and makes for splendid skating and skiing. ~ Route 3A, Bridgewater; 603-744-9111, 800-745-7990, fax 603-744-3894; www.newfoundlake.com, e-mail inonlk@metrocast.net. DELUXE.

The Inn on Golden Pond took its moniker from the movie (not vice versa), and its serene ambience does resemble the restful house depicted in the film. Stationed in a 50-acre wooded glen near Squam Lake—not on it—the graceful white clapboard house offers eight comfortable units enhanced by country decor with contemporary touches. Early American dressers and braided rugs contrast nicely with lace curtains and sleek bathrooms. Out back, a breezy lawn provides solace. ~ Route 3, Holderness; 603-968-7269, fax 603-968-9226; www.innongoldenpond.com, e-mail innkeepers@innongoldenpond.com. DELUXE.

Shielded from a busy road by a string of giant rocks, the **Boulders Motel and Cottages** fits the standard motor court genre with one exception: every room claims a fabulous view of Squam Lake. There's also a small but pristine sandy beach out back, a great place to gape at passing boats. Accommodations range from 12 clean but sparse rooms to six efficiencies and three rustic cottages. Closed November through April. ~ Route 3, Holderness; 603-968-3600, 800-968-3601; www.bouldermotel.com. MODERATE TO DELUXE.

Greystone Inn & Motel Suites has two very important virtues: It's hidden down a scenic, little-traveled side road, and it's right on gorgeous Lake Winnipesaukee. There are two buildings with basic but clean accommodations ranging from inn rooms to waterfront motel suites. There's also a five-room farmhouse rented by the week. The name of the game here is boating, fishing and outstanding panoramas. ~ 132 Scenic Drive, off Route 11, Gilford; 603-293-7377; www.greystoneinn-nh.com, e-mail info@greystoneinn.nh.com. MODERATE TO DELUXE.

◄ HIDDEN

Wolfeboro's premier lodging establishment is undoubtedly **The Wolfeboro Inn**, a rambling, Cape Cod–like manor resting beside Lake Winnipesaukee. The lobby is a fusion of wood beams, carpeted floors and leather sofas, while 44 rooms feature modern touches of sleek oak and pine furniture and pedestal sinks. A 150-passenger paddlewheel boat is available for charters. ~ 90 North Main Street, Wolfeboro; 603-569-3016, 800-451-2389, fax 603-569-5375; www.wolfeboroinn.com, e-mail info@wolfeboroinn.com. ULTRA-DELUXE.

AUTHOR FAVORITE

Lake views, dreamy Colonial architecture, shops and restaurants right outside your door. Sound enticing? Then **The Inns and Spa at Mill Falls** is where you want to be. This spiffy resting place has 158 designer rooms, most with fireplaces and lake-view balconies. Relax in the indoor pool, jacuzzi, spa or sauna. A busy road is all that separates guests from Lake Winnipesaukee. ~ Route 3 in the Mill Falls Marketplace, Meredith; 603-279-7006, 800-622-6455, fax 603-279-6797; www.millfalls.com, e-mail info@millfalls.com. DELUXE TO ULTRA-DELUXE.

Wolfeboro is lucky enough to border three lakes, and you can catch views of two at **The Lake Motel.** Nestled on the picturesque corner of Lake Winnipesaukee and Crescent Lake, the motor court takes advantage of its surroundings with an enormous lawn stretching to the shorelines. Some of the 35 rooms and five efficiency apartments offer water views and all have wall-to-wall carpets. Closed mid-October to mid-May. ~ Route 28, Wolfeboro; 603-569-1100, fax 603-515-9006; www.thelakemotel.com, e-mail info@thelakemotel.com. MODERATE.

DINING

The Common Man enjoys a sterling reputation around the lakes, undoubtedly for its steadfast, uncomplicated cuisine and nostalgic surroundings. Old farm tools and classic *Life* and *Saturday Evening Post* covers are parked on the walls of this two-story brick eatery, formerly an early-1800s home. Go for the steaks (the prime rib is heady stuff) or the fresh fish and seafood. There's also pineapple-ginger chicken stir-fry, rack of lamb and vegetable lasagna. ~ Main Street, Ashland; 603-968-7030; www.thecman.com, e-mail info@thecman.com. MODERATE TO DELUXE.

If you want to splurge on a special meal, consider making a reservation at **The Manor on Golden Pond.** In this mansion overlooking Squam Lake, you can feast on New England specialities (with quite a few international touches) in what was the original billiards room or in the very elegant original dining room. The á la carte menu changes weekly; prix-fixe meals are served nightly. ~ Route 3, Holderness; 603-968-3348, 800-545-2141, fax 603-968-2116; www.manorongoldenpond.com, e-mail info@manorongoldenpond.com. ULTRA-DELUXE.

Lago Trattoria aims to deliver an old-world Italy feel with its decor and food. A casual restaurant on the water expected fare includes ciabatta bread, pastas, fresh fish and meat entrées. Dinner only. ~ Route 25, Meredith; 603-279-2253, fax 603-279-1160. MODERATE.

It's not hard to figure out why **West Lake Asian Cuisine** stays perpetually packed. Snuggled in a wooded area along Lake Wentworth, the eatery headlines over 100 different and delicious dishes that make choosing extremely difficult. You'll find seafood, poultry, beef and pork dunked in steamy sauces with garlic, chili or black beans, along with specials like mala lamb. Closed Monday from October through April. ~ Route 28, Wolfeboro; 603-569-6700, fax 603-569-8050. MODERATE.

The dining room at the **Tamworth Inn** is bright and elegant with linen tablecloths, candlelight and sweeping floral curtains. Entrées are upscale and creative, including dishes such as chicken mole with organic pumpkin seeds, craisins, cocoa, chile and spices; and mojito swordfish marinated in rum, lime and mint and topped with a habanero-mango salsa. Closed Sunday through

Wednesday from mid-September to mid-June, closed Sunday and Monday from mid-June to mid-September, closed in April and the first two weeks of November. ~ Tamworth Village; 603-323-7721, 800-642-7352, fax 603-323-2026; www.tamworth.com, e-mail inn@tamworth.com. DELUXE TO ULTRA-DELUXE.

The monument called the Endicott Rock at Weirs Beach marks what used to be the most northerly point of Massachusetts before New Hampshire became a state.

Lake residents frequently mob **The Yankee Smokehouse**, a modest cinderblock joint parked on the corner of a rural intersection. Smoke trundles out the top, and an old air conditioner hums away while diners scarf down massive portions of ribs and chicken that hang off plastic plates. Also known for its sliced beef and pork and killer barbecue sauce, the smokehouse offers summer outdoor dining on picnic tables. ~ Junction of Routes 16 and 25, West Ossipee; 603-539-7427; www.yankeesmokehouse.com. BUDGET TO MODERATE.

SHOPPING

Bud's Cards specializes in autographed goods—photos, jerseys, balls and the like—but also stocks more than a million trading cards from baseball and hockey to X-men and Batman. Saturday and evening hours only from Labor Day to July. Closed Sunday. ~ 4 Oak Street, Meredith; 603-279-7603; www.budscards.com.

Mill Falls Marketplace is a pretty lakeside complex where Christmas and bath shops mingle with sports stores, art galleries and candy kitchens. One of the largest stores here is **Country Carriage** (603-279-6790; www.countrycarriage.com), a purveyor of American folk art, Yankee candles and other fine New England gifts. ~ Route 3, Meredith; www.millfalls.com/marketplace.

NIGHTLIFE

On some Friday and Saturday summer nights, don't miss the wide variety of lively music at **The Common Man**, a lively place featuring comfortable couches and swag lamps. ~ The Common Man restaurant, Main Street, Ashland; 603-968-7030, fax 603-968-2123; www.thecman.com.

The Barnstormers, the country's oldest summer professional stock theater group was formed in 1931. They now perform a variety of comedy, mystery and drama year round. ~ Main Street off Route 113, Tamworth; 603-323-8661; www.barnstormerstheatre.org.

BEACHES & PARKS

WELLINGTON STATE PARK AND BEACH Secluded pine coves, strings of granite boulders and a brow of chestnut sand amble around Newfound Lake at this ultra-scenic spot. Lying on a peninsula and framed by small peaks and isles of evergreens, Wellington has the views. The lake's white sandy bottom and gentle shores make it one of the best swimming holes in New Hampshire. Facilities include a picnic area, pavilions, a snack bar, bathhouses, restrooms and a playground. Closed Columbus Day through Memorial Day. Day-use fee, $3 per person. ~ Off Route 3A, four miles north of Bristol; phone/fax 603-744-2197.

WEIRS BEACH This *is* the paradigm of summertime family vacations. It rests in an elbow of Lake Winnipesaukee and bears a half moon of amber granules bordered by grassy slopes. Though the lake views are pretty spectacular, the beach itself is nothing to write home about. Still, crowds flock here for the carnival mood stirred up by the adjacent boardwalk and amusement centers. There's also excellent fishing for lake trout and salmon. The monument called the Endicott Rock marks what used to be the most northerly point of Massachusetts before New Hampshire became a state. Facilities include a picnic area, restrooms, lifeguards and a playground. Closed after Labor Day to Memorial Day. Parking fee, $10. ~ Off Route 3 at Lakeside Avenue, Weirs Beach; 603-524-5531, fax 603-524-5534; www.weirsbeach.com, e-mail webmaster@weirsbeach.com.

ELLACOYA STATE PARK AND BEACH The only state park on Lake Winnipesaukee and one of its few parcels of public land, Ellacoya combines a 600-foot beach with birch groves and fabulous sunsets. Mocha-colored sand, flecked with pine needles and cones, weaves about the lake and courts sublime views of the Ossipee and Sandwich mountain ranges. Lake trout and salmon fishing is excellent. There are picnic areas, restrooms and bathhouses. Closed Labor Day through Memorial Day. Day-use fee, $3 per person. ~ Route 11, Gilford; 603-293-7821; www.nhparks.org, e-mail ellacoyastatepark@yahoo.com.

▲ There's an RV campground with 37 full hookups; $42 per night. Closed October through May. Reservations: 603-271-3628.

White Mountain Region

A bold sweep of compelling peaks hovers against New Hampshire's northern horizon. The White Mountains, which cover more than 760,000 acres, were named by 19th-century sailors for their brilliant crowns of snow framed by blue sky. Their drama—for centuries painted on landscape canvases—lies amid swift waterfalls, rocky gorges, rugged passes, granite silhouettes and one of the most stirring foliage displays in all of New England.

Towering above the region, broad Mount Washington is etched with jagged ravines and topped with rock-strewn grassy lawns. At 6288 feet, it's the highest peak east of the Mississippi and north of the Carolinas.

For the sightseer, the White Mountains ensure exploration at its height. Roads are scenic, usually remote and almost always dotted with hidden treasure. Even short distances can take a while to cover on mountain roads, so always allow extra travel time.

Franconia Notch must be one of New England's seven wonders. At first glance, it is entirely overwhelming, offering dozens of natural phenomena and activities that could fill several days. A dramatic mountain gap caused by eons of glacial and river erosion, the notch lies within **Franconia Notch State Park**'s 6500 acres and draws more than two million visitors annually. Off Route 93, Franconia.

Most sights can be accessed by scenic **Franconia Notch Parkway,** which *is* Route 93 for the eight-mile length of the park. The best place to start is **Park Headquarters,** which will help organize the numerous activities. ~ Tramway main building, Exit 2; 603-823-8800.

From the park headquarters, board the **Cannon Mountain Aerial Tramway** for a ten-minute cable car ride with panoramic views into Canada, Vermont, Maine and New York. The mountain, whose rocky profile resembles the barrels of a cannon, has the first engineered ski slopes in the United States. Closed November through April. Admission. ~ 603-823-5563, fax 603-823-8088; www.cannonmt.com, e-mail info@cannonmt.com.

Here also is the trail leading to pretty **Profile Lake,** headwaters of the Pemigewasset River. Pemigewasset, Indian for "swift waters," provided a reflecting basin for the granite profile of **Old Man of the Mountains,** whose gnarled eyebrows and prominent chin loomed 1200 feet up and kept watch over the notch until 2003 when this 30,000-year-old geologic formation collapsed.

The Flume Visitors Center is a state-of-the-art complex with historic films and photographs of the park. It's also the entrance to The Flume (admission), a dramatic chasm that plummets 800 feet to the base of Mount Liberty. Carved before the Ice Age by the rushing waters of the Pemigewasset River, The Flume is banked in rare flowers and mosses and takes one and a half hours to visit fully. Closed late October to mid-May. ~ Franconia Notch State Park; 603-745-8391, fax 603-745-4951; www.flumegorge.com, e-mail info@cannonmt.com.

After you leave the park, head northward to the town of **Franconia,** a lovely mountain burg where you'll find **The Frost**

A BATH FIT FOR A GODDESS

South on the Franconia Notch Parkway, turn off for a look at **The Basin.** Formed 25,000 years ago, this large pothole of whirling azure waters and smooth rock is bored 15 feet into the Pemigewasset River. It has long intrigued spectators, including Henry David Thoreau in 1839 and Samuel Eastman in 1858, the latter calling it "a luxurious and delicious bath fit for the ablutions of a goddess."

Place. An old mailbox with the inscription "R. Frost" rests against a shady dirt lane, marking the modest frame home where Robert Frost lived and visited for many years. Here he penned many poems for which he's famous, gleaning inspiration from a backyard filled with sugar maples, an apple orchard and wildflowers. A Poetry Trail winds through the surrounding wooded area. Closed weekdays from Memorial Day through June; closed Tuesday from July to Columbus Day; and closed from mid-October to Memorial Day. Admission. ~ On Ridge Road off Route 116, Franconia; 603-823-5510; www.frostplace.org, e-mail rfrost@ncia.net.

Sugar Hill, Franconia's sister town, is just as charming and bucolic. The Abenaki Indians once hunted in this area, which today is sprinkled with whitewashed Colonial buildings and country stores. The **Sugar Hill Historical Museum** traces local ancestry to the late 1700s and has two barns filled with farm tools, old photographs and horse-drawn wagons and sleighs. The main building houses the genealogy library and changing exhibits. Closed Sunday through Wednesday and from late October through May. ~ Route 117, Sugar Hill; 603-823-5336, fax 603-823-8431; www.franconianotch.org, e-mail harwrw@aol.com.

Work your way eastward to Route 302, a picturesque mountain trail that crawls to Crawford Notch. A nice side trip from here, **Santa's Village** is a tot's fairytale world. The place is laid out like a fantasyland, with gingerbread houses and miniature trains, sleigh rides, a "Rudolph-Go-Round" carousel, log rides and a rollercoaster. There are musical shows, sing-a-longs and, of course, Santa and his reindeer. Open daily from Father's Day through Labor Day. Open weekends only from Memorial Day through Columbus Day; closed from Columbus Day to mid-June (except for Thanksgiving weekend and weekends in December). Admission. ~ Route 2, Jefferson; 603-586-4445, fax 603-586-7025; www.santasvillage.com, e-mail santa@santasvillage.com.

Then on to **Crawford Notch**. Moose hunter Timothy Nash discovered the pass in 1771, reporting his find to Governor John Wentworth. Nash could have a large piece of land, Wentworth said, if he took his horse through the treacherous notch. Nash and a friend got the horse through, sometimes hoisting him over ledges with ropes. In 1775, the first notch road opened.

The geographical pinnacle here is the big guy himself, **Mount Washington**. Sighted from the ocean back in 1605, the mountain soars 6288 snow-capped feet across the skyline. It's reputed to be the world's most dangerous small mountain, with wind-chill temperatures tantamount to those in Antarctica.

Perhaps this fierce reputation only heightens the mountain's intrigue, as several hundred thousand people scale its slopes each year. One of the most popular ascents is on the **Mount Washing-**

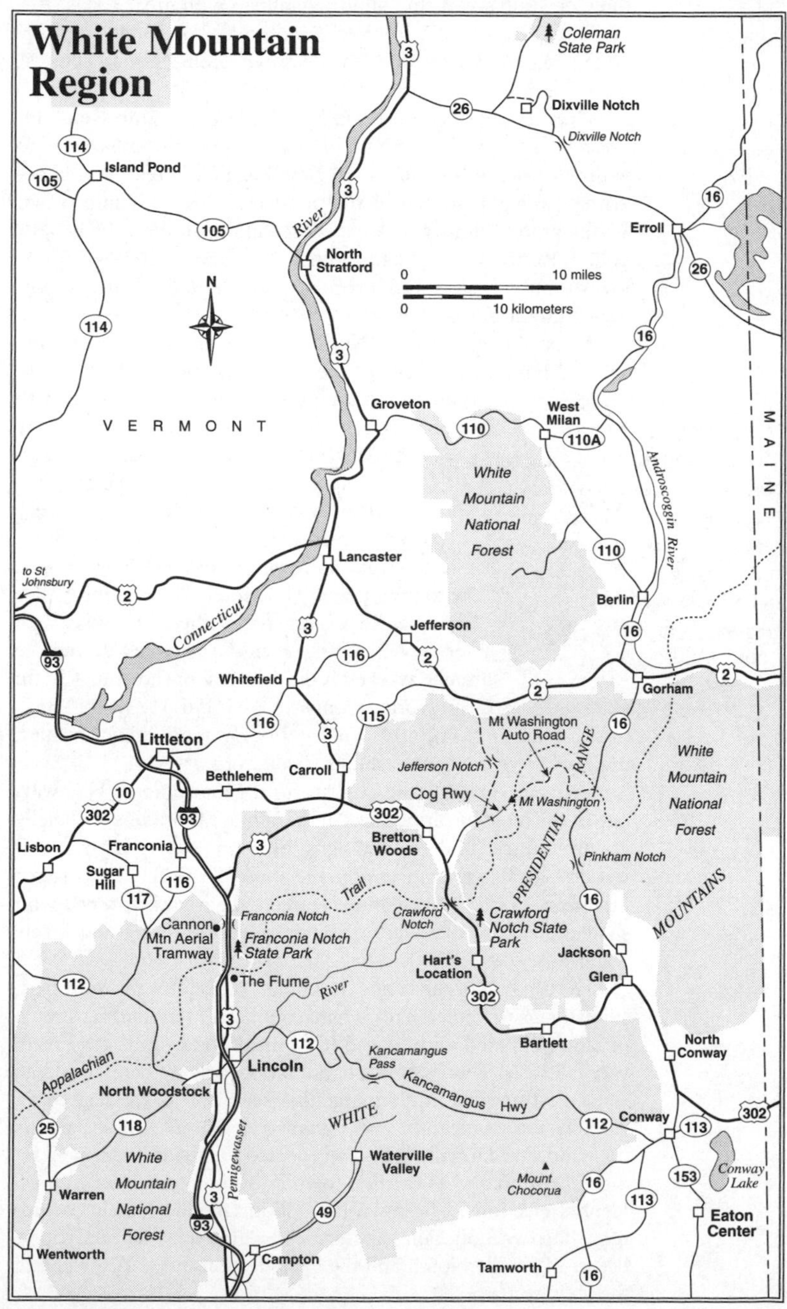
White Mountain Region
Coleman State Park
Dixville Notch
Dixville Notch
Island Pond
Erroll
North Stratford
River
0
10 miles
0
10 kilometers
N
VERMONT
Groveton
West Milan
White Mountain National Forest
Androscoggin River
MAINE
Lancaster
to St Johnsbury
Berlin
Connecticut
Jefferson
Whitefield
Gorham
Mt Washington Auto Road
Littleton
Carroll
Bethlehem
Jefferson Notch
Cog Rwy
Mt Washington
RANGE
PRESIDENTIAL
White Mountain National Forest
Bretton Woods
Lisbon
Franconia
Sugar Hill
Pinkham Notch
Trail
Franconia Notch
Crawford Notch
Crawford Notch State Park
MOUNTAINS
Cannon Mtn Aerial Tramway
Franconia Notch State Park
Hart's Location
Jackson
Glen
The Flume
River
Bartlett
North Conway
Appalachian
Lincoln
Kancamangus Pass
Kancamangus Hwy
North Woodstock
Conway
WHITE
Pemigewasset
White Mountain National Forest
Waterville Valley
Mount Chocorua
Conway Lake
Warren
Eaton Center
Wentworth
Campton
Tamworth
114
105
105
114
3
3
3
26
16
26
16
110
110A
110
2
16
3
116
2
2
2
93
116
3
115
16
10
302
93
302
3
116
117
16
112
302
3
112
25
118
112
113
302
153
16
113
3
49
93
16

ton Cog Railway, a three-hour roundtrip with great vistas. Admission. ~ Route 302, Bretton Woods; 603-278-5404, 800-922-8825, fax 603-278-5830; www.thecog.com, e-mail doug@thecog.com.

The other easy climb is via **Mt. Washington Auto Road,** located between Jackson and Gorham. This steep mountain road without guardrails is unique in New England, a real driving adventure and the source of the popular "This car climbed Mt. Washington" bumper stickers. Closed mid-October to mid-May. Toll. ~ Route 16, Pinkham Notch in Gorham; 603-466-3988; www.mountwashingtonautoroad.com, e-mail info@mountwashingtonautoroad.com.

About 25 miles south, **North Conway** and **Conway** are the White Mountains' tokens of modern development. Actually it's the stretch of Route 16 *between* the two towns—jammed with outlet stores, fast-food joints, tacky tourist centers and condos—that seems so out of place in this earthy setting.

The state's most spectacular fall foliage displays occur in White Mountain National Forest, and one of the best places to see the changing colors is along the 34-mile Kancamagus Highway from Route 302 to Route 3A.

North Conway, which stays very crowded year-round, features quaint shops, restaurants and century-old buildings ringed with mountains. The **Mount Washington Valley Chamber of Commerce** is there to assist with your travels. Open seven days a week during the summer, weekends only the rest of the year. ~ Main Street, North Conway; 603-356-3171, 800-367-3364, fax 603-356-7069; www.mtwashingtonvalley.org, e-mail visitor@mtwashingtonvalley.org.

Smaller Conway is the gateway for the **Kancamagus Highway,** one of the most inspiring treks in the White Mountains. Officially it's pronounced Kan-ka-MAW-gus, but don't worry if you get it wrong—locals are quite used to the abuse of this Indian word for "the fearless one." Cool and evergreen, the road is rimmed with shaded glens, scenic overlooks, ponds, rocky gorges and lovely waterfalls.

The top half of the White Mountains region, for the most part, still belongs to nature. This is wild country, an unremitting stretch of land peppered with jagged hills, lucid ponds and very green, very tall trees. There's only a handful of people up here, including some old-timers so firmly rooted they seem part of the very earth.

Between civilization and Canada, several geographic points do stand out. **Dixville** is known for two things: its extremely remote location and as the first town in the nation to vote in presidential elections. The town lies within **Dixville Notch,** a stunning, narrow mountain pass formed by glaciers. Mention you've been to Dixville Notch and the likely response is: "You went all the way up *there*?"

Indeed, this area truly is "at the end of the world"—New Hampshire's world, that is.

LODGING

A rustic old-time air fills the **Woodstock Inn,** a homey kind of resting place that beckons to the late 1800s. Rosy wallpaper, pine floors and lacy Victorian draperies frame the 33 rooms, many of which face the Pemigewasset River and some of which share baths. The inn also boasts a microbrewery and pub. Full breakfast is included. ~ Route 3, North Woodstock; 603-745-3951, 800-321-3985, fax 603-745-3701; www.woodstockinnnh.com, e-mail relax@woodstockinnnh.com. MODERATE TO DELUXE.

Wild winds whip through a slender valley, become trapped in a narrow opening and whirl backward to form what's known as a bungay jar. This explains the moniker of **The Bungay Jar,** a beautifully renovated 18th-century barn positioned at the mouth of just such a "tunnel valley." Set in a wooded mountain nest, this cozy bed and breakfast features six rooms decorated with antiques. Stroll through the garden and see the water lily pond and stream. Guests enjoy the use of a small library, sauna and living room. Closed November and April. ~ Route 116, just south of Sugar Hill Road, Franconia; 603-823-7775, 800-421-0701, fax 603-823-5620; www.bungayjar.com, e-mail info@bungayjar.com. DELUXE TO ULTRA-DELUXE. ◄HIDDEN

You'll enjoy taking in the view from a chair on the front porch of the **Ammonoosuc Inn,** on the western edge of the White Mountains. This B&B has been a tourist destination for nearly a century; along with that porch, guests love the spacious parlor and the sunny, roomy bedrooms (all with pretty coverlets on the beds and private bathrooms, most with clawfoot tubs). For summer visitors, there's a scenic nine-hole golf course next door. If you're here in the winter, the White Mountain ski areas aren't far away. The inn has three eateries that happen to feature the culinary skills of the owner. ~ Bishop Road, Lisbon; 603-838-6118, 888-546-6118, fax 603-838-5591; e-mail info@amminn.com. MODERATE TO DELUXE.

Perhaps it's the dozens of nostalgic curios, or the cozy feel of the six bedrooms, or even the hardwood floors that glide so smoothly under bare feet. Regardless of the reason, **The Hilltop Inn** is sure to make you feel at home. Situated along a secluded byroad, the inn is run by an amiable couple that loves to work around the house. Dogs are welcome. The rates include a full breakfast. ~ Route 117, Sugar Hill; 603-823-5695, 800-770-5695, fax 603-823-5518; www.hilltopinn.com, e-mail info@hilltopinn.com. DELUXE TO ULTRA-DELUXE. ◄HIDDEN

Owned and run by lesbians, **The Highlands Inn** has three separate buildings with a total of 19 guest accommodations. Thirteen of the rooms are in the main inn; the rest are in the farmhouse and a cottage. Each room has its own identity and is thoughtfully decorated with antiques and special touches; some have private decks, spas or fireplaces. It's a beautiful property sprawling over 100 mountain acres. There's a heated swimming pool, two jacuzzis (indoors and outdoors) and 15 miles of trails. Full breakfast is included. ~ Valley View Lane, Bethlehem; 603-869-3978, 877-537-2466; www.highlandsinn-nh.com, e-mail vacation@highlandsinn-nh.com. MODERATE TO DELUXE.

By far one of New England's grandest retreats, the **Mount Washington Hotel and Resort** has been displaying its magical opulence ever since 1902. Set at the foot of the Presidential Range, the imposing, red-roofed mansion rests on 1200 acres and is striking from miles away. Inside, an expansive lobby is heavy with archways, Doric columns and ornate chandeliers, and a rear porch seems to stretch for miles. The staff numbers 400, the rooms 200. Expect room decor ranging from simple to extravagant. ~ Route 302, Bretton Woods; 603-278-1000, 877-873-0626, fax 603-278-8838; www.mtwashington.com, e-mail hotelinfo@mtwashington.com. ULTRA-DELUXE.

At the Mount Washington Hotel and Resort, horse-drawn carriages meander through rolling manicured hills sprinkled with flower and rock gardens.

In Mount Washington Valley, **The Notchland Inn** is a converted Victorian mansion with 14 rooms; all but one have fireplaces. In addition to 11 rooms in the main house—built of granite in the 1860s—there's a converted schoolhouse with two suites, as well as a separate cottage with a deck and kitchen. The inn is owned and run by gay men and welcomes a mixed clientele. The dining room is open to the public for dinner from Wednesday through Sunday. Full breakfast is included. Pets are welcome in the cottage. Closed the last week in November. ~ Route 302, Hart's Location; 603-374-6131, 800-866-6131, fax 603-374-6168; www.notchland.com, e-mail innkeepers@notchland.com. ULTRA-DELUXE.

All 11 individually themed rooms at the tranquil **Inn at Crystal Lake & Pub Bed and Breakfast** include a private bath and specially chosen furnishings. The cool-colored, dog- friendly Birdhouse Room features a cottage bed, a CD player and a garden view, while the Coach Room offers a queen iron-frame bed, a shared balcony and a seasonal lake view. Full country breakfasts can showcase orange-honey french toast or three-mushroom quiche. ~ 2356 Eaton Road, Eaton Center; 603-447-2120, 800-343-7336; www.innatcrystallake.com, e-mail stay@innatcrystallake.com. DELUXE TO ULTRA-DELUXE

Accommodations may be minimal, but you can't beat the price of the dorms at **Cranmore Mountain Lodge**, an independent hostel. Full country breakfast is included. ~ 859 Kearsarge Road, North Conway; 603-356-2044, 800-356-3596, fax 603-356-

4498; www.cml1.com. BUDGET. You'll also find super-low-budget dorm beds and private rooms at **Hostelling International—White Mountains.** The rates include use of their bicycles and full kitchen. ~ 36 Washington Street, Conway; 603-447-1001; www.conwayhostel.com, e-mail conwayhostel@yahoo.com. BUDGET.

Logs stay stacked on the stone porch of **The 1785 Inn**, a gracious old house that seems to say, "Do drop in." One of the oldest homesteads in Mount Washington Valley, the inn was built as a "publick house" by Revolutionary War veteran Elijah Dinsmore. These days, 17 rooms offer simple accommodations featuring country wallpaper, antique bed frames and ample mountain scenery. A full breakfast is included. ~ Route 16, two miles north of North Conway; 603-356-9025, 800-421-1785, fax 603-356-6081; www.the1785inn.com, e-mail the1785inn@aol.com. DELUXE.

The **Inn at Thorn Hill** is a Stanford White–inspired building. The main inn and private cottages are elegantly furnished with period pieces. There are 25 rooms with private baths plus a restaurant, lounge and deluxe spa. Breakfast is included. ~ Thorn Hill Road, Jackson; 603-383-4242, 800-289-8990, fax 603-383-8062; www.innatthornhill.com, e-mail stay@thornhillinn.com. DELUXE TO ULTRA-DELUXE.

The quintessence of New England lodging exists at the **Christmas Farm Inn**, a tranquil place tucked high in the mountains. Resembling a quaint Colonial village, the inn includes a main house built in 1786, plus a cozy log cabin, a 1778 saltbox and a honeymoon cottage. Fourty-two rooms are carefully accented with canopy beds, vaulted ceilings, whirlpool tubs and beautiful quilts. Congenial innkeepers make Christmastime here special, organizing caroling, eggnog breaks and visits from Santa. Breakfast and dinner are included. ~ Route 16B, Jackson; 603-383-4313, 800-443-5837, fax 603-383-6495; www.christmasfarminn.com, e-mail info@christmasfarminn.com. MODERATE.

The Balsams Grand Resort Hotel is one of those places that makes you wonder how guests can ever bring themselves to leave. This self-contained mini-city sprawls across 15,000 acres of exquisite landscape. This is escapism at its height, a reveling in alpine ridges, thick forests and spectacular lakes and rivers. Stashed way up in New Hampshire's northern boondocks, the rambling, castlelike resort boasts 202 rooms decorated in French provincial style. There's a movie theater, 27 holes of golf, an Olympic swimming pool, croquet and tennis courts, and an outstanding restaurant. The price includes meals and the use of facilities. ~ Route 26, Dixville Notch; 603-255-3400, 800-255-0600, fax 603-255-4221; www.thebalsams.com. ULTRA-DELUXE.

DINING

A popular town spot that's just plain fun, **Truants Taverne** has an upstairs game room with billiards, fooseball, shuffleboard and darts. The decor is casual wood-lined pub, the food is basic, with items such as chicken parmigiana, sandwiches and prime rib. ~ Main Street, North Woodstock; 603-745-2239. MODERATE.

HIDDEN ► Stationed along a wooded mountain backroad, **Horse and Hound Inn** abounds in Colonial gentility. Lofty pine beams and large hearths are accented by a hunting motif in the 1840 farmhouse. The menu includes filling fare like veal marsala, lamb chops and roast duckling. On warm summer days, opt for the breezy outdoor terrace overlooking the forest. Dinner only. Reservations required. Closed Monday and Tuesday, closed mid-April to late May, and from mid-October to Thanksgiving. ~ 205 Wells Road off Route 18, Franconia; phone/fax 603-823-5501; e-mail info@horseandhoundnh.com. MODERATE TO ULTRA-DELUXE.

Polly's Pancake Parlor was little more than a backwoods diner before the "Good Morning, America" crew wandered in one day. Ever since, the place has been invaded by tourists who line up outside the 1830 red-shingled carriage shed for home-style breakfast and lunch goodies. Polly's is still out in the boondocks, but views of the countryside are special. Ditto the griddle cakes, made from whole wheat and cornmeal batters and smothered in a choice of maple syrup, maple sugar or maple spread. Closed mid-October to Mother's Day. ~ Route 117, Sugar Hill; 603-823-5575, fax 603-823-5576; www.pollyspancakeparlor.com, e-mail info@pollyspancakeparlor.com. BUDGET.

The views are superb, the surroundings intimate and the cuisine sublime at **The 1785 Inn**. The restaurant, a pretty, glassed-in porch that scans a broad mountain range, resides in a venerable 18th-century inn. French dishes are served with flair and understated elegance and include appetizers like lobster crepe and entrées like raspberry duckling and shrimp and scallop Provençal. Dinner only for general public. ~ Route 16, North Conway; 603-356-9025, 800-421-1785, fax 603-356-6081; www.the1785inn.com, e-mail the1785inn@aol.com. MODERATE TO DELUXE.

GET IN HERE!

Mount Washington Valley's premier noshing post is **Horsefeathers**, a downtown pub with awnings that command "Get in Here!" There is an extensive menu with a focus on Continental and regional dishes that changes twice a year. Items may include pan-blackened salmon and New England lobster pie, as well as basic burgers, steaks and munchies. But the main reason you go here is to see and be seen. Get there early—lines are known to form at the drop of a "feather." ~ Main Street, North Conway; 603-356-2687, fax 603-356-9368; www.horsefeathers.com, e-mail info@horsefeathers.com. MODERATE.

Small gas lanterns flicker on linen tablecloths and beautiful valanced draperies hover across walls at the **Christmas Farm Inn.** The romantic mountain hideout purveys New England cuisine with a twist—exceptional dishes such as grilled rack of lamb with rosemary glaze, filet mignon, and honey soy glazed salmon. For breakfast, there are waffles with bananas in yogurt cream and corned beef hash. No lunch. ~ Route 16B, Jackson; 603-383-4313, 800-443-5837, fax 603-383-6495; www.christmasfarminn.com, e-mail info@christmasfarminn.com. MODERATE TO DELUXE.

SHOPPING

Conway and North Conway extend endless shopping opportunities. Quaint, eclectic marts line Main Street in North Conway, while Route 16 between the two towns is shoulder-to-shoulder with factory outlets and novelty stores.

North Country Angler will accommodate all your flyfishing needs. This is also your spot for expert local advice, as well as guided flyfishing trips. Closed Monday from mid-October to mid-April. ~ 2888 White Mountain Highway, North Conway; 603-356-6000; www.northcountryangler.com, e-mail angler@ncia.net.

If it's nippy out, drop by **Jack Frost** for earmuffs, colorful sweaters and skiwear. ~ Main Street, Jackson; 603-383-4391; www.jackfrostshop.com.

NIGHTLIFE

The **North Country Center for the Arts,** located in a partially rehabbed 1800s paper mill, presents musicals and children's theater in the summer. ~ Route 112, Lincoln; 603-745-2141; www.papermilltheatre.org.

The Red Parka Steakhouse & Pub is a wildly popular après-ski bar and restaurant that hosts rock bands that keep things cranking. Live music is featured on Thursday, Friday and Saturday. Monday is open-mic night. ~ Route 302, Glen; 603-383-4344; www.redparkapub.com, e-mail info@redparkapub.com.

Horsefeathers wins hands-down as the hippest mountain restaurant and neighborhood pub, a genuine rooting place with sports decor, crazy bartenders and a rough pine bar where patrons stand three deep. Live bands play soft rock, blues and jazz Friday and Saturday in the Up Bar, the upstairs watering hole. ~ Main Street, North Conway; 603-356-2687; www.horsefeathers.com, e-mail info@horsefeathers.com.

Looking like a low-slung barn, **Up Country Family Restaurant and Tavern** jams with live cover music from the '70s to '90s and mixes Tiffany lamps and greenery with a shuffle board table, pool table and a rambling oak bar. Thursday is karaoke night; live deejays on Friday and Saturday. Occasional cover. ~ Route 16, North Conway; 603-356-3336; www.upcountryrestaurant.com, e-mail upcountryrestaurant@adelphia.net.

BEACHES & PARKS

WHITE MOUNTAIN NATIONAL FOREST A colossal land mass draped across northern New Hampshire, the forest is New England's largest piece of public land and one of the country's most popular forests. It's so all-encompassing that you soon realize it *is* much of New Hampshire. Its 800,000 acres (45,000 lie in Maine) include several state parks and 1200 miles of hiking trails, 50 lakes and ponds, 750 miles of fishing streams and 23 campgrounds. Most of the Northeast's highest peaks call this forest home, as do whitetail deer, black bear, moose, beaver and a host of other wildlife. There are endless possibilities for trout, bass, perch and pickerel in ponds, lakes and streams. Some of the best are Basin, Russell, Sawyer and Long ponds. Hiking trails, including part of the Appalachian Trail, are scattered throughout the forest. Picnic areas are found throughout. Parking fee, $3 per vehicle. ~ The national forest stretches more or less from Percy southward to Rumney, and from Benton eastward into Maine. Several main routes cut through, including Routes 93/3, 302, 16 and 112 (Kancamagus Highway); 603-528-8721, fax 603-528-8783.

▲ Permitted in 23 campgrounds, including tent and trailer camps (no hookups); RVs can go into many of the sites. Fees range from $16 to $20 per night. Reservations: 877-444-6777.

FRANCONIA NOTCH STATE PARK This is the flagship of New Hampshire parks, the one that everyone raves about. A truly incredible place, Franconia blankets 6500 acres, hosts more than 2 million visitors a year and boasts a dizzying array of natural and manmade wonders that make it seem like the Disney World of parklands. Flanked by rocky peaks and riddled with rivers and lakes, the park encompasses the Cannon Mountain ski area and tramway, an intriguing rock pool called the Basin, a minicanyon known as the Flume, and the Old Man of the Mountain Museum. Then there are sandy beaches, miles of hiking trails, swimming and fishing (especially in Echo Lake; canoe and paddleboat rentals are available), beautiful fern grottos and some of the finest bike paths in New Hampshire. The best advice here? Plan to spend some time. (For more information, see the "White Mountains Region" sightseeing section in this chapter.) There are picnic areas, restrooms, a bathhouse, cafeterias, snack bars and the New England Ski Museum. ~ Located north of North Woodstock. Access all sights from Franconia Notch Parkway, which is also Route 93 for the eight-mile length of the park; 603-823-8800, fax 603-823-8088.

▲ Lafayette Campground (603-823-9513) has 97 sites, most accommodating RVs (no hookups), and includes showers; $19 per night. There are seven full hookups at Cannon Mountain

State RV Park (603-823-8800); $29 per night. Facilities are closed Columbus Day to mid-May.

CRAWFORD NOTCH STATE PARK A rugged mountain pass navigates some of the most untamed forest and rocks in New Hampshire. It forms a six-mile shear through the U-shaped Saco River Valley and harbors numerous ponds, trails and cascades, including Arethusa Falls, the highest in the state. Several log cabins commemorate the Willey Family, some of the area's first settlers who were killed in 1826 while fleeing a horrible landslide. Picnic areas, restrooms, a visitors center, a gift shop and a snack bar are available. Closed mid-October to mid-May. ~ Along Route 302, eight miles north of Bartlett; 603-374-2272.

▲ Dry River Campground features 36 tent sites (a few take RVs); $13 per night. Closed mid-October to mid-May. Reservations: 603-271-3628.

MOUNT WASHINGTON STATE PARK This 59-acre park wraps around the hood of Mount Washington, the highest peak in the northeastern United States. The summit—some 6288 feet up—tingles the spine as you peer across a cosmos of mountains and forests that seem to fall off the horizon. The mountain itself has long been the subject of curiosity and wonder. Its sometimes freakish weather can change from toasty to blizzard-like (or vice versa) in a matter of minutes, and its plant life is an unusual mix of sparse lichens, shrubs and rare wildflowers. You'll find more on this uncanny butte at the Mount Washington Museum (admission), parked right on the treeless, rocky crest. Amenities here include restrooms, a snack bar, a museum, a gift shop and a post office. Closed mid-October to early May. ~ On Route 16 in Pinkham Notch, off Route 302 southeast of Crawford Notch; 603-466-3347, fax 603-466-2705.

Back in 1934, Mount Washington endured the highest wind velocity (231 miles per hour) ever recorded on earth.

COLEMAN STATE PARK It's safe to say that this place is virtually at the end of the planet. Purists will find the surroundings heady stuff, a coalition of thick timbers, broad mountains and sparkling lakes. Much of the activity (though there's really not much) centers around Little Diamond Pond, sprinkled with small fishing boats and surrounded by rolling hills. You'll find a picnic area and a recreation building. The day-use area is open from Memorial Day to Labor Day. ~ From Route 26 in Kidderville, take Diamond Pond Road north into the park; 603-237-5382 or 603-538-6707.

◄ HIDDEN

▲ Permitted in 30 sites (most take RVs; no hookups); $18 per night. Self-service camping available during the off-season. Reservations: 603-271-3628.

Outdoor Adventures

SKIING

Downhill and cross-country skiing are pursued with a vengeance in New Hampshire. Ski centers are sprinkled along highways and a few rural roads, while backwoods trails exist everywhere. The length of the skiing season varies from December to April depending on the altitude.

For ski information, write to the **New Hampshire Office of Travel and Tourism.** A wintertime report on current ski conditions can be obtained by calling 800-887-5464. ~ 172 Pembroke Road, Box 1856, Concord, NH 03302; 603-271-2665, 800-386-4664; www.visitnh.gov.

SEACOAST Though the region has no downhill facilities, you can ski through the countryside along the eastern corridor. One of the best (and least-known) cross-country spots is **Applecrest Farm Orchards**, where 8 kilometers of trails cut through hills of apple orchards. ~ Route 88, Hampton Falls; 603-926-3721; www.applecrest.com.

HIDDEN ►

MERRIMACK VALLEY **Pats Peak**, just outside Concord, is the largest downhill ski facility in the valley. They offer 22 trails (40 percent are beginner runs) and a 710-foot vertical drop. There's also a snowboard park. ~ Off Route 114, Henniker; 603-428-3245; www.patspeak.com. **Nashoba Valley Ski Area** has 17 trails and the largest snow tubing park in New England. Closed April through November. ~ 79 Powers Road, Westford; (978) 692-3033; www.skinashoba.com

MONADNOCK REGION **Crotched Mountain** has 17 trails through 75 acres with wide slopes and glades that run on a 875-vertical drop. Closed from late March to mid-November. ~ 615 Francestown Road, Bennington; 603- 588-3668; www.crotchedmountain.com.

LAKE SUNAPEE–DARTMOUTH AREA **Mount Sunapee Resort** has 60 downhill trails and a 1510-foot drop. Its snowboard park has a half-pipe. ~ Route 103, Newbury; 603-763-2356; www.mtsunapee.com, e-mail info@mtsunapee.com. **Eastman Cross Country Center** has nine Nordic trails totaling 36 kilometers. ~ Off Exit 13 at Routes 89 and 10, Grantham; 603-863-6772, 603-863-4500 (winter); www.eastmannh.com. **Norsk Touring Center** has more than 40 kilometers of trails. Guided moonlight tours are available. ~ Fairway Lane, off Route 11, New London; www.skinorsk.com.

LAKES REGION **Gunstock** features 46 trails, a 1400-foot vertical drop, a tubing park, and 50 kilometers of cross-country skiing. ~ Route 11A, Gilford; 603-293-4341; www.gunstock.com. **Nordic Skier** has 30 kilometers of trails. Lessons are available. ~ 47 North Main Street, Wolfeboro; 603-569-3151; www.wolfeboroxc.org; e-mail info@wolfeboroxc.org.

WHITE MOUNTAINS REGION Five of the largest downhill ski centers run along the spine of Route 93. The **Waterville Valley Ski Area** has 52 trails served by 11 lifts. For snowboarders, there's a half-pipe on the Exhibition run. Cross-country skiers can choose between 70 kilometers of groomed and tracked trails or 35 kilometers of backcountry trails. ~ 1 Ski Area Road off Route 49, Waterville Valley; 603-236-8311; www.waterville.com. **Loon Mountain**'s ten lifts serve 280 acres with 44 trails, nearly two-thirds rated intermediate. A 15-acre snowboard park sports a half-pipe. Cross-country skiers can trek on 35 kilometers of groomed trails. ~ Kancamagus Highway, Lincoln; 603-745-8111, 800-229-5666; www.loonmtn.com. In Franconia Notch State Park, **Cannon Mountain** has six lifts and 40 runs, with the range of difficulty divided equally between beginner, intermediate and expert. ~ Route 93; 603-823-7771; www.cannonmt.com. **Bretton Woods** offers some good slopes; nine lifts serve 66 trails. Also here are 100 kilometers of Nordic trails and a snowpark for boarders. ~ Route 302, Bretton Woods; 877-873-0626; www.brettonwoods.com.

FISHING

Aficionados of both saltwater and freshwater fishing will find a bounty of opportunities in New Hampshire. Since lakes and ponds in this area freeze over in the winter, the best time for freshwater fishing is from April to October. Many tour companies only offer their services during these months; it is best to call ahead.

SEACOAST Deep-sea fishing charters are offered by **Eastman's Fishing Fleet and Whale Watching.** Excursions to Jeffrey's Ledge will likely reel in cod and haddock. Closed November through March. ~ River Road, Seabrook Beach; 603-474-3461; www.eastmansdocks.com. **Al Gauron Deep Sea Fishing** provides half- and full-day charters. Closed November through March. ~ Hampton Beach State Pier on Ocean Boulevard, Hampton Beach; 603-926-2469, 800-905-7820; www.algauron.com. **Smith & Gilmore Fishing Pier**'s two-hour, half- and full-day trips angle for pollock, striped bass, cod, mackerel and bluefish. ~ P.O. Box 2353, Hampton, State Pier; 603-926-3503; www.smithandgil

AUTHOR FAVORITE

I love the desolate solitude of cross-country skiing. Way up in the northern wilderness, the **BALSAMS Wilderness** is one such marvelous setting with 5 lifts, 16 runs and a 1000-foot vertical drop. There are also more than 95 kilometers of cross-country trails. ~ Route 26, Dixville Notch; 603-255-3951, 800-255-0600 , fax 603-255-3952; www.thebalsams.com.

more.com. In Rye Harbor, **Atlantic Fishing & Whale Watching** offers half- and full-day trips aboard an 80-foot boat. Closed Columbus Day to mid-April. ~ Route 1A, Rye; 603-964-5220, 800-942-5364; www.atlanticwhalewatch.com.

Fishing fans will be happy in New Hampshire. Angle for pollack, cod, mackerel and bluefish off the seacoast, or for trout, salmon, cusk, perch and bass in one of hundreds of ponds and lakes.

LAKES REGION **Landlocked Fishing Guide Service** books five-hour-long trips on Lake Winnipesaukee and at other prime fishing spots. Closed October through March. ~ Lake Winnipesaukee, Center Harbor; 603-253-6119; www.rickforge.com. Fish for landlocked Atlantic salmon, rainbow trout and lake trout with **YOAdrien Fishing Charters** ~ Lake Winnipesaukee; 603-785-6660; www.yoadriencharters.com.

BOATING

LAKES REGION In Laconia, **Winni Sailboarders' School** rents boats of all varieties and offer instruction in windsurfing and kayaking. Open weekends only. ~ 687 Union Avenue; 603-528-4110. **Fay's Boat Yard** rents boats from May to October. ~ 71 Varney Point Road, Gilford; 603-293-8000; www.faysboatyard.com. In Weirs Beach, there's **Thurston's Marina**, where you can rent boats from May through September. Closed Tuesday. ~ Route 3; 603-366-4811; www.thurstonsmarina.com.

WHALE WATCHING

Humpbacks, finbacks, minke and other Atlantic whales are known to put on quite a show. In Hampton Beach, **Al Gauron Deep Sea Fishing** provides half- and full-day trips. Closed November through March. ~ Hampton Beach State Pier, Ocean Boulevard; 603-926-2469, 800-905-7820; www.algauron.com. In Rye Harbor, **Granite State Whale Watch** offers expeditions from May to the end of September. ~ Route 1A; 603-964-5545; www.whales-rye.com.

GOLF

Golf enthusiasts will happily take to New Hampshire's scenic greens. In general, depending on the weather, courses shut down from mid-November to mid-April. Most rent clubs and carts.

SEACOAST Visit **Sagamore Hampton Golf Club**, a walking course with 18 holes that is open to the public. ~ 101 North Road, North Hampton; 603-964-5341; www.sagamorehampton.com.

MERRIMACK VALLEY The **Derryfield Country Club**'s terrain ranges from a hilly front nine to a flat back nine on a municipal course. ~ 625 Mammoth Road, Manchester; 603-669-0235; www.derryfieldgolf.com. Or you can tee off at **Passaconaway Country Club**, a public 18-hole course that is flat and very lengthy. There's a putting green. ~ 12 Midway Avenue, Litchfield; 603-424-4653.

MONADNOCK REGION Try **Bretwood Golf Course**, with two 18-hole public courses. ~ East Surry Road, Keene; 603-352-7626; www.bretwoodgolf.com.

LAKE SUNAPEE–DARTMOUTH AREA The Sugar River meanders through the 18-hole **Newport Golf Club.** ~ Unity Road, off Route 11, Newport; 603-863-7787; www.newport-golf.com.

LAKES REGION Enjoy the scenic views of the White Mountains and Red Hill as you putt your way though the semiprivate 18-hole **Waukewan Golf Club.** ~ Waukewan Road, West Center Harbor; 603-279-6661; www.waukewan.com.

WHITE MOUNTAINS REGION Surrounded by the White Mountains, **Waterville Valley Golf Club** has nine holes open to the public. ~ Route 49, Waterville Valley; 603-236-4805. In Bretton Woods, **Mount Washington Hotel and Resort** offers a nine-hole and an 18-hole course, both with spectacular views of Mt. Washington. There's also a driving range. ~ Route 302; 603-278-1000.

TENNIS

SEACOAST You'll find seven outdoor public courts at **Exeter Recreation Park.** Lessons are available. ~ The park is on Hampton Road, Exeter; 603-778-0591. Public courts in Portsmouth are on the **South Mill Pond.** ~ Junkins Avenue.

MERRIMACK VALLEY **Memorial Field** has ten outdoor public courts. ~ South Fruit Street, Concord; 603-225-8690.

MONADNOCK REGION **Wheelock Park**'s two outdoor courts are lighted. ~ Park Avenue, Keene; 603-357-9829.

LAKE SUNAPEE–DARTMOUTH AREA **Dartmouth College Athletic Complex** offers indoor and outdoor courts. The outdoor courts are free, while the indoor courts cost $17 for non-students. During the indoor months, you may want to call ahead for a reservation. ~ Wheelock and South Park streets, Hanover; 603-646-1387.

LAKES REGION Try one of the public courts at **Prescott Park.** ~ Route 3, Meredith; 603-279-8197. **Moultonboro Tennis Courts** has four courts available to the public. ~ Playground Drive, Moultonboro; 603-476-8868.

WHITE MOUNTAINS REGION Enjoy a view of the White Mountains while playing outdoors in one of **Waterville Valley Tennis Court's** 18 red clay courts. Fee. ~ Route 49, Waterville Valley; 603 236-4840; www.wvtennis.com. Play on one of 18 outdoor clay courts during the summer, or two indoor hardtop courts during winter at **White Mountain Athletic Club.** Reservations are recommended for the indoor courts. Lessons are available. Fee. ~ Route 49, Waterville Valley; 603-236-8303; www.wmacwv.com.

RIDING STABLES

What better way to take in New Hampshire scenery than on horseback?

MERRIMACK VALLEY The trail rides at the **Wingedspur Farm** take you along country roads where you may catch a glimpse of moose or deer. Highlights include Bear Brook Reservation. Lessons are offered, and there are day camps. ~ 24 Currier Road, Candia; 603-483-5960. **Cobble Mountain Stables** offers guided horseback tours through scenic woodlands; you'll see plenty of wildlife. Open mid-June to mid-October. ~ Route 11A, Gilford; 603-293-4341; 800-486-78625, ext. 153; www.cobblemountain stables.com.

WHITE MOUNTAINS REGION **The Stables at the Farm By the River** leads one-hour guided tours through 70 acres located in the Mount Washington Valley year round. Children's pony rides, sleigh and carriage rides are also available. Reservations are strongly recommended. ~ 2555 West Side Road, North Conway; 603-356-6640. **Mount Washington Hotel and Resort Stables** offers trail rides over the cross-country ski trails at the base of Mount Washington. Closed late October to May. ~ Route 302, Bretton Woods; 603-278-1000; www.mtwashington.com.

BIKING

This state of grand mountains, vast lakes and rocky coastline is truly a bicyclist's nirvana.

SEACOAST One of the most popular routes in all New Hampshire, the 18-mile **Atlantic Shoreline** wends along the rugged seacoast on Route 1A from Massachusetts to Portsmouth. Caution: during summer months, traffic is extremely heavy.

> Seven miles of bikeable rolling hills and apple orchards await along Route 88 between Exeter and Hampton Falls.

MERRIMACK VALLEY The 34-mile trek from **Milford to Concord** along Route 13 is lined with old red barns, rivers and streams, and superb vistas.

MONADNOCK REGION For a picturesque, less-traveled odyssey, take Route 149 from **South Weare to Hillsboro.** The 12-mile excursion slices through archetypical New England villages and rambling farmlands.

LAKES REGION With its gorgeous water and mountain views, the 62-mile loop around **Lake Winnipesaukee** is a favorite among bicyclists. The terrain varies from flat to very hilly, and roads can be congested in the summer. Stick to Routes 28, 109, 25B and 11.

WHITE MOUNTAINS REGION The strong at heart will opt for a very steep 10-mile journey on Hurricane Mountain Road from **North Conway to the Maine Border**. An easier mountain route that's just as scenic, Route 16 and Side Road follow the Androscoggin River for 29 miles from **Errol to Berlin**.

Bike Rentals Because of high liability insurance rates, bike rental centers are scarce across New Hampshire. A full-service shop, **Piche's** rents mountain and road bikes in the Lakes Region. ~ 318 Gilford Avenue, Gilford; 603-524-2068; www.piches.com. The **Adventure Center** rents, sells and services bikes. Closed Columbus Day to Memorial Day. ~ Town Square, Waterville Valley;

603-236-4666, 800-468-2553; www.waterville.com. In Lincoln, call **Loon Mountain Bike Center**, which rents, sells and services bikes. Shuttle service to Franconia Notch is available; there you can take a self-guided bike tour and see refreshing waterfalls. Closed mid-October to mid-May. ~ Kancamagus Highway (Route 112); 603-745-8111, 800-229-5666; www.loonmtn.com.

HIKING

New Hampshire's vast timberlands and lakes, wide mountains and ravines make it a hiker's haven. For information on many of the state's trails, contact the **White Mountain National Forest.** ~ 719 Main Street, Laconia, NH 03246; 603-528-8721.

The Appalachian Mountain Club's **White Mountain Guide**, considered the hiker's bible, is available through the club. ~ Box 298, Gorham, NH 03581; 603-466-2721, 800-262-4455; www.outdoors.org. For inn-to-inn hikes and treks through Franconia Notch and Mount Washington, get in touch with **New England Hiking Holidays.** Tours are available from May through October. ~ P.O. Box 1648, North Conway, NH 03860; 603-356-9696, 800-869-0949; www.nehikingholidays.com.

The weather here can be highly unpredictable: you should always carry a flashlight and food essentials. Weather and trail conditions can be checked easily by calling parks ahead of time.

All distances listed for hiking trails are one way unless otherwise noted.

SEACOAST Though you won't scale any significant peaks along the coast, you can explore some very scenic footpaths. One of the best spots is **Odiorne Point State Park**, where trails wander along gentle shoreline, rocky beaches and stands of pines, oaks and wild roses.

A few miles inland, the **University of New Hampshire's College Woods** offers a labyrinth of nature trails that crisscross more than 200 thickly forested acres. There's also the **College Brook Ravine** trail (1 mile), which follows a brook through a 15-acre ravine and offers peeks at 155 species of plants.

MERRIMACK VALLEY The **Uncanoonuc Mountain Trail** (.75 mile) cuts through a stone wall and hemlock forest and passes a small cave on the way to the summit, where views of Manchester await. To find the rather obscure trailhead, take Route 114 east from Goffstown to Mountain Road. Go south for a mile, then bear left for a mile and a half.

MONADNOCK REGION Isolated Mount Monadnock, often called "the world's most-hiked mountain," offers more than a dozen trails with all levels of difficulty. For detailed information, stop by the visitors center (off Route 124, four miles west of Jaffrey). **White Arrow Trail** (1 mile), one of the mountain's oldest footpaths, ambles across brooks, ledges and narrow gullies to the summit. It commences at the end of the mountain toll road.

Pumpelly Trail (4.5 miles) zigzags up Monadnock, following a ridge and passing a huge rectangular boulder and several glacial carvings. The trailhead starts on Old Marlboro Road off Route 101, just west of Dublin.

Hikers took the **Marlboro Trail** (2 miles) as early as 1850, tackling the steep nose of Monadnock's ridges to open ledges. Start on the dirt road located off Route 124, west of Monadnock State Park.

The popular **White Dot Trail** (2 miles), a steep and rocky course, is the most direct route to the summit.

Wapack Trail (21 miles) is a popular skyline trek along the Wapack Range, running from Watatic Mountain in Ashburnham, Massachusetts, across the Pack Monadnocks in New Hampshire. With many open ledges and beautiful views, it navigates a large spruce forest.

LAKE SUNAPEE–DARTMOUTH AREA The **Monadnock-Sunapee Greenway** (49 miles) crawls across ridgetops between Mounts Monadnock and Sunapee. You can also scale **Mount Sunapee** via its ski slopes (2 miles), which plow through heavy forests to gorgeous, secluded Lake Solitude and then go on to the summit.

LAKES REGION With its marvelous union of mountains and water, the Lakes Region provides some of the most scenic hiking in New Hampshire. On the north end of Squam Lake, a pair of low-lying mountains called the Rattlesnakes feature easy treks with unparalleled views.

Old Bridle Path (.9 mile), off Route 113 near Center Sandwich, meanders along an old cart road to the summit of West Rattlesnake. **Ridge Trail** (1 mile) connects East and West Rattlesnakes, beginning northeast of the cliffs on the western mountain.

In the Red Hill area of Squam Lake, **Eagle Cliff Trail** (2.5 miles) ambles through a thicket and dense woods, scales the steep cliff and ends at the fire tower for great views from Red Hill. The trailhead is in Sandwich on Square Lake Road (which is called Bean Road in Center Harbor). Four-tenths of a mile past the Sandwich–Moultonboro line you'll come to a "Traffic Turning and Entering" sign. The trailhead is across the street from the sign. For a comprehensive $6 trail guide of Squam Lake, contact the Squam Lakes Association. ~ 603-968-7336, fax 603-968-7444; www.squamlakes.org, e-mail info@squamlakes.org.

For excellent vistas of Lake Winnipesaukee, try the **Mount Shaw Trail** (3.5 miles), which travels through a hemlock forest and past several streams and brooks to an open knob. It starts at a dirt road on the north side of Route 171 west of Tuftonboro.

East Gilford Trail (2.1 miles) begins on Wood Road off Route 11A, climbs Belknap Mountain and affords several fine outlooks over Lake Winnipesaukee.

WHITE MOUNTAINS REGION Spectacular hiking is found everywhere in the White Mountains Region.

Offering splendid scenery, **Welch Dickey Loop Trail** (4.5 miles) follows rock outcroppings and gives you the feeling that you're above the timberline. The trailhead is beside the Mad River on Orris Road, off Upper Mad River Road from Route 49.

Forests cover 84 percent of New Hampshire, and the White Mountain National Forest alone has over 1200 miles of trails.

Along the beautiful Kancamagus Highway near Conway, you'll find **Boulder Loop Trail** (2.8 miles), a gradual climb with panoramas of Mount Chocorua and the Swift River Valley. The easy **Sabbaday Falls Trail** (.4 mile), a spur path off the **Sabbaday Brook Trail** (4.9 miles), wanders to a series of cascades in a narrow chasm. The Brook Trail offers easy grades, numerous brook crossings and views of the falls.

The Franconia Notch area is a maze of trails for all hiking levels. The more experienced hiker should check out the **Falling Waters Trail** (3.2 miles), which navigates lovely cascades and brooks, shady glens and narrow gorges, and offers great vistas of the notch. It starts at Lafayette Place.

The **Whitehouse Trail** (.8 mile) connects to the **Pemi Trail** (6 miles), which winds along the Pemigewasset River, making a nice trek through Franconia Notch State Park. Pick up the trail at the Flume Visitors Center.

Bald Mountain–Artists Bluff Trail (.8 mile) makes a panoramic loop in the notch, starting at Peabody Base on Route 18. Nestled in the mountains, **Lonesome Lake Trail** (1.6 miles) offers commanding views of surrounding peaks. It commences at the Lafayette Campground off Route 93.

Often overlooked, **Cascade Brook Trail** (5 miles) is a stroll through verdant foliage along Cascade Brook. The trail begins at the Whitehouse Bridge in Franconia Notch State Park and ends at the Kingsman Pond Shelter.

One of the state's most popular hikes, **Tuckerman Ravine Trail** (2.3 miles) is a rugged cirque with bare slopes and sheer cliffs on Mount Washington. A moderately difficult path, it starts at the Appalachian Mountain Club's Pinkham Notch Camp on Route 16.

Thompson Falls Trail (.8 mile) clambers up the south side of Wildcat Brook to cascades and views of the Presidential mountain range. The trailhead starts at Wildcat Ski Area on Route 16.

Transportation

CAR

The fastest means of road travel are the interstate highways. **Route 93** scoots up the north–south center of the state, while **Route 95** cuts in from Massachusetts, follows the seacoast, then heads out into southern Maine.

On the west corridor, **Route 91** actually lies in Vermont but is used by many New Hampshire drivers as a major north–south artery.

There's no quick way to reach the state's northern wilderness, but **Route 16** and **Route 3** will take you there while skirting some spectacular scenery.

AIR

New Hampshire's air traffic flows through **Manchester Airport**, a small but quite convenient facility in Manchester. Several major carriers provide service, including Air Canada, Continental Airlines, Delta Air Lines, Northwest Airlines, Southwest Airlines, United Airlines and US Airways. ~ 603-324-6539; www.flymanchester.com.

Boston's **Logan International Airport**, about 30 miles from New Hampshire's seacoast, is also a major air gateway for the state (see Chapter Four).

Satisfaction Transportation transports passengers from Logan to most points in southern New Hampshire, including Nashua, Merrimack and Manchester. ~ 603-881-3724, 800-252-7754; www.satisfactiontrans.com.

BUS

Concord Trailways operates a broad network across New Hampshire. Buses start from Boston's Logan Airport and stop in Manchester, Concord and smaller towns as far north as Littleton. ~ 603-228-3300, 800-639-3317; www.concordtrailways.com, e-mail info@concordtrailways.com.

TRAIN

Train travel is practically nonexistent here, though **Amtrak** does provide service to Vermont's White River Junction and Bellows Falls, along New Hampshire's western border. The trains make direct routes from Washington, D.C., New York and Montreal. ~ 800-872-7245; www.amtrak.com.

CAR RENTALS

Arriving at Manchester Airport, you'll find the following rental companies: **Avis Rent A Car** (800-831-2847), **Budget Rent A Car** (800-527-0700), **Dollar Rent A Car** (800-800-4000), **Hertz Rent A Car** (800-654-3131), **National Car Rental** (800-227-7368) and **Thrifty Car Rental** (800-367-2277).

TEN

Maine

Mention you're going to Maine and you get all sorts of envious looks. People automatically envision the Andrew Wyeth landscapes, the pine-scented woods, the candy-striped lighthouses, the huge platters of lobster and baskets of steamers. Over the years, its name has practically become synonymous with the word "vacation." License plates even read "Vacationland." Indeed, visitors can find many opportunities to vacate cluttered lives in this spectacularly scenic New England state.

Maine has the Ice Age to thank for its smashingly good looks. Massive glaciers left over 6000 lakes and ponds and 32,000 miles of rivers and streams in their wake as well as the towering peaks of Cadillac Mountain and Mt. Katahdin (the latter stretches about a mile high). The coast is made up of a series of deeply cut indentations and narrow peninsulas and has more offshore islands than you can count. Measure the seaboard in a straight line and you come up with about 230 miles. Count every inch of shoreline and it's an amazing 3478 miles.

The state's name supposedly came from sailors' use of the term "main" for the mainland apart from the offshore islands. In later years, Maine was given the nickname "Pine Tree State" because nearly 90 percent of its land is covered with fragrant evergreens.

Maine's beauty, however, is not skin deep. The people who live here are really what make this state so special. Real Mainers—or State-of-Mainers as the most patriotic refer to themselves—are full of pride. They're also very individualistic and don't put on any airs. They are who they are, whether you like it or not. And they're tough. While carloads of tourists and summer residents pack up and head south at the end of the summer, they prepare for the long, cold winters ahead. Many Mainers also devotedly preserve the traditions of the past. You see crafts such as wooden boatbuilding, quilting and weaving still very much alive all over the state.

The biggest concentration of the population is clustered around the harbor-perched city of Portland, the state's commercial and cultural center. Established in 1624, Portland was destroyed four times: twice by the Indians in the 1600s, once by the British in 1775 and again by the great fire of 1866. Today the phoenix—the mythical Egyptian bird that rises from the ashes of destruction—is the city symbol.

A very progressive city, Portland has attracted people from across America as well as immigrants from Greece, Cambodia, Jamaica, Finland and a host of other countries. Maine's statewide residents are a mix of ethnicities as well. These include Abenaki Indians, whose ancestors can be traced back 2000 years, and Europeans, whose forefathers settled along the coast in the beginning of the 1600s.

Most historians believe that Maine was sighted by Vikings as early as the year 1000, but since no real evidence can be found, the credit for discovering the area has been passed along to others. It is believed that John Cabot saw the Maine coast on his second voyage to the New World in 1498, thereby establishing all future British claims to the land. However, the first European colony was established at the mouth of the St. Croix River in 1604 by French explorers Sieur de Monts, Pierre du Guast and Samuel de Champlain. The colony didn't last very long, however. In 1605, England's King James I included the area in the land grant given the Plymouth Colony.

The years that followed were marked by territorial struggles between the English, French and Indians. In spite of its bitterly cold winters, Maine had an abundance of natural assets to fight over, including dozens of deep-water harbors, timber-filled forests, navigable inland rivers and waters teeming with fish. The fighting eventually led to the 18th-century French and Indian Wars. After the British were victorious, what would be the State of Maine became a part of the Commonwealth of Massachusetts. Not until 1820 was Maine admitted to the union as a free state.

About 50 years later, word got out that Mount Desert Island and its then-sleepy little fishing village of Bar Harbor was an exceptionally beautiful place. Indeed, with its rock-hewn shores and sky-poking mountains, it's certainly spectacular. Before long, the island became an exclusive retreat for wealthy and powerful American families who came by steamboat and train. Folks with names like Rockefeller and Vanderbilt built sprawling summer "cottages" on bluffs overlooking the sea. They hired locals to staff these homes and the well-appointed yachts on which they hosted glamorous cocktail parties. By the turn of the 20th century, there were over 200 magnificent mansions on Mount Desert Island. Other areas along the coast south of Bar Harbor started to become popular summering spots as well, as trains brought in the moneyed people looking to build by the sea.

These golden years did pass, however, their demise brought by the Depression and World War II. But the final blow to Bar Harbor's days of grandeur came when a fire broke out in 1947 and burned over a third of Mount Desert Island, including nearly 70 of its estates. The island was eventually rebuilt but in a less-opulent fashion. Affordable motels and hotels sprouted like mushrooms after a rain, making the area much more accessible to average tourists.

Maine's coastal beauty is still what attracts most travelers today. Dozens of little fishing villages here burst with character. Some have gone a little overboard trying to attract tourists and are a bit too gussied up. If you're interested in seeing places that haven't sprung into tourist hubs, you have to be willing to go an extra yard. Follow the little roads that turn off like stray thoughts. They may take you to a tiny village on the sea. Consider taking a boat trip out to an island you've never heard of. And go north! The coast above Mount Desert Island is still largely undiscovered.

Text continued on page 578.

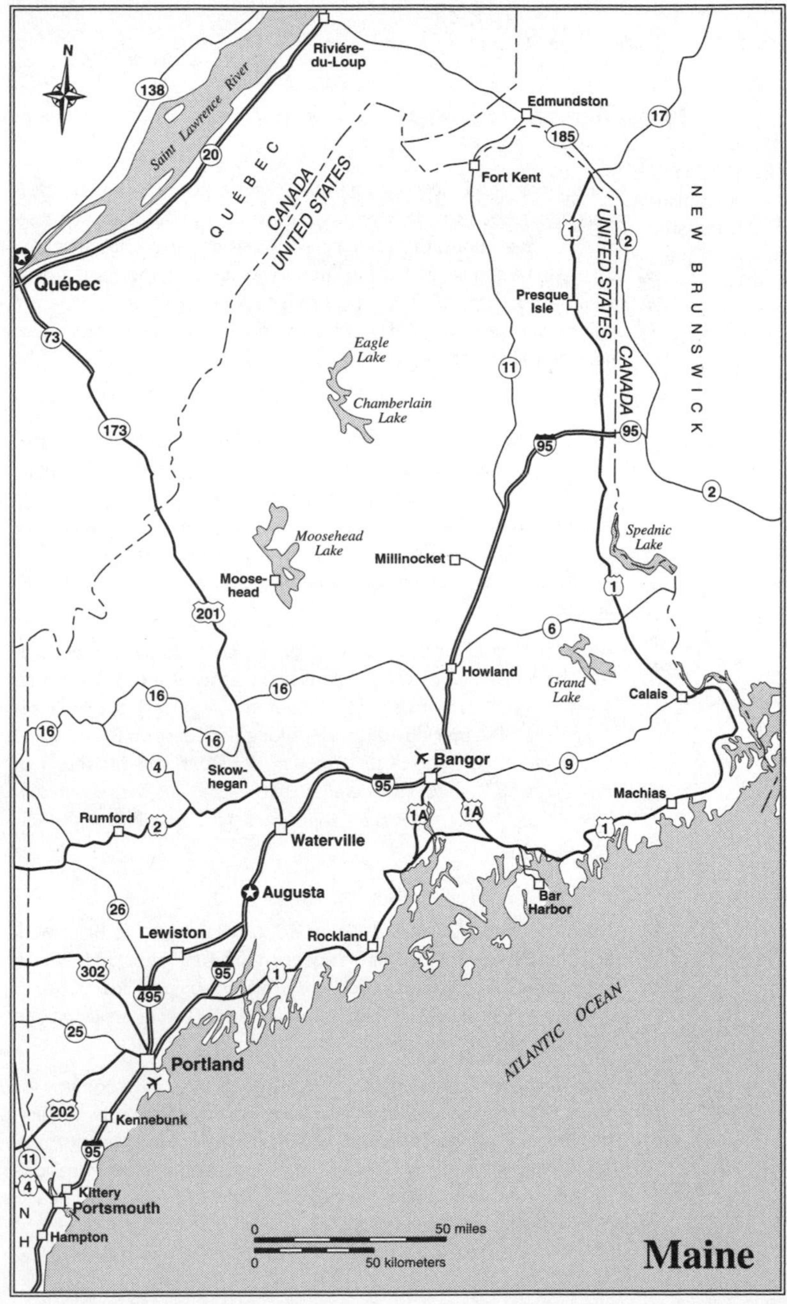
Maine
N
Rivière-du-Loup
Saint Lawrence River
QUÉBEC
CANADA
UNITED STATES
Edmundston
Fort Kent
Québec
NEW BRUNSWICK
Presque Isle
Eagle Lake
Chamberlain Lake
Moosehead Lake
Moose-head
Millinocket
Spednic Lake
Howland
Grand Lake
Calais
Skow-hegan
Bangor
Machias
Rumford
Waterville
Augusta
Bar Harbor
Lewiston
Rockland
Portland
ATLANTIC OCEAN
Kennebunk
Kittery
Portsmouth
Hampton
N H
0 50 miles
0 50 kilometers

Three-day Weekend

The *Maine Art Museum Trail*

Coastal Maine is a motorist's paradise, where Route 1 and countless small side roads provide access to more than 3000 miles of coastline. For generations, the scenery along this shoreline has attracted more painters than any other nonurban area of the East Coast, resulting in a rich artistic heritage to match its scenic beauty. You can explore both in a three-day weekend that connects Maine's seven major art museums.

Day 1

- Leaving Boston early, take Route 95 north for about 75 miles to the Maine state line and get off at Exit 1, just before the Main Turnpike toll booth. Follow coastal Route 1 north for eight miles to **Ogunquit**, one of America's first art colonies. Spend the morning at the **Ogunquit Museum of American Art** (page 580), which features paintings and sculptures by 20th- and 21st-century artists.
- After lunch in Ogunquit, continue up the coast to the city of Portland. It's a distance of about 50 miles on either Route 95 or Route 1 (which veers away from the coast on this segment), but you'll get a big dose of scenery by detouring along the coast on Route 9 and still arrive in Portland in time to visit the **Portland Museum of Art** (page 583), a five-story edifice that gives Maine native Winslow Homer top billing over such superstars as Degas, Monet, Renoir and Picasso.

Day 2

- From Portland, a 23-mile drive on Route 1 takes you to Brunswick and the **Bowdoin College Museum of Art** (page 584), which showcases Colonial and Federal portraits, including Gilbert Stuart's *Thomas Jefferson,* along with Roman and Greek artifacts and Winslow Homer memorabilia.
- From Brunswick, follow Route 196 inland through farm country for about 15 miles to Lewiston, Marsden Hartley's hometown. Here, the **Bates College Museum of Art** (page 585) features not only a generous sampling of Hartley's work but also an exceptional collection of contemporary works on paper with a focus on pencil, pen and charcoal drawings.

• Return to Brunswick the way you came. After lunch, rejoin Route 1 and drive north, crossing a number of inlets along 55 miles of the picturesque southern coast, to the touristy fishing village of Rockland and the **Farnsworth Art Museum and Wyeth Center** (page 587). One of the country's finest regional art museums, it has works by leading artists including the "first family" of Maine painting, with more than 4000 works by N.C., Andrew and Jamie Wyeth on rotating display.

Day 3 • From Rockland, drive 38 miles along the coast on Route 1. At Bucksport, turn north onto Route 1A and follow the Penobscot River for 27 miles to Bangor, where the **University of Maine Museum of Art** (page 588) has a 6000-piece collection of regional and international, classic and contemporary works.

• Returning south from Bangor on Route 95, a drive of 53 miles will bring you to Waterville, where the **Colby College Museum of Art** (page 588) has 13 galleries tracing the development of American art from the mid-18th century to the present. From here, the return trip to Boston takes about two and a half hours.

Bear in mind that Maine is enormous, so taking on a little piece at a time is all any visitor should do. We've broken it up into four areas, each of which might be seen in about a week's time. The coast is divided into two sections: the Southern Coast (between Kittery and Bucksport) and the Downeast Coast (from Castine to Calais). Maine's most visited area, the Southern Coast is well endowed with hotels, restaurants and other facilities geared for tourists. It's also home to some of the state's most beautiful beaches. Downeast Coast is not quite as busy and less developed, with the exception of Bar Harbor, an enormously popular vacation hub. This chapter follows Route 1 up the coast, taking you to the major tourist towns as well as the little-known villages and islands.

Our third section takes you through the northern woods, which Henry Thoreau praises endlessly in his book *The Maine Woods*. An area of unmatched wild beauty, it's home to the state's highest peak (Mt. Katahdin), the biggest state park (Baxter) and the largest lake (Moosehead). Its year-round residents include hearty-souled State of Mainers and a large black bear population, in addition to moose, bobcats and scores of birds.

Our final section—the western lakes and mountains—is an excursion to the White Mountains and the sprawling Indian-named lakes that are set in hills like precious gems. The woods that wrap around them teem with moose, deer and all sorts of songbirds. There are also several picture-perfect little villages crammed with antique and craft shops.

Like all the New England states, Maine has four distinctly different seasons. Summer—especially July and August—is the customary time to visit. That's when the bays swell with pleasure boats and towns open up like roses. Though the weather is predictably unpredictable (one day the harbor is bundled in mist, the next it's clear as a window), it's always lovely. Temperatures all over the state remain comfortable, hovering around 70° in the daytime. Nights, however, can get nippy, especially along the coast where the breezes off the sea can be chilling.

Some say autumn is the very best time to visit Maine. The summer-only residents have packed up and left. The partying vacationers are back at work and in school. The real full-time Mainers reappear. You're no longer one of many tourists but an appreciated guest. The weather is often phenomenally beautiful, with blue skies and sunshine. And, of course, you can see the fall colors. Spring, too, is appealing, as new life appears.

Winter brings on a whole array of snow-based activities, including great skiing, especially in the northern and western parts of the state. Maine's long and cold winters create a died-and-gone-to-heaven land for winter sports enthusiasts.

In this chapter, we introduce you to just some of Maine's attractions. In many ways, this is a very American state, but in others it feels almost like a foreign country. One visit and you'll inevitably feel compelled to return.

Southern Coast

Many people cross the New Hampshire border into the state of Maine expecting to find what they've always pictured: postcard fishing villages with salty characters, sprawling farms, pine forests. Well, dear readers, you have to look a little to find these pictures in southern Maine. What you are most likely to notice first along the Southern Coast—besides scores of factory outlets that line Route 1—is a profusion of hotels, motels, inns and every other kind of tourist accommodation conceivable, along with clam shacks and lobster joints broadcasting their low, low prices.

This is the gateway to the Vacation State. Just about everybody passes through the narrow southern tip on their way to the big tourist hubs like Boothbay Harbor and Mount Desert Island as well as the never-heard-of-before villages and hamlets that line the coast and lie scattered around the northern and western parts of the state. Interstate 95 can get you up north much faster, but we're going to take it slow, meandering up Route 1.

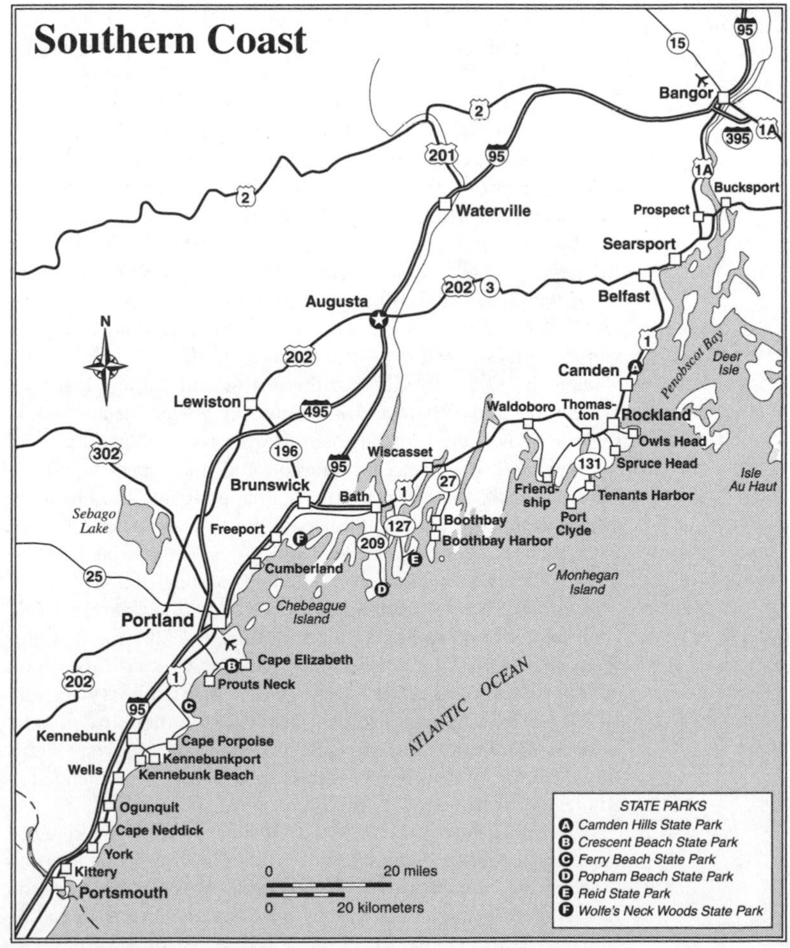

SIGHTS

Southern Maine has an abundance of something the rest of the state can envy—sandy beaches. In fact, even though Maine boasts nearly 3500 miles of coastline, sandy beaches skirt fewer than 100 of those miles, and the majority lie below Portland. They start almost immediately around Kittery, Maine's southernmost town. As you drive along Route 1, don't hesitate to detour along shore roads and Route 1A, which lead right by the beaches.

You can pull over at any time (why not, everybody else does—the traffic problem is part of the fun) to gaze out at the fury of the sea and the beach crowd. Beachgoers in this part of the world dress the gamut from string bikinis to down parkas and wool socks in August (the winds can really send chills racing through your body). If you want to take a swim, you can have your pick of beaches in Kittery, York, Cape Neddick, Ogunquit, Wells and other spots (see "Beaches & Parks" below).

Check out www.rideshare maine.org for comprehensive information on all your southern Maine transportation needs.

These southern towns are also rife with worthwhile attractions. In **Kittery**, you might want to take a look around the **Kittery Historical and Naval Museum**. It's filled with naval relics representing the earliest shipbuilding days through modern submarine construction at the Portsmouth Navel Shipyard nearby. Open June through Columbus Day. Call ahead for hours. Admission. ~ Route 1, just north of the Route 236 Rotary, Kittery; phone/fax 207-439-3080; e-mail kitterymuseum@netzero.net.

In **York**, 8 historic museum buildings have been nicely restored. Guides or self-guided tours take you through buildings including the **Old Schoolhouse**, the 18th-century **John Hancock Warehouse and Wharf** and the **Emerson–Wilcox House** (a tavern/family-dwelling-turned-general-store-turned-tailor-shop) and the oldest jail in Maine. Orientation and tours start at **Jefferds Tavern**, which houses the visitors center, on Route 1A. For more information, contact the Old York Historical Society. Closed Columbus Day to mid-June. Admission. ~ 207-363-4974, fax 207-363-4021; www.oldyork.org, e-mail oyhs@oldyork.org.

One of the more intriguing of York's historic sights, the **Old Gaol** first opened its doors and dungeons in 1720. Today a museum and part of the historic tour, the gaol gives visitors a look at its gruesome relics—cramped cells, the disciplinary pit and jailer's quarters. You'll also find displays of Indian and pioneer artifacts. Gaol breaks are recreated on Friday and Saturday nights July through August. Reservations are strongly recommended. ~ Route 1A, York Street; York.

Ogunquit, north of York, is named for an Abenaki word meaning "beautiful place by the sea." Set in a gorgeous location overlooking Narrow Cove, the **Ogunquit Museum of American Art** exhibits works by 19th- to 21st-century artists including Marsden Hartley, Edward Hopper and Walt Kuhn. Closed October through June. Admission. ~ 543 Shore Road, Ogunquit; 207-646-4909, fax 207-646-6903; www.ogunquitmuseum.org, e-mail ogunquitmuseum@aol.com.

If you can drag yourselves away from the beaches in **Wells,** you'll find good attractions for children. The **Wells Auto Museum** features over 80 antique cars are displayed along with antique music boxes and arcade games (precursors to today's video games). Closed late September to Memorial Day. Admission. ~ 1181 Post Route 1, Wells; 207-646-9064; e-mail wellsauto@aol.com.

Birdwatchers can log in some remarkable sightings at Wells' **Rachel Carson National Wildlife Refuge**. See the "Beaches & Parks" section below. ~ Off Route 9, Wells. Another public preserve is the **Wells National Estuarine Research Reserve,** which attracts both birdwatchers and hikers to its seven miles of trails. Day-use fee, $2 per adult year round. ~ 342 Laudholm Farm Road, off Route 1, Wells; 207-646-1555, fax 207-641-2036; www.wellsreserve.org.

Just north of Wells, you'll come to the Kennebunks—the commercial center of **Kennebunk** and the port town, **Kennebunkport**. Both towns were early shipbuilding and fishing settlements. The latter is now referred to as **Bush Country**, since it's home to the first President Bush's summer home. The little town itself is a bit too gussied up for tourists (with prices to match), but it's a worthwhile stop nonetheless. Consider putting the car in a lot for a good part of the day and picking up a copy of the *Strolling Through the Port*, the Kennebunkport walking guide, which is available at the **Kennebunkport Historical Society**. Closed Sunday and Monday from mid-June to Columbus Day; closed Saturday through Monday the rest of the year. ~ 125 North Street, Kennebunkport; 207-967-2751; www.kporthistory.org, e-mail kporths@gwi.net. The **Kennebunk–Kennebunkport Chamber of Commerce** will guide you to the best sights. Closed weekends. ~ Yellow House, 17 Western Avenue, Kennebunk; 207-967-0857, fax 207-967-2827; www.visitthekennebunks.com, e-mail info@visitthekennebunks.com.

Tom's of Maine is the pride of the state. For over 30 years, this family business has been making well-known natural bath and body care products. If you want to take a peek at how it's done, take a guided tour of the surprisingly small factory. The factory can get loud, however, and tours are not particularly recommended for young children. Tours available by appointment only. Seasonal hours vary, call ahead. ~ 302 Lafayette Center, Kennebunk; 207-985-2944, 800-367-8667, fax 207-985-2196; www.tomsofmaine.com, e-mail info@tomsofmaine.com. ◄ HIDDEN

In summer months, there are walking tours of Kennebunkport's historical area. They start at **Nott House**, a Greek Revival building that dates back to 1853. Closed mid-October to mid-June.

Closed Sunday and Monday. Admission. ~ 8 Maine Street, Kennebunkport; 207-967-2751. The **History Center of Kennebunkport**, home to the Kennebunkport Historical Society, offers more information and exhibits about Kennebunkport's history. Closed Sunday and Monday from mid-June to Columbus Day; closed Saturday through Monday the rest of the year. Admission. ~ 125 North Street, Kennebunkport; 207-967-2751; www.kporthistory.org, e-mail kporths@gwi.net.

If you want to get a glimpse of the former president's compound, take a drive along mansion-dotted **Ocean Avenue. Walker's Point** is the name of the Bush compound. It's a beautiful promontory surrounded by the horizonless waters of the Atlantic. The brown-shingled house is the centerpiece.

While you're in the neighborhood, you might want to stop at the **Seashore Trolley Museum.** Its comprehensive collection of antique electric trolley cars includes samples from around the world—Japan, Germany, New Zealand and Budapest. And visitors can hop aboard a trolly for a half-hour journey. Closed weekdays from May to mid-June and early October to November. Closed November through April. Admission. ~ Log Cabin Road, Kennebunkport; 207-967-2800, fax 207-967-0867; www.trolleymuseum.org.

Back inland, you can take an architectural walking tour of Kennebunk's **National Register District**. It includes **The Brick Store Museum,** located in a block of restored early-19th-century commercial buildings. Closed Sunday and Monday. Walking tours in summer by appointment. Admission. ~ 117 Main Street, Kennebunk; 207-985-4802, fax 207-985-6887; www.brickstoremuseum.org.

One of the most well-known attractions in southern Maine is the **Wedding Cake House**. As the name implies, it's a yellow house with intricate white latticework that looks like lace. A local sea captain fashioned his house after cathedrals he saw in Milan, Italy. The public is not welcome inside, however. ~ Summer Street, Kennebunk.

sights

AUTHOR FAVORITE

To glimpse a retail business that's dramatically different than the Freeport scene down the coast, pull off in Woolwich (just beyond Bath) at the **Montsweagg Flea Market**. One of the state's biggest flea markets, Montsweagg features nearly a hundred of dealers peddling everything from old postcards to used trailers. Even if you're not in the market for anything, it's worth stopping just for the shot of local color. Closed mid-October to mid-May. ~ Route 1, Woolwich; 207-443-2809; e-mail fleamarket@suscom-maine.net.

As you continue north from the Kennebunks, you can either pick up Route 1 (at Kennebunk) or opt for the more scenic Route 9 from Kennebunkport. The latter takes you past several sun-soaked beaches. When you reach the town of Scarborough, turn right onto Route 207, which leads to **Prouts Neck.** This oddly shaped peninsula juts into Saco Bay about eight miles south of Portland. Much of its coastal scenery—steep cliffs, swirling surf and dwarfish rock-clinging trees—can be seen on the canvases of American painter Winslow Homer, who lived and worked here. His studio, a converted stable overlooking the ocean, is open to the public, by appointment, for touring. There's also the **Prouts Neck Bird Sanctuary** at the tip, where all sorts of exotic birds have been spotted.

Portland, Maine's largest city, is the next stop. Often called "The Little San Francisco of the East," it's a lovely city of hills surrounded by water. Many of Portland's streets are lined with beautifully preserved Victorian buildings. Very progressive, the city boasts a horde of museums, galleries, shops and restaurants.

Five stories house works from the 18th century to the present at the **Portland Museum of Art.** Winslow Homer, Andrew Wyeth, Claude Monet, Pablo Picasso and Auguste Renoir are a few of the American and European artists represented here. Closed Monday from Columbus Day to Memorial Day. Admission. ~ 7 Congress Square; 207-775-6148, fax 207-773-7324; www.portlandmuseumofart.org, e-mail pma@maine.rr.com.

Just down the street is the **Wadsworth-Longfellow House,** where the poet spent his childhood. Guided tours available May through October. Call for winter hours. Closed January through April. Admission. ~ Congress Street, Portland; 207-774-1822, fax 207-775-4301; www.mainehistory.org, info@mainehistory.org.

One of the most interesting districts in the city is the **Old Port Exchange,** between Exchange and Pearl streets, on the waterfront. Here you'll see old brick and granite buildings that were erected during the early 19th century, when Portland was a major rail center and shipping port. Many now house restaurants, taverns and shops.

For exploring Portland's historic districts, consider stopping by the Portland Convention and Visitors Bureau's **Visitors Information Center.** Here you can pick up self-guided walking tours of the Old Port Exchange, **Congress Street** (Portland's most important commercial street since the early 1800s), **State Street** (a wealthy residential district with large Federal-style mansions) and the **Western Promenade** (a fascinating selection of architectural styles, including high Victorian Gothic, shingle-style and Italianate mansions). There are also guided tours of "Historic Portland" that leave from the same site (tours run July to mid-October). Admission. ~ 245 Commercial Street, Portland; 207-772-5800.

For a wonderful view of the city and island-dotted Casco Bay, climb the 103 steps up the **Portland Observatory**, the last remaining 19th-century marine signal tower in the United States, built in 1807. Guided tours run every half hour. Closed Columbus Day to Memorial Day. Admission. ~ 138 Congress Street, Portland; 207-774-5561, fax 207-774-2509; www.portlandlandmarks.org, e-mail info@portlandlandmarks.org.

For a seal's-eye view of the bay, take a guided boat tour from Commercial Street. You can contact **Casco Bay Lines**, the oldest continually operating ferry system in the United States. ~ Casco Bay Ferry Terminal, Commercial Street, Portland; 207-774-7871, fax 207-774-7875; www.cascobaylines.com, e-mail info@cascobaylines.com. **Bay View Cruises** operates tours from May to late October. Admission. ~ Fisherman's Wharf, 184 Commercial Street, Portland; 207-761-0496, fax 207-761-0118.

HIDDEN ►

For something completely different, spend a few days on **Chebeague Island.** One of the 365 Calendar Islands scattered across Casco Bay, Chebeague (pronounced "sha-BEEG") is a small forested island with only a few hundred hardy year-round residents. They earn their living from the sea or commute by ferry to the mainland and then on to Portland, which is approximately a half-hour's drive from the ferry parking area. Chebeague is a place for people who love to walk or bike along quiet roads. You can easily visit the island as a day trip. In Yarmouth, call **Chebeague Transportation Company**. ~ 207-846-3700; www.chebeaguetrans.com. In Portland, call **Casco Bay Lines**. ~ 207-774-7871.

About 20 miles north of Portland along Route 1 is the world-famous town of **Freeport**, home of the legendary **L. L. Bean**. The mall-like shop looks just like the catalogs: it's wall-to-wall camping gear, outdoor wear and sporting equipment. Aside from Bean's, the whole town has sprouted into a factory-outlet hub. You'll find all the big-name designers (Polo–Ralph Lauren, Calvin Klein, Laura Ashley) have set up shop here. This is definitely the place to come with your shopping lists. ~ Route 1, Freeport; 800-865-1212, 800-809-7057; www.llbean.com, www.freeportusa.com.

A few miles down the road, Brunswick is home to **Bowdoin College**, founded in 1794. Such luminaries as Nathaniel Hawthorne and Henry Wadsworth Longfellow have walked the halls of this venerable school. ~ College Street, Brunswick; 207-725-3000; www.bowdoin.edu.

The **Bowdoin College Museum of Art**, one of the most comprehensive collections in the state, is a must-see on campus. Thousands of objects hail from the ancient world to modern times. Highlights include Gilbert Stuart's portrait of Thomas Jefferson and the extensive Winslow Homer gallery. Though paintings predominate the offerings, you'll also find decorative arts, sculptures, miniatures and drawings. The Walker Art Building is undergoing renovations and is expected to reopen in fall 2007. Until then, selected exhibits may be viewed at the Bliss Room in Hubbard Hall. Closed Sunday and Monday. ~ Walker Art Building; 207-725-3275, fax 207-725-3762; www.bowdoin.edu/artmuseum, e-mail artmuseum@bowdoin.edu.

Bowdoin College is the spot where Harriet Beecher Stowe wrote *Uncle Tom's Cabin*, reportedly after seeing a vision.

If you take Route 196 inland from Brunswick, the highway will lead you to **Lewiston**, birthplace of Marsden Hartley and home to the **Bates College Museum of Art**. Hartley's works form the centerpiece of the museum's collection, which also features prints, photographs and paintings by contemporary artists. Closed Sunday and Monday. ~ 75 Russell Street, Lewiston; 207-786-6158, fax 207-786-8335; www.bates.edu/museum.xml.

Returning to Route 1, the next town along the coast is **Bath**, which holds in its borders a wealth of shipbuilding history. In the days of wooden ships, many of the world's seacraft came from Bath's shipyards. For a journey back to that era, stop by the **Maine Maritime Museum**. From June to October, visiting vessels are docked here and open to visitors. The museum's galleries and small shipyard are open year-round. A bookstore and gift shop is also on the premises. Admission. ~ 243 Washington Street, Bath; 207-443-1316, fax 207-443-1665; www.maritimemuseum.org, e-mail maritime@bathmaine.com.

Wiscasset is a very worthwhile stop as you travel north on Route 1. This lovely little village of sea captains' houses and beautifully maintained old brick buildings was a very prosperous shipping port between the years of the American Revolution and the War of 1812.

Musical Wonder House has a collection of over 5000 antique music boxes, Victrolas, player pianos, singing birdcages, musical porcelains, talking machines and advertising icons such as the RCA Victor dog. The museum, located in a 32-room sea captain's house, which boasts a flying staircase, is one of the authentic treasures of the Maine Coast. Don't miss it. Closed November to Memorial Day weekend. Admission. ~ 18 High Street, Wiscasset; 207-882-7163, fax 207-882-6373; www.musicalwonderhouse.com, e-mail music@musicalwonderhouse.com. ◄ HIDDEN

There's something incredibly lovable about the seaport of **Boothbay Harbor**, down a peninsula south of Wiscasset. Admittedly, it's about as overripe as a tourist town can be—and it's hit by around 500,000 visitors each summer. But Boothbay (which started life as a tiny lobstering and fishing town) definitely has a personality of its own.

If you've come to Maine for the serenity of the sea, you're best off totally skipping Boothbay. Though there are the customary seaside elements (soaring seagulls, lobster traps, bobbing buoys), this village leans more to manmade amusements. Just pause on the footbridge that stretches across the harbor and you'll hear bowling balls trundling down alleys, the ringing and dinging of pinball machines and the smack of a cue stick hitting a pool ball. The beauty of Boothbay, however, extends far beyond the footbridge. Walk into any restaurant, and you're sure to be served by a genuinely cheery college waiter or waitress about whom—by the end of the meal—you'll know absolutely everything.

Besides popping in and out of the dozens of shops and galleries that crowd around the hilly little streets, there are several ways to amuse yourself in Boothbay. One of the very best is by taking a boat trip. Several booths on the wharf sell tickets for anything from a one-hour sunset cruise to an all-day outing to nearby Monhegan (see the "Beaches & Parks" section in this chapter). If time is limited, at least go out on a short trip. You'll glide by tiny islands covered with spruce and fir trees, colonies of seals lounging around with their bellies up and the kinds of birds you've seen on the pages of *National Geographic*. If you're lucky, you'll spot a great blue heron standing in the water like a caryatid.

You can spend three to six days on a windjammer, eating hearty home-cooked meals and flitting about from one gorgeous island to another.

The sweet little village of **Waldoboro** is one of the next towns you'll come to as you continue up Route 1. It has several old homes and a Lutheran church that dates back to 1771. Farther out on that peninsula (following Route 220) is **Friendship**, a picturesque lobstering port. You have to go around the inlet and then out to the tip of St. George Peninsula to get to **Port Clyde**, launching site for the mail boat to Monhegan Island. You can head out to the island from here or take a boat from Boothbay Harbor. **Monhegan Island**, a mere smidgen on the map (less than two miles long and one mile wide), has been known as a popular artists and writers retreat for years. Its scenery is striking: steep cliffs thrashed by Atlantic surf and graced with pine forests and golden meadows. The lighthouse was built in 1824. The island's many hiking trails give the visitor on foot a chance to scout out its lovely terrain.

On your way back to Route 1, take time to visit the picture-perfect waterfront towns of **Tenants Harbor** and **Spruce Head**. Around this point of the coast—at **Penobscot Bay**—you start to see the Maine coastline everyone has always raved about. There are startlingly beautiful islands rising abruptly out of the choppy waters with sparkling sailboats gracefully skimming the waves.

Most beautiful, though, are the tall-masted **windjammers** that are famous in this area. The main departure points are located in the Rockland, Rockport and Camden areas. ~ For further information, contact the **Maine Windjammer Association**, P.O. Box

1144, Blue Hill, ME 04614; 800-807-9463, fax 207-374-2952; www.sailmainecoast.com, e-mail captains@sailmainecoast.com

The towns of **Rockland** and **Camden** are fishing villages that have been discovered by tourists. They are "cute" and can be counted on for restaurants, shops and inns. Some say they're too cute and have given in to the pressures of pleasing tourists, therefore losing their original charms.

One very worthwhile attraction in the area is the **Farnsworth Art Museum and Wyeth Center**. Founded in 1948 with a bequest from Lucy Farnsworth, the museum showcases American art with a focus on the state of Maine. Among its holdings are works by Thomas Eakins, Winslow Homer and Edward Hopper. Two gallery buildings are devoted to the works of the Wyeth family. Between them, they hold more than 4000 works by Andrew, N.C. and Jamie Wyeth. The Morehouse wing showcases works by contemporary Maine artists as well as the Maine in America collection. In addition to the art museums, the complex includes the adjacent Farnsworth family homestead (one of the finest Victorian-era residences on the East Coast) and the nearby Olson house, where Andrew Wyeth's masterpiece, *Christina's World,* was painted. Closed Monday from Columbus Day through Memorial Day. Admission. ~ 16 Museum Street, Rockland; 207-596-6457, fax 207-596-0509; www.farnsworthmuseum.org, e-mail farnsworth@midcoast.com.

You should also visit the **Owls Head Transportation Museum**, which houses one of the country's most impressive collections of operating antique planes and cars, as well as engines, bicycles and carriages. Here you can see an exact replica of the Wright Brothers' flyer, along with displays explaining the technological advances that the brothers made. Admission. ~ Route 73, just south of Rockland; 207-594-4418, fax 207-594-4410; www.ohtm.org.

As you continue up the coast, you'll come to **Searsport**, an old shipping port with stately old sea captains' homes and a multitude of antique shops. Before you cross the Waldo-Hancock bridge to Bucksport, take Route 174 to the **Fort Knox State Historic Site,** a very impressively constructed fort that was manned during the Civil and Spanish-American wars. Tours available in the summer. Closed November through April. Admission. ~ On Route 174, just off Route 1 west of the Waldo-Hancock Bridge, Prospect; phone/fax 207-469-7719; www.fortknox.maineguide.com, e-mail ffriends@midcoast.com.

Cross the bridge to Bucksport. From here, you can take Route 15 right into **Bangor,** Maine's third-largest city and a commercial and lumbering center. Take time to stroll around the **West Market Square Historic District** (a mid-19th-century block of shops) and the **Broadway Area**, where you'll see one lumber baron's mansion after another lined up as if contestants in a beauty contest. Then, jumping from the sublime to the unusual, you can spot the huge—31-foot-tall, 3000-pound—statue of **Paul Bunyan** (Main Street), which commemorates the town's great logging past.

Winslow Homer, Marsden Hartley, Roy Lichtenstein, Marc Chagall and Francisco Goya are a few of the artists represented in the **University of Maine Museum of Art**'s 6000-piece collection, the majority of which is 20th-century works on paper. Closed Sunday. Admission. ~ Norumbega Hall, 40 Harlow Street, Bangor; 207-561-3350, fax 207-561-3351; umma.umaine.edu, e-mail umma@umit.maine.edu.

The **Colby College Museum of Art**, located about 50 minutes southwest of Bangor via Route 95, focuses on American art from early portraits to 21st-century works. The museum also shows examples of European art, Chinese ceramics, Japanese woodcuts, Indian miniatures and over 300 Asian ceramics. ~ Bixler Art and Music Center, Colby College, Waterville; 207-872-3228, fax 207-872-3807; www.colby.edu/museum, e-mail museum@colby.edu.

LODGING

Maine accommodations come in all sizes and shapes, from conventional sea-viewing motels to European-style inns. Most are concentrated along the coast, predominantly in the southern and midcoast regions. Many places are seasonal, open only during the warm-weather months, so you should call ahead if you're traveling during the late fall or winter.

You have two options at **Dockside Guest Quarters**. You can stay either in the "Maine House" (a stately 19th-century building with five guest rooms) or in one of the 20 modern shore-hugging units. If it's charm you're after, go for the former, where rooms are individually decorated with antiques and floral fabrics. Open weekends only from November through May. Closed January to mid-February. ~ Harris Island Road, York; 207-363-2868, 800-270-1977, fax 207-363-1977; www.docksidegq.com, e-mail info@docksidegq.com. DELUXE TO ULTRA-DELUXE.

Perched atop a peninsula where the York River spills into the Atlantic Ocean, the secluded **Stage Neck Inn** offers spectacular views of the rocky Maine coastline. Each of its 58 rooms is decorated with European furnishings and provides a private terrace or balcony. The oceanside pool is perfect for a dip after a stroll along the coastline to nearby York Harbor, past cheerful cottages that pepper the hillside. Other amenities include tennis courts, an exercise room, an indoor pool and hot tub, and two restaurants. Full buffet breakfast. Closed in January. ~ 8 Stage Neck Road, York; 207-363-3850, 800-340-1130, fax 207-363-2221; www.stageneck.com, e-mail reserve@stageneck.com. ULTRA-DELUXE.

Located on a quiet street near Marginal Way (a footpath on the ocean's edge), **The Heritage of Ogunquit** is a Victorian reproduction. A gay-friendly establishment, its clientele is predominately women. All five guest rooms have private baths. There is an indoor hot tub and giant cedar deck plus a common room with a refrigerator and cooking facilities. ~ Ogunquit; 207-646-7787, 888-623-2647; www.heritageogunquit.com, e-mail heritage@maine.rr.com. MODERATE TO DELUXE.

The Inn at Two Village Square is a gay-owned and -operated 1886 inn propped up on a hillside. It attracts a mixed clientele that enjoys its close proximity to all of Ogunquit's resort activities. There's a heated pool and hot tub. Sunday cocktail parties and Wednesday night pool parties are included during the season. Closed November through April. ~ 14 Village Square Lane, Ogunquit; 207-646-5779; www.twovillagesquare.com, e-mail twovillagesquare@aol.com. MODERATE TO DELUXE.

A former Catholic church, **Haven By The Sea** is now a delightful bed and breakfast lovingly operated by John and Susan Jarvis. All rooms have private baths and cable TV; some have fireplaces, and the common areas include a lobby with a three-story cathedral ceiling. You'll find a direct view of the ocean and a beach only steps away. Closed in January and February. ~ 59 Church Street, Wells; 207-646-4194, fax 207-646-6883; www.havenbythesea.com, e-mail jarvis@havenbythesea.com. DELUXE TO ULTRA-DELUXE.

Situated on three and a half acres two miles north of Kennebunk, **Arundel Meadows Inn** is a gay-friendly bed and breakfast. Seven guest rooms in this restored farmhouse (it dates back to 1827) are decorated with antiques and original artwork. Each has its own bathroom; three have fireplaces. A full breakfast is served. ~ 1024 Portland Road, Arundel; phone/fax 207-985-3770; www.arundelmeadowsinn.com. DELUXE.

AUTHOR FAVORITE

Serenely situated on Westport Island, the **Squire Tarbox Inn** offers 11 guest rooms. Four of them are located in the main Federal-style house dating back to 1820. The others, well, er .... they're in the barn. But don't panic—it's a lovely barn dating back to 1763. And it's spanking clean. Meals in the Colonial dining room are a big part of any stay at the Squire Tarbox Inn. They are prepared by the Swiss owner and chef. Closed January to mid-May. ~ 1181 Maine Road, Westport Island; 207-882-7693, 800-818-0626, fax 207-882-7107; www.squiretarboxinn.com, e-mail innkeepers@squiretarboxinn.com. DELUXE.

One of the most wonderful things about the **Captain Lord Mansion** is that it successfully combines impeccably good taste with true comfort. Designed by Captain Lord, a wealthy merchant and shipbuilder, it's a stunning three-story Federal-style building that dates back to 1812. There is also a smaller 1807 house with additional guest rooms. Inside, it has all the hallmarks of a ship carpenter's craft, including a suspended elliptical staircase, blown-glass windows and mahogany doors with brass locks. Each of its 20 newly remodeled guest rooms has been decorated with period-reproduction wallpaper, exquisite antiques and four-poster and canopy beds. They all have gas fireplaces and private baths. ~ Pleasant and Green streets, Kennebunkport; 207-967-3141, 800-522-3141, fax 207-967-3172; www.captainlord.com, e-mail innkeeper@captainlord.com. ULTRA-DELUXE.

When George Bush, Sr. was president, the **Cape Arundel Inn** was *the* place to be—it overlooks the Bush family compound. But even if you couldn't care less about what was once the Summer White House, it's a good choice. Propped up on cliff-hanging Ocean Avenue, it's just one of several eye-poppingly beautiful shingle-style buildings that line the road. From the wraparound porch and some of the 14 rooms of this 1895 Victorian house, you have a wide-angle view of Walker's Point and the Atlantic all around. Continental breakfast included. Closed January and February. ~ 208 Ocean Avenue, Kennebunkport; 207-967-2125, fax 207-967-1199; www.capearundelinn.com, e-mail cai@capearundelinn.com. ULTRA-DELUXE.

Back in the late 1800s when wealthy out-of-staters were flocking to Maine to build their summer houses, the **Black Point Inn** came into being. Like many of its neighbors, it's a massive shingled building complete with a front porch and far-reaching ocean views. The main house has 58 guest rooms, and there are another 26 in cottages on the grounds. Two meals served. Closed November through May. ~ Prouts Neck; 207-883-2500, 800-258-0003, fax 207-883-9976; www.blackpointinn.com, e-mail public@blackpointinn.com. ULTRA-DELUXE.

The 1840 **Inn at Park Spring** is the type of place that doesn't have to advertise. This elegantly furnished three-story Greek Revival townhouse's six rooms are usually filled with found-it-by-word-of-mouthers. All rooms have private baths. A full breakfast,which includes fresh fruit, croissants, homemade muffins and French toast, tops the bill. ~ 135 Spring Street, Portland; 207-774-1059, 800-437-8511, fax 207-774-3455; www.innatparkspring.com, e-mail info@innatparkspring.com. MODERATE TO DELUXE.

The **West End Inn** is a six-room bed and breakfast in a 19th-century brick townhouse that was built in 1871. There are three king and three queen-size guest rooms, all with private baths and cable televisions. Each room is beautifully decorated in Waverly or Ralph Lauren decor. There is also a living room available for guests. The inn is located on the historic Western Prom minutes away from the old port. ~ 146 Pine Street, Portland; 207-772-1377, 800-338-1377, fax 207-828-0984; www.westendbb.com, e-mail innkeeper@westendbb.com. MODERATE TO DELUXE.

The **Inn on Carleton** not only sounds like a place you'd find in London but looks like it, too. This townhouse in the Western Promenade part of town offers six rooms lavishly decorated with Victorian antiques; all have private baths. ~ 46 Carleton Street, Portland; 207-775-1910, 800-639-1779, fax 207-761-0956; www.innoncarleton.com, e-mail innkeeper@innoncarleton.com. DELUXE TO ULTRA-DELUXE.

If peace and quiet in a remote country setting sounds good to you, spend a few days at **Chebeague Orchard Bed and Breakfast.** The 1876 Greek Revival home sits behind an impressive stone wall that borders a two-acre apple orchard. The five bedrooms and one apartment are comfortably appointed and tastefully decorated. Three of the rooms have private baths. The hospitable owners are only too happy to suggest walks or bike rides (rentals are available if you didn't bring your own); guests can play a game of croquet, relax on the swing, or look around in the organic flower and vegetable garden. The inn runs a series of retreats and workshops that range from kayaking to art. A full breakfast, which you can choose to eat on the sunporch, is included. ~ 66 North Road, Chebeague Island; phone/fax 207-846-9488; www.chebeague-orchard.com, e-mail orchard@nlis.net. MODERATE TO DELUXE.

Earmuffs, appropriately enough, were invented in Maine.

If you want to be near L. L. Bean and the profusion of factory outlets that have taken over the once very New England (now almost mall-like) town of Freeport, consider booking a room at the **Harraseeket Inn.** This Colonial-style inn is within walking distance of all the shops and outlets. There are 84 guest rooms, some with jacuzzis, quarter-canopied beds and working fireplaces. Eight of the rooms are in the lovely older section of the building dating from the 1850s. There are also two ballrooms and an exercise area. Rates include a full buffet breakfast and afternoon tea. ~ 162 Main Street, Freeport; 207-865-9377, 800-342-6423, fax 207-865-1684; www.harraseeketinn.com, e-mail harraseeke@aol.com. ULTRA-DELUXE.

Though the **Boothbay Harbor Inn** is clearly a motel (and not an inn as the name leads one to believe), it does have some personality. For one thing, it's smack-dab on the water. You walk into your room, roll open the glass doors and *voilà!* The bobbing buoys, the wooden fishing boats, the screaming gulls—you feel as if you've just walked into the postcard you bought down at the desk. Don't get your hopes up about the rooms, however. They are about as generic as motel rooms get. All 60 rooms have private baths, though. Closed late October to mid-May. ~ 31 Atlantic Avenue, Boothbay Harbor; 207-633-6302, 800-533-6302; www.boothbayharborinn.com, e-mail info@boothbayharbor inn.com. DELUXE.

One look at the cluttered little streets of Boothbay Harbor and you'll be happy you're staying at the **Spruce Point Inn**. It's set apart from the ongoing carnival of town, on a 100-acre peninsula at the eastern end of the harbor. There's a main inn as well as a handful of cottages and lodges scattered around the grounds; some offer ocean views and all rooms have private decks. Sports are big here, with two pools, clay tennis courts, a putting green, a playground and some lawn games with a spa to unwind in afterward. Closed mid-October to mid-May. ~ Spruce Point on Atlantic Avenue, Boothbay Harbor; 207-633-4152, 800-553-0289, fax 207-633-7138; www.spruce pointinn.com, e-mail reservations@sprucepointinn.com. DELUXE TO ULTRA-DELUXE.

Maine is home to some 1.2 million year-round residents, a startlingly small number when you consider it's as big as all of the other New England states put together.

You can walk to the center of the village in minutes from the **Broad Bay Inn & Gallery**, a lovely Colonial house built in 1830 offering bed and breakfast. The five rooms are very New England with canopy beds and brightly polished antiques. There is a back deck and a garden with a hammock. Take time to stroll around the art gallery and art library, which is run by innkeeper Libby Hopkins. Breakfasts are wonderful and include plum tarts, soufflés and blueberry puddings. Several art classes are offered in the summer. Closed in winter. ~ 1014 Main Street, Waldoboro; 207-832-6668, 800-736-6769; www.broadbayinn.com, e-mail innkeeper@broadbayinn.com. MODERATE.

Set amongst the historic seaport buildings of Rockland is the **Captain Lindsey House Inn**, a nine-room inn that was built in 1837. All of the rooms are decorated with antiques and furnishings from around the world. Great attention is given to comfortable details including down comforters and European-style pillows on all the beds. There's a large living room with a fireplace and soft down couches plus a library with comfortable reading chairs and a computer port. Guests also have access to a courtyard garden. ~ 5 Lindsey Street, Rockland; 207-596-7950, 800-523-2145, fax 207-596-2758; www.lindseyhouse.com, e-mail lindsey@midcoast.com. DELUXE TO ULTRA-DELUXE.

Choosing just one inn in Camden is like picking one chocolate out of a whole box. There are many you'll want to try. Be that as it may, you definitely won't be sorry if you stay at the **Blue Harbor House**, a restored 1810 New England Cape (and carriage house) with ten guest rooms. All are beautifully furnished with soft colors, country fabrics, comfortable antiques and hand-fashioned quilts. Some have canopy beds or gas fireplaces; all have private baths. Breakfast—which includes specialties such as lobster quiche, cheese soufflé and blueberry pancakes—are included and always memorable affairs. Dinner is also available. The inn is a short walk from the waterfront. ~ 67 Elm Street, Camden; 207-236-3196, 800-248-3196, fax 207-236-6523; www.blueharborhouse.com, e-mail info@blueharborhouse.com. DELUXE.

◄HIDDEN

For years, **The Trailing Yew** has been a favorite among artists visiting Monhegan. It's a friendly place where returning guests are welcomed as if family. Its 34 guest rooms—in four houses and one private cottage—are basic, with kerosene lamps and shared baths. Breakfast and dinner are hearty, home-cooked and served family-style. Special rates for children. Closed from mid-October to mid-May. ~ Monhegan Island; 207-596-0440, fax 207-596-7636; www.trailingyew.com. DELUXE.

The 19th-century **East Wind Inn** looks like something right out of Sarah Orne Jewett's *Country of the Pointed Firs*. Indeed, the author wrote the book in nearby Martinville. The inn is composed of a former sea captain's house, a sail loft and a more modern building. All of the 25 rooms are beautifully furnished with antiques and gaze out over the harbor. This view brings you the Maine coast just as you've pictured it—lobster traps piled high and wooden boats gently undulating with the tide. Closed December through Good Friday. ~ Mechanic Street, Tenants Harbor; 207-372-6366, 800-241-8439, fax 207-372-6320; www.eastwindinn.com, e-mail info@eastwindinn.com. MODERATE TO DELUXE.

The beautiful, four-story **Charles Inn at West Market Square** is located in the heart of historic Bangor. This 1873 brick structure, listed on the National Historic Registry, was lovingly restored and renovated. The European Victorian interior motif features mahogany and leather antique reproduction furnishings. A continental breakfast is included. ~ West Market Square, 20 Broad Street, Bangor; 207-992-2820, fax 207-992-2826; www.thecharlesinn.com, e-mail thecharlesinn@aol.com. MODERATE.

DINING

Back in 1896, Edward and Mattie Talpey started **The Goldenrod**. As more visitors came to the area—thanks to the arrival of the electric trolleys coming into York Beach from Portsmouth and Kittery—word got around, and before long it became a tradition to stop for a meal and watch saltwater taffy being made. Indeed, the Goldenrod prides itself on its Goldenrod Kisses (selling homemade candy is 50 percent of their business)—but it's also one of the most popular family restaurants you'll find in Maine. Menu items include American favorites such as soups, salads and sandwiches plus dinner specialties (fresh haddock, meatloaf). Closed Labor Day to late May. ~ Route 1A, York Beach; 207-363-2621; www.thegoldenrod.com. BUDGET.

The **Cape Neddick Lobster Pound** is not just lobster and clams. It boasts an array of other dishes such as reef and beef kebab, a mix of skewered shrimp, scallops, steak and vegetables. Its setting is fairly predictable in these parts—a shingled building right on the water. Closed mid-December to mid-March and Tuesday in the fall. ~ Shore Road off Route 1A, Cape Neddick; 207-363-5471; www.capeneddick.com, e-mail info@capeneddick.com. MODERATE TO ULTRA-DELUXE.

Follow your nose into **Pie in the Sky Bakery** if you're looking for a snack. Baker/owners John and Nancy Stern seem to be on a never-ending roll of creating one yummy treat after another, including muffins and, of course, gourmet pies. Closed Tuesday and Wednesday. Closed the first six weeks of the year. ~ Route 1 and River Road, Cape Neddick; 207-363-2656, 800-869-2656. BUDGET TO DELUXE.

For a quiet, elegant dinner in Ogunquit, try **Tavern at Clay Hill Farm**. It's a lovely New England restaurant located in an old farmhouse just west of the village. The menu is rather refined, offering items like pan-seared salmon with seasonal variations, and roast duckling. A pianist provides the dreamy background music throughout dinner. Dinner only. Closed Monday and Tuesday from January through March. ~ 220 Clay Hill Road, Ogunquit; 207-646-2272; www.clayhillfarm.com, e-mail info@clayhillfarm.com. DELUXE TO ULTRA-DELUXE.

Look for crowds outside **Barnacle Billy's**, a basic Maine lobster joint where you pull a number, wait to be called and then settle in for a feast. You can sit in the dining room, which has the air of a bustling fish house, or on the deck, where you can gaze out at boats while you eat. Closed mid-October to mid-April. ~ Perkins Cove, Ogunquit; 207-646-5575, 800-866-5575, fax 207-646-1219; www.barnbilly.com, e-mail info@barnbilly.com. MODERATE TO DELUXE.

The menu is what drew us into the **White Barn Inn**, a barn-turned-restaurant. The cuisine is somewhat of a departure from the norm in these parts; the prix-fixe four-course dinners change seasonally and may feature Maine lobster and sweetbreads ragout, grilled tenderloin of beef with a carmel potato custard, and grilled vegetables with tomato coulis and basil oil. All this in a lovely candlelit barn. Gentlemen, wear a jacket—it's required. Dinner only. Closed the second and third weeks in January. ~ 37 Beach Avenue, Kennebunk Beach; 207-967-2321, fax 207-967-1100; www.whitebarninn.com, e-mail innkeeper@whitebarninn.com. ULTRA-DELUXE.

Expect perfection at the Kennebunkport Inn's **Port Tavern & Grille**. This ultra-elegant restaurant prides itself on making sure everything is just right. The hushed Colonial dining room is a fitting background for a candlelight dinner of flawlessly grilled native salmon, baked scallops, pork tenderloin or roasted duck. In the summer months, you can opt to eat on the outdoor patio. There is also a turn-of-the-20th-century pub with a piano bar. Closed Sunday through Tuesday during the winter. ~ 1 Dock Square, Kennebunkport; 207-967-2621, fax 207-967-3705; www.porttavern.com, e-mail dine@porttavern.com. MODERATE TO ULTRA-DELUXE.

Windows on the Water has a major-league claim to fame. Its chef—John—was one of 52 who prepared food for former President Bush's inauguration. Admittedly, the food is right up there with the best, including seasonal dishes such as lobster ravioli drizzled with drambuie cream and grilled prosciutto-wrapped shrimp. The view almost one-ups the meal, however. Diners look out at the busy little port through the arched windows or from the terrace during warm-weather months. ~ 12 Chase Hill Road, Kennebunk; 207-967-3313, fax 207-967-5377; www.windowsonthewater.com, e-mail info@windowsonthewater.com. DELUXE TO ULTRA-DELUXE.

For some real down-to-earth Maine dining, head to **Nunan's Lobster Hut**. Here you can stuff yourselves on ultra-fresh lobster and piles of steamers and top it all off with homemade apple or blueberry pie. It's a typically casual Maine restaurant, housed in a low-slung shed. Dinner only. Closed the Saturday following Columbus Day through the first Thursday of May. ~ Mill Road, Cape Porpoise; 207-967-4362, fax 207-967-4362. MODERATE TO DELUXE.

The **Back Bay Grill** is in a novel location: a restored 1888 pharmacy. But apart from the original pressed-tin ceiling, how-

AUTHOR FAVORITE

A trip to Maine would not be complete without at least one meal at a diner. That's where you see the real characters, the perennial Mainers. One of our favorites is **Moody's Diner**. It's been passed down through the Moody family for generations. The décor is authentic dineresque. The menu is mainstream but good enough to make you want to go back several times—especially for breakfast! ~ 1185 Atlantic Highway, Waldoboro; 207-832-7468; www.moodysdiner.com, e-mail info@moodysdiner.com. BUDGET.

ever, it retains no hint of its earlier incarnation. Now, it's a very elegant-looking restaurant (complete with white tablecloths). Local art adorns the walls, including a lively 22-foot mural of the restaurant in one dining room. One of the two dining areas is open to the kitchen. The New American menu is seasonal and has many offerings, including duck, lamb, filet mignon and fresh seafood. The kitchen does its own baking; try the crème brûlée. The extensive wine list won the board of excellence from *Wine Spectator* magazine. Dinner only. Closed Sunday. ~ 65 Portland Street, Portland; 207-772-8833; www.backbaygrill.com. MODERATE TO ULTRA-DELUXE.

Learn your lobster lingo: A "lobster car" is a storage system for live lobsters and consists of a raft with an underwater cage.

David's Creative Cuisine offers a range of food including seafood, such as lobster and salmon, vegetarian dishes, gourmet pizzas, filet mignon and their special pork Oscar. ~ 22 Monument Square, Portland; 207-773-4340, fax 207-773-4425; www.davidsrestaurant.com, e-mail davidsrest@aol.com. MODERATE TO DELUXE.

If you want to combine dining with a bit of partying, find your way to the **Great Lost Bear**. This is one of Portland's most popular bar-cum-restaurants where you can count on getting old standbys like chili, burgers, steaks and salads. ~ 540 Forest Avenue, Portland; 207-772-0300, fax 207-871-1384; www.greatlostbear.com, e-mail bear@greatlostbear.com. BUDGET TO MODERATE.

HIDDEN ►

Lots of Portlanders go to **Norm's** when they want to have a nice casual meal and not break the bank. Next door to the State Theater, it's a lively place with red walls, checkerboard floors and a busy bar scene. The menu includes a large variety of dishes, from Thai-spiced chicken wings and steamed mussels to pork chops, burgers and steaks. ~ 617 Congress Street, Portland; 207-828-9944. MODERATE.

For Northern Italian cuisine, you can't go wrong with **The Roma**. Located in a Victorian mansion (circa 1887), it has six dining rooms—some with fireplaces. Especially good are the seafood dishes, including lobster. Dinner only Monday through Saturday. Closed Sunday. ~ 769 Congress Street, Portland; 207-773-9873, fax 207-756-6768; www.theromacafe.com, e-mail romacafe@aol.com. MODERATE TO ULTRA-DELUXE.

The owners of **Le Garage** have a good sense of humor. After all, this really is a 1920s-era garage-turned-restaurant. You'd hardly know it though, since they've gussied the place up and added on a glassed-in porch. The food is very good (predominately seafood, but lamb, steaks and chicken, too) and the value unmatchable. Closed Monday from September through May. Closed January. ~ 15 Water Street, Wiscasset; 207-882-5409, fax 207-882-6370. MODERATE TO DELUXE.

In spite of its magnet-for-tourists location, **Andrew's Harborside Restaurant** attracts quite a few locals for all three meals. Lines form outside for the breakfasts, which are prefaced by large cinnamon rolls fresh out of the oven and dripping with a glassy icing. Lunch and dinner dishes are largely of the seafood variety, though you can get meat and poultry dishes as well. The restaurant is unimaginatively decorated, but the setting—inches from the water's edge—makes it enormously appealing. Closed mid-October to mid-May. ~ 12 Bridge Street, Boothbay Harbor; 207-633-4074, fax 207-563-2899. MODERATE.

In the mood for yet more seafood? Then make a beeline for **Harborview Tavern.** Graze on appetizers like fried mozzarella or fried mushrooms. Then move in on mussels in cream, scallops au gratin, sirloin or nightly seafood and steak specials. There's prime rib on weekends. Ask for a seat on the enclosed deck or open terrace and you'll enjoy a great view. Closed Sunday in the summer. ~ 1 Water Street, Thomaston; 207-354-8173. MODERATE TO DELUXE.

The **Waterworks Pub and Restaurant** is locally famed for its super-fresh seafood and pub fare. Its long mahogany bar (where Maine-brewed ales, single malts, brandies and wines are served) is also a local favorite. The restaurant is part of a completely restored building that belonged to a waterworks company. The menu always includes the freshest seafood available as well as vegetarian dishes and plenty of meat choices, including a delicious meatloaf. For dessert, the apple crisp served with cinnamon ice cream is not to be missed. ~ 7 Lindsey Street, Rockland; 207-596-2753, fax 207-596-2443. MODERATE.

Even the most self-assured diners can't make up their mind what to order at **The Waterfront.** The dinner menu lists an inviting selection of specialties including crabcakes. And, of course, there are lobsters and steamers to further throw you into a tizzy. The setting—right on the harbor—is unmatchable. ~ 40 Bayview Street, Camden; 207-236-3747, fax 207-236-3815; e-mail wtrfront@midcoast.com. MODERATE TO DELUXE.

Scooping up spoonfuls of clam chowder at **Cappy's Chowder House** is close to having a spiritual experience. But that's just the chowder. Cappy's is also famed for its seafood dishes, pasta, burgers—you name it. It's a pubby kind of place with nautical decor, always abuzz with both out-of-towners and salty locals. Sunday brunch. Closed Wednesday in the winter. ~ 1 Main Street, Camden; 207-236-2254, fax 207-236-6472; www.cappyschowder.com, e-mail goodeats@cappyschowder.com. BUDGET TO MODERATE.

SHOPPING

The most southern part of Maine, along Route 1, seems to be suffering—actually, prospering would be a more accurate term—

from factory-outlet- and mall-itis. Discount stores are everywhere. Unless you've come specifically to scout out bargains, you might be better off sniffing out the small shops, especially those that specialize in Maine arts and crafts. (See "State of the Artists" in this chapter.)

In York, stop by **The Old York Historical Society Museum and Gift Shop**. It offers a delightful array of traditional Maine crafts along with a large collection of Maine books. Closed Sunday and from Columbus Day through May. ~ 196 York Street, York; 207-363-4974, fax 207-363-4021; www.oldyork.org, e-mail oyhs@oldyork.org.

R. Jorgensen Antiques is definitely worth stopping at, unlike some of the faux-antiques shops that have staked out prime tourist territory on the coast. There's a little bit of everything here, including genuine Americana and 18th- and 19th-century antiques and accessories. Closed Wednesday. ~ 502 Post Road, Route 1, Wells; 207-646-9444, fax 207-646-4954; www.rjorgensen.com, e-mail office@rjorgensen.com.

If you're in the market for some pottery, stop by **The Good Earth**. It's filled with decorative stoneware and cooking pieces in a fascinating array of designs—all produced by local potters. Closed December 25 through May 15. ~ Dock Square, Kennebunkport; 207-967-4635.

Some very attractive wood carvings, wooden boxes and other functional wares are found at **Gerard Craft Woodproducts**. They are all skillfully handcrafted by Gerry and Linda Laberge. Open by appointment or by chance. ~ 510 Mitchell Road, Cape Elizabeth; 207-799-3526; www.gerardcraft.com, e-mail gerardcraft@maine.rr.com.

In Portland, the best shopping can be found at the **Old Port Exchange**, along Fore and Exchange streets. For American crafts, make your way to **Abacus**. Over 600 of the country's craftspeople are represented here. (There are also galleries in Boothbay Harbor, Kennebunkport and Freeport.) Call ahead for hours as some locations close seasonally. ~ 44 Exchange Street, Portland; 207-772-4880, 800-206-2166; www.abacusgallery.com, e-mail info@abacusgallery.com.

The Maine Potters Market is just as it sounds: a cooperative where you can shop for clay works created by local potters. In fact, it's the largest potters co-op in the state. You'll find more than a dozen artists displaying a wonderful selection of traditional pieces as well as avant-garde finds. Call for winter hours. ~ 376 Fore Street, Portland; 207-774-1633; www.mainepottersmarket.com, e-mail info@mainepottersmarket.com.

Pick up sandwiches and other provisions at **Doughty's Island Market**, Chebeague Island's only store, where you're sure to meet the owner, congenial Chebeague native Ed Doughty. Closed Wednesday from September to May. ~ South Road, Chebeague Island; 207-846-9997.

You'll find an amazing selection of wonderfully detailed maps of Maine (as well as other areas) at **The DeLorme Map Store**. ~ 2 DeLorme Drive, Yarmouth; 800-642-0970; www.delorme.com.

It's been called the preppy mecca, among other things. But love it or not, don't deny yourself the privilege of seeing **L. L. Bean**. Today, the quality of the rugged outdoor clothes and equipment is legendary, and the store—a huge mall-like building—is open 24 hours a day, 7 days a week, 365 days a year. L. L. Bean's success comes largely from marketing the image of Maine (outdoors, fresh air, healthy) and the Maine people (hardworking, rugged, independent). ~ Route 1, Freeport; 207-865-4761; www.llbean.com.

Pop into the Boothbay Harbor branch of **Abacus** just to take a quick look around and an hour later, you realize you're still there. It has a captivating selection of crafts by a variety of American artisans. Check out the oak bentwood rocking chairs by Paul Miller. Closed November through April. ~ 12 McKown Street, Boothbay Harbor; 207-633-2166, fax 207-633-7401; www.abacusgallery.com, e-mail abacusmail@aol.com.

It may never have occurred to you that you needed a chowder mug. But one look at the selection of **Edgecomb Potters'** mugs and you can't live without one. But that's not all. The Potters' high-gloss, berry-colored pieces come in all sizes and shapes, from very attractive creamer and sugar sets to huge bowls. You'll also find a wide selection of jewelry, iron and glass products in the store. ~ Route 27, Edgecomb; 207-882-9493; www.edgecombpotters.com.

L. L. Bean was started by an avid outdoorsman who built up a mail-order business for his Maine hunting shoe.

The floor of **Enchantments** is littered with colored metallic stars. This is the place to go for crystals and healing gemstones. It also has a book section that's broken into categories such as Findhorn, New Age, Astrology, Kabbalah, Runes and Fairies and Lore. ~ 10 Boothbay House Hill, Boothbay Harbor; 207-633-4992.

A delicious array of mohair, fine wool, cotton, silk and cotton handwoven scarves, stoles and throws are the results of **Nancy Lubin Designs** hard work. A very worthwhile stop. Open by appointment only. ~ 13 Trim Street, Camden; 207-236-4069; e-mail nancy@intention.com.

Étienne Perret and Company specializes in fine designer jewelry. Though somewhat pricey, they're cherishable works of art. Jewelry can be viewed by appointment only. ~ 14 Sea Street, Cam-

Text continued on page 602.

State of the Artists

Like all beautiful places, Maine draws artists like a magnet. Along the shore, you'll spot painters studying the colors of the sea before easels firmly rooted in the sand. Shops often display watercolors, sculpture and jewelry by local artisans. Even in rural villages, you'll find artwork as impressive as that of sophisticated urban areas and European capitals. In fact, many resident Maine artists hold national or international reputations. Some of their studios and workshops are open to the public. Here's a sampling of what you'll find.

In Portland's Old Port District lies the **Maine Potters Market**, a cooperative gallery featuring the work of more than a dozen potters from the state of Maine. ~ 376 Fore Street; 207-774-1633; www.mainepotters market.com, e-mail info@mainepottersmarket.com.

Of course, you won't want to miss the prominent **Portland Museum of Art**, the state's oldest art museum. Its rooms are filled with the work of Maine natives Wyeth, Homer and Hartley. You'll also view pieces by Monet, Renoir, Degas and Picasso. Daily tours are available. Closed Monday from Columbus Day to Memorial Day. Admission. ~ 7 Congress Square, Portland, ME 04101; 207-775-6148, fax 207-773-7324; www.portlandmuseum.org, e-mail pma@maine.rr.com.

It may be just a barn, but that building behind the **Broad Bay Inn & Gallery** features watercolor paintings and hosts several workshops and art classes during the summer. The gallery sells gift items such as jewelry made from sea shells and books on Maine. Several art classes are also offered. Closed in winter. ~ 1014 Main Street, Waldoboro, ME 04572; 207-832-6668, 800-736-6769; www.broadbayinn.com, e-mail broadbayinn@verizon.net.

Center for Maine Contemporary Art, located in a historic firehouse, is a nonprofit organization dedicated to advancing contemporary Maine art through exhibits and educational programs. Closed Monday. Admission. ~ 162 Russell Avenue, P.O. Box 147, Rockport, ME 04856; 207-236-2875; www.cmcanow.org, e-mail info@cmcanow.org.

A self-taught artist, Jud Hartmann has created a series of bronze sculptures depicting the Amerindians of the Northeast. You can view them at the **Jud Hartmann Gallery and Sculpture Studio**, along with paintings by Jerry Rose, Barron Krody and others. Closed mid-September to June. Also closed Sunday during the summer if it is sunny weather. ~ 79 Main Street, P.O. Box 753, Blue Hill, ME 04614; 207-374-9917; www.judhartmann gallery.com, e-mail hartmann@hypernet.com.

Works by over 30 contemporary artists are on view at the well-known **Leighton Gallery**. The exhibit changes monthly, and the grounds also feature a sculpture garden. Closed mid-October to late May. ~ Parker Point Road, Blue Hill; 207-374-5001; www.leightongallery.com, e-mail leighton gallery@verizon.net.

A large number of artists and craftspeople live and work on Deer Isle. For starts, you'll find **Ronald Hayes Pearson's Studio/Gallery**. This is definitely a high-risk zone if you're trying not to spend money; his sterling silver and gold jewelry pieces are stunning. By appointment only on Sunday. ~ Old Ferry Road; 207-348-2535; www.ronaldhayespearson.com. The **Turtle Gallery** features works by regional artists and craftspeople. In the summer, the gallery offers two- and three-week exhibitions in a wide variety of media, including watercolors, oils, glassworks, collage, sculpture and clay. Closed October to Memorial Day. ~ Just north of Deer Isle on Route 15; 207-348-9977; www.turtlegallery.com, e-mail person@turtle gallery.com.

On that same serene little island, at the end of a bumpy dirt road, you'll find the **Haystack Mountain School of Crafts**. Here artists of all skill levels from around the world gather to produce works in metal, textiles, wood, glass, pottery and paper. The school is housed in a series of studios designed by noted architect Edward Larrabee Barnes. Works created here can be bought in a silent auction benefitting the school's scholarship fund, or you can purchase them at various studios and galleries around the island, including the Blue Heron Gallery and Studio in Deer Isle Village. From June through August, a free tour of the school is conducted on Wednesday at 1 p.m. Call ahead for information. Closed September through May. ~ South of Deer Isle Village, turn left off Route 15 onto Sunshine Road and follow signs for about seven miles; 207-348-2306, fax 207-348-2307; www.haystack-mtn.org, e-mail haystack@haystack-mtn.org.

As one Eastport artist put it, "All great places are discovered—or rediscovered—by artists." Such is the case with this former sardine-canning town on the northernmost coast of Maine. Here, the painters and potters are the prominent citizens, and the works of around 30 local artists are on display at the **Eastport Gallery**. Closed October to mid-June. ~ 74 Water Street, Eastport, ME 04631; 207-853-4166; www.eastportgallery.com, e-mail eastportgallery@yahoo.com.

With this list in hand, visitors will surely have a great deal of Maine art to choose from or simply to browse through. But travelers in these parts will undoubtedly find worthwhile art throughout the state, sometimes where they least expect it—in a hole-in-the-wall café, perhaps. Or you might discover the next Andrew Wyeth standing right next to you on a scenic stretch of beach, touching up his canvas.

den; 207-236-9696, 800-426-4367, fax 207-236-9698; www.etienneperret.com, e-mail etienne@etienneperret.com.

Crafts, crafts and more crafts can be found at the **Maine Gathering**. Over 100 of the state's craftspeople and artisans are shown here. Camden Falls Fine Art Gallery is also located here. ~ 21 Main Street, Camden; 207-236-9004, fax 207-230-0767; www.mainegathering.com, e-mail megather@midcoast.com.

NIGHTLIFE The **Ogunquit Playhouse**, which started in 1932, still brings in theatergoers from all over the country. Its season runs from June through August every summer, and features Broadway musicals. ~ Route 1, Ogunquit; 207-646-5511, 207-646-4732; www.ogunquitplayhouse.org.

Portland is where you'll find the most to do after dark in southern Maine. It's rife with cultural diversions, including the **Portland Stage Company**, which puts on about half a dozen plays per season (September through May). ~ Portland Performing Arts Center, 25-A Forest Avenue, Portland; 207-774-1043, fax 207-774-0576; www.portlandstage.com, e-mail info@portlandstage.com.

The **Portland Players** have the distinction of being Maine's oldest community theater. The season's five productions are performed in an intimate community theater environment. Their season runs from September through June. ~ 207-799-7337, fax 207-767-6208; www.portlandplayers.org, e-mail info@portlandplayers.org. If musicals are your thing, the small **Lyric Music Theater** puts on four of them in a September-to-May season. ~ 176 Sawyer Street, Portland; 207-799-6509 or 207-799-1421; www.lyricmusictheater.com.

The **Portland Symphony Orchestra** offers classical, chamber pops and holiday concerts from October to July. ~ 477 Congress Street, Portland (administration); 207-773-6128, fax 207-773-6089; www.portlandsymphony.com. **PCA Great Performances** puts on a variety of concerts—opera, jazz, chamber music and dance—as well as Broadway performances from October through May. ~ 207-773-3150; www.pcagreatperformances.org. Both companies perform in the Merrill Auditorium, in the Portland City Hall at 20 Myrtle Street. For tickets, call **PorTix**. ~ 207-842-0800.

Portland has quite a few thriving nightspots, such as **Gritty McDuff's Brew Pub**, where you can chomp on fish and chips and down some beers brewed right on the premises. It's a rowdy spot, especially on Saturday nights, when you may have to scream your order across the copper-topped bar. There's live music on Saturday and Sunday nights. ~ 396 Fore Street, Portland; 207-772-2739, fax 207-772-6204; www.grittys.com, e-mail grittys@grittys.com.

Another good pub is **Three Dollar Dewey's**, an English-style tavern that prides itself on its wide selection of draught beers and three-alarm chili. A large following of fanatical regulars really whoops it up here, knocking 'em down at long tavern tables. ~ 241 Commercial Street, Portland; 207-772-3310, fax 207-879-7424; www.3dollardeweys.com.

If your timing is right, someone famous—like James Taylor—will be putting on a show at the **Cumberland County Civic Center**. ~ 1 Civic Center Square, Portland; 207-775-3458; www.the civiccenter.com.

If you're in the Freeport area, check out some of **L. L. Bean's Outdoor Discovery Schools'** workshops and clinics at their retail stores. They offer a vast variety of programs including instruction in flyfishing, kayaking, canoeing, outdoor photography, wilderness survival and more. Call ahead for details and reservations. ~ Main Street, Freeport; 888-552-3261; www.llbean.com/odp, e-mail outdoor.discovery@llbean.com.

On Friday and Saturday, **Gilbert's Publick House** has live bands playing mostly rock-and-roll but also R&B, jazz and pop in a maritime bar setting. Cover on Friday and Saturday. ~ Sharp's Wharf, Bayview Street, Camden; 207-236-4320, fax 207-236-6068.

BEACHES & PARKS

RACHEL CARSON NATIONAL WILDLIFE REFUGE This 5300-acre refuge spans approximately 50 miles of Maine's southern coast from Kittery to Cape Elizabeth. Each of ten divisions protects rivers that form salt marshes where they meet the Atlantic. The wheelchair-accessible Carson Trail (1 mile), located at the Wells headquarters, makes it easy to view the coast and adjacent woodlands. You'll also find a picnic area and restrooms. This unit is also adjacent to the Wells National Estuarine Research Reserve/Laudholm Farm, a public facility offering seven miles of trails. ~ Headquarters is on Route 9, west of Kennebunkport; 207-646-9226, fax 207-646-6554; www.fws.gov/northeast/rachelcarson.

OGUNQUIT BEACH Driving along Route 1, turn onto Beach Street and gasp at the beauty of this spacious beach. It's utterly magnificent. You see the wild ocean crashing in, waves breaking in a series of prismatic explosions. On a good day, the sky's a beautiful blue punctuated with perfect white clouds. Wide and smooth, the beach stretches for three miles and divides into three main areas. You'll find the most popular expanse at the foot of Beach Street. The Footbridge area, slightly less crowded, is off Ocean Street. Moody Beach, off Eldridge Road, is even less peopled. Fishing and whale watching are popular activities here. Since the water temperature rarely exceeds 65° even in July and August, not all people would say swimming is good here. However, for northern Mainers and Canadians, it's tepid. There are restrooms in all three areas, and lifeguards are on duty in summer. ~ Near Ogunquit, off Route 1; 207-646-2939, fax 207-641-0856; www.ogunquit.org.

WELLS BEACH Just north of the wave-slapped sands of Ogunquit Beach, this is similar in its natural beauty. The beach is wide and smooth and has great bodysurfing waves but, ooooh, is the water chilly. It does, however, go a bit overboard with the tourist clutter. There are motels, cottages, condos and restaurants lining the beach. Facilities include toilets, playgrounds, a parking area. ~ Off Mile Road in the village of Wells Beach; 207-646-2451.

GOOCH'S BEACH One look at this beach and you'll understand why former President Bush lives nearby and why everyone else bought summer cottages in this area. It's wildly spacious, long and wide (some fine sand areas, some shingle patches) and smashed by waves that drown out any conversation you might try to have. Add a couple of diving gulls and an invigorating breeze and what more could you possibly want? There are portable toilets. Lifeguards. Parking permit required. ~ On Beach Avenue, one and a half miles southwest of Kennebunkport; 207-967-0857, fax 207-967-2867.

ARUNDEL (COLONY) BEACH This small sandy pocket has a marvelous air of exclusivity in spite of its Bush Country location. It's backed by huge rocks that are fun to climb on. It's also right down the coast from Walker's Point, where former President Bush's Summer White House is located. No lifeguards. You can catch a tour trolley (fee) to the beaches at designated stops starting at the head of Ocean Avenue. ~ Off Ocean Avenue across from the Colony Hotel, Kennebunkport; 207-967-0857, fax 207-967-2867.

FERRY BEACH STATE PARK Hugging the coastline, this 117-acre preserve is densely scenic. Along with patches of pines and other northern trees, there's a surprising stand of tupelo trees, which are rare at this latitude. The whole park is threaded with trails that are wheelchair accessible. Guided nature walks are offered upon request and on Sunday. The beach—a sweep of white smashed by Atlantic waves—is perhaps its biggest attraction. Facilities include picnic tables, grills, toilets, a large shelter, changing rooms and lifeguards in summer. Closed October through Memorial Day. Day-use fee, $4 per person. ~ Off Route 9 on Bayview Road, between Camp Ellis and Old Orchard Beach; phone/fax 207-283-0067.

HIDDEN ►

SCARBOROUGH BEACH PARK Just before following Route 207 out to Prouts Neck (a funny-shaped little peninsula), you can turn off and find yourselves face to face with a gorgeous sandy beach that's backed by dunes and marshes. It's not big, and it's not heavily populated, thanks to limited parking. There are good bodysurfing waves and almost no undertow. You will find changing rooms, restrooms, drinking water, a snack bar and lifeguards. Day-use fee, $4 per person. ~ Take Route 207, three miles south of Route 1, from the town of Scarborough; 207-883-2416.

Wolfe's Neck Woods State Park is largely covered with woods colonized by birds that belt out arias as if they were opera singers.

▲ There are two campgrounds near this park. **Bayley's Camping Resort** has 500 tent/RV sites (with hookups). Tents cost $40 to $45 per night and RV sites run from $50 to $60. ~ Route 9W, Scarborough; 207-883-6043; www.bayleys-camping.com. **Wild Duck Campground** has 15 tent sites and 70 RV sites (with hookups); $32 to $47 per night. Closed Columbus Day to May 10. ~ Route 9, south of Scarborough; 207-883-4432; www.wildduckcampground.com, e-mail info@wildduckcampground.com.

CRESCENT BEACH STATE PARK Located in Cape Elizabeth, this 235-acre park is known for its sandy beach that sprawls on for a mile. It attracts lots of Portlanders, especially during summer weekends. They come to swim in the sudsy surf and to soak up rays. There are also many water sports to enjoy, mostly at crowded Kettle Cove at one end of the park. The beach is situated so that you're protected from the really cool Atlantic and northern breezes. Elsewhere in the park, you'll find a rocky headland, tidal pools, a freshwater marsh, a spruce and oak forest, and abundant wildlife and birds. Amenities include picnic tables, grills, changing rooms with showers, a playground and a snack bar. Wheelchair accessible. Closed Columbus Day to Memorial Day. Day-use fee, $4.50 per adult, $1 per child 5 and up. Handicap accessible. ~ Along Route 77, eight miles south of Portland; 207-799-5871, fax 207-767-2078.

WOLFE'S NECK WOODS STATE PARK You don't have to go very far from L. L. Bean's to try out your new hiking boots or cross-country skis. This 250-acre park is in Freeport, about five miles away. It's woven with five miles of well-maintained trails that offer achingly beautiful views of Casco Bay, its spruce and fir-covered islands and the coast's rocky shoreline. Picnic tables, restrooms and nature programs are available. Gates may be closed off-season but visitors are welcome year-round during daylight hours. Day-use fee, $3 per person. ~ Follow Bow Street to Wolf Neck Road; phone/fax 207-865-4465.

▲ Nearby **Recompence Shores** has 100 woodsy or oceanfront tent sites, including seven RV sites with hookups; $19 to $38 per night. Two cabins rent for $75 per night. ~ Burnett

Road, south of Freeport; 207-865-9307; www.freeportcamping.com, e-mail info@freeportcamping.com.

POPHAM BEACH STATE PARK Seemingly at the end of the world, this park offers an array of beachy pleasures. Along with a spacious sandy beach, there are tidal pools, smooth rocks to climb on and a sand bar to explore when the tide goes out. It's right at the mouth of the Kennebec River. You'll find bathhouses, freshwater showers and charcoal grills. No pets allowed. Closed mid-October through March. Day-use fee, $1 to $4 per person. ~ Off Route 209, south of Phippsburg; 207-389-1335.

▲ One half mile south of the park entrance is **Ocean View Park** (Route 209, Phippsburg; 207-389-2564), which has 48 RV sites (with hookups); $38 per night.

REID STATE PARK The centerpiece here is a great expanse of sand beach that stretches nearly a mile and a half and is backed by dunes and marshes. In addition to ocean swimming, there's a saltwater lagoon that is especially great for young children. Fortunately, the area never seems to get too crowded. There are also cross-country trails and ocean fishing for striped bass and mackerel. Facilities include bathhouses with freshwater showers, grills and a snack bar. There are lifeguards in summer. Day-use fee, $3.50 per person. ~ Off Route 127, 14 miles south of Woolwich; phone/fax 207-371-2303.

RACHEL CARSON SALT POND PRESERVE Named for the author of *Silent Spring*, this lovely Pemaquid Peninsula refuge offers a wide range of habitats to explore. Located a few peninsulas north of Boothbay Harbor, the one-quarter-acre salt pond is encircled by rocks and home to a multitude of marine species, ducks and other waterfowl. ~ From New Harbor, follow Route 32 for about a mile and look for the entrance sign.

CAMDEN HILLS STATE PARK A huddle of gentle hills, this park is always lovely whether bundled in mist or reflective as mica. It's laced with wooded trails that wrap around the hills like vines, offering beautiful views of Penobscot Bay, the windswept mountain scenery and the piney forests. There's a picnic area and restrooms. Day-use fee, $3 per person. Closed second half of November. ~ Two miles north of Camden on Route 1; 207-236-3109, fax 207-236-0849.

▲ There are 107 tent/RV sites (no hookups); $15 to $20 per night.

Downeast Coast

Maine's Downeast Coast extends roughly from the east side of Penobscot Bay up to Calais on the Canadian border. Except in patches, it's not quite as built up as the Southern Coast. The farther north you go, the more apt you are to find hidden places and Mainers (who, up here, are called Downeasterners) who are still genuinely curious about travelers. Don't expect to find lots of restaurants, nightlife and that sort of thing. The Downeast Coast—especially in the northern parts—is worlds away from big-city life. We continue up Route 1, veering off to several villages. Our first stop is Castine, poised on the tip of a peninsula about half an hour's drive from Bucksport.

SIGHTS

If the state of Maine were to have a Tidy Village Award (like the Cotswolds in England), it would probably go to the village of

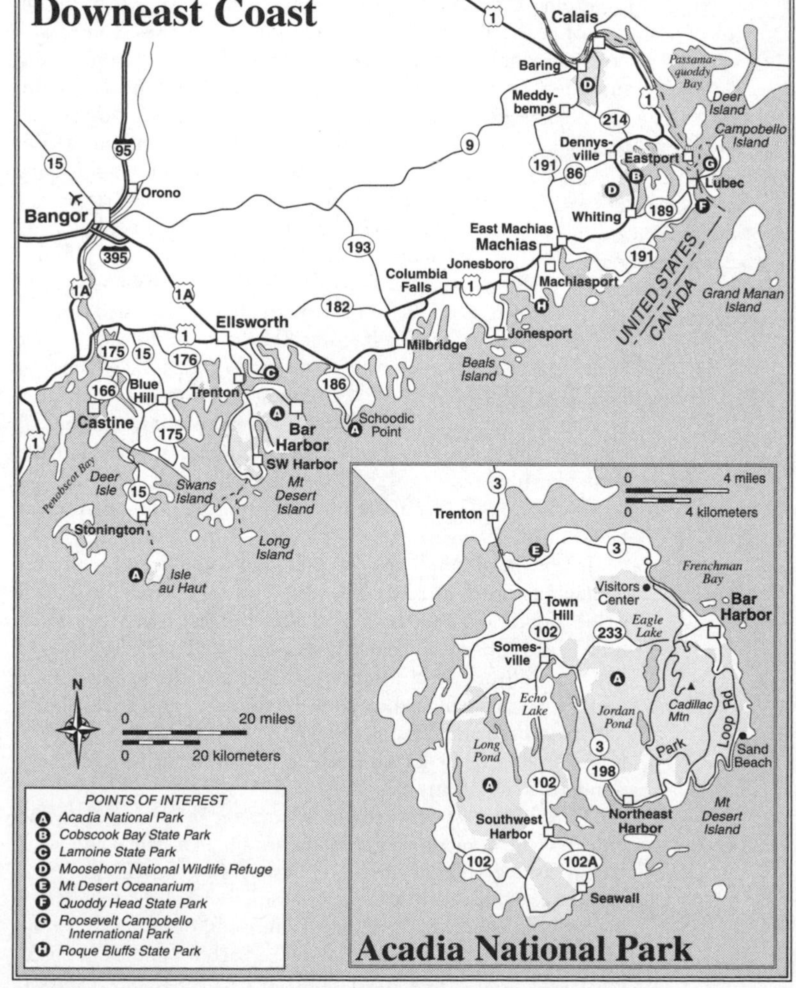

HIDDEN ► **Castine.** The attraction here is the town itself: a community of 18th- and 19th-century Georgian and Federalist houses standing in impeccable condition. Most of these were originally erected in the mid-19th century when Castine was a prosperous shipbuilding town. Many have since been restored by people "from away" (in other words, big-city folks with money to invest). Much to the objection of some natives, the town is beginning to look and feel like an open-air museum. Like most of these small coastal villages, Castine is best seen *à pied*. For information call the **Town Office.** ~ 67 Court Street, Castine; 207-326-4502, fax 207-326-9465; www.castine.me.us, e-mail castine@verizon.com.

From Castine, it's a short, steadily scenic drive over to the village of **Blue Hill.** You'll pass storybook farmhouses, ponies with tangled manes, shiny blue coves surrounded by firs and golden meadows rippling off in every direction. Blue Hill is not for everyone. In fact, many neighboring towns consider it snobby and pretentious. Indeed, it does have a big summer home–owning community, and you're likely to see BMWs, Mercedes Benzes and Saabs with New York or Massachusetts plates.

Think twice about riding bikes on Deer Isle. With the narrow, shoulderless roads, it's not only dangerous, apparently the locals abhor bikers slowing down traffic.

The name Blue Hill comes from the hill that looms up behind, covered with blueberry bushes. The town itself is home to 76 buildings listed on the National Historic Register. Take time out to walk around and poke in the pottery and crafts shops for which Blue Hill is well-known (see the "Shopping" section in this chapter) or enjoy an eclectic mix of dining options. For information call the **Blue Hill Peninsula Chamber of Commerce**. Closed Saturday through Monday. ~ 20 Water Street, P.O. Box 520, Blue Hill, ME 04614; 207-374-3242; www.bluehillpeninsula.org, e-mail chamber@bluehillpeninsula.org.

If you head southwest of Blue Hill, you'll eventually cut through a corner of Little Deer Isle and then climb an arching suspension bridge that takes you over to **Deer Isle**, a wonderful little island almost too beautiful to promote. Thanks to its seemingly end-of-the-world location, it gets only the serious Maine visitors. For a small island, it's well endowed with attractions—both manmade and natural. One of the nicest ways to enjoy Deer Isle is on foot or by kayak (see the "Outdoor Adventures" section at the end of this chapter).

HIDDEN ► Tops on our list of worthwhile stops on Deer Isle is the sweet little town of **Stonington** at the southern tip. In a state where once-quaint fishing villages turn into Disneyesque attractions seemingly overnight, this town is a welcome relief. It has everything you've been expecting in Maine—shingled houses, lobster traps piled high, seagulls screeching above, a harbor bundled in mist—but hasn't been completely colonized by the "Kennebushport" crowd. Ask one of the locals to point you in the direction of **Ames Pond**, about a two-minute drive east from the center of town. During the summer months, the rare pink lilies in the pond bloom, turning it into a meadow of pink blossoms.

If you're visiting from June through August, plan on arriving for the Wednesday tour that starts at 1 p.m. at the **Haystack Mountain School of Crafts**. Dramatically situated amidst deep piney woods right on the water, the shingled buildings house artists' studios where you can observe devoted artisans skillfully manipulating clay, blowing glass or working in other media. Closed September through May. Fee. ~ South of Deer Isle Village, turn left off Route 15 onto Sunshine Road, and follow signs for about seven miles; 207-348-2306, fax 207-348-2307; www.haystack-mtn.org, e-mail haystack@haystack-mtn.org.

As you drive back in the direction of the mainland, go slow where you probably missed the turnoff on the way out to **Nervous Nellie's Jams and Jellies**, a jam and jelly kitchen surrounded by landscape sculptures by one of the owners. You're welcome to sample the jams and jellies. We took home a jar of blue-razz conserve and instantly became hooked. Thank goodness they do mail order. ~ 598 Sunshine Road, Deer Isle; 207-348-6182, 800-777-6845, fax 800-804-7698; www.nervousnellies.com, e-mail jam@nervousnellies.com.

Ever since the mid-19th century, **Mount Desert Island** has been one of Maine's most popular destinations. Once you cross the bridge connecting it to the mainland, it's easy to see why. The island (New England's third-largest) is home to **Cadillac Mountain**, at 1530 feet the highest point on the Atlantic coast of the United States. Looming all around are 16 other mountains that drop right down into the sea. Fortunately, most of the island (35,000 acres) is under the protection of **Acadia National Park**, which is threaded with miles of hiking, driving and biking trails.

Wherever your peregrinations take you, there's plenty to keep you enormously busy for at least a couple of days on Mount Desert Island. By the way, Mount Desert Island is pronounced like "dessert," the sweet course that follows a meal. It was given the name by French explorer Samuel de Champlain, who discovered the island in 1604. He named it *L'Isle des Monts Déserts* because of its bare, desertlike mountaintops.

Start by heading to **Acadia National Park's Hulls Cove Visitors Center** to pick up a copy of the *Official Map and Guide to Acadia*. There's also a 15-minute introductory video and several racks of nature books. Ask for a copy of *Acadia's Beaver Log*, a park newspaper, if you're interested in finding out that week's ranger-led activities. The Hulls Cove location is open mid-April through October; the rest of the year, visitor information can be found at the park headquarters near Bar Harbor. ~ Off

Route 3 in Hulls Cove; 207-288-3338, fax 207-288-8813; www.nps.gov/acad, e-mail acadia_information@nps.gov.

The **Park Loop Road** takes in the major sights of the park, including Frenchman Bay Overlook, a scenic lookout that faces Schoodic Peninsula; Sieur de Monts Spring, with its nature center; the Wild Gardens of Acadia, a lovely patch featuring local flowers, trees and shrubs; Sand Beach, made partially of the crushed shells of marine animals; the Robert Abbe Museum (admission), showcasing prehistoric artifacts of the area's original Indian tribes; and the summit of Cadillac Mountain. The road traverses approximately 27 miles up mountains, by the sea, through forests and past ponds and lakes, taking in the park's highlights (see "Beaches & Parks" below). For a closer look at the park's multitude of attractions, consider hiking along the many foot trails or signing up for a ranger-led program. There are also boat trips, fishing opportunities and places to swim. In winter, there's cross-country skiing, snowmobiling, ice fishing and winter hiking. Most of the road is closed from about mid-November to mid-April. For more information, contact: Superintendent, Acadia National Park, P.O. Box 177, Bar Harbor, ME 04609; 207-288-3338, fax 207-288-8813; www.nps.gov/acad, e-mail acadia_information@nps.gov.

The island's main town is **Bar Harbor**, which, back in the late 1800s, was a thriving resort community for very wealthy and powerful American families. They built more than 200 enormous summer homes along the sea that were just as opulent as the Newport mansions. The Depression years and two world wars really took a toll on the community, however. And finally, the Great Fire of 1947 all but wiped it out. Many of the grand old hotels and about 70 mansions were destroyed.

Bar Harbor did recover, but it emerged as a more middle-class resort. Today, during summer months, it's crawling with tourists. The main street is a tangle of T-shirt shops, motels and restaurants busy with teeny-boppers and young families. We recommend visiting the **Bar Harbor Historical Society**, which features a collection of early photographs of the town before the big fire. Closed Sunday from June through October. Open by appointment only the rest of the year. ~ 33 Ledgelawn Avenue, Bar Harbor; 207-288-0000, 207-288-3807 (for appointments); www.barharborhistorical.org.

We also encourage a visit to the **Natural History Museum**, which showcases taxidermied birds and animals done by students. It also features complete whale skeletons and a marine touch tank. Closed Sunday in September and October, and from November to mid-June. Admission. ~ College of the Atlantic, Route 3, Bar Harbor; 207-288-5015; www.coa.org.

A quartet of other towns on the island—Northeast Harbor, Southwest Harbor, Seal Harbor and Somesville—are likely to appeal more to the traveler in search of hidden attractions. They're quintessential Maine fishing villages. One especially worthwhile stop to make is the **Asticou Gardens**, a lovely spot devoted to azalea and Japanese gardens. ~ Route 3, near the junction of Route 198, Northeast Harbor; 207-276-5040.

You must also stop at the **Wendell Gilley Museum** if you're interested in seeing bird carvings. Closed Monday from June through October, Monday through Thursday in May, and from November to mid-December. There are no visitor hours from mid-December through April. Call ahead for hours. Admission. ~ Corner of Harrick Road and Route 102, Southwest Harbor; 207-244-7555; www.wendellgilleymuseum.org, e-mail info@wendellgilleymuseum.org.

Families with children will want to stop at the **Mount Desert Oceanarium**, where you'll find plenty of hands-on exhibits, live sea animals and a touch-tank with sea snails, starfish and horseshoe crabs. Closed mid-October to mid-May. Admission. ~ 172 Clark Point Road, Southwest Harbor; 207-244-7330; www.theoceanarium.com, e-mail theoceanarium@pananax.com.

Back on the mainland, in busy Ellsworth, try not to miss the **Woodland Museum**, a startlingly beautiful 1820s Federal estate filled with the original furnishings and decorative pieces of the Black family. Closed Monday from May through October. Closed November through April. Admission. ~ Route 172 (Surry Road), Ellsworth; 207-667-8671, fax 207-667-7950; www.woodlawnmuseum.com, e-mail info@woodlawnmuseum.com.

Also worth visiting is the **Stanwood Wildlife Sanctuary (Birdsacre)**, a 200-acre nature preserve centerpieced by a homestead that dates back to 1850. The grounds are open year round, but the house hours are seasonal. ~ Route 3, Ellsworth; 207-667-8460.

As you work your way up the coast, you'll see less traffic, fewer commercial buildings and increasingly beautiful scenery (rolling

DAY TRIP TO ISLE AU HAUT

From the dock at the corner of Sea Breeze Avenue and Bayview Street in Stonington, you can catch the mail boat, *Miss Lizzie* (207-367-5193), for a day trip over to elf-sized **Isle au Haut**. Since you've come this far, you might as well not miss it. Part of Acadia National Park, it has some mapped-out trails to explore and picnic areas. It's also home to a one-room schoolhouse and a general store.

farmlands, pine forests, glimpses of the sea). You'll also notice fewer tourists—here they're chiefly RV families and rugged outdoor sports enthusiasts en route to the dense wilderness of Baxter State Park. Your chances of meeting real, hard-working, homespun locals are much greater here than along the Southern Coast, where everyone grows up learning how to treat "people from away" properly so they'll come back. You'll find Downeasterners love to strike up a conversation with a "foreigner," and have a wonderful sense of humor.

Continue to follow Route 1, veering off whenever a road looks appealing. There are several interesting detours to watch for, including **Jonesport** and **Beals Island**, which you have to squint to find on most maps. Ask any Maine aficionado which are their favorite coastal villages and they're sure to mention this little duet of lobstering and fishing towns at the end of Route 187. The two are connected by a bridge and in people's minds—rarely do you hear someone mention one without the other. Your best bet is to park in Jonesport and wander around aimlessly. You'll find a handful of restaurants, antique stores and other salty little shops.

HIDDEN ►

Back on Route 1, don't miss the **Ruggles House**. Built for a wealthy lumber dealer named Thomas Ruggles in 1818, it's an extravagant Federal-style building with a flying staircase and meticulously carved woodwork throughout. Closed mid-October through May. Admission. ~ Columbia Falls; 207-483-4637; www.ruggleshouse.org, e-mail etenan@ruggleshouse.org.

The Quoddy Head Lighthouse's claim to fame is that it sits on the easternmost point of the land in the continental United States.

Machias is one of the next towns you'll come to. It's worth pulling over and getting out to take a stroll around. An old commercial center, it now has a handful of shops and restaurants and is home to the **Maine Wild Blueberry Company**.

Machias is supposedly an Indian word meaning "bad little falls," named because of the falls that run through the middle of town, where you'll also find a nice picnicking spot. Less than 15 minutes away is **Machiasport**, another photogenic village.

At East Machias, you can either continue on Route 1 or sidetrack to Route 191, taking in the little fishing village called **Cutler**. Consider taking a trip to see the puffins on **Machias Seal Island** (from May through August) on **Captain Norton's** excursions. Captain Norton has been taking visitors to the island since 1939. Closed Labor Day through Memorial Day. Fee. ~ 118 Main Street, P.O. Box 330, Jonesport; 207-497-5933; www.machiassealisland.com, e-mail puffins@downeast.net.

Next stop is **Lubec**, a once-very-active sardine-canning town. Today, it has sort of a lonely, end-of-the-world feel to it, but it's lovable nonetheless. It's the country's most easterly town and a stepping-stone to **Campobello Island**, noted as the summer home of Franklin Roosevelt's family (which is actually in New Brunswick, Canada). You don't need passports, special papers or even toll change to cross the bridge and spend the afternoon visiting FDR's house. From late May to October, visitors can tour **Roosevelt Campobello International Park**, the 34-room "cottage" where Roosevelt spent his boyhood summers from 1905 to 1921. Start by watching the excellent 15-minute movie. Then explore the house, which has been maintained exactly as the family left it. The grounds are landscaped with flower beds and woven with over eight miles of trails through piney woods and along the shore. Closed mid-October to mid-May. ~ 506-752-2922 (house), fax 506-752-6000; www.fdr.net, e-mail info@fdr.net.

Back in Lubec, follow South Lubec Road to the end to get to the **Quoddy Head State Park**. You've undoubtedly seen the **Quoddy Head Lighthouse** before: the candy-striped, red-and-white tower is practically an emblem for the state of Maine. The perfect-snapshot lighthouse is at the end of a long bumpy dirt road. Signs warn visitors not to venture out when the tide is coming in. It rises five feet per hour and could leave you stranded for hours. There are more than four miles of hiking trails to wander along as well as benches if you feel like sitting and waiting for the sun to come up.

Route 189 will take you back out to Route 1 and up through West Pembroke, where you can detour off to see Reversing Falls (see "Beaches & Parks" below).

You might also consider taking another detour along Route 214 to **Meddybemps**. The road stretches out like a canvas over one waterslide of a hill after another, edged by wheaty fields right out of an Andrew Wyeth painting. One little hill-clinging farm has a stand of vegetables with a self-service sign. Meddybemps itself is an adorable little village with a white church, white houses and a general store. There's also a pier on Meddybemps Lake and a small beach where you can swim.

It's worth arranging to spend a few days in **Eastport**, an intriguing port city set on Moose Island in Passamaquoddy Bay. For years, it's had a statewide reputation of being somewhat down and out, but actually it's quite charming and those who have discovered—or rediscovered—the spot keep it to themselves. At one time, Eastport was a bustling town with 18 sardine canneries. The population had reached 5300 by the turn of the 20th century. But between 1937 and 1943, it went bust. Canneries closed, and people moved out, leaving houses standing empty. Today, grand old Federal and Victorian houses remain as testimony to its better days. The skeletal population (maybe 2000) is a combination of old-timers remaining from the town's heyday, a thriving artist population and a small infusion of investment-seeking out-of-towners. ◄ HIDDEN

The best way to get acquainted with Eastport and the Eastporters is to wander along its streets. Water Street is the hub, with more empty commercial space than filled. The town has been slowly upgrading and has completed a revival of the 19th-century storefronts on the waterfront. Unfortunately, few tenants have moved in. However, many say Eastport is the next frontier. The next Bar Harbor. We hope not. The star attraction is the **Eastport Gallery**, a highly respected and lovingly cared for showcase of local art. The 27-person artist collective features rotating exhibits of the members' work. Closed October to mid-June. ~ 74 Water Street, Eastport; 207-853-4166; www.eastportgallery.com, e-mail eastportgallery@yahoo.com.

One way to take in a big bite of this part of the coast is to drive the **Quoddy Loop**. Also known as "The Loop," it's a network of car-ferry services linking the New Brunswick mainland with Campobello Island, Deer Island (not to be confused with Deer Isle, farther down the coast), Lubec and Eastport. Ferry service is available late June to mid-September.

Calais (pronounced CAL-lus) is the last real stop along this stretch of coast, and actually it's set on the St. Croix River a little inland. It's a jumping-off spot for many outdoors sportspeople since it lies near **Grand Lake**, one of Maine's most beautiful and salmon-rich lakes. While in the area, stop at the **St. Croix Island Overlook** at Red Beach. It's a view of the island on which French explorers established the first European settlement in North America north of Florida (in 1604).

Another worthwhile stop in this area is the **Moosehorn National Wildlife Refuge**. Managed by the U.S. Fish and Wildlife Service, it's the northeast end of a chain of migratory bird refuges that extend all the way up the East Coast. Two divisions make up the refuge, the largest (20,000 acres) in Baring, north of Calais, and the other (9000 acres) about 20 miles south near Edmunds. These wilderness areas are crisscrossed by hiking trails that can also be used for cross-country skiing and snow-shoeing. There

LEISURE READING

Try to get your hands on the Portland-based magazine called *Salt* (sold in various shops in town). It sometimes has beautiful essays about Eastport's wonderful characters. Another publication to pick up is the *Quoddy Tides*, a bimonthly newspaper highlighting all the area's goings-on, including the new titles the Lubec Library has added. Don't laugh. Some people love this little tabloid so much, they end up getting a subscription sent to their Park Avenue apartment.

are old logging roads that are suitable for biking, too. ~ Baring; 207-454-3521, fax 207-454-2550; moosehorn.fws.gov.

LODGING

If you're looking for the perfect New England inn in the perfect New England village, consider detouring off Route 1 to Castine and **The Castine Inn**. The 1898 bed-and-breakfast inn is ideally situated in town minutes from the water's edge. Its 17 guest rooms are bright, decent-sized and lovingly maintained by innkeepers Tom and Amy Gutow. Some have views of the harbor. Full breakfast included. Closed October through April. ~ Main Street, Castine; 207-326-4365, fax 207-326-4570; www.castineinn.com, e-mail relax@castineinn.com. MODERATE TO ULTRA-DELUXE.

Poised on Castine's stately Main Street is the main building of the **Pentagoet Inn**, a large old Victorian bed and breakfast. Guests can stay either in that house or at neighboring Perkins Cottage, a late-18th-century building where all guest rooms have country antiques. Between the two, there are 16 rooms, all with private baths. Closed November through April. A full breakfast and bikes are included in the rates. ~ Main Street, Castine; 207-326-8616, 800-845-1701, fax 207-326-9382; www.pentagoet.com, e-mail stay@pentagoet.com. MODERATE TO ULTRA-DELUXE.

Snugly set on 48 acres, **Blue Hill Farm Country Inn** seems to attract a healthy, life-loving crowd. There are seven guest rooms in the farmhouse and seven in the renovated barn, all looking as though they might have been photographed for *Country Living* magazine. The rooms in the barn have private baths. The highlight every morning is breakfast: fresh-out-of-the-oven breads and muffins, homemade granola, fresh fruits and various cheeses. ~ 578 Pleasant Street, Blue Hill; 207-374-5126; www.bluehillfarminn.com, e-mail bluehillfarm@gwi.net. MODERATE.

The **Pilgrim's Inn** has found its way into travel and gourmet publications all over the United States and Canada. It's not surprising. Perched on a shiny millpond directly opposite Northwest Harbor, this 1793 house is impeccably maintained. Recently renovated rooms—a total of 12, plus 3 housekeeping units in the neighboring guest cottage—are decorated simply with antiques and artwork and crafts by local artists, who are numerous in these parts. Tourists and Mainers from as far as Bar Harbor come for the dinners here, which are among the best in the midcoast area. Closed mid-October to mid-May. ~ Deer Isle Village; phone/fax 207-348-6615, 888-778-7505; www.pilgrimsinn.com, e-mail innkeeper@pilgrimsinn.com. DELUXE TO ULTRA-DELUXE.

As one totally satiated guest said while stretching his legs in a lounge chair and peering out at the fog-bundled sea with its hooting vessels, "This may not be five-star, but you can't beat the setting." The **Inn on the Harbor** features 13 rooms of varying sizes, most of which are smack-dab on the water with ocean views. All are furnished with antiques and some feature private decks, sitting areas and fireplaces. There's also a two-bedroom apartment with a wood stove and a private deck. Stepping out on the deck that hangs over the harbor is like walking right into a painting. Expanded continental breakfast is included. ~ Main Street, Stonington; 207-367-2420, 800-942-2420, fax 207-367-5165; www.innontheharbor.com, e-mail info@innontheharbor.com. DELUXE.

HIDDEN ►

Though many visitors take the mail boat out just to spend the day on Isle au Haut, you can overnight there. **The Keeper's House** is a stucco lighthouse-keeper's-cottage-turned-inn that still uses kerosene and candles for its lighting, although it does use some solar- and wind-generated electricity. There are two large, airy and simply decorated bedrooms along with a dining room in the main cottage, as well as a separate accommodation in the tiny Oil House with its own outdoor shower and an outhouse (there's no indoor plumbing in the Oil House). Three meals are provided. Bicycles are available for guests' use. Closed late October to mid-May. ~ Robinson's Point, Isle au Haut; 207-460-0257; www.keepershouse.com. ULTRA-DELUXE.

You can spend hours—no, days—roaming around the rooms of **Cleftstone Manor**, filled with period antiques collected over the years. The house is a huge mansion built in 1880 that quickly became a favorite summer home for visiting Washington dignitaries. Its 17 ornately decorated guest rooms, with private baths, are named for people who have had an interest in or ownership of the building. The grandly proportioned Cleftstone room, with its wooden canopy bed, beamed ceilings and fireplace, is worth taking a peek at if you happen to be staying in one of the others. However, all are jaw-droppingly impressive. A full-service, gourmet breakfast is included. Closed November through April. ~ 92 Eden Street, Bar Harbor; 207-288-4951, 888-288-4951, fax 207-288-2089; www.cleftstone.com, e-mail innkeeper@cleftstone.com. DELUXE.

ON JORDAN POND

When driving the Park Loop Road in Acadia National Park, you couldn't ask for a better place to stop for lunch, tea or dinner than **Jordan Pond House**. Along with a mountain view, it offers Maine specialties such as lobster stew and Maine crab cakes—in a setting of classical music warmed by the fireplace. Closed mid-October to mid-May. ~ Park Loop Road, Bar Harbor; 207-276-3316, fax 207-288-1263; www.jordanpond.com. MODERATE.

If you want to glimpse what life was like in turn-of-the-20th-century Bar Harbor summer cottages, consider staying at the **Ledgelawn Inn**. You can have your pick of rooms in either the main house or the Carriage House. There are 33 rooms, some with working fireplaces, verandas and, for a modern touch, whirlpool baths and saunas. All are handsomely decorated with beautiful antiques. Closed late October to mid-May. ~ 66 Mount Desert Street, Bar Harbor; 207-288-4596, 800-274-5334, fax 207-288-9968; www.ledgelawninn.com, e-mail desk@ledgelawninn.com. DELUXE TO ULTRA-DELUXE.

Listed in the National Register of Historic Places, the **Manor House Inn** is yet another summer cottage that has been restored and preserved. This lovely 22-room Victorian mansion, built in the late 1800s, has 18 guest quarters, all with private baths and Victorian furnishings, some with working fireplaces. A full breakfast is included in the price. Closed November through April. ~ 106 West Street, Bar Harbor; 207-288-3759, 800-437-0088, fax 207-288-2974; www.barharbormanorhouse.com, e-mail manor@acadia.net. MODERATE TO ULTRA-DELUXE.

Fortunately, some things never change. Such is the case with the **Claremont**, Mount Desert Island's oldest summer hotel (it dates to 1884). Of course, this grande dame (listed on the National Register of Historic Places) has been renovated—heavily. But it still manages to preserve the old Maine vacation traditions such as dressing for dinner (that means jackets are suggested) and socializing with fellow guests. The large, rambling, clapboard building has a wide veranda lined with wicker rocking chairs. The view of Somes Sound is nonpareil. The food—lots of lobster and seafood—is unfailingly good. The rooms (a total of 43 units, 13 of them cottages) are homey and comfortable. On top of all that, guests can sample the many on-site sporting facilities, including clay tennis courts, bikes, rowboats, and croquet courts. Credit cards are not accepted. Closed November to mid-May. ~ Claremont Road, Southwest Harbor; 207-244-5036, 800-244-5036, fax 207-244-3512; www.theclaremonthotel.com, e-mail clmhotel@adelphia.net. ULTRA-DELUXE.

Many guests intending to spend one or two nights at the **Weston House** end up extending their stay. From what we could tell, it was the combination of the bed and breakfast itself (it feels very European) and the enormously interesting town of Eastport. There are four guest rooms and two baths on the upper level of the house, a stately old Federal built in 1810. All the rooms are thoughtfully furnished with comfortable beds along with tasteful antique pieces and little touches like fresh flowers in season. The house is within walking distance of everything. The breakfasts are unmatchable, featuring all sorts of inspired recipes. ~ 26 Boynton Street, Eastport; 207-853-2907, 800-853-2907, fax 207-853-0981; ◄ HIDDEN www.westonhouse-maine.com, e-mail westonhouseinn@prexar.com. MODERATE.

DINING

In a little town as amphibious as Castine, it's surprising to find just one restaurant on the water. Fortunately, the food at **Dennett's Wharf**, a net-hung, bustling fish house, is just as appealing as the view of the sailboat-dotted harbor. It features 120 feet of float space out in front of the deck to accommodate visiting yachts. A lunch of freshly cracked oysters followed by a grilled crab sandwich and one of ten Maine microbrewed drafts on tap is deliriously good. Also try the mussels marinara, seafood linguine or one of the surf-and-turf specials. Dennett's is ultracasual, with waitresses sporting khakis. Don't forget to check out the ceiling covered with dollar bills. If you want to know how they got there, ask Gary. His response: "If you've got a dollar, I'll show you!" Closed mid-October through April. ~ Sea Street, Castine; 207-326-9045; www.dennettswharf.com, e-mail info@dennettswharf.com. MODERATE TO ULTRA-DELUXE.

The Castine Inn is elegantly accoutred with pretty table settings and wall murals depicting harbor scenes. The menu changes weekly, and may feature innovative entrées such as butter-bathed lobster with corn tortellini and basil and slow-roasted salmon with green apple, celery and radish sprouts. Be sure to try the crabcakes, grilled foie gras or any of the delicious desserts. Budget-priced traditional pub fare is available at their attached tavern. Closed Columbus Day through April. ~ Main Street, Castine; 207-326-4365; www.castineinn.com, e-mail relax@castineinn.com. DELUXE TO ULTRA-DELUXE.

If you can't stay at **Pilgrim's Inn**, by all means do have dinner there. Their restaurant, The Whale's Rib Tavern, is housed in a converted timber-beamed barn and features a wide range of options from sandwiches to fine-dining specials such as blue cheese encrusted beef tenderloin with shiitake mushrooms or sesame-seared yellowfin tuna with gingered sweet-potato mash. Among the other courses are local chowders, salads made from locally grown vegetables, and homemade desserts. Dinner only. Closed mid-October to mid-May. ~ Deer Isle Village; phone/fax 207-348-6615; www.pilgrimsinn.com, e-mail innkeeper@pilgrimsinn.com. ULTRA-DELUXE.

HIDDEN ►

The light-of-wallet but discriminating seafood eater won't find a better value than **Fisherman's Friend Restaurant**. Go when you are starving—the place prides itself on its generous servings of spanking fresh fish and seafood. The diner decor could use some gussying up, but with a platter piled high with clams, who cares? Call ahead for winter hours. ~ Main Street, Stonington; 207-367-2442. BUDGET TO MODERATE.

We sat for hours at our window seat in the **Reading Room Restaurant** at the Bar Harbor Inn, mesmerized by the view. Breakfast and dinner are available at this expansive dining room with a circular view of the bay. The food is lovely, too, with specialties like fresh lobster pie and grilled seafood. In addition, an outdoor waterfront terrace dining area offers lunch and light suppers. Closed December through March. ~ Newport Drive, Bar Harbor; 207-288-3351, 800-248-3351, fax 207-288-8548; www.barharborinn.com. DELUXE TO ULTRA-DELUXE.

Children are in their glory in the delightfully decorated **Route 66**. The restaurant is decorated with antique toys: everywhere you spot old toys, tools and other gadgets, each having a story of its own. The food is good old Americana, with standard favorites like grilled steaks and boiled lobster. And there are more innovative dishes as well, including shrimp fettuccine and baked stuffed haddock. Closed mid-October to mid-April. ~ 21 Cottage Street, Bar Harbor; 207-288-3708, fax 207-288-0318; www.bhroute66.com, e-mail info@bhroute66.com. MODERATE TO DELUXE.

Simple yet dignified, **Guinness and Porcellis** offers premier Italian cuisine served on candle-lit tables brightened by fresh flowers. Light canary walls and sleek lighting create a chic ambience that pairs easily with the extensive menu. Indulge in entrées such as gorgonzola-dolce-encrusted filet with Chianti demiglace served with truffled mashed potatoes. Closed Sunday. ~ 191 Main Street, Bar Harbor; 207-288-0030; www.guinnessporcellis.com. MODERATE TO ULTRA-DELUXE.

If hunger strikes while you're driving north on Route 1, stop in Milbridge at **The Red Barn**, a very casual, knotty pine–paneled spot with some counter seats, booths and separate dining rooms. It has a mainstream menu (pastas, burgers, steak, seafood)

AUTHOR FAVORITE

Since I'd always associated Maine with lobsters, I was surprised to find that most are exported. Maine restaurants typically serve them—if at all—shredded into a stew, bisque or salad. A tasty exception is **Beal's Lobster Pier**, where you can eat them fresh or ship them home. It's also an outstanding place to stuff yourself on clams. It's super casual, with picnic tables set outside in nice weather. They'll pack lobsters in ice to go and arrange air freight as well. Closed mid-October to mid-May. ~ Clark Point Road, Southwest Harbor; 207-244-7178, 800-245-7178, fax 207-244-9479; www.bealslobster.com, e-mail beals@acadia.net. MODERATE TO ULTRA-DELUXE.

as well as some house specialties like the seafood stew, a delicious concoction of shrimp, scallops, haddock and crabmeat. ~ 5 North Main Street, Milbridge; 207-546-7721; e-mail hleighton@nemaine.com. BUDGET TO DELUXE.

Design your own submarine sandwich, pizza or burger at **Bank Square Pizza & Deli**. Even burgers come in small, medium or large. But if you'd prefer to order a meal without customization, there are salads, chicken dishes and vegetarian options on the lengthy menu. ~ 34 Water Street, Eastport; 207-853-2709; www.banksquarepizza.com, e-mail mari_maine@yahoo.com. BUDGET TO MODERATE.

Nervous Nellie's Jams and Jellies produces about 40,000 jars a year of the homemade stuff out of their little white clapboard building.

The **Waco Diner**, Maine's oldest restaurant, solves the pesky problem of wanting a shot of local color. Here you'll see all the local Eastport characters, including salty seafaring types and former sardine cannery workers. The food—standard diner fare—is nothing to get excited about, but that's not the point. You're here for the Eastport atmosphere. There is also a more upscale dining room overlooking the water that serves pasta, seafood, beef and poultry. Outdoor deck seating is available. No dinner on Sunday during the winter. ~ Water Street, Eastport; 207-853-4046. MODERATE.

Before taking off for the northern woods, do yourself a favor and have a meal at **Chandler House Restaurant**. This warm and popular restaurant is well known in these parts for its prime rib and seafood dishes. All the baking is done right here. Closed Monday. ~ 20 Chandler Street, Calais; 207-454-7922. MODERATE TO DELUXE.

SHOPPING

Though you probably won't find any bargains in the little shops and art galleries of Castine, you can find yourself happily occupied looking at all the truly original fashions, the nautical gifts and the New England crafts and artwork. The bookstore **Compass Rose** has a good selection of Maritime and Maine-themed volumes. Closed Monday through Wednesday from January through April. ~ 3 Main Street, Castine; 207-326-9366, fax 207-326-0694; www.compassrosebooks.com, e-mail compassrosebookstore@verizon.net. The **McGrath Dunham Gallery** showcases New England artists from May through October. ~ 9 Main Street, Castine; 207-326-9175; www.mcgrathdunhamgallery.com, e-mail art@mcgrathdunhamgallery.com.

The village of Blue Hill is known in the area for its profusion of potters and artisans. For functional pottery, especially dinnerware, stop by **Rowantrees Pottery**. Closed Sunday. ~ Union Street, Blue Hill; 207-374-5535. The family-aimed **Rackliffe Pottery** has been producing earthenware for three generations. Closed Sunday from Labor Day through July 4. ~ Route 172,

Blue Hill; 207-374-2297, 888-631-3321; www.rackliffepotter.com, e-mail info@rackliffepotter.com. **Handworks Gallery** has pottery, fine art and diverse Maine-made items such as jewelry and furniture. Closed Sunday in spring and fall, closed January through mid-May. ~ Main Street, Blue Hill; 207-374-5613; www.handworksgallery.org, e-mail artwork@handworksgallery.org.

You could easily plan your entire trip around visiting the studios and galleries of Deer Isle. Start by going to the **Deer Isle Artists Association**, a 150-member cooperative gallery with exhibits changing every two weeks. There you can pick up studio maps and postcards and plan a route. ~ 6 Dow Road, Deer Isle Village; 207-348-2330; www.deerisleartists.com.

William Mor Oriental Rugs is the place for oriental and vegetable-dyed tribal rugs. Closed mid-October through April. ~ 663 Reach Road, Deer Isle; 207-348-2822; www.williammororientalrugs.com, e-mail rugs@williammororientalrugs.com.

Any visitor to Maine really ought to stop at **Nervous Nellie's Jams and Jellies**. Though it's a small company, walk-in customers can sample the goods—hot tomato chutney, strawberry rhubarb conserve, cherry peach conserve, just to name a few—before deciding what to buy. May through October, the company also serves as a café offering coffee, tea, homemade scones and other goodies. The store is located next to the owner's sculpture studio, resulting in a property dotted with whimsical installations. The salesroom is closed from October through May, but Nellie's still sells jams and jellies right out of the kitchen, as well as by mail order. ~ 598 Sunshine Road, Deer Isle; 207-348-6182, 800-777-6845; www.nervousnellies.com, e-mail jam@nervousnellies.com.

Bar Harbor is chockablock with shops, many of them purveying standard tourist goods—T-shirts that say "Baa-Haa-Bah" (the way Mainers pronounce it), multicolored wind socks (a craze here) and Maineana books, calendars and cards. However, there are some galleries and shops to make a point of finding.

Birdnest Gallery has oils, watercolors, graphics and woodcarvings by contemporary New England artists. Closed November to mid-May. Call for fall hours. ~ 12 Mount Desert Street, Bar Harbor; 207-288-4054; www.birdsnestgallery.com. **Island Artisans** features works by local artists. Closed December through April. ~ 99 Main Street, Bar Harbor; 207-288-4214, fax 207-288-8051; www.islandartisans.com, e-mail artisans@downeast.com. **A Lone Moose** is the oldest made-in-Maine gallery on the island. They offer wildlife sculptures in wood and bronze, pottery, watercolors, limited-edition wood blockprints, collectible miniature teapots and jewelry. Closed November through April. ~ 78 West Street, Bar Harbor; 207-288-4229; www.finemainecrafts.com, e-mail gallery@finemainecrafts.com. Another interesting shop in the area is **The Woodshop Cupolas**, where you can buy handcrafted cupolas and weathervanes. They're located on Route 3 in Trenton during the summer, and on Route 102 in Bar Harbor during the winter. ~ 207-667-6331, 207-288-5530 (winter), 800-698-5538; www.woodshopcupolas.com.

If you're interested in pottery, be sure to get to **Connie's Clay of Fundy**, where you'll find museum-quality contemporary porcelain and raku. If you're lucky, you may see the artist at work in her adjoining studio. ~ Route 1, East Machias; 207-255-4574, 888-255-8131; www.clayoffundy.com, e-mail connie@clayoffundy.com.

In the business of concocting mustard since 1903, **Raye's Mustard Mill** is also a working museum where condiment afficionados can watch their mustard being ground before choosing from the dozens of varieties that Raye's sells. Closed on Sunday during the winter. ~ 83 Washington Street, Eastport; 207-853-4451, 800-853-1903; www.rayesmustard.com, e-mail mustards@rayesmustard.com.

NIGHTLIFE One look at Castine and it's clear: no neon-zapped discos here. Not even a sleazy bar. Most visitors plan their nights around a big, satiating seafood dinner.

The big night out in Blue Hill is attending concerts at the **Kneisel Hall Chamber Music Festival**. From late June to late August, string and ensemble performances are held on Friday evenings and Sunday afternoons. Kneisel Hall also features student and amateur concerts. ~ For information, write: P.O. Box 648, Blue Hill, ME 04614; 207-374-2811; www.kneisel.org, e-mail festival@kneisel.org.

Lights go off early on Deer Isle and Isle au Haut, as well.

In Bar Harbor, we managed to scrounge up a couple of things to do after dark. The liveliest pub spot is **Geddy's**, a magnet for families. This is also a good spot to pick up pizzas or burgers. There's also ribs, lobster and pasta dishes. ~ 19 Main Street, Bar Harbor; 207-288-5077, fax 207-288-3986; www.geddys.com, e-mail info@geddys.com.

Like many parts of the Maine coast, Mount Desert Island has a flourishing cultural life. Check the local papers to find out what performances are on while you're on the island. The **Acadia Repertory Theatre** puts on four main stage plays and one children's production a season in the Somesville Masonic Hall. Their season runs from July to September. ~ Route 102, Somesville; 207-244-7260, 888-362-7480; www.acadiarep.com, e-mail arep@acadia.net. The **Deck House Restaurant Cabaret Theatre** features outstanding summer cabaret shows in an ocean-view setting. ~ Southwest Harbor; 207-244-5044, fax 207-244-7678; www.thedeckhouse.com, e-mail robin@acadia.net. Between the first weekend in July through the first weekend in August, the **Bar Harbor Music Festival** is in full swing with concerts of all strains—recitals, pops, opera, string and up-and-coming artists—performed at sites around town, including the outdoor amphitheater at Acadia National Park. There are also occasional jazz concerts. ~ 207-288-5744, 212-222-1026 (winter), fax 207-288-5886; www.barharbormusicfestival.org, e-mail info@barharbormusicfestival.org. Also from mid-July to mid-August, there's the **Mount Desert Festival of Chamber Music**, a series of chamber concerts. ~ Neighborhood House, Main Street, Northeast Harbor; 207-276-3988; www.mtdesertfestival.org, e-mail info@mtdesertfestival.org. **The Arcady Music Festival** draws a big crowd with summer and winter performances ranging from small ensembles to chamber orchestras in locations throughout Bangor, Bar Harbor and the down east region. ~ 207-669-4225, fax 207-449-1331; www.arcady.org, e-mail arcady@arcady.org.

Once you get north of Ellsworth, you'll find even less to do after the sun goes down. This is real Maine country, where going to the movies constitutes the big night out.

In July and August, there are a series of chamber music concerts hosted by the **Bay Chamber Concerts**. ~ Centre Street Congregational Church, Machias; 207-255-3889.

In Eastport, check to see what is going on at the **Eastport Arts Center**. In 2005 the center relocated to a charming 1837 church building, which allowed it to greatly expand. It is now home to numerous community organizations, including a small orchestra, a film society, multiple dance troupes and a very active community theater that stages three or four productions each season. There is also an art gallery and a wing dedicated to art education. ~ 36 Washington Street, Eastport; 207-853-2358; www.eastportartscenter.com, e-mail info@eastportartscenter.com.

STROLL BENEATH THE STARS

Acadia National Park offers all sorts of nocturnal diversions, including ranger-led walks that focus on "Stargazing over Sand Beach," a "Night Walk" or learning about the life of a beaver on a dusk walk. There are also slide presentations in the amphitheaters at Seawall and Blackwoods Campgrounds. Programs are listed in the *Beaver Log*, the official park newspaper. Ranger-led programs are offered from mid-May through mid-October. ~ 207-288-3338, fax 207-288-8813; www.nps.gov/acad, e-mail acadia_information@nps.gov.

BEACHES & PARKS

Sand Beach at Acadia National Park is made up of the crushed shells of marine animals.

ACADIA NATIONAL PARK One of Maine's most scenic areas, Acadia National Park encompasses a large portion of Mount Desert Island, the Schoodic Peninsula on the mainland and teeny Isle au Haut. For exploring on Mount Desert, consider driving the Park Loop Road. It hits the major highlights, including Frenchman Bay Overlook, a spectacular lookout point complete with interpretive signs pointing out the islands before you; the Wild Gardens of Acadia, a colorful wildflower garden; Champlain Mountain Overlook, another jaw-dropping view of the island-dotted Frenchman Bay area; and the summit of Cadillac Mountain, an above-the-clouds view of it all. The Schoodic Peninsula provides a good day-long side trip. A one-way road wraps around the peninsula, with sweeping views of Frenchman Bay, the Atlantic Ocean and the Mount Desert Mountains, while another climbs to the top of Schoodic Mountain. It takes a bit of planning to reach Isle au Haut, but once there, you can go hiking and birding. To fish within the park, try Jordan Pond for salmon and lake trout; Long Pond for landlocked salmon; Eagle Lake for brook trout, salmon and lake trout; Echo Lake for brook trout and salmon; and Upper and Lower Hadlock Pond for brook trout. You can swim at Sand Beach or in freshwater Echo Lake. Among the many amenities are an information center, picnic areas, restrooms and souvenir shops. ~ The best way to approach Mount Desert Island is via Route 3 from Route 1 at Ellsworth. Isle au Haut is reached by a mail boat (fee; 207-367-5193) that makes regular trips from Stonington. The Schoodic Point peninsula is farther up the coast, off Route 186; 207-288-3338, fax 207-288-8813; www.nps.gov/acad, e-mail acadia_information@nps.gov.

▲ There are two campgrounds in the park. Blackwoods has 310 tent/RV sites (no hookups); free in winter, $20 per night in season. Seawall, open from late May through September, has 212 tent/RV sites (no hookups); $14 to $20 per night. ~ 207-288-3338.

LAMOINE STATE PARK Located on Frenchman Bay, Lamoine State Park offers spectacular views of the dramatic peaks of Mount Desert Island. Its own 55 acres of woods and waterfront are popular for camping and picnicking. You can swim at nearby Lamoine Beach (no lifeguard) in the cold water. There are picnic tables, restrooms, a playground, a sand volleyball court, a fishing dock and a boat launch. Day-use fee, $3 per person. ~ Follow Route 184 from Ellsworth to Lamoine; 207-667-4778, fax 207-664-0487.

▲ There are 61 tent/RV sites (no hookups) with flush toilets and hot showers; $15 to $20 per night. Campgrounds are closed

October 15 to May 15. Reservations: 207-287-3824; www.campwithme.com.

ROQUE BLUFFS STATE PARK Carved out of Englishman Bay, Roque Bluffs is a 300-acre park with both a saltwater and freshwater beach. One beach skirts the edge of a sheltered freshwater pond, ideal for fishing. There are eight miles of hiking trails, perfect for spotting all kinds of wildlife, including eagles. Picnic and changing areas, toilets and a playground are the facilities here. Closed mid-October through Memorial Day. Day-use fee, $3 per person. ~ About six miles off Route 1; turn off Route 1 just beyond Jonesboro; 207-255-3475.

COBSCOOK BAY STATE PARK An extremely scenic park, Cobscook (an Indian word that means "boiling tide") sits on the shores of Whiting Bay, where tides can reach 24 feet. Its 888 acres are covered with spruce and fir trees and snaked by hiking and cross-country ski trails. It's also a good place to spot bald eagles. Fishing and clamming are permitted in the bay, but it is not an ideal spot for fishing as compared to surrounding areas. Among the facilities are a picnic area, restrooms and hot showers. There is also a dump station for RVs. Day-use fee, $3 per person. ~ Route 1, South Edmunds; phone/fax 207-726-4412; www.maine.gov/doc.

▲ There are 106 tent/RV sites (no hookups); $14 to $19 per night. Campgrounds are closed October 15 to May 15.

QUODDY HEAD STATE PARK Dramatically situated at the easternmost point of land in the continental United States, Quoddy Head State Park offers some magnificent views of the Atlantic Ocean and Grand Manan Island. The biggest attraction here is the red-and-white-striped lighthouse that surveys the Bay of Fundy, known for its extreme tides. More than four miles of hiking trails ribbon through spruce groves; one skirts a high ledge along steep cliffs that drop into the sea. Picnic tables and fireplaces are available. Day-use fee, $2 for adults, $1 for children. Closed October 15 through May 15. ~ From Route 1, take Route 189 to the town of Lubec and follow the signs; phone/fax 207-733-0911.

REVERSING FALLS PARK You're not alone if you're wondering what reversing falls are. This is definitely one of those go-see-for-yourself situations. The falls are actually a field of rapids dramatically galloping in the middle of the waterway. The Baltic scenery around it is part of a 140-acre park with hiking trails and picnic sites. Picnic tables and grills are available for the barbecue crowd. Restroom facilities are limited to outhouses. ~ Traveling north on Route 1, you'll pass the turn-off for Cobscook Bay State Park. Continue on for nine and a half miles and turn right at Antone's Triangle Store. Almost immediately, you'll turn right again at the red building. Follow that for three and a half miles, then turn right again. Follow for almost three miles, bearing left at the water. It's easier than it sounds, but none of these dirt roads have names.

Northern Woods

Dense wilderness is what you'll find in this part of Maine. Mountains holding shiny blue lakes as if they were precious gems. Thick woods that seem to go on forever. Rivers roaring through canyons. The air here is invigoratingly fresh. Hiking, fishing, camping and other outdoor pastimes abound. For serious nature lovers, the northern woods provide the ultimate nirvana.

Not until you actually go to northern Maine can you understand how big the state really is. You can go for hours passing only an occasional farmhouse or two. You can't take anything (such as service stations and restaurants) for granted. Once you decide to travel up here, be sure to take a good map (you'll really need one, since there's often nobody to bail you out of jams). Your best bet is to pick a destination for the day and take your time getting there.

SIGHTS

Continuing on from Calais, you can stay on Route 1, which turns from a coastal road into an inland route and can be taken to **Aroostook County**, where lakes and forests reign. **Presque Isle** is the hub up in this region and also the commercial center of Maine's potato country.

We will, however, head for Baxter State Park and the northern lakes area in the central northern part of the state. It'll take several hours to get to **Millinocket** (pronounced the proper Maine way, it's Mill-a-NORK-it), and there's not much in between. You can finally leave Route 1 at Topsfield, turning onto Route 6E and following the network of roads that eventually get you into the heart of Millinocket, where every one of the main streets is dirt.

Don't get your hopes up for much here. Look at it as a good place to stock up on supplies and gas before heading off to the wilderness areas. In fact, do yourselves a favor and stop by the **Baxter State Park Headquarters** for some detailed maps. Millinocket is also a popular takeoff point for canoe trips to the Allagash Wilderness Waterway. This 95-mile passage comprises 200,000 acres of interconnected lakes and rivers that run from Telos Lake to the Canadian border. Before attempting to canoe the waterway, one should have some experience (see "Beaches & Parks" below). ~ 64 Balsam Drive, Millinocket; 207-287-3821, fax 207-287-8111; www.main.gov/doc/parks.

You'll find the main entrance to **Baxter State Park** about 20 miles north of Millinocket. Sprawling majestically over 204,733 acres, this largest of Maine's parks is awe-inspiring. It was a gift to the state in 1931 by Percival Baxter, who, while serving as a legislator and as governor of Maine, urged creation of a park around Mt. Katahdin. Rebuffed, the governor bought the land with his own capital and deeded to the state of Maine the land "to be forever left in its natural, wild state." No overnight use from mid-October to December and from April to mid-May.

The centerpiece is, indisputably, **Mt. Katahdin**. At 5267 feet, it's the highest peak in Maine. It's also the northern terminus for the **Appalachian Trail**. Open mid-May to mid-October and December through March, the park has 45 other peaks and over 175 miles of well-marked trails. You can drive around the perimeter in less than three hours. (See "Beaches & Parks" below.)

As you continue west of the park, you'll come to **Ripogenus Dam**, where the mighty waters of several interconnected lakes

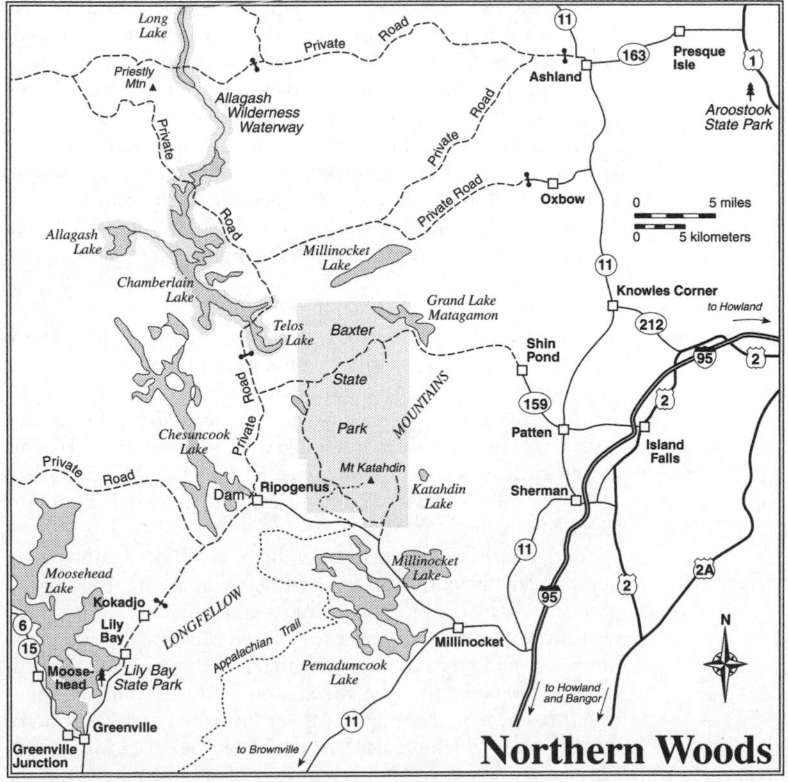

are halted and washed out the other side in a narrow river that races triumphantly through a deep gorge. This is the departure point for several whitewater rafting trips. It's also the turnoff point for those driving into the Allagash Wilderness Waterway.

A dirt road takes you south of Ripogenus Dam to **Kokadjo,** an adorable little complex of camps and a general store that was built as the headquarters for a lumber company in the early 1900s.

Continue south, stopping at **Lily Bay** (see "Beaches & Parks" below) and **Greenville**, a major New England seaplane base. You can stuff yourselves on local steamboat history at the latter's **Moosehead Marine Museum,** which displays local memorabilia and paintings as well as the restored steamship *Katahdin*, now a floating museum. Cruises are available. Closed Columbus Day through May. Admission. ~ Greenville; 207-695-2716, fax 207-695-2367; www.katahdincruises.com, e-mail info@katahdincruises.com.

Millinocket's biggest claim to fame is very big indeed. Being the home of Bowater Inc., it is one of the largest producers of newsprint in the United States.

From there, drive up the western coast of **Moosehead Lake** to the waterfront towns of Moosehead (a lumberman's depot and departure point for wilderness excursions) and Rockwood. The whole area is mesmerizingly beautiful, with mountains looming all around and evergreens perfectly reflected in the lake. It's very common to see moose in these parts.

Moosehead Lake is the center for the state's wilderness sports and the source of the Kennebec River. For more information, contact the **Moosehead Lake Chamber of Commerce.** ~ P.O. Box 581, Greenville, ME 04441; 207-695-2702, 888-876-2778, fax 207-695-3440; www.mooseheadlake.org, e-mail info@mooseheadlake.org.

LODGING

Several of the lodging options in this area are so remote you'll need to fly or boat in—or jump on a pack horse and ride.

Before setting out into the wilderness of Baxter State Park, you can fuel up for a night by staying at **Pamola Motor Lodge**. It's just as it sounds, a basic motor lodge with 30 generic motel rooms and efficiencies. ~ 973 Central Street, Millinocket; 207-723-9746, 800-575-9746, fax 207-723-9746 ext. 63; www.pamolamotorlodge.com. BUDGET TO MODERATE.

Like a little nest hidden up in the trees, **Pray's Cottages** is a homey spot tucked away in the thick woods. It's the takeoff point for many bear-hunting groups and whitewater rafters, as well as a civilization-stopover for rugged campers desiring some hot water and electricity for a change. There are four one-bedroom efficiency units in a ranch-style building and two separate three-bedroom cottages. All are furnished with the kind of things you might have used to decorate your first apartment, but they're comfortable nonetheless. They also have all the modern kitchen conveniences. Closed in winter after hunting season. ~ 101 Morgan Lane, Millinocket, ME 04462; 207-723-3582. BUDGET.

At **Big Moose Cabins** guests can sleep under the stars in a lean-to, enjoy an antique-filled suite or reside in a rustic cabin by the lake. Five newly remodeled suites boast private baths and vintage furniture; the largest one includes large windows and two queen-sized beds. The two-story Katahdin House features a fireplace and a full dining area with cooking tools and linens. ~ P.O. Box 98, Millinocket; 207-723-8391, 877-666-7346, fax 207-723-8199; www.bigmoosecabins.com, e-mail info@bigmoose cabins.com.BUDGET TO DELUXE.

Anglers are the biggest fans of **Frost Pond Camps**. It's a group of ten campsites and seven rustically furnished housekeeping cabins set on Frost Pond, which is loaded with trout. It's also a great place for families and hunters (in the fall). ~ Three miles beyond Ripogenus Dam near Baxter State Park; 207-852-4700; www. frostpondcamps.com, e-mail info@frostpondcamps.com. BUDGET.

Remotely situated within the Allagash Wilderness Waterway (50 miles north of Millinocket), **Nugent's Chamberlain Lake Camps** is a collection of six rustic log cabins. The best way to reach them is to fly in (contact Folsom's Air Service, 207-695-2821). Otherwise, it's a five-mile boat (or snowmobile) trip up Chamberlain Lake. This is a year-round sporting camp with fishing, canoeing, cross-country skiing and snowmobiling. Closed April and December. ~ Greenville; 207-944-5991; www.nugent-mc nallycamps.com. BUDGET TO MODERATE.

McNally's Ross Stream Camps on Chemquasabamticook Stream boast five cabins with wood stoves and running water. Canoes and kayaks are available to rent. Although used year round, there is no running water in the winter. ~ Greenville; 207-944-5991; www.nugent-mcnallycamps.com. MODERATE.

Try to get one of the three rooms that has a fireplace at the **Greenville Inn**. But if you can't, don't worry. All 13 guest rooms at this former lumber baron's 1890 home are wonderful. Antiques are scattered throughout the bed and breakfast, and in the common rooms cherrywood and mahogany panels warm up all the corners. Best of all are the views of Moosehead Lake and the encircling mountains from the porch and the dining room. Breakfast is included. ~ Norris Street, Greenville; 207-695-2206, 888-695-6000, fax 207-695-0735; www.greenvilleinn.com, e-mail innkeeper@greenvilleinn.com. DELUXE.

You can stay right in Chesuncook, a 19th-century lumberman's village that's on the National Register of Historic Places, at the **Chesuncook Lake House and Cabins**. It's a beautifully maintained 1864 farmhouse with four rooms. The living and dining rooms have gas lamps. The three rustic, fully equipped cabins can sleep up to six. To reach it, you can be picked up by boat at

◄ HIDDEN

Allagash Gateway Campsites or fly in. Three meals a day are included in the farmhouse. Closed in April. ~ Mailing address: Box 656, Route 76, Greenville, ME 04441; 207-745-5330; www.chesuncooklakehouse.com. ULTRA-DELUXE.

If images of a palace and castles run through your head when you hear about **Chalet Moosehead Lakefront Motel**, forget them. It's just a motel with a bizarre name. It's ideally situated, however, overlooking Moosehead Lake. The "chalet" is also an inexpensive way to settle into the area, with eight efficiencies and seven standard rooms as well as a slew of diversions to keep you happily occupied (including a dock to swim off of or dock your boat, and free use of canoes and paddle boats). Twelve new deluxe rooms sport balconies and whirlpool tubs. ~ On Moosehead Lake, off Routes 6 and 15, Greenville Junction; 207-695-2950, 800-290-3645; www.mooseheadlodging.com, e-mail info@mooseheadlodging.com. MODERATE TO DELUXE.

Poised on the shores of Moosehead Lake, **The Birches** is a string of 15 log cabins privately spaced out in a grove of birch trees. All of them have porches woodburning stoves and kitchens; some have fireplaces. There's a main lodge with an open-timbered dining room where the fare is wholesome and good. Major pastimes include hiking, fishing, swimming, canoeing, boating and snowmobiling. There's also tennis and golf nearby. In winter, there's more than 25 miles of cross-country trails. ~ Two miles from Rockwood; 207-534-7305, 800-825-9453, fax 207-534-8835; www.birches.com, e-mail wwld@aol.com. MODERATE TO DELUXE.

Gazing over at Mt. Kineo on Moosehead Lake are the **Rockwood Cottages**. Eight cottages come with fully equipped kitchens, baths with showers and screened porches. There's a long list of activities to enjoy, including snowmobiling, cross-country skiing, snowshoeing, fishing, hunting, whitewater rafting, seaplane rides, tennis and hiking. Closed December through April. ~ Rockwood; phone/fax 207-534-7725; www.mooseheadlakelodging.com. MODERATE.

Maynards in Maine is one of Moosehead Lake's oldest established sporting camps. The centerpiece of it all is a grand old lodge filled with memorabilia from earlier hunting trips (such as stuffed fish and moose heads) and comfortable sofas and chairs that date back to the early 1900s. The dining room is always abuzz with outdoor lovers who congregate for two hearty meals a day. The camp has 13 cabins, with one to four bedrooms and full baths. Closed Columbus Day through April. ~ 131 Maynards Road, Rockwood; 207-534-7703; www.maynardsinmaine.com, e-mail gmaynards@hotmail.com. BUDGET.

There are just seven units at **Sundown Cabins**, so be sure to reserve yours early. Located on Moosehead Lake, these one- to-three-bedroom units with full kitchens are ideally located for water sports, hunting, snowmobiling and fishing. ~ Route 15 (Rockwood Road), Rockwood; 207-534-7357, fax 207-534-7395; www.sundowncabins.com, e-mail sundown@prexar.net. BUDGET TO MODERATE.

DINING

In this neck of the woods, you'll find most meals are included in the price at camps and lodges. They're often served family-style and consist of good solid home cooking. But there are a handful of restaurants you might want to try.

The Black Frog is clearly a second home for the locals. Ask for a seat in the atrium, which looks right onto the lake. You'll enjoy ordering things like the "Looks Like Steak, Smells Like Steak, Must Be Steak" steak. They've thoughtfully provided a vegetarian option (a portobello mushroom burger), known as the "Tree Hugger." For dessert, they recommend asking someone in the kitchen for a suggestion. If no one there can help, "check out the reach-in refrigerators. If there's nothing there, go across the street to Jamo's and get a Ring Ding." That pretty much sums up The Black Frog. Good luck. ~ Pritham Avenue, Greenville; 207-695-1100; www.theblackfrog.com, e-mail info@theblackfrog.com. MODERATE TO DELUXE.

Moosehead Lake is 40 miles long and 20 miles wide—the biggest of Maine's countless lakes.

HIDDEN

One of the most elegant meals you can have in the northern woods is at the **Greenville Inn**. In its graciously decorated dining room, there's a good selection of Continental dishes, all enhanced by festive sauces created by an adept kitchen. Dinner only. Closed Sunday through Thursday from November through May, and Sunday from June through October. ~ Norris Street, Greenville; 207-695-2206, 888-695-6000, fax 207-695-0335; www.greenvilleinn.com, grlinn@moosehead.net. DELUXE.

If you're in the mood for a hamburger, lobster roll or a big bowl of chili or broasted chicken, make your way to **Flatlander's Pub**. They serve heaping platters of Americana. It's a casual spot, attracting plain folks and family types. ~ 36 Pritham Avenue, Greenville; 207-695-3373. BUDGET TO MODERATE.

Kelly's Landing is a great diner-style spot for breakfast. It opens at 8 a.m. and has a traditional American menu all day long. ~ Greenville Junction; 207-695-4438, fax 207-695-0280. BUDGET TO DELUXE.

SHOPPING

There's not much in the way of shopping in the northern woods, unless you're into hunting gear and camouflage hats.

BEACHES & PARKS

BAXTER STATE PARK Maine's grande dame of parks, this 204,733-acre wilderness preserve is magnificent. Over 180 miles of hiking trails take you through pine forests, by rivers of rapids, alongside blue lakes and up mountains—including Mt. Katahdin (5267 feet), the highest in Maine. Katahdin is the northern terminus for the Appalachian Trail. Wildlife and birds are abundant here, as are a phenomenal variety of trees and plants. You can fish or swim (if you can stand the cold) in the park's streams and lakes. Once you're in the park, there's no food, fuel or supplies. Stock up in Millinocket or Patten. In the winter, roads are only plowed halfway between Millinocket and the park. Closed to overnight use from October 15 to December 1, and from March 31 to May 15. ~ You can't miss this place. Look at any map, it's that huge green area in the central north section. The easiest approach is from Millinocket. Park headquarters: 207-723-5140, fax 207-723-4758.

Most of the Allagash Wilderness outfitters are in Allagash Village. If you're on your own, a good put-in point is Chamberlain Thoroughfare at the junction of Chamberlain and Telos lakes.

▲ There are hundreds of sites in ten campgrounds, two of which are accessible only to backpackers. Among the other campgrounds are 72 lean-to sites, 80 tent sites and 21 cabins; prices range from $9 to $25 per night per person, but minimum rates do apply to sites. Permit and reservations are required; procedure and application vary by season. For information, write: Reservation Clerk, Baxter State Park, 64 Balsam Drive, Millinocket, ME 04462; 207-723-5140; www.baxterstateparkauthority.com.

AROOSTOOK STATE PARK Maine's first and northernmost state park, Aroostook covers nearly 800 thickly wooded acres on the shores of Echo Lake. It's an outdoor lover's paradise, with hiking and secluded glassy coves for swimming in summer and cross-country ski trails and snowshoe trails in winter. There's good stocked trout fishing on Echo Lake. There are picnic sites, charcoal grills, changing facilities, paddleboat and canoe rentals, and a boat launch. Day-use fee, $2 for adults and $1 for children. ~ Off Route 1, five miles south of Presque Isle; phone/fax 207-768-8341.

▲ There are 28 tent/RV sites (no hookups); $12 per night for Maine residents, $15 per night for nonresidents. The campground includes hot showers, toilets and a kitchen shelter. Closed mid-October to mid-May. Reservations: 207-287-3824, 800-332-1501 (within Maine); e-mail frank.appleby@maine.gov.

ALLAGASH WILDERNESS WATERWAY Stretching for 92 miles from Telos Lake (north of Ripogenus Dam) to the far north near Fort Kent, this famous corridor of lakes and rivers is most well known for its flatwater/whitewater canoe trips. It's quite beautiful and known as "God's Country." The strip also boasts good fishing waters and snowmobiling in winter. You can swim the clear lakes as well, but there are no lifeguards or formal safety measures. Remember, this is an extremely remote area, so prepare accordingly. If you plan to canoe, it's necessary to register at the gate when you enter the waterway. For information, write the Allagash Wilderness Waterway, c/o Bureau of Parks and Lands, 106 Hogan Road, Bangor, ME 04401. ~ You'll find rangers at Allagash Lake, Chamberlain Thoroughfare, Eagle Lake, Churchill Dam, Long Lake Thoroughfare and the Michaud Farm; 207-941-4014, fax 207-941-4222; www.state.me.us/doc/prkslands/alla.htm.

▲ There are 100 sites for tents only; $4 per night for Maine residents, $5 per night for nonresidents. Most campsites are accessible only by water.

LILY BAY STATE PARK This is a beautiful wilderness area on the shores of 40-mile-long Moosehead Lake. The lake really does sparkle and is framed by evergreen forests and mountains that look like waves plastered against the sky. There is a hiking trail, but most of the activity revolves around the water—swimming, fishing or boating. Moosehead Lake is well known for its brook trout, salmon and lake trout. During the winter, snowmobiling and skiing takes over. There are two boat launches with berths, as well as a dump station and potable water. Showers are available. Closed mid-October to mid-May. Day-use fee, $3 per person. ~ About nine miles north of Greenville on the eastern shore of Moosehead Lake; phone/fax 207-695-2700 (in season), 207-941-4014 (off season).

▲ There are 90 tent/RV sites (no hookups); $14 to $19 per night.

Western Lakes and Mountains

Stretching along the New Hampshire border right up to Quebec, the western lakes and mountains of Maine are unusually scenic. This area is home to dozens of lakes (in the Rangeley area alone there are about 40) and mountains (including Sugarloaf). The southern reaches—Waterford, Bridgton and the Sebago Lake area—are within easy reach of Portland and other coastal destinations, and they attract lots of visitors, especially during the summer months. The northern parts such as Bethel and Rangeley take a bit longer to get to and feel as if they're worlds away. These areas tend to attract skiers in winter and wilderness-seeking vacationers in summer.

SIGHTS

The star winter attraction in the western region is **Sugarloaf/USA**, the state's second-highest mountain and its biggest ski mountain (see the "Outdoor Adventures" section at the end of this chapter). At the top, you'll find New England's largest self-contained ski village, complete with hotels, restaurants, shops and a church. Below is **Carrabassett Valley**, home to the Carrabassett Valley Ski Touring Center, an enormous network of cross-country trails. The town of **Kingfield**, at the southern entrance to the Carrabassett Valley, was founded in 1816. It has a fine collection of shops, restaurants and inns.

Year-round, however, inland Maine is becoming more and more popular, especially the **Rangeley Lakes** region. Like the northern woods, this whole western area is almost solid wilderness punctuated with an occasional town (by town, we often mean a post office, a church and a general store). Moose, bear, wildflowers that look as strange as their Latin names, and birds who know a good thing when they spot one, are the most abundant residents. Some of the biggest lakes have names that are almost impossible to pronounce, but go ahead, try. They're Mooselookmeguntic, Kennebago, Aziscohos, Cupsuptic and Umbagog. Okay, we'll throw in a few easy ones: Rangeley and Richardson. They're all busy with boaters and anglers in summer months. And scattered along the shores are small camps with rustic log cabins hidden behind thick pine trees or in birch groves.

The town of **Rangeley** is evolving fast. Too fast, according to some old-timers. Seemingly overnight, it has gone from a sleepy backwoods town to an up-and-coming tourist center. Besides the little town of Oquossoc down the road, it's really the only place where you'll find restaurants, a handful of shops, gas stations and, of course, ice cream parlors. The truth is, however, that Rangeley can't hold a candle to the real tourist towns on the coast. It's still a little town in the middle of the woods, no matter how many out-of-state license plates you count.

Rangeley does have some wonderful attributes on top of being one of the only signs of civilization for miles. It's *right* on the water. The silky ripples of Rangeley Lake practically slosh up onto the main street. It also has a landmark **library** (in the middle of town) that, according to one resident, "still smells the way it used to in the '40s."

As you move south of the Rangeley Lakes region, you come to the **Bethel** area, which is in the Oxford Hills, not far from the White Mountain National Forest on the New Hampshire border. Bethel itself is a lovely 19th-century village with a meticulously maintained green and stately old houses. Come winter, Bethel is a thriving cross-country skiing area.

One of the town's highlights is the **Bethel Historical Society's Regional History Center**, featuring a restored Federal-style house displaying period furnishings and the Robinson House, which

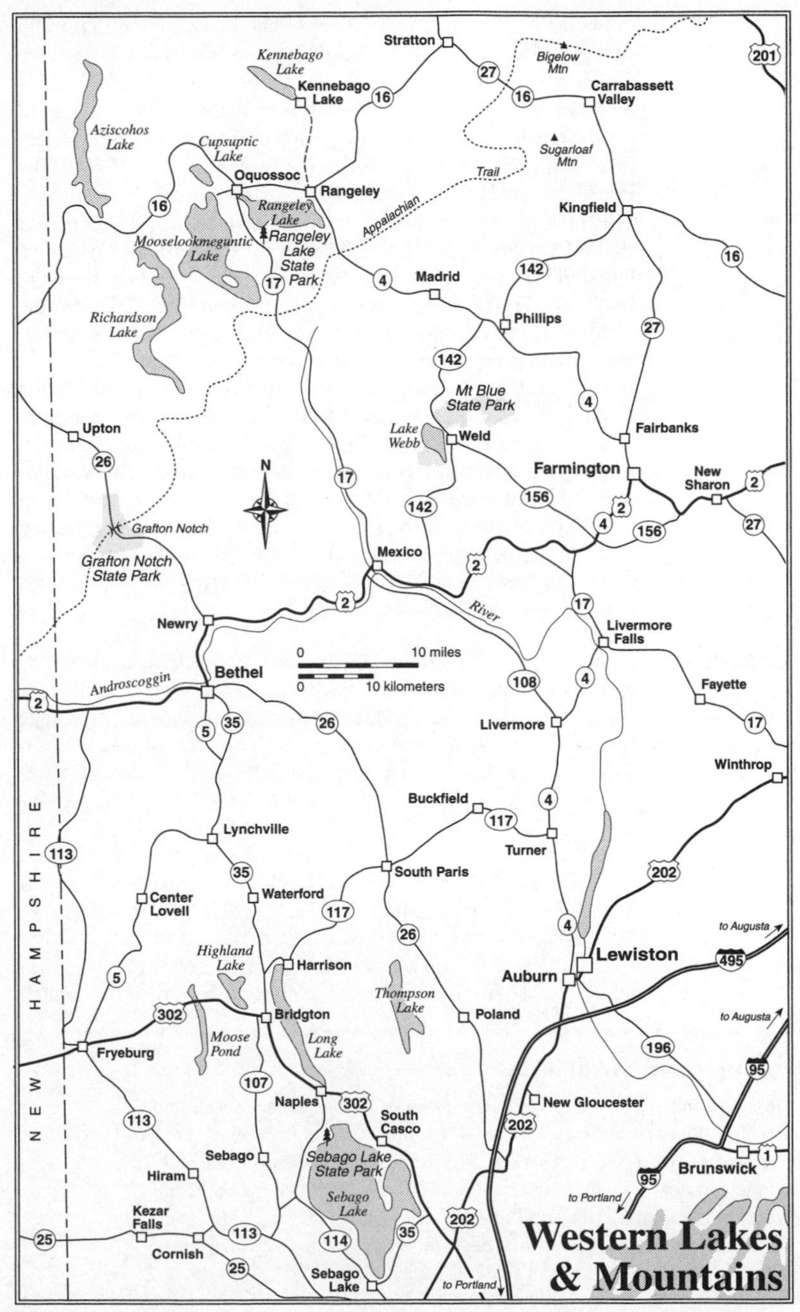
Western Lakes & Mountains
Stratton
Kennebago Lake
Kennebago Lake
Bigelow Mtn
Carrabassett Valley
Aziscohos Lake
Cupsuptic Lake
Sugarloaf Mtn
Oquossoc
Rangeley
Rangeley Lake
Rangeley Lake State Park
Appalachian Trail
Mooselookmeguntic Lake
Kingfield
Madrid
Phillips
Richardson Lake
Mt Blue State Park
Lake Webb
Weld
Fairbanks
Upton
Farmington
New Sharon
N
Grafton Notch
Grafton Notch State Park
Mexico
River
Newry
Livermore Falls
Androscoggin
Bethel
0 10 miles
0 10 kilometers
Fayette
Livermore
Winthrop
Buckfield
Lynchville
Turner
South Paris
Waterford
Center Lovell
NEW HAMPSHIRE
to Augusta
Highland Lake
Harrison
Lewiston
Auburn
Thompson Lake
Bridgton
Poland
Moose Pond
Long Lake
to Augusta
Fryeburg
Naples
New Gloucester
South Casco
Sebago
Sebago Lake State Park
Brunswick
Hiram
Sebago Lake
to Portland
Kezar Falls
Cornish
Sebago Lake
to Portland
201
27
16
16
4
142
16
17
27
142
4
17
142
156
2
4
156
2
27
26
2
2
17
108
4
2
5
35
26
17
113
35
117
4
202
117
26
495
5
302
196
95
107
302
113
202
1
95
25
113
25
114
35
202

holds local and regional historic exhibits. Closed Saturday through Monday. Open weekends in July, August and December. Admission. ~ 10–14 Broad Street, Bethel; 207-824-2908, 800-824-2910, fax 207-824-0082; www.bethelhistorical.org, e-mail info@bethelhistorical.org. The **Gould Academy** is a very widely respected prep school. ~ 39 Church Street; 207-824-7700. The **Broad Street Historic District** is lined with historic homes.

The area south of Bethel (including Waterford, Bridgton and the towns near Sebago Lake) is loved mostly for its profusion of lakes and rivers (see "Beaches & Parks" below). In fact, from the summit of **Pleasant Mountain**, you can see about 50 lakes. These include crystal-clear **Sebago Lake,** Maine's second largest, popular with anglers and city folk from nearby Portland.

In addition to water sports, the area is rife with *terra firma* attractions, including the **Sabbathday Lake Shaker Community and Museum,** an active Shaker settlement and one of the oldest in the United States, including a Shaker store and exhibit buildings representing Shaker life through the ages. It also features an exhibit on the lives of children in the community. Closed Sunday and from Columbus Day through Memorial Day. Admission. ~ Route 26, New Gloucester; 207-926-4597; www.shaker.lib.me.us, e-mail usshakers@aol.com.

LODGING

There are over 300 condominium units available through **Sugarloaf Mountain Corporation.** Each has its advantages. Some are close to the lifts, others to the restaurants and shops. They range from very modern accommodations with all sorts of new conveniences to ones that are older but more affordable. Some are bare-bones hotel rooms, others full-fledged homes. ~ Sugarloaf Mountain; 207-237-2000, 800-843-5623, fax 207-237-3768; www.sugarloaf.com, e-mail info@sugarloaf.com. DELUXE TO ULTRA-DELUXE.

The **Sugarloaf Grand Summit Hotel** is a six-story building with one- to three-bedroom suites. ~ 207-237-2222, 800-527-9879, fax 207-237-2874; www.sugarloaf.com. DELUXE TO ULTRA-DELUXE.

Fanatical skiers on a budget have a choice of bare-bones motels to choose from in this area, including **White Wolf Inn,** which

TRAINS AND TIMBER

About 18 miles from Rangeley is the town of Phillips, where you'll find the **Phillips Historical Society.** There's an interesting collection of pictures and artifacts from the area's early days when a narrow-gauge railroad connected nearby lumbering communities. Ask about summer and fall rides on the Sandy River and Rangeley Lakes Railroad. Open first and third Sundays from June through September and by appointment in winter months. ~ Pleasant Street, Phillips; 207-639-3111.

actually is quite homey in spite of its generic looks. The ten rooms are ultra-basic but can accommodate between two and five guests. It's great for a pack of friends. ~ Route 27, Main Street, Stratton; 207-246-2922; www.thewhitewolfinn.com. BUDGET.

Low-priced lodgings with sophistication are something of an anomaly these days, but **Mountain Village Inn** offers deluxe suites without the high price tag. All seven modern country-style guest rooms boast private baths, some include whirlpool tubs and/or cedar showers. Queen- or king-sized beds and mountain views add romance to the earth-toned suites. There are dogs, chickens, a horse and a donkey on the premises. Pet-friendly. ~ 164 Main Street, Kingfield; 207- 265-2030, 866-577-0741, fax 207-265-2216; www.mountainvillageinn.com, e-mail innkeeper@mountainvillageinn.com. MODERATE TO DELUXE.

About 15 miles south of Sugarloaf Mountain stands the **Herbert Grand Hotel**, an alternative to the mountain condos. It's a grand old hotel with 26 tastefully decorated guest rooms. The main lobby area offers a warm reprieve, and it's often filled with rosy-cheeked skiers who don't feel guilty about taking an afternoon off from the slopes to sit in front of the fireplace and listen to piano music. Continental breakfast is included. ~ 246 Main Street, Kingfield; 207-265-2000, 888-656-9922; www.herbertgrandhotel.com, e-mail innkeeper@herbertgrandhotel.com. MODERATE TO DELUXE.

Named after Amos Winter, the founder of the Sugarloaf ski area, the **Inn on Winter's Hill** is a Georgian Revival mansion with 20 charming antique-filled rooms in the main house and connecting barn. Registered as a National Historic Property, the Inn's lavishly decorated common rooms look as if they should be roped off like a museum, but actually they're very comfortable. Additional amenities include a pool, hot tub and tennis court. ~ Winter Hill Road, Kingfield; 207-265-5421, 800-233-9687, fax 207-265-5424; www.wintershill.com, e-mail wntrhill@somtel.com. BUDGET TO DELUXE.

Right on the water, the **Rangeley Inn and Motor Lodge** is a Rangeley landmark. The older building—erected in 1907—is a three-story shingled structure with 35 remodeled rooms. There's also a newer motel wing with 15 rooms, some offering fireplaces or woodburning stoves, waterbeds and whirlpool baths. Two cabins on the water sleep up to five people. ~ Main Street, Rangeley; 207-864-3341, 800-666-3687, fax 207-864-3634; www.rangeleyinn.com, e-mail rangeinn@rangeley.org. MODERATE TO DELUXE.

Magnificently situated on a hill overlooking Rangeley Lake and surrounded by an 18-hole golf course, the **Country Club Inn** is a grand old summer resort built by a wealthy sportsman back in the 1920s. The living room is lavishly endowed with two immense fireplaces that face each other. The 20 rooms are rather ordinary for this extraordinary setting, but all have great views and private baths. Breakfast is included; dinner is included for an additional fee. Closed mid-October to late December and April to mid-May. ~ Country Club Road, Rangeley; phone/fax 207-864-3831; www.countryclubinnrangeley.com, e-mail ccinn@rangeley.org. MODERATE.

HIDDEN ▶ **Sunset Point Cottages** could be in Sweden. As the name implies, Sunset Point is a sprig of land jutting into spectacularly scenic Mooselookmeguntic Lake. It's colonized by a quintet of housekeeping cottages (with one, two or three bedrooms), all inches from the water's edge. Though satisfyingly rugged (woodburning stoves, gas lights), the place provides real plumbing and hot showers (!) in one common bathhouse. All cottages but one have private bathrooms as well. Weekly rentals only. Closed mid-September to mid-June. ~ On Mooselookmeguntic Lake, outside of Rangeley; 207-864-5387; e-mail tutatkaman@yahoo.com. MODERATE TO DELUXE.

Bald Mountain Camps are the woods of Maine just as you pictured them. They're right on Mooselookmeguntic Lake, surrounded by hundreds of miles of dense wilderness. Guests stay in cabins (there are 15, all with fireplaces) that are warm and homey. No fancy furnishings here—you never have to worry about the kids spilling things. Meals are taken in the log dining room, which is always alive with vacationers who come back to their same cabin year after year. Three meals are included. Closed mid-September to mid-May. ~ Bald Mountain Road, Oquossoc; phone/fax 207-864-3671, 888-392-0072; www.baldmountaincamps.com, e-mail info@baldmountaincamps.com. DELUXE.

A lovely old Victorian house surrounded by four piney acres, **A Prodigal Inn & Gallery** is situated in the small mountain town of Bethel. There are six guest rooms, all attractively decorated with Victorian antiques that exude elegance. Guests are welcome to use the three common rooms as well, including the television and movie room with woodburning fireplace, living rooms, den, jacuzzi and screened-in gazebo. A full gourmet breakfast and afternoon tea are included. ~ 162 Mayville Road, Route 2, Bethel; 207-824-8884, 800-320-9201, fax 207-824-8884; www.prodigalinn.com, e-mail info@prodigalinn.com. DELUXE.

The **Bethel Inn and Country Club** is a large resort-type place that has everything. By everything, we mean 45 traditional inn rooms, 52 two-bedroom townhouses (all with their own telephones, TVs and bathrooms), as well as luxury rooms (with balconies) and suites, a well-respected dining room and an array of sporting options including golf on the 18-hole course, tennis, fishing, swimming, exercise rooms, sauna and cross-country skiing in winter. A huge, sprawling yellow building right on the town's common, it's impossible to miss. The individual rooms are decorated in a ho-hum style with all the modern comforts.

The common rooms are formally attired in antiques. Breakfast and dinner are included. ~ On the Common, Bethel; 207-824-2175, 800-654-0125, fax 207-824-2233; www.bethelinn.com, e-mail info@bethelinn.com. MODERATE TO ULTRA-DELUXE.

Within walking distance of the town's shops and restaurants, **L'Auberge Country Inn & Bistro** is the kind of place you fall in love with and then hesitate to tell even your best friends about. Formerly a barn, it has seven guest rooms simply but elegantly furnished with country antiques. Guests are free to roam about the common rooms, which include a living room with a hearth and the kind of chairs and couches you sink into. During the winter months, you can cross-country ski right from the door. Country-style breakfast is included. ~ On the Common, Bethel; 207-824-2774, 800-760-2774, fax 207-824-3108; www.laubergecountryinn.com, e-mail info@laubergecountryinn.com. MODERATE TO DELUXE.

The Noble House offers nine guest rooms in a 1903 Queen Anne. Set on a hill, this bed and breakfast is comfortably furnished with antiques. The majority of the rooms and suites come with whirlpool baths and porches. You're welcome to play the grand piano or the pump organ. Explore the adjacent public beach with canoes or foot-pedal boats, or just watch the sunset from the comfort of your own hammock. Full gourmet breakfast is included. ~ 37 Highland Road, Bridgton; 207-647-3733, 888-237-4880; www.noblehousebb.com, e-mail noblehse@adelphia.net. DELUXE TO ULTRA-DELUXE.

Surrounded by 25 lakeside acres, the **Tarry-A-While Resort** is a grand old "Maine" summer resort with rooms in the main house and five private cottages that punctuate the grounds. The innkeepers pride themselves on their unending hospitality. You almost feel as if you're guests in a private home. There's an array of diversions nearby, including water sports (a 500-foot lakefront beach with canoes, rowboats and kayaks), tennis and golf.

THE MAINE THING

If you've never experienced a real Maine lodge, consider staying at the **Kawanhee Inn**. It has the works: exposed timber beams, an immense stone fireplace, woodsy smelling rooms. Guests can stay in one of nine rooms with basic furnishings in the main lodge or settle into a cabin (each accommodates two to six people). All ten cabins have their own fireplaces and screened-in porches. The setting is lovely—on a hill overlooking Lake Webb—and guests can use the small beach and boats. Closed mid-October to mid-May. ~ Weld; 207-585-2000; www.lakeinn.com, e-mail info@lakeinn.com. MODERATE TO ULTRA-DELUXE.

There's a three-night minimum for the rooms; one-week for cottages. Closed Labor Day to mid-June. ~ Tarry-a-While Road, on Highland Lake, Bridgton; 207-647-2522, 800-451-9076, fax 207-647-5512; www.tarryawhileresort.com, e-mail tarryayl@megalink.net. MODERATE TO DELUXE.

DINING

For a quick but satiating meal between ski runs, try **Gepetto's**. You can warm up with a bowl of seafood chowder or a thick slice of pizza, or settle in for fresh chicken and seafood dishes. From its windowed walls (it's the greenhouse style) you can sit and watch skiers schussing down the mountain. Closed from early spring to July 4th. ~ Village West at Sugarloaf; 207-237-2192, fax 207-237-2190; e-mail gepettos@somtel.com. MODERATE TO DELUXE.

Julia's, an ornate dining room at the Inn on Winter's Hill, is as romantic and handsomely decorated as the rest of the historic building it occupies. The restaurant offers intriguing cuisine. Closed Sunday and Monday from December to mid-April;. closed mid-April to December. ~ Winter Hill Road, Kingfield; 207-265-5421, fax 207-265-5424. DELUXE.

The area's most highly regarded restaurant is **One Stanley Avenue**. It's housed in a Queen Anne–style Victorian building and offers classic regional cuisine (maple-cider chicken, saged rabbit with raspberry sauce). Desserts can be counted on to elicit oohs and aahs. Dinner only. Open mid-December to mid-April. Closed Monday. ~ 1 Stanley Avenue, Kingfield; 207-265-5541; www.stanleyavenue.com. ULTRA-DELUXE.

The food at the **Country Club Inn** is almost upstaged by the view. From your table you can look out over Rangeley Lake, often as smooth as glass and interrupted only by a lone canoe. All around loom mountains that seem to change colors as often as you change courses. Fortunately, the food holds its own, with a selection of traditional American dishes along with some French recipes. Closed April and November. Breakfast and dinner only. ~ Country Club Road, Rangeley; phone/fax 207-864-3831; www.countryclubinnrangeley.com, e-mail ccinn@rangeley.org. DELUXE.

When locals want to celebrate birthdays or anniversaries, they usually go to the **Rangeley Inn**. It has a formal, late-19th-century dining room where you can feast on French or American specialties. Closed in April, May, November and December. ~ Main Street, Rangeley; 207-864-3341, 800-666-3687; www.rangeleyinn.com; e-mail rangeinn@rangeley.org. MODERATE TO DELUXE.

If you just don't feel like cooking in your housekeeping cottage yet you're not in the mood to dress up for dinner out, pull up to the **Red Onion**. It's your basic pizza and subs kind of place that's crammed with locals and tourists alike. Don't be surprised if you have to wait a few minutes for a table to free up. Deck dining in summer months. Closed first week in December and first week in April. ~ Main Street, Rangeley; 207-864-5022, fax 207-864-5042. BUDGET TO MODERATE.

If you're not staying at the **Bethel Inn**, at least treat yourself to dinner there. The fare at this lovely country resort is traditional New England served in the formal dining room (with views of the golf course and hills), in the Mill Brook Tavern and Grille downstairs or on the screened-in veranda during the summer. Closed November and April upstairs. ~ On the Common, Bethel; 207-824-2175, 800-654-0125; www.bethelinn.com, e-mail info@bethelinn.com. DELUXE.

For a quick health booster, check out **Mountain Dew Natural Foods Grocery & Deli.** A small natural foods store, Mountain Dew has a deli where you can grab a quick lunch or some healthy picnic fixings. In addition to fresh soups daily, there is a large selection of vegetarian wraps and sandwiches. Meat eaters take heart: there's also a turkey sandwich or two. ~ 19 Sandy Creek Road; Bridgton; phone/fax 207-647-4003. BUDGET.

Stephen King, author of legendary horror novels *Carrie*, *Misery* and *The Shining* (among others), is a Maine native and still resides here today.

True gourmands find their way to the **Oxford House Inn**, a 1913 house that faces the White Mountains. It has a lovely repertoire of dishes including a champagne-poached salmon with a fresh herb sauce and grilled pork tenderloin with a plum, cinnamon and port wine sauce, fresh Maine seafood, steaks and nightly specials. During the summer, cocktails are served on the piazza. Dinner only. Reservations required. Closed Monday through Wednesday in the winter. ~ Main Street, Fryeburg; 207-935-3442, 800-261-7206; www.oxfordhouseinn.com, e-mail innkeeper@oxfordhouseinn.com. DELUXE TO ULTRA-DELUXE.

SHOPPING

If you lose your ski hat or mittens, head straight for **Sugarloaf Sports Outlet**, where you can find all sorts of great bargains. ~ Main Street, Kingfield; 207-265-2011.

Bonnema Potters specializes in lamps, but they also have a beautiful assortment of functional stoneware pieces and porcelain pottery. Ask about seconds. Closed Wednesday. ~ 146 Main Street, Bethel; 207-824-2821; e-mail bonnema@megalink.net.

If you're in the market for a handmade quilt, consider making your way to Bridgton in mid-July. At the annual **Quilt Show**, you'll find all sorts of wonderful quilts—both antique and new—and supplies for sale, plus demonstrations. ~ Location varies. Contact the Greater Bridgton Lakes Region Chamber of Commerce, Portland Road, Bridgton; 207-647-3472; www.mainelakes chamber.com, e-mail info@mainelakeschamber.com.

The **United Society of Shakers** sells reproduction Shaker furniture, herbs, tea and handcrafted items. It also offers workshops and demonstrations, as well as community events throughout the year. Closed Columbus Day through Memorial Day. ~ Route 26, New Gloucester; 207-926-4597; www.shaker.lib.me.us, e-mail usshakers@aol.com.

NIGHTLIFE

Nightlife in this area is also limited. In many towns, you're lucky if there's even a movie theater.

However, if you're in the Rangeley Lakes region, you might be able to see a performance sponsored by **Rangeley Friends of the Arts**. They're put on throughout July and August at local churches, lodges and the high school. Contact the chamber of commerce (207-864-5364) for this year's program. ~ P.O. Box 333, Rangeley, ME 04970; www.rangeleyme.com/rangeleyarts.

The **Sebago-Long Lake Region Chamber Music Festival** is a series of Tuesday night concerts held in July and August. Call for information. ~ Deertrees Theatre, Harrison; 207-583-6747 or 207-781-3202; www.sebagomusicfestival.org.

BEACHES & PARKS

RANGELEY LAKE STATE PARK This is unadulterated wilderness. Pine trees point to the sky, while white birch are perfectly reflected in the glassy lake. Moose are seen here frequently. The park covers 869 acres, taking in lots of forest and approximately three miles of shoreline on the southern rim of Rangeley Lake. Anglers love to try for trout and land-locked salmon. People that know about the Rangeley Lake State Park usually keep it to themselves. Facilities include picnic sites, a bathhouse and a children's play area. Day-use fee, $3 per person. Closed October to early May. ~ Off Route 17 on South Shore Drive, south of Oquossoc; phone/fax 207-864-3858.

In South Casco, you can visit Nathaniel Hawthorne's boyhood home on Hawthorne Road, where the 19th-century author spent his early years.

▲ There are 50 tent/RV sites (no hookups); $15 to $20 per night; 207-287-3824 (reservations).

MOUNT BLUE STATE PARK A 7500-acre park that encompasses Mount Blue and Webb Lake, Mount Blue offers one jaw-droppingly beautiful vista (mountains, lakes, more mountains) after another. There are plenty of hiking trails, as well as boating opportunities on Webb Lake. The lake also has good fishing for bass, perch and trout. The park offers guided nature walks in the summer. Facilities include a picnic area, a bathhouse, an amphitheater, a nature center and canoe, paddleboat and rowboat rentals. Day-use fee, $4 per person. ~ Off Route 156, Weld; 207-585-2347.

▲ There are 136 tent/RV sites (no hookups) and shower facilities are available; $17 per night. From May 20 to September 15, call 207-287-3824 or visit www.campwithme.com for reservations.

GRAFTON NOTCH STATE PARK Over on the Maine–New Hampshire border, between Upton and Newry, is Grafton Notch. The 2000-mile Appalachian Trail passes through it on the way to its northern terminus, Mt. Katahdin. Throughout the park, you'll see waterfalls, caves and beautiful mountain scenery (it's at the end of the Mahoosuc Range). There are picnic tables, grills, toilets and a water pump. Day-use fee, $2 per person. ~ Route 26, 16 miles north of Bethel; 207-824-2912, fax 207-824-7638.

▲ Nearby, Stoney Brook offers 30 tent/RV sites with hookups; $20 to $30 per night. ~ Route 2, six miles from Bethel; 207-824-2836, fax 207-824-6898; www.stoneybrookrec.com.

SEBAGO LAKE STATE PARK Some days, this gigantic lake shines like one huge sheet of tin foil. You'll find the water deliciously clear (it's Portland's main water supply). Many people come just for the day to swim and play on and off the sandy beaches. Some stay at the campsites that are spread out along the shores and in the woods on the northern end. You can fish for salmon and togue. Amenities include picnic sites with tables and grills, bathhouses, playgrounds, an amphitheater and lifeguards in season. Day-use fee, $4.50 for adults, $1 for children. ~ Off Route 302, between Naples and South Casco; 207-693-6613 (summer), 207-693-6231.

▲ There are 250 RV/tent sites (no hookups); $15 to $20 per night. Closed October 15 to May 1. Reservations can be made through www.campwithme.com.

Outdoor Adventures

SPORT-FISHING

Opportunities to get out on deep-sea fishing boats abound on Maine's coast.

SOUTHERN COAST **Bigger n' Better** has trips on a 35-foot boat from early May to late September. Catches include cod, haddock, pollack, shark and tuna. ~ Town Dock #2, York Harbor; 207-363-7406; www.biggernbetter.com. From mid-June through Labor Day, the **Ugly Anne** offers half-day fishing trips in search of cod and bottom fish. Cash only. Closed Labor Day to May. ~ Ogunquit; 207-646-7202; www.uglyanne.com. **Charger Charters** goes out on half- and full-day trips for mackerel, shark, cod and whatever else the ocean yields. If you wish to go out on your own, they have one sailboat and two motorboats for rent. Closed October to mid-June. ~ Tugboat Inn, Boothbay Harbor; 207-882-9309 or 207-380-4556.

DOWNEAST COAST **Seafari Charters** on Badger's Island offers private fishing charters up to 100 miles offshore. Catches range from cod, bluefish and stripers to sharks and giant bluefin tuna. Closed December through February. ~ 7 Island Avenue, Badger's Island, Kittery; 207-439-5068; www.seafaricharters.com.

CANOEING & KAYAKING

In a state where the sea, lakes and rivers sparkle like diamonds, you couldn't ask for a better way to explore than in a canoe.

SOUTHERN COAST Rent canoes and motorboats from **Sally Mountain Cabins** for exploring Big Woods Lake. ~ Off Route 201, Jackman; 207-668-5621; www.sallymtcabins.com. **Maine Sport Outfitters** rents canoes and kayaks. Nice spots to boat in the area are Megunticook Lake and Penobscot Bay. ~ Route 1, Rockport; 207-236-8797, 800-722-0826; www.mainesport.com. **Coastal Kayaking Tours** leads sea kayak trips around Mount Desert Island. Closed November through April. ~ 48 Cottage Street, Bar Harbor; 207-288-5483, 800-526-8615; www.acadiafun.com.

DOWNEAST COAST In Southwest Harbor, rent sailboats at **Mansell Boat Rentals.** Lessons are also available. Closed late October to late May. ~ 135 Shore Road; 207-244-5625; www.mansellboatrentals.com.

NORTHERN WOODS Up in Millinocket, call **Katahdin Outfitters** to rent a canoe or touring kayak. Tours are also available. Closed late October to late May. ~ 207-723-5700, 800-862-2663; www.katahdinoutfitters.com.

WESTERN LAKES AND MOUNTAINS **Saco River Canoe & Kayak** rents canoes and kayaks. Closed mid-October to mid-May. ~ 1009 Main Street, Fryeburg; 207-935-2369, 888-772-6573; www.sacorivercanoe.com.

SAILING

You'll find every kind of sailboat imaginable in Maine's waters, from simple Sunfish to tall-masted windjammers.

SOUTHERN COAST In Rockport, the **Schooner Timberwind** runs three-, four- and six-day trips. Children ages five and up welcome. Closed mid-October to Memorial Day. ~ P.O. Box 247, Rockport, ME 04856; 207-236-0801, 800-759-9250; www.

AUTHOR FAVORITE

I know of few experiences as sublime as canoeing silently through Maine's north woods. Although I daydream of paddling the 95-mile length of the Allagash Wilderness Waterway sometime, I'm glad to have had the chance to canoe a stretch of the Moose River with a little help from **Wilderness Expeditions**. They rent sea kayaks, motorboats and sailboats. They also lead white-water rafting trips and kayak tours. Popular rivers in the area are the Penobscot (Class V), the Dead (Class III to V) and Kennebeck (Class III and IV). ~ P.O. Box 41, Rockwood, ME 04478; 207-534-2242, 800-825-9453, fax 207-534-8835; www.birches.com.

schoonertimberwind.com. **Great Harbor Charters** will take you out for three-hour trips in a 33-foot sloop. Half- and full-day charters are also available. Closed mid-September to mid-June. ~ Municipal Pier, Northeast Harbor; 207-244-9159. Sailing lessons are offered by the **Camden Yacht Club Sailing Program**. Closed in winter. ~ Bayview Street, Camden; 207-236-4575.

GOLF

The central part of the coast is where you'll find Maine's largest concentration of golf courses.

SOUTHERN COAST With a scenic course bordering Arcadia National Park, the **Kebo Valley Golf Club** is listed as one of the top 100 classical courses in the country. Its 18 holes will challenge even the most skilled golfer. Closed November through April. ~ Eagle Lake Road, Bar Harbor; 207-288-3000; www.kebovalleyclub.com. The Jordan River flows alongside the scenic, championship 18-hole **Bar Harbor Golf Course.** Watch out for the 18th hole; it has a reputation of being untouchable due to its 29-yard stretch. Closed October through March. ~ Junction of Routes 3 and 204, Trenton; 207-667-7505. On Deer Isle, tee off at **Island Country Club**'s moderately challenging nine-hole green. Closed November through April. ~ Route 15A, Sunset; 207-348-2379. In Hancock, the nine-hole **White Birches Golf Course** has two holes over water. ~ Thorsen Road; 207-667-3621, 800-435-1287; www.wbirches.com.

DOWNEAST COAST **Castine Golf Club**'s nine-hole, par-35 course was built in 1897 and designed by Willie Park, Jr. in 1923. The green is fashioned in the old Scottish way, links-style. Closed mid-October to mid-May. ~ Battle Avenue, Castine; 207-326-8844; www.castinegolfclub.com. The **Causeway Club**'s nine-hole course is located on the waterfront of Norewood Cove, affording beautiful water views. Watch out for the fourth and seventh holes—they are on the water. Weather permitting. ~ Fernald Point Road, Southwest Harbor; 207-244-3780. The **Northeast Harbor Golf Club** has an 18-hole course with stunning views of the surrounding mountains. The green is par 69, and their signature hole is the fifth, with a stream running through it. Weather permitting. ~ Sargent Drive, Northeast Harbor; 207-276-5335. One of the nine holes at **St. Croix Country Club** is on the St. Croix River. The seventh hole is their signature, featuring an eagle's nest above the green. Closed November through April. ~ River Road, Calais; 207-454-8875; www.stcroixcc.com. The quaint coastal **Grindstone Neck Golf Course** has nine holes right along the ocean, with the second green located on the rocks of the shore. Closed October through May. ~ Grindstone Avenue, Winter Harbor; 207-963-7760; www.grindstonegolf.com.

BOAT TOURS

Hundreds of boat companies along the Maine coast offer excursions that range from one-hour cocktail cruises to day-long whale-watching expeditions to week-long cruises on historic windjammers. You'll find the biggest concentrations of such companies in Kennebunkport, Boothbay Harbor, Rockland and Rockport, and on Mount Desert Island. Keep in mind that these are generally offered only in the summer months. Here are a few to try:

In Kennebunkport, take a two-hour trip on the high seas aboard the **Schooner Eleanor.** It leaves from the Arundel Wharf Restaurant from mid-May to mid-October. ~ Ocean Avenue; 207-967-8809; www.gwi.net/schoonersails, e-mail schoonersails@gwi.net.

Second Chance Cruiselines offers a scenic lobster cruise that glides by George Bush's summer home and past lolling harbor seals. The captain even provides a lobster-trapping demonstration. It also runs whale-watching cruises four times a day. Closed November through April. ~ 4 Western Avenue, Kennebunk Lower Village; 207-967-5507, 800-767-2628; www.firstchance whalewatch.com, e-mail whales@gwi.net.

Cap'n Fish Boat Trips is just one of many excursion companies competing for your attention on the Boothbay Harbor wharf. They offer nature-viewing trips that spot seals, whales, exotic birds and whatever else decides to fly or swim by. Closed November through April. ~ Pier 1, Boothbay Harbor; 207-633-3244; www.mainewhales.com.

Tidal Transit offers guided kayak tours on the bay in Boothbay Harbor. Choose either the wildlife, lighthouse or sunset trip. Closed in October. ~ 18 Granary Way, Footbridge; 207-633-7140; www.kayakboothbay.com.

Penobscot Bay is where you'll find Maine's tall-masted windjammers. You can spend three days or a week sailing on one, staying in comfortable cabins and eating like royalty. Contact the **Maine Windjammer Association** for a complete listing of all the possibilities. ~ P.O. Box 1144, Blue Hill, ME 04614; 800-807-9463; www.sailmainecoast.com.

From Stonington, **Miss Lizzie**, Isle au Haut's mail boat, doubles as a sightseeing cruise boat. During the summer, hour-long cruises depart from the dock at the corner of Sea Breeze Avenue and Bayview Street. ~ P.O. Box 709, Stonington, ME 04681; 207-367-5193; www.isleauhaut.com.

On Mount Desert Island, there are a number of boating possibilities, including whale watching with **Bar Harbor Whale Watch Co.**; they also offer seal and lobster watching. Closed November through May. ~ 1 West Street, Bar Harbor; 207-288-2386, 800-942-5374; www.whalesrus.com. There's also nature-viewing with **Sea Princess Naturalist Cruises.** Closed mid-October to late May. ~ Northeast Harbor; 207-276-5352; www.barharborcruises.com.

DOWNHILL SKIING

Maine offers a number of full-service resorts—including New England's biggest ski mountain—that'll keep you happily schussing the slopes. All facilities listed here rent equipment and offer lessons.

SOUTHERN COAST Hit the slopes at **Camden Snow Bowl** on the side of Ragged Mountain, with a summit of 1300 feet and a vertical drop of 800 feet. Snowboarders and skiers are welcome on all 11 trails. Equipped with one double lift, two T-lifts, and a handle-tow beginners lift, seven miles of groomed trails are easily accessible. There's night skiing on over half the trails; the park tends to cater to the intermediate skier (only 15 percent of the trails are for beginners and 15 percent for experts). The season runs from approximately December to March. The Bowl also features cross-country ski trails, a tubing hill and the only toboggan chute in New England. Closed Monday. ~ 20 Barnestown Road, Camden; 207-236-3438 (office), 207-236-4418 (conditions), fax 207-230-0490; www.camdensnowbowl.com, e-mail info@camdensnow bowl.com.

WESTERN LAKES AND MOUNTAINS Maine's downhill skiing revolves largely around **Sugarloaf/USA**, the biggest ski mountain in New England. With a base elevation of 1417 and a vertical drop of 2820 feet, there are challenges to be found on this hill for even the most experienced skier. Snowboarders will be thrilled with the 500-foot-long superpipe and the snow park's jumps, rolls and spines. The season runs from approximately November to April. ~ Carrabassett Valley, Kingfield; 207-237-2000, 800-843-5623; www.sugarloaf.com, e-mail info@sugarloaf.com.

At a base elevation of 2290 feet, **Saddleback Mountain** has three lifts and two T-bars that cover 40 runs equally divided between beginner, intermediate and expert. The summit is at 4120 feet and the mountain has a vertical drop of 2000 feet. A snow park features jumps and snow ramps for boarders. ~ Rangeley;

SMOOTH SAILING

For a scenic cruise to the legendary artist colony of Monhegan Island, head south from Thomaston to Port Clyde and board the **Laura B.** or the **Elizabeth Ann.** The cruises lead past Allen and Benner Island to idyllic Monhegan Island. Here you'll explore the historic artists' colony set amid a thriving fishing community. Visitors can walk Monhegan's scenic trails, visit artists' studios and peruse displays at the lighthouse museum. There is also a lighthouse and nature cruise and a trip to watch the puffins. ~ P.O. Box 238, Port Clyde, ME 04855; 207-372-8848, fax 207-372-8542; www.monheganboat.com, e-mail barstow@monheganboat.com.

207-864-3380; www.saddlebackmaine.com, e-mail saddleback@saddlebackmaine.com.

Sunday River Skiway has 18 lifts servicing slopes that are 25 percent beginner, 35 percent intermediate and 40 percent expert. Snowboarders have a chance to test their skills on one of three half-pipes and four terrain parks. The summit elevation of the resort is 3140 feet, with a vertical drop of 2340 feet. ~ Bethel; 207-824-3000, 800-543-2754, fax 207-824-5110; www.sundayriver.com, e-mail info@sundayriver.com.

Skiing aficionados and layfolk alike should visit www.skimaine.com for a helpful list of local surface conditions, snowfall statistics and kilometers of trails open.

Downhill skiers, telemarkers and snowboarders share **Shawnee Peak**, which has a base elevation of 600 feet and a vertical drop of 1300 feet. The resort has four lifts and one surface lift, with more than 40 trails crisscrossing the mountain. Night skiing is permitted on 19 of the runs. A terrain park keeps snowboarders busy with jumps, rolls and spines. Half the runs are intermediate. ~ Bridgton; 207-647-8444, fax 207-647-3203; www.shawneepeak.com, e-mail ski@shawneepeak.com.

CROSS-COUNTRY SKIING

Gliding through Maine's miles and miles of pine-scented cross-country trails on skis is a compelling way to experience the essence of the state's winters. The season generally begins at the end of November and lasts well into April. The ski centers listed have rentals and lessons unless noted.

NORTHERN WOODS **Birches Ski Touring Center** has 25 kilometers of groomed trails, and offers rentals and lessons. ~ P.O. Box 41, Rockwood, ME 04478; 207-534-7305, 800-825-9453; www.birches.com.

WESTERN LAKES AND MOUNTAINS In Carrabassett Valley try the **Sugarloaf Outdoor Center.** With more than 105 kilometers of groomed trails to explore, plus an ice-skating rink and a short track to ski at night, there is plenty to keep the whole family happy. ~ Carrabassett Valley; 207-237-2000, 800-843-5623; www.sugarloaf.com. In Rangeley, snowboarders and downhill and cross-country skiers share the mountain at the **Ski Nordic Touring Center at Saddleback.** Some 20 kilometers of groomed trails and 20 kilometers of backcountry trails are for the Nordic skiers. ~ 207-864-5671; www.saddlebackskiarea.com. **Bethel Inn and Country Club** has 40 kilometers of trails that wind through beautiful woods and over brooks. Sleigh rides are offered. ~ Bethel; 207-824-2175; www.bethelinn.com. Or you can try the 40 kilometers of trails at the **Sunday River Cross Country Ski Center.** ~ Bethel; 207-824-2410; www.sundayriverinn.com.

RIVER RUNNING

The northern woods are laced with choppy-water rivers. **Wilderness Rafting Expeditions** leads one-day and overnight trips on the Kennebec, Dead and Penobscot rivers. Levels of difficulty range from beginner to experienced, and you can go down the river in a raft, canoe or kayak. They also rent inflatable kayaks, motorboats, pontoon boats and sailboats. Fly-fishing classes are available. ~ P.O. Box 41, Rockwood, ME 04478; 207-534-2242, 800-825-9453; www.birches.com, e-mail wwld@aol.com. The experienced guides at **Northern Outdoors, Inc.** lead one- or two-day trips down the rapids of the Kennebec (Class III and IV), the Dead (Class III and IV) or Penobscot (Class IV and V) rivers. ~ The Forks; 207-663-4466, 800-765-7238; www.northernoutdoors.com. For an excursion down the Kennebec, Deerfield, Miller's Dead or West rivers, contact **Crab Apple Whitewater.** Take a full-day trip in a raft; rapids range from Class I to Class V. They also offer half-day funyak rentals. Closed mid-October to late March. ~ The Forks; 207-663-2218, 800-553-7238; www.crabappleinc.com.

BIKING

One of the best ways to see the coast is by pedaling along it. You can pick a spot—any spot—and start riding; just watch out for summer traffic.

SOUTHERN COAST A lovely 22-mile loop on Cape Elizabeth, just south of Portland, starts and finishes at the **Scarborough Public Library** on Route 207. It winds through Scarborough Marsh, past several beaches (including Scarborough Beach and Crescent Beach State Park) and through Lights State Park and Prouts Neck Bird Sanctuary.

The **Boothbay Harbor** area is a lot more manageable on two wheels than four. From Boothbay Harbor itself, try pedaling east to East Boothbay and then south to Ocean Point (about 14 miles roundtrip). Or do the loop around Southport Island (about 16 miles, starting and finishing in Boothbay Harbor).

DOWNEAST COAST On Deer Isle, there are several bicycling possibilities. From the center of the village, you can ride through silent woods out to the Haystack Mountain School of Crafts (7 miles one-way) or to the little lobstering village of Stonington (6.5 miles one-way). Or take your bikes over on the mail boat to Isle au Haut and ride along the sea for a couple of miles.

There are more than 50 miles of carriage paths on **Mount Desert Island** to cycle on. One of the most exhilarating trips is the 28-mile **Acadia National Park Loop** (the car route with detours). The steep ascent of Cadillac Mountain, however, is not for everyone.

NORTHERN WOODS You may find some pleasant inland trips though distances tend to be long and—in the western region—hilly or mountainous. A stunningly beautiful trip for big-time bikers can be had up at **Baxter State Park.** It's about 46 miles between Ripogenus Dam and Spencer Cove. You pass waterfalls, whitewater rivers and miles of majestically beautiful forest and you can see Mt. Katahdin looming on the horizon.

Bike Rentals In Kennebunkport, the full-service **Cape-able Bike Shop** rents mountain, hybrid, children's and tandem bikes. Closed Monday and Tuesday. ~ 83 Arundel Road; 207-967-4382; www.capeablebikes.com. In Rockport, you can rent hybrids and children's bikes, baby trailers and tag-a-longs at **Maine Sport Outfitters.** They also do repairs and carry biking maps. ~ Route 1; 207-236-7120, 888-236-8797; www.mainesport.com. To rent 24-speed mountain bikes in Bar Harbor, contact **Acadia Bike.** Reduced hours in winter. ~ 48 Cottage Street; 207-288-5483, 800-526-8615; www.acadiabike.com. At Moosehead Lake in the Northern Woods, mountain bikes are available at **The Birches.** ~ The Birches, Birches Road, Rockwood; 207-534-7305; www.birches.com.

HIKING

All distances listed for hiking trails are one way unless otherwise noted.

SOUTHERN COAST The **Fore River Trail** (1 mile) goes through the heart of Portland's Fore River Sanctuary. It's an easy walk, weaving through woods and marshes to a 30-foot waterfall. Several other trails veer off the main loop.

The whole of Monhegan Island is prime hiking territory, but if time is limited, follow **Cliff Trail** (about 2 miles). It takes you through the most densely scenic part of the island, over the dramatic headlands and coves that make up the eastern shore. You'll probably spend about half the day following it, but the views (plunging cliffs, deeply indented coves, open sea) are worth it.

The hike to the top of **Bald Rock Mountain** (.5 mile) in Camden Hills State Park rewards trekkers with glorious views of Penobscot Bay, Blue Hill, Mount Desert Island and the islands anchored offshore. To reach the trailhead, take Route 1 north of Camden to Lincolnville Beach. Turn left on Route 173 and take another left when you reach Young Town Road. The trailhead is near a fire road.

DOWNEAST COAST **Duck Harbor Mountain** (1 mile) is a delightful short hike on Isle au Haut. From its peak, you can see much of the island—it's largely covered with dense stands of spruce and fir, marshlands, streams and ponds and some spectacular cliffs.

From atop **Blue Hill** (1 mile) you won't be able to take your eyes off the view. Like a painting, the peaks of Mount Desert Island and the sailboat-dotted waters of the Blue Hill Bay spread out before you. On a clear day, you can see the villages of Penobscot and Castine and the Camden Hills. The trail itself passes through thick spruce and fir forests. To reach it, turn west on the Mountain Road opposite the entrance to the Blue Hill Fairgrounds; you'll see the trailhead about a mile down on the right.

Acadia National Park has an enormous network of hiking trails that attracts hikers and rock climbers from around the world. The Visitors Center has an information sheet, profiling many of the trails, which range in difficulty from very easy paths to strenuous hikes.

The **North Ridge of Cadillac Mountain** (2.2 miles) in Acadia National Park is a moderate trail with some steep grades and level stretches. By and large, though, it's a gradual ascent with exhilarating views of the island-dotted bays, coastline and clouds—below you.

If you feel up to it, consider climbing **Acadia Mountain** (1.3 miles), also in Acadia National Park. It's fairly strenuous but offers achingly beautiful views of the mountains, the offshore islands (from the top they look like croutons floating in soup) and Somes Sounds, the only fjord of the eastern U.S. seaboard.

The trail up to Bald Rock Mountain is a fairly easy climb that passes through forests ablaze with wildflowers in the spring.

Another good, though strenuous, hike inside Acadia National Park is **Beachcroft Trail** (1.2 miles), whose trailhead is along Route 3 at the northern end of the Tarn.

Beech Mountain (.6 mile) over in Southwest Harbor is our personal favorite. As you ascend, the land seems to fall off all around you, revealing increasingly magnificent views of the sea and islands. There's a fire tower at the summit, if you really want to stuff yourself on gorgeous scenery.

NORTHERN WOODS Baxter State Park's **Owl Trail** (6.6 miles) begins gradually, passing through woods and by streams. However, it does get steep in patches, taking you through bouldery cliff areas. If you've got the physical fortitude, it's worth it for views of Katahdin. From the wind-slapped summit, you can see the lakes and streams that wash through this startlingly beautiful chunk of Maine. To reach the Owl Trail, start off on the Hunt Trail at the Katahdin Stream Campground. You'll see blue markers indicating where the Owl Trail turns off.

One of the most spectacular routes to Baxter Peak on Katahdin is the **Cathedral Trail.** It is very steep and rocky, though, so be forewarned. Its name comes from the cathedrals you'll see—huge outcroppings of vertical rock slabs. To reach the summit of Katahdin, Baxter Peak, you will need to park at Roaring Brook campground and hike 3.3 miles uphill to Chimney Pond campground. From Chimney, you can take the Cathedral Trail 1.8 miles to Baxter Peak. To return, you can descent via Saddle Trail 2.2 miles to Chimney Pond, featuring a steep, loose slide about 1 mile downhill from the peak. Be warned that all hiking in Katahdin takes a *minimum* of eight hours. There are limits for children and regulations for hikers. ~ 207-732-5140; www.baxterstateparkauthority.com.

Along the Allagash Waterway at Umsaskis Lake begins the trail up **Priestly Mountain** (3.5 miles). From the fire tower that crowns its peak (about 1900 feet), you'll have far-reaching views of the whole water-webbed Allagash area. To reach the trail, leave your canoe at the park ranger's camp about halfway down the western shore. You'll see a sign.

Two trails lead to the summit of **Mount Kineo**, which rises dramatically from the middle of Moosehead Lake. **The Indian Trail** (1 mile) is the tougher of the two, taking you along steep cliffs. The **Bridle Trail** (1 mile) is easier but not half as beautiful. Whichever way you choose, the views from the bald summit will make your heart throb. To reach the mountain, you have to boat in. There are motorboats for rent along the Moose River, in Rockwood, and on the western shore of Moosehead Lake; shuttle boats depart every other hour from Kineo House.

The Beachcroft Trail takes you steeply up the side of an ice-carved valley where you can read the glacial record.

If you take just one hike while in New England, let it be at **Gulf Hagas** (8 miles roundtrip), otherwise known as "Maine's Grand Canyon." This area is perhaps the most scenic in the state, taking in the three-mile canyon, five major waterfalls and 40-foot-high vertical walls. The only catch is finding this place. It's east of Greenville and west of Katahdin Iron Works. Your best bet is to consult *The Maine Atlas*, where it's clearly indicated. If you're game for a hunt, follow these directions: From Routes 6 and 15 in Greenville, take a right on Pleasant Street and follow it for two miles. Pleasant takes a sharp right and becomes a dirt road; follow it for ten miles and you'll come to Hedgehog Check Point gate. The attendant will guide you from there.

The **Sally Trail** (3 miles) winds its way up Sally Mountain through forests of birch hardwoods and fir trees. From the summit, you can see island-dotted Attean Pond and other mountains that loom up all around. To reach the trail, drive two miles south from Jackman on Route 201 to Attean Road. Turn right and follow the road for about two miles to the Attean Lake Resort. The trail starts near the lake landing, by the railroad tracks. Look for signal post #770.

WESTERN LAKES AND MOUNTAINS A good "starter" mountain in the Rangeley Lakes area is **Bald Mountain** (1 mile), where the trail gradually ascends through hardwood forests. From the top at the observation deck, you can see portions of Mooselookmeguntic Lake and nearby lakes. You'll see the Kennebago Mountains to the north, the Azis cohos and Deer Mountains to the west and Saddleback Mountain to the east. To reach the trailhead, follow Route 4 from the Oquossoc Post Office for a mile and take a sharp left onto Bald Mountain Road.

The moderately tricky trail up **Little Jackson Trail** (3.3 miles) climbs above the timberline through pretty woods and patches of blueberry and cranberry bushes. The view of the Weld area from the summit is worth the hike. To get there, follow the unmarked road that heads west out of Weld Corner. Stay on it until you see a cemetery. Just beyond that, turn right onto the bumpy dirt road (Byron Road).

Step Falls (1 mile) is a long, dramatic string of cascades and icy pools. During summer months (even late August), take along your bathing suit for a dip in the thrilling natural water slide. The falls are off Route 26, about 15 miles northwest of Bethel. There's no sign, but you'll see cars parked at the trailhead.

A simple walk recommended for young families is the trail to the summit of **Sabattus Mountain** (.75 mile), which passes through silent woods on gentle inclines. At the top, you'll find wide-angle views of the mountains. To reach the trail, follow Route 5 to just north of Center Lovell; turn right on the dirt road. When you come to a fork, stay right. Continue past a white house to the parking area.

Transportation

CAR

The most common way to enter Maine is from the south, on **Route 95**, the interstate. It's the fastest way to reach Portland, Augusta and Bangor. It's also the quickest way to get to most of the coastal resort areas between the border of New Hampshire and Mount Desert Island, and to the edge of the northern woods.

An alternative to Route 95 is **Route 1**, which roughly runs along the coast from Kittery to Calais. At Calais, it turns north and follows the Canadian border all the way up to Fort Kent in the state's northern reaches. A word of caution: Route 1 is notoriously slow, especially in the south in the summer months, when tourists are traveling and stopping at the scores of factory outlets that line it. It's also hilly in parts (especially in the north), which makes passing quite dangerous.

You can easily reach towns in the southern half of the state on the well-maintained webwork of roads that cover it. The north is a bit more difficult, however. There are times when you may have to go north, south, north, south just to get from a western town to an eastern town. Fortunately, the scenery in these parts more than compensates. One more note about the north. Once you get north and west of Millinocket, you'll spend most of your time on dirt roads. Some are downright rough and rugged. And some are private and require permits.

AIR

There are two major airports in the state: the Portland International Jetport and the Bangor International Airport.

Portland International Jetport is served by American Airlines, Continental Airlines, Delta Air Lines, Northwest, United Airlines and US Airways, plus several regional airlines. ~ www.portland jetport.org.

Flying into **Bangor International Airport** are American Eagle, Delta Air Lines, Boston-Maine Airways, Continental Airlines and US Airways. ~ www.flybangor.com.

At both, you'll find plenty of taxis to take you into town. In Portland, you can bus in with the **Metro Bus Company** (207-774-0351; www.metrobus.com). There are also small airports in Auburn/Lewiston, Augusta, Bar Harbor, Frenchville, Presque Isle, Rockland and Waterville—all serviced by either Continental Express or Valley Airlines.

BUS

Concord Trailways cruises up Route 1, stopping in Brunswick, Bath, Wiscasset, Lincolnville, Waldoboro, Rockland, Camden and Belfast. ~ Thompson Point Road, Portland; 207-828-1151, 800-639-3317; www.concordtrailways.com, e-mail info@concord trailways.com. **Vermont Transit/Greyhound** has service from Portland to Lewiston, Bangor, Augusta and Waterville. In summer, they also stop in Bar Harbor. ~ 950 Congress Street, Portland; 207-772-6587, 800-231-2222; www.greyhound.com.

FERRY

You can tour the Portland Harbor aboard a bright-yellow half-truck, half-boat. The amphibious **SuperDuck** combines tours of Old Port with a dip in the bay right off Commercial Street. ~ 207-773-3825.

CAR RENTALS

Unless you're planning to stay put in one hotel or in one city for the duration of your trip, you'll most likely need a car in Maine.

At the Portland and Bangor airports, you'll find **Avis Rent A Car** (800-331-1212), **Budget Rent A Car** (800-527-0700), **Hertz Rent A Car** (800-654-3131), **National Car Rental** (800-328-4567) and **Alamo Rent A Car** (800-462-5266).

PUBLIC TRANSIT

For getting around Portland on your own, there's a very good bus system called the **Metro**. It has regularly scheduled routes throughout the greater Portland area. ~ 207-774-0351; www.tran sportme.com.

TAXIS

Several taxi companies serve the Portland International Jetport. In Bangor, try **Town Taxi** (207-945-5671).

Index

Lodging Index

HOSTELS

LODGING SERVICES

Dining Index

HIDDEN GUIDES

Adventure travel or a relaxing vacation?—"Hidden" guidebooks are the only travel books in the business to provide detailed information on both. Aimed at environmentally aware travelers, our motto is "Where Vacations Meet Adventures." These books combine details on unique hotels, restaurants and sightseeing with information on camping, sports and hiking for the outdoor enthusiast.

PARADISE FAMILY GUIDES

Ideal for families traveling with kids of any age—toddlers to teenagers—Paradise Family Guides offer a blend of travel information unlike any other guides to the Hawaiian islands. With vacation ideas and tropical adventures that are sure to satisfy both action-hungry youngsters and relaxation-seeking parents, these guides meet the specific needs of each and every family member.

Ulysses Press books are available at bookstores everywhere. If any of the following titles are unavailable at your local bookstore, ask the bookseller to order them.

You can also order books directly from Ulysses Press
P.O. Box 3440, Berkeley, CA 94703
800-377-2542 or 510-601-8301
fax: 510-601-8307
www.ulyssespress.com
e-mail: ulysses@ulyssespress.com

HIDDEN GUIDEBOOKS

____ Hidden Arizona, $16.95
____ Hidden Baja, $15.95
____ Hidden Belize, $15.95
____ Hidden Big Island of Hawaii, $13.95
____ Hidden Boston & Cape Cod, $14.95
____ Hidden British Columbia, $18.95
____ Hidden Cancún & the Yucatán, $16.95
____ Hidden Carolinas, $17.95
____ Hidden Coast of California, $18.95
____ Hidden Colorado, $15.95
____ Hidden Disneyland, $13.95
____ Hidden Florida, $19.95
____ Hidden Florida Keys & Everglades, $13.95
____ Hidden Georgia, $16.95
____ Hidden Hawaii, $19.95
____ Hidden Idaho, $14.95
____ Hidden Kauai, $13.95
____ Hidden Los Angeles, $14.95
____ Hidden Maine, $15.95
____ Hidden Maui, $14.95
____ Hidden Miami, $14.95
____ Hidden Montana, $15.95
____ Hidden New England, $19.95
____ Hidden New Mexico, $15.95
____ Hidden Oahu, $14.95
____ Hidden Oregon, $15.95
____ Hidden Pacific Northwest, $19.95
____ Hidden Philadelphia, $14.95
____ Hidden Puerto Vallarta, $14.95
____ Hidden Salt Lake City, $14.95
____ Hidden San Diego, $14.95
____ Hidden San Francisco & Northern California, $19.95
____ Hidden Seattle, $14.95
____ Hidden Southern California, $19.95
____ Hidden Southwest, $19.95
____ Hidden Tahiti, $18.95
____ Hidden Tennessee, $16.95
____ Hidden Utah, $16.95
____ Hidden Walt Disney World, $13.95
____ Hidden Washington, $15.95
____ Hidden Wine Country, $14.95
____ Hidden Wyoming, $15.95

PARADISE FAMILY GUIDES

____ Paradise Family Guides: Kaua'i, $17.95
____ Paradise Family Guides: Maui, $17.95
____ Paradise Family Guides: Big Island of Hawai'i, $17.95

Mark the book(s) you're ordering and enter the total cost here ⇨ ☐

California residents add 8.75% sales tax here ⇨ ☐

Shipping, check box for your preferred method and enter cost here ⇨ ☐

❑ BOOK RATE — FREE! FREE! FREE!

❑ PRIORITY MAIL/UPS GROUND — cost of postage

❑ UPS OVERNIGHT OR 2-DAY AIR — cost of postage

Billing, enter total amount due here and check method of payment ⇨ ☐

❑ CHECK ❑ MONEY ORDER

❑ VISA/MASTERCARD ______________________ EXP. DATE __________

NAME ______________________ PHONE __________

ADDRESS ______________________________

CITY ______________________ STATE ______ ZIP __________

MONEY-BACK GUARANTEE ON DIRECT ORDERS PLACED THROUGH ULYSSES PRESS.

ABOUT THE AUTHOR

SUSAN FAREWELL has written about New England for newlyweds (*Bride's*), young parents (*Child*) and Japanese travelers (*Gulliver*). Farewell is the author of Hidden Maine *How to Make a Living as a Travel Writer*, *Quick Escapes from New York City* and several other travel books.

ABOUT THE ILLUSTRATOR

TIM CARROLL, the illustrator for *Hidden New England*, has illustrated several Ulysses Press titles, including *Hidden Florida*. His artwork has appeared in *Esquire*, *GQ*, the *Boston Globe*, Parco, *Disney On-Line* and the *Washington Post*. He has also done animation for Nickelodeon.